# COMPUTER GRAPHICS

Annual Conference Series 1999

SIGGRAPH 99
Conference Proceedings
August 8–13, 1999
Papers Chair: Alyn Rockwood

A Publication of ACM SIGGRAPH

Sponsored by the ACM's Special Interest Group on Computer Graphics

PROCEEDINGS

**The Association for Computing Machinery, Inc.**
1515 Broadway
New York, NY 10036



Sample Citation Information:
...Proceedings of SIGGRAPH 99 (Los Angeles, California, August 8–13, 1999). In *Computer Graphics* Proceedings, Annual Conference Series, 1999, ACM SIGGRAPH, pp. xx – yy.

**Orders from members of ACM:**

**U.S.A. and Canada:**
ACM Order Department
P.O. Box 12114
Church Street Station
New York, NY 10257
Telephone: +1-800-342-6626
Telephone: +1-212-626-0500
Fax: +1-212-944-1318
E-mail: orders@acm.org
URL: http://www.acm.org/

**All other countries:**
ACM European Service Center
108 Cowley Road
Oxford OX4 1JF
United Kingdom
Telephone: +44-1-865-382338
Fax: +44-1-865-381338
E-mail: acm_europe@acm.org

ACM Order Number: 428990
ACM ISBN: 0-201-48560-5
ACM ISSN: 1069-529X

**Orders from nonmembers of ACM:**

Addison-Wesley will pay postage and handling on orders accompanied by check. Credit card orders may be placed by mail or by calling the Addison-Wesley Order Department at the number above. Followup inquiries should be directed at the same number. Please include the Addison-Wesley ISBN with your order:
A-W Softcover Proceedings and CD-ROM Package ISBN: 0-201-48560-5

**United States:**
Addison-Wesley Publishing Company
Order Department
Jacob Way
Reading, MA 01867
Telephone: +1-800-447-2226

**Europe/Middle East:**
Addison-Wesley Publishing Group
Concertgebouwplein 25
1071 LM Amsterdam
The Netherlands
Telephone: +31-20-6717296
Fax: +31-20-6645334

**Germany/Austria/Switzerland:**
Addison-Wesley Verlag Deutschland GmbH
Hildachstraße 15d
Wachsbleiche 7-12
53111 Bonn
Germany
Telephone: +49-228-98-515-0
Fax: +49-228-98-515-99

**United Kingdom/Africa:**
Addison-Wesley Publishers Ltd.
Finchampstead Road
Wokingham, Berkshire RG11 2NZ
United Kingdom
Telephone: +44-734-794000
Fax: +44-734-794035

**Asia:**
Addison-Wesley Singapore Pte. Ltd.
15 Beach Road
#05-02/09/10 Beach Centre
Singapore 0718
Telephone: +65-339-7503
Fax: +65-339-9709

**Japan:**
Addison-Wesley Publishers Japan Ltd.
Nichibo Building
1-2-2 Sarugakucho
Chiyoda-ku, Tokyo 101
Japan
Telephone: +81-33-2914581
Fax: +81-33-2914592

**Australia/New Zealand:**
Addison-Wesley Publishers Pty. Ltd.
6 Byfield Street
North Ryde, N.S.W. 2113
Australia
Telephone: +61-2-878-5411
Fax: +61-2-878-5830

**Latin America:**
Addison-Wesley Iberoamericana S.A.
Boulevard de las Cataratas #3
Colonia Jardines del Pedregal
Delegacion Alvaro Obregon
01900 Mexico D.F.
Telephone: +52-5-660-2695
Fax: +52-5-660-4930

**Canada:**
Addison-Wesley Publishing (Canada) Ltd.
26 Prince Andrew Place
Don Mills, Ontario M3C 2T8 Canada
Telephone: +1-416-447-5101
Fax: +1-416-443-0948

# Contents

## Papers Sessions, Friday, 13 August 1999

# Papers Preface

Good thoughts, empowered and embrained with fit words [and images],
Walk the earth like a living soul. -after Whitaker

Since January I have spent considerable time absorbing the papers submitted this year and musing over their content. I am impressed. Not only do the fundamental algorithms keep improving, sometimes dramatically, but I also see a couple of other noteworthy trends. First, we continue to mine new application areas for graphics and interactive techniques. It is not unlike the pervasiveness of the computer itself. If you believe as I that every intelligent human endeavor can be improved and enhanced by computer, then it is not a far jump to say the same thing about computer graphics and interactive techniques. We are, after all, talking about how the human and computer interact.

Second, I see engaging new syntheses. We are not only broadening the foundations, but we are stretching the scaffolding higher and catching a glimpse of glowing new horizons. Read these proceedings and see if you agree with me. There is a vision embedded herein. Those with imagination should step forward and grab hold.

The SIGGRAPH papers review process is a singular undertaking. This year's review was even more so because of the record 320 papers submitted. It is a difficult task to get 1600+ extensive reviews accomplished in two and one half months. It is a tribute to the SIGGRAPH community that this is possible. On March 13-15, 1999, in Colorado Springs in an intense meeting, 35 senior reviewers chose 52 papers for the conference. Undoubtedly, many fine papers did not make it for a number of reasons, but for anyone involved in the process, the dedication, effort and evenhanded attempt to find the best work by committee members is imposing. No paper was chosen for the program without a consensus of those reviewers who had read and considered the paper. The committee chose three papers as "impact" papers this year. They will be presented in a special papers/course session with an extended format, as well as in the regular papers venue. Look for them.

This year we also had the special category of visionary papers. An august board of reviewers considered these. In spite of many provocative and insightful thoughts, none of these contained the enduring, long-range vision the board had hoped to achieve. This topic will be investigated further by a Special Session panel at SIGGRAPH 99. My especial thanks to several people who worked hard, very hard behind the scenes. Vicki Schaefer was the papers coordinator, who ably handled mountains of detail. Janet McAndless jumped in whenever it got too frenetic and needed some calming competence. They had the unenviable tasks of reassuring some understandably excitable submitters, and keeping me so I appeared organized. Kurt Akeley (next year's papers chair), Eugene Fiume and Michael Cohen served as my advisory board, helping with everything from selecting jury members to sorting papers. Stephen Spencer, SIGGRAPH Director for Publications, is ultimately responsible for the physical product you now hold in your hands.

It is now yours. Enjoy it. Learn from it. Get excited by it!

Alyn Rockwood
SIGGRAPH 99 Papers Chair

## 1999 ACM SIGGRAPH Awards

# Steven A. Coons Award for Outstanding Creative Contributions to Computer Graphics

# James F. Blinn

Dr. James F. Blinn is an artist of picture, word, and science. In SIGGRAPH's twenty-six year history, he has made our community richer and more interesting with his wit, technical discoveries, animated productions of math and physics, and many graphics columns. His writing has a personal style and clarity that have made them a joy to read.

While working on his Ph.D. at the University of Utah he developed bump mapping and, along with Martin Newell, reflection mapping - techniques that are still widely used today. During the same period he consulted with the New York Institute of Technology and with Information International Inc, where he participated in foundational work for computer graphics in feature films.

In 1977 Jim moved to the Jet Propulsion Laboratory and the California Institute of Technology, where he made, along with his collaborators, a series of educational and scientific films. These included the Voyager Fly-by Animations, computer graphics animations for COSMOS (Carl Sagan's PBS series), The Mechanical Universe (animated sequences for a Caltech college-level physics telecourse), and Project Mathematics! (a series of video tapes to teach high school mathematics). Excerpts of these animations, awaited with great anticipation, were shown annually at SIGGRAPH.

In 1987, Jim began to write "Jim Blinn's Corner," a regular column for IEEE Computer Society's Computer Graphics and Applications. While his primary motivation was to share his bag of computer graphics tricks, his articles were personal, humorous, and above all, models of clear exposition. They have since been collected in two books, A Trip Down the Graphics Pipeline and Dirty Pixels.

Through the years Jim has also taught courses in computer graphics at institutions as diverse as the Universities of Michigan, Utah, and California (Berkeley), Caltech, West Coast College and the Pasadena Art Center's College of Design.

Jim has been recognized numerous times for his contributions. He was the first recipient of the SIGGRAPH Computer Graphics Achievement Award for his work in lighting and surface modeling. He was awarded a MacArthur Fellowship to support his work in educational animation. NASA gave him the Exceptional Service medal for the Voyager Fly-By animations, the IEEE gave him the Outstanding Contribution Award for his column, and he received an Honorary Doctor of Fine Arts from the Parsons School of Design.

In accepting his honorary Doctorate, Jim stated: "I think that the most import result of the computer graphics revolution is that it has helped heal the gulf between art and science." One cannot talk of the revolution or of the diminishing gulf without thinking of Jim. He has used his vision and deep understanding of the creative process in art and science to dramatically and permanently improve both disciplines.

SIGGRAPH now awards the Steven Anson Coons Award in recognition of his long-term contributions to Computer Graphics.

Major Publications

Blinn, J. F. and Newell, M. E., Texture and Reflection in Computer Generated Images, CACM, 19(10), October 1976, pp. 542-547. (The original teapot paper. Introduces reflection mapping.)

Blinn, J. F., Models of Light Reflection for Computer Synthesized Pictures, Proceedings of SIGGRAPH 77, pp. 192-198. (Introduces the Torrance-Sparrow highlight model.)

Blinn, J. F., Simulation of Wrinkled Surfaces, Proceedings of SIGGRAPH 78, pp. 286-292. (Introduces bump mapping.)

Blinn, J. F., A Generalization of Algebraic Surface Drawing, ACM Transactions on Graphics, 1(3), July 1982, pp. 235-256. (Introduces blobby modeling.)

Blinn, J. F., Light Reflection Functions for the Simulation of Clouds and Dusty Surfaces, Proceedings of SIGGRAPH 82, pp. 21-29.(Lighting model for rings of Saturn.)

Smith, A. R. and Blinn, J. F., Blue Screen Matting. Proceedings of SIGGRAPH 96, pp. 259-268. (Mathematical model of blue screen matte extraction.)

Books

Jim Blinn's Corner: A Trip Down The Graphics Pipeline, Morgan Kauffman Publishers Inc., San Francisco CA, 214 pp., 1996.

Bloomenthal, J., Bajaj, C., Blinn, J., Cani-Gascuel, M., Rockwood, A., Wyvill, B., and Wyvill, G., Introduction to Implicit Surfaces, Morgan Kauffman Publishers Inc, San Francisco CA, 323 pp., 1997.

Jim Blinn's Corner: Dirty Pixels, Morgan Kauffman Publishers Inc., San Francisco, CA, 247 pp., 1998.

**Previous Award Recipients**

| | |
|---|---|
| 1997 | James Foley |
| 1995 | Jose Luis Encarnação |
| 1993 | Ed Catmull |
| 1991 | Andries van Dam |
| 1989 | David C. Evans |
| 1987 | Donald P. Greenberg |
| 1985 | Pierre Bézier |
| 1983 | Ivan E. Sutherland |

## 1999 ACM SIGGRAPH Awards

# Computer Graphics Achievement Award

# Tony DeRose

ACM SIGGRAPH recognizes Anthony D. DeRose with the 1999 Computer Graphics Achievement Award for his seminal work in making subdivision surfaces a practical geometric modeling technique. Although there are many hopefuls waiting in the wings, there are only two widely accepted geometric primitives in computer graphics-polygons and parametric patches. DeRose's work, and the wide range of activity that it has sparked, will surely add another primitive to the geometric modeler's pantheon-subdivision surfaces.

Tony's work spans a wide range of topics in geometric modeling starting with a characterization of Geometric Continuity in terms of differential geometry. A series of papers set up the basic framework and mathematical foundation for transforming clouds of scanned 3D points into useful geometric objects, and for the connection between subdivision and multi-resolution wavelet techniques. He has published on many other phases of geometric design.

Tony has been a versatile collaborator, both with his students-many of whom have gone on to establish major research reputations-as well as with colleagues. Aside from work on geometric design, he's collaborated on global illumination using wavelets, VLSI CAD systems, image based rendering, user interface mechanisms, discontinuity meshing, parallel computing, and ray tracing. Perhaps the most fascinating and under appreciated work has been his creation of an elegant and powerful system for programming geometric systems in a coordinate-free manner.
Holding an undergraduate degree in Physics from the University of California, Davis, and a Ph.D. from the University of California, Berkeley under Brian Barsky, Tony's graphics work quickly helped to put the University of Washington on the map in the decade he spent there. Tony is currently a Senior Scientist at Pixar Animation Studios where he was a major contributor to "Geri's Game," winner of the 1997 Academy award for a short animated film.

Tony has consistently demonstrated a style concentrating on important fundamental groundwork rather than on flashy but shallow results. His creativity, his wide collaboration, and his impressive list of students marks Tony as a major contributor to our field in a quiet, but yet outstanding way.

Consequently SIGGRAPH is pleased to award Tony DeRose the 1999 Computer Graphics Achievement Award.

Major Publications

T. DeRose, and B. Barsky, Geometric Continuity, Shape Parameters, and Geometric Constructions for Catmull-Rom Splines, ACM Transactions on Graphics, Vol. 7, No. 1, January 1988, pp. 1-41.

C. Loop and T. DeRose, A Multisided Generalization of Bezier Surfaces, ACM Transactions on Graphics, Vol. 8, No. 3, July 1989, pp. 204-234.

T. DeRose, A Coordinate-Free Approach to Geometric Programming, pp. 291-305 in Theory and Practice of Geometric Modeling, edited by W. Strasser and H.-P. Seidel, Springer-Verlag, Berlin, 1989.

C. Loop and T. DeRose, Generalized B-spline Surfaces of Arbitrary Topology, Proceedings of SIGGRAPH 90, pp. 347-356.

H. Hoppe, T. DeRose, T. Duchamp, J. McDonald, and W. Stuetzle, Surface Reconstruction from Unorganized Points, Proceedings of SIGGRAPH 92, pp. 71-78.

H. Hoppe, T. DeRose, T. Duchamp, J. McDonald, and W. Stuetzle, Mesh Optimization, Proceedings of SIGGRAPH 93, pp. 19-26.

E. Bier, M. Stone, K. Pier, W. Buxton, and T. DeRose, Tool Glass and Magic Lenses: The See-Through Interface, Proceedings of SIGGRAPH '93, pp. 73-80.

M. Halstead, M. Kass, and T. DeRose, Efficient, Fair Interpolation using Catmull-Clark Surfaces, Proceedings of SIGGRAPH 93, pp. 35-44.

H. Hoppe, T. DeRose, T. Duchamp, H. Jin, M. Halstead, J. McDonald, J. Schweitzer, and W. Stuetzle, Piecewise Smooth Surface Reconstruction, Proceedings of SIGGRAPH 94, pp. 295-302.

M. Eck, T. DeRose, T. Duchamp, H. Hoppe, M. Lounsbery, and W. Stuetzle, Multiresolution Analysis of Arbitrary Meshes, Proceedings of SIGGRAPH 95, pp. 173-182.

A. Certain, J. Popovic, T. DeRose, T. Duchamp, D. Salesin, and W. Stuetzle, Interactive Viewing of Multiresolution Surfaces, Proceedings of SIGGRAPH 96, pp. 91-98.

J. Shade, D. Lischinski, D. Salesin, T. DeRose, and J. Snyder, High-Performance Hierarchical Image Caching for Accelerated Walkthroughs of Complex Environments. Proceedings of SIGGRAPH 96, pp. 75-82.

E. Stollnitz, T. DeRose, and D. Salesin, Wavelets for Computer Graphics: Theory and Applications, Morgan-Kaufmann, 1996.

P. Christensen, E. Stollnitz, D. Salesin, and T. DeRose, Global Illumination of Glossy Environments using Wavelets and Importance, ACM Transactions on Graphics, Vol. 15, No. 1, January 1996, pp. 37-71.

M. Lounsbery, T. DeRose, and J. Warren, Multiresolution Analysis for Surfaces of Arbitrary Topological Type, ACM Transactions on Graphics, Vol. 16, No. 1, January 1997, pp. 34-73.

T. DeRose, M. Kass, T. Truong, Subdivision Surfaces in Character Animation, Proceedings of SIGGRAPH 98, pp. 85-94.

**Previous Award Recipients**

| | |
|---|---|
| 1998 | Michael F. Cohen |
| 1997 | Przemyslaw Prusinkiewicz |
| 1996 | Marc Levoy |
| 1995 | Kurt Akeley |
| 1994 | Kenneth E. Torrance |
| 1993 | Pat Hanrahan |
| 1992 | Henry Fuchs |
| 1991 | James T. Kajiya |
| 1990 | Richard Shoup and Alvy Ray Smith |
| 1989 | John Warnock |
| 1988 | Alan H. Barr |
| 1987 | Robert Cook |
| 1986 | Turner Whitted |
| 1985 | Loren Carpenter |
| 1984 | James H. Clark |
| 1983 | James F. Blinn |

# Physically Based Motion Transformation

Zoran Popović        Andrew Witkin*

Computer Science Department
Carnegie Mellon University

## Abstract

We introduce a novel algorithm for transforming character animation sequences that preserves essential physical properties of the motion. By using the spacetime constraints dynamics formulation our algorithm maintains realism of the original motion sequence without sacrificing full user control of the editing process.

In contrast to most physically based animation techniques that synthesize motion from scratch, we take the approach of *motion transformation* as the underlying paradigm for generating computer animations. In doing so, we combine the expressive richness of an input animation sequence with the controllability of spacetime optimization to create a wide range of realistic character animations. The spacetime dynamics formulation also allows editing of intuitive, high-level motion concepts such as the time and placement of footprints, length and mass of various extremities, number of body joints and gravity.

Our algorithm is well suited for the reuse of highly-detailed captured motion animations. In addition, we describe a new methodology for mapping a motion between characters with drastically different numbers of degrees of freedom. We use this method to reduce the complexity of the spacetime optimization problems. Furthermore, our approach provides a paradigm for controlling complex dynamic and kinematic systems with simpler ones.

**CR Categories:** I.3.7 [Computer Graphics]: Three-Dimensional Graphics and Realism—Animation; G.1.6 [Numerical Analysis]: Optimization.

**Keywords:** Human Body Simulation, Physically Based Animation, Animation with Constraints

## 1 Introduction

Controllable automatic synthesis of realistic character motion is a difficult problem. The motion of a character with many degrees of freedom (DOFs) needs to be consistent with the laws of physics. More importantly, in order for the motion to look realistic, the entire musculoskeletal structure must be taken into account. Controlling this complex motion generation process adds further difficulties. In this paper, we present a solution to the problem of generating both controllable and realistic character animations. Instead of motion synthesis, we take the approach of motion transformation. For example, we transform a human running sequence by restricting the range of motion for a knee joint to obtain a realistic run with a limp.

Any dynamically sound motion, such as captured motion or the result of a physical simulation, can be used as an input to our transformation algorithm. The first step of our algorithm constructs a simplified character model and fits the motion of the simplified model to the captured motion data. From this fitted motion we obtain a physical spacetime optimization solution that includes the body's mass properties, pose, and footprint constraints, muscles and the objective function. To edit the animation we modify the constraints and physical parameters of the model and other spacetime optimization parameters (e.g. limb geometry, footprint positions, objective function, gravity.) From this altered spacetime parameterization we compute a transformed motion sequence. Finally, we map the *motion change* of the simplified model back onto the original motion to produce a final animation sequence.

Once the spacetime model has been constructed from the input data, our algorithm can be turned into a motion library, since each change in the physical formulation of the model produces a new motion sequence. Thus, a captured motion sequence of a human run can be turned into a running motion library capable of generating all possible runs that fit the needs of the animator.

Our algorithm presents the first solution to the problem of editing captured motion taking dynamics into consideration. We also describe a novel methodology for mapping motion between characters with drastically different kinematic structure. In addition, we introduce a method for simplification of complex dynamic systems without losing the fundamental dynamic properties of motion.

The next section describes how this work relates to other research efforts. We follow with the algorithm outline, and proceed to describe each stage of the algorithm in detail. In Section 8 we report the results of the algorithm's application on two human captured motion sequences. We conclude the paper with the main contributions and future research directions.

## 2 Related Work

Forward dynamics methods compute motions of objects that obey the laws of physics. For rigid objects (e.g. [5, 4, 21]), or secondary motion of cloth (e.g. [12, 6]), forward dynamics techniques are ideal because obeying physical laws is synonymous with realism. However, active characters create motion with their own muscles. The specific motion of real creatures depends on their intricate musculoskeletal structure. Determining exact muscle forces that would make the animation look realistic is extremely difficult. In addition, with dynamics methods each animation frame depends on the previous frame (and consequently on all other preceding frames). The smallest change of dynamic properties of any single frame drastically affects all consecutive frames, resulting in lack of controllability.

*Spacetime constraints* approach effectively addresses the need for both realism and controllability of character motion [33, 9, 20, 28]. In the spacetime framework the user first specifies *pose constraints* that must be satisfied by the resulting motion sequence (e.g.

*now at Pixar Animation Studios.

the character pose at the beginning and end of the animation). In addition to these constraints, the user also specifies an *objective function* that is a metric of performance or style such as total power consumption of all of the character's muscles. The algorithm takes this spacetime specification and finds the motion trajectories that minimize the objective function while satisfying the constraints. High realism and intuitive control give this method great appeal. The downside, however, is that the current algorithms do not scale up to the complexity of characters one would like to animate. The time complexity of the spacetime formulation and convergence difficulties remain a huge impediment. Another problem of these methods is that they are extremely sensitive to the starting position of the optimization process — if optimization begins far away from the solution, the optimization methods often cannot converge to the optimal motion. As a result, spacetime optimization methods have not been successfully applied to automatic generation of human motion. Our work draws from the ideas of spacetime constraints and tries to address the issues that prevent this method from being applied to complex character models.

Robot controller design has also been applied to the domain of realistic computer animation (e.g. [26, 32, 31, 18]). These methods use controllers that drive the actuator forces based on the current state of the environment. These forces, in turn, produce desired motion. Intuitively, controllers can be thought of as a set of instinctual reflexes that control muscles and collectively produce a character's continuous motion. Once the controllers have been fine-tuned and synchronized to each other, this method can produce a wide range of expressive animations [26, 19]. Furthermore, a number of different animations can be created without any additional work, because the controllers adjust to the changes in the environment. Recently, van de Panne introduced an interesting method for generating motion from footsteps that includes some rudimentary physical properties[30]. Although a controller transformation algorithm has been reported [17], determining controllers that produce realistic character motion is extremely difficult, and has not been formalized.

Another way to generate realistic motion is to attain it from the real world. Recent availability of real-time 3-D motion capture systems provides such an alternative. Motion capture systems use sensors to record absolute positions of key points on the character's body over a period of time. Not surprisingly, the resulting clip motion is convincing and rich with expressive detail that is almost impossible to generate by any computer methods. Although this type of animation is quite realistic, it yields highly unstructured and uncorrelated motion, even when converted to joint angles within a hierarchical character model.

Recently, a number of motion capture editing methods have been proposed [34, 8, 15, 14, 16, 27]. These methods don't generate motion "from scratch" like earlier described methods, but transform existing motion sequences. Even though some of the methods solve for the entire transformed motion sequence (and thus use the term spacetime), they do not include any notion of dynamics. Recently Gleicher [16] introduced a method for remapping captured motion onto drastically different characters. While his method is capable of producing many interesting motions, it has no means of making the motion physically realistic. For example, a tall and lanky character would utilize his muscles (and therefore move) in very different ways than a more compact character. A property of all motion editing methods that ignore inherent dynamics is that while they can effectively transform motion by small amounts, larger deformations reveal undesirable, unrealistic artifacts.

An alternative approach to editing realistic motion sequences is to extract the physical model from captured data, and perform all editing on the computer model instead. Spacetime optimization is a good candidate for this task. Of course, the primary problem of spacetime methods is that they do not guarantee a solution for motion problems of complex characters such as humans. We circumvent this issue by developing smaller, abstracted models. This model simplification is motivated by biomechanics research [7]. Blickhan and Full demonstrate the similarity in the multi-legged locomotion of kinematically different animals. They show striking similarities between a human run, a horse run and the monopode bounce (i.e. pogostick). This similarity motivates our approach to reducing the DOF count of complex kinematic structures such as humans.

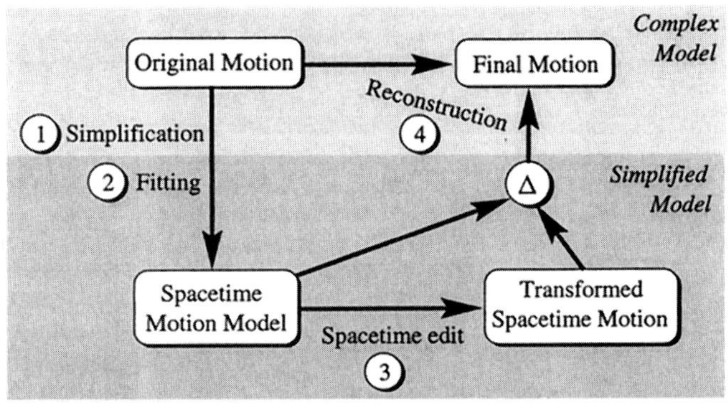


Figure 1: Algorithm outline.

Biomechanics also studies the postulated optimality of motion in nature [1, 2, 24]. There has been a considerable amount of work in the area of human performance in sports [22]. This work also reaffirms that spacetime optimization is a good choice for realistic motion synthesis.

## 3 Algorithm Outline

Much like the motion capture editing methods, our algorithm does not synthesize motion from ground zero. Instead, it transforms the input motion sequence to satisfy the needs of the animation. Although our algorithm was motivated by the desire to enable realistic high-level control of high quality captured motion sequences, the same methods can be applied to motion of arbitrary source.

At its core our algorithm uses spacetime optimization because the spacetime formulation maintains the dynamic integrity of motion and provides intuitive motion control. Because such methods have not been shown to be feasible for human motion models, we must also find a way to simplify the character model.

The entire transformation process breaks down to four main stages (Figure 1):

**Character Simplification.** Create an abstract character model containing the minimal number of degrees of freedom necessary to capture the essence of the input motion. Map the input motion onto the simplified model.

**Spacetime Motion Fitting.** Find the spacetime optimization problem whose solution closely matches the simplified character motion.

**Spacetime Edit.** Change spacetime motion parameters, introduce new pose constraints, change the character kinematics, objective function, etc.

**Motion Reconstruction.** Remap the change in motion introduced by the spacetime edit onto the original motion to produce the final animation.

The *character simplification* and *spacetime motion fitting* stages require a significant amount of human intervention. However, once

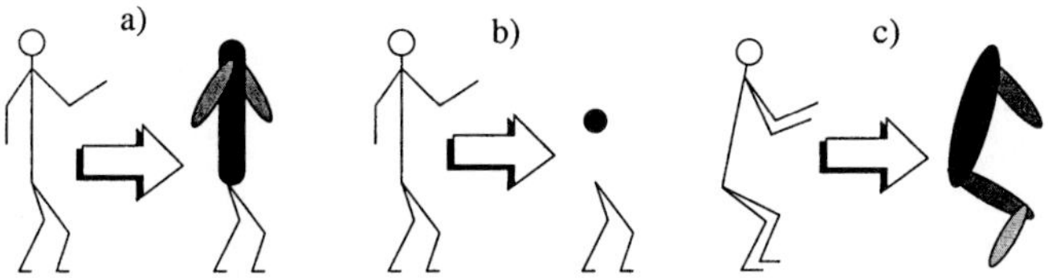


Figure 2: Kinematic character simplification: a) elbows and spine are abstracted away, b) upper body reduced to the center of mass, c) symmetric movement abstraction.

the spacetime model is computed it can be reused to generate a wide range of different animations. The *spacetime edit* and *motion reconstruction* stages are fully automated. They also take much less time to compute than the first two stages, which enables computation of transformed motion sequences at near-interactive speeds.

# 4 Character Simplification

Instead of solving spacetime constraint optimizations on the full character, we first construct a simpler character model which we then use for all spacetime optimizations. There are two important reasons for character simplification:

- DOF reduction improves performance and facilitates convergence of the spacetime optimization.
- creation of an abstract model that contains only DOFs essential for the given motion captures the more fundamental properties of the body movement. As a result, detailed motion in the input sequence will be preserved during the transformation process.

Simplified models capture the minimum amount of structure necessary for the input motion task, and therefore capture the "essence" of the input motion. Subsequent motion transformations modify this abstract representation while preserving the specific feel and uniqueness of the original motion. Our simplification process draws from certain ideas in the biomechanics research [7]. We take the view that, abstractly speaking, highly dynamic natural motion is created by "throwing the mass around," or changing the *relative position* of body mass. With this in mind a human arm with more than 10 DOFs can be represented by a rigid object with only three shoulder DOFs without losing much of the mass displacement ability. Simplification of certain body parts also depends on the type of the input motion. For example, while the above mentioned arm simplification may work well for the human run motion, it would not appropriately represent the ball-throwing motion.

Simplification reduces the number of kinematic DOFs, as well as muscle DOFs by a factor of two to five. Since each DOF is represented by hundreds of unknown coefficients during the optimization, simplification can reduce the size of the optimization by as many as 1000 unknowns. More importantly, a character with fewer DOFs also creates constraints with significantly smaller nonlinearities. In practice, the optimization has no convergence problems with the simplified character models.

Character simplification is performed manually. We apply three basic principles during this process:

**DOF removal.** Some body parts are fused together removing DOFs that link them together. Elbow and wrist DOFs are usually removed for running and walking motion sequences where they have little impact on the motion.

**Node subtree removal.** In some cases of high-energy motion the entire subtree of the character hierarchy can be replaced with a single object, usually a mass point with three translational DOFs. For example, the upper body of a human character can be reduced to a mass point for various jumping motion sequences where the upper body catapults in the direction of the jump.

**Exploit symmetric movement.** Broad jump motions contain inherent symmetry since both legs move in unison. Thus, we can abstract both legs with one, turning the character into a monopode.

The simplification process ensures that the overall mass distribution is preserved, so if a number of nodes are represented with a single object we match the mass, center of mass and moments of inertia of the new structure to be as close to the original as possible.

Once the character model has been simplified the original motion can be mapped onto it. Since the simplified character has significantly fewer DOFs, this mapping is over-determined. We define *handles* to aid us in the motion transfer process by correlating essential properties between complex and simplified motion sequences.

## 4.1 Handles

Handles are multi-valued time-varying functions that can be evaluated on both complex and simplified character models. All handles depend on the character pose defined by the vector of values for each DOF $\mathbf{q}(t_i)$. They represent intuitive measurements of various body properties such as 3D point positions, 3D directions, distance between two assigned body points.

Some 3D position handles are simply points on the character's body (e.g. the foot-ground contact position). Others, like the center of mass position handle, depend on a much larger set of DOFs. Direction handles are often used to represent the orientation of the character. When kinematic topology has been drastically changed during the simplification, it is often useful to use distance handles to correlate various body points.

In order to match two animations, we ensure equality between the corresponding handles. For example, if we reduced the human upper body down to a mass point, we would use the center of mass handle to correlate two animations. When two legs are reduced to one, we would use the foot-floor contact point handle, defined as the midpoint between two foot contact points and equate it with the foot point handle of the monopode.

Let us define the collection of all handles of the original (complex) motion as $\mathbf{h}_o(\mathbf{q}_o(t))$, and let $\mathbf{h}_s(\mathbf{q}_s(t))$ be the corresponding simplified motion handles. We find the motion of the simplified character by solving

$$E_d = [\mathbf{h}_o(\mathbf{q}_o(t_i)) - \mathbf{h}_s(\mathbf{q}_s(t_i))]^2 \quad (1)$$

$$\min_{\mathbf{q}_s(t_i)} E_d \quad (2)$$

for each frame $t_i$. This process is equivalent to solving an inverse kinematics problem for each time frame of the animation. Naturally, there should be *at least* as many handles as there are DOFs in the simplified character. That way the simplified motion is fully determined by $\mathbf{h}_s(\mathbf{q}_s(t))$.

# 5 Spacetime Motion Fitting

Handles help us map the original motion onto the simplified character. However, the resulting motion is no longer dynamically correct. Before we can edit the motion with spacetime constraints we need to create not only dynamically correct but also realistic motion of the simplified model. In other words, we need to find the spacetime optimization problem whose solution comes very close to the simplified model motion we computed in section 4.1. Section 5.1 describes the spacetime constraints formulation of motion. Subsequent sections describe our approach to finding the appropriate muscles, spacetime constraints and the objective function which would yield the motion closely matching the input sequence.

### 5.1 Spacetime Constraints Formulation

We obtain the body dimensions and mass distributions from biomechanics sources [11, 23]. All other concepts of spacetime optimization have their intuitive counterparts in real-life.

A *character* is an object performing motion of its own accord. It has a finite number of kinematic DOFs and a number of *muscles*. DOFs usually represent joint angles of the character's extremities, while muscles exert forces or torques on different parts of the body, thus actuating locomotion. Given that both body and muscle DOFs change through time we refer to them collectively as $\mathbf{q}(t)$, or separately as kinematic $\mathbf{q}_k(t)$, and muscle DOFs $\mathbf{q}_m(t)$.

The task of motion synthesis is to find the desired motion of a character. This "goal motion" is rarely uniquely specified; rather, one looks for a motion that satisfies some set of requirements. Generally these requirements are represented either through constraints, external forces or through the objective function.

For instance, the requirements of a sequence that animates a person getting up from a chair would include the fact that the person is sitting in the chair at time $t_0$ and standing up at final time $t_1$. We refer to such requirements as *pose constraints* ($\mathbf{C}_p$), and we insist that the character must use its own muscles to satisfy these constraints.

In addition to pose constraints, the environment imposes a number of *mechanical constraints* ($\mathbf{C}_m$) onto the body. For example, in order to enforce the upright position of a human, we need to constrain both of her feet to the floor. The floor exerts forces onto the feet ensuring that the feet never penetrate the floor surface. All mechanical constraints provide external forces necessary to satisfy the constraints. There may also be other external forces within the environment such as gravity and wind.

Finally, we also need to ensure dynamic correctness of the motion. We do this by constraining the acceleration of each DOF. Intuitively, we make sure that $F = ma$ holds for all degrees of freedom at all times. In this document we call such constraints *dynamics constraints* ($\mathbf{C}_d$). As long as these constraints are satisfied, we know that the resulting motion is physically possible, given the muscles' ability to generate forces.

When motion is defined in this way, it straightforwardly maps onto a non-linearly constrained optimization problem: we optimize the objective function $E(\mathbf{q}(t), t)$ parameterized in space and time, subject to the pose, mechanical and dynamics constraints:

$$\min_{\mathbf{q}(t)} E(\mathbf{q}(t), t) \qquad \text{subject to} \qquad \begin{cases} \mathbf{C}_p(\mathbf{q}(t), t) = 0 \\ \mathbf{C}_m(\mathbf{q}(t), t) = 0 \\ \mathbf{C}_d(\mathbf{q}(t), t) = 0 \end{cases} \tag{3}$$

This optimization is a variational calculus problem, as we solve for functions, not values. Such problems are solved by continuous optimization methods, which require computation of first derivatives of all constraints and the objective function. We use a sparse SQP [13] method to solve spacetime optimization problems.

The following sections describe specifics of determining muscles, constraints and the objective function that produce realistic motion and closely match the input animation.

### 5.2 Muscles

*Muscles* are the primary source of character locomotion. The biomechanics community has developed a number of complex muscle models, which closely match empirical data [29, 10, 3]. While these models tend to be very accurate, their complexity makes them difficult to differentiate and use in full body optimizations. Since our character model is drastically simplified, it would not make much sense to apply realistic muscles on simplified kinematic structure. Instead, we use simple structures that account for entire muscle groups, yet still induce forces onto DOFs similar to those of real muscles.

We use *generalized muscle forces* $Q$ to represent the abstract muscle. These muscles apply accelerations directly onto DOFs, much like robotic servo-motors positioned at joints apply forces on robotic limbs. Having a generalized muscle at each character DOF presents the minimum set of muscles that ensures the full range of character motion. Unfortunately, the ability to apply arbitrary generalized force onto each joint is a poor model of natural muscles. For example, sudden non-smooth muscle forces generate extremely jerky, unnatural motion much like motion generated by bang-bang controllers [25].

In addition, arbitrary impulse muscle forces tend to produce highly unstable spacetime optimization problems with poor convergence properties, because the problem becomes badly scaled. This becomes apparent when we compare the relative change in motion resulting from changing a single coefficient of a kinematic DOF $q_k(t)$ and a generalized muscle DOF $q_m(t)$ by the same fixed amount $\delta q$. Naturally, motion changes are orders of magnitude more drastic when we displace $q_m(t)$ coefficients, since muscles directly affect accelerations of many kinematic DOFs. This imbalance in sensitivity between the coefficients of kinematic and generalized muscle DOFs makes it difficult for any optimization methods to converge to a solution.

To circumvent the problems of simple generalized force muscles described above, yet still maintain a simple and differentiable muscle model, we use a damped servo model often used in robotic simulations [26, 19]. Each kinematic DOF $q_{k_i}$ has a corresponding damped generalized muscle force

$$Q_{k_i} = k_s(q_{k_i} - q_{m_i}) - k_d(\dot{q}_{k_i} - \dot{q}_{m_i}) \tag{4}$$

where $q_{m_i}$ is the additional muscle DOF that is often interpreted as the desired value of $q_{k_i}$. Differentiation with respect to DOFs and their velocities is straightforward. This formulation does not exhibit scaling problems since $q_{m_i}$ is of the same scale as $q_{k_i}$, and the velocity dependent damping encourages smoothness. To further ensure smooth muscle forces akin to those found in nature, we always include a muscle smoothness metric within the objective function (see Section 5.4.)

### 5.3 Constraints

Most of the pose and mechanical constraints fall out of the nature of the input motion. For example, in a run or walk sequence we specify mechanical point constraints during each period the foot is in contact with the floor. Similarly, a leg kick animation defines a pose constraint at the time the leg strikes the target. We avoid specifying extraneous constraints that are not essential for the input motion, since they reduce the flexibility of the subsequent spacetime editing process.

The model simplification process may also introduce additional constraints. For example, if the upper body was reduced to a mass point, the mass point DOFs need to be restricted to stay within the bounds of the upper body center of mass. This ensures that movement of mass points can never cause an improper human configuration.

Additional pose constraints can be introduced for further control during motion editing. For example, we can introduce a hurdle obstacle into the human jump motion environment, which forces the character to clear a certain height during flight.

### 5.4 Objective Function

There has been much research into the optimality of motion in nature [1, 2, 24]. We, however, avoid guessing the right objective function altogether. Instead, we rely on the fact that the starting motion is very close to the optimum. At first, our objective measured the deviation from the original motion ($E_d$) as described by Equation 1. We also include the muscle smoothness objective component $E_m = \ddot{\mathbf{q}}_m^2$ at all times. The spacetime objective is a weighted sum of the two objective components.

$$E = w_d \int E_d + \int E_m \tag{5}$$

Once the Newtonian constraint residuals become small, we gradually decrease $w_d$ all the way to zero. The existence of the $E_d$ component early in the optimization process prevents the optimization method from diverging from the initial motion until the spacetime constraints are satisfied (i.e. until the dynamics integrity of the motion has been established). This approach ensures that the spacetime minimization process stays near the input motion, while at the same time keeps the muscle forces smooth.

Upon convergence, we end up with a spacetime problem definition whose solution is very close to the original motion. With the spacetime optimization problem successfully constructed, the intuitive "control knobs" of the spacetime constraints formulation can be edited to produce a nearly inexhaustible number of different realistic motion sequences.

## 6 Spacetime Edit

A spacetime constraints parameterization provides powerful and intuitive control of many aspects of the dynamic animation: pose and environment constraints, explicit kinematic and dynamic properties of the character, and the objective function.

By changing existing constraints the user can rearrange foot placements both in space and time. For example, a human run sequence can be changed into a zig-zag run on an uphill slope by moving the floor contact constraints wider apart and progressively elevating them. The constraint timing can also be changed: extending the floor contact time duration of one leg creates an animation that gives the appearance of favoring one leg. We can also introduce new obstacles along the running path, producing new constraints that, for example, require legs to clear a specified height during the flight phase of the run. We can also affect the environment of the run by changing the gravity constant, producing a human running sequence on the moon surface, for example.

Changes can also be made on the character model itself. We can change the limb dimensions or their mass distribution characteristics, and observe the resulting dynamic change of the motion. We can remove body parts, restrict various DOFs to specific ranges, or remove DOFs altogether, effectively placing certain body parts in a cast. For example, we can create different gimpy run sequences by shortening the leg, making one leg heavier, reducing the range of motion for the knee DOF, removing the knee DOF. Various muscle properties of the character can also affect the look of transformed motion. We can limit the force output of the muscles, forcing the character to compensate by using other muscles.

Finally, the overall "feel" of the motion can be changed by adding additional appropriately weighted objective components. For example, we can produce a softer looking run by adding an objective component that minimizes floor impact forces. Or we can make the run look more stable by including a measure of static balance in the objective.

After each edit we re-solve the spacetime optimization problem and produce a new transformed animation. Since the optimization starting point is near the desired solution, and all dynamic constraints are satisfied at the outset, optimization converges rapidly. In practice, while the initial spacetime optimization may take more than 15 minutes to converge, the spacetime optimizations during the editing process take less than two minutes.

## 7 Motion Reconstruction

In order to create the transformed animation of the full character model, we reconstruct the final motion from the original motion and two simplified spacetime motions. We apply the transformation to the original sequence so that we modify the fundamental dynamic properties of motion, while preserving the specific intricate details in the original.

The reconstruction relies on both spacetime constraints and motion handles as described in Section 4.1. All spacetime constraints are mapped to their full character equivalents. For example, foot placement constraints are mapped onto foot constraints of the full character. Having completed the spacetime editing stage, we have three distinct sets of handles[1]

- original motion handles $\mathbf{h}_o(\mathbf{q}_o)$
- spacetime fit handles $\mathbf{h}_s(\mathbf{q}_s)$
- transformed spacetime handles $\mathbf{h}_t(\mathbf{h}_t)$

We define the final motion handles as

$$\mathbf{h}_f(\mathbf{q}_f) = \mathbf{h}_o(\mathbf{q}_o) + (\mathbf{h}_t(\mathbf{q}_t) - \mathbf{h}_s(\mathbf{q}_s)) \tag{6}$$

essentially displacing the original handles by the difference between the two spacetime solutions. Since the right side of the equation is known, it would seem that solving for the inverse-kinematics-like problem of finding $\mathbf{q}_f$ that satisfies equation 6 would complete the reconstruction. Unfortunately, the number of handles is *considerably smaller* than the number of DOFs in the full character, so this problem is highly under-determined, and we cannot directly solve for $\mathbf{q}_f$ without accounting for the extra DOFs.

We formulate the reconstruction process as a sequence of per-frame subproblems:

$$\begin{array}{ll} \min_{\mathbf{q}_f} & E_{dm}(\mathbf{q}_o, \mathbf{q}_f) \\ \text{subject to} & \left\{ \begin{array}{l} \mathbf{C}(\mathbf{q}) = 0 \\ \mathbf{h}_f(\mathbf{q}_f) = \mathbf{h}_o(\mathbf{q}_o) + (\mathbf{h}_t(\mathbf{q}_t) - \mathbf{h}_s(\mathbf{q}_s)) \end{array} \right. \end{array} \tag{7}$$

Simply stated, we follow the transformed handles and satisfy all constraints ($\mathbf{C}(\mathbf{q})$) while we try to be as close as possible to the original motion.

We first formulate a measure of closeness to the original motion. A simple objective function that measures the deviation of each DOF $E_{dd} = (\mathbf{q}_f - \mathbf{q}_o)^2$ produces undesirable results. Each DOF needs to be carefully scaled both with respect to what it measures (joint angles measure radians, translational DOFs measure meters), and with respect to its importance within the character hierarchy. For example, the change of the hip joint DOF affects the overall motion significantly more than the same amount of change applied to the ankle joint. In order to avoid these problems, we designed a completely new objective $E_{dm}$ that measures the amount of displaced mass between the two poses.

[1] For clarity, we omit the explicit time dependency of handles and DOFs.

## 7.1 Minimum Displaced Mass

Given two character poses described by the DOF values $\bar{\mathbf{q}}$ and $\mathbf{q}$ we compute the total amount of displaced mass $E_{dm}(\bar{\mathbf{q}}, \mathbf{q})$ when transforming from pose $\bar{\mathbf{q}}$ to pose $\mathbf{q}$. This metric is loosely analogous to the measurement of dynamic power consumption, with the exception that we compare two kinematic (not dynamic) states. Total displaced mass is the sum of mass displacements for each node $k$ in the hierarchy $E_{dm} = \sum_k E_k$.

We compute the node mass displacement $E_k$ as a body point $p_i$ displacement scaled with its mass $\mu_i$ integrated over all body points of the node $k$

$$E_k = \iiint_i \mu_i(\mathbf{p}_i - \bar{\mathbf{p}}_i)^2 \, dx\, dy\, dz,$$

where each "bar"-ed symbol refers to quantities computed at pose $\bar{\mathbf{q}}$.

Since we are only interested in the *relative* mass displacement, we compute the body positions invariant of the global rotation and translation. In other words, if

$$\mathbf{p}'_i = \mathbf{R}_0\mathbf{R}_1 \cdots \mathbf{R}_{j-1}\mathbf{R}_j\mathbf{x}_i$$

is the world space position of the body point $\mathbf{x}_i$ in the node $j$ of the character hierarchy, and transformation $\mathbf{R}_0$ contains the global rotation and translation of the hierarchy, we define

$$\mathbf{p}_i = \mathbf{R}_1 \cdots \mathbf{R}_{j-1}\mathbf{R}_j\mathbf{x}_i = \mathbf{W}_j\mathbf{x}_i$$

This notation allows us to simplify $E_k$

$$\begin{aligned} E_k &= \iiint_i \mu_i(\mathbf{W}_i\mathbf{x}_i\mathbf{W}_i\mathbf{x}_i - 2\mathbf{W}_i\mathbf{x}_i\overline{\mathbf{W}}_i\mathbf{x}_i + \overline{\mathbf{W}}_i\mathbf{x}_i\overline{\mathbf{W}}_i\mathbf{x}_i) \; dx\, dy\, dz \\ &= \mathrm{tr}\left(\mathbf{W}_i\mathbf{M}_i\mathbf{W}_i^T - 2\mathbf{W}_i\mathbf{M}_i\overline{\mathbf{W}}_i^T + \overline{\mathbf{W}}_i\mathbf{M}_i\overline{\mathbf{W}}_i^T\right) \\ &= \mathrm{tr}\left(\mathbf{W}_i\mathbf{M}_i(\mathbf{W}_i - 2\overline{\mathbf{W}}_i)^T\right) \end{aligned}$$

where tr() is a matrix trace operator and the mass matrix tensor $\mathbf{M}_i$ of node $i$ is computed as the integral over body points $\mathbf{x}_j$ of outer products scaled by the node mass $m_i$

$$\mathbf{M}_i = m_i \iiint_j \mathbf{x}_j\mathbf{x}_j^T \, dx\, dy\, dz.$$

Note that because $\overline{\mathbf{W}}_i\mathbf{M}_i\overline{\mathbf{W}}_i^T$ is a constant expression (it does not depend on $\mathbf{q}$) we remove it from the final expression.

We also compute derivatives with respect to kinematic DOFs

$$\begin{aligned} \frac{\partial E_k}{\partial q_j} &= \mathrm{tr}\left(\frac{\partial \mathbf{W}_i}{\partial q_j}\mathbf{M}_i(\mathbf{W}_i - 2\overline{\mathbf{W}}_i)^T + \mathbf{W}_i\mathbf{M}_i\frac{\partial \mathbf{W}_i^T}{\partial q_j}\right) \\ &= \mathrm{tr}\left(2(\mathbf{W}_i - \overline{\mathbf{W}}_i)\,\mathbf{M}_i\frac{\partial \mathbf{W}_i^T}{\partial q_j}\right) \end{aligned}$$

Both $E_k$ and $\frac{\partial E_k}{\partial q_j}$ can be computed efficiently by recursively computing the subexpressions $\mathbf{M}_i\mathbf{W}_i^T$ and $\mathbf{M}_i\frac{\partial \mathbf{W}_i^T}{\partial q_j}$ for each node in the hierarchy. We find that $E_{dm}$ performs extremely well as a measure of closeness between two motions.

Since the reconstruction process is performed separately for each frame the resulting motion may, on occasion, appear non-smooth. We correct this by defining intervals of animation where improved smoothness is required. The problem defined in Equation 7 is then solved collectively over the entire interval with the added smoothness objective $E_{smooth} = \ddot{\mathbf{q}}^2$.

| Jump | | Run | |
|---|---|---|---|
| Name | Minutes | Name | Minutes |
| Fitting | 21 | Fitting | 16 |
| Twist | 1.6 | Wide | 0.9 |
| Diagonal | 1.4 | Crossed | 1.3 |
| Unbalanced | 0.6 | Limp | 1.7 |
| Obstacle | 1.4 | Short-leg Limp | 1.9 |
| | | Moon | 1.5 |
| | | Neptune | 1.3 |

Figure 3: SGI Octane computation times for the run and the jump motion transformations.

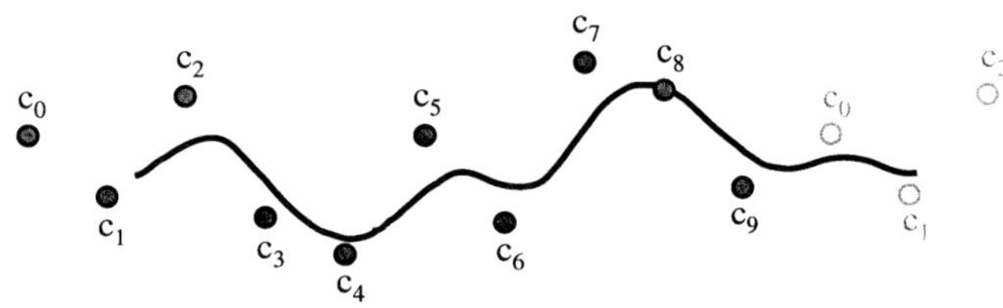


Figure 4: Representation of the cyclical B-spline DOFs.

# 8 Results

We have created two different motion libraries from which we generated a number of different animations. We used high detail (120Hz) motion capture data as input sequences. During the fitting stage, we used drastically different simplification approaches for the libraries in order to show the versatility of our algorithm.

All of the described motion sequences would be difficult to create with existing motion editing tools. While it is conceivable that a number of constraints could be introduced to enhance realism, for some sequences it would require an overwhelming amount of work, on par with creating a realistic motion sequence from scratch with keyframing. In contrast, our approach requires minimal number of intuitive changes for each transformed sequence.

## 8.1 Human Run

We extracted a single gait from a human run motion sequence, and made all DOFs cyclic so that the motion could be concatenated into a continuous run sequence of arbitrary length. We represented each DOF with a cyclical B-spline, where the first three coefficients influence the beginning and the end of the DOF values (Figure 4). This formulation forces endpoint values and their time derivatives to coincide.

In the character simplification stage we removed all hand, foot and elbow DOFs reducing the entire arm into one rigid object. Similarly, the foot and shin are represented with a single object. We also preserved only a few upper body DOFs. The torso, head and shoulders have been fused into a single object that has a quaternion ball joint at the waist. Each shoulder has a single Euler hinge joint that allows the arm to move back and forth. This is a significant reduction from the original configuration with a ball joint at each shoulder. Hip joints are the only ball joints that have been preserved during the simplification. (Figure 5). We should note that reducing the arms to a single object with only one DOF significantly restricts the amount of change each resulting motion can undertake. If we wanted to allow greater ability to alter the movement of arms, we would allow for additional DOFs at each shoulder.

In order to map the human motion onto the biped we introduce several types of handles:

**Foot contact points.** On the human character the floor contact points for each foot are located at the ball of the foot. On the

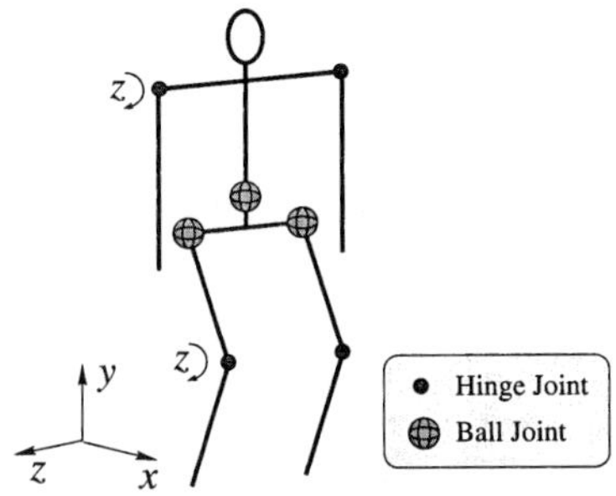


Figure 5: Biped: Simplified character for the human run motion library.

biped these points are shin endpoints. The handles are tracked throughout the entire animation, not just while the foot is on the ground.

**Character mass center.** The mass centers for the human and the biped follow the same trajectories.

**Upper body mass center.** We define the upper body as the character subtree rooted at the waist joint. Again, the mass centers follow the same trajectories.

**Arm mass centers.** The character subtree rooted at the shoulder joint is a three link chain for the human character and a single object for the biped. We correlate the mass centers for both the left and the right arm subtree.

**Torso orientation.** The body direction is tracked the orientation of the lower abdomen node.

**Shoulder orientation.** The shoulder orientation handle is defined as the unit vector formed by the two points located at the left and right shoulder.

We also defined two mechanical constraints corresponding to the foot-ground contact events. These constraints need to be mechanical since the floor exerts forces onto the body keeping the foot in place. We also constrained the forces produced by the floor constraints so that they are non-negative in the upward direction. This effectively indicates that the floor provides forces which prevent floor penetration, but not floor separation. In addition, we provided a muscle for each kinematic DOF of the biped character. The muscle coefficients were identical for each muscle: $k_s = 4.0$ and $k_d = -0.04$. Our experiments showed that different coefficients affected the speed of convergence for the optimization, but not the resulting motion itself.

We used the objective function described in Section 5.4. Optimizations during the spacetime model fit stage took about 21 minutes to compute on an SGI Octane. Once the spacetime model was completed we created numerous realistic animations by editing various spacetime formulation parameters.

**Wide Footsteps.** We repositioned the footprint mechanical constraints to be wider apart so that the character would have to leap significantly farther to the side at each step. We kept the constraint time intervals unchanged. Since each step now covered more distance, the overall resulting motion had leaps of smaller height (Figure 8). The appropriate change in the upper body orientation was apparent in the resulting motion.

**Crossed Footsteps.** We moved footprints to the opposite side of the body, forcing the character to twist at each step, criss-crossing the feet. Again we kept the constraint time intervals unchanged. We also introduced the "slippery floor" objective component, which penalized the component of the floor reaction forces in the floor plane. This effectively forced the character to rely less on the floor friction during landing.

**Moon Run.** In order to create a human run sequence on the moon, we reduced the gravity constant to $1.6m/s^2$, and we allowed for more time to elapse by applying a global time warp. The resulting run was slower and had much higher leaps appropriate for the low gravity environment.

**Neptune Run.** We also increased the Earth's gravity by tenfold to see how the running sequence would adjust to such extreme gravitational field[2]. Naturally, no human muscle forces could possibly produce a running motion under such extreme gravitational field. Consequently we removed any existing bounds on the muscle actuation forces. The resulting flight phase of the run was so low to the ground that the running character had the appearance of speed walking.

**Limp Run.** We removed the left knee DOF, creating the appearance of the leg being put in a cast. We also reduced the duration of the left footstep mechanical constraint, while we increased the duration of the right footstep. The advent of a straight leg introduced a new problem.

The stiff leg can move either to the outside or to the inside during the flight phase to avoid hitting the ground. These are two distinct local minima. If a leg were to move towards the inside, a more dynamically stable option, it would inevitably collide with the other leg. To prevent this, we included the objective component which penalizes for the closeness of the two foot points during the small time period just as the stiff leg leaves the ground. Effectively, we are biasing the solution towards the one where the legs do not go through each other. We do not need to include this objective during the entire animation since we only need to intervene at the specific point of the solution space bifurcation. We note that this problem would not be solved with the collision detection since the choice to go inside or outside occurs far before the actual collision. In the final motion sequence the character leans to the side and swings the right leg in a more dramatic fashion, creating a realistic (albeit painful) limp run.

**Short-Legged Limp Run.** In order to test the limits of character model modifications, we shortened the shin of the right leg and fixed the left knee DOF as in the *limp run*. We also kept the non-penetration inequality constraint for the feet during flight. The output running sequence has an extreme limp, with the leg in the cast swinging more to the side due to the shorter right leg. The motion has an extreme lean towards the shorter leg. The lean appears to be right on the edge of falling. The motion maintains the dynamic balance by significantly increasing the push-off forces of the shortened leg.

## 8.2 Broad Jump

We created the broad jump motion library to explore how far we could simplify the character without losing the dynamic essence of the jump. In order to demonstrate the power and the flexibility of the simplification tools, we used drastically different simplification approach than the one used on the human running motion (Figure 6).

[2] Neptune's gravitational acceleration is $88.98m/s^2$

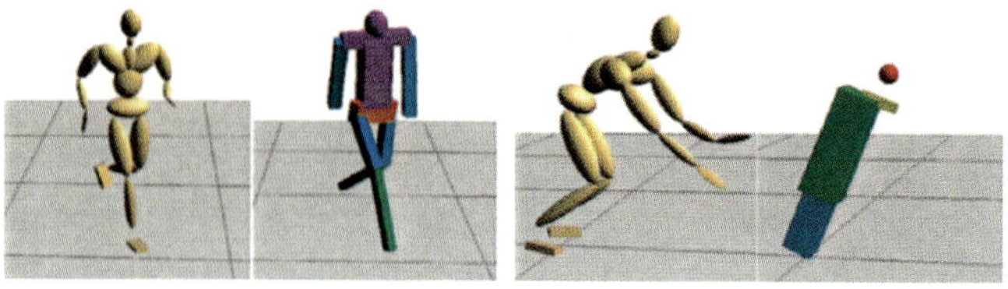

Figure 6: Full and simplified characters for the human run and broad jump.

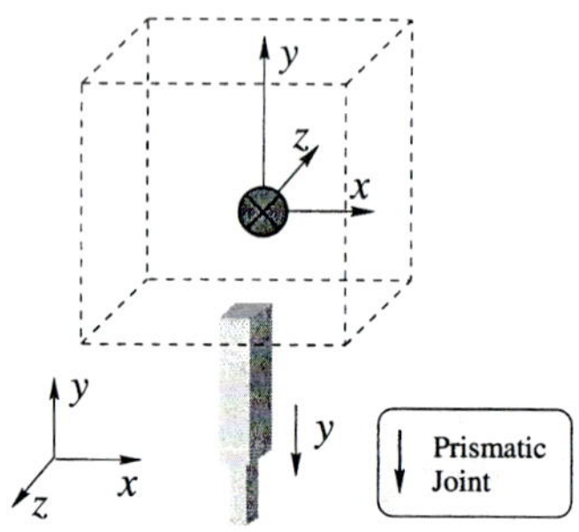


Figure 7: Hopper: Simplified character for the broad jump motion transformation.

The entire upper body structure is reduced to a single mass point. The mass point moves with three prismatic muscles that push off from the rest of the body (Figure 7). Since the legs move together during a broad jump, we turned them into a single leg. Although it was not necessary, we also turned the knee hinge joint into a prismatic joint, to show that even with this completely changed character model the dynamic properties of the broad jump are preserved. The simplified character (hopper) has *ten* DOFs of which six are the global position and orientation of the model. It does not contain any angular joints.

The broad jump motion sequence lasts more than two seconds, which is more than twice as long as the run gait cycle. Since the sequence duration is linearly proportional to the size of the problem it would appear that optimization would take considerably longer. However, due to fewer DOFs, the spacetime fitting optimization converges within 16 minutes. Subsequent transformation optimizations all finish within 2 minutes on an SGI Octane (Figure 3).

In order to fit the human broad jump motion onto the hopper we defined a number of handles:

**Foot position.** For the human character, we defined the foot handle as the midpoint between the two balls of the feet. The hopper's foot is located at the shin's endpoint.

**Leg extension.** For the human character, the leg extension is measured as a distance handle between the foot handle and the midpoint between the two hips. For the hopper, this handle is measured as a distance between the foot handle and the location of the prismatic hip.

**Body mass center.** For both the human and the hopper, the body mass center point is the center of mass for the entire hierarchy.

**Upper body mass center.** For the human character the upper body mass center is the center of mass of the subtree rooted at the lower abdomen. The hopper's upper body mass center is identical to the location of the upper body mass point.

**Torso orientation.** We preserved the body orientation by tracking the orientation of the lower abdomen character node. For both the human and the hopper character, this is the direction of the unit vector pointing down the forward direction in the local frame of the lower abdomen node.

In addition to handles, we also defined a number of constraints. Again, we used mechanical constraints for the foot-ground constraints. We also specified the initial and the final upright pose constraint. These constraints are needed to make the endpoints of the animation invariant. We also restricted the freedom of movement for the upper body mass point, with simple bound constraints in each dimension. Without these constraints, the upper body mass point would be free to move outside the range of motion of a human upper body center of mass. The rest of this section describes each transformed jump in more detail.

**Twist Jump.** We introduced the torso orientation pose constraint at the end of the animation, which mandates a 90 degree turn. The output motion clearly shows the change in the anticipation and the introduction of the body twist during the flight stage. The landing stage has also changed to accommodate the sideways landing position.

**Diagonal Jump.** We displaced the landing position to the side and constrained the torso orientation to point straight ahead at all times. This change realigned the push-off and anticipation stages in the direction of the jump. Since the jump length was increased, the entire resulting motion appears more impulsive.

**Obstacle Jump.** We raised the landing position and introduced a hurdle, which forces a raising of legs during the flight stage. As a result, the character push-off is more vertical, and the legs tuck in during the flight.

**Unbalanced Jump.** We removed the final pose constraint that imposed the upright position. In the resulting sequence, the character never uses its muscles to stand up upon landing, since this would require extra energy. Instead of straightening up the character tumbles forward giving the appearance of poor landing balance.

In conclusion, our experiments show that, despite the extreme simplification, the hopper spacetime model still encapsulates the realistic properties of the broad jump with surprising accuracy.

### 8.3 Limitations

Although our algorithm has been effective for a number of input motion sequences and for a wide spectrum of transformed motion animation sequences, a number of possibilities for improvement remain.

It appears that our methodology is best suited for the animation sequences containing high-energy, dynamic character movement. Other motion sequences that are more lethargic or kinematic, like picking up an object or getting up from the chair are not well suited for our dynamic transformation framework. Of course, it is still possible to apply our technique to such animations, but the benefits of a full-blown dynamics representation would not be large. In general, the non-realism for such motions is much less of an issue. The more a particular motion contains visible dynamic properties, the more suitable it would be for our motion transformation algorithm.

The main shortcoming of our approach is that large portions of the motion fitting algorithm stage are performed manually. We have found the simplification process quite intuitive. The simplification is performed only once per input motion sequence, so the effort spent by the motion library creator is amortized over the large number of possible transformed animation sequences. Nevertheless, automating this manual decision-making process would enable on-the-fly construction of a physically based spacetime formulation from an input animation.

Furthermore, specific decisions in the motion fitting stage directly affect the types of modifications that can be performed on the motion. For example, if we wanted to add a waving gesture to the human running sequence we could not simplify the waving arm to a single rigid object as we did in the biped model. Consequently, a modification of the simplification process might be necessary in order to achieve a transformation which was unforeseen during the motion fitting process. Such modifications break down the motion library concept.

Since all dynamics computations are performed on the simplified model, there is no guarantee that the reconstruction stage of the algorithm would preserve the dynamics properties. In fact, the final motion sequence is *not* physically realistic in the absolute sense, simply due to the fact that no dynamics computations are done on the full character model. Our algorithm preserves the *essential* physical properties of the motion. This makes our algorithm ill-suited for applications which require that a resulting motion contains all the forces involved in the character locomotion.

## 9 Conclusion

Our algorithm presents the first solution to the problem of editing captured motion that takes dynamics into consideration.

We also describe a novel methodology for mapping motion between characters with drastically different kinematic structures which broadens the applicability of motion capture data to animation of characters that do not exist in nature.

The paper also presents a method for control of complex dynamic systems with simpler ones. These ideas can be further developed into a realtime optimal robot control planner.

Lastly, these methods can be used for motion analysis in biomechanics and perhaps help prove the very ideas that motivated this algorithm.

## 10 Acknowledgements

This research was supported by the Schlumberger Foundation Fellowship and National Science Foundation award IRI9502464. The authors wish to thank R.J. Full for motivating certain biomechanics aspects of this work. We also thank Sebastian Grassia, Jovan Popović, Andrew Willmott, Elly Winner and our reviewers for the valuable comments during the preparation of this paper.

## References


[1] R. M. Alexander. Optimum walking techniques for quadrupeds and bipeds. *J. Zool., London*, 192:97–117, 1980.

[2] R. M. Alexander. Optimum take-off techniques for high and long jumps. *Phil. Trans. R. Soc. Lond.*, 329:3–10, 1990.

[3] K.N. An, B.M. Kwak, E.Y. Chao, and B.F. Morrey. Determination of muscle and joint forces: A new technique to solve the indeterminate problem. *J. of Biomech. Eng.*, 106:663–673, November 1984.

[4] David Baraff. Curved surfaces and coherence for non-penetrating rigid body simulation. In *Computer Graphics (SIGGRAPH '90 Proceedings)*, volume 24, pages 19–28, August 1990.

[5] David Baraff. Fast contact force computation for nonpenetrating rigid bodies. In *Computer Graphics (SIGGRAPH '94 Proceedings)*, July 1994.

[6] David Baraff and Andrew Witkin. Large steps in cloth simulation. In Michael Cohen, editor, *Computer Graphics (SIGGRAPH '98 Proceedings)*, pages 43–54, July 1998.

[7] R. Blickhan and R. J. Full. Similarity in multilegged locomotion: bouncing like a monopode. *J Comp. Physiol. A*, 173:509–517, 1993.

[8] Armin Bruderlin and Lance Williams. Motion signal processing. In *Computer Graphics (SIGGRAPH '95 Proceedings)*, pages 97–104, August 1995.

[9] Michael F. Cohen. Interactive spacetime control for animation. In *Computer Graphics (SIGGRAPH '92 Proceedings)*, volume 26, pages 293–302, July 1992.

[10] Roy D. Crowninshield and Richard A. Brand. A physiologivcallly based criterion of muscle force prediction in locomotion. *J. Biomechanics*, 14(11):793–801, 1981.

[11] Paolo de Leva. Adjustments to Zatsiorsky-Seluyanov's segment inertia parameters. *J. of Biomechanics*, 29(9):1223–1230, 1996.

[12] Tony DeRose, Michael Kass, and Tien Truong. Subdivision surfaces in character animation. In Michael Cohen, editor, *Computer Graphics (SIGGRAPH '98 Proceedings)*, pages 85–94, July 1998.

[13] P.E. Gill, M.A. Saunders, and W. Murray. SNOPT: An SQP algorithm for large-scale constrained optimization. Technical Report NA 96-2, University of California, San Diego, 1996.

[14] Michael Gleicher. Motion editing with spacetime constraints. In Michael Cohen and David Zeltzer, editors, *1997 Symposium on Interactive 3D Graphics*, pages 139–148. ACM SIGGRAPH, April 1997. ISBN 0-89791-884-3.

[15] Michael Gleicher. Retargeting motion to new characters. In *Computer Graphics (SIGGRAPH '98 Proceedings)*, pages 33–42, July 1998.

[16] Michael Gleicher and Peter Litwinowicz. Constraint-based motion adaptation. *The Journal of Visualization and Computer Animation*, 9(2):65–94, 1998.

[17] J. K. Hodgins and N. S. Pollard. Adapting simulated behaviours for new characters. *SIGGRAPH 97*, pages 153–162, 1997.

[18] Jessica K. Hodgins. Animating human motion. *Scientific American*, 278(3):64–69, March 1998.

[19] Jessica K. Hodgins, Paula K. Sweeney, and David G. Lawrence. Generating natural-looking motion for computer animation. In *Proceedings of Graphics Interface '92*, pages 265–272, May 1992.

[20] Zicheng Liu, Steven J. Gortler, and Michael F. Cohen. Hierarchical spacetime control. In *Computer Graphics (SIGGRAPH '94 Proceedings)*, July 1994.

[21] Matthew Moore and Jane Wilhelms. Collision detection and response for computer animation. In *Computer Graphics (SIGGRAPH '88 Proceedings)*, volume 22, pages 289–298, August 1988.

[22] M.G. Pandy, F. E. Zajac, E. Sim, and W. S. Levine. An optimal control model of maximum-height human jumping. *J. Biomechanics*, 23:1185–1198, 1990.

[23] D.J. Pearsall, J.G. Reid, and R. Ross. Inertial properties of the human trunk of males determined from magnetic resonance imaging. *Annals of Biomed. Eng.*, 22:692–706, 1994.

[24] A. Pedotti, V. V. Krishnan, and L. Stark. Optimization of muscle-force sequencing in human locomotion. *Math. Biosci.*, 38:57–76, 1978.

[25] L. S. Pontryagin, V. G. Boltyanskii, R. V. Gamkrelidze, and E. F. Mishchenko. *The Mathematical Theory of Optimal Processes*. John Wiley and Sons, New York, N.Y., 1962.

[26] Marc H. Raibert and Jessica K. Hodgins. Animation of dynamic legged locomotion. In *Computer Graphics (SIGGRAPH '91 Proceedings)*, volume 25, pages 349–358, July 1991.

[27] C. Rose, M. F. Cohen, and B. Bodenheimer. Verbs and adverbs: Multidimensional motion interpolation. *IEEE Computer Graphics & Applications*, 18(5), September – October 1998.

[28] C. Rose, B. Guenter, B. Bodenheimer, and M. Cohen. Efficient generation of motion transitions using spacetime constraints. In *Computer Graphics (SIGGRAPH '96 Proceedings)*, pages 147–154, 1996.

[29] A. Seireg and R. J. Arvikar. The prediction of muscular load sharing and joint forces in the lower extremities during walking. *J. Biomechanics*, 8:89–102, 1975.

[30] M. van de Panne. From footprints to animation. *Computer Graphics Forum*, 16(4):211–224, 1997.

[31] Michiel van de Panne and Eugene Fiume. Sensor-actuator networks. In *Computer Graphics (SIGGRAPH '93 Proceedings)*, volume 27, pages 335–342, August 1993.

[32] Michiel van de Panne and Eugene Fiume. Virtual wind-up toys. In *Proceedings of Graphics Interface '94*, May 1994.

[33] Andrew Witkin and Michael Kass. Spacetime constraints. In *Computer Graphics (SIGGRAPH '88 Proceedings)*, volume 22, pages 159–168, August 1988.

[34] Andrew Witkin and Zoran Popović. Motion warping. In *Computer Graphics (SIGGRAPH '95 Proceedings)*, August 1995.

Figure 8: Frames from the crossed footsteps, limp, wide footsteps run; and the diagonal, obstacle, unbalanced, and twist jump.

# Voice Puppetry

Matthew Brand

MERL — a Mitsubishi Electric Research Laboratory
201 Broadway, Cambridge, MA 02139

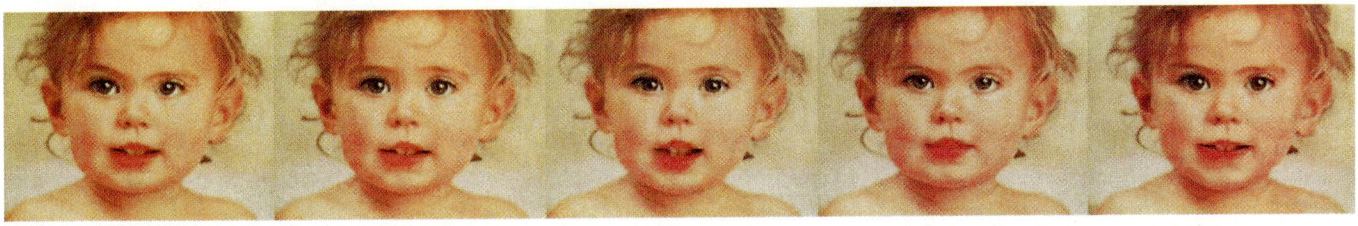

Frames from a voice-driven animation, computed from a single baby picture and an adult model of facial control. Note the changes in upper facial expression. See figures 5, 6 and 7 for more examples of predicted mouth shapes.

## Abstract

We introduce a method for predicting a control signal from another related signal, and apply it to *voice puppetry*: Generating full facial animation from expressive information in an audio track. The voice puppet learns a facial control model from computer vision of real facial behavior, automatically incorporating vocal and facial dynamics such as co-articulation. Animation is produced by using audio to drive the model, which induces a probability distribution over the manifold of possible facial motions. We present a linear-time closed-form solution for the most probable trajectory over this manifold. The output is a series of facial control parameters, suitable for driving many different kinds of animation ranging from video-realistic image warps to 3D cartoon characters.

**CR Categories:** I.3.7 [Computer Graphics]: Three-Dimensional Graphics and Realism—Animation; I.2.9 [Artificial Intelligence]: Robotics—Kinematics and Dynamics; I.4.8 [Image Processing and Computer Vision]: Scene Analysis—Time-varying images; G.3 [Mathematics of Computing]: Probability and Statistics—Time series analysis; E.4 [Data]: Coding and Information Theory—Data compaction and compression; J.5 [Computer Applications]: Arts and Humanities—Performing Arts

**Keywords:** Facial animation, lip-syncing, control, learning, computer vision and audition.

## 1 Face-syncing and control

As rendering techniques begin to deliver realistic-looking scenes, people are beginning to expect realistic-looking behavior. Therefore control is an increasingly prominent problem in animation. This is especially true in character facial animation, where good lip-syncing and dynamic facial expression are necessary to make a character look lively and believable. Viewers are highly attentive to facial action, quite sophisticated in their judgments of realism, and easily distracted by facial action that is inconsistent with the voice track.

We introduce methods for learning a control program for speech-based facial action from video, then driving this program with an audio signal to produce realistic whole-face action, including lip-syncing and upper-face expression, with correct dynamics, co-articulation phenomena, and ancillary deformations of facial tissues. In principle this method can be used to reconstruct any process from a related signal, for example, to synthesize dynamically correct 3D body motion from a sequence of shadows. We demonstrate with facial animation because of the obvious complexity of the process being modeled—the human face has many degrees of freedom, many nonlinear couplings, and a rather complicated control program, the mind.

Voice puppetry provides a low-cost quick-turnaround alternative to motion capture, with the additional flexibility that an actor's facial manner can be re-used over and over again to "face-sync" completely novel audio by other speakers and at other frame rates. It is fully automatic but an animator can intercede at any level to add detail. All algorithms have time complexity linear in the length of the input sequence; production time is slightly faster than utterance-time on a contemporary mid-level workstation.



## 2 Background

Psychologists and storytellers alike have observed that there is a good deal of mutual information between vocal and facial gesture [27]. Facial information can add significantly to the observer's comprehension of the formal [3] and emotional content of speech, and is considered by some a necessary ingredient of successful speech-based interfaces. Conversely, the difficulty of synthesizing believable faces is a widely-noted obstacle to producing acceptable digital avatars and animations. People are highly specialized for interpreting facial action; a poorly animated face can be disturbing and even can interfere with the comprehension of speech [20].

Lip-syncing alone is a laborious process: The voice track is dissected (often by hand) to identify features such as stops and vowels, then matched mouth poses are scheduled in the animation track, 2-10 per second. Because it can overwhelm production schedules, lip-syncing has been the focus of many attempts at quasi-automation. Nearly all lip-syncing systems are based on an intermediate phonemic representation, whether obtained by hand [23, 24], from text [9, 12, 1, 17] or, with varying degrees of success, via speech recognition [18, 28, 7, 8, 29]. Typically, phonemic or visemic tokens are mapped directly to lip poses, ignoring dynamical factors. Efforts toward dynamical realism have been heuristic and use limited contextual information (e.g., [10, 7]). Consider the problem of co-articulation—the interaction between nearby speech segments due to latencies in tissue motion. To date, all attempts at co-articulation have depended on heuristic formulæ and *ad hoc* smoothing methods. E.g., BALDY [9] is a phoneme-driven computer graphics head that uses hand-designed vocal co-articulatory models inspired by the psychological literature. Although VIDEO REWRITE [7] works by re-ordering existing video frames rather than by generating animations, it deserves mention because it partially models vocal (but not facial) co-articulation with triphones—phonemes plus one 1 unit of left and right context. The quality of a video rewrite is determined by the amount of video that is available to be provide triphone examples and how successfully it is analyzed; smoothing is necessary because triphones don't fully constrain the solution and no video will provide an adequate stock of triphones.

Considerable information can be lost when discretizing to phonemic or visemic representations. The international phonetic alphabet is often mistaken for a catalog of the sounds and articulations humans make while communicating; in fact, phonemes are designed only to provide the acoustic features thought necessary to distinguish pronunciations of higher, meaning-carrying language elements. Phonemic representations are useful for analysis but quite suboptimal for synthesis because they obliterate predictive relationships such as those of vocal prosody to upper facial gesture, vocal energy to gesture magnitude, and vocal phrasing to lip articulation. There have been attempts to circumvent phonemes and generate lip poses directly from the audio signal (e.g., [22, 19]) but these are limited to predicting instantaneous vowel shapes.

None of these methods address the actual dynamics of the face. Facial muscles and tissues contract and relax at different rates. There are co-articulations at multiple time-scales—50-250 milliseconds in the vocal apparatus [21], possibly longer on the face. Furthermore, there is evidence that lips alone convey less than half of the visual information that human subjects can use to disambiguate noisy speech [3]. Much of the expressive and emotional content of facial gesture occurs in the upper half of the face. This is not addressed at all in speech-driven systems; some text-driven systems attempt upper-face animation, usually via hand annotations or *ad hoc* rules that exploit clues to sentence meaning such as punctuation.

We propose a more realistic mapping from voice to face by learning a model of a face's *observed* dynamics during speech, then learning a mapping from vocal patterns to facial motion trajectories. Animation is accomplished by using voice information to steer the model. This strategy has several appealing properties:

- Voice is analyzed with regard to learned (equivalently, optimized) categories of facial gesture, rather than with regard to hypothesized categories of speech perception.
- A consistent probabilistic framework allows us to find the optimal face trajectory for a whole utterance, making full use of forward and backward context and avoiding unjustified shortcuts such as smoothing or windowing.
- Video is analyzed just once, for training; the resulting model can be used re-used to face-sync any other person or creature to novel audio.
- The puppet animates speech and non-speech sounds.
- It predicts full facial motion from the neck to the hairline.
- The output is a sequence of facial motion vectors that can be used to drive 2D, 3D, or image-based animations.

## 3 Modeling the facial behavior manifold

It is useful to think of control in terms of the face's true behavioral manifold—a surface of all possible facial pose and velocity configurations embedded in a high-dimensional measurement space, like crumpled paper in 3-space. Actual performances are trajectories over this manifold. Our learning strategy is to piecewise approximate this manifold with quasi-linear submanifolds, then glue together these pieces with transition probabilities. Approximation is unavoidable because there isn't enough information in a finite training set to determine the shape of the true manifold. Therefore our control model is a probabilistic finite state machine, in which each state has an "output" probability distribution over facial poses and velocities, including how they covary. E.g., for every instantaneous pose each state predicts a unique most likely instantaneous velocity. The states are glued together with a distribution of transition probabilities that specify state-to-state switching dynamics and, implicitly, expected state durations.

Formally, this is a *hidden Markov model* (HMM)—Markov because all the context needed to do inference can be summed up in a vector of current state probabilities, and hidden because we never actually observe the states; we must infer them from the signal. For this we have the Viterbi algorithm [13], which identifies the most likely state sequence given a signal. The related Baum-Welch algorithm [2] estimates parameter values, given training data and a prior specification of the model's finite state machine. Both algorithms are based on dynamic programming and give locally optimal results in linear time. For this reason, HMMs dominate the literature of speech and gesture recognition.

Unfortunately, even for very small problems such as individual phoneme recognition, finding an adequate state machine is a matter of guesswork. This limits the utility of HMMs for more complex modeling because the structure of the state machine (pattern of available transitions) is the most important determinant of a model's success. Structure also determines the machine's ability to carry context; the rate at which an HMM forgets context is determined by how easily it can transition between any two states.

Voice puppetry features two significant innovations in the theory of HMMs: In §4.2 we outline the mathematical basis for training algorithms that estimate both the HMM parameter values *and* the structure of its finite state machine. This substantially generalizes Baum-Welch. In §4.5 we introduce an efficient solution for synthesizing the most probable signal from a state sequence. This can be thought of as an inverse Viterbi. Together, these techniques allow us to turn HMMs—traditionally only good enough for classification—into models of behavioral manifolds that are accurate enough for synthesis. As such, they can be trained to predict any nonrandom time-varying signal from a coordinated signal.

## 4 System overview

Figure 1 schematically outlines the main phases of voice puppetry. In **training** (first line), video is analyzed to yield a probabilistic finite state machine; a mapping from states into regions of facial configuration space; and an occupancy matrix giving state probabilities for each frame of the training sequence. In

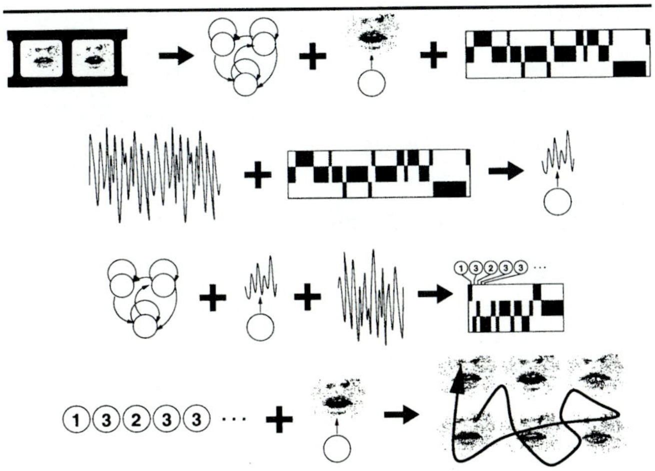

Figure 1: Schematic of the training, remapping, analysis, and synthesis steps of voice puppetry. See §4 overview.

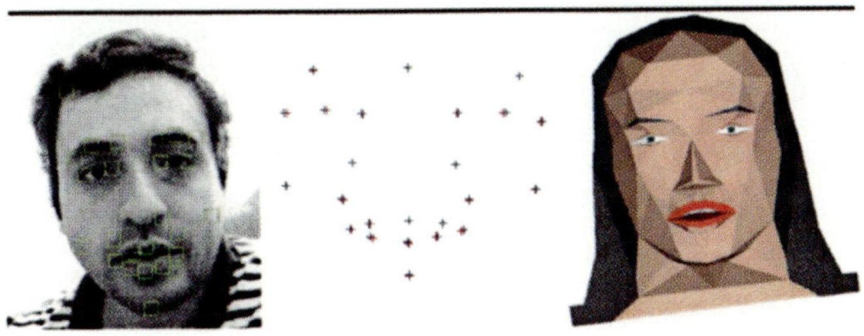

A. tracking B. reconstruction C. control

Figure 2: (A) Tracking of facial features for training data. See §4.1. (B) Voice-predicted facial feature locations (blue) superimposed over ground-truth locations (red). See §4.5. (C) A 3D model articulated via vertex motions. See §4.6.

**remapping** (second line), the occupancy matrix is combined with the synchronized audio to give each state a dual mapping into acoustic feature space. These two steps define a puppet. In **analysis** of novel audio (third line), the state machine and the vocal distributions are combined to form an HMM which is used to analyze control audio, resulting in a most likely facial state sequence. This is much like speech recognition, except that the units of interest are facial states rather than phonemes. In **synthesis** (last line), the system solves for a trajectory through facial configuration space that is optimal with regard to the state sequence and learned facial output distributions.

## 4.1 Signal processing

To obtain facial articulation data, we developed a computer vision system that simultaneously tracks many individual features on the face, such as corners and creases of the lips. Taking Hager's SSD texture-based tracker [15] as a starting point, we developed a mesh of such trackers to cover the face. Figure 2A shows the system tracking 26 points on a face. We assigned spring tensions to each edge connecting a pair of trackers, and the entire system was made to relax by simultaneously minimizing the spring energies and the residuals of the individual trackers. If a tracker falls off its landmark feature, spring forces from its neighbors tend to push it back into place. To estimate spring lengths and stiffnesses for a specific sequence, we run the video through the system, record the mean and variance of the distance between pairs of trackers, and use this to re-estimate the spring properties. A few repetitions sufficed to obtain stable and accurate tracking in our training videos. By tracking from two views we can also obtain stereo estimates of 3D depth. Our tracker can track on unmarked faces but depends on high-quality video to deliver facial texture, e.g., wrinkles or beard shadow. Since obtaining accurate data was more important than stress-testing our tracker, we marked low-texture facial areas and asked subjects to reduce head motions.

To obtain a useful vocal representation, we calculate a mix of LPC and RASTA-PLP audio features [16]. These are known to be useful to speech recognition and somewhat robust to variations between speakers and recording conditions. However, they are designed for phonemic analysis and aren't necessarily good indicators of facial activity. We also extract some prosodic features such as the formant frequencies and the energy in sonorant frequency bands.

Note that the puppet may work equally well with other representations of vocal and facial signals, and even different kinds of signals. Indeed, the success of our experiments notwithstanding, "Where in the signal is the information?" is still an open question for voice-driven facial animation and more generally for face perception and speech recognition.

## 4.2 Learning by entropy minimization

The mapping from vocal configurations to facial configurations is many-to-many: Many sounds are compatible with one facial pose; many facial poses are compatible with one sound. Were it not for this ambiguity, we could use a regression method such as a neural network or radial basis function network. Since much of the complexity arises from causal factors such as co-articulation, the best remedy is to use context from before and after the frame of interest. The fact that the disambiguating context has no fixed length or proximity to the current frame strongly recommends that we use a hidden Markov model, which (if properly trained) can make optimal use of context across an entire utterance, regardless of its length. An HMM uses its hidden states to carry contextual information forward and backward in time; a sufficiently powerful training algorithm will naturally assign some states to that task.

Since the hidden state changes in each frame under the influence of the observed data, it is important for the probability matrix governing state transitions to be sparse, otherwise a context-carrying state will easily transition to a data-driven state, and the contextual information will be lost. We have developed a framework for training probabilistic models that minimizes their internal entropy; in HMMs that translates to maximizing compactness, sparsity, capacity to carry contextual information, and specificity of the states. The last property is also important because conventionally trained HMMs typically express the content of a frame as a mixture of states, making it impossible to say that the system was in any one state.

We briefly review the entropic training framework here, and refer readers to [5, 4] for details and derivations. We begin with a dataset $\boldsymbol{X}$ and a model whose parameters and structure are specified by the vector $\boldsymbol{\theta}$. In conventional training, one guesses the sparsity structure of $\boldsymbol{\theta}$ in advance and merely re-estimates nonzero parameters to maximize the likelihood function $f(\boldsymbol{X}|\boldsymbol{\theta})$. In entropic training, we learn the size of the $\boldsymbol{\theta}$, its sparsity structure, and its parameter values simultaneously by maximizing the posterior probability given by Bayes' rule,

$$\boldsymbol{\theta}^* = \underset{\boldsymbol{\theta}}{\operatorname{argmax}} \left[ P(\boldsymbol{\theta}|\boldsymbol{X}) \propto f(\boldsymbol{X}|\boldsymbol{\theta}) P_e(\boldsymbol{\theta}) \right] \tag{1}$$

Bayes' rule tells us how the probability of a hypothesis $\boldsymbol{\theta}$ changes after we have seen some evidence $\boldsymbol{X}$. The key to entropic estimation is that we derive the prior probability of a hypothesis from its entropy,

$$P_e(\boldsymbol{\theta}) \propto e^{-H(\boldsymbol{\theta})} \tag{2}$$

where $H(\cdot)$ is an entropy measure defined on the model's parameters. Entropy measures uncertainty, thus we are seeking the least ambiguous model that can explain the data. The entropic prior can be understood as a mathematization of Occam's razor: Choose the simplest hypothesis that adequately explains the data. Simpler models are less ambiguous because they allow fewer alternatives. Entropic estimation has interpretations as optimal compression and free energy minimization [5], depending on the formulation of $H(\boldsymbol{\theta})$. The free energy interpretation derives from the differential entropy $H_{\mathcal{F}}(\boldsymbol{\theta}) = -\int P(\boldsymbol{X}|\boldsymbol{\theta}) \log P(\boldsymbol{X}|\boldsymbol{\theta})\, d\boldsymbol{X}$ or the more tractable expected entropy; algorithmic complexity theory recommends that we use the compression formulation, which upper-bounds $H_{\mathcal{F}}$ with the sum the entropies of the model's component distributions. For discrete-state Gaussian-output HMMs, the likelihood function and compression entropy are:

$$f(\boldsymbol{X}|\boldsymbol{\theta}) = \sum_{S} \prod_{t}^{T} \theta_{s(t)|s(t-1)} \mathcal{N}(\boldsymbol{x}_t; \boldsymbol{\mu}_{s(t)}, \boldsymbol{K}_{s(t)}), \tag{3}$$

$$H_C(\boldsymbol{\theta}) = \sum_{i} \sum_{j} \theta_{j|i} \log 1/\theta_{j|i} + \tfrac{1}{2} \log(2\pi e)^d |\boldsymbol{K}_i|, \tag{4}$$

where $\theta_{j|i}$ are transition probabilities and $\boldsymbol{\mu}_i, \boldsymbol{K}_i$ are the $d$-dimensional mean and covariance of the $i^{\text{th}}$ state's Gaussian output probability density function.

Given a factorizable model such as an HMM, the maximum *a posteriori* (MAP) problem decomposes into a separate equation for each independent parameter, each having its own entropic prior. In [5] we present exact solutions for a wide variety of such equations, yielding very fast learning algorithms; the case of HMMs is extensively treated in [4]. MAP estimation extinguishes excess parameters and maximizes the information content of the surviving parameters. Consequently, if we begin with a large fully-connected HMM, the training procedure whittles away all parts of the model that are not in accord with the hidden structure of the signal. This allows us to learn the proper size and sparsity structure of a model. Frequently, entropic estimation of HMMs recovers a finite-state machine that is very close to the mechanism that generated the data.

#### 4.2.1 Example

The topmost illustration in figure 4 shows an HMM entropically estimated from very noisy samples of a system that orbits in a figure-eight. The true system is a 2D manifold (phase and its rate of change) embedded in a 4D measurement space (observed 2D position and velocity); the HMM approximates this manifold with neighborhoods of locally consistent curvature in which velocity covaries linearly with position. Note that even though the data is noisy and has a continuation ambiguity where it crosses itself, the entropically estimated HMM recovers the deterministic structure of the system. A conventionally estimated HMM will get "lost" at the crossing, bunching states at the ambiguity and leaving many of them incorrectly over-connected, thus allowing multiple circuits on either loop as well as small circuits on the crossing itself. It is this additional concision and precision of entropic models makes them significantly outperform their conventionally estimated counterparts in traditional inference tasks, and enables novel applications such as voice puppetry.

### 4.3 Training and remapping

Using entropic estimation, we learn a facial dynamical model from the time-series of poses and velocities output by the vision system.

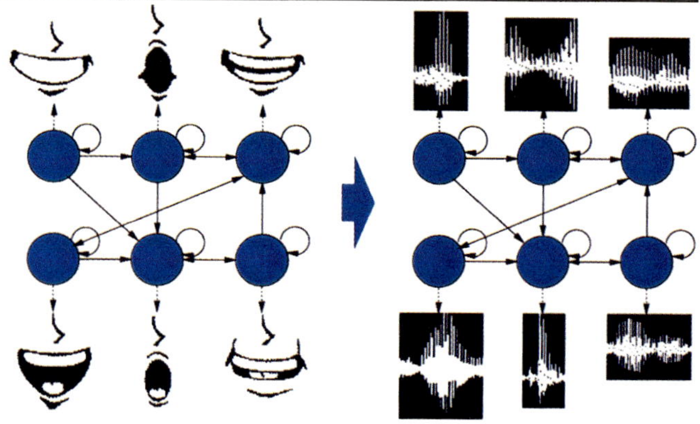

Figure 3: Reuse of the facial HMM's internal state machine in constructing the vocal HMM. Circles signify hidden states; arrows signify conditional probabilities; icons signify regions of facial and vocal configuration space contained within each output distribution. See §4.3.

The learning algorithm gives us an HMM plus an occupancy matrix $\gamma_{i,t}$ = Prob(HMM hidden state $i$ explains frame $t$) of the training video. We use $\gamma$ to estimate a second set of output probabilities, given each state, of the synchronized audio track. This associates audio features to each facial state, resulting in a new vocal HMM which has the dynamics of the face, but is driven by the voice (figure 3).

### 4.4 Analysis

Given a new vocal track, we apply the Viterbi algorithm to the vocal HMM to find the most likely sequence of predicted facial states. Although it is steered by information in the new vocal track, the Viterbi sequence is constrained to follow the natural dynamics of the face.

### 4.5 Synthesis

We use the facial output probabilities to make a mapping from the Viterbi states to actual facial configurations. Were we to simply pick the most probable configuration for each state—its mean face—the animation would jerk from pose to pose. Most phoneme- and viseme-based lip-sync systems address this problem by interpolating or splining between poses. This might ameliorate the jerkiness, but it is an *ad hoc* solution that ignores the face's natural dynamics.

A proper solution should yield a short, smooth trajectory that passes through regions of high probability density in configuration space at the right time—in our framework, a geodesic on the facial behavior manifold. Prior approaches to trajectory estimation typically involve optimizing an objective function having a likelihood term plus penalty terms for excess length and/or kinkiness and/or point clumpiness. The user must choose a parameterization and weighting for each term. This leads to variational algorithms that are often approximate and computationally intensive (e.g., [26]); often the objective function is nonconvex and one cannot tell whether the found optimum is global or mediocre.

Our current setting constrains the problem so significantly that a globally optimal closed-form solution is available. Because we model both pose and velocity, the facial output probabilities alone contain enough information to completely specify the smooth trajectory that is most consistent with the facial dynamics and a given facial state sequence.

The formulation is quite clean: We assume that each state has Gaussian outputs that model positions and velocities. For simplicity of exposition, we'll assume a single Gaussian per state, but our treatment trivially generalizes to Gaussian mixtures. Let $\boldsymbol{\mu}_i, \dot{\boldsymbol{\mu}}_i$ be the mean position and velocity for state $i$, and $\boldsymbol{K}_i^{-1} = \begin{bmatrix} \boldsymbol{K}_i^{xx} & \boldsymbol{K}_i^{x\dot{x}} \\ \boldsymbol{K}_i^{\dot{x}x} & \boldsymbol{K}_i^{\dot{x}\dot{x}} \end{bmatrix}$ be a full-rank covariance matrix relating positions and velocities in all dimensions. Furthermore, let $s(t)$ be the state governing frame $t$ and let $\boldsymbol{Y} = \{\boldsymbol{y}_1, \boldsymbol{y}_2, \boldsymbol{y}_3, \ldots\}^\top$ be the variable of interest, namely, the points the trajectory passes through at frame 1,2,3,... (All vectors in this paper are row-major.) We seek the maximum likelihood trajectory

$$\begin{aligned} \boldsymbol{Y}^* &= \operatorname*{argmax}_{\boldsymbol{Y}} \log \prod_t \mathcal{N}(\tilde{\boldsymbol{y}}_t; \boldsymbol{K}_{s(t)}) \\ &= \operatorname*{argmin}_{\boldsymbol{Y}} \sum_t \tilde{\boldsymbol{y}}_t \boldsymbol{K}_{s(t)}^{-1} \tilde{\boldsymbol{y}}_t^\top / 2 + c \end{aligned} \quad (5)$$

where $\mathcal{N}(\boldsymbol{x}; \boldsymbol{K})$ is the Gaussian probability of $\boldsymbol{x}$ given covariance $\boldsymbol{K}$; and $\tilde{\boldsymbol{y}}_t = [\boldsymbol{y}_t - \boldsymbol{\mu}_{s(t)}, (\boldsymbol{y}_t - \boldsymbol{y}_{t-1}) - \dot{\boldsymbol{\mu}}_{s(t)}]$ is a vector of the mean-subtracted facial position and velocity at time $t$. Eqn. 5 is a quadratic form having a single global optimum. Setting its derivative to zero yields a block-banded system of linear equations:

$$\begin{bmatrix} \boldsymbol{K}_{s(t)}^{xx} + \boldsymbol{K}_{s(t)}^{\dot{x}x} \\ \boldsymbol{K}_{s(t)}^{\dot{x}x} + \boldsymbol{K}_{s(t)}^{\dot{x}\dot{x}} \\ \boldsymbol{K}_{s(t+1)}^{\dot{x}x} + \boldsymbol{K}_{s(t+1)}^{\dot{x}\dot{x}} \\ \boldsymbol{K}_{s(t+1)}^{\dot{x}x} \\ \boldsymbol{K}_{s(t+1)}^{\dot{x}\dot{x}} \end{bmatrix}^\perp \begin{bmatrix} \boldsymbol{y}_t - \boldsymbol{\mu}_{s(t)} \\ \boldsymbol{y}_t - \boldsymbol{y}_{t-1} - \dot{\boldsymbol{\mu}}_{s(t)} \\ \boldsymbol{y}_t - \boldsymbol{y}_{t+1} \\ \boldsymbol{\mu}_{s(t+1)} \\ \dot{\boldsymbol{\mu}}_{s(t+1)} \end{bmatrix}^{\perp\top} = \boldsymbol{0} \quad (6)$$

where the block-transpose $\begin{bmatrix} \boldsymbol{A} \boldsymbol{B} \\ \boldsymbol{C} \boldsymbol{D} \end{bmatrix}^\perp = \begin{bmatrix} \boldsymbol{A} \boldsymbol{C} \\ \boldsymbol{B} \boldsymbol{D} \end{bmatrix} \neq \begin{bmatrix} \boldsymbol{A}^\top \boldsymbol{C}^\top \\ \boldsymbol{B}^\top \boldsymbol{D}^\top \end{bmatrix}$ and $\boldsymbol{K}_i^{\dot{x}x} = (\boldsymbol{K}_i^{x\dot{x}} + \boldsymbol{K}_i^{\dot{x}x})/2$. For $T$ frames and $D = \dim(\boldsymbol{y}_t)$ dimensions, the system can be LU-decomposed and solved in time $O(TD^3)$ [14, §4.3.1]. By scaling the velocity terms, one may also solve for this trajectory at frame rates other than that of the training video.

Figure 4 shows various ways of estimating trajectories from an HMM model of the manifold of motion in a figure-eight. Increasing the number of HMM states improves the quality of the synthesized trajectory, provided there is sufficient data to support estimates of the additional parameters. Entropic estimation will automatically remove insufficiently supported parameters.

Eqn. 5 is only justified when the Viterbi sequence $\mathcal{V} = \{s(1), s(2), \ldots, s(T)\}$ strongly dominates the distribution of probable sequences. The Viterbi sequence, while most likely, may only represent a small fraction of the total probability mass—there may be thousands of slightly different state sequences that are nearly as likely. If this were to happen in the voice puppet, $\mathcal{V}$ would be a very poor representation of the relevant information in the audio, and the animation quality would suffer greatly. Consequently, we found that voice puppetry works very poorly with conventionally estimated HMMs. These problems are virtually banished with entropically estimated models because entropy minimization concentrates the probability mass on the optimal Viterbi sequence. (see §5, paragraph 2 for an empirical example). In [6] we present a full Bayesian MAP solution which considers *all* possible state sequences and show that it and the maximum likelihood solution are only valid for low-entropy models, where they give almost identical results inferring 3D full-body pose and motion from shadows.

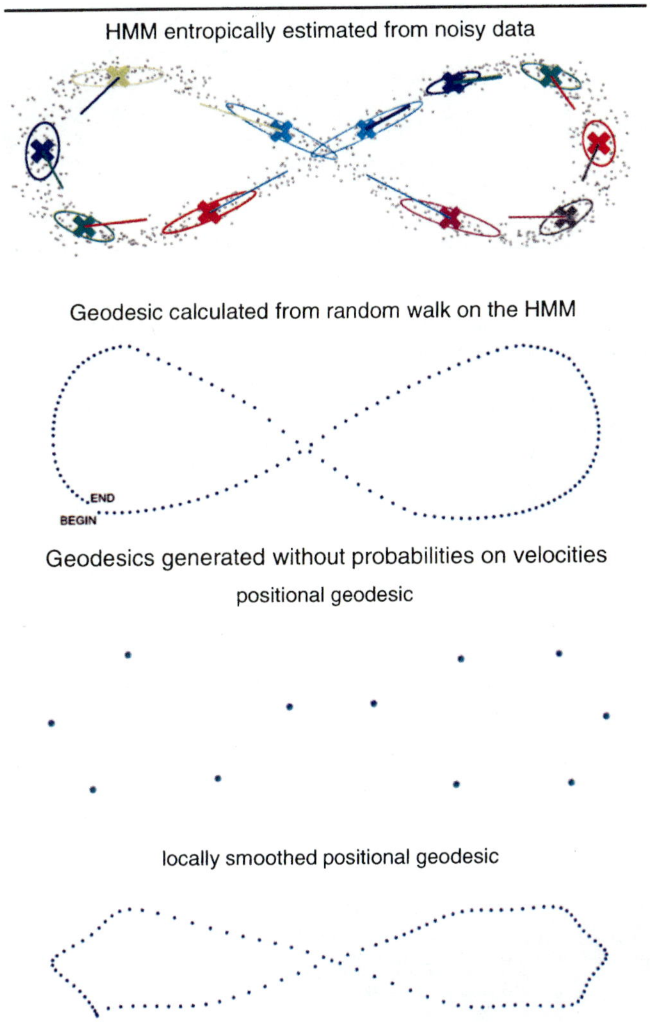


Figure 4: TOP: An entropically estimated HMM projected onto synthetic training data. An × indicates the mean output of a state; an ellipse indicates its covariance; and arcs indicate allowable transitions. See §4.2.1. SECOND: A trajectory generated using our method based on positional and velocity distributions. The state sequence is obtained from a random walk through the HMM. (Irregularities are due to variations between state dwells in the random walk.) See §4.5. THIRD: If one solves for a geodesic using just positional constraints, all control points clump on the means. BOTTOM: Traditionally, clumpiness is ameliorated by smoothing terms, but the trajectory is still unacceptable. (This could be improved if one is able and willing to hand-tune the objective function.)

### 4.6 Animation

The puppet synthesizes would-be facial tracking data—what most likely would have been seen had the training subject produced the input vocalization. This can be used to control a 3D animated head model or to warp a 2D face image to give the appearance of motion. Or, by learning an inverse mapping from tracking data back to training video, we can directly synthesize new video. We chose a versatile solution which provides a surprisingly good illusion—a 2D image such as a photograph is texture-mapped onto a 3D model having a low triangle count—roughly 200 (figure 2C). Deformations of the 3D model give a naturalistic illusion of facial motion while the smooth shading of the image gives the illusion of smooth surfaces. The deformations can be applied directly by moving vertices according to puppet output, or indirectly by projecting synthesized facial configurations onto a basis set of

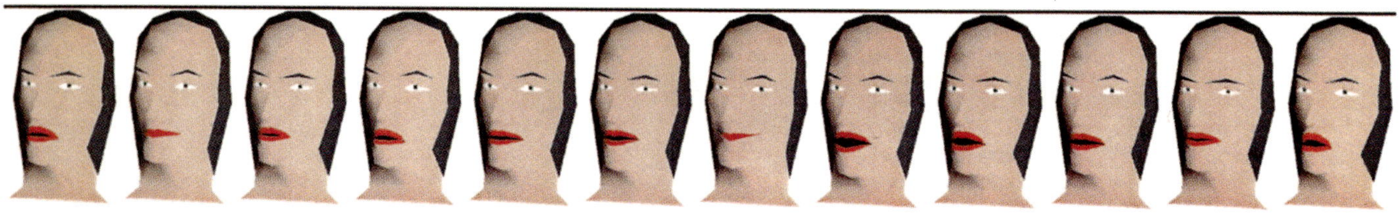

Figure 5: Visualization of the mean configuration for some of the learned states. Dynamical content is not shown.

motion vectors (a.k.a. facial action units) that are defined on the model (e.g., [25]). The latter approach has the advantage of giving us full 3D control of a model even when the training data is only 2D. Action units are also commonly used for facial animation and image coding, e.g., MPEG-4.

# 5 Examples

We recorded subjects telling a variety of children's stories and processed 180 seconds of video, tracking 25 features on the face, mostly around the mouth and eyes. Roughly 60 seconds of the data were modeled with a 26-state entropically estimated HMM. Many of the learned states had mean outputs resembling visemes and common facial morph targets, augmented with dynamical content (figure 5). The perplexity (average branching factor) of the learned facial state machine was 2.08, indicating that the model is carrying context effects such as co-articulation an average of $\approx 4.5$ frames ($\approx$ 150 milliseconds) in either temporal direction[1]. In practice, we have seen this model carry context over 330 milliseconds, indicating that the system has discovered facial co-articulation phenomena that last longer than vocal co-articulations (and have yet to be mentioned in the speech psychology literature). These properties are due to entropic estimation; an HMM conventionally trained from the same initialization carried context an average of slightly under 2 frames.

Figure 6 shows this model animating Mt. Rushmore under the control of novel voice data. In this synthesis task, the predicted face state sequence had an entropy rate of 0.0315. This means that roughly one out of every 22 predictions in the facial state sequence had a single plausible alternative. By contrast, a conventionally trained HMM yielded an entropy rate of 0.875—roughly 2.4 plausible alternatives for *every* prediction in the facial state sequence. As expected, the most probable sequence from the conventionally estimated HMM yielded an unacceptably degraded animation, while the properly weighted combination of all such sequences produced only a slight improvement.

## 5.1 Evaluation via error and coding measures

Remarkably, we found that the training data could be quite accurately reconstructed (via the model) from its most probable state sequence. After string compression, this works out to facial motion coding of less than 4 bits per frame. Reconstruction of facial motion from the vocal track was almost as good. We quantified this with a squared error measure of divergence between ground-truth ($\boldsymbol{x}$) and reconstructed ($\boldsymbol{y}$) facial motion vectors, weighted to penalize motions in the wrong direction:

$$\mathrm{Err}(\boldsymbol{x},\boldsymbol{y}) = (\boldsymbol{x}-\boldsymbol{y})(\boldsymbol{x}-\boldsymbol{y})^{\top}/(\boldsymbol{x}+\boldsymbol{y})(\boldsymbol{x}+\boldsymbol{y})^{\top} \quad (7)$$

We reconstructed facial motion from (1) most probable state sequences of the ground-truth motion; (2) the vocal track; and (3) a minimum squared error coding of the data via activations of action units of the facial action coding system (FACS[2] [11, 25]). The table below shows mean errors as well as coding costs for storing and transmitting animations:

| coding | model Kbytes | bits/ frame | reconstruction error train | test |
|---|---|---|---|---|
| state sequence | $\approx 1.1$ | $\approx 4$ | 0.1255 | 0.1698 |
| vocal features | $\approx 2.0$ | $<500$ | 0.1731 | 0.2115 |
| FACS | $\approx 0.6$ | $>600$ | 0.4735 | 0.4692 |

The same ranking obtains if one switches to an unweighted squared-error measure. Note that synthesis from voice is significantly better than the reconstruction from action unit codings, indicating that the learned representation of the HMM is superior to the psychologically-motivated but heuristic representation of FACS.

We obtained even better results by training and using separate models for the lower and upper face (e.g., eyes and up). Surprisingly, even with a single model, motion in the upper face is more accurately predicted than motion around the mouth. One possible explanation is that upper facial behavior is a much less complicated phenomenon, even though it seems less directly linked to vocal behavior.

## 5.2 Evaluation by naive viewers

In order to judge the subjective quality of the animations, we designed a set of blind trials in which naive observers tried to distinguish synthesized from real facial motion. We took 1500 frames of tracked video that had not been used for training, set the tracking data aside, and synthesized new facial motion from the audio. We generated animations from both the synthesized motion and the "ground-truth" tracked motion, broke each animation into three segments, and presented all segments in random order to naive observers. The subjects were asked to select the "more natural" animations. Three observers consistently preferred the synthesized animation; three consistently preferred the ground-truth animation; and one preferred the ground-truth animation in two out of three segments. This modest experiment indicates that while true and synthesized facial action can be distinguished (real facial action is more varied); they are almost equally plausible to naive viewers.

# 6 Discussion

The main determinant of puppetry quality is the extent and variety of speech behavior in the training video. With 12 seconds of

[1] More precisely, $\log_{2.08} 26 \approx 4.5$ is the average number of transitions the state machine takes to go between any two states. We use this as a heuristic indicator of the model's memory. The actual amount of time the HMM takes to forget that it was in any particular state is a function of the data and the output distributions, and can be determined empirically from differences between the most likely state sequence and the set of states that are most likely to output the observed data.

[2] FACS, like phonemes and visemes, was designed for psychological analysis, but has been pressed into service for modeling and coding by computer scientists.

Figure 6: President Jefferson at rest and face-syncing to novel audio. Animation runs from neck to hairline. On contemporary hardware, compute time is less than the duration of the utterance.

training video we can produce tolerable animation; with 3 minutes we approach video-realism. The quality of puppeteering degrades gracefully as we increase acoustic noise levels or change to microphones or speakers unlike those in the training set. E.g., when trained on adult men, the puppet has some difficulty with children's and women's voices. We would recommend separate models for each group because of large differences in facial manner and spectral profiles between gender and age groups. It is possible to train one large model on all groups, but this requires more data than needed for separate models.

We have used French-trained puppets to produce English animations and English-trained puppets to produce Russian and Japanese animations. This compares favorably with phoneme-based systems, which typically use an English subset of phonemes. We have also found it reasonably easy, via projection, to animate heads with substantially varied geometries, e.g., toddlers and animals (figure 7).

We currently train with NTSC 29.97Hz video—a sampling rate too low to reliably capture fast facial transients such as plosives and blinks. The puppet can infer most plosives from context, but true film-quality puppetry will probably require higher-resolution training data, tracking a hundred or so points on the face over tens of minutes of 100Hz video. In addition, we currently make no effort to track and model the shape of the tongue; we are currently looking into using archival X-ray films to complement the training set. Finally, for photo-realism we must handle wrinkling and changes in skin translucency; we are exploring variants of voice puppetry that predict changes in both the facial geometry and the texture map.

The voice puppet is fully automatic. Animators, on the other hand, want full control of an animation. Aside from adjusting the raw vertex motions predicted by the voice puppet, there are several ways an animator could intercede to customize the animation. Here we list a few, beginning with the easiest: (1) Choose from a palette of puppets, each trained on a different style of speech and facial mannerisms. (2) Increase the variance of the training data, which produces a cartoon-like exaggerated range of motion in facial expression. (3) Add whole-face expression vectors (e.g., a grin) to those generated by the voice puppet. (4) Edit the facial state sequence. Options 3&4 are analogous to the present-day practices of superimposing multiple morph targets and editing a phoneme sequence, respectively.

## 7 Summary

Voice puppetry combines the voice, face, and facial mannerisms of three different people into a realistic speaking animation. Given novel audio, the system accurately generates lip and whole-face motions in the style of the training performance, even reproducing subtle effects such as co-articulation. This purely data-driven approach stands on two innovations: An entropy-minimization algorithm learns extremely compact and accurate probabilistic models of the facial behavior manifold from training video; a closed-form solution for geodesics on this manifold yields facial motion sequences that are optimally compatible with new audio and with learned facial behavior.

## 8 Acknowledgments

Thanks to interns and code contributors: The HMM and geodesic code was optimized by Ken Shan. The face renderer [25] was graciously provided to us by Robert Forchheimer, and modified for real-time animation by Ilya Baran. The texture tracker [15] was obtained from Greg Hager and modified to include mesh constraints by Ken Shan and Jon Yedidia. Ilya Baran, Jane Maduram, and Ken Mathews performed for training data and helped to process and analyze it. Thanks to the Rickover Science Institute for providing these talented high school interns. The acoustic analysis code [16] was obtained from the Berkeley International Computer Science Institute web site. Finally, thanks to anonymous reviewers and to colleagues who previewed this work at the 1998 Workshop on Perceptual User Interfaces for their comments and questions.

## References

[1] J.E. Ball and D.T. Ling. Spoken language processing in the Persona conversational assistant. In *Proc. ESCA Workshop on Spoken Dialogue Systems*, 1995.

[2] L. Baum. An inequality and associated maximization technique in statistical estimation of probabilistic functions of Markov processes. *Inequalities*, 3:1–8, 1972.

[3] C. Benoit, C. Abry, M.-A. Cathiard, T. Guiard-Marigny, and T. Lallouache. Read my lips: Where? How? When? And so... What? In *8th Int. Congress on Event Perception and Action*, Marseille, France, July 1995. Springer-Verlag.

[4] M. Brand. Structure discovery in conditional probability models via an entropic prior and parameter extinction. *Neural Computation (accepted 8/98)*, October 1997.

[5] M. Brand. Pattern discovery via entropy minimization. In *Proc. Artificial Intelligence and Statistics #7*, Morgan Kaufmann Publishers. January 1999.

[6] M. Brand. Shadow puppetry. Submitted to *Int. Conf. on Computer Vision, ICCV '99*, 1999.

[7] C. Bregler, M. Covell, and M. Slaney. Video Rewrite: Driving visual speech with audio. In *Proc. ACM SIGGRAPH '97*, 1997.

[8] T. Chen and R. Rao. Audio-visual interaction in nultimedia communication. In *Proc. ICASSP '97*, 1997.

Figure 7: The many faces of a voice puppet.


[9] M.M. Cohen and D.W. Massaro. Modeling coarticulation in synthetic visual speech. In N.M. Thalmann and D. Thalmann, editors, *Models and Techniques in Computer Animation.* Springer-Verlag, 1993.

[10] S. Curinga, F. Lavagetto, and F. Vignoli. Lip movement sythesis using time delay neural networks. In *Proc. EUSIPCO '96*, 1996.

[11] P. Ekman and W.V. Friesen. *Manual for the Facial Action Coding System.* Consulting Psychologists Press, Inc., Palo Alto, CA, 1978.

[12] T. Ezzat and T. Poggio. MikeTalk: A talking facial display based on morphing visemes. In *Proc. Computer Animation Conference*, June 1998.

[13] G.D. Forney. The Viterbi algorithm. *Proc. IEEE*, 6:268–278, 1973.

[14] G.H. Golub and C.F. van Loan. *Matrix Computations.* Johns Hopkins, 1996. 3rd edition.

[15] G. Hager and K. Toyama. The XVision system: A general-purpose substrate for portable real-time vision applications. *Computer Vision and Image Understanding*, 69(1) pp. 23–37. 1997.

[16] H. Hermansky and N. Morgan. RASTA processing of speech. *IEEE Transactions on Speech and Audio Processing*, 2(4):578–589, October 1994.

[17] I. Katunobu and O. Hasegawa. An active multimodal interaction system. In *Proc. ESCA Workshop on Spoken Dialogue Systems*, 1995.

[18] J.P. Lewis. Automated lip-sync: Background and techniques. *J. Visualization and Computer Animation*, 2:118–122, 1991.

[19] D.F. McAllister, R.D. Rodman, and D.L. Bitzer. Speaker independence in lip synchronization. In *Proc. CompuGraphics '97*, December 1997.

[20] H. McGurk and J. MacDonald. Hearing lips and seeing voices. *Nature*, 264:746–748, 1976.

[21] K. Stevens (MIT). Personal communication., 1998.

[22] S. Morishima and H. Harashima. A media conversion from speech to facial image for intelligent man-machine interface. *IEEE J. Selected Areas in Communications*, 4:594–599, 1991.

[23] F.I. Parke. A parametric model for human faces. Technical Report UTEC-CSc-75-047, University of Utah, 1974.

[24] F.I. Parke. A model for human faces that allows speech synchronized animation. *J. Computers and Graphics*, 1(1):1–4, 1975.

[25] M. Rydfalk. CANDIDE, a parameterised face. Technical Report LiTH-ISY-I-0866, Department of Electrical Engineering, Linköping University, Sweden, October 1987. Java demo available at http://www.bk.isy.liu.se/candide/candemo.html.

[26] L.K. Saul and M.I. Jordan. A variational principle for model-based interpolation. Technical report, MIT Center for Biological and Computational Learning, 1996.

[27] E.F. Walther. *Lipreading.* Nelson-Hall Inc., Chicago, 1982.

[28] K. Waters and T. Levergood. DECface: A system for synthetic face applications. *Multimedia Tools and Applications*, 1:349–366, 1995.

[29] E. Yamamoto, S. Nakamura, and K. Shikano. Lip movement synthesis from speech based on hidden Markov models. In *Proc. Int. Conf. on automatic face and gesture recognition, FG '98*, pages 154–159, Nara, Japan, 1998. IEEE Computer Society.

# Cognitive Modeling:
## Knowledge, Reasoning and Planning for Intelligent Characters

John Funge
Intel Corporation

Xiaoyuan Tu (涂晓媛)
Intel Corporation

Demetri Terzopoulos
University of Toronto

## Abstract

Recent work in behavioral animation has taken impressive steps toward autonomous, self-animating characters for use in production animation and interactive games. It remains difficult, however, to *direct* autonomous characters to perform specific tasks. This paper addresses the challenge by introducing *cognitive modeling*. Cognitive models go beyond behavioral models in that they govern what a character knows, how that knowledge is acquired, and how it can be used to plan actions. To help build cognitive models, we develop the cognitive modeling language CML. Using CML, we can imbue a character with domain knowledge, elegantly specified in terms of actions, their preconditions and their effects, and then direct the character's behavior in terms of goals. Our approach allows behaviors to be specified more naturally and intuitively, more succinctly and at a much higher level of abstraction than would otherwise be possible. With cognitively empowered characters, the animator need only specify a behavior outline or "sketch plan" and, through reasoning, the character will automatically work out a detailed sequence of actions satisfying the specification. We exploit interval methods to integrate sensing into our underlying theoretical framework, thus enabling our autonomous characters to generate action plans even in highly complex, dynamic virtual worlds. We demonstrate cognitive modeling applications in advanced character animation and automated cinematography.

**Keywords:** Computer Animation, Character Animation, Intelligent Characters, Behavioral Animation, Cognitive Modeling, Knowledge, Sensing, Action, Reasoning, Planning

**CR Categories:** I.3.7 [Computer Graphics]: Three-Dimensional Graphics and Realism—Animation; I.2.4 [Artificial Intelligence]: Knowledge Representation Formalisms and Methods—Representation languages, Modal logic, Temporal logic, Predicate logic; I.2.8 [Artificial Intelligence]: Problem Solving, Control Methods, and Search—Graph and tree search strategies, Heuristic methods; I.6.8 [Simulation and Modeling]: Types of Simulation—Animation

[0]For contact information see www.cs.toronto.edu/∼{funge,tu,dt}.



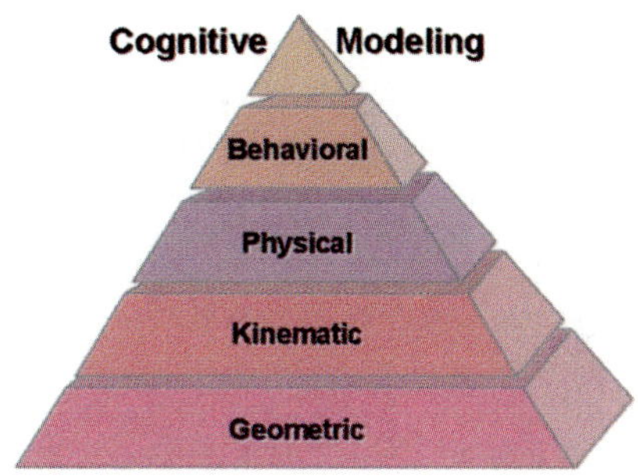


Figure 1: Cognitive modeling is the new apex of the CG modeling hierarchy.

## 1 Making Them Think

Modeling for computer animation addresses the challenge of automating a variety of difficult animation tasks. An early milestone was the combination of geometric models and inverse kinematics to simplify keyframing. Physical models for animating particles, rigid bodies, deformable solids, fluids, and gases have offered the means to generate copious quantities of realistic motion through dynamic simulation. Biomechanical modeling employs simulated physics to automate the lifelike animation of animals with internal muscle actuators. Research in behavioral modeling is making progress towards self-animating characters that react appropriately to perceived environmental stimuli. It has remained difficult, however, to *direct* these autonomous characters so that they satisfy the animator's goals. Hitherto absent in this context has been a substantive apex to the computer graphics modeling pyramid (Fig. 1), which we identify as *cognitive modeling*.

This paper introduces and develops cognitive modeling for computer animation and interactive games. Cognitive models go beyond behavioral models in that they govern what a character knows, how that knowledge is acquired, and how it can be used to plan actions. Cognitive models are applicable to directing the new breed of highly autonomous, quasi-intelligent characters that are beginning to find use in production animation and interactive computer games. Moreover, cognitive models can play subsidiary roles in controlling cinematography and lighting.

We decompose cognitive modeling into two related sub-tasks: *domain knowledge specification* and *character direction*. This is reminiscent of the classic dictum from the field of artificial intelligence (AI) that tries to promote modularity of design by separating out knowledge from control. Domain (knowledge) specification involves administering knowledge to the character about its world and how that world can change. Character direction involves instructing the character to try to behave in a certain way within its world in order to achieve specific goals. Like other advanced modeling tasks, both of these steps can be fraught with difficulty unless animators are given the right tools for the job. To this end, we develop the cognitive modeling language, CML.

### 1.1 CML: knowledge + directives = intelligent behavior

CML rests on a solid foundation grounded in theoretical AI. This high-level language provides an intuitive way to give characters, and also cameras and lights, knowledge about their domain in terms of actions, their preconditions and their effects. We can also endow characters with a certain amount of "common sense" within their domain and we can even leave out tiresome details from the directives we give them. The missing details are automatically filled in at run-time by the character's reasoning engine which decides what must be done to achieve the specified goal.

Traditional AI style planning [1] certainly falls under the broad umbrella of this description, but the distinguishing features of CML are the intuitive way domain knowledge can be specified and how it affords an animator familiar control structures to focus the power of the reasoning engine. This forms an important middle ground between regular logic programming (as represented by Prolog) and traditional imperative programming (as typified by C). Moreover, this middle ground turns out to be crucial for cognitive modeling in animation and computer games. In one-off animation production, reducing development time is, within reason, more important than fast execution. The animator may therefore choose to rely more heavily on the reasoning engine. When run-time efficiency is also important, our approach lends itself to an incremental style of development. We can quickly create a working prototype. If this prototype runs too slowly, it may be refined by including increasingly detailed knowledge to narrow the focus of the reasoning engine.

### 1.2 Related work

Tu and Terzopoulos [25, 24] have taken major strides towards creating realistic, self-animating graphical characters through biomechanical modeling and the principles of behavioral animation introduced in the seminal work of Reynolds [21]. A criticism sometimes leveled at behavioral animation methods is that, robustness and efficiency notwithstanding, the behavior controllers are hardwired into the code. Blumberg and Galyean [7] begin to address such concerns by introducing mechanisms that give the animator greater control over behavior, and Blumberg's superb thesis considers interesting issues such as behavior learning [6]. While we share similar motivations, our research takes a different route. One of its unique features is the emphasis we place on investigating important higher-level cognitive abilities, such as knowledge representation, reasoning, and planning, which are the domain of AI. The research teams led by Badler [3], Bates [4], Hayes-Roth [13], and the Thalmanns [17] have applied AI techniques to produce inspiring results with animated humans or cartoon characters.

The theoretical basis of our work is new to the graphics community and we consider some novel applications. We employ an AI formalism known as the situation calculus. The version we use is a recent product of the cognitive robotics community [15]. A noteworthy point of departure from existing work in cognitive robotics is that we render the situation calculus amenable to animation within highly dynamic virtual worlds by introducing interval valued fluents [10, 12, 11] to deal with sensing.

Perlin [19] describes fascinating work aimed at providing animators with useful behavior modeling tools. Our work on defining and implementing the cognitive modeling language CML complements these efforts by encapsulating some of the basic concepts and techniques that may soon enough be incorporated into advanced tools for animation. Autonomous camera control for animation is particularly well suited to our cognitive modeling approach because there already exists a large body of widely accepted rules upon which we can draw [2]. This fact has also been exploited by a recent paper on the subject which implement hierarchical finite state machines for camera control [14]. Our approach to camera control employs CML.

### 1.3 Overview

The remainder of the paper is organized as follows. Section 2 covers the theoretical foundations of our research and presents our cognitive modeling language CML. Section 3 presents our work on automated cinematography, the first of three case studies. Here, our primary aim is to show how separating out the control information from the background domain knowledge makes it easier to understand and maintain controllers. Our camera controller is ostensibly reactive, making minimal use of CML's planning capabilities, but it demonstrates that cognitive modeling subsumes conventional behavioral modeling as a limiting case. Section 4 presents two case studies in character animation that highlight the ability of our approach to generate intelligent behavior consistent with goal-directed specification by exploiting domain knowledge and reasoning. In a "prehistoric world" case study, we show how our tools can simplify the development of cognitive characters that autonomously generate knowledge-based, goal-directed behavior. In an "undersea world" case study, we produce an elaborate animation which would overwhelm naive goal-directed specification approaches. We demonstrate how cognitive modeling allows the animator to provide a loose script for the characters to follow; some of the details of the animation are provided by the animator while the rest are filled in automatically by the character. Section 5 presents conclusions and suggestions for future work.

## 2 Theoretical Background

The *situation calculus* is an AI formalism for describing changing worlds using sorted first-order logic. Mathematical logic is somewhat of a departure from the repertoire of mathematical tools commonly used in computer graphics. We shall therefore overview in this section the salient points of the situation calculus, whose details are well-documented elsewhere (e.g., [10, 11, 15]). We emphasize that from the user's point of view the underlying theory is *hidden*. In particular, a user is *not* required to type in axioms written in first-order mathematical logic. Instead, we have developed an intuitive high-level interaction language CML whose syntax employs descriptive keywords, but which has a clear and precise mapping to the underlying formalism.

### 2.1 Domain modeling

A *situation* is a "snapshot" of the state of the world. A domain-independent constant $\mathsf{S}_0$ denotes the initial situation. Any property of the world that can change over time is known as a *fluent*. A fluent is a function, or relation, with a situation term (by convention) as its last argument. For example $\mathsf{Broken}(x, s)$ is a fluent that keeps track of whether an object $x$ is broken in a situation $s$.

*Primitive actions* are the fundamental instrument of change in our ontology. The sometimes counter-intuitive term "primitive" serves only to distinguish certain atomic actions from the "complex", compound actions that we will define in Section 2.3. The situation $s'$ resulting from doing action $a$ in situation $s$ is given by the distinguished function *do*, so that $s' = do(a, s)$. The possibility of performing action $a$ in situation $s$ is denoted by a distinguished predicate $Poss(a, s)$. Sentences that specify what the state of the world must be before performing some action are known as *precondition axioms*. For example, it is possible to drop an object $x$ in a situation $s$ if and only if a character is holding it, $Poss(drop(x), s) \Leftrightarrow \mathsf{Holding}(x, s)$. In CML, this axiom can be expressed more intuitively without the need for logical connectives and the explicit situation argument as follows:[1]

[1]To promote readability, all CML keywords will appear in bold type, actions (complex and primitive) will be italicized, and fluents will be underlined. We will also use various other predicates and functions that are not

**action** *drop*($x$) **possible when** Holding($x$);

The effects of an action are given by *effect axioms*. They give necessary conditions for a fluent to take on a given value after performing an action. For example, the effect of dropping an object $x$ is that the character is no longer holding the object in the resulting situation, and vice versa for picking up an object. This is stated in CML as follows:

**occurrence** *drop*($x$) **results in** !Holding($x$); ("!" denotes negation)
**occurrence** *pickup*($x$) **results in** Holding($x$);

Surprisingly, a naive translation of the above statements into the situation calculus does not give the expected results. In particular, stating what does not change when an action is performed is problematic. This is called the "frame problem" in AI [18]. That is, a character must consider whether dropping a cup, for instance, results in, say, a vase turning into a bird and flying about the room. For mindless animated characters, this can all be taken care of implicitly by the programmer's common sense. We need to give our thinking characters this same common sense. They need to be told that they should assume things stay the same unless they know otherwise. Once characters in virtual worlds start thinking for themselves, they too will have to tackle the frame problem. The frame problem has been a major reason why approaches like ours have not previously been used in computer animation or until recently in robotics. Fortunately, the frame problem can be solved provided characters represent their knowledge with the assumption that effect axioms enumerate all the possible ways that the world can change. This so-called closed world assumption provides the justification for replacing the effect axioms with *successor state axioms* [20].[2]

## 2.2 Sensing

Artificial life in a complex, dynamic virtual world should appear as thrilling and unpredictable to the character as it does to the human observer. Compare the excitement of watching a character run for cover from a falling stack of bricks to one that accurately precomputes brick trajectories and, realizing that it is in no danger, stands around nonchalantly while bricks crash down around it. On a more practical note, the expense of performing multiple speculative high fidelity forward simulations could easily be prohibitive. Usually it makes far more sense for a character to decide what to do using a simplified mental model of its world, sense the outcome, and perform follow up actions if things don't turn out as expected.

We would therefore like characters that can realize when they have some outdated information and can then perform a sensing action to get more current information so that they can replan a new course of action. A simple way to sidestep the issue of when to sense is to have characters replan periodically. One problem with this is that it is wasteful when there is no real need to replan. Even worse a character might not be replanning enough at certain critical times. Consequently, we would like characters that can replan *only when necessary*.

To this end, we must come up with a way for a character to represent its uncertainty about aspects of the world. Previous approaches to the problem in AI used modal logic to represent what a character knows and doesn't know. The so-called epistemic K-fluent

fluents. These will not be underlined and will have names to indicate their intended meaning. The convention in CML is that fluents to the right of the **when** keyword refer to the current situation.

[2]For example, the CML statements given above can now be effectively translated into the following successor state axiom that CML uses internally to represent how the character's world can change. The axiom states that, provided the action is possible, then a character is holding an object $x$ if and only if it just picked up the object or it was holding the object before and it did not just drop the object: *Poss* $(a, s) \Rightarrow$ [Holding($x$, *do*($a, s$)) $\Leftrightarrow a =$ *pickup*($x$) $\vee$ ($a \neq$ *drop*($x$) $\wedge$ Holding($x, s$))].

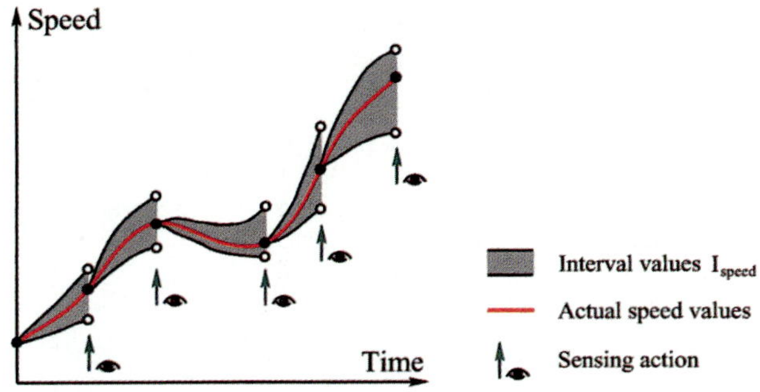


Figure 2: Sensing narrows IVE fluents bounding the actual value.

allows us, at least in principle, to express an agent's uncertainty about the value of a fluent in its world [22]. Unfortunately, the result is primarily of theoretical interest as there are as yet no clear ideas regarding its practical implementation.[3] Next, we shall instead propose the practicable concept of interval-valued epistemic fluents [10, 12, 11].

### 2.2.1 Interval-valued epistemic (IVE ) fluents

Interval arithmetic is relatively well-known to the graphics community [23, 26]. It can be used to express uncertainty about a quantity in a way that circumvents the problem of using a finite representation for an uncountable number of possibilities. It is, therefore, natural to ask whether we can also use intervals to replace the troublesome epistemic K-fluent. The answer, as we show in [10, 12, 11], is affirmative. In particular, for each sensory fluent $f$, we introduce an interval-valued epistemic (IVE ) fluent $\mathcal{I}_f$. The IVE fluent $\mathcal{I}_f$ is used to represent an agent's uncertainty about the value of $f$. Sensing now corresponds to making intervals narrower.[4]

Let us introduce the notion of *exogenous* actions (or events) that are generated by the environment and not the character. For example, we can introduce an action *setSpeed* that is generated by the underlying virtual world simulator and simply sets the value of a fluent speed that tracks an object's speed. We can introduce an IVE fluent $\mathcal{I}_{\mathsf{speed}}$ that takes on values in $\mathcal{I}_{\mathbb{R}^{\star+}}$, which denotes the set of pairs $\langle u, v \rangle$ such that $u, v \in \mathbb{R}^{\star+}$ (the extended positive real numbers) and $u \leqslant v$). Intuitively, we can now use the interval $\mathcal{I}_{\mathsf{speed}}(\mathrm{S}_0) = \langle 10, 50 \rangle$ to state that the object's speed is initially known to be between 10 and 50 m/sec. Now, as long as we have a bound on how fast the speed can change, we can always write down logically true statements about the world. Moreover, we can always bound the rate of change. That is, in the worst case we can choose our rate of change as infinite so that, except after sensing, the character is completely ignorant of the object's speed in the current situation: $\mathcal{I}_{\mathsf{speed}}(s) = \langle 0, \infty \rangle$. Figure 2 depicts the usual case when we do have a reasonable bound. The solid line is the actual speed speed and the shaded region is the interval guaranteed to bound the object's speed. Notice that the character's uncertainty about the object's speed increases over time (i.e., the intervals grow wider) until a sensing action causes the interval to once again col-

[3]Potential implementations of the epistemic K-fluent are plagued by combinatorial explosion. In general, if we have $n$ relational fluents whose values may be learned through sensing, then we must list potentially $2^n$ initial possible worlds. Things get even worse with functional fluents whose range is the real numbers $\mathbb{R}$, since we cannot list out the uncountably many possible worlds associated with uncertainty about their value.

[4]IVE fluents represent *uncertainty intervals* about time-dependent variables. They do not represent and are unrelated to *time intervals* of the sort that have been used in the underlying semantics of various temporal logics (for example see [16]).

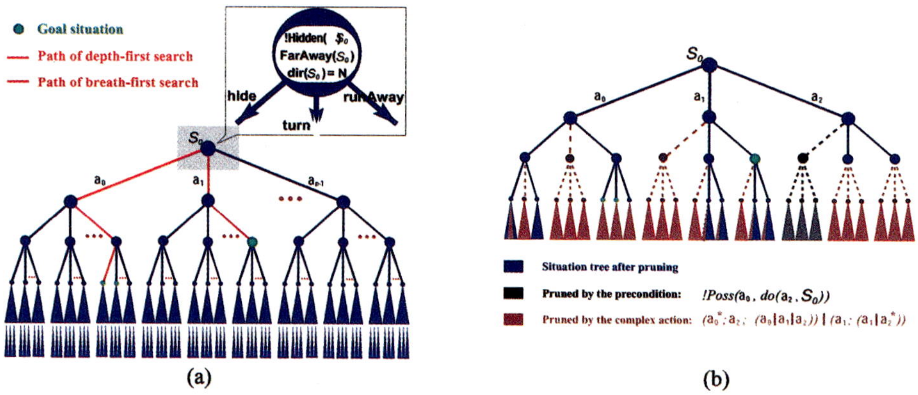


Figure 3: The situation tree (a). Pruning the tree (b).

lapse to its actual value (assuming noise-free sensing). Whenever the interval is less than a certain width, we say that the character "knows" the property in question. We can then write precondition axioms based not only upon the state of the world, but also on the state of the character's knowledge of its world. For example, we can state that a character cannot calculate its travel time unless it knows its speed. So, if a character wishes to know when it will arrive somewhere, but does not know its speed (i.e., $\mathcal{I}_{\text{speed}}(s)$ is too wide), then it can infer that it must perform a sensing action. In [10, 12, 11] we prove several theorems that allow us to justify formally our IVE fluent as a replacement for the troublesome K-fluent.

## 2.3 Complex actions

The actions, effect axioms and preconditions we have described so far can be thought of as a tree (Fig. 3(a)). The nodes of the tree represent situations. Effect axioms describe the characteristics of each situation. At the root of the tree is the initial situation and each path through the tree represents a possible sequence of actions. The precondition axioms mean that some sequences of actions are not possible. This is represented in the picture by the black portion of the tree. If some situations are desired "goals" then we can use a conventional logic programming approach to automatically search the tree for a sequence of actions that takes us to the goal. The green nodes in the figure represent goal situations and we can use various search strategies to come up with an appropriate sequence of actions to perform. The red path shows the sequence of actions that result from a breadth-first search of the tree, and the magenta path from depth-first search.

The problem with the exhaustive search approach is that the search space is exponential in the length of the plan. Much of the planning literature has sought to address this problem with more sophisticated search algorithms, such as the well known $A^\star$ algorithm, or stochastic planning techniques. We shall introduce a different approach. In particular, we shall be looking at how to speed up planning by "pruning" the search space. How we choose to search the remaining space is an important but independent problem for which all the previous work on planning is equally applicable.

It is interesting to note that conventional imperative style programming can be regarded as a way to prune the tree down to a single path. That is, there is no "searching" and the programmer bears the sole responsibility for coming up with a program that generates the desired sequence of actions. However, by defining what we refer to as "complex actions" we can prune part of the search tree. Figure 3(b) represents the complex action $(a_0\star \,⨟\, a_2 \,⨟\, (a_0|a_1|a_2))|(a_1 \,⨟\, (a_1|a_2)\star)$ and its corresponding effect of reducing the search space to the blue region of the tree. In what follows we shall see more examples of complex actions and their definitions. For now, it is important to understand that the purpose of complex actions is to give us a convenient tool for encoding any heuristic knowledge we have about the problem. In general, the search space will still be exponential, but reducing the search space can make the difference between a character that can tractably plan only 5 steps ahead and one that can plan 15 steps ahead. That is, we can get characters that appear a lot more intelligent!

The theory underlying *complex actions* is described in [15]. Complex actions consist of a set of recursively defined operators. Any primitive action is also a complex action. Other complex actions are composed using various control structures. As a familiar artifice to aid memorization, the control structure syntax of CML is designed to resemble C. Fig. 4 gives the complete list of operators for specifying complex actions. Together, these operators define the instruction language we use to issue direction to characters.

Although the syntax of CML is similar to a conventional programming language, CML is a strict superset in terms of functionality. The user can give characters instructions based on behavior outlines, or "sketch plans". In particular, a behavior outline can be nondeterministic. By this we mean that we can cover multiple possibilities in one instruction, not that the behavior is random. As we shall explain, this added freedom allows many behaviors to be specified more naturally, more simply, more succinctly and at a much higher level of abstraction than would otherwise be possible. Using its background knowledge, the character can decide for itself how to fill in the necessary missing details.

As a first serious example of a powerful complex action, the one to the left below,[5] with its corresponding CML code on the right, defines a depth-bounded (to $n$ steps) depth-first planner:

```
proc planner(n)
  goal? |
  [(n > 0)? ⨟
     (π a)(primitiveAction(a)? ⨟ a) ⨟
     planner(n − 1)]
end
```

```
proc planner(n) {
  choose test(goal);
  or {
    test(n > 0);
    pick(a) {
      primitiveAction(a);
      do(a); }
    planner(n − 1); }}
```

We have written a Java application, complete with documentation, that is publicly available to further assist the interested reader in mastering this novel language [8].

[5] Adopted from R. Reiter's forthcoming book "Knowledge in Action".

(Primitive Action)
If $\alpha$ is a primitive action then, provided the precondition axiom states it is possible, do the action.
[same syntax in CML i.e. <ACTION>; except we must use an explicit **do** when the action is a variable.]

(Sequence)
$\alpha \fatsemi \beta$ means do action $\alpha$, followed by action $\beta$.
[<ACTION> ; <ACTION> ; (note the semi-colon is used as a statement terminator to mimic C)]

(Test)
$p?$ succeeds if $p$ is true, otherwise it fails.
[**test**(<EXPRESSION>)]

(Nondeterministic choice of actions)
$\alpha \mid \beta$ means do action $\alpha$ or action $\beta$.
[**choose** <ACTION> **or** <ACTION>]

(Conditionals)
**if** $p$ $\alpha$ **else** $\beta$ **fi**, is just shorthand for $p? \fatsemi \alpha \mid (\neg p)? \fatsemi \beta$.
[**if** (<EXPRESSION>) <ACTION> **else** <ACTION>]

(Non-deterministic iteration)
$\alpha\,\star$, means do $\alpha$ zero or more times.
[**star** <ACTION>]

(Iteration)
**while** $p$ **do** $\alpha$ **od** is just shorthand for $p?\ \alpha\,\star$.
[**while** (<EXPRESSION>) <ACTION>]

(Nondeterministic choice of arguments)
$(\pi\ x)\ \alpha$ means pick some argument $x$ and perform the action $\alpha(x)$.
[**pick**(<EXPRESSION>) <ACTION>]

(Procedures)
**proc** $P(x_1, \ldots, x_n)$ $\alpha$ **end** declares a procedure that can be called as $P(x_1, \ldots, x_n)$.
[**void** $P$(<ARGLIST>) <ACTION>]

Figure 4: Complex action operators. Following each definition, the equivalent CML syntax is given in square brackets. The mathematical definitions for these operators are given in [15]. It is straightforward to modify the complex action definitions to include a check for any exogenous actions and, if necessary, include them in the sequence of resulting actions (see [10, 11] for more details).

# 3 Automated Cinematography

At first it might seem strange to advocate building a cognitive model for a camera. We soon realize, however, that it is natural to capture in a cognitive model the knowledge of the director and cameraperson who control the camera. In effect, we want to treat all the elements of a scene, be they lights, cameras, or characters as "actors". CML is ideally suited to realizing this approach.

To appreciate what follows, the reader may benefit from a rudimentary knowledge of cinematography. The exposition on principles of cinematography given in Section 2.3 of [14] is an excellent starting point. In [14], the authors discuss one particular formula for filming two characters conversing. The idea is to flip between "external" shots of each character, focusing on the character doing the talking (Fig. 5). To break the monotony, the shots are interspersed with reaction shots of the other character. In [14], the formula is encoded as a finite state machine. We will show how elegantly we can capture the formula using the instruction facilities of CML. First, however, we need to specify the domain. For conciseness, we restrict ourselves to explaining only the principal aspects of the specification (see [10, 9, 11] for the details).

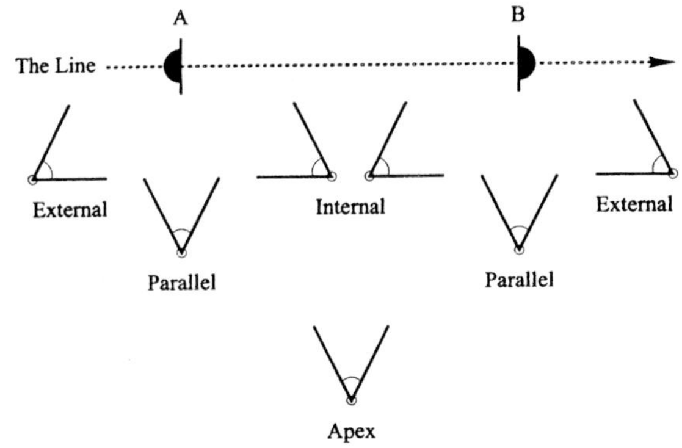


Figure 5: Common camera placements relative to characters $A$, $B$.

## 3.1 Camera domain

Assuming that the motion of all the objects in the scene has been computed, our task is to decide the vantage point from which each frame is to be rendered. The fluent <u>frame</u> keeps track of the current frame number, and a *tick* action causes it to be incremented. The precomputed scene is represented as a lookup function scene which completely specifies the position, orientation, and shape of each object in each frame.

The most common camera placements used in cinematography will be modeled in our formalization as primitive actions. These actions are referred to in [14] as "camera modules". This is a good example where the term "primitive" is misleading. As described in [5], low-level camera placement is a complex and challenging task in its own right. Here we shall make some simplifications to clarify our exposition. More realistic equations are easily substituted, but the principles remain the same. For now, we specify the camera with two fluents <u>lookFrom</u>, and <u>lookAt</u>. Let us assume that up remains constant and also make the simplifying assumption that the viewing frustrum is fixed. Despite our simplifications, we still have a great deal of flexibility in our specifications. We will now give examples of effect axioms for some of the primitive actions in our ontology.

The *fixed* action is used to specify explicitly a particular camera configuration. We can, for example, use it to provide an overview shot of the scene:

**occurrence** *fixed*$(e,c)$ **results in** <u>lookFrom</u> $= e$ && <u>lookAt</u> $= c$;

A more complicated action is *external*. It takes two arguments, character $A$, and character $B$ and places the camera so that $A$ is seen over the shoulder of $B$. One effect of this action, therefore, is that the camera is looking at character $A$:

**occurrence** *external*$(A,B)$ **results in** <u>lookAt</u> $= p$ **when**
scene($A$(upperbody,centroid)) $= p$;

The other effect is that the camera is located above character $B$'s shoulder. This could be done with an effect axiom such as:

**occurrence** *external*$(A,B)$ **results in**
<u>lookFrom</u> $= p + k_2 *$ up $+ k_3 *$ normalize$(p - c)$ **when**
scene($B$(shoulder,centroid)) $= p$ && scene($A$(upperbody,centroid)) =

where $k_2$ and $k_3$ are some suitable constants. There are many other possible camera placement actions. Some of them are listed in [14], and others may be found in [2].

The remaining fluents are concerned with more esoteric aspects of the scene, but some of their effect axioms are mundane and so we shall only explain them in English. For example, the fluent <u>Talking</u> ($A$,$B$) (meaning $A$ is talking to $B$) becomes true after a *startTalk*

($A$,$B$) action, and false after a *stopTalking* ($A$,$B$) action. Since we are currently only concerning ourselves with camera placement, it is the responsibility of the application that generates the scene descriptions to produce the start and stop talking actions (i.e., the start and stop talking actions are represented as exogenous actions within the underlying formal semantics).

A more interesting fluent is silenceCount, which keeps count of how long it has been since a character spoke:

**occurrence** *tick* **results in** silenceCount $= n - 1$
  **when** silenceCount $= n$ && !Talking($A$,$B$);
**occurrence** *stopTalk*($A$,$B$) **results in** silenceCount $= k_a$;
**occurrence** *setCount* **results in** silenceCount $= k_a$;

Note that $k_a$ is a constant ($k_a = 10$ in [14]), such that the counter will be negative after $k_a$ ticks of no-one speaking. A similar fluent filmCount keeps track of how long the camera has been pointing at the same character:

**occurrence** *setCount* || *external*($A$,$B$) **results in** filmCount $= k_b$
  **when** Talking($A$,$B$);
**occurrence** *setCount* || *external*($A$,$B$) **results in** filmCount $= k_c$
  **when** !Talking($A$,$B$);
**occurrence** *tick* **results in** filmCount $= n - 1$ **when** filmCount $= n$;

where $k_b$ and $k_c$ are constants ($k_b = 30$ and $k_c = 15$ in [14]) that state how long we can continue the same shot before the counter becomes negative. Note that the constants for the case of looking at a non-speaking character are lower. We will keep track of which constant we are using with the fluent tooLong.

For convenience, we now introduce two defined fluents that express when a shot has become boring because it has gone on too long, and when a shot has not gone on long enough. We need the notion of a minimum time for each shot to avoid annoying flitter between shots:[6]

**defined** Boring := filmCount $< 0$;
**defined** TooFast := tooLong - $k_s \leqslant$ filmCount; (where $k_s$ is a constant)

Finally, we introduce a fluent Filming to keep track of the character at whom the camera is pointing.

Until now we have not mentioned any preconditions for our actions. Unless stated otherwise, we assume that actions are always possible. In contrast, the precondition axiom for the *external* camera action states that we only want to point the camera at character $A$ if we are already filming $A$ and it has not yet gotten boring, or if we are not filming $A$, and $A$ is talking, and we have stayed with the current shot long enough:

**action** *external*($A$,$B$) **possible when** (!Boring && Filming($A$)) ||
  (Talking($A$,$B$) && !Filming($A$) && !TooFast);

We are now in a position to define the controller that will move our "cognitive camera" to shoot the character doing the talking, with occasional respites to focus on the other character's reactions:

*setCount*;
**while** ($0 <$ silenceCount) {
  **pick**($A$,$B$) *external*($A$,$B$);
  *tick*; }

This specification makes heavy use of the ability to nondeterministically choose arguments. The reader can contrast our specification with the encoding given in [14] to achieve the same result.

[6]A *defined* fluent is defined in terms of other fluents, and therefore, its value changes implicitly as the fluents on which it depends change. The user must be careful to avoid any circular definitions when using defined fluents. A defined fluent is indicated with the keyword "**defined**" and symbol ":=".

Figure 6: The "Cinemasaurus" autonomous camera animation. (top) External shot of the T-Rex. (center) Internal shot of the Raptor. (bottom) Apex shot of the actors.

## 4 Character Animation

We now turn our attention to the main application of our work, character animation. Our first example is a prehistoric world and the second is an undersea world. The two worlds are differentiated by the complexity of their underlying models, the undersea world model being significantly more complex.

### 4.1 Prehistoric world

The prehistoric world, comprising a volcanic territory and a jungle territory, is inhabited by a Tyrannosaurus Rex (T-Rex) and Velociprators (Raptors). It is implemented as a game engine API which runs in real-time any modern PC. The dinosaur characters are animated by keyframed footprints and inverse kinematics to position the legs onto the ground. To add some physical realism, the body is modeled as a point mass that moves dynamically in response to the leg movements.

We interfaced the game engine to a reasoning engine implemented in C++.[7] The performance of the cognitive modeling aug-

[7]We first tried compiling our CML specifications into Prolog using our

mented prehistoric world remains real-time on average, but we see occasional pauses when the reasoning engine takes longer than usual to plan a suitable behavior. We will present two cognitive modeling animations. The first one demonstrates our approach to camera control and the second demonstrates plan-based territorial behavior.

The action in the camera control demonstration consists of a T-Rex and a Raptor "conversing" by roaring at each other. The camera always films the dinosaur that is roaring unless it roars for too long, in which case it will get a reaction shot from the other dinosaur. The T-Rex has an additional behavior—if it gets bored listening to a yapping Raptor, it will attack! The camera will automatically track moving creatures. Sample frames from the resulting animation "Cinemasaurus", which was filmed automatically in the jungle territory by our cognitive camera, are shown in figure 6. The cognitive camera uses essentially the same CML code as the example in Section 3, although some of the camera angles are programmed a bit differently.

In the territorial T-Rex animation our challenge is to administer enough knowledge to the T-Rex about its world, especially about the reactive behavior of the Raptors (which behave not unlike Reynold's "boids" [21]), so that the T-Rex knows enough to automatically formulate plans for expelling Raptors out of its volcanic territory and into the neighboring jungle territory. To this end, the T-Rex must herd Raptors through a narrow passage that connects the two territories. The passage is marked by a stone arch at the northwest corner of the volcanic territory.

The Raptors have good reason to fear the larger, stronger and highly vicious T-Rex should it come close. The following code shows how we use CML to instruct the T-Rex that the Raptors will become frightened when it approaches them:

**occurrence** *move*(direction) **results in** Frightened(Raptor($i$))
  **when** position(T-Rex) $= p$ && position(Raptor($i$)) $= q$ &&
    $|q -$ adjacent($p$, direction)$| \leqslant \Delta$;

The code we used in the demonstration was slightly more complicated in that we also instructed the T-Rex that even less proximal Raptors would also become frightened if it roared. A second CML expression tells the T-Rex that frightened Raptors will run away from it:

**defined** heading(Raptor($i$)) = direction
  **where** (Frightened(Raptor($i$)) &&
    direction = opposite(directionT-Rex)) ||
    (!Frightened(Raptor($i$)) && direction = directionOld)
  **when** relativeDirectionOfT-Rex (Raptor($i$)) = directionT-Rex &&
    heading(Raptor($i$)) = directionOld;

Here, relativeDirectionOfT-Rex is a fluent that is easily defined in terms of the relative positions of the T-Rex and Raptor $i$.

With a third CML expression, we instruct the T-Rex to plan paths that avoid obstacles:[8]

**action** *move*(direction) **possible**
  **when** position(T-Rex) $= p$ && Free(adjacent($p$, direction));

Given enough patience, skill and ingenuity, it is conceivable that one could successfully program herding behavior using sets of stimulus-response rules. Using CML, we can do the same thing with relative ease through much higher-level, goal-directed specification. Suppose we want to get some Raptors heading in a particular direction. Then, we simply give the T-Rex the goal of getting more Raptors heading in the right direction than are initially heading that way. Here is how this goal is specified in CML:

**defined** goal := NumRaptorsInRightDirection $= n$ && $n \geqslant n_0 + k$
  **when initially** $n_0 =$ NumRaptorsInRightDirection;

This goal along with our previous instructions enable the T-Rex to plan its actions like a smart sheepdog. It autonomously plans collision-free paths to maneuver in and around groups of Raptors in order to frighten them in the desired direction.

The T-Rex plans up to 6 moves ahead of its current position. Longer duration plans degrade real-time performance. They are also rarely useful in a highly kinetic world about which the T-Rex has only partial knowledge. A better strategy is adaptive herding through periodic re-planning. To speed things up we also defined undesirable situations using the fluent Undesirable. These are the antithesis of goals in that they represent situations that, although not illegal, are undesirable. For example, if the Raptors are too far away there is no point in roaring as it will have no effect. Therefore a situation in which the T-Rex roars without anticipating any Raptors changing direction is useless, hence undesirable:

**defined** Undesirable **after** *roar* := NumRaptorsInRightDirection $= n$
  **when** NumRaptorsInRightDirection $= n_0$ && $n_0 \geqslant n$;

The T-Rex need not consider this or its subsequent situations when searching for appropriate behavior.

The pack of reactive Raptors prefer to stay away from the passage under the arch, but the smarter, cognitively empowered T-Rex succeeds in expelling this unruly mob from its territory.[9] Some frames from the corresponding animation are shown in figure 7.

## 4.2 Undersea world

Our undersea world is entirely physics-based. It is inhabited by mermen, fabled creatures of the sea with the head and upper body of a man and the tail of a fish. Its other inhabitants are predator sharks. An artificial life simulator implements the virtual creatures as fully functional (pre-cognitive) autonomous agents. The modeling is similar to that in [25, 24]. It provides a *graphical display model* that captures the form and appearance of our characters, a *biomechanical model* that captures their anatomical structure, including internal muscle actuators, and simulates the deformation and physical dynamics of the character's body, and a *behavioral control model* that implements the character's brain and is responsible for motor, perception and low-level behavior control. A merman's reactive behavior system interprets his intentions and generates coordinated muscle actions. These effect locomotion by deforming the body to generate propulsion-inducing forces against the virtual water. The sharks are animated likewise.

Our goal is to equip the mermen with a cognitive model that enables them to reason about their world based on acquired knowledge, thus enabling them to interpret high-level direction from the animator. Fig. 8 depicts the relationship between the user, the reasoning system and the reactive system.

The simulated dynamics makes it hard for a merman to reason precisely about his world because, as is the case in the real world, it is possible to predict only approximately the ultimate effect of one's actions. However, the reactive behavior model helps by mediating between the reasoning engine and the physics-based environment. Thus at the higher level we need only consider actions

online Java applet [8] and then linking the compiled Prolog code with the API using Quintus Prolog's ability to link with Visual C++. Although convenient, this approach adversely affected the real-time performance, so we abandoned it in favor of a complete C++ implementation of the reasoning engine.

[8] In fact, the T-Rex autonomously maps out all the obstacles by exploring its world in a preprocessing step. When it encounters an obstacle, the T-Rex remembers the location of the obstacle in a mental map of its world.

[9] Note that all a "reactive T-Rex" (i.e. a cognitive T-Rex allowed to plan only a single move ahead) can do is aimlessly chase the agile Raptors around. Only by sheer luck can it eventually chase a few Raptors through the narrow passage under the arch and out of its territory.

Figure 7: The "Territorial T-Rex" animation. A cognitively empowered T-Rex herds Raptors like a smart sheepdog.

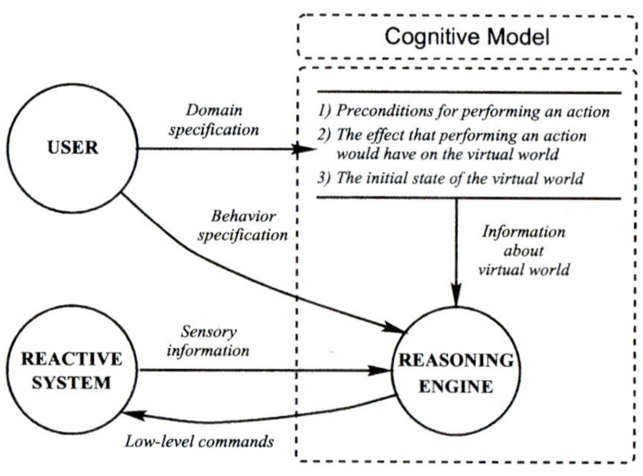


Figure 8: Interaction between cognitive model, user and low-level reactive behavior system.

such as "swim forward" and "turn left". The reactive system translates these commands down to the necessary detailed muscle actions. It also includes sensorimotor control loops that enable the agent to approximately satisfy commands, such as "go to a given position". The reactive system furthermore acts as a fail-safe should the reasoning system temporarily fall through. In the event that the character cannot decide upon an intelligent course of action in a reasonable amount of time, the reactive layer continually tries to prevent the character from doing anything stupid, such as bashing into obstacles. Typical default reactive behaviors are "turn right", "avoid collision" and "swim for your life".

Even so, short of performing precise multiple forward simulations, it is impossible for his reasoning system to predict the exact position that a merman will end up after he executes a plan of action. A typical solution would be to re-initialize the reasoning engine every time it is called, but this makes it difficult to pursue long term goals as we are tossing out all the character's knowledge instead of just the outdated knowledge. The solution is for the characters to represent positions using the IVE fluents that we described in Section 2.2.1. After sensing, the positions of all the visible objects are known. The merman can then use this knowledge to replan his course of action, possibly according to some long-term strategy. Regular fluents are used to model the merman's internal state, such as his goal position, fear level, etc.

#### 4.2.1 Undersea animations

The undersea animations revolve around pursuit and evasion behaviors. The hungry sharks try to catch and eat the mermen and the mermen try to use their superior reasoning abilities to avoid this grisly fate. For the most part, the sharks are instructed to chase mermen they see. If they cannot see any mermen, they go to where they last saw one. If all else fails, they start to forage systematically. Figure 9 shows selected frames from two animations.

The first animation verifies that because the shark is a larger and faster swimmer, it has little trouble catching merman prey in open water. In the second animation, we introduce some large rocks in the underwater scene and things get a lot more interesting. Now, when a merman is in trouble, cognitive modeling enables him to come up with short term plans to take advantage of the rocks and frequently evade capture. He can hide behind the rocks and hug them closely so that a shark has difficulty seeing or reaching him.

We were able to use the control structures of CML to encode a great deal of heuristic knowledge. For example, consider the problem of trying to come up with a plan to hide from the predator. A traditional planning approach will be able to perform a search of various paths according to criteria such as whether the path routes through hidden positions, or leads far from a predator, etc. Unfortunately, this kind of planning is prohibitively expensive. By contrast, the control structures of CML allow us to encode heuristic knowledge to help overcome this limitation. For example, we can specify a procedure that encodes the following heuristic: If the current position is good enough then stay where you are, else search the area around you (the expensive planning part); otherwise, check out the obstacles (hidden positions are more likely near obstacles); finally,

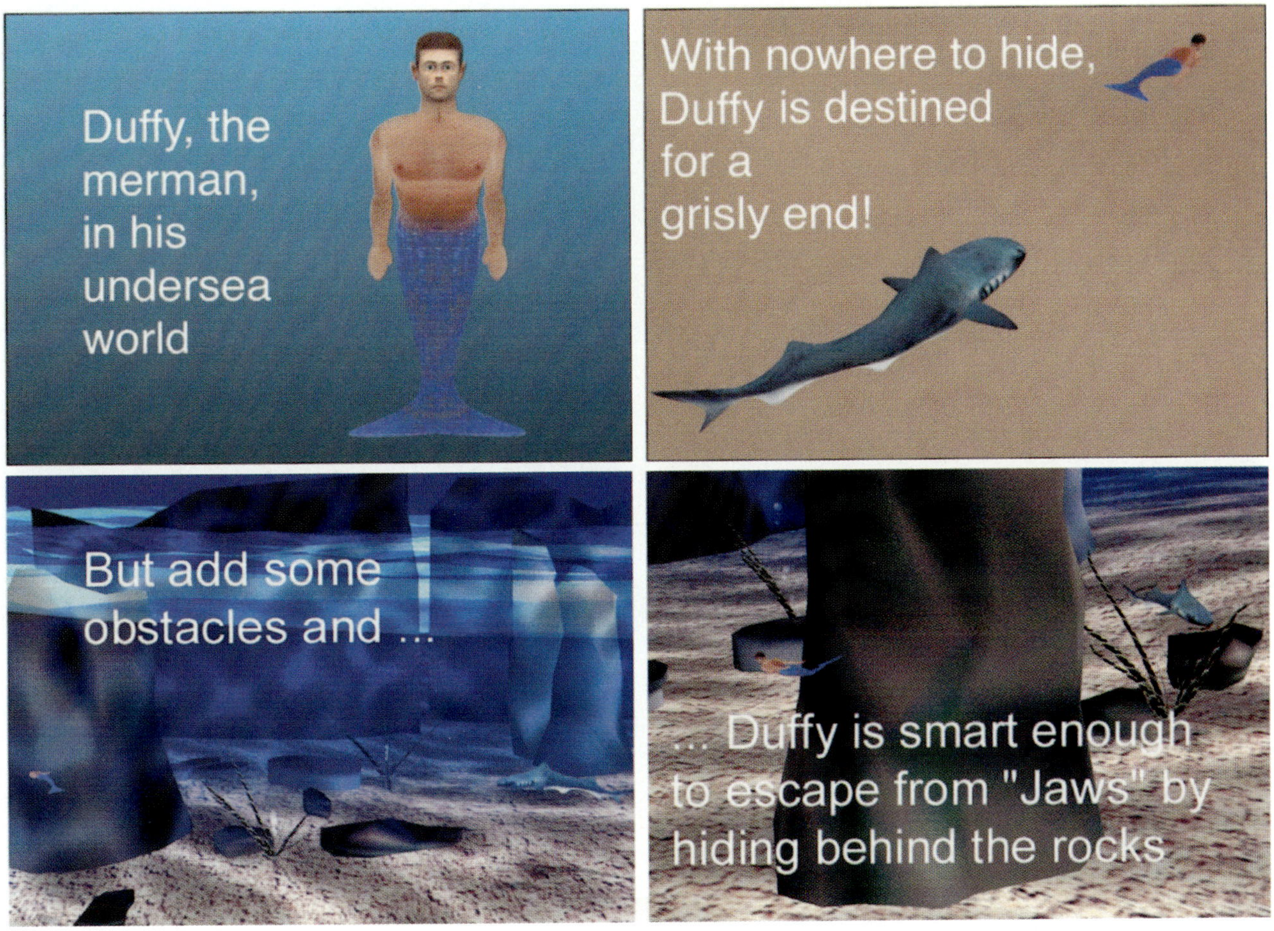


Figure 9: The undersea animations. Duffy the merman cleverly evades a predator shark.

if all else fails and danger looms, panic and flee in a random direction. With a suitable precondition for *pickGoal*, which prevents the merman selecting a goal until it meets certain minimum criteria, the following CML procedure implements the above heuristic for character $i$:

```
proc evade(i) {
    choose testCurrPosn(i);
    or search(i);
    or testObstacles(i);
    or panic(i); }
```

In turn, the above procedure can be part of a larger program that directs a merman to hide from sharks while, say, trying to visit the other rocks in the scene whenever it is safe to do so. Of course, planning is not always a necessary, appropriate or possible way to generate every aspect of an animation. This is especially so if an animator has something highly specific in mind. In this regard, it is important to remember that CML can also support detailed behavioral programming because it offers a full range of control structures that are customary in regular programming languages.

We used CML's control structures to make the animation "The Great Escape". This was done by simply instructing the merman to avoid being eaten, and whenever it appears reasonably safe to do so, to make a break for a large rock in the scene. The particular rock to which we want to get the merman to go proffers a narrow crack through which the merman, but not the larger-bodied shark, can pass. We wanted an exciting animation in which the merman eventually gets to that special rock with the shark in hot pursuit. The merman's *evade* procedure should then swing into action, hopefully enabling him to evade capture by finding and slipping through the crack. Although we do not specify exactly how or when, we have a mechanism to heavily stack the deck toward getting the desired animation. As it turns out, we got what we wanted on our first attempt (after debugging). However, if the animation that we desired remained elusive, we can use CML to further constrain what happens all the way down to scripting an entire sequence if necessary.

As an extension to behavioral animation, our approach enables us to linearly scale our cognitive modeling efforts for a single character in order to create multiple similarly-behaved characters. Each character will behave autonomously according to its own unique perspective of its world. In a third animation, we demonstrate that numerous cognitive characters may also cooperate with one another to try to survive in shark infested waters. We have specified that some mermen are brave and others are timid. When the timid ones are in danger of becoming shark food, they cry for help (telepathically for now) and the brave ones come to their rescue provided it isn't too dangerous for them. Once a brave rescuer has managed to attract a shark's attention away from a targeted victim, the hero tries to escape.

## 5 Conclusion

We have introduced the idea of cognitive modeling as a substantive new apex to the computer graphics modeling pyramid. Unlike behavioral models, which are reactive, cognitive models are deliberative. They enable an autonomous character to exploit acquired knowledge to formulate appropriate plans of action. To assist the animator or game developer in implementing cognitive models, we have created the cognitive modeling language CML. This powerful language gives us an intuitive way to afford a character knowledge about its world in terms of actions, their preconditions and their effects. When we provide a high-level description of the desired goal of the character's behavior, CML offers a general, automatic mechanism for the character to search for suitable action sequences. At the other extreme, CML can also serve like a conventional programming language, allowing us to express precisely how we want the character to act. We can employ a combination of the two extremes and the whole gamut in between to build different parts of a cognitive model. This combination of convenience and automation makes our cognitive modeling approach in general, and CML in particular, a potentially powerful tool for animators and game developers.

### 5.1 Future work

Cognitive modeling opens up numerous opportunities for future work. For example, we could incorporate a mechanism to learn reactive rules that mimic the behavior observed from the reasoning engine. Other important issues arise in the user interface. As it stands CML is a good choice as the underlying representation that a developer might want to use to build a cognitive model. An animator or other end users, however, would probably prefer a graphical user interface front-end. In order to make such an interface easy to use, we might limit possible interactions to supplying parameters to predefined cognitive models, or perhaps we could use a visual programming metaphor to specify the complex actions.

Cognitive modeling is a potentially vast topic whose riches we have only just begun to explore. In our prehistoric world, for instance, we concentrated on endowing the T-Rex with CML-based cognition. There is no reason why we could not similarly endow the Raptors as well. This would allow the animation of much more complex dinosaur behavior.[10] A lone Raptor is no match for the T-Rex, but imagine the following scenario in which a pack of cunning Raptors conspire to fell their large opponent. Through cognitive modeling, the Raptors hatch a strategic plan—the ambush! Based on their domain knowledge, the Raptors have inferred that the T-Rex's size, his big asset in open terrain, would hamper his maneuverability within the narrow passage under the arch. The leader of the pack plays the decoy, luring their unsuspecting opponent into the narrow passage. Her pack mates, who have assumed their positions near both ends of the passage, rush into it on command. Some Raptors jump on the T-Rex and chomp down on his back while others bite into his legs. Thus the pack overcomes the brute through strategic planning, cooperation, and sheer number. Coordinating multiple Raptors in this way would significantly increase the branching factor in the situation trees of the cognitive models. A solution would be to control them as intelligent subgroups. We could also exploit complex actions to provide a loose script that would specify some key intermediate goals, such as the decoy stratagem.

## Acknowledgments

We would like to thank Eugene Fiume for many helpful comments and for originally suggesting the application of CML to cinematography, Steve Rotenberg and Andy Styles at Angel Studios (Carlsbad, CA) and Steve Hunt for developing the low-level "Demosaurus Rex" API, Steven Shapiro and Hector Levesque for technical assistance on the situation calculus, and Jeffrey Tupper for technical assistance on interval arithmetic. JF thanks Ramesh Subramonian for his benevolent support during the final stages of this work.

[10] See Robert T. Bakker's captivating novel *Raptor Red* (Bantam, 1996).

## References


[1] J. Allen, J. Hendler, and A. Tate, editors. *Readings in Planning*. Morgan Kaufmann, 1990.

[2] D. Arijon. *Grammar of the Film Language*. Communication Arts Books, Hastings House Publishers, New York, 1976.

[3] N. I. Badler, C. Phillips, and D. Zeltzer. *Simulating Humans*. Oxford University Press, 1993.

[4] J. Bates. *The Role of Emotion in Believable Agents*. *Communications of the ACM*, 37(7), 1994, 122–125.

[5] J. Blinn. Where am I? What am I looking at? *IEEE Computer Graphics and Applications*, **8**(4), 1988, 76–81.

[6] B. Blumberg. *Old Tricks, New Dogs: Ethology and Interactive Creatures*. PhD thesis, MIT Media Lab, MIT, Cambridge, MA, 1996.

[7] B. M. Blumberg and T. A. Galyean. Multi-level direction of autonomous creatures for real-time environments. *Proceedings of SIGGRAPH 95*, Aug. 1995, 47–54.

[8] J. Funge. CML compiler. `www.cs.toronto.edu/~funge/cml`, 1997.

[9] J. Funge. Lifelike characters behind the camera. *Lifelike Computer Characters '98 Snowbird, UT*, Oct. 1998.

[10] J. Funge. *Making Them Behave: Cognitive Models for Computer Animation*. PhD Thesis, Department of Computer Science, University of Toronto, Toronto, Canada, 1998. Reprinted in SIGGRAPH 98 Course Notes #10, Orlando, Florida.

[11] J. Funge. *AI for Games and Animation: A Cognitive Modeling Approach*. A.K. Peters, 1999.

[12] J. Funge. Representing knowledge within the situation calculus using interval-valued epistemic fluents. *Journal of Reliable Computing*, 5(1), 1999.

[13] B. Hayes-Roth, R. v. Gent, and D. Huber. Acting in character. In R. Trappl and P. Petta, editors, *Creating Personalities for Synthetic Actors*. Lecture Notes in CS No. 1195. Springer-Verlag: Berlin, 1997.

[14] L. He, M. F. Cohen, and D. Salesin. The virtual cinematographer: A paradigm for automatic real-time camera control and directing. *Proceedings of SIGGRAPH 96*, Aug. 1996, 217–224.

[15] H. Levesque, R. Reiter, Y. Lespérance, F. Lin, and R. Scherl. Golog: A logic programming language for dynamic domains. *Journal of Logic Programming*, 31, 1997, 59–84.

[16] C. Pinhanez, K. Mase, and A. Bobick. Interval scripts: A design paradigm for story-based interactive systems *Proceedings of CHI'97*, Mar. 1997.

[17] N. Magnenat-Thalmann and D. Thalmann. *Synthetic Actors in Computer-Generated Films*. Springer-Verlag: Berlin, 1990.

[18] J. McCarthy and P. Hayes. Some philosophical problems from the standpoint of artificial intelligence. In B. Meltzer and D. Michie, editors, *Machine Intelligence 4*, pages 463–502. Edinburgh University Press, Edinburgh, 1969.

[19] K. Perlin and A. Goldberg. IMPROV: A system for scripting interactive actors in virtual worlds. *Proceedings of SIGGRAPH 96*, Aug. 1996, 205–216.

[20] R. Reiter. The frame problem in the situation calculus: A simple solution (sometimes) and a completeness result for goal regression. In V. Lifschitz, editor, *Artificial Intelligence and Mathematical Theory of Computation*. Academic Press, 1991.

[21] C. W. Reynolds. Flocks, herds, and schools: A distributed behavioral model. *Proceedings of SIGGRAPH 87*, Jul. 1987, 25–34.

[22] R. Scherl and H. Levesque. The frame problem and knowledge-producing actions. *Proceedings of AAAI-93*, AAAI Press, Menlo Park, CA, 1993.

[23] J. Snyder. Interval analysis for computer graphics. *Proceedings of SIGGRAPH 92*, Jul. 1992, 121–130.

[24] X. Tu. *Artificial animals for computer animation: Biomechanics, locomotion, perception and behavior.* ACM Distinguished Dissertation Series, Springer-Verlag, Berlin, 1999.

[25] X. Tu and D. Terzopoulos. Artificial fishes: Physics, locomotion, perception, behavior. *Proceedings of SIGGRAPH 94*, Jul. 1994, 24–29.

[26] J. Tupper. Graphing Equations with Generalized Interval Arithmetic. MSc Thesis, Department of Computer Science, University of Toronto, Toronto, Canada, 1996. See also GRAFEQ from Pedagoguery Software `www.peda.com`.

# A Hierarchical Approach to Interactive Motion Editing for Human-like Figures

Jehee Lee †  Sung Yong Shin ‡

Computer Science Department
Korea Advanced Institute of Science and Technology §

## Abstract

This paper presents a technique for adapting existing motion of a human-like character to have the desired features that are specified by a set of constraints. This problem can be typically formulated as a spacetime constraint problem. Our approach combines a hierarchical curve fitting technique with a new inverse kinematics solver. Using the kinematics solver, we can adjust the configuration of an articulated figure to meet the constraints in each frame. Through the fitting technique, the motion displacement of every joint at each constrained frame is interpolated and thus smoothly propagated to frames. We are able to adaptively add motion details to satisfy the constraints within a specified tolerance by adopting a multilevel B-spline representation which also provides a speedup for the interpolation. The performance of our system is further enhanced by the new inverse kinematics solver. We present a closed-form solution to compute the joint angles of a limb linkage. This analytical method greatly reduces the burden of a numerical optimization to find the solutions for full degrees of freedom of a human-like articulated figure. We demonstrate that the technique can be used for retargetting a motion to compensate for geometric variations caused by both characters and environments. Furthermore, we can also use this technique for directly manipulating a motion clip through a graphical interface.

**CR Categories:** I.3.7 [Computer Graphics]: Three-dimensional Graphics—Animation; G.1.2 [Numerical Analysis]: Approximation—Spline and piecewise polynomial approximation

**Keywords:** Motion Editing, Motion Adaptation, Spacetime Constraints, Hierarchical Techniques, Inverse Kinematics

## 1 Introduction

Animating human-like characters is a recurring issue in computer graphics. Recently, motion capture has become one of the most promising technologies in character animation. Realistic motion data can be captured by recording the movement of a real actor with an optical or magnetic motion capture system. A motion library, that is an archive of reusable motion clips, is also commercially available. Much of the recent research in motion control has been devoted to developing various kinds of editing tools to produce a convincing motion from prerecorded motion clips. To reuse motion-captured data, animators often adapt them to a different character, i.e., retargetting a motion from one character to another [13], or to a different environment to compensate for geometric variations [3, 37]. Animators also combine two motion clips in such a way that the end of one motion is seamlessly connected to the start of the other [28].

The core of the motion manipulation can be modeled as a spacetime constraint problem [12, 13, 28]. Each kinematic constraint specifies the desired position or orientation of an end-effector, such as a foot and a hand, of an articulated figure at a specific time. The important features of the target motion are specified interactively as constraints, and the captured motion is deformed to satisfy those constraints.

Motion data consist of a bundle of motion signals. Each signal represents a sequence of sampled values for each degree of freedom. Those signals are sampled at a sequence of discrete time instances with a uniform interval to form a motion clip that consists of a sequence of frames. In each frame, the sampled values from the signals determine the configuration of an articulated figure at that frame, and thus they are related to each other by kinematic constraints. This structure yields two relationships among sampled values: *inter-frame* and *intra-frame relationships*. Through the use of an inverse kinematics solver, the intra-frame relationship, that is, the configuration of an articulated figure within each frame can be adjusted to meet the kinematic constraints. However, if each frame is considered independently, then there could be an undesirable jerkiness between consecutive frames. Therefore, we have to take account of the inter-frame relationship as well. For this purpose, we employ the multilevel B-spline fitting technique. We also present an efficient inverse kinematics algorithm which is used in conjunction with the fitting technique. Our approach is distinguished from the work of Gleicher [13] who addressed the same problem. He provided a unified approach to fuse both relationships into a very large non-linear optimization problem, which is cumbersome to handle. Instead, we decouple the problem into manageable subproblems each of which can be solved very efficiently.

Multilevel B-spline fitting techniques have been investigated to design smooth surfaces which interpolate scattered features within a specified tolerance [10, 20, 21, 34]. Among them, we extend the technique presented by Lee *et al.* [21] for adapting a motion to satisfy the constraints which are scattered over the frames. The multilevel B-splines make use of a coarse-to-fine hierarchy of knot sequences to generate a series of uniform cubic B-spline curves whose sum approaches the desired function. At each level in the hierarchy, the control points of the B-spline curve are computed locally with a least-squares method which provides an interactive performance. With this fitting technique, we cannot only manipulate a curve adaptively to satisfy a large set of constraints within a specified error tolerance, but also edit a curve at any level of detail to allow an arbitrary portion of the motion to be affected through direct manipulation. Exploiting these favorable properties of the

†jehee@jupiter.kaist.ac.kr, http://tclab.kaist.ac.kr/~jehee
‡syshin@cs.kaist.ac.kr, http://tclab.kaist.ac.kr/~syshin
§KAIST, 373-1 Kusung-dong Yusung-gu, Taejon, Republic of Korea

multilevel B-spline curves, we conveniently derive a hierarchy of displacement maps which are applied to the original motion data to obtain a new, smoothly modified motion. Because of this displacement mapping, the detail characteristics of the original motion can be preserved [3, 37].

The performance of our approach is further enhanced by our new inverse kinematics solver. It is commonplace to formulate the inverse kinematics with multiple targets as a constrained non-linear optimization for which the computational cost is expensive [28, 38]. As noticed by Korein and Badler [19], we can find a closed-form solution to the inverse kinematics problem for a limb linkage which consists of three joints, for example, shoulder-elbow-wrist for the arm and hip-knee-ankle for the leg. We combine this analytical method with a numerical optimization technique to compute the solutions for full degrees of freedom of a human-like articulated figure. Our hybrid algorithm enables us to edit the motions of a 37 DOF articulated figure, interactively.

The remainder of the paper is organized as follows. After a review of previous works, we give an introduction to the displacement mapping and the multilevel B-spline fitting technique in Section 3. In Section 4, we present our motion editing technique. In Section 5, we describe two inverse kinematics algorithms: One is designed to manipulate a general tree-structured articulated figure and the other is specialized to a human-like figure with limb linkages. In Section 6, we demonstrate how our technique can be used for interactive motion capture-based animation which includes adapting a motion from one character to another, fitting a recorded walk onto a rough terrain and performing seamless transitions among motion clips. Finally, we conclude this paper in Section 7.

# 2 Previous Works

## 2.1 Motion Editing

There have been an abundance of research results to develop motion editing tools. Bruderlin and Williams [3] showed that techniques from the signal processing domain can be applied to manipulating animated motions. They introduced the idea of displacement mapping to alter a motion clip. Witkin and Popović [37] presented a motion warping technique for the same purpose. Bruderlin and Williams also presented a multi-target interpolation with dynamic time warping to blend two motions. Unuma *et al.* [33] used Fourier analysis techniques to interpolate and extrapolate motion data in the frequency domain. Wiley and Hahn [35] and Guo and Robergé [14] investigated spatial domain techniques to linearly interpolate a set of example motions. Rose *et al.* [27] adopted a multidimensional interpolation technique to blend multiple motions all together.

Witkin and Kass [36] proposed a spacetime constraint technique to produce the optimal motion which satisfies a set of user-specified constraints. Brotman and Netravali [2] achieved a similar result by employing optimal control techniques. The spacetime formulation leads to a constrained non-linear optimization problem. Cohen [5] developed a spacetime control system which allows a user to interactively guide a numerical optimization process to find an acceptable solution in a feasible time. Liu *et al.* [22] used a hierarchical wavelet representation to automatically add motion details. Rose *et al.* [28] adopted this approach to generate a smooth transition between motion clips. Gleicher [12] simplified the spacetime problem by removing the physics-related aspects from the objective function and constraints to achieve an interactive performance for motion editing. He also applied this technique for motion retargetting [13].

## 2.2 Hierarchical Curve/Surface Manipulation

There is a vast amount of literature devoted to investigating hierarchical representations of curves and surfaces. Schmitt *et al.* [29] presented an adaptive subdivision method to produce a smooth surface from sampled data. Forsey and Bartels [9] introduced a hierarchical B-spline representation to enhance surface modeling capability. This representation allows details to be adaptively added to the surface through local refinement. They also employed the hierarchical representation for fitting a spline surface to the regular data sampled at grid points [10]. Welch and Witkin [34] proposed a variational approach to directly manipulate a B-spline surface with scattered features, such as points and curves. Lee *et al.* [20, 21] suggested an efficient method for interpolating scattered data points. They also demonstrated that image warping applications can be cast as a surface fitting problem by adopting the idea of displacement mapping. Although authors used different terms, such as hierarchical and multilevel B-spline surfaces, to refer to their hierarchical structures, their underlying ideas are the same, that is, a coarse-to-fine hierarchy of control lattices. Another class of approaches is due to multiresolution analysis and wavelets. Finkelstein and Salesin [8] used B-spline wavelets for multiresolution editing of curves. Many authors have investigated multiresolution analysis for manipulating spline surfaces and polygonal meshes [4, 6, 23, 30].

## 2.3 Inverse Kinematics

Traditionally, inverse kinematics solvers can be divided into two categories: *analytic* and *numerical solvers*. Most industrial manipulators are designed to have analytic solutions for efficient and robust control. Kahan [16] and Paden [24] independently discussed methods to solve an inverse kinematics problem by reducing it into a series of simpler subproblems whose closed-form solutions are known. Korein and Badler [19] showed that the inverse kinematics problem of a human arm and leg allows an analytic solution. Actual solutions are derived by Tolani and Badler [32].

A numerical method relies on an iterative process to obtain a solution. Girard and Maciejewski [11] addressed the locomotion of a legged figure using Jacobian matrix and its pseudo inverse. Koga *et al.* [18] made use of results from neurophysiology to achieve an "experimentally" good initial guess and then employed a numerical procedure for fine tuning. Zhao and Badler [38] formulated the inverse kinematics problem of a human figure as a constrained non-linear optimization problem. Rose *et al.* [28] extended this formulation to handle variational constraints that hold over an interval of motion frames.

# 3 Preliminary

## 3.1 Displacement Mapping

The configuration of an articulated figure is specified by its joint angles in addition to the position and orientation of the root segment. We will denote the position of the root by a 3-dimensional vector and the others by unit quaternions. It is well-known that unit quaternions can represent 3-dimensional orientations smoothly and compactly without singularity [31]. This representation can also describe a human joint conveniently.

A motion is a time-varying function which provides the configuration of an articulated figure at a time. We denote a motion by $\mathbf{m}(t) = (\mathbf{p}(t), \mathbf{q}^1(t), \cdots, \mathbf{q}^n(t))^T$, where $\mathbf{p}(t) \in \mathbb{R}^3$ and $\mathbf{q}^1(t) \in \mathbb{S}^3$ describe the translational and rotational motion of the root segment, and $\mathbf{q}^i(t) \in \mathbb{S}^3$ gives the rotational motion of the $(i-1)$-th joint for $2 \leq i \leq n$.

A displacement map (also called a warp function) describes the difference between two motions [3, 37]. Gleicher [13] provided a good explanation to introduce this technique into a spacetime formulation. In our mathematical setting, the displacement map is defined as $\mathbf{d}(t) = \mathbf{m}(t) \ominus \mathbf{m}_0(t)$, where $\mathbf{d}(t) = (\mathbf{v}^0(t), \cdots, \mathbf{v}^n(t))^T$ and $\mathbf{v}^i(t) \in \mathbb{R}^3$ for $0 \leq i \leq n$. Thus, a new motion can be obtained by applying the displacement map to the original motion as $\mathbf{m}(t) = \mathbf{m}_0(t) \oplus \mathbf{d}(t)$, that is,

$$\begin{pmatrix} \mathbf{p} \\ \mathbf{q}^1 \\ \vdots \\ \mathbf{q}^n \end{pmatrix} = \begin{pmatrix} \mathbf{p}_0 \\ \mathbf{q}_0^1 \\ \vdots \\ \mathbf{q}_0^n \end{pmatrix} \oplus \begin{pmatrix} \mathbf{v}^0 \\ \mathbf{v}^1 \\ \vdots \\ \mathbf{v}^n \end{pmatrix} = \begin{pmatrix} \mathbf{p}_0 + \mathbf{v}^0 \\ \mathbf{q}_0^1 \exp(\mathbf{v}^1) \\ \vdots \\ \mathbf{q}_0^n \exp(\mathbf{v}^n) \end{pmatrix}. \quad (1)$$

Here, $\exp(\mathbf{v})$ denotes a 3-dimensional rotation about the axis $\frac{\mathbf{v}}{\|\mathbf{v}\|} \in \mathbb{R}^3$ by angle $\|\mathbf{v}\| \in \mathbb{R}$. We refer the readers to Kim *et al.* [17] for details of quaternion algebra and the exponential map. With the displacement mapping, we are able to deal with both position and orientation data in a uniform way; the displacement map is a homogeneous array of 3-dimensional vectors, while the configuration of an articulated figure is represented as a heterogeneous array of a vector and unit quaternions.

## 3.2 Multilevel B-spline Approximation

Lee *et al.* [21] proposed a multilevel B-spline approximation technique for fitting a spline surface to scattered data points. In this section, we give a brief summary to introduce their fitting technique. Since we need to manipulate a curve rather than a surface, our derivation focuses on curve fitting.

Let $\Omega = \{t \in \mathbb{R} | 0 \le t < n\}$ be a domain interval. Consider a set of scattered data points $\mathcal{P} = \{(t_i, x_i)\}$ for $t_i \in \Omega$. To interpolate the data points, we formulate an approximation function $f$ as a B-spline function which is defined over a uniform knot sequence overlaid on the domain $\Omega$. The function $f(t) = \sum_{k=0}^{3} B_k(t - \lfloor t \rfloor) b_{\lfloor t \rfloor + k - 1}$ can be described in terms of its control points and uniform cubic B-spline basis functions $B_k$, $0 \le k \le 3$. Here, $b_i$ is the $i$-th control point on the knot sequence for $-1 \le i \le n+1$. With this formulation, the problem of deriving function $f$ is reduced to that of finding the control points that best approximate the data points in $\mathcal{P}$.

Since each control point $b_j$ is influenced by the data points in its neighborhood, we can define the *proximity set* $\mathcal{P}_j = \{(t_i, x_i) \in \mathcal{P} | j - 2 \le t_i < j + 2\}$ which affect the value of $b_j$. Simple linear algebra using pseudo inverse provides a least-squares solution

$$b_j = \frac{\sum_{(t_i, x_i) \in \mathcal{P}_j} \omega_{ij}^2 \beta_{ij}}{\sum_{(t_i, x_i) \in \mathcal{P}_j} \omega_{ij}^2} \quad (2)$$

which minimizes a local approximation error $\sum_{(t_i, x_i) \in \mathcal{P}_j} \|f(t_i) - x_i\|^2$. Here, $\omega_{ij} = B_{j+1-\lfloor t_i \rfloor}(t_i - \lfloor t_i \rfloor)$ comes from a B-spline basis function, and $\beta_{ij} = \frac{\omega_{ij} x_i}{\sum_{k=0}^{3} B_k(t_i - \lfloor t_i \rfloor)}$ takes an effect to pull the curve toward a data point $(t_i, x_i)$.

There is a trade-off between the shape smoothness and accuracy of the approximation function. If the knot spacing of the approximation function is too coarse, it may leave large deviations at the data points. Conversely, if the function is defined over an excessively fine knot sequence, its shape would undulate through the data points. Multilevel B-spline approximation uses a series of B-spline functions with different knot spacings to achieve a smooth shape while accurately approximating given data points in $\mathcal{P}$. The function from the coarsest knot sequence provides a rough approximation, which is further refined in accuracy by the functions derived from subsequent finer knot sequences.

A multilevel B-spline function is a sum of cubic B-spline functions $f_0, \cdots, f_h$ which are defined over uniform knot sequences overlaid on domain $\Omega$. The knot sequences yield a coarse-to-fine hierarchy. Without loss of generality, we assume that the knot spacing of $f_i$ is coarser than that of $f_j$ for any $i < j$. The multilevel B-spline approximation begins by determining the control points of

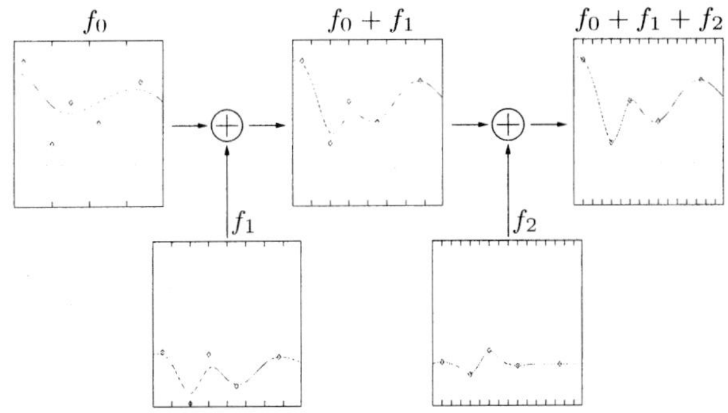


Figure 1: Hierarchical curve fitting to scattered data through multilevel B-spline approximation

$f_0$ with Equation (2), which serves as a smooth initial approximation. $f_0$ may leave a deviation $\Delta^1 x_i = x_i - f_0(t_i)$ for each point $(t_i, x_i)$ in $\mathcal{P}$. The next finer function $f_1$ is used to approximate the difference $\mathcal{D}_1 = \{(t_i, \Delta^1 x_i)\}$. Then, the sum $f_0 + f_1$ yields a smaller deviation $\Delta^2 x_i = x_i - f_0(t_i) - f_1(t_i)$ for each point $(t_i, x_i)$. At a level $k$ of the hierarchy, function $f_k$ is derived to approximate $\mathcal{D}_k = \{(t_i, \Delta^k x_i)\}$ where $\Delta^k x_i = x_i - \sum_{l=0}^{k-1} f_l(t_i)$. By repeating this process to the finest level, we can incrementally derive the final approximation function $f = \sum_{k=0}^{h} f_k$.

# 4 Hierarchical Motion Editing

## 4.1 Basic Idea

Given the original motion $\mathbf{m}_0$ and a set $\mathcal{C}$ of constraints, our problem is to derive a smooth displacement map $\mathbf{d}$ such that a target motion $\mathbf{m} = \mathbf{m}_0 \oplus \mathbf{d}$ satisfies the constraints in $\mathcal{C}$. Current motion editing techniques represent the displacement map as an array of spline curves defined over a common knot sequence [13, 37]. Each spline curve gives the time-varying motion displacement of its corresponding joint. With a finer knot sequence, we can possibly find a solution that accurately satisfies all the constraints in $\mathcal{C}$. However, we have to pay a higher computational cost for the accuracy due to the finer knot sequence. Ideally, we wish to determine the density of knots to yield just enough shape freedom for an exact solution. However, the target motion is not known in advance and thus we require the displacement map which allows details to be added by adaptively refining the knot sequence.

We adopt the hierarchical structure [21] reviewed in Section 3.2 to perform this adaptive refinement. The multilevel B-spline approximation technique was employed to derive a warp function for image morphing and geometry reconstruction. In our context, we extend this technique to handle motion data. From the displacement map $\mathbf{d}$, we derive a series of successively finer submaps $\mathbf{d}_1, \cdots, \mathbf{d}_h$ that give the corresponding series of incrementally refined motions, $\mathbf{m}_1, \cdots, \mathbf{m}_h$.

$$\mathbf{m}_h = (\cdots((\mathbf{m}_0 \oplus \mathbf{d}_1) \oplus \mathbf{d}_2) \oplus \cdots \oplus \mathbf{d}_h). \quad (3)$$

Here, $\mathbf{d}_k$, $1 \le k \le h$, is represented by an array of cubic B-spline curves in the 3-dimensional vector space. The component curves of $\mathbf{d}_k$ are defined over a common sequence $\tau_k$ of knots that are uniformly spaced. The knot sequences $\tau_k$, $1 \le k \le h$, form a coarse-to-fine hierarchy. $\tau_1$ is placed on the coarsest level in the hierarchy and $\tau_h$ is on the finest level. The motion $\mathbf{m}_1 = \mathbf{m}_0 \oplus \mathbf{d}_1$ provides a rough approximation to a target motion, which is further refined by applying $\mathbf{d}_2$ to give a more accurate approximation $\mathbf{m}_2$. By applying the submaps one by one, we can incrementally obtain the final motion. Be aware that it is a very frequent mistake to have

$\mathbf{d} = \sum_{k=1}^{h} \mathbf{d}_k$ from an erroneous derivation, that is, to substitute $\exp(\mathbf{v}_1)\exp(\mathbf{v}_2)\cdots\exp(\mathbf{v}_h)$ for $\exp(\mathbf{v}_1+\mathbf{v}_2+\cdots+\mathbf{v}_h)$ in Equation (1) and (3). This derivation is not correct, since the quaternion multiplication is not commutative.

## 4.2 Constraints

To specify the desired features of the target motion, two categories of constraints are employed: The ones in the first category are used to describe an articulated figure itself, such as a joint limit and an anatomical relationship among joints. Those in the other category are for placing end-effectors of the figure at particular positions and orientations which are interactively specified by the user or automatically derived from the interaction between the figure and its environment. For example, we first specify the contact point between the foot and the ground through a graphical interface and automatically modify the point later in accordance with the geometric variation of the ground. We assume that a constraint in either category is defined at a particular instance of time. A variational constraint that holds over an interval of motion frames can be realized by a sequence of constraints for the time interval. An ordered pair $(t_j, C_j)$ specifies the set $C_j$ of constraints at a frame $t_j$.

## 4.3 Motion Fitting

In order to compute a displacement map, it is necessary to estimate the motion displacement of each joint at every constrained frame. The displacement of the joint at a particular frame is interpolated by the corresponding component curve of the displacement map and thus smoothly propagated to the neighboring frames. Suppose that we are now at the $k$-th level for $1 \leq k \leq h$. At each constrained frame $t_j$, our inverse kinematics solver gives the configuration $\mathbf{m}^{t_j}$ of the character, that meets a given set of constraints $(t_j, C_j)$. Since there may exist many possible configurations that satisfy all constraints in $C_j$, we consistently choose the one that is minimally deviated from the motion $\mathbf{m}_{k-1}$ at the previous level. That is, we minimize

$$\begin{aligned} \|\mathbf{d}^{t_j}\|_\alpha^2 &= \|\mathbf{m}^{t_j} \ominus \mathbf{m}_{k-1}(t_j)\|_\alpha^2 \qquad (4) \\ &= \sum_{i=0}^{n} \alpha_i \|\mathbf{v}^i\|^2, \end{aligned}$$

where $\mathbf{d}^{t_j} = (\mathbf{v}^0, \cdots, \mathbf{v}^n)$. We can control the rigidity of an individual joint by adjusting its weight value.

Combining the inverse kinematics solver with the hierarchical structure given in Equation (3), we give the following motion fitting algorithm:

**Algorithm 1** Hierarchical motion fitting

INPUT : the original motion $\mathbf{m}_0$, the set $\mathcal{C}$ of constraints
OUTPUT : a new motion $\mathbf{m}_h$

1: **for** $k := 1$ **to** $h$ **do**
2: $\quad\mathcal{D} := \emptyset$
3: $\quad$**for each** $(t_j, C_j) \in \mathcal{C}$ **do**
4: $\quad\quad\mathbf{m}^{t_j} := \text{IK\_solver}(C_j, \mathbf{m}_{k-1}(t_j))$
5: $\quad\quad\mathbf{d}^{t_j} := \mathbf{m}^{t_j} \ominus \mathbf{m}_{k-1}(t_j)$
6: $\quad\quad\mathcal{D} := \mathcal{D} \cup (t_j, \mathbf{d}^{t_j})$
7: $\quad$**end for**
8: $\quad$Compute $\mathbf{d}_k$ by curve fitting to $\mathcal{D}$
9: $\quad\mathbf{m}_k := \mathbf{m}_{k-1} \oplus \mathbf{d}_k$
10: **end for**

This algorithm evaluates $\mathbf{d}_k$, $1 \leq k \leq h$, in the coarse-to-fine order. At each level $k$ in the hierarchy, we compute the motion displacement $\mathbf{d}^{t_j} = \mathbf{m}^{t_j} \ominus \mathbf{m}_{k-1}(t_j)$ for all $(t_j, C_j)$ in $\mathcal{C}$ using the inverse kinematics solver (See lines 2–7). Here, $\mathbf{m}_{k-1}$ is either the original motion ($k = 1$) or has been already obtained in the previous level ($k > 1$). The newly computed displacements in $\mathcal{D} = \{(t_j, \mathbf{d}^{t_j})\}$ are used as the keyframes for deriving the displacement map $\mathbf{d}_k$(See line 8). Several techniques are available for computing $\mathbf{d}_k$ that interpolates the displacements. One possible solution is to employ an iterative numerical method that may give an optimal solution. However, we choose a curve fitting method given in Equation (2) to achieve an interactive performance. Our method is extremely fast, since the solution can be obtained analytically unlike the numerical method that normally requires a heavy computational cost for iterations. In general, local curve fitting with B-splines may have several drawbacks. The resulting curve may be less accurate and could have undulations because of the lack of the global propagation of a displacement. Fortunately, our hierarchical structure can compensate for such drawbacks by globally propagating the displacement at a coarse level and performing the later tuning at fine levels.

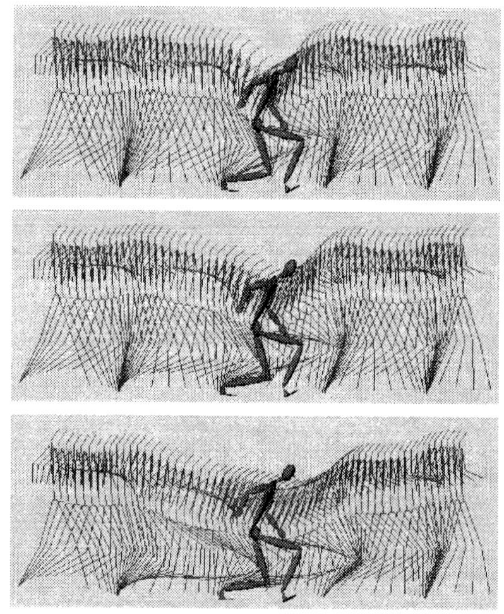

Figure 2: A live-captured walking motion was interactively modified at the middle frame such that the character bent forward and lowered the pelvis. The character is depicted at the modified frame. The range of deformation is determined by the density of the knot sequences. The knots in $\tau_1$ are spaced every (top) 4, (middle) 6, and (bottom) 12 frames.

## 4.4 Knot Spacing

For simplicity, our implementation doubles the density of a knot sequence from one level to the next. Therefore, if $\tau_k$ has $(n+3)$ control points on it, then the next finer knot sequence $\tau_{k+1}$ will have $(2n+3)$ control points. The density of a knot sequence $\tau_k$, $1 \leq k \leq h$, determines the range of influence of a constraint on the displacement map at a level $k$. This is of great importance for direct manipulation. For example, consider the situation that we interactively adjust the configuration of an articulated figure by dragging one of its segments at a certain frame through a graphical interface. The user input is interpreted as constraints which are immediately added to the set of prescribed constraints. Then, our system smoothly deforms a portion of the motion clip around this modified frame. Here, the range of influence on the motion clip is mainly dependent on the spacing of $\tau_k$. The larger spacing between

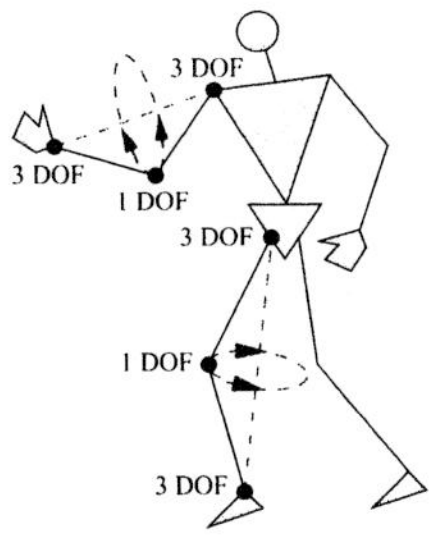


Figure 3: A human-like figure that has explicit redundancies at its limb linkages

knots yields the wider range of deformation (See Figure 2). Therefore, the displacement map $\mathbf{d}_1$, that is derived from the coarsest sequence $\tau_1$, has non-zero values over the widest range to smoothly propagate the change of the motion. The subsequent finer displacement maps $\mathbf{d}_k$, $2 \leq k \leq h$, perform successive tunings to satisfy the constraints.

The density of the finest knot sequence $\tau_h$ controls the precision of the final motion $\mathbf{m}_h$. If $\tau_h$ is sufficiently fine to accommodate the distribution of constraints in the time domain, $\mathbf{m}_h$ can exactly satisfy all constraints. However, our algorithm may leave a small deviation for each constraint in $C$ even with several levels in the hierarchy. In our experiments, we need just four or five levels for visually pleasing results, that can be further enhanced to achieve an exact interpolation by enforcing each constraint independently with the inverse kinematics solver.

### 4.5 Initial Guesses

For a spacetime problem, a good initial guess on the desired solution is very important to improve both the convergence of numerical optimization and the quality of the result [13]. We obtain an initial guess for motion fitting by shifting the position of the root segment in the original motion. To motivate this, consider the walking motion that is adapted to the rough terrain as shown in Figures 5 (a) and (b). The position of a stance foot, that touches the surface of the terrain, is pulled upward at a small hill on the terrain, and thus the character is unwantedly forced to squat. Even though the inverse kinematics solver tries to minimize the deviation of joint angles, it cannot prevent the knee bending completely. To reduce this artifact, we change the position of the root segment due to the change of geometry. Specifically, we displace the root segment by the average shift of the contact positions at each frame. The shift of the root segment position at a frame can also be smoothly propagated to the neighboring frames using the multilevel B-spline fitting method.

## 5 Inverse Kinematics

The most time consuming component in the motion fitting algorithm is the inverse kinematics solver which is invoked very frequently at each level of the fitting hierarchy. Therefore, the overall performance of a hierarchical fitting critically depends on the performance of the inverse kinematics solver. We describe, in this section, two inverse kinematics algorithms. In Section 5.1, we introduce an inverse kinematics algorithm for a general tree-structured figure with spherical joints based on numerical optimization techniques. In Section 5.2, we present a faster specialized algorithm for a human-like figure with limb linkages. The latter algorithm combines the numerical techniques with an analytical method illustrated in Section 5.3.

### 5.1 A Numerical Approach

Our inverse kinematics solver is based on a constrained non-linear optimization technique that minimizes the objective function subject to a set $C$ of constraints. We have an additional burden to enforce the unitariness of each quaternion parameter $\mathbf{q} = (w, x, y, z)$. One possible solution would be to augment the set $C$ with a new constraint $w^2 + x^2 + y^2 + z^2 - 1 = 0$ for the unit quaternion parameter. We circumvent this extra constraint from the observation that every orientation $\mathbf{q}$ can be expressed as a rotation $\exp(\mathbf{v}) \in \mathbb{S}^3$ from a fixed reference orientation $\mathbf{q}_0 \in \mathbb{S}^3$, that is, $\mathbf{q} = \mathbf{q}_0 \exp(\mathbf{v})$. Therefore, we can parameterize $(\mathbf{p}, \mathbf{q}^1, \cdots, \mathbf{q}^n)$ by a simple vector $\mathbf{x} = (x_0, \cdots, x_{3n+2}) \in \mathbb{R}^{3n+3}$ using the displacement $\mathbf{d} = (\mathbf{v}^0, \cdots, \mathbf{v}^n)$ from a given reference configuration $(\mathbf{p}_0, \mathbf{q}_0^1, \cdots, \mathbf{q}_0^n)$ as follows:

$$\begin{aligned} \mathbf{p} &= \mathbf{p}_0 + \mathbf{v}^0, \quad \text{and} \\ \mathbf{q}^i &= \mathbf{q}_0^i \exp(\mathbf{v}^i), \quad 1 \leq i \leq n, \end{aligned} \tag{5}$$

where $\mathbf{v}^i = (x_{3i}, x_{3i+1}, x_{3i+2})$ for $0 \leq i \leq n$. Letting the reference configuration be $\mathbf{m}_{k-1}(t_j)$ in Equation (4), we reduce the objective function to a quadratic form of $\mathbf{x}$. Accordingly, our constrained optimization problem is formulated as follows:

$$\begin{aligned} \text{minimize} \quad & f(\mathbf{x}) = \frac{1}{2}\mathbf{x}^T \mathbf{M}\mathbf{x}, \\ \text{subject to} \quad & c_i(\mathbf{x}) = 0, \quad i \in N_e, \\ & c_i(\mathbf{x}) > 0, \quad i \in N_i, \end{aligned}$$

where $\mathbf{M}$ is a diagonal matrix that determines the rigidity of individual parameters in $\mathbf{x}$.

A typical approach to the constrained optimization is to transform the constrained problem into an unconstrained version with extra parameters (the Lagrange multipliers) or extra energy terms (penalty functions). We avoid illegal configurations by employing the penalty method that allows us to handle the equality and inequality constraints in a uniform way [25]. The objective function for the unconstrained version is

$$g(\mathbf{x}) = f(\mathbf{x}) + \sum_{i \in N_e} \omega_i c_i(\mathbf{x})^2 + \sum_{i \in N_i} \omega_i (\min(c_i(\mathbf{x}), 0))^2, \tag{6}$$

where $\omega_i$ weights each individual constraint. We adopt the conjugate gradient method to minimize this function [26].

### 5.2 A Hybrid Approach

The major difficulty of solving an inverse kinematics problem stems from the excessive DOFs of an articulated figure. A reasonable human model may have about 40 DOFs for computer animation, while we specify much fewer constraints for manipulating the figure. For a figure of $n$ DOFs, we can remove $c$ of those DOFs with a set of $c$ independent constraints imposed on it. The remaining $(n - c)$ DOFs span the solution space of the problem.

A reduced-coordinate formulation parameterizes the redundant DOFs with a reduced set of $(n - c)$ variables. One explicit redundancy in the human body is the "elbow circle" that was first mentioned in Korein and Badler [19]. Even though the shoulder and the wrist are firmly planted, we can still afford to move the elbow along a circle with its axis through the shoulder and the wrist (See Figure 3). The human figure has four limbs, two from arms and two from legs. The redundant DOF for the $i$-th limb linkage can be parameterized with a rotation angle $\theta_i$, $1 \leq i \leq 4$, about the axis.

Without loss of generality, we assume that the positions and orientations of hands and feet are fixed by constraints. If there is a free hand or foot, the DOFs in the corresponding limb are left unchanged. Let $\mathbf{m} = (\mathbf{p}, \mathbf{q}^1, \cdots, \mathbf{q}^r, \mathbf{q}^{r+1}, \cdots, \mathbf{q}^n)$ be the configuration of a human-like figure. Its rear part $(\mathbf{q}^{r+1}, \cdots, \mathbf{q}^n)$ denotes the DOFs for the limbs and the fore part $(\mathbf{p}, \mathbf{q}^1, \cdots, \mathbf{q}^r)$ does the remaining DOFs. Since the constraints restrain the DOFs in the limb linkages, the reduced set of parameters $(\mathbf{p}, \mathbf{q}^1, \cdots, \mathbf{q}^r, \theta_1, \cdots, \theta_4)$ span all possible configurations of the figure under the constraints.

Incorporating the idea of reduced-coordinate formulation into the numerical optimization framework, we can solve an inverse kinematics problem using a fewer number of optimization parameters $\hat{\mathbf{x}} = (x_0, \cdots, x_{3r+2}, \theta_1, \cdots, \theta_4) \in \mathbb{R}^{3r+7}$. Note that we have replaced the rear part of $\mathbf{x}$ with the elbow circle parameters $\theta_1, \cdots, \theta_4$ for limb linkages. Whenever we evaluate the objective function with new parameters $\hat{\mathbf{x}}$, the parameters $(\mathbf{p}, \mathbf{q}^1, \cdots, \mathbf{q}^r)$ are computed first by Equation (5), and then the others for $(\mathbf{q}^{r+1}, \cdots, \mathbf{q}^n)$ are uniquely determined by an analytical solver which takes $(\mathbf{p}, \mathbf{q}^1, \cdots, \mathbf{q}^r)$ and $\theta_i$, $1 \leq i \leq 4$, as input. Then, we extract the unknown part $(x_{3r+3}, \cdots, x_{3n+2})$ of $\mathbf{x}$ from $(\mathbf{q}^{r+1}, \cdots, \mathbf{q}^n)$ to evaluate the objective function in Equation (6). The reduced-coordinate formulation uses a fewer number of parameters to yield faster convergence and fewer iterations to enhance the overall performance.

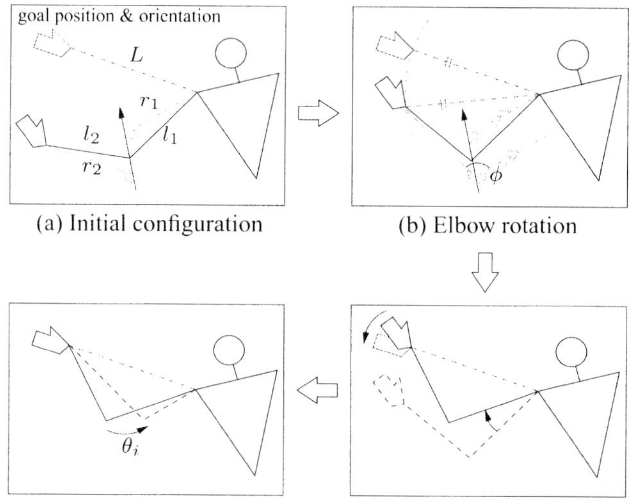


(a) Initial configuration (b) Elbow rotation (c) Shoulder & Wrist rotation (d) Redundancy

Figure 4: The process for adjusting the arm posture

### 5.3 Arm and Leg Postures

Consider a limb linkage, for example, an arm linkage. Starting from an initial configuration, we sequentially adjust the joint angles for the elbow, the shoulder and the wrist of the arm linkage to place the hand at the desired position and orientation. We assume that the torso and the shoulder positions are given. Let $l_1$, $l_2$, $r_1$, $r_2$ and $L$ be defined as follows (See Figure 4(a)):

$l_1$ = the length of the upper arm,
$l_2$ = the length of the fore arm,
$r_1$ = the distance from the elbow rotation axis to the shoulder,
$r_2$ = the distance from the elbow rotation axis to the wrist, and
$L$ = the distance between the shoulder and the wrist.

To place the wrist at a position distant from the shoulder by $L$ (See Figure 4(b)), the angle $\phi$ between upper and lower arms is given by

$$\phi = \cos^{-1}\left(\frac{l_1^2 + l_2^2 + 2\sqrt{l_1^2 - r_1^2}\sqrt{l_2^2 - r_2^2} - L^2}{2r_1r_2}\right), \tag{7}$$

as illustrated in the appendix. Then, we bring the wrist to the goal position by adjusting the shoulder angles (See Figure 4(c)). In the subsequent step, we rotate the wrist angles to coincide with the goal orientation. Once one feasible solution is given, the other solutions can be obtained by rotating the elbow about the axis that passes through the shoulder and the wrist positions. Given $\theta_i$, we can determine the arm posture uniquely (See Figure 4(d)). Similarly, we can determine a leg posture.

If $L$ is longer than the arm length, $l_1 + l_2$, the elbow stretches as far as possible. On the other hand, if $L$ is too small, then the elbow angle could violate its lower limit and thus is pulled back into the allowable range. In both cases, we cannot place the wrist at the exact position and thus the corresponding penalty function yields a positive value for the given torso configuration.

## 6 Experimental Results

Our human model has 6 DOFs for the pelvis position and orientation, 3 DOFs for the (either rigid or flexible) spine, and 7 DOFs for each limb to yield the total of 37 parameters for the inverse kinematics problem. Other parameters for the head, the neck, and the fingers are not used for resolving kinematic constraints. Through the reduced-coordinate formulation, we can remove 6 DOFs for each limb and thus we have at most 13 DOFs to be computed by a numerical optimization method. The motion clips for our experiments have been sampled at the rate of 30 frames per second.

The walking motion of Figure 5(a) is produced by performing a sequence of transitions among a set of motion-captured clips, which include "walk straight", "turn left", "turn right", "start", and "stop". We interactively specify the moments of heel-strikes and toe-offs for the motion clips. This information is used for establishing the kinematic constraints that enforce the foot contacts for the entire motion. The terrain of Figure 5(b) is represented as a NURBS surface of which control points are placed on a regular grid with a spacing of 80 % of the height of the character, and their y-coordinates (heights) are randomly perturbed within 120 % of the height. To adapt the motion onto the rough terrain with doorways, we first adjust the constraints such that the contact positions are shifted along the y-axis to be placed on the terrain, and add new constraints to bend the character under the doorways. Then, we use our motion fitting algorithm to warp the motion to satisfy the constraints. The original and the adapted motions are depicted in Figures 5(a) and 5(b), respectively.

The "climbing a rope" example in Figure 5(c) gives constraints on both hands and feet. A physically simulated rope is used to explicitly illustrate the moments of grasping and releasing the rope by a hand, which correspond to the initiation and termination, respectively, of a variational constraint for that hand. We adapt this motion to a different character with longer legs and a shorter body and arms. For the character morphing example shown in Figure 5(d), the size of a character smoothly changes to have extremely long legs and a short body, and then to have extremely short legs and a long body. The original walking motion is warped to preserve its uniform stride against the change of character size.

Our motion fitting method is also useful for generating a smooth transition between motion clips. Figure 5(e) shows the transitions from walking to sneaking and from sneaking to walking. The basic approach is very similar to the one presented by Rose *et al.* [27] We seamlessly connect the motion data by fading one out while fading the other in. Over the fading duration, Hermite interpolation and time warping techniques are used to smoothly blend the joint parameters of the motion data. Since joint parameter blending may cause foot sliding, we enforce foot contact constraints with the motion fitting method.

(a) The original walking motion on the flat ground

(b) The adapted motion for the rough terrain

(c) Climbing a rope for different characters

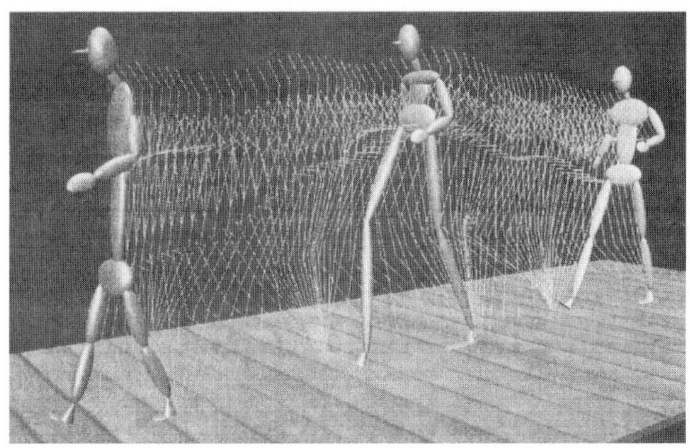

(d) Character morphing

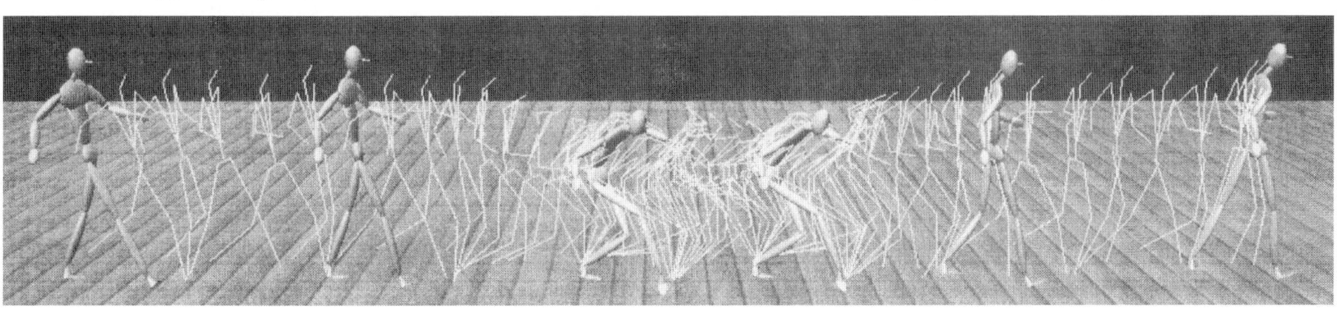

(e) Transitions between walking and sneaking

Figure 5: Examples

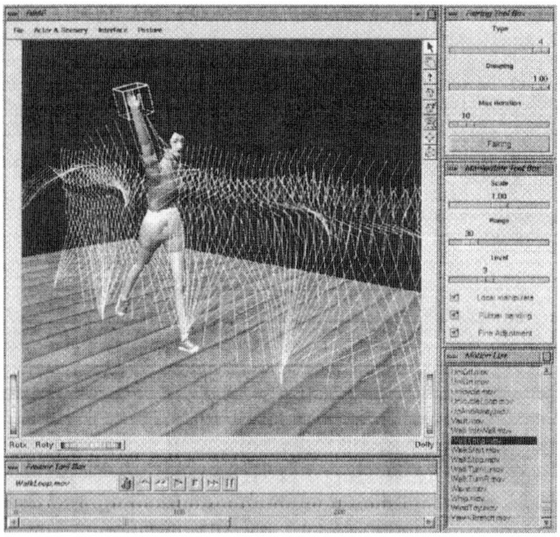

Figure 6: Graphical user interface

Table 1 gives a performance summary of the examples. Timing information is obtained on a SGI Indigo2 workstation with an R10000 195 MHz processor. The execution time for each example is not only influenced by quantitative factors such as the number of frames, constraints and parameters, but also by qualitative factors such as the difficulty of achieving desired features specified by constraints and the quality of initial estimates. In particular, well-chosen initial estimates provide great speedups for most of examples. One promising observation is that both execution times and maximum errors rapidly decrease level by level. This implies that the performance of our algorithm is not critically dependent on the error tolerance. In all examples, every constraint is satisfied within or slightly over 1 % of the height of the character by the hierarchical fitting of four levels. A few more levels may result in a more accurate solution. As shown in experimental data, we can anticipate that the computation cost for an additional level is much cheaper than the cost for the prior level.

Our prototype system is implemented in C++ on top of X-windows/MOTIF$^{TM}$ and Open Inventor$^{TM}$ that facilitates developing interactive 3D user interfaces. In particular, Open Inventor$^{TM}$ provides convenient toolkits to support direct manipulation in the 3D space. With this toolkits, an animator can interactively modify the pose of a character by dragging one of its segments. Our user interface allows the user to edit a desired portion of the motion by adjusting the spacing of knots over which the displacement map is defined. Since we use cubic B-splines to represent the displacement map, the change of the pose at a frame could affect the poses at the neighboring frames covered by seven knots at the current level in the hierarchy [1, 7].

## 7 Discussion

In this section, we compare our motion fitting algorithm to the previous approaches at several viewpoints.

**Interpolating splines vs. Multilevel B-splines:** An interpolating spline is a possible choice to represent the displacement map [3, 37]. However, the interpolating spline could undulate rapidly for a dense distribution of constraints so that it often fails to preserve the detail characteristics of the original motion. Instead, we use a series of uniform B-splines that form a hierarchy of motion displacements. Since uniform B-splines approximate different details of displacements according to knot spacings, we are able to edit the motion at any level of detail; fitting at the coarsest level makes a gross deformation and then fine details are incrementally added at the finer levels.

**Global vs. Local least-squares:** Fitting a B-spline curve to scattered data points can be formulated as a least-squares approximation problem for solving an over-determined or under-determined system of linear equations [26]. To obtain the optimal solution in the least-squares sense, we can use the pseudo inverse of a large matrix that accommodates the data points all together [15]. However, this global method often suffers from over-shooting that may give an undesirable curve shape. Ironically, the less accurate local method in Equation (2) is preferred in a hierarchical framework. Since approximation errors at one level are incrementally canceled out in the later levels, the accuracy at each level is not critical. This local method is much more efficient and less prone to over-shooting than the global method.

**Single large optimization vs. Many small optimizations:** Gleicher [13] cast motion retargetting as a large optimization problem. Based on the "divide-and-conquer" strategy, however, we partition his optimization problem into many smaller inverse kinematics optimizations and then solve each of them very efficiently by adopting specialized techniques such as the hybrid inverse kinematics solver. Finally, we combine the poses at constrained frames employing the hierarchical curve fitting technique. This divide-and-conquer approach provides a noticeable speedup to satisfy the performance requirement of our interactive motion editing system.

**Limitation of our approach:** Our motion fitting algorithm requires additional work to handle an inter-frame constraint that enforces the relationship among parameters scattered over multiple frames. This kind of constraints are used for avoiding foot sliding between the heel-strike of a foot and its toe-off while allowing the absolute coordinates of the foot to be altered. We address this problem by incorpolating the intra-frame inverse kinematics constraints at those co-related frames into a larger optimization problem that includes inter-frame constraints among those frames as well. In the extreme case where all frames are related to each other, this approach is reduced to Gleicher's so that we have to solve one large optimization problem to derive the displacement map at each level in the hierarchy.

## 8 Conclusion

We have presented a new approach to adapting existing motion of a human-like character to have desired features that are specified by a set of constraints. The key idea of our approach is to introduce a hierarchical motion representation by which we cannot only manipulate a motion adaptively to satisfy a large set of constraints within a specified error tolerance, but also edit an arbitrary portion of the motion through direct manipulation.

The performance of our algorithm is greatly improved by employing a curve fitting technique that minimizes a local approximation error. The hierarchical structure compensates for the possible drawbacks of the local approximation method by globally propagating the displacement at a coarse level and later tuning at fine levels. Further performance gain is achieved by the new inverse kinematics solver. Our hybrid algorithm performs much faster than a pure numerical algorithm. We also present a simple yet effective formulation to optimize orientation parameters without yielding extra constraints.

Table 1: Performance data. # of parameters counts the DOFs of a character used for resolving kinematic constraints. A number in ( ) indicates that of reduced parameters. The maximum error is measured in percentages of the height of the character.

| | walking on rough terrain | | | | climbing a rope | | | |
|---|---|---|---|---|---|---|---|---|
| # of parameters | 20 (8) | | | | 37 (13) | | | |
| # of frames | 464 | | | | 275 | | | |
| # of constraints (except joint limits) | 5568 | | | | 5898 | | | |
| preprocessing time (CPU sec.) | 0.17 | | | | 0.21 | | | |
| level | 1st | 2nd | 3rd | 4th | 1st | 2nd | 3rd | 4th |
| # of frames/knot | 16 | 8 | 4 | 2 | 16 | 8 | 4 | 2 |
| execution time (CPU sec.) | 2.50 | 1.67 | 1.31 | 1.10 | 6.50 | 3.51 | 1.32 | 0.70 |
| maximum error (%) | 14.31 | 9.24 | 3.48 | 1.06 | 11.09 | 7.51 | 3.57 | 1.11 |

| | character morphing | | | | transition | | | |
|---|---|---|---|---|---|---|---|---|
| # of parameters | 20 (8) | | | | 20 (8) | | | |
| # of frames | 62 | | | | 119 | | | |
| # of constraints (except joint limits) | 420 | | | | 834 | | | |
| preprocessing time (CPU sec.) | 0.02 | | | | . | | | |
| level | 1st | 2nd | 3rd | 4th | 1st | 2nd | 3rd | 4th |
| # of frames/knot | 16 | 8 | 4 | 2 | 16 | 8 | 4 | 2 |
| execution time (CPU sec.) | 0.18 | 0.13 | 0.09 | 0.06 | 0.18 | 0.15 | 0.15 | 0.14 |
| maximum error (%) | 6.98 | 5.35 | 3.08 | 1.10 | 7.17 | 4.71 | 2.14 | 0.74 |

## Acknowledgments

We would like to thank Michael Cohen at Microsoft Research for his careful reading and constructive criticism. We are also grateful to Hyun Joon Shin and Min Gyu Choi who helped edit the accompanying video tape. We thank Korean Broadcasting System (KBS) for supplying the model in Figures 5(a) and 5(b). This research was supported in part by the Ministry of Information and Communication (MIC) and the Electronics and Telecommunications Research Institute (ETRI).

## References

[1] R. H. Bartels, J. C. Beatty, and B. Barsky. *An Introduction to Splines for Use in Computer Graphics and Geometric Modeling*. Morgan Kaufmann, 1979.

[2] L. S. Brotman and A. N. Netravali. Motion interpolation by optimal control. *Computer Graphics (Proceedings of SIGGRAPH 88)*, 22(4):309–315, August 1988.

[3] A. Bruderlin and L. Williams. Motion signal processing. *Computer Graphics (Proceedings of SIGGRAPH 95)*, 29:97–104, August 1995.

[4] A. Certain, J. Popović, T. DeRose, T. Duchamp, D. Salesin, and W. Stuetzle. Interactive multiresolution surface viewing. *Computer Graphics (Proceedings of SIGGRAPH 96)*, 30:97–115, August 1996.

[5] M. F. Cohen. Interactive spacetime control for animation. *Computer Graphics (Proceedings of SIGGRAPH 92)*, 26(2):293–302, July 1992.

[6] M. Eck, T. DeRose, T. Duchamp, H. Hoppe, M. Lounsbery, and W. Stuetzle. Multiresolution analysis of arbitrary meshes. *Computer Graphics (Proceedings of SIGGRAPH 95)*, 29:173–182, August 1995.

[7] G. Farin. *Curves and Surfaces for Computer Aided Geometric Design – A Practical Guide*. Academic Press, 4th edition, 1997.

[8] A. Finkelstein and D. H. Salesin. Multiresolution curves. *Computer Graphics (Proceedings of SIGGRAPH 94)*, 28:261–268, July 1994.

[9] D. R. Forsey and R. H. Bartels. Hierarchical B-spline refinement. *Computer Graphics (Proceedings of SIGGRAPH 88)*, 22(4):205–212, August 1988.

[10] D. R. Forsey and R. H. Bartels. Surface fitting with hierarchical splines. *ACM Transactions of Graphics*, 14(2):134–161, April 1995.

[11] M. Girard and A. A. Maciejewski. Computational modeling for the computer animation of legged figures. *Computer Graphics (Proceedings of SIGGRAPH 85)*, pages 263–270, July 1985.

[12] M. Gleicher. Motion editing with spacetime constraints. In *Proceedings of Symposium on Interactive 3D Graphics*, pages 139–148, 1997.

[13] M. Gleicher. Retargetting motion to new characters. *Computer Graphics (Proceedings of SIGGRAPH 98)*, 32:33–42, July 1998.

[14] S. Guo and J. Robergé. A high-level control mechanism for human locomotion based on parametric frame space interpolation. In *Proceedings of Computer Animation and Simulation '96, Eurographics Animation Workshop*, pages 95–107. Springer-Verlag, 1996.

[15] W. M. Hsu, J. F. Hughes, and H. Kaufman. Direct manipulation of free-form deformations. *Computer Graphics (Proceedings of SIGGRAPH 92)*, 26:177–184, July 1992.

[16] W. Kahan. Lectures on computational aspects of geometry. *Unpublished manuscripts*, 1983.

[17] M. J. Kim, M. S. Kim, and S. Y. Shin. A general construction scheme for unit quaternion curves with simple high order derivatives. *Computer Graphics (Proceedings of SIGGRAPH 95)*, 29:369–376, August 1995.

[18] Y. Koga, K. Kondo, J. Kuffer, and J. Latombe. Planning motions with intentions. *Computer Graphics (Proceedings of SIGGRAPH 94)*, 28:395–408, July 1994.

[19] J. U. Korein and N. I. Badler. Techniques for generating the goal-directed motion of articulated structures. *IEEE CG&A*, pages 71–81, Nov. 1982.

[20] S. Lee, K.-Y. Chwa, S. Y. Shin, and G. Wolberg. Image metamorphosis using snakes and free-form deformations. *Computer Graphics (Proceedings of SIGGRAPH 95)*, 29:439–448, August 1995.

[21] S. Lee, G. Wolberg, and S. Y. Shin. Scattered data interpolation with multilevel b-splines. *IEEE Transactions on Visualization and Computer Graphics*, 3(3):228–244, 1997.

[22] Z. Liu, S. G. Gortler, and M. F. Cohen. Hierarchical spacetime control. *Computer Graphics (Proceedings of SIGGRAPH 94)*, pages 35–42, July 1994.

[23] M. Lounsbery, T. D. DeRose, and J. Warren. Multiresolution analysis for surfaces of arbitrary topological type. *ACM Transactions on Graphics*, 16(1):34–73, 1997.

[24] B. Paden. *Kinematics and Control Robot Manipulators*. PhD thesis, University of California, Berkeley, 1986.

[25] J. C. Platt and A. H. Barr. Constraint methods for flexible models. *Computer Graphics (Proceedings of SIGGRAPH 88)*, 22(4):279–288, August 1988.

[26] W. H. Press, Saul A. Teukolsky, W. T. Vetterling, and B. P. Flannery. *Numerical Recipes in C: The Art of Scientific Computing*. Cambridge University Press, second edition, 1992.

[27] C. Rose, M. F. Cohen, and B. Bodenheimer. Verbs and Adverbs: Multidimensional motion interpolation. *IEEE CG&A*, 18(5):32–40, October 1998.

[28] C. Rose, B. Guenter, B. Bodenheimer, and M. F. Cohen. Efficient generation of motion transitions using spacetime constraints. *Computer Graphics (Proceedings of SIGGRAPH 96)*, 30:147–154, August 1996.

[29] F. J. M. Schmitt, B. A. Barsky, and W. Du. An adaptive subdivision method for surface-fitting from sampled data. *Computer Graphics (Proceedings of SIGGRAPH 86)*, 20(4):179–188, August 1986.

[30] P. Schröder and W. Sweldens. Spherical wavelets: Efficiently representing functions on the sphere. *Computer Graphics (Proceedings of SIGGRAPH 95)*, 29:161–172, August 1995.

[31] K. Shoemake. Animating rotation with quaternion curves. *Computer Graphics (Proceedings of SIGGRAPH 85)*, 19:245–254, 1985.

[32] D. Tolani and N. I. Badler. Real-time inverse kinematics of the human arm. *Presence*, 5(4):393–401, 1996.

[33] M. Unuma, K. Anjyo, and R. Takeuchi. Fourier principles for emotion-based human figure animation. *Computer Graphics (Proceedings of SIGGRAPH 95)*, 29:91–96, August 1995.

[34] W. Welch and A. Witkin. Variational surface modeling. *Computer Graphics (Proceedings of SIGGRAPH 92)*, 26(2):157–166, July 1992.

[35] D. J. Wiley and J. K. Hahn. Interpolation synthesis for articulated figure motion. In *Proceedings of IEEE Virtual Reality Annual International Symposium '97*, pages 157–160. IEEE Computer Society Press, 1997.

[36] A. Witkin and M. Kass. Spacetime constraints. *Computer Graphics (Proceedings of SIGGRAPH 88)*, 22(4):159–168, August 1988.

[37] A. Witkin and Z. Popović. Motion warping. *Computer Graphics (Proceedings of SIGGRAPH 95)*, 29:105–108, August 1995.

[38] J. Zhao and N. I. Badler. Inverse kinematics positioning using nonlinear programming for highly articulated figures. *ACM Transactions on Graphics*, 13(4):313–336, 1994.

## Appendix: Derivation for Equation (7)

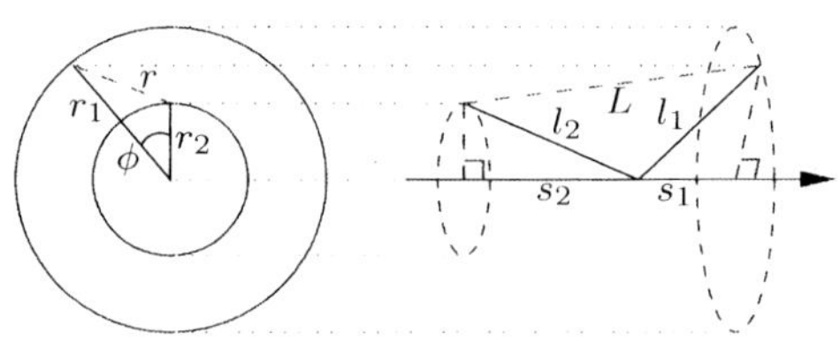

To identify the angle between the upper and fore arms, we project the joint positions onto a plane perpendicular to the elbow rotation axis. Then, the projections for the shoulder and the wrist are placed on two concentric circles whose center coincides with the projection for the elbow. The distance $r$ between the projections is given in terms of $r_1$, $r_2$ and the angle $\phi$ between them.

$$r^2 = r_1^2 + r_2^2 - 2r_1r_2\cos\phi.$$

Letting $s_1 = \sqrt{l_1^2 - r_1^2}$ and $s_2 = \sqrt{l_2^2 - r_2^2}$, respectively, the distance $L$ between the shoulder and the wrist positions is

$$\begin{aligned} L^2 &= (s_1 + s_2)^2 + r^2 \\ &= l_1^2 + l_2^2 + 2\sqrt{l_1^2 - r_1^2}\sqrt{l_2^2 - r_2^2} - r_1^2 - r_2^2 + r^2 \\ &= l_1^2 + l_2^2 + 2\sqrt{l_1^2 - r_1^2}\sqrt{l_2^2 - r_2^2} - 2r_1r_2\cos(\angle r_1r_2). \end{aligned}$$

Therefore, $\cos\phi = \frac{l_1^2+l_2^2+2\sqrt{l_1^2-r_1^2}\sqrt{l_2^2-r_2^2}-L^2}{2r_1r_2}$.

# Robust Mesh Watermarking

Emil Praun* Hugues Hoppe† Adam Finkelstein*

*Princeton University †Microsoft Research

## Abstract

We describe a robust method for watermarking triangle meshes. Watermarking provides a mechanism for copyright protection of digital media by embedding information identifying the owner in the data. The bulk of the research on digital watermarks has focused on media such as images, video, audio, and text. Robust watermarks must be able to survive a variety of "attacks", including resizing, cropping, and filtering. For resilience to such attacks, recent watermarking schemes employ a "spread-spectrum" approach – they transform the document to the frequency domain and perturb the coefficients of the perceptually most significant basis functions. We extend this spread-spectrum approach to work for the robust watermarking of arbitrary triangle meshes.

Generalizing spread spectrum techniques to surfaces presents two major challenges. First, arbitrary surfaces lack a natural parametrization for frequency-based decomposition. Our solution is to construct a set of scalar basis function over the mesh vertices using multiresolution analysis. The watermark perturbs vertices along the direction of the surface normal, weighted by the basis functions. The second challenge is that simplification and other attacks may modify the connectivity of the mesh. We use an optimization technique to resample an attacked mesh using the original mesh connectivity. Results show that our watermarks are resistant to common mesh operations such as translation, rotation, scaling, cropping, smoothing, simplification, and resampling, as well as malicious attacks such as the insertion of noise, modification of low-order bits, or even insertion of other watermarks.

**CR Categories:** I.3.5 [Computer Graphics]: Computational Geometry and Object Modeling—Surface Representations.

**Keywords:** copyright protection, steganography.

## 1 Introduction

We describe a robust watermarking scheme suitable for proving ownership claims on triangle meshes representing surfaces in 3D. The explosive growth of the Web has led to a blossoming interest in the electronic publication of various media. Unfortunately, many owners of digital materials, such as images, video, audio, text, and 3D models, are reluctant to distribute their documents on the Web or other networked environment, because the ease of duplicating digital material facilitates copyright violation. Digital watermarks provide a mechanism for copyright protection of digital media by allowing people to permanently mark their documents and thereby prove claims of authenticity or ownership.

http://www.cs.princeton.edu/gfx/proj/meshwm



The bulk of the research into digital watermarks has focused on media such as images, video, audio, and text, because these media dominate the proprietary material distributed on the Web. As of the writing of this paper, there are eight commercial Web sites offering watermarking technologies or services for images, video, or audio. In contrast, the problem of watermarking 3D models has received less attention from researchers, in part because the technology that has emerged for watermarking images, video, and audio cannot be easily adapted to work for arbitrary surfaces.

### 1.1 Background

The field of *steganography* addresses the problem of hiding information within digital documents. The information, called the embedded object, is inserted into the original document, called the cover object, to produce a stego object. The term *watermarking* loosely refers to the use of steganography in the application areas of ownership assertion, authentication, content labeling, content protection, and distribution channel tracing [1, 4, 13, 15, 21]. Note that no single watermarking scheme is suitable for all of these applications, as some of their goals are incompatible. We limit the scope of this paper to the use of watermarking triangle meshes for ownership assertion.

To be effective for ownership claims, the watermarking scheme must minimize the probability of *false-positive* results – asserting incorrectly that a document is watermarked when it is not. To decrease the probability of false-positive claims, the watermark is usually encoded in the document using a vector of coefficients. This vector is compared to that observed in the suspect document, and the ownership claim is based on their statistical correlation.

The probability of *false-negative* results, that of failing to detect a watermarked document, is of lesser importance, and is more difficult to analyze since it depends on the type and magnitude of attacks. Such attacks may include inadvertent alterations like compression, blurring, sharpening, cropping, scaling, darkening, and format conversion, but may also include malicious operations like intentional addition of noise, modification of low-order bits, or even insertion of other watermarks.

According to their resilience, watermarks can be *fragile* or *robust*. Fragile watermarks are used for authentication and for localization of modifications. Like digital signatures, their goal is to detect the slightest change to the document. In contrast, robust watermarks are designed to survive (remain detectable) through most attacks. While an attack of sufficient magnitude could erase the watermark, the hope is that an attacker would have to significantly degrade the document in order to destroy the watermark (i.e. achieve false-negative results).

Watermarks can be *perceptible* or *imperceptible*, depending on whether they are directly detectable by the human senses. Perceptible watermarks are often used to display copyright notices or to lower the commercial value of public or preview documents. In contrast, imperceptible watermarks can only be detected using a computational algorithm, which may or may not require the original unwatermarked document. Typically, imperceptible watermarks are advantageous because they are more robust to malicious attacks.

A particularly mischievous approach to defeating ownership claims is for an attacker to manufacture a counterfeit original and to allege that the true original document contains the *attacker's watermark*. This scenario can be prevented by requiring the watermarking scheme to be *non-invertible*: forcing the watermark to be a non-invertible function of the original document [5].

Another application of watermarking is tracing distribution channels. In this case, the document is provided to each recipient with a distinct watermark, referred to as a *fingerprint*, which encodes enough data bits to uniquely identify the recipient. Unfortunately, such an approach is susceptible to collusion attacks, in which several recipients compare their fingerprinted documents to produce a new, seemingly unwatermarked document [22].

The method we present is a robust, imperceptible, non-invertible watermarking scheme designed to serve ownership claims.

### 1.2 Modus Operandi

Here is a typical scenario for creation and detection of a watermark:

1. The owner, Alice, starts with the original mesh. (Figure 1a)
2. Alice embeds a watermark into the original mesh, creating the watermarked mesh. (Figure 1b)
3. Alice hides the original mesh and the watermark information in a safe place, and publishes the watermarked mesh.
4. An attacker, Bob, takes a copy of the watermarked mesh and alters it – either inadvertently or deliberately attacking the watermark – thereby creating the suspect mesh. (Figure 1d)
5. Bob publishes the suspect mesh, claiming it to be his own. Alice obtains a copy of the suspect mesh, believing it is hers.
6. Alice compares (Figure 1f) the suspect mesh to the original mesh in order to extract a suspect watermark. Alice demonstrates that the suspect watermark and the original (secret) watermark are essentially identical, proving that Bob's model is derived from hers.
7. Bob pays Alice a lot of money.

### 1.3 Previous watermarking methods

In this section we describe previous watermarking efforts for other media, followed by related work specifically in the area of meshes.

**Image, audio and video watermarking.** Early watermarking techniques for images and sound used the least significant bits of the document to encode the watermark [21]. Somewhat more robust techniques encode the watermark in the differences of numerous pairs of pixel values [14].

To date, the most robust watermarking schemes for images, video, and sound are based on the *spread-spectrum* method of Cox *et al.* [4], which embeds the watermark in the most perceptually salient features of the data. More precisely, their scheme transforms the data to the frequency domain using a discrete cosine transform (DCT) or wavelet transform, and identifies the largest coefficients, which correspond to the basis functions with the most "energy" in the data. A randomly chosen watermark $w = \{w_1 \dots w_m\}$ is inserted by scaling the $m$ largest coefficients by small perturbations $(1 + \alpha w_i)$. Given a suspect document, an extracted watermark $w^*$ is computed as the difference on the same set of frequency coefficients between the suspect data and the original unwatermarked data. The watermark is declared to be present based on the statistical correlation of $w^*$ and $w$. The robustness of this scheme derives from hiding the watemark in many different frequencies, and from targeting those frequencies with the most energy. Podilchuk and Zeng [17] achieve greater robustness by employing visual models based on JPEG and wavelet image compression to focus the watermark in regions of high perceptual impact. Our method also relies on a compression scheme to identify significant features in the model.

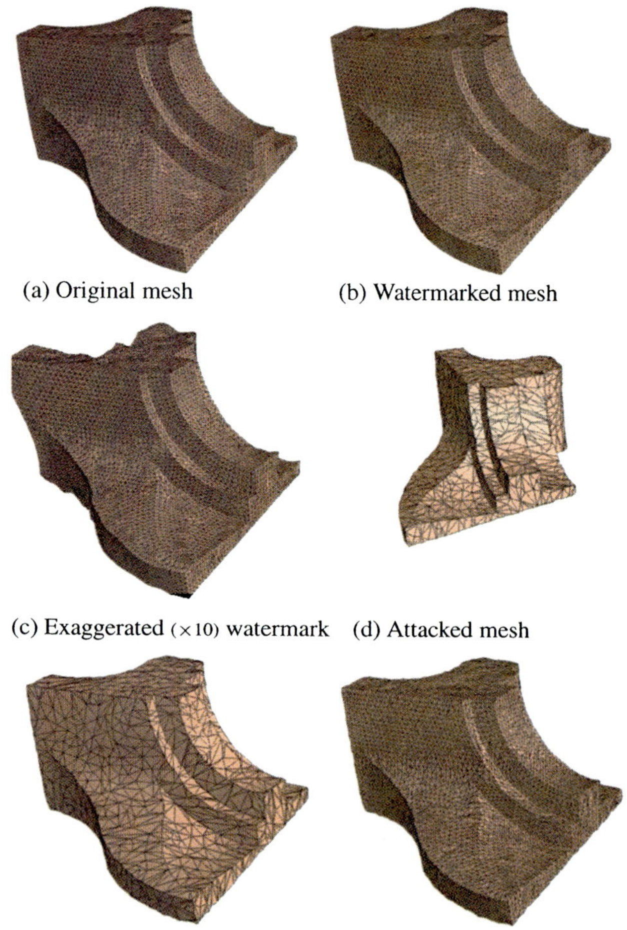

(a) Original mesh (b) Watermarked mesh

(c) Exaggerated (×10) watermark (d) Attacked mesh

(e) After registration (f) After resampling

Figure 1: Given an arbitrary triangle mesh, our robust digital watermarking scheme applies small perturbations to the mesh geometry along the surface normal direction. To detect the presence of the watermark, we register the attacked mesh and project it onto the original mesh using a resampling process.

**Mesh watermarking.** While watermarking image, video, and audio has been the subject of much research (and a number of commercial systems), only recently have a few papers addressed watermarking 3D models.

Yeung and Yeo [25] present a scheme for fragile watermarking. They slightly perturb the vertices such that a certain hash function of each vertex's coordinates matches another hash function applied to the centroid of its neighboring vertices. Note that the goals of fragile watermarking are different from those of robust watermarking, and accordingly, successful approaches to these two problems have little in common.

Ohbuchi *et al.* [15] introduce several schemes for watermarking polygonal models. One scheme embeds information using groups of four adjacent triangles: they perturb the vertex coordinates to obtain certain desired values for ratios of edge lengths in the group or for ratios of triangle height over triangle base. Another scheme they propose uses ratios of tetrahedra volumes. The tetrahedra are formed by the three vertices of each face and a common apex vertex that is computed by averaging a few fixed mesh vertices. Finally they propose a way of visually embedding information by subdividing some triangles of the mesh so as to produce recognizable patterns in the wireframe rendering of the model.

These schemes provide high steganographic bandwidth and are therefore useful for model annotation, and for carrying ownership information when faced with benevolent users. However, they are not robust against many of the attacks addressed here, particularly simplification, remeshing, and the addition of noise.

Our strategy is perhaps most similar to that of Benedens [1], who also embeds watermark information in surface geometry. His discussion addresses many of the challenges and properties of *any* system using surface geometry to embed information in a 3D model. Benedens maps surface normals onto the unit sphere, and then subtly alters groups of similar normals in order to embed the individual bits of the watermark sequence. However, he demonstrates robustness only with simplification attacks. His results seem roughly comparable to some of the tests we describe in Section 6 (although it is very difficult to compare quantitatively since even if we used the same models there is a subjective aspect to choosing the strength of an "invisible" watermark.)

Like Ohbuchi *et al.* and Benedens, we address the problem of robust watermarking of polygonal meshes. Our approach differs in that it is based on the principles of spread-spectrum watermarking as previously developed for images, sound, and video. The spread-spectrum method, which embeds the watermark at multiple scales into the perceptually salient features of the model, is robust against a much broader range of attacks (see Section 6) than are reported by previous efforts.

## 2 Our approach

Surface models come in a variety of representations, such as meshes, B-spline patches, subdivision surfaces, implicit surfaces. We opt to perform the watermarking process on meshes, because they are considered the "lowest common denominator" of surface representations – it is easy to convert other representations to meshes.

There are a number of obvious techniques for embedding information within meshes. For example, one can use comments inside the file containing the mesh, or permute the order of vertices, the order of faces, and even the order of vertices within faces. However, such information is easily lost, even during innocent mesh processing operations.

As in the previous work on images, robust watermarking requires that the watermark be embedded deep within the content data, in this case the mesh geometry. Given a mesh with vertex positions $\mathbf{v} = (\mathbf{v}_1 \dots \mathbf{v}_n)^T$ and arbitrary connectivity (Figure 1a), we propose to embed a random watermark $w = (w_1 \dots w_m)^T$ by letting each coefficient $w_i$ induce small displacements on a subset of the vertices (Figure 1b-c). These displacements are achieved by generalizing the spread-spectrum approach of Cox *et al.* [4] described briefly in Section 1.3.

Generalizing the spread-spectrum approach to the case of arbitrary triangle meshes presents two major challenges. The first is that arbitrary meshes lack a natural parametrization for frequency-based decomposition. Fortunately, recent advances in analysis of meshes have led to multiresolution surface representations that share similar properties to traditional wavelet transforms [6, 8, 10, 11]. Moreover, many of these constructions (particularly those that focus on approximation or compression) automatically identify significant features in the surface. We develop a technique derived from *progressive meshes* [8] to construct a multiresolution set of scalar basis function $\Phi = (\phi^1 \dots \phi^m)$ over the mesh (Section 3). The watermarking scheme should perturb vertices without changing the mesh connectivity. Therefore we define the basis functions on the original set of vertices in the mesh, instead of on a resampled set as in other multiresolution schemes [6, 11]. Section 4 describes how the basis functions $\Phi$ are used to insert and extract the watermark $w$ in a given mesh.

The other challenge in watermarking arbitrary meshes is that the attacker may modify not only the geometry coefficients (the vertex positions), but also the structure of the vertex sampling itself. By comparison, in image watermarking, the image may be misregistered through a *similarity transform* (translation, rotation, and uniform scaling), but the image format always consists of a Cartesian grid sampling. With meshes, besides misregistration, the mesh connectivity may have been modified by the attacker. To address this challenge, we develop an optimization technique to resample the attacked mesh using the original mesh connectivity (Figure 1d-f), as described in Section 5.

Finally, Section 6 shows the resilience of the watermark under a variety of attacks.

Thus, the contributions of this paper can be summarized as follows. First, we provide a scheme for constructing a set of scalar basis functions over the mesh vertices. We then adapt the spread-spectrum principles used in image watermarking to embed information into the basis functions corresponding to perceptually significant features of the model. Finally we provide a method for resampling a suspect mesh in order to obtain a mesh with the same geometry but with a given connectivity. These contributions combine to form a robust scheme suitable for watermarking 3D models.

## 3 Surface basis functions

For each coefficient $w_i$ of the watermark, we construct a scalar basis function $\phi^i_j$ over the mesh vertices $v_j$, and associate with it a global displacement direction $\mathbf{d}_i$. During the watermarking process (Section 4), the effect of the watermark coefficient $w_i$ is to perturb each vertex $v_j$ by a vector proportional to $w_i \phi^i_j \mathbf{d}_i$. In this section, we describe the construction of these basis functions $\Phi = (\phi^1 \dots \phi^m)$.

For the watermarking scheme to be robust, the basis functions $\Phi$ should correspond to large, perceptually significant features of the model. Recall that in earlier image watermarking work, these were obtained as the DCT basis functions with the largest amplitude. We also need information about how much change can be inserted using a given basis function without perceptibly degrading the model. This information was provided by the magnitude of the selected DCT coefficients.

Our approach is to convert the original triangle mesh into a multiresolution format, consisting of a coarse base mesh and a sequence of refinement operations. We identify the $m$ refinement operations that cause the greatest geometric change to the model. For each of these $m$ refinements, we define a scalar basis function over its corresponding neighborhood in the original mesh. These $m$ basis functions form $\Phi$, and are used to insert the watermark. The same basis functions $\Phi$, computed on the original mesh, are later used for the extraction of the watermark (see Section 4). We now describe in more detail the steps for creating $\phi^i$.

Our first step is to simplify the given mesh through a sequence of *restricted edge collapse* operations. Each operation collapses an edge to one of its endpoints [9, 18]. The edge collapses are chosen deterministically with the goal of preserving the geometric shape of the original mesh [8]. Recording this simplification sequence gives rise to a *progressive mesh* (PM) representation [8], which encodes the mesh as a coarse base mesh together with a sequence of *vertex split* operations (Figure 2a-d).

We measure the geometric "magnitude" $h$ of a vertex split operation as follows. First, we predict the position of the newly introduced vertex using the centroid of its immediate neighbors. Next, we compute a surface normal based on these neighbors. Finally, $h$ is computed as the dot product between the surface normal and the difference between the actual and predicted positions. Intuitively, $h$ measures the distance between the new vertex and the coarser mesh.

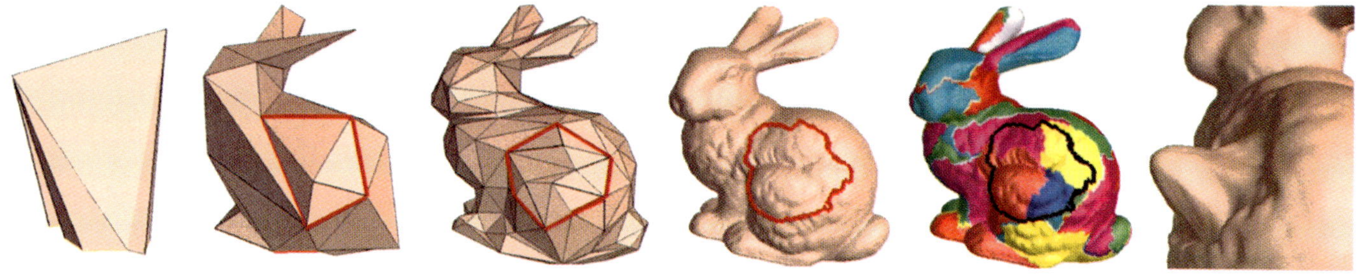

(a) Base mesh (b) 1-ring area (c) Some refinement (d) Finest mesh (e) 50 basis functions (f) Sombrero $\times 200$

Figure 2: Progressive mesh representation, tracking of a basis function boundary through successive vertex splits, 50 overlapping basis functions, and the sombrero basis function (exaggerated by a factor of 200) applied to the original mesh.

We select the $m$ vertex splits with the largest geometric magnitude $h$, and proceed to construct their associated basis functions $\phi^i$. In addition, the magnitude $h_i$ is used later to scale the contribution of the watermark coefficient $w_i$. Because we use restricted edge collapses, each vertex split $i$ of a vertex $c_i$ is naturally associated with a neighborhood in the original mesh. The neighborhood is taken to be the ring of edges about the collapsed vertex (Figure 2b), and these edges are tracked through the subsequent vertex split refinements. In particular, each edge of a mesh is naturally mapped onto one or two edges by a vertex split operation. After all refinements are applied, the edges define the boundary $B_i$ of the neighborhood in the original mesh (Figure 2d). Figure 2e shows the support neighborhoods of 50 overlapping basis functions, drawn from coarse to fine.

In each neighborhood we construct a basis function by mapping a radially symmetric function to this region. To begin, we define a "radius" function $r_j^i$ on the vertices $v_j$ such that it is 0 at the center vertex $c_i$, is 1 on and outside the boundary $B_i$, and varies linearly in between. More precisely, for vertices $v_j$ in the neighborhood:

$$r_j^i = \frac{d(v_j, \{c_i\})}{d(v_j, \{c_i\}) + d(v_j, B_i)}$$

where $d(v, S)$ is the length of the shortest path between $v$ and any vertex in the set $S$.

The distances $d(v_j, \{c_i\})$ and $d(v_j, B_i)$ are computed using two instances of Dijkstra's algorithm on the edges of the mesh graph. The cost of each edge equals its length, and the search is constrained within the interior of the boundary $B_i$. For notational simplicity we shall henceforth refer to $r_j^i$ as $r$.

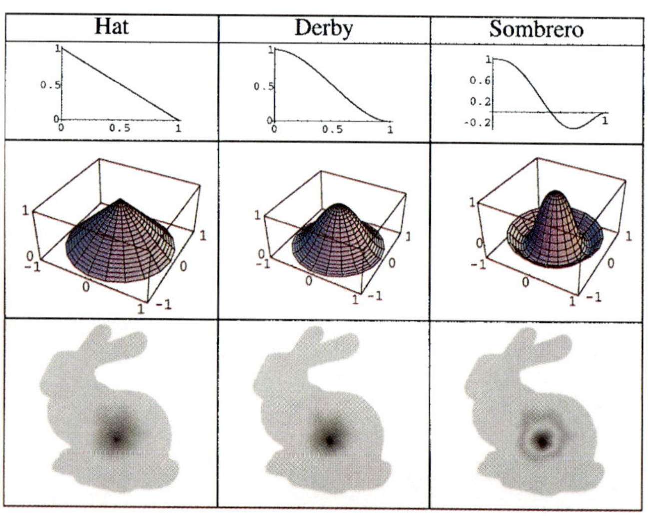


Figure 3: Basis functions

There are two main considerations to take into account when designing basis functions: the changes induced on the mesh should be unnoticeable to a human observer, and the functions should not result in a translation or scale bias when we register the model.

We explore the use of three types of basis functions. Section 6 compares their effectiveness.

**Hat.** The linear mapping $\phi_j^i = 1 - r$ creates the usual *hat function*.

**Derby.** We obtain smoother-looking functions using higher degree polynomials. In considering the goal of imperceptibility, we note that since the polygonal mesh itself has only $C^0$ continuity, we do not really need $C^\infty$ basis functions. However, the human eye is very good at picking up derivative discontinuities, so basis functions that do not have $C^1$ continuity are easily noticed when rendering the model flat-shaded. Derivative discontinuities can appear at the apex and at the boundary of the hat function. We eliminate these discontinuities using a third degree polynomial: $\phi_j^i = 2r^3 - 3r^2 + 1$ . This basis function, applied on a disc, looks like a smooth bump, or colonial ("derby") hat.

**Sombrero.** We would like a function that does not induce a translation bias during mesh registration, so we now add the constraint that the area integral over the unit disc $r \leq 1$ be zero. This results in a sombrero-like function with a somewhat narrow middle. When this function is discretized on a mesh with few faces, the center is visibly pointy. We smooth the function with the additional constraint of zero second derivative at the apex. The resulting polynomial is $\phi_j^i = -21r^5 + 45r^4 - 25r^3 + 1$ .

In our watermarking application, we only construct basis functions for vertex splits with the largest magnitudes $h$. However, if we were to construct basis functions associated with all vertex splits, these, together with the vertices of the base mesh, would form a basis for scalar functions defined on all vertices. A sketch of the proof goes as follows. If one considers the basis functions in reverse order of the vertex splits, each basis function includes a vertex not referenced by any of the previous ones. Therefore, they are linearly independent. Also, the number of vertex splits added to the number of vertices of the base mesh equals the number of original vertices, thus the basis functions also form a complete set.

## 4 Watermarking process

We now use the basis functions to insert the watermark vector into the mesh and to later extract it.

First we generate the watermark vector $w = (w_1 \dots w_m)^T$. Its coefficients $w_i$ are real numbers sampled from a Gaussian distribution with zero mean and variance 1. To make the watermark a non-invertible function of the original document (in order to prevent false ownership claims [5]), the original document (possibly concatenated with some extra information like serial number, date, owner's name, etc) is passed through a cryptographic hash function (like MD5, or SHA-1 [20]). The result is used to seed a cryptographic random number generator, that produces the watermark with the required length.

**Insertion.** The watermark is inserted as follows. Each basis function is multiplied by a coefficient, and added to the 3D coordinates of the mesh vertices. Each basis function $i$ has a scalar effect $\phi_j^i$ at each vertex $j$ and a global displacement direction $\mathbf{d}_i$. We express this process as a matrix multiplication:

For each of the three spatial coordinates X, Y, and Z:

$$\begin{bmatrix} \\ v'_{\mathrm{x}} \\ \\ \end{bmatrix} = \begin{bmatrix} \\ v_{\mathrm{x}} \\ \\ \end{bmatrix} + \epsilon * \begin{bmatrix} \\ \Phi \\ \\ \end{bmatrix} * \begin{bmatrix} h_1 d_{1\mathrm{x}} & & 0 \\ & \ddots & \\ 0 & & h_m d_{m\mathrm{x}} \end{bmatrix} * \begin{bmatrix} \\ w \\ \\ \end{bmatrix}$$

where $v'_{\mathrm{x}}$ are the X coordinates of watermarked mesh vertices,
$v_{\mathrm{x}}$ are the X coordinates of original vertices $\mathbf{v}$,
$\epsilon$ is a user-provided global parameter that scales the energy of the watermark,
$\Phi$ is an $n \times m$ matrix with the scalar functions $\phi^i$ as columns,
$hd_{\mathrm{x}}$ is an $m \times m$ diagonal matrix whose entries are the X components of the displacement directions $\mathbf{d}_i$ scaled by the basis function heights $h_i$, and
$w$ is the watermark.

By concatenating the rows of the matrices and vectors corresponding to the three coordinate components (X,Y,Z) we can express the insertion process as a single equation

$$\mathbf{v}' = \mathbf{v} + \mathbf{B} * w \; .$$

The original document $\mathbf{v}$, along with the watermark $w$ are stored and kept secret, and the watermarked document $\mathbf{v}'$ is published.

**Extraction.** Before we can check for watermark presence in a suspect mesh, we have to both bring it into the same coordinate frame as the original, and resample it in order to produce a mesh with the same connectivity as the original (see Section 5). By taking the difference between the 3D coordinates of the vertices of this resampled mesh and those of the original, we accumulate a vector of 3D residuals. Next, we extract a watermark from these residuals by solving the sparse linear least squares system

$$\mathbf{B}\, w^* = (\mathbf{v}^* - \mathbf{v})$$

where $w^*$ is the extracted watermark,
$\mathbf{v}^*$ are the vertex coordinates of the resampled attacked mesh
$\mathbf{v}$ are the vertex coordinates of the original mesh.

**Analysis.** We compare the inserted and extracted watermarks using a statistical analysis. First, like Cox *et al.*[4] we filter the extracted coefficients. Since they are expected to have a normal distribution with mean 0 and deviation 1, we discard coefficients whose absolute value exceeds a given threshold.[1] We then compute the linear correlation [19] between the remaining coefficients and their corresponding values in the inserted watermark:

$$\rho = \frac{\sum_i (w_i^* - \overline{w^*})(w_i - \overline{w})}{\sqrt{\sum_i (w_i^* - \overline{w^*})^2 \times \sum_i (w_i - \overline{w})^2}}$$

where $\overline{w}$ denotes the average of the vector elements. The result $\rho$ is a number between -1 and 1.

Finally, we turn the correlation $\rho$ into a probabilistic answer using a standard statistical analysis. We compute the probability $P_{fp}$ that the correlation of $w^*$ with a randomly generated watermark would be as high as the observed $\rho$, using Student's $t$-test [19].

If a yes/no answer is required, we compare $P_{fp}$ with a given threshold $P_{\mathrm{thresh}}$: we answer *yes* iff $P_{fp} < P_{\mathrm{thresh}}$. Since the argument is probabilistic, we may sometimes be wrong. The risk of declaring a false positive (saying that the watermark is present when in fact it is not) can be computed analytically, and is in fact, $P_{fp}$. The risk of declaring a false negative (the watermark is there but we fail to identify it) cannot be computed analytically in general, since it depends on the specific attack that was applied. By changing the decision threshold $P_{\mathrm{thresh}}$ we can trade off false positives against false negatives. An analysis of this trade-off using real data is provided in the appendix in the electronic version of the paper.

## 5 Registration and Resampling

**Registration.** When including a mesh within a graphical scene, it is common to apply a similarity transform: the object is translated, rotated, and scaled uniformly (Figure 1d). While such a transformation is often kept separate from the object, an attacker might fold the transformation directly into the vertex coordinates. In order to extract the watermark, we need to bring the object back to its original location and scale (Figure 1e).

Several methods have been developed for the rigid registration of meshes (e.g. [2, 3, 7]). We use the algorithm by Chen and Medioni [3], but we allow one additional degree of freedom: uniform scaling of the mesh. The algorithm can deal with meshes that represent only parts of the object, which is useful when our watermarked mesh has been cropped during an attack.

The registration algorithm is an iterative process and requires a reasonable initial condition. Sometimes user intervention is required to provide the initial alignment, especially for cropped objects or for objects with strong symmetries.

Note that the alignment process must be performed between the attacked mesh and the original, unwatermarked mesh. The reason is that if we align against the watermarked model, we might falsely increase the apparent presence of the watermark in an unwatermarked model.

**Resampling.** As part of the attack, the topology of the mesh (number and order of vertices, and the number, order and connectivity of the faces) may have changed (Figure 1d-e). In this case, for the watermark extraction process, we need to obtain a mesh with the topology of the original and the geometry of the attacked object (after alignment). This gives rise to a resampling problem. The basic question we need to answer is: for a given initial mesh vertex $\mathbf{v}_j$, what is the corresponding point $\mathbf{v}_j^*$ on the surface of the attacked mesh? The residuals vector $(\mathbf{v}^* - \mathbf{v})$ provides the input for the extraction process (see Section 4). A very simple answer to the question can be obtained by pairing each original mesh vertex with the closest point on the attacked surface. If the residual is larger than a given threshold, we assume that the object has been cropped, and the vertex has no corresponding point.

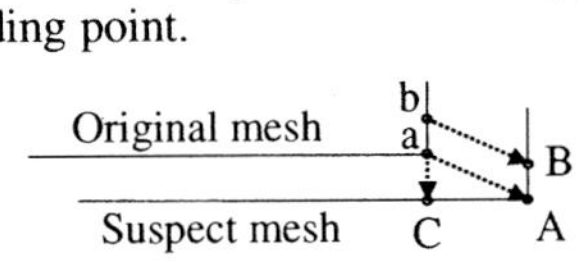


Closest point projection may give rise to problems, as shown on the right. In the picture, the watermark followed by the attack moved the surface right and down, but the corner $a$ projects to point $C$ instead of the corner $A$. Furthermore, point $b$ also projects to $C$ instead of $B$, causing a degeneracy.

In general, any local technique that only considers one vertex at a time may encounter problems. We cast the resampling problem as the fitting of the original mesh to the suspect mesh while minimally

[1] We use a threshold of 2.5 for rejecting outliers. Given the normal distribution, we expect to reject about 1.24% of the elements of our watermark vector, which has minimal impact on the analysis.

deforming it. We implement this as an energy-minimization, which we solve using a *conjugate gradient* method [19]. The energy functional has three terms:

$$E(\mathbf{v}^*) = E_{\text{dist}}(\mathbf{v}^*) + c_d * E_{\text{deform}}(\mathbf{v}^*) + c_f * E_{\text{flip}}(\mathbf{v}^*)$$

where

$E_{\text{dist}}$ measures the distance between the meshes. Specifically, it is the sum of squared distances between points randomly sampled on the attacked mesh and their projections onto the original mesh.

$E_{\text{deform}}$ measures the deformation of the original mesh. A spring is placed on each mesh edge, with rest length equal to the original edge length, as done in [12].

$E_{\text{flip}}$ is a term that penalizes surface flipping. The term $E_{\text{deform}}$ penalizes surface stretching and contraction, but fails to prevent the surface from "buckling" in areas of high contraction [12]. We let $E_{\text{flip}}$ be a sum of penalties over each face. On each face, we compute the dot product of its normal with the the corresponding face normal of the original mesh. If the result is positive, the penalty is zero. Otherwise it is the square of this dot product.

$c_d$ and $c_f$ give relative weights to the terms. Empirically we have found that $c_d = 10^{-3}$ and $c_f = 10^7$ give a reasonable tradeoff.

As a final note, in the extraction process, one can try to skip the registration and/or the resampling steps if the object appears to be in the same location and/or to have the same topology. Multiple attempts at extracting the watermark can be made with or without registration and/or resampling, and the lowest $P_{fp}$ value is kept. As noted by Cox *et al.* [4], since the probability of declaring a false positive when we can choose from several extraction variants is lower than the sum of the individual probabilities, a conservative approach is to divide our proposed false-positive decision threshold by the number of extraction schemes.

## 6 Results

In this section, we demonstrate that our watermarking scheme is effective in the presence of various real-world attacks. We first present quantitative results for a variety of attacks and then we motivate the choice of parameters used in the tests and describe some typical running times.

Since the watermarking process and the attacks depend on random numbers, there is variability in the results. We therefore ran each test 5 times, using different random seeds, and report the median value.

**Battery of attacks.** Table 1 shows the detection results for a host of attacks. The second and third columns specify if the registration and/or resampling steps were used as part of watermark detection. Entries with asterisks correspond to the attacked meshes pictured in Figure 4.

Row B (the reorder attack) shows the impact of the resampling process on the detection scheme. Even though the geometry of the watermarked model is not changed by the attack, the recovered false-positive probabilities are nonzero. The reason is that the resampling process is not given any knowledge of the watermarked mesh, in order to prevent any information from the watermark to "leak" into the suspect mesh. For the same reason, the probabilities in row G are also nonzero.

Rows C-E demonstrate the resilience of the watermark under the addition of white noise. The percentage represents the noise amplitude as a fraction of the largest dimension of the object.

| Attack | Reg | Res | Fandisk | Head | Dragon | Bunny |
|---|---|---|---|---|---|---|
| A. No attack | | | 0 | 0 | 0 | 0 |
| B. Vertex reorder | | √ | $10^{-14}$ | $10^{-15}$ | $10^{-16}$ | $10^{-21}$ |
| C. Noise 0.2% | | | $10^{-14}$ | $10^{-12}$ | $10^{-17}$ | $10^{-35}$ |
| D. Noise 0.45% | | | $10^{-5}$ | $\mathbf{10^{-6}}$ * | $10^{-9}$ | $10^{-21}$ |
| E. Noise 0.7% | | | $10^{-3}$ | $10^{-5}$ | $10^{-5}$ | $10^{-15}$ |
| F. Smoothing | | | $\mathbf{10^{-12}}$ * | $10^{-38}$ | $10^{-32}$ | 0 |
| G. Transform | √ | | $10^{-33}$ | $10^{-24}$ | $\mathbf{10^{-29}}$ * | $10^{-29}$ |
| H. Simplify 1/2 | | √ | $10^{-12}$ | $10^{-9}$ | $\mathbf{10^{-7}}$ * | $10^{-17}$ |
| I. Simplify 1/8 | | √ | $10^{-11}$ | $10^{-3}$ | $10^{-2}$ | $\mathbf{10^{-13}}$ * |
| J. 2nd watermark | | | $10^{-8}$ | $\mathbf{10^{-7}}$ * | $10^{-17}$ | $10^{-6}$ |
| K. Crop | | | 0 | 0 | 0 | **0** * |
| L. B + C | | √ | $10^{-12}$ | $10^{-6}$ | $10^{-11}$ | $10^{-28}$ |
| M. B + G | √ | √ | $10^{-12}$ | $10^{-12}$ | $10^{-15}$ | $10^{-20}$ |
| N. C + G | √ | | $10^{-11}$ | $10^{-12}$ | $10^{-15}$ | $10^{-24}$ |
| O. G + L | √ | √ | $10^{-22}$ | $10^{-9}$ | $10^{-20}$ | $10^{-18}$ |
| P. B + C + G | √ | √ | $10^{-12}$ | $10^{-4}$ | $10^{-14}$ | $10^{-22}$ |
| Q. B + G + H | √ | √ | $10^{-13}$ | $10^{-9}$ | $10^{-6}$ | $10^{-17}$ |
| R. All (B,C,F,G,H,J,K) | √ | √ | $\mathbf{10^{-2}}$ * | $10^{-2}$ | $10^{-2}$ | $10^{-5}$ |

Table 1: Median of 5 tests for various attacks. Entries show the false-positive probability $P_{fp}$. Entries with asterisks correspond to pictures in Figure 4.

Row F shows the results of applying 10 iterations of the Taubin smoothing filter [23] to the vertex coordinates. The effect can be seen in the rounded edges of Figures 4e and 4i. Since the head and bunny models are already relatively smooth, this attack has little impact on them.

The simplification scheme used for rows H and I is based on full edge collapse operations, which replace a mesh edge with a vertex at an optimized location. For simplification factors less than 1/2, it is likely that few vertices keep their original positions, so this can attack can be considered an instance of "remeshing". We note that the head and the dragon suffer most from this kind of attack, which can be explained by the fact that these models have a higher ratio of detail to number of faces. The watermark coefficients hidden in the fine details of the ears, eyes and lips of the mannequin head and in the head, legs and tail of the dragon are lost during aggressive simplification. Of course, the visual appearance of the models is also degraded by such severe attacks.

Row J addresses to the addition of a second watermark. Because the watermarked geometry is different from the original, the sequence of edge collapses used for inserting the second watermark is different from that used in the initial watermark. By inserting a third and fourth watermark the attacker may further degrade the original watermark, so we believe that a barrage of many watermarks would form an effective attack. However, such an attack would impose changes on the mesh that, if still imperceptible, might have been used to strengthen the original watermark.

The crop attack presented in row K consists of discarding all vertices in the right third of the object's bounding box. As mentioned in Section 5, the registration algorithm can handle incomplete meshes. The resampling step declares any vertex in the optimized mesh to be missing if it lacks a corresponding point on the attacked mesh. During watermark extraction, equations corresponding to missing vertices are deleted from the system. Watermark coefficients that only affect removed vertices (zero columns in the **B** matrix) are also removed. Since missing vertices may cause some columns to become linearly dependent, the remaining system is solved using SVD. We observe that the surviving watermark coefficients are perfectly recovered, so the false-positive probability for this attack is 0.

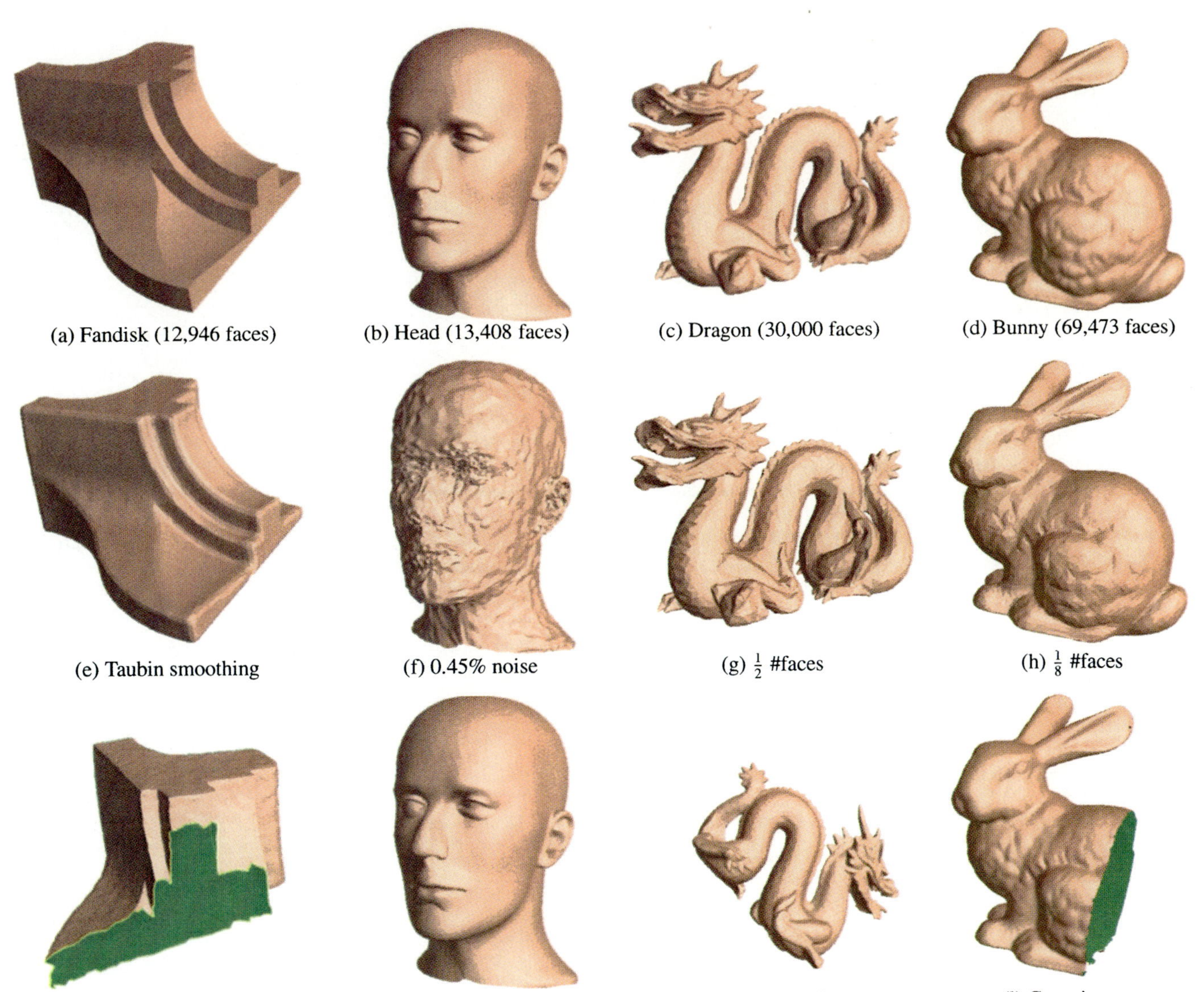

(a) Fandisk (12,946 faces) (b) Head (13,408 faces) (c) Dragon (30,000 faces) (d) Bunny (69,473 faces)

(e) Taubin smoothing (f) 0.45% noise (g) $\frac{1}{2}$ #faces (h) $\frac{1}{8}$ #faces

(i) All attacks (j) Second watermark (k) Similarity transform (l) Cropping

Figure 4: Watermarked models (top row) and various attacks.

**Parameter settings.** The test results in this section were obtained using a watermark length of $m$=50 coefficients, an energy scale factor $\epsilon$=0.01, and the sombrero basis function.

We experimented with different watermark lengths. Ideally, the length of the watermark should be maximized so that an observed correlation value corresponds to a low false-positive probability $P_{fp}$. However, making the watermark long requires that we include basis functions that correspond to features of low significance, and such features have high frequency components which are most affected by many types of attacks. We find that using more than 100 coefficients yields results that are significantly worse than the ones reported here. A watermark length of 50 coefficients is comparable to the lengths (16 and 50) used by Benedens [1] but much smaller than the length (1000) used by Cox *et al.* [4] when watermarking images. One explanation is that photographs contain much more detail than the relatively smooth surfaces present in our test models. Ultimately, the number of coefficients should be model-specific, based on some "information complexity" of the model, and should be carefully selected to maximize robustness.

We determined the value $\epsilon$=0.01 experimentally, as providing reasonable robustness while still leaving the watermark imperceptible, as demonstrated in Figures 1b and 4. At levels above $\epsilon$=0.03 the watermark became noticeable.

Table 2 compares the three choices of basis function. The letters preceding the attacks are the same as in Table 1. For a noise attack, the three basis functions give similar results. The sombrero outperforms its counterparts under the similarity transform attack, as well as under simplification, which requires a resampling step. We conjecture that accurate resampling expects that the mesh be least deformed from its original shape, and that, of the three basis functions, the sombrero induces the least overall distortion.

| Model | Attack | Hat | Derby | Sombrero |
|---|---|---|---|---|
| Fandisk | C. Noise 0.2% | $10^{-13}$ | $\mathbf{10^{-15}}$ † | $10^{-14}$ |
| | E. Noise 0.7% | $10^{-2}$ | $10^{-2}$ | $\mathbf{10^{-3}}$ † |
| | G. Similarity transform | $10^{-17}$ | $10^{-6}$ | $\mathbf{10^{-33}}$ † |
| | H. Simplify 1/2 # faces | $10^{-7}$ | $10^{-5}$ | $\mathbf{10^{-12}}$ † |
| Head | C. Noise 0.2% | $\mathbf{10^{-18}}$ † | $10^{-12}$ | $10^{-12}$ |
| | E. Noise 0.7% | $\mathbf{10^{-5}}$ † | $10^{-3}$ | $10^{-5}$ |
| | G. Similarity transform | $10^{-1}$ | $10^{-3}$ | $\mathbf{10^{-24}}$ † |
| | H. Simplify 1/2 # faces | $10^{-2}$ | $10^{-1}$ | $\mathbf{10^{-9}}$ † |

Table 2: Resilience of the three basis function types. Each entry shows the false-positive probability $P_{fp}$ for the median of 5 tests. Entries with daggers highlight the best result for each attack.

| Stage | Fandisk | Head | Dragon | Bunny |
|---|---|---|---|---|
| Conversion to PM | 3 | 3 | 9 | 24 |
| Watermark insertion | 0.1 | 0.1 | 0.1 | 0.5 |
| Registration | 2 | 3 | 6 | 13 |
| Resampling | 15 | 15 | 45 | 120 |
| Watermark extraction | 0.2 | 0.2 | 0.8 | 2 |

Table 3: Typical running times in minutes (MIPS R10000 195MHz) for various stages of the pipeline.

Table 3 shows some typical running times for various steps in the watermark insertion and extraction processes. We have not tried to optimize for execution time in this work.

## 7 Summary and future work

In this paper, we address the problem of robustly watermarking 3D models. We present a practical method for encoding information in the model geometry by imperceptibly displacing the vertices. To maximize robustness, the watermark is hidden in the perceptually significant features of the model, which are identified using a multiresolution approach.

To detect the watermark in a suspect mesh, we first optionally register this mesh with the original and/or resample it. The watermark is then extracted using a sparse linear least-squares solution. Finally, we compare the inserted and extracted watermarks in order to determine the probability that the suspect model was created independently of the watermarked model.

Our scheme has proven to be robust against a wide variety of attacks, including vertex reordering, addition of noise, similarity transforms, cropping, smoothing, simplification, and insertion of a second watermark.

This project suggests a number of areas for future work:

**Fast rejection.** Given a suspect model, it would be desirable to more quickly determine that it does not match an owner's set of watermarked models. This would enable an automated agent (such as a web crawler) to search for possible stolen watermarked documents, without having to run the complete, high-accuracy detection scheme.

**Other surface representations.** We would like to investigate the direct watermarking of other surface representations such as subdivision surfaces, CSG, and Bezier/B-spline patches. The challenge is that such representations often contain fewer coefficients.

**Other attacks.** It is impossible to anticipate all possible attacks to a 3D model. It is also difficult to assess the degree of damage that a certain attack inflicts upon a model. Some attacks we have not considered thus far include general affine transforms, projective transforms, and free-form deformations. It would be easy to extend the registration algorithm to handle arbitrary affine transforms or even projective transforms. Handling free-form deformations (FFD) is more problematic, however, since these can have an arbitrary number of degrees of freedom. A watermark detection algorithm would have the task of separating vertex motion due to the watermark from vertex motion due to the FFD, without knowledge of either the watermark sequence or the FFD parameters. An alternative would be to create a watermarking scheme that is orthogonal to FFD. We note that to date FFD seems to be the most successful attack against image watermarks [16].

## Acknowledgements

This work was supported in part by Microsoft Research and the National Science Foundation. For the use of the 3D models we would like to thank Stanford University, Pratt & Whitney, and Technical Arts Co. Special thanks go to Talal Shamoon and Harold Stone for many helpful discussions.

## References

[1] BENEDENS, O. Geometry-based watermarking of 3d models. *IEEE Computer Graphics and Applications* (Jan. 1999), 46–55.

[2] BESL, P. J., AND MCKAY, N. D. A method for registration of 3-d shapes. *IEEE Transactions on Pattern Analysis and Machine Intelligence 14*, 2 (Feb. 1992), 239–256.

[3] CHEN, Y., AND MEDIONI, G. Object modelling by registration of multiple range images. *Image and Vision Computing 10*, 3 (Apr. 1992), 145–155.

[4] COX, I. J., KILLIAN, J., LEIGHTON, T., AND SHAMOON, T. Secure spread spectrum watermarking for multimedia. *IEEE Transactions on Image Processing 12*, 6 (1997), 1673–1687.

[5] CRAVER, S., MEMON, N., YEO, B.-L., AND YEUNG, M. M. Resolving rightful ownership with invisible watermarking techniques: Limitations, attacks, and implications. *IEEE Journal on Selected Areas in Communications 16*, 4 (May 1998), 573–586.

[6] ECK, M., DEROSE, T., DUCHAMP, T., HOPPE, H., LOUNSBERY, M., AND STUETZLE, W. Multiresolution analysis of arbitrary meshes. In *ACM SIGGRAPH 95 Conference Proceedings* (Aug. 1995), pp. 173–182.

[7] FAUGERAS, O. D. The representation, recognition, and locating of 3-d objects. *International Journal on Robotic Research 5*, 3 (1986), 27–52.

[8] HOPPE, H. Progressive meshes. In *ACM SIGGRAPH 96 Conference Proceedings* (Aug. 1996), pp. 99–108.

[9] KOBBELT, L., CAMPAGNA, S., AND SEIDEL, H.-P. A general framework for mesh decimation. In *Proceedings of Graphics Interface* (1998).

[10] KOBBELT, L., CAMPAGNA, S., VORSATZ, J., AND SEIDEL, H.-P. Interactive multi-resolution modeling on arbitrary meshes. In *ACM SIGGRAPH 98 Conference Proceedings* (July 1998), pp. 105–114.

[11] LEE, A. W. F., SWELDENS, W., SCHRÖDER, P., COWSAR, L., AND DOBKIN, D. MAPS: Multiresolution adaptive parameterization of surfaces. In *ACM SIGGRAPH 98 Conference Proceedings* (July 1998), pp. 95–104.

[12] MAILLOT, J., YAHIA, H., AND VERROUST, A. Interactive texture mapping. In *Computer Graphics (SIGGRAPH 93 Proceedings)*, vol. 27, pp. 27–34.

[13] MEMON, N., AND WONG, P. W. Protecting digital media content. *Communications of the ACM 41*, 7 (July 1998), 35–43.

[14] NIKOLAIDIS, N., AND PITAS, I. Copyright protection of images using robust digital signatures. In *Proceedings of the IEEE International Conference on Acoustics, Speech and Signal Processing* (May 1996), pp. 2168–2171.

[15] OHBUCHI, R., MASUDA, H., AND AONO, M. Watermarking three-dimensional polygonal models through geometric and topological modifications. *IEEE Journal on Selected Areas in Communications 16*, 4 (May 1998), 551–559.

[16] PETITCOLAS, F. A., ANDERSON, R. J., AND KUHN, M. G. Attacks on copyright marking systems. In *Second Workshop on Information Hiding* (Apr. 1998).

[17] PODILCHUK, C. I., AND ZENG, W. Image-adaptive watermarking using visual models. *IEEE Journal on Selected Areas in Communications 16*, 4 (May 1998), 525–539.

[18] POPOVIĆ, J., AND HOPPE, H. Progressive simplicial complexes. In *ACM SIGGRAPH 97 Conference Proceedings* (Aug. 1997), pp. 217–224.

[19] PRESS, W. H., TEULKOLSKY, S. A., VETTERLING, W. T., AND FLANNERY, B. P. *Numerical Recipes in C*, 2nd ed. Cambridge University Press, 1996.

[20] SCHNEIER, B. *Applied Cryptography: protocols, algorithms, and source code in C*, 2nd ed. John Wiley & Sons, Inc., 1996.

[21] SCHYNDEL, R. V., TIRKEL, A., AND OSBORNE, C. A digital watermark. In *Proceedings of ICIP* (Nov. 1994), IEEE Press, pp. 86–90.

[22] STONE, H. S. Analysis of attacks on image watermarks with randomized coefficients. Tech. rep., NEC Research Institute, May 1996.

[23] TAUBIN, G. A signal processing approach to fair surface design. In *ACM SIGGRAPH 95 Conference Proceedings* (Aug. 1995), pp. 351–358.

[24] WOODS, K. Generating ROC curves for artificial neural networks. *IEEE Transactions on medical imaging 16*, 3 (June 1997), 329–337.

[25] YEUNG, M. M., AND YEO, B.-L. Fragile watermarking of 3d objects. In *International Conference on Image Processing* (1998).

**Note:** The electronic version of the paper contains an appendix.

# Interpolating Nets Of Curves By Smooth Subdivision Surfaces

Adi Levin*

Tel Aviv University

## Abstract

A subdivision algorithm is presented for the computation and representation of a smooth surface of arbitrary topological type interpolating a given net of smooth curves. The algorithm belongs to a new class of subdivision schemes called *combined subdivision schemes*. These schemes can exactly interpolate a net of curves given in any parametric representation. The surfaces generated by our algorithm are $G^2$ except at a finite number of points, where the surface is $G^1$ and has bounded curvature. The algorithm is simple and easy to implement, and is based on a variant of the famous Catmull-Clark subdivision scheme.

**CR Categories and Subject Descriptors:** I.3.5 [Computer Graphics]: Computational Geometry and Object Modeling—Curve,surface, solid and object modeling.

**Additional Keywords:** Subdivision, Interpolation, Combined Subdivision schemes, Net of curves.

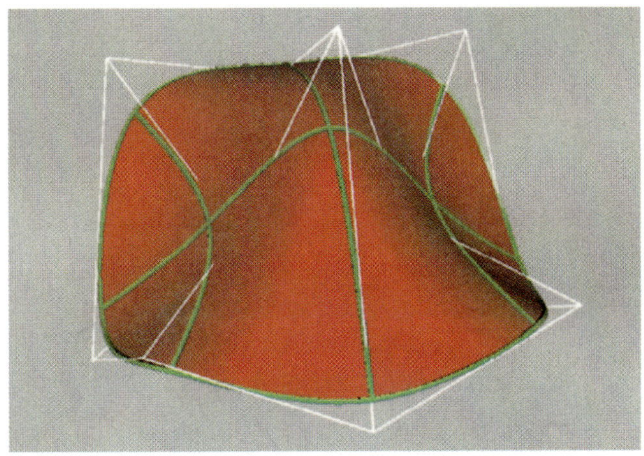

Figure 1: Interpolation of a net of curves

## 1 INTRODUCTION

Subdivision schemes provide efficient algorithms for the design, representation and processing of smooth surfaces of arbitrary topological type. Their simplicity and their multiresolution structure make them attractive for applications in 3D surface modeling, and in computer graphics [2, 4, 5, 6, 11, 18].

A common task in surface modeling is that of interpolating a given net of smooth curves by a smooth surface. A typical solution, using either subdivision surfaces or NURBS surfaces (or other kinds of spline surfaces), is based on establishing the connection between parts of the control net which defines the surface, and certain curves on the surface. For example, the boundary curves of NURBS surfaces are NURBS curves whose control polygon is the boundary polygon of the NURBS surface control net. Hence, curve interpolation conditions are translated into conditions on the control net. Fairing techniques [5, 15, 17] can be used to calculate a control net satisfying those conditions. Using subdivision surfaces, this can be carried out, in general, for given nets of arbitrary topology (see [12, 13]).

However, the curves that can be interpolated using that approach are restricted by the representation chosen for the surface. NURBS surfaces are suitable for interpolating NURBS curves; Doo-Sabin surfaces can interpolate quadratic B-spline curves [12, 13]; Other kinds of subdivision surfaces can be shown to interpolate specific kinds of subdivision curves. Furthermore, interpolation of curves that have small features requires a large control net, making the fairing process slower and more complicated.

This paper presents a new subdivision scheme specially designed for the task of interpolating nets of curves. This scheme falls into the category of *combined subdivision schemes* [7, 8, 10], where the underlying surface is represented not only by a control net, but also by given parametric curves (or in general, given interpolation conditions or boundary conditions). The scheme repeatedly applies a subdivision operator to the control net, which becomes more and more dense. In the limit, the vertices of the control net converge to a smooth surface. Point-wise evaluations of the given curves participate in every iteration of the subdivision, and the limit surface interpolates the given curves, regardless of their representation.

Figure 1 illustrates a surface generated by our algorithm. The surface is defined by an initial control net that consists of 11 vertices, and by a net of intersecting curves, shown in green. The edges of the control net are shown as white lines.

The combined subdivision scheme presented in this paper is based on the famous Catmull-Clark subdivision scheme. Our algorithm applies Catmull-Clark's scheme almost everywhere on the control net. The given curves affect the control net only locally, at parts of the control net that are near the given curves.

The motivation behind the specific subdivision rules, and the smoothness analysis of the scheme are presented in [9]. In the following sections, we describe Catmull-Clark's scheme, and we present the details of our scheme.

*adilev@math.tau.ac.il, http://www.math.tau.ac.il/~adilev



## 2 CATMULL-CLARK'S SCHEME

Camull Clark's subdivision scheme is defined over closed nets of arbitrary topology, as an extension of the tensor product bi-cubic B-spline subdivision scheme (see [1, 3]). Variants of the original scheme were analyzed by Ball and Storry [16]. Our algorithm employs a variant of Catmull-Clark's scheme due to Sabin [14], which generates limit surfaces that are $G^2$ everywhere except at a finite number of irregular points. In the neighborhood of those points the surface curvature is bounded. The irregular points come from vertices of the original control net that have valency other than 4, and from faces of the original control net that are not quadrilateral.

A net $N = (V, E)$ consists of a set of vertices $V$ and the topological information of the net $E$, in terms of edges and faces. A net is closed when each edge is shared by exactly two faces.

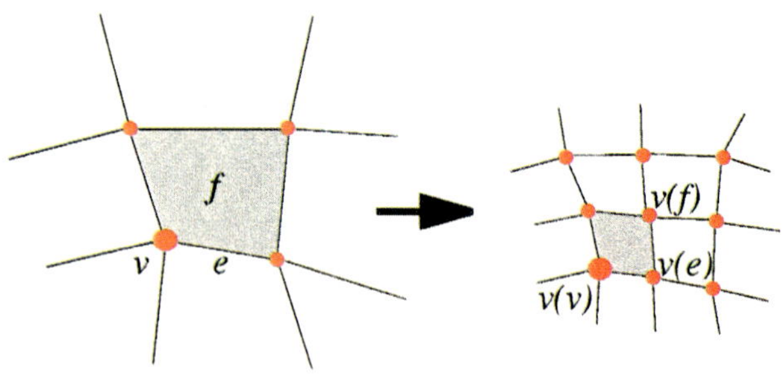


Figure 2: Catmull-Clark's scheme.

The vertices $V'$ of the new net $N' = (V', E')$ are calculated by applying the following rules on $N$ (see figure 2):

1. For each old face $f$, make a new face-vertex $v(f)$ as the weighted average of the old vertices of $f$, with weights $W_n$ that depend on the valency $n$ of each vertex.

2. For each old edge $e$, make a new edge-vertex $v(e)$ as the weighted average of the old vertices of $e$ and the new face vertices associated with the two faces originally sharing $e$. The weights $W_n$ (which are the same as the weights used in rule 1) depend on the valency $n$ of each vertex.

3. For each old vertex $v$, make a new vertex-vertex $v(v)$ at the point given by the following linear combination, whose coefficients $\alpha_n, \beta_n, \gamma_n$ depend on the valency $n$ of $v$:

   $\alpha_n \cdot$ (the centroid of the new edge vertices of the edges meeting at v) + $\beta_n \cdot$ (the centroid of the new face vertices of the faces sharing those edges) + $\gamma_n \cdot v$.

The topology $E'$ of the new net is calculated by the following rule:

> For each old face $f$ and for each vertex $v$ of $f$, make a new quadrilateral face whose edges join $v(f)$ and $v(v)$ to the edge vertices of the edges of $f$ sharing $v$ (see figure 2).

The formulas for the weights $\alpha_n, \beta_n, \gamma_n$ and $W_n$ are given in the appendix.

# 3 THE CONTROL NET

Our subdivision algorithm is defined both on closed nets and on open nets. In the case of open nets, we make a distinction between *boundary vertices* and *internal vertices* (and between *boundary edges* and *internal edges*). The control net that is given as input to our scheme consists of vertices, edges, faces and given smooth curves. We assume that these are $C^2$ parametric curves. An edge which is associated with a segment of a curve, is called a *c-edge*. Both of its vertices are called *c-vertices*. All the other edges and vertices are *ordinary vertices* and *ordinary edges*.

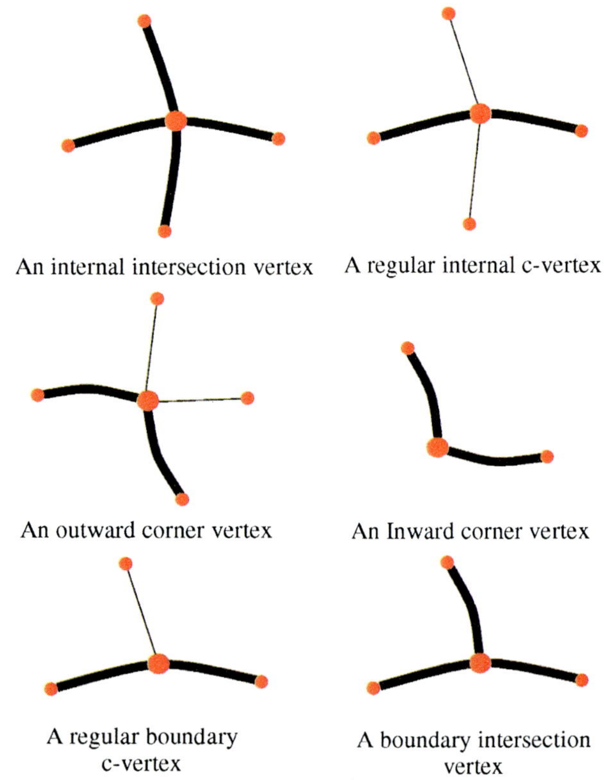


Figure 3: The different kinds of c-vertices. C-edges are marked by bold curved lines. Usual edges are shown as thin lines.

In case two c-edges that share a c-vertex are associated with two different curves, the c-vertex is associated with two curves, and we call it an *intersection vertex*. Every *c-vertex* is thus associated with a parameter value on a curve, while *intersection vertices* are associated with two curves and two different parameter values. In case of intersection vertices, we require that the two curves intersect at those parameter values.

Every *c-edge* contains a pointer to a curve $c$, and to a segment on that curve designated by a parameter interval $[u_0, u_1]$. The vertices of that edge are associated with the points $c(u_0)$ and $c(u_1)$ respectively. We require that in the original control net, the parameter intervals be all of constant length for all the c-edges associated with a single curve $c$, namely $|u_1 - u_0| = \text{const}$. In order to fulfill this requirement, the c-vertices along a curve $c$ can be chosen to be evenly spaced with respect to the parameterization of the curve $c$, or the curve $c$ can be reparameterized appropriately such that the c-vertices of $c$ are evenly spaced with respect to the new parameterization.

The restrictions on the control net are that every boundary edge is a c-edge (i.e. the given net of curves contains all the boundary curves of the surface), and that we allow only the following types of *c-vertices* to exist in the net (see figure 3):

**A regular internal c-vertex** A c-vertex with four edges emanating from it: Two c-edges that are associated with the same curve, and two ordinary edges from opposite sides of the curve.

**A regular boundary c-vertex** A c-vertex with 3 edges emanating from it: Two boundary edges that are associated with the same curve, and one other ordinary internal edge.

**An internal intersection vertex** A c-vertex with 4 edges emanating from it: Two c-edges that are associated with the same curve, and two other c-edges that are associated with a second curve, from opposite sides of the first curve.

**A boundary intersection vertex** A c-vertex with 3 edges emanating from it: Two c-edges that are associated with the same curve, and another c-edge associated with a different curve.

**An inward corner vertex** A c-vertex with 2 c-edges emanating from it, each associated with a different curve.

**An outward corner vertex** A c-vertex with 4 edges emanating from it: Two consequent c-edges that are associated with two different curves and two ordinary edges.

In particular, we do not handle more than two curves intersecting at one point.

In our algorithm, there is an essential difference between c-vertices and ordinary vertices: While the location $p(v)$ of ordinary vertices of the original control net is determined by the designer, the location of c-vertices is calculated in a preprocessing stage of the algorithm (the exact procedure is described in §4).

Every c-vertex $v$ which is associated with a parameter value $u$ on the curve $c$, has associated with it a three-dimensional vector $d(v)$, which determines the second partial derivative of the limit surface at the point $c(u)$ in the cross-curve direction (The differentiation is made with respect to a local parameterization that is induced by the subdivision process. The cross-curve direction at a c-vertex $v$ is the limit direction of the ordinary edge emanating for $v$). We call the value $d(v)$ the *cross-curve second derivative* associated with the vertex $v$.

Every intersection vertex $v$ has associated with it two three-dimensional vectors $d_1(v), d_2(v)$ that correspond to the two curves $c_1, c_2$ that are associated with $v$. At the intersection between two curves, the surface second derivatives in the two curve directions are determined by the curves, therefore the user does not have control over the cross-curve second derivatives there. Their initialization procedure is described below.

For c-vertices that are not intersection vertices, the vectors $d(v)$ in the initial control net are determined by the designer and they affect the shape of the limit surface. Several ways of initializing the values $d(v)$ are discussed in §5.

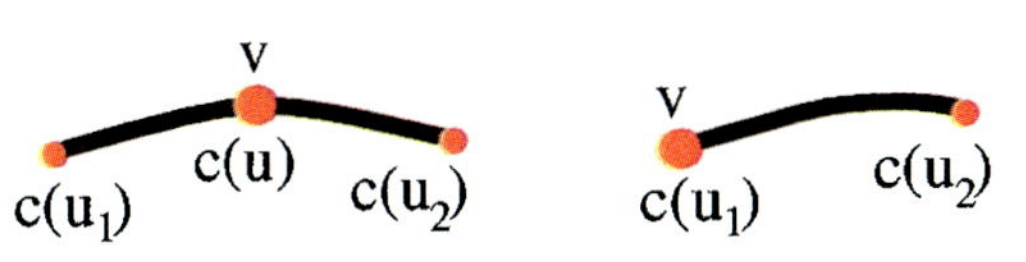


Figure 4: For each c-vertex $v$ that is associated with a curve $c$ we define the second difference $\Delta^2 c(v)$.

Throughout the scheme we apply second difference operators to the given curves. Let $v$ denote a c-vertex associated with a curve $c$. We define the *second difference of $c$ at $v$*, denoted by $\Delta^2 c(v)$ as follows (see figure 4): If $v$ is associated with the end of the curve $c$, then there is a single c-edge emanating from $v$ that is associated with the parameter interval $[u_1, u_2]$ on $c$. In this case

$$\Delta^2 c(v) = 4c(u_1) - 8c\left(\frac{u_1 + u_2}{2}\right) + 4c(u_2).$$

In case there are two c-edges emanating from $v$ that are associated with the parameter intervals $[u_1, u], [u, u_2]$ on $c$, we define

$$\Delta^2 c(v) = c(u_1) - 2c(u) + c(u_2).$$

The values $d_1(v), d_2(v)$ at the intersection vertex $v$ which is associated with two curves $c_1$ and $c_2$, are initialized by

$$\begin{aligned} d_1(v) &= \Delta^2 c_1(v) \\ d_2(v) &= \Delta^2 c_2(v). \end{aligned} \tag{1}$$

We say that $d_1(v)$ is the cross-curve second derivative associated with $v$ with respect to the curve $c_2$. Similarly, $d_2(v)$ is the cross-curve second derivative associated with $v$ with respect to the curve $c_1$.

## 4 THE COMBINED SCHEME

In the preprocessing stage of our algorithm, we calculate $p(v)$ for every c-vertex of the original control net, according to the following rules: In case $v$ is an intersection vertex which is associated with the point $c(u)$, its location is given by

$$p(v) = c(u) - \frac{d_1(v) + d_2(v)}{6}. \tag{2}$$

In case $v$ is not an intersection vertex, its location is given by

$$p(v) = c(u) - \frac{\Delta^2 c(v) + d(v)}{6}. \tag{3}$$

From (2) and (3) it is clear why the c-vertices do not necessarily lie on the given curves. Notice, for example, in figure 8 how the boundary vertices of the original control net are 'pushed away' from the given boundary curve, due to the term $\Delta^2 c(v)$ in (3).

Each iteration of the subdivision algorithm consists of the following steps: First, Catmull-Clark's scheme as described in §2 is used to calculate the new ordinary vertices. Next, the new c-vertices are calculated (this includes all the boundary vertices). Finally, we perform local 'corrections' on new ordinary vertices that are neighbors of c-vertices.

### 4.1 Calculation Of Ordinary Vertices

Step 1 of the combined scheme creates the new control net topology, and calculates all the new ordinary vertices, by applying Catmull-Clark's scheme. Since Catmull-Clark's scheme was designed for closed nets, we adapt it a little bit near the surface boundaries, by considering the boundary vertices to have valency 4 when calculating new ordinary vertices that are affected by the boundary vertices.

### 4.2 Calculation Of C-Vertices

In step 2, the data associated with the new c-vertices is calculated, by the following procedure:

Let $e$ denote a c-edge on the old control net, which corresponds to the parameter interval $[u_0, u_1]$ of the curve $c$. Let $v_0, v_1$ denote the vertices of $e$. We associate the vertex $v(e)$ with $c\left(\frac{u_0+u_1}{2}\right)$, and we calculate the new cross-curve second derivative for $v(e)$ by the following simple rule:

$$d(v(e)) = \frac{d(v_0) + d(v_1)}{8}. \tag{4}$$

In case $v_0$ or $v_1$ are intersection vertices (and therefore, contain two cross-curve second derivative vectors $d_1$ and $d_2$), the one taken in (4) should be the cross-curve second derivative with respect to the curve $c$.

Let $v$ denote a c-vertex on the old control net. We associate $v(v)$ with the same curve and the same parameter value on that curve,

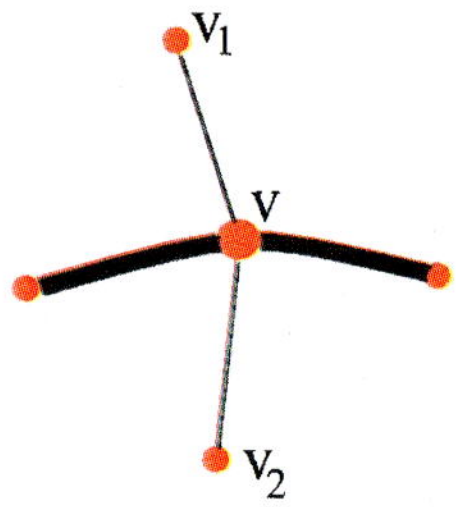


Figure 5: Local corrections near a regular internal c-vertex

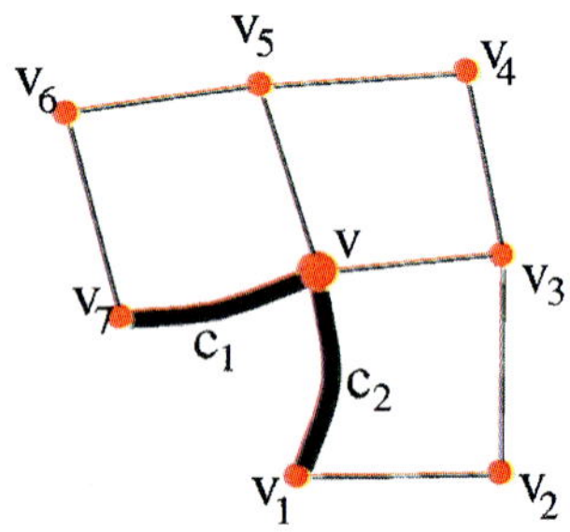


Figure 6: Local corrections near an outward corner.

as $v$ had. In case $v$ is an intersection vertex, we set $d_1(v(v))$ and $d_2(v(v))$ by (1). Otherwise, the new cross-curve second derivative at $v(v)$ is inherited from $v$ by the following rule:

$$d(v(v)) = \frac{d(v)}{4}. \tag{5}$$

Step 2 is completed by calculating the location of every c-vertex using (2) and (3).

As the subdivision iterations proceed, the values $d(v)$ and $\Delta^2 C(v)$ decay at a rate of $4^{-k}$, where $k$ is the level of subdivision. Therefore the c-vertices converge to points on the curves, which provides the interpolation property (see figure 8).

### 4.3 Local Corrections Near C-Vertices

Step 3 performs local modifications to the resulting control net near regular internal c-vertices, and near outward corners. Ordinary vertices that are neighbors of regular internal c-vertices are recalculated by the following rule: Let $v$ denote a regular internal c-vertex, and let $v_1$ and $v_2$ denote its two neighboring ordinary vertices (see figure 5). Let $p(v_1), p(v_2)$ denote the locations of $v_1$ and $v_2$ that resulted from step 1 of the algorithm. Let $p(v)$ denote the location of $v$ that resulted from step 2 of the algorithm. We calculate the *corrected* locations $\hat{p}(v_1), \hat{p}(v_2)$ by

$$\hat{p}(v_1) = p(v) + \frac{d(v)}{2} + \frac{p(v_1) - p(v_2)}{2},$$
$$\hat{p}(v_2) = p(v) + \frac{d(v)}{2} + \frac{p(v_2) - p(v_1)}{2}. \tag{6}$$

A different correction rule is applied near outward corner vertices. Let $v$ denote an outward corner vertex, and let $v_1, \ldots, v_7$ denote its neighboring vertices (see figure 6). The vertex $v$ corresponds to the curve $c_1$ at the parameter value $u_1$, and to the curve $c_2$ at the parameter value $u_2$. In particular, $c_1(u_1) = c_2(u_2)$.

Let $p(v), p(v_1), \ldots, p(v_7)$ denote the locations of $v, v_1, \ldots, v_7$ that resulted from steps 1 and 2 of the algorithm. Let $a$ be the vector $a = \frac{1}{4}(1, -1, -1, 2, -1, -1, 1)$. We calculate the corrected locations for $v_2, \ldots, v_6$ by the following rules:

$$\begin{aligned}
t &= \sum_{i=1}^{7} a_i p(v_i), \\
\hat{p}(v_3) &= \frac{1}{3}p(v_3) + \frac{2}{3}\left(2p(v) - p(v_7) + \Delta^2 c_1(v)\right), \\
\hat{p}(v_5) &= \frac{1}{3}p(v_5) + \frac{2}{3}\left(2p(v) - p(v_1) + \Delta^2 c_2(v)\right). \\
\hat{p}(v_2) &= \frac{1}{3}p(v_2) + \frac{2}{3}\left(\hat{p}(v_3) + p(v_1) - p(v) - t\right) \\
\hat{p}(v_6) &= \frac{1}{3}p(v_6) + \frac{2}{3}\left(\hat{p}(v_5) + p(v_7) - p(v) - t\right) \\
\hat{p}(v_4) &= \frac{1}{3}p(v_4) + \frac{2}{3}\left(\hat{p}(v_5) + \hat{p}(v_3) - p(v) + t\right)
\end{aligned} \tag{7}$$

There are cases when a single vertex has more than one corrected location, for example an ordinary vertex which is a neighbor of several c-vertices. In these cases we calculate all the corrected locations for such a vertex, using (6) or (7) and define the new location of that vertex to be the arithmetic mean of all the corrected locations. Situations like these occur frequently at the first level of subdivision. The only possibility for a vertex to have more than one corrected location after the first subdivision iteration, is near intersection vertices; The vertex always has two corrected locations, and its new location is taken to be their arithmetic mean.

## 5 DISCUSSION

The cross-curve second derivatives $d(v)$ of the original control net as determined by the designer, play an important role in determining the shape of the limit surface. As part of constructing the initial control net, a 3D vector $d(v)$ should be initialized by the designer, for every *regular internal c-vertex* and for every *regular boundary c-vertex*.

In case the initial control net contains only intersection vertices (such as the control net in figure 1), (1) determines all the cross-curve second derivatives. Otherwise they can be initialized by any kind of heuristic method.

We suggest the following heuristic approach to initialize $d(v)$ in case $v$ is a regular internal c-vertex: Let $v$ be associated with the curve $c$ at the parameter value $u$, and let $v_1, v_2$ denote the two ordinary vertices that are neighbors of $v$ (see figure 5). It seems reasonable to calculate $d(v)$ such that

$$p(v_1) + p(v_2) - 2p(v) = d(v),$$

because we know that this relation holds in the limit. Since $p(v)$ itself depends on $d(v)$ according to (3), we get the following formula for $d(v)$:

$$d(v) = \frac{3}{2}\left(p(v_1) + p(v_2)\right) - 3c(u) + \frac{1}{2}\Delta^2 c(v). \tag{8}$$

In case $v$ is a regular boundary c-vertex, which lies between two boundary intersection vertices $v_1, v_2$ (see figure 7), one should probably consider the second derivatives at $v_1, v_2$ when determining $d(v)$. The following heuristic rule can be used:

$$d(v) = \frac{\Delta^2 c_1(v) + \Delta^2 c_2(v)}{2}, \tag{9}$$

where $v_1, v_2$ are associated with $c_1(u_1)$ and $c_2(u_2)$ respectively.

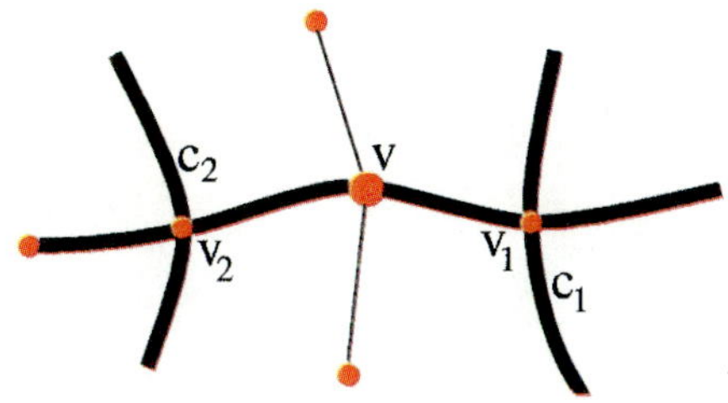


Figure 7: A regular boundary c-vertex between two boundary intersection vertices

The are many cases when the choice $d(v) = 0$ generates the nicest shapes when $v$ is a regular boundary c-vertex. Recall that the natural interpolating cubic spline has zero second derivative at its ends.

Other ways of determining $d(v)$ may employ variational principles. One can choose $d(v)$ such as to minimize a certain fairness measure of the entire surface.

# 6 CONCLUSIONS

With *combined subdivision schemes* that extend the notion of the known subdivision schemes, it is simple to generate surfaces of arbitrary topological type that interpolate nets of curves given in any parametric representation. The scheme presented in this paper is easy to implement and generates nice looking and almost $G^2$ surfaces, provided that the given curves are $C^2$. These surfaces are suitable for machining purposes since they have bounded curvature.

The current algorithm is restricted to nets of curves where no more than two curves intersect at one point, which is a considerable restriction for many applications. However, we believe that the basic idea of applying subdivision rules that explicitly involve the given curve data, and the general theory of combined subdivision schemes can be extended to handle nets where three or more curves intersect at one point, as well as nets with irregular c-vertices.

The proposed scheme can work even if the given curves are not $C^2$, since it only uses point-wise evaluations. In case the curves are $C^1$, for example, the limit surface will be only $G^1$. Moreover, in case a given curve has a local 'fault', and otherwise it is $C^2$, the local 'fault' will have only a local effect on the limit surface.

Creases in the limit surface can be introduced along a given curve by avoiding the corrections made to vertices near that curve in step 3 of the subdivision. This causes the curve to act as a boundary curve to the surface on both sides of the curve.

Concerning the computation time, notice that most of the computational work in each iteration is spent in the first step of the subdivision iteration, namely, in applying Catmull-Clark's scheme. The local corrections are very simple, and apply only near c-vertices (whose number, after a few iterations, is much lower than that of the ordinary vertices).

Using the analysis tools we have developed in [7, 8], other combined subdivision schemes can be constructed to perform other tasks, such as the generation of surfaces that satisfy certain boundary conditions, including tangent plane conditions [10], and even curvature continuity conditions.

Figures 8-19 show several surfaces created by our algorithm.

# Acknowledgement

This work is sponsored by the Israeli Ministry of Science. I thank Nira Dyn for her guidance and many helpful comments, and Peter Schröder for his constant encouragement and advice.

# References

[1] E. Catmull and J. Clark. Recursively generated b-spline surfaces on arbitrary topological meshes. *Computer Aided Design*, 10:350–355, 1978.

[2] T. DeRose, M. Kass, and T. Truong. Subdivision surfaces in character animation. In *SIGGRAPH 98 Conference Proceedings*, Annual Conference Series, pages 85–94. ACM SIGGRAPH, 1998.

[3] D. Doo and M. Sabin. Behaviour of recursive division surface near extraordinary points. *Computer Aided Design*, 10:356–360, 1978.

[4] N. Dyn, J. A. Greogory, and D. Levin. A butterfly subdivision scheme for surface interpolation with tension control. *ACM Transactions on Graphics*, 9:160–169, 1990.

[5] M. Halstead, M. Kass, and T. DeRose. Efficient, fair interpolation using catmull-clark sutfaces. In *SIGGRAPH 93 Conference Proceedings*, Annual Conference Series, pages 35–44. ACM SIGGRAPH, 1993.

[6] L. Kobbelt, T. Hesse, H. Prautzsch, and K. Schweizerhof. Interpolatory subdivision on open quadrilateral nets with arbitrary topology. *Computer Graphics Forum*, 15:409–420, 1996. Eurographics '96 issue.

[7] A. Levin. Analysis of combined subdivision schemes 1. in preparation, available on the web at http://www.math.tau.ac.il/~adilev, 1999.

[8] A. Levin. Analysis of combined subdivision schemes 2. in preparation, available on the web at http://www.math.tau.ac.il/~adilev, 1999.

[9] A. Levin. Analysis of combined subdivision schemes for the interpoation of curves. SIGGRAPH'99 CDROM Proceedings, 1999.

[10] A. Levin. Combined subdivision schemes for the design of surfaces satisfying boundary conditions. To appear in CAGD, 1999.

[11] C. Loop. Smooth spline surfaces based on triangles. Master's thesis, University of Utah, Department of Mathematics, 1987.

[12] A. H. Nasri. Curve interpolation in recursively generated b-spline surfaces over arbitrary topology. *Computer Aided Geometric Design*, 14:No 1, 1997.

[13] A. H. Nasri. Interpolation of open curves by recursive subdivision surface. In T. Goodman and R. Martin, editors, *The Mathematics of Surfaces VII*, pages 173–188. Information Geometers, 1997.

[14] M. Sabin. Cubic recursive division with bounded curvature. In P. J. Laurent, A. le Mehaute, and L. L. Schumaker, editors, *Curves and Surfaces*, pages 411–414. Academic Press, 1991.

[15] J. Schweitzer. *Analysis and Applications of Subdivision Surfaces*. PhD thesis, University of Washington, Seattle, 1996.

[16] D. J. T. Storry and A. A. Ball. Design of an n-sided surface patch. *Computer Aided Geometric Design*, 6:111–120, 1989.

[17] G. Taubin. A signal processing approach to fair surface design. In Robert Cook, editor, *SIGGRAPH 95 Conference Proceedings*, Annual Conference Series, pages 351–358. ACM SIGGRAPH, Addison Wesley, August 1995. held in Los Angeles, California, 06-11 August 1995.

[18] D. Zorin, P. Schröder, and W. Sweldens. Interpolating subdivision for meshes with arbitrary topology. *Computer Graphics Proceedings (SIGGRAPH 96)*, pages 189–192, 1996.

## Appendix

We present the procedure for calculating the weights mentioned in §2, as formulated by Sabin in [14].

Let $n > 2$ denote a vertex valency. Let $k := \cos(\pi/n)$. Let $x$ be the unique real root of

$$x^3 + (4k^2 - 3)x - 2k = 0,$$

satisfying $x > 1$. Then

$$\begin{aligned} W_n &= x^2 + 2kx - 3, \qquad (10) \\ \alpha_n &= 1, \\ \gamma_n &= \frac{kx + 2k^2 - 1}{x^2(kx+1)}, \\ \beta_n &= -\gamma_n. \end{aligned}$$

| $n$ | $W_n$ | $\gamma_n$ |
|---|---|---|
| 3 | 1.23606797749979... | 0.06524758424985... |
| 4 | 1 | 0.25 |
| 5 | 0.71850240323974... | 0.40198344690335... |
| 6 | 0.52233339335931... | 0.52342327689253... |
| 7 | 0.39184256502794... | 0.61703187134796... |

Table 1: The weights used in Sabin's variant of Catmull-Clark's subdivision scheme

The original paper by Sabin [14] contains a mistake: the formulas for the parameters $\alpha, \beta$ and $\gamma$ that appear in §4 there, are $\beta := 1,\ \gamma := -\alpha$.

The weights $W_n$ and $\gamma_n$ for $n = 3, \ldots, 7$ are given in table 1.

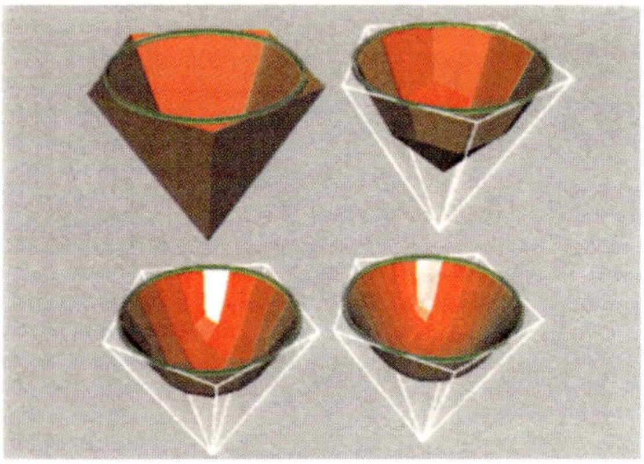

Figure 8: Three iterations of the algorithm. We have chosen $d(v) = 0$ for every c-vertex $v$, which results in parabolic points on the surface boundary.

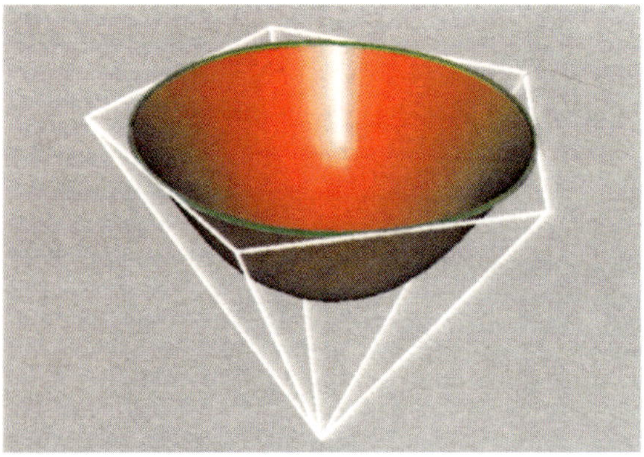

Figure 9: The limit surface of the iterations shown in figure 8

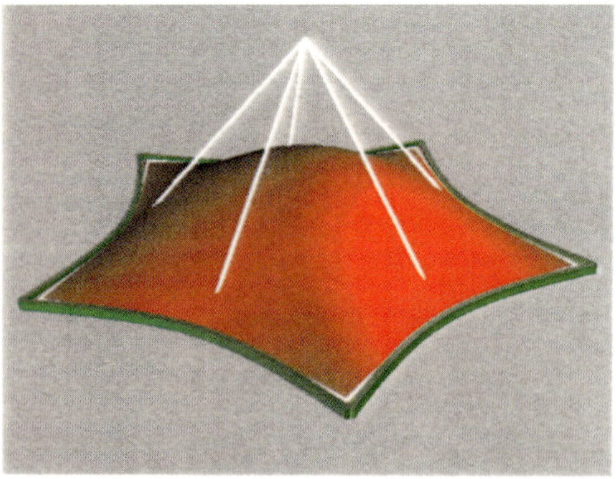

Figure 10: A 5-sided surface generated from a simple control net, with zero $d(v)$ for all c-vertices $v$. Our algorithm easily fills arbitrary N-sided patches.

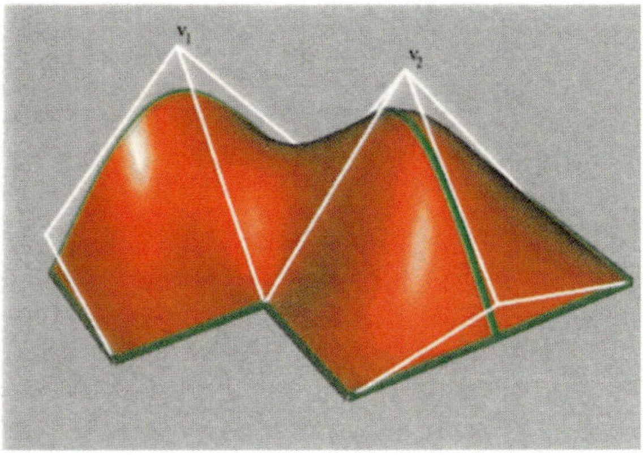

Figure 11: A surface with an outward corner. We used (8) to calculate $d(v_2)$, and set $d(v_1) = 0$.

Figure 12: A surface with non smooth boundary curves, and zero cross-curve second derivatives

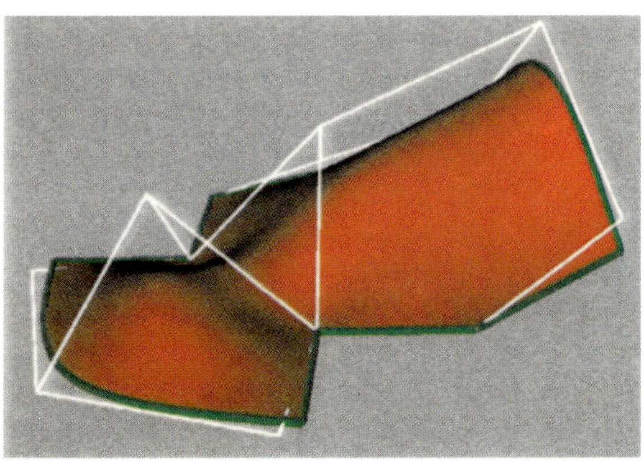

Figure 13: A surface with non smooth boundary curves, and zero cross-curve second derivatives

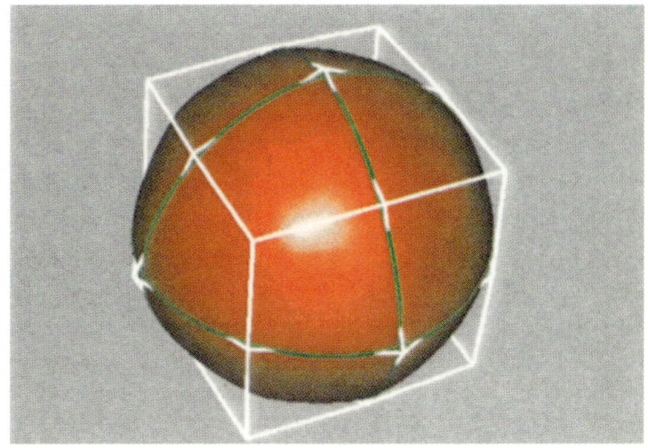

Figure 14: A closed surface. The cross curve second derivatives for regular internal c-vertices were calculated using (9).

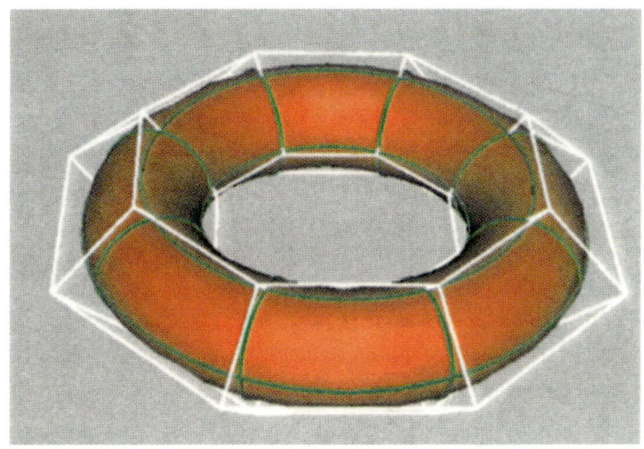

Figure 15: A Torus-like surface, from a net of circles.

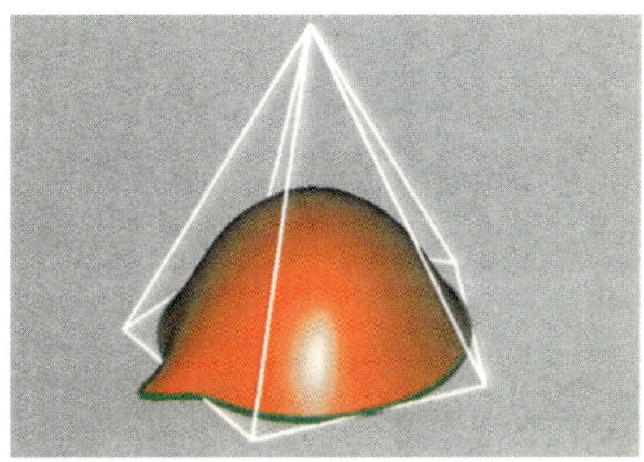

Figure 16: Introducing small perturbations to the given curves results in small and local perturbations of the limit surface. Notice that the original control net does not contain the information of the small perturbations. These come directly from the data of the curves.

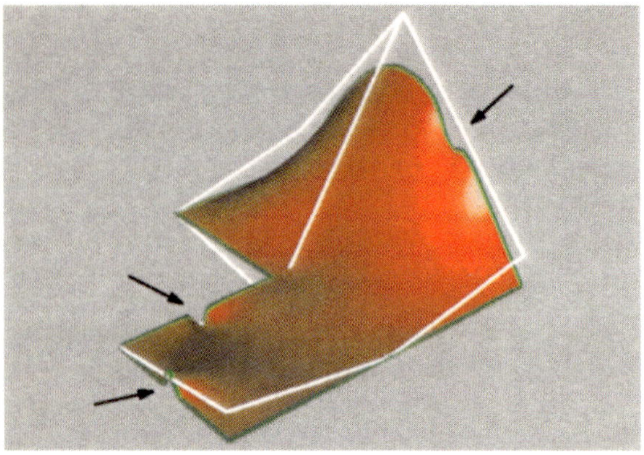

Figure 17: Small perturbations to the given curves result in small and local deformation of the limit surface.

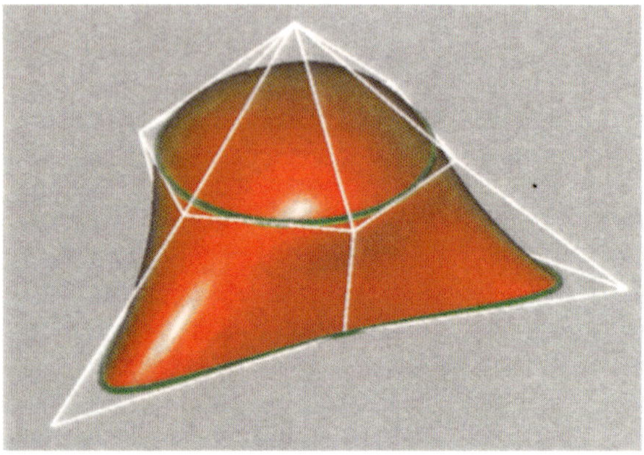

Figure 18: A surface constructed from two given sections. The cross curve second derivatives for the regular internal c-vertices were calculated using (8). For boundary vertices, we took $d(v) = 0$.

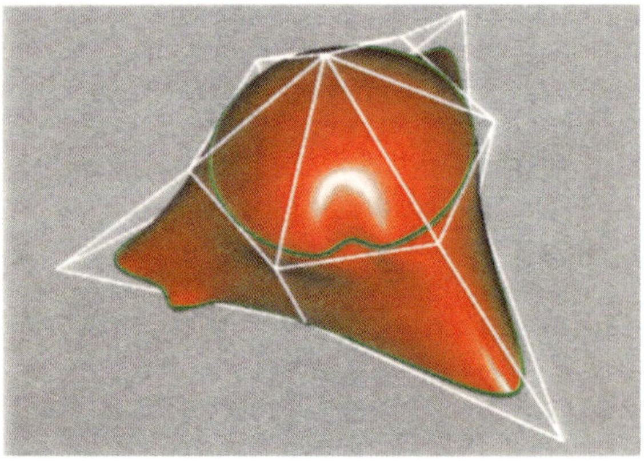

Figure 19: the same surface as in figure 18 after introducing small perturbations in the section curves.

# ArtDefo
# Accurate Real Time Deformable Objects

Doug L. James[1] and Dinesh K. Pai[1,2]

University of British Columbia

## Abstract

We present an algorithm for fast, physically accurate simulation of deformable objects suitable for real time animation and virtual environment interaction. We describe the boundary integral equation formulation of static linear elasticity as well as the related Boundary Element Method (BEM) discretization technique. In addition, we show how to exploit the coherence of typical interactions to achieve low latency; the boundary formulation lends itself well to a fast update method when a few boundary conditions change. The algorithms are described in detail with examples from ArtDefo, our implementation.

Figure 1: Example of interactive simulation with ArtDefo. Here, a human-like character is being tickled by its alien abductors. The body is rendered as a Loop subdivision surface.

## 1 Introduction

Simulation of deformable objects is a key challenge, with a long history in computer graphics. Deformable object models are important because so much of our physical world can not be modeled as rigid bodies. The most important examples are, of course, humans, human tissue, and human-like characters. We conjecture that one reason for the preponderance of robotic, wooden, and chitinous characters in recent computer animation is the difficulty of realistic deformable object simulation.

Simulating deformable objects for graphics is difficult because of the conflicting demands of interactivity and accuracy. In animation, the simulation must be fast enough to provide useful feedback to the animator. In virtual environments, the objects must deform in real time, in response to user input. In surgical training and games with haptic force feedback, forces due to the deformation must also be computed in real time.

On the other hand, physical accuracy is important since it allows users to treat deformable objects as "black boxes" and focus on the their primary objectives. In animation, it allows an animator to focus on the action rather than on surface tweaking. In surgical simulation, the contact forces felt by the surgeon must be accurate — this increases the likelihood that the surgeon has acquired useful manual skills for real surgeries, rather than skill at a new video game.

As a result of these conflicting demands, work to date can be broadly classified into two categories. (1) Interactive models: in these models, speed and low latency are paramount and physical accuracy is secondary. Typical examples include mass-spring models and spline surfaces used as deformable models. (2) Accurate models: in these models, physical accuracy is paramount; the models start with the constitutive laws of the material and solve the resulting boundary value PDE's numerically using, for instance, the Finite Element Method (FEM). The models are computationally expensive and are typically simulated off-line.

In this paper we describe a physically based algorithm for deformable object simulations which makes this tradeoff unnecessary for many applications in which linear elastic models are sufficient. Interactive speeds as well as accuracy are attained by exploiting the fact that a linear model allows many system responses (Green's functions) to be precomputed and then combined later in real time using an incremental low-rank update solution reconstruction approach. Our linear elastic model is based on boundary integrals and the Boundary Element Method (BEM). While the low rank update approach could in fact be applied to any discrete linear system, it is particularly convenient and instructive using a BEM discretization. The solver's low latency success is due in part to the limited amount of nonzero boundary data associated with typical interactions.

This model has been implemented in our system, ArtDefo, using Java. We chose Java for integration into our software environment and for easy accessibility from the Internet. Despite the performance penalty imposed by current Java virtual machines for numerical array-based computations, our system provides good interactive performance for the examples described in this paper. Visit `www.cs.ubc.ca/~djames/deformable` for online demos.

Figure 1 shows an interactive simulation in which the torso of the character is deformable. The deformation and resulting contact forces due to a virtual finger or medical instrument touching a location on the torso were computed in approximately a millisecond after an initial cost of several milliseconds on an ordinary 350MHz PC. The global deformation is accurately computed and important phenomena such as the upward bulging of the torso due to the preservation of volume are automatically produced.

An important feature is that since our model is physically

[1] Institute of Applied Mathematics

[2] Dept. of Computer Science, 2366 Main Mall, UBC, Vancouver, Canada. {djames|pai}@cs.ubc.ca. This work was supported in part by IRIS NCE and NSERC.

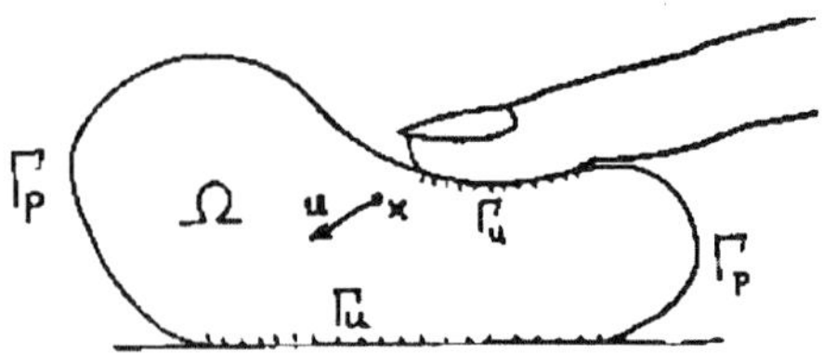

Figure 2: Notation

based, deformable objects are also easier to create and modify; the object's deformation behavior is specified using a few material properties rather than by adjusting a large number of spring constants and other parameters. Material properties for standard objects can be looked up in a handbook, and properties can be modified in intuitive ways by making it "more compressible (sponge-like)" "less stiff," "more dense" etc. We can easily represent physical constraints, such as incompressibility, which are difficult for deformable models based on spring networks and splines.

Finally, even though the technique has somewhat complex mathematical foundations, it is easy to implement. We describe the basic algorithms in sufficient detail to allow implementation. We bring out the connections between deformation computations and radiosity methods in global illumination. This will allow rendering professionals to easily understand and implement fast simulations of deformation.

The paper is organized as follows. In §2 we present an overview of all the important techniques in this paper. Connections to related work are discussed in §3. In subsequent sections §4–7 we provide details of the algorithms, with specific integrals needed for the constant element case collected in the Appendix.

# 2 Overview

We describe the key ideas in our system in this section, at a high level. Details are provided in the sections that follow.

## 2.1 Linear Elasticity

Our model is physically based and starts with the physics of static linear elastic deformation. Linear elasticity accurately models small deformations of objects and is commonly used in engineering analysis. Biological tissues and large deformations will involve additional non-linear effects; nevertheless, linear models can play an important role in a hybrid simulation given that they can be significantly cheaper to evaluate.

We use the following notation (see Figure 2) which is standard (e.g., [5]). The domain of the deformable object is denoted $\Omega \subset \mathbb{R}^3$ with boundary $\Gamma$. A point $\mathbf{x} \in \Omega$ undergoes a displacement $\mathbf{u}$ due to deformation. The deformation is governed locally by Navier's equation (described in §4) which is a generalization of Hooke's law from high school physics. It is written

$$\mathbf{N}\mathbf{u} + \mathbf{b} = 0, \tag{1}$$

where $\mathbf{N}$ is a linear second-order differential operator, and $\mathbf{b}$ is a term due to "body forces" like gravity which act everywhere in the body. Navier's equation must be satisfied at all points $\mathbf{x} \in \Omega$; $\mathbf{N}$, $\mathbf{u}$, and $\mathbf{b}$ are functions of $\mathbf{x}$. $\mathbf{N}$ encodes all the elastic material properties of the object. For simplicity, we will assume $\mathbf{b} = 0$ in the remainder of this section.

## 2.2 Boundary Value Problem

To specify the deformation, we must also describe how the object interacts with the environment at its boundary $\Gamma$. We may want to specify *displacement boundary conditions* on some parts of the boundary (denoted $\Gamma_u$). For instance, we can indicate that the boundary is in contact with a rigid table or is being poked by a virtual finger whose motion is known (e.g., through a motion tracker attached to the user's hand). In other parts of the boundary (denoted $\Gamma_p$), it may be more natural to specify the force or rather the *traction*, $\mathbf{p}$, which is defined as the force per unit area (and has the same units as pressure). These *traction boundary conditions* are useful for specifying that the boundary is free to move (zero traction).

The boundary conditions, along with Navier's equation, constitute the boundary value problem (BVP). Changing the type of a boundary condition changes the BVP significantly, which is an important consideration we will return to in §2.5.

## 2.3 Boundary Integral Formulation

In graphics applications, we are primarily interested in determining the displacement $\mathbf{u}$ and traction $\mathbf{p}$ on the boundary of the body. The boundary displacement $\mathbf{u}$ is needed for rendering while the boundary traction $\mathbf{p}$ is needed for force feedback user interfaces. Therefore it is possible to use a boundary integral formulation of Navier's equation,

$$\mathbf{c}\mathbf{u} + \int_\Gamma \mathbf{p}^* \mathbf{u} \, d\Gamma = \int_\Gamma \mathbf{u}^* \mathbf{p} \, d\Gamma. \tag{2}$$

Here $\mathbf{c}$ is a (known) function that depends only on the geometry of the boundary, and $\mathbf{u}^*$ and $\mathbf{p}^*$ are *fundamental solutions* which depend only on known elasticity properties.

A key advantage of the boundary integral formulation is that all the unknowns are on the boundary $\Gamma$, and are exactly the quantities we are interested in. In contrast, the FEM has unknowns in the interior as well.

For an excellent survey of boundary integral equation issues we refer the reader to [2].

We remark that boundary integral equations also arise in global illumination in the form of the Rendering Equation [17], where it is derived from the physics of radiative energy transport. Therefore many of the same issues arise in solving such integral equations. There are also important differences; equation 2 is a vector integral equation instead of a scalar equation, and far from being a Fredholm integral equation of the second kind, the vector equation involves both single and double layer potential integral operators [2].

## 2.4 Numerical Discretization

To solve equation 2 numerically, it is discretized by approximating $\mathbf{u}$, $\mathbf{u}^*$, etc., in finite dimensional function spaces. We discuss the choice of these spaces in §6 when we discuss the BEM, but in the end the integral equation is reduced to a matrix equation of the form

$$\mathsf{H}\mathsf{u} = \mathsf{G}\mathsf{p}, \tag{3}$$

where $\mathsf{u}$ is a vector of displacements $\mathsf{u}_i = \mathbf{u}(\mathbf{x}_i)$, sampled at a finite set of nodes $\mathbf{x}_i, i = 1, \ldots, n$, on the boundary, and $\mathsf{p}$ are the corresponding tractions at these nodes. For the constant boundary element we describe in §6, $\mathbf{x}_i$ are the centroids of boundary triangles.

The $3n \times 3n$ dense matrices $\mathsf{H}$ and $\mathsf{G}$ are discretized versions of the operators on the left and right and sides of (2), respectively. They are analogous to the form factors computed in radiosity methods.

Finally, specifying boundary conditions, either $\mathbf{u}$ or $\mathbf{p}$, at each of the $n$ nodes, yields a system of equations for the unknown nodal quantities:

$$\mathsf{A}\mathsf{v} = \mathsf{z}. \tag{4}$$

Since A depends on the BVP specified, it is not possible to simply invert A ahead of time. Nor is it realistic to invert and store all possible matrices ahead of time.

### 2.5 Interactive Deformation

Equation 4 is still prohibitively expensive to solve at interactive rates for even moderate size problems consisting of a few hundred surface nodes. This is so even though fast transform and iterative methods are available for solving (4). Therefore solving the discrete equations directly in real time is not necessarily suitable for an interactive method. This is especially true when it is possible to do much of the work ahead of time.

In a typical situation a user may, say, poke the deformable object with a virtual finger, and then move the finger along its surface. As mentioned, this process is accompanied by a sequence of different matrix problems to be solved.

We address this issue by observing that, for example, as the user makes or breaks contact with a surface node only 3 columns of A change. This implies that there is a great degree of similarity between these matrix BVP problems. We can then compute the solution to the new problem efficiently using results obtained directly from using the Sherman-Morrison-Woodbury formula [12]. We describe this procedure in detail in §7 — we mention here that if $s$ boundary conditions change, we spend $O(s^3)$ time updating a set of weights, after which correct solutions can be computed, with each using an additional $O(ns)$ time. While complexity analysis isn't indicative of interactivity, we find that these solution methods are very fast in practice. Also, since this is a *direct* solution method, latency bounds are strictly related to $s$. Hence the real-time performance can be easily predicted.

With the boundary integral formulation and our optimizations, we are able to accurately simulate deformation problems on ordinary PCs at interactive rates, even with changing boundary conditions. The high cost usually associated with deformation computations is relegated to precomputation and storage of the database used by the fast run-time solver.

## 3 Related Work

There has been considerable work in the area of deformable models in graphics. We refer the reader to a recent, thorough survey [10] which describes much of this work. We mention some relevant physically based models here, which include cloth models (e.g., [4]), linked volumetric objects [11], modal models [23] and the pioneering work of Terzopoulos and colleagues [26, 24, 25, 22]. In the following we focus mainly on models specifically designed to simulate physical deformation of objects, rather than purely geometric deformable models.

Among physically-based models, the most popular are mass-spring models (e.g., [4, 19, 28]). They divide the domain $\Omega$ into set of mass points connected by springs. The technique is effective for several applications, can be used for static as well as dynamic deformations, and has been extended to model non-linear materials and even liquids [27]. However, despite the simplicity of formulation, the resulting systems can be expensive to solve; the inaccuracy of the method implies that a larger number of nodes are required for realistic simulations (compared to FEM and BEM techniques), and these result in larger system matrices. Numerical stiffness is also a problem [3]. The model parameters are difficult to tune and can easily produce undesired Jello-like or putty-like behavior. Worse, common properties of materials like incompressibility are difficult to model. In contrast our model (and others explicitly based on Navier's equation) can be tuned using a few, well-known material properties; incompressibility is trivial to specify using Poisson's ratio $\nu = \frac{1}{2}$.

The Finite Element Method (FEM), a widely used, flexible and accurate method for solving Navier's equations, has seen application in graphics [13, 7, 8, 6]. However, its use has been limited by the complexity of the method and the cost of solving the resulting linear system.

While FEM techniques are effective general tools for (especially nonlinear) elasticity, we believe that the BEM, on which our technique is based, has certain features which will be of interest to the graphics community. These methods also have a long history in engineering analysis (e.g., [5, 9]). Radiosity methods for global illumination are closely related and are essentially boundary element methods [1, 20]. To our knowledge, BEM techniques have not been used in computer graphics for the simulation of deformable objects.

In BEM, the unknowns are only the boundary displacements and forces — exactly the quantities we need in graphics and haptics. This is in contrast with many engineering applications, in which stresses and deformations inside the body are important for determining properties of a structure, making FEM more natural. The BEM leads to a small but dense set of well-conditioned equations which are simple to solve; the FEM leads to a larger, but sparse, set of equations which can be solved efficiently using sparse matrix techniques. Fast solution methods exist for FEM, e.g., multigrid; numerous fast integral transform methods exist for BEM [2]. The BEM is also more accurate for computing contact forces than the FEM since forces are solved for just like displacements, instead of being derived from displacements using difference formulas [5]. As a result, the BEM easily handles mixed boundary conditions. And, perhaps of greatest interest, the BEM can use the same boundary discretization as used for rendering — no separate meshing is required; in FEM the interior has to be meshed as well. However, while the boundary-only nature of the BEM is a selling point, it also restricts the class of materials which it can handle to those with homogeneous material properties. A few regions with different material properties can be handled using BEM by introducing internal boundaries, but for complicated inhomogeneities a domain method, such as the FEM, is better.

Our use of the Sherman-Morrison-Woodbury formula to exploit coherence between deformable is related to the technique used in the FEM community called "structural reanalysis" [14, 18]. Unfortunately, due to the overhead introduced by internal domain nodes, these methods are not necessarily suitable for interactive applications. A notable exception is the work of [6] and colleagues; they perform various linear system optimizations, similar to those presented here, and eliminate interior nodes, using a technique called condensation, to achieve a boundary-only representation.

## 4 Navier's Equation

Linear elastostatic objects with isotropic and homogeneous material properties, have displacements satisfying the well-known Navier's equation on $\Omega$,

$$G\sum_{k=1}^{3}\left(\frac{\partial^2 u_i}{\partial x_k^2}+\frac{1}{1-2\nu}\frac{\partial^2 u_k}{\partial x_k \partial x_i}\right)+b_i=0, \tag{5}$$

which is conveniently written in a vector operator form as

$$(\mathbf{N}\mathbf{u})(\mathbf{x})+\mathbf{b}(\mathbf{x})=0, \qquad \mathbf{x}\in\Omega. \tag{6}$$

Here $\nu$ is Poisson's ratio and $G$ is the shear modulus. These are material properties which can be found in handbooks for many materials. Suitable values for Poisson's ratio are $0<\nu\leq\frac{1}{2}$, with $\nu=\frac{1}{2}$ corresponding to an incompressible material. The shear modulus $G$ is positive, with larger values resulting in larger forces accompanying a given deformation. Figure 4 shows the effect of changing $\nu$; see also Figure 3.

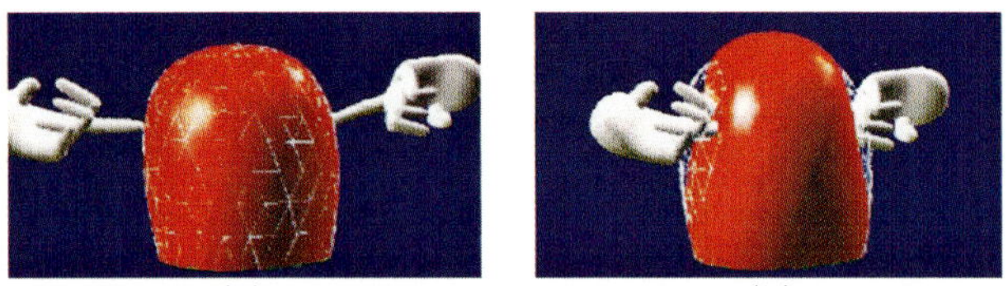

(a) (b)

Figure 3: A test nodule is pinched between two fingers. The nodule is a Loop subdivision surface, whose control polyhedron is an octahedron. The boundary of one face of the octahedron is tagged as "sharp" [16] and leads to a sharp edge around the bottom face of the object. We impose a zero-displacement boundary condition on this face, and zero traction everywhere else, except for the two finger contacts.

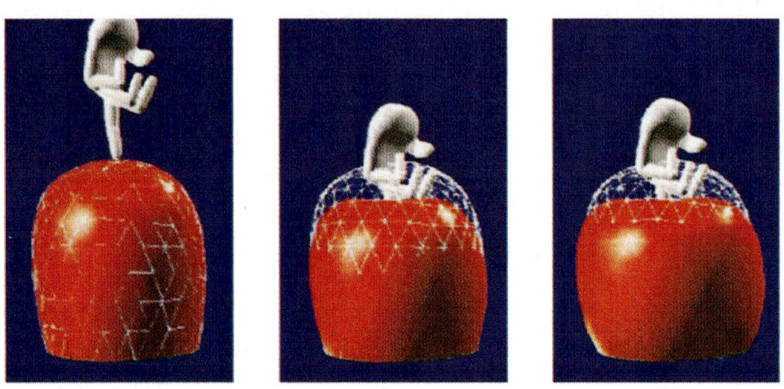

(a) (b) (c)

Figure 4: Poisson's ratio, $\nu$, provides an easy way to describe the compressibility of a material. Figure (a) shows the example nodule in its rest state. A coarse reference mesh is also shown in white on the surface. In figure (b), $\nu=0.01$, making the material very compressible; the nodule exhibits a sponge-like behavior, deforming mainly in the vicinity of the contact. In Figure (c) $\nu=0.5$, making the material incompressible; the sides of the nodule bulge to conserve volume.

The traction at a point on the surface is

$$p_i=p_i(\mathbf{x})=G\sum_{j=1}^{3}\left(\frac{\partial u_i}{\partial x_j}+\frac{\partial u_j}{\partial x_i}\right)n_j+\frac{2G\nu}{1-2\nu}n_i\left(\sum_{k=1}^{3}\frac{\partial u_k}{\partial x_k}\right)$$

where $n_i$ are the direction cosines of the outward normal. In a vector operator notation this becomes

$$\mathbf{p}(\mathbf{x})=(\mathbf{P}\mathbf{u})(\mathbf{x}), \qquad \mathbf{x}\in\Gamma. \tag{7}$$

## 5 Boundary Integral Formulation

Similar to Laplace's equation, Navier's equation on a domain may be converted to an integral equation defined on the boundary of that domain. At the heart of the derivation is integration by parts, which produces boundary integrals from volume integrals. The end result is that Navier's equations (5) on, for example, a bounded domain may be converted into a set of integral equations. The direct boundary integral equation formulation yields the vector integral equation

$$\begin{aligned}\mathbf{c}(\mathbf{x})\mathbf{u}(\mathbf{x})+\int_\Gamma \mathbf{p}^*(\mathbf{x},\mathbf{y})\mathbf{u}(\mathbf{y})\,d\Gamma(\mathbf{y}) \\ =\int_\Gamma \mathbf{u}^*(\mathbf{x},\mathbf{y})\mathbf{p}(\mathbf{y})\,d\Gamma(\mathbf{y})+\int_\Omega \mathbf{u}^*(\mathbf{x},\mathbf{y})\mathbf{b}(\mathbf{y})\,d\Omega(\mathbf{y})\end{aligned} \tag{8}$$

valid at a point $\mathbf{x}$ on the boundary $\Gamma$ [5]. Three matrix functions occur in this equation:

$$\begin{aligned}\mathbf{c} &= \mathbf{c}(\mathbf{x}) &&= [c_{ij}],\\ \mathbf{u}^* &= \mathbf{u}^*(\mathbf{x},\mathbf{y}) &&= [u^*_{ij}],\\ \mathbf{p}^* &= \mathbf{p}^*(\mathbf{x},\mathbf{y}) &&= [p^*_{ij}].\end{aligned}$$

The integral kernel functions $u^*_{ij}(\mathbf{x},\mathbf{y})$ and $p^*_{ij}(\mathbf{x},\mathbf{y})$ are known fundamental solutions and tractions, respectively, and are provided in the next section. The coefficient $c_{ij}(\mathbf{x})$ depends on the smoothness properties of the boundary at $\mathbf{x}$, but is not needed explicitly (see Appendix A.2.1).

### 5.1 Fundamental Solutions

The fundamental solutions of Navier's equation, $u^*_{ij}(\mathbf{x},\mathbf{y})$, correspond to the displacement in the $j^{th}$ direction at a field point, $\mathbf{y}$, as produced by a unit point load applied in each of the $i$ directions at a specified load point, $\mathbf{x}$, in an infinite linear elastic medium. This corresponds to the fundamental solution due to Kelvin [21]. Conceptually, this point load fundamental solution plays an analogous role in elasticity as the familiar $\frac{1}{r}$ Coulomb potential solution accompanying a point charge in electrostatics. In both cases, the fundamental solutions are highly localized and decay very quickly, e.g., the fundamental displacements have a typical $\frac{1}{r}$ character while the fundamental tractions behave like $\frac{1}{r^2}$. Mathematically, $u^*_{ij}(\mathbf{x},\mathbf{y})$ is the $j^{th}$ component of the displacement solution to

$$(\mathbf{N}\mathbf{u})(\mathbf{y})+\delta(\mathbf{x}-\mathbf{y})\hat{\mathbf{e}}_i=0,$$

where the vector operator notation from (6) has been used. The fundamental tractions are related to the fundamental displacements via (7), that is

$$\mathbf{p}^*=\mathbf{P}\mathbf{u}^*.$$

Expressions for the fundamental solutions are [5]

$$\begin{aligned}u^*_{ij}(\mathbf{x},\mathbf{y}) &= \frac{1}{16\pi(1-\nu)G}\left\{\frac{(3-4\nu)\,\delta_{ij}}{r}+\frac{r_i r_j}{r^3}\right\}\\ p^*_{ij}(\mathbf{x},\mathbf{y}) &= \frac{(1-2\nu)}{8\pi(1-\nu)}\left[\frac{(r_i n_j-r_j n_i)}{r^3}-\left\{\frac{\delta_{ij}}{r^2}+\frac{3 r_i r_j}{(1-2\nu)\,r^4}\right\}\frac{\partial r}{\partial \mathbf{n}(\mathbf{y})}\right]\end{aligned}$$

where

$$\mathbf{r} = \mathbf{y}-\mathbf{x} \qquad r = |\mathbf{r}|$$
$$r_i = (\mathbf{r})_i \qquad \frac{\partial r}{\partial \mathbf{n}(\mathbf{y})} = \frac{\mathbf{r}\cdot\mathbf{n}(\mathbf{y})}{r}$$

and $\mathbf{n}(\mathbf{y})$ is the outward unit normal at $\mathbf{y} \in \Gamma$.

### 5.2 Internal Body Forces

Any user-specified body forces mildly complicate the boundary-only character of the integral equations, as they introduce a volume integral term in (8). However, for certain classes of functions, e.g., polynomials, it is possible to analytically convert the volume integral into a boundary integral using essentially repeated integration by parts via the Multiple Reciprocity Method [5]. For example, a constant gravitational force, $\mathbf{b}=\rho\mathbf{g}$, may be evaluated as a boundary integral. More simply, concentrated force loads, $\mathbf{b}=\mathbf{b}_0\delta(\mathbf{x}-\mathbf{x}_0)$, are trivial to integrate, and are useful for introducing internal body articulation. Due to space limitations, the body force term will not be mentioned hereafter.

## 6 The Boundary Element Method

The Boundary Element Method (BEM) is a straight-forward approach to discretizing integral equations defined on the boundary via a collocation method. There are three main steps when implementing the BEM in 3D:

1. Discretize the boundary $\Gamma$ into a set of $N$ non-overlapping elements which represent the displacements and tractions by functions which are piecewise interpolated between the element's nodal points.
2. Apply the integral equation(s) at each of the $n$ boundary nodes, and perform the resulting integrals over each boundary element in order to generate an undetermined system of $3n$ equations involving the $3n$ nodal displacements and $3n$ nodal tractions.
3. Apply the boundary conditions of the desired boundary value problem, fixing $n$ nodal values (either displacement or traction) per direction. The remaining linear system of $3n$ equations is determined and may be solved to obtain the unknown nodal boundary values.

Drawing on the notation from [5], the discretization of (8), dropping the body force, may be summarized as follows. The piecewise interpolated displacement and traction functions evaluated at the point $\mathbf{x}$ may be written as

$$\begin{aligned} \mathbf{u} &= \mathbf{u}(\mathbf{x}) = (u_1,u_2,u_3)^T = \mathbf{\Phi}(\mathbf{x})\mathsf{u} \\ \mathbf{p} &= \mathbf{p}(\mathbf{x}) = (p_1,p_2,p_3)^T = \mathbf{\Phi}(\mathbf{x})\mathsf{p} \end{aligned} \tag{9}$$

where $\mathbf{\Phi}(\mathbf{x})$ is an interpolation matrix and $\mathsf{u}$ and $\mathsf{p}$ are $n$-vectors of the nodal displacement and traction 3-vectors, respectively, e.g., $\mathsf{u} = [\mathsf{u}_1,\ldots,\mathsf{u}_n]^T$.

The displacement, traction and $c$ vectors at the $i^{th}$ node, $\mathbf{x}_i$, will be denoted by

$$\mathsf{u}_i = \mathbf{u}(\mathbf{x}_i), \qquad \mathsf{p}_i = \mathbf{p}(\mathbf{x}_i), \qquad \mathsf{c}_i = \mathbf{c}(\mathbf{x}_i),$$

respectively. Substituting (9) into the elasticity integral equation (8) applied at $\mathbf{x}_i$ and converting the surface integrals into sums of integrals over each boundary element, one obtains

$$\mathsf{c}_i\mathbf{u}_i + \sum_{j=1}^{N}\left(\int_{\Gamma_j} \mathbf{p}^*(\mathbf{x}_i,\mathbf{y})\,\mathbf{\Phi}(\mathbf{y})\,d\Gamma(\mathbf{y})\right)\mathsf{u} = \sum_{j=1}^{N}\left(\int_{\Gamma_j} \mathbf{u}^*(\mathbf{x}_i,\mathbf{y})\,\mathbf{\Phi}(\mathbf{y})\,d\Gamma(\mathbf{y})\right)\mathsf{p}$$

which, in an obvious notation, may be written as

$$\mathsf{c}_i\mathsf{u}_i + \sum_{j=1}^{n}\hat{\mathsf{h}}_{ij}\mathsf{u}_j = \sum_{j=1}^{n}\mathsf{g}_{ij}\mathsf{p}_j. \tag{10}$$

For convenience, define off-diagonal $\mathsf{h}_{ij}$ as $\hat{\mathsf{h}}_{ij}$, but let

$$\mathsf{h}_{ii} = \mathsf{c}_i + \hat{\mathsf{h}}_{ii}.$$

Assembling the equations at all nodes into a block matrix system yields

$$\sum_{j=1}^{n}\mathsf{h}_{ij}\mathsf{u}_j = \sum_{j=1}^{n}\mathsf{g}_{ij}\mathsf{p}_j \quad \text{or} \quad \mathsf{Hu} = \mathsf{Gp}. \tag{11}$$

The final step is to specify the boundary conditions at each of the $n$ nodes, then bring the unknowns to the left-hand side, and the knowns to the right-hand side to obtain the final linear system

$$\mathsf{Av} = \mathsf{z}, \tag{12}$$

which may be solved for the unknown nodal quantities, $\mathsf{v}$.

All that remains is to determine the integrals for the matrix entries of $\mathsf{H}$ and $\mathsf{G}$. Indeed, this is the part of the BEM which takes the majority of a computation. Complete formulae for constant boundary elements, are provided in the Appendix for those who are interested in constructing their own elasticity solver. It is the simplest element for the reader to implement and understand. Formulae for linear elements may be found in [15].

### 6.1 Constant Element Case

Analogous to the midpoint rule for integrating a univariate function, integration of a triangular constant element is accomplished using data located at the centroid. This corresponds to a centroid collocation scheme, as the $j^{th}$ node, $\mathbf{x}_j$, is identified as the centroid of the $j^{th}$ element, and is where the elastic state is represented accurately. In this case $n = N$. Since the collocation node lies in the element's interior, it is called a *nonconforming* element. This happens to make the element particular easy to implement, as connectivity is not required. It also has the convenient casual property that special care need not be taken to accommodate corners or sharp edges [5].

## 7 Interactive simulation

To solve equation 12 at interactive rates, we exploit the coherence of typical deformable object interactions. This allows us to achieve low latency at the expense of memory and precomputation.

### 7.1 Precomputation

Suppose $\mathsf{A_0}$ is the matrix in (12) corresponding to a particular reference BVP. In the following, we assume that we have precomputed $\mathsf{A}_0^{-1}\mathsf{H}$ and $\mathsf{A}_0^{-1}\mathsf{G}$. Note that only half of the columns from the last two matrices require storage since $\mathsf{A_0}$ consists of columns of $\mathsf{G}$ and $\mathsf{H}$, and $\mathsf{A}_0^{-1}\mathsf{A_0} = \mathsf{I}$. In general, several such reference BVPs can be precomputed and it is possible to perform this computation adaptively in a low priority thread.

We remind the reader that to simplify indexing, $\mathsf{A_0}$, $\mathsf{H}$, etc., are $3 \times 3$ block matrices; similarly $\mathsf{v}$, $\mathsf{z}$, etc., are block column matrices whose elements are 3D vectors.

### 7.2 Changing boundary values

The simplest case of coherence occurs for the reference BVP when there is a change in some boundary values of the reference BVP. The new solution can be computed in time $O(n(|S_u| + |S_p|))$ as

$$\mathsf{v}^{(0)} = \mathsf{v}_{\mathsf{unchanged}} + \sum_{j \in S_u} (-\mathsf{A}_0^{-1}\mathsf{H}_j)\, \delta\bar{\mathsf{u}}_j + \sum_{j \in S_p} (\mathsf{A}_0^{-1}\mathsf{G}_j)\, \delta\bar{\mathsf{p}}_j \quad (13)$$

where $\delta\bar{\mathsf{u}}_j$ and $\delta\bar{\mathsf{p}}_j$ are changes in the specified boundary values, $\mathsf{G}_j$ (respectively $\mathsf{H}_j$) represents the $j^{th}$ column of $\mathsf{G}$ (resp. $\mathsf{H}$), and $S_u$ and $S_p$ are mutually exclusive sets indicating where specified displacements and tractions, respectively, are changing. The term $\mathsf{v}_{\mathsf{unchanged}}$ represents already computed contributions from unchanged or previous boundary values, and provides a way to avoid somewhat redundant vector summations. If present, (un)changing parameterized body forces are handled in a similar manner.

### 7.3 Changing boundary conditions

The more difficult case occurs if the type of a boundary condition changes; for instance, a new contact between a rigid virtual finger and deformable object will change a traction condition to a displacement one. The system matrix $\mathsf{A_0}$ itself changes and can introduce unacceptable latencies if we have to solve the linear system afresh.

The key to fast computation is to realize: (1) Typically only a few columns of $\mathsf{A_0}$ change; and (2) the columns change in very specific ways: a column of $\mathsf{A_0}$ which originated in $(-\mathsf{H})$ is replaced by the corresponding column of $\mathsf{G}$, or vice-versa. We exploit (1) by using the Sherman-Morrison-Woodbury formula; we exploit (2) by extracting large parts of the formula from the precomputed matrices listed in §7.1

#### 7.3.1 The Sherman-Morrison-Woodbury Formula

Expressions relating the inverse of a matrix to the inverse of the matrix after it has undergone some minor changes are well-known from linear algebra and have enjoyed numerous applications [14]. Essentially, given our square block matrix $\mathsf{A_0}$ and its inverse $\mathsf{A}_0^{-1}$, as well as a second square matrix $\mathsf{A_S}$ which is related to the first matrix by a rank $3s$ change,

$$\mathsf{A_S} = \mathsf{A_0} + \mathsf{R}\mathsf{S}^\mathsf{T},$$

where $\mathsf{R}$ and $\mathsf{S}$ have $s$ block columns, the Sherman-Morrison-Woodbury (SMW) formula [12], provides an expression for the inverse of the second matrix as

$$\mathsf{A}_\mathsf{S}^{-1} = \mathsf{A}_0^{-1} - \mathsf{A}_0^{-1}\mathsf{R}\left[\mathsf{I} + \mathsf{S}^\mathsf{T}\mathsf{A}_0^{-1}\mathsf{R}\right]^{-1}\mathsf{S}^\mathsf{T}\mathsf{A}_0^{-1}. \quad (14)$$

However, explicit calculation of the inverse is not our intent. We can do better by using the formula to efficiently evaluate $\mathsf{A}_\mathsf{S}^{-1}\mathsf{z}$ matrix-vector multiplications as shown below.

#### 7.3.2 The Fast Update Process

If the type of boundary condition on node $j$ changes, only the $j^{th}$ column of $\mathsf{A_0}$ changes; let $\mathsf{L}_j$ denote the column that is replaced, and let $\mathsf{M}_j$ be its replacement. As described in §6, these columns are either $(-\mathsf{H}_j)$ or $\mathsf{G}_j$. Now suppose $s$ boundary conditions change (corresponding to nodes $j \in S$, where $S$ is an index set). Let $\mathsf{L}$ be the $n \times s$ matrix whose columns are replaced by those of $\mathsf{M}$, and let $\delta\mathsf{A_S} = \mathsf{M} - \mathsf{L}$. Formally, we can write the change in $\mathsf{A_0}$ as

$$\mathsf{A_S} = \mathsf{A_0} + \delta\mathsf{A_S}\, \mathsf{E}^\mathsf{T}$$

where $\mathsf{E}$ is the $n \times s$ submatrix of the $n \times n$ identity matrix, consisting of columns $j \in S$.

Applying the SMW formula to $\mathsf{A}_\mathsf{S}^{-1}\mathsf{z}$ and grouping terms,

$$\mathsf{A}_\mathsf{S}^{-1}\mathsf{z} = (\mathsf{A}_0^{-1}\mathsf{z}) - (\mathsf{A}_0^{-1}\delta\mathsf{A_S})\left[\mathsf{I} + \mathsf{E}^\mathsf{T}(\mathsf{A}_0^{-1}\delta\mathsf{A_S})\right]^{-1}\mathsf{E}^\mathsf{T}(\mathsf{A}_0^{-1}\mathsf{z}), \quad (15)$$

we obtain a formula that can be transcribed into an efficient algorithm for computing the new solution $\mathsf{v}$ for general boundary data when $s$ boundary conditions have changed.

The first step is to construct the portion independent of $\mathsf{z}$ that may be reused for other BVPs with $\mathsf{A} = \mathsf{A_S}$:

1. "Compute" $\mathsf{W} = \mathsf{A}_0^{-1}\delta\mathsf{A_S}$. Since $\delta\mathsf{A_S} = \mathsf{M} - \mathsf{L}$ and $\mathsf{A}_0^{-1}\mathsf{L} = \mathsf{E}$, obtaining $\mathsf{W}$ only consists of looking up $\mathsf{A}_0^{-1}\mathsf{M}$ in the precomputed $\mathsf{A}_0^{-1}\mathsf{G}$ and $\mathsf{A}_0^{-1}\mathsf{H}$ matrices.

2. Construct the s-by-s matrix
$$\mathsf{C_S} = \mathsf{I} + \mathsf{E}^\mathsf{T}\mathsf{W}$$
by extracting rows from $\mathsf{W}$. The matrix $\mathsf{C_S}$ is traditionally called the *capacitance matrix* [14].

3. Compute the LU factors of $\mathsf{C_S}$ [12] and store them for future use. Denote the LU decomposition by $\mathsf{C}_\mathsf{S}^{-1}$.

The total cost is $O(s^3)$. Once this has been done, particular BVPs may be solved efficiently as follows:

1. Construct $\mathsf{v}^{(0)} = \mathsf{A}_0^{-1}\mathsf{z}$ efficiently as in (13).

2. Extract rows of $\mathsf{v}^{(0)}$ to make $\mathsf{E}^\mathsf{T}\mathsf{v}^{(0)}$.

3. Apply $\mathsf{C}_\mathsf{S}^{-1}$ to the $s$-vector $\mathsf{E}^\mathsf{T}\mathsf{v}^{(0)}$.

4. Apply $\mathsf{W}$ to the $s$-vector $(\mathsf{C}_\mathsf{S}^{-1}\mathsf{E}^\mathsf{T}\mathsf{v}^{(0)})$ and subtract the result from $\mathsf{v}^{(0)}$ to obtain the final solution $\mathsf{v}$.

After the initial construction of $\mathsf{v}^{(0)}$, whose cost is $O(n(|S_u| + |S_p|))$, the solve only costs $O(ns)$ operations.

## 8 Conclusions

We have described a fast method for simulating linear elastic deformable objects in interactive applications. We have used the boundary element method for linear elasticity, and have shown that it is a useful tool for graphics applications, due to its boundary-only nature, accuracy, and simplicity of implementation. It is particularly useful for interactive

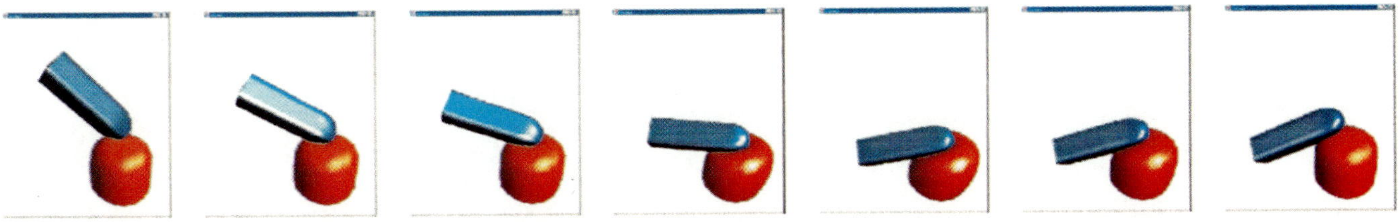

Figure 5: Simulation of a kinematically constrained rigid object contacting a deformable object. This is a difficult problem because the contact boundary conditions keep changing during the motion. ArtDefo solves such a sequence of problems quickly by combining precomputed system responses using a rank update procedure. It is possible to perform multiple solves each frame in order to guarantee unilateral contact constraints are satisfied.

simulation because of the ease of combination with low-rank update solution approaches derived from the Sherman-Morrison-Woodbury formula.

Specifically, for the small localized changes in boundary conditions which are typical of user interaction, the algorithm is linear in the complexity of the boundary discretization. It is also fast in practice; we have demonstrated these results in our system ArtDefo. By precomputing and updating the solver's component matrices, we can quickly compute the deformation and contact forces during user interaction, with low latency. In addition, it is a direct solution method — this allows accurate prediction of solution costs which is essential for real time applications. Using our method, we believe it is now possible to simulate more realistic deformable models with real-time user interaction.

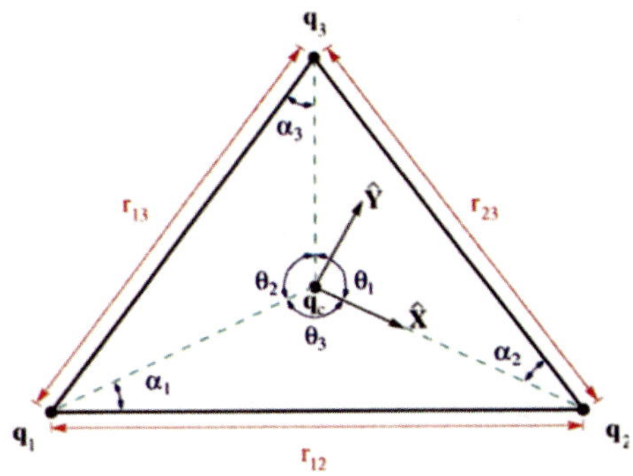


Figure 6: Notation

## A Constant Element Influence Coefficients

When implementing boundary elements, there are always a number of singular integrals which the user must acquire or spend some time calculating. In the relatively simple case of triangular constant elements with centroid collocation, there are only a few integrals, and they are presented here for completeness.

### A.1 Inter-element Effects

These are integrals corresponding to interactions where the load point lies at the centroid of a triangle other than the one being integrated over, i.e., $\mathbf{x}_i \notin \Gamma_j$. This includes the elements of the $3 \times 3$ matrices $\mathbf{g}_{ij}$ and $\hat{\mathbf{h}}_{ij}$, for $i \neq j$, and therefore corresponds to the majority of the integrals. Since $r = |\mathbf{x}_i - \mathbf{y}|$ is never zero, these are nonsingular integrals which may easily be calculated using standard numerical quadrature (see Brebbia [5]).

### A.2 Self-effects

Self-effects correspond to the integrals in the diagonal terms of equation 11 such as $\mathbf{g}_{ii}$ and $\hat{\mathbf{h}}_{ii}$. Since the load point lies in the center of the triangle being integrated over, these are singular integrals, as the fundamental solutions are unbounded as $r \to 0$. The first integral is only weakly singular, while the second integral is strongly singular and only exists in a Cauchy principle value sense.

#### A.2.1 Calculation of $\mathbf{h}_{ii}$

Despite $\hat{\mathbf{h}}_{ii}$ being strongly singular, it is easy to calculate indirectly using rigid body translations by considering a bounded object with all nodes subjected to any arbitrary constant displacement boundary conditions, $\mathbf{u}_j = \bar{\mathbf{u}}, \forall j$. Since this body necessarily experiences no induced surface tractions, $\mathbf{p}_j = 0, \forall j$. It follows from (11) that

$$\mathbf{h}_{ii} = -\sum_{j \neq i} \mathbf{h}_{ij} \tag{16}$$

and therefore *neither* $\hat{\mathbf{h}}_{ii}$ *nor* $\mathbf{c}_i$ *need be calculated explicitly.* Note that (16) implies that $H$ is a singular matrix.

#### A.2.2 Calculation of $\mathbf{g}_{ii}$

The elements of

$$(\mathbf{g}_{ii})_{kl} = \frac{1}{16\pi(1-\nu)G} \int_{\Gamma_i} \left( \frac{(3-4\nu)\,\delta_{kl}}{r} + \frac{r_k r_l}{r^3} \right) d\Gamma(\mathbf{y})$$

will be expressed for a triangle $\Delta$, using the notation in figure 6, i.e., with vertices at $\mathbf{q}_1$, $\mathbf{q}_2$, $\mathbf{q}_3$, centroid at $\mathbf{q}_c$, area $A$, and an outward unit normal $\hat{\mathbf{n}}$. Omitting any constant factors, the first integral is $J_1^\Delta$, and the second is

$$\hat{\mathbf{X}}_k \hat{\mathbf{X}}_l J_1^\Delta + \frac{1}{2}\left(\hat{\mathbf{X}}_k \hat{\mathbf{Y}}_l + \hat{\mathbf{X}}_l \hat{\mathbf{Y}}_k\right) J_2^\Delta + \left(\hat{\mathbf{Y}}_k \hat{\mathbf{Y}}_l - \hat{\mathbf{X}}_k \hat{\mathbf{X}}_l\right) J_3^\Delta.$$

with

$$\hat{\mathbf{X}} = \frac{\mathbf{q}_2 - \mathbf{q}_c}{|\mathbf{q}_2 - \mathbf{q}_c|}, \quad \hat{\mathbf{Y}} = \hat{\mathbf{n}} \times \hat{\mathbf{X}},$$

and

$$J_m^\Delta = \frac{2A}{3}\left[\frac{J_m(\theta_1, \alpha_2, 0)}{r_{23}} + \frac{J_m(\theta_2, \alpha_3, 0)}{r_{31}} + \frac{J_m(\theta_3, \alpha_1, \theta_1 + \theta_2)}{r_{12}}\right]$$

where

$$J_1(\Delta\theta, \alpha, \theta_{\min}) = \ln\left[\frac{\tan\left(\frac{\Delta\theta + \alpha}{2}\right)}{\tan\left(\frac{\alpha}{2}\right)}\right]$$

$$J_2(\Delta\theta,\alpha,\theta_{\min}) = \sin\left(\frac{\theta_{\min}-\alpha}{2}\right)\ln\left[\frac{\tan\left(\frac{\Delta\theta+\alpha}{4}\right)}{\tan\left(\frac{\alpha}{4}\right)}\right]$$
$$+\cos\left(\frac{\theta_{\min}-\alpha}{2}\right)\ln\left[\frac{\left[1-\tan\left(\frac{\alpha}{4}\right)\right]\left[1+\tan\left(\frac{\Delta\theta+\alpha}{4}\right)\right]}{\left[1+\tan\left(\frac{\alpha}{4}\right)\right]\left[1-\tan\left(\frac{\Delta\theta+\alpha}{4}\right)\right]}\right]$$

$$J_3(\Delta\theta,\alpha,\theta_{\min}) = 2\sin\left(2\theta_{\min}-\alpha+\frac{\Delta\theta}{2}\right)\sin\left(\frac{\Delta\theta}{2}\right)$$
$$-\sin^2(\theta_{\min}-\alpha)\ln\left[\frac{\tan\left(\frac{\alpha}{2}\right)}{\tan\left(\frac{\Delta\theta+\alpha}{2}\right)}\right].$$

## References


[1] James Arvo, Kenneth Torrance, and Brian Smits. A framework for the analysis of error in global illumination algorithms. In Andrew Glassner, editor, *Computer Graphics (SIGGRAPH 94 Conference Proceedings)*, pages 75–84. ACM SIGGRAPH, ACM Press, July 1994. ISBN 0-89791-667-0.

[2] Kendall Atkinson. The numerical solution of boundary integral equations. In I. Duff and G. Watson, editors, *The State of the Art in Numerical Analysis*, Clarendon Press, pages 223–259, 1997.

[3] David Baraff and Andrew Witkin. Dynamic simulation of non-penetrating flexible bodies. In Edwin E. Catmull, editor, *Computer Graphics (SIGGRAPH 92 Conference Proceedings)*, volume 26, pages 303–308, July 1992.

[4] David Baraff and Andrew Witkin. Large steps in cloth simulation. In Michael Cohen, editor, *Computer Graphics (SIGGRAPH 98 Conference Proceedings)*, pages 43–54. ACM SIGGRAPH, Addison Wesley, July 1998. ISBN 0-89791-999-8.

[5] C. A. Brebbia, J. C. F. Telles and L. C. Wrobel *Boundary Element Techniques: Theory and Applications in Engineering*, Springer-Verlag, New York, 1984.

[6] Morten Bro-Nielsen and Stephane Cotin. Real-time volumetric deformable models for surgery simulation using finite elements and condensation. *Computer Graphics Forum*, 15(3):57–66, August 1996. Proceedings of Eurographics '96. ISSN 1067-7055.

[7] George Celniker and Dave Gossard. Deformable curve and surface finite elements for free-form shape design. In Thomas W. Sederberg, editor, *Computer Graphics (SIGGRAPH 91 Conference Proceedings)*, volume 25, pages 257–266, July 1991.

[8] David T. Chen and David Zeltzer. Pump it up: Computer animation of a biomechanically based model of muscle using the finite element method. In Edwin E. Catmull, editor, *Computer Graphics (SIGGRAPH 92 Conference Proceedings)*, volume 26, pages 89–98, July 1992.

[9] S. L. Crouch and A. M. Starfield *Boundary Element Methods in Solid Mechanics*, Unwin Hyman Inc., London, 1990.

[10] Sarah F. Gibson and Brian Mirtich. A survey of deformable models in computer graphics. Technical Report TR-97-19, Mitsubishi Electric Research Laboratories, Cambridge, MA, November 1997.

[11] Sarah F. F. Gibson. 3D chainmail: a fast algorithm for deforming volumetric objects. In Michael Cohen and David Zeltzer, editors, *1997 Symposium on Interactive 3D Graphics*, pages 149–154. ACM SIGGRAPH, April 1997. ISBN 0-89791-884-3.

[12] G. H. Golub and C. F. Van Loan *Matrix Computations* . Second Edition, The John Hopkins University Press, Baltimore, 1989.

[13] Jean-Paul Gourret, Nadia Magnenat Thalmann, and Daniel Thalmann. Simulation of object and human skin deformations in a grasping task. In Jeffrey Lane, editor, *Computer Graphics (SIGGRAPH 89 Conference Proceedings)*, volume 23, pages 21–30, July 1989.

[14] W. W. Hager. Updating the Inverse of a Matrix. In *SIAM Review*, volume 31, no. 2, pages 221-239, 1989.

[15] Friedel Hartmann. *Introduction to Boundary Elements: Theory and Applications*. Springer-Verlag, Berlin, 1989.

[16] H. Hoppe, T. DeRose, T. Duchamp, M. Halstead, H. Jin, J, McDonald and J. Schweitzer and W. Stuetzl. Piecewise Smooth Surface Reconstruction. *Computer Graphics (SIGGRAPH 94 Conference Proceedings)*, pages 24–29, July 1994.

[17] James T. Kajiya. The rendering equation. In David C. Evans and Russell J. Athay, editors, *Computer Graphics (SIGGRAPH 86 Conference Proceedings)*, volume 20, pages 143–150, August 1986.

[18] J. H. Kane, B. L. Kumar and R. H. Gallagher Boundary Element Direct Reanalysis for Continuum Structures In *Journal of Engineering Mechanics*, volume 118, pages 1679-1691, 1992.

[19] Yuencheng Lee, Demetri Terzopoulos, and Keith Waters. Realistic modeling for facial animation. In *Computer Graphics (SIGGRAPH 95 Conference Proceedings)*, pages 55–62, August 1995.

[20] Dani Lischinski, Brian Smits, and Donald P. Greenberg. Bounds and error estimates for radiosity. In Andrew Glassner, editor, *Computer Graphics (SIGGRAPH 94 Conference Proceedings)*, pages 67–74. ACM SIGGRAPH, ACM Press, July 1994. ISBN 0-89791-667-0.

[21] A. E. H. Love. *A Treatise on the Mathematical Theory of Elasticity*. Dover, New York, 1944.

[22] Dimitri Metaxas and Demetri Terzopoulos. Dynamic deformation of solid primitives with constraints. In Edwin E. Catmull, editor, *Computer Graphics (SIGGRAPH 92 Conference Proceedings)*, volume 26, pages 309–312, July 1992.

[23] Alex Pentland and John Williams. Good vibrations: Modal dynamics for graphics and animation. In Jeffrey Lane, editor, *Computer Graphics (SIGGRAPH 89 Conference Proceedings)*, volume 23, pages 215–222, July 1989.

[24] Demetri Terzopoulos and Kurt Fleischer. Deformable models. *The Visual Computer*, 4(6):306–331, December 1988.

[25] Demetri Terzopoulos and Kurt Fleischer. Modeling inelastic deformation: Viscoelasticity, plasticity, fracture. In John Dill, editor, *Computer Graphics (SIGGRAPH 88 Proceedings)*, volume 22, pages 269–278, August 1988.

[26] Demetri Terzopoulos, John Platt, Alan Barr, and Kurt Fleischer. Elastically deformable models. In Maureen C. Stone, editor, *Computer Graphics (SIGGRAPH 87 Conference Proceedings)*, volume 21, pages 205–214, July 1987.

[27] Demetri Terzopoulos, John Platt, and Kurt Fleischer. Heating and melting deformable models (from goop to glop). In *Proceedings of Graphics Interface '89*, pages 219–226, June 1989.

[28] Xiaoyuan Tu and Demetri Terzopoulos. Artificial fishes: Physics, locomotion, perception, behavior. In Andrew Glassner, editor, *Computer Graphics (SIGGRAPH 94 Conference Proceedings)*, pages 43–50. ACM SIGGRAPH, ACM Press, July 1994. ISBN 0-89791-667-0.

[29] Keith Waters. A muscle model for animating three-dimensional facial expression. In Maureen C. Stone, editor, *Computer Graphics (SIGGRAPH 87 Conference Proceedings)*, volume 21, pages 17–24, July 1987.

# A Perceptually Based Physical Error Metric for Realistic Image Synthesis

Mahesh Ramasubramanian Sumanta N. Pattanaik Donald P. Greenberg

Program of Computer Graphics *
Cornell University

## Abstract

We introduce a new concept for accelerating realistic image synthesis algorithms. At the core of this procedure is a novel *physical* error metric that correctly predicts the *perceptual* threshold for detecting artifacts in scene features. Built into this metric is a computational model of the human visual system's loss of sensitivity at high background illumination levels, high spatial frequencies, and high contrast levels (visual masking). An important feature of our model is that it handles the luminance-dependent processing and spatially-dependent processing independently. This allows us to *precompute* the expensive spatially-dependent component, making our model extremely efficient.

We illustrate the utility of our procedure with global illumination algorithms used for realistic image synthesis. The expense of global illumination computations is many orders of magnitude higher than the expense of direct illumination computations and can greatly benefit by applying our perceptually based technique. Results show our method preserves visual quality while achieving significant computational gains in areas of images with high frequency texture patterns, geometric details, and lighting variations.

**CR Categories:** I.3.3 [Computer Graphics]: Picture/Image Generation; I.3.7 [Computer Graphics]: Three-Dimensional Graphics and Realism.

**Keywords:** Realistic Image Synthesis, Global Illumination, Adaptive Sampling, Perception, Visual Masking, Error Metric, Visual Threshold.

## 1 INTRODUCTION

*Realistic Image Synthesis* is an important area of research in computer graphics and has been widely studied in the last few decades. It aims at producing synthetic images that are visually indistinguishable from the actual scene it seeks to reproduce. Earlier work attempted to simulate this realism by modeling only the direct illumination of the scene by light sources, but this approach failed to capture many important visual cues: indirect illumination, soft shadows, color bleeding, and caustics. *Global Illumination* algorithms developed in recent years have been able to accurately render these effects in addition to the direct illumination [12]. These algorithms physically simulate accurate light reflection and the complex light interactions between surfaces in the environment. Unfortunately, these simulations make global illumination algorithms computationally very expensive, with execution times many orders of magnitude slower than simple direct illumination algorithms. The research described in this paper is focused on improving the efficiency of computing global illumination.

*Perceptually based techniques* promise dramatic performance gains. As the final result of a global illumination algorithm is an image interpreted by the human eye, it is sufficient to aim for perceptual accuracy. Due to the limitations of the human visual system, the degree of effort required to attain acceptable perceptual accuracy varies over the image. Perceptually based rendering algorithms take advantage of this phenomenon and attempt to expend only "just-necessary" effort over the image to meet this perceptual accuracy criteria. To accomplish this a computational model of the visual system [7, 17, 21] is necessary. Such vision models typically predict the visual sensitivity variations with background illumination levels, spatial frequency, and scene contrast features. These predictions can then be used to make image quality judgements. The vision model is applied as the image is being generated and additional efforts are then expended only in areas with detectable visual artifacts, thereby reducing the overall computation time.

Vision models are normally expensive to evaluate as some of their components perform multiscale spatial processing. Moreover, in a progressive image synthesis algorithm, image quality judgements are required at every iteration and the vision model is invoked many times. Hence, although perceptually based algorithms show significant potential for acceleration, they also involve considerable amount of additional overhead due to the repeated vision model evaluation.

In this paper we introduce a new framework for perceptually based rendering that drastically reduces the overhead of incorporating a perceptual basis. *We develop a threshold model which defines a physical error metric that correctly predicts the perceptual threshold for detecting artifacts in scene features. This allows image quality judgements to be made in the physical domain using the perceptually based physical error metric.* This framework opens new avenues for using a perceptual basis in speeding up global illumination computations.

A key ingredient for realism in synthesized images is *complexity* [5]. Realistic images tend to be richly detailed. This richness and detail take many forms, such as texture patterns, geometric details, and lighting variations, and contain high spatial frequency content. But since the visual system's threshold and suprathreshold sensitivity to high spatial frequency content is poor [10], more artifacts can be tolerated in these areas. Our framework takes advantage of these phenomena to reduce global illumination computation time. The texture patterns and geometric detail are inherent in the scene specification and can be captured during direct illumination computation. Direct illumination algorithms also capture most of the high spatial frequency of the image due to lighting variations. From this solution, we "precompute" the spatially-dependent component of our threshold model before the indirect illumination computation

*580 Rhodes Hall, Ithaca, NY 14853, USA.
WWW: http://www.graphics.cornell.edu/
E-mail: {mahesh,sumant,dpg}@graphics.cornell.edu

(a) reference global illumination solution (b) sample density pattern (c) adaptive global illumination solution

Figure 1: An illustration of our framework applied to an adaptive global illumination algorithm. Image (b) is the sample density pattern used for the indirect illumination computation (darker areas indicate fewer samples), and image (c) is the final solution resulting from the adaptive global illumination computation. For comparison, image(a) is a reference global illumination solution generated using uniformly high sampling density. While it may seem counterintuitive, areas with higher spatial frequency content require less computational effort.

stage and thus avoid recomputing this complex component over subsequent iterations. As computing this component of the threshold model involves the expensive multiscale spatial processing, we benefit enormously by this precomputation. Figure 1 illustrates the sampling density pattern when our threshold model is used to direct the sampling in an adaptive global illumination algorithm. Notice that the sampling density reflects the psychophysical observation that our visual system is less sensitive in areas with higher spatial frequency content.

The remainder of this paper is organized as follows: Section 2 reviews the previous approaches to perceptually based rendering. In Section 3 we introduce our new framework. At the core of this framework is the *threshold model* which defines a perceptually based physical error metric. The perceptual basis and implementation of this model are described in Section 4. In Section 5 we illustrate the utility of our framework by applying it to an adaptive global illumination algorithm. We conclude the paper with a summary of our framework and the future directions for this research.

## 2 PREVIOUS WORK

Many researchers have attempted to develop perceptually based rendering algorithms. Bolin and Meyer [3] present an excellent survey of the early algorithms. Our discussion concentrates on the algorithms most relevant to our work.

All of these algorithms attempt to exploit the limitations of the human visual system to speed up rendering computations without sacrificing visual quality. They differ in the extent to which they model the visual system and the way they apply this vision model to the rendering algorithms. Mitchell [19] defined an adaptive sampling strategy for his ray tracing algorithm by taking advantage of the poor sensitivity of the visual system to high spatial frequency, to absolute physical error (threshold sensitivity), and to the high and low wavelength content of the scene. Meyer and Liu [18] took into account the human visual system's poor color spatial acuity in developing an adaptive image synthesis algorithm. Bolin and Meyer [2] developed a frequency based ray tracer using a simple vision model which incorporated the visual system's spatial processing behavior and sensitivity change as a function of luminance. Myszkowski [20] and Bolin and Meyer [3] applied sophisticated vision models to guide Monte Carlo based ray tracing algorithms. The models they used incorporated the visual system's threshold sensitivity, spatial frequency sensitivity, and contrast masking behavior. Gibson and Hubbold [11] and Hedley *et al.* [14] have applied the threshold sensitivity of the visual system to speed up radiosity computations.

Of all the approaches described above, the recent work by Myszkowski [20] and Bolin and Meyer [3] needs special mention for two reasons. First, they used sophisticated vision models which incorporate the most recent advances in the understanding of the human visual system [7, 17]. Thus in principle their algorithms can take maximum advantage of the limitations of the visual system. Second, they introduced a perceptual error metric into their rendering algorithms. Thus their algorithms were able to adaptively allocate additional computational effort to areas where errors remained above perceivable thresholds and stop computation elsewhere.

Both approaches were conceptually similar and used a *visual difference predictor* [7, 17] to define a perceptual error metric. A visual difference predictor takes a pair of images and transforms them to multidimensional visual representations by applying a vision model. It then computes the "distance" between this pair of visual representations in a multidimensional space, producing the form of a local visual difference map. This is compared against a perceptual threshold value to ascertain the "perceivability" of the difference. Figure 2 illustrates the functioning of such a predictor.

When one of the two input images to the predictor is the final converged image and the other is the image at any intermediate stage of computation, then the visual difference map becomes an error estimate for that stage and the visual difference predictor functions as an estimator of the perceived error. Myszkowski, and Bolin and Meyer used such an estimator during their image computation and used this information to direct subsequent computational effort. Unfortunately, during the image synthesis process one does not have the luxury of accessing the final converged image at an intermediate stage. Myszkowski assumed that two intermediate images obtained at consecutive time steps of computation could be used as input to the visual difference predictor to get a functional error estimate. Bolin and Meyer computed the upper and lower bound images from the computation results at intermediate stages and applied the predictor to get the error estimate for that stage. Their approach thus estimates the error bounds.

These algorithms achieve the ability to focus computational efforts in areas with perceivable errors, but only at considerable cost. They use the perceptual error metric at every stage of image computation which requires repeated evaluation of the embedded vision model. The vision model is very expensive to compute as some of its components require multiscale spatial processing, and this over-

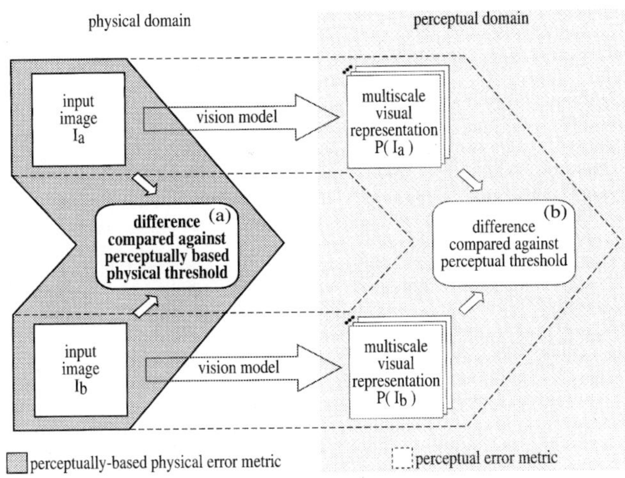


Figure 2: Conceptual difference between a perceptually based physical error metric and a perceptual error metric. A perceptual metric operates in the perceptual domain. Images to be compared are first transformed into their multi-scale visual representation and the perceptual metric is applied to the difference of the visual representation (b). In contrast, a perceptually based physical error metric operates in the physical domain. The metric is applied to the physical luminance difference between the images (a). Our metric is non-uniform over the physical space of the image.

head offsets some of the advantages gained by using the perceptual error metric to speed up the rendering algorithm.

# 3 NEW FRAMEWORK

We propose a new framework for perceptually based rendering which drastically reduces the overhead of introducing the perceptual basis while still gaining maximum advantage from the limitations of the human visual system. To achieve this we first develop a *threshold model* which incorporates the human visual system's threshold sensitivity, spatial frequency sensitivity, and contrast sensitivity (masking) to predict the perceptual threshold for detecting artifacts in scene features. The threshold model $T$ operates on an image $I$ to generate a *threshold map* $T(I)$ which is an index to the maximum physical luminance error that can be tolerated at any location on the image, while preserving visual quality.

We call our framework a *perceptually based physical error metric* to emphasize the fact that once the threshold map is computed, the pair of images can be compared directly in the physical luminance domain, while still accounting for the limitations of the visual system. Figure 2 illustrates the conceptual difference between the perceptual error metric and our perceptually based physical error metric. A major advantage of our approach is that we can precompute the expensive components of our threshold model at an earlier rendering computation stage and thus avoiding the recomputation that has hindered earlier approaches.

# 4 THRESHOLD MODEL

In this section we develop a model for computing a threshold map for any given image. The threshold map predicts the maximum luminance error that can be tolerated at every location over the image. This model makes use of three main characteristics of the visual system, namely: threshold sensitivity, contrast sensitivity, and contrast masking. An important feature of this model is that it handles the luminance-dependent processing and the spatially-dependent processing independently. The luminance-dependent processing computes a starting threshold map $\Delta L_{tvi}$ for the luminance distribution using the *threshold-vs-intensity* (TVI) function. The spatially-dependent processing computes a map containing elevation factors $F_{spatial}$ for the spatial pattern using the *contrast sensitivity function* (CSF) and *masking function*. From these two we derive the final threshold map $\Delta L_T(x, y)$ as:

$$\boxed{\Delta L_T(x, y) = \Delta L_{tvi}(x, y) \times F_{spatial}(x, y)} \quad (1)$$

The separate handling of luminance distributions and spatial patterns allows us to precompute the expensive spatially-dependent component of the threshold model, making our model extremely efficient when used in perceptually-based rendering algorithms. Figure 3 provides an overview of the model.

## 4.1 Model Description

**Threshold Sensitivity** The *threshold-vs-intensity* (TVI) function describes the threshold sensitivity of the visual system as a function of background luminance. The threshold, as defined by this function, is the minimum amount of incremental luminance, $\Delta L$, by which a test spot should differ from a uniform background of luminance $L$ to be detectable. Figure 3(b) plots thresholds computed from this function at different background luminance values. The two curves in the figure represent the thresholds of the rod and cone systems. The linear part of each curve follows Weber's law, which means that the threshold increases linearly with luminance. The threshold from this TVI function, $\Delta L_{tvi}$, provides the luminance-dependent starting values from which we build our final threshold map.

**Contrast Sensitivity** The threshold given by the TVI function predicts sensitivity in uniform visual fields. However, the luminance distribution in any complex image is far from uniform. The *contrast sensitivity function* (CSF) [21] provides us with a better understanding of the visual sensitivity in such situations. The sensitivity is highest at frequencies in the range of 2 to 4 cycles per degree (cpd) of visual angle and drops off significantly at higher and lower spatial frequencies. The peak sensitivity is normally predicted by the TVI function. What the TVI function does not predict is the loss of sensitivity as the frequency deviates from this range. The relation between contrast sensitivity, $S_{csf}$, and visual threshold, $\Delta L_{csf}$, at any frequency $f$ is derived as:

$$S_{csf}(f) = \frac{1}{\Delta C_{csf}(f)} = \frac{1}{(\Delta L_{csf}(f)/L)} \quad (2)$$

where $\Delta C_{csf}$ is the threshold contrast, and $L$ is the background luminance. From this we get:

$$\Delta L_{csf}(f) = \frac{L}{S_{csf}(f)} \quad (3)$$

Thus, the CSF function gives us the threshold $\Delta L_{csf}(f)$ for detecting a sinusoidal grating pattern of any given frequency from a background luminance $L$. The threshold predicted by CSF for a grating is conceptually different from the threshold from TVI function. The difference lies in the fact that the threshold itself is a pattern of the same frequency with a peak value of $\Delta L_{csf}(f)$ and defined around a mean value of zero[1].

[1] This difference derives from the fact that in psychophysics two types of contrast definitions are used: Weber contrast is used in experiments with aperiodic signals (spot on background tests), which is $\frac{\Delta L}{L_{background}}$ and Michaelson contrast is used in experiments with periodic signals (tests with sinusoidal gratings) which is $\frac{L_{max}-L_{min}}{L_{max}+L_{min}} = \frac{\Delta L_{peak}}{L_{mean}} \approx \frac{\Delta L_{peak}}{L_{background}}$.

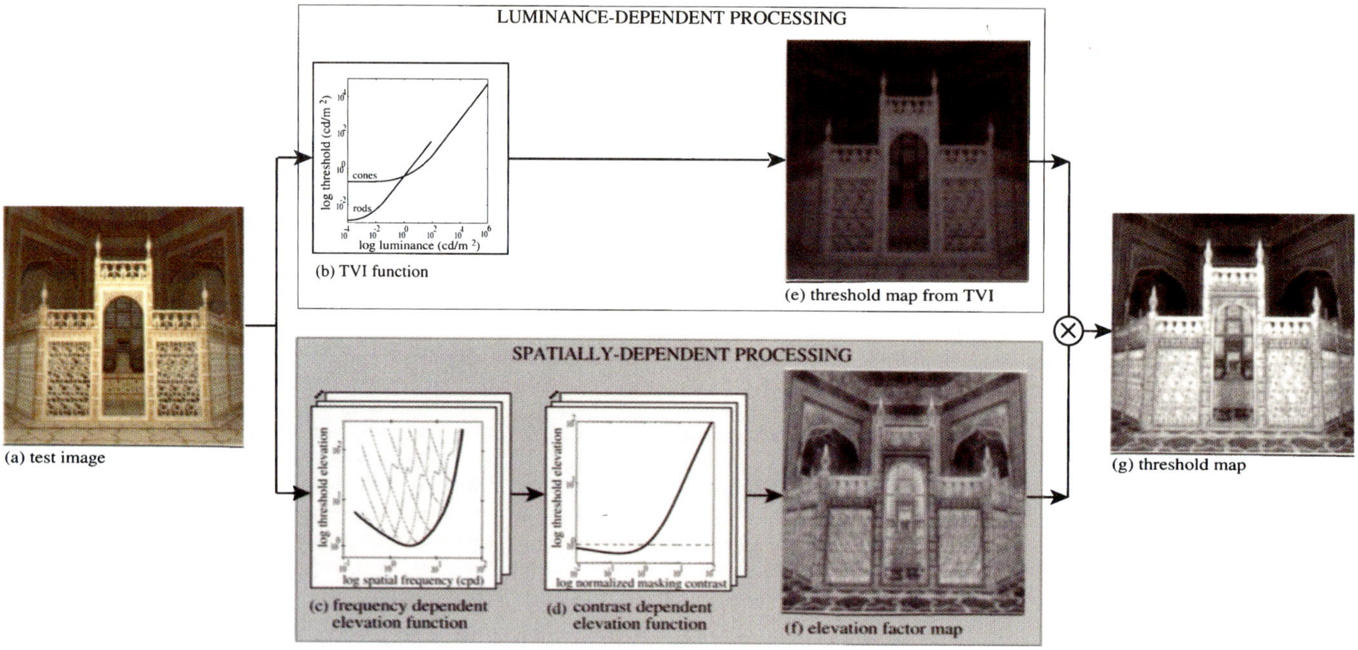


Figure 3: Flow chart outlining the computational steps of our threshold model.

As the sensitivity decreases for frequencies outside the range of 2 to 4 cpd, this $\Delta L_{csf}$ increases. We write this increase in threshold for any frequency $f$, as compared to the threshold at peak of the CSF function as:

$$F_{csf}(f) = \frac{\Delta L_{csf}(f)}{\Delta L_{csf}^{peak}} \tag{4}$$

We refer to this relative increase as the *threshold elevation factor* due to contrast sensitivity, $F_{csf}(f)$. Figure 3(c) plots this elevation factor as a solid line. The peak contrast sensitivity is normally predicted by the TVI function i.e. $\Delta L_{csf}^{peak} = \Delta L_{tvi}$. Thus from the TVI and $F_{csf}$ functions we can compute the threshold for patterns at any frequency $f$ as:

$$\Delta L_{csf}(f) = \Delta L_{tvi} \times F_{csf}(f) \tag{5}$$

where $\Delta L_{tvi}$ is the threshold for the background luminance $L$ of the frequency pattern.

**Multi-scale Spatial Processing** The CSF behavior of the visual system is believed to be the result of the spatial processing of the frequency patterns by multiple bandpass mechanisms. Each mechanism processes only a small band of spatial frequencies from the range over which the visual system is sensitive. The inverse of the response curves of these bandpass mechanisms normalized with respect to the peak CSF value are shown by the curves drawn in broken lines in Figure 3(c). As can be inferred from the figure, the peak sensitivity of each mechanism is equal to the CSF sensitivity at their peak frequencies.

Most of the frequencies in the range over which the visual system is sensitive are processed by multiple bandpass mechanisms. We can describe the contribution of each mechanism to the threshold elevation factor for a grating of frequency $f$ as:

$$F_{csf}^{i}(f) = F_{csf}(f_{peak}^{i}) \times fraction^{i}(f) \tag{6}$$

$$fraction^{i}(f) = \frac{C^{i}(f)}{\sum_i C^{i}(f)} \tag{7}$$

where $f_{peak}^{i}$ is the peak frequency of the $i^{th}$ bandpass mechanism, and $C^{i}$ is the band-limited contrast of the grating pattern at the $i^{th}$ bandpass mechanism.

The elevation factor for the grating of frequency $f$ due to all the bands is then given by:

$$\begin{aligned} F_{csf}(f) &= \sum_i F_{csf}^{i}(f) \\ &= \sum_i (F_{csf}(f_{peak}^{i}) \times fraction^{i}(f)) \end{aligned} \tag{8}$$

Similar summation techniques are used to compute the distance in multi-dimensional perceptual space [7, 17]. Equation 4 and Equation 8 are two different representations of the elevation function for a sinusoidal grating of frequency $f$. Equation 8 is more useful for deriving elevation from complex patterns. Any complex pattern can be represented as a sum of sinusoidal grating patterns of various wavelength, amplitude, orientation and phase. We can use the same summation technique given in the above equation to compute the elevation factor map for complex patterns. However, to account for the complexity of the patterns we redefine Equation 7 as:

$$fraction^{i}(x,y) = \frac{C^{i}(x,y)}{\sum_i C^{i}(x,y)} \tag{9}$$

where $C^{i}(x,y)$ is the band-limited Weber contrast of the complex pattern at the $i^{th}$ bandpass mechanism at every point $(x,y)$ of the pattern. (Computation of this band-limited Weber contrast is described in the next section.) Consequently, the elevation factor in Equation 8 for complex patterns becomes an elevation factor map $F_{csf}(x,y)$ which is given by:

$$\begin{aligned} F_{csf}(x,y) &= \sum_i (F_{csf}^{i}(x,y)) \\ &= \sum_i F_{csf}(f_{peak}^{i}) \times fraction^{i}(x,y) \end{aligned} \tag{10}$$

(a) test image (b) noise map (c) test image + noise map

Figure 4: Testing the threshold model. Our threshold model computes a threshold map, shown in Figure 3(g) for the test image shown in (a). The threshold map is used to create a noise map. The absolute luminance value at every pixel in the noise map is below the threshold value given for that pixel in the threshold map. Image (b) shows the "absolute values" of this noise map. Image (c) is obtained by adding this noise to the test image. This image, though now containing noise, is visually indistinguishable from the original test image.

**Contrast Masking** The multiple bandpass mechanisms of the visual system are known to have non-linear response to pattern contrast. This compressive non-linearity results in further elevation of threshold with increases in the contrast of the pattern. Such behavior of the visual system is known as visual masking [10]. The elevation of threshold as a function of contrast is shown in Figure 3(d). We combine this elevation due to masking with the elevation due to CSF to compute a cumulative elevation factor map as:

$$F_{spatial}(x,y) = \sum_i (F_{csf}(f^i_{peak}) \times F^i_{masking}(x,y) \times fraction^i(x,y)) \quad (11)$$

where $F_{csf}(f^i_{peak})$ is the elevation factor due to contrast sensitivity, and $F^i_{masking}(x,y)$ is the elevation factor due to masking which is computed for the band-limited contrast at location $(x,y)$ for the $i^{th}$ band.

From the elevation factor derived in Equation 11 and the $\Delta L_{tvi}$ derived from the TVI function, our model computes a threshold map for any complex image patterns as given by Equation 1.

## 4.2 Implementation

In this section we describe the specific computational procedures that were used to implement each of the components of the model. Input to the model is a luminance image and output is the threshold map containing the threshold luminance values in $cd/m^2$. We use the scene luminance image as input to the threshold model with the assumption that whatever tone reproduction operator is used to display the final image will preserve its appearance [22]. To find the threshold map we need to evaluate Equation 1 over the image.

The first step of the model is to find the luminance-dependent threshold ($\Delta L_{tvi}$) from the TVI function. We employ Ward's [16] piecewise approximation of the TVI curves given by Ferwerda *et al.* [9]. Computation of $\Delta L_{tvi}(x,y)$ at a pixel using this function requires the adaptation luminance at that pixel. Following the procedure adopted by Ward *et al.* [16] we computed the adaptation luminance by averaging the luminance over a $1°$ diameter solid angle centered around the pixel.

The next step is to evaluate the cumulative elevation factor $F_{spatial}$ given in Equation 11. The terms in this equation require spatial decomposition of the image to "band-limited contrast responses". We use Lubin's approach [17] for this spatial decomposition. First, the image is decomposed into a Laplacian pyramid (Burt and Adelson [4]), resulting in six bandpass levels with peak frequencies at 1, 2, 4, 8, 16, and 32 cycles/degree (cpd). Then, a *contrast pyramid* is created by dividing the Laplacian value at each point in each level by the corresponding point upsampled from the Gaussian pyramid level two levels down in resolution. The resulting contrast measure in the bands is equivalent to the *band-limited Weber contrast* [17] referred to in Equation 9.

The first term in Equation 11 is the band-limited peak elevation factor $F_{csf}$. This factor is derived from Barten's CSF formula [1]:

$$S_{csf}(f,L) = af\exp(-bf)\sqrt{1+0.06\exp(bf)} \quad (12)$$

$$\begin{aligned} where \quad S_{csf} &= \text{contrast sensitivity} \\ a &= 440(1+0.7/L)^{-0.2} \\ b &= 0.3(1+100/L)^{0.15} \\ L &= \text{display luminance in } cd/m^2 \\ f &= \text{spatial frequency in cycles per degree (cpd)} \end{aligned}$$

We use the normalized CSF curve at 100 $cd/m^2$. Measurements by van Nes [25] show that the CSF is relatively independent of luminance level for levels above 100 $cd/m^2$, so the shape of the CSF curve at 100 $cd/m^2$ is a good match for higher luminance levels. At lower levels of illumination there is a proportionate decrease in sensitivity. However, the relative falloff in sensitivity at low spatial frequencies, as normally observed in a CSF curve, reduces with lowering of illumination level. To avoid any overestimation of threshold at lower frequencies we set the normalized CSF sensitivity factor below 4 cpd to be one. The reciprocal of the normalized CSF sensitivity values gives us the threshold elevation factors at various frequencies. The elevation factors at the discrete frequencies from 1 through 32 cpd are:

| $f^i_{peak}$ (cpd) | 1 | 2 | 4 | 8 | 16 | 32 |
|---|---|---|---|---|---|---|
| $F_{csf}(f^i_{peak})$ | 1.00 | 1.00 | 1.02 | 1.57 | 4.20 | 31.32 |

(13)

Next we need to evaluate the elevation factor due to masking in the bands, $F^i_{masking}(x,y)$. This elevation factor is determined using a masking function. These functions are usually given as compressive transducers [17] and can be converted to a threshold elevation function using numerical inversion methods. In the current

(a) test scene (b) direct illumination solution (c) direct illumination solution + ambient term

Figure 5: The direct illumination solution plus an approximate ambient term capture most of the high spatial frequency and contrast content in the scene.

implementation we have used the simpler analytic function given by Daly [7]:

$$F_{masking}(C_n) = (1 + (0.0153(392.498 \cdot C_n)^{0.7})^4)^{1/4} \quad (14)$$

$$where \quad F_{masking} = \text{threshold elevation factor due to masking}$$
$$C_n = \text{normalized masking contrast}$$

Before using this function the contrasts in the bands are first normalized by the CSF function evaluated at luminance values from the low pass Gaussian pyramid.

Finally, the term $fraction^i(x, y)$ is evaluated using Equation 9. In this equation, $C^i(x, y)$ is the band-limited Weber contrast at point $(x, y)$ in the $i^{th}$ band.

The map in each band is spatially pooled by a disc-shaped kernel of diameter 5 [17] before applying Equation 11. This is to account for the influence of the number of cycles in the various frequencies present in the image on the elevation functions, as suggested by Lubin [17].

Figure 4 shows the threshold map for a test image and verifies our claim that the threshold map is an index to the maximum physical luminance error that can be tolerated at any location on the image.

# 5 APPLICATION TO GLOBAL ILLUMINATION ALGORITHMS

The threshold model described in the previous section operates on an input image to generate a threshold map which predicts the maximum luminance error that can be tolerated at every location over the input image, while preserving perceived visual quality. We can use this threshold map to predict the visible differences of another image relative to the input image; the areas in which the luminance difference between these images is below the threshold map are visually indistinguishable. In a progressive global illumination algorithm, we can use the threshold model to compare intermediate rendered images at two consecutive time steps to locate areas where the global illumination solution has not perceptually converged and concentrate computational effort in those areas. Computation can be stopped in areas where the luminance differences are below threshold. This perceptually based error metric could potentially lead to a significant savings in computation time, but as we saw in the previous section, the threshold model includes components which perform multiscale processing and are quite expensive to evaluate at each intermediate stage of a progressive algorithm. This adds considerable additional overhead to the global illumination algorithm. However, as we shall see in the next subsection, we exploit the representation of our threshold model and information from an earlier stage of the global illumination, to apply the threshold model in a global illumination framework and drastically reduce this overhead.

## 5.1 Precomputing the expensive components of the threshold model

The most expensive component in the threshold model is the processing of the input image with band-limited multi-scale visual filters. As shown in Figure 3, this operation is required for computing the frequency-dependent elevation function and the contrast-dependent elevation function. These functions predict the loss of sensitivity to scene features with high spatial frequencies and high contrast regions. If we can capture these scene features at an early stage of global illumination computation, these two functions could be evaluated once and reused at later stages.

Our target application provides a structure in which we can evaluate these functions once and re-use them to avoid repetitive model evaluations. Global illumination computation has two major components: direct illumination computation and indirect illumination computation. Indirect illumination computation involves simulating complex light interactions between the surfaces in the scene and is many orders of magnitude more expensive than direct illumination computation. Fortunately, indirect illumination generally varies only gradually over the surfaces and accounts for more subtle effects. Direct illumination computation is comparatively less expensive, but captures most of the higher spatial frequency and contrast content in the scene, such as texture patterns, geometric details, and shadow patterns. These two features make the direct illumination solution a perfect candidate for use in the precomputation stage. In order to ensure capturing the high spatial frequency and contrast present in shadowed portions of the scene, we add an approximate ambient term. This ambient term is computed in much the same way as the ambient term in radiosity algorithms [11, 6]. As shown in Figure 5, the direct illumination solution plus an approximate ambient term capture most of the high spatial frequency and contrast content even in scenes with large portions in shadow. This ambient term is not included while computing global illumination and does not affect the physical accuracy of the global illumination solution.

The scene rendered by direct illumination plus an approximate ambient term is used to evaluate the elevation factor map (the shaded parts of Figure 3) in a precomputation stage prior to the expensive indirect illumination computation. This serves two purposes: the expensive components of the threshold model are evaluated only once and can be reused, and the noise patterns introduced during the indirect illumination computation do not influence the evaluation of the elevation factor map. The indirect illumination solution is generally "soft" and causes only gradual variation in lighting patterns. The components we precompute only predict the elevation factor due to high frequency content in the scene and are not affected much by the variations in the low frequency content. These components need not be recomputed during the indirect illumination computation. However, the indirect illumination solution does add significantly to the luminance distribution and hence we need to recompute the luminance-dependent threshold during the indirect illumination computation. Fortunately, evaluation of this component of the threshold model is cheap.

## 5.2 An adaptive global illumination algorithm

We applied our framework to speed up a path tracing algorithm [15]. Path tracing is a type of stochastic ray tracing that traces random paths through the scene to compute the illumination value for each pixel on the image plane. The variance for computing indirect illumination is generally much higher than for computing direct illumination, so a large number of samples have to be taken over the image plane to obtain an acceptable estimate for the indirect illumination component. The algorithm we implemented attempts to reduce the number of samples required for the indirect illumination computation by adaptively refining this component using our threshold model.

The algorithm proceeds through a few basic steps as illustrated in the flowchart in Figure 6. First, the direct illumination solution is computed and an approximate ambient term is added. This is used as an input to the threshold model to generate the elevation factor map which involves precomputing the spatially-dependent functions. This completes the precomputation stage. Next, the computationally expensive indirect illumination solution is progressively computed. At every iteration, the computed indirect illumination solution is added to the direct illumination solution to get an intermediate global illumination solution. The current solution is used to compute the luminance-dependent threshold by evaluating only the TVI function which is not spatially-dependent and is much simpler to compute. The precomputed elevation factor map is then used to scale this luminance-dependent threshold to generate the threshold map which guides the refinement. The luminance difference between the global illumination solutions at the $i^{th}$ iteration and the $(i-1)^{th}$ iteration is compared against the threshold map evaluated at the $(i-1)^{th}$ stage to locate the regions where the solution has perceptually converged. In the next iteration, the regions where the difference remains above threshold are refined. The iteration is continued until the difference over the entire image plane is below the threshold map.

During each iteration the refinement can be carried out by uniformly distributing samples, but it is more advantageous to vary the number of samples in a region based on its "perceptual importance". Higher ratios between the luminance difference map and the threshold map reflect higher perceivability of error. Alternatively, the threshold map at the current stage can be treated as a predictor of the perceivability of error on areas of the image plane, where lower thresholds imply higher perceivability and indicate greater need to sample. In our implementation we used the latter approach to determine the distribution of samples over the regions which need further refining.

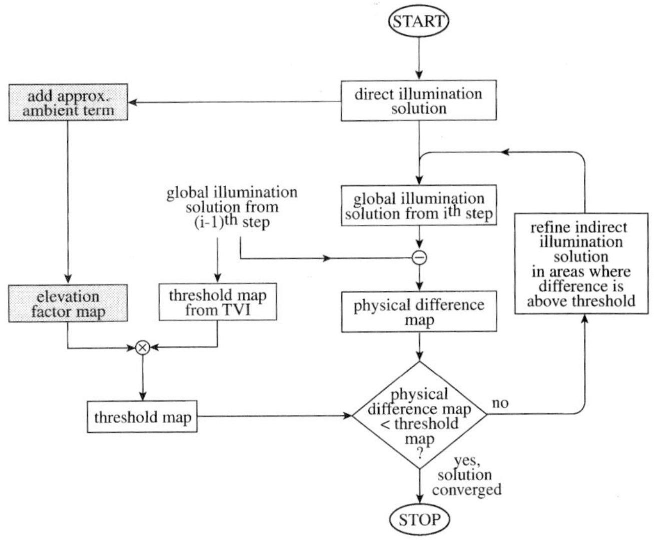


Figure 6: Flow chart of the adaptive global illumination algorithm.

## 5.3 Results

The adaptive path tracing algorithm described above was applied to several test scenes.

In Figure 7 we show some of the results on the test scene shown in Figure 7(a). The elevation factor map is computed from Figure 7(b). This is used to evaluate the threshold map at every iteration to guide the refinement of the indirect illumination solution. Figure 7(c) is the threshold map at an intermediate iteration. Notice that it has correctly predicted larger thresholds in areas with high spatial frequency and contrast content, indicating the poor sensitivity of the eye in such image features. Figures 7(d-f) show the results from the final iteration of the algorithm. The computed adaptive indirect illumination solution is shown in Figure 7(e) and the sample density pattern it traced is shown in Figure 7(d). Figure 7(f) is the final adaptive global illumination solution. Notice that because our adaptive sampling technique uses smaller number of samples on the areas with high frequency and contrast, the indirect illumination solution for the wall painting and floor carpet shown in Figure 7(e) is noisy. But this noise is completely masked in the final global illumination solution in Figure 7(f). This demonstrates that our threshold model correctly predicted the loss of sensitivity in these textured areas and that we did not have to compute a very accurate solution in these areas. The number of samples taken over the entire image plane required for this solution was approximately 6% of those of the reference solution (Figure 7(a)) computed using uniform sample density, where the number of samples for each pixel is the maximum of all the pixels in the corresponding sampling density map. Notice that these two solutions are visually indistinguishable. (Subtle differences might be noticeable as the threshold model was calibrated to our display device, and the perceivability of differences depends on the image reproduction method and ratio of physical image size to observer viewing distance.)

The two test scenes in Figure 8 were selected to illustrate the computational savings in areas of the image plane which contain texture patterns, geometric detail, and shadow patterns with high spatial frequency and high contrast. The two images on the right, image (c) and image (f), are global illumination solutions obtained using sample density patterns shown in image (b) and image (e) respectively. In the sampling pattern shown here, lighter areas indicate more samples and darker area indicate fewer samples. The sample density patterns result from applying the threshold model

(a) reference global illumination solution (b) direct illumination solution + ambient term (c) threshold map

(d) sample density pattern (e) adaptive indirect illumination solution (f) direct illumination solution + adaptive indirect illumination solution

Figure 7: Applying the threshold model in an adaptive global illumination algorithm.

to our adaptive path tracing algorithm. In image (b), observe that fewer samples were taken on the texture patterns and geometric detail in the scene. Image(e) shows that fewer samples were taken on the shadow pattern on the floor. The two images on the left, image (a) and image (d), are the solutions computed using uniform sample density, where the number of samples for each pixel is the maximum value of all the pixels in the corresponding sampling density map. Notice that the image pairs (a), (c) and (d), (f) are indistinguishable even though the number of samples required by our algorithm was approximately 5% of those of the reference solution in the scene on the top left and approximately 10% of the reference solution in the scene on the bottom left.

We have tested the algorithm on a number of test scenes and all results show that we can correctly exploit the limitations of the visual system at high frequency and contrast to reduce the expensive global illumination computations. Timing tests reveal that it has given us great benefit at very little extra cost. This is because the expensive components of the threshold model were evaluated only once at a precomputation stage and reused during the rendering iterations. The cost of computing the spatially-dependent component on an image of resolution 512 by 512 is 12 seconds (or, 0.05 ms per pixel) on a 400 MHz processor. In comparison, the luminance-dependent component takes only 0.1 seconds (or, 0.4 $\mu$s per pixel) for the same image resolution. These figures are independent of the specific global illumination algorithm used to generate the direct and indirect illumination solutions. Comparisons with uniform sampling methods and adaptive approaches with purely physical error metrics showed that our approach took many fewer samples for computing images of similar visual quality.

### 5.4 Discussion

The adaptive technique we described above makes very few assumptions about the underlying global illumination computation algorithm. The illumination at each sample on the image plane could be computed using most image-space global illumination algorithms. We only require that the direct illumination solution be computed first, before the indirect illumination solution. There are many methods already developed which make direct illumination computation very efficient [23, 8, 26, 13] and we concentrate on speeding up the relatively expensive indirect illumination computation.

Further research is necessary to better capture details in shadowed areas. Using an approximate ambient term has certain drawbacks. If the ambient term is overestimated then it affects the contrast in the scene and the contrast-dependent elevation function is no longer conservative. One possible approach is to compute the elevation factor map in shadowed areas using only the frequency-dependent elevation function. Another approach is to use a very small ambient term which is sufficiently conservative. The ambient term also fails to capture the high spatial frequencies caused purely by geometric detail in the areas under shadow. For example, in Figure 5(c) the ambient term captured the texture patterns in shadowed areas (the carpet) but overlooked high frequencies caused purely by geometric detail (features of the statue).

In scenes with significant specular-to-diffuse light transfers, high frequency patterns may result at later stages of global illumination (e.g. mirror reflections and caustics). In such cases the spatially-dependent component of the threshold model can be recomputed after these effects become apparent.

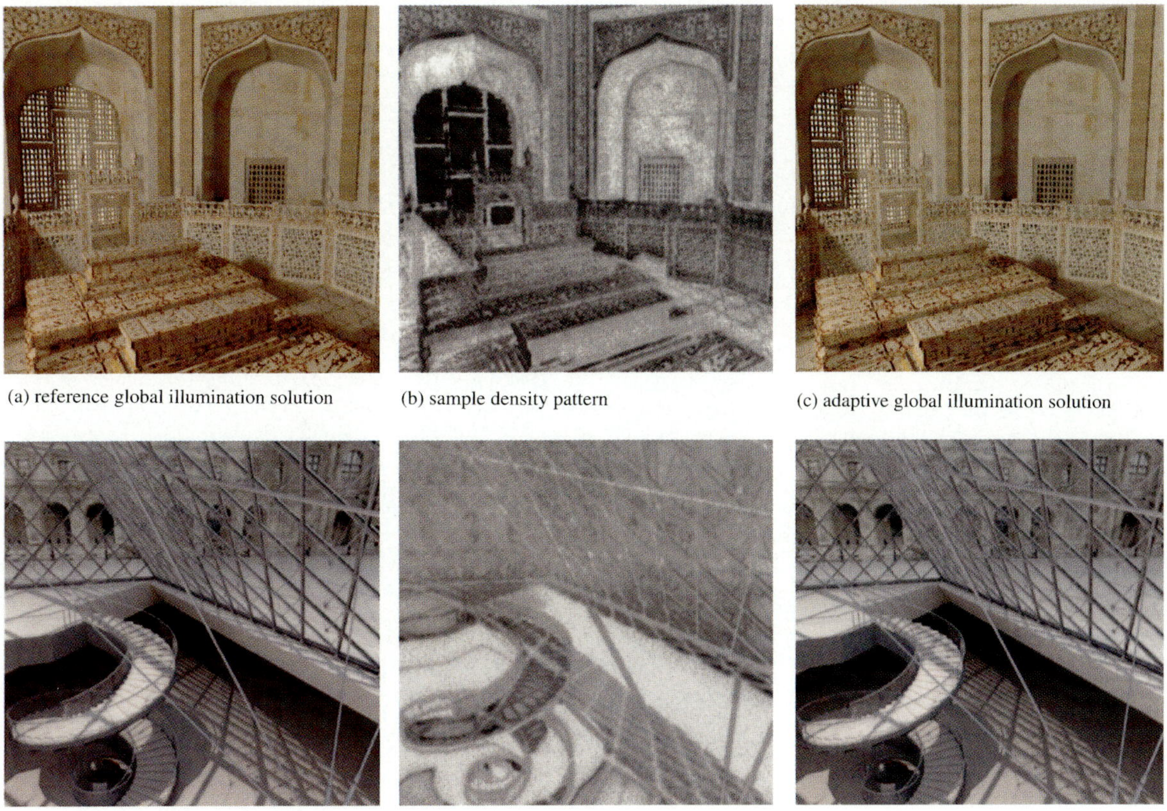

(a) reference global illumination solution (b) sample density pattern (c) adaptive global illumination solution

(d) reference global illumination solution (e) sample density pattern (f) adaptive global illumination solution

Figure 8: Sample density patterns and adaptive global illumination solutions for two test scenes.

# 6 CONCLUSIONS AND FUTURE WORK

In this paper we have described a new framework for perceptually based image synthesis. The objective of this framework was twofold:

- To speed up realistic image synthesis using a perceptual basis which exploits the limitations of the human visual system, and
- To reduce the overhead (in terms of both memory and time) of incorporating such a perceptual basis in the image synthesis algorithm.

To achieve these objectives, we modeled the visual system as a number of components that affect the visual threshold for detecting artifacts depending on the image features. These components together form the threshold model which was used in our framework. Tests on an adaptive global illumination algorithm showed that our threshold model exploits texture patterns, geometric details, and lighting variations in the image to enormously reduce computation time, while preserving image fidelity. By precomputing the expensive spatial components of our threshold model before the more expensive indirect illumination computations, we nearly eliminated all visual processing during the later iterations and also minimized memory requirements. Incorporating the threshold model added an overall insignificant overhead over our standard global illumination algorithm.

In summary, we have vastly improved the computation times for view dependent global illumination solutions using a perceptually based physical error metric.

Through this framework, we have introduced three fundamentally new concepts which have been independently tested and together hold promise for making realistic image synthesis more efficient. These concepts are:

- Predicting the maximum physical luminance error that can be tolerated at any location in an image while preserving perceptual quality.
- Guiding image synthesis algorithms with a perceptually based physical error metric.
- Precomputing expensive components of the vision model essential to perceptually based image synthesis algorithms.

A major goal while designing the framework presented in this paper was to keep it sufficiently general for application to most view dependent realistic image synthesis algorithms.

There is still much work to be done. Our threshold model does not include color, orientation, or temporal processing. Temporal extension to the model is particularly important and would be very useful for dynamic image sequences such as animations or architectural walkthroughs.

Our framework is also especially suited for architectures which switch between model-based and image-based rendering, such as Talisman [24]. These systems render and transform objects as image layers (image-based rendering) instead of re-rendering their geometry (model-based rendering). We could precompute our threshold model from the scene and use it as a perceptual guide for establishing distortion criteria. This could improve performance as it would correctly predict locally higher acceptable distortions due to loss of visual sensitivity.

## ACKNOWLEDGEMENTS

Special thanks to James Ferwerda and Jonathan Corson-Rikert for help in preparing this paper.

This work was supported by the NSF Science and Technology Center for Computer Graphics and Scientific Visualization (ASC-8920219) and by NSF grant ASC-9523483, and performed on workstations generously donated by the Intel Corporation and by the Hewlett-Packard Corporation.

## References

[1] Peter G. J. Barten. The Square Root Integral (SQRI): A New Metric to Describe the Effect of Various Display Parameters on Perceived Image Quality. In *Human Vision, Visual Processing, and Digital Display*, volume 1077, pages 73–82. Proc. of SPIE, 1989.

[2] Mark R. Bolin and Gary W. Meyer. A Frequency Based Ray Tracer. In *SIGGRAPH 95 Conference Proceedings*, pages 409–418, Los Angeles, California, August 1995.

[3] Mark R. Bolin and Gary W. Meyer. A Perceptually Based Adaptive Sampling Algorithm. In *SIGGRAPH 98 Conference Proceedings*, pages 299–310, Orlando, Florida, July 1998.

[4] Peter J. Burt and Edward H. Adelson. The Laplacian Pyramid as a Compact Image Code. *IEEE Transactions on Communications*, 31(4):532–540, April 1983.

[5] Kenneth Chiu and Peter Shirley. Rendering, Complexity and Perception. In *Proceedings of the Fifth Eurographics Workshop on Rendering*, pages 19–33, Darmstadt, Germany, June 1994.

[6] Michael Cohen, Donald P. Greenberg, Dave S. Immel, and Philip J. Brock. An Efficient Radiosity Approach for Realistic Image Synthesis. *IEEE Computer Graphics and Applications*, 6(3):26–35, March 1986.

[7] Scott Daly. The Visible Differences Predictor: An Algorithm for the Assessment of Image Fidelity. In A. B. Watson, editor, *Digital Images and Human Vision*, pages 179–206. MIT Press, 1993.

[8] George Drettakis and Eugene Fiume. A Fast Shadow Algorithm for Area Light Sources Using Backprojection. In *SIGGRAPH 94 Conference Proceedings*, pages 223–30, Orlando, Florida, July 1994.

[9] James A. Ferwerda, Sumanta N. Pattanaik, Peter Shirley, and Donald P. Greenberg. A Model of Visual Adaptation for Realistic Image Synthesis. In *SIGGRAPH 96 Conference Proceedings*, pages 249–258, New Orleans, Louisiana, August 1996.

[10] James A. Ferwerda, Sumanta N. Pattanaik, Peter Shirley, and Donald P. Greenberg. A Model of Visual Masking for Computer Graphics. In *SIGGRAPH 97 Conference Proceedings*, pages 143–152, Los Angeles, California, August 1997.

[11] S. Gibson and R. J. Hubbold. Perceptually-Driven Radiosity. *Computer Graphics Forum*, 16(2):129–141, 1997.

[12] Donald P. Greenberg, Kenneth E. Torrance, Peter Shirley, James Arvo, James A. Ferwerda, Sumanta N. Pattanaik, Eric P. F. Lafortune, Bruce Walter, Sing-Choong Foo, and Ben Trumbore. A Framework for Realistic Image Synthesis. In *SIGGRAPH 97 Conference Proceedings*, pages 477–494, Los Angeles, California, August 1997.

[13] David Hart, Philip Dutré, and Donald Greenberg. Direct Illumination with Lazy Visibility Evaluation. In *SIGGRAPH 99 Conference Proceedings*, Los Angeles, California, August 1999.

[14] David Hedley, Adam Worrall, and Derek Paddon. Selective Culling of Discontinuity Lines. In *Proceedings of the Eighth Eurographics Workshop on Rendering*, pages 69–80, St.Etienne, France, June 1997.

[15] James T. Kajiya. The Rendering Equation. In *Computer Graphics (SIGGRAPH 86 Proceedings)*, volume 20, pages 143–150, Dallas, Texas, August 1986.

[16] Gregory Ward Larson, Holly Rushmeier, and Christine Piatko. A Visibility Matching Tone Reproduction Operator for High Dynamic Range Scenes. *IEEE Transactions on Visualization and Computer Graphics*, 3(4):291–306, October 1997.

[17] Jeffrey Lubin. A Visual Discrimination Model for Imaging System Design and Evaluation. In E. Peli, editor, *Vision Models for Target Detection and Recognition*, pages 245–283. World Scientific, 1995.

[18] Gary W. Meyer and Aihua Liu. Color Spatial Acuity Control of a Screen Subdivision Image Synthesis Algorithm. In Bernice E. Rogowitz, editor, *Human Vision, Visual Processing, and Digital Display III*, volume 1666, pages 387–399. Proc. SPIE, 1992.

[19] Don P. Mitchell. Generating Antialiased Images at Low Sampling Densities. In *Computer Graphics (SIGGRAPH 87 Proceedings)*, volume 21, pages 65–72, Anaheim, California, July 1987.

[20] Karol Myszkowski. The Visible Differences Predictor: Applications to Global Illumination Problems. In *Proceedings of the Ninth Eurographics Workshop on Rendering*, pages 223–236, Vienna, Austria, June 1998.

[21] Sumanta N. Pattanaik, James A. Ferwerda, Mark D. Fairchild, and Donald P. Greenberg. A Multiscale Model of Adaptation and Spatial Vision for Realistic Image Display. In *SIGGRAPH 98 Conference Proceedings*, pages 287–298, Orlando, Florida, July 1998.

[22] Holly Rushmeier, Greg Ward, C. Piatko, P. Sanders, and B. Rust. Comparing Real and Synthetic Images: Some Ideas About Metrics. In *Proceedings of the Sixth Eurographics Workshop on Rendering*, pages 213–222, Dublin, Ireland, June 1995.

[23] Peter Shirley, Chang Yaw Wang, and Kurt Zimmerman. Monte Carlo Techniques for Direct Lighting Calculations. *ACM Transactions on Graphics*, 15(1):1–36, January 1996.

[24] Jay Torborg and Jim Kajiya. Talisman: Commodity Real-time 3D Graphics for the PC. In *SIGGRAPH 96 Conference Proceedings*, pages 353–364, New Orleans, Louisiana, August 1996.

[25] F. L. van Nes and M. A. Bouman. Spatial Modulation Transfer in the Human Eye. *J. Opt. Soc. Am.*, 57:401–406, 1967.

[26] Andrew Woo, Pierre Poulin, and Alain Fournier. A Survey of Shadow Algorithms. *IEEE Computer Graphics and Applications*, 10(6):13–32, November 1990.

# LCIS: A Boundary Hierarchy For Detail-Preserving Contrast Reduction

Jack Tumblin and Greg Turk

Georgia Institute of Technology

## Abstract

High contrast scenes are difficult to depict on low contrast displays without loss of important fine details and textures. Skilled artists preserve these details by drawing scene contents in coarse-to-fine order using a hierarchy of scene boundaries and shadings. We build a similar hierarchy using multiple instances of a new *low curvature image simplifier* (LCIS), a partial differential equation inspired by anisotropic diffusion. Each LCIS reduces the scene to many smooth regions that are bounded by sharp gradient discontinuities, and a single parameter $K$ chosen for each LCIS controls region size and boundary complexity. With a few chosen $K$ values $(K_1 > K_2 > K_3 ...)$ LCIS makes a set of progressively simpler images, and image differences form a hierarchy of increasingly important details, boundaries and large features.

We construct a high detail, low contrast display image from this hierarchy by compressing only the large features, then adding back all small details. Unlike linear filter hierarchies such as wavelets, filter banks, or image pyramids, LCIS hierarchies do not smooth across scene boundaries, avoiding "halo" artifacts common to previous contrast reducing methods and some tone reproduction operators. We demonstrate LCIS effectiveness on several example images.

**CR Descriptors:** I.3.3 [**Computer Graphics**]: Picture/image generation - *Display algorithms*; I.4.1 [**Image Processing and Computer Vision**]: Enhancement *-Digitization and Image Capture*

Keywords: Signal Processing, Displays, Non-Realistic Rendering, Level Of Detail Algorithms, Radiosity, Weird Math.

## 1 Introduction

Local adaptation, the ensemble of local sensitivity-adjusting processes in the visual system, reveals visible details almost everywhere in a viewed scene. Even while driving at night, we see few shadows that are truly featureless black. We can read the tiny lettering on the dazzling surface of a frosted incandescent bulb in a desk lamp, yet we also see the dark room around us. Mechanisms of visual appearance often cause us to underestimate large scene contrasts. For example, we measured a piece of paper on a desk to find it was 1,200 times brighter than the dark carpet in the foot-well beneath it, yet we could easily see the fibrous textures of both simultaneously. Making an image such as Figure 1 that captures both the high contrast appearance of a scene and its small low-contrast details is contradictory and difficult, and currently the best, most satisfying depictions of these scenes may be the creations of skilled artists.

Figure 1: This low contrast image of a streetlight on a foggy night was made by LCIS methods from an extremely high contrast radiance map [2]; Small images show the original scene radiances scaled by progressive factors of 10. Despite scene contrasts greater than 100,000:1, LCIS methods preserve details impossible to capture in a single photograph, including long, dramatic fog streaks, asphalt texture, and tree details in highlight and shadow.

For three important reasons listed here, cameras and computer graphics renderings have severe difficulties capturing, preserving, and displaying the subtle textures and details in high contrast scenes. First, available display contrasts are small and are easily overwhelmed by the scene contrasts, where contrast is the ratio between two measured light intensities. Newspaper photographs achieve a maximum contrast of about 30:1, typically CRT displays offer contrasts of no more than 100:1, and only the best photographic prints can provide contrasts as high as 1000:1. However, scenes that include visible light sources, deep shadows, and specu-

College of Computing, Georgia Institute of Technology,
Atlanta, GA 30332-0280. ccsupjt@cc.gatech.edu, turk@cc.gatech.edu.

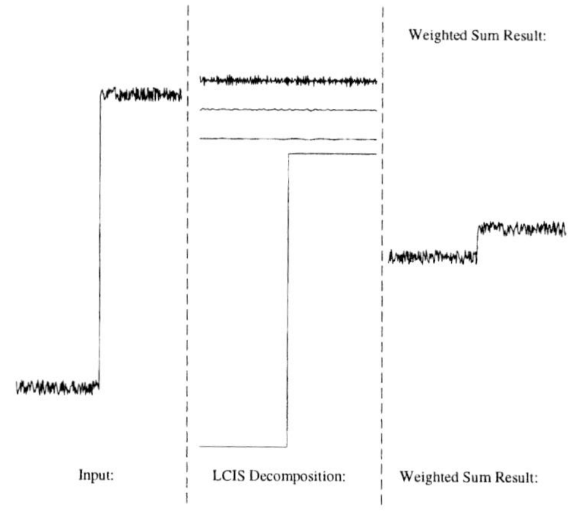


Figure 2: Applied to a scanline from a high contrast scene, an LCIS hierarchy separates large features and fine details as an artist might. Compressing only its simplest features reduces contrasts but preserves details.

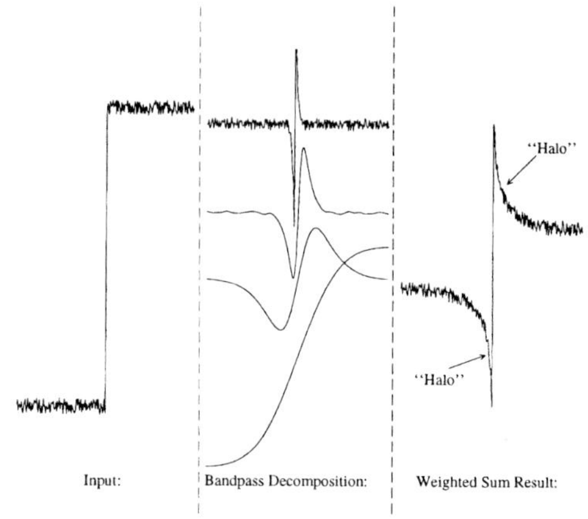


Figure 3: A linear filter hierarchy does not adequately separate fine details from large features. Compressing only the low-frequency components to reduce contrasts causes halo artifacts.

lar highlights can reach contrasts of 100,000:1 or much more.

Second, the simplest ways to adjust scene intensities for display will usually damage or destroy important details and textures. Most commonly used adjustments are borrowed from photography, and are given by

$$I_d = F(m \cdot I_s^{\gamma}) \tag{1}$$

where $I_d, I_s$ are display and scene intensities in $cd/m^2$, $m$ is a scale factor from film exposure, $\gamma$ is contrast sensitivity and will compress contrasts for values $< 1.0$, and $F()$ limits the output to display intensity abilities. The simplest, default $F()$ truncates out-of-range intensities to the display limits, but this discards the fine details and textures in the scene's shadows, highlights, or both, depending on "exposure" or scale factor $m$. Compressing all scene contrasts uniformly by adjusting film gamma $\gamma$ may compress large contrasts sufficiently for display, but will also reduce smaller contrasts to invisibility. Choosing a better limiting function $F()$ such as the S-shaped response of film can help by gracefully compressing contrasts of scene highlights and shadows, but any function choice forces a tradeoff between preserving details at mid-range and destroying them in shadows and highlights.

Third and most importantly, understanding of the human visual system has not advanced sufficiently to allow construction of a definitive, verifiable, quantitative model of visual appearance, especially for high contrast scenes where local adaptation effects are strong. With these uncertainties, artists offer valuable guidance. Skilled artists learn effective and pleasing ways to convey visual appearance with limited display media, and for some uses their methods are more appropriate than current visual appearance models built from psychophysical measurements and small-signal models. Accordingly, LCIS is an attempt to mathematically mimic a well-known artistic technique for rendering high contrast scenes.

When drawing or painting, many artists capture visual appearance with a "coarse-to-fine" sequence of boundaries and shading. Many begin with a sketch of large, important scene features and then gradually add finer, more subtle details. Initial sketches hold sharply defined boundaries around large, smoothly shaded regions for the largest, highest contrast, and most important scene features. The artist then adds more shadings and boundaries to build up fine details and "fill in" the visually empty regions and capture rich detail everywhere.

This method works particularly well for high contrast scenes because it permits separate contrast adjustments at every stage of increasing detail and refinement. An artist drastically compresses the contrasts of large features, then adds the fine details and textures with little or no attenuation to ensure they are visible in the final image. The artist may also emphasize or mute scene components, to control their prominence and direct the viewer's attention.

An artist's progressive image refinement is quite different from widely used linear filter hierarchies, such as wavelets, filter banks, MIP-maps, and steerable image pyramids. Instead of a hierarchy of sinusoids, artists use a hierarchy of boundaries and shadings. For example, consider a simple high contrast scene made from two adjacent sheets of rough-textured paper. A black-colored sheet on the left is dimly but uniformly lit, but the white sheet on the right is illuminated by a strong white light source sharply masked to fall only on the white paper. To an artist, the scene has only one strong boundary and one faint texture everywhere, as in the scanline plots of Figure 2 (created by LCIS), but to a linear filter decomposition this is a rich, broad-band scene, as in Figure 3. At its largest scale, the linear filter hierarchy is a blurred wash from black to white showing only that the left and right intensities differ greatly. Each finer level contains a strong, zero-mean, ripple-like "detail" that sharpens and narrows the transition from black to white, as if each were improving the focus of a camera. At the finest levels these focus-like "details" overwhelm the much weaker components of the paper texture. Reducing scene contrast by compressing only these coarsest levels fails badly for linear filter methods because some parts of the scene's step-like "large feature" have escaped compression by mixing with fine details of the paper texture. The resulting display image, as shown in Figure 3, suffers from artifacts known variously as "halos" [1], "overshoot-undershoot" or "gradient reversals" [19].

We have devised a new hierarchy that more closely follows artistic methods for scene renderings. Each level of the hierarchy is made from a "simplified" version of original scene made of sharp boundaries and smooth shadings. We named the sharpening and smoothing method "low curvature image simplifiers," or LCIS, and will show in Section 5 how to use it in a hierarchy to convert high contrast scenes to low contrast, highly detailed display images such as Figure 1.

## 2 Previous Work

Detail-preserving contrast reduction is a small but central part of a broader problem: how can we accurately recreate the visual appearance of all scenes within the narrow limits of existing displays? As discussed by Tumblin and Rushmeier [16], light levels dramatically affect scene appearance; a forest by starlight looks very different in daylight because of complex, light dependent changes in human ability to sense contrast, color, detail, and movement. They advocated "tone reproduction operators" built from mathematical models of human visual perception to improve displayed images by imitating the light-dependent changes our eyes would experience on viewing the actual scene. We must emphasize that the LCIS method presented here is not true tone reproduction operator, but a sensitive detail extractor for high contrast scenes; it does not determine whether these details would be visible to a human viewer.

Soon afterwards Ward [17] published a simple and practical operator to adjust display brightness by analytically finding scale factor $m$ from scene luminance. Building on this, Ferwerda and colleagues [3] used further psychophysical data to model global adaptation in both cone- and rod-mediated vision, and included changes in sensitivity to color, luminance and spatial resolution in their model. None of these papers have addressed display contrast limitations.

Limited display contrast causes perhaps the worst part of the tone reproduction problem, because most sensations of scene contents, color, acuity, and movements can be directly evoked by the display outputs, but large contrasts cannot. High contrasts must be reduced for display, yet somehow retain a high contrast appearance, perhaps from secondary effects. Papers by Nakamae [7] and Spencer [13] and their colleagues present careful models of the optics of the eye responsible for glare, diffraction, and blooming effects, but as Spencer concluded, these methods must be combined with a perceptually valid method for contrast reduction. Globally applied compression functions ($F$ in Equation 1) such as the S-shaped response of photographic film work well for moderate-contrast scenes, but can easily obliterate details in highlights and shadows. The rational function given by Schlick [12] is an excellent compromise, as it adjusts to keep highlight compression minimal, is fast and simple to compute, and can be calibrated without measuring instruments.

Very large contrasts are much more troublesome because compressive functions destroy important details in highlights and shadows unless adjusted according to local image features. Photographers use "dodging and burning" (moving hand-held masks) to locally adjust print exposure in a darkroom, inspiring an early paper by Chiu *et al.* [1] that constructs a locally varying attenuation factor $m$ by repeatedly clipping and low-pass filtering the scene. Though their method works well in smoothly shaded regions, any small, bright scene feature causes strong attenuation of neighboring pixels and surrounds the feature with a noticeable dark band or halo artifact as in Figure 3. Schlick's attempts to vary his compression function locally also found halos [12], and he suggested local image attenuation should change abruptly at feature boundaries to avoid them. Tanaka and Ohnishi [14] later published a contrast reducing display method similar to Chiu *et al.*, except they used retinal receptive field measurements to design their linear filters. Their method also produces halos. Jobson, Rahman and colleagues [5, 11] devised a contrast reduction method in accordance with Land's "retinex" theory of lightness (perceived reflectance) and color adaptation, but they use linear filters on the logarithm of scene intensities to find local attenuating factors. Their multi-scale extensions help reduce halos by merging results from three manually selected filters.

Ward-Larson *et al.* [19] entirely avoided halos by using iterative histogram adjustment to reduce scene contrasts as part of their tone reproduction operator. Their operator produces very appealing results, and includes locally adjusted models of glare, color sensitivity, and acuity well supported by psychophysical data. However, their computed mapping from scene to display intensities is strictly monotonic, while artists and the LCIS method presented here often use overlapping intensity ranges in different scene regions to achieve greater displayed contrasts for some features. In another halo-free approach, Tumblin and colleagues [15] made computer graphics renderings of separate "layers" of lighting and reflectance and combined them after compressing illumination. They also proposed an interactive display method for high contrast scenes that recomputes the displayed image according to "foveal" neighborhood near the viewer's direction of gaze in the scene.

Building on a rigorous paper on perceptual image metrics [4], last year Pattanaik and colleagues [9] presented a tone reproduction operator that performed contrast reduction using an intricate model of local adaptation assembled from extensive psychophysical data, including acuity, chromatic adaptation, and many measured nonlinearities of vision. However, contrast reduction is chiefly due to attenuation in a linear filter hierarchy; despite many admirable qualities, their method is still susceptible to strong halo components.

## 3 LCIS Method: Shocks and Smoothing

The central importance of boundaries and shadings in artistic renderings suggests a new image decomposition method. To an artist, shadings usually refer to regions of nearly uniform intensity gradient. Because the gradients change smoothly and gradually with position, the region has low curvature. An image made entirely of low curvature regions has boundaries defined by gradient discontinuities, and these may include both ridge-like and step-like features, but only ridges are necessary, as a step may be regarded as two adjacent ridge-like features.

The intensities and locations of these boundaries alone are sufficient to construct an interesting form of simplified image by interpolating between the boundaries with a curvature-minimizing process. The result has an interesting physical analogy; imagine image boundary intensities as a height field made from a frame of thin wires. Dipping the wires in soapy water forms low-curvature bubble membranes between the wires. By adding more wires we may encode the entire scene by boundaries and their intensities. Such an artist-like coarse-to-fine hierarchy is possible if we create a well-behaved method to find these boundaries and smooth away their intervening details.

Anisotropic diffusion has shown great success as a boundary-finding intra-region smoothing method [10] and gathered widespread attention in the image processing literature. Mathematically, it is a gradual, time-dependent evolution of an image towards a piecewise-constant approximation, as shown in Figure 5. The change in image intensity over time is determined by the same class of partial differential equations (PDEs) that govern diffusion of heat or other fluids through solids. For example, if we regard the image intensity $I(x, y)$ as the temperature of a large flat plate of uniform thin material, and also treat temperature as a measure of heat fluid per unit area, then the change in $I$ over time is given by:

$$I_t = \nabla \cdot (-\Phi) = \nabla \cdot (C \nabla I) \tag{2}$$

Subscripts denote partial derivatives such that $I_t$ is $(\partial/\partial t) I(x, y, t)$, the time rate of change in temperature, $I_x$ is $(\partial/\partial x) I(x, y, t)$, $I_{xx}$ is $(\partial^2/\partial x^2) I(x, y, t)$, and so forth. $C$ is the heat conductance scalar, and $\Phi$ is the heat flux, the velocity vector for heat fluid.

In this classic heat equation, heat flows "downhill" from hot regions to cold regions, from larger $I$ to smaller $I$, as permitted by material conductance $C$; $0 \leq C \leq 1$, and all heat fluid movements are described by their flux vector $\Phi$. The flux is caused by a "motive force" pushing the fluid in the hot-to-cold direction given by the negative gradient vector $-\nabla I = (I_x, I_y)$, and by the material's conductance $C$. If conductance is a constant, $C_0$, the equation reduces to $I_t = C_0(I_{xx} + I_{yy})$; as time passes the image changes in the same way it would if repeatedly convolved with a Gaussian filter kernel, smoothing away differences between neighboring points and asymptotically approaching a uniform temperature. The conductance $C$ determines how fast this smoothing occurs, and if C is constant the behavior is known as isotropic diffusion.

In anisotropic diffusion the conductance depends on the image, and both the image and the conductance evolve over time in more interesting ways. In their seminal 1990 paper, Perona and Malik [10] noted that conductance controls the rate of local image

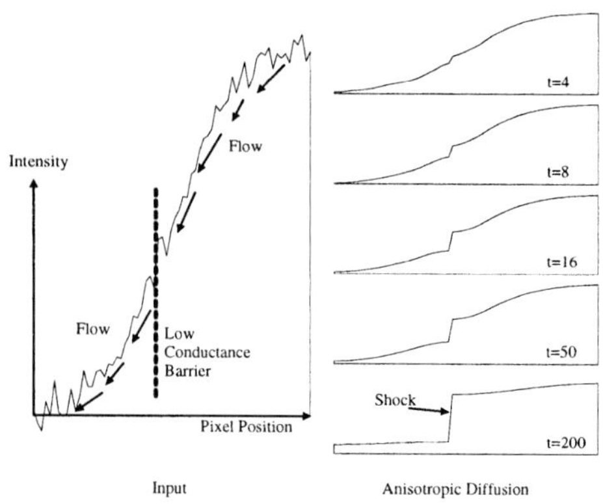


Figure 4: Anisotropic diffusion rapidly forms step discontinuities or "shocks" in high gradient regions.

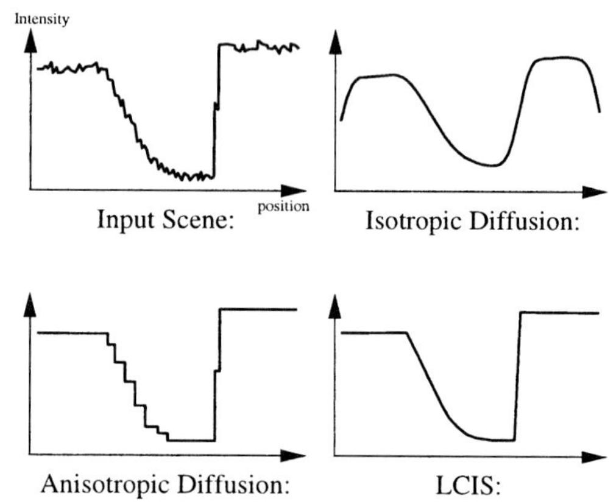


Figure 5: Isotropic diffusion uniformly smoothes the entire image; anisotropic diffusion forms step-like shocks at persistent high gradients and smoothes away all intensity variations between them, sometimes forming "stair-steps" [20]; but LCIS forms ridge-like shocks at persistent high curvatures and smoothes away the gradient variations between them.

smoothing, and proposed that conductance should vary inversely with a local "edginess" estimate to find, preserve, and sharpen image edges. This edginess value is a measure of the likelihood that a point is near an edge or boundary. Low conductance at likely edge locations and high conductances elsewhere preserves 'edgy' features, yet rapidly smoothes away the details and textures between them, and simple edginess estimates work well. They used gradient magnitude scalar $||\nabla I||$ and offered two inverse functions to find variable conductance $C(x, y, t)$. Thus anisotropic diffusion is:

$$I_t = \nabla \cdot (C(x,y,t)\nabla I) \tag{3}$$

$$= \frac{\partial}{\partial x}(CI_x) + \frac{\partial}{\partial y}(CI_y) \tag{4}$$

where $C(x,y,t) = g(||\nabla I||) = g\left(\sqrt{I_x^2 + I_y^2}\right)$, and (chosen from Perona and Malik [10]):

$$g(m) = \frac{1}{1 + \left(\frac{m}{K}\right)^2}, \tag{5}$$

where $K$ is the "conductance threshold" for $m$.

Anisotropic diffusion is especially interesting because both its edge-preserving and its smoothing abilities are self-reinforcing, as illustrated in Figure 4. Small-gradient regions have high conductance, allowing easy fluid flow that further reduces gradients. Large-gradient regions have low conductance, discouraging flow as if forming a weak barrier. However, higher conductances of its surroundings let fluid erode and steepen the already large gradients. Heat fluid seeps inwards towards the "uphill" side of the barrier, and fluid quickly drains away from the "downhill" side, making the large gradient region narrower and steeper, strengthening its barrier effect. The region quickly evolves into a step-wise discontinuity with infinite gradient and zero conductance known as a "shock.". As a result, anisotropic diffusion transforms an image into a piecewise constant approximation with step-like discontinuities in regions of high 'edginess'.

More importantly, the self-reinforcing behaviors of anisotropic diffusion improve its performance as a boundary finder. Gradient magnitudes much larger than the "gradient threshold" $K$ in Equation 5 will consistently form shocks, but the boundary/not-boundary decision is not a simple threshold testing process. Image behavior at points where gradient magnitude is near $K$ is strongly influenced by image surroundings; gradients less than $K$ may still form shocks if another shock is forming nearby, and small, isolated fine details with gradients greater than $K$ are still smoothed away. Thus anisotropic diffusion finds boundaries according to both their gradients and their surroundings, sharpens the boundaries to create shocks, and smoothes away all textures and details between them.

Though numerically stable and guaranteed to converge to a piecewise-constant solution as $t \to \infty$, Nitzberg and Shiota [8] and others have shown that anisotropic diffusion is ill-posed; infinitesimal changes in input can cause very large changes in output due to the shock-forming process. Shocks usually form at local gradient maxima and follow image boundaries closely, but this is not always true. Regions of high, approximately uniform gradient may develop shocks anywhere within the region. Instead of a single large, centrally placed shock, anisotropic diffusion may develop multiple shocks placed seemingly at random, causing "stairsteps" in the region as shown in Figure 4 and explored by Whitaker and Pizer [20].

Inspired by anisotropic diffusion, we have created a related set of PDEs that capture its self-reinforced smoothing and shock-forming behavior, but is driven by higher derivatives of the image $I$. Instead of evolving an image towards a piecewise constant approximation by driving all gradients towards zero or infinity, our equations smooth and sharpen an image towards a piecewise linear approximation by driving all curvatures towards zero or infinity. Because boundary conditions usually prevent a zero curvature solution, we call our method a "low curvature image simplifier"(LCIS).

As with anisotropic diffusion, LCIS equations describe fluid flow, but both the motive force pushing the fluid and the variable conductances permitting flow are computed differently. The "motive force" of anisotropic diffusion is the negative gradient $-\nabla I$, but LCIS pushes fluids to encourage uniform gradients; it pushes outwards from intensity peaks or ridges with negative curvature and inwards towards pits or hollows with positive curvature. Therefore the LCIS motive force vector should follow positive derivatives of curvature, but these form a tensor with no obvious single direction. Instead, we define the motive force vector using simpler directional derivatives and vector integration. To evaluate the motive force at image point $I(x_0, y_0)$, we first define a 1-D line $L$ through the point with orientation $\theta$ and signed distance parameter $\alpha$ along line $L$. We evaluate the image $I$ along line $L$ and find its third derivative $I_{\alpha\alpha\alpha}$ as a measure of curvature change in the direction given by $\theta$:

$$A = x_0 + \alpha \cos\theta, \tag{6}$$

$$B = y_0 + \alpha \sin\theta. \tag{7}$$

$$I_\alpha(A,B) = I_x(A,B)\cos\theta + I_y(A,B)\sin\theta$$

$$= \left(\left(\frac{\partial}{\partial x}\right)\cdot\cos\theta + \left(\frac{\partial}{\partial y}\right)\cdot\sin\theta\right) I. \quad (8)$$

$$I_{\alpha\alpha\alpha} = \left(\left(\frac{\partial}{\partial x}\right)\cdot\cos\theta + \left(\frac{\partial}{\partial y}\right)\cdot\sin\theta\right)^3 I, \quad (9)$$

where $(A, B)$ are $(x, y)$ coordinates of line $L(\alpha)$, $I_\alpha$ is the directional derivative of $I$ along line $L$, and $I_{\alpha\alpha\alpha}$ is the third derivative of $I$ along line $L$.

If $I_{\alpha\alpha\alpha} > 0$, then the curvature $I_{\alpha\alpha}$ is increasing along line $L$ as it passes through point $(x_0, y_0)$; flow in that direction would help equalize curvatures on either side of the point and reduce $I_{\alpha\alpha\alpha}$. Accordingly, we let $I_{\alpha\alpha\alpha}$ define the strength of an infinitesimal motive force vector along line $L$, and we sum up these tiny forces for all orientations $\theta$ to find the force vector's $x$ and $y$ components, labeled "East" and "North" to avoid confusion with partial derivatives, and given by: $\boldsymbol{F} = (f_E, f_N)$;

$$f_E = \frac{1}{\pi}\int_0^{2\pi} I_{\alpha\alpha\alpha}\cos\theta d\theta = \frac{3}{4}(I_{xxx} + I_{yyx}), \quad (10)$$

$$f_N = \frac{1}{\pi}\int_0^{2\pi} I_{\alpha\alpha\alpha}\sin\theta d\theta = \frac{3}{4}(I_{xxy} + I_{yyy}). \quad (11)$$

For LCIS conductance, we use Equation 5 from anisotropic diffusion, but now the $m$ argument is given by a new "edginess" estimate. As our desired ridge-like shocks have infinite curvature, we construct $m$ from a non-directional measure of curvature magnitude: $m^2 = 0.5(I_{xx}^2 + Iyy^2) + I_{xy}^2$. Our "low curvature image simplifier" is then defined as:

$$I_t(x, y, t) = \nabla \cdot (C(x, y, t)\boldsymbol{F}(x, y, t)) \quad (12)$$

where $\boldsymbol{F}(x, y, t)$ is the motive force vector computed from partial derivatives and given by $\boldsymbol{F} = (f_E, f_N) = (I_{xxx} + I_{yyx}, I_{xxy} + I_{yyy})$, and conductance $C(x, y, t) = g(m)$ is computed from "edginess" $m$ using Equation 5.

Low curvature image simplifiers (LCIS) share several important properties with anisotropic diffusion. Equation 12 is adiabatic; intensity neither created nor destroyed. LCIS meets the goals set forth by Perona and Malik [10]; varying its conductance threshold $K$ defines a continuous scale space that exhibits causality, immediate localization, and piecewise smoothing. Conductance is inversely linked with the motive force, causing rapid shock formation at image boundaries, and smoothing between boundaries is self-reinforcing, though asymptotic. Unlike anisotropic diffusion, LCIS shocks are discontinuities in gradient instead of intensity; they form ridge-like features that appear step-like when adjacent. Just as large high gradient regions can cause multiple shocks or "stairstepping" in anisotropic diffusion results, LCIS can also form multiple shocks unpredictably in large regions of uniform high curvature. However, high curvature regions tend to be smaller due to the larger intensity range they require, and we have found that multiple ridge-like shocks are far less visually apparent than stairsteps. Finally, both anisotropic diffusion and LCIS are formally defined for continuously variable $(x, y)$. Any practical implementations must use discrete approximations.

## 4 LCIS Implementation

Our pixel-based LCIS approximation is straightforward to implement. We use explicit integration with a fixed timestep to find $I(t)$, compute a new image on each timestep, assume constant conductance and flux during each timestep, and compute flux only between 4-connected neighboring pixels. The computation is entirely local; each new image is computed only from pixels in the previous timestep's image, and each new pixel is computed from a fixed set of neighboring pixels in the previous image.

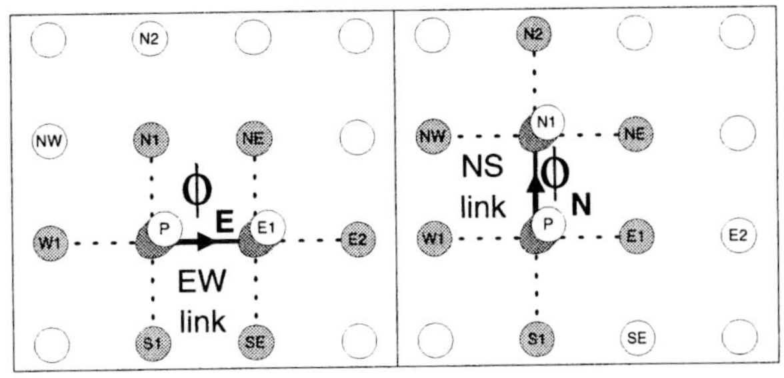


Figure 6: LCIS transfers intensity through "links" between pixels. On each timestep, flux $\phi_E$,$\phi_N$ flows through $EW$ and $NS$ links respectively, computed from the gray-shaded pixels.

Continuing with the fluid flow analogy, imagine that each pixel is a tank holding a fluid volume equal to the pixel intensity. Each pixel reservoir is tied to each of its four-connected neighbors through separate pipelines or "links." As shown in Figure 6, pixel $P$ has links to pixels $E1$, $N1$, $W1$, and $S1$. During a fixed timestep $T$ we transfer a fluid quantity "flux" $\phi$ through a link, decreasing the source pixel intensity and increasing the destination. On each timestep we compute flux for each link and then adjust the current image by the flux amounts to create a new output image.

The left and right sides of Figure 6 show the two types of links. The drawing on the left shows an $EW$ link connecting pixels $P$ and $E1$. The flux $\phi_E$ that flows through this $EW$ link is computed from the values of eight neighborhood pixels shown in gray and connected by dotted lines. The sign of $\phi$ determines flow direction: $\phi_E > 0$ flows in the $+x$ direction, which lowers the intensity of pixel $P$ and increases pixel $E1$ by the same amount. Similarly, link $NS$ connects pixels $P$ and $N1$, and positive flux $\phi_N$ flows in $+y$ direction to diminish $P$ and increase $N1$.

Motive force through each link is found from forward-difference estimates of third partial derivatives of the image at each link center. For the $EW$ link between pixels $P$ and $E1$:

$$I_{xxx} = (E2 - W1) + 3(P - E1), \quad (13)$$
$$I_{yyx} = (NE - N1) + (SE - S1) + 2(P - E1), \quad (14)$$

and for the $NS$ link between $P$ to $N1$,

$$I_{yyy} = (N2 - S1) + 3(P - N1), \quad (15)$$
$$I_{xxy} = (NE - E1) + (NW - W1) + 2(P - N1). \quad (16)$$

Conductance of each link is found from forward difference estimates of second partial derivatives. We define:

$$P_{xx} = E1 + W1 - 2P, \qquad P_{yy} = N1 + S1 - 2P,$$
$$E_{xx} = E2 + P - 2E1, \qquad E_{yy} = NE + SE - 2E1,$$
$$N_{xx} = NE + NW - 2N1, \qquad N_{yy} = N2 + P - 2N1,$$

and

$$N_{xy} = (NE - E1) - (N1 - P),$$
$$S_{xy} = (E1 - SE) - (P - S1),$$
$$W_{xy} = (N1 - P) - (NW - W1).$$

Thus

$$m_{EW}^2 = (P_{xx}^2 + P_{yy}^2 + E_{xx}^2 + E_{yy}^2)/4 + (N_{xy}^2 + S_{xy}^2)/2 \text{ for EW links, and} \quad (17)$$

$$m_{NS}^2 = (P_{xx}^2 + P_{yy}^2 + N_{xx}^2 + N_{yy}^2)/4 + (W_{xy}^2 + N_{xy}^2)/2 \text{ for NS links.} \quad (18)$$

Assuming constant curvatures and flow rates during each timestep, the flux through each link is the product of timestep length, motive force, and conductance, given by $\phi_E = TF_EC_E$ and $\phi_N = TF_NC_N$. We recommend a timestep of $T \leq 1/32$ for stability. $F_E$ and $F_N$ are the motive forces driving $EW$ and $NS$ flux, given by $F_E = (I_{xxx} + I_{yyx})$ and $F_N = (I_{xxy} + I_{yyy})$. Conductances through $NS$ and $EW$ links are

$$C_E = \frac{1}{1 + \left(\frac{m_{EW} D_E}{K}\right)^2} \tag{19}$$

and

$$C_N = \frac{1}{1 + \left(\frac{m_{NS} D_N}{K}\right)^2}. \tag{20}$$

where $m_{EW}$, $m_{NS}$ are edginess estimates from Equations 17 and 18, $D_E$, $D_N$ are leakfix multipliers explained below, initialized to 1.0.

Estimating image derivatives with adjacent pixel differences causes "leakage" problems. Shocks in continuous images form perfectly impermeable boundaries to prevent any fluid flow across them. Though discrete images also form shocks, neither the gradients nor the curvature estimates reach infinity due to the fixed, finite spacing between pixels, allowing small fluid flows or "leaks" across boundaries that should be impermeable. Small leaks over many timesteps gradually erode the image boundaries and eventually destroy them all. Though several papers (*e.g.* [6]) offer strategies for stopping the time evolution before boundary erosion is too large, any chosen stopping time is a compromise between adequate intra-region smoothing and minimal leakage. Instead, we devised a simple leakage fix that works quite well for both discrete LCIS and anisotropic diffusion.

Our leakage fix is a single self-adjusting "leakfix multiplier" value $D_E$ or $D_N$ stored for each $EW$ or $NS$ link respectively and used in Equations 19 and 20. We noticed in Equation 5 that shock forming drives all the edginess estimates $m$ rapidly away from the conductance threshold $K$ in the earliest timesteps. Edginess estimates at boundaries are boosted towards infinity by shock formation, and self-reinforced smoothing drives all other $m$ below $K$ and towards zero. To identify and prevent leakage as an image evolves, we continually compare $m$ against $K$ to find links that cross image boundaries and should hold shocks, and we adjust $D_E$ or $D_N$ of these links to amplify their edginess estimates $m$ and drive conductance towards zero. Leakfix multipliers grow exponentially with time in links where $m$ is consistently larger than $K$, but settles rapidly back towards 1.0 if edginess falls below $K$. In our implementation, initially $D_E = 1.0$ and $D_N = 1.0$ for all pixels, then for each timestep:

$$D_E = \begin{cases} D_E(1.0 + m_{EW}) & \text{if}(m_{EW} > K), \\ 0.8D_E + 0.2 & \text{otherwise, and} \end{cases} \tag{21}$$

$$D_N = \begin{cases} D_N(1.0 + m_{NS}) & \text{if}(m_{NS} > K), \\ 0.8D_N + 0.2 & \text{otherwise.} \end{cases} \tag{22}$$

The leakage fix also provides a convenient marker for boundaries; we label any link with a leakfix multiplier greater than 10.0 as a "boundary link" that may cross a ridge-like boundary shock in the image. Even though conductance drops to zero at LCIS shocks, our analysis of continuous LCIS showed ridge-like shocks should not evolve into step-like shocks during intra-region smoothing. To prevent this divergence in our discrete implementation, we also mark the pixels on either end of a boundary link as "boundary pixels" and stop all subsequent flux into or out of these pixels; see the Proceedings CD-ROM for source code. With this simple two-part fix we have not encountered any noticeable problems with leakage or boundary erosion.

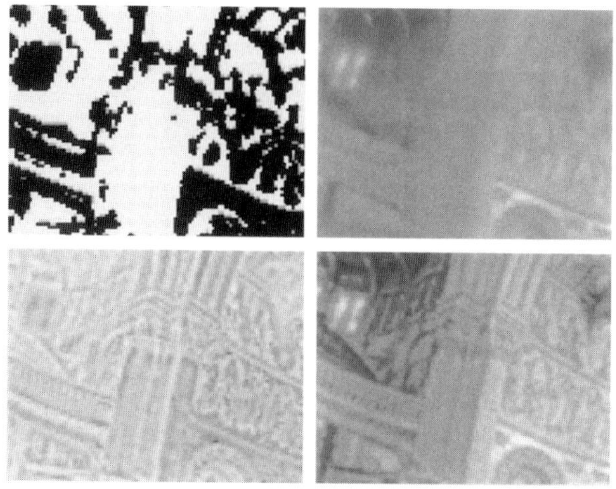

Figure 7: Images from an LCIS hierarchy reveal its methods. From a part of the church scene of Figure 9, LCIS creates a boundary pixel map (top left), and a simplified image (top right), shown after contrast compression to make it displayable. A detail image (lower left) holds the input minus the simplified image. A detailed displayable image(lower right) is the sum of images at upper right and lower left.

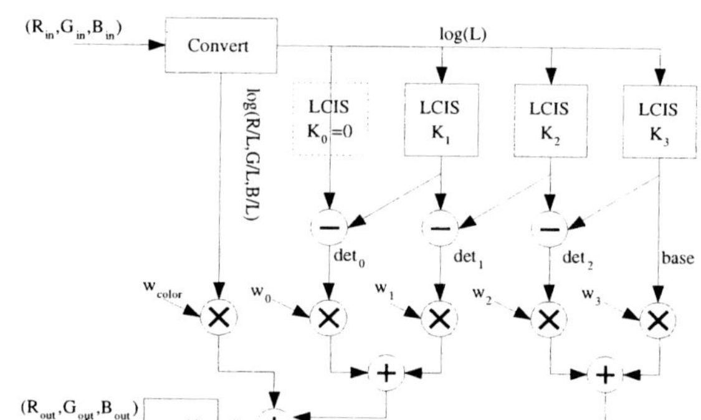


Figure 8: Detail-preserving contrast reduction method using an LCIS hierarchy, as used for Figures 1 and 9.

## 5 Contrast Reduction: LCIS Hierarchy

Discrete LCIS mimics the artist's drawing process in reverse; it selectively removes details from a scene to leave only smoothly shaded regions separated by sharp boundaries. We can easily recover the removed details by subtracting the LCIS-smoothed image from the original scene, and then follow the artists scheme for detail-preserving contrast reduction: we strongly compress the contrasts of the simplified image, then add in the details with little or no compression, as shown in Figure 7.

The LCIS hierarchy shown in Figure 8 shows the expandable multiscale form we used to make Figures 1 and 9. Just as an artist may create an image by progressive refinement, the LCIS hierarchy extracts preserved scene details with a progressive set of LCIS settings. We first convert the scene to its base-10 logarithm so that pixel differences directly correspond to contrasts (intensity ratios). Our handling of color here is rudimentary: we apply LCIS only to scene luminances and reconstruct color outputs using color ratios as suggested by Schlick [12]. Next, we make a set of progressively simpler images by applying LCIS with progressively larger $K$ values starting from zero: when $K = 0$, LCIS has no effect on the

Figure 9: These low contrast, highly detailed display images were made using an LCIS hierarchy as diagrammed in Figure 8. In the Stanford Memorial Church scene (radiance map courtesy Paul Debevec, University of California at Berkeley; see [2]), note the visible floor tile seams, wood grain, gold inlay texture, and stone arch fluting. Vast contrasts ($> 250,000 : 1$) prevent capturing all these details within a single photograph. The hotel room image, from a radiometrically accurate high contrast scene ($> 70,000 : 1$) designed and rendered by Simon Crone using RADIANCE [18], shows rich detail everywhere, even in highlights and shadows; note the floor lamp bulb and glass shade still plainly visible against the brilliant window shades, and the complex shadows on the wall and ceiling. Source Image: Proposed Burswood Hotel Suite Refurbishment (1995). Interior Design – The Marsh Partnership, Perth, Australia. Computer Simulation – Lighting Images, Perth, Australia. Copyright © 1995 Simon Crone.

input image. For the church scene in Figure 9 we used $K_1 = 0.06$, $K_2 = 0.10$ and $K_3 = 0.16$. LCIS with the largest $K$ value makes the simplest or "base" image, and we extract a graduated set of "detail" images ($det_0, det_1, ...$) by subtraction, with the finest details in $det_0$. Next, we compress their contrasts by scaling (for the church image in Figure 9 we chose $w_{0,1,2,3} = 1.0, 0.8, 0.4, 0.16$, $w_{color} = w_3$) and then add and exponentiate to find display intensities. Our test-bed software allows us to interactively adjust the parameters $K$, $w$, and the number of LCIS timesteps, and by trial and error we found 100 to 1000 timesteps and $K$ from $0.02$ to $0.32$ spanned our entire range of interest for all our test scenes. Though $w_{base}$ is dictated by desired display contrast, $w_0$ is usually best around 1.0 with intervening $w$ values between the two, none are critical; a wide range of settings provides a pleasing visual appearance and small changes are not easy to notice. Usually $w_{color} = w_{base}$ looked pleasant, but some images looked better with exaggerated values: we set $w_{base} = 0.2$ in the hotel room scene, but used $w_{color} = 0.6$ to avoid a "washed out" appearance.

## 6 Results

As shown in Figures 1 and 9, the LCIS hierarchy reveals an astonishing amount of subtle detail and scene content. Though we think the histogram-based result of Ward-Larson *et al.* [19] (also seen in [2]) is a more beautiful and natural-looking depiction of Debevec's Stanford Church radiance map, it does not include many features clearly visible in the LCIS result. For example, note the intricate gold filigree in the ceiling dome. Linear filter-based methods have difficulties with strong halo artifacts cause by the skylight nearby. LCIS also reveals rich detail in the hotel room scene; previous depictions of this scene often made the carpet and bed covering look muted and subtle, here we see strong wood, bedspread and carpet textures. The elaborate shadow details behind the plant and on the ceiling also suggests the sun and sky lighting was approximated with several point sources.

We confirmed that these details exist at these contrasts in the scene by using simple scaling and truncation to display scene radiances. In Figures 1 and 9 we include tiny versions of scaled, truncated scene radiances with $\gamma = 1.0$ and scale factor $m$ (Equation 1) increasing by a factor of 10 for each successive image to help viewers understand the scenes' huge contrasts.

Computing costs for LCIS results are moderate in our current implementation. Written in Visual C++ without regard for speed or efficiency, using 32-bit floating point values for all images and computations, our code required 14 minutes 47 seconds to compute a 187x282-pixel image of Figure 1 on a 200 MHz Pentium Pro with 128MB RAM running Windows NT4.0. This timing result includes five LCIS simplifiers computing 500 timesteps each, the auxiliary calculations diagrammed in Figure 8, and windowing and display overhead of an interactive data-flow application. Most of our tests of LCIS behavior and our choices of parameters such as curvature thresholds $K$, weighting factors $w$, and the number of timesteps were made interactively on much smaller images (often 128 x 192) where computing delays rarely exceeded 30 seconds. We found that parameter choices at low resolutions invariably worked well for much larger images, and no parameter settings needed extensive or critical tuning. Better integration methods and software tuning may also greatly improve these initial LCIS speed ratings.

## 7 Discussion and Future Work

LCIS smoothing and LCIS hierarchies offer a new way to decompose an image reversibly into a multiscale set of large features, boundaries and fine details. It permits a novel form of detail-preserving contrast reduction that avoids halo artifacts common to previous methods based on linear filtering. Detail extraction problems arise in many domains, and LCIS may also be useful for viewing other high contrast signals such as data from astronomy, radiology or seismology. The initial results images presented here are promising, but our LCIS work has many open questions and opportunities for further research. Though we found the $K$ and $w$ controls of the LCIS hierarchy easy to use, they affect the image globally; would localized, paint-box-like controls to vary them within the scene be a useful artistic tool? Conversely, how could we best apply psychophysical data to control an LCIS hierarchy automatically and perform as a true tone reproduction operator? How could a more thoughtful treatment of color better exploit the boundary and detail information it contains?

We have also discovered that even though LCIS forms sharp boundaries without smoothing across them, sometimes weak, "residual halo" artifacts can appear with strong contrast reductions. However, even the worst residual halos are far weaker than those from linear filters, and are caused by a different mechanism. Residual halos seem to form only in blurred image regions with high contrast, sparse shocks and low curvature such as a badly out-of-focus step image. If shocks do not form at the blurred boundary, LCIS further smoothes the region and reduces its curvature, causing a broad low-curvature component to appear in one or more "detail" images in Figure 8. Weak residual halos are visible in Figure 1 under the left lowermost tree branches. We are currently investigating a solution for this anomaly.

We do not yet fully understand the relationship between curvature, spatial scale, contrast, and shock formation for a given $K$, but suspect that the extensive published studies of anisotropic diffusion may offer help. Large scale, high contrast scene features such as soft shadows may have very low curvatures obscured by small scale high curvature textures; can LCIS-like methods find shocks for both? Can we ensure "reasonable" behavior for LCIS for all possible images?

Finally, extending LCIS to higher dimensions appears straightforward, and may be useful for revealing fine details in high contrast 3D scalar and vector fields or for motion estimation in high contrast scenes.

## 8 Acknowledgements

Thanks to Arno Schödl for thoughtful discussions on the continuous version of LCIS in Equation 12, and to Huong Q. Dinh for critical and timely work on image alignment for Figure 1. This work was supported in part by NSF CAREER grant CCR-9703265.

## References

[1] K. Chiu, M. Herf, P. Shirley, S. Swamy, C. Wang, and K. Zimmerman. Spatially nonuniform scaling functions for high contrast images. In *Proceedings of Graphics Interface '93*, pages 245–254, May 1993.

[2] P. E. Debevec and J. Malik. Recovering high dynamic range radiance maps from photographs. In *SIGGRAPH 97*, pages 369–378, August 1997.

[3] James. A. Ferwerda, Sumant N. Pattanaik, Peter Shirley, and Donald P. Greenberg. A model of visual adaptation for realistic image synthesis. In Holly Rushmeier, editor, *SIGGRAPH 96*, Annual Conference Series, pages 249–258, August 1996.

[4] James A. Ferwerda, Sumanta N. Pattanaik, Peter Shirley, and Donald P. Greenberg. A model of visual masking for computer graphics. In Turner Whitted, editor, *SIGGRAPH 97*, Annual Conference Series, pages 143–152, August 1997.

[5] D. J. Jobson, Z. Rahman, and G. A. Woodell. A multiscale retinex for bridging the gap between color images and the human observation of scenes. *IEEE Transactions on Image Processing*, 6(7):965–976, July 1997.

[6] X. Li and T. Chen. Nonlinear diffusion with multiple edginess thresholds. *Pattern Recognition*, 27(8):1029–1037, August 1994. Pergamon Press.

[7] E. Nakamae, K. Kaneda, T. Okamoto, and T. Nishita. A lighting model aiming at drive simulators. In *Computer Graphics (SIGGRAPH 90 Conference Proceedings)*, Annual Conference Series, pages 395–404, August 1990.

[8] M. Nitzberg and T. Shiota. Nonlinear image filtering with edge and corner enhancement. *IEEE Transactions on Pattern Analysis and Machine Intelligence*, 14(8):826–833, August 1992.

[9] Sumanta N. Pattanaik, James A. Ferwerda, Mark D. Fairchild, and Donald P. Greenberg. A multiscale model of adaptation and spatial vision for realistic image display. In Michael Cohen, editor, *SIGGRAPH 98*, Annual Conference Series, pages 287–298, July 1998.

[10] P. Perona and J. Malik. Scale-space and edge detection using anisotropic diffusion. *IEEE Transactions on Pattern Analysis and Machine Intelligence*, 12(7):629–639, July 1990.

[11] Z. Rahman, D. J. Jobson, and G. A. Woodell. Multi-scale retinex for color image enhancement. In *Proceedings, International Conference on Image Processing*, volume 3, pages 1003–1006, June 1996. Held in Lausanne, Switzerland 16-19 September 1996.

[12] C. Schlick. Quantization techniques for visualization of high dynamic range pictures. In G. Sakas, P. Shirley, and S. Mueller, editors, *Photorealistic Rendering Techniques*, Proceedings of the 5th Eurographics Rendering Workshop 13-15 June 1994, pages 7–20, Berlin, 1995. Springer Verlag.

[13] G. Spencer, P. Shirley, K. Zimmerman, and D. P. Greenberg. Physically-based glare effects for digital images. In *SIGGRAPH 95*, Annual Conference Series, pages 325–334, August 1995.

[14] T. Tanaka and N. Ohnishi. Painting-like image emphasis based on human vision systems. In D. Fellner and L Szirmay-Kalos, editors, *EUROGRAPHICS '97*, volume 16(3), pages C253–C260. The Eurographics Association, 1997.

[15] J. Tumblin, J. Hodgins, and B. Guenter. Two methods for display of high contrast images. *ACM Transactions On Graphics*, 18(1):(to appear), January 1999.

[16] J. Tumblin and H. Rushmeier. Tone reproduction for computer generated images. *IEEE Computer Graphics and Applications*, 13(6):42–48, November 1993.

[17] G. Ward. A contrast-based scalefactor for luminance display. In Paul S. Heckbert, editor, *Graphics Gems IV*, chapter Frame Buffer Techniques: VII.2, pages 415–421. AP Professional, Cambridge MA 02139, 1994.

[18] G. Ward. The RADIANCE Lighting simulation and rendering system. In *SIGGRAPH 94*, Annual Conference Series, pages 459–472, July 1994.

[19] G. Ward Larson, H. Rushmeier, and C. Piatko. A visibility matching tone reproduction operator for high dynamic range scenes. *IEEE Transactions on Visualization and Computer Graphics*, 3(4):291–306, October-December 1997.

[20] R. Whitaker and S Pizer. A multi-scale approach to nonuniform diffusion. *CVGIP: Image Understanding*, 57(1):99–110, January 1993.

# A Practical Analytic Model for Daylight

A. J. Preetham Peter Shirley Brian Smits

University of Utah www.cs.utah.edu

Figure 1: *Left: A rendered image of an outdoor scene with a constant colored sky and no aerial perspective. Right: The same image with a physically-based sky model and physically-based aerial perspective.*

## Abstract

Sunlight and skylight are rarely rendered correctly in computer graphics. A major reason for this is high computational expense. Another is that precise atmospheric data is rarely available. We present an inexpensive analytic model that approximates full spectrum daylight for various atmospheric conditions. These conditions are parameterized using terms that users can either measure or estimate. We also present an inexpensive analytic model that approximates the effects of atmosphere (aerial perspective). These models are fielded in a number of conditions and intermediate results verified against standard literature from atmospheric science. These models are analytic in the sense that they are simple formulas based on fits to simulated data; no explicit simulation is required to use them. Our goal is to achieve as much accuracy as possible without sacrificing usability.

**CR Categories:** I.3.7 [Computing Methodologies ]: Computer Graphics—Three-Dimensional Graphics and RealismColor, shading, shadowing, and texture

**Keywords:** sunlight, skylight, aerial perspective, illumination



## 1 Introduction

Most realistic rendering research has dealt with indoor scenes. Increased computing power and ubiquitous measured terrain data has made it feasible to create increasingly realistic images of outdoor scenes. However, rendering outdoor scenes is not just a matter of scaling up rendering technology originally developed for indoor scenes. Outdoor scenes differ from indoor scenes in two important aspects other than geometry: most of their illumination comes directly from the sun and sky; and the distances involved make the effects of air visible. These effects are manifested as the desaturation and color shift of distant objects and is usually known as *aerial perspective*. In this paper we present an efficient closed form approximation that captures the visually salient aspects of these phenomena and is easy to incorporate into a rendering system. Our approach is motivated by the desire to generate images of real terrain, so we pay attention to maintaining physically-based radiometry, and use input parameters that are readily available to computer graphics researchers. We feel that current approaches are either far too general and expensive to be easily used, or include too many simplifications to generate a sufficiently realistic appearance.

The importance of the phenomena modeled in this paper is emphasized in the psychology and art literature. Psychologists assert that aerial perspective is a fundamental depth cue that humans use to estimate distances, and the only absolute depth cue available for distant unfamiliar objects [10]. Painters use aerial perspective and variation in sky color in almost all landscape paintings. Da Vinci devoted an entire chapter of his notebooks to the painting of these effects [6]. He stated several characteristics that painters should capture including the whitening of the sky toward the horizon, the increasing density of aerial perspective toward the ground, and the hue shift of distant objects. Any models of the sky and aerial perspective should make sure they capture these subjective effects. The model presented in this paper does capture these effects and is careful to predict their magnitude and color as well. Rendered images with and without these effects are shown in Figure 1. The image on the right of Figure 1 was rendered using the techniques from this paper.

To produce a realistic outdoor image, we need to model the aspects of atmosphere that produce the color of the sky and the effects of aerial perspective. To be most convenient and efficient for rendering, two formulas are needed. The first should describe the spectral radiance of the sun and sky in a given direction. The second should describe how the spectral radiance of a distant object is changed as it travels through air to the viewer. Although computer graphics researchers have captured these effects by explicit modeling, there has so far been no such compact formulas that do not introduce gross simplifications (e.g., the sky is a uniform color).

While it is possible to directly simulate the appearance of a particular sky given particular detailed conditions, this is inconvenient because it is a complex and CPU-intensive task, and data for detailed conditions is generally not available. It would be more convenient to have a parameterized formula that takes input data that is generally available, or is at least possible to estimate. While such formulas exist for sky luminance, there have not been any for sky spectral radiance. Given a sky spectral radiance formula, there have been no closed-form formulas that account for accurate aerial perspective. This paper presents such a set of formulas that are parameterized by geographic location, time and date, and atmospheric conditions. The formulas are for clear and overcast skies only. While we do not present results for partially cloudy skies, our clear sky results should be useful for developing such a model.

Our formulas are parametric fits to data from simulations of the scattering in the atmosphere. These models are analytic in the sense that they are simple formulas based on fits to simulated data; no explicit simulation is required to use them. We will downplay the mechanics of our simulation which is based largely on previous work in computer graphics. Instead we emphasize a careful discussion on its underlying assumptions and accuracy as well as all material needed to implement our model. In Section 2 we review previous work on modeling the atmospheric phenomena that are responsible for the appearance of the sky and objects under natural illumination. In Section 3 we describe a new model for the spectral radiance of the sun and sky. In Section 4 we extend that model to include the effects of aerial perspective. We present images created using these models in Section 5. We discuss limitations of the models and future work in Section 6. All needed formulas and data for implementing the model are given in the appendices.

# 2 Background

Many applications use estimates of energy levels of skylight and sunlight to aid in simulation. For this reason modeling skylight has been studied in many fields over several decades. For rendering, we need a function of the form:

$$\mathit{sky} : \text{(direction, place, date/time, conditions)} \rightarrow \text{spectral radiance}.$$

Here "place" is the geographic coordinates (e.g., latitude/longitude) of the viewer. Such a formula would allow a renderer to query the sky for a color in a specific direction for either display or illumination computation. The spectral radiance of the sun should in principle be given by a compatible formula.

In this section we review previous approaches to generating formulas related to the sky function above. We will see that no efficient formula of the form of *sky* has previously appeared, but that many techniques are available that bring us close to that result.

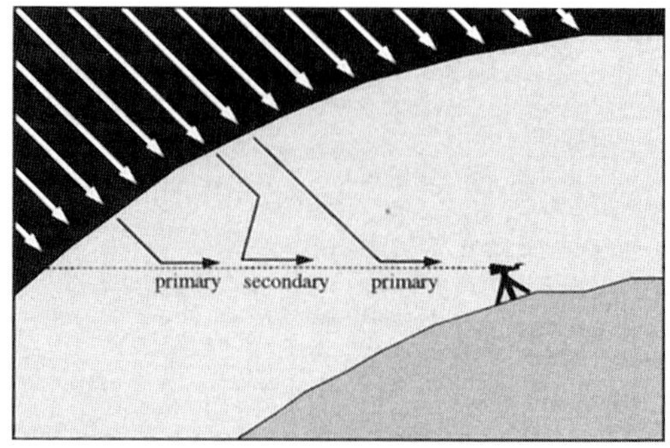


Figure 2: *The earth's atmosphere receives almost parallel illumination from the sun. This light is scattered into the viewing direction so that the sky appears to have an intrinsic color. Light may scatter several times on the way to the viewer, although primary scattering typically dominates.*

## 2.1 Atmospheric Phenomena

The visually rich appearance of the sky is due to sunlight scattered by a variety of mechanisms (Figure 2). These mechanisms are described in detail in the classic book by Minnaert [22], and with several extensions in the more recent book by Lynch and Livingston [19]. For a clear sky, various types of atmospheric particles are responsible for the scattering. Because the scattering is not necessarily the same for all light wavelengths, the sky takes on varying hues.

The details of the scattering depend on what types of particles are in the atmosphere. Rayleigh developed a theory for scattering by air molecules less than $0.1\lambda$ in diameter [28]. The crux of the theory is that the monochromatic optical extinction coefficient varies approximately as $\lambda^{-4}$, and this has been verified experimentally. This means that blue light (400nm) is scattered approximately ten times as much as red light (700nm), which is the usual explanation for why the sky is blue. Because the short wavelengths in sunlight are preferentially scattered by the same effect, sunlight tends to become yellow or orange, especially when low in the sky because more atmosphere is traversed by the sunlight on the way to the viewer.

Although Rayleigh scattering does explain much of the sky's appearance, scattering from haze is also important. The term *haze* refers to an atmosphere that scatters more than molecules alone, but less than fog [21]. Haze is often referred to as a *haze aerosol* because the extra scattering is due to particles suspended in the molecular gas. These particles are typically much bigger than molecules, and Mie scattering models the scattering behavior of these particles. Because the haze particles typically scatter more uniformly than molecules for all wavelengths, haze causes a whitening of the sky. The actual particles come from many sources – volcanic eruptions, forest fires, cosmic bombardment, the oceans – and it is very difficult to precisely characterize the haze of a given sky. Many researchers, starting with Angstrom, have attempted to describe haze using a single heuristic parameter. In the atmospheric sciences literature, the parameter *turbidity* is used [21].

Turbidity is a measure of the fraction of scattering due to haze as opposed to molecules. This is a convenient quantity because it can be estimated based on visibility of distant objects. More formally, turbidity $T$ is the ratio of the optical thickness of the haze atmosphere (haze particles and molecules) to the optical thickness of the atmosphere with molecules alone:

$$T = (t_m + t_h)/t_m,$$

where $t_m$ is the vertical optical thickness of the molecular atmosphere, and $t_h$ is the vertical optical thickness of the haze atmosphere. Optical thickness for a given path is given by $\int_0^s \beta(x)dx$

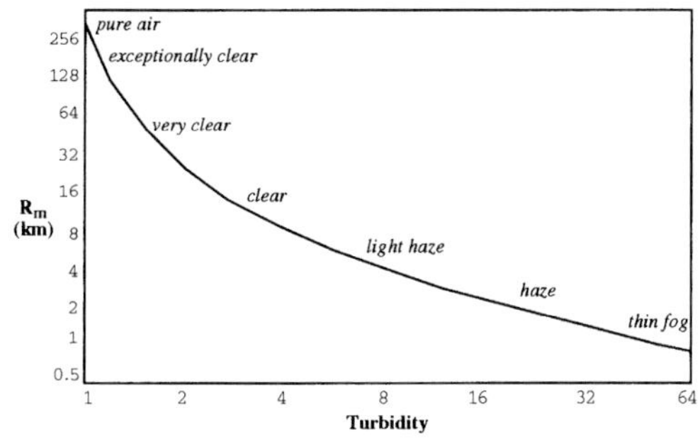


Figure 3: *Meteorological range $R_m$ for various turbidity values. Values computed from source data in McCartney [21]*

where $\beta(x)$ is the scattering coefficient (fraction scattered per meter of length traveled) which may vary along the path. Several other definitions of turbidity are used in various fields, so some care must be taken when using reported turbidity values. Since turbidity varies with wavelength, its value at 550nm is used for optical applications [21]. Turbidity can also be estimated using meteorologic range, as is shown in Figure 3. Meteorological range $R_m$ is the distance under daylight conditions at which the apparent contrast between a black target and its background (horizon sky) becomes equal to the threshold contrast ($\epsilon = 0.02$) of an observer, and it roughly corresponds to the distance to most distant discernible geographic feature.

Although turbidity is a great simplification of the true nature of the atmosphere, atmospheric scientists have found it a practical measure of great utility. Because it does not require complex instrumentation to estimate turbidity, it is particularly well-suited for application in graphics, and we use it to characterize atmospheric conditions throughout the rest of this paper.

## 2.2 Atmospheric Measurements and Simulation

One way to develop a sky model is to use measured or simulated data directly. The CIE organized the International Daylight Measurement Program (IDMP) to collect worldwide information on daylight availability. Several other efforts have collected measured data that can be used directly. The data sources do not include spectral radiance measurements, so they are not directly useful for our purposes. Ineichen et al. surveyed these data sources and compared them to analytic sky luminance models [12]. They did find that existing sky luminance models are reasonably predictive for real skies in a variety of locations around the world.

Various computer graphics researchers have simulated atmospheric effects. Blinn simulated scattering for clouds and dusty surfaces to generate their appearance [1]. Klassen used a planar layer atmospheric model and single scattering to simulate sky color [18]. Kaneda et al. employed a similar simulation using a spherical atmosphere with air density changing exponentially with altitude [15]. Nishita et al. extended this to multiple scattering to display sky color [25] and also simulated atmospheric scattering to display earth and atmosphere from space [26]. All of these methods require a lengthy simulation for a given sky condition, but they have the advantage of working with arbitrarily complex atmospheric conditions.

## 2.3 Analytic Sky Models

For simpler sky conditions, various researchers have proposed parametric models for the sky. Pokrowski proposed a formula for sky luminance (no wavelength information) based on theory and sky measurements. Kittler improved this luminance formula which was later adopted as a standard by the CIE [4]:

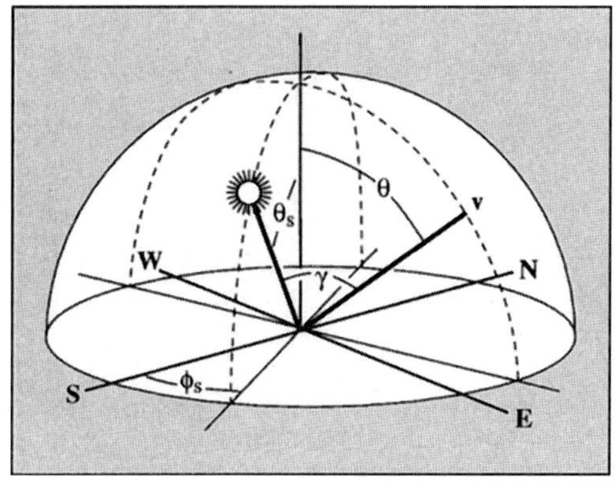


Figure 4: *The coordinates for specifying the sun position and the direction* **v** *on the sky dome.*

$$Y_z \frac{\left(0.91 + 10e^{-3\gamma} + 0.45\cos^2\gamma\right)\left(1 - e^{-0.32/\cos\theta}\right)}{\left(0.91 + 10e^{-3\theta_s} + 0.45\cos^2\theta_s\right)\left(1 - e^{-0.32}\right)}, \quad (1)$$

where $Y_z$ is the luminance at the zenith, and the geometric terms are defined in Figure 4. The zenith luminance $Y_z$ can be found in tables [17], or can be based on formulas parameterized by sun position and turbidity [4, 16].

In computer graphics, the CIE luminance formula has been used by several researchers (e.g., [23, 30]). To get spectral data for values returned by the CIE luminance formula, Takagi et al. inferred associated color temperature with luminance levels using empirical data for Japanese skies, and used this color temperature to generate a standard daylight spectrum [29]. In the *Radiance* system the luminance is multiplied by a unit luminance spectral curve that is approximately the average sky color [31].

Moon and Spencer developed a formula for the luminance distribution of overcast skies which was later adopted by the CIE [4]:

$$Y_z\left(1 + 2\cos\theta\right)/3, \quad (2)$$

There are various more complicated formulas for overcast sky luminance, but they vary only subtly from Equation 2 [17]. The zenith values for luminance of overcast skies can be found from tables [17] or from analytic results adopted by CIE [4].

To gain efficiency over brute-force simulations, while retaining the efficiency of the CIE representation, researchers have used basis functions on the hemisphere to fit simulation data. Dobashi et al. used a series of Legendre basis functions for specific sky data [7]. These basis functions can be used to fit any sky data, and does not supply a specific analytic sky model. Rather, it provides a representation and a fitting methodology for some arbitrary data set. These basis functions have the advantage of being orthogonal, but have the associated property that care must be taken to keep the approximation nonnegative everywhere. Because these basis functions are not tailored specifically for sky distributions, many terms might be needed in practice. Our work differs from that of Dobashi et al. in the choice of basis functions. More importantly, we supply the parameters resulting from our simulations, so the formulas in this paper can be used directly.

Nimeroff et al. used steerable basis functions to fit various sky luminance models including the CIE clear sky model [24]. They demonstrated that the steerable property yielded great advantage in rendering applications. They used approximately ten basis functions for their examples.

Brunger used the SKYSCAN data to devise a sky radiance model [2]. His model represented the sky radiance distribution as a

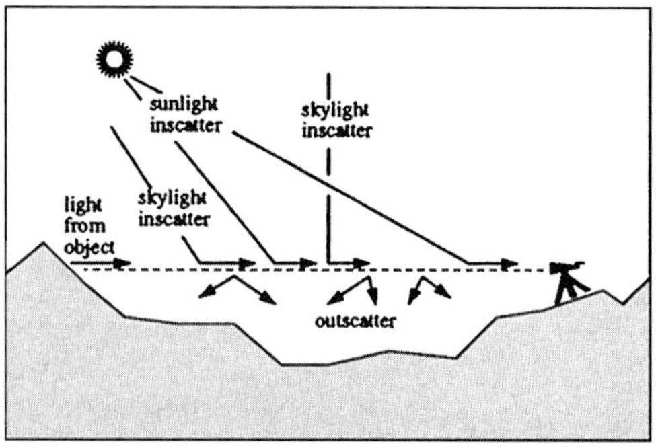


Figure 5: *The color of a distant object changes as the viewer moves away from the object. Some light is removed by out-scattering, and some is added by in-scattering.*

composition of two components, one depending on viewing angle from zenith and the other on scattering angle. An analytic radiance model is very useful for illumination engineers for energy calculations, but what the graphics community needs is a spectral radiance model and not a radiance model.

Perez et al. developed a five parameter model to describe the sky luminance distribution [27]. Each parameter has a specific physical effect on the sky distribution. The parameters relate to (a) darkening or brightening of the horizon, (b) luminance gradient near the horizon, (c) relative intensity of the circumsolar region, (d) width of the circumsolar region and (e) relative backscattered light. These basis functions can be fit to any data, and are designed to capture the overall features of sky distributions without ringing or a data explosion. Perez et al.'s model is given by:

$$\mathcal{F}(\theta,\gamma) = (1 + Ae^{B/\cos\theta})(1 + Ce^{D\gamma} + E\cos^2\gamma), \quad (3)$$

where $A, B, C, D$ and $E$ are the distribution coefficients and $\gamma$ and $\theta$ are the angles shown in Figure 4. The luminance $Y$ for sky in any viewing direction depends on the distribution function and the zenith luminance and is given by

$$Y = Y_z \mathcal{F}(\theta,\gamma)/\mathcal{F}(0,\theta_s). \quad (4)$$

The Perez model is similar to the CIE model, but has been found to be slightly more accurate if the parameters $A$ through $E$ are chosen wisely [12]. The Perez formula has been used in graphics with slight modification by Yu et al. [33].

What would be most convenient for computer graphics applications is a spectral radiance analog of Equation 1 that captures the hue variations suggested by real skies and full simulations. Such a form will be introduced in Section 3.

### 2.4 Aerial Perspective

A sky model is useful for both direct display and illuminating the ground. However, it is not directly applicable to how the atmosphere changes the appearance of distant objects (Figure 5). Unlike a sky model, aerial perspective effects cannot be stored in a simple function or precomputed table because they vary with distance and orientation. A subtlety of aerial perspective is that it can cause color shifts in any direction. Typically, it causes a blue-shift, but when the viewing direction is near the sun, it can cause a yellow-shift. It is hard to predict such color shifts without a physically-based model.

Max presented an analytic single scattering model for light scattering through haze with uniform density and a generalized result for the case of layered fog [20]. Kaneda et al. presented analytical results for fog effects where density variation of fog was exponential [15] which is a special case of Max's layered fog model. However, it is not possible to analytically solve for the extended case of air combined with haze.

Several researchers have simulated aerial perspective using explicit modeling [15, 18]. This in fact is just a particular instance of general light scattering simulation. While such techniques have the advantage of working on arbitrary atmospheric conditions, they are also computationally expensive.

Ward-Larson has implemented a simpler version of aerial perspective in the *Radiance* system [30]. He assumes a constant ambient illumination that does not vary with viewing direction. This produces an efficient global approximation to aerial perspective, but does not allow the changes in intensity and hue effects for changing viewer or sun position.

In Ebert et al., the aerial perspective effect is modeled through a simulation of single Rayleigh scattering [8]. The color of distant mountains is a linear combination of the mountain color and sky color whose weighting varies with distance. They include a sophisticated discussion of how to numerically integrate the resulting expressions. Although they restrict themselves to pure air (turbidity 1), their techniques could easily be extended to include haze because they use numeric techniques. The only shortcoming of their method is that the quadrature they perform is intrinsically costly, although they minimize that cost as much as possible.

## 3 Sunlight and Skylight

This section describes our formulas for the spectral radiance of the sun and the sky. The input to the formulas is *sun position* and *turbidity*. Sun position can be computed from latitude, longitude, time, and date using formulas given in the Appendix. We assume the *U.S. Standard Atmosphere* for our simulations. We use Elterman's data for the density profile for haze up to 32km [9].

### 3.1 Sunlight

For sunlight we use the sun's spectral radiance outside the earth's atmosphere, which is given in the Appendix. To determine how much light reaches the earth's surface we need to compute the fraction removed by scattering and absorption in the atmosphere. Sunlight is scattered by molecular and dust particles and absorbed by ozone, mixed gases and water vapor. In what order, this attenuation takes place does not matter because attenuation is multiplicative and thus commutative. Iqbal gives direct radiation attenuation coefficients for the various atmospheric constituents [13], so we can compute the total attenuation coefficient if we know the accumulated densities along the illumination path.

The sun's extraterrestrial spectral radiance is multiplied with the spectral attenuation due to each atmospheric constituents to give us the sun's spectral radiance at earth's surface. Transmissivity due to these constituents are given in the Appendix. To test our formulas we compared the sunlight results at turbidity two with measured values of sun chromaticity and luminance given by Wyszecki and Stiles [32]. These numbers were with two percent of each other.

### 3.2 Skylight Model

Skylight is much more complicated to model than sunlight. Given a model for the composition of the atmosphere, we can run a simulation using the methods of previous researchers. However, we would then have the data for only one turbidity and sun position. What we do is compute the sky spectral radiance function for a variety of sun positions and turbidities, and then fit a parametric function. Basic issues that must be addressed are the assumptions used for the simulation, and the parametric representation we use to fit the data.

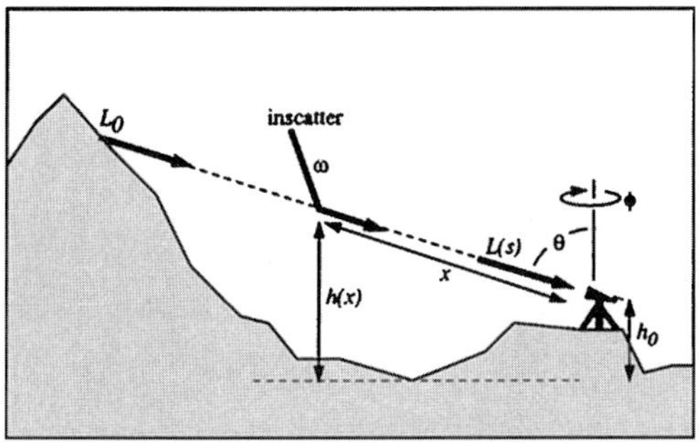


Figure 6: *The variables used to compute aerial perspective.*

For the simulation we used the method of Nishita et al. [25]. The earth was assumed flat for zenith angles less than seventy degrees and spherical for other angles. This allowed several terms to be evaluated analytically for the smaller angles. Third and higher order scattering terms were ignored as their contribution to skylight is not significant. Reflectance of light from the earth's surface was also ignored. This simulation was run for twelve sun positions and five different turbidities (2 through 6). The spectral radiance was computed for 343 directions in a sky dome for each of these combinations. Because the amount of computation required was large (about 600 CPU hours in all) a number of careful optimizations were employed to make the computation feasible such as an aggressive use of lookup tables and adaptive sampling of directions.

For our parametric formula for luminance we use Perez et al.'s formulation (Equation 4). This formulation has been battle-tested and has few enough variable that the optimization stage of the fitting process is likely to converge. We use this in preference to the CIE model because it has a slightly more general form and can thus capture more features of the simulated data. To account for spectral variation, we also fit chromatic variables. We found Perez's formulation to be a poor way to represent the CIE $X$ and $Z$ variables, but the chromaticities $x$ and $y$ are well represented with this five parameter model. The functions were fit using *Levenberg-Marquardt* non-linear least squares method in MATLab [11]. A linear function in turbidity was obtained to describe the five parameters for $Y$, $x$ and $y$. The zenith values for $Y$, $x$ and $y$ were also fit across different sun positions and turbidities.

Chromaticity values $x$ and $y$ are similarly behaved and are given by the same model. Thus,

$$x = x_z \frac{\mathcal{F}(\theta,\gamma)}{\mathcal{F}(0,\theta_s)}, \text{ and } y = y_z \frac{\mathcal{F}(\theta,\gamma)}{\mathcal{F}(0,\theta_s)},$$

where $\mathcal{F}$ is given by Equation 3 with different values of $(A, B, C, D, E)$ for $x$ and $y$. The distribution coefficients and zenith values for luminance $Y$, and chromaticities $x$ and $y$ are given in the Appendix. The luminance $Y$ and chromaticities $x$ and $y$ can be converted to spectral radiance on the fly using the CIE daylight curve method described in the Appendix.

# 4 Aerial Perspective Model

Unlike the sun and sky, aerial perspective cannot be precomputed for a given rendering. At every pixel it is a complex integral that must be evaluated numerically. Because we want to capture the subjective hue and intensity effects of aerial perspective we must preserve a reasonable degree of accuracy. But to make the problem tractable we assume a slightly simpler atmospheric model than we did for skylight: we approximate the density of the particles as exponential with respect to height. The rate of decrease is different for the two gas constituents. This does not make the aerial perspective equations solvable analytically, but it does make them tractable enough to be approximated accurately. This approximation will be described for the rest of this section. We assume that the earth is flat, which is a reasonable assumption for viewers on the ground.

Aerial perspective results when the light $L_0$ from a distant object is attenuated on the way to the viewer. In addition, light from the sun and sky can be scattered towards the viewer. This is shown in Figure 6. If $\tau$ is the extinction factor as $L_0$ travels a distance $s$ to reach the eye, and $L_{\text{in}}$ is the in-scattered light, then $L(s) = L_0\tau + L_{in}$.

Both the extinction factor $\tau$ and the in-scattered light $L_{\text{in}}$ are a result of the scattering properties of the different particles in the atmosphere. Because the scattering coefficients of particles is proportional to the density of particles, the scattering coefficients also decrease exponentially with height. Thus, $\beta(h) = \beta^0 e^{-\alpha h}$, where $\beta^0$ is the value of scattering coefficient at earth's surface and $\alpha$ is the exponential decay constant. In our case, $h$ is a function of the distance from the viewer, as shown in Figure 6, and can be represented as $h(x) = h_0 + x\cos\theta$. We can now write the expression for $\beta$ as

$$\beta(h(x)) = \beta^0 u(x), \tag{5}$$

where $u(x) = e^{-\alpha(h_0 + x\cos\theta)}$ is the ratio of density at point $x$ to the density at earth's surface. The other scattering term we need must describe the fraction of light scattered into the viewing direction $(\theta, \phi)$ from a solid angle $\omega$. This is commonly denoted $\beta(\omega, \theta, \phi, h)$. Using the same trick as for $\beta(h)$, it can be rewritten as

$$\beta(\omega, \theta, \phi, h(x)) = \beta^0(\omega, \theta, \phi)u(x). \tag{6}$$

## 4.1 Extinction Factor

The extinction factor $\tau$ can be determined directly given our assumptions of an exponential density of particles. Attenuation of light due to particles with total scattering coefficient $\beta$ over a distance $s$ is given by $e^{-\int_0^s \beta dx}$. Using equation 5 and integrating, we have

$$\tau = e^{-\int_0^s \beta^0 u(x)dx} = e^{-\beta^0 e^{-\alpha h_0} \frac{(1-e^{-\alpha\cos\theta s})}{\alpha\cos\theta}}.$$

For convenience, we make the substitutions $K = -\frac{\beta^0}{\alpha\cos\theta}$ and $H = e^{-\alpha h_0}$, allowing the extinction factor to be neatly written as $e^{-K(H-u(s))}$ for a single type of particle.

Atmosphere contains both molecules and haze, both of which scatter light. The scattering properties of a particle is independent of the presence of other particles and therefore the total attenuation due to the presence of two types of particles is equal to the product of the attenuation by each individual particles. This means the total extinction due to both these particles is

$$\tau = e^{-K_1(H_1-u_1(s))}e^{-K_2(H_2-u_2(s))}, \tag{7}$$

where the subscript "1" denotes haze particles and the subscript "2" denotes molecular particles.

## 4.2 Light Scattered into Viewing Ray

At every point on the ray, light from the sun/sky is scattered into the viewing direction. Let $L^s(\omega)$ denote the spectral radiance of sun and sky in the direction $\omega$. We can assume that the spectral radiance from sun and sky, $L^s(\omega)$ does not depend on altitude because the viewer and source are close to the earth's surface. Let $S(\theta, \phi, x)$ be the term to denote the light scattered into the viewing direction $(\theta, \phi)$ at point $x$. Using the angular scattering coefficient from equation 6, we can express the light scattered into the viewing direction at $x$ as

$$\begin{aligned} S(\theta,\phi,x) &= \int L^s(\omega)\beta(\omega,\theta,\phi,h)d\omega \\ &= \int L^s(\omega)\beta^0(\omega,\theta,\phi)u(x)d\omega \\ &= S^0(\theta,\phi)u(x), \end{aligned}$$

where $S^0(\theta,\phi) = \int L^s(\omega)\beta^0(\omega,\theta,\phi)d\omega$ is the light scattered into the viewing direction $(\theta,\phi)$ at ground level.

If we denote attenuation (equation 7) from 0 to $x$ along viewing ray as $\tau(0..x)$ then, the total light scattered into the viewing direction for a single type of particle is:

$$L_{\text{in}} = \int_0^s S(\theta,\phi,x)\tau(0..x)dx = \int_0^s S^0(\theta,\phi)u(x)\tau(0..x)dx.$$

Since there are two kinds of particles (haze and molecules), the total light scattered into viewing direction is:

$$\begin{aligned} L_{\text{in}} &= \int_0^s S_1^0(\theta,\phi)u_1(x)\tau(0..x)dx + \\ &\quad \int_0^s S_2^0(\theta,\phi)u_2(x)\tau(0..x)dx \\ &= S_1^0(\theta,\phi)I_1 + S_2^0(\theta,\phi)I_2, \end{aligned} \tag{8}$$

where $I_i = \int_0^s u_i(x)\tau(0..x)dx$. A table of $S_1^0(\theta,\phi)$ and $S_2^0(\theta,\phi)$ for different $\theta$ and $\phi$ can be precomputed thus avoiding expensive computation for every pixel.

We show how to solve $I_1$ in this paper; the solution for $I_2$ is analogous. First we expand $\tau(0..x)$ and examine the results.

$$I_1 = \int_0^s u_1(x)e^{-K_1(H_1-u_1(x))}e^{-K_2(H_2-u_2(x))}dx. \tag{9}$$

If $|\alpha s\cos\theta| \ll 1$ which would happen when the viewing ray is close to horizon or the distances considered are small, the term $e^{-K(H-u(x))} = e^{-\beta H\frac{1-e^{-\alpha x\cos\theta}}{\alpha\cos\theta}} \approx e^{-\beta Hx}$. Thus

$$\begin{aligned} I_1 &= \int_0^s u_1(x)e^{-K_1(H_1-u_1(x))}e^{-K_2(H_2-u_2(x))}dx \\ &= \int_0^s e^{-H_1}e^{-\alpha_1 x\cos\theta}e^{-\beta_1 H_1 x}e^{-\beta_2 H_2 x}dx \\ &= e^{-H_1}\frac{1-e^{-(\alpha_1\cos\theta+\beta_1 H_1+\beta_2 H_2)s}}{\alpha_1\cos\theta+\beta_1 H_1+\beta_2 H_2}. \end{aligned} \tag{10}$$

Otherwise, two different approaches could be taken to solving these integrals. The simplest and most accurate method of calculating the integrals $I_1$ and $I_2$ are by numerical integration techniques. This is too expensive for the model to remain practical. We make approximations to the expressions above to present the results in closed form. In Equation 9 we make the following substitution, $v = u_1(x) = e^{-\alpha_1(h_0+x\cos\theta)}$. Therefore, $dv = -\alpha_1\cos\theta u_1(x)dx$. We now have

$$I_1 = -\frac{1}{\alpha_1\cos\theta}\int_{u_1(0)}^{u_1(s)} e^{-K_1(H_1-v)}e^{-K_2(H_2-u_2(x))}dv.$$

We replace the term $f(x) = e^{-K_2(H_2-u_2(x))}$ with a Hermite cubic polynomial $g(v) = av^3 + bv^2 + cv + d$ so that $I_1$ is integrable in closed form. The coefficients $a$, $b$, $c$ and $d$ for the cubic equivalent are determined such that $g(v)$ interpolates the position and slope of the endpoints of $f(x)$. The resulting integral,

$$I_1 = -\frac{1}{\alpha_1\cos\theta}\int_{u_1(0)}^{u_1(s)} e^{-K_1(H_1-v)}g(v)dv, \tag{11}$$

can be integrated by parts, leaving an analytic approximation for $I_1$. This result and the coefficients for the polynomial are given in the Appendix.

## 5 Results

Our model was implemented in a C++ path tracer [14] that accepts 30m digital elevation data. All images are of a constant albedo terrain skin of approximately 4000km$^2$. The 30m resolution cells visible in the foreground of the images give an idea of scale. The implementation of the model was not carefully optimized, and slowed down the program by approximately a factor of two on a MIPS R10000 processor. The images are 1000 by 750 pixels and were run with 16 samples per pixel.

Figure 7 shows the same landscape at different times of day and turbidities for a viewer looking west. Note that near sunset, there is much warm light visible in the aerial perspective for the higher turbidities. This is as expected because the high concentrations of aerosols present at high turbidities tend to forward scatter the sunlight which has had much of the blue removed by the thick atmosphere for shallow sun angles.

We used a high value for turbidity for the last picture of Figure 7. For these high values, we would typically expect an overcast sky for such high turbidities, and this is shown in the figure using the CIE overcast sky luminance and a flat spectral curve. For intermediate turbidities our model and the overcast model should be interpolated between as recommended for the CIE luminance models. These unusual conditions are the "hazy, hot, and humid" weather familiar to the inland plains.

Figure 8 shows a comparison between the model used by Ward-Larson in the *Radiance* package and our model for a summer sky a half hour before sunset with turbidity 6. Our implementation of Ward-Larson's model uses the correct luminance but the relative spectral curve of the zenith. It correctly sets the attenuation at one kilometer and uses an exponential interpolant elsewhere. For in-scattering it uses the product of the zenith spectral radiance and the complement of the attenuation factor. This is our best estimate for setting the "ambient" in-scattering term suggested by Ward-Larson. We could certainly hand-tune this in-scattering term to produce better results for one view, but it would cause problems for other views because Ward-Larson's model does not take view direction into account. Note that for our model at sunset the east view always has a blue-shift in the hue (because of backward Rayleigh scattering), and a yellowish shift for west views depending upon turbidity. This effect is not possible to achieve with a model that does not vary with direction.

## 6 Conclusions and Future Work

We have presented a reasonably accurate analytic model of skylight that is relatively easy to use. It captures the effects of different atmospheric conditions and times of day. In the same spirit, we have presented a model for aerial perspective. The use of both models greatly enhances the realism of outdoor rendering with minimal performance penalties, which may allow widespread use of these effects for rendering.

Our models use uniform (exponential or nearly exponential) density distributions of particles. These assumptions do not hold for cloudy (or partly cloudy) skies. They also do not hold for fog or

Figure 7: *The new model looking west at different times/turbidities. Top to bottom: morning, tubididity 2; evening, turbidity 2; evening, turbidity 6; overcast, turbidity 10.*

Figure 8: *Top: the CIE clear sky model using constant chromaticity coordinates and Ward-Larson's aerial perspective approximation for east viewing directions and the same viewpoint. Bottom: the new model. Note the change in hue for different parts of the sky for the new model.*

the effects of localized pollution sources and inversion effects that often occur near some large cities. In these cases the density distribution of particles is much more complicated than in our model. In these cases, our model can be used as boundary conditions for more complex simulations.

## 7 Acknowledgments

Thanks to Sumant Pattanaik for the original CIE sky model implementation, to Chuck Hansen and the Los Alamos ACL lab for enabling computer runs, to Bill Thompson and Simon Premoze for supplying digital terrain data, and to the Utah SGI Visual Supercomputing Center for thousands of hours of CPU time. This work was supported by NSF awards 9731859 and 9720192, and the NSF STC for Computer Graphics & Visualization.

## A Appendix

Although much of the data in this appendix is available in the literature, it is not in sources readily accessible to most graphics professionals. The information here should allow users to implement our model without sources other than this paper.

## A.1 Transmittance expressions for atmospheric constituents

Simple results are given describing the attenuation of direct radiation by various atmospheric constituents using the data given by Iqbal [13]. The formulas permit atmospheric parameters such as ozone layer thickness, precipitable water vapor and turbidity to be varied independently. These results are used in the computation of sunlight received at earth's surface.

Relative optical mass $m$ is given by the following approximation, where sun angle $\theta_s$ is in radians:

$$m = \frac{1}{\cos\theta_s + 0.15 * (93.885 - \theta_s \frac{180}{\pi})^{-1.253}}.$$

Transmittance due to Rayleigh scattering of air molecules ($\tau_{r,\lambda}$), Angstrom's turbidity formula for aerosol ($\tau_{a,\lambda}$), transmittance due to ozone absorption ($\tau_{o,\lambda}$), transmittance due to mixed gases absorption ($\tau_{g,\lambda}$) and transmittance due to water vapor absorption ($\tau_{wa,\lambda}$) are given by:

$$\begin{aligned}
\tau_{r,\lambda} &= e^{-0.008735\lambda^{-4.08m}}, \\
\tau_{a,\lambda} &= e^{-\beta\lambda^{-\alpha m}}, \\
\tau_{o,\lambda} &= e^{-k_{o,\lambda} lm}, \\
\tau_{g,\lambda} &= e^{-1.41k_{g,\lambda}m/(1+118.93k_{g,\lambda}m)^{0.45}}, \\
\tau_{wa,\lambda} &= e^{-0.2385k_{wa,\lambda}wm/(1+20.07k_{wa,\lambda}wm)^{0.45}},
\end{aligned}$$

where $\beta$ is Angstrom's turbidity coefficient, $\alpha$ is the wavelength exponent, $k_{o,\lambda}$ is the attenuation coefficient for ozone absorption, $l$ is the amount of ozone in $m$ at NTP, $k_{g,\lambda}$ is the attenuation coefficient of mixed gases absorption, $k_{wa,\lambda}$ is the attenuation coefficient of water vapor absorption, $w$ is the precipitable water vapor in $m$ and $\lambda$ is the wavelength in $\mu m$. The coefficient $\beta$ varies with turbidity $T$ and is approximately given by $0.04608T - 0.04586$. As originally suggested by Angstrom, we use $\alpha = 1.3$. A value of 0.0035m for $l$ and 0.02m for $w$ is commonly used.

The spectrums $k_{o,\lambda}$, $k_{g,\lambda}$ and $k_{wa,\lambda}$ are found in Table 2.

## A.2 Skylight Distribution Coefficients and Zenith Values

The distribution coefficients vary with turbidity and the zenith values are functions of turbidity and sun position.

The coefficients for the $Y$, $x$ and $y$ distribution functions are:

$$\begin{bmatrix} A_Y \\ B_Y \\ C_Y \\ D_Y \\ E_Y \end{bmatrix} = \begin{bmatrix} 0.1787 & -1.4630 \\ -0.3554 & 0.4275 \\ -0.0227 & 5.3251 \\ 0.1206 & -2.5771 \\ -0.0670 & 0.3703 \end{bmatrix} \begin{bmatrix} T \\ 1 \end{bmatrix}$$

$$\begin{bmatrix} A_x \\ B_x \\ C_x \\ D_x \\ E_x \end{bmatrix} = \begin{bmatrix} -0.0193 & -0.2592 \\ -0.0665 & 0.0008 \\ -0.0004 & 0.2125 \\ -0.0641 & -0.8989 \\ -0.0033 & 0.0452 \end{bmatrix} \begin{bmatrix} T \\ 1 \end{bmatrix}$$

$$\begin{bmatrix} A_y \\ B_y \\ C_y \\ D_y \\ E_y \end{bmatrix} = \begin{bmatrix} -0.0167 & -0.2608 \\ -0.0950 & 0.0092 \\ -0.0079 & 0.2102 \\ -0.0441 & -1.6537 \\ -0.0109 & 0.0529 \end{bmatrix} \begin{bmatrix} T \\ 1 \end{bmatrix}$$

Absolute value of zenith luminance in K cd m$^{-2}$:

$$Y_z = (4.0453T - 4.9710)\tan\chi - 0.2155T + 2.4192,$$

| $\theta\backslash\lambda$ | 400 | 450 | 550 | 650 | 850 |
|---|---|---|---|---|---|
| 1 | 4.192 | 4.193 | 4.177 | 4.147 | 4.072 |
| 4 | 3.311 | 3.319 | 3.329 | 3.335 | 3.339 |
| 7 | 2.860 | 2.868 | 2.878 | 2.883 | 2.888 |
| 10 | 2.518 | 2.527 | 2.536 | 2.542 | 2.547 |
| 30 | 1.122 | 1.129 | 1.138 | 1.142 | 1.147 |
| 60 | 0.3324 | 0.3373 | 0.3433 | 0.3467 | 0.3502 |
| 80 | 0.1644 | 0.1682 | 0.1730 | 0.1757 | 0.1785 |
| 90 | 0.1239 | 0.1275 | 0.1320 | 0.1346 | 0.1373 |
| 110 | 0.08734 | 0.09111 | 0.09591 | 0.09871 | 0.10167 |
| 120 | 0.08242 | 0.08652 | 0.09179 | 0.09488 | 0.09816 |
| 130 | 0.08313 | 0.08767 | 0.09352 | 0.09697 | 0.10065 |
| 150 | 0.09701 | 0.1024 | 0.1095 | 0.1137 | 0.1182 |
| 180 | 0.1307 | 0.1368 | 0.1447 | 0.1495 | 0.1566 |

Table 1: Scattering term $\eta(\theta)$ for Mie scattering.

where $\chi = (\frac{4}{9} - \frac{T}{120})(\pi - 2\theta_s)$.

Zenith chromaticity ($x_z$, $y_z$):

$$x_z = \begin{bmatrix} T^2 & T & 1 \end{bmatrix} \begin{bmatrix} 0.0017 & -0.0037 & 0.0021 & 0.000 \\ -0.0290 & 0.0638 & -0.0320 & 0.0039 \\ 0.1169 & -0.2120 & 0.0605 & 0.2589 \end{bmatrix} \begin{bmatrix} \theta_s^3 \\ \theta_s^2 \\ \theta_s \\ 1 \end{bmatrix}$$

$$y_z = \begin{bmatrix} T^2 & T & 1 \end{bmatrix} \begin{bmatrix} 0.0028 & -0.0061 & 0.0032 & 0.000 \\ -0.0421 & 0.0897 & -0.0415 & 0.0052 \\ 0.1535 & -0.2676 & 0.0667 & 0.2669 \end{bmatrix} \begin{bmatrix} \theta_s^3 \\ \theta_s^2 \\ \theta_s \\ 1 \end{bmatrix}$$

## A.3 Scattering Coefficients

In scattering theory, the angular scattering coefficient and the total scattering coefficient determine how the light is scattered by particles. For our work Rayleigh scattering is used for gas molecules and Mie scattering theory is used for haze particles. Here we give the scattering coefficients for gas molecules and haze. Notice that the total scattering coefficient is the integral of angular scattering coefficient in all directions, for example $\beta = \int \beta(\theta) dw$. For an elaborate discussion on scattering, see [21, 28].

The angular and total scattering coefficients for Rayleigh scattering for molecules are:

$$\begin{aligned}
\beta_m(\theta) &= \frac{\pi^2(n^2-1)^2}{2N\lambda^4}(\frac{6+3p_n}{6-7p_n})(1+\cos^2\theta), \\
\beta_m &= \frac{8\pi^3(n^2-1)^2}{3N\lambda^4}(\frac{6+3p_n}{6-7p_n}),
\end{aligned}$$

where $n$ is refractive index of air and is 1.0003 in the visible spectrum, $N$ is number of molecules per unit volume and is 2.545x10$^{25}$ for air at 228.15K and 1013mb, $p_n$ is the depolarization factor and 0.035 is considered standard for air.

The angular and total scattering coefficients for Mie scattering for haze are:

$$\begin{aligned}
\beta_p(\theta) &= 0.434c(\frac{2\pi}{\lambda})^{v-2}\frac{1}{2}\eta(\theta), \\
\beta_p &= 0.434c\pi(\frac{2\pi}{\lambda})^{v-2}K,
\end{aligned}$$

where $c$ is the concentration factor that varies with turbidity $T$ and is $(0.6544T - 0.6510)$x10$^{-16}$ and $v$ is Junge's exponent with a value of 4 for the sky model. A table for $\eta(\theta, \lambda)$ for $v = 4$ (Source: [3]) is given in Table 1, and the spectrum for $K$ is given in Table 2.

## A.4 Aerial Perspective Formulas

The expression for aerial perspective is $L(s) = L_0\tau + L_{\text{in}}$, where $L_0$ is the spectral radiance of the distant object. The extinction factor $\tau$ is given by equation 7. The light scattered into the ray is handled differently depending upon the viewing angle $\theta$ and distance $s$. For $|\alpha s \cos\theta| \ll 1$ we use equations 10 and 8. Otherwise we need to integrate the expression from equation 11. First the integration:

$$
\begin{aligned}
I_1 &= -\frac{1}{\alpha_1 \cos\theta} \int_{u_1(0)}^{u_1(s)} e^{-K_1(H_1 - v)} g(v)\,dv \\
&= -\frac{1}{\alpha_1 \cos\theta} [e^{-K_1(H_1-v)} (\frac{g(v)}{K_1} - \frac{g'(v)}{K_1^2} + \frac{g''(v)}{K_1^3} - \frac{g'''(v)}{K_1^4})]_{H_1}^{u_1(s)} \\
&= -\frac{1}{\alpha_1 \cos\theta} ((e^{-K_1(H_1 - u_1(s))}) \times \\
&\quad (\frac{g(u_1(s))}{K_1} - \frac{g'(u_1(s))}{K_1^2} + \frac{g''(u_1(s))}{K_1^3} - \frac{g'''(u_1(s))}{K_1^4}) - \\
&\quad (\frac{g(H_1)}{K_1} - \frac{g'(H_1)}{K_1^2} + \frac{g''(H_1)}{K_1^3} - \frac{g'''(H_1)}{K_1^4}))
\end{aligned}
$$

The values of $a$, $b$, $c$, and $d$ for the function $g(v) = av^3 + bv^2 + cv + d$ to approximate $f(x) = e^{-K_2(H_2 - u_2(x))}$ where $v = u_1(x)$ are determined by the solution to the following system of linear equations:

$$
\begin{bmatrix} H_1^3 & H_1^2 & H_1 & 1 \\ u_1(s)^3 & u_1(s)^2 & u_1(s) & 1 \\ 3H_1^2 & 2H_1 & 1 & 0 \\ 3u_1(s)^2 & 2u_1(s) & 1 & 0 \end{bmatrix} \begin{bmatrix} a \\ b \\ c \\ d \end{bmatrix} = \begin{bmatrix} 1 \\ f(s) \\ f'(0) \\ f'(s) \end{bmatrix}
$$

The values for the exponential decay constant $\alpha$ are: $\alpha_{haze} = 0.8333\ \text{km}^{-1}$ and $\alpha_{molecules} = 0.1136\ \text{km}^{-1}$.

## A.5 Converting Tristimulous Values to Spectral Radiance

From Wyszecki and Stiles [32], the relative spectral radiant power $S_D(\lambda)$ of a D-illuminant is given by a linear combination of mean spectral radiant power $S_0(\lambda)$ and first two eigen vector functions $S_1(\lambda)$ and $S_2(\lambda)$ used in calculating daylight illuminants. $S_D(\lambda) = S_0(\lambda) + M_1 S_1(\lambda) + M_2 S_2(\lambda)$. Scalar multiples $M_1$ and $M_2$ are functions of chromaticity values $x$ and $y$ and are given by

$$
\begin{aligned}
M_1 &= \frac{-1.3515 - 1.7703x + 5.9114y}{0.0241 + 0.2562x - 0.7341y}, \\
M_2 &= \frac{0.0300 - 31.4424x + 30.0717y}{0.0241 + 0.2562x - 0.7341y}.
\end{aligned}
$$

## A.6 Sun Position

Sun position is given by angle from zenith ($\theta_s$) and azimuth angle ($\phi_s$) and they depend on the time of the day, date, latitude and longitude (see Figure 4). Solar time can be calculated from the standard time by using the formula

$$
t = t_s + 0.170 \sin(\frac{4\pi(J - 80)}{373}) - 0.129 \sin(\frac{2\pi(J - 8)}{355}) + \frac{12(SM - L)}{\pi},
$$

where $t$ is solar time in decimal hours, $t_s$ is standard time in decimal hours, $SM$ is standard meridian for the time zone in radians, $L$ is site longitude in radians and $J$ is Julian date (the day of the year as an integer in the range 1 to 365).

The solar declination ($\delta$) in radians is approximated by

$$
\delta = 0.4093 \sin(\frac{2\pi(J - 81)}{368}).
$$

| $\lambda$ $(nm)$ | $K$ | $S_0$ | $S_1$ | $S_2$ | Sun rad. | $k_o$ | $k_{wa}$ | $k_g$ |
|---|---|---|---|---|---|---|---|---|
| 380 | 0.650 | 63.4 | 38.5 | 3 | 16559 | - | - | - |
| 390 | 0.653 | 65.8 | 35 | 1.2 | 16233.7 | - | - | - |
| 400 | 0.656 | 94.8 | 43.4 | -1.1 | 21127.5 | - | - | - |
| 410 | 0.658 | 104.8 | 46.3 | -0.5 | 25888.2 | - | - | - |
| 420 | 0.661 | 105.9 | 43.9 | -0.7 | 25829.1 | - | - | - |
| 430 | 0.662 | 96.8 | 37.1 | -1.2 | 24232.3 | - | - | - |
| 440 | 0.663 | 113.9 | 36.7 | -2.6 | 26760.5 | - | - | - |
| 450 | 0.666 | 125.6 | 35.9 | -2.9 | 29658.3 | 0.3 | - | - |
| 460 | 0.667 | 125.5 | 32.6 | -2.8 | 30545.4 | 0.6 | - | - |
| 470 | 0.669 | 121.3 | 27.9 | -2.6 | 30057.5 | 0.9 | - | - |
| 480 | 0.670 | 121.3 | 24.3 | -2.6 | 30663.7 | 1.4 | - | - |
| 490 | 0.671 | 113.5 | 20.1 | -1.8 | 28830.4 | 2.1 | - | - |
| 500 | 0.672 | 113.1 | 16.2 | -1.5 | 28712.1 | 3 | - | - |
| 510 | 0.673 | 110.8 | 13.2 | -1.3 | 27825 | 4 | - | - |
| 520 | 0.674 | 106.5 | 8.6 | -1.2 | 27100.6 | 4.8 | - | - |
| 530 | 0.676 | 108.8 | 6.1 | -1 | 27233.6 | 6.3 | - | - |
| 540 | 0.677 | 105.3 | 4.2 | -0.5 | 26361.3 | 7.5 | - | - |
| 550 | 0.678 | 104.4 | 1.9 | -0.3 | 25503.8 | 8.5 | - | - |
| 560 | 0.679 | 100 | 0 | 0 | 25060.2 | 10.3 | - | - |
| 570 | 0.679 | 96 | -1.6 | 0.2 | 25311.6 | 12 | - | - |
| 580 | 0.680 | 95.1 | -3.5 | 0.5 | 25355.9 | 12 | - | - |
| 590 | 0.681 | 89.1 | -3.5 | 2.1 | 25134.2 | 11.5 | - | - |
| 600 | 0.682 | 90.5 | -5.8 | 3.2 | 24631.5 | 12.5 | - | - |
| 610 | 0.682 | 90.3 | -7.2 | 4.1 | 24173.2 | 12 | - | - |
| 620 | 0.683 | 88.4 | -8.6 | 4.7 | 23685.3 | 10.5 | - | - |
| 630 | 0.684 | 84 | -9.5 | 5.1 | 23212.1 | 9 | - | - |
| 640 | 0.684 | 85.1 | -10.9 | 6.7 | 22827.7 | 7.9 | - | - |
| 650 | 0.685 | 81.9 | -10.7 | 7.3 | 22339.8 | 6.7 | - | - |
| 660 | 0.685 | 82.6 | -12 | 8.6 | 21970.2 | 5.7 | - | - |
| 670 | 0.685 | 84.9 | -14 | 9.8 | 21526.7 | 4.8 | - | - |
| 680 | 0.686 | 81.3 | -13.6 | 10.2 | 21097.9 | 3.6 | - | - |
| 690 | 0.686 | 71.9 | -12 | 8.3 | 20728.3 | 2.8 | 1.6 | - |
| 700 | 0.687 | 74.3 | -13.3 | 9.6 | 20240.4 | 2.3 | 2.4 | - |
| 710 | 0.687 | 76.4 | -12.9 | 8.5 | 19870.8 | 1.8 | 1.25 | - |
| 720 | 0.688 | 63.3 | -10.6 | 7 | 19427.2 | 1.4 | 100 | - |
| 730 | 0.688 | 71.7 | -11.6 | 7.6 | 19072.4 | 1.1 | 87 | - |
| 740 | 0.689 | 77 | -12.2 | 8 | 18628.9 | 1 | 6.1 | - |
| 750 | 0.689 | 65.2 | -10.2 | 6.7 | 18259.2 | 0.9 | 0.1 | - |
| 760 | 0.689 | 47.7 | -7.8 | 5.2 | - | 0.7 | 1e-03 | 3.0 |
| 770 | 0.689 | 68.6 | -11.2 | 7.4 | - | 0.4 | 1e-03 | 0.21 |
| 780 | 0.689 | 65 | -10.4 | 6.8 | - | - | 0.06 | - |

Table 2: Spectral quantities used in the model (SI units).

Solar position ($\theta_s$, $\phi_s$) can be computed from the solar declination angle, latitude and longitude.

$$
\begin{aligned}
\theta_s &= \frac{\pi}{2} - \arcsin(\sin l \sin\delta - \cos l \cos\delta \cos\frac{\pi t}{12}), \\
\phi_s &= \arctan(\frac{-\cos\delta \sin\frac{\pi t}{12}}{\cos l \sin\delta - \sin l \cos\delta \cos\frac{\pi t}{12}}),
\end{aligned}
$$

where $\theta_s$ is solar angle from zenith in radians, $\phi_s$ is solar azimuth in radians, $l$ is site latitude in radians, $\delta$ is solar declination in radians and $t$ is solar time in decimal hours. Solar angles from zenith are between 0 and $\pi/2$ and angles above $\pi/2$ indicate sun below horizon. Positive solar azimuthal angles represent direction west of south.

## A.7 Spectra

There are several spectral quantities used in the model: K for $v = 4$ used in the calculation of Mie scattering coefficient; $S_0, S_1, S_2$ spectrums [32]; the sun's spectral radiance in $\text{Wm}^{-2}\text{nm}^{-1}\text{sr}^{-1}$. The latter was calculated from the spectral distribution of solar radiation incident at top of the atmosphere as adopted by NASA as a standard for use in engineering design [5]. These quantities can be found in Table 2. The spectral curves $k_o$ in $\text{m}^{-1}$, $k_{wa}$ in $\text{m}^{-1}$ and $k_g$ used in the sunlight computation are also listed (Source: [13]).

## References


[1] BLINN, J. F. Light reflection functions for simulation of clouds and dusty surfaces. vol. 16, pp. 21–29.

[2] BRUNGER, A. P., AND HOOPER, F. C. Anisotropic sky radiance model based on narrow field of view measurements of shortwave radiance. *Solar Energy* (1993).

[3] BULLRICH, K. Scattered radiation in the atmosphere. In *Advances in Geophysics*, vol. 10. 1964.

[4] CIE-110-1994. Spatial distribution of daylight - luminance distributions of various reference skies. Tech. rep., International Commission on Illumination, 1994.

[5] COULSON, K. L. *Solar and Terrestrial Radiation*. Academic Press, 1975.

[6] DA VINCI, L. *The Notebooks of Leonardo da Vinci*, vol. 1. Dover, 1970.

[7] DOBASHI, Y., NISHITA, T., KANEDA, K., AND YAMASHITA, H. Fast display method of sky color using basis functions. In *Pacific Graphics '95* (Aug. 1995).

[8] EBERT, D., MUSGRAVE, K., PEACHEY, D., PERLIN, K., AND WORLEY. *Texturing and Modeling: A Procedural Approach*, second ed. Academic Press, 1998.

[9] ELTERMAN, L. Aerosol measurements in the troposphere and stratosphere. *Applied Optics 5*, 11 (November 1966), 1769–1776.

[10] GOLDSTEIN, E. B. *Sensation and Perception*. Wadsworth, 1980.

[11] GRACE, A. *Optimization Toolbox for use with MATLAB: User's Guide*. The Math Works Inc., 1992.

[12] INEICHEN, P., MOLINEAUX, B., AND PEREZ, R. Sky luminance data validation: comparison of seven models with four data banks. *Solar Energy 52*, 4 (1994), 337–346.

[13] IQBAL, M. *An Introduction to Solar Radiation*. Academic Press, 1983.

[14] KAJIYA, J. T. The rendering equation. In *Computer Graphics (SIGGRAPH '86 Proceedings)* (Aug. 1986), D. C. Evans and R. J. Athay, Eds., vol. 20, pp. 143–150.

[15] KANEDA, K., OKAMOTO, T., NAKAME, E., AND NISHITA, T. Photorealistic image synthesis for outdoor scenery under various atmospheric conditions. *The Visual Computer 7*, 5 and 6 (1991), 247–258.

[16] KARAYEL, M., NAVVAB, M., NE'EMAN, E., AND SELKOWITZ, S. Zenith luminance and sky luminance distributions for daylighting calculations. *Energy and Buildings 6*, 3 (1984), 283–291.

[17] KAUFMAN, J. E., Ed. *The Illumination Engineering Society Lighting Handbook, Reference Volume*. Waverly Press, Baltimore, MD, 1984.

[18] KLASSEN, R. V. Modeling the effect of the atmosphere on light. *ACM Transactions on Graphics 6*, 3 (1987), 215–237.

[19] LYNCH, D. K., AND LIVINGSTON, W. *Color and Light in Nature*. Cambridge University Press, 1995.

[20] MAX, N. L. Atmospheric illumination and shadows. In *Computer Graphics (SIGGRAPH '86 Proceedings)* (Aug. 1986),' vol. 20, pp. 117–24.

[21] MCCARTNEY, E. J. *Optics of the Atmosphere*. Wiley publication, 1976.

[22] MINNAERT, M. *Light and Color in the Open Air*. Dover, 1954.

[23] NAKAMAE, E., KANEDA, K., OKAMOTO, T., AND NISHITA, T. A lighting model aiming at drive simulators. In *Computer Graphics (SIGGRAPH '90 Proceedings)* (Aug. 1990), F. Baskett, Ed., vol. 24, pp. 395–404.

[24] NIMEROFF, J., DORSEY, J., AND RUSHMEIER, H. Implementation and analysis of an image-based global illumination framework for animated environments. *IEEE Transactions on Visualization and Computer Graphics 2*, 4 (Dec. 1996). ISSN 1077-2626.

[25] NISHITA, T., DOBASHI, Y., KANEDA, K., AND YAMASHITA, H. Display method of the sky color taking into account multiple scattering. In *Pacific Graphics '96* (1996), pp. 117–132.

[26] NISHITA, T., SIRAI, T., TADAMURA, K., AND NAKAMAE, E. Display of the earth taking into account atmospheric scattering. In *Computer Graphics (SIGGRAPH '93 Proceedings)* (Aug. 1993), J. T. Kajiya, Ed., vol. 27, pp. 175–182.

[27] R. PEREZ, R. SEALS, J. M., AND INEICHEN, P. An all-weather model for sky luminance distribution. *Solar Energy* (1993).

[28] RAYLEIGH, L. On the scattering of light by small particles. *Philosophical Magazine 41* (1871), 447–454.

[29] TAKAGI, A., TAKAOKA, H., OSHIMA, T., AND OGATA, Y. Accurate rendering technique based on colorimetric conception. In *Computer Graphics (SIGGRAPH '90 Proceedings)* (Aug. 1990), F. Baskett, Ed., vol. 24, pp. 263–272.

[30] WARD, G. J. The RADIANCE lighting simulation and rendering system. In *Proceedings of SIGGRAPH '94 (Orlando, Florida, July 24–29, 1994)* (July 1994), A. Glassner, Ed., Computer Graphics Proceedings, Annual Conference Series, ACM SIGGRAPH, ACM Press, pp. 459–472. ISBN 0-89791-667-0.

[31] WARD-LARSON, G. Personal Communication, 1998.

[32] WYSZECKI, G., AND W.S.STILES. *Color Science*. Wiley-Interscience publication, 1982.

[33] YU, Y., AND MALIK, J. Recovering photometric properties of architectural scenes from photographs. In *SIGGRAPH 98 Conference Proceedings* (July 1998), M. Cohen, Ed., Annual Conference Series, ACM SIGGRAPH, Addison Wesley, pp. 207–218. ISBN 0-89791-999-8.

# Diffraction Shaders

Jos Stam*

Alias | wavefront

## Abstract

The reflection of light from surfaces is a fundamental problem in computer graphics. Although many reflection models have been proposed, few take into account the wave nature of light. In this paper, we derive a new class of reflection models for metallic surfaces that handle the effects of diffraction. Diffraction is a purely wave-like phenomenon and cannot be properly modeled using the ray theory of light alone. A common example of a surface which exhibits diffraction is the compact disk. A characteristic of such surfaces is that they reflect light in a very colorful manner. Our model is also a generalization of most reflection models encountered in computer graphics. In particular, we extend the He-Torrance model to handle anisotropic reflections. This is achieved by rederiving, in a more general setting, results from surface wave physics which were taken for granted by other researchers. Specifically, our use of Fourier analysis has enabled us to tackle the difficult task of analytically computing the Kirchhoff integral of surface scattering.

**CR Categories:** I.3.7 [Computer Graphics]: Three-Dimensional Graphics and Realism—Color, shading, shadowing, and texture J.2 [Physical Sciences and Engineering]: Physics

**Keywords:** shading models, diffraction, Fourier transform, Kirchhoff theory, rough surface scattering, random processes

## 1 Introduction

The modeling of the interaction of light with surfaces is one of the main goals of computer graphics. Over the last thirty years many reflection models have been proposed that have considerably improved the quality of computer graphics imagery. Almost all of these reflection models are either empirical or based on the ray theory of light. Surprisingly little attention has been devoted to the purely wave-like character of light. It is well known from physical optics that ray theory is only an approximation of the more fundamental wave theory. Why then has wave theory been so neglected ? The main reason is that the ray theory is sufficient to visually capture the reflected field from many commonly occurring surfaces. This observation is usually true when the surface detail is much larger than the wavelength of visible light (roughly 0.5 microns ($10^{-6}$ meters)). Another reason for this neglect is the common belief that models based on wave theory are computationally too expensive to be of any use in computer graphics. In this paper we challenge this point of view by introducing a new class of analytical reflection models which simulate the effects of *diffraction*. Diffraction is a purely wave-like phenomenon which cannot be modeled using the standard ray theory of light. Diffraction occurs when the surface detail is comparable to the wavelength of light. A common example of a surface that produces visible diffraction patterns is the compact disk (CD). By rotating a CD under a steady light source, one can fully appreciate the visual complexity of diffraction. To capture these subtle changes in color and intensity requires a wave-like description of light. In this paper we derive analytical reflection models based on the wave theory that capture the effects of diffraction. In addition, our model is both easy to implement as a standard "shader" and computationally efficient. The derivation which leads to our new model, however, is not simple. This is because the wave theory is mathematically much more complex than the ray theory of light.

Scanning through the computer graphics literature, we found only a few references which explicitly use the wave description of light. In 1981 Moravec proposed solving the global illumination problem using the wave theory of light [11]. For his method to give acceptable results, both a very fine resolution (on the order of the wavelength of light) and a large ensemble of simulations (to model incoherent natural light sources) are required. This makes his approach unsuitable for practical computer graphics applications. Later in 1985, Kajiya proposed to numerically solve the Kirchhoff integral[1] to simulate the light reflected from anisotropic surfaces [9]. His approach, although less ambitious than Moravec's, suffers from the same limitations. In this context it would appear to be more promising to solve directly for the coherence functions associated with the waves, which are second order statistical averages of the wave fields. Some work in this area has been pursued by Tannenbaum et al. [20]. The coherence functions can also be employed to define generalized radiances [23].

A more practical use of the wave theory in computer graphics is to employ it to derive analytical reflection models. This approach, which has a long history in the applied optics literature, e.g., [2], was first seriously introduced to computer graphics by Bahar and Chakrabarti [1]. Using Bahar's full wave theory, they were able to fit analytical distributions to their computations for surfaces having a large isotropic surface roughness. The full wave theory has the advantage over the Kirchhoff theory in that it takes into account the global shape of the object. However, in practice analytical expressions are known only for simple objects such as spheres. Also the *global* shapes of surfaces in computer graphical models are usually much larger than the wavelength of light. Later in 1991, He and collaborators derived a general reflection model based on the electro-magnetic wave theory to predict the reflection of light from isotropic surfaces of any surface roughness [8]. At about the same time, a very similar model was proposed in the computer vision literature by Nayar [13]. As in Kajiya's work, these two models are essentially based on the Kirchhoff approximation of surface reflection [2]. We also note that Blinn already used some asymptotic results from Beckmann's monograph [3]. However, Blinn's model does not account for wave-like effects.

*Alias | wavefront, 1218 Third Ave, 8th Floor, Seattle, WA 98101, U.S.A. jstam@aw.sgi.com

[1]This integral will be defined more precisely below.

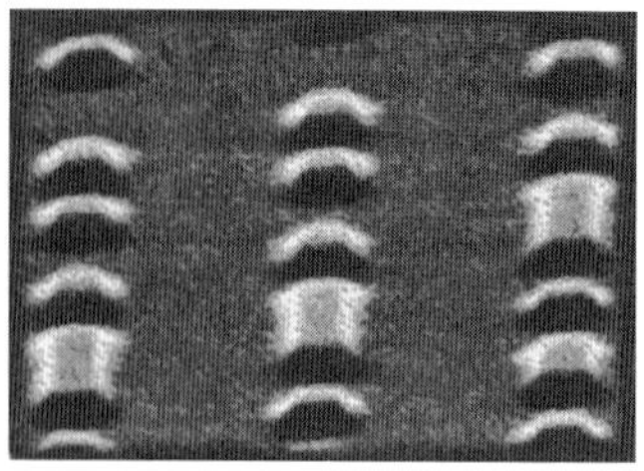

Figure 1: Close-up "view" of the micro-geometry of the surface of a compact disk.

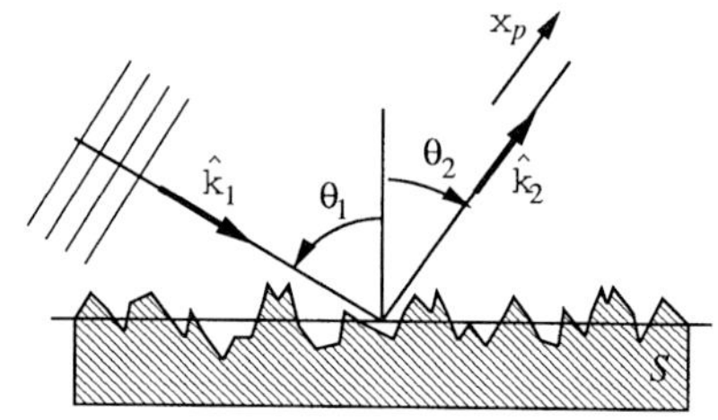


Figure 2: Basic geometry of the surface wave reflection problem.

Although the analytical models just discussed are based on wave theory, none of them is able to capture the visual complexity of the light reflected off of a compact disk, for example. The main reason is that these models assume the surface detail to be isotropic, i.e., the surface "looks the same" in every direction. Interesting diffraction phenomena, however, occur mostly when the surface detail is highly *anisotropic*, viz. non-isotropic. Fig. 1 shows that this is certainly the case for the CD. Other examples include brushed metals and colorful diffraction gratings. In computer graphics, both empirical and ray optics models have been proposed to model the reflection from anisotropic surfaces [15, 17, 22]. However, since these models are not based on wave theory, they failed to capture the effects of diffraction. To the best of our knowledge, reflection models that handle colorful diffraction effects have not appeared in the computer graphics literature or in any commercially available graphics software before. The phenomenon of diffraction was used, however, by Nakamae et al. to model the fringes caused when viewing bright light sources through the pupil and eyelashes [12].

In this paper, we derive various analytical anisotropic reflection models using the scalar Kirchhoff wave theory and the theory of random processes. In particular, we show that the reflected intensity is equal to the spectral density of a simple function $p = e^{i\alpha h}$ of the (random) surface height $h$. We show that the spectral density can be computed for a large class of surfaces not considered in previous models. We believe that our approach is novel, since the "classic" monographs on scattering from statistical surfaces do not mention such an approach [2, 14].

Diffraction should not be confused with the related phenomenon of *interference*. Interference produces colorful effects due to the phase differences caused by a wave traversing thin media of different indices of refraction, e.g., a soap bubble. Interference effects, unlike diffraction, can be modeled using the ray theory of light alone [7].

To fully understand the derivations in this paper the reader should have a background in Fourier analysis, distribution theory and random processes. Due to a lack of space we refer the reader not versed in these areas to the relevant literature, e.g., [16, 24]. The reader might also want to consult the longer version of this paper available on the CDROM proceedings which contains appendices summarizing the main results from these disciplines. The remainder of this paper is organized as follows. A reader who is interested solely in implementing our new shaders can go directly to Section 6 where the model is stated "as is". Section 2 summarizes the main results from wave theory which are required in this paper. Section 3 presents our derivation. Subsequently, Sections 4 and 5 present several applications of our new reflection model. Section 6 addresses implementation issues and can be read without any advanced mathematical knowledge. Section 7 discusses several results created using our new shaders. Finally, Section 8 concludes, outlining possible directions for future research.

## 2 Wave Theory and Computer Graphics

In this section we briefly outline some results and concepts from the wave theory necessary to understanding the derivation of our reflection model. We employ the so-called "scalar wave theory of diffraction" [4]. In this approximation the light wave is assumed to be a complex valued scalar disturbance $\psi$. This theory completely ignores the polarization of light, so its results are therefore restricted to unpolarized light. Fortunately, most common light sources such as the sun and light bulbs are totally unpolarized. The waves generated by these sources also have the property that they fluctuate very rapidly over time. Typical frequencies for such waves are on the order of $10^{14}\ s^{-1}$. In practice this means that we cannot take accurate "snapshots" of a wave. Light waves are thus essentially random and only statistical averages of the wave function have any physical significance. The averaging, denoted by $\langle . \rangle$, can be interpreted either as an average over a long time period or equivalently (via ergodicity) as an ensemble average. An example of a statistical quantity associated with waves is the *irradiance*, $I = \langle |\psi|^2 \rangle$.

We also assume that the waves emanating from the source are stationary. This means that the wave is a superposition of independent monochromatic waves. Consequently, we can restrict our analysis to a wave having a definite wavelength $\lambda$ associated with it. For visible light, the wavelengths range from the ultraviolet (0.3 microns) to the infrared (0.8 microns) region. Each of these waves satisfies a Helmholtz's wave equation:

$$\nabla^2 \psi + k^2 \psi = 0,$$

where $k$ is the *wavenumber* equal to the reciprocal of the wavelength, $k = 2\pi/\lambda$.

The main task in the theory of diffraction is to solve this wave equation for different geometries. In our case we are interested in computing the reflected waves from various types of surfaces. More precisely, we want to compute the wave $\psi_2$ equal to the reflection of an incoming planar monochromatic wave $\psi_1 = e^{ik\hat{\mathbf{k}}_1 \cdot \mathbf{x}}$ traveling in the direction $\hat{\mathbf{k}}_1$ from a surface $S$. Fig. 2 illustrates this situation. The equation relating the reflected field to the incoming field is known as the *Kirchhoff integral.* This equation is a formalization of Huygen's well-known principle that states that if one knows the wavefront at a given moment, the wave at a later time can be deduced by considering each point on the first wave as the source of a new disturbance. This principle implies that once the field on the surface is known, the field everywhere else away from the surface can be computed. The field on the surface is usually related to the incoming field $\psi_1$ using the *tangent plane* approximation. For a planar surface, the wave theory predicts that a fraction $F$ of the incoming light is specularly reflected. The fraction $F$ is equal to the Fresnel factor for unpolarized light (see p. 48 of [4]). The tangent approximation states that the wave field on the surface is equal to the incoming field plus the field reflected off of the tangent plane at the surface point. Using this relation and the assumption that the "observation point" is sufficiently far removed from the surface, the

Kirchhoff integral is ([2], p. 22):

$$\psi_2 = \frac{ike^{ikR}}{4\pi R}\,(F\mathbf{v} - \mathbf{p}) \cdot \int_S \hat{\mathbf{n}}\, e^{ik\mathbf{v}\cdot\mathbf{s}}\, ds, \qquad (1)$$

where $R$ is the distance from the center of the patch to the receiving point $\mathbf{x}_p$, $\hat{\mathbf{n}}$ is the normal of the surface at $\mathbf{s}$ and the vectors

$$\mathbf{v} = \hat{\mathbf{k}}_1 - \hat{\mathbf{k}}_2 \text{ and } \mathbf{p} = \hat{\mathbf{k}}_1 + \hat{\mathbf{k}}_2.$$

The vector $\hat{\mathbf{k}}_2$ is equal to the unit vector pointing from the origin of the surface towards the point $\mathbf{x}_p$. To obtain this result it is also assumed that the Fresnel coefficient $F$ is replaced by its average value over the normal distribution of the surface and can thus be taken out of the integral. Eq. 1 is the starting point for our derivation. We will show below that it can be evaluated analytically for a large class of interesting surface profiles. Before we do so, we will also outline how the reflected wave is related to the usual reflection nomenclature used in computer graphics.

In computer graphics, the reflected properties are often modeled using the bidirectional reflection distribution function (BRDF) which is defined as the ratio of the reflected radiance to the incoming irradiance. In this paper we will provide in every case the BRDF corresponding to our reflection model. The relationship between the BRDF and the waves can be shown to be [21]:

$$\text{BRDF} = \lim_{R\to\infty} \frac{R^2}{A\cos\theta_1} \frac{\langle|\psi_2|^2\rangle}{\langle|\psi_1|^2\rangle\cos\theta_2}, \qquad (2)$$

where $A$ is the area of the surface and $\theta_1$ and $\theta_2$ are the angles that the vectors $\hat{\mathbf{k}}_1$ and $\hat{\mathbf{k}}_2$ make with the vertical direction (see Fig. 2).

## 3 Derivation

In this section we demonstrate that the Kirchhoff integral of Eq. 1 can be computed analytically. In this paper, as in related work, we restrict ourselves to the reflection of waves from height fields. We assume that the surface is defined as an elevation over the $(x, y)$ plane. Each surface point is then parameterized by the equation

$$\mathbf{s} \to \mathbf{s}(x, y) = (x, y, h(x, y)), \qquad (3)$$

where $h(x, y)$ is a (random) function. The normal to the surface at each point then admits an analytical expression in terms of the partial derivatives $h_x$ and $h_y$ of the height function:

$$\hat{\mathbf{n}}\, ds \to \hat{\mathbf{n}}(x, y)\, ds = (-h_x(x, y), -h_y(x, y), 1)\, dxdy.$$

Introducing the notation $\mathbf{v} = (u, v, w)$, it then follows directly that the integral in Eq. 1 acquires the following form:

$$\mathbf{I}(ku, kv) = \int\!\!\int (-h_x, -h_y, 1)\, e^{ikwh} e^{ik(ux+vy)}\, dxdy. \qquad (4)$$

The integrand can be further simplified by noting that:

$$(-h_x, -h_y, 1)e^{ikwh} = \frac{1}{ikw}(-p_x, -p_y, ikwp),$$

where

$$p(x, y) = e^{ikwh(x,y)}. \qquad (5)$$

We now use the common assumption (e.g., [2, 8]) that the integration can be extended over the entire plane. This assumption is usually justified on the grounds that the surface detail is much smaller than the distances over which the surface is viewed. In doing so we observe that the integral of Eq. 4 is now a two-dimensional Fourier transform:

$$\mathbf{I}(ku, kv) = \int\!\!\int \frac{1}{ikw}(-p_x, -p_y, ikwp)e^{ik(ux+vy)}dxdy.$$

This important observation can be implemented. Let $P(ku, kv)$ be the Fourier transform of the function $p$. We observe that differentiation with respect to $x$ (resp. $y$) in the Fourier domain is equivalent to a multiplication of the Fourier transform by $-iku$ (resp. $-ikv$). This leads to the simple relationship

$$\mathbf{I}(ku, kv) = \frac{1}{w}\, P(ku, kv)\, \mathbf{v}.$$

We have thus related the integral of Eq. 1 directly to the Fourier transform of the function $p$. Now, since

$$(F\mathbf{v} - \mathbf{p}) \cdot \mathbf{v} = 2F\,(1 - \hat{\mathbf{k}}_1 \cdot \hat{\mathbf{k}}_2),$$

the scattered wave of Eq. 1 is equal to

$$\psi_2 = \frac{ike^{ikR}}{2\pi R} \frac{F(1 - \hat{\mathbf{k}}_1 \cdot \hat{\mathbf{k}}_2)}{w} P(ku, kv). \qquad (6)$$

This result shows that the scattered wave field is proportional to the Fourier transform of a simple function of the surface height. Consequently, from Eq. 2, it follows that the BRDF is

$$\text{BRDF} = \frac{k^2F^2G}{4\pi^2Aw^2}\,\langle|P(ku, kv)|^2\rangle, \qquad (7)$$

where

$$G = \frac{(1 - \hat{\mathbf{k}}_1 \cdot \hat{\mathbf{k}}_2)^2}{\cos\theta_1\cos\theta_2}. \qquad (8)$$

This result and the derivation that leads to it are remarkably simple when compared to derivations that do not employ the Fourier transform, e.g., [2]. More importantly, this treatment is more general, since we have not made any assumptions regarding the function $P$ yet.

We now specialize our results for a homogeneous random function [16]. Homogeneity is a natural assumption since we are interested in the bulk reflection from a large portion of the surface having a certain profile. For example, the portion of the CD depicted in Fig. 1 could have been taken from any part of the CD. However, and this is important, we do not assume that the surface is isotropic. This is mainly where we depart from previous wave physics models in computer graphics. Referring again to Fig. 1 we observe that the CD is clearly not isotropic.

From the definition of the function $p$ (Eq. 5) it follows immediately that this function is also homogeneous. In particular, its correlation function depends only on the separation between two locations:

$$C_p(x', y') = \langle p^*(x, y)p(x + x', y + y')\rangle - |\langle p\rangle|^2,$$

independently of the location $(x, y)$. The Fourier transform of the correlation function is known as the *spectral density* ([16], p. 338):

$$S_p(u, v) = \int\!\!\int C_p(x', y')e^{i(ux'+vy')}dx'dy'.$$

The spectral density is a non-negative function which gives the relative contribution of each wavenumber $(u, v)$ to the entire energy. We now show that the average in Eq. 7 is directly related to the spectral density. Indeed, let $\xi = (x, y)$, $\xi' = (x', y')$ and $\zeta = (ku, kv)$, then

$$\langle|P(\zeta)|^2\rangle = \langle P^*(\zeta)P(\zeta)\rangle = \int\!\!\int \langle p^*(\xi)p(\eta)\rangle e^{-i\zeta\cdot\xi}e^{i\zeta\cdot\eta}d\xi d\eta.$$

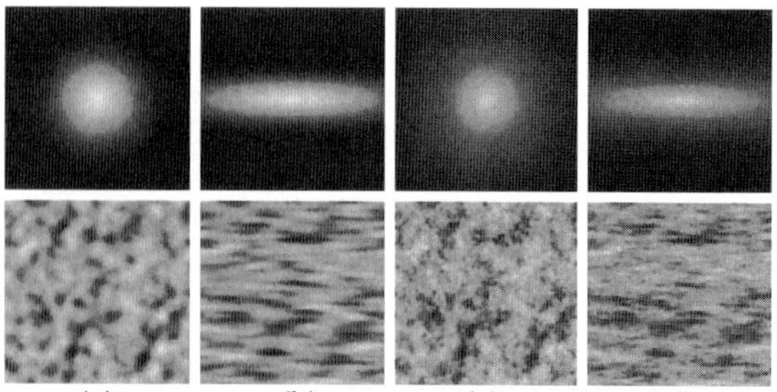

(a) (b) (c) (d)

Figure 3: Effect of the correlation function on the appearance of a random surface. The pictures at the top show plots of different correlation functions with a realization of the corresponding random surface below. The surface types are: (a) isotropic Gaussian, (b) anisotropic Gaussian, (c) isotropic fractal and (d) anisotropic fractal.

With the change of variable $\eta = \xi + \xi'$, this integral becomes

$$\begin{aligned} \iint \langle p^*(\xi)p(\xi+\xi')\rangle e^{i\zeta\cdot\xi'}d\xi d\xi' &= \\ \int d\xi \int (C_p(\xi') + |\langle p\rangle|^2)e^{i\zeta\cdot\xi'}d\xi' &= A\left(S_p(\eta) + 4\pi^2\delta(\zeta)\right), \end{aligned}$$

where $\delta$ is the two-dimensional Dirac delta function. Consequently, the average in Eq. 7 is a function of the spectral density of the function $p$:

$$\frac{1}{A}\langle |P(ku,kv)|^2\rangle = S_p(ku,kv) + 4\pi^2|\langle p\rangle|^2\delta(ku,kv).$$

Substituting this result back into Eq. 7 we get:

$$\mathrm{BRDF} = \frac{F^2G}{w^2}\left(\frac{k^2}{4\pi^2}S_p(ku,kv) + |\langle p\rangle|^2\delta(u,v)\right), \quad (9)$$

where we have used the fact that $\delta(ku,kv) = \delta(u,v)/k^2$ [24]. Eq. 9 is the main theoretical result of this paper. It shows that the reflection from a random surface is proportional to the spectral density of the random function $e^{ikwh}$. In the next two sections we apply this result to the derivation of reflection models for various types of surfaces.

# 4 Anisotropic Rough Surfaces

## 4.1 General Case

Every surface depicted in Fig. 3 is a realization of a *Gaussian random process*. These processes are entirely defined by their corresponding correlation function depicted in the upper part of Fig. 3. From the figure it is clear that the correlation function determines the general appearance of the random surface. Radially symmetrical correlation functions correspond to isotropic surfaces, c.f., surfaces (a) and (c), while the derivative of the correlation function at the origin also determines smoothness of the surfaces. Consequently, surfaces (a) and (b) are smooth, while surfaces (c) and (d) have a fractal appearance. In this section we further clarify the fact that the reflection from these surfaces is intimately related to the correlation function. Gaussian random processes have the nice property that their characteristic functions admit analytical expressions [2]. These functions are exactly what we require in order to compute the spectral density $S_p$ and the variance $|\langle p\rangle|^2$ appearing in Eq. 9. Indeed, for Gaussian random processes these quantities are related to their surface height counterparts as follows. Firstly, we have the following identities ([16], p. 255):

$$\begin{aligned} \langle p\rangle &= \langle e^{ikwh}\rangle = e^{-g/2} \quad \text{and} && (10) \\ C_p(x,y) &= e^{-g}\left(e^{gC_h(x,y)} - 1\right), && (11) \end{aligned}$$

where $g = (kw\sigma_h)^2$, and $\sigma_h$ is the standard deviation of the height fluctuations. Secondly, the spectral density $S_p$ is the Fourier transform of the correlation function $C_p$ ([16], p. 338). To compute this Fourier transform analytically we can use the expansion of the exponential function into an infinite series [2]:

$$e^{gC_h(x,y)} = \sum_{m=0}^{\infty}\frac{g^m}{m!}C_h(x,y)^m.$$

Then using the linearity of the Fourier transform, we can compute the spectral density as

$$S_p = \mathcal{F}\{C_p\} = e^{-g}\sum_{m=1}^{\infty}\frac{g^m}{m!}\mathcal{F}\{(C_h)^m\}. \quad (12)$$

This requires the computation of the Fourier transform of the surface correlation to a power $m$. We now give analytical results for the two correlation functions corresponding to the surfaces depicted in Fig. 3. These surfaces are defined by the following two correlation functions:

$$C_1(x,y) = e^{-\frac{x^2}{T_x^2}-\frac{y^2}{T_y^2}} \text{ and } C_2(x,y) = e^{-\sqrt{\frac{x^2}{T_x^2}+\frac{y^2}{T_y^2}}}.$$

In all cases, the *correlation lengths* $T_x$ and $T_y$ control the anisotropy of the surface. Fig. 3.(a) and (b) both correspond to the correlation function $C_1$. This function is infinitely smooth at the origin, which accounts for the smoothness of the corresponding surfaces. In Fig. 3.(a) $T_x = T_y$ and the surfaces are isotropic. Most previous wave-based models considered only the isotropic case. Fig. 3.(c) and (d) correspond to the correlation function $C_2$. The corresponding surfaces have a fractal appearance. They are thus good models for very rough materials. In the results section we will see that these surfaces give rise to reflection patterns which are visually different from the smooth case.

For each correlation function, we can compute its Fourier transforms to a power $m$ analytically. They are equal to

$$D_1^m = \frac{\pi T_x T_y}{m}e^{-\frac{U^2+V^2}{4m}} \text{ and } D_2^m = \frac{2\pi T_x T_y m}{(m^2+U^2+V^2)^{3/2}}, \quad (13)$$

respectively, where $U = kuT_x$ and $V = kvT_y$. By substituting these expressions back into the infinite sum of Eq. 12, we get an analytical expression for the BRDF:

$$\mathrm{BRDF} = \frac{F^2G}{w^2}e^{-g}\left(\frac{k^2}{4\pi^2}\sum_{m=1}^{\infty}\frac{g^m}{m!}D^m + \delta(u,v)\right), \quad (14)$$

where $D^m$ is any one of the functions of Eq. 13.

## 4.2 Discussion

In this section we demonstrate that most previous models in computer graphics are special cases of our new shading model.

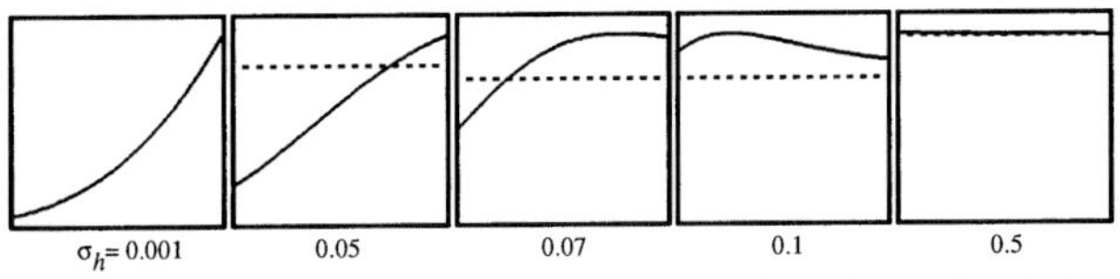


Figure 4: Plots of the BRDF for $k$ ranging from the infrared ($8.06\mu^{-1}$) to the ultraviolet region ($16.53\mu^{-1}$). The reflection is in the specular direction: $\theta_1 = \theta_2 = 45^o$. The plots show the effect of the standard deviation $\sigma_h$ on the color of the reflection. For low deviations the reflection is bluish, while for higher roughness it tends to flatten out. The dashed line is the geometrical optics approximation.

### Born Approximation

When $g << 1$, the infinite sum appearing in Eq. 12 can be truncated to its first term. This is equivalent to the approximation $e^{ikwh} \approx 1 + ikwh$ often taken in physical theories. This approximation should be valid whenever the scales of the surfaces are much smaller than the wavelength of light.

$$\mathrm{BRDF}_{Born} = F^2 G\, e^{-g} \left( \frac{\sigma_h^2 k^4}{4\pi^2} S_h(ku, kv) + \delta(u, v) \right).$$

This result is described in the *Handbook of Optics* [5]. Notice that the BRDF is dependent on the fourth power of the inverse of the wavelength. This means that generally "bluish" light is more strongly scattered than "reddish" light. These surfaces should therefore have a bluish appearance. An interesting feature of this approximation is that one can actually "see" the spectral density of the random surface in its highlight, i.e., any of the plots in Fig. 3 (top).

### Geometrical Optics

In the opposite limit when $g >> 1$, an approximate expression for the sum of Eq. 12 can also be derived. This case corresponds to a situation usually encountered in computer graphics when the surface detail is much larger than the wavelength of light. For large $g$, the Fourier integral only depends on the behavior of the function $e^{gC_h}$ near the origin (see [2, 1] for details):

$$e^{gC_h(x,y)} \approx e^g e^{-g(x^2/T_x^2 + y^2/T_y^2)}.$$

The Fourier transform of this function can be computed analytically and is equal to:

$$S_p(ku, kv) = \frac{\pi T_x T_y}{g}\, e^{-\frac{U^2}{4g}}\, e^{-\frac{V^2}{4g}}.$$

The BRDF in this case is equal to ($e^{-g} \approx 0$):

$$\mathrm{BRDF}_{geom} = \frac{F^2 G}{4\pi w^4 r_x r_y}\, e^{-\frac{u^2}{4w^2 r_x^2}}\, e^{-\frac{v^2}{4w^2 r_y^2}}, \qquad (15)$$

where $r_x = \sigma_h / T_x$ and $r_y = \sigma_h / T_y$. This distribution is a generalization of the isotropic distributions found in the Blinn and Cook-Torrance models where there is only one roughness parameter "$m$". In fact, our model closely resembles Ward's anisotropic reflection model [22]. As in the Cook-Torrance model, $\mathrm{BRDF}_{geom}$ is only dependent on the wavelength of light through the Fresnel factor $F$, as there is no other explicit dependence on wavelength: $k$ does not explicitly appear in the distribution.

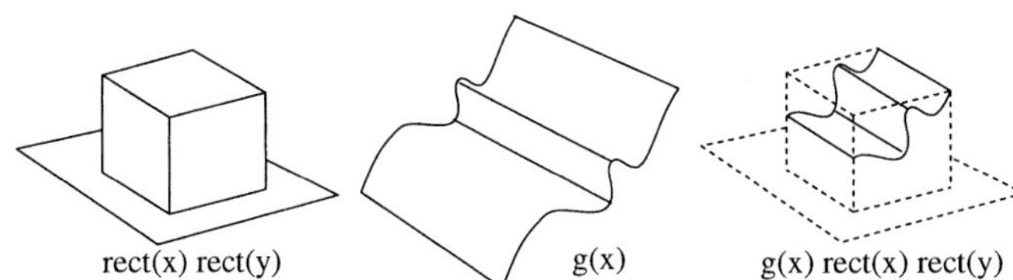


Figure 5: Each bump is defined as the multiplication of a function $g(x, y)$ with the product of box-like functions.

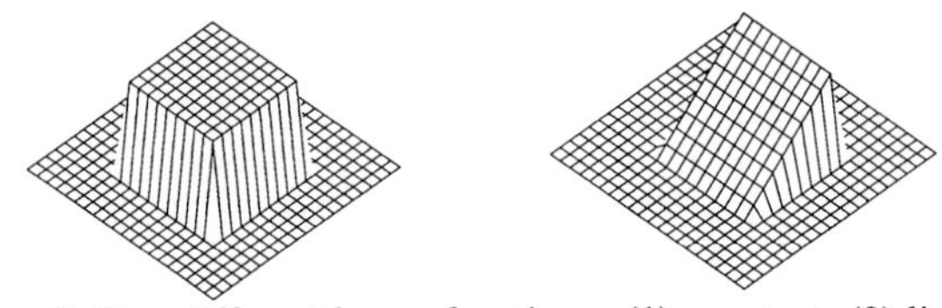

Figure 6: Two different bump functions: (1) constant, (2) linear in one coordinate.

### Isotropic Distributions

The He-Torrance [8] and the Nayar [13] reflection models are obtained when our model is restricted to the class of isotropic surfaces corresponding to Fig. 3.(a). Using our result for the correlation function $C_1$ with $T_x = T_y$, we essentially recover both of these models. It is worth noting that one of the versions of the He-Torrance model handles polarization effects while our model doesn't. This is because they used the vector valued version of the Kirchhoff integral. However, in practice it seems He-Torrance have only used their unpolarized version to create the pictures accompanying their paper. The dependence on wavelength (as in our model) is a function of the Fresnel factor $F$ and the function $k^2\, S_p(ku, kv)$. In Fig. 4 we illustrate the dependence of this function on wavenumber $k$ for different surface deviations $\sigma_h$. The reflection goes from a $k^2$ dependence to a flat spectrum. Notice that in the midrange we actually get a small yellowish hue. The figure also demonstrates that for $\sigma_h > 0.5$ the geometrical optics model, shown as a dashed line, is a very good approximation. In practice we have found that whenever $g > 10$ the pictures generated with the geometrical optics approximation are visually indistinguishable from pictures generated using the exact model.

## 5 Diffraction from Periodic-like Surfaces

We now turn to an application that most clearly demonstrates the power of our new reflection model.

Many surfaces have a micro-structure that is made out of similar "bumps". A good example is a compact disk which has small bumps that encode the information distributed over each "track". Fig. 1 is a magnified view of the actual surface of a compact disk. Notice in particular that the distribution of bumps is random along each track but that the tracks are evenly spaced. In this section we derive general formulae for certain shapes of bumps, and then specialize the results for a CD-shader.

| symbol | description | size |
|---|---|---|
| $h_0$ | height of a bump | 0.15 $\mu m$ |
| $a$ | width of a bump | 0.5 $\mu m$ |
| $b$ | length of a bump | 1 $\mu m$ |
| $\Delta x$ | separation between the tracks | 2.5 $\mu m$ |
| $\nu_y$ | density of bumps on each track | 0.5 $(\mu m)^{-1}$ |

Table 1: Typical dimensions of a compact disk.

We assume that the surface is given by a superposition of bumps:

$$h(x,y) = \sum_{n=-\infty}^{\infty} \sum_{m=-\infty}^{\infty} b(x - x_n, y - y_m), \quad (16)$$

where the locations $(x_n, y_m)$ are assumed to be either regularly spaced or randomly (Poisson) distributed. To handle the two cases simultaneously, we assume that $x_n$ is evenly spaced and that $y_n$ is Poisson distributed. Extensions to the case where both locations are evenly spaced or where both are Poisson distributed should be obvious from our results. Let $\Delta x$ be the constant spacing between the $x$-locations: $x_n = n\Delta x$. The random Poisson distribution of the locations $y_m$ is entirely specified by a density $\nu_y$ of bumps per unit length. The function $b(x,y)$ appearing in Eq. 16 is a "bump function": a function with (small) finite support. We will assume that the bump function has the following simple form:

$$b(x,y) = h_0 \; g(x/a)\mathrm{rect}(x/a)\mathrm{rect}(y/b), \quad (17)$$

where $a$, $b$ and $h_0$ define the width, length and height of each bump respectively ($a \le \Delta x$). Typical values of these parameters for a CD are provided in Table 1. The function rect equals one on the interval $[-1/2, 1/2]$ and zero elsewhere. Fig. 5 illustrates our definition of a bump. Our derivation is valid for arbitrary $g$, however, we provide an analytical expression only for the following two functions:

$$g^0(x) = 1 \quad \text{and} \quad g^1(x) = 1/2 + x. \quad (18)$$

The bumps corresponding to these functions are depicted in Fig. 6. The function $g^0$ is a good approximation of the bumps found on a CD and the function $g^1$ can be used to model diffraction gratings.

The function $p(x,y)$ defined by Eq. 5 in our case is equal to:

$$p(x,y) = \sum_{n=-\infty}^{\infty} \sum_{m=-\infty}^{\infty} \phi((x - x_n)/a, (y - y_m)/b), \quad (19)$$

where $\phi(x,y) = e^{i\alpha g(x)}\mathrm{rect}(x)\mathrm{rect}(y)$ and $\alpha = kwh_0$. We dropped a constant term "1" that accounts for the space between the bumps and only adds a delta spike in the specular direction.

A simple computation shows that the Fourier transform of the function $p(x,y)$ is equal to

$$P(u,v) = \sigma_x(u)\sigma_y(v)\; ab\; \Phi(au, bv),$$

where $\Phi(u,v)$ is the Fourier transform of $\phi(x,y)$ and

$$\sigma_x(u) = \sum_{n=-\infty}^{\infty} e^{iun\Delta x} \quad \text{and} \quad \sigma_y(v) = \sum_{m=-\infty}^{\infty} e^{ivy_m}. \quad (20)$$

To compute the spectral density of Eq. 9 we note that:

$$S_p(u,v) = (ab)^2 |\Phi(au,bv)|\; |\sigma_x(u)|^2\; S_{\sigma_y}(v).$$

The spectral density and the average of the sum of random Poisson distributed locations are both equal to the density $\nu_y$ (see [16] p. 561):

$$S_{\sigma_y}(v) = \nu_y \quad \text{and} \quad \langle \sigma_y \rangle = \nu_y.$$

The sum of evenly spaced location $x_n$ is a bit harder to deal with. First we need the following two results from the theory of distributions (see pp. 54-55 of reference [24]):

$$\sum_{n=-\infty}^{\infty} e^{iun} = 2\pi \sum_{n=-\infty}^{\infty} \delta(u - 2\pi n) \quad \text{and} \quad \delta(sz+t) = \frac{1}{s}\delta(z + t/s),$$

where $s > 0$ and $t$ are real numbers. The first of these two equalities is known as "Poisson's summation formula". Using these results we can express the square of the sum $\sigma_x$ in terms of delta distributions only:

$$|\sigma_x(u)|^2 = \frac{(2\pi)^2}{\Delta x^2} \sum_{n=-\infty}^{\infty} \delta(u - 2\pi n/\Delta x).$$

We can now compute the spectral density $S_p$ by putting all these computations together:

$$S_p(ku, kv) = b^2 \nu_y \lambda \sum_{n=-\infty}^{\infty} |\Phi_n(kv)|^2 \delta(u - n\lambda/\Delta x), \quad (21)$$

where

$$|\Phi_n(kv)|^2 = \frac{a^2}{\Delta x^2} |\Phi(2\pi na/\Delta x, kv)|^2. \quad (22)$$

The function $|\Phi|^2$ can be computed analytically for the two bumps depicted in Fig. 6:

$$|\Phi^0(au,bv)|^2 = 2(1 - \cos(\alpha))\mathrm{sinc}^2(au/2)\mathrm{sinc}^2(bv/2), \quad (23)$$

$$|\Phi^1(au,bv)|^2 = \big(\mathrm{sinc}^2(\alpha_0/2) - 2\mathrm{sinc}(\alpha_0/2)\times \mathrm{sinc}(au/2)\cos(\alpha/2) + \mathrm{sinc}^2(au/2)\big)\,\mathrm{sinc}^2(bv/2), \quad (24)$$

where $\alpha_0 = \alpha + au$. Putting all these pieces together we get the following expression for the BRDF:

$$\mathrm{BRDF} = \frac{F^2 G}{w^2} b^2 \nu_y \sum_{n=-\infty}^{\infty} |\Phi_n(kv)|^2 \delta(u - n\lambda/\Delta x)(k + \nu_y \delta(u)).$$

# 6 Implementation

We have implemented our reflection models as various shaders in our MAYA animation system. Any model created in that package can be rendered using our new shaders. The fact that our shaders have been included in a commercial product should be a sufficient proof of their practicality.

As in [9], we model the anisotropy of the surface by assigning an orthonormal frame at each point of the surface. In the case of a parametric surface, the most natural choice for this frame is to take the normal and the two vectors tangent to the iso-parameter lines. We have also added an additional rotation angle to the frame around the normal. When this angle is texture mapped, it allows us to create effects such as brushed metal (Fig. 8.(a)).

The general form of our shader is

$$\mathrm{BRDF} = |F(\theta_1')|^2\; G(\mathbf{k}_1, \mathbf{k}_2)\; S(\mathbf{k}_1, \mathbf{k}_2)\; (D(\mathbf{v}, \lambda) + r\mathrm{Env}),$$

where $F$ is the Fresnel factor [6], $S$ is a shadowing function [8], $G$ is a geometrical factor defined by Eq. 8 in Section 3 and $D$ is a distribution function that is related to the micro-geometry of the surface. The function "Env" returns the color in the mirror direction of $\mathbf{k}_2$ from an environment map and the factor $r$ accounts for how much the surface reflects direct illumination. The vector $\mathbf{v} = (u, v, w)$ is the angle midway between $-\mathbf{k}_1$ and $\mathbf{k}_2$. The Fresnel factor is evaluated at the angle $\theta_1'$ that the direction $\mathbf{k}_1$ makes with the vector $\mathbf{v}$. The Fresnel factor varies with the index of refraction of the metallic surface and is wavelength dependent [6]. We do not use the He-Torrance shadowing function since it is restricted to isotropic surfaces. Instead, we employ a model introduced by Sancer [18]. For convenience, we have included this model in Appendix A. The distribution $D$ is the most important component of our model and is now described in more detail.

In the previous sections we have derived distribution functions for both the random surfaces depicted in Fig. 3 and for periodic-like profiles such as the one shown in Fig. 1. When the surface is random, the distribution is defined by the three parameters $\sigma_h$, $T_x$ and $T_y$. The variance $\sigma_h^2$ models the average height fluctuations of the surface and the parameters $T_x$ and $T_y$ model the amount of correlation of the micro-surface in the directions of the local frame. See Section 3 for further details on these quantities. When $T_x = T_y$, the surface is isotropic. In the most general case, the distribution $D$ is computed by the infinite sum appearing in Eq. 14. In Appendix B, we provide a stable implementation of this sum. As pointed out in Section 4.2, the sum is very well approximated by the geometrical optics approximation of Eq. 15, when $g = (kw\sigma_h)^2$ is large (see also Fig. 4). The factor "$r$" is equal to $\exp(-g)$. The smoother the surface, the more indirect illumination is directly reflected off of it.

The implementation of periodic-like profiles giving rise to colorful diffraction patterns is different. When evaluating the distribution $D$, the values $u$ and $v$ (and $w$) are determined by the incoming and outgoing angles. The incoming light is usually assumed to be an incoherent sum of many monochromatic waves whose number is proportional to the distribution $L(\lambda)$ of the light source. To determine the intensity and the color of the light reflected in the outgoing direction, we first compute the wavelengths $\lambda_n$ for which $L(\lambda)$ is non zero and for which the delta spikes in Eq. 21 are non-zero. This only occurs when $\lambda_n = \Delta x u/n$ and $n \neq 0$. When $n = 0$, all wavelengths contribute intensities in the specular direction $u = 0$. In general, visible light is comprised only of waves with wavelengths between $\lambda_{min} = 0.4\mu m$ and $\lambda_{max} = 0.7\mu m$. This means that the indices $n$ are constrained to lie in the range $\Delta x u[1/\lambda_{max}, 1/\lambda_{min}]$ if $u > 0$ and in the range $\Delta x u[1/\lambda_{min}, 1/\lambda_{max}]$ when $u < 0$. Once these wavelengths are determined, the red, green and blue components of the distribution $D$ are computed as follows

$$D_{rgb} = b^2 \nu_y \sum_{n=N_{min}}^{N_{max}} \frac{1}{\lambda_n} \mathrm{Spec}_{rgb}(\lambda_n) L(\lambda_n) \left| \Phi_n \left( \frac{2\pi v}{\lambda_n} \right) \right|^2,$$

where $\mathrm{Spec}_{rgb}$ is a function that for each wavelength returns the corresponding color. This function can either be constructed from psychophysical experiments or simply set by an animator as a "ramp". In our implementation we constructed a ramp function from standard RGB response curves. See Eq. 22 for a definition of the function $\Phi_n$.

## 7 Results

Once the shaders were implemented in MAYA, it was an easy task to generate results demonstrating the power of our new shading model. In Fig. 7 we show the effect of some of the parameters of our model on the appearance of the surfaces. In each rendering we chose to have a spectrally flat Fresnel factor to demonstrate the dependence of the distribution on wavelength. For the Gaussian correlations the reflection is more bluish for small roughness and becomes whiter for larger roughness, in accordance with the analysis of Section 4.2. The reflection from fractal surfaces is quite interesting: bluish for small roughness, then yellowish for intermediate roughness and finally white for large roughness. The third row of spheres exhibits the effect of the separation and twist angle parameters of our diffraction shader. We used a different texture map for the twist angle of each one of the three "diffraction cones" at the bottom of Fig. 7.

Fig. 8 shows several renderings created in this manner. In each case we have texture mapped the directions of anisotropy to add more interesting visual detail. Fig. 8.(a) demonstrates that this can be employed to create a "brushed metal" look. In Fig. 8.(b) we textured both the roughness and the degree of anisotropy of the surface. Fig. 8.(c) is a picture of a CD illuminated by a directional light source. Notice that all the highlights appear automatically in the correct places when the data from Table 1 is used. Fig. 8.(d) is an example of the use of our diffraction grating model. Notice all the subtle coloring effects that result (especially when viewing the corresponding animation). These colorful effects would be hard to model by trial and error without properly modeling the wave properties of light.

The effects of the anisotropy and of diffraction are most pronounced in an animation when moving either the object or the light sources. For this reason we have included some animations on the CDROM proceedings.

## 8 Conclusions

In this paper we have proposed a new class of reflection models that take into account the wave-like properties of light. For the first time in computer graphics, we have derived reflection models that properly simulate the effects of diffraction. We have shown that our models can be easily implemented as standard shaders in our MAYA animation software. Our derivations, while mathematically involved, are simpler and more general than previously published results in this area. In particular, our use of the Fourier transform has proven to be a very powerful tool in deriving new reflection models.

In future work, we hope to extend our model to an even wider class of surfaces by relaxing some of the assumptions in our model. Presently, our model only accounts for the reflection from metallic surfaces and ignores multiple-scattering. It would be interesting to derive more general models that take into account subsurface scattering by waves. It seems unlikely that the effects of multiple scattering might be captured by an analytical model. An alternative would be to fit analytical models to either the results from a Monte-Carlo wave simulation or to experimentally measured data.

As well, we wish to extend our work to the computation of the fluctuations of the intensity field [10]. In this manner we can compute exact texture maps for given surface profiles. We could achieve this by deriving analytical expressions for the higher order statistics of the reflected intensity field. More specifically, we hope to extend our previous work on stochastic rendering of density fields to surfaces [19].


## Acknowledgments

Thanks to Duncan Brinsmead for suggesting the "twist angle", for helping me write the MAYA plugin and for creating Figs. 8.(a) and (b). Thanks to Greg Ward for encouraging me to study the wave theory and for commenting on the first draft of this paper. Thanks also to Pamela Jackson for proofreading the paper.


## A A Shadowing Function

The shadowing function used in He's model applies only to isotropic surfaces. For this reason we have used a different model derived by Sancer [18]. The shadowing function is valid for a Gaussian random surface having a correlation function $C_h$ and standard deviation $\sigma_h$:

$$S = \begin{cases} (C_1+1)^{-1} & \text{if } u = v = 0 \text{ and } \theta_1 \leq \theta_2 \\ (C_2+1)^{-1} & \text{if } u = v = 0 \text{ and } \theta_2 \leq \theta_1 \\ (C_1+C_2+1)^{-1} & \text{else} \end{cases},$$

where

$$C_i = \sqrt{\frac{2|\beta_i|}{\pi}} \tan\theta_i \exp\left(-\frac{\cot^2\theta_i}{2|\beta_i|}\right) - \operatorname{erfc}\left(\frac{\cot\theta_i}{\sqrt{2|\beta_i|}}\right)$$

$$\beta_i = \sigma_h^2 \left(C_{h,xx}\cos^2\phi_i + C_{h,xy}\sin 2\phi_i + C_{h,yy}\sin^2\phi_i\right),$$

where $i = 1, 2$ and $C_{h,xx}$ is the second derivative with respect to $x$ of the correlation function at the origin. Since the derivatives of the correlation function depend on the correlation lengths $T_x$ and $T_y$, this clearly shows that this shadowing function takes into account the anisotropy of the surface.

# B Computing Infinite Sums

The following piece of code will compute the distribution of reflected light from the surface:

```
compute_D (lambda,u,v,w,s_h,Tx,Ty)
  k = 2*PI/lambda;
  g = k*s_h*w; g *= g;
  if ( g>10 )
    return D_geom(u,v,w,s_h/Tx,s_h/Ty);
  tmp=1; sum=log_g=0;
  for(m=1;abs(tmp)>EPS||m<3*g;m++) {
    log_g += log(g/m); tmp = exp(log_g-g);
    sum += tmp*D(m,k*u,k*v,Tx,Ty);
  }
  return lambda*lambda*sum
```

The function `D()` is any one of the functions of Equation 13. This routine is a stable implementation of the infinite sum appearing in Equation 14. A naive implementation of the sum results in numerical overflows. The condition "`m<3*g`" is there to make sure that we do not exit the loop too early. This is an heuristic which has worked well in practice.

# References


[1] E. Bahar and S. Chakrabarti. Full-Wave Theory Applied to Computer-Aided Graphics for 3D Objects. *IEEE Computer Graphics and Applications*, 7(7):46–60, July 1987.

[2] P. Beckmann and A. Spizzichino. *The Scattering of Electromagnetic Waves from Rough Surfaces*. Pergamon, New York, 1963.

[3] J. F. Blinn. Models of Light Reflection for Computer Synthesized Pictures. *ACM Computer Graphics (SIGGRAPH '77)*, 11(3):192–198, August 1977.

[4] M. Born and E. Wolf. *Principles of Optics. Sixth (corrected) Edition*. Cambridge University Press, Cambridge, U.K., 1997.

[5] E. L. Church and P. Z. Takacs. *Chapter 7. Surface Scattering*. In *Handbook of Optics (Second Edition). Volume I: Fundamentals, Techniques and Design*. McGraw Hill, New York, 1995.

[6] R. L. Cook and K. E. Torrance. A Reflectance Model for Computer Graphics. *ACM Computer Graphics (SIGGRAPH '81)*, 15(3):307–316, August 1981.

[7] J. S. Gondek, G. W. Meyer, and J. G. Newman. Wavelength dependent reflectance functions. In *Computer Graphics Proceedings, Annual Conference Series, 1993*, pages 213–220, 1994.

[8] X. D. He, K. E. Torrance, F. X. Sillion, and D. P. Greenberg. A Comprehensive Physical Model for Light Reflection. *ACM Computer Graphics (SIGGRAPH '91)*, 25(4):175–186, July 1991.

[9] J. T. Kajiya. Anisotropic Reflection Models. *ACM Computer Graphics (SIGGRAPH '85)*, 19(3):15–21, July 1985.

[10] W. Krueger. Intensity Fluctuations and Natural Texturing. *ACM Computer Graphics (SIGGRAPH '88)*, 22(4):213–220, August 1988.

[11] H. P. Moravec. 3-D Graphics and the Wave Theory. *ACM Computer Graphics (SIGGRAPH '81)*, 15(3):289–296, August 1981.

[12] E. Nakamae, K. Kaneda, and T. Nishita. A Lighting Model Aiming at Drive Simulators. *ACM Computer Graphics (SIGGRAPH '90)*, 24(4):395–404, August 1990.

[13] S. K. Nayar, K. Ikeuchi, and T. Kanade. Surface Reflection: Physical and Geometrical Perspectives. *IEEE Transactions on Pattern Analysis and Machine Intelligence*, 13(7):611–634, July 1991.

[14] J. A. Ogilvy. *Theory of Scattering from Random Rough Surfaces*. Adam Hilger, Bristol, U.K., 1991.

[15] Tomohiro Ohira. A Shading Model for Anisotropic Reflection. *Technical Report of The Institute of Electronic and Communication Engineers of Japan*, 82(235):47–54, 1983.

[16] A. Papoulis. *Probability, Random Variables, and Stochastic Processes*. McGraw-Hill, Systems Science Series, New York, 1965.

[17] P. Poulin and A. Fournier. A Model for Anisotropic Reflection. *ACM Computer Graphics (SIGGRAPH '90)*, 24(4):273–282, August 1990.

[18] M. I. Sancer. Shadow Corrected Electromagnetic Scattering from Randomly Rough Surfaces. *IEEE Transactions on Antennas and Propagation*, AP-17(5):577–585, September 1969.

[19] J. Stam. Stochastic Rendering of Density Fields. In *Proceedings of Graphics Interface '94*, pages 51–58, Banff, Alberta, May 1994.

[20] D. C. Tannenbaum, P. Tannenbaum, and M. J. Wozny. Polarization and Birefringency Considerations in Rendering. In *Computer Graphics Proceedings, Annual Conference Series, 1994*, pages 221–222, July 1994.

[21] K. Tomiyasu. Relationship Between and Measurement of Differential Scattering Coefficient ($\sigma^0$) and Bidirectional Reflectance Distribution Function (BRDF). *SPIE Proceedings. Wave Propagation and Scattering in Varied Media*, 927:43–46, 1988.

[22] G. J. Ward. Measuring and Modelling Anisotropic Reflection. *ACM Computer Graphics (SIGGRAPH'92)*, 26(2):265–272, July 1992.

[23] E. Wolf. Coherence and Radiometry. *Journal of the Optical Society of America*, 68(1), January 1978.

[24] A. H. Zemanian. *Distribution Theory and Transform Analysis: An Introduction to Generalized Functions, with Applications*. Dover, New York, 1987.

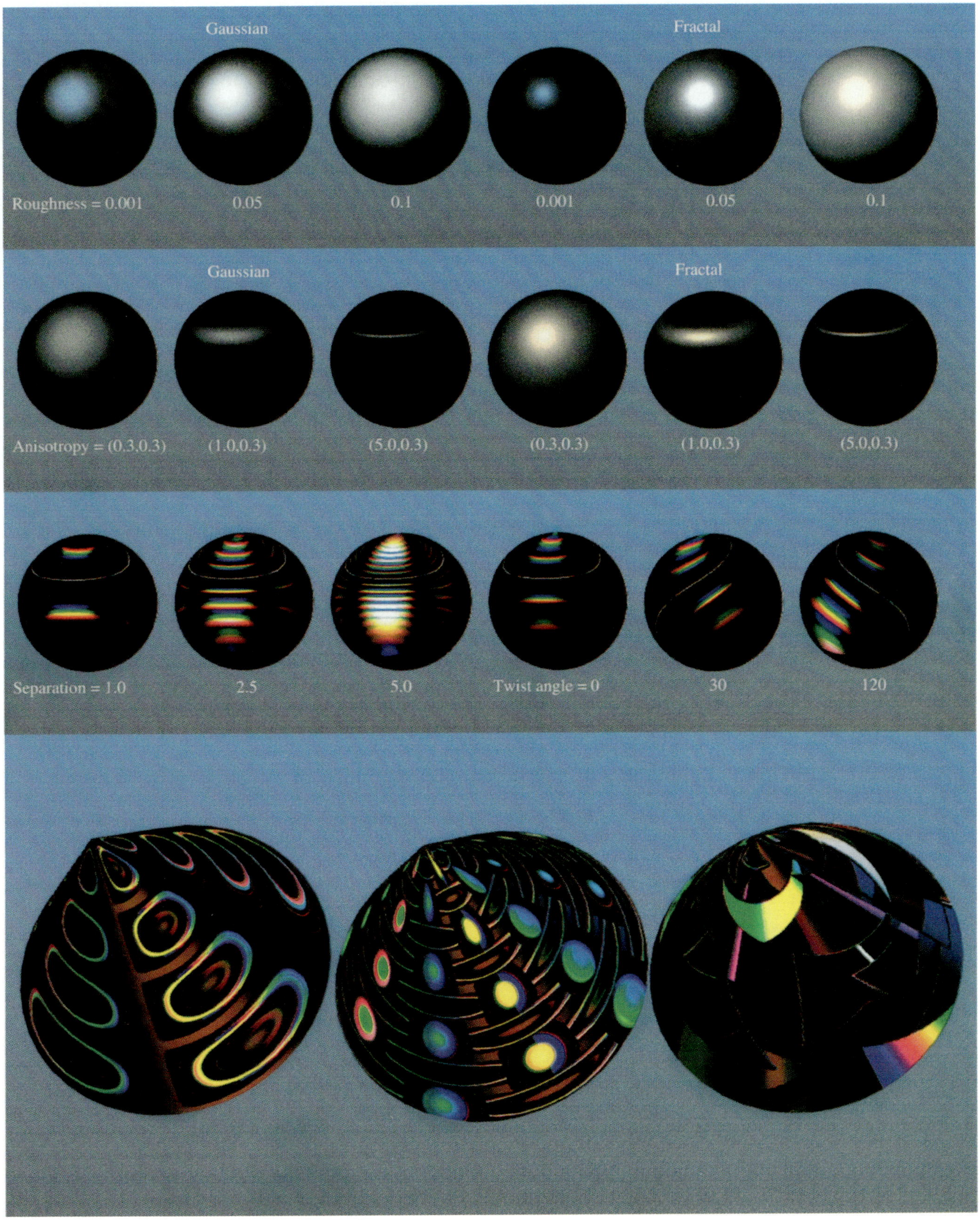


Figure 7: Effect of some of the parameters.

(a)

(b)

(c)

(d)

Figure 8: More pictures.

# Subdivision Schemes for Fluid Flow

Henrik Weimer* Joe Warren

Rice University

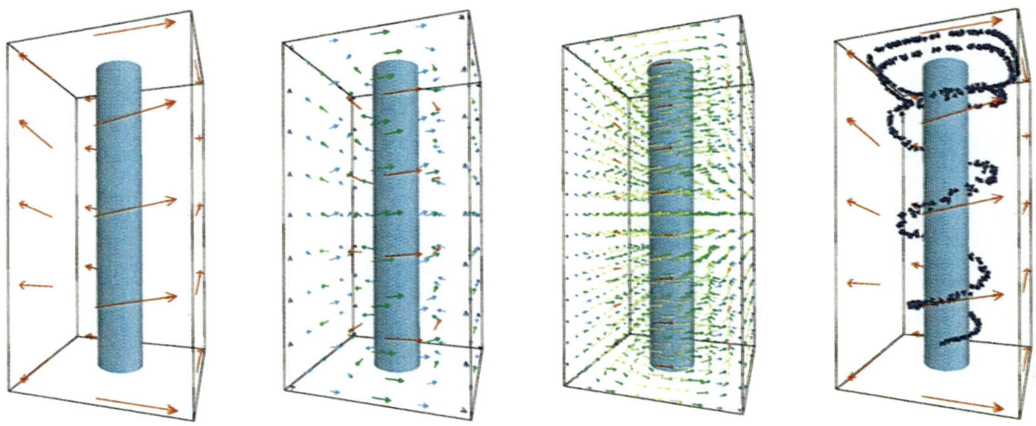

Figure 1: Modeling a helical flow using subdivision.

## Abstract

The motion of fluids has been a topic of study for hundreds of years. In its most general setting, fluid flow is governed by a system of non-linear partial differential equations known as the Navier-Stokes equations. However, in several important settings, these equations degenerate into simpler systems of linear partial differential equations. This paper will show that flows corresponding to these linear equations can be modeled using subdivision schemes for vector fields. Given an initial, coarse vector field, these schemes generate an increasingly dense sequence of vector fields. The limit of this sequence is a continuous vector field defining a flow that follows the initial vector field. The beauty of this approach is that realistic flows can now be modeled and manipulated in real time using their associated subdivision schemes.

**CR Categories:** I.3.5 [Computer Graphics]: Computational Geometry and Object Modeling— Physically based modeling; I.6.5 [Simulation and Modeling]: Model Development—Modeling Methodologies

**Keywords:** CAD, subdivision, multi-grid, fluid simulations, fractals, physically based animation, physically based modeling

*Rice University, Department of Computer Science, P.O. Box 1892, Houston, TX 77251-1892, {henrik, jwarren}@rice.edu



## 1 Introduction

This paper describes an application of an increasingly popular modeling technique, subdivision, to a traditional problem in computer graphics, generating realistic fluid flows. Given that the physical behavior of a flow is governed by a system of partial differential equations (PDEs), one standard approach is to use some type of multi-level solver to compute solutions for these PDEs. One of the most efficient multi-level methods currently in use is multi-grid. Multi-grid recursively generates increasingly dense approximations to the exact continuous flow using a nested sequence of domain grids. This method provides exceptionally good convergence rates and has found many successful applications [2].

While multi-grid solvers are very efficient compared to standard iterative solvers, they remain too costly to permit interactive modeling in many situations. One alternate technique that has proven very useful in surface modeling is subdivision. Subdivision schemes have been used to model a variety of surface types [3, 8, 7, 14, 24]. More recent work has applied subdivision to the modeling of surfaces with variational definitions [18, 19, 27, 28]. Due to their simplicity, subdivision schemes are easy to implement and permit interactive modeling of the resulting surfaces.

This paper has two goals, one practical and one theoretical: The practical goal of this paper is to demonstrate that subdivision can be extended beyond the domain of surface modeling to that of modeling flows. Modeling fluid flow through subdivision provides the user with an intuitive modeling metaphor. She defines a coarse initial vector field as a small set of vectors. The subdivision process produces an arbitrarily dense discrete vector field which follows the initial field and satisfies the underlying partial differential equations. Application of the subdivision scheme is conceptually simple, easy to implement and efficient because subdivision is in essence a local weighted averaging process. In particular, implementation of a subdivider based on these schemes is much simpler than implementation of any flow solver with comparable stability. Furthermore, should a denser solution be required than has previously been computed, the subdivision scheme can simply be applied a few extra rounds with no need to re-run the entire solving process.

The theoretical goal of this paper is to expose an intrinsic link between linear systems of PDEs and subdivision. Given a linear system of PDEs, there exists an associated subdivision scheme that produces solutions to these equations. In particular, this scheme is a variant of a more general multi-grid process. The next section of the paper briefly reviews multi-grid and derives the basic relationship between multi-grid and subdivision. The following section then re-derives a known subdivision scheme for polynomial splines as an illustrative example. After introducing the partial differential equations for fluid flow, the paper uses the same methodology to derive subdivision schemes for flow. The resulting subdivision schemes are finally used to construct an interactive modeling system for fluid flow and for real time fluid flow animation.

## 2 Multi-Resolution Methods

Multi-resolution methods typically compute a sequence of discrete approximations to some continuous limit shape. In this paper, this shape is characterized as the solution to a system of partial differential equations. At an abstract level, the method computes a continuous shape $\mathbf{u}$ that satisfies the equation $\mathbf{D}\,\mathbf{u} = 0$, where $\mathbf{D}$ is a continuous differential operator. Since $\mathbf{u} = 0$ is a trivial solution to this equation, extra *boundary conditions* are added to disallow this trivial solution. Instead, the continuous problem consists of finding the shape $\mathbf{u}$ that satisfies

$$\mathbf{D}\,\mathbf{u} = \mathbf{b} \tag{1}$$

where $\mathbf{b}$ is determined by the boundary conditions.

Because computation with continuous quantities is cumbersome, a common approach is to discretize the continuous shape $\mathbf{u}$ over some type of domain grid $T$ yielding a discrete representation $u$. [1] Similarly, the continuous differential operator $\mathbf{D}$ is represented by a discrete counterpart $D$ and the boundary conditions $\mathbf{b}$ are replaced by their discrete analog $b$. Now, the discrete analog of equation 1 is

$$D\,u = b. \tag{2}$$

If the discretization is chosen appropriately, the discrete solution $u$ of equation 2 approximates the continuous solution $\mathbf{u}$ of equation 1.

Equation 2 can be solved using a direct method such as Gauß elimination. However, this approach is impractical for large problems. An alternate approach is to exploit the local structure of the discrete operator $D$ and to solve equation 2 using an iterative method such as Jacobi smoothing. Varga [26] and Young [30] provide background material on several iterative smoothing methods. Unfortunately, these iterative methods tend to converge very slowly for large problems. Multi-grid solvers converge much more rapidly and provide an efficient method for recursively solving large systems of linear equations [2].

In multi-grid, the domain grid $T$ is replaced by a sequence of nested grids $T_0 \subseteq T_1 \subseteq \ldots \subseteq T_n$. Similarly, the discrete entities $D$, $u$ and $b$ are replaced by corresponding entities $D_k$, $u_k$ and $b_k$, defined over the associated domain grid $T_k$. Consequently, the problem now consists of solving the sequence of linear systems

$$D_k\,u_k = b_k. \tag{3}$$

Again, if the discretizations are chosen appropriately, the limit of these discrete solutions $u_k$ converges to the desired continuous solution $\mathbf{u}$.

[1] Note that we follow the convention of using bold roman notation such as $\mathbf{u}$ for continuous entities and italics such as $u$ for their discrete counterparts.

Multi-grid is a recursive method for computing $u_0, u_1, u_2, \ldots$ . Given the solution $u_{k-1}$, multi-grid computes $u_k$ using the following three steps:

1. **Prediction:** Compute an initial guess of the solution $u_k$ using a prediction operator $S_k$,

   $$u_k = S_{k-1} u_{k-1}.$$

   In multi-grid terminology, this step is also referred to as *prolongation*. A common choice for the prediction operator $S_k$ is piecewise linear interpolation.

2. **Smoothing:** Use a traditional iterative method such as Jacobi or Gauß-Seidel smoothing to improve the current solution for $u_k$.

3. **Coarse grid correction:** Restrict the current residual $D_k\,u_k - b_k$ to the next coarser grid $T_{k-1}$. There, solve for an error correction term $e_{k-1}$ that is then added back into the solution using $u_k = u_k + S_{k-1}e_{k-1}$.

Note that both steps 2 and 3 serve to improve the accuracy of the solution $u_k$. If the operator $S_{k-1}$ used in the prediction phase of multi-grid produces an exact initial guess, i.e. $D_k S_{k-1} u_{k-1} = b_k$, then both the smoothing steps and coarse grid correction steps can be omitted. Such an operator $S_{k-1}$ is a *perfect predictor*. A multi-grid scheme based on perfect predictors consists of repeated applications of $S_k$ to produce finer and finer solutions that converge to the exact, continuous solution. Such a multi-grid scheme is exactly a subdivision scheme, where the perfect predictor takes the role of the subdivision operator! The remainder of this section focuses on characterizing perfect predictors in terms of the discrete operators $D_k$.

To be useful in practice, application of the perfect predictor should not be too costly. Therefore, the perfect predictors should have a local structure. To this end, we suggest a specific choice for the right-hand side $b_k$ of equation 3 based on upsampling. Let $R_{k-1}$ be the discrete *upsampling (replication) operator* that converts data defined over the coarse grid $T_{k-1}$ into data defined over the next finer grid $T_k$. $R_{k-1}$'s action is very simple: data associated with grid points in $T_{k-1}$ are replicated; the remaining data associated with grid points in $T_k - T_{k-1}$ are set to zero. Choosing the right-hand side $b_k$ to have the form

$$b_k = R_{k-1} R_{k-2} \ldots R_0 D_0 u_0$$

results in equation 3 having the form

$$D_k u_k = R_{k-1} R_{k-2} \ldots R_0 D_0 u_0. \tag{4}$$

This particular choice of $b_k$ can be interpreted as follows: $u_k$ is determined so that the discrete differences $D_0 u_0$ over the coarsest grid $T_0$ are replicated onto the fine grids $T_k$; all the remaining entries in $D_k u_k$ are forced to zero. Intuitively, the limit of this process, as $k \to \infty$, is an object $\mathbf{u}$ that satisfies the continuous partial differential equation $\mathbf{D}\,\mathbf{u} = 0$ everywhere except at the coarsest grid points. At these coarsest grid points $\mathbf{D}\,\mathbf{u}$ exactly reproduces the differences $D_0\,u_0$.

Based on equation 4, a predictor $S_{k-1}$ is perfect if it satisfies the *fundamental multi-grid relation*

$$D_k S_{k-1} = R_{k-1} D_{k-1}. \tag{5}$$

To verify this assertion, let $u_{k-1}$ be a solution to equation 4, i.e. $D_{k-1}\,u_{k-1} = R_{k-2}\,R_{k-3} \ldots R_0\,D_0\,u_0$. Multiplying both sides of this equation by $R_{k-1}$ yields that $R_{k-1}\,D_{k-1}\,u_{k-1} = R_{k-1}\,R_{k-2}\,R_{k-3} \ldots R_0\,D_0\,u_0$. Replacing $R_{k-1} D_{k-1}$ by $D_k S_{k-1}$ (due to equation 5) yields $D_k S_{k-1}\, u_{k-1} = R_{k-1}\, R_{k-2}\, R_{k-3} ... R_0\, D_0\, u_0$. Finally, since $u_k = S_{k-1} u_{k-1}$, $u_k$ also satisfies equation 4.

At a high level, our approach to building subdivision schemes for linear systems of PDEs can be outlined as follows: First, we construct discrete analogs of the continuous differential operators involved in the problem. Next, we determine the relationship between the grids of different levels, and define the upsampling and concrete discrete difference operators for these grids. Finally, we solve for the perfect predictor using the fundamental relation 5. The result of this process is a perfect predictor, or subdivision scheme, which converges to solutions of the original, continuous problem.

The next section fills in more of the details of this process. In particular, we derive a subdivision scheme for the simple differential equation that characterizes piecewise polynomial splines. Later in the paper, the same methodology is used to construct subdivision schemes for the PDEs that characterize fluid flow.

# 3 Subdivision for Polynomial Splines

A polynomial spline $\mathbf{u}[\mathbf{x}]$ of order $m$ is a piecewise polynomial function of degree $m-1$ in a real variable $\mathbf{x}$. For uniform grids (i.e. $T$ is the integer grid, $\mathbb{Z}$), the spline $\mathbf{u}[\mathbf{x}]$ satisfies the differential equation

$$\mathbf{D}[\mathbf{x}]^m \mathbf{u}[\mathbf{x}] = 0 \qquad (6)$$

for all $\mathbf{x} \notin \mathbb{Z}$. Here, the differential operator $\mathbf{D}[\mathbf{x}]$ computes the derivative of $\mathbf{u}[\mathbf{x}]$ with respect to $\mathbf{x}$. $\mathbf{D}[\mathbf{x}]^m$ takes the $m$th derivative of $\mathbf{u}[\mathbf{x}]$ with respect to $\mathbf{x}$. Our task is to derive the subdivision rules for these polynomial splines using equation 5.

## 3.1 A multi-grid scheme

Moving to the multi-grid setting, we consider a sequence of domain grids $T_k$ of the form $T_k = \frac{1}{2^k}\mathbb{Z}$. Note that the grids $T_k$ grow dense in the domain $\mathbb{R}$ as $k \to \infty$. Given the continuous spline $\mathbf{u}[\mathbf{x}]$, let $u_k$ be a vector whose $i$th entry approximates $\mathbf{u}\left[\frac{i}{2^k}\right]$. The vectors $u_k$ are discrete approximations to $\mathbf{u}[\mathbf{x}]$. As $k \to \infty$, these vectors $u_k$ should converge to the continuous function $\mathbf{u}[\mathbf{x}]$.

In the uniform case, generating functions provide a particularly concise and powerful representation for the vectors $u_k$. Let $u_k[x]$ denote the generating function of the form

$$u_k[x] = \sum_i (u_k)_i x^i$$

where $(u_k)_i$ is the coefficient of the vector $u_k$ with grid point $i$. For example, the vector $u_0 = \{4, 12, 10, 5, 8\}$ over the integer grid points $\{0, 1, 2, 3, 4\}$ can be represented by the generating function $u_0[x] = 4 + 12x + 10x^2 + 5x^3 + 8x^4$. (Note that the generating functions used in this paper may posses negative and even fractional exponents.)

To discretize the left-hand side of equation 6, we next derive the discrete counterpart of the continuous $m$th derivative operator $\mathbf{D}[\mathbf{x}]^m$. On the initial grid $T_0 = \mathbb{Z}$, the discrete analog of $\mathbf{D}[\mathbf{x}]$ is the generating function

$$\mathrm{D}[\mathrm{x}] = \frac{1-\mathrm{x}}{\mathrm{x}^{1/2}}.$$

(Note the power $x^{-1/2}$ centers the difference operator $\mathrm{D}[\mathrm{x}]$ over the origin.) On finer grids $T_k = \frac{1}{2^k}\mathbb{Z}$, this generating function $\mathrm{D}[\mathrm{x}]$ is scaled by a factor of $2^k$. Application of the differential operator $\mathbf{D}[\mathbf{x}]$ to $\mathbf{u}[\mathbf{x}]$ has a simple discrete analog: multiplication of $u[x]$ by $\mathrm{D}[\mathrm{x}]$. Repeated application of $\mathbf{D}[\mathbf{x}]$ is equivalent to repeated multiplication by $\mathrm{D}[\mathrm{x}]$. Thus, on the grid $T_k$, the discrete analog of the left-hand side of equation 6 is

$$(2^k \mathrm{D}[\mathrm{x}])^m u_k[x].$$

This expression forms the left-hand side of the fundamental multi-grid relation of equation 4. Our next task is to build a generating function that models the right-hand side of these equations. Recall that the upsampling operator $R_k$ replicated data on $T_k$ and inserted zero on $T_{k+1} - T_k$. If $u_k[x]$ is the generating function associated with the vector $u_k$, then the expression $R_k u_k$ corresponds to the generating function $u_k[x^2]$. Likewise, the action of the combined operator $R_{k-1} ... R_0$ can be modeled by replacing $x$ by $x^{2^k}$. Thus, equation 4 can be expressed in terms of generating functions as

$$(2^k \mathrm{D}[\mathrm{x}])^m u_k[x] = 2^k \mathrm{D}[\mathrm{x}^{2^k}]^m u_0[x^{2^k}]. \qquad (7)$$

Note that an extra factor of $2^k$ appears on the right-hand side of equation 7. This factor reflects the effect of the varying grid spacing on $R_k$. By scaling each upsampling operator $R_k$ by $2^d$ (where $d$ is the dimension of the underlying domain), the resulting normalized equation defines a sequence of solutions $u_k$ that converges to the desired polynomial spline $\mathbf{u}[\mathbf{x}]$.

## 3.2 The associated subdivision scheme

Given this multi-grid framework, we can now apply equation 5 and derive a perfect predictor for this scheme. In the uniform setting, the predictor (subdivision matrix) $S$ is a 2-slanted matrix whose columns are all shifts of a single vector. If we let $s[x]$ denote the generating function associated with this vector, then equation 5 has the form:

$$(2^k \mathrm{D}[\mathrm{x}])^m s[x] = 2\left(2^{k-1} \mathrm{D}[\mathrm{x}^2]\right)^m. \qquad (8)$$

The beauty of equation 8 is that we can now directly solve for the subdivision mask $s[x]$. In particular, $s[x]$ is independent of $k$ and has the form:

$$s[x] = 2\left(\frac{\mathrm{D}[\mathrm{x}^2]}{2\mathrm{D}[\mathrm{x}]}\right)^m = \frac{1}{2^{m-1}} \frac{(1+x)^m}{x^{m/2}}. \qquad (9)$$

To verify this fact, recall that $\mathrm{D}[\mathrm{x}] = \frac{1-\mathrm{x}}{\mathrm{x}^{1/2}}$. Therefore, $\mathrm{D}[\mathrm{x}^2] = \frac{1-\mathrm{x}^2}{\mathrm{x}}$ and $\frac{\mathrm{D}[\mathrm{x}^2]}{\mathrm{D}[\mathrm{x}]} = \frac{1+x}{x^{1/2}}$. Substituting this expression into equation 9 yields a mask of the form $s[x] = \frac{1}{2^{m-1}} \frac{(1+x)^m}{x^{m/2}}$. This mask exactly captures the subdivision rule for polynomial splines of order $m$. In the case of cubic splines, i.e. $m = 4$, equation 9 correctly yields the subdivision mask $s[x] = \frac{(1+x)^4}{8x^2} = \frac{1}{8}\left(x^{-2} + 4x^{-1} + 6 + 4x + x^2\right)$ due to Lane and Riesenfeld [21].

Given the mask $s[x]$, subdivision can be expressed very concisely in terms of generating functions. The coefficient vectors $u_{k-1}$ and $u_k$ are related by

$$u_k[x] = s[x] u_{k-1}[x^2].$$

As $k \to \infty$, the coefficients of $u_k[x]$ form increasingly dense approximations to a continuous limit function $\mathbf{u}[\mathbf{x}]$. In particular, the coefficient of $x^i$ in $u_k[x]$ acts as a discrete approximation to a continuous function value $\mathbf{u}\left[\frac{i}{2^k}\right]$. Figure 2 shows three rounds of subdivision for a cubic spline.

The upper left curve in figure 2 depicts the coefficients $u_0 = \{4, 12, 10, 5, 8\}$ plotted over the integer grid points $\{0, 1, 2, 3, 4\}$. This coefficient sequence can be represented by the generating function $u_0[x] = 4 + 12x + 10x^2 + 5x^3 + 8x^4$. The upper right curve shows the coefficients of $u_1[x] = s[x] u_0[x^2]$,

$$u_1[x] = \frac{1}{8}\left(\frac{1}{x^2} + \frac{4}{x} + 6 + 4x + x^2\right)\left(4 + 12\,x^2 + 10\,x^4 + 5\,x^6 + 8x^8\right),$$

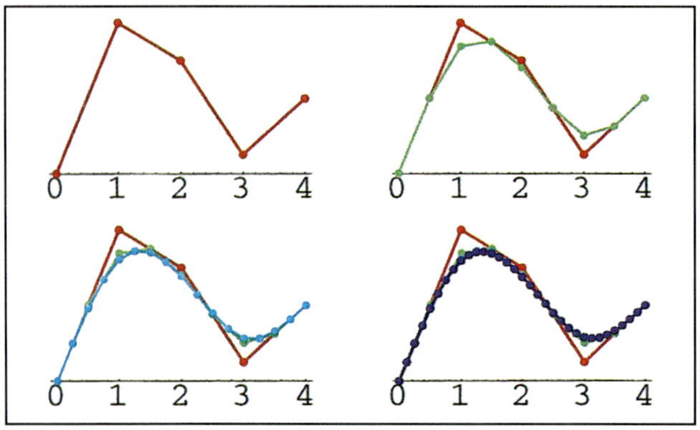


Figure 2: Subdivision for cubic splines.

plotted over the half-integer sequence, $\left\{0,\frac{1}{2},1,\frac{3}{2},2,\frac{5}{2},3,\frac{7}{2},4\right\}$. (Remember, the coefficients of $x^i$ in $u_k[x]$ is plotted at $\mathbf{x} = \frac{i}{2^k}$.) The lower figures show the coefficients of $u_2[x] = s[x]u_1[x^2]$ and $u_3[x] = s[x]u_2[x^2]$ plotted over the quarter and one eighth integers, respectively. Observe that this process quickly converges to the desired polynomial spline.

Figure 3 shows plots of the discrete differences $\mathrm{D}[x]^4 u_k[x]$ for $k = 0,1,2,3$. Note that these differences are identically zero except at the original integer grid points, $\{0,1,2,3,4\}$.

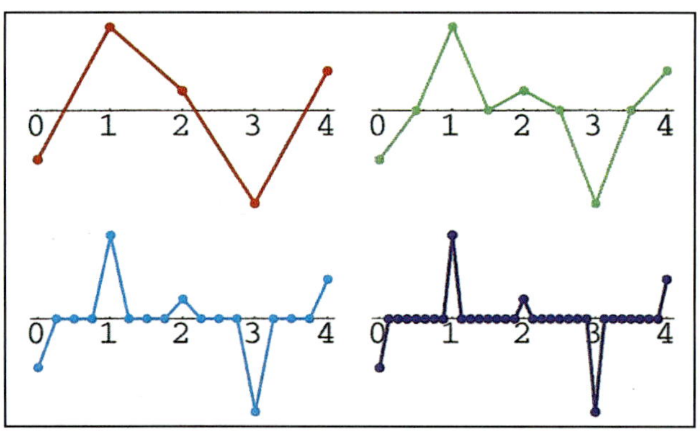


Figure 3: Fourth order discrete differences for cubic splines.

This univariate subdivision scheme can be extended to two-dimensional meshes in a variety of ways. Much of subdivision's popularity as a modeling technique is due to the landmark papers by Doo and Sabin [8] and Catmull and Clark [3]. Hoppe, DeRose and co-workers [14],[7] and Sederberg et al. [24] developed subdivision schemes that can incorporate curvature discontinuities such as creases. Zorin and Schroeder [31] and Kobbelt et al. [20] show that subdivision is well suited for interactive multi-resolution editing of smooth models. Finally, recent work by Kobbelt [18, 19] and the authors [28] investigates the link between subdivision and variational problems.

# 4 A Brief Introduction to Fluid Mechanics

Fluid mechanics is a field of study that can occupy an entire career. Our goal in this section is to give a brief introduction suitable for the mathematically savvy non-specialist. The source for most of the material in this paper is *Fluid Mechanics* by Liggett [17]. Our approach is to develop most of the theory for flows in two-dimensions. Later in the paper, we extend the theory to three dimensions.

A flow in two dimensions is a vector-valued function $(\mathbf{u}[\mathbf{x},\mathbf{y}],\mathbf{v}[\mathbf{x},\mathbf{y}])^T$ in two parameters $\mathbf{x}$ and $\mathbf{y}$. Flows can be visualized in a number of ways. Perhaps the simplest method is to evaluate $(\mathbf{u}[\mathbf{x},\mathbf{y}],\mathbf{v}[\mathbf{x},\mathbf{y}])^T$ at a grid of parameter values $(\mathbf{x}_i,\mathbf{y}_j)$. Each resulting vector $(\mathbf{u}[\mathbf{x}_i,\mathbf{y}_j],\mathbf{v}[\mathbf{x}_i,\mathbf{y}_j])^T$ is then plotted with its tail placed at $(\mathbf{x}_i,\mathbf{y}_j)$.

The behavior of flows is governed by a set of PDEs known as the *Navier-Stokes equations*. In the most general setting, this set of equations is non-linear. As a result, the behavior of many types of flows is very hard to predict. However, in several important settings, the Navier-Stokes equations reduce to a much simpler set of linear PDEs. In the next sections, we consider two such cases: perfect flow and slow flow. Later, we derive subdivision schemes for slow flow, noting that the exact same methodology can be used to build schemes for perfect flow.

## 4.1 Perfect flows

Perfect flows are characterized by two properties: *incompressibility* and *zero viscosity*. A flow $(\mathbf{u}[\mathbf{x},\mathbf{y}],\mathbf{v}[\mathbf{x},\mathbf{y}])^T$ is *incompressible* if it satisfies the partial differential equation:

$$\mathbf{u}^{(1,0)}[\mathbf{x},\mathbf{y}] + \mathbf{v}^{(0,1)}[\mathbf{x},\mathbf{y}] = 0.$$

The superscript $(i,j)$ denotes the $i$th derivative with respect to $\mathbf{x}$ and the $j$th derivative with respect to $\mathbf{y}$. Flows $(\mathbf{u}[\mathbf{x},\mathbf{y}],\mathbf{v}[\mathbf{x},\mathbf{y}])^T$ satisfying this equation are said to be *divergence-free*. In most flows, viscosity induces rotation in the flow. However, if the fluid has zero viscosity, then its flows are free of rotation. Such flows are often referred to as *irrotational*. Irrotational flows are characterized by the partial differential equation:

$$\mathbf{u}^{(0,1)}[\mathbf{x},\mathbf{y}] = \mathbf{v}^{(1,0)}[\mathbf{x},\mathbf{y}].$$

Together, these two equations in two functions $\mathbf{u}$ and $\mathbf{v}$ uniquely characterize perfect flow:

$$\begin{aligned} \mathbf{u}^{(1,0)}[\mathbf{x},\mathbf{y}] + \mathbf{v}^{(0,1)}[\mathbf{x},\mathbf{y}] &= 0, \\ \mathbf{u}^{(0,1)}[\mathbf{x},\mathbf{y}] - \mathbf{v}^{(1,0)}[\mathbf{x},\mathbf{y}] &= 0. \end{aligned} \qquad (10)$$

To facilitate manipulations involving such systems of PDEs, we use two important tools. As in the univariate case, we express various derivatives using the differential operators $\mathbf{D}[\mathbf{x}]$ and $\mathbf{D}[\mathbf{y}]$. Left multiplication by the differential operator $\mathbf{D}[\mathbf{z}]$ is simply a shorthand for taking a continuous derivative in the $\mathbf{z}$ direction. For example, $\mathbf{D}[\mathbf{x}]\mathbf{u}[\mathbf{x},\mathbf{y}] = \mathbf{u}^{(1,0)}[\mathbf{x},\mathbf{y}]$ and $\mathbf{D}[\mathbf{y}]\mathbf{v}[\mathbf{x},\mathbf{y}] = \mathbf{v}^{(0,1)}[\mathbf{x},\mathbf{y}]$. Our second tool is matrix notation. After replacing the derivatives in equation 10 by their equivalent differential operators, the two linear equations in two unknowns can be written in matrix form as:

$$\begin{pmatrix} \mathbf{D}[\mathbf{x}] & \mathbf{D}[\mathbf{y}] \\ \mathbf{D}[\mathbf{y}] & -\mathbf{D}[\mathbf{x}] \end{pmatrix} \begin{pmatrix} \mathbf{u}[\mathbf{x},\mathbf{y}] \\ \mathbf{v}[\mathbf{x},\mathbf{y}] \end{pmatrix} = 0. \qquad (11)$$

In conjunction, these techniques allow generation of subdivision schemes from systems of PDEs using the same strategy as was employed for polynomial splines in the previous section.

## 4.2 Slow flows

As we saw in the previous section, perfect flows are governed by a simple set of linear PDEs. Another important class of linear flow is *slow flow*. A slow flow is an incompressible flow in which the viscous behavior of the flow dominates any inertial component of the flow. For example, the flow of viscous fluids such as asphalt, sewage sludge or molasses is governed almost entirely by its viscous nature. Other examples of slow flow include the movement of small particles through water or air and the swimming of micro organisms [17].

Slow flow may also be viewed as a minimum energy elastic deformation applied to an incompressible material. This observation is based on the fact that the flow of an extremely viscous fluid is essentially equivalent to an elastic deformation of a solid. One byproduct of this view is that any technique for creating slow flows can also be applied to create minimum energy deformations.

Slow flows in two dimensions are also governed by two partial differential equations. The first partial differential equation corresponds to incompressibility. However, due to their viscosity, slow flows have a rotational component. This rotational component is governed by the partial differential equation:

$$\mathbf{u}^{(2,1)}[\mathbf{x},\mathbf{y}]+\mathbf{u}^{(0,3)}[\mathbf{x},\mathbf{y}]-\mathbf{v}^{(3,0)}[\mathbf{x},\mathbf{y}]-\mathbf{v}^{(1,2)}[\mathbf{x},\mathbf{y}]=0$$

For a complete derivation of this equation, see Liggett [17], p.161. If $\mathbf{L}[\mathbf{x},\mathbf{y}]=\mathbf{D}[\mathbf{x}]^2+\mathbf{D}[\mathbf{y}]^2$ denotes the continuous Laplacian, then these two partial differential equations can now be written together in matrix form as:

$$\begin{pmatrix} \mathbf{D}[\mathbf{x}] & \mathbf{D}[\mathbf{y}] \\ \mathbf{L}[\mathbf{x},\mathbf{y}]\mathbf{D}[\mathbf{y}] & -\mathbf{L}[\mathbf{x},\mathbf{y}]\mathbf{D}[\mathbf{x}] \end{pmatrix} \begin{pmatrix} \mathbf{u}[\mathbf{x},\mathbf{y}] \\ \mathbf{v}[\mathbf{x},\mathbf{y}] \end{pmatrix} = 0. \tag{12}$$

In this form, the similarity between the governing equations for perfect flow and slow flow is striking: The second equation in 12 corresponds to the equation for irrotational flow multiplied by the Laplacian $\mathbf{L}[\mathbf{x},\mathbf{y}]$. The effect of this extra factor of $\mathbf{L}[\mathbf{x},\mathbf{y}]$ on the rotational component of slow flows is easy to explain: Perfect flows exhibit infinite velocities at sources of rotational flow. The extra factor of $\mathbf{L}[\mathbf{x},\mathbf{y}]$ smoothes the velocity field at rotational sources and causes slow flows to be continuous everywhere.

Due to limited space, our main focus in this paper is on developing subdivision schemes for slow flows based on equation 12. Slow flows define smooth vector fields and relate to other interesting problems such as minimum energy deformations. However, we remind the reader that all of the techniques described here are equally applicable to perfect flows.

### 4.3 Previous work on flows

Traditionally, fluid flow has been modeled either through explicit or numerical solutions of the associated PDEs. Explicit solutions for perfect flow are known for a number of primitives such as sources, sinks and rotors. These can be combined into more complex fields using simple linear combinations (see [17] for more details).

Numerical solutions for the modeling and simulation of flow is a very active research area. Commonly, such solutions involve approximation using either finite difference or finite element schemes. Brezzi and Fortin [1] provide an introduction to some of the standard numerical techniques used for modeling flow. Recently, cellular automata have been applied with some success for the discrete modeling of physical problems, including gas and fluid flow [6, 23].

On the computer graphics side, Kass and Miller [16] simulate surface waves in water by approximately solving a two-dimensional shallow water problem. Chen and Lobo [4] solve the Navier Stokes equations in two dimensions and use the resulting pressure field to define a fluid surface. Chiba et al. [5] simulate water currents using a particle based behavioral model. Miller and Pearce [22] model viscous fluids through a connected particle system. Wejchert and Haumann [29] introduce notions from aerodynamics to the graphics community. Stam and Fiume [25] model turbulent wind fields for animation based on solving the underlying PDEs. Foster and Metaxas [11] suggest solving the Navier-Stokes equations on a coarse grid in three dimensions using a finite difference approach and then interpolating the coarse solution locally as needed. They also extended their method to handle turbulent steam [12].

## 5 A Subdivision Scheme for Slow Flow

Following the same approach as in the polynomial case, we first build discrete analogs of the continuous PDEs for slow flow and then employ the fundamental multi-grid relation of equation 5 to solve for the subdivision scheme. Given a coarse vector field $(u_0, v_0)^T$, the resulting subdivision scheme defines a sequence of increasingly dense vector fields $(u_k,\ v_k)^T$. These fields converge to a continuous vector field $(\mathbf{u}[\mathbf{x},\mathbf{y}],\mathbf{v}[\mathbf{x},\mathbf{y}])^T$ that follows the original coarse vector field $(u_0, v_0)^T$.

As for polynomial splines, we represent a discrete vector field by a 2-vector of generating functions:

$$\begin{pmatrix} u_k[x,y] \\ v_k[x,y] \end{pmatrix} = \sum_{i,j} \begin{pmatrix} u_k \\ v_k \end{pmatrix}_{ij} x^i y^j.$$

Again, the vectors comprising $(u_k, v_k)^T$ act as discrete approximations to the continuous limit field $(\mathbf{u}[\mathbf{x},\mathbf{y}],\mathbf{v}[\mathbf{x},\mathbf{y}])^T$. In particular, the $ij$th entry of $(u_k, v_k)^T$ acts at $(\mathbf{x},\mathbf{y}) = \left(\frac{i}{2^k}, \frac{j}{2^k}\right)$. The subdivision scheme $s[x,y]$ is the linear operator that relates $(u_{k-1}[x], v_{k-1}[x])^T$ and $(u_k[x], v_k[x])^T$ according to

$$\begin{pmatrix} u_k[x,y] \\ v_k[x,y] \end{pmatrix} = s[x,y] \begin{pmatrix} u_{k-1}[x^2,y^2] \\ v_{k-1}[x^2,y^2] \end{pmatrix}.$$

Thus, $s[x,y]$ is a $2\times 2$ matrix of generating functions.

In practice, interesting flows depend on boundary conditions which drive the flow. Our approach to boundary conditions is similar to that for polynomial splines. In particular, we enforce the flow PDEs everywhere except on the initial integer grid, $\mathbb{Z}^2$. The coarse, initial vector field encoded by $(u_0[x,y], v_0[x,y])^T$ determines the boundary conditions at $\mathbb{Z}^2$. Denser vector fields are represented by the generating functions $(u_k[x], v_k[x])^T$ and determined so as to satisfy the PDEs for flow.

### 5.1 A multi-grid scheme

Following the polynomial case, we consider slow flows $(\mathbf{u}[\mathbf{x},\mathbf{y}],\mathbf{v}[\mathbf{x},\mathbf{y}])^T$ that satisfy the differential equations (in matrix form)

$$\begin{pmatrix} \mathbf{D}[\mathbf{x}] & \mathbf{D}[\mathbf{y}] \\ \mathbf{L}[\mathbf{x},\mathbf{y}]\mathbf{D}[\mathbf{y}] & -\mathbf{L}[\mathbf{x},\mathbf{y}]\mathbf{D}[\mathbf{x}] \end{pmatrix} \begin{pmatrix} \mathbf{u}[\mathbf{x},\mathbf{y}] \\ \mathbf{v}[\mathbf{x},\mathbf{y}] \end{pmatrix} = 0$$

for all $(\mathbf{x},\mathbf{y}) \notin \mathbb{Z}^2$. On the grid $T_k = \frac{1}{2^k}\mathbb{Z}^2$, the discrete version of this equation (left-hand side only) has the form:

$$\begin{pmatrix} 2^k \mathrm{D}[x] & 2^k \mathrm{D}[y] \\ 8^k L[x,y]\mathrm{D}[y] & -8^k L[x,y]\mathrm{D}[x] \end{pmatrix} \begin{pmatrix} u_k[x,y] \\ v_k[x,y] \end{pmatrix}$$

where $L[x,y] = \mathrm{D}[x]^2 + \mathrm{D}[y]^2$ is the discrete version of the Laplacian. The various powers of two are necessary for the discrete differences to converge to the appropriate continuous derivatives as $k \to \infty$. Based on this observation, the fundamental multi-grid equation (equation 4) can be expressed in terms of generating functions as:

$$\begin{pmatrix} 2^k \mathrm{D}[x] & 2^k \mathrm{D}[y] \\ 8^k L[x,y]\mathrm{D}[y] & -8^k L[x,y]\mathrm{D}[x] \end{pmatrix} \begin{pmatrix} u_k[x,y] \\ v_k[x,y] \end{pmatrix} = 4^k \begin{pmatrix} 0 & 0 \\ L\left[x^{2^k}, y^{2^k}\right]\mathrm{D}[y^{2^k}] & -L\left[x^{2^k}, y^{2^k}\right]\mathrm{D}[x^{2^k}] \end{pmatrix} \begin{pmatrix} u_0\left[x^{2^k}, y^{2^k}\right] \\ v_0\left[x^{2^k}, y^{2^k}\right] \end{pmatrix}. \tag{13}$$

As before, the left-hand side of equation 13 is a discrete approximation to the PDEs for slow flow on $T_k$. On the right-hand side, the top row of the difference matrix, corresponding to divergence, is zero. The bottom row of the difference matrix computes a discrete approximation to the rotational component of the flow on $\mathbb{Z}^2$. This rotational component is then upsampled (via $x \to x^{2^k}$ and $y \to y^{2^k}$) to the grid $\frac{1}{2^k}\mathbb{Z}^2$. (The extra factor of $4^k$ on the right-hand side is due to the scaling of the upsampling matrices.)

As $k \to \infty$, the discrete flows $(u_k[x], v_k[x])^T$ satisfying equation 13 converge to a continuous slow flow $(\mathbf{u}[\mathbf{x},\mathbf{y}], \mathbf{v}[\mathbf{x},\mathbf{y}])^T$ satisfying equation 12. The appendix demonstrates this convergence by deriving an analytic representation for the limit flow directly from equation 13. This analytic representation for $(\mathbf{u}[\mathbf{x},\mathbf{y}], \mathbf{v}[\mathbf{x},\mathbf{y}])^T$ is especially useful in understanding the behavior of the resulting flows. For example, the resulting slow flows are divergence-free everywhere and rotation-free everywhere except at the initial grid points $\mathbb{Z}^2$. The flow is driven by rotational sources that are positioned to drive a flow that follows the initial vector field $(u_0, v_0)^T$. Figure 4 depicts two flows, each generated by a single unit vector in the $\mathbf{x}$ and $\mathbf{y}$ direction, respectively. Note that each flow is driven by a pair of rotational source located on grid points in $\mathbb{Z}^2$. More complex flows are formed by taking linear combinations of translates of these flows on $\mathbb{Z}^2$.

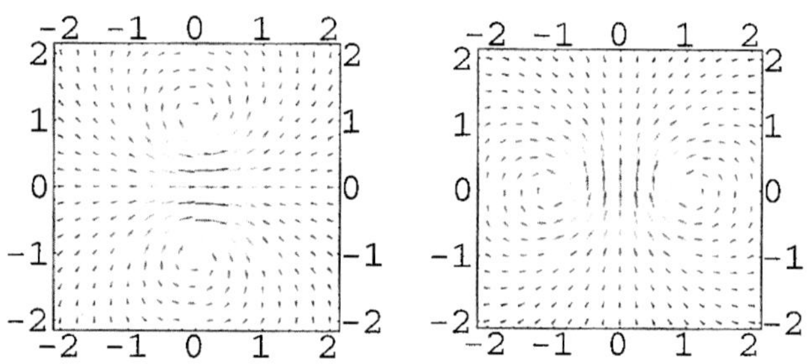

Figure 4: Vector basis functions for slow flow

## 5.2 The associated subdivision scheme

In analogy with the case of polynomial splines, we next apply our characterization for perfect predictors (equation 5) and derive the subdivision scheme associated with this multi-grid process.

$$\begin{pmatrix} \frac{1}{2}\mathrm{D}[x] & \frac{1}{2}\mathrm{D}[y] \\ 2L[x,y]\mathrm{D}[y] & -2L[x,y]\mathrm{D}[x] \end{pmatrix} s[x,y] = \begin{pmatrix} 0 & 0 \\ L[x^2,y^2]\mathrm{D}[y^2] & -L[x^2,y^2]\mathrm{D}[x^2] \end{pmatrix}. \quad (14)$$

Solving for $s[x,y]$ in equation 14 yields a two by two matrix of generating functions of the form

$$s[x,y] = \frac{L[x^2,y^2]}{2L[x,y]^2} \begin{pmatrix} \mathrm{D}[y]\,\mathrm{D}[y^2] & -\mathrm{D}[x^2]\,\mathrm{D}[y] \\ -\mathrm{D}[x]\,\mathrm{D}[y^2] & \mathrm{D}[x]\,\mathrm{D}[x^2] \end{pmatrix}.$$

The matrix $s[x,y]$ encodes the subdivision scheme for slow flow. Note that this subdivision scheme is a true vector scheme: $u_k[x,y]$ depends on both $u_{k-1}[x,y]$ and $v_{k-1}[x,y]$. Such schemes, while rare, have been the object of some theoretical study. Dyn [10] investigates some of the properties of such vector schemes.

Unfortunately, our analogy with polynomials is not complete. The generating function $L[x,y]^2$ fails to divide into the numerators of $s[x,y]$. In reality, this difficulty is to be expected. Polynomial splines are known to have locally supported bases (B-splines). This observation is consistent with the subdivision scheme $s[x]$ having finitely supported subdivision rules. On the other hand, the vector basis functions in figure 4 do not have local support. Therefore, the generating function $s[x,y]$ can not be expected to divide out and yield finite rules.

Fortunately, all is not lost. The vector basis functions depicted in figure 4 do have two important properties: they are highly localized (i.e. decay rapidly towards zero as $\mathbf{x},\mathbf{y} \to \infty$) and form a partition of unity. As a result, these vector basis functions can be approximated to any desired degree of accuracy via a locally supported vector subdivision scheme. The next section describes an algorithm for finding the subdivision scheme with fixed support that nearly satisfies equation 14.

# 6 Locally Supported Approximations

Before computing approximations to the matrix mask $s[x,y]$, we make an important adjustment to the subdivision scheme for slow flow. Uniform subdivision schemes for univariate splines come in two types: primal and dual. *Primal* schemes have subdivision masks of odd length that position new coefficients both over old coefficients and between adjacent pairs of old coefficients. *Dual* schemes have masks of even length that position two new coefficients between each adjacent pair of old coefficients. In the bivariate setting, each dimension of a uniform scalar subdivision scheme can be either primal or dual. For vector subdivision schemes, the situation can be even more complex. Each dimension of each component can be primal or dual. In particular, distinct components of a vector scheme need not share the same primal/dual structure.

Indeed, this situation is the case for slow flow. Its vector subdivision scheme has the remarkable property that the $\mathbf{u}$ component is primal in $\mathbf{x}$ and dual in $\mathbf{y}$, and the $\mathbf{v}$ component is dual in $\mathbf{x}$ and primal in $\mathbf{y}$. This observation can be verified by checking the size of the masks in the numerator of $s[x,y]$. In practice, this property makes computing with the given vector subdivision scheme unpleasant. The indexing for schemes with such mixed structure is difficult and prone to errors. In practice, we desire a subdivision scheme for slow flows that is purely primal.

To this end, we adjust equation 14 slightly. In particular, we approximate the differential operators $\mathbf{D}[\mathbf{x}]$ and $\mathbf{D}[\mathbf{y}]$ in equation 12 by $\mathrm{D}[x^2]$ and $\mathrm{D}[y^2]$ instead of $\mathrm{D}[x]$ and $\mathrm{D}[y]$. The resulting subdivision scheme $s[x,y]$ has the form

$$\begin{pmatrix} \frac{1}{2}\mathrm{D}[x^2] & \frac{1}{2}\mathrm{D}[y^2] \\ 2L[x,y]\mathrm{D}[y^2] & -2L[x,y]\mathrm{D}[x^2] \end{pmatrix} s[x,y] = \begin{pmatrix} 0 & 0 \\ L[x^2,y^2]\mathrm{D}[y^4] & -L[x^2,y^2]\mathrm{D}[x^4] \end{pmatrix}. \quad (15)$$

Note that the scheme still converges to slow flows. However, the associated subdivision scheme is now primal with a matrix generating function of the form:

$$\frac{1}{2L[x,y]} \begin{pmatrix} \mathrm{D}[y^2]\,\mathrm{D}[y^4] & -\mathrm{D}[x^4]\,\mathrm{D}[y^2] \\ -\mathrm{D}[x^2]\,\mathrm{D}[y^4] & \mathrm{D}[x^2]\,\mathrm{D}[x^4] \end{pmatrix}. \quad (16)$$

Our final goal is to compute a matrix of finitely supported generating functions

$$\begin{pmatrix} s_{11}[x,y] & s_{12}[x,y] \\ s_{21}[x,y] & s_{22}[x,y] \end{pmatrix}$$

that nearly satisfy equation 15. By treating each coefficient of the masks $s_{ij}[x,y]$ as an unknown, the values for these unknowns can be computed as the solution to an optimization problem. In particular, the matrix of approximations $s_{ij}[x,y]$ should nearly satisfy equation 15:

$$\begin{pmatrix} \frac{1}{2}\mathrm{D}[x^2] & \frac{1}{2}\mathrm{D}[y^2] \\ 2L[x,y]\mathrm{D}[y^2] & -2L[x,y]\mathrm{D}[x^2] \end{pmatrix} \begin{pmatrix} s_{11}[x,y] & s_{12}[x,y] \\ s_{21}[x,y] & s_{22}[x,y] \end{pmatrix} \approx \begin{pmatrix} 0 & 0 \\ L[x^2,y^2]\mathrm{D}[y^4] & -L[x^2,y^2]\mathrm{D}[x^4] \end{pmatrix} \quad (17)$$

The maximum of the matrix difference between the two sides of equation 17 can easily be expressed as a linear program. In practice, the size of this program can be reduced by noting that $s_{11}[x,y] = s_{22}[y,x]$ and $s_{21}[x,y] = s_{12}[y,x]$ due to structure of expression 16. Likewise, due to expression 16, the coefficients of $s_{11}[x,y]$ are symmetric in $x$ and $y$ while the coefficients of $s_{21}[x,y]$ are anti-symmetric in $x$ and $y$. As a final modification, we constrain the $s_{ij}[x,y]$ to define a vector scheme with constant precision, i.e. $s[x,y]$ applied to a coarse, constant field should produce the same constant on the finer grid. This extra constraint is necessary for the scheme to be convergent (see Dyn [10]) and is consistent with the observation that the vector basis functions for slow flow have constant precision.

Using a standard linear programming code *(CPLEX,* http://www.cplex.com/), we have precomputed approximations $s_{ij}[x,y]$ for matrix masks of size $5 \times 5$ to size $15 \times 15$. Figure 5 shows a plot of the maximum differences in equation 17 for masks of various sizes. Note the rapid convergence of this residual to zero. This convergence is due to the fact that the basis functions for slow flow decay to zero as $\mathbf{x}, \mathbf{y} \to \infty$.

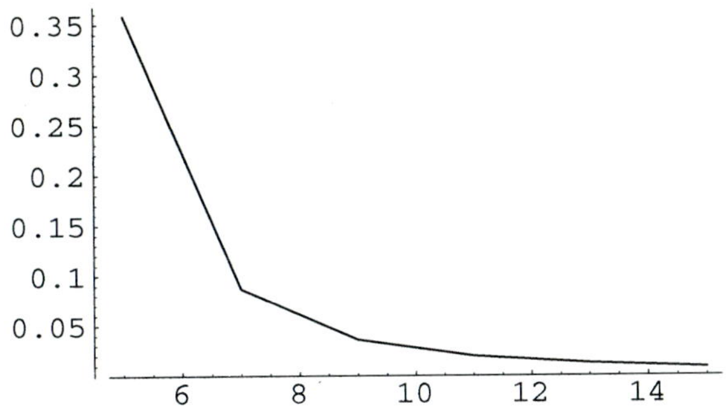


Figure 5: Residuals for finite matrix masks of various sizes.

Given these precomputed masks $s_{ij}[x,y]$, we can apply the vector subdivision scheme to an initial, coarse vector field $(u_0, v_0)^T$ and generate increasingly dense vector fields $(u_k, v_k)^T$ via the matrix relation

$$\begin{pmatrix} u_k[x,y] \\ v_k[x,y] \end{pmatrix} = \begin{pmatrix} s_{11}[x,y] & s_{12}[x,y] \\ s_{12}[y,x] & s_{11}[y,x] \end{pmatrix} \begin{pmatrix} u_{k-1}[x^2,y^2] \\ v_{k-1}[x^2,y^2] \end{pmatrix}.$$

If the vector field $(u_{k-1}, v_{k-1})^T$ is represented as a pair of arrays, then the polynomial multiplications in this expression can be implemented very efficiently using discrete convolution. The resulting implementation allows us to model and manipulate flows in real time. Although matrix masks as small as $5 \times 5$ yield nicely behaved vector fields, we recommend the use of $9 \times 9$ or larger matrix masks if visually realistic approximations to slow flows are desired. Figure 6 shows a plot of several rounds of subdivision applied to a vector basis function defined in the **x**-direction (using a matrix mask of size $9 \times 9$). Note the similarity to the plot of the exact analytic representation in the left-hand side of figure 4.

The proceedings video tape contains a demonstration of an interactive flow modeler based on these subdivision schemes and discusses some further issues. More material, including the actual local subdivision masks of various sizes, can be found on the conference CDROM as well as on our web page under http://www.cs.rice.edu/CS/Graphics/S99.

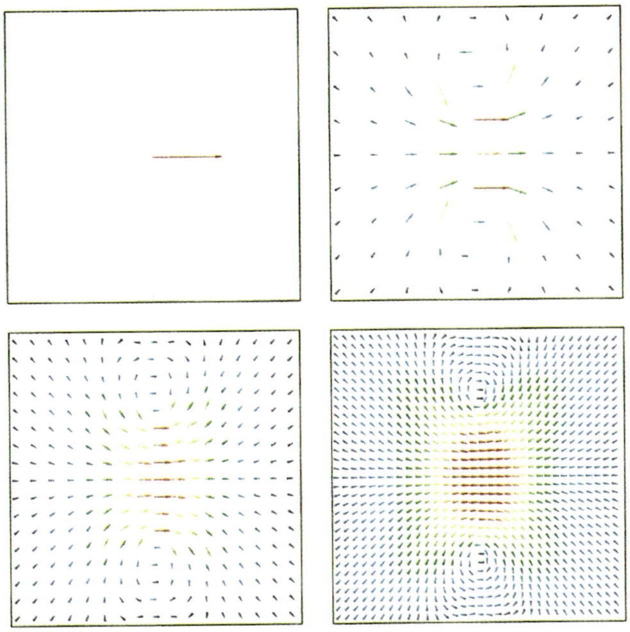

Figure 6: Three rounds of subdivision for a basis vector.

## 7 Extension to Three Dimensions

Three-dimensional flow is a vector-valued function $(\mathbf{u}[\mathbf{x},\mathbf{y},\mathbf{z}], \mathbf{v}[\mathbf{x},\mathbf{y},\mathbf{z}], \mathbf{w}[\mathbf{x},\mathbf{y},\mathbf{z}])^T$ in three variables $\mathbf{x},\mathbf{y},\mathbf{z}$. Three-dimensional slow flow is characterized by two sets of partial differential equations modeling the same conditions as in the two-dimensional case. The first partial differential equation forces the flow to be incompressible. The incompressibility condition is given by

$$\mathbf{D}[\mathbf{x}]\mathbf{u}[\mathbf{x},\mathbf{y},\mathbf{z}] + \mathbf{D}[\mathbf{y}]\mathbf{v}[\mathbf{x},\mathbf{y},\mathbf{z}] + \mathbf{D}[\mathbf{z}]\mathbf{w}[\mathbf{x},\mathbf{y},\mathbf{z}] = 0.$$

The second set of partial differential equations characterizes the rotational behavior of the flow. These conditions are slightly more complicated in three dimensions. For perfect flow these conditions are:

$$\begin{aligned} \mathbf{D}[\mathbf{y}]\mathbf{u}[\mathbf{x},\mathbf{y},\mathbf{z}] &= \mathbf{D}[\mathbf{x}]\mathbf{v}[\mathbf{x},\mathbf{y},\mathbf{z}], \\ \mathbf{D}[\mathbf{z}]\mathbf{u}[\mathbf{x},\mathbf{y},\mathbf{z}] &= \mathbf{D}[\mathbf{x}]\mathbf{w}[\mathbf{x},\mathbf{y},\mathbf{z}], \\ \mathbf{D}[\mathbf{z}]\mathbf{v}[\mathbf{x},\mathbf{y},\mathbf{z}] &= \mathbf{D}[\mathbf{y}]\mathbf{v}[\mathbf{x},\mathbf{y},\mathbf{z}]. \end{aligned} \tag{18}$$

For slow flows, each equation is multiplied by a factor of $\mathbf{L}[\mathbf{x},\mathbf{y},\mathbf{z}]$. Notice that these three continuous equations are linearly dependent. Thus, a continuous solution to these four equations in three unknowns is possible. Unfortunately, the multi-grid approach used in equation 14 fails to yield a subdivision scheme for this set of equations. However, modifying the PDEs for the rotational component of the flow makes subdivision possible. Multiplying each equation of 18 by $\mathbf{D}[\mathbf{z}]$, $\mathbf{D}[\mathbf{y}]$, and $\mathbf{D}[\mathbf{x}]$, respectively yields an new system of partial differential equations:

$$\begin{aligned} \mathbf{D}[\mathbf{z}]\mathbf{D}[\mathbf{y}]\mathbf{u}[\mathbf{x},\mathbf{y},\mathbf{z}] &= \mathbf{D}[\mathbf{x}]\mathbf{D}[\mathbf{z}]\mathbf{v}[\mathbf{x},\mathbf{y},\mathbf{z}], \\ \mathbf{D}[\mathbf{y}]\mathbf{D}[\mathbf{z}]\mathbf{u}[\mathbf{x},\mathbf{y},\mathbf{z}] &= \mathbf{D}[\mathbf{x}]\mathbf{D}[\mathbf{y}]\mathbf{w}[\mathbf{x},\mathbf{y},\mathbf{z}], \\ \mathbf{D}[\mathbf{x}]\mathbf{D}[\mathbf{z}]\mathbf{v}[\mathbf{x},\mathbf{y},\mathbf{z}] &= \mathbf{D}[\mathbf{x}]\mathbf{D}[\mathbf{y}]\mathbf{v}[\mathbf{x},\mathbf{y},\mathbf{z}]. \end{aligned}$$

Note that any solution to these equations is also a solution to equations 18. Given these new equations, we can apply the same

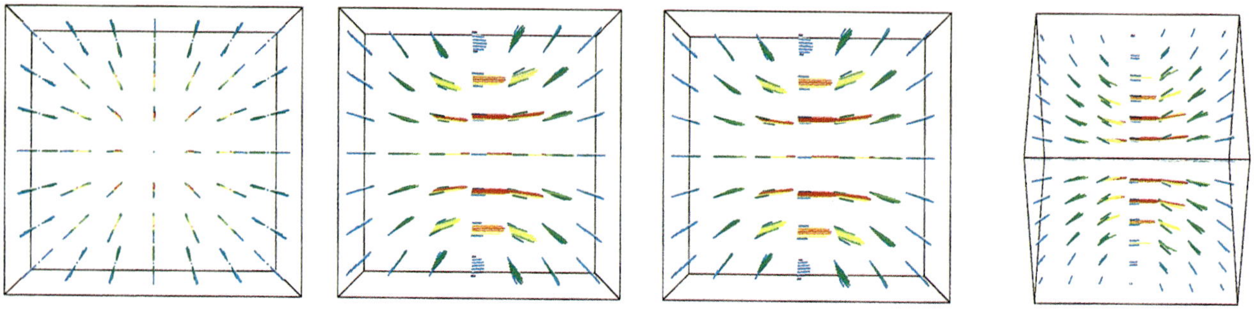

Figure 7: Four views of a 3D vector basis function for slow flow.

derivation used in the two-dimensional case. First, we set up a discrete version of this continuous system of PDEs. Next, we derive the associated subdivision scheme and its analytic bases from the fundamental equation 5. Finally, we compute approximations to the matrix subdivision mask for the scheme using linear programming. Again, the actual subdivision masks can be found on the conference CDROM and on our web page under http://www.cs.rice.edu/CS/Graphics/S99.

The resulting subdivision scheme shares all of the nice properties of the two-dimensional scheme. Given a coarse, initial vector field $(u_0, v_0, w_0)^T$, the limit of the scheme is a continuous vector field $(\mathbf{u}[\mathbf{x},\mathbf{y},\mathbf{z}], \mathbf{v}[\mathbf{x},\mathbf{y},\mathbf{z}], \mathbf{w}[\mathbf{x},\mathbf{y},\mathbf{z}])^T$ that follows $(u_0, v_0, w_0)^T$. Figure 7 shows four plots of a vector basis function in the **x**-direction. The respective plots show views of the vector basis along the **x**-axis, the **y**-axis, the **z**-axis and the vector $(0,1,1)^T$. The basis defines a localized slow flow driven by a toroidal flow around a unit square orthogonal to the **x**-axis.

We conclude with a snapshot from the video proceedings. Figure 8 depicts a stream of particles flowing down a drain. This flow was computed by applying several rounds of subdivision to an initial $3 \times 3 \times 3$ grid of vectors.

## 8 Conclusion and Future Work

This paper developed vector subdivision schemes for slow flows. These subdivision schemes were special instances of more general multi-grid schemes for solving the PDEs that characterize slow flow. Just as subdivision has revolutionized the process of polyhedral modeling, we feel that these schemes have the potential to revolutionize the process of modeling flow. We have several strong reasons for this belief. First and foremost, the speed of these subdivision schemes allows examination and manipulation of interesting flow fields at interactive rates. Next, the simplicity of these subdivision schemes allow graphics enthusiasts who are not specialist in flow to experiment with creating realistic flows. For example, many of the stability problems that arise in conventional solvers are not an issue here. Subdivision also provides a modeling paradigm even if other simple methods such as potential fields fail (i.e. flows in three dimensions). Finally, subdivision can also be incorporated as an add-on to an existing flow package with the subdivision rules used to refine an existing solution and provide more local detail. Because the subdivision scheme models solutions to the Navier-Stokes PDEs, this approach is far superior to polynomial interpolation, which is usually used to locally refine the solutions of a flow package.

On the other hand, there are limitations to the modeling of fluid flow with the methodology developed here. First, subdivision is an intrinsically linear process. Therefore, subdivision can only be applied to modeling solutions to linear systems of PDEs. In the case of flow, this restriction forces the focus onto modeling linear flows such as slow flows and perfect flows. For now, modeling non-linear flows seems beyond the reach of this method. Second, the system of linear PDEs used here describes steady, time independent flows. Thus, the resulting subdivision scheme models steady, time independent flows. However, there is no fundamental limitation to applying the methodology to derive subdivision schemes for time dependent problems as long as the associated PDEs remain linear. Finally, the derivations in this paper are based on regular grids, modeled through generating functions. Hence, the subdivision schemes only model flows on regular grids. However, the same methodology using linear algebra in place of generating functions can be employed to derive subdivision schemes for irregular grids. The main obstacle to this approach is the enumeration and computation of subdivision rules for each distinct geometric configuration in the underlying grid.

Our future plans focus on two problems. The first problem is to use these schemes as the building block for an interactive system for designing flows. Ideally, the user would sketch approximate streamlines and obstacles for the flow. The modeler would then use subdivision to create a physically accurate flow that approximates the sketch. Our second task is to consider an extension of this work to time varying flows. One simple approach would be to modify the initial, coarsest vector field smoothly over time. Since the underlying basis functions are highly localized and smooth, the resulting limit flow should change smoothly. A more physically realistic approach for time-dependent flows would be to add an extra dimension corresponding to time to the discrete vector fields. Time slices of the initial vector field $(u_0, v_0)^T$ would be viewed as key flow configurations (analogous to key frames). The vector subdivision scheme would then define a sequence of increasingly dense (in both time and space) vector fields $(u_k, v_k)^T$ that converge to the true time-dependent flow.

## Acknowledgments

We would like to thank the anonymous reviewers of the paper for the many constructive suggestions. This work was supported in part under National Science Foundation grants CCR-9500572 and CCR-9732344.

## References

[1] F. Brezzi, M. Fortin: *Mixed and Hybrid Finite Element Methods*, Springer, 1991.

[2] W. L. Briggs: *A Multigrid Tutorial*. Society for Industrial and Applied Mathematics, 1987.

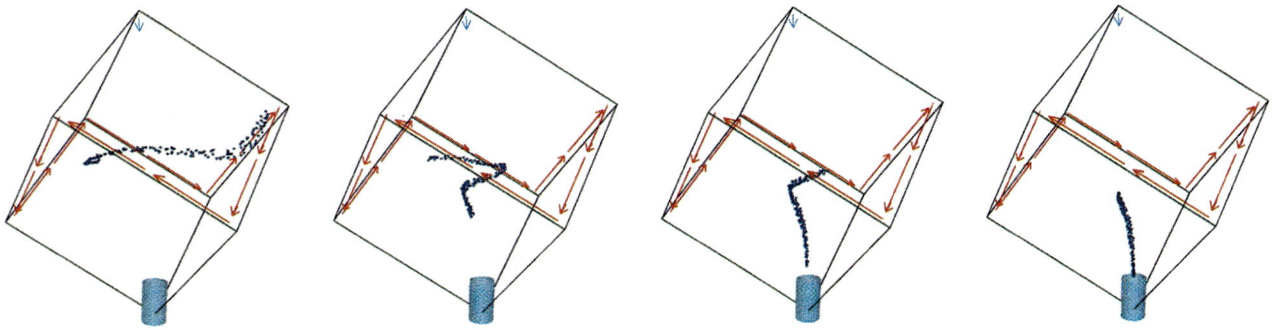

Figure 8: Particles flowing down a drain.


[3] E. Catmull, J. Clark: *Recursive generated B-spline surfaces on arbitrary topological meshes.* Computer Aided Design 10(6), pp. 350-355, 1978.

[4] J. Chen, N. Lobo: *Toward interactive-rate simulation of fluid with moving obstacles using Navier-Stokes equations.* Graphical Models and Image Processing, 57(2), pp. 107-116, 1995.

[5] N. Chiba et al.: *Visual simulation of water currents using a particle-based behavioral model.* Journal of Visualization and Computer Animation 6, pp. 155-171, 1995.

[6] B. Chopard, M. Droz: *Cellular Automata Modeling of Physical Systems.* Cambridge University Press, 1998.

[7] T. DeRose, M. Kass, T. Truong: *Subdivision surfaces in character animation.* Proceedings of SIGGRAPH 98. In *Computer Graphics* Proceedings, Annual Conference Series, pp. 85-94, 1998.

[8] D. Doo, M. Sabin: *Behavior of recursive division surfaces near extraordinary points.* Computer Aided Design 10(6), pp. 356-360, 1978.

[9] N. Dyn: *Interpolation of scattered data by radial functions.* In C. K. Chui et al. (eds.): *Topics in Multivariate Approximation*, Academic Press, pp. 47-61, 1987.

[10] N. Dyn: *Subdivision schemes in computer aided geometric design.* In W. Light (ed.): *Advances in Numerical Analysis II*, Oxford University Press, , pp. 36-104, 1992.

[11] N. Foster, D. Metaxas: *Realistic animation of liquids.* Graphical Models and Image Processing, 58 (5), pp. 471-483, 1996.

[12] N. Foster, D. Metaxas: *Modeling the motion of a hot, turbulent gas.* Proceedings of SIGGRAPH 97. In *Computer Graphics* Proceedings, Annual Conference Series, pp. 181-188, 1997.

[13] J. Hosckek, D. Lasser: *Fundamentals of Computer Aided Geometric Design.* A K Peters, 1993.

[14] H. Hoppe, T. DeRose, T. Duchamp, M. Halstead, H. Jin, J. McDonald, J. Schweitzer, W. Stuetzle: *Piecewise smooth surface reconstruction.* Proceedings of SIGGRAPH 94. In *Computer Graphics* Proceedings, Annual Conference Series, pp. 295-302, 1994.

[15] Z. Kadi, A. Rockwood: *Conformal maps defined about polynomial curves.* Computer Aided Geometric Design 15, pp. 323-337, 1998.

[16] M. Kass, G. Miller: *Rapid, stable fluid dynamics for computer graphics.* Proceedings of SIGGRAPH 89. In Computer Graphics Proceedings, Annual Conference Series, pp. 49-57, 1989.

[17] J. Liggett: *Fluid Mechanics.* McGraw Hill, 1994.

[18] L. Kobbelt: *A variational approach to subdivision.* Computer Aided Geometric Design 13, pp. 743-761, 1996.

[19] L. Kobbelt: *Variational design with parametric meshes of arbitrary topology.* To appear, http://www9.informatik.uni-erlangen.de/Persons/Kobbelt/papers/design.ps.gz, 1998.

[20] L. Kobbelt, S. Campagna, J. Vorsatz, H.-P. Seidel: *Interactive multi-resolution modeling on arbitrary meshes.* Proceedings of SIGGRAPH 98. In *Computer Graphics* Proceedings, Annual Conference Series, pp. 105-114, 1998.

[21] J. Lane, R. Riesenfeld. *A theoretical development for the computer generation and display of piecewise polynomial surfaces.* IEEE Transactions on Pattern Analysis and Machine Intelligence 2, 1, pp. 35-46, 1980.

[22] G. Miller, A. Pearce: *Globular dynamics: A connected particle system for animating viscous fluids.* Computers and Graphics 13 (3), pp. 305-309, 1989.

[23] D. H. Rothman, S. Zaleski: *Lattice-Gas Cellular Automata.* Cambridge University Press, 1997.

[24] T. W. Sederberg, J. Zheng, D. Sewell, M. Sabin: *Non-uniform recursive subdivision surfaces.* Proceedings of SIGGRAPH 98. In *Computer Graphics* Proceedings, Annual Conference Series, pp. 387-394, 1998.

[25] J. Stam, E. Fiume: *Turbulent Wind Fields for Gaseous Phenomena.* Proceedings of SIGGRAPH 93. In *Computer Graphics* Proceedings, Annual Conference Series, pp. 369-376, 1993.

[26] R. S. Varga: *Matrix Iterative Analysis.* Prentice-Hall, 1962.

[27] J. Warren, H. Weimer: *A cookbook for variational subdivision.* in D. Zorin (ed.): *Subdivision for Modeling and Animation*, SIGGRAPH 99 course-notes number 37, 1999.

[28] H. Weimer, J. Warren: *Subdivision schemes for thin plate splines.* Computer Graphics Forum 17, 3, pp. 303-313 & 392, 1998.

[29] J. Wejchert, D. Haumann: *Animation Aerodynamics.* Proceedings of SIGGRAPH 91. Computer Graphics 25 (3), pp. 19-22, 1991.

[30] D. M. Young: *Iterative Solution of Large Linear Systems.* Academic Press, 1971.

[31] D. Zorin, P. Schröder, W. Sweldens: *Interactive multiresolution mesh editing.* Proceedings of SIGGRAPH 97. In *Computer Graphics* Proceedings, Annual Conference Series, pp. 259-168, 1997.

## Appendix: Analytic Bases for Slow Flow

This appendix derives an analytic representation for the limiting flows of equation 13. Due to the linearity of the process, the limiting vector field defined by the multi-grid scheme can be written as a linear combination of translates of two vector basis functions $(\phi_{\mathbf{x}}[\mathbf{x},\mathbf{y}], \phi_{\mathbf{y}}[\mathbf{x},\mathbf{y}])$ (shown in figure 4) times the vectors of the initial field $(u_0, v_0)^T$. Specifically, the limiting field $(\mathbf{u}[\mathbf{x},\mathbf{y}], \mathbf{v}[\mathbf{x},\mathbf{y}])^T$ has the form:

$$\begin{pmatrix} \mathbf{u}[\mathbf{x},\mathbf{y}] \\ \mathbf{v}[\mathbf{x},\mathbf{y}] \end{pmatrix} = \sum_{i,j=-\infty}^{\infty} \left( \phi_{\mathbf{x}}[\mathbf{x}-i,\mathbf{y}-j] \,,\ \phi_{\mathbf{y}}[\mathbf{x}-i,\mathbf{y}-j] \right) \begin{pmatrix} u_0 \\ v_0 \end{pmatrix}_{ij}$$

Note again that both $\phi_{\mathbf{x}}[\mathbf{x},\mathbf{y}]$ and $\phi_{\mathbf{y}}[\mathbf{x},\mathbf{y}]$ are vector-valued functions. Our goal is to find a simple, closed-form expression for these functions.

### A rotational generator of slow flow

Recall that the continuous field $(\mathbf{u}[\mathbf{x},\mathbf{y}], \mathbf{v}[\mathbf{x},\mathbf{y}])^T$ is the limit of the discrete fields$(u_k, v_k)^T$ as $k \to \infty$. By solving equation 13 we can express $(u_k, v_k)^T$ directly in terms of $(u_0, v_0)^T$,

$$\begin{pmatrix} u_k[x,y] \\ v_k[x,y] \end{pmatrix} = \frac{L\left[x^{2^k}, y^{2^k}\right]}{2^k L[x,y]^2} \begin{pmatrix} \mathrm{D}[y] \\ -\mathrm{D}[x] \end{pmatrix} \left( \mathrm{D}[y^{2^k}],\ -\mathrm{D}[x^{2^k}] \right) \begin{pmatrix} u_0[x,y] \\ v_0[x,y] \end{pmatrix}.$$

This matrix of generating functions relating $(u_0, v_0)^T$ and $(u_k, v_k)^T$ can be re-written in the form:

$$\frac{1}{4^k L[x,y]^2} L\left[x^{2^k}, y^{2^k}\right] \begin{pmatrix} 2^k \mathrm{D}[y] \\ -2^k \mathrm{D}[x] \end{pmatrix} \left( \mathrm{D}[y^{2^k}],\ -\mathrm{D}[x^{2^k}] \right). \qquad (19)$$

Our next task is to find continuous analogs of various parts of this matrix expression as $k \to \infty$. We first analyze the most difficult part of the expression, $\frac{1}{4^k L[x,y]^2}$. Consider a sequence of generating functions $r_k[x,y]$ such that $4^k L[x,y]^2 r_k[x,y] = 1$ for all $k$. The coefficients of the $r_k[x,y]$ are discrete approximations to a continuous function $\mathbf{r}[\mathbf{x},\mathbf{y}]$ satisfying the differential equation,

$$\mathbf{L}[\mathbf{x},\mathbf{y}]^2 \mathbf{r}[\mathbf{x},\mathbf{y}] = 0$$

everywhere except at $(\mathbf{x},\mathbf{y}) = 0$. Fortunately, a closed form solution to this partial differential equation is known. The function $\mathbf{r}[\mathbf{x},\mathbf{y}]$ is a radial basis function of the form:

$$\mathbf{r}[\mathbf{x},\mathbf{y}] = \frac{1}{16\pi}(\mathbf{x}^2+\mathbf{y}^2)\log[\mathbf{x}^2+\mathbf{y}^2].$$

Hoschek and Lasser [13] and Dyn [9] give a brief introduction to radial basis functions and discuss some of their properties. The factor of $4^k$ normalizes the coefficients of the sequence $r_k[x,y]$ so that their limit $\mathbf{r}[\mathbf{x},\mathbf{y}]$ satisfies $\int \mathbf{L}[\mathbf{x},\mathbf{y}]^2 \mathbf{r}[\mathbf{x},\mathbf{y}] = 1$.

The other components of expression 19 are easier to interpret. Differences of the form $2^k \mathrm{D}[z]$ taken on $\frac{1}{2^k}\mathbb{Z}^2$ converge to the continuous derivative $\mathbf{D}[\mathbf{z}]$. Differences of the form $\mathrm{D}[z^{2^k}]$ taken on $\frac{1}{2^k}\mathbb{Z}^2$ correspond to unit differences taken on $\mathbb{Z}^2$. Based on these two observations, we can convert successively larger portions of expression 19.

Let $g_k[x,y]$ denote $r_k[x,y] L\left[x^{2^k}, y^{2^k}\right] \left( 2^k \mathrm{D}[y] \,,\ -2^k \mathrm{D}[x] \right)^T$. The continuous analog of $L\left[x^{2^k}, y^{2^k}\right]$ is a sequence of differences on $\mathbb{Z}^2$ corresponding to the discrete difference mask $L[x,y]$. The continuous analog of the vector of discrete operators $\left( 2^k \mathrm{D}[y],\ -2^k \mathrm{D}[x] \right)^T$ is the vector of differential operators $\left( \mathbf{D}[\mathbf{y}],\ -\mathbf{D}[\mathbf{x}] \right)^T$. Based on these observations, the corresponding vector function $\mathbf{g}[\mathbf{x},\mathbf{y}]$ has the form:

$$\begin{aligned} \mathbf{g}[\mathbf{x},\mathbf{y}] \;=\; & \begin{pmatrix} \mathbf{d}[\mathbf{y}] \\ -\mathbf{d}[\mathbf{x}] \end{pmatrix} \Big( -4\mathbf{r}[\mathbf{x},\mathbf{y}] + \mathbf{r}[\mathbf{x}+1,\mathbf{y}] + \\ & \mathbf{r}[\mathbf{x}-1,\mathbf{y}] + \mathbf{r}[\mathbf{x},\mathbf{y}+1] + \mathbf{r}[\mathbf{x},\mathbf{y}-1] \Big). \end{aligned}$$

The behavior of $\mathbf{g}[\mathbf{x},\mathbf{y}]$ gives us our first insight into the structure of slow flow. In fact, $\mathbf{g}[\mathbf{x},\mathbf{y}]$ is a generator for a localized, rotational slow flow. We can verify that $\mathbf{g}[\mathbf{x},\mathbf{y}]$ is truly a slow flow by substituting the definition of $\mathbf{g}[\mathbf{x},\mathbf{y}]$ into equation 12. Likewise, we can verify that this flow is highly localized (i.e. decays to zero very fast away from the origin) based on the analytic representation. Figure 9 shows a plot of $\mathbf{g}[\mathbf{x},\mathbf{y}]$ on the domain $[-2,2]^2$.

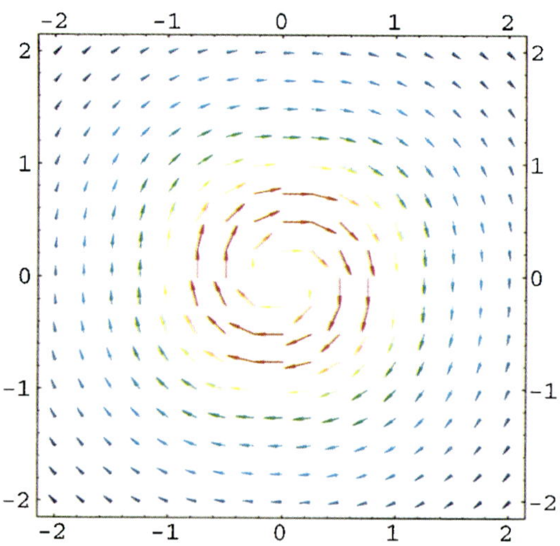


Figure 9: A rotational generator for slow flow

### Vector basis functions for slow flow

Finally, expression 19 can be written as $g_k[x,y]\left( \mathrm{D}[y^{2^k}] \,,\ -\mathrm{D}[x^{2^k}] \right)$. The coefficients of this sequence converge to differences of the rotational generator $\mathbf{g}[\mathbf{x},\mathbf{y}]$ taken in the $\mathbf{y}$-direction and $\mathbf{x}$-direction, respectively. The resulting functions are the vector basis functions for our subdivision scheme:

$$\begin{aligned} \phi_{\mathbf{x}}[\mathbf{x},\mathbf{y}] &= \mathbf{g}\left[\mathbf{x},\mathbf{y}+\tfrac{1}{2}\right] - \mathbf{g}\left[\mathbf{x},\mathbf{y}-\tfrac{1}{2}\right], \\ \phi_{\mathbf{y}}[\mathbf{x},\mathbf{y}] &= -\mathbf{g}\left[\mathbf{x}+\tfrac{1}{2},\mathbf{y}\right] + \mathbf{g}\left[\mathbf{x}-\tfrac{1}{2},\mathbf{y}\right]. \end{aligned}$$

Figure 4 contains plots of these basis functions in the $\mathbf{x}$ and $\mathbf{y}$ directions, respectively. Note that the vector basis consists of a pair of rotational sources positioned so as to drive a flow along the appropriate axis. Again, this flow is localized in the sense that it decays rapidly to zero away from the origin. More complex flows can be constructed by taking linear combinations of these vector basis functions. Due to the normalizing constant of $\frac{1}{16\pi}$ used in defining the original radial basis function $\mathbf{r}[\mathbf{x},\mathbf{y}]$, the scheme has constant precision. In particular, choosing the coarse vector field $(u_0, v_0)^T$ to be translates of a constant vector defines a constant flow of the same magnitude in the same direction.

# Stable Fluids

Jos Stam*

Alias | wavefront

## Abstract

Building animation tools for fluid-like motions is an important and challenging problem with many applications in computer graphics. The use of physics-based models for fluid flow can greatly assist in creating such tools. Physical models, unlike key frame or procedural based techniques, permit an animator to almost effortlessly create interesting, swirling fluid-like behaviors. Also, the interaction of flows with objects and virtual forces is handled elegantly. Until recently, it was believed that physical fluid models were too expensive to allow real-time interaction. This was largely due to the fact that previous models used unstable schemes to solve the physical equations governing a fluid. In this paper, for the first time, we propose an unconditionally stable model which still produces complex fluid-like flows. As well, our method is very easy to implement. The stability of our model allows us to take larger time steps and therefore achieve faster simulations. We have used our model in conjuction with advecting solid textures to create many fluid-like animations interactively in two- and three-dimensions.

**CR Categories:** I.3.7 [Computer Graphics]: Three-Dimensional Graphics and Realism—Animation

**Keywords:** animation of fluids, Navier-Stokes, stable solvers, implicit elliptic PDE solvers, interactive modeling, gaseous phenomena, advected textures

## 1 Introduction

One of the most intriguing problems in computer graphics is the simulation of fluid-like behavior. A good fluid solver is of great importance in many different areas. In the special effects industry there is a high demand to convincingly mimic the appearance and behavior of fluids such as smoke, water and fire. Paint programs can also benefit from fluid solvers to emulate traditional techniques such as watercolor and oil paint. Texture synthesis is another possible application. Indeed, many textures result from fluid-like processes, such as erosion. The modeling and simulation of fluids is, of course, also of prime importance in most scientific disciplines and in engineering. Fluid mechanics is used as the standard mathematical framework on which these simulations are based. There is a consensus among scientists that the *Navier-Stokes* equations are a very good model for fluid flow. Thousands of books and articles have been published in various areas on how to compute these equations numerically. Which solver to use in practice depends largely on the problem at hand and on the computing power available. Most engineering tasks require that the simulation provide accurate bounds on the physical quantities involved to answer questions related to safety, performance, etc. The visual appearance (shape) of the flow is of secondary importance in these applications. In computer graphics, on the other hand, the shape and the behavior of the fluid are of primary interest, while physical accuracy is secondary or in some cases irrelevant. Fluid solvers, for computer graphics, should ideally provide a user with a tool that enables her to achieve fluid-like effects in real-time. These factors are more important than strict physical accuracy, which would require too much computational power.

In fact, most previous models in computer graphics were driven by visual appearance and not by physical accuracy. Early flow models were built from simple primitives. Various combinations of these primitives allowed the animation of particles systems [15, 17] or simple geometries such as leaves [23]. The complexity of the flows was greatly improved with the introduction of random turbulences [16, 20]. These turbulences are mass conserving and, therefore, automatically exhibit rotational motion. Also the turbulence is periodic in space and time, which is ideal for motion "texture mapping" [19]. Flows built up from a superposition of flow primitives all have the disadvantage that they do not respond dynamically to user-applied external forces. Dynamical models of fluids based on the Navier-Stokes equations were first implemented in two-dimensions. Both Yaeger and Upson and Gamito et al. used a vortex method coupled with a Poisson solver to create two-dimensional animations of fluids [24, 8]. Later, Chen et al. animated water surfaces from the pressure term given by a two-dimensional simulation of the Navier-Stokes equations [2]. Their method unlike ours is both limited to two-dimensions and is unstable. Kass and Miller linearize the shallow water equations to simulate liquids [12]. The simplifications do not, however, capture the interesting rotational motions characteristic of fluids. More recently, Foster and Metaxas clearly show the advantages of using the full three-dimensional Navier-Stokes equations in creating fluid-like animations [7]. Many effects which are hard to key frame manually such as swirling motion and flows past objects are obtained automatically. Their algorithm is based mainly on the work of Harlow and Welch in computational fluid dynamics, which dates back to 1965 [11]. Since then many other techniques which Foster and Metaxas could have used have been developed. However, their model has the advantage of being simple to code, since it is based on a finite differencing of the Navier-Stokes equations and an explicit time solver. Similar solvers and their source code are also available from the book of Griebel et al. [9]. The main problem with explicit solvers is that the numerical scheme can become unstable for large time-steps. Instability leads to numerical simulations that "blow-up" and therefore have to be restarted with a smaller time-step. The instability of these explicit algorithms sets serious limits on speed and interactivity. Ideally, a user should be able to interact in real-time with a fluid solver without having to worry about possible "blow ups".

In this paper, for the first time, we propose a stable algorithm that solves the full Navier-Stokes equations. Our algorithm is very

*Alias | wavefront, 1218 Third Ave, 8th Floor, Seattle, WA 98101, U.S.A. jstam@aw.sgi.com

easy to implement and allows a user to interact in real-time with three-dimensional fluids on a graphics workstation. We achieve this by using time-steps much larger than the ones used by Foster and Metaxas. To obtain a stable solver we depart from Foster and Metaxas' method of solution. Instead of their explicit Eulerian schemes, we use both Lagrangian and implicit methods to solve the Navier-Stokes equations. Our method cannot be found in the computational fluids literature, since it is custom made for computer graphics applications. The model would not be accurate enough for most engineering applications. Indeed, it suffers from too much "numerical dissipation", i.e., the flow tends to dampen too rapidly as compared to actual experiments. In a computer graphical application, on the other hand, this is not so bad, especially in an interactive system where the flow is "kept alive" by an animator applying external forces. In fact, a flow which does not dampen at all might be too chaotic and difficult to control. As our results demonstrate we are able to produce nice swirling flows despite the numerical dissipation.

In this paper we apply our flows mainly to the simulation of gaseous-like phenomena. We employ our solver to update both the flow and the motion of densities within the flow. To further increase the complexity of our animations we advect texture coordinates along with the density [13]. In this manner we are able to synthesize highly detailed "wispy" gaseous flows even with low resolution grids. We believe that the combination of physics-based fluid solvers and solid textures is the most promising method of achieving highly complex flows in computer graphics.

The next section presents the Navier-Stokes equations and the derivation which leads to our method of solution. That section contains all the fundamental ideas and techniques needed to obtain a stable fluids solver. Since it relies on sophisticated mathematical techniques, it is written in a mathematical physics jargon which should be familiar to most computer graphics researchers working in physics-based modeling. The application oriented reader who wishes only to implement our solver can skip Section 2 entirely and go straight to Section 3. There we describe our implementation of the solver, providing sufficient information to code our technique. Section 4 is devoted to several applications that demonstrate the power of our new solver. Finally, in Section 5 we conclude and discuss future research. To keep this within the confines of a short paper, we have decided not to include a "tutorial-type" section on fluid dynamics, since there are many excellent textbooks which provide the necessary background and intuition. Readers who do not have a background in fluid dynamics and who wish to fully understand the method in this paper should therefore consult such a text. Mathematically inclined readers may wish to start with the excellent book by Chorin and Marsden [3]. Readers with an engineering bent on the other hand can consult the didactic book by Abbott [1]. Also, Foster and Metaxas' paper does a good job of introducing the concepts from fluid dynamics to the computer graphics community.

# 2 Stable Navier-Stokes

## 2.1 Basic Equations

In this section we present the Navier-Stokes equations along with the manipulations that lead to our stable solver. A fluid whose density and temperature are nearly constant is described by a velocity field $\mathbf{u}$ and a pressure field $p$. These quantities generally vary both in space and in time and depend on the boundaries surrounding the fluid. We will denote the spatial coordinate by $\mathbf{x}$, which for two-dimensional fluids is $\mathbf{x} = (x, y)$ and three-dimensional fluids is equal to $(x, y, z)$. We have decided not to specialize our results for a particular dimension. All results are thus valid for both two-dimensional and three-dimensional flows unless stated otherwise. Given that the velocity and the pressure are known for some initial time $t = 0$, then the evolution of these quantities over time is given by the Navier-Stokes equations [3]:

$$\nabla \cdot \mathbf{u} = 0 \tag{1}$$

$$\frac{\partial \mathbf{u}}{\partial t} = -(\mathbf{u} \cdot \nabla)\mathbf{u} - \frac{1}{\rho}\nabla p + \nu \nabla^2 \mathbf{u} + \mathbf{f}, \tag{2}$$

where $\nu$ is the kinematic viscosity of the fluid, $\rho$ is its density and $\mathbf{f}$ is an external force. Some readers might be unfamiliar with this compact version of the Navier-Stokes equations. Eq. 2 is a vector equation for the three (two in two-dimensions) components of the velocity field. The "$\cdot$" denotes a dot product between vectors, while the symbol $\nabla$ is the vector of spatial partial derivatives. More precisely, $\nabla = (\partial/\partial x, \partial/\partial y)$ in two-dimensions and $\nabla = (\partial/\partial x, \partial/\partial y, \partial/\partial z)$ in three-dimensions. We have also used the shorthand notation $\nabla^2 = \nabla \cdot \nabla$. The Navier-Stokes equations are obtained by imposing that the fluid conserves both mass (Eq. 1) and momentum (Eq. 2). We refer the reader to any standard text on fluid mechanics for the actual derivation. These equations also have to be supplemented with boundary conditions. In this paper we will consider two types of boundary conditions which are useful in practical applications: *periodic* boundary conditions and *fixed* boundary conditions. In the case of periodic boundaries the fluid is defined on an $n$-dimensional torus ($n = 2, 3$). In this case there are no walls, just a fluid which wraps around. Although such fluids are not encountered in practice, they are very useful in creating evolving texture maps. Also, these boundary conditions lead to a very elegant implementation that uses the fast Fourier transform as shown below. The second type of boundary condition that we consider is when the fluid lies in some bounded domain $D$. In that case, the boundary conditions are given by a function $\mathbf{u}_D$ defined on the boundary $\partial D$ of the domain. See Foster and Metaxas' work for a good discussion of these boundary conditions in the case of a hot fluid [7]. In any case, the boundary conditions should be such that the normal component of the velocity field is zero at the boundary; no matter should traverse walls.

The pressure and the velocity fields which appear in the Navier-Stokes equations are in fact related. A single equation for the velocity can be obtained by combining Eq. 1 and Eq. 2. We briefly outline the steps that lead to that equation, since it is fundamental to our algorithm. We follow Chorin and Marsden's treatment of the subject (p. 36ff, [3]). A mathematical result, known as the *Helmholtz-Hodge Decomposition*, states that any vector field $\mathbf{w}$ can uniquely be decomposed into the form:

$$\mathbf{w} = \mathbf{u} + \nabla q, \tag{3}$$

where $\mathbf{u}$ has zero divergence: $\nabla \cdot \mathbf{u} = 0$ and $q$ is a scalar field. Any vector field is the sum of a mass conserving field and a gradient field. This result allows us to define an operator $\mathbf{P}$ which projects any vector field $\mathbf{w}$ onto its divergence free part $\mathbf{u} = \mathbf{P}\mathbf{w}$. The operator is in fact defined implicitly by multiplying both sides of Eq. 3 by "$\nabla$":

$$\nabla \cdot \mathbf{w} = \nabla^2 q. \tag{4}$$

This is a Poisson equation for the scalar field $q$ with the Neumann boundary condition $\frac{\partial q}{\partial n} = 0$ on $\partial D$. A solution to this equation is used to compute the projection $\mathbf{u}$:

$$\mathbf{u} = \mathbf{P}\mathbf{w} = \mathbf{w} - \nabla q.$$

If we apply this projection operator on both sides of Eq. 2 we obtain a single equation for the velocity:

$$\frac{\partial \mathbf{u}}{\partial t} = \mathbf{P}\left(-(\mathbf{u} \cdot \nabla)\mathbf{u} + \nu \nabla^2 \mathbf{u} + \mathbf{f}\right), \tag{5}$$

where we have used the fact that $\mathbf{P}\mathbf{u} = \mathbf{u}$ and $\mathbf{P}\nabla p = 0$. This is our fundamental equation from which we will develop a stable fluid solver.

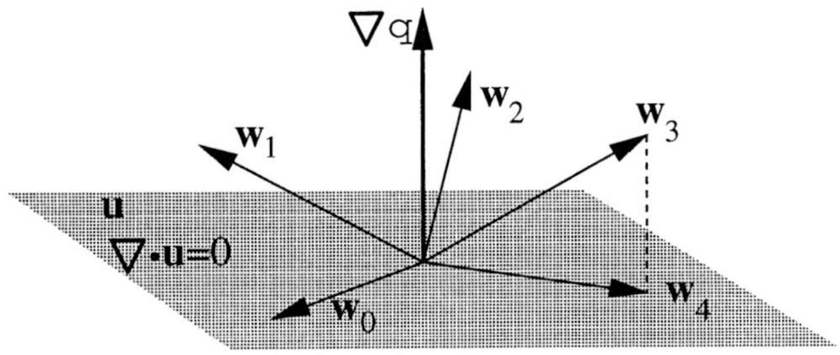


Figure 1: One simulation step of our solver is composed of steps. The first three steps may take the field out of the space of divergent free fields. The last projection step ensures that the field is divergent free after the entire simulation step.

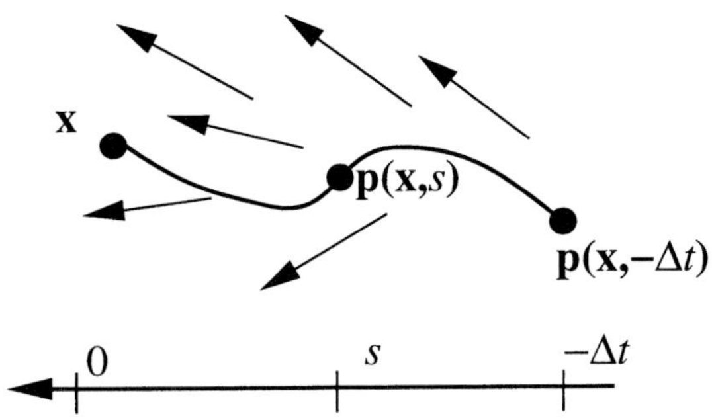


Figure 2: To solve for the advection part, we trace each point of the field backward in time. The new velocity at $\mathbf{x}$ is therefore the velocity that the particle had a time $\Delta t$ ago at the old location $\mathbf{p}(\mathbf{x}, -\Delta t)$.

## 2.2 Method of Solution

Eq. 5 is solved from an initial state $\mathbf{u}_0 = \mathbf{u}(\mathbf{x}, 0)$ by marching through time with a time step $\Delta t$. Let us assume that the field has been resolved at a time $t$ and that we wish to compute the field at a later time $t + \Delta t$. We resolve Eq. 5 over the time span $\Delta t$ in four steps. We start from the solution $\mathbf{w}_0(\mathbf{x}) = \mathbf{u}(\mathbf{x}, t)$ of the previous time step and then sequentially resolve each term on the right hand side of Eq. 5, followed by a projection onto the divergent free fields. The general procedure is illustrated in Figure 1. The steps are:

$$\mathbf{w}_0(\mathbf{x}) \overset{\text{add force}}{\longrightarrow} \mathbf{w}_1(\mathbf{x}) \overset{\text{advect}}{\longrightarrow} \mathbf{w}_2(\mathbf{x}) \overset{\text{diffuse}}{\longrightarrow} \mathbf{w}_3(\mathbf{x}) \overset{\text{project}}{\longrightarrow} \mathbf{w}_4(\mathbf{x}).$$

The solution at time $t + \Delta t$ is then given by the last velocity field: $\mathbf{u}(\mathbf{x}, t + \Delta t) = \mathbf{w}_4(\mathbf{x})$. A simulation is obtained by iterating these steps. We now explain how each step is computed in more detail.

The easiest term to solve is the addition of the external force $\mathbf{f}$. If we assume that the force does not vary considerably during the time step, then

$$\mathbf{w}_1(\mathbf{x}) = \mathbf{w}_0(\mathbf{x}) + \Delta t\ \mathbf{f}(\mathbf{x}, t)$$

is a good approximation of the effect of the force on the field over the time step $\Delta t$. In an interactive system this is a good approximation, since forces are only applied at the beginning of each time step.

The next step accounts for the effect of advection (or convection) of the fluid on itself. A disturbance somewhere in the fluid propagates according to the expression $-(\mathbf{u} \cdot \nabla)\mathbf{u}$. This term makes the Navier-Stokes equations non-linear. Foster and Metaxas resolved this component using finite differencing. Their method is stable only when the time step is sufficiently small such that $\Delta t < \Delta\tau/|\mathbf{u}|$, where $\Delta\tau$ is the spacing of their computational grid. Therefore, for small separations and/or large velocities, very small time steps have to be taken. On the other hand, we use a totally different approach which results in an unconditionally stable solver. No matter how big the time step is, our simulations will never "blow up". Our method is based on a technique to solve partial differential equations known as the *method of characteristics*. Since this method is of crucial importance in obtaining our stable solver, we provide all the mathematical details in Appendix A. The method, however, can be understood intuitively. At each time step all the fluid particles are moved by the velocity of the fluid itself. Therefore, to obtain the velocity at a point $\mathbf{x}$ at the new time $t + \Delta t$, we backtrace the point $\mathbf{x}$ through the velocity field $\mathbf{w}_1$ over a time $\Delta t$. This defines a path $\mathbf{p}(\mathbf{x}, s)$ corresponding to a partial streamline of the velocity field. The new velocity at the point $\mathbf{x}$ is then set to the velocity that the particle, now at $\mathbf{x}$, had at its previous location a time $\Delta t$ ago:

$$\mathbf{w}_2(\mathbf{x}) = \mathbf{w}_1(\mathbf{p}(\mathbf{x}, -\Delta t)).$$

Figure 2 illustrates the above. This method has several advantages. Most importantly it is unconditionally stable. Indeed, from the above equation we observe that the maximum value of the new field is never larger than the largest value of the previous field. Secondly, the method is very easy to implement. All that is required in practice is a particle tracer and a linear interpolator (see next Section). This method is therefore both stable and simple to implement, two highly desirable properties of any computer graphics fluid solver. We employed a similar scheme to move densities through user-defined velocity fields [19]. Versions of the method of characteristics were also used by other researchers. The application was either employed in visualizing flow fields [13, 18] or improving the rendering of gas simulations [21, 5]. Our application of the technique is fundamentally different, since we use it to update the velocity field, which previous researchers did not dynamically animate.

The third step solves for the effect of viscosity and is equivalent to a diffusion equation:

$$\frac{\partial \mathbf{w}_2}{\partial t} = \nu \nabla^2 \mathbf{w}_2.$$

This is a standard equation for which many numerical procedures have been developed. The most straightforward way of solving this equation is to discretize the diffusion operator $\nabla^2$ and then to do an explicit time step as Foster and Metaxas did [7]. However, this method is unstable when the viscosity is large. We prefer, therefore, to use an implicit method:

$$\left(\mathbf{I} - \nu \Delta t \nabla^2\right) \mathbf{w}_3(\mathbf{x}) = \mathbf{w}_2(\mathbf{x}),$$

where $\mathbf{I}$ is the identity operator. When the diffusion operator is discretized, this leads to a sparse linear system for the unknown field $\mathbf{w}_3$. Solving such a system can be done efficiently, however (see below).

The fourth step involves the projection step, which makes the resulting field divergence free. As pointed out in the previous subsection this involves the resolution of the Poisson problem defined by Eq. 4:

$$\nabla^2 q = \nabla \cdot \mathbf{w}_3 \qquad \mathbf{w}_4 = \mathbf{w}_3 - \nabla q.$$

The projection step, therefore, requires a good Poisson solver. Foster and Metaxas solved a similar equation using a relaxation scheme. Relaxation schemes, though, have poor convergence and usually require many iterations. Foster and Metaxas reported that they obtained good results even after a very small number of relaxation steps. However, since we are using a different method to resolve for the advection step, we must use a more accurate method.

Indeed, the method of characteristics is more precise when the field is close to divergent free. More importantly from a visual point of view, the projection step forces the fields to have vortices which result in more swirling-like motions. For these reasons we have used a more accurate solver for the projection step.

The Poisson equation, when spatially discretized, becomes a sparse linear system. Therefore, both the projection and the viscosity steps involve the solution of a large sparse system of equations. Multigrid methods, for example, can solve sparse linear systems in linear time [10]. Since our advection solver is also linear in time, the complexity of our proposed algorithm is of complexity $O(N)$. Foster and Metaxas' solver has the same complexity. This performance is theoretically optimal since for a complicated fluid, any algorithm has to consult at least each cell of the computational grid.

## 2.3 Periodic Boundaries and the FFT

When we consider a domain with periodic boundary conditions, our algorithm takes a particularly simple form. The periodicity allows us to transform the velocity into the Fourier domain:

$$\mathbf{u}(\mathbf{x}, t) \longrightarrow \hat{\mathbf{u}}(\mathbf{k}, t).$$

In the Fourier domain the gradient operator "$\nabla$" is equivalent to the multiplication by $i\mathbf{k}$, where $i = \sqrt{-1}$. Consequently, both the diffusion step and the projection step are much simpler to solve. Indeed the diffusion operator and the projection operators in the Fourier domain are

$$\mathbf{I} - \nu\Delta t\nabla^2 \longrightarrow 1 + \nu\Delta t k^2 \quad \text{and}$$
$$\mathbf{P}\mathbf{w} \longrightarrow \hat{\mathbf{P}}\hat{\mathbf{w}}(\mathbf{k}) = \hat{\mathbf{w}}(\mathbf{k}) - \frac{1}{k^2}(\mathbf{k}\cdot\hat{\mathbf{w}}(\mathbf{k}))\mathbf{k},$$

where $k = |\mathbf{k}|$. The operator $\hat{\mathbf{P}}$ projects the vector $\hat{\mathbf{w}}(\mathbf{k})$ onto the plane which is normal to the wave number $\mathbf{k}$. The Fourier transform of the velocity of a divergent free field is therefore always perpendicular to its wavenumbers. The diffusion can be interpreted as a low pass filter whose decay is proportional to both the time step and the viscosity. These simple results demonstrate the power of the Fourier transform. Indeed, we are able to completely transcribe our solver in only a couple of lines. All that is required is a particle tracer and a fast Fourier transform (FFT).

FourierStep($\mathbf{w}_0$,$\mathbf{w}_4$,$\Delta t$):
  add force: $\mathbf{w}_1 = \mathbf{w}_0 + \Delta t\ \mathbf{f}$
  advect: $\mathbf{w}_2(\mathbf{x}) = \mathbf{w}_1(\mathbf{p}(\mathbf{x}, -\Delta t))$
  transform: $\hat{\mathbf{w}}_2 = \text{FFT}\{\mathbf{w}_2\}$
  diffuse: $\hat{\mathbf{w}}_3(\mathbf{k}) = \hat{\mathbf{w}}_2(\mathbf{k})/(1 + \nu\Delta t k^2)$
  project: $\hat{\mathbf{w}}_4 = \hat{\mathbf{P}}\hat{\mathbf{w}}_3$
  transform: $\mathbf{w}_4 = \text{FFT}^{-1}\{\hat{\mathbf{w}}_4\}$

Since the Fourier transform is of complexity $O(N \log N)$, this method is theoretically slightly more expensive than a method of solution relying on multi-grid solvers. However, this method is very easy to implement. We have used this algorithm to generate the "liquid textures" of Section 4.

## 2.4 Moving Substances through the Fluid

A non-reactive substance which is injected into the fluid will be advected by it while diffusing at the same time. Common examples of this phenomenon include the patterns created by milk stirred in coffee or the smoke rising from a cigarette. Let $a$ be any scalar quantity which is moved through the fluid. Examples of this quantity include the density of dust, smoke or cloud droplets, the temperature of a fluid and a texture coordinate. The evolution of this scalar field is conveniently described by an advection diffusion type equation:

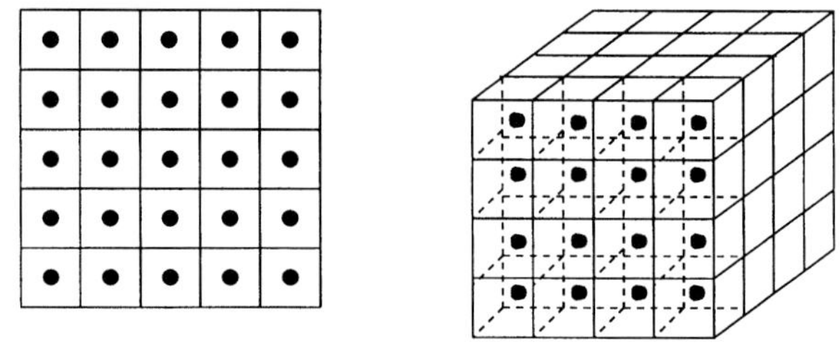

Figure 3: The values of the discretized fields are defined at the center of the grid cells.

$$\frac{\partial a}{\partial t} = -\mathbf{u}\cdot\nabla a + \kappa_a\nabla^2 - \alpha_a a + S_a,$$

where $\kappa_a$ is a diffusion constant, $\alpha_a$ is a dissipation rate and $S_a$ is a source term. This equation is very similar in form to the Navier-Stokes equation. Indeed, it includes an advection term, a diffusion term and a "force term" $S_a$. All these terms can be resolved exactly in the same way as the velocity of the fluid. The dissipation term not present in the Navier-Stokes equation is solved as follows over a time-step:

$$(1 + \Delta t\alpha_a)a(\mathbf{x}, t + \Delta t) = a(\mathbf{x}, t).$$

Similar equations were used by Stam and Fiume to simulate fire and other gaseous phenomena [21]. However, their velocity fields were not computed dynamically.

We hope that the material in this section has convinced the reader that our stable solver is indeed based on the full Navier-Stokes equations. Also, we have pointed to the numerical techniques which should be used at each step of our solver. We now proceed to describe the implementation of our model in more detail.

# 3 Our Solver

## 3.1 Setup

Our implementation handles both the motion of fluids and the propagation by the fluid of any number of substances like mass-density, temperature or texture coordinates. Each quantity is defined on either a two-dimensional (`NDIM=2`) or three-dimensional (`NDIM=3`) grid, depending on the application. The grid is defined by its physical dimensions: origin `O[NDIM]` and length `L[NDIM]` of each side, and by its number of cells `N[NDIM]` in each coordinate. This in turn determines the size of each voxel `D[i]=L[i]/N[i]`. The definition of the grid is an input to our program which is specified by the animator. The velocity field is defined at the center of each cell as shown in Figure 3. Notice that previous researchers, e.g., [7], defined the velocity at the boundaries of the cells. We prefer the cell-centered grid since it is more straightforward to implement. We allocate two grids for each component of the velocity: `U0[NDIM]` and `U1[NDIM]`. At each time step of our simulation one grid corresponds to the solution obtained in the previous step. We store the new solution in the second grid. After each step, the grids are swapped. We also allocate two grids to hold a scalar field corresponding to a substance transported by the flow. Although our implementation can handle any number of substances, for the sake of clarity we present only the algorithm for one field in this section. This scalar quantity is stored in the grids `S0` and `S1`. The speed of interactivity is controlled by a single time step `dt`, which can be as large as the animator wishes, since our algorithm is stable.

The physical properties of the fluid are a function of its viscosity `visc` alone. By varying the viscosity, an animator can simulate a wide range of substances ranging from glue-like matter to highly turbulent flows. The properties of the substance are modeled by a diffusion constant `kS` and a dissipation rate `aS`. Along with these parameters, the animator also must specify the values of these fields on the boundary of the grid. There are basically two types: periodic or fixed. The boundary conditions can be of a different type for each coordinate. When periodic boundary conditions are chosen, the fluid wraps around. This means that a piece of fluid which leaves the grid on one side reenters the grid on the opposite side. In the case of fixed boundaries, the value of each physical quantity must be specified at the boundary of the grid. The simplest method is to set the field to zero at the boundary. We refer the reader to Foster and Metaxas' paper for an excellent description of different boundary conditions and their resulting effects [7]. In the results section we describe the boundary conditions chosen for each animation. For the special case when the boundary conditions are periodic in each coordinate, a very elegant solver based on the fast Fourier transform can be employed. This algorithm is described in Section 2.3. We do not repeat it here since the solver in this section is more general and can handle both types of boundary conditions.

The fluid is set into motion by applying external forces to it. We have written an animation system in which an animator with a mouse can apply directional forces to the fluid. The forces can also be a function of other substances in the fluid. For example, a temperature field moving through the fluid can produce buoyant and turbulent forces. In our system we allow the user to create all sorts of dependencies between the various fields, some of which are described in the results section of this paper. We do not describe our animation system in great detail since its functionality should be evident from the examples of the next section. Instead we focus on our simulator, which takes the forces and parameters set by the animator as an input.

## 3.2 The Simulator

Once we worked out the mathematics underlying the Navier-Stokes equations in Section 2, our implementation became straightforward. We wish to emphasize that the theoretical developments of Section 2 are in no way gratuitous but are immensely useful in coding compact solvers. In particular, casting the problem into a mathematical setting has allowed us to take advantage of the large body of work done in the numerical analysis of partial differential equations. We have written the solver as a separate library of routines that are called by the interactive animation system. The entire library consists of only roughly 500 lines of C code. The two main routines of this library update either the velocity field `Vstep` or a scalar field `Sstep` over a given time step. We assume that the external force is given by an array of vectors `F[NDIM]` and that the source is given by an array `Ssource` for the scalar field. The general structure of our simulator looks like

```
while ( simulating ) {
  /* handle display and user interaction */
  /* get forces F and sources Ssource from the UI */
  Swap(U1,U0); Swap(S1,S0);
  Vstep ( U1, U0, visc, F, dt );
  Sstep ( S1, S0, kS, aS, U1, Ssource, dt );
}
```

The velocity solver is composed of four steps: the forces are added to the field, the field is advected by itself, the field diffuses due to viscous friction within the fluid, and in the final step the velocity is forced to conserve mass. The general structure of this routine is:

```
Vstep ( U1, U0, visc, F, dt )
  for(i=0;i<NDIM;i++)
    addForce ( U0[i], F[i], dt );
  for(i=0;i<NDIM;i++)
    Transport ( U1[i], U0[i], U0, dt );
  for(i=0;i<NDIM;i++)
    Diffuse ( U0[i], U1[i], visc, dt );
  Project ( U1, U0, dt );
```

The general structure of the scalar field solver is very similar to the above. It involves four steps: add the source, transport the field by the velocity, diffuse and finally dissipate the field. The scalar field solver shares some of the routines called by the velocity solver:

```
Sstep ( S1, S0, k, a, U, source, dt )
  addForce ( S0, source, dt );
  Transport ( S1, S0, U, dt );
  Diffuse ( S0, S1, k, dt );
  Dissipate ( S1, S0, a, dt );
```

The `addForce` routine adds the force field multiplied by the time step to each value of the field. The dissipation routine `Dissipate` divides each element of the first array by `1+dt*a` and stores it in the new array. The `Transport` routine is a key step in our simulation. It accounts for the movement of the substance due to the velocity field. More importantly it is used to resolve the non-linearity of the Navier-Stokes equations. The general structure of this routine (in three-dimensions) is

```
Transport ( S1, S0, U, dt )
  for each cell (i,j,k) do
    X = O+(i+0.5,j+0.5,k+0.5)*D;
    TraceParticle ( X, U, -dt, X0 );
    S1[i,j,k] = LinInterp ( X0, S0 );
  end
```

The routine `TraceParticle` traces a path starting at `X` through the field `U` over a time `-dt`. The endpoint of this path is the new point `X0`. We use both a simple second order Runge-Kutta (RK2) method for the particle trace [14] and an adaptive particle tracer, which subsamples the time step only in regions of high velocity gradients, such as near object boundaries. The routine `LinInterp` linearly interpolates the value of the scalar field `S` at the location `X0`. We note that we did not use a higher order interpolation, since this might lead to instabilities due to the oscillations and overshoots inherent in such interpolants. On the other hand, higher order spline approximants may be used, though these tend to smooth out the resulting flows.

To solve for the diffusion (`Diffuse`) and to perform the projection (`Project`) we need a sparse linear solver `SolveLin`. The best theoretical choice is the multi-grid algorithm [10]. However, we used a solver from the FISHPAK library since it was very easy to incorporate into our code and gave good results [22][1]. In practice, it turned out to be faster than our implementation of the multi-grid algorithm. In Appendix B, we show exactly how these routines are used to perform both the `Diffuse` step and the `Project` step. These routines are ideal for domains with no internal boundaries. When complex boundaries or objects are within the flow, one can either use a sophisticated multi-grid solver or a good relaxation routine [9]. In any case, our simulator can easily accomodate new solvers.

[1] FISHPAK is available from `http://www.netlib.org`.

## 4 Results

Our Navier-Stokes solver can be used in many applications requiring fluid-like motions. We have implemented both the two- and the three-dimensional solvers in an interactive modeler that allows a user to interact with the fluids in real-time. The motion is modeled by either adding density into the fluid or by applying forces. The evolution of the velocity and the density is then computed using our solver. To further increase the visual complexity of the flows, we add textural detail to the density. By moving the texture coordinates using the scalar solver as well, we achieve highly detailed flows. To compensate for the high distortions that the texture maps undergo, we use three sets of texture coordinates which are periodically reset to their initial (unperturbed) values. At every moment the resulting texture map is the superposition of these three texture maps. This idea was first suggested by Max et al. [13].

Figure 4.(a) shows a sequence of frames from an animation where the user interacts with one of our liquid textures. The figure on the backcover of the SIGGRAPH proceedings is another frame of a similar sequence with a larger grid size ($100^2$).

Figures 4.(b) through 4.(g) show frames from various animations that we generated using our three-dimensional solver. In each case the animations were created by allowing the animator to place density and apply forces in real-time. The gases are volume rendered using the three-dimensional hardware texture mapping capabilities of our SGI Octane workstation. We also added a single pass that computes self-shadowing effects from a directional light source in a fixed position. It should be evident that the quality of the renderings could be further improved using more sophisticated rendering hardware or software. Our grid sizes ranged from $16^3$ to $30^3$ with frame rates fast enough to monitor the animations while being able to control their behavior. In most of these animations we added a "noise" term which is proportional to the amount of density (the factor of proportionality being a user defined parameter). This produced nice billowing motions in some of our animations. In Figures 4.(d)-(e) we used a fractal texture map, while in Figure 4.(g) we used a texture map consisting of evenly spaced lines.

All of our animations were created on an SGI Octane workstation with a R10K processor and 192 Mbytes of memory.

## 5 Conclusions

The motivation of this paper was to create a general software system that allows an animator to design fluid-like motions in real time. Our initial intention was to base our system on Foster and Metaxas' work. However, the instabilities inherent in their method forced us to develop a new algorithm. Our solver has the property of being unconditionally stable and it can handle a wide variety of fluids in both two- and three-dimensions. The results that accompany this paper clearly demonstrate that our solver is powerful enough to allow an animator to achieve many fluid-like effects. We therefore believe that our solver is a substantial improvement over previous work in this area. The work presented here does not, however, discredit previous, more visually oriented models. In particular, we believe that the combination of our fluid solvers with solid textures, for example, may be a promising area of future research [4]. Our fluid solvers can be used to generate the overall motion, while the solid texture can add additional detail for higher quality animations.

Also we have not addressed the problem of simulating fluids with free boundaries, such as water [6]. This problem is considerably more difficult, since the geometry of the boundary evolves dynamically over time. We hope, however, that our stable solvers may be applied to this problem as well. Also, we wish to extend our solver to finite element boundary-fitted meshes. We are currently investigating such extensions.

## Acknowledgments

I would like to thank Marcus Grote for his informed input on fluid dynamics and for pointing me to reference [3]. Thanks to Duncan Brinsmead for his constructive criticisms all along. Thanks also to Pamela Jackson for carefully proofreading the paper and to Brad Clarkson for his help with creating the videos.

## A Method of Characteristics

The method of characteristics can be used to solve advection equations of the type

$$\frac{\partial a(\mathbf{x},t)}{\partial t} = -\mathbf{v}(\mathbf{x}) \cdot \nabla a(\mathbf{x},t) \quad \text{and} \quad a(\mathbf{x},0) = a_0(\mathbf{x}),$$

where $a$ is a scalar field, $\mathbf{v}$ is a steady vector field and $a_0$ is the field at time $t=0$. Let $\mathbf{p}(\mathbf{x}_0,t)$ denote the *characteristics* of the vector field $\mathbf{v}$ which flow through the point $\mathbf{x}_0$ at $t=0$:

$$\frac{d}{dt}\mathbf{p}(\mathbf{x}_0,t) = \mathbf{v}(\mathbf{p}(\mathbf{x}_0,t)) \quad \text{and} \quad \mathbf{p}(\mathbf{x}_0,0) = \mathbf{x}_0.$$

Now let $\bar{a}(\mathbf{x}_0,t) = a(\mathbf{p}(\mathbf{x}_0,t),t)$ be the value of the field along the characteristic passing through the point $\mathbf{x}_0$ at $t=0$. The variation of this quantity over time can be computed using the chain rule of differentiation:

$$\frac{d\bar{a}}{dt} = \frac{\partial a}{\partial t} + \mathbf{v} \cdot \nabla a = 0.$$

This shows that the value of the scalar does not vary along the streamlines. In particular, we have $\bar{a}(\mathbf{x}_0,t) = \bar{a}(\mathbf{x}_0,0) = a_0(\mathbf{x}_0)$. Therefore, the initial field and the characteristics entirely define the solution to the advection problem. The field for a given time $t$ and location $\mathbf{x}$ is computed by first tracing the location $\mathbf{x}$ back in time along the characteristic to get the point $\mathbf{x}_0$, and then evaluating the initial field at that point:

$$a(\mathbf{p}(\mathbf{x}_0,t),t) = a_0(\mathbf{x}_0).$$

We use this method to solve the advection equation over a time interval $[t, t+\Delta t]$ for the fluid. In this case, $\mathbf{v} = \mathbf{u}(\mathbf{x},t)$ and $a_0$ is any of the components of the fluid's velocity at time $t$.

## B FISHPAK Routines

The linear solver `POIS3D` from FISHPAK is designed to solve a general system of finite difference equations of the type:

```
K1*(S[i-1,j,k]-2*S[i,j,k]+S[i+1,j,k]) +
K2*(S[i,j-1,k]-2*S[i,j,k]+S[i,j+1,k]) +
A[k]*S[i,j,k-1]+B[k]*S[i,j,k]+     .
```

For the diffusion solver, the values of the constants on the left hand side are:

```
K1 = -dt*k/(D[0]*D[0]),
K2 = -dt*k/(D[1]*D[1]),
A[k] = C[k] = -dt*k/(D[2]*D[2]) and
B[k] = 1+2*dt*k/(D[2]*D[2]),
```

while the right hand side is equal to the grid containing the previous solution: `F=S0`. In the projection step these constants are equal to

```
K1 = 1/(D[0]*D[0]),K2 = 1/(D[1]*D[1]),
A[k] = C[k] = 1/(D[2]*D[2]) and
B[k] = -2/(D[2]*D[2]),
```

while the right hand side is equal to the divergence of the velocity field:

```
F[i,j,k] = 0.5*((U[i+1,j,k]-U[i-1,j,k])/D[0]+
    (U[i,j+1,k]-U[i,j-1,k])/D[1]+
    (U[i,j,k+1]-U[i,j,k-1])/D[2]).
```

The gradient of the solution is then subtracted from the previous solution:

```
U1[0][i,j,k] = U0[0][i,j,k] -
   0.5*(S[i+1,j,k]-S[i-1,j,k])/D[0],
U1[1][i,j,k] = U0[1][i,j,k] -
   0.5*(S[i,j+1,k]-S[i,j-1,k])/D[1],
U1[2][i,j,k] = U0[2][i,j,k] -
   0.5*(S[i,j,k+1]-S[i,j,k-1])/D[2].
```

The FISHPAK routine is also able to handle different types of boundary conditions, both periodic and fixed.

## References


[1] M. B. Abbott. *Computational Fluid Dynamics: An Introduction for Engineers.* Wiley, New York, 1989.

[2] J. X. Chen, N. da Vittoria Lobo, C. E. Hughes, and J. M. Moshell. Real-Time Fluid Simulation in a Dynamic Virtual Environment. *IEEE Computer Graphics and Applications*, pages 52–61, May-June 1997.

[3] A. J. Chorin and J. E. Marsden. *A Mathematical Introduction to Fluid Mechanics.* Springer-Verlag. Texts in Applied Mathematics 4. Second Edition., New York, 1990.

[4] D. Ebert, K. Musgrave, D. Peachy, K. Perlin, and S. Worley. *Texturing and Modeling: A Procedural Approach.* AP Professional, 1994.

[5] D. S. Ebert, W. E. Carlson, and R. E. Parent. Solid Spaces and Inverse Particle Systems for Controlling the Animation of Gases and Fluids. *The Visual Computer*, 10:471–483, 1994.

[6] N. Foster and D. Metaxas. Realistic Animation of Liquids. *Graphical Models and Image Processing*, 58(5):471–483, 1996.

[7] N. Foster and D. Metaxas. Modeling the Motion of a Hot, Turbulent Gas. In *Computer Graphics Proceedings, Annual Conference Series, 1997*, pages 181–188, August 1997.

[8] M. N. Gamito, P. F. Lopes, and M. R. Gomes. Two-dimensional Simulation of Gaseous Phenomena Using Vortex Particles. In *Proceedings of the 6th Eurographics Workshop on Computer Animation and Simulation*, pages 3–15. Springer-Verlag, 1995.

[9] M. Griebel, T. Dornseifer, and T. Neunhoeffer. *Numerical Simulation in Fluid Dynamics: A Practical Introduction.* SIAM, Philadelphia, 1998.

[10] W. Hackbusch. *Multi-grid Methods and Applications.* Springer Verlag, Berlin, 1985.

[11] F. H. Harlow and J. E. Welch. Numerical Calculation of Time-Dependent Viscous Incompressible Flow of Fluid with Free Surface. *The Physics of Fluids*, 8:2182–2189, December 1965.

[12] M. Kass and G. Miller. Rapid, Stable Fluid Dynamics for Computer Graphics. *ACM Computer Graphics (SIGGRAPH '90)*, 24(4):49–57, August 1990.

[13] N. Max, R. Crawfis, and D. Williams. Visualizing Wind Velocities by Advecting Cloud Textures. In *Proceedings of Visualization '92*, pages 179–183, Los Alamitos CA, October 1992. IEEE CS Press.

[14] W. H. Press, B. P. Flannery, S. A. Teukolsky, and W. T. Vetterling. *Numerical Recipes in C. The Art of Scientific Computing.* Cambridge University Press, Cambridge, 1988.

[15] W. T. Reeves. Particle Systems. A Technique for Modeling a Class of Fuzzy Objects. *ACM Computer Graphics (SIGGRAPH '83)*, 17(3):359–376, July 1983.

[16] M. Shinya and A. Fournier. Stochastic Motion - Motion Under the Influence of Wind. In *Proceedings of Eurographics '92*, pages 119–128, September 1992.

[17] K. Sims. Particle Animation and Rendering Using Data Parallel Computation. *ACM Computer Graphics (SIGGRAPH '90)*, 24(4):405–413, August 1990.

[18] K. Sims. Choreographed Image Flow. *The Journal Of Visualization And Computer Animation*, 3:31–43, 1992.

[19] J. Stam. A General Animation Framework for Gaseous Phenomena. *ERCIM Research Report*, R047, January 1997. http://www.ercim.org/publications/technical_reports/047-abstract.html.

[20] J. Stam and E. Fiume. Turbulent Wind Fields for Gaseous Phenomena. In *Proceedings of SIGGRAPH '93*, pages 369–376. Addison-Wesley Publishing Company, August 1993.

[21] J. Stam and E. Fiume. Depicting Fire and Other Gaseous Phenomena Using Diffusion Processes. In *Proceedings of SIGGRAPH '95*, pages 129–136. Addison-Wesley Publishing Company, August 1995.

[22] P. N. Swarztrauber and R. A. Sweet. Efficient Fortran Subprograms for the Solution of Separable Elliptic Partial Differential Equations. *ACM Transactions on Mathematical Software*, 5(3):352–364, September 1979.

[23] J. Wejchert and D. Haumann. Animation Aerodynamics. *ACM Computer Graphics (SIGGRAPH '91)*, 25(4):19–22, July 1991.

[24] L. Yaeger and C. Upson. Combining Physical and Visual Simulation. Creation of the Planet Jupiter for the Film 2010. *ACM Computer Graphics (SIGGRAPH '86)*, 20(4):85–93, August 1986.

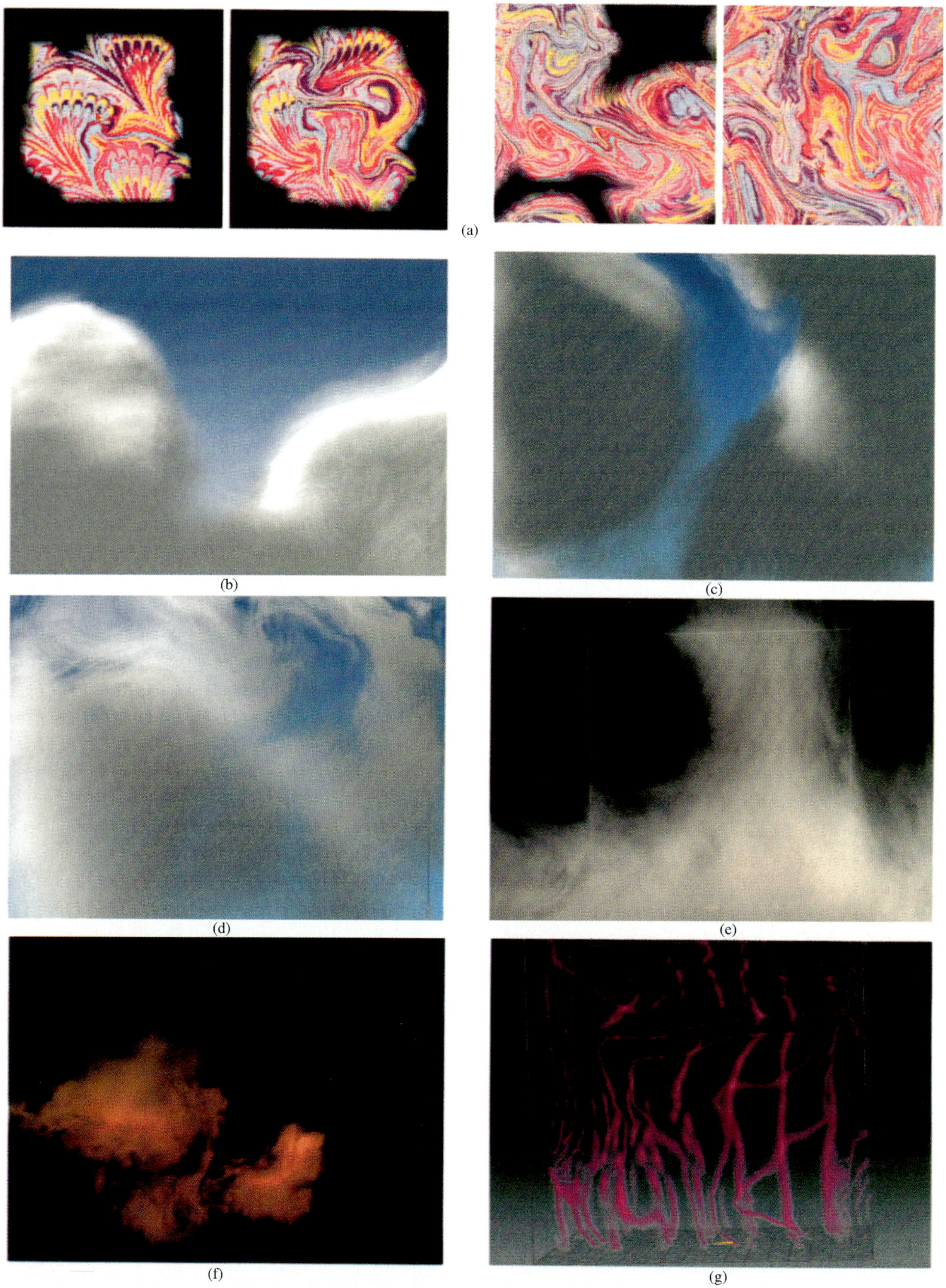


Figure 4: Snapshots from our interactive fluid solver.

# Computational Fluid Dynamics in a Traditional Animation Environment

Patrick Witting*

DreamWorks Feature Animation and Squeaky Cat

## Abstract

This paper presents a system that uses computational fluid dynamics to produce smoke, water, and other effects for traditionally-animated films. The system was used in over twenty scenes in the animated feature film *The Prince of Egypt.* Animators use images and animation sequences to drive two-dimensional numerical simulations of the time-dependent compressible Navier-Stokes equations. For instance, images can be used to initialize temperature fields which cause dynamic buoyancy-driven vortices to evolve. In addition to being image-driven, the system is unique in allowing for compressibility of the fluid, and in its use of partial differential equations for texture mapping.

**Keywords:** animation, animation systems, applications, fluid simulations, natural phenomena, numerical analysis, physically based animation, physically based modeling, scientific visualization, texture mapping

## 1 Introduction

Computer graphics simulations of fluid behavior are in demand in filmmaking for depicting gases, liquids, smoke, dust, fire, and other natural phenomena. Methods for creating these simulations vary widely, depending on the requirements for realism, controllability, rendering style, and complexity. This paper describes a system, which utilizes numerical simulations of the full equations of fluid dynamics, that is being used at DreamWorks Feature Animation Studios in the production of traditionally-animated films. The system employs techniques from both the scientific and computer graphics communities in order to be both efficient and accessible to animators.

### 1.1 Motivation

Of the many ways of incorporating simulation into the creation of fluids animations, one end of the spectrum in a traditional animation environment is to use no simulation at all, and draw every frame of the animation. This approach gives a wide range of flexibility and control, but is a tedious process with realistic limits on the complexity that can be achieved. At the other extreme, there are many advantages to numerically solving the full equations of motion for fluids, usually referred to as the Navier-Stokes equations, to create animations of fluid behavior. With simple user set-ups, the physically accurate equations take over, generating lots of high quality animation, rich in complexity and guaranteed realistic motion.

*3763 Lockerbie Lane Glendale, CA 91208
patrick@squeakycat.com



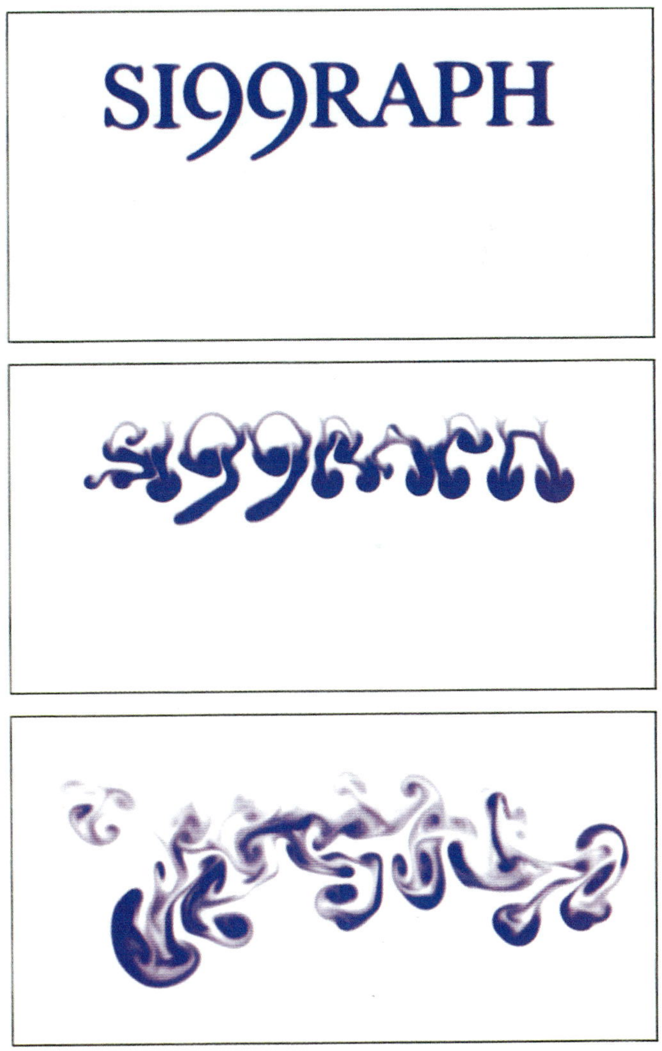


Figure 1: Temperature distribution - after 0, 100 and 400 time steps.

Figure 1 shows the results of a buoyancy-driven simulation created by simply interpreting the luminance of an image supplied by the user as the initial condition for the temperature field. The fluid inside the letters is colder and more dense than the surrounding fluid, causing it to sink. This is typical of the type of simulation that was used to generate smoke for *The Prince of Egypt*, where contours of temperature were rendered from a simulation driven by buoyant instabilities. This and other examples are discussed in more detail in

### 1.2 Modeling Fluid Behavior for the Sciences

Compared to computer graphics, the equations of fluid motion and solution methods for them have a long history. Equations expressing conservation of mass, momentum, and energy, often referred to as the Navier-Stokes equations, have been around since the early 1800's. Sir Horace Lamb's *Hydrodynamics* [11], from 1932, is still regarded as one of the best sources for fundamental theorems, equations, and solutions in fluid mechanics. The equations of motion cannot be solved analytically, except in simplified situations, and therefore need to be solved numerically. Numerical integration methods for systems of equations predate the modern computer as well, and John von Neumann envisioned using the computer to solve the equations of motion for weather prediction in the 1940's.

Today, the use of computers to solve the Navier-Stokes equations is widespread, with descriptions of particular models and their solutions filling the pages of journals such as *Journal of Fluid Mechanics* and *Journal of the Atmospheric Sciences*. Although computational fluid dynamics is a fairly mature subject, the emphasis so far has been on accurately simulating physical situations for scientific purposes, rather than creating images and animations as the end goal, which has different concerns and motivations. One simple example of this is the use of artificial compressibility, employed in the equation set presented in section 3, as a means of speeding up the calculations. For scientific work, the non-physical compressibility effects introduced need to be rigorously justified, whereas for the creation of imagery and animation, the guiding standard is how the images look.

When the emphasis is on the look of the final images, there are new sets of concerns about how to control and modify the simulation dynamics, and what and how to render. These concerns move us into the territory of computer graphics, with the highly practical production environment driving the process forward.

### 1.3 Modeling Fluid Behavior for Computer Graphics

Previous work in the graphics literature [2, 4, 6, 7, 9, 12, 13, 14, 16, 19] has modeled various aspects of fluid behavior with an emphasis on efficiency and controllability issues. Some of this work makes use of existing velocity fields or allows users to create their own in a variety of ways, rather than have a simulation determine the velocity field. The emphasis in this paper is on the use of the full Navier-Stokes equations to solve for the dynamic velocity and temperature fields numerically. Kass and Miller [9] solve the shallow water equations, which reduce the Navier-Stokes equations down to solving for an evolving height field for the surface of a shallow body of liquid. Yaeger, Upson, and Myers [19], used two-dimensional time-dependent vorticity equations to model the atmosphere of Jupiter. The strongest advocacy for use of the full Navier-Stokes equations so far in the graphics literature is from Foster and Metaxas [7], who solve the three-dimensional equations of motion to model smoke.

There may be no right or wrong answer as to what level of physical modeling is appropriate, in general, but there is usually a decision making process based on the imagery needed to guide this choice. Creative control and the level of realism desired are two of the main concerns. The decision making process is well illustrated in [19], where the end goal, creating animations of Jupiter's atmosphere for the film *2010*, guided aspects from the equations being solved to their final rendering method. This paper is of that same style, describing a system built at DreamWorks to support the use of fluid dynamics simulations in the creation of special effects for the animated feature film *The Prince of Egypt*.

### 1.4 Contributions of this Paper

Some of the unique features of the system described in this paper include: a compressible version of the equations of motion; the use of images and animations for controlling the dynamics; fast accurate texture mapping features; and finally, a complete production system.

The compressible formulation, unlike any in the graphics literature, allows for the modeling of compressible effects, such as shock waves, and also provides a mechanism for speeding up flow calculations by an order of magnitude or more. Another unique feature of the system is the use of images and animations as input devices, which allows animators to control initial conditions, source terms, and movable internal boundaries in an easy and flexible way. The inclusion of texture mapping differential equations, another new concept developed here, makes it possible to precalculate particle paths on a fixed grid which can be used in a straight-forward manner at render time.

The system also provides fast turn around time. Fourth order accuracy allows animators to use coarser grids, thus saving time. The use of two-dimensional simulations, the compressible formulation, and coarser grids, results in fast, useful simulations. Simulations performed on a 100 by 100 grid are detailed enough for film work and can be calculated at a rate of one frame per second. Additional production components make the overall process efficient for the animator.

## 2 Design Goals

Desirable characteristics of a useful production system which incorporates fluid dynamics simulations include the following:

- **Simulating a Variety of Flow Situations:** The equations being solved and the solution method should be capable of modeling a wide variety of flow situations, i.e. shear flow instabilities (Kelvin-Helmholtz), vortex motions, buoyant instabilities (Rayleigh-Taylor), Coriolis effects, gravity waves, compressible effects, etc. In addition, arbitrary forcing functions, or source terms, would be desirable to make many more situations possible, even those without any physical justification. Users should have easy access to setting up the various flow situations.

- **Control Throughout the Process:** The biggest difference between simulation systems for scientific purposes and simulation systems for production purposes is the level of control required in production work. Ideally, animators would control many aspects of the simulation dynamics and be able to incorporate the results into the final scene in a variety of ways.

- **Speed:** Speed is always a consideration in production work, because it usually translates into more iterations of the creative design cycle and a better final result.

- **Pipeline:** The overall process must make sense within the context of the production environment. The system should be able to make use of other scene elements, produce scene elements in the most convenient formats, and should be part of an efficient work flow.

- **A Variety of Rendering Styles:** The rendering style plays an important role in the overall process. A wide variety of rendering styles increases the expressive power of scene elements and their interpretation.

## 3 The Model

The equation set used was derived for a meteorology application, the study of clouds [10, 18]. The equation set presented in section 3.2 is a simplification of that system which meets the needs discussed in section 2 in a variety of ways discussed throughout.

### 3.1 Important Aspects of the Equation Set

Because this formulation of the equations of motion will be unfamiliar to many readers, this section has been included to characterize the equation set in a qualitative manner.

- **Conservation of Mass, Momentum, Energy:** The system of five equations and five unknowns is used to express conservation of mass, conservation of the 3 components of momentum, and conservation of energy. Along with the equation of state, which is an equation for one thermodynamic quantity as a function of two others, this forms a complete description of the fluid, i.e. the velocity and thermodynamic state of the fluid at any point. Given appropriate initial conditions and boundary conditions, the equations can be used to advance the solution forward in time. At the boundaries, a well-posed problem can be formed by specifying information for all the variables except the pressure, where the solution needs to be calculated [8].

- **Compressibility:** One of the most important aspects of the equation set is that there is no assumption of incompressibility. Not only does this mean that compressibility effects can be modeled, but the equations can be solved much faster. When an incompressible formulation is used, there is an elliptical partial differential equation involved, corresponding to an "infinite" speed of propagation of pressure waves. This typically translates into solving a large matrix equation, usually by iterative techniques, to ensure the pressure field is consistent with the velocity field. This is usually a time consuming part of the solution method and does not scale well as grid resolution is increased. Using the compressible formulation means that calculation times for each time step are essentially linear in the number of grid points.

- **Pressure Equation:** Because of the lengthy derivation, the pressure equation is presented as is. In summary, conservation of mass is expressed in the compressible equations by the mathematical statement that changes in density for a parcel of fluid are the result of divergence in the velocity field.

- **Buoyancy:** Some systems of equations make an assumption that the fluid has the same density everywhere, which simplifies the equation set at the expense of not modeling buoyancy effects. The equations being used here do not make that assumption and buoyancy effects dominate the dynamics in most of the examples presented.

- **Potential Temperature:** Potential temperature is used in meteorology as the appropriate measure of static stability, instead of density, temperature, or other variables which are not conserved in the atmosphere. For instance, a situation of having a colder fluid on top of a hotter fluid is not necessarily an unstable arrangement, due to the stratified hydrostatic pressure in the atmosphere. This concept is defined in most meteorology texts [3]. Throughout this paper "temperature" is often used in place of "potential temperature" for ease of reading.

- **Forcing:** The equations also allow for arbitrary forcing functions to each of the equations, except the pressure equation, corresponding to localized source terms for momentum and energy. These forcing functions can be analytical functions of the other variables, such as coriolis or buoyancy terms, or can come from other sources, such as images and animations.

- **Diffusion:** Each of the equations includes a diffusion term, which has the effect of damping out the high frequency waves. These terms have many interpretations, from molecular diffusion, to turbulence modeling, to numerical stability devices. Most ODE solvers (ordinary differential equation), including the fourth order Runge-Kutta scheme employed here, require some level of diffusion to avoid nonlinear instabilities.

- **Passive Scalar:** As discussed later, the system can also be augmented with additional equations, for things such as passive scalars which advect with the flow. Equations are derived for including texture mapping information, so that particle trajectories don't need to be computed via integration later.

### 3.2 Equation Set

The equations being solved are essentially those in [10]. The subgrid scale model is replaced by diffusion terms with constant diffusion coefficients, and the rain processes and coriolis terms are neglected. Also, the coefficient for the sound speed is multiplied by a constant, introducing artificial compressibility, so that the time step requirement is less severe. The primary variables being advanced forward in time are $u$, $v$, and $w$, which are the velocity components in the $x$, $y$, and $z$ directions, respectively, the pressure perturbation variable, $\pi$, defined in equation 9, and the potential temperature, $\theta$, defined in equation 8. The meteorology convention of using $z$ as the *up* direction is used here.

$$\frac{Du}{Dt} = -c_p\overline{\theta}\frac{\partial\pi}{\partial x} + \nu\Delta u + f_u \tag{1}$$

$$\frac{Dv}{Dt} = -c_p\overline{\theta}\frac{\partial\pi}{\partial y} + \nu\Delta v + f_v \tag{2}$$

$$\frac{Dw}{Dt} = -c_p\overline{\theta}\frac{\partial\pi}{\partial z} + g\left(\frac{\theta-\overline{\theta}}{\overline{\theta}}\right) + \nu\Delta w + f_w \tag{3}$$

$$\frac{\partial\pi}{\partial t} = \frac{\overline{c}^2}{c_p\overline{\rho}\overline{\theta}^2}\left(\frac{\partial}{\partial x}(\overline{\rho}\overline{\theta}u) + \frac{\partial}{\partial y}(\overline{\rho}\overline{\theta}v) + \frac{\partial}{\partial z}(\overline{\rho}\overline{\theta}w)\right) \tag{4}$$

$$\frac{D\theta}{Dt} = \nu_\theta\Delta\theta + f_\theta \tag{5}$$

$\frac{D}{Dt}$ is the material derivative operator $\frac{\partial}{\partial t} + u\frac{\partial}{\partial x} + v\frac{\partial}{\partial y} + w\frac{\partial}{\partial z}$, and $\Delta$ is the Laplacian operator $\frac{\partial^2}{\partial x^2} + \frac{\partial^2}{\partial y^2} + \frac{\partial^2}{\partial z^2}$. $g$ is the acceleration of gravity, $\nu$ and $\nu_\theta$ are diffusion coefficients, $c_p$ is the specific heat at constant pressure, $c$ is the speed of sound, and $f_u$, $f_v$, $f_w$, and $f_\theta$ are forcing functions, or source terms for their respective equations. Base state variables, denoted by overbars, are time-invariant functions of $z$, the vertical coordinate.

The equation of state is the perfect gas law,

$$p = \rho RT, \tag{6}$$

where p is the pressure, $\rho$ is the density of the fluid, $R$ is the gas constant, and $T$ is the temperature. Using $p_0$ as a reference pressure, a non-dimensional pressure, $\Pi$, is defined by

$$\Pi = \left(\frac{p}{p_0}\right)^{\frac{R}{c_p}}, \tag{7}$$

and a potential temperature, $\theta$, by

$$\theta = T\left(\frac{p}{p_0}\right)^{\frac{-R}{c_p}}. \tag{8}$$

Defining a pressure perturbation variable $\pi$ by

$$\Pi = \overline{\Pi} + \pi, \tag{9}$$

we assume the base state profiles obey the hydrostatic relationship

$$\frac{\partial \overline{\Pi}}{\partial z} = \frac{-g}{c_p \overline{\theta}}, \tag{10}$$

which reflects that the hydrostatic pressure of a parcel of air is caused by the weight of a column of air above it.

A two-dimensional version of the above equations can be derived by assuming that in one of the horizontal directions there is no flow and no change in any of the variables. Taking $y$ to be the flowless direction, equation 2 is no longer needed, and simplifications are made to equation 4 and to the material derivative and Laplacian operators to account for zero derivatives in the $y$ direction.

In addition to the basic equations of fluid motion, equations can be appended to the system which may or may not have feedback into the basic equations. Equation 11 is the prototypical passive scalar equation, which models an arbitrary scalar $\psi$ being advected along with the fluid, and optionally diffusing through the non-negative diffusion coefficient $\nu_\psi$.

$$\frac{D\psi}{Dt} = \nu_\psi \Delta \psi \tag{11}$$

Derivations of the equations of motion from first principles can be found in many textbooks for the interested reader [3, 11, 15, 17].

### 3.2.1 Texture Mapping Equations

Figure 2: Texture mapping after 0 and 400 time steps.

A convenient way to record the flow field history is through the dynamic evolution of texture map information. The idea is to initialize passive scalar variables with the original positions of the fluid parcels. These variables would obey equation 11, and let you know the original location of the parcel at any stage in the simulation, at the fixed grid locations. This *Eulerian* description is particularly useful in the rendering phase, since the texture mapping coordinate information is evenly spaced in the output image space. This technique is shown in figure 2 for the same simulation used to produce figure 1.

Suppose we are running a two-dimensional simulation on a rectangular domain of physical dimensions $L_x$ by $L_z$. Define a horizontal texture map variable, $\psi_x$, with initial condition $\psi_x(x, z, 0) = x/L_x$ and a vertical texture map variable, $\psi_z$, with initial condition $\psi_z(x, z, 0) = z/L_z$. If both of these variables obey equation 11, then at a later time, $t$, $\psi_x(x, z, t)$ and $\psi_z(x, z, t)$ will contain the texture map coordinates at time $t = 0$ for the parcel at location $x$, $z$ at time $t$, that is, they tell where the parcel of fluid "came from."

When implementing periodic boundary conditions, it is more desirable to keep track of displacement offsets from $\psi_x$ and $\psi_z$ because of the discontinuity of $\psi_x$ and $\psi_z$ as you cross periodic boundaries. Defining $p_x = \psi_x - x/L_x$ and $p_z = \psi_z - z/L_z$, we arrive at the following equations

$$\frac{Dp_x}{Dt} = -u/L_x + \nu_p \Delta p_x \tag{12}$$

$$\frac{Dp_z}{Dt} = -w/L_z + \nu_p \Delta p_z \tag{13}$$

## 3.3 Solution Method

The solution method for solving the system of equations is the fourth order Runge-Kutta scheme, using fourth order centered finite differencing for spatial derivatives on a regular grid with equal grid spacing. At boundary points and one point away, one-sided differencing is used. This solution method is briefly described below:

Ordinary differential equation solvers, such as the Runge-Kutta methods, solve the vector equation

$$\mathbf{y}' = \mathbf{f}(\mathbf{y}), \tag{14}$$
$$\mathbf{y}(t_0) = \mathbf{y}_0$$

The equation set 1 through 5 can be written in this form for the solution vector $\mathbf{y} = [u \; v \; w \; \pi \; \theta\,]^T$ by moving the advective terms in the material derivatives over to the right hand side of their respective equations. The advective terms are those not involving partial derivatives with respect to time. The equations will now look like equation 14 where the prime in equation 14 denotes differentiation with respect to time. The right hand side of the equations become $\mathbf{f}(\mathbf{y})$.

The solution vector is initialized with values at the regularly spaced grid locations, then advanced forward in time according to the time integration scheme. This involves evaluating the function $\mathbf{f}(\mathbf{y})$ at each of the grid points, making use of the solution vector in a stencil of grid points surrounding the grid point being evaluated.

First and second derivative terms are replaced by their fourth order finite difference approximations, which can be found in [1]. The overall method is globally fourth order accurate in space and time, provided that the initial conditions, boundary conditions, and forcing functions are sufficiently smooth.

The fourth order accuracy is not required for production purposes, but the effort in achieving this added accuracy is not significant, and the increased accuracy allows for the use of coarser grids. For instance, comparing Runge-Kutta fourth order with Euler's method, four function evaluations per time step are required for Runge-Kutta compared with one for Euler, but this is almost offset by the time steps which can be 2.82 times larger, according to equation 15.

The time step limitation for stability for the advection problem, i.e. negligible diffusion, is

$$\Delta t < \frac{2\sqrt{2}}{c_* \sqrt{nm}} \Delta x, \tag{15}$$

where $\Delta t$ is the time step, $\Delta x$ is the grid spacing, $n$ is the number of space dimensions, $c_*$ is the speed of the fastest moving wave in the system, and $m$ is a factor that accounts for the spatial differencing method. For fourth order centered first derivatives, this factor turns out to be 1.372, compared with 1.0 for second order centered first derivatives.

Numerical methods for fluid dynamics can be found in a variety of places [5, 8], and an extensive book list and summary of available codes can be found at `http://chemengineer.miningco.com/msub74.htm` .

# 4 The Production System

This section describes the actual system built, which reflects the design goals of section 2, makes use of the model described in section 3, and also takes into account additional considerations specific to the traditional animation environment and the needs of *The Prince of Egypt.* In a traditional animation studio, most artwork and animation is two dimensional; the illusion of depth comes from the drawn or painted perspective, along with the camera moves and techniques available in the compositing software.

Many simulation and rendering techniques were used in the visual development stage of the film. Test animation resulted from three-dimensional simulations with temperature being visualized via volume rendering, two-dimensional simulations creating velocity fields used for line integral convolution of source imagery, as well as other techniques. By far, the biggest success was two-dimensional simulations of buoyant instabilities, where the temperature field was visualized as smoke. The plan was to use this technique to create "magical smoke" for the sequence *Playing with the Big Boys*, and the process was streamlined with this in mind.

Figure 3: Reactionary elements created by simple transformations.

## 4.1 Design Decisions

The components described in sections 4.2-4.4 were built to support two-dimensional simulations which use images and animations as input. The simulations output information at regular intervals which is later used in the compositor for rendering. Some of the advantages of these decisions are described below.

- **Control Through Layering:** Animators can build up libraries of elements produced by simulations, all of which can be easily repositioned, scaled, and even put into perspective within the compositor. The bottom of figure 3 shows two layers and how they were integrated into the final image above. The top element was scaled and had animating transforms to match to the motion of one of the magician's hands. The lower element had an animating transform to react to the sliding of one of his feet. Individual layers allow artists to make independent decisions for colors, opacities, rendering parameters, and transforms.

- **Speed:** Two-dimensional simulations allow for good interactivity in creating elements for later use. Some of the lower resolution final elements used in the film were created in under two minutes, and even the highest resolution simulations could be set up using the information gathered in simulations taking only a few minutes.

- **Deferred Rendering:**

  The texture mapping differential equations developed in section 3.2.1 and periodic output from the simulations allow for deferred rendering, using only a small fraction of the disk space required to save final images. Deferred rendering means that no rendering decisions need to be made at simulation time, and no simulation time is required at render time.

  This allows for a flexible system, where simulations can be run with a specific flow situation and final element in mind, such as rising smoke. Artists choose rendering parameters later, e.g. to alter final timing or to animate contour levels that make the smoke slowly dissipate. At render time, a library of potentially useful simulations is already built up, and rendering involves little more than appropriate resampling (see section 4.4).

## 4.2 Setting Up and Running Simulations

Although the code is capable of handling more general situations, such as analytically defined forcing functions, gravitational fields, and diffusion coefficients, only a subset of the functionality is available via the user interface. Images define the initial conditions for velocity and temperature. Scalar variables on the interface aid the software in interpreting the images, e.g. assigning values to the black and white limits of the images. Similarly, images and animations are employed to apply forcing terms to the momentum and energy equations. In addition, two images are used to optionally assign profiles to the horizontal velocity and the temperature as functions of $z$. This makes it easy to set up shear flows and stratified layers of density. Figure 4 shows the interface for starting simulations.

Using the simulation starting interface, animators can set other parameters such as the resolution, boundary condition types, output frequency, etc., and can monitor simulations in the viewer described below. If a simulation is evolving unsatisfactorily, an animator can quickly restart it using modified images or parameter settings. Before the simulation is run, the system performs a preprocessing step on the images, essentially resampling them and slightly smoothing them for the appropriate simulation resolution, and enforcing periodic conditions if needed. It also calculates the initial pressure field from the temperature field, ensuring that the hydrostatic relationship is satisfied for vertical columns of fluid. Figure 5 shows the input image summary before the preprocessing steps. Figures 4 through 6 are taken from example 2 discussed in section 5.

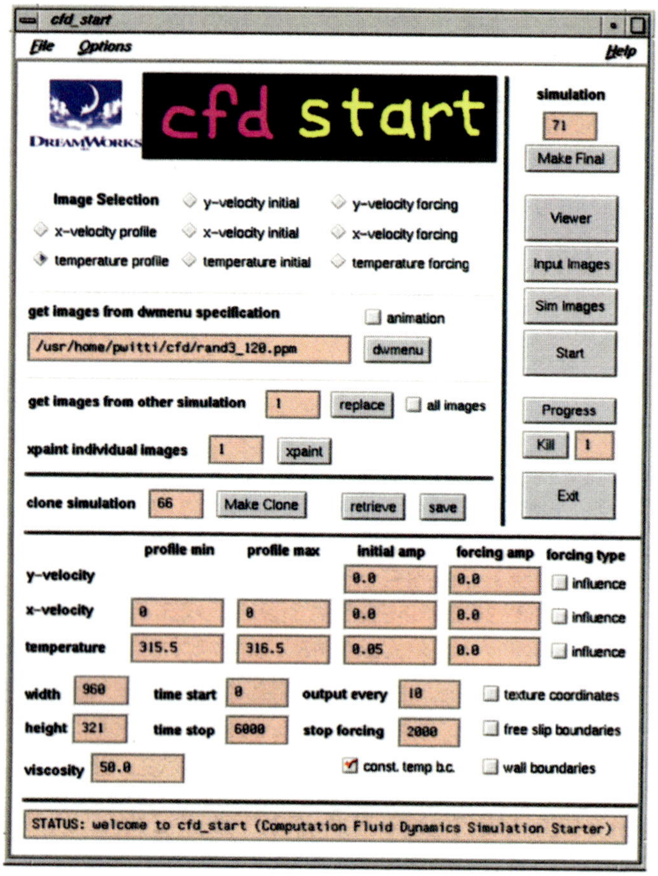


Figure 4: Simulation starter.

## 4.3 Previewing Simulations

As the simulations are running, or afterward, animators can preview and optionally render the results to disk via the interface shown in figure 6. This previewer is a simple mapping of the temperature values to the luminance of the black and white images. More rendering options described below are available in the compositor.

## 4.4 Rendering Simulations

The compositor is a graph-based system (DAG) where rendering operations are "nodes" in the graph.

- **Temperature Contours:** Two image generation nodes are provided in the compositor for rendering the temperature field, with temperature being mapped in a linear fashion to transparency. Values outside the linear range are clamped to "clear" or "solid." One node maps the results of simulations done on a rectangle with periodic sides onto a circle, as in middle of figure 8, and the other renders the rectangular temperature field.

  All of the parameters, such as the timing and threshold values, have animation curves. The rendering process involves reading the data from disk at the simulation resolution and performing resampling with a two-pass, one-dimensional cubic convolution kernel. It is important to do periodic extensions *before* resampling to avoid seams at the periodic boundaries, and to do thresholding *after* resampling to avoid stair-step effects for magnification near the threshold values.

- **Volume Rendering:** Volume rendering of the thresholded temperature field was supported for three-dimensional simulations in the visual development phase, but not in the production system.

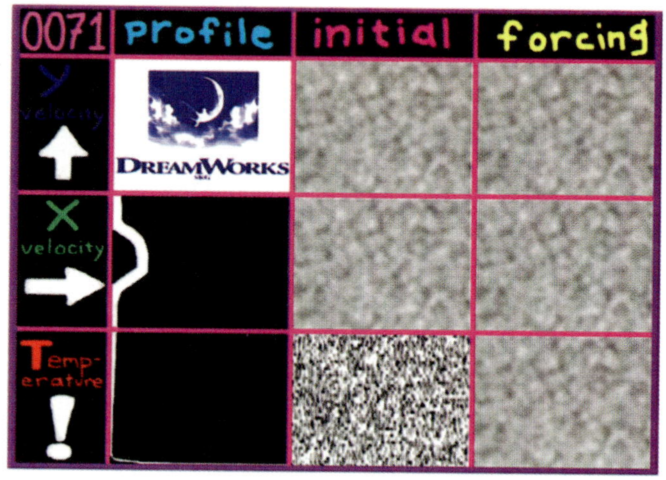


Figure 5: Input summary before preprocessing.

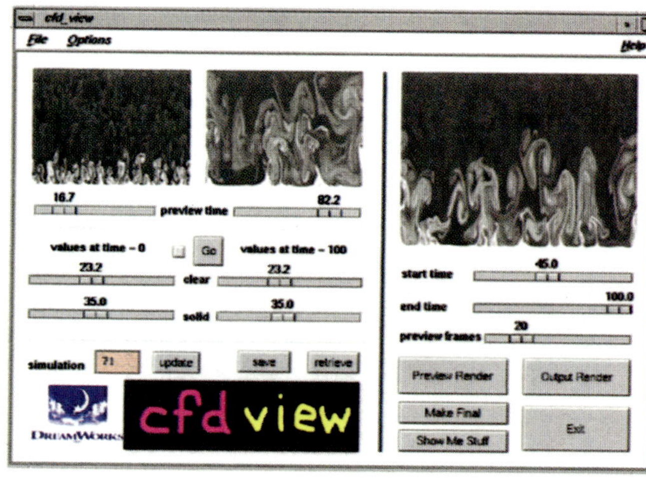


Figure 6: Simulation viewer.

- **Texture Mapping:** As described in section 3.2.1 and seen in figure 2, texture mapping is supported in the compositor. Inputs to this node are an image to be distorted, a simulation number, a reference time, and a current time. The image is distorted based on the flow field evolution between the reference time and the current time, using the texture mapping data for those two times.

- **Image Smearing:** Another rendering option supported in the compositor is the smearing of an image via line integral convolution using two-dimensional flow fields provided by the simulation. A single smearing uses one static flow field and a time range for the integration, provided by the user. Each output pixel receives its color from the colors visited along a flow integration path passing through the output pixel between the two specified times.

# 5 Examples

The example times quoted below are for a single processor SGI O2 with R10K floating point chip and processor chip. Calculation times are given for simulation time steps. Simulation time steps and simulation time between final frames are roughly equal, for comparison purposes, using the following logic: According to equation 15, if a Mach number of 0.4 is used and the largest possible stable time step is used, then the fluid speed will travel the distance of about one grid point per time step. Unless the grid is extremely large, structures moving by one grid point corresponds to a reasonable speed for an animation. For render times, the quote is for producing 640 by 480 images.

Figure 7: top) Temperature field. middle) Composition in scene. bottom) Final scene.

### 5.1 Example 1 - Image Used for Initial Temperature

In the first example, an image defines the initial temperature distribution and drives the dynamics of the simulation. The lettering in "SI99RAPH" is colder than the surrounding fluid, which causes it to sink. Conservation of mass dictates that there be areas of return flow as the cold fluid sinks, creating vortices. There is enough variation in the initial distribution such that the nonlinear equations result in pleasing graphic shapes and interesting dynamics.

This simulation was run on a 400 by 300 grid, with periodic sides. Figure 1 shows the temperature distribution at the start of the simulation and at two later times. Calculation time between time steps is 19.8 seconds, which include the texture mapping calculations. Render time for frames such as figure 1 is 3.16 seconds per frame.

As described in section 3.2.1, texture mapping information can be calculated along with the simulation to provide rendering information. Particle advection through the dynamically evolving velocity field is thus precalculated, eliminating the need to calculate particle trajectories at render time. Figure 2 shows the result of advecting the colors in an image along with the fluid for the simulation used to produce figure 1. An average render time for distortions such as those depicted in figure 2 is 9.8 seconds per frame.

### 5.2 Example 2 - Constant Heat Flux from Below

The second example simulates heat being introduced at the bottom of the domain creating "magical smoke" (see figure 7). The initial temperature distribution is a random noise pattern with an overall average temperature which is essentially constant except in a narrow layer near the bottom, where it is hotter. The images used for defining the initial conditions are shown in figure 5 and the other input values are the same as those shown in figure 4. The only images that are not scaled by zero, are the images used to define the unstable profile and the random perturbations in the initial temperature.

The simulation is performed on a 960 by 321 grid, with the rendering aspect ratio adjusted to make the shapes look taller and thinner than the actual simulation, which would otherwise promote rising plumes with essentially round circulation patterns. One time step calculation takes 36.3 seconds, and one rendered frame such as at the top of figure 7 takes 4.7 seconds to render.

### 5.3 Example 3 - Periodic Boundary Conditions in Action

In figure 8, "magical blood" is created by a simulation driven by a random forcing function in the temperature equation, defined by one of the input images. Using the circular rendering option and a periodic simulation domain creates a seamless texture mapping with the appearance of blood emanating from the center of the bowl. The final composite shows the circular shape being repositioned in perspective, registered to the bowl. Everything can be defined and rendered in one pass within the compositing package, including the animating perspective transformation. The simulation resolution is 150 by 151. Time step calculation time is 2.7 seconds per time step and rendering time is 1.57 seconds per frame.

## 6 Summary

This paper presents a complete production system which enables animators to access the beauty and realism embodied in the physically accurate equations of motion, the Navier-Stokes equations. With this system, animators can express themselves by controlling the simulation dynamics through a familiar user interface—the use of images and animations. Texture mapping features allow deferred rendering of flow distortions, with no need to recompute particle trajectories through a time-evolving velocity field. A compressible formulation and two-dimensional simulations allow for quick turnaround time in the creative cycle of creating/modifying simulations and applying the results within the compositor to the final scene.

While this production system emphasizes the needs of a traditional animation environment, many of the concepts apply outside

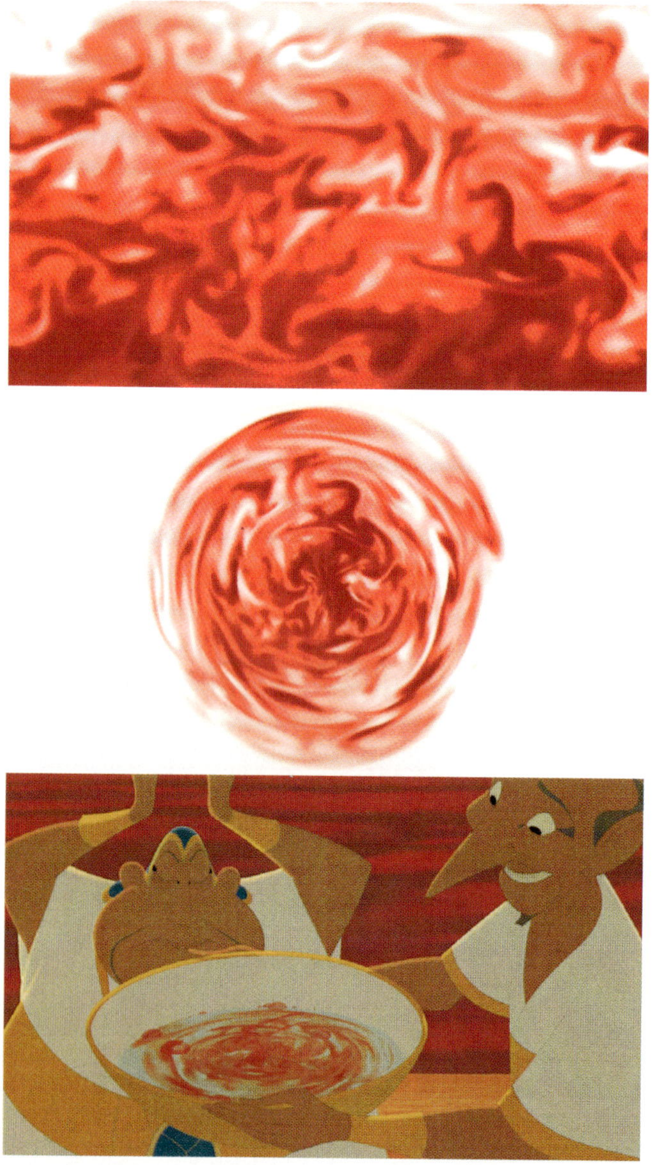

Figure 8: top) Temperature on periodic rectangular domain. middle) Circular domain remapping. bottom) Final scene.

this context as well. All of the equations, including the texture mapping equations, extend to three dimensions. One of the most useful ideas presented here for three-dimensional simulations is the implementation of an artificial speed of sound through the compressible formulation of the equations. Atmospheric researchers often use the compressible formulation because of its computational advantages over the incompressible formulation, even when using the actual speed of sound for pressure waves. For computer graphics purposes, an artificial speed of sound of an order of magnitude less than the actual one is often justified, and provides a mechanism for dramatic speed increases.

## References


[1] Milton Abramowitz and Irene A. Stegun. *Handbook of Mathematical Functions, With Formulas, Graphs, and Mathematical Tables.* Dover, 1974.

[2] Cassidy J. Curtis, Sean E. Anderson, Joshua E. Seims, Kurt W. Fleischer, and David H. Salesin. Computer-Generated Watercolor. In *Computer Graphics*, pages 421–430. ACM SIGGRAPH, 1997.

[3] John A. Dutton. *The Ceaseless Wind.* Dover, 1986.

[4] David S. Ebert and Richard E. Parent. Rendering and Animation of Gaseous Phenomena by Combining Fast Volume and Scanline A-buffer Techniques. In *Computer Graphics*, volume 24(4), pages 357–366. ACM SIGGRAPH, 1990.

[5] C.A.J. Fletcher. *Computational Techniques for Fluid Dynamics.* Springer, 1990.

[6] Nick Foster and Dimitris Metaxas. Realistic Animation of Liquids. In *Graphical Models and Image Proc.*, volume 58(5), pages 471–483, 1996.

[7] Nick Foster and Dimitris Metaxas. Modeling the Motion of a Hot, Turbulent Gas. In *Computer Graphics*, pages 181–188. ACM SIGGRAPH, 1997.

[8] Bertil Gustafsson, Heinz-Otto Kreiss, and Joseph Oliger. *Time Dependent Problems and Difference Methods.* Wiley, 1995.

[9] Michael Kass and Gavin Miller. Rapid, Stable Fluid Dynamics for Computer Graphics. In *Computer Graphics*, volume 24(4), pages 49–57. ACM SIGGRAPH, 1990.

[10] Joseph B. Klemp and Robert B. Wilhelmson. The Simulation of Three-Dimensional Convective Storm Dynamics. *Journal of the Atmospheric Sciences*, 35:1070–1096, 1978.

[11] Sir Horace Lamb. *Hydrodynamics.* Dover, 1932.

[12] Karl Sims. Particle Animation and Rendering Using Data Parallel Computation. In *Computer Graphics*, volume 24(4), pages 405–413. ACM SIGGRAPH, 1990.

[13] Jos Stam and Eugene Fiume. Turbulent Wind Fields for Gaseous Phenomena. In *Computer Graphics*, pages 369–376. ACM SIGGRAPH, 1993.

[14] Jos Stam and Eugene Fiume. Depicting Fire and Other Gaseous Phenomena Using Diffusion Processes. In *Computer Graphics*, pages 129–136. ACM SIGGRAPH, 1995.

[15] Philip A. Thompson. *Compressible-Fluid Dynamics.* Rensselaer Polytechnic Institute Press, 1988.

[16] Jakub Wejchert and David Haumann. Animation Aerodynamics. In *Computer Graphics*, volume 25(4), pages 19–22. ACM SIGGRAPH, 1991.

[17] Frank M. White. *Viscous Fluid Flow.* McGraw-Hill, Inc., 1991.

[18] Patrick Witting. *Numerical Investigation of Stratus Cloud Layer Breakup by Cloud Top Instabilities.* PhD thesis, Stanford University, 1995.

[19] Larry Yaeger, Craig Upson, and Robert Myers. Combining Physical and Visual Simulation - Creation of the Planet Jupiter for the Film "2010". In *Computer Graphics*, volume 20(4), pages 85–93. ACM SIGGRAPH, 1986.

# Graphical Modeling and Animation of Brittle Fracture

James F. O'Brien Jessica K. Hodgins

GVU Center and College of Computing
Georgia Institute of Technology

## Abstract

In this paper, we augment existing techniques for simulating flexible objects to include models for crack initiation and propagation in three-dimensional volumes. By analyzing the stress tensors computed over a finite element model, the simulation determines where cracks should initiate and in what directions they should propagate. We demonstrate our results with animations of breaking bowls, cracking walls, and objects that fracture when they collide. By varying the shape of the objects, the material properties, and the initial conditions of the simulations, we can create strikingly different effects ranging from a wall that shatters when it is hit by a wrecking ball to a bowl that breaks in two when it is dropped on edge.

**CR Categories:** I.3.5 [Computer Graphics]: Computational Geometry and Object Modeling—Physically based modeling; I.3.7 [Computer Graphics]: Three-Dimensional Graphics and Realism—Animation; I.6.8 [Simulation and Modeling]: Types of Simulation—Animation

**Keywords:** Animation techniques, physically based modeling, simulation, dynamics, fracture, cracking, deformation, finite element method.

## 1 Introduction

With the introduction in 1998 of simulated water in *Antz* [5, 14] and clothing in *Geri's Game* [4, 15], passive simulation was clearly demonstrated to be a viable technique for commercial animation. The appeal of using simulation for objects without an internal source of energy is not surprising, as passive objects tend to have many degrees of freedom, making keyframing or motion capture difficult. Furthermore, while passive objects are often essential to the plot of an animation and to the appearance or mood of the piece, they are not characters with their concomitant requirements for control over the subtle details of the motion. Therefore, simulations in which the motion is controlled only by initial conditions, physical equations, and material parameters are often sufficient to produce appealing animations of passive objects.

College of Computing, Georgia Institute of Technology, Atlanta, GA 30332. job@acm.org, jkh@cc.gatech.edu.

Figure 1: Slab of simulated glass that has been shattered by a heavy weight.

Our approach to animating breaking objects is based on linear elastic fracture mechanics. We model three-dimensional volumes using a finite element method that is based on techniques presented in the computer graphics and mechanical engineering literature [3, 6, 18]. By analyzing the stresses created as a volumetric object deforms, the simulation determines where cracks should begin and in what directions they should propagate. The system accommodates arbitrary propagation directions by dynamically retesselating the mesh. Because cracks are not limited to element boundaries, the models can form irregularly shaped shards and edges as they shatter.

We demonstrate the power of this approach with the following examples: a glass slab that shatters when a weight is dropped onto it (Figure 1), an adobe wall that crumbles under the impact of a wrecking ball (Figure 9), a series of bowls that break when they hit the floor (Figure 11), and objects that break when they collide with each other (Figure 14). To assess the realism of this approach, we compare high-speed video images of a physical bowl dropping onto concrete and a simulated version of the same event (Figure 13).

## 2 Background

In the computer graphics literature, two previous techniques have been developed for modeling dynamic, deformation-induced fracture. In 1988, Terzopoulos and Fleischer [18, 19] presented a general technique for modeling viscoelastic and plastic deformations. Their method used three fundamental metric tensors to define energy functions that measured deformation over curves, surfaces, and volumes. These energy functions provided the basis for a continuous deformation model that they simulated using a variety of discretization methods. One of their methods made use of a finite differencing technique defined by controlled continuity splines [17]. This formulation allowed them to demonstrate how certain fracture effects could be modeled by setting the elastic coefficients between adjacent nodes to zero whenever the distance between the nodes exceeded a threshold. They demonstrated this technique with sheets paper and cloth that could be torn apart.

In 1991, Norton and his colleagues presented a technique for animating 3D solid objects that broke when subjected to large strains [12]. They simulated a teapot that shattered when dropped onto a table. Their technique used a spring and mass system to model the behavior of the object. When the distance between two attached mass points exceeded a threshold, the simulation severed the spring connection between them. To avoid having flexible strings of partially connected material hanging from the object, their simulation broke an entire cube of springs at once.

Two limitations are inherent in both of these methods. First, when the material fails, the exact location and orientation of the fracture are not known. Rather the failure is defined as the entire connection between two nodes, and the orientation of the fracture plane is left undefined. As a result, these techniques can only realistically model effects that occur on a scale much larger than the inter-node spacing.

The second limitation is that fracture surfaces are restricted to the boundaries in the initial mesh structure. As a result, the fracture pattern exhibits directional artifacts, similar to the "jaggies" that occur when rasterizing a polygonal edge. These artifacts are particularly noticeable when the discretization follows a regular pattern. If an irregular mesh is used, then the artifacts may be partially masked, but the fractures will still be forced onto a path that follows the element boundaries so that the object can break apart only along predefined facets.

Other relevant work in the computer graphics literature includes techniques for modeling static crack patterns and fractures induced by explosions. Hirota and colleagues described how phenomena such as the static crack patterns created by drying mud can be modeled using a mass and spring system attached to an immobile substrate [8]. Mazarak et al. use a voxel-based approach to model solid objects that break apart when they encounter a spherical blast wave [9]. Neff and Fiume use a recursive pattern generator to divide a planar region into polygonal shards that fly apart when acted on by a spherical blast wave [10].

Fracture has been studied more extensively in the mechanics literature, and many techniques have been developed for simulating and analyzing the behavior of materials as they fail. A number of theories may be used to describe when and how a fracture will develop or propagate, and these theories have been employed with various numerical methods including finite element and finite difference methods, boundary integral equations, and molecular particle simulations. A comprehensive review of this work can be found in the book by Anderson [1] and the survey article by Nishioka [11].

Although simulation is used to model fracture both in computer graphics and in engineering, the requirements of the two fields are very different. Engineering applications require that the simulation predict real-world behaviors in an accurate and reliable fashion. In computer animation, what matters is how the fracture looks, how difficult it was to make it look that way, and how long it took. Although the technique presented in this paper was developed using traditional engineering tools, it is an animation technique and relies on a number of simplifications that would be unacceptable in an engineering context.

# 3 Deformations

Fractures arise in materials due to internal stresses created as the material deforms. Our goal is to model these fractures. In order to do so, however, we must first be able to model the deformations that cause them. To provide a suitable framework for modeling fractures, the deformation method must provide information about the magnitude and orientation of the internal stresses, and whether they are tensile or compressive. We would also like to avoid deformation methods in which directional artifacts appear in the stress patterns and propagate to the resulting fracture patterns.

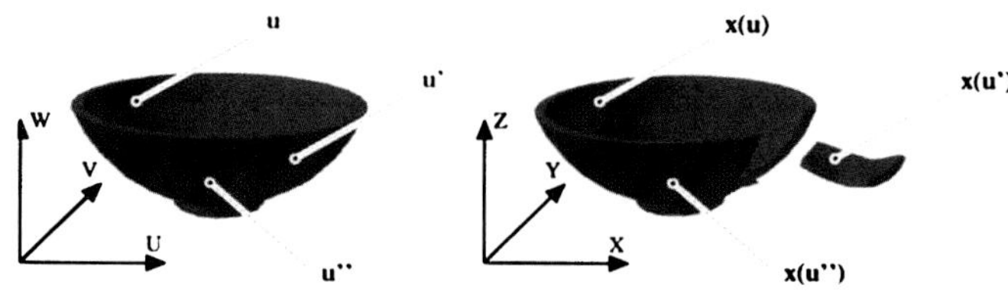


Figure 2: The material coordinates define a 3D parameterization of the object. The function $\boldsymbol{x}(\boldsymbol{u})$ maps points from their location in the material coordinate frame to their location in the world coordinates. A fracture corresponds to a discontinuity in $\boldsymbol{x}(\boldsymbol{u})$.

We derive our deformation technique by defining a set of differential equations that describe the aggregate behavior of the material in a continuous fashion, and then using a finite element method to discretize these equations for computer simulation. This approach is fairly standard, and many different deformation models can be derived in this fashion. The one presented here was designed to be simple, fast, and suitable for fracture modeling.

## 3.1 Continuous Model

Our continuous model is based on continuum mechanics, and an excellent introduction to this area can be found in the text by Fung [7]. The primary assumption in the continuum approach is that the scale of the effects being modeled is significantly greater than the scale of the material's composition. Therefore, the behavior of the molecules, grains, or particles that compose the material can be modeled as a continuous media. Although this assumption is often valid for modeling deformations, macroscopic fractures can be significantly influenced by effects that occur at small scales where this assumption may not be valid. Because we are interested in graphical appearance rather than rigorous physical correctness, we will put this issue aside and assume that a continuum model is adequate.

We begin the description of the continuous model by defining material coordinates that parameterize the volume of space occupied by the object being modeled. Let $\boldsymbol{u} = [u, v, w]^\mathsf{T}$ be a vector in $\Re^3$ that denotes a location in the material coordinate frame as shown in Figure 2. The deformation of the material is defined by the function $\boldsymbol{x}(\boldsymbol{u}) = [x, y, z]^\mathsf{T}$ that maps locations in the material coordinate frame to locations in world coordinates. In areas where material exists, $\boldsymbol{x}(\boldsymbol{u})$ is continuous, except across a finite number of surfaces within the volume that correspond to fractures in the material. In areas where there is no material, $\boldsymbol{x}(\boldsymbol{u})$ is undefined.

We make use of Green's strain tensor, $\epsilon$, to measure the local deformation of the material [6]. It can be represented as a $3 \times 3$ symmetric matrix defined by

$$\epsilon_{ij} = \left( \frac{\partial \boldsymbol{x}}{\partial u_i} \cdot \frac{\partial \boldsymbol{x}}{\partial u_j} \right) - \delta_{ij} \tag{1}$$

where $\delta_{ij}$ is the Kronecker delta:

$$\delta_{ij} = \begin{cases} 1 & : \ i = j \\ 0 & : \ i \neq j \, . \end{cases} \tag{2}$$

This strain metric only measures deformation; it is invariant with respect to rigid body transformations applied to $\boldsymbol{x}$ and vanishes when the material is not deformed. It has been used extensively in the engineering literature. Because it is a tensor, its invariants do not depend on the orientation of the material coordinate or world systems. The Euclidean metric tensor used by Terzopoulos and Fleischer [18] differs only by the $\delta_{ij}$ term.

In addition to the strain tensor, we make use of the strain rate tensor, $\boldsymbol{\nu}$, which measures the rate at which the strain is changing.

It can be derived by taking the time derivative of (1) and is defined by

$$\nu_{ij} = \left(\frac{\partial \boldsymbol{x}}{\partial u_i} \cdot \frac{\partial \dot{\boldsymbol{x}}}{\partial u_j}\right) + \left(\frac{\partial \dot{\boldsymbol{x}}}{\partial u_i} \cdot \frac{\partial \boldsymbol{x}}{\partial u_j}\right) \tag{3}$$

where an over dot indicates a derivative with respect to time such that $\dot{\boldsymbol{x}}$ is the material velocity expressed in world coordinates.

The strain and strain rate tensors provide the raw information that is required to compute internal elastic and damping forces, but they do not take into account the properties of the material. The stress tensor, $\boldsymbol{\sigma}$, combines the basic information from the strain and strain rate with the material properties and determines forces internal to the material. Like the strain and strain rate tensors, the stress tensor can be represented as a $3 \times 3$ symmetric matrix. It has two components: the elastic stress due to strain, $\boldsymbol{\sigma}^{(\epsilon)}$, and the viscous stress due to strain rate, $\boldsymbol{\sigma}^{(\nu)}$. The total internal stress, is the sum of these two components with

$$\boldsymbol{\sigma} = \boldsymbol{\sigma}^{(\epsilon)} + \boldsymbol{\sigma}^{(\nu)} . \tag{4}$$

The elastic stress and viscous stress are respectively functions of the strain and strain rate. In their most general linear forms, they are defined as

$$\sigma^{(\epsilon)}_{ij} = \sum_{k=1}^{3}\sum_{l=1}^{3} C_{ijkl}\, \epsilon_{kl} \tag{5}$$

$$\sigma^{(\nu)}_{ij} = \sum_{k=1}^{3}\sum_{l=1}^{3} D_{ijkl}\, \nu_{kl} \tag{6}$$

where $\boldsymbol{C}$ is a set of the 81 elastic coefficients that relate the elements of $\epsilon$ to the elements $\boldsymbol{\sigma}^{(\epsilon)}$, and $D$ is a set of the 81 damping coefficients.[1]

Because both $\epsilon$ and $\boldsymbol{\sigma}^{(\epsilon)}$ are symmetric, many of the coefficients in $\boldsymbol{C}$ are either redundant or constrained, and $\boldsymbol{C}$ can be reduced to 36 independent values that relate the six independent values of $\epsilon$ to the six independent values of $\boldsymbol{\sigma}^{(\epsilon)}$. If we impose the additional constraint that the material is isotropic, then $\boldsymbol{C}$ collapses further to only two independent values, $\mu$ and $\lambda$, which are the Lamé constants of the material. Equation (5) then reduces to

$$\sigma^{(\epsilon)}_{ij} = \sum_{k=1}^{3} \lambda \epsilon_{kk} \delta_{ij} + 2\mu\epsilon_{ij} . \tag{7}$$

The material's rigidity is determined by the value of $\mu$, and the resistance to changes in volume (dilation) is controlled by $\lambda$.

Similarly, $\boldsymbol{D}$ can be reduced to two independent values, $\phi$ and $\psi$ and (6) then reduces to

$$\sigma^{(\nu)}_{ij} = \sum_{k=1}^{3} \phi \nu_{kk} \delta_{ij} + 2\psi\nu_{ij} . \tag{8}$$

The parameters $\mu$ and $\lambda$ will control how quickly the material dissipates internal kinetic energy. Since $\boldsymbol{\sigma}^{(\nu)}$ is derived from the rate at which $\epsilon$ is changing, $\boldsymbol{\sigma}^{(\nu)}$ will not damp motions that are locally rigid, and has the desirable property of dissipating only internal vibrations.

Once we have the strain, strain rate, and stress tensors, we can compute the elastic potential density, $\eta$, and the damping potential density, $\kappa$, at any point in the material using

$$\eta = \frac{1}{2}\sum_{i=1}^{3}\sum_{j=1}^{3} \sigma^{(\epsilon)}_{ij} \epsilon_{ij} , \tag{9}$$

[1]Actually $\boldsymbol{C}$ and $D$ are themselves rank four tensors, and (5) and (6) are normally expressed in this form so that $\boldsymbol{C}$ and $\boldsymbol{D}$ will follow the standard rules for coordinate transforms.

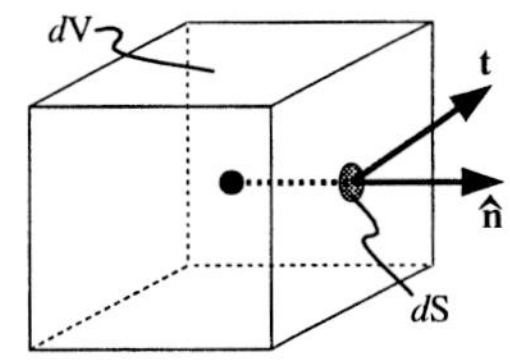


Figure 3: Given a point in the material, the traction, $\boldsymbol{t}$, that acts on the surface element, $dS$, of a differential volume, $dV$, centered around the point with outward unit normal, $\hat{\boldsymbol{n}}$, is given by $\boldsymbol{t} = \boldsymbol{\sigma}\,\hat{\boldsymbol{n}}$.

$$\kappa = \frac{1}{2}\sum_{i=1}^{3}\sum_{j=1}^{3} \sigma^{(\nu)}_{ij} \nu_{ij} . \tag{10}$$

These quantities can be integrated over the volume of the material to obtain the total elastic and damping potentials. The elastic potential is the internal elastic energy of the material. The damping potential is related to the kinetic energy of the material after subtracting any rigid body motion and normalizing for the material's density.

The stress can also be used to compute the forces acting internal to the material at any location. Let $\hat{\boldsymbol{n}}$ be an outward unit normal direction of a differential volume centered about a point in the material. (See Figure 3.) The traction (force per unit area), $\boldsymbol{t}$, acting on a face perpendicular to the normal is then given by

$$\boldsymbol{t} = \boldsymbol{\sigma}\,\hat{\boldsymbol{n}} . \tag{11}$$

The examples in this paper were generated using this isotropic formulation. However, these techniques do not make use of the strain or strain rate tensors directly; rather they rely only on the stress. Switching to the anisotropic formulation, or even to a nonlinear stress to strain relation, would not require any significant changes.

### 3.2 Finite Element Discretization

Before we can model a material's behavior using this continuous model, it must be discretized in a way that is suitable for computer simulation. Two commonly used techniques are the finite difference and finite element methods.

A finite difference method divides the domain of the material into a regular lattice and then uses numerical differencing to approximate the spatial derivatives required to compute the strain and strain rate tensors. This approach is well suited for problems with a regular structure but becomes complicated when the structure is irregular.

A finite element method partitions the domain of the material into distinct sub-domains, or elements as shown in Figure 4. Within each element, the material is described locally by a function with some finite number of parameters. The function is decomposed into a set of orthogonal shape, or basis, functions that are each associated with one of the nodes on the boundary of the element. Adjacent elements will have nodes in common, so that the mesh defines a piecewise function over the entire material domain.

Our discretization employs tetrahedral finite elements with linear polynomial shape functions. By using a finite element method, the mesh can be locally aligned with the fracture surfaces, thus avoiding the previously mentioned artifacts. Just as triangles can be used to approximate any surface, tetrahedra can be used to approximate arbitrary volumes. Additionally, when tetrahedra are split along a fracture plane, the resulting pieces can be decomposed exactly into more tetrahedra.

We chose to use linear elements because higher-order elements are not cost effective for modeling fracture boundaries. Although higher-order polynomials provide individual elements with many

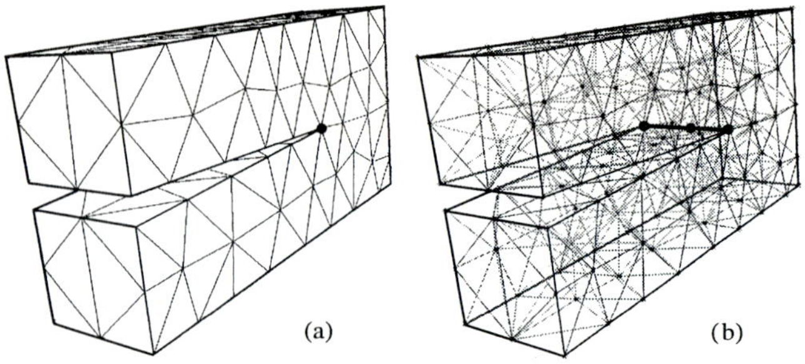

Figure 4: Tetrahedral mesh for a simple object. In **(a)**, only the external faces of the tetrahedra are drawn; in **(b)** the internal structure is shown.

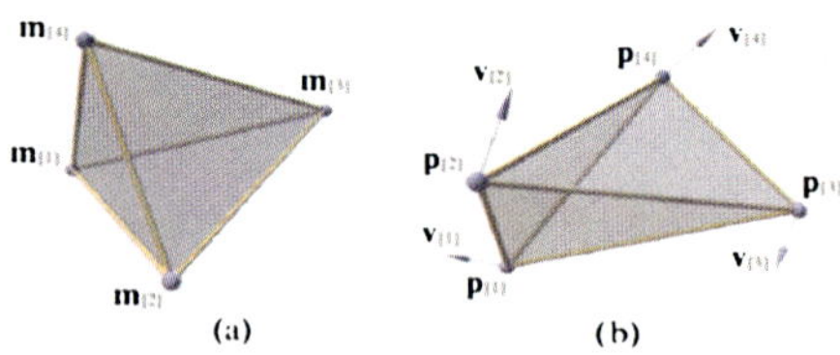

Figure 5: A tetrahedral element is defined by its four nodes. Each node has **(a)** a location in the material coordinate system and **(b)** a position and velocity in the world coordinate system.

degrees of freedom for deformation, they have few degrees of freedom for modeling fracture because the shape of a fracture is defined as a boundary in material coordinates. In contrast, with linear tetrahedra, each degree of freedom in the world space corresponds to a degree of freedom in the material coordinates. Furthermore, whenever an element is created, its basis functions must be computed. For high-degree polynomials, this computation is relatively expensive. For systems where the mesh is constant, the cost is amortized over the course of the simulation. However, as fractures develop and parts of the object are remeshed, the computation of basis matrices can become significant.

Each tetrahedral element is defined by four nodes. A node has a position in the material coordinates, $\boldsymbol{m}$, a position in the world coordinates, $\boldsymbol{p}$, and a velocity in world coordinates, $\boldsymbol{v}$. We will refer to the nodes of a given element by indexing with square brackets. For example, $\boldsymbol{m}_{[2]}$ is the position in material coordinates of the element's second node. (See Figure 5.)

Barycentric coordinates provide a natural way to define the linear shape functions within an element. Let $\boldsymbol{b} = [b_1, b_2, b_3, b_4]^{\mathsf{T}}$ be barycentric coordinates defined in terms of the element's material coordinates so that

$$\begin{bmatrix}\boldsymbol{u}\\1\end{bmatrix} = \begin{bmatrix}\boldsymbol{m}_{[1]} & \boldsymbol{m}_{[2]} & \boldsymbol{m}_{[3]} & \boldsymbol{m}_{[4]}\\ 1 & 1 & 1 & 1\end{bmatrix}\boldsymbol{b}\,. \tag{12}$$

These barycentric coordinates may also be used to interpolate the node's world position and velocity with

$$\begin{bmatrix}\boldsymbol{x}\\1\end{bmatrix} = \begin{bmatrix}\boldsymbol{p}_{[1]} & \boldsymbol{p}_{[2]} & \boldsymbol{p}_{[3]} & \boldsymbol{p}_{[4]}\\ 1 & 1 & 1 & 1\end{bmatrix}\boldsymbol{b} \tag{13}$$

$$\begin{bmatrix}\dot{\boldsymbol{x}}\\1\end{bmatrix} = \begin{bmatrix}\boldsymbol{v}_{[1]} & \boldsymbol{v}_{[2]} & \boldsymbol{v}_{[3]} & \boldsymbol{v}_{[4]}\\ 1 & 1 & 1 & 1\end{bmatrix}\boldsymbol{b}\,. \tag{14}$$

To determine the barycentric coordinates of a point within the element specified by its material coordinates, we invert (12) and obtain

$$\boldsymbol{b} = \boldsymbol{\beta}\begin{bmatrix}\boldsymbol{u}\\1\end{bmatrix} \tag{15}$$

where $\boldsymbol{\beta}$ is defined by

$$\boldsymbol{\beta} = \begin{bmatrix}\boldsymbol{m}_{[1]} & \boldsymbol{m}_{[2]} & \boldsymbol{m}_{[3]} & \boldsymbol{m}_{[4]}\\ 1 & 1 & 1 & 1\end{bmatrix}^{-1}. \tag{16}$$

Combining (15) with (13) and (14) yields functions that interpolate the world position and velocity within the element in terms of the material coordinates:

$$\boldsymbol{x}(\boldsymbol{u}) = \boldsymbol{P}\,\boldsymbol{\beta}\begin{bmatrix}\boldsymbol{u}\\1\end{bmatrix} \tag{17}$$

$$\dot{\boldsymbol{x}}(\boldsymbol{u}) = \boldsymbol{V}\,\boldsymbol{\beta}\begin{bmatrix}\boldsymbol{u}\\1\end{bmatrix} \tag{18}$$

where $\boldsymbol{P}$ and $\boldsymbol{V}$ are defined as

$$\boldsymbol{P} = \begin{bmatrix}\boldsymbol{p}_{[1]}\, \boldsymbol{p}_{[2]}\, \boldsymbol{p}_{[3]}\, \boldsymbol{p}_{[4]}\end{bmatrix} \tag{19}$$

$$\boldsymbol{V} = \begin{bmatrix}\boldsymbol{v}_{[1]}\, \boldsymbol{v}_{[2]}\, \boldsymbol{v}_{[3]}\, \boldsymbol{v}_{[4]}\end{bmatrix}\,. \tag{20}$$

Note that the rows of $\boldsymbol{\beta}$ are the coefficients of the shape functions, and $\boldsymbol{\beta}$ needs to be computed only when an element is created or the material coordinates of its nodes change. For non-degenerate elements, the matrix in (16) is guaranteed to be non-singular, however elements that are nearly co-planar will cause $\boldsymbol{\beta}$ to be ill-conditioned and adversely affect the numerical stability of the system.

Computing the values of $\boldsymbol{\epsilon}$ and $\boldsymbol{\nu}$ within the element requires the first partials of $\boldsymbol{x}$ with respect to $\boldsymbol{u}$:

$$\frac{\partial \boldsymbol{x}}{\partial u_i} = \boldsymbol{P}\,\boldsymbol{\beta}\,\boldsymbol{\delta}_i \tag{21}$$

$$\frac{\partial \dot{\boldsymbol{x}}}{\partial u_i} = \boldsymbol{V}\,\boldsymbol{\beta}\,\boldsymbol{\delta}_i \tag{22}$$

where

$$\boldsymbol{\delta}_i = [\delta_{i1}\; \delta_{i2}\; \delta_{i3}\; 0]^{\mathsf{T}}\,. \tag{23}$$

Because the element's shape functions are linear, these partials are constant within the element.

The element will exert elastic and damping forces on its nodes. The elastic force on the $i$th node, $\boldsymbol{f}^{(\epsilon)}_{[i]}$, is defined as the partial of the elastic potential density, $\eta$, with respect to $\boldsymbol{p}_{[i]}$ integrated over the volume of the element. Given $\boldsymbol{\sigma}^{(\epsilon)}$, $\boldsymbol{\beta}$, and the positions in world space of the four nodes we can compute the elastic force by

$$\boldsymbol{f}^{(\epsilon)}_{[i]} = \frac{\text{vol}}{2}\sum_{j=1}^{4}\boldsymbol{p}_{[j]}\sum_{k=1}^{3}\sum_{l=1}^{3}\beta_{jl}\beta_{ik}\sigma^{(\epsilon)}_{kl} \tag{24}$$

where

$$\text{vol} = \frac{1}{6}[(\boldsymbol{m}_{[2]} - \boldsymbol{m}_{[1]}) \times (\boldsymbol{m}_{[3]} - \boldsymbol{m}_{[1]})] \cdot (\boldsymbol{m}_{[4]} - \boldsymbol{m}_{[1]})\,. \tag{25}$$

Similarly, the damping force on the $i$th node, $\boldsymbol{f}^{(\nu)}_{[i]}$, is defined as the partial of the damping potential density, $\kappa$, with respect to $\boldsymbol{v}_{[i]}$ integrated over the volume of the element. This quantity can be computed with

$$\boldsymbol{f}^{(\nu)}_{[i]} = \frac{\text{vol}}{2}\sum_{j=1}^{4}\boldsymbol{p}_{[j]}\sum_{k=1}^{3}\sum_{l=1}^{3}\beta_{jl}\beta_{ik}\sigma^{(\nu)}_{kl}\,. \tag{26}$$

Summing these two forces, the total internal force that an element exerts on a node is

$$\boldsymbol{f}^{\text{el}}_{[i]} = \frac{\text{vol}}{2}\sum_{j=1}^{4}\boldsymbol{p}_{[j]}\sum_{k=1}^{3}\sum_{l=1}^{3}\beta_{jl}\beta_{ik}\sigma_{kl}\,, \tag{27}$$

and the total internal force acting on the node is obtained by summing the forces exerted by all elements that are attached to the node.

As the element is compressed to less than about 30% of its material volume, the gradient of $\eta$ and $\kappa$ start to vanish causing the resisting forces to fall off. We have not found this to be a problem as even the more squishy of the materials that we have modeled conserve their volume to within a few percent.

Using a lumped mass formulation, the mass contributed by an element to each one of its nodes is determined by integrating the material density, $\rho$, over the element shape function associated with that node. In the case of tetrahedral elements with linear shape functions, this mass contribution is simply $\rho\,\mathrm{vol}/4$.

The derivations above are sufficient for a simulation that uses an explicit integration scheme. Additional work, including computing the Jacobian of the internal forces, is necessary for implicit integration scheme. (See for example [2] and [3].)

### 3.3 Collisions

In addition to the forces internal to the material, the system computes collision forces. The collision forces are computed using a penalty method that is applied when two elements intersect or if an element violates another constraint such as the ground. Although penalty methods are often criticized for creating stiff equations, we have found that for the materials we are modeling the internal forces are at least as stiff as the penalty forces. Penalty forces have the advantage of being very fast to compute. We have experimented with two different penalty criteria: node penetration and overlap volume. The examples presented in this paper were computed with the node penetration criteria; additional examples on the conference proceedings CD-ROM were computed with the overlap volume criteria.

The node penetration criteria sets the penalty force to be proportional to the distance that a node has penetrated into another element. The penalty force acts in the direction normal to the penetrated surface. The reaction force is distributed over the penetrated element's nodes so that the net force and moment are the negation of the penalty force and moment acting at the penetrating node. This test will not catch all collisions, and undetected intersecting tetrahedra may become locked together. It is however, fast to compute, easy to implement, and adequate for situations that do not involve complex collision interactions.

The overlap volume criteria is more robust than the node penetration method, but it is also slower to compute and more complex to implement. The intersection of two tetrahedral elements is computed by clipping the faces of each tetrahedron against the other. The resulting polyhedron is then used to compute the volume and center of mass of the intersecting region. The area weighted normals of the faces of the polyhedron that are contributed by one of the tetrahedra are summed to compute the direction that the penalty force acts in. A similar computation can be performed for the other tetrahedra, or equivalently the direction can be negated. Provided that neither tetrahedra is completely contained within the other, this criteria is more robust than the node penetration criteria. Additionally, the forces computed with this method do not depend on the object tessellation.

Computing the intersections within the mesh can be very expensive, and we use a bounding hierarchy scheme with cached traversals to help reduce this cost.

## 4 Fracture Modeling

Our fracture model is based on the theory of linear elastic fracture mechanics [1]. The primary distinction between this and other theories of fracture is that the region of plasticity near the crack tip[2] is neglected. Because we are not modeling the energy dissipated by this plastic region, modeled materials will be brittle. This statement does not mean that they are weak; rather the term "brittle" refers to the fact that once the material has begun to fail, the fractures will have a strong tendency to propagate across the material as they are driven by the internally stored elastic energy.

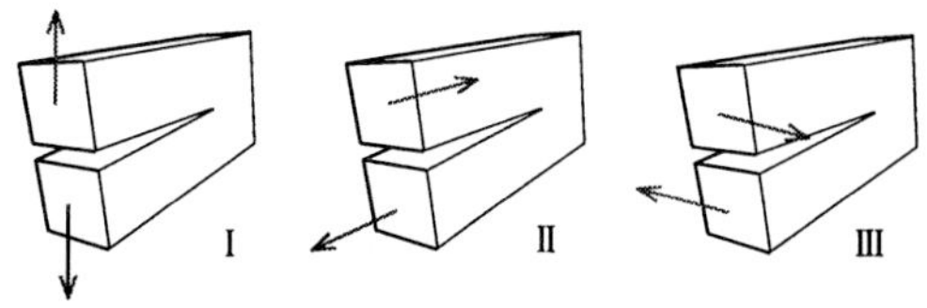


Figure 6: Three loading modes that can be experienced by a crack. Mode I: Opening, Mode II: In-Plane Shear, and Mode III: Out-of-Plane Shear. Adapted from Anderson [1].

There are three loading modes by which forces can be applied to a crack causing it to open further. (See Figure 6.) In most circumstances, some combination of these modes will be active, producing a mixed mode load at the crack tip. For all three cases, as well as mixed mode situations, the behavior of the crack can be resolved by analyzing the forces acting at the crack tip: tensile forces that are opposed by other tensile forces will cause the crack to continue in a direction that is perpendicular to the direction of largest tensile load, and conversely, compressive loads will tend to arrest a crack to which they are perpendicular.

The finite element model describes the surface of a fracture with elements that are adjacent in material coordinates but that do not share nodes across the internal surface. The curve that represents the crack tip is then implicitly defined in a piecewise linear fashion by the nodes that border the fracture surface, and further extension of the crack may be determined by analyzing the internal forces acting on these nodes.

We will also use the element nodes to determine where a crack should be initiated. While this strategy could potentially introduce unpleasant artifacts, we note that because the surface of an object is defined by a polygonal boundary (the outer faces of the tetrahedra) there will always be a node located at any concavities. Because concavities are precisely the locations where cracks commonly begin, we believe that this decision is acceptable.

Our fracture algorithm is as follows: after every time step, the system resolves the internal forces acting on all nodes into their tensile and compressive components, discarding any unbalanced portions. At each node, the resulting forces are then used to form a tensor that describes how the internal forces are acting to separate that node. If the action is sufficiently large, the node is split into two distinct nodes and a fracture plane is computed. All elements attached to the node are divided along the plane with the resulting tetrahedra assigned to one or the other incarnations of the split node, thus creating a discontinuity in the material. Any cached values, such as the node mass or the element shape functions, are recomputed for the affected elements and nodes. With this technique, the location of a fracture or crack tip need not be explicitly recorded unless this information is useful for some other purpose, such as rendering.

[2] The term "crack tip" implies that the fracture will have a single point at its tip. In general, the front of the crack will not be a single point; rather it will be a curve that defines the boundary of the surface discontinuity in material coordinates. (See Figure 4.) Nevertheless, we will refer to this front as the crack tip.

### 4.1 Force Decomposition

The forces acting on a node are decomposed by first separating the element stress tensors into tensile and compressive components. For a given element in the mesh, let $\mathrm{v}^i(\boldsymbol{\sigma})$, with $i \in \{1,2,3\}$, be the $i$th eigenvalue of $\boldsymbol{\sigma}$, and let $\hat{\mathbf{n}}^i(\boldsymbol{\sigma})$ be the corresponding unit length eigenvector. Positive eigenvalues correspond to tensile stresses and negative ones to compressive stresses. Since $\boldsymbol{\sigma}$ is real and symmetric, it will have three real, not necessarily unique, eigenvalues. In the case where an eigenvalue has multiplicity greater than one, the eigenvectors are selected arbitrarily to orthogonally span the appropriate subspace [13].

Given a vector $\boldsymbol{a}$ in $\Re^3$, we can construct a $3 \times 3$ symmetric matrix, $\mathbf{m}(\boldsymbol{a})$ that has $|\boldsymbol{a}|$ as an eigenvalue with $\boldsymbol{a}$ as the corresponding eigenvector, and with the other two eigenvalues equal to zero. This matrix is defined by

$$\mathbf{m}(\boldsymbol{a}) = \begin{cases} \boldsymbol{a}\,\boldsymbol{a}^{\mathsf{T}}/|\boldsymbol{a}| & : \ \boldsymbol{a} \neq \mathbf{0} \\ \mathbf{0} & : \ \boldsymbol{a} = \mathbf{0}\,. \end{cases} \tag{28}$$

The tensile component, $\boldsymbol{\sigma}^+$, and compressive component, $\boldsymbol{\sigma}^-$, of the stress within the element can now be computed by

$$\boldsymbol{\sigma}^+ = \sum_{i=1}^{3} \max(0, \mathrm{v}^i(\boldsymbol{\sigma}))\, \mathbf{m}(\hat{\mathbf{n}}^i(\boldsymbol{\sigma})) \tag{29}$$

$$\boldsymbol{\sigma}^- = \sum_{i=1}^{3} \min(0, \mathrm{v}^i(\boldsymbol{\sigma}))\, \mathbf{m}(\hat{\mathbf{n}}^i(\boldsymbol{\sigma}))\,. \tag{30}$$

Using this decomposition, the force that an element exerts on a node can be separated into a tensile component, $\boldsymbol{f}^+_{[i]}$, and a compressive component, $\boldsymbol{f}^-_{[i]}$. This separation is done by reevaluating the internal forces exerted on the nodes using (27) with $\boldsymbol{\sigma}^+$ or $\boldsymbol{\sigma}^-$ substituted for $\boldsymbol{\sigma}$. Thus the tensile component is

$$\boldsymbol{f}^+_{[i]} = \frac{\mathrm{vol}}{2} \sum_{j=1}^{4} \boldsymbol{p}_{[j]} \sum_{k=1}^{3} \sum_{l=1}^{3} \beta_{jl}\beta_{ik}\sigma^+_{kl}\,. \tag{31}$$

The compressive component can be computed similarly, but because $\boldsymbol{\sigma} = \boldsymbol{\sigma}^+ + \boldsymbol{\sigma}^-$, it can be computed more efficiently using $\boldsymbol{f}_{[i]} = \boldsymbol{f}^+_{[i]} + \boldsymbol{f}^-_{[i]}$.

Each node will now have a set of tensile and a set of compressive forces that are exerted by the elements attached to it. For a given node, we denote these sets as $\{\boldsymbol{f}^+\}$ and $\{\boldsymbol{f}^-\}$ respectively. The unbalanced tensile load, $\boldsymbol{f}^+$ is simply the sum over $\{\boldsymbol{f}^+\}$, and the unbalanced compressive load, $\boldsymbol{f}^-$, is the sum over $\{\boldsymbol{f}^-\}$.

### 4.2 The Separation Tensor

We describe the forces acting at the nodes using a stress variant that we call the separation tensor, $\varsigma$. The separation tensor is formed from the balanced tensile and compressive forces acting at each node and is computed by

$$\varsigma = \frac{1}{2}\left( -\mathbf{m}(\boldsymbol{f}^+) + \sum_{\boldsymbol{f} \in \{\boldsymbol{f}^+\}} \mathbf{m}(\boldsymbol{f}) + \mathbf{m}(\boldsymbol{f}^-) - \sum_{\boldsymbol{f} \in \{\boldsymbol{f}^-\}} \mathbf{m}(\boldsymbol{f}) \right)\,. \tag{32}$$

It does not respond to unbalanced actions that would produce a rigid translation, and is invariant with respect to transformations of both the material and world coordinate systems.

The separation tensor is used directly to determine whether a fracture should occur at a node. Let $\mathrm{v}^+$ be the largest positive eigenvalue of $\varsigma$. If $\mathrm{v}^+$ is greater than the material toughness, $\tau$, then the material will fail at the node. The orientation in world coordinates of the fracture plane is perpendicular to $\hat{\mathbf{n}}^+$, the eigenvalue of $\varsigma$ that corresponds to $\mathrm{v}^+$. In the case where multiple eigenvalues are greater than $\tau$, multiple fracture planes may be generated by first generating the plane for the largest value, remeshing (see below), and then recomputing the new value for $\varsigma$ and proceeding as above.

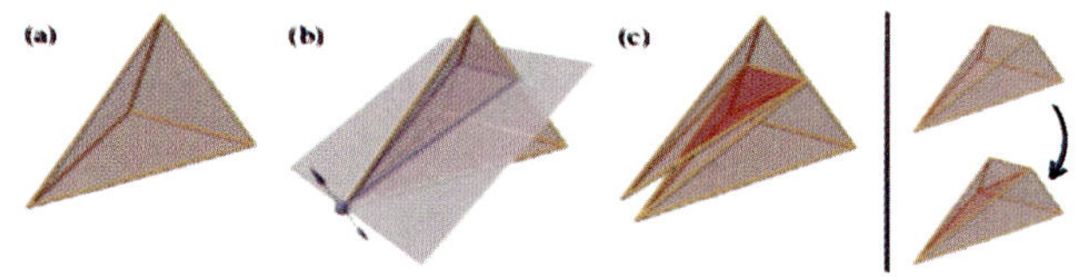


Figure 7: Diagram showing how an element is split by the fracture plane. **(a)** The initial tetrahedral element. **(b)** The splitting node and fracture plane are shown in blue. **(c)** The element is split along the fracture plane into two polyhedra that are then decomposed into tetrahedra. Note that the two nodes created from the splitting node are co-located, the geometric displacement shown in **(c)** only illustrates the location of the fracture discontinuity.

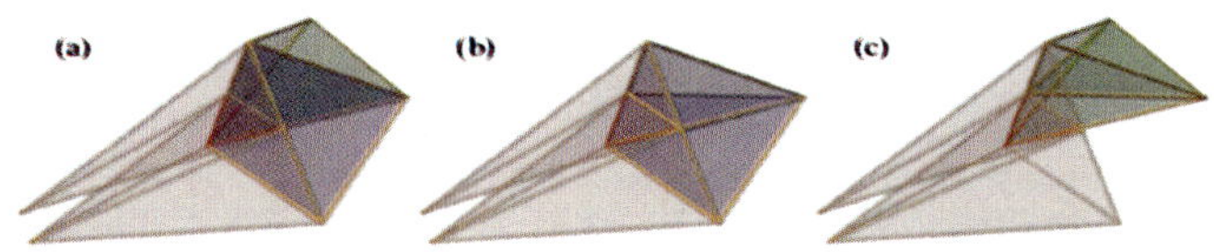


Figure 8: Elements that are adjacent to an element that has been split by a fracture plane must also be split to maintain mesh consistency. **(a)** Neighboring tetrahedra prior to split. **(b)** Face neighbor after split. **(c)** Edge neighbor after split.

### 4.3 Local Remeshing

Once the simulation has determined the location and orientation of a new fracture plane, the mesh must be modified to reflect the new discontinuity. It is important that the orientation of the fracture be preserved, as approximating it with the existing element boundaries would create undesirable artifacts. To avoid this potential difficulty, the algorithm remeshes the local area surrounding the new fracture by splitting elements that intersect the fracture plane and modifying neighboring elements to ensure that the mesh stays self-consistent.

First, the node where the fracture originates is replicated so that there are now two nodes, $n^+$ and $n^-$ with the same material position, world position, and velocity. The masses will be recalculated later. The discontinuity passes "between" the two co-located nodes. The positive side of the fracture plane is associated with $n^+$ and the negative side with $n^-$.

Next, all elements that were attached to the original node are examined, comparing the world location of their nodes to the fracture plane. If an element is not intersected by the fracture plane, then it is reassigned to either $n^+$ or $n^-$ depending on which side of the plane it lies.

If the element is intersected by the fracture plane, it is split along the plane. (See Figure 7.) A new node is created along each edge that intersects the plane. Because all elements must be tetrahedra, in general each intersected element will be split into three tetrahedra. One of the tetrahedra will be assigned to one side of the plane and the other two to the other side. Because the two tetrahedra that are on the same side of the plane both share either $n^+$ or $n^-$, the discontinuity does not pass between them.

In addition to the elements that were attached to the original node, it may be necessary to split other elements so that the mesh

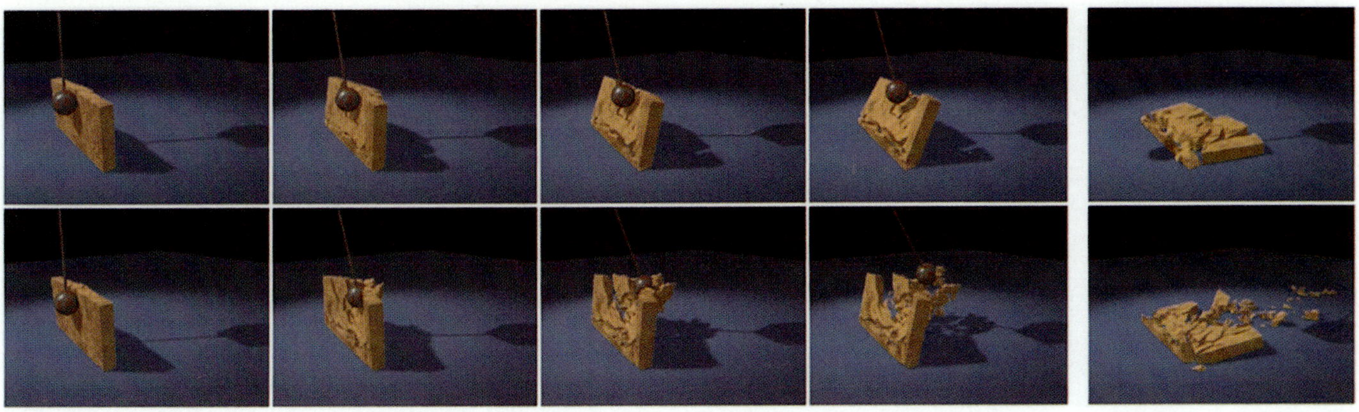

Figure 9: Two adobe walls that are struck by wrecking balls. Both walls are attached to the ground. The ball in the second row has $50\times$ the mass of the first. Images are spaced apart 133.3 ms in the first row and 66.6 ms in the second. The rightmost images show the final configurations.

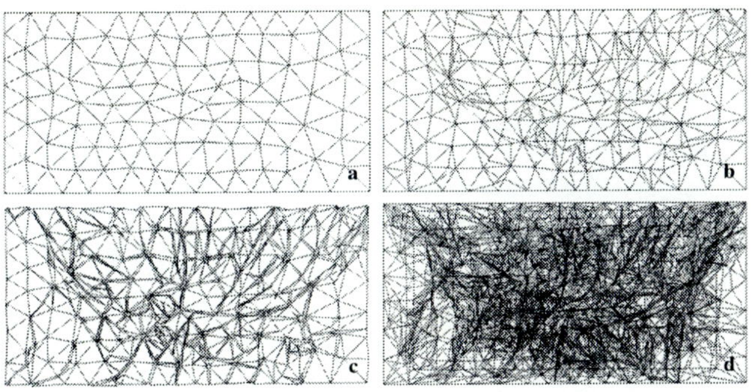


Figure 10: Mesh for adobe wall. **(a)** The facing surface of the initial mesh used to generate the wall shown in Figure 9. **(b)** The mesh after being struck by the wrecking ball, reassembled. **(c)** Same as (b), with the cracks emphasized. **(d)** Internal fractures shown as wireframe.

stays consistent. In particular, an element must be split if the face or edge between it and another element that was attached to the original node has been split. (See Figure 8.) To prevent the remeshing from cascading across the entire mesh, these splits are done so that the new tetrahedra use only the original nodes and the nodes created by the intersection splits. Because no new nodes are created, the effect of the local remeshing is limited to the elements that are attached to the node where the fracture originated and their immediate neighbors. Because the tetrahedra formed by the secondary splits do not attach to either $n^+$ or $n^-$, the discontinuity does not pass between them.

Finally, after the local remeshing has been completed, any cached values that have become invalid must be recomputed. In our implementation, these values include the element basis matrix, $\boldsymbol{\beta}$, and the node masses.

Two additional subtleties must also be considered. The first subtlety occurs when an intersection split involves an edge that is formed only by tetrahedra attached to the node where the crack originated. When this happens, the fracture has reached a boundary in the material, and the discontinuity should pass through the edge. Remeshing occurs as above, except that two nodes are created on the edge and one is assigned to each side of the discontinuity.

Second, the fracture plane may pass arbitrarily close to an existing node producing arbitrarily ill-conditioned tetrahedra. To avoid this, we employ two thresholds, one the distance between the fracture plane and an existing node, and the other on the angle between the fracture plane and a line from the node where the split originated to the existing node. If either of these thresholds are not met, then the intersection split is snapped to the existing node. In our results, we have used thresholds of 5 mm and 0.1 radians.

## 5 Results and Discussion

To demonstrate some of the effects that can be generated with this fracture technique, we have animated a number of scenes that involve objects breaking. Figure 1 shows a plate of glass that has had a heavy weight dropped on it. The area in the immediate vicinity of the impact has been crushed into many small fragments. Further away from the weight, a pattern of radial cracks has developed.

Figure 9 shows two walls being struck by wrecking balls. In the first sequence, the wall develops a network of cracks as it absorbs most of the ball's energy during the initial impact. In the second sequence, the ball's mass is $50\times$ greater, and the wall shatters when it is struck. The mesh used to generate the wall sequences is shown in Figure 10. The initial mesh contains only 338 nodes and 1109 elements. By the end of the sequence, the mesh has grown to 6892 nodes and 8275 elements. These additional nodes and elements are created where fractures occur; a uniform mesh would require many times this number of nodes and elements to achieve a similar result.

Figure 11 shows the final frames from four animations of bowls that were dropped onto a hard surface. Other than the toughness, $\tau$, of the material, the four simulations are identical. The first bowl develops only a few cracks; the weakest breaks into many pieces.

Because this system works with solid tetrahedral volumes rather than with the polygonal boundary representations created by most modeling packages, boundary models must be converted before they can be used. A number of systems are available for creating tetrahedral meshes from polygonal boundaries. The models that we used in these examples were generated either from a CSG description or a polygonal boundary representation using NETGEN, a publicly available mesh generation package [16].

Although our approach avoids the "jaggy" artifacts in the fracture patterns caused by the underlying mesh, there remain ways in which the results of a simulation are influenced by the mesh structure. The most obvious is that the deformation of the material is limited by the degrees of freedom in the mesh, which in turn limits how the material can fracture. This limitation will occur with any discrete system. The technique also limits where a fracture may ini-

Figure 11: Bowls with successively lower toughness values, $\tau$. Each of the bowls were dropped from the same height. Other than $\tau$, the bowls have same material properties.

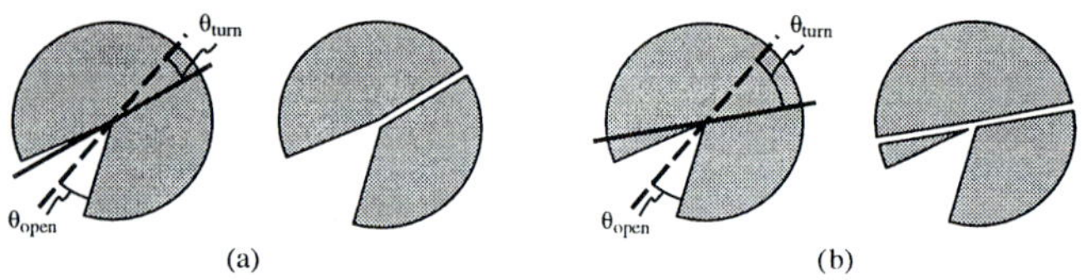


Figure 12: Back-cracking during fracture advance. The dashed line is the axis of the existing crack. Cracks advance by splitting elements along a fracture plane, shown as a solid line, computed from the separation tensor. **(a)** If the crack does not turn sharply, then only elements in front of the tip will be split. **(b)** If the crack turns at too sharp an angle, then the backwards direction may not fall inside of the existing failure and a spurious bifurcation will occur.

tiate by examining only the existing nodes. This assumption means that very coarse mesh sizes might behave in an unintuitive fashion. However, nodes correspond to the locations where a fracture is most likely to begin; therefore, with a reasonable grid size, this limitation is not a serious handicap.

A more serious limitation is related to the speed at which a crack propagates. Currently, the distance that a fracture may travel during a time step is determined by the size of the existing mesh elements. The crack may either split an element or not; it cannot travel only a fraction of the distance across an element. If a crack were being opened slowly by an applied load on a model with a coarse resolution mesh, this limitation would lead to a "button popping" effect where the crack would travel across one element, pause until the stress built up again, and then move across the next element. A second type of artifact may occur if the crack's speed should be significantly greater than the element width divided by the simulation time step. In this case, a high stress area will race ahead of the crack tip, causing spontaneous failures to occur in the material. Although we have not observed these phenomena in our examples, developing an algorithm that allows a fracture to propagate arbitrary distances is an area for future work.

Another limitation stems from the fact that while the fracture plane's orientation is well defined, the crack tip's forward direction is not. As shown in Figure 12, if the cracks turns at an angle greater than half the angle at the crack tip, then a secondary fracture will develop in the opposite direction to the crack's advance. While this effect is likely present in some of our examples, it does not appear to have a significant impact on the quality of the results. If the artifacts were to be a problem, they could be suppressed by explicitly tracking the fracture propagation directions within the mesh.

The simulation parameters used to generate the examples in this paper are listed in Table 1 along with the computation time required to generate one second of animation. While the material density values, $\rho$, are appropriate for glass, stone, or ceramic, we used values for the Lamé constants, $\lambda$ and $\mu$, that are significantly less than those of real materials. Larger values would make the simulated materials appear stiffer, but would also require smaller time steps. The values that we have selected represent a compromise between realistic behavior and reasonable computation time.

Our current implementation can switch between either a forward Euler integration scheme or a second order Taylor integrator. Both of these techniques are explicit integration schemes, and subject to stability limits that require very small time steps for stiff materials. Although semi-implicit integration methods have error bounds similar to those of explicit methods, the semi-implicit integrators tend to drive errors towards zero rather than infinity so that they are stable at much larger time steps. Other researchers have shown that by taking advantage of this property, a semi-implicit integrator can be used to realize speed ups of two or three orders of magnitude when modeling object deformation [2]. Unfortunately, it may be difficult to realize these same improvements when fracture propagation is part of the simulation. As discussed above, the crack speed is limited in inverse proportion to the time step size, and the large time steps that might be afforded by a semi-implicit integrator could cause spontaneous material failure to proceed crack advance. We are currently investigating how our methods may be modified to be compatible with large time step integration schemes.

Many materials and objects in the real world are not homogeneous, and it would be interesting to develop graphical models for animating them as they fail. For example, a brick wall is made up of mortar and bricks arranged in a regular fashion, and if simulated in a situation like our wall example, a distinct pattern would be created. Similarly, the connection between a handmade cup and its handle is often weak because of the way in which the handle is attached.

One way to assess the realism of an animation technique is by comparing it with the real world. Figure 13 shows high-speed video footage of a physical bowl as it falls onto its edge compared to our imitation of the real-world scene. Although the two sets of fracture patterns are clearly different, the simulated bowl has some qualitative similarities to the real one. Both initially fail along the leading edge where they strike the ground, and subsequently develop vertical cracks before breaking into several large pieces.

## Acknowledgments

The authors would like to thank Wayne L. Wooten of Pixar Animation Studios for lighting, shading, and rendering the images for many of the figures in this paper. We would also like to thank Ari Glezer and Bojan Vukasinovic of the School Mechanical Engineering at the Georgia Institute of Technology for their assistance and the use of the high-speed video equipment. Finally, we would like to thank those in the Animation Lab who lent a hand to ensure that we made the submission deadline.

This project was supported in part by NSF NYI Grant No. IRI-9457621, Mitsubishi Electric Research Laboratory, and a Packard Fellowship. The first author was supported by a Fellowship from the Intel Foundation.

| | | Material Parameters | | | | | | Minutes of Computation Time per Simulation Second | | |
|---|---|---|---|---|---|---|---|---|---|---|
| Example | Figure | $\lambda\,(N/m^2)$ | $\mu\,(N/m^2)$ | $\phi\,(Ns/m^2)$ | $\psi\,(Ns/m^2)$ | $\rho\,(kg/m^3)$ | $\tau\,(N/m^2)$ | Minimum | Maximum | Average |
| Glass | 1 | $1.04 \times 10^8$ | $1.04 \times 10^8$ | 0 | 6760 | 2588 | 10140 | 75 | 667 | 273 |
| Wall #1 | 9.a | $6.03 \times 10^8$ | $1.21 \times 10^8$ | 3015 | 6030 | 2309 | 6030 | 75 | 562 | 399 |
| Wall #2 | 9.b | 0 | $1.81 \times 10^8$ | 0 | 18090 | 2309 | 6030 | 75 | 2317 | 1098 |
| Bowl #1 | 11.a | $2.65 \times 10^6$ | $3.97 \times 10^6$ | 264 | 397 | 1013 | 52.9 | 90 | 120 | 109 |
| Bowl #2 | 11.b | $2.65 \times 10^6$ | $3.97 \times 10^6$ | 264 | 397 | 1013 | 39.6 | 82 | 135 | 115 |
| Bowl #3 | 11.c | $2.65 \times 10^6$ | $3.97 \times 10^6$ | 264 | 397 | 1013 | 33.1 | 90 | 150 | 127 |
| Bowl #4 | 11.d | $2.65 \times 10^6$ | $3.97 \times 10^6$ | 264 | 397 | 1013 | 13.2 | 82 | 187 | 156 |
| Comp. Bowl | 13 | 0 | $5.29 \times 10^7$ | 0 | 198 | 1013 | 106 | 247 | 390 | 347 |
| The End | 14 | 0 | $9.21 \times 10^6$ | 0 | 9.2 | 705 | 73.6 | 622 | 6667 | 4665 |

Table 1: Material parameters and simulation times for examples. The times listed reflect the total number of minutes required to compute one second of simulated data, including graphics and file I/O. Times were measured on an SGI O2 with a 195 MHz MIPS R10K processor.

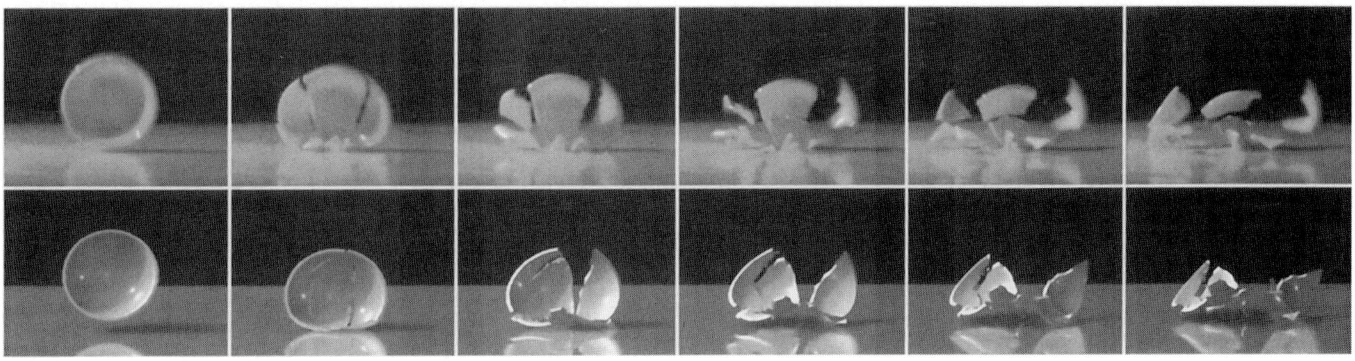

Figure 13: Comparison of a real-world event and simulation. The top row shows high-speed video images of a physical ceramic bowl dropped from approximately one meter onto a hard surface. The bottom row is the output from a simulation where we attempted to match the initial conditions of the physical bowl. Video images are 8 ms apart. Simulation images are 13 ms apart.

## References

Figure 14: Several breakable objects that were dropped from a height.


[1] T. L. Anderson. *Fracture Mechanics: Fundamentals and Applications*. CRC Press, Boca Raton, second edition, 1995.

[2] D. Baraff and A. Witkin. Large steps in cloth simulation. In *SIGGRAPH 98 Conference Proceedings*, Annual Conference Series, pages 43–54. ACM SIGGRAPH, Addison Wesley, July 1998.

[3] R. D. Cook, D. S. Malkus, and M. E. Plesha. *Concepts and Applications of Finite Element Analysis*. John Wiley & Sons, New York, third edition, 1989.

[4] T. DeRose, M. Kass, and T. Truong. Subdivision surfaces in character animation. In *SIGGRAPH 98 Conference Proceedings*, Annual Conference Series, pages 85–94. ACM SIGGRAPH, Addison Wesley, July 1998.

[5] N. Foster and D. Metaxas. Realistic animation of liquids. In *Graphics Interface '96*, pages 204–212, May 1996.

[6] Y. C. Fung. *Foundations of Solid Mechanics*. Prentice-Hall, Englewood Cliffs, N.J., 1965.

[7] Y. C. Fung. *A First Course in Continuum Mechanics*. Prentice-Hall, Englewood Cliffs, N.J., 1969.

[8] K. Hirota, Y. Tanoue, and T. Kaneko. Generation of crack patterns with a physical model. *The Visual Computer*, 14:126–137, 1998.

[9] O. Mazarak, C. Martins, and J. Amanatides. Animating exploding objects. In *Graphics Interface '99*, June 1999.

[10] M. Neff and E. Fiume. A visual model for blast waves and fracture. In *Graphics Interface '99*, June 1999.

[11] T. Nishioka. Computational dynamic fracture mechanics. *International Journal of Fracture*, 86:127–159, 1997.

[12] A. Norton, G. Turk, B. Bacon, J. Gerth, and P. Sweeney. Animation of fracture by physical modeling. *The Visual Computer*, 7:210–217, 1991.

[13] W. H. Press, B. P. Flannery, S. A. Teukolsky, and W. T. Vetterling. *Numerical Recipes in C.* Cambridge University Press, second edition, 1994.

[14] B. Robertson. Antz-piration. *Computer Graphics World*, 21(10), 1998.

[15] B. Robertson. Meet Geri: The new face of animation. *Computer Graphics World*, 21(2), 1998.

[16] J. Schöberl. NETGEN – An advancing front 2D/3D–mesh generator based on abstract rules. *Computing and Visualization in Science*, 1:41–52, 1997.

[17] D. Terzopoulos. Regularization of inverse visual problems involving discontinuities. *IEEE Transactions on Pattern Analysis and Machine Intelligence*, 8(4):413–424, July 1986.

[18] D. Terzopoulos and K. Fleischer. Deformable models. *The Visual Computer*, 4:306–331, 1988.

[19] D. Terzopoulos and K. Fleischer. Modeling inelastic deformation: Viscoelasticity, plasticity, fracture. In *Computer Graphics (SIGGRAPH '88 Proceedings)*, volume 22, pages 269–278, August 1988.

# Direct Illumination with Lazy Visibility Evaluation

David Hart Philip Dutré Donald P. Greenberg

Program of Computer Graphics*
Cornell University

## Abstract

In this paper we present a technique for computing the direct lighting in a three-dimensional scene containing area light sources. Our method correctly handles partial visibility between luminaires and receivers, and is able to efficiently generate accurate soft shadows in scenes modeled with general bidirectional reflectance distribution functions. In most current algorithms, the form factor between a light source and receiver is computed using a stochastic ray casting approach which evaluates partial visibility. Such an approach often leads to noisy artifacts or aliasing problems. Generating significantly more rays is often the only solution to improving image quality. Our approach first stores visibility information in the image plane, using lazy evaluation of the visibility function. In a second phase, illumination values for each pixel are generated, using analytic or stochastic integration. Soft shadows and other shading effects are generated with high accuracy in less time than with existing shading algorithms. Coherence in specific blocker-light source relationships across the image plane is exploited to amortize the cost of analytic form factor calculations. By storing information in the image plane, our method is currently designed for generating a single image, and is thus view-dependent.

**CR Categories:** I.3.3 [Computer Graphics]: Picture/Image Generation; I.3.7 [Computer Graphics]: Three-Dimensional Graphics and Realism - color, shading, shadowing.

**Additional Keywords:** Rendering, Illumination Effects, Monte Carlo Techniques, Shadow Algorithms, Visibility Determination.

## 1 INTRODUCTION

In order to compute the direct illumination in a three-dimensional scene, it is necessary to be able to determine the visibility between any surface point and an area light source. Since changes in visibility between a surface point and an area light source are the cause of penumbra and umbra regions on the receiver surface, an efficient processing of the visibility function is often the key for rendering fast and accurate soft shadows. Once the visibility has been processed, the illumination can then be computed by integrating the incoming radiance function due to the light source, taking into account the bidirectional reflectance distribution function at the receiving surface, as expressed by the rendering equation [10].

In this paper we split the direct illumination computation into two distinct phases. A first phase evaluates the visibility function; the second phase computes the actual illumination by evaluating the rendering equation.

As contrasted with some existing techniques for computing soft shadows from direct illumination (e.g. [6]), we do not construct a complete discontinuity mesh in object space. Constructing such a mesh is computationally expensive, and many of the resulting mesh elements do not affect the final image quality. Moreover, implementing a robust algorithm that handles all possible cases often leads to numerical difficulties.

Our visibility pass instead detects, for each pixel in the image, any blocker-light source pairs which affect the illumination for the surface point visible through that pixel. We find such pairs by casting one or more shadow rays from the visible point towards the light source. Once such a pair is found, we exploit coherence by examining adjacent pixels to determine whether the same blocker-light source pair shows up for their respective visible points. The resulting image-space occluder- or blocker-map encodes the necessary visibility events that will be used in the next phase of the algorithm.

The second phase computes the illumination for each visible point. For each point, the stored blockers are clipped against the light source. The remaining light source area defines the integration domain for the illumination integral. Analytic or stochastic integration can then be employed to compute the actual radiance values to be attributed to each pixel.

The algorithm, therefore, passes over all pixels in the image twice and can be summarized as follows:

**First pass.** (Construction of the blocker-map):
- Compute the nearest point visible through each pixel using a classic ray-casting technique. By casting shadow rays to each light source, blockers are detected and relevant blocker-light source pairs are stored with the pixel.
- Project each blocker onto the light source, to determine whether the same blocker-light source pair appears in neighboring pixels. Neighboring pixels are found by using a flood-fill algorithm.

**Second pass.** (Evaluation of the illumination):
- For each pixel, the stored blockers are projected and clipped onto their paired light sources using the visible surface point through the pixel as the center of projection.
- Given the clipped area light sources, the illumination is computed to acquire a radiance value for each pixel. Integration can be done analytically, stochastically, or by any other suitable method.

The main advantage of our approach is that we do not need an elaborate examination of all possible visibility events. Blocker-

*Program of Computer Graphics, 580 Rhodes Hall, Cornell University, Ithaca NY 14850, USA. URL: http://www.graphics.cornell.edu/

light source pairs are included in the blocker-map only if detected by a shadow-ray. If detected, coherence is exploited by flood-filling the blocker-light source pair to neighboring pixels. This procedure replaces the construction of a discontinuity mesh or a visibility skeleton. We store no visibility information that will not be needed during the illumination computations.

## 2 PREVIOUS WORK

The generation of shadows from area light sources is a long standing problem in computer graphics. Several algorithms for generating sharp shadows due to point light sources have been published. A good survey of such shadow algorithms can be found in Woo et al. [24].

Stochastic ray tracing algorithms [5,15] compute the direct illumination shadow at any point by sampling the area of the light source with shadow rays. Various optimization techniques based on importance sampling [16] can be used, but the fact remains that the shadow rays still have to evaluate both illumination and visibility.

Radiosity algorithms [4,17] intrinsically compute soft shadows as part of the full global illumination solution. Discontinuity meshing [11] provides an accurate way of computing soft shadows, but requires substantial amounts of computation time. Moreover, discontinuity meshing is usually driven by an exhaustive algorithm, as each possible discontinuity is considered as a potential candidate for subdividing the mesh. A constructed discontinuity mesh can also be used in pixel-based ray tracing algorithms. Drettakis and Fiume [6], constructed the complete discontinuity mesh, after which the exact illumination for a surface point visible through a pixel is computed analytically. Similar ideas for computing shadow boundaries are presented by Stewart and Ghali [19].

The visibility skeleton [7] encodes all possible visibility events that cause discontinuities in visibility or shading at considerable computational cost. It can be used to compute accurate illumination due to area light sources for any surface point in the scene.

A space subdivision based on ray directions emanating from the light sources was proposed by Tanaka and Takahashi [21], allowing a fast detection of possible blockers for a surface point to be shaded. Casting rays from surface points to detect blockers is also proposed in other algorithms for computing soft shadows [20,23].

Soler and Sillion [18] presented a method for interactive soft shadows based on convolution operators and using scan-conversion hardware. Although their method is restricted in computing exact soft shadows in a limited number of cases, the results are quite convincing and can be applied in real-time.

## 3 DIRECT ILLUMINATION

### 3.1 Rendering Equation

In order to compute the direct illumination in a scene, we have to integrate the incoming radiance at a surface point according to the rendering equation [10]. The exitant radiance $L(x \to \Theta)$ leaving a surface point $x$ in a direction $\Theta$, due to direct illumination from the light sources, is given by:

$$L(x \to \Theta) = \int_A L_e(y \to x) f_r(\Theta \leftrightarrow \overline{xy}) \frac{\cos\Theta \cos\overline{yx}}{r_{xy}^2} V(x, y) d\mu_y \quad (1)$$

where $L_e(y \to x)$ is the emitted radiance of the light source from a surface point $y$ to $x$, $A$ is the area of all light sources, $d\mu_y$ is a differential surface area around $y$, $f_r(\Theta \leftrightarrow \overline{xy})$ is the bidirectional reflectance distribution function (BRDF) at $x$, $\cos\Theta$ is the cosine of the angle between $\Theta$ and the surface normal at $x$, $\overline{xy}$ is the direction vector connecting $x$ and $y$, $r_{xy}$ is the distance between $x$ and $y$, and $V(x, y)$ is the visibility function, having a value of 1 if $x$ and $y$ are mutually visible, 0 otherwise.

By summing over light sources explicitly, and by folding the visibility function into the integration domain, equation (1) can also be written as:

$$L(x \to \Theta) = \sum_{i=1}^{N_L} \int_{A_i} L_{ei}(y \to x) f_r(\Theta \leftrightarrow \overline{xy}) \frac{\cos\Theta \cos\overline{yx}}{r_{xy}^2} d\mu_y \quad (2)$$

where $N_L$ is the number of different light sources, and $A_i$ is the visible part of the light source as seen from point $x$. The use of this equation implies that we can determine $A_i$, before carrying out the actual integration.

### 3.2 Analytic Integration

We now describe a set of conditions for which equation (2) can be worked out analytically:

- The luminaires are a (disjoint) set of polygons;
- The exitant radiance is a constant for a given light source ($L_e(x \to \Theta) = L_{ei}$);
- The receiving surface is diffuse.

Using Stoke's theorem, the continuous integral over the area $A_i$ can be converted into an integral over the boundaries of the polygonal light source [12,3]:

$$L(x \to \Theta) = \frac{f_r}{2} \sum_{i=1}^{N_L} L_{ei} \sum_{j=1}^{E_i} N \cdot \Gamma_j \quad (3)$$

where $E_i$ is the number of boundaries for light source $i$ and $N$ is the normal vector at $x$. $\Gamma_j$ is a vector with magnitude equal to the angle gamma, as illustrated in figure 1, whose direction is given by the cross-product of vectors $R_j$ and $R_{j+1}$. A more detailed derivation of this formula can be found in [9].

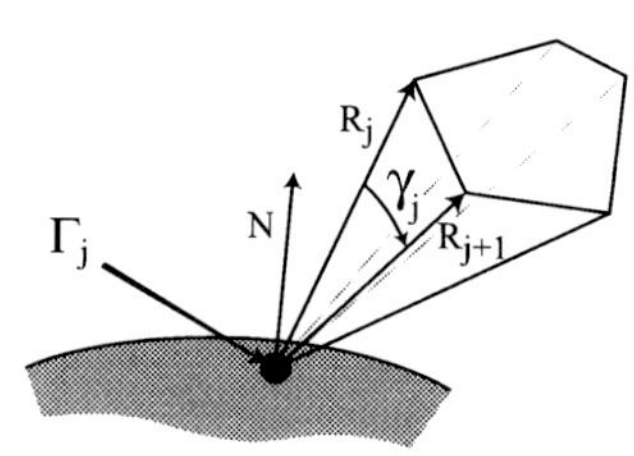


**Figure 1:** Geometry for analytically evaluating illumination.

Equation (3) is only valid for the visible part of the light source, $A_i$. In the event where occlusion occurs between $x$ and the light source, and if we have a way to remove the occluded parts from the light source so that only non-occluded parts remain, we can successfully use the above closed form to compute the radiance exactly.

If the receiving surface is not diffuse, an analytic computation of the direct illumination is more difficult. Arvo [1] gave a derivation that makes it possible to integrate equation (2) if the BRDF is composed of a linear combination of Phong-lobes [13]. This method also transforms the area integral into a line integral. Again, this method assumes the integration only takes place over the unoccluded parts of the light source.

## 3.3 Monte Carlo Integration

Monte Carlo integration techniques can also be used to compute the direct illumination [16], regardless of the type of BRDF. A number of sample points are generated over the area of the light sources, and the integrand has to be evaluated for each point. By taking the weighted average of these evaluations, an unbiased estimator for the direct illumination is obtained. Since the visibility function is part of the integrand, a fraction of the generated samples will evaluate to zero causing significant noise in the image. A reduction of the integration domain to the visible parts of the light sources would decrease noise significantly, using the same number of sampling points.

Moreover, the integration domain can be transformed from the area of the light sources to the solid angle subtended by the light sources on the hemisphere around $x$. This reduces noise even further since the inverse distance and one cosine factor are folded into the integration variable.

The overall effect of using domain reduction and solid angle sampling is that we can achieve the same image quality with a reduced number of shadow rays, therefore speeding up the rendering algorithm.

# 4 ALGORITHM

## 4.1 Construction of the blocker-map.

The purpose of the first pass, which constructs the blocker-map, is to identify relevant blocker-light source pairs for each pixel. We use a combination of shadow rays and a flood-fill algorithm in the image plane to identify the necessary pairs for each pixel. A ray is cast through the center of each pixel in order to find the nearest visible point on a surface. The location of this visible point, along with its surface normal, is stored with the pixel for future reference.

Once the visible point is found, a number of shadow rays starting from this point are generated for each light source by using a uniform sampling function over the solid angle subtended by the light source as seen from the visible point [2]. If one of these rays hits an intervening object, this blocker-light source pair is stored in the blocker-map for that pixel. A blocker will be found with a probability proportional to its subtended solid angle covering the subtended solid angle of the light source. Figures 2a and 2b illustrate the identification and storage of the blockers in the blocker-map.

Since for each shadow-ray, we find at most one blocker, we probably do not find all relevant blockers for a pixel. We assume that the umbra-penumbra region of a single blocker extends over multiple pixels in the image plane. Therefore, once a blocker-light source pair is found, neighboring pixels are examined to check whether the same blocker shows up, using an eight-connect recursive flood-fill mechanism. For each pixel visited during the flood-fill, the blocker is projected onto the light source, using the visible point in that pixel as the center of projection. If a simple test indicates that the two polygons (blocker and light source) overlap, the pair will be added to the blocker-map for the visited pixel. The flood-fill stops if there is no overlap for the current pixel, or if the blocker-

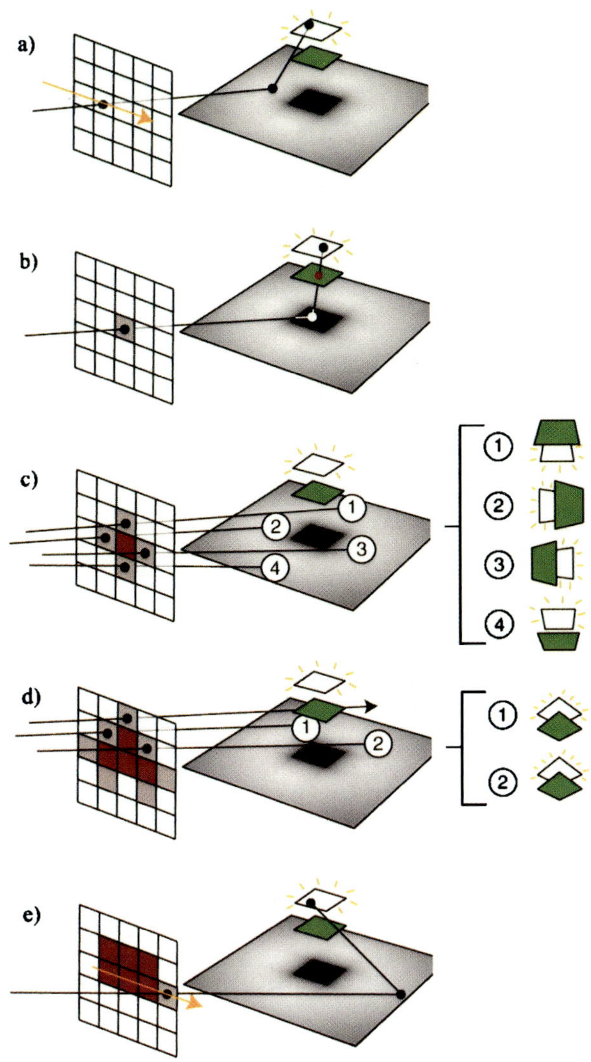


**Figure 2: a)** A shadow-ray is sent to the area light source, but is not blocked by any blocker. The orange arrow indicates the order in which the pixels are visited. **b)** The shadow-ray generated for this pixel is blocked by the blocker. The blocker-light pair is added to the blocker-map. **c)** A 4-connect flood-fill tests whether the same pair shows up in adjacent pixels. The blocker is projected on the light source plane, and their relative position indicates whether the blocker is added to the blocker-map for the tested pixel (pixels 1, 2 and 3) or the flood-fill is stopped (pixel 4). **d)** The flood-fill continues recursively and stops if the blocker-light source pair was already stored in the blocker-map for that pixel, or if no overlap between projected blocker and light source is detected. **e)** Once the flood-fill has stopped, regular testing is resumed with the next eligible pixel.

light source pair already has been stored for that pixel. Figures 2c, 2d and 2e illustrate this part of the algorithm. Pseudo-code for the construction of the blocker-map is given in Figure 3.

Using the flood-fill algorithm makes it sufficient to detect the blocker in any of the pixels covered by the umbra-penumbra region, in order to take it into account for all those pixels during the illumination pass. Note that the blocker-map accumulates all possible blocker-light source pairs, and does not just store the last one encountered.

The result of this first pass is that we have constructed a blocker-map in the image plane. For each pixel, we have stored blocker-

```
floodFillBlocker(int x, y; light l; blocker b)

// if blocker already is stored in pixel, return
if (b,l) is in bMap(x,y) return;

// clip blocker behind light and visible point
cBlocker = clipBlocker(b, l, bMap(x,y).point);

// project the blocker on the light source
pBlocker =
   projectBlocker(cBlocker, l, bMap(x,y).point);

// check if the blocker overlaps the light source

if triangleOverlap(pBlocker, l) then

   // store the pair in the blocker-map
   bMap(x,y).store(b,l);

   // flood-fill the surrounding pixels
   if (x > 1)       floodFillBlocker(x-1,y,l,b);
   if (x < width)   floodFillBlocker(x+1,y,l,b);
   if (y > 1)       floodFillBlocker(x,y-1,l,b);
   if (y < height)  floodFillBlocker(x,y+1,l,b);
endif

return;
```

**Figure 3:** Pseudo-code for the flood-fill algorithm in the image plane.

light source pairs which affect the illumination of the point visible through that pixel. Figure 4 shows what a blocker-map looks like for a simple example. The color values indicate how many blocker-light source pairs are stored in each pixel, with white indicating 15 pairs and black indicating 0. Red regions indicate detected umbra regions (see Discussion). No visibility information is stored in the black pixels, therefore, no clipping or visibility tests are needed during the illumination phase for those areas. The blocker-map can, therefore, also be considered as an indicator of which pixels demand the most amount of work. This indicator could be worthwhile information for parallelizing the algorithm and achieving a good load-balancing amongst different processors.

## 4.2 Illumination Pass

After construction of the blocker-map, a second pass computes the illumination in each pixel. Equation (2) has to be evaluated for the visible point seen through the pixel. As described above, both analytic and Monte Carlo integration benefit from a more elaborate handling of the visibility function, by eliminating the non-visible parts of the light sources from the integration domain. For each pixel, each blocker in the blocker-map is projected onto its paired light source using the visible point as the center of projection. Each light source is clipped accordingly, such that only the visible parts remain.

Integrating the direct illumination can then be done using the reduced integration domain. In general, when using arbitrary BRDFs or non-diffuse luminaires, Monte Carlo integration is the preferred method. A suitable probability density function that samples all visible parts of the light sources produces an unbiased estimator. The variance on this estimator can always be reduced by increasing the number of samples.

Analytic integration is limited to a few cases where the BRDF is diffuse or is described as a linear combination of Phong-lobes. Equation (3), or the methods described in [1], are applied to all visible parts of the light sources. If no blockers are missed in the blocker-map, analytic integration gives the correct answer for the direct illumination.

**Figure 4:** The top-left image shows a simple scene consisting of a ground-plane and several polyhedra. Two light-sources are present, casting soft shadows. The bottom images show the blocker-maps for the two light sources separately, the top-right image shows the combined blocker-map.

## 4.3 Polygon Clipping

The efficiency and generality of the polygon clipping algorithm determines the overall efficiency of the integration pass. There is a large number of approaches to polygon clipping found in the literature [22]. Many well-known polygon clippers have constraints which make general clipping (e.g. with concave, self-intersecting, or overlapping polygons) difficult or numerically unstable. Our current algorithm constrains the scene to be composed of triangles only, which is possible without loss of generality. The advantage is that we can uniformly sample the projection of a triangle on a hemisphere [2] to compute the illumination integral with Monte Carlo integration.

## 4.4 Anti-Aliasing

Since the list of blockers constructed for each pixel is only valid for a single surface point visible at the center of that pixel, aliasing artifacts will occur if we compute the illumination only at this single point (e.g. jagged edges when more than one object is visible in a pixel). If more than one ray per pixel is generated for illumination computations as part of an anti-aliasing algorithm, the blocker-light source list stored for this pixel might not be valid for each surface point hit by these rays, since the surface points might be located in very different positions in object space. Nevertheless, we need a strategy that allows us to perform anti-aliasing.

The coherency of the penumbra regions over the image plane can again be exploited. Due to the flood-fill, we know that a blocker is at least valid for the center location of all covered pixels. Pixels located in the middle of the flood-fill area are completely covered with the penumbra region. Therefore, we can assume that the blocker is valid for all surface points seen through such pixels. For pixels located at the edge of the flood-fill area, the penumbra might extend up to the center of the first pixel outside the flood-filled region. Therefore, if we allow the flood-fill algorithm to include the boundary pixels for which the flood-fill test fails, we can safely assume that we have stored all possible blockers in a pixel that are needed for computing the illumination for any point visible through the pixel. This is illustrated in figure 5.

This strategy allows us to generate multiple sample rays for illumination computations, without increasing the number of rays used for constructing the blocker-map. Therefore, a suitable anti-aliasing algorithm can be employed. In the current implementation, adaptive anti-aliasing is carried out in adjacent pixels whose visible points show different polygons with different surface normals or whose illumination computations based on the first point show sufficiently different spectral radiance values. This strategy will capture most aliasing artefacts. Note however, that high-frequency geometry, such as small objects, might be overlooked.

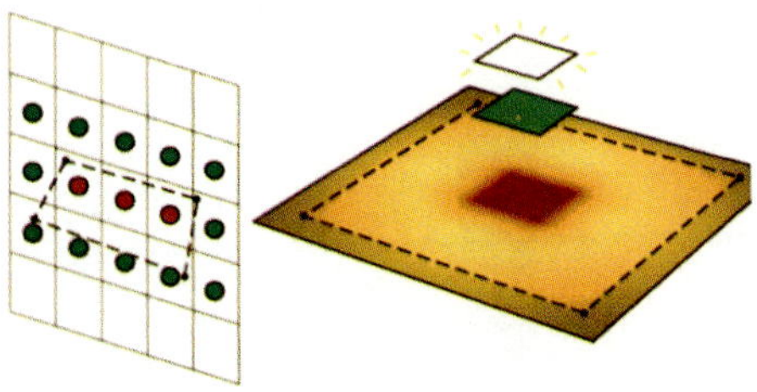

**Figure 5:** The flood-fill algorithm stores the blocker in the red pixels where the penumbra is detected, and also in the green pixels, where the penumbra might show up.

## 5 DISCUSSION

**Missing blockers.** During the construction of the blocker-map, some blockers might be overlooked. Because of the flood-fill algorithm, a blocker is only missed if it is not intersected by any of the shadow rays starting from visible points covered by the penumbra or umbra caused by that blocker. If a blocker is missing, some pixels will be too bright because invisible parts of the light sources are taken into account. By increasing the number of shadow rays, the probability of missing blockers decreases. This implies that the analytic integration method is consistent: the possible error can be made arbitrarily small by generating more shadow rays.

The probability of missing blockers or computing insufficient shadows is further diminished by the fact that we locate the nearest polygon intersected by each shadow ray. We are therefore assured that the polygon causing the most significant shadow on a receiver point is stored in the blocker-map. This is no less efficient than a more traditional approach where any intersecting polygon found is sufficient to conclude the receiver point lies in a shadow, since we use a regular voxel-based spatial subdivision technique (with an average of one polygon per voxel), and all polygons in the traversed voxel are tested for intersection [8].

**Receiver Surfaces.** Because we do not use any form of texture-map to display soft shadows, our method produces soft shadows on any surface type that can be handled by a ray tracing algorithm. The number of receiver surfaces or polygons is not a limiting factor for generating the correct direct illumination and soft shadows.

**Small Blockers.** Small objects or small polygons causing shadows create small blockers in the blocker-map. Such blockers probably only clip a very small piece of the light source and, therefore, do not affect the shading by a large amount. One might be tempted to dismiss small blockers without computing their influence on the illumination. However, a whole set of small blockers might significantly affect the visibility of a light source, thus they cannot be ignored. Each of these small blockers requires a full clipping operation. In the limit, this is a worst-case scenario for our current algorithm. A possible solution might be to use some form of clustering as in radiosity algorithms, although with loss of exact visibility; or construct the silhouette polygon of a collection of smaller polygons, and use that as the blocker.

**Umbra Regions.** One straightforward optimization is to make a distinction between penumbra and umbra regions. When testing whether a blocker overlaps with a light source as seen from a visible point, a triangle-triangle "surround" test indicates if the point lies in the umbra or penumbra region. By storing this information in the blocker-map, we know that this particular light source does not have to be included in the illumination computations, and expensive clipping operations are avoided. Also, it prevents other blockers associated with the same light source from being stored in those pixels.

## 6 RESULTS

We have implemented the algorithm as outlined above, including umbra detection and anti-aliasing using the flood-fill extension. Timings were performed on one Intel Pentium II 400Mhz processor. All images were computed at a resolution of 512x512 pixels.

Figure 6 shows three different views of the interior of the Church of the Year 2000 in Rome, consisting of 64,216 triangles and one large light source, split in two triangles. All surfaces are diffuse. The top row shows an overview of the chapel, looking from the back towards the altar. The light source is located in the upper right, and casts shadows from the benches on the floor. The middle row shows a close-up of the cross at the altar. The third row shows a view from a small anteroom into the main chapel through a number of slats. The light is shining through the slats and causes shadows to fall on the floor of the anteroom. For each viewpoint, three pictures are shown. The middle column shows pictures generated using the blocker-map, and analytic evaluation of the direct illumination. The first and third columns are generated using standard Monte Carlo rendering of the direct lighting term. Visibility is evaluated by casting shadow rays from each visible point to the light sources, and the shadow rays are generated by sampling the solid angles subtended by the light source. The number of shadow rays, as well as the execution times, are mentioned below each picture. The first column executes in roughly equal time compared to the second column; the third column produces roughly equal image quality as the second column. From these comparisons, it is obvious that for an equal execution time, our algorithm generates significantly better quality pictures. The Monte Carlo solutions show significant noise in the soft shadow regions. The special geometrical case of the anteroom can be handled by our algorithm efficiently; all slats are clipped from the light source and, therefore, we have an almost exact visibility computation although the execution time is quite high. The equal quality comparisons indicate that our algorithm, while providing very accurate soft shadows, executes up to 20 times faster compared to the standard Monte Carlo method.

Figure 7 shows a different scene, with a somewhat more complex set-up. The scene consists of 556 polygons and four light sources. The four images on the right are a close-up of the area marked in red, all generated by different algorithms. Picture (a) is generated using the blocker-map and analytic integration; picture (b) used Monte Carlo integration with 4 sample rays and shadow rays per pixel, using the blocker-map to restrict the integration domain. Picture (c) and (d) are generated using standard Monte Carlo integration with 30 and 100 sample rays per pixel respectively. In each of the pictures, one shadow ray was generated per sample ray for each

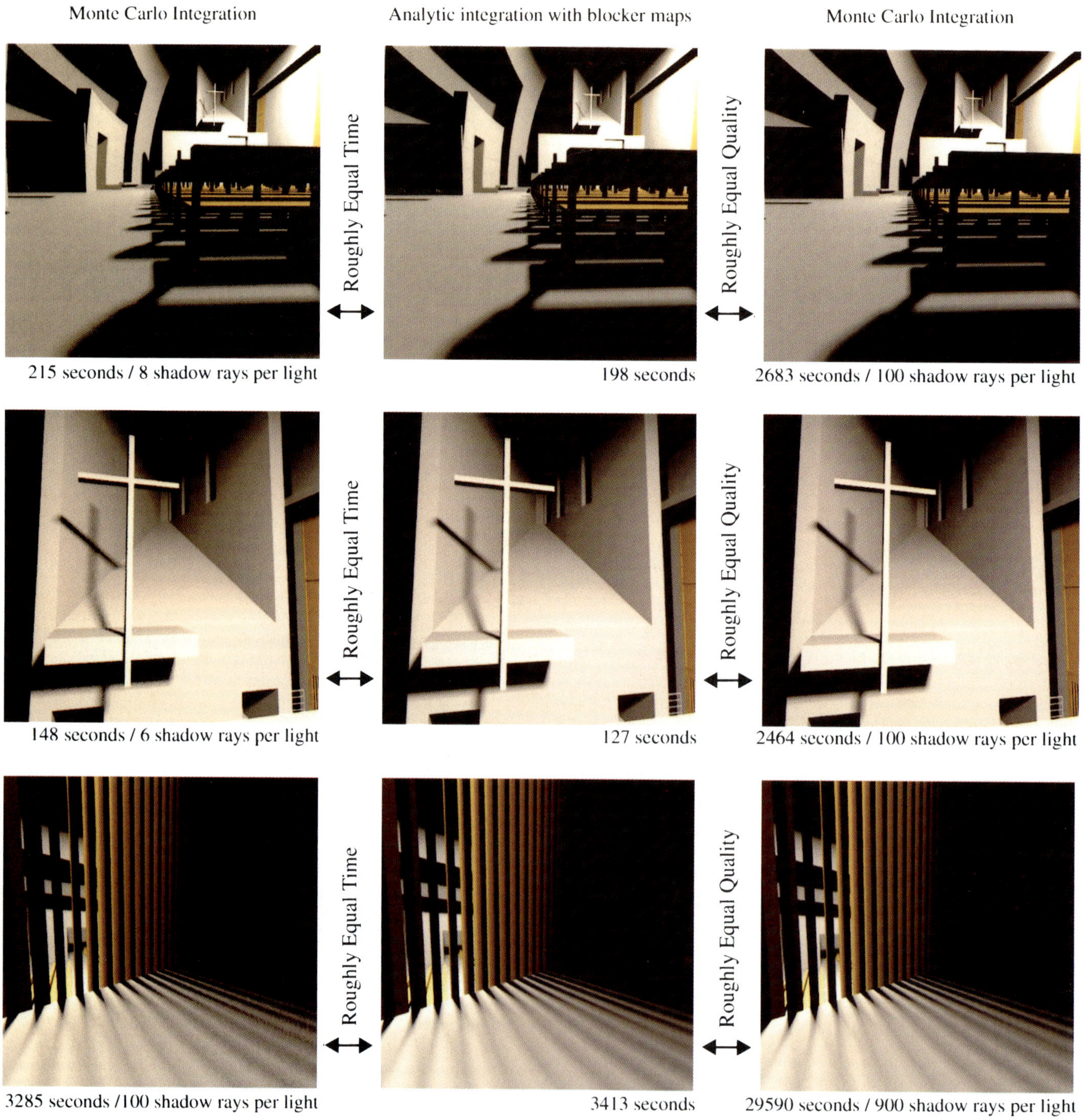


**Figure 6:** Three different viewpoints for the Church of the Year 2000 in Rome. The middle column is rendered using the blocker map and analytic integration; the left column is generated using standard Monte Carlo integration and shows pictures generated in roughly equal time; the right column shows pictures generated with roughly equal quality.

light source. Again it is clear that our algorithm, using analytic integration, provides the best quality in the least time. Picture (c) give an equal time comparison with (a), while (d) provides an equal quality comparison. Picture (b) indicates that Monte Carlo integration benefits from using the blocker-map to reduce the integration domain: the noise on the back wall is almost completely gone, and the only noise that is left on the green cubes is due to one remaining cosine factor in the integral. Note that the execution times for this scene are higher than for the church scene, although the number of polygons in this scene is far less than in the church scene. This is mainly due to the more complex soft shadows and, therefore, the higher number of blockers stored in the blocker-map. Execution times are comparable to the anteroom pictures of the church. Nevertheless, by comparing images (a) and (d), our algorithm provides the same image quality in about one-tenth the time.

Figure 8 shows that glossy surfaces can also be successfully handled by our algorithm. Both pictures are computed using the blocker-map and analytic evaluation of the illumination. The float-

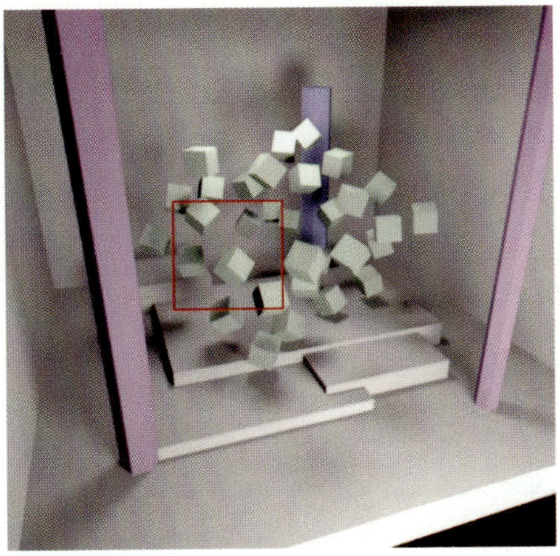

(a) 1256 seconds / analytic integration

(b) 3366 seconds / 4 sample rays per pixel

(c) 1238 seconds / 30 sample rays per pixel

(d) 16526 seconds / 400 sample rays per pixel

**Figure 7:** The pictures on the right are close-ups from the red area on the left, and are rendered with different algorithms: (a) Analytic integration using the blocker map; (b) Monte Carlo integration using the blocker-map to reduce the integration domain; (c,d) Standard Monte Carlo integration. Pictures (a) and (c) are an equal time comparison, pictures (a) and (d) an equal quality comparison. Picture (b) shows the effect of domain reduction on the Monte Carlo integration.

ing cubes scene on the left has a glossy back wall. One can clearly see the soft shadows cast in the glossy highlight of the light source. In the picture on the right, the SIGGRAPH 99 title floats above a spherical surface. One light source is positioned in front, another placed in the back. Two different shadows are visible: the diffuse shadow caused by the diffuse component of the BRDF, and the specular shadows caused by the glossy component. In the second case, the viewer is inside the Phong-lobe of light reflected from the light source in the back. Although no indirect illumination component is computed, the geometry of where the reflection should occur is handled correctly and shows up as a specular shadow.

## 7 FUTURE WORK

Even though the algorithm seems to perform well in our test cases, there are areas where improvement can be achieved:

**Silhouette Polygons and Clustering.** In our current implementation, polygons are considered as blockers without looking at the higher-level object of which they are part. By substituting a collection of polygons by its silhouette polygon, only the silhouette needs to be clipped. It is likely that the complexity will be lowered in this case, although the silhouette needs to be recomputed for every new visible point.

**Non-polygonal surfaces.** Computing analytic visibility for non-polygonal surfaces (e.g. spline surfaces) could be a very interesting direction for future research. It is conceivable that when a point needs to be shaded, the silhouette of an object could itself be computed as a spline curve. If the clipping pass could handle two-dimensional spline-polygon and spline-spline boolean operations, soft shadows could be computed for smooth surfaces.

**Reprojection of blocker maps.** Because a blocker map contains per pixel information, the blocker-map can be reprojected to a new viewpoint, using an image-warping function which is common in image-based rendering algorithms. This would open possibilities for faster image generation in animation or interactive sequences.

**Load balancing & Perception.** The blocker-map gives an indication of how much work is needed to render individual pixels. This could be used to achieve better load balancing in parallel rendering algorithms or distribute work according to some perceptual error metric [14].

## 8 CONCLUSION

We have presented an efficient and fast algorithm to compute accurate direct illumination in a general polygonal environment. Two passes over the image plane are used. A first pass identifies blocker-light source pairs on a per pixel basis. A limited number of shadow rays combined with a flood-fill algorithm in the image plane gives a highly reliable method for detecting the correct blockers. A second pass computes the actual illumination for each pixel by performing analytic or stochastic integration.

Timing results indicate that the algorithm runs faster than more classic Monte Carlo illumination techniques. Although there is a probability that some shadow effects may be missed, there is in general no visible differences between the rendered images with our method and highly accurate reference solutions.

Our results indicate that clipping the light sources with blockers is a viable and acceptable tactic to be used for direct illumination computations or, more generally, for global illumination algorithms.

**Figure 8:** In the top picture, soft shadows are visible in the glossy highlight on the back wall. In the bottom picture, specular shadows are visible on the ground plane.

## Acknowledgements

This work was supported by the NSF Science and Technology Center for Computer Graphics and Scientific Visualization (ASC-8920219) and by NSF grant ASC-9523483, and performed on workstations generously donated by the Intel Corporation.

Richard Meier & Partners, Architects, generously provided us with the model of the "Church of the Year 2000".

## References

[1] James Arvo. Applications of irradiance tensors to the simulation of non-lambertian phenomena. In Robert Cook, editor, *SIGGRAPH 95 Conference Proceedings*, Annual Conference Series, pages 335-342. ACM SIGGRAPH, Addison Wesley, August 1995.

[2] James Arvo. Stratified sampling of spherical triangles. In Robert Cook, editor, *SIGGRAPH 95 Conference Proceedings*, Annual Conference Series, pages 437-438. ACM SIGGRAPH, Addison Wesley, August 1995.

[3] Daniel R. Baum, Holly E. Rushmeier, and James M. Winget. Improving radiosity solutions through the use of analytically determined form-factors. In Jeffrey Lane, editor, *Computer Graphics (SIGGRAPH 89 Conference Proceedings)*, volume 23, pages 325-334. Addison Wesley, July 1989.

[4] Michael F. Cohen and John R. Wallace. *Radiosity and Realisitc Image Synthesis*. Academic Press Professional, San Diego, CA, 1993.

[5] Robert L. Cook, Thomas Porter, and Loren Carpenter. Distributed Ray tracing. In *Computer Graphics (SIGGRAPH 84 Conference Proceedings)*, volume 18, pages 137-145. Addison Wesley, July 1984.

[6] George Drettakis and Eugene Fiume. A fast shadow algorithm for area light sources using back-projection. In Andrew Glassner, editor, *SIGGRAPH 94 Conference Proceedings*, Annual Conference Series, pages 223-230. ACM SIGGRAPH, Addison Wesley, July 1994.

[7] Frédo Durand, George Drettakis, and Claude Puech. The visibility skeleton: A powerful and efficient multi-purpose global visibility tool. In Turner Whitted, editor, *SIGGRAPH 97 Conference Proceedings*, Annual Conference Series, pages 89-100. ACM SIGGRAPH, Addison Wesley, August 1997.

[8] Tanaka T., Fujimoto A. and Iwata K. Arts: Accelerated ray tracing system. *IEEE Computer Graphics and Applications*, 6(6):16-26, April 1986.

[9] Adel F. Sarofim Hotte, Hoyt C. *Radiative Transfer.* McGraw Hill, New York, NY, 1967.

[10] James T. Kajiya. The rendering equation. In David Evans and Russel Athay, editors, *Computer Graphics (SIGGRAPH 86 Conference Proceedings)*, volume 20, pages 143-150. Addison Wesley, August 1986.

[11] Daniel Lischinski, Filippo Tampieri, and Donald P. Greenberg. Discontinuity meshing for accurate radiosity. *IEEE Computer Graphics and Applications*, 12(6):25-39, November 1992.

[12] Tomoyuki Nishita and Eihachiro Nakamae. Continous tone representation of three-dimensional objects taking account of shadows and interreflection. In Brian Barsky, editor, *Computer Graphics (SIGGRAPH 85 Conference Proceedings)*, volume 19, pages 23-30. Addison Wesley, July 1985.

[13] Bui-T. Phong. Illumination for computer generated pictures. *Communications of the ACM*, 18(6):311-317, June 1975.

[14] Mahesh Ramasubramanian, Sumanta N. Pattanaik, and Donald P. Greenberg. A Perceptually Based Physical Error Metric for Realistic Image Synthesis. In Alyn Rockwood, editor, *SIGGRAPH 99 Conference Proceedings*, Annual Conference Series. ACM SIGGRAPH, Addison Wesley, August 1999.

[15] Peter Shirley and Chang Yaw Wang. Distribution ray tracing: Theory and practice. *Proceedings of the Third Eurographics Workshop on Rendering*, pages 33-43, May 1992.

[16] Peter Shirley, Chang Yaw Wang, and Kurt Zimmerman. Monte Carlo methods for direct lighting calculation. *ACM Transactions on Graphics*, January 1996.

[17] François Sillion and Claude Puech. *Radiosity and Global Illumination*. Morgan Kaufmann, San Francisco, 1994.

[18] Cyril Soler and François X. Sillion. Fast calculation of soft shadow textures using convolution. In Michael Cohen, editor, *SIGGRAPH 98 Conference Proceedings*, Annual Conference series, pages 321-332. ACM SIGGRAPH, Addison Wesley, July 1998.

[19] James Stewart, Sherif Ghali. Fast Computation of Shadow Boundaries Using Spatial Coherence and Backprojections. In Andrew Glassner, editor, *SIGGRAPH 94 Conference Proceedings*, Annual Conference Series, pages 231-238. ACM SIGGRAPH, Addison Wesley, July 1994.

[20] Wolfgang Stürzlinger. Adaptive Mesh Refinement with Discontinuities for the Radiosity Method. *Photorealistic Rendering Techniques (Proceedings of the 5th Eurographics Workshop on Rendering)*, G. Sakas, P. Shirley, S. Müller (eds.), Springer-Verlag 1995.

[21] Toshimitsu Tanaka, Tokiichiro Takahashi. Fast Analytic Shading and Shadowing for Area Light Sources. *Computer Graphics Forum (Proceedings of Eurographics 1997)*, volume 16, 3.

[22] B.R. Vatti. A generic solution to polygon clipping. *Communications of the ACM*, 35(7):56-63, July 1992.

[23] Christophe Vedel. Computing Illumination from Area Light Sources by Approximate Contour Integration. *Proceedings of Graphics Interface '93*, pages 237-244.

[24] Andrew Woo, Pierre Poulin, and Alain Fournier. A survey of shadow algorithms. *IEEE Computer Graphics and Applications*, 10(6):13-32, November 1990.

# Computing Exact Shadow Irradiance Using Splines

Michael M. Stark
University of Utah

Elaine Cohen
University of Utah

Tom Lyche
University of Oslo

Richard F. Riesenfeld
University of Utah

## Abstract

We present a solution to the general problem of characterizing shadows in scenes involving a uniform polygonal area emitter and a polygonal occluder in arbitrary position by manifesting shadow irradiance as a spline function. Studying generalized prism-like constructions generated by the emitter and the occluder in a four-dimensional (shadow) space reveals a simpler intrinsic structure of the shadow as compared to the more complicated 2D projection onto a receiver. A closed form expression for the spline shadow irradiance function is derived by twice applying Stokes' theorem to reduce an evaluation over a 4D domain to an explicit formula involving only 2D faces on the receiver, derived from the scene geometry. This leads to a straightforward computational algorithm and an interactive implementation. Moreover, this approach can be extended to scenes involving multiple emitters and occluders, as well as curved emitters, occluders, and receivers. Spline functions are constructed from these prism-like objects. We call them generalized polyhedral splines because they extend the classical polyhedral splines to include curved boundaries and a density function. The approach can be applied to more general problems such as some of those occurring in radiosity, and other related topics.

**CR Categories:** I.3.0 [Computer Graphics]: General; I.3.7 [Computer Graphics]: Three-Dimensional Graphics and Realism;

**Keywords:** rendering, shadow algorithms, illumination, visibility determination

## 1 INTRODUCTION

While computing shadows from a single point source is relatively simple and goes back to the early days of graphics when the light source was moved away from the eye position, the accurate representation of shadows resulting from area sources is quite complicated, as Soler and Sillion [38] point out:

> The calculation of detailed shadows remains one of the most difficult challenges in computer graphics, especially in the case of extended (linear or area) light sources.

University of Utah Department of Computer Science, 50 S. Central Campus Dr., 3190 MEB, Salt Lake City, UT 84112
Institutt for informatikk, Universitetet i Oslo, Postboks 1080 Blindern, 0316 Oslo
Email: {mstark,cohen,rfr}@cs.utah.edu, tom@ifi.uio.no



In this paper we present a solution to the general differential area to polygon form factor in the presence of a polygonal occluder, by representing the induced irradiance as a spline function. We generalize the polyhedral spline [4, 16, 32] to obtain our result. The polyhedral spline is defined as a distribution. A geometric interpretation of this definition involves regarding the splines as cross-sectional volumes of higher dimensional polyhedra [14]. The more familiar univariate and tensor product B-splines are special cases of the polyhedral spline.

To introduce the fundamental ideas of our approach, we begin with an analysis in Flatland [26], where the higher dimension construction can be directly visualized and more easily understood. Then we work through the construction of a generalized perspective prism in 4D associated with an element that can be either an emitter or an occluder. The 4D perspective prism is defined so that the 2D cross-section taken through any point $(x, y)$ is a perspective view of the element from the point $(x, y, 0)$. A shadow function can be built by considering boolean operations on such prisms. In the case where the emitter $E$, occluder $O$, and receiver $R$ are all parallel, the intersection region of the $E$ and $O$ prisms is isomorphic to the 4D Cartesian product $O \times E$, where $O$ and $E$ are taken as 2D polygons. To bolster confidence for looking into 4D, we observe that the projection of $O \times E$ onto $R$ generates all the discontinuity lines of the shadow structure.

The boolean combination of the $O$- and $E$-prisms gives a polyhedron-like object in 4D which is used to define a polyhedral spline function. At each point $(x, y)$ in the plane the value of the spline is obtained by integrating a density function over the 2D cross-section at $(x, y)$. With a proper definition of the density function this spline gives us the exact partially occluded irradiance at $(x, y)$. Using Stokes' theorem we derive a recurrence relation that yields a closed form solution for the irradiance function.

### 1.1 Related Work

Accurate computation of shadows has been a rich and active area of graphics research since near the beginning of the field. In 1990 Woo *et al.* [44] made an extensive survey of relevant techniques. Since then many techniques have been aimed at faster or more accurate computation.

Methods that are based on a single point light source create hard shadows. A typical example of such a method is used in ray tracing, where a ray is cast between a point lying on the surface and a specified light source. The algorithm must determine if there is an occluder between it and the light source [42]. Soft shadows caused by area light sources are simulated by stochastically selecting a set of sample points on the source and casting several rays towards them from the surface [11, 36]. Exact evaluation can be obtained by clipping all the occluders against the area source [18, 33].

Several methods consider the view from a point light source. The shadow buffer creates a discrete depth image from the point light source view [43], using only a single point. Shadow volumes are constructed from a point light source and polygonal occluders [13] or curved boundary occluders [27], from which a point can be tested for its visibility in object space. Soft shadows can be approximated in a similar manner to the ray tracing method, by breaking the light source into several point samples [7].

The radiosity method theoretically includes the computation of soft shadows. However, the method requires the reconstruction of irradiance functions, for which no general closed form is known. Methods to compute radiosity use a mesh of finite surface elements, then "form factors" representing the exchange of energy between mesh elements are computed. Frequently, the implementation assumes a constant radiosity distribution across each surface patch and finite element, then the values are interpolated across each mesh element. Meshing surfaces without considering the shadow structure can lead to inaccurate solutions and "shadow leaks". The discontinuity meshing approach [17, 25, 30] was developed to avoid these problems. For each source, a discontinuity mesh is created on the scenes surfaces (receivers). The mesh includes all lines where the illumination function has discontinuities, including the effects of boundaries of multiple occluders. Meshing concerns have been a principal driving force behind shadow research.

It was recognized quite early that solutions could be improved if the form factors could be computed analytically. Analytical solutions have been determined for specific geometries [28, 35]. Generally such solutions assume that each surface is flat and fully visible from the other. Baum *et al* [3] proposed computing the unoccluded point to polygon form factor analytically. To avoid violation of visibility assumptions, they proposed that each source patch be subdivided until all components were either fully visible or fully hidden from all elements in the environment.

Many current methods to compute form factors approximate them with an upper bound calculation, that is, they assume that an unoccluded radiosity kernel can be multiplied against a visibility factor, which gives the fraction of the area of the light source element visible from the receiver [9, 24, 40]. The point to polygon form factor is assumed to have constant exitance on the source. Then it is separated into the unoccluded point to polygon form factor integral and a visibility factor integral.

Arvo [1] provided hope that a closed-form formula for shadow irradiance might exist by developing a clean, elegant closed-form formula for the irradiance Jacobian due to a partially occluded polygonal source. Recently Soler and Sillion [38] showed that when polygonal emitter, occluder, and receiver are all parallel to each other, shadow computations on the receiver can be written exactly as a convolution. This method uses the characteristic functions of both the emitter and the occluder, and computationally uses fast Fourier transforms to compute convolutions. When the elements are not parallel to each other, the method requires approximating the elements by parallel elements, called virtual geometry. Since the error can be estimated, it is suggested that when the error is too large, the elements should be subdivided and new orientations and approximating parallel sub-elements should be chosen until the error is within bounds. They compute irradiance using the radiosity kernel-visibility factor approximation.

Polyhedral splines have been well studied for special polyhedra like simplices, boxes, and cones; de Boor and Höllig's original paper [4] contains references and a recurrence relation valid for more general polyhedra than simplices, boxes, and cones. Simplex and box splines have been used in geometric modeling [19]. McCool has used polyhedral splines for signal processing and rendering analytically antialiased polygons, and also suggested they might be used for penumbral approximation [31, 32].

## 2 FLATLAND

We begin by carrying through our formulation in Edwin Abbott's "Flatland." In Flatland, surfaces become plane curves, planes become lines, and polygons become line segments [26]. Irradiance is

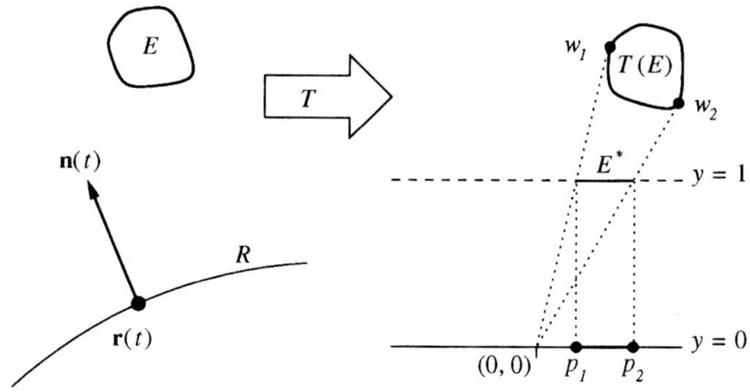


Figure 1: A general irradiance situation in Flatland. To compute the irradiance at $\mathbf{r}(t)$, we transform to the origin and rotate so that the surface normal is $(0, 1)$. Then the transformed emitter is projected onto the line $y = 1$, where it is a line segment projectively equivalent to the apparent silhouette of $T(E)$. The transformation and resulting objects are all functions of $t$.

computed from the integral

$$I(r) = \int_C L(r, \theta) \cos\theta \, d\theta \tag{1}$$

where $L(r, \theta)$ is the radiance coming into $r$ from direction $\theta$, and $C$ is the open semi-circle above the surface at $r$.

### 2.1 Formulation of Irradiance

Consider a receiver surface $R$ described by a plane parametric curve $\mathbf{r}(t) = (x(t), y(t))$ and a normal vector $\mathbf{n}(t) = (n_x(t), n_y(t))$. Let $E$ be a uniformly emitting surface, situated above the receiver $R$, as shown in Figure 1. In order to compute the irradiance at a point $\mathbf{r}(t_0) = (x_0, y_0)$ on $R$ corresponding to a parameter value $t = t_0$ we proceed as follows:

1. Transform the scene such that $(x_0, y_0)$ is mapped to the origin, and such that the unit normal $\mathbf{n}(t_0)$ becomes parallel to the $y$-axis. This transformation, which we call $T$, is a translation followed by a rotation, which transforms $E$ into a new position $T(E)$.

2. Let $E^*$ be the perspective projection of $T(E)$ onto the line $y = 1$ with the origin as the center of projection.

We then have

$$E^* = \{(x, 1) : p_1^*(t) \le x \le p_2^*(t)\}$$

where

$$p_i^*(t) = \frac{w_{i,1}(t)}{w_{i,2}(t)}, \quad i = 1, 2,$$

and $w_i(t) = (w_{i,1}(t), w_{i,2}(t))$ are the silhouette points of $T(E)$ as seen from the origin. The object $T(E)$ and the projection $E^*$ produce the same irradiance at the origin, which is the irradiance at $\mathbf{r}(t)$. Denoting this irradiance $I_E(\mathbf{r}(t))$ by $I(t)$, we have

$$I(t) = K \left| \int_{p_1^*(t)}^{p_2^*(t)} \frac{\cos\theta \cos\theta'}{d(x)} dx \right|,$$

where $K$ is a constant, $d(x)$ the distance between the origin and the point $(x, 1)$, $\theta$ the angle between the ray $(0, 0) \to (x, 1)$ and the $y$-axis, and $\theta'$ the angle between the same ray and the normal to $E^*$.

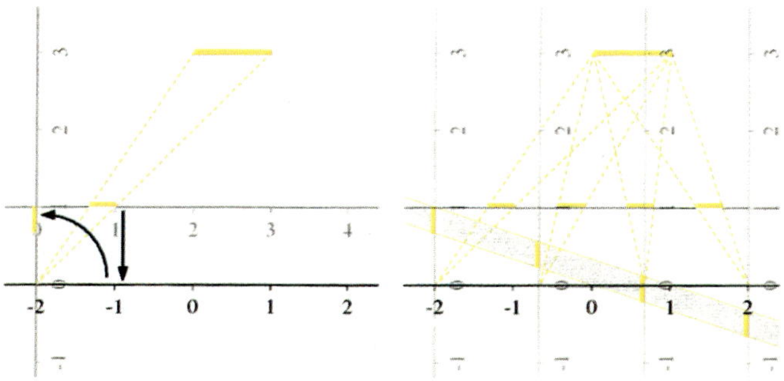


(a) (b)

Figure 2: Construction of the strip for a parallel polygon in Flatland. (a) For irradiance at $x = -2$, $E$ is projected to $E^*$ through $x = -2$, then $E^*$ is rotated to the slice of the $M_E$ prism; (b) The slices as a function of $x$ sweep out $M_E$.

Since $E^*$ is normal to the $y$-axis we have $\theta' = \theta$, $\cos\theta = 1/d(x)$, and $d(x)^2 = 1 + x^2$. It follows that

$$I(t) = K \left| \int_{p_1^*(t)}^{p_2^*(t)} \frac{dx}{(1+x^2)^{\frac{3}{2}}} \right| = K \left| \Omega(p_2^*(t)) - \Omega(p_1^*(t)) \right|, \tag{2}$$

where

$$\Omega(x) = \frac{x}{\sqrt{1+x^2}}.$$

The function $I(t)$ can be interpreted geometrically. Suppose for simplicity that $p_2^*(t) \geq p_1^*(t)$ for all $t$. We consider the integral

$$\int_{p_1^*(t)}^{p_2^*(t)} \omega(y)dy,$$

where

$$\omega(y) = \frac{1}{(1+y^2)^{\frac{3}{2}}}.$$

Let $M_E$ be the 2-dimensional strip

$$M_E = \{(t, y) : -\infty < t < \infty, p_1^*(t) \leq y \leq p_2^*(t)\}.$$

For fixed $t$ the integral is obtained by taking a vertical cut through $M_E$ at $t$ and integrating the density function from the lower boundary of $M_E$ to the upper boundary of $M_E$. Thus $I(t)$ is the weighted length of this cut at $t$.

## 2.2 Irradiance in the Presence of Occluders

Suppose that we extend the scene above by also including an occluder $O$. In the same way as we did for $E$ we obtain an infinite strip $M_O$ corresponding to the occluder. Where the occluder strip overlaps the emitter strip, the covered portion of the emitter is not visible. The occluded irradiance can be computed from the integral of the same density function $\omega(y)$ over the uncovered portion of the strip. This portion of the strip is the set difference $M_E - M_O$.

If the set difference $M_E - M_O$ is endowed with the density function $\omega(y)$, the integral over each slice of the strip produces the unoccluded irradiance at that point, as in Figure 4(b). This approach generalizes. Suppose we have $n$ occluders $O_1, \ldots, O_n$ situated below $E$. The irradiance at $r(t)$ can be found by integrating the same density function over the set

$$M_E - M_{O_1} - \cdots - M_{O_n}.$$

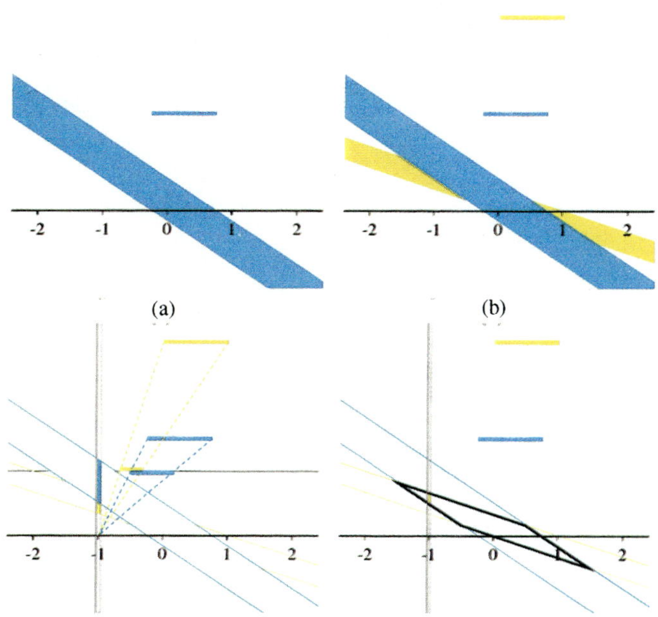


(a) (b) (c) (d)

Figure 3: Any Flatland polygon parallel to the floor generates a strip. (a) A polygon closer to the floor generates a thicker and more steeply sloped strip. (b) The cyan strip covers the yellow strip in a way that encodes the occlusion of the yellow emitting polygon by the occluding cyan polygon. (c) A vertical slice of the two strips (shown at $x = -1$) contains a snapshot of the scene. The uncovered portion of the yellow slice corresponds to the unoccluded portion of the emitter. (d) Slices of the intersection of the strips (the black parallelogram) give the occluded portion of the emitter.

If there are also multiple emitters, the total irradiance is computed by summing the contributions from the individual emitters; however, all other emitters must be treated as potential occluders, and there is also the issue of front-and-back culling.

The advantage of this construction is that all the local visibility calculations can be replaced by a single set operation that handles the occlusion geometry for the entire floor. Set differences may not be easy to compute in general, but in the restricted case where the receiver is a line and the objects line segments, the geometry turns out to be very clean.

## 2.3 Polygonal Objects

Suppose now $E$ and $O$ are one-dimensional polygons (line segments) and the receiver is the line $y = 0$ in Flatland. In this case, the parameterization of $\mathbf{r}(t)$ is simply $\mathbf{r}(t) = (t, 0)$ and we simply use $x$ for the position on the receiver. The transformation $T$ becomes merely a translation by $x$ and the subsequent projection $E \to E^*$ can be computed directly: if $E$ has vertices $(x_i', y_i')$, $i = 1, 2$ then

$$p_i^* = \frac{x_i' - x}{y_i'}, \quad i = 1, 2.$$

Equation (2) can now be evaluated in closed form. Furthermore, each $p_i^*$ as a function of $x$ traces out a line, so the strip for $M_E$ is an (unbounded) polygon.

To take occlusion by $O$ into account, the strip $M_O$ is constructed for $O$. The partially-occluded irradiance can be computed from

$$I(x) = S_{E^*}(x) - S_{E^* \cap O^*}(x),$$

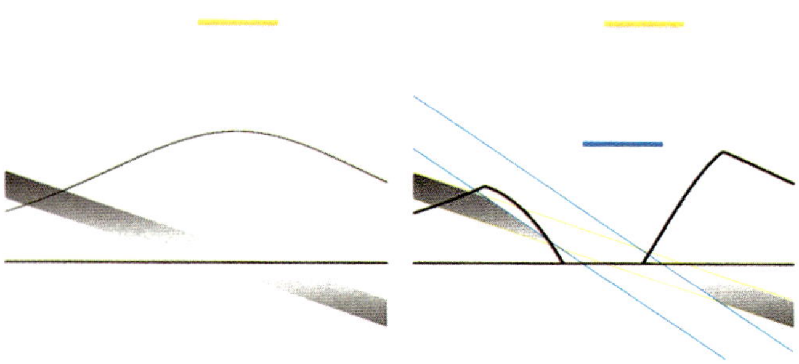


Figure 4: (a) When endowed with the appropriate density function, the integral over each slice produces the irradiance (the smooth curve). (b) The occluded irradiance is the integral over the set difference of the emitter strip and the occluder strip. The removed portion, the intersection of the strips, is a parallelogram.

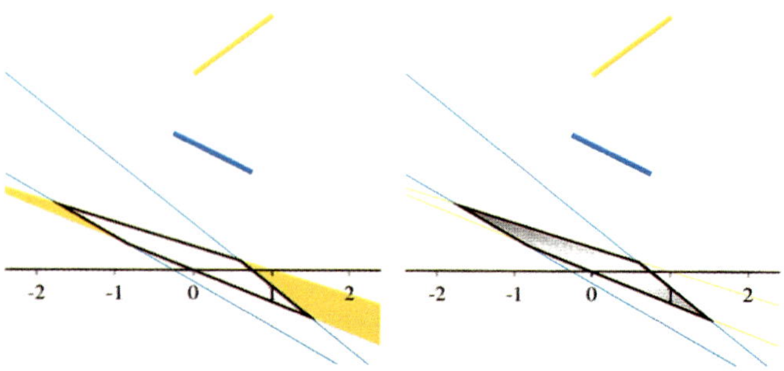


Figure 5: A non-parallel situation. (a) The strips are actually Flatland cones, but their intersection remains a four-sided quadrilateral. (b) The integral of the density function over cross-sections of the intersection (outlined in black) produces the subtractive shadow irradiance. One advantage of this geometry is that the density function is independent of $x$.

where

$$S_Q(x) = \int_{a(x)}^{b(x)} \omega(y)dy$$

in case $Q$ is the line segment from $(a(x), 1)$ to $(b(x), 1)$.

The value of $S_{E^* \cap O^*}(x)$ is therefore the integral of the irradiance density function $\omega(y)$ over the cut at $x$ of the *intersection* of the strips $M_O \cap M_E$. This intersection has four vertices, one for each pair of edges of $M_O$ and $M_E$. In the special case where $O$ and $E$ both happen to be parallel to the $x$-axis, $M_O$ and $M_E$ are both strips of constant width and the intersection $M_O \cap M_E$ is a parallelogram as shown in Figure 2. In the more general case, the intersection $M_O \cap M_E$ can be shown to be a quadrilateral, as in Figure 5. The quadrilateral is not self-intersecting as long as the line containing $E$ do not intersect $O$, and vice-versa.

The formulation of irradiance as the integral over a cut of a two-dimensional object casts it as a weighted polyhedral spline. The constructions in this subsection show that both unoccluded and partially occluded irradiance have this formulation. What is the advantage? First of all, the formulation of irradiance in terms of a polyhedron encodes all the visibility information from the receiver in to a single, easily described two-dimensional object, as suggested in Figure 6. Second, and more importantly, polyhedral splines can be evaluated in closed form without actually finding the intersection of the cut [4].

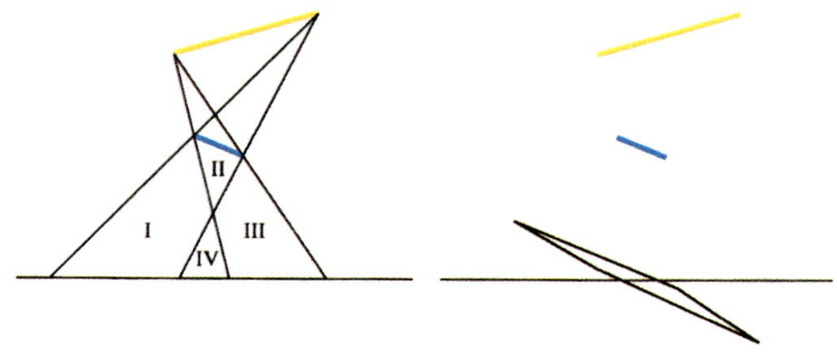


Figure 6: (a) An occluder partitions space into regions of visibility. In this figure, the umbra does not reach the receiver. (b) The regions of visibility on the plane are stored in the intersection quadrilateral. The projection of the edges of the quadrilateral onto $y = 0$ give visibility information for each object vertex; the projected vertices are the points of discontinuity of the irradiance.

## 3 THE PERSPECTIVE PRISM

In this section we construct the perspective prism analogous to the one in flatland, which stores the apparent geometry of an arbitrary polygon in $\mathbb{R}^3$ at every point on the floor $z = 0$. The construction pertains to a scene element $Q$ which is either an emitter or an occluder.

### 3.1 Definition by Cross-Section

Suppose $Q$ is a planar polygon having vertices $\mathbf{v}_i = (x_i, y_i, z_i)$ for $i = 1, \ldots, n$. Furthermore, assume $Q$ is situated strictly above the floor, so that each $z_i > 0$. We define a subset $M_Q$ of $\mathbb{R}^4$ in terms of its 2D cross-sections $\mathcal{P}_{(x,y)} \cap M_Q$, where for fixed $(a, b)$

$$\mathcal{P}_{(a,b)} = \{(a, b, z, w) : z, w \in \mathbb{R}\}$$

is an $(a, b)$-slice.

For each $(x, y)$ the cross-section is given by the polygon $\langle \mathcal{V}_1, \ldots, \mathcal{V}_n \rangle$ including its interior, where

$$\mathcal{V}_i = (x, y, \frac{x_i - x}{z_i}, \frac{y_i - y}{z_i}), \quad i = 1, \ldots, n. \qquad (3)$$

We observe that the last two components of $\mathcal{V}_i$ are the perspective transformation of $(x_i, y_i)$ with the origin moved to $(x, y)$.

For later use we define $Q^*$ as the polygon with vertices $((x_i - x)/z_i, (y_i - y)/z_i, 1)$ for $i = 1, \ldots, n$. Thus $Q^* = Q^*(x, y)$ is a perspective transformation of $Q$ including its interior to $z = 1$ with the origin moved to $(x, y)$.

### 3.2 The Geometric Structure of the Perspective Prism

Describing the cross-sections of $M_Q$ is sufficient to properly define the prism as a point set, but the slices give only a local characterization, and, for our purpose, we need a quantitative understanding of the boundary of all of $M_Q$.

Suppose $i$ is fixed. As $(x, y)$ varies, the $i$th vertex $\mathcal{V}_i = \mathcal{V}_i(x, y)$ can be interpreted as a 2-surface in $\mathbb{R}^4$ that is in fact a 2-plane.

Each apparent edge of $Q$ is a line segment that is a function of $(x, y)$, and can be parameterized by

$$\mathcal{E}_i(x, y, t) = (1 - t)\mathcal{V}_i(x, y) + t\mathcal{V}_{i+1}(x, y). \qquad (4)$$

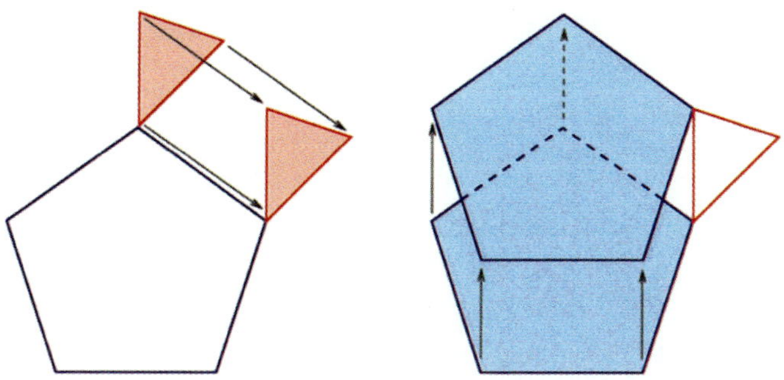

Figure 7: The product polyhedron $O \times E$ is formed by sweeping a copy of $E$ (the red triangle) across $O$ (the blue pentagon) or vice-versa. The boundary is thus formed by sweeping each object along each edge of the other, resulting in three-dimensional prisms. Occluder prism $j$ shares a rectangular "side" with emitter prism $i$.

Equation (4) is a parameterized 3-surface in $\mathbb{R}^4$ with $x, y \in \mathbb{R}$ and $t \in [0, 1]$. That is, each apparent edge of $Q$ "sweeps out" a 3-surface in $\mathbb{R}^4$. Each slice is a polygon, and the boundary of the polygon consists exactly of its edges, so the boundary of $M_Q$ is therefore the union of the sweep-surfaces of all the apparent edges. This shows that $M_Q$ is actually a four-dimensional *manifold with boundary* embedded in $\mathbb{R}^4$.

$M_Q$ has even simpler structure if $Q$ happens to be parallel to the floor. In this case, $z_i = h$ for each $i$, where $h$ is the height of $Q$ above the floor, and the vertex surface functions $\mathcal{V}_i$ becomes

$$\begin{bmatrix} x \\ y \\ \dfrac{x_i - x}{z_i} \\ \dfrac{y_i - y}{z_i} \end{bmatrix} = \frac{1}{h}\begin{bmatrix} 0 \\ 0 \\ x_i \\ y_i \end{bmatrix} + \begin{bmatrix} x \\ y \\ -\dfrac{x}{h} \\ -\dfrac{y}{h} \end{bmatrix}$$

Thus $M_Q$ can be viewed as $Q$ rotated so that it is parallel to the $zw$-plane, scaled by $1/h$, and swept along a 2-plane in $\mathbb{R}^4$. The edge surface functions, from (4)

$$\mathcal{E}_i(x, y, t) = \begin{bmatrix} x \\ y \\ \dfrac{x_i - x}{h} + t\dfrac{x_{i+1} - x_i}{h} \\ \dfrac{y_i - y}{h} + t\dfrac{y_{i+1} - y_i}{h} \end{bmatrix} \qquad (5)$$

with the domain of $t$ extended to all of $\mathbb{R}$, become proper hyperplanes (affine images of $\mathbb{R}^3$) in $\mathbb{R}^4$. Therefore the perspective prism $M_Q$ is a genuine, albeit unbounded, four-dimensional polyhedron.

# 4 THE OCCLUDER AND EMITTER PRISM

We now proceed to the situation where there is an occluding polygon in the scene. Suppose we have in $\mathbb{R}^3$ a uniformly emitting polygon $E = \langle e_1, \ldots, e_m \rangle$ and an occluding polygon $O = \langle o_1, \ldots, o_n \rangle$. We assume that $E$ lies strictly above the plane of $O$, and also that both $E$ and $O$ lie strictly above the floor.

## 4.1 Algebra of Perspective Prisms

To analyze partially occluded emitters we need a 4D object $M$ whose $(x, y)$ cross-sections stores the geometry of the *visible* portion of the emitter. At each floor point $(x, y)$ the *visible portion* of the apparent emitting polygon is simply $E^* - O^*$, where $E^*$ and

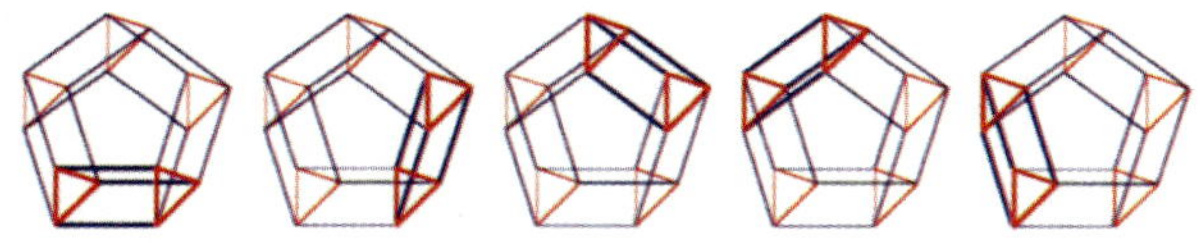

Figure 8: The five emitter-prism facets of $O \times E$. Adjacent emitter prisms share a common emitter face.

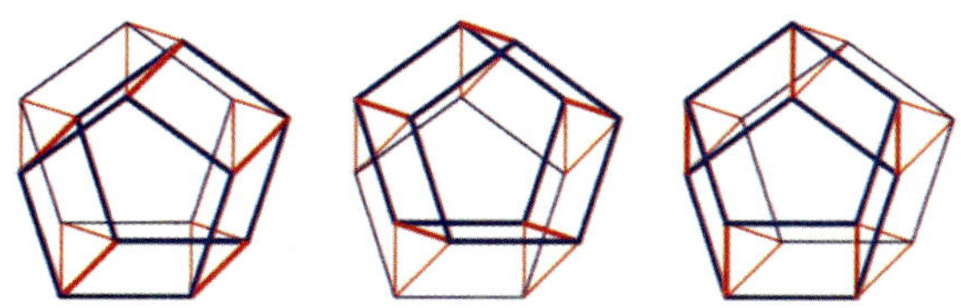

Figure 9: The three occluder-prism facets of $O \times E$. Adjacent occluder prisms share a common occluder face.

$O^*$ are $E$ and $O$ projectively transformed through $(x, y)$. From the definition of the perspective prism it follows immediately that

$$M = M_E - M_O.$$

Dealing with occlusion is now reduced to a tractable problem of performing booleans of the prisms.

## 4.2 The Structure of $O \times E$

If $E$ and $O$ are both parallel to the floor, then $M_O$ and $M_E$ are both four-dimensional "prism" polyhedra, and consequently their intersection is another polyhedron. It can be shown that the intersection of the two "prisms" is isomorphic to the product polyhedron $O \times E$, as in Flatland. In the more general case of non-parallel polygons the boundary structure is topologically equivalent to $O \times E$.

The product polyhedron $O \times E$ can be constructed by sweeping $E$, rotated to the $zw$-plane across all of $O$, or vice-versa. The boundary of $O \times E$ can be viewed as $E$ swept along each edge of $O$, and vice-versa, as suggested in Figure 7. (Of course, the object is really four-dimensional, so these figures are only a representation.) Sweeping $E$ along an edge of $O$ produces a prism in the shape of $E$, a three-dimensional polyhedron embedded in $\mathbb{R}^4$. Similarly, sweeping $O$ along an edge of $E$ produces an "occluder" prism. The boundary of $O \times E$ therefore consists of $n$ emitter prisms, and $m$ occluder prisms, each a three-dimensional polyhedron situated in $\mathbb{R}^4$. These prisms are the $n + m$ *facets* of $O \times E$.

Each emitter prism has two emitter *faces*, which are two-dimensional polygons situated in $\mathbb{R}^4$. Adjacent emitter prisms share a facet, and there is thus exactly one emitter face for each occluder vertex, and vice-versa. The rectangular *sides* of the prisms are also proper two-dimensional polygons situated in $\mathbb{R}^4$. Occluder prism $j$ shares exactly one side with emitter prism $i$, hence there are $m \times n$ sides. The $n$ emitter faces, the $m$ occluder faces, and the $m \times n$ sides together form the boundaries of the facets of $O \times E$.

## 5 IRRADIANCE

Our goal is to build a shadow function that produces exact irradiance everywhere. We review what the irradiance quantity is for a scene with polygonal occluders and emitters.

We recall that the irradiance from a uniformly emitting surface $S$, which is not self-occluding as viewed from a point $(x_0, y_0)$ on a receiver, can be computed [1] from the surface integral

$$I(x_0, y_0) = K \int_S \frac{\cos\theta_0 \cos\theta}{\|r(x,y)\|^2}\, dS, \tag{6}$$

where $r(x, y) = (x - x_0, y - y_0)$ is the ray from $(x_0, y_0)$ to a point $(x, y)$ on $S$, $\theta_0$ is the angle between the normal to the receiver at $(x_0, y_0)$ and $r(x, y)$, while $\theta$ is the angle between $r(x, y)$ and the normal to $S$ at $(x, y)$. The constant $K$ is a physical parameter of $S$. For simplicity we hereafter assume that $K = 1$.

When the emitting surface is a polygon, the integral in (6) can be shown to be equal to

$$I(x_0, y_0) = \int_{E^*} \frac{1}{(1 + x^2 + y^2)^2}\, dx\, dy \tag{7}$$

where $E^* = E^*(x_0, y_0)$ is the perspective transformation of $E$ onto the plane $z = 1$ with the origin moved to $(x_0, y_0)$. For each polygon $Q^*$ in the plane $z = 1$ we define the function

$$S_{Q^*} = \int_{Q^*} \frac{1}{(1 + x^2 + y^2)^2}\, dx\, dy. \tag{8}$$

In an unoccluded scene with a emitter $E$ the irradiance at a point $(x_0, y_0)$ on the receiver is simply $I(x_0, y_0) = S_{E^*}(x_0, y_0)$. In a scene which in addition has an occluder $O$ it follows from the algebra of perspective prisms that

$$I(x_0, y_0) = S_{E^* - O^*} = S_{E^*} - S_{E^* \cap O^*}. \tag{9}$$

This is another way of saying that the net irradiance at the point $(x_0, y_0)$ on the receiver is obtained by subtracting the occluded irradiance from the full unoccluded quantity.

## 6 GENERALIZED POLYHEDRAL SPLINES

In this section we develop some mathematical tools that are needed to describe shadows. Suppose $B$ is a bounded convex polyhedral body in $\mathbb{R}^n$ whose boundary $\partial B$ is a disjoint union of finitely many hyperplanes $F_i$ , and suppose $\omega = \omega(\mathbf{y}) = \omega(y_1, \ldots, y_n)$ is a function of $n$ variables which is continuous and integrable over $B$ . Given an integer $s \le n$ let $Q$ be the projection $\mathbb{R}^n \to \mathbb{R}^s$ given by $P(y_1, \ldots, y_n) = (y_1, \ldots, y_s)$. We define a generalized polyhedral spline $N_{B,\omega}(x)$ of $s$ variables such that for all sufficiently smooth functions $\phi$ of $s$ variables with local support

$$\int_{\mathbb{R}^s} N_{B,\omega}(\mathbf{x})\phi(\mathbf{x})d\mathbf{x} = \int_B \omega(\mathbf{y})\phi(P\mathbf{y})d\mathbf{y}. \tag{10}$$

Note that (10) defines $N_{B,\omega}$ as a distribution which we assume can be defined as a continuous function. If $n = s$ we then have

$$N_{B,\omega}(\mathbf{x}) = \chi_B(\mathbf{x})\omega(\mathbf{x}), \tag{11}$$

where $\chi_B(\mathbf{x}) = 1$ if $\mathbf{x} \in B$ and 0 otherwise.

If $\omega = 1$ the function $N_{B,\omega}$ is the multivariate polyhedral spline [4, 32]. We will use more general densities $\omega$ for the definition of our shadow irradiance functions.

By writing the right-hand side of (10) as an iterated integral we obtain a common geometric interpretation of $N_{B,\omega}$

$$N_{B,\omega}(\mathbf{x}) = \int_{\mathbb{R}^{n-s}} \chi_B(\mathbf{x}, \mathbf{z})\, \omega(\mathbf{x}, \mathbf{z})\, d\mathbf{z}. \tag{12}$$

In this interpretation the value of the spline at a point $\mathbf{x} \in \mathbb{R}^s$ is obtained by integrating the density function $\omega$ over a $n - s$-dimensional cross-section of $B$ located at $\mathbf{x}$. This cross-section is the intersection of $B$ and an $\mathbf{x}$-slice in $\mathbb{R}^n$.

To make the above formula tractable for evaluation we apply Stokes' theorem to (10) and obtain

$$N_{B,\omega}(\mathbf{x}) = \sum_i \operatorname{sgn}(v_i) N_{P^n_{n-1}(F_i), \Omega \circ \Phi_i}(\mathbf{x}). \tag{13}$$

Here $F_i$ is facet $i$ of $B$, having outward normal $\mathbf{n}_i$, $v_i$ is the $n$th component of $\mathbf{n}_i$, $\operatorname{sgn}(t)$ is equal to 1,0,-1 if $t > 0, t = 0, t < 0$, respectively, $\Omega$ is an anti-derivative of $\omega$ with respect to the last variable, $P^n_{n-1}(F_i)$ is the canonical projection of $F_i$ to $\mathbb{R}^{n-1}$, and $\Phi_i$ is a function of $n - 1$ variables describing $F_i$ in the form $\Phi_i(y_1, \ldots, y_{n-1}) = (y_1, \ldots, y_{n-1}, y_n)$, where $y_n$ is an equation for the hyperplane $F_i$ in terms of $y_1, \ldots, y_{n-1}$. The sgn function handles a reversal of the orientation of facet $F_i$ in the projection to the lower space.

We note that the functions on the right of (13) are splines of $s$ variables defined using objects in $\mathbb{R}^{n-1}$. We can apply this formula recursively to reduce $n$. The recurrence stops when $n$ reaches $s$, in which case the spline is given by (11).

The unweighted polyhedral spline recurrence ($\omega = 1$) developed by de Boor and Höllig [4], as well as the polynomially weighted recurrence of McCool [32] both are derived following an identity of Hakopian. Ours takes a different approach, based directly on Stokes' theorem. The main use for our formula is to derive the explicit shadow irradiance function in the next section.

### 6.1 Extension to Non-Polyhedral Objects

The recurrence (13) can be extended beyond proper polyhedra, to certain general manifolds having the same general structure as polyhedra, inasmuch as their boundaries consist of facet-like manifolds, each of one lower dimension. As we shall see, the general occluded polygonal irradiance problem leads to manifolds of this form. The primary difficulty of this extension is that the "facets" may not be expressible as explicit surfaces of their projections, and when they are, they are no longer the simple affine hyperplane functions as in the polyhedron case. Problems such as this can sometimes be circumvented by partitioning the boundary facets into disjoint pieces; however, in the object we are about to develop, it happens that we can effectively ignore this potential problem.

### 6.2 The Irradiance Function

In Section 5 we gave an explicit formula for the irradiance functions based on the geometry of prisms in $\mathbb{R}^4$. In this section we have developed the appropriate spline theory to construct the irradiance functions. The remaining task is to combine the two approaches to show that the irradiance function is, in fact, a spline. First consider a scene with an unoccluded emitter. The irradiance at a point $(x_0, y_0)$ on the receiver is given in (7), which we write in the form

$$I(x_0, y_0) = \int_{E^*} \omega(x_0, y_0, z, w) dz\, dw,$$

with

$$\omega(x_0, y_0, z, w) = \frac{1}{(1 + z^2 + w^2)^2}. \tag{14}$$

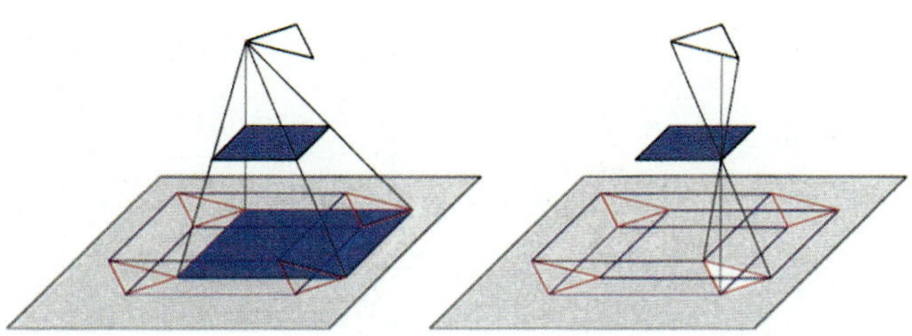

Figure 10: The shadow discontinuity lines consist of $E$ projected through each point of $O$, and vice-versa.

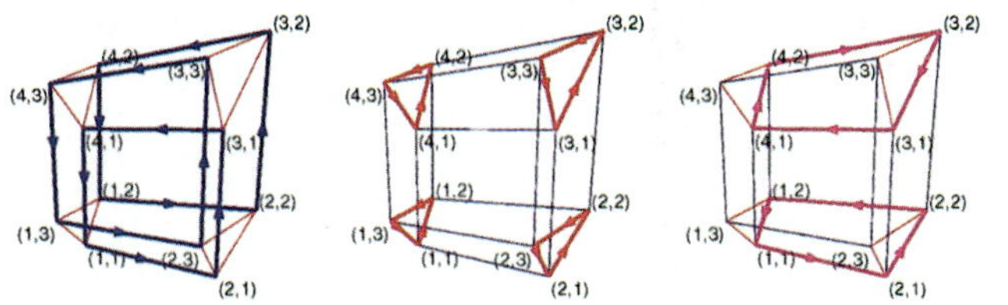


(a) (b) (c)

Figure 11: The floor shadow structure for a non-parallel configuration. Here $n = 4$ and $m = 3$. (a) The three occluder images; each has a counter-clockwise orientation. (b) The four emitter images; each has a counter-clockwise orientation. (c) Two of the side images: $S_{1,1}$ has a negative (clockwise) orientation, $S_{3,1}$ is positively oriented.

Since $E^*$ is essentially the cross-section of the prism $M_E$ at $(x_0, y_0)$ we obtain

$$I(x_0, y_0) = \int_{\mathbb{R}^2} \chi_{M_E}(x_0, y_0, z, w)\omega(x_0, y_0, z, w)\, dz\, dw.$$

Hence from (12) with $n = 4$, $s = 2$ we obtain

$$I(x_0, y_0) = N_{M_E,\omega}(x_0, y_0), \tag{15}$$

and we have demonstrated that the irradiance function is a spline. This agrees with the fact that a shadow is a piecewise smooth function with jumps in derivatives across the discontinuity lines, and the nature of spline functions. The above derivation holds equally well in the more general situation including multiple elements. For example in the situation described in (9) we have

$$I(x_0, y_0) = N_{M_E - M_O,\omega}(x_0, y_0). \tag{16}$$

## 7 THE SHADOW EQUATION

Using the recurrence relation (13) we can actually give a closed-form expression for the irradiance function corresponding to a scene with a single planar polygonal emitter and a planar polygonal occluder, in terms of the space coordinates of the vertices

$$\begin{aligned} O &= \langle (x_1, y_1, z_1), \ldots, (x_n, y_n, z_n) \rangle \\ E &= \left\langle (x'_1, y'_1, z'_1), \ldots, (x'_m, y'_m, z'_m) \right\rangle. \end{aligned}$$

We assume $O$ and $E$ are convex, and $O$ lies strictly above the floor, and the plane of $O$ lies strictly below $E$. We define the direction of the normal $\mathbf{n}_E$ of $E$ to be opposite the direction of emittance. (This is the opposite of the usual convention, but we need the emitter projections onto the plane to have counter-clockwise orientation.) The region on the plane in which the emitting side of $E$ is visible is the set

$$R_E \equiv \left\{ (x, y) \in \mathbb{R}^2 : (x, y, 0) \cdot (\mathbf{n}_E - (x_1, y_1, z_1)) > 0 \right\} \tag{17}$$

The formula presented in this section is valid on the planar region $R_O \cap R_E$.

The shadow equation is expressed in terms of the characteristic functions of the projected 2D boundary faces of $O \times E$. To define these polygons, first define the *shadow nodes*

$$\mathbf{v}_{ij} \equiv \left( \frac{z'_j x_i - z_i x'_j}{z'_j - z_i}, \frac{z'_j y_i - z_i y'_j}{z'_j - z_i} \right). \tag{18}$$

Geometrically, $\mathbf{v}_{i,j}$ is the point on the floor where $\mathbf{o}_i$ and $\mathbf{e}_j$ appear to coincide. The shadow polygons consist of $m$ occluder images $O_j$, $n$ emitter images $E_i$, and $mn$ quadrilaterals $S_{ij}$, as shown in Figures 10 and 11. In terms of the shadow nodes,

$$\begin{aligned} E_i &= \langle \mathbf{v}_{i,1}, \ldots, \mathbf{v}_{i,m} \rangle \\ O_j &= \langle \mathbf{v}_{1,j}, \ldots, \mathbf{v}_{n,j} \rangle \\ S_{ij} &= \langle \mathbf{v}_{i,j}, \mathbf{v}_{i+1,j}, \mathbf{v}_{i+1,j+1}, \mathbf{v}_{i,j+1} \rangle, \end{aligned}$$

The $z$ and $w$ coordinates of the vertices of the $(x, y)$-slices of the objects give the apparent geometry from $(x, y)$. Define (cf. Section 3.1.)

$$p_i(x, y) = (p_{i,1}, p_{i,2}) = \left( \frac{x_i - x}{z_i}, \frac{y_i - y}{z_i} \right) \tag{19}$$

$$p'_j(x, y) = (p'_{j,1}, p'_{j,2}) = \left( \frac{x'_j - x}{z'_j}, \frac{y'_j - y}{z'_j} \right). \tag{20}$$

It is convenient to introduce

$$\begin{aligned} e_i(x, y) &= (e_{i,1}, e_{i,2}) = p_{i+1}(x, y) - p_i(x, y) \\ e'_j(x, y) &= (e'_{j,1}, e'_{j,2}) = p'_{j+1}(x, y) - p'_j(x, y). \end{aligned}$$

For the evaluation of the spline, the function defining the $i$th facet must be written in the form $w_i(x, y, z) = m_i(x, y)z + b_i(x, y)$, where for $O$,

$$\begin{aligned} m_i(x, y) &= \frac{e_{i,2}}{e_{i,1}} \\ b_i(x, y) &= p_{i,2} - \frac{e_{i,2}}{e_{i,1}} p_{i,1}, \end{aligned}$$

and for $E$,

$$\begin{aligned} m'_j(x, y) &= \frac{e'_{j,2}}{e'_{j,1}} \\ b'_j(x, y) &= p_{j,2} - \frac{e'_{j,2}}{e'_{j,1}} p_{j,1}. \end{aligned}$$

The second iteration of (13) requires the equations for the boundary of the facets of $M_O$ which are the 2-surfaces traced out by the vertices of $O^*$ and $E^*$ in $M_O$ and $M_E$. These are essentially given by (3). There are also the extra boundary 2-surfaces traced by the intersection of edges $i$ of $O^*$ and $j$ of $E^*$, which can be computed from

$$\psi_{ij}(x, y) = \frac{e_{i,1}e'_{j,2}p_{j,1} - e'_{j,1}(e_{i,2}p_{i,1} + e_{i,1}(p_{j,2} - p_{i,2}))}{e_{i,1}e'_{j,2} - e_{i,2}e'_{j,1}} \tag{21}$$

Finally, we need the twice-integrated density function

$$F(z, u, v) = \frac{v \arctan\left(\frac{uv + z + u^2 z}{\sqrt{1+u^2+v^2}}\right)}{2\sqrt{1 + u^2 + v^2}} + \frac{z \arctan\left(\frac{v + uz}{\sqrt{1+z^2}}\right)}{2\sqrt{1 + z^2}} \tag{22}$$

The irradiance on the plane $z = 0$ is then

$$I(x, y) = N_{M_E,\omega}(x, y) - N_{M_O \cap M_E,\omega}(x, y)$$

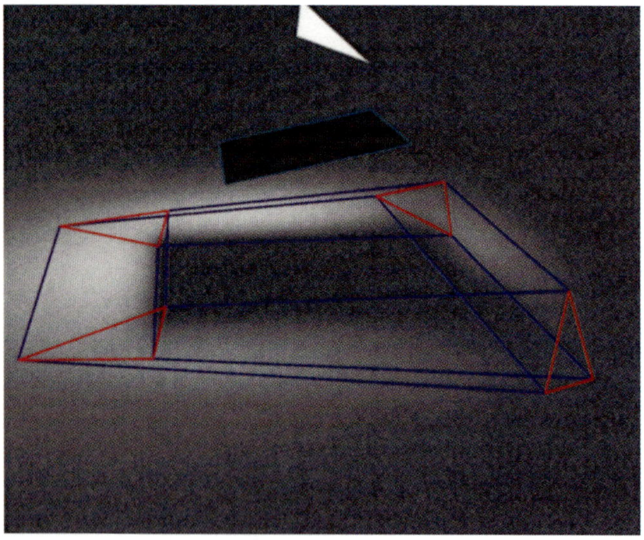

Figure 12: A non-parallel emitter/occluder configuration, showing the irradiance with discontinuity lines. Both $E$ and $O$ are outlined for clarity.

where $\omega$ is given by (14). Applying (13) twice it can be shown that

$$\begin{aligned} N_{M_O \cap M_E,\omega}(x,y) = \\ & \sum_{j=1}^{m} \chi_{\hat{O}_j}(x,y)\left[F(p'_{j,1},m'_j,b'_j) - F(p'_{j,1},m'_{j-1},b'_{j-1})\right] \\ + & \sum_{i=1}^{n} \chi_{\hat{E}_i}(x,y)\left[F(p_{i,1},m_i,b_i) - F(p_{i,1},m_{i-1},b_{i-1})\right] \\ + & \sum_{i=1}^{n}\sum_{j=1}^{m} o(S_{ij})\chi_{\hat{S}_{ij}}(x,y)\left[F(\psi_{ij},m_i,b_i) - F(\psi_{ij},m'_j,b'_j)\right] \end{aligned} \tag{23}$$

Here $\hat{Q}$ is the polygon $Q$ excluding edges whose oriented angle with the $x$-axis is greater than zero, and less than $\pi$. The $o(Q)$ function is the orientation of the polygon $Q$: $o(Q)$ is 1 if the vertices are in counter-clockwise order, and $-1$ otherwise.

Inspection of the equation for $N_{M_O \cap M_E,\omega}(x,y)$ reveals the first summation is in fact the unoccluded irradiance, hence the irradiance can be expressed directly in the following shadow equation.

$$\begin{aligned} I(x,y) = \\ & \sum_{j=1}^{m} \left[1 - \chi_{\hat{O}_j}(x,y)\right]\left[F(p'_{j,1},m'_j,b'_j) - F(p'_{j,1},m'_{j-1},b'_{j-1})\right] \\ - & \sum_{i=1}^{n} \chi_{\hat{E}_i}(x,y)\left[F(p_{i,1},m_i,b_i) - F(p_{i,1},m_{i-1},b_{i-1})\right] \\ - & \sum_{i=1}^{n}\sum_{j=1}^{m} o(S_{ij})\chi_{\hat{S}_{ij}}(x,y)\left[F(\psi_{ij},m_i,b_i) - F(\psi_{ij},m'_j,b'_j)\right]. \end{aligned} \tag{24}$$

The shadow spline function $I(x,y)$ is therefore a collection of smooth functions supported on the shadow polygons $O_j$, $E_i$ and $S_{i,j}$.

Images demonstrating the formula are shown in Figures 12, 13.

Figure 13: A typical difficult case, where the $O$ (nearly) touches the floor. The direct shadow formula fails if the objects actually touch, but they may come arbitrarily close. Here the occluder has been lifted slightly, to reveal the $C^0$ discontinuity along the line of contact.

These images were rendered using ray tracing, with the irradiance on the surfaces calculated directly using the shadow equation.

The formula extends to multiple occluders as long as their shadows do not interact. The facets of a convex polyhedral occluder meet this, and the requirements of the shadow equation (if the normals point inward), so the formula can be extended to convex polyhedral emitters and occluders, as demonstrated in Figures 14 and 15.

## 8 FUTURE WORK AND CONCLUSION

The general formulation presented in this paper is rich in possibilities worthy of deeper investigation. As a first step, we hope to generalize the non-interfering occluder formula to take into account multiple objects and their interactions with each other. Beyond this, we are encouraged by the possibility of producing an analytic formula for objects more general than polygons, and receivers more general than portions of a plane. Furthermore, the ideas generalize to non-uniform emittance and arbitrary BRDFs.

### 8.1 Conclusion

In this paper we analyze the essential mathematical structure of shadows on a surface and show that the natural place to understand them is in a higher dimensional space. We show that the general problem of calculating the irradiance function for the shadow cast by a single polygonal occluder $O$ from a polygonal emitter $E$ in general position leads to a weighted (generalized) polyhedral spline function, and that the Cartesian product $O \times E$ provides the structure necessary to compute the shadow. To compute the irradiance for non-parallel configurations of $E$ and $O$, ordinary polyhedral splines must be generalized. The resulting splines are built on objects which are deformations of polyhedra in higher dimensions, instead of the usual flat-faced structures.

Figure 14: The shadow of a regular dodecahedron cast by a triangular emitter. The irradiance is computed by subtracting the value of (23) for each face from the unoccluded irradiance; this works for convex polyhedra, because the edges do not interact under the emitter.

Figure 15: The shadow of a dodecahedron cast by three symmetrically placed emitters colored red, green, and blue. The total irradiance is the sum of the contributions from each emitter.

Using Stokes' theorem to reduce the Euclidean dimension of the integration problem, we arrive at a closed-form formula for evaluating the irradiance function, not just the partial visibility quantity, as an exact analytical expression. The wire frame structure of the 4D object by itself produces the shadow discontinuity lines when projected to the floor. That is, the projection method naturally specializes to the produce the discontinuity graph described by Nishita and Nakamae [33]. When $E$, $O$, and the floor are all parallel and a constant weighting function is specified, the spline specializes to an $O \times E$ (prism) polyhedral spline that yields the convolution presented by Soler and Sillion in their shadow algorithm [38]. Although it is a common simplifying approximation to factor out visibility from the irradiance integral, there is no penalty in our method for doing it exactly.

Although exact shadows may not be necessary in many situations, they are important because their structure gives fundamental understanding. Knowing their exact behavior also provides a way to compute the error in approximate methods. And finally, the direct evaluation of the explicit formula is fast enough to compete with approximate algorithms.

A benefit of studying shadows in the higher dimensional context with the constructions provided is that the approach generalizes beyond the solution for a single emitter and occluder in arbitrary configuration. This approach also generalizes theoretically in a straightforward manner to more complicated situations involving curved and multiple emitter and occluder elements, at the expense of complicating the geometry. To carry forward this approach for curved and nonuniform elements we must again use generalized polyhedral splines.

Computing irradiance quantities for shadow functions is equivalent to computing the differential area to polygon form factor in the presence of an occluder. Although we do not take the space to develop the details, one can see that this approach may be used in radiosity. There is also a connection between the 4D emitter or occluder prisms and some image based rendering algorithms.

Considering shadow irradiance functions as higher dimension generalized polyhedral splines has lead to several advances in understanding and computation. Although somewhat abstract, the approach described herein, which appears to be quite general and powerful, seems rather promising as a basis from which to do further work in this area and related problems.

## Acknowledgments

This work was supported in part by DARPA (F33615-96-C-5621) and the NSF Science and Technology Center for Computer Graphics and Scientific Visualization (ASC-89-20219). The authors wish to thank John Hughes, Brian Smits, and Peter Shirley for reading earlier drafts of this paper, and the reviewers for their comments.

## References

[1] James Arvo. The irradiance Jacobian for Partially Occluded Polyhedral Sources. In Andrew Glassner, editor, *SIGGRAPH 94 Conference Proceedings*, Annual Conference Series, pages 343–350. ACM SIGGRAPH, ACM Press, July 1994. ISBN 0-89791-667-0.

[2] James Arvo. *Analytic Methods for Simultated Light Transport*. PhD thesis, Yale University, 1995.

[3] Daniel R. Baum, Holly E. Rushmeier, and James M. Winget. Improving Radiosity Solutions Through the Use of Analytically Determined Form-Factors. In Jeffrey Lane, editor, *Computer Graphics (SIGGRAPH 89 Conference Proceedings)*, volume 23, pages 325–334, July 1989. ISBN 0-89791-746-4.

[4] C. de Boor and K. Höllig. Recurrence Relations for Multivariate B-Splines. *Proc. Amer. Math. Soc.*, pages 397–400, 1982.

[5] C. de Boor, K. Höllig, and S. Riemenschneider. *Box Splines*. Springer-Verlag, 1993.

[6] Arne Brøndsted. *An Introduction to Convex Polytopes*. Springer-Verlag, New York, 1983.

[7] A. T. Campbell, III and Donald S. Fussell. Adaptive Mesh Generation for Global Diffuse Illumination. In Forest Baskett, editor, *Computer Graphics (SIGGRAPH 90 Conference Proceedings)*, volume 24, pages 155–164, August 1990. ISBN 0-89791-344-2.

[8] Elaine Cohen, Tom Lyche, and Richard Riesenfeld. Discrete Box Splines and Refinement Algorithms. *Computer Aided Geometric Design*, 1(2):131–148, 1984.

[9] Michael F. Cohen and Donald P. Greenberg. The Hemi-Cube: A Radiosity Solution for Complex Environments. In B. A. Barsky, editor, *Computer Graphics (SIGGRAPH 85 Conference Proceedings)*, volume 19, pages 31–40, August 1985.

[10] Michael F. Cohen and John R. Wallace. *Radiosity and Realistic Image Synthesis*. Academic Press Professional, San Diego, CA, 1993.

[11] Robert L. Cook, Thomas Porter, and Loren Carpenter. Distributed Ray Tracing. In Hank Christiansen, editor, *Computer Graphics (SIGGRAPH 84 Conference Proceedings)*, volume 18, pages 137–45, July 1984.

[12] H. S. M. Coxeter. *Regular Complex Polytopes, Second Edition*. Cambridge University Press, New York, 1991.

[13] Franklin C. Crow. Summed-area Tables for Texture Mapping. In Hank Christiansen, editor, *Computer Graphics (SIGGRAPH 84 Conference Proceedings)*, volume 18, pages 207–212, July 1984.

[14] H. B. Curry and I. J. Schoenberg. On Pólya frequency functions IV: the fundamental spline functions and their limits. *J. Analyse Math.*, 17:71–107, 1966.

[15] M. Dæhlen and T. Lyche. Box Splines and Applications. *Geometric Modelling, Methods and Applications*, pages 35–93, 1991.

[16] W. Dahmen and C. A. Micchelli. Recent Progress in Multivariate Splines. In C. Chui, L. Schumaker, and J. Ward, editors, *Approximation Theory IV*, pages 27–121. Academic Press, New York, 1983.

[17] George Drettakis. *Structured Sampling and Reconstruction of Illumination for Image Synthesis*. PhD thesis, University of Toronto, 1994.

[18] George Drettakis and Eugene Fiume. A Fast Shadow Algorithm for Area Light Sources Using Backprojection. In Andrew Glassner, editor, *SIGGRAPH 94 Conference Proceedings*, Annual Conference Series, pages 223–230. ACM SIGGRAPH, ACM Press, July 1994. ISBN 0-89791-667-0.

[19] P. Fong and Hans-Peter Seidel. Modeling with multivariate B-spline surfaces over arbitrary triangulations. In M. Silbermann and H. Tagare, editors, *Curves and Surfaces in Computer Vision and Graphics II*, pages 97–108. SPIE, 1992.

[20] Philip Fong and Hans-Peter Seidel. An implementation of multivariate B-spline surfaces over arbitrary triangulations. In *Proceedings of Graphics Interface '92*, pages 1–10, May 1992.

[21] Cindy M. Goral, Kenneth E. Torrance, Donald P. Greenberg, and Bennett Battaile. Modelling the Interaction of Light Between Diffuse Surfaces. In Hank Christiansen, editor, *Computer Graphics (SIGGRAPH 84 Conference Proceedings)*, volume 18, pages 212–22, July 1984.

[22] Steven J. Gortler, Peter Schroder, Michael F. Cohen, and Pat Hanrahan. Wavelet Radiosity. In *Computer Graphics Proceedings, Annual Conference Series, 1993*, pages 221–230, 1993.

[23] Branko Grünbaum. *Convex Polytopes*. John Wiley & Sons, 1967.

[24] Pat Hanrahan, David Salzman, and Larry Aupperle. A Rapid Hierarchical Radiosity Algorithm. In Thomas W. Sederberg, editor, *Computer Graphics (SIGGRAPH 91 Conference Proceedings)*, volume 25, pages 197–206, July 1991. ISBN 0-89791-436-8.

[25] Paul Heckbert. Discontinuity Meshing for Radiosity. *Third Eurographics Workshop on Rendering*, pages 203–226, May 1992.

[26] Paul Heckbert. Radiosity in Flatland. *Computer Graphics Forum (Eurographics '92)*, 11(3):181–192, September 1992.

[27] G. Heflin and G. Elber. Shadow Volume Generation from Free Form Surfaces. In *Communicating with Virtual Worlds, Proceedings of CGI'93 (Lausanne, Switzerland)*, pages 115–126. Springer-Verlag, June 1993.

[28] J. R. Howell. *A Catalog of Radiation Configuration Factors*. McGraw Hill, 1982.

[29] Marc Levoy and Pat Hanrahan. Light Field Rendering. In Holly Rushmeier, editor, *SIGGRAPH 96 Conference Proceedings*, Annual Conference Series, pages 31–42. ACM SIGGRAPH, Addison Wesley, August 1996. ISBN 0-89791-746-4.

[30] Daniel Lischinski, Filippo Tampieri, and Donald P. Greenberg. Discontinuity Meshing for Accurate Radiosity. *IEEE Computer Graphics and Applications*, 12(6):25–39, November 1992.

[31] Michael D. McCool. Analytic Antialiasing With Prism Splines. In Robert Cook, editor, *SIGGRAPH 95 Conference Proceedings*, Annual Conference Series, pages 429–436. ACM SIGGRAPH, Addison Wesley, August 1995. ISBN 0-89791-701-4.

[32] Michael D. McCool. *Analytic Signal Processing for Computer Graphics using Multivariate Polyhedral Splines*. PhD thesis, University of Toronto, 1995.

[33] Tomoyuki Nishita and Eihachiro Nakamae. Continuous Tone Representation of Three-Dimensional Objects Taking Account of Shadows and Interreflection. In B. A. Barsky, editor, *Computer Graphics (SIGGRAPH 85 Conference Proceedings)*, volume 19, pages 23–30, July 1985.

[34] William T. Reeves, David H. Salesin, and Robert L. Cook. Rendering Antialiased Shadows with Depth Maps. In Maureen C. Stone, editor, *Computer Graphics (SIGGRAPH 87 Conference Proceedings)*, volume 21, pages 283–291, July 1987. ISBN 0-89791-227-6.

[35] Peter Schröder and Pat Hanrahan. On the Form Factor Between Two Polygons. In James T. Kajiya, editor, *SIGGRAPH 93 Conference Proceedings*, Annual Conference Series, pages 163–164, 1993. ISBN 0-89791-601-8.

[36] Peter Shirley, Chang Yaw Wang, and Kurt Zimmerman. Monte Carlo Techniques for Direct Lighting Calculations. *ACM Transactions on Graphics*, 15(1):1–36, January 1996. ISSN 0730-0301.

[37] François Sillion and Claude Puech. *Radiosity and Global Illumination*. Morgan Kaufmann, San Francisco, 1994.

[38] Cyril Soler and François X. Sillion. Fast Calculation of Soft Shadow Textures Using Convolution. In Michael Cohen, editor, *SIGGRAPH 98 Conference Proceedings*, Annual Conference Series, pages 321–332. ACM SIGGRAPH, Addison Wesley, July 1998. ISBN 0-89791-999-8.

[39] Seth J. Teller. Computing the Antipenumbra of an Area Light Source. UCB/CSD 91 6, Computer Science Division, University of California, Berkeley, 1991.

[40] John R. Wallace, Kells A. Elmquist, and Eric A. Haines. A Ray Tracing Algorithm for Progressive Radiosity. In Jeffrey Lane, editor, *Computer Graphics (SIGGRAPH 89 Conference Proceedings)*, volume 23, pages 315–324, July 1989.

[41] Gregory J. Ward and Paul Heckbert. Irradiance Gradients. *Third Eurographics Workshop on Rendering*, pages 85–98, May 1992.

[42] Turner Whitted. An Improved Illumination Model for Shaded Display. *Communications of the ACM*, 23(6):343–349, July 1980.

[43] Lance Williams. Casting Curved Shadows on Curved Surfaces. In *Computer Graphics (SIGGRAPH 78 Conference Proceedings)*, volume 12, pages 270–274, Aug 1978.

[44] Andrew Woo, Pierre Poulin, and Alain Fournier. A Survey of Shadow Algorithms. *IEEE Computer Graphics and Applications*, 10(6):13–32, November 1990.

# Reflection Space Image Based Rendering

Brian Cabral, Marc Olano, Philip Nemec*
SGI

## Abstract

High quality, physically accurate rendering at interactive rates has widespread application, but is a daunting task. We attempt to bridge the gap between high-quality offline and interactive rendering by using existing environment mapping hardware in combination with a novel Image Based Rendering (IBR) algorithm. The primary contribution lies in performing IBR in reflection space. This method can be applied to ordinary environment maps, but for more physically accurate rendering, we apply reflection space IBR to radiance environment maps. A radiance environment map pre-integrates a Bidirectional Reflection Distribution Function (BRDF) with a lighting environment. Using the reflection-space IBR algorithm on radiance environment maps allows interactive rendering of arbitrary objects with a large class of complex BRDFs in arbitrary lighting environments. The ultimate simplicity of the final algorithm suggests that it will be widely and immediately valuable given the ready availability of hardware assisted environment mapping.

**CR categories and subject descriptors:** I.3.3 [Computer Graphics]: Picture/Image generation; I.3.7 [Image Processing]: Enhancement.

**Keywords:** interactive rendering and shading, texture mapping, reflection mapping, image based rendering.

## 1 INTRODUCTION

Offline rendering algorithms have to a great extent conquered physically accurate photo-realism and complex synthetic shading. A result of over twenty years of research [1, 4, 5, 12, 15, 19, 21, 23], these techniques all solve the lighting or rendering equation [16] in some manner. The outstanding rendering challenge now becomes how to increase the performance of sophisticated shading algorithms without losing the advancements made in quality. Specifically, we are interested in interactive algorithms that change the nature and work-flow of artists, designers and scientists.

This implies that many orders of magnitude in performance improvements must be found. Traditionally, this has been accomplished by vastly simplifying the approximations used in the shading and lighting equations – resulting in a significant loss in complexity and quality. We take a modest, intermediate step toward interactive photo-realistic rendering – an algorithm that uses IBR techniques to approximate the integral lighting equation.

*e-mail: {cabral,olano,nemec}@sgi.com



Environment mapping is one method used to improve the realism of interactive rendering. As originally described by Newell and Blinn [1], a simple environment map is used to quickly find reflections of distant objects from a perfectly mirrored surface. Other researchers refined this notion by generalizing the BRDF used [3, 11, 19, 21], though some of these refinements lost the interactivity of simple environment mapping.

Another method used to bridge the gap between realism and interactivity is image based rendering [18]. IBR avoids solving the lighting equation during interactive rendering by warping existing photographs or images. These images can be thought of as radiance maps [8], and generalized to light fields [17] and lumigraphs [10]. This works well for predefined scenes or images, but not for dynamically changing synthetic objects.

Recently Debevec [5] combined captured environment maps and synthetic objects to produce compelling renderings with both synthetic objects and image based environments. His techniques do not work at interactive rates since he computes the lighting equation integration as he renders using RADIANCE [25].

We build upon the work of Debevec by pre-integrating the lighting equation to allow interactive rendering – in part by constraining the geometry of the global radiance environment maps. This introduces a view-dependence in the generated maps, which we overcome with a new form of IBR in reflection space. The result is interactive rendering of synthetic objects using a wide range of BRDFs in arbitrary lighting environments.

There are two primary contributions in this paper. The first is the application of IBR techniques in reflection space. We call this method reflection space IBR – even though we are not operating on normal images, nor is the result a rendered image. Second is our hybrid rendering algorithm. While we use IBR techniques, our algorithm and the nature of environment maps allows us to to use new BRDFs and new geometry not found in the original source images – thus extending the class of renderings possible with interactive IBR algorithms.

## 2 RADIANCE ENVIRONMENT MAPS

A traditional environment map records the incident radiance, $L_i$, from each direction. The two most common representations are the sphere map and cube map. A sphere map is a view-dependent representation, equivalent to an orthographic view of a reflective sphere. Note that it is not necessary to render an orthographic view when using a sphere map, for example the sphere mapping in OpenGL 1.2 includes the appropriate correction for perspective views. A cube map is a view-independent representation, created by projecting the environment onto the faces of a cube. Other representations are also possible, for example the parabolic map used by Heidrich and Seidel [13].

Instead of recording incoming radiance, a radiance environment map records the total reflected radiance, $L_r$, for each possible surface orientation. It is defined by the classic lighting equa-

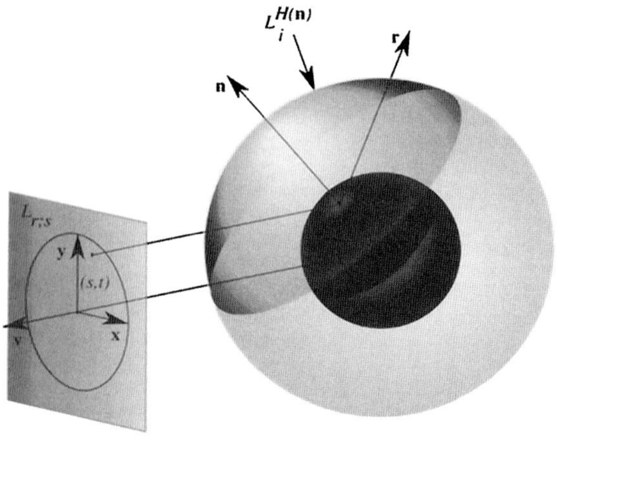


Figure 1: A radiance environment sphere map, $L_{r;s}$, is defined on the image plane shown on the left. Each point $(s,t)$ in $L_{r;s}$ is associated with a normal, $\mathbf{n}$, and a reflection vector, $\mathbf{r}$. The normal specifies the hemisphere, $H(\mathbf{n})$ over which $L_i^{H(\mathbf{n})}$ is defined.

tion [14]:

$$L_r(\theta_r,\phi_r) = \int_H f_r(\theta_i,\phi_i;\theta_r,\phi_r)L_i(\theta_i,\phi_i)\cos\theta_i d\omega_i$$

Thus, $L_r$ is the environment ($L_i$) modulated by the BRDF ($f_r$). $H$ is the hemisphere above the surface, which varies with surface orientation (see figure 1). Each texel in a radiance environment map captures the pre-integrated value for $L_r$ for one possible orientation of $H$. Since the radiance environment map is indexed by orientation, we can choose any of the storage representations used for traditional environment mapping. Figure 1 shows a sphere map representation. Heidrich and Seidel [13] use a similar technique of pre-integrating a BRDF and environment.

The pre-integrated radiance environment map introduces a couple of restrictions for rendering. Since all surface points that have a common normal use the same reflected radiance, only the lighting contribution from a distant environment can be captured, not reflections of local objects or inter-reflections of a single surface. Also, we are restricted to isotropic BRDFs; with only a single reflected radiance stored in the map per surface normal there is no way to record BRDF variation with rotation around the normal.

We also introduce an approximation to the true lighting equation. A radiance environment map is computed with a single view direction, so it is incorrect to use it with a perspective view, where the view direction changes from pixel to pixel. While graphics hardware corrects for perspective-induced changes in mirror reflection direction, this correction is not always appropriate for the radiance environment map. We render perspective views anyway and accept the (usually minor) resulting errors as part of the price for interactivity.

## Obtaining Radiance Environment Maps

One method to obtain radiance environment maps is to take photographs in the desired environment of a physical sphere whose surface BRDF matches that of the target object. The photographs should be taken with a narrow field of view lens to approximate an orthographic projection and to minimize the reflection of the camera. The resulting images are the radiance environment maps, with the integration done by nature. Our algorithm requires several radiance environment maps, so we require several such images along with the camera orientation for each.

A second method is to compute the lighting integral numerically given a desired BRDF and lighting environment. The lighting environment should be known with high dynamic range for good integration results. Such environments can be captured through photographs by the methods of Debevec [6], or rendered with a package like RADIANCE [25]. We have used six photographs or images to represent $L_i$, arranged as a cube environment map [24]. Since the BRDF and the environment map, $L_i$, are decoupled the lighting environment can be reused to compute $L_r$ for many different surface types. Results using maps computed in this way are shown in figure 3.

## 3 REFLECTION SPACE IBR

With conventional IBR, the light field is sampled by a discrete set of images. For our algorithm, these samples are a set of radiance environment maps taken from different viewpoints. These maps must be warped to match a new point of view, then blended together.

In addition to matching the viewpoint, the warping correlates features on the different maps. For traditional IBR, the image correlation may require only an affine or projective warp [22]. For general light fields it can require gathering light rays in a variety of discontinuous patterns [17].

Since each point in a radiance environment map is an integration of the environment and BRDF, the warp that best correlates features in the environment can vary from BRDF to BRDF. By choosing a warp that models the BRDF well, we can significantly reduce the number of radiance environment maps required for good reconstruction. If the BRDF is a perfect mirror and the warp models it as a perfect mirror, we need only sample well enough to catch the highest frequencies in the environment. If the warp does not match the BRDF, we must sample well enough for the product of the highest frequencies in the BRDF and environment. This is because the lighting integral is essentially a convolution of the BRDF with the environment.

For BRDFs that are principally reflective, we use a warp that matches the reflection directions of the different maps. So a point on the source image warps to the point on the destination image that reflects in the same direction. Primarily diffuse BRDFs suggest a warp that matches surface normal directions. We can find a well-matched warp for any BRDF that is radially symmetric about a principal direction and does not change shape across the surface. With such a BRDF, the same area of the environment will be integrated for corresponding points from different views.

Lambertian diffuse reflection and Phong specular reflection both satisfy this restriction, but most more realistic BRDFs do not. Fortunately, since the radiance environment maps sample a smooth, continuous function, we can effectively handle a much wider class of BRDFs that are close to the symmetric ideal without requiring a large number of sample maps. For example, we have used a numerically computed BRDF with Fresnel effects and diffuse, specular and backscatter components. For this BRDF, we use a warp that matches mirror reflections. It works because the specular lobe is the only high-frequency component of the BRDF and its shape does not vary too much from texel to texel. The Fresnel effects are naturally handled by the method and the other components do not require a large number of sample maps because they are low frequency.

Once the sample maps have been warped to the new viewpoint, they must be combined with some reconstruction filter. Oppenheim and Schafer [20] describe many sampling and reconstruction choices. For simplicity and efficiency, we use linear interpolation between neighboring images. The linear interpolation uses a spherical form of barycentric weights, presented in section 3.4. Thus, for any given viewpoint, the three nearby radiance environment maps are warped and blended to create an approximation to the new map (see figure 4).

## 3.1 Sampling View Directions

Certain environment map representations (e.g. cube maps) are viewpoint independent, while others (e.g. sphere maps) depend on the viewpoint. In contrast, each radiance environment map, whether it is stored in cube map, sphere map or another form, is correct for only a single viewpoint. This is because the radiance environment map captures Fresnel reflectance and other view-dependent effects.

As alluded to above, the view-dependence does limit the use of each map to only one view. This limitation is overcome by precomputing a set of maps – denoted $L_{r,j}, j \in \{0...N-1\}$ – at various viewpoints. The unit view vectors can be thought of as points lying on a sphere. We use reflection-space IBR to reconstruct the map for rendering from the $L_{r,j}$ maps, but we still require reasonable coverage of the sphere of possible view directions to avoid aliasing artifacts. We have used one $L_r$ for each viewpoint defined at the vertices of an icosahedron. This number of samples has been sufficient for the environments and BRDF we have employed and is desirable because its symmetry means that each viewpoint is handled in an unbiased manner.

## 3.2 Map Warping

Each warp is between a source map, $L_{r;s}$ (from the precomputed set $L_{r,j}$) and a destination map, $L_{r;d}$ (for the current rendering viewpoint). Points in these maps will be called $\mathbf{p}_s$ and $\mathbf{p}_d$ respectively.

For each map point, $\mathbf{p}$, there is a vector $\mathbf{r}$ along the central reflection direction of the BRDF. For Phong specular or perfect mirror reflectors, $\mathbf{r}$ is the geometric reflection vector. For diffuse surfaces $\mathbf{r}$ is the surface normal. To assist in the warp, we define an invertible function

$$g : \mathbf{p} \to \mathbf{r}$$

$g(\mathbf{p})$ depends on both the BRDF and the map representation. It is most easily defined in terms of a local coordinate system for each map, so we also have a transformation per map to convert the local coordinate system to a common global space

$$T : \mathbf{r} \to \bar{\mathbf{r}}$$

The composition of these functions defines the full warp from $\mathbf{p}_s$ to $\mathbf{p}_d$:

$$\mathbf{p}_d = g_d^{-1} \circ T_d^{-1} \circ T_s \circ g_s(\mathbf{p}_s)$$

This takes a point in $L_{r;s}$ (defined by s and t texture coordinates for a sphere map representation). It is converted first to a 3D reflection vector in the local coordinate system associated with $L_{r;s}$. This 3D vector is transformed to the global space, then to a vector in the local coordinate system associated with $L_{r;d}$. Finally, the resulting vector is converted to a point in $L_{r;d}$ (once again given by two texture coordinates if we use the sphere map representation).

## 3.3 Specific Warps

We will derive two specific warp functions. Both use a sphere-map representation for $L_{r;s}$ and $L_{r;d}$. The first is for BRDFs where the central reflection direction is the surface normal. The second is for BRDFs where the central reflection direction aligns with the mirror reflection direction.

For both warps, the local coordinate system associated with each map is aligned with the camera used to create the map. The x-axis points right, the y-axis points up and the z-axis points from the origin toward the camera. Thus transformations $T_s$ and $T_d$ are defined as 3x3 matrices with columns equal to three axes expressed in global coordinates.

The surface normal warp uses $g_{normal}$:

$$\begin{aligned} g_{normal}(s,t) &= \begin{pmatrix} 2s-1 \\ 2t-1 \\ \sqrt{1-(2s-1)^2+(2t-1)^2} \end{pmatrix} \\ g_{normal}^{-1}(x,y,z) &= (x/2+.5, y/2+.5) \end{aligned}$$

We base the mirror reflection warp, $g_{mirror}$ on the $x$, $y$ and $z$ produced by $g_{normal}$:

$$\begin{aligned} g_{mirror}(s,t) &= \begin{pmatrix} 2xz \\ 2yz \\ 2z^2-1 \end{pmatrix} \\ g_{mirror}^{-1}(x,y,z) &= g_{normal}^{-1}\left(\frac{(x,y,z+1)}{\sqrt{x^2+y^2+(z+1)^2}}\right) \end{aligned}$$

Since we have graphics hardware to do mirror reflections with a sphere map, we modify the final stage of both warps to use $g_{mirror}^{-1}$. The following functional composition chains define the two warps:

$$\mathbf{p}_d = g_{mirror}^{-1} \circ T_d^{-1} \circ T_s \circ g_{normal}(\mathbf{p}_s)$$
$$\mathbf{p}_d = g_{mirror}^{-1} \circ T_d^{-1} \circ T_s \circ g_{mirror}(\mathbf{p}_s)$$

Performing three of these warps per texel in the target map for every rendered frame is expensive and impractical for an interactive application. A fast, accurate approximation is possible by rendering the destination sphere map as a tessellated disk. Texture coordinates at each mesh vertex are chosen according to the warping function, and the source image is used as a texture while rendering the disk into the frame buffer. To account for the non-linearity of the warp functions, the mesh is finer toward the edges of the disk and coarser near the center. The 3D coordinate system associated with the destination map changes as the view moves, but the same disk tessellation can always be used. The reflection vectors, $\mathbf{r}_d$, also remain constant for each mesh vertex and can be precomputed.

The piecewise linear approximation to the warp is accurate for most of the sphere map area. Because we use a sphere map representation, the mirror warp has a singularity at the limit of extreme grazing reflections around the edge of the map – the reflection direction exactly opposite the view vector. The warp equation from $L_{r;s}$ to $L_{r;d}$ fails at this singularity.

We can locate $\mathbf{p}_d$ for the singularity by warping the problem reflection direction (the negated source map view vector) into the destination map. Near this point in the destination map, the source map will become pinched and unreliable instead of warping cleanly. We use a simple distance from $\mathbf{p}_d$ in the destination map to weight our confidence in the warped source image. This weight is used to fade the contribution of each source near its respective singularity.

The textured disk method accelerates the warping operation in two ways. First, $s$ and $t$ are not explicitly calculated for all the

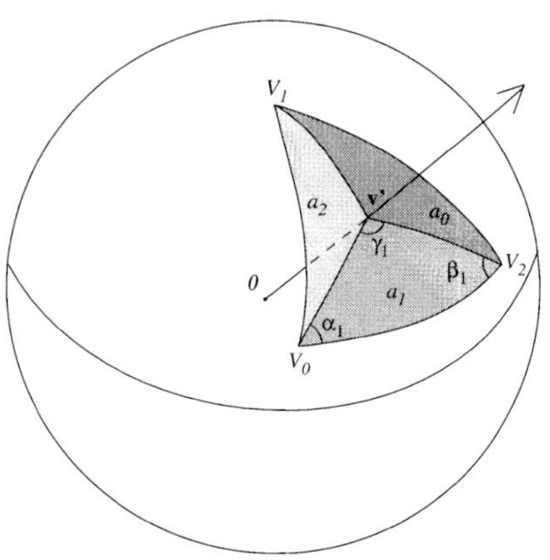


Figure 2: Illustrated is the spherical patch defined by $\mathbf{v}_0$, $\mathbf{v}_1$, and $\mathbf{v}_2$ associated with a particular point of view given by $\mathbf{v}_d$. By definition $\mathbf{v}_d$ defines in the line of sight of the viewer and in general forms three spherical triangles within the larger spherical triangle patch. Areas $a_0, a_1$ and $a_2$ represent the three weights for the sphere maps associated with vertices $\mathbf{v}_0$, $\mathbf{v}_1$ and $\mathbf{v}_2$ respectively, where $\alpha_1, \beta_1$, and $\gamma_1$ are the dihedral angles used to compute $a_1$.

points on the sphere map, only at the vertices of the mesh. Second, a major bottleneck in performing the warp is accessing memory associated with the source and destination maps. We leverage the rendering and texturing hardware to solve this memory bottleneck.

### 3.4 Spherical Barycentric Interpolation

Once the warps have taken place the warped images must be blended. Our interpolation scheme is a spherical variant of classic affine barycentric interpolation, as defined in Farin [7]. Classic barycentric interpolation uses the ratio of the areas of triangles, we instead use the ratio of spherical triangles.

Any given view vector, $\mathbf{v}_d$, will in general lie within a spherical patch as illustrated in figure 2. Each vertex, $\mathbf{v}_i$ of this spherical triangle is the view vector for one of the source images that have been warped to match $\mathbf{v}_d$. $\mathbf{v}_d$ is used to form three interior spherical triangles. The weight for the source image at vertex $i$ is a ratio of the areas of the spherical triangle opposite $\mathbf{v}_i$ and the overall spherical triangle. The area of an interior spherical triangle, $a_i$, on a unit sphere is given by the spherical excess formula [2]:

$$a_i = \alpha_i + \beta_i + \gamma_i - \pi; i \in 0, 1, 2$$

The dihedral angles $\alpha_i$, $\beta_i$, and $\gamma_i$ are defined as:

$$\begin{aligned}
\alpha_i &= \cos^{-1}((\mathbf{v}_d \otimes \mathbf{v}_{(i-1)\oslash 3}) \cdot (\mathbf{v}_{(i+1)\oslash 3} \otimes \mathbf{v}_{(i-1)\oslash 3})) \\
\beta_i &= \cos^{-1}((\mathbf{v}_{(i+1)\oslash 3} \otimes \mathbf{v}_d) \cdot (\mathbf{v}_{(i+1)\oslash 3} \otimes \mathbf{v}_{(i-1)\oslash 3})) \\
\gamma_i &= \cos^{-1}((\mathbf{v}_{(i+1)\oslash 3} \otimes \mathbf{v}_d) \cdot (\mathbf{v}_{(i-1)\oslash 3} \otimes \mathbf{v}_d))
\end{aligned}$$

Where $\otimes$ is the normalized cross product and $\oslash$ is an index-wrapping operator, defined as

$$a \oslash b = \begin{cases} b-1 & \text{if } a < 0 \\ 0 & \text{if } a \geq b \\ a & \text{otherwise} \end{cases}$$

## 4 RENDERING ALGORITHM

This leads to a straightforward interactive rendering algorithm. Pseudo-code for the algorithm is given here. It leverages texture mapping graphics hardware in two ways: once to perform the warping and blending between the sample images; and again using the generated sphere map in the final rendering.

```
main()
// Set up radiance maps and sphere geometry
G_v ← LoadGeodesicLocations(); v ∈ {(θ_0, φ_0)...(θ_{N-1}, φ_{N-1})}
L_{r,j} ←LoadSphereMaps( G, L_i, f_r ); j ∈ {0...N − 1}
// Viewpoint tracking loop
loop for each frame
    (x_d, y_d, v_d) ← ComputeViewCoordinateSystem( )
    (v_0, v_1, v_2) ← FindSubtendedTriangle( G, v_d )
    (a_0, a_1, a_2) ← ComputeWeights( (v_0, v_1, v_2), v_d )
    glClearAccum( 0, 0, 0, 0 )
    // Warp and blending loop
    loop for each of the three vertices, i
        mesh ← ComputeMesh( v_i, v_d)
        drawMesh(mesh, L_{r,i})
        glAccum(GL_ACCUM, a_i)
    end vertex loop
    glAccum(GL_RETURN, 1.0/(a_0 + a_1 + a_2))
    LoadNewSphereMap()
    RenderObject()
end frame loop
```

The interactive rendering program outlined above reads in a set of sphere maps at a prescribed set of geodesic locations along with the associated triangle faces. This decouples the interactive program from any specific choice of sphere map sampling view directions.

## 5 EXAMPLES

We have validated our technique with several examples. One is shown in figure 3. This example shows the recently introduced Mercedes-Benz S-Class automobile in an outdoor environment. The car shows an isotropic BRDF modeling automobile paint, computed using techniques similar to that found in Gondek [9]. We modeled the clear polyurethane coat over a paint substrate containing paint particles. Using a custom offline ray tracer we directly solve the lighting integral for each point in twelve pre-computed radiance environment maps. Thus the under coat of the paint and the clear coat are both modeled with high fidelity. Each sphere map takes several minutes to create. Figure 5 shows all of the textures used to render the car example.

Our software is available online[1]. On a Silicon Graphics(R) Onyx2(TM) InfiniteReality2(TM), the interactive viewing program runs at a sustained frame rate of 20Hz.

## 6 CONCLUSION

Interactive photo-realistic rendering is difficult to achieve because solving the lighting integral is computationally expensive. We precompute this integral into several view-dependent radiance environment maps, each of which would allow realistic rendering of arbitrary geometry from one fixed viewpoint. We dynamically create new maps for new viewpoints by combining the precomputed maps using an application of IBR techniques in reflection space. The resulting algorithm is readily implementable on most texture mapping

[1] http://www.sgi.com/software/rsibr/

capable graphics hardware. This technique allows rendering quality similar to that presented in Debevec [5], but at interactive rates and from arbitrary viewpoints.

Some areas of future work to improve this technique are apparent. We would like to perform the reflection-space IBR warp on a per pixel basis. We would also like to extend the range of BRDFs that can be accurately rendered. For example, we could handle arbitrary isotropic BRDFs with multiple high-frequency lobes in multiple passes, though admittedly with a loss in interactive performance. We would decompose the BRDF using a basis of symmetric lobes. Each basis function would be independently integrated with the environment and warped in a separate pass. We would also like to handle anisotropic BRDFs.

A broader area of future research is opened by the idea of reflection-space IBR. Traditional IBR could not have achieved these results; it is limited to rendering geometry contained in the source images. Traditional rendering, even using radiance environment maps, could also not have achieved these results; it could not provide the viewpoint independence without a fast way to create new intermediate maps. By applying IBR to an intermediate image representation in traditional rendering, it becomes possible to produce new algorithms that combine the strengths of both.

## 7 ACKNOWLEDGMENTS

The authors would like to thank all the individuals who helped us with the writing and development of this work. We are very grateful for the incredible S-Class data set from Andreas Fischer at DiamlerChrysler – he and DiamlerChrysler have been invaluable colleagues and partners in our research into interactive surface rendering. During the writing and review process the anonymous reviewers provided valuable insight and suggestions. Also, Peter Shirley and Gavin Miller helped with guidance and clarifications to refine many of the key ideas in the paper. Mark Peercy helped out with technical inspiration, ideas, and proofreading throughout the paper writing endeavor. We would also like to thank Gosia Kulczycka at General Motors for the numerous paint samples and feedback on the viability and quality of our technique. Greg Larson-Ward was extremely helpful with advice, technical proofreading and energy balanced synthetic images from RADIANCE. And thanks to Dany Galgani who provided the excellent figure 1 illustration on very short notice.

## References


[1] Blinn, J. F., and Newell, M. E. Texture and reflection in computer generated images. *Communications of the ACM 19* (1976), 542–546.

[2] Bronshtein, I., and Semendyayev, K. *Handbook of Mathematics*. Van Nostrand Reinhold Company, 1985.

[3] Cabral, B., Max, N., and Springmeyer, R. Bidirectional reflection functions from surface bump maps. In *Computer Graphics (SIGGRAPH '87 Proceedings)* (July 1987), M. C. Stone, Ed., vol. 21, pp. 273–281.

[4] Cook, R. L., Carpenter, L., and Catmull, E. The Reyes image rendering architecture. In *Computer Graphics (SIGGRAPH '87 Proceedings)* (July 1987), M. C. Stone, Ed., pp. 95–102.

[5] Debevec, P. Rendering synthetic objects into real scenes: Bridging traditional and image-based graphics with global illumination and high dynamic range photography. In *SIGGRAPH 98 Conference Proceedings* (July 1998), M. Cohen, Ed., Annual Conference Series, ACM SIGGRAPH, Addison Wesley, pp. 189–198. ISBN 0-89791-999-8.

[6] Debevec, P. E., and Malik, J. Recovering high dynamic range radiance maps from photographs. In *SIGGRAPH 97 Conference Proceedings* (Aug. 1997), T. Whitted, Ed., Annual Conference Series, ACM SIGGRAPH, Addison Wesley, pp. 369–378. ISBN 0-89791-896-7.

[7] Farin, G. *Curves and Surfaces for Computer Aided Geometric Design*. Academic Press, 1990.

[8] Gershbein, R., Schröder, P., and Hanrahan, P. Textures and radiosity: Controlling emission and reflection with texture maps. In *Proceedings of SIGGRAPH '94 (Orlando, Florida, July 24–29, 1994)* (July 1994), A. Glassner, Ed., Computer Graphics Proceedings, Annual Conference Series, ACM SIGGRAPH, ACM Press, pp. 51–58. ISBN 0-89791-667-0.

[9] Gondek, J. S., Meyer, G. W., and Newman, J. G. Wavelength dependent reflectance functions. In *Proceedings of SIGGRAPH '94 (Orlando, Florida, July 24–29, 1994)* (July 1994), A. Glassner, Ed., Computer Graphics Proceedings, Annual Conference Series, ACM SIGGRAPH, ACM Press, pp. 213–220. ISBN 0-89791-667-0.

[10] Gortler, S. J., Grzeszczuk, R., Szeliski, R., and Cohen, M. F. The lumigraph. In *SIGGRAPH 96 Conference Proceedings* (Aug. 1996), H. Rushmeier, Ed., Annual Conference Series, ACM SIGGRAPH, Addison Wesley, pp. 43–54. held in New Orleans, Louisiana, 04-09 August 1996.

[11] Greene, N. Applications of world projections. In *Proceedings of Graphics Interface '86* (May 1986), M. Green, Ed., pp. 108–114.

[12] He, X. D., Torrance, K. E., Sillion, F. X., and Greenberg, D. P. A comprehensive physical model for light reflection. In *Computer Graphics (SIGGRAPH '91 Proceedings)* (July 1991), T. W. Sederberg, Ed., vol. 25, pp. 175–186.

[13] Heidrich, W., and Seidel, H.-P. Realistic, hardware-accelerated shading and lighting. In *Proceedings of SIGGRAPH '99 (Los Angeles, California, August 8–13, 1999)* (Aug. 1999), Computer Graphics Proceedings, Annual Conference Series, ACM SIGGRAPH, ACM Press.

[14] Immel, D. S., Cohen, M. F., and Greenberg, D. P. A radiosity method for non-diffuse environments. In *Computer Graphics (SIGGRAPH '86 Proceedings)* (Aug. 1986), D. C. Evans and R. J. Athay, Eds., vol. 20, pp. 133–142.

[15] Jensen, H. W., and Christensen, P. H. Efficient simulation of light transport in scenes with participating media using photon maps. In *SIGGRAPH 98 Conference Proceedings* (July 1998), M. Cohen, Ed., Annual Conference Series, ACM SIGGRAPH, Addison Wesley, pp. 311–320. ISBN 0-89791-999-8.

[16] Kajiya, J. T. The rendering equation. In *Computer Graphics (SIGGRAPH '86 Proceedings)* (Aug. 1986), D. C. Evans and R. J. Athay, Eds., vol. 20, pp. 143–150.

[17] Levoy, M., and Hanrahan, P. Light field rendering. In *SIGGRAPH 96 Conference Proceedings* (Aug. 1996), H. Rushmeier, Ed., Annual Conference Series, ACM SIGGRAPH, Addison Wesley, pp. 31–42. held in New Orleans, Louisiana, 04-09 August 1996.

[18] McMillan, L., and Bishop, G. Plenoptic modeling: An image-based rendering system. In *SIGGRAPH 95 Conference Proceedings* (Aug. 1995), R. Cook, Ed., Annual Conference Series, ACM SIGGRAPH, Addison Wesley, pp. 39–46. held in Los Angeles, California, 06-11 August 1995.

[19] Miller, G. S., and Hoffman, C. R. Illumination and reflection maps: Simulated objects in simulated and real environments. In *SIGGRAPH '84 Advanced Computer Graphics Animation seminar notes*. July 1984.

[20] Oppenheim, A. V., and Schafer, R. W. *Digital Signal Processing*. Prentice-Hall, Englewood Cliffs, NJ, 1975.

[21] Poulin, P., and Fournier, A. A model for anisotropic reflection. In *Computer Graphics (SIGGRAPH '90 Proceedings)* (Aug. 1990), F. Baskett, Ed., vol. 24, pp. 273–282.

[22] Seitz, S. M., and Dyer, C. R. View morphing: Synthesizing 3D metamorphoses using image transforms. In *SIGGRAPH 96 Conference Proceedings* (Aug. 1996), H. Rushmeier, Ed., Annual Conference Series, ACM SIGGRAPH, Addison Wesley, pp. 21–30. held in New Orleans, Louisiana, 04-09 August 1996.

[23] Veach, E., and Guibas, L. J. Metropolis light transport. In *SIGGRAPH 97 Conference Proceedings* (Aug. 1997), T. Whitted, Ed., Annual Conference Series, ACM SIGGRAPH, Addison Wesley, pp. 65–76. ISBN 0-89791-896-7.

[24] Voorhies, D., and Foran, J. Reflection vector shading hardware. In *Proceedings of SIGGRAPH '94 (Orlando, Florida, July 24–29, 1994)* (July 1994), A. Glassner, Ed., Computer Graphics Proceedings, Annual Conference Series, ACM SIGGRAPH, ACM Press, pp. 163–166. ISBN 0-89791-667-0.

[25] Ward, G. J. The RADIANCE lighting simulation and rendering system. In *Proceedings of SIGGRAPH '94 (Orlando, Florida, July 24–29, 1994)* (July 1994), A. Glassner, Ed., Computer Graphics Proceedings, Annual Conference Series, ACM SIGGRAPH, ACM Press, pp. 459–472. ISBN 0-89791-667-0.

Figure 3: Mercedes-Benz S-Class automobile in an outdoor environment.

Figure 4: The outer images are source radiance environment maps for a test environment and a mirror BRDF. The next layer of images show each map warped to the new viewpoint with appropriate spherical barycentric weighting. The center image is the final generated radiance environment map.

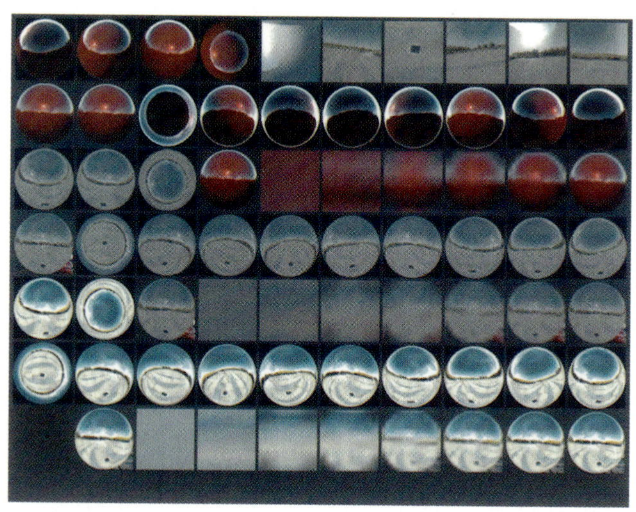

Figure 5: All of the textures used for figure 3. Includes the environment, source radiance environment maps for several surface types on the car, and generated MIP mapped radiance environment maps.

# Realistic, Hardware-accelerated Shading and Lighting

Wolfgang Heidrich* Hans-Peter Seidel

Max-Planck-Institute for Computer Science

## Abstract

With fast 3D graphics becoming more and more available even on low end platforms, the focus in hardware-accelerated rendering is beginning to shift towards higher quality rendering and additional functionality instead of simply higher performance implementations based on the traditional graphics pipeline.

In this paper we present techniques for realistic shading and lighting using computer graphics hardware. In particular, we discuss multipass methods for high quality local illumination using physically-based reflection models, as well as techniques for the interactive visualization of non-diffuse global illumination solutions. These results are then combined with normal mapping for increasing the visual complexity of rendered images.

Although the techniques presented in this paper work at interactive frame rates on contemporary graphics hardware, we also discuss some modifications of the rendering pipeline that help to further improve both performance and quality of the proposed methods.

**CR Categories:** I.3.1 [Computer Graphics]: Hardware Architecture—Graphics processors; I.3.3 [Computer Graphics]: Picture/Image Generation—Bitmap and frame buffer operations; I.3.6 [Computer Graphics]: Methodology and Techniques—Standards I.3.7 [Computer Graphics]: Three-Dimensional Graphics and Realism—Color, Shading, Shadowing and Texture

**Keywords:** reflectance functions, illumination effects, shading, texture mapping, rendering hardware, frame buffer techniques

## 1 Introduction

Until recently, the major concern in the development of new graphics hardware has been to increase the performance of the traditional rendering pipeline. Today, graphics accelerators with a performance of several million textured, lit triangles per second are within reach even for the low end. As a consequence, we see that the emphasis is beginning to shift away from higher performance towards higher quality renderings and an increased feature set that makes graphics hardware applicable to more demanding applications.

Despite this development, most current graphics hardware still only uses a local Phong illumination model, which was shown to be inappropriate a long time ago [4]. Moreover, techniques for visualizing non-diffuse global illumination are not widely applied, although several researchers have worked on such methods.

In this paper, we present a class of techniques to improve the quality of shading and lighting in hardware-accelerated computer graphics. We start with algorithms for high-quality local illumination using alternative lighting models such as the one by Torrance and Sparrow [39]. This approach is based on an analytic factorization of the respective model into bivariate terms that can be represented as texture maps. We then discuss methods for visualizing non-diffuse global illumination solutions based on environment maps. We introduce both a Fresnel term for simulating reflections in non-metallic objects, as well as a pre-filtering method for environment maps. To this end, we also review an alternative parameterization for environment maps that we recently introduced [20], and that allows us to use one map for all viewing positions and directions. These techniques are finally combined with normal mapping to increase the visual complexity of the scene.

Although the techniques presented here produce renderings at interactive frame rates on contemporary graphics hardware, a more direct support by future hardware could be achieved through some modifications of the rendering pipeline. These will be outlined at the end of this paper.

## 2 Previous Work

Most of today's graphics hardware uses either the Phong [7], or the Blinn-Phong [4] illumination model. Many other, physically more plausible models have been proposed, but have so far only been used in software rendering systems or by hardware that has programmable shaders, such as [30]. The most important of these models are the ones by Torrance and Sparrow [39] and Cook and Torrance [11]. The Torrance-Sparrow model uses a Gaussian micro facet distribution function and a geometric attenuation factor based on the assumption of v-shaped grooves on the surface. Other distribution functions have been proposed, for example, by Beckmann and Spizzichino [3], while Smith [36] presented a more accurate geometry term under the assumption of a Gaussian facet distribution. He et al. [18] proposed the HTSG model based directly on the Kirchhoff theory of electromagnetic fields. This model is capable of simulating even more physical effects, although at significantly increased computational cost.

In addition to the isotropic models listed above, anisotropic models have also been proposed. Banks [1] described a very simple model based on results from the illumination of lines in 3-space, while Cabral et al. [8] and Poulin and Fournier [32] use simulations of different kinds of micro geometry. Ward [42] modified the Torrance-Sparrow model by using an anisotropic micro facet distribution function.

Several different methods for interactively visualizing non-diffuse global illumination have been suggested in the literature. Environment maps as a means of computing a mirror term were proposed by Blinn [6], while the spherical parameterization used by most graphics hardware today was presented by Haeberli and Segal [16]. Diefenbach [13] demonstrated a multipass method for rendering mirror and glossy reflections on planar surfaces. Ofek and

*Computer Graphics Group, Im Stadtwald, 66123 Saarbrücken, Germany, {heidrich,hpseidel}@mpi-sb.mpg.de

Rappoport [29] interactively compute mirror reflections off curved reflectors by warping the reflected geometry. Miller et al. [28] propose an approach where the glossy reflection on a surface is stored in a compressed light field, and Walter et al. [41] place virtual lights in the scene to simulate glossy reflections. Stürzlinger and Bastos [38] employ multipass rendering to visualize the result of a photon tracing algorithm. Finally, in some work developed in parallel to ours, Bastos et al. [2] use textures and filtering techniques to render reflections in planar objects based on physically correct reflection models, and Cabral et al. [9] propose an environment mapping technique for glossy reflections not unlike ours.

Bump maps, originally introduced by Blinn [5], have recently found their way into hardware-accelerated rendering. Some researchers [14, 26, 31] built or proposed dedicated graphics hardware to implement bump maps, while others [25] use multipass techniques to realize bump maps with traditional graphics hardware. In contrast to bump maps, which define the variation of the surface normal in terms of a bump height, normal maps directly specify the direction of the surface normal. On the one hand, normal maps are less expensive to compute than bump maps, and can also be generated more easily, for example by measurements [33], or surface simplification [10]. On the other hand, normal maps are attached to the underlying geometry, while bump maps can be applied to any surface.

# 3 Alternative Lighting Models for Local Illumination

In this section we describe techniques for applying physically accurate reflection models to the computation of local illumination in hardware-based rendering. Rather than replacing the standard Phong model by another single, fixed model, we seek a method that allows us to utilize a wide variety of different models so that the most appropriate model can be chosen for each application.

To achieve this flexibility without introducing procedural shading, a sample-based representation of the BRDF seems most promising. However, a faithful sampling of 3D isotropic or 4D anisotropic BRDFs requires too much storage to be useful on contemporary graphics hardware. Wavelets or spherical harmonics could be used to store this data more compactly, but these representations do not easily lend themselves to hardware implementations.

## 3.1 Isotropic Models

We propose a different approach. It turns out that most lighting models in computer graphics can be factored into independent components that only depend on one or two angles. Consider, for example the model by Torrance and Sparrow [39]:

$$f_r(\vec{l} \rightarrow \vec{v}) = \frac{F \cdot G \cdot D}{\pi \cdot \cos\alpha \cdot \cos\beta}, \quad (1)$$

where $f_r$ is the BRDF, $\alpha$ is the angle between the surface normal $\vec{n}$ and the vector $\vec{l}$ pointing towards the light source, while $\beta$ is the angle between $\vec{n}$ and the viewing direction $\vec{v}$. The geometry is depicted in Figure 1.

For a fixed index of refraction, the Fresnel term $F$ in Equation 1 only depends on the angle $\theta$ between the light direction $\vec{l}$ and the micro facet normal $\vec{h}$, which is the halfway vector between $\vec{l}$ and $\vec{v}$. Thus, the Fresnel term can be seen as a univariate function $F(\cos\theta)$.

The micro facet distribution function $D$, which defines the percentage of facets oriented in direction $\vec{h}$, depends on the angle $\delta$ between $\vec{h}$ and the surface normal $\vec{n}$, as well as a roughness parameter.

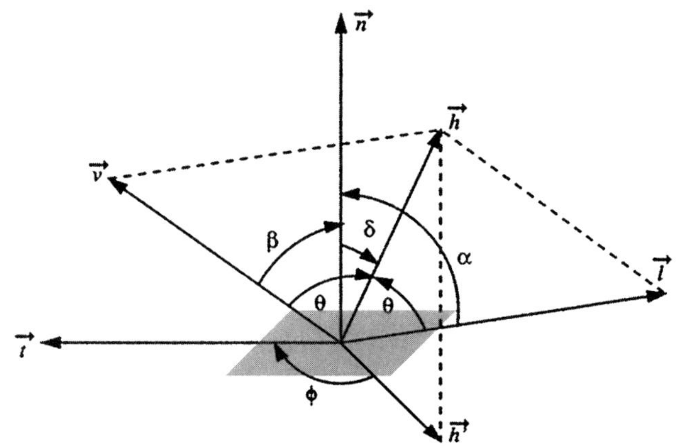


Figure 1: The local geometry of reflection at a rough surface.

This is true for all widely used choices of distribution functions, including a Gaussian distribution of $\delta$ or of the surface height, as well as the distribution by Beckmann [3]. Since the roughness is generally assumed to be constant for a given surface, this is again a univariate function $D(\cos\delta)$.

Finally, when using the geometry term $G$ proposed by Smith [36], which describes the shadowing and masking of light for surfaces with a Gaussian micro facet distribution, this term is a bivariate function $G(\cos\alpha, \cos\beta)$.

The contribution of a single point- or directional light source with intensity $I_i$ to the intensity of the surface is given as $I_o = f_r(\vec{l} \rightarrow \vec{v}) \cos\alpha \cdot I_i$. The term $f_r(\mathbf{x}, \vec{l} \rightarrow \vec{v}) \cos\alpha$ can be split into two bivariate parts $F(\cos\theta) \cdot D(\cos\delta)$ and $G(\cos\alpha, \cos\beta)/(\pi \cdot \cos\beta)$, which are then stored in two independent 2-dimensional lookup tables.

Regular 2D texture mapping can be used to implement the lookup process. If all vectors are normalized, the texture coordinates are simple dot products between the surface normal, the viewing and light directions, and the micro facet normal. These vectors and their dot products can be computed in software and assigned as texture coordinates to each vertex of the object.

The interpolation of these texture coordinates across a polygon corresponds to a linear interpolation of the vectors without renormalization. Since the reflection model itself is highly nonlinear, this is much better than simple Gouraud shading, but not as good as evaluating the illumination in every pixel (Phong shading). The interpolation of normals without renormalization is commonly known as *fast Phong shading*.

This method for looking up the illumination in two separate 2-dimensional textures requires either a single rendering pass with two simultaneous textures, or two separate rendering passes with one texture each in order to render specular reflections on an object. If two passes are used, their results are multiplied using alpha blending. A third rendering pass with hardware lighting (or a third simultaneous texture) is applied for adding a diffuse term.

If the light and viewing directions are assumed to be constant, that is, if a directional light and an orthographic camera are assumed, the computation of the texture coordinates can even be done in hardware. To this end, light and viewing direction as well as the halfway vector between them are used as row vectors in the texture matrix for the two textures:

$$\begin{bmatrix} 0 & 0 & 0 & \cos\theta \\ h_x & h_y & h_z & 0 \\ 0 & 0 & 0 & 0 \\ 0 & 0 & 0 & 1 \end{bmatrix} \cdot \begin{bmatrix} n_x \\ n_y \\ n_z \\ 1 \end{bmatrix} = \begin{bmatrix} \cos\theta \\ \cos\delta \\ 0 \\ 1 \end{bmatrix} \quad (2)$$

$$\begin{bmatrix} l_x & l_y & l_z & 0 \\ v_x & v_y & v_z & 0 \\ 0 & 0 & 0 & 0 \\ 0 & 0 & 0 & 1 \end{bmatrix} \cdot \begin{bmatrix} n_x \\ n_y \\ n_z \\ 1 \end{bmatrix} = \begin{bmatrix} \cos\alpha \\ \cos\beta \\ 0 \\ 1 \end{bmatrix} \quad (3)$$

Figure 2 shows a torus rendered with two different roughness settings using this technique. The assumption of an orthographic camera for lighting purposes is quite common in hardware-accelerated rendering, since it saves the normalization of the viewing vector for each vertex. APIs like OpenGL have a separate mode for applications where this simplification cannot be used, and the viewing direction has to be computed for every vertex. This case is called a *local viewer*.

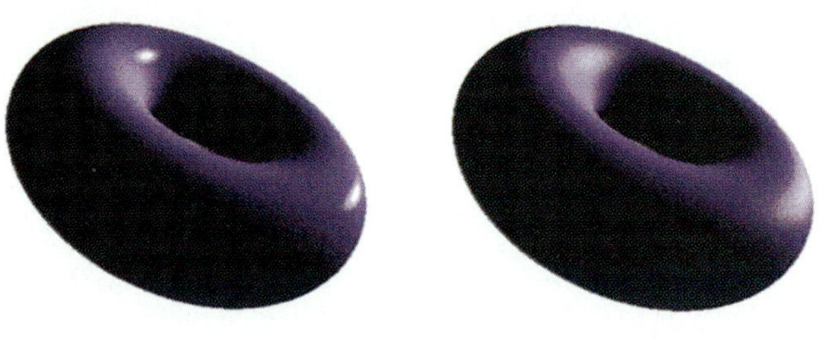

Figure 2: A torus rendered with the Torrance-Sparrow reflection model and two different settings for the surface roughness.

We would like to note that the use of textures for representing the lighting model introduces an approximation error: while the term $F \cdot D$ is bounded by the interval $[0, 1]$, the second term $G/(\pi \cdot \cos\beta)$ exhibits a singularity for grazing viewing directions ($\cos\beta \to 0$). Since graphics hardware typically uses a fixed-point representation of textures, the texture values are clamped to the range $[0, 1]$. When these clamped values are used for the illumination process, areas around the grazing angles can be rendered too dark, especially if the surface is very shiny. This artifact can be reduced by dividing the values stored in the texture by a constant which is later multiplied back onto the final result. In practice, however, these artifacts are hardly noticeable.

The same methods can be applied to all kinds of variations of the Torrance-Sparrow model, using different distribution functions and geometry terms, or the approximations proposed in [34]. With varying numbers of terms and rendering passes, it is also possible to come up with similar factorizations for all kinds of other models. For example the Phong, Blinn-Phong and Cosine Lobe models can all be rendered in a single pass with a single texture, which can even already account for an ambient and a diffuse term in addition to the specular one.

### 3.2 Anisotropy

Although the treatment of anisotropic materials is somewhat harder, similar factorization techniques can be applied here. For anisotropic models, the micro facet distribution function and the geometrical attenuation factor also depend on the angle $\phi$ between the facet normal and a reference direction in the tangent plane. This reference direction is given in the form of a tangent vector $\vec{t}$.

For example, the elliptical Gaussian model [42] introduces an anisotropic facet distribution function specified as the product of two independent Gaussian functions, one in the direction of $\vec{t}$, and one in the direction of the binormal $\vec{n} \times \vec{t}$. This makes $D$ a bivariate function in the angles $\delta$ and $\phi$. Consequently, the texture coordinates can be computed in software in much the same way as described above for isotropic materials. This also holds for the other anisotropic models in computer graphics literature.

Since anisotropic models depend on both a normal and a tangent per vertex, the texture coordinates cannot be generated with the help of a texture matrix, even if light and viewing directions are assumed to be constant. This is due to the fact that the anisotropic term can usually not be factored into a term that only depends on the surface normal, and one that only depends on the tangent.

One exception to this rule is the model by Banks [1], which is mentioned here despite the fact that it is an *ad-hoc* model which is not based on physical considerations. Banks defines the reflection off an anisotropic surface as

$$I_o = \cos\alpha \cdot (k_d < \vec{n'}, \vec{l} > + k_s < \vec{n'}, \vec{h} >^{1/r}) \cdot I_i, \quad (4)$$

where $\vec{n'}$ is the projection of the light vector $\vec{l}$ into the plane perpendicular to the tangent vector $\vec{t}$. This vector is then used as a shading normal for a Blinn-Phong lighting model with diffuse and specular coefficients $k_d$ and $k_s$, and surface roughness $r$. In [37], it has been pointed out that this Phong term is really only a function of the two angles between the tangent and the light direction, as well as the tangent and the viewing direction. This fact was used for the illumination of lines in [37].

Applied to anisotropic reflection models, this means that this Phong term can be looked up from a 2-dimensional texture, if the tangent $\vec{t}$ is specified as a texture coordinate, and the texture matrix is set up as in Equation 3. The additional term $\cos\alpha$ in Equation 4 is computed by hardware lighting with a directional light source and a purely diffuse material, so that the Banks model can be rendered with one texture and one pass per light source. Figure 3 shows two images rendered with this reflection model.

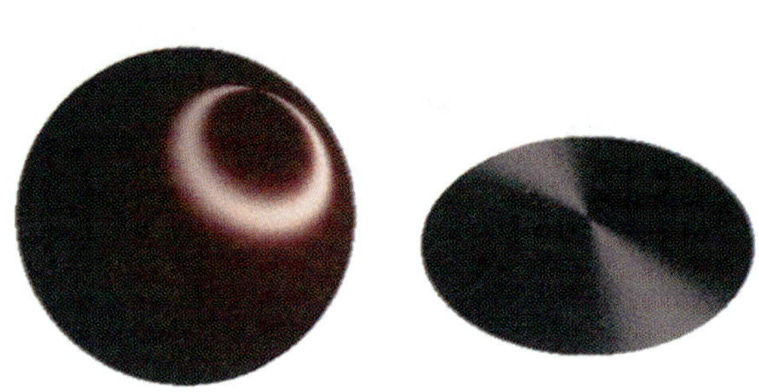

Figure 3: Sphere and disk rendered with Banks' anisotropic reflection model.

## 4 Visualizing Global Illumination with Environment Maps

The presented techniques for applying alternative reflection models to local illumination computations can significantly increase the realism of synthetic images. However, true photorealism is only possible if global effects are also considered. Since texture mapping techniques for diffuse illumination are widely known and applied, we concentrate on non-diffuse global illumination, in particular mirror- and glossy reflection.

Our approach is based on environment maps, because they offer a good compromise between rendering quality and storage requirements. With environment maps, 2-dimensional textures instead of the full 4-dimensional radiance field [28] can be used to store the illumination.

### 4.1 View-independent Environment Maps

The first step for using environment maps is the choice of an appropriate parameterization. The spherical parameterization [16] used in most of today's graphics hardware is based on the simple analogy of a infinitely small, perfectly mirroring ball centered around the object. The environment map is the image that an orthographic camera sees when looking at this ball along the negative $z$-axis. The sampling rate of this map is maximal for directions opposing the viewing direction (that is, objects behind the viewer), and goes towards zero for directions close to the viewing direction. Moreover, there is a singularity in the viewing direction, since all points where the viewing vector is tangential to the sphere show the same point of the environment.

With these properties, it is clear that this parameterization is not suitable for viewing directions other than the original one. Maps using this parameterization have to be regenerated for each change of the view point, even if the environment is otherwise static. The major reason why spherical maps are used anyway, is that the lookup can be computed efficiently with simple operations in hardware: the texture coordinates for a given reflection direction are simply the $x$ and $y$ components of the normalized halfway vector between the reflection vector and the $z$-axis, which acts as a reference viewing direction (see Figure 4). For orthographic cameras, this halfway vector simplifies to the surface normal.

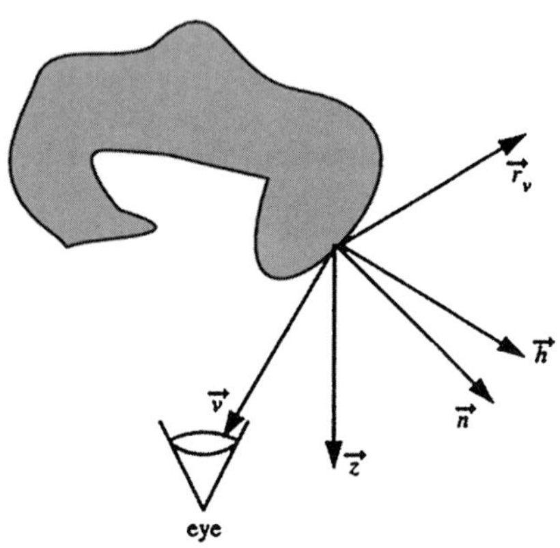


Figure 4: Spherical environment maps are indexed by the $x$ and $y$ components of the halfway vector $\vec{h}$ between the viewing direction $\vec{v}$ and the $z$-axis.

A parameterization which avoids the problems of spherical maps is cubical environment mapping, which consist of 6 independent perspective images from the center of a cube through each of its faces. The sampling of these maps is fairly good, as the sampling rates for the directions differ by a factor of $3\sqrt{3} \approx 5.2$. However, although hardware implementations of this parameterization have been proposed [40], these are not available at the moment. The reason for this is probably that the handling of six independent textures poses problems, and that anti-aliasing across the image borders is difficult.

We use a different parameterization that is both view independent and easy to implement on current and future hardware, and that we first described in [20]. A detailed description of its properties can be found in [19]. The parameterization is based on an analogy similar to the one used to describe spherical maps. Assume that the reflecting object lies in the origin, and that the viewing direction is along the negative $z$ axis. The image seen by an orthographic camera when looking at the paraboloid

$$f(x, y) = \frac{1}{2} - \frac{1}{2}(x^2 + y^2), \quad x^2 + y^2 \leq 1 \tag{5}$$

contains the information about the hemisphere facing towards the viewer (see Figure 5). The complete environment is stored in two separate textures, each containing the information of one hemisphere.

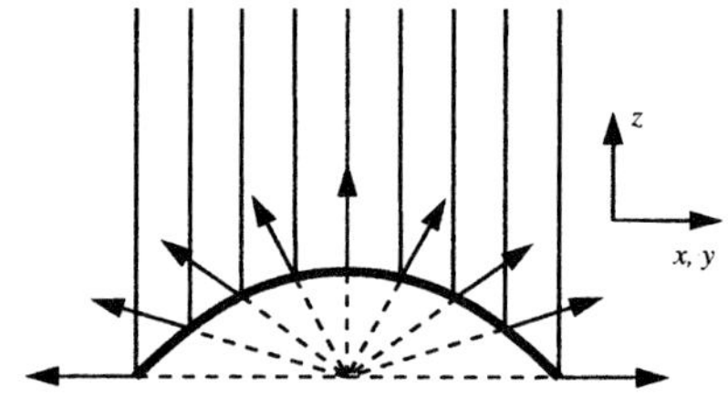


Figure 5: The reflections off a paraboloid can be used to parameterize the incoming light from a hemisphere of directions.

One useful property of this parameterization is a very uniform sampling of the hemisphere of directions. The differential solid angle covered by a pixel at location $(x, y)$ is given as

$$d\omega(x, y) = \frac{dA}{|(x, y, f(x, y))^T|^2} \cdot sr, \tag{6}$$

where $dA$ is the differential area of the pixel. From this formula, it is easy to derive the fact that the sampling rate only varies by a factor of 4, which is even better than for cubical maps [19].

Another big advantage of this parameterization is that it can be used very efficiently in hardware implementations. Since the normal of the paraboloid in Equation 5 is the vector $[x, y, 1, 0]^T$, the texture coordinates for this parameterization are given as $h_x/h_z$ and $h_y/h_z$. Thus, if the reflection vector $\vec{r}_v$ in eye space is specified as the initial set of texture coordinates, the coordinates needed for the environment lookup can be computed using a projective texture matrix:

$$\begin{bmatrix} x \\ y \\ 1 \\ 1 \end{bmatrix} = \mathbf{P} \cdot \mathbf{S} \cdot \mathbf{M}^{-1} \cdot \begin{bmatrix} r_{v,x} \\ r_{v,y} \\ r_{v,z} \\ 1 \end{bmatrix}, \tag{7}$$

where $\mathbf{M}$ is a linear transformation mapping the environment map space into eye space. The environment map space is the space in which the environment is defined, that is, the one, in which the paraboloid is given by Equation 5. The inverse of $\mathbf{M}$ thus maps the $\vec{r}_v$ back into this space. Then the matrix $\mathbf{S}$ adds the vector $[0, 0, 1, 0]^T$ to compute the halfway vector $\vec{h}$, and finally $\mathbf{P}$ copies the $z$-component into the homogeneous component $w$ to perform the perspective division.

In order to specify $\vec{r}_v$ as the initial set of texture coordinates, this vector has to be computed per vertex. This can be achieved either in software, or by a hardware extension allowing for the automatic computation of these texture coordinates, which we proposed in [20]. Kilgard [23] has implemented this extension for Mesa and the new drivers for the Riva TNT graphics chip.

What remains to be done is to combine frontfacing and backfacing regions of the environment into a single image. To this end, we mark those pixels inside the circle $x^2 + y^2 \leq 1$ of one of the two maps with an alpha value of 1, the others with 0. The second map does not need to contain an alpha channel. Then, with either a single rendering pass and two texture maps, or two separate rendering passes, the object is rendered with the two different maps applied, and the alpha channel of the first map is used to select which map should be visible for each pixel.

Figure 6 shows the two images comprising an environment map in this parameterization, as well as two images rendered with these maps under different viewing directions. The environment maps were generated using a ray-caster. The marked circular regions contain the information for the two hemispheres of directions. The regions outside the circles are, strictly speaking, not part of the environment map, but are useful for avoiding seams between the two hemispheres of directions, as well as for generating mipmaps of the environment. These parts have been generated by extending the paraboloid from Equation 5 to the domain $[-1, 1]^2$.

Figure 6: Top: two parabolic images comprising one environment map. Bottom: rendering of a torus using this environment map.

## 4.2 Mip-map Level Generation for Parabolic Maps

Anti-aliasing of parabolic environment maps can be performed using any of the known prefiltering algorithms, such as mip-mapping [43]. For correct prefiltering, the front- and backfacing maps need to contain valid information for the whole domain $[-1, 1]^2$, as in Figure 6.

The next level in the mip-map hierarchy is then generated by computing a weighted sum for each $2 \times 2$ block of texels. The weight for each texel is proportional to the solid angle it covers (Equation 6). The sum of these solid angles is the solid angle covered by the texel in the new mip-map level, and is used as a weight for the next iteration step.

Mip-mapping is, of course, an isotropic filtering technique, and therefore produces excessive blurring for grazing viewing angles. These problems, are, however in no way specific to environment maps. By weighting each pixel with its solid angle, filtering is correct within the limits of the mip-mapping approach, since each texel in the map is correctly anti-aliased, and each pixel on the object is textured by exactly one hemispherical map.

## 4.3 Mirror and Diffuse Terms with Environment Maps

Once an environment map is given in the parabolic parameterization, it can be used to add a mirror reflection term to an object. Due to the view-independent nature of this parameterization, one map suffices for all possible viewing positions and directions. Using multi-pass rendering and either alpha blending or an accumulation buffer [17], it is possible to add a diffuse global illumination term through the use of a precomputed texture. Two methods exist for the generation of such a texture. One way is, that a global illumination algorithm such as Radiosity is used to compute the diffuse global illumination in every surface point.

The second approach is purely image-based, and was proposed by Greene [15]. The environment map used for the mirror term contains information about the incoming radiance $L_i(\mathbf{x}, \vec{l})$, where $\mathbf{x}$ is the point for which the environment map is valid, and $\vec{l}$ the direction of the incoming light. This information can be used to prefilter the environment map to represent the diffuse reflection of an object for all possible surface normals. Like regular environment maps, this texture is only valid for one point in space, but can be used as an approximation for nearby points.

## 4.4 Fresnel Term

A regular environment map without prefiltering describes the incoming illumination in a point in space. If this information is directly used as the outgoing illumination, as with regular environment mapping, only metallic surfaces can be modeled. This is because for metallic surfaces (surfaces with a high index of refraction) the Fresnel term is almost one, independent of the angle between light direction and surface normal. Thus, for a perfectly smooth (i.e. mirroring) surface, incoming light is reflected in the mirror direction with a constant reflectance.

For non-metallic materials (materials with a small index of refraction), however, the reflectance strongly depends on the angle of the incoming light. Mirror reflections on these materials should be weighted by the Fresnel term for the angle between the normal and the viewing direction $\vec{v}$.

Similar to the techniques for local illumination presented in Section 3, the Fresnel term $F(\cos\theta)$ for the mirror direction $\vec{r}_v$ can be stored in a texture map. Since here only the Fresnel term is required, a 1-dimensional texture map suffices for this purpose. This Fresnel term is rendered to the framebuffer's alpha channel in a separate rendering pass. The mirror part is then multiplied with this term in a second pass, and a third pass is used to add the diffuse part. This yields an outgoing radiance of $L_o = F \cdot L_m + L_d$, where $L_m$ is the contribution of the mirror term, while $L_d$ is the contribution due to diffuse reflections.

In addition to simply adding the diffuse part to the Fresnel-weighted mirror reflection, we can also use the Fresnel term for blending between diffuse and specular: $L_o = F \cdot L_m + (1 - F)L_d$. This allows us to simulate diffuse surfaces with a transparent coating: the mirror term describes the reflection off the coating. Only light not reflected by the coating hits the underlying surface and is there reflected diffusely.

Figure 7 shows images generated using these two approaches. In the top row, the diffuse term is simply added to the Fresnel-weighted mirror term (the glossy reflection is zero). For a refractive index of 1.5 (left), which approximately corresponds to glass, the object is only specular for grazing viewing angles, while for a high index of refraction (200, right image), which is typical for metals, the whole object is highly specular.

The bottom row of Figure 7 shows two images generated with the second approach. For a low index of refraction, the specular term is again high only for grazing angles, but in contrast to the image above, the diffuse part fades out for these angles. For a high index of refraction, which, as pointed out above, corresponds to metal, the diffuse part is practically zero everywhere, so that the object is a perfect mirror for all directions.

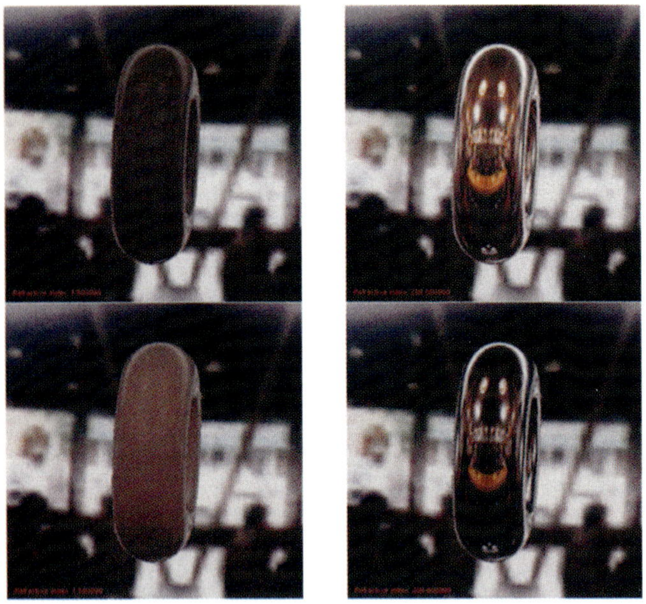

Figure 7: Mirror and diffuse reflections weighted by a Fresnel term for a varying index of refraction. Top: constant diffuse coefficient, bottom: diffuse reflection fading out with the Fresnel term.

Figure 8: Top: original parabolic map used in this figure and Figure 7, as well as prefiltered map with a roughness of 0.01. Bottom: application of the filtered map to a reflective torus (left) and a transmissive rectangle (right).

### 4.5 Precomputed Glossy Reflection and Transmission

We would now like to extend the concept of environment maps to glossy reflections. The idea is similar to the diffuse prefiltering proposed by Greene [15] and the approach by Voorhies and Foran [40] to use environment maps to generate Phong highlights from directional light sources. These two ideas can be combined to precompüte an environment map containing the glossy reflection of an object with a Phong material. With this concept, effects similar to the ones presented by Debevec [12] are possible in real time.

As shown in [24], the Phong BRDF is given by

$$f_r(\vec{l} \to \vec{v}) = k_s \cdot \frac{<\vec{r}_l, \vec{v}>^{1/r}}{\cos\alpha} = k_s \cdot \frac{<\vec{r}_v, \vec{l}>^{1/r}}{\cos\alpha}, \quad (8)$$

where $\vec{r}_l$, and $\vec{r}_v$ are the reflected light- and viewing directions, respectively.

Thus, the specular global illumination using the Phong model is

$$L_o(\vec{r}_v) = k_s \cdot \int_{\Omega(\vec{n})} <\vec{r}_v, \vec{l}>^{1/r} L_i(\vec{l})\, d\omega(\vec{l}), \quad (9)$$

which is only a function of the reflection vector $\vec{r}_v$ and the environment map containing the *incoming* radiance $L_i(\vec{l})$. Therefore, it is possible to take a map containing $L_i(\vec{l})$, and generate a filtered map containing the *outgoing* radiance for a glossy Phong material. Since this filtering is relatively expensive, it cannot be redone for every frame in an interactive application. Thus, it is important to use a view-independent parameterization such as our parabolic maps.

Figure 8 shows such a map generated from the original environment in Figure 6, as well as a glossy sphere textured with this map. The same technique can be applied to simulate glossy transmission on thin surfaces. This is also depicted in Figure 8.

If the original environment map is given in a high-dynamic range format, then this prefiltering technique allows for effects similar to the ones described by Debevec [12]. Although reflections of an object onto itself cannot be modeled by environment maps, the renderings are quite convincing, considering that these images can be rendered at frame rates of about 20Hz even on low end workstations such as an SGI O2.

## 5 Normal Maps

Bump maps are becoming popular for hardware-accelerated rendering, because they allow us to increase the visual complexity of a scene without requiring excessive amounts of geometric detail.

Normal maps can be used for achieving the same goal, and have the advantage that the expensive operations (computing the local surface normal by transforming the bump into the local coordinate frame) have already been performed in a preprocessing stage. All that remains to be done is to use the precomputed normals for shading each pixel. Another advantage of normal maps is that recently methods have shown up for measuring them directly [33], or for generating them as a by-product of mesh simplification [10]. Although we only handle normal maps here, some of these results could also be useful for implementations of bump maps, as will be discussed in Section 6.

In this section, we first describe how normal maps can be lit according to the Blinn-Phong illumination model using a set of so-called *imaging operations*. These have been formally defined in OpenGL version 1.2 [35], and it can therefore be expected that they will be available on a wide variety of future graphics hardware.

Afterwards, we discuss how the techniques for other local illumination models from Section 3, as well as the environment mapping techniques from Section 4 can be used together with normal maps. This part relies on the *pixel texture* extension that is currently only available from Silicon Graphics [22]. It has been shown elsewhere [21], that this extension is so powerful and versatile, that it might be implemented by other vendors in future systems.

The methods described here assume an orthographic camera and directional light sources. The artifacts introduced by these assumptions are usually barely noticeable for surfaces with bump maps, because the additional detail hides much of them.

### 5.1 Normal Maps with local Blinn-Phong Illumination

Among many other features (see [35] for details), the imaging operations make it possible to apply a $4 \times 4$ matrix to each pixel in an image, as it is transferred to or from the frame buffer or to texture RAM. Following this color matrix transformation, a lookup table may be applied to each individual color component.

With these two mechanisms and a given normal map in the form of a color coded image, the map can be lit in two rendering passes. First, a color matrix is specified, which maps the normal from object space into eye space and then computes the diffuse illumination (which is essentially given by the dot product with the light direction). When the normal image is now loaded into texture RAM, the lighting computations are performed. Afterwards the loaded, lit texture is applied to the object using texture mapping.

A similar second rendering pass draws the specular part. This time, however, the matrix computes the dot product between normal and the halfway vector $\vec{h}$ from Figure 1. The exponentiation by $1/r$, where $r$ is the surface roughness, is performed by a color lookup table.

Figure 9 shows two images where one polygon is rendered with this technique. On the left side, a simple exponential wave function is used as a normal map. The normal map for the image on the right side has been measured from a piece of wallpaper with the approach presented in [33].

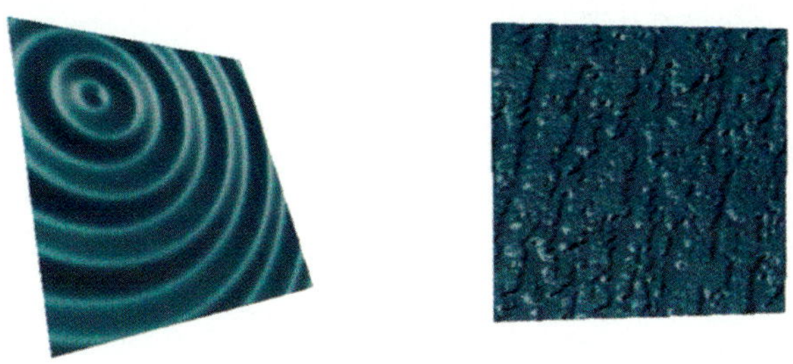

Figure 9: Two Phong-lit normal maps. The right one has been measured from a piece of wallpaper using the approach presented in [33].

### 5.2 Normal Maps with Other Reflection Models and Environment Maps

The techniques from Sections 3 and 4 could also be applied to normal maps, if the texture lookup could be performed per pixel instead of only per vertex. This can be achieved using the pixel texture extension from Silicon Graphics. It adds an additional stage to the rendering pipeline directly after the color matrix and the color table described above. This stage allows to interpret each of the color components as a texture coordinate pointing into a 1-, 2-, 3-, or 4-dimensional texture (see [22] for details).

This leads to the following algorithm for applying alternative lighting models:

- Render the object with the color coded normal map as a texture, thereby marking each visible pixel in the stencil buffer.
- Copy the frame buffer to main memory. This yields an image which contains the normal vector for each pixel.
- For each pass described in Section 3, set up the color matrix and blending as required by the respective illumination model, and copy the normal image from main memory into the frame buffer. Copy only those pixels marked in the stencil buffer.

For environment maps, the situation is somewhat more difficult, because the parabolic parameterization requires the use of projective textures, which are currently not supported by the pixel texture extension. As has been pointed out in [21], this limitation also prevents the use of pixel textures in other interesting applications, such as shadow maps. Hopefully this restriction will be removed in the future. Until then, pixel textures can still be used for environment mapping from a fixed viewing direction, which of course defeats the point of introducing the parabolic parameterization.

The images in Figure 10 were generated using the pixel texture extension and a single, view-dependent environment map.

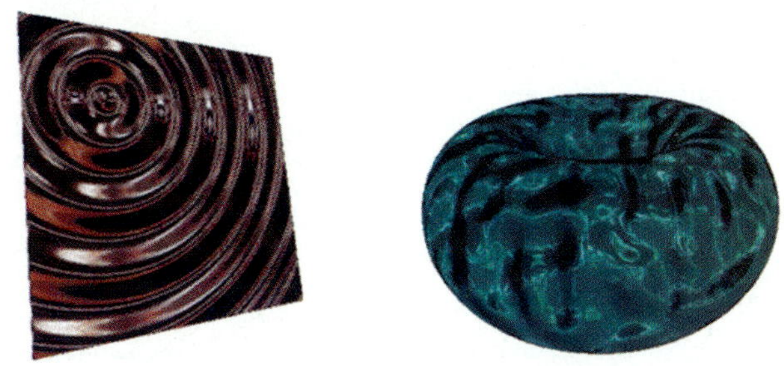

Figure 10: Combination of environment mapping and normal mapping. Left: environment map only. Right: Local Phong illumination plus environment map.

## 6 Discussion and Conclusions

The methods described in this paper provide means for generating realistic shading and lighting effects with computer graphics hardware. We have concentrated on concepts that can be implemented on current graphics hardware. All the techniques presented here run at frame rates of 15-20Hz on an SGI O2 (except for the ones requiring pixel textures, which the O2 does not support), and $> 20$ Hz on an SGI Octane MXE.

To conclude, we would now like to mention some issues which we deem important for the design of future graphics hardware:

The number of required rendering passes is reduced dramatically if the hardware has support for multiple textures. This is a feature which is beginning to appear on PC boards, and will probably be universally available soon.

Pixel textures are a very valuable tool and should be available on more platforms (see [21] for other applications than presented here). They should also support projective textures.

The easiest way to directly support our techniques in future hardware is to add more automatic texture generation modes. For local illumination with isotropic lighting models, the cosines between surface normal, facet normal, light direction and viewing direction are required. Except for orthographic viewing and directional light sources, these angles need to be computed in software, which requires the transformation of all vectors into eye space. For hardware lighting, these vectors are available in eye space anyway, so if the hardware could generate these cosine values automatically, this would both improve the performance and simplify the implementation. Automatic texture coordinate generation is also useful for generating the reflection vector required for the parabolic environment map parameterization. As pointed out above, this extension is already available in some implementations of OpenGL [23].

A more ambitious change to the rendering pipeline would be to replace the traditional hardware Phong lighting with a customizable sampling-based approach. In this case, the programmer would specify the material as a set of two or three 2-dimensional tables that can be downloaded to the hardware. The geometry processing hardware can then compute the indices into these tables for multiple light sources at the same time.

Although we have only discussed normal maps, the shading and lighting techniques presented here could also be applied to bump mapping hardware, by allowing an additional texture access after the normal for a pixel has been computed. This would, in particular, be a transparent implementation of environment maps for bump mapping hardware.

## 7 Acknowledgments

This work was done while the authors worked at the University of Erlangen. The cafe environment map used in this paper is a resampled version of the spherical map used in [16]. We would like to thank Mark Kilgard for implementing the extension for parabolic environment maps for Mesa and Riva TNT.

## References

[1] D. C. Banks. Illumination in diverse codimensions. In *Computer Graphics (Proceedings of SIGGRAPH '94)*, pages 327–334, July 1994.

[2] R. Bastos, K. Hoff, W. Wynn, and A. Lastra. Increased photorealism for interactive architectural walkthroughs. In *Symposium on Interactive 3D Graphics*. ACM Siggraph, 1999.

[3] P. Beckmann and A. Spizzichino. *The Scattering of Electromagnetic Waves from Rough Surfaces*. McMillan, 1963.

[4] J. F. Blinn. Models of light reflection for computer synthesized pictures. In *Computer Graphics (SIGGRAPH '77 Proceedings)*, pages 192–198, July 1977.

[5] J. F. Blinn. Simulation of wrinkled surfaces. In *Computer Graphics (SIGGRAPH '78 Proceedings)*, pages 286–292, August 1978.

[6] J. F. Blinn and M. E. Newell. Texture and reflection in computer generated images. *Communications of the ACM*, 19:542–546, 1976.

[7] P. Bui-Tuong. Illumination for computer generated pictures. *Communications of the ACM*, 18(6):311–317, June 1975.

[8] B. Cabral, N. Max, and R. Springmeyer. Bidirectional reflection functions from surface bump maps. In *Computer Graphics (SIGGRAPH '87 Proceedings)*, pages 273–281, July 1987.

[9] B. Cabral, M. Olano, and P. Nemec. Reflection space image based rendering. In *Computer Graphics (SIGGRAPH '99 Proceedings)*, August 1999.

[10] J. Cohen, M. Olano, and D. Manocha. Appearance-preserving simplification. In *Computer Graphics (SIGGRAPH '98 Proceedings)*, pages 115–122, July 1998.

[11] R. L. Cook and K. E. Torrance. A reflectance model for computer graphics. In *Computer Graphics (SIGGRAPH '81 Proceedings)*, pages 307–316, August 1981.

[12] P. Debevec. Rendering synthetic objects into real scenes: Bridging traditional and image-based graphics with global illumination and high dynamic range photography. In *Computer Graphics (SIGGRAPH '98 Proceedings)*, pages 189–198, July 1998.

[13] P. J. Diefenbach. *Pipeline Rendering: Interaction and Realism Through Hardware-based Multi-Pass Rendering*. PhD thesis, University of Pennsylvania, 1996.

[14] I. Ernst, H. Rüsseler, H. Schulz, and O. Wittig. Gouraud bump mapping. In *Eurographics/SIGGRAPH Workshop on Graphics Hardware*, pages 47–54, 1998.

[15] N. Greene. Applications of world projections. In *Proceedings of Graphics Interface '86*, pages 108–114, May 1986.

[16] P. Haeberli and M. Segal. Texture mapping as A fundamental drawing primitive. In *Fourth Eurographics Workshop on Rendering*, pages 259–266, June 1993.

[17] P. E. Haeberli and K. Akeley. The accumulation buffer: Hardware support for high-quality rendering. In *Computer Graphics (SIGGRAPH '90 Proceedings)*, pages 309–318, August 1990.

[18] X. D. He, K. E. Torrance, F. X. Sillion, and D. P. Greenberg. A comprehensive physical model for light reflection. In *Computer Graphics (SIGGRAPH '91 Proceedings)*, pages 175–186, July 1991.

[19] W. Heidrich. *High-quality Shading and Lighting for Hardware-accelerated Rendering*. PhD thesis, University of Erlangen-Nürnberg, April 1999.

[20] W. Heidrich and H.-P. Seidel. View-independent environment maps. In *Eurographics/SIGGRAPH Workshop on Graphics Hardware*, pages 39–45, 1998.

[21] W. Heidrich, R. Westermann, H.-P. Seidel, and Th. Ertl. Applications of pixel textures in visualization and realistic image synthesis. In *Symposium on Interactive 3D Graphics*, 1999. (Accepted for publication).

[22] Silicon Graphics Inc. *Pixel Texture Extension*, December 1996. Specification document, available from http://www.opengl.org.

[23] M. Kilgard. Personal communication, April 1999.

[24] R. R. Lewis. Making shaders more physically plausible. In *Fourth Eurographics Workshop on Rendering*, pages 47–62, June 1993.

[25] T. McReynolds, D. Blythe, B. Grantham, and S. Nelson. Advanced graphics programming techniques using OpenGL. In *Siggraph 1998 Course Notes*, July 1998.

[26] G. Miller, M. Halstead, and M. Clifton. On-the-fly texture computation for real-time surface shading. *IEEE Computer Graphics & Applications*, 18(2):44–58, March–April 1998.

[27] G. Miller and C. Hoffman. Illumination and reflection maps: Simulated objects in simulated and real environments. In *ACM SIGGRAPH '84 Course Notes - Advanced Computer Graphics Animation*, July 1984.

[28] G. Miller, S. Rubin, and D. Ponceleon. Lazy decompression of surface light fields for precomputed global illumnation. In *Rendering Techniques '98 (Proceedings of Eurographics Rendering Workshop)*, pages 281–292, March 1998.

[29] E. Ofek and A. Rappoport. Interactive reflections on curved objects. In *Computer Graphics (SIGGRAPH '98 Proceedings)*, pages 333–342, July 1998.

[30] M. Olano and A. Lastra. A shading language on graphics hardware: The PixelFlow shading system. In *Computer Graphics (SIGGRAPH '98 Proceedings)*, pages 159–168, July 1998.

[31] M. Peercy, J. Airey, and B. Cabral. Efficient bump mapping hardware. In *Computer Graphics (SIGGRAPH '97 Proceedings)*, pages 303–306, August 1997.

[32] P. Poulin and A. Fournier. A model for anisotropic reflection. In *Computer Graphics (SIGGRAPH '90 Proceedings)*, volume 24, pages 273–282, August 1990.

[33] H. Rushmeier, G. Taubin, and A. Guéziec. Applying shape from lighting variation to bump map capture. In *Rendering Techniques '97 (Proceedings of Eurographics Rendering Workshop)*, pages 35–44, June 1997.

[34] C. Schlick. A customizable reflectance model for everyday rendering. In *Fourth Eurographics Workshop on Rendering*, pages 73–83, June 1993.

[35] M. Segal and K. Akeley. *The OpenGL Graphics System: A Specification (Version 1.2)*, 1998.

[36] B. G. Smith. Geometrical shadowing of a random rough surface. *IEEE Transactions on Antennas and Propagation*, 15(5):668–671, September 1967.

[37] D. Stalling, M. Zöckler, and H.-C. Hege. Fast display of illuminated field lines. *IEEE Transactions on Visualization and Computer Graphics*, 3(2):118–128, 1997.

[38] W. Stürzlinger and R. Bastos. Interactive rendering of globally illuminated glossy scenes. In *Rendering Techniques '97*, pages 93–102, 1997.

[39] K. E. Torrance and E. M. Sparrow. Theory for off-specular reflection from roughened surfaces. *Journal of the Optical Society of America*, 57(9):1105–1114, September 1967.

[40] D. Voorhies and J. Foran. Reflection vector shading hardware. In *Computer Graphics (SIGGRAPH '94 Proceedings)*, pages 163–166, July 1994.

[41] B. Walter, G. Alppay, E. Lafortune, S. Fernandez, and D. P. Greenberg. Fitting virtual lights for non-diffuse walkthroughs. *Computer Graphics (SIGGRAPH '97 Proceedings)*, pages 45–48, August 1997.

[42] G. J. Ward. Measuring and modeling anisotropic reflection. *Computer Graphics (SIGGRAPH '92 Proceedings)*, pages 265–273, July 1992.

[43] L. Williams. Pyramidal parametrics. In *Computer Graphics (SIGGRAPH '83 Proceedings)*, pages 1–11, July 1983.

# Tracing Ray Differentials

Homan Igehy

Computer Science Department

Stanford University

## Abstract

Antialiasing of ray traced images is typically performed by supersampling the image plane. While this type of filtering works well for many algorithms, it is much more efficient to perform filtering locally on a surface for algorithms such as texture mapping. In order to perform this type of filtering, one must not only trace the ray passing through the pixel, but also have some approximation of the distance to neighboring rays hitting the surface (i.e., a ray's footprint). In this paper, we present a fast, simple, robust scheme for tracking such a quantity based on *ray differentials*, derivatives of the ray with respect to the image plane.

**CR Categories and Subject Descriptors:** I.3.7 [Computer Graphics]: Three-Dimensional Graphics and Realism – color, shading, shadowing, and texture; raytracing.

## 1 INTRODUCTION

Ray tracing [18] is an image generation technique that is able to accurately model many phenomena which are difficult or impossible to produce with a traditional graphics pipeline. As with any image synthesis algorithm, ray tracing is prone to aliasing, and antialiasing is typically performed by tracing rays at multiple sub-pixel offsets on the image plane (e.g., [12, 18]). By stochastically point sampling each of many variables per ray [6], one may filter over multiple phenomena simultaneously. For some algorithms, however, it is much more efficient to filter over a more local domain. For example, in texture mapping, a texture will often be viewed under high minification so that the entire texture falls under a small number of pixels. Filtering such a texture by taking bilinear samples for a set of stochastic rays requires the tracing of a correspondingly large number of rays. This is problematic because the cost of tracing a ray is relatively high, and the minification factor can be arbitrarily high. On the other hand, if we knew the distance between a ray and the rays for a neighboring pixel when the ray hit the texture map (i.e., a ray's footprint), then we could efficiently filter the texture by using a fast, memory coherent algorithm such as mip mapping [19]. Tracing such a quantity in a polygon rendering pipeline is straightforward because primitives are drawn in raster order, and the transformation between texture space and image space is described by a linear projective map [10]. In a ray tracer, however, the primitives are accessed according to a pixel's ray tree, and the transformation between texture space and image space is non-linear (reflection and refraction can make rays converge, diverge, or both), making the problem substantially more difficult.

homan@graphics.stanford.edu



Tracing a ray's footprint is also important for algorithms other than texture mapping. A few of these algorithms are listed below:

- Geometric level-of-detail allows a system to simultaneously antialias the geometric detail of an object, bound the cost of tracing a ray against an object, and provide memory coherent access to the data of an object. However, to pick a level-of-detail, one must know an approximation of the ray density when a ray is intersected against an object.
- When ray tracing caustics, the intensity attributed to a sampled light ray depends upon the convergence or divergence of the wavefront [13]. Similarly, in illumination mapping, the flux carried by a ray from a light source must be deposited over an area on a surface's illumination map based on the density of rays [5].
- Dull reflections may be modeled by filtering textures over a kernel which extends beyond the ray's actual footprint [2].

In this paper, we introduce a novel approach for quickly and robustly tracking an approximation to a ray's footprint based on *ray differentials*. Ray tracing can be viewed as the evaluation of the position and direction of a ray as the ray propagates through the scene. Because a ray is initially parameterized in terms of image space coordinates, in addition to tracing the ray, we can also trace the value of its derivatives with respect to the image plane. A first-order Taylor approximation based on these derivatives gives an estimate of a ray's footprint. A few techniques for estimating ray density have been presented in the literature [2, 5, 13, 16], but ray differentials are faster, simpler, and more robust than these algorithms. In particular, because ray differentials are based on elementary differential calculus rather than on differential geometry or another mathematical foundation that has an understanding of the 3D world, the technique may be readily applied to non-physical phenomena such as bump mapping and normal-interpolated triangles. General formulae for tracing ray differentials are derived for transfer, reflection, and refraction, and specific formulae are derived for handling normal-interpolated triangles. Finally, we demonstrate the utility of ray differentials in performing texture filtering.

## 2 RELATED WORK

Several algorithms have been developed for estimating a texture filtering kernel in polygon rendering pipelines (e.g., [1, 10]). Similar algorithms have been used in ray tracers that calculate the projection of texture coordinates onto the image plane [8], but such a projection is only valid for eye rays. This technique can be extended to reflected and refracted rays by computing the total distance traveled, but such an approximation is invalid because curved surfaces can greatly modify the convergence or divergence of rays. A few algorithms have been developed that take this into account, and we will review them briefly.

Within the context of a ray tracer, finite differencing has been used to calculate the extent over which a light ray's illuminance is deposited on an illumination map by examining the illumination map coordinates of neighboring rays [5]. The main advantage of finite differencing is that it can easily handle any kind of surface. The main disadvantages, however, are the difficult problems associated with robustly handling neighboring eye rays whose ray trees differ. The algorithm must detect when a neighboring ray does not hit the same primitives and handle this case specially. One plausible method of handling such a case is to send out a special neighboring ray that follows the same ray tree and intersects the plane of the same triangles beyond the triangle edges, but this will not work for spheres and other higher-order primitives. Additionally, this special case becomes the common case as neighboring rays intersect different primitives that are really part of the same object (e.g., a triangle mesh). Our algorithm circumvents these difficulties by utilizing the differential quantities of a single ray independently of its neighbors.

Cone tracing [2] is a method in which a conical approximation to a ray's footprint is traced for each ray. This cone is used for edge antialiasing in addition to texture filtering. The main problem with a conical approximation is that a cone is isotropic. Not only does this mean that pixels must be sampled isotropically on the image plane, but when the ray footprint becomes anisotropic after reflection or refraction, it must be re-approximated with an isotropic footprint. Thus, this method cannot be used for algorithms such as anisotropic texture filtering. In addition, extending the technique to support surfaces other than planar polygons and spheres in not straightforward.

Wavefront tracing [9] is a method in which the properties of a differentially small area of a ray's wavefront surface is tracked, and it has been used to calculate caustic intensities resulting from illumination off of curved surfaces [13]. Wavefronts have also been used to calculate the focusing characteristics of the human eye [11]. Although highly interrelated, the main difference between wavefronts and our method of ray differentials is that our method tracks the directional properties of a differentially small distance while wavefront tracing tracks the surface properties of a differentially small area. Thus, wavefronts cannot handle anisotropic spacing between pixel samples. Additionally, because a differential area is an inherently more complex quantity, the computational steps associated with wavefront tracing are more complicated. Wavefront tracing is based on differential geometry while our algorithm is based on elementary differential calculus, and a technical consequence of this is that we can readily handle non-physically based phenomena such as normal-interpolated triangles, bump mapped surfaces, and other algorithms that are self-contradicting in the framework of differential geometry. A practical consequence of being based on the simpler field of elementary differential calculus is that our formulation is easier to understand, and extending the technique to handle different phenomena is straightforward.

Paraxial ray theory [4] is an approximation technique originally developed for lens design, and its application to ray tracing is known as pencil tracing [16]. In pencil tracing, paraxial rays to an axial ray are parameterized by point-vector pairs on a plane perpendicular to the axial ray. The propagation of these paraxial rays is approximated linearly by a system matrix. As with wavefront tracing, the computational complexity of pencil tracing is significantly higher than our method. Additionally, pencil tracing makes a distinct set of simplifying assumptions to make each phenomenon linear with respect to the system matrix. An approximation is made even on transfer, a phenomenon that is linear with respect to a ray. Furthermore, the handling of non-physical phenomena is unclear. By comparison, the single unified approximation we make is simply that of a first-order Taylor approximation to a ray function.

# 3 TRACING RAY DIFFERENTIALS

One way to view ray tracing is as the evaluation of the position and direction of a ray function at discrete points as it propagates through the scene. Any value $v$ that is computed for the ray (e.g., luminance, texture coordinate on a surface, etc.) is derived by applying a series of functions to some initial set of parameters, typically the image space coordinates $x$ and $y$:

$$v = \mathrm{f}_n\left(\mathrm{f}_{n-1}\left(\ldots \mathrm{f}_2\left(\mathrm{f}_1(x, y)\right)\right)\right) \tag{1}$$

We can compute the derivative of this value with respect to an image space coordinate (e.g., $x$) by applying the Chain Rule:

$$\frac{\partial v}{\partial x} = \frac{\partial \mathrm{f}_n}{\partial \mathrm{f}_{n-1}} \cdots \frac{\partial \mathrm{f}_2}{\partial \mathrm{f}_1}\frac{\partial \mathrm{f}_1}{\partial x} \tag{2}$$

As transformations are applied to a ray to model propagation through a scene, we are just applying a set of functions $\mathrm{f}_i$ to keep track of the ray. We can also keep track of *ray differentials*, derivatives of the ray with respect to image space coordinates, by applying the derivatives of the functions. These ray differentials can then be used to give a first-order Taylor approximation to the ray as a function of image space coordinates. In the forthcoming derivations, we express scalars in italics and points, directions, and planes with homogeneous coordinates in bold.

A ray can be parameterized by a point representing a position on the ray and unit vector representing its direction:

$$\vec{\mathbf{R}} = \langle \mathbf{P} \quad \mathbf{D} \rangle \tag{3}$$

The initial values for a ray depend on the parameterization of the image plane: a pinhole camera is described by an eye point, a viewing direction, a right direction, and an up direction. The direction of a ray going through a pixel on the image plane can be expressed as a linear combination of these directions:

$$\mathbf{d}(x, y) = \mathbf{View} + x\mathbf{Right} + y\mathbf{Up} \tag{4}$$

Thus, the eye ray is given by:

$$\begin{aligned} \mathbf{P}(x, y) &= \mathbf{Eye} \\ \mathbf{D}(x, y) &= \frac{\mathbf{d}}{(\mathbf{d} \cdot \mathbf{d})^{1/2}} \end{aligned} \tag{5}$$

We can now ask the question, given a ray, if we were to pick a ray slightly above or to the right of it on the image plane, what ray would result? Each of these differentially offset rays can be represented by a pair of directions we call *ray differentials*:

$$\begin{aligned} \frac{\partial \vec{\mathbf{R}}}{\partial x} &= \left\langle \frac{\partial \mathbf{P}}{\partial x} \quad \frac{\partial \mathbf{D}}{\partial x} \right\rangle \\ \frac{\partial \vec{\mathbf{R}}}{\partial y} &= \left\langle \frac{\partial \mathbf{P}}{\partial y} \quad \frac{\partial \mathbf{D}}{\partial y} \right\rangle \end{aligned} \tag{6}$$

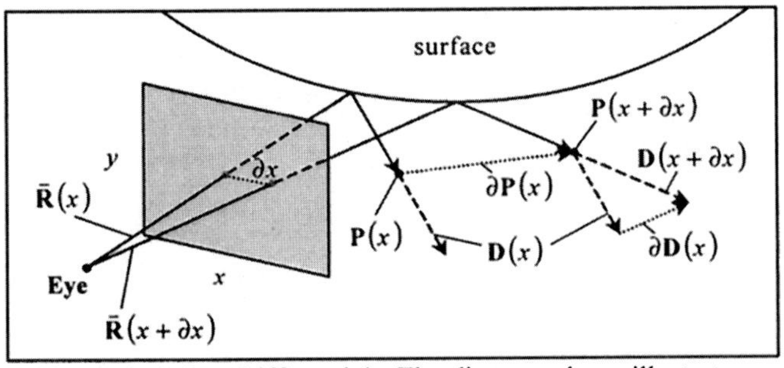


**Figure 1:** A Ray Differential. The diagram above illustrates the positions and directions of a ray and a differentially offset ray after a reflection. The difference between these positions and directions represents a ray differential.

A ray differential is illustrated in Figure 1. If we evaluate the ray differentials as a ray propagates in addition to the position and direction of the ray, then the distance between neighboring rays (and hence the ray's footprint) can be estimated with a first-order differential approximation:

$$\left[\bar{\mathbf{R}}(x+\Delta x,y)-\bar{\mathbf{R}}(x,y)\right]\approx \Delta x\frac{\partial\bar{\mathbf{R}}(x,y)}{\partial x}$$
$$\left[\bar{\mathbf{R}}(x,y+\Delta y)-\bar{\mathbf{R}}(x,y)\right]\approx \Delta y\frac{\partial\bar{\mathbf{R}}(x,y)}{\partial y} \qquad (7)$$

We can compute the initial value of the ray differential in the $x$ direction by differentiating (5) with respect to $x$:

$$\frac{\partial\mathbf{P}}{\partial x}=\mathbf{0}$$
$$\frac{\partial\mathbf{D}}{\partial x}=\frac{(\mathbf{d}\cdot\mathbf{d})\ \mathbf{Right}-(\mathbf{d}\cdot\mathbf{Right})\ \mathbf{d}}{(\mathbf{d}\cdot\mathbf{d})^{3/2}} \qquad (8)$$

A similar expression can be derived for the $y$ direction. Although we only track first-order derivatives, higher-order derivatives could be computed as well for a better approximation or for error bounding. However, we have found that discontinuities limit the effectiveness of higher-order approximations and that a first-order approximation is sufficient in practice.

## 3.1 Propagation

Given an expression for the propagation of a ray for any phenomenon (i.e., how a phenomenon affects the ray's value), then we can find the expression for the propagation of a ray differential by simply differentiating the expression. Here, we will derive the formulae for the three common ray tracing operations: transfer, reflection, and refraction. We will express our formulae as derivatives with respect to $x$ without any loss in generality.

### 3.1.1 Transfer

Transfer is the simple operation of propagating a ray through a homogenous medium to the point of intersection with a surface. The equation for transfer onto a surface at a distance $t$ is given by:

$$\mathbf{P}'=\mathbf{P}+t\mathbf{D}$$
$$\mathbf{D}'=\mathbf{D} \qquad (9)$$

For a ray differential, we differentiate (9) to get:

$$\frac{\partial\mathbf{P}'}{\partial x}=\left(\frac{\partial\mathbf{P}}{\partial x}+t\frac{\partial\mathbf{D}}{\partial x}\right)+\frac{\partial t}{\partial x}\mathbf{D}$$
$$\frac{\partial\mathbf{D}'}{\partial x}=\frac{\partial\mathbf{D}}{\partial x} \qquad (10)$$

For a planar surface $\mathbf{N}$ (defined as the locus of points $\mathbf{P}'$ such that $\mathbf{P}'\bullet\mathbf{N}=0$), $t$ is given by:

$$t=-\frac{\mathbf{P}\cdot\mathbf{N}}{\mathbf{D}\cdot\mathbf{N}} \qquad (11)$$

Differentiating this and re-expressing it in terms of $t$, we get:

$$\frac{\partial t}{\partial x}=-\frac{\left(\frac{\partial\mathbf{P}}{\partial x}+t\frac{\partial\mathbf{D}}{\partial x}\right)\cdot\mathbf{N}}{\mathbf{D}\cdot\mathbf{N}} \qquad (12)$$

Note that the fourth component of $\mathbf{N}$ is irrelevant in this equation (its dot product is taken with directions only), and it can thus be viewed as the normal of the surface. Equations (10) and (12) actually have a geometric interpretation: the first two terms of the first equation in (10) express the fact that as a ray travels through homogeneous space, the positional offset of a differentially offset ray changes according to its directional offset and the distance traveled. Then, the third term orthographically projects this positional offset in the direction of the ray onto the plane.

Although a formal proof is beyond the scope of this paper, (12) is not only valid for a plane, but is also correct for an arbitrary surface. In the case of an arbitrary surface, $\mathbf{N}$ is just the normal of the surface at the point of intersection. The intuition behind this is that a surface has a fixed shape and curvature at an intersection point. As we intersect an offset ray against this surface by smaller and smaller offsets, the surface will look more and more like the tangent plane at the intersection point. In the limit, a differentially offset ray intersects the surface in the tangent plane of the intersection point.

### 3.1.2 Reflection

Given a ray that has been transferred onto a surface by (9), the equation for a reflection ray [7] is given by:

$$\mathbf{P}'=\mathbf{P}$$
$$\mathbf{D}'=\mathbf{D}-2(\mathbf{D}\cdot\mathbf{N})\mathbf{N} \qquad (13)$$

For a ray differential, reflection is given by:

$$\frac{\partial\mathbf{P}'}{\partial x}=\frac{\partial\mathbf{P}}{\partial x}$$
$$\frac{\partial\mathbf{D}'}{\partial x}=\frac{\partial\mathbf{D}}{\partial x}-2\left[(\mathbf{D}\cdot\mathbf{N})\frac{\partial\mathbf{N}}{\partial x}+\frac{\partial(\mathbf{D}\cdot\mathbf{N})}{\partial x}\mathbf{N}\right] \qquad (14)$$

where:

$$\frac{\partial(\mathbf{D}\cdot\mathbf{N})}{\partial x}=\frac{\partial\mathbf{D}}{\partial x}\cdot\mathbf{N}+\mathbf{D}\cdot\frac{\partial\mathbf{N}}{\partial x} \qquad (15)$$

This equation requires the evaluation of the derivative of the normal at the point of intersection, a topic that will be addressed in Sections 3.2 and 3.3.

### 3.1.3 Refraction

Once a ray has been transferred onto a surface, the equation for a refracted ray [7] can be expressed as:

$$\mathbf{P}'=\mathbf{P}$$
$$\mathbf{D}'=\eta\mathbf{D}-\mu\mathbf{N} \qquad (16)$$

where we use the shorthand notation:

$$\mu=\left[\eta(\mathbf{D}\cdot\mathbf{N})-(\mathbf{D}'\cdot\mathbf{N})\right]$$
$$\mathbf{D}'\cdot\mathbf{N}=-\sqrt{1-\eta^2\left[1-(\mathbf{D}\cdot\mathbf{N})^2\right]} \qquad (17)$$

and $\eta$ is the ratio of the incident index of refraction to the transmitted index of refraction. Differentiating, we get:

$$\frac{\partial \mathbf{P}'}{\partial x} = \frac{\partial \mathbf{P}}{\partial x}$$
$$\frac{\partial \mathbf{D}'}{\partial x} = \eta \frac{\partial \mathbf{D}}{\partial x} - \left( \mu \frac{\partial \mathbf{N}}{\partial x} + \frac{\partial \mu}{\partial x} \mathbf{N} \right) \tag{18}$$

where (referring to (15) from Section 3.1.2):

$$\frac{\partial \mu}{\partial x} = \left[ \eta - \frac{\eta^2 (\mathbf{D} \cdot \mathbf{N})}{(\mathbf{D}' \cdot \mathbf{N})} \right] \frac{\partial (\mathbf{D} \cdot \mathbf{N})}{\partial x} \tag{19}$$

## 3.2 Surface Normals

The formulae derived for reflection and refraction of ray differentials in Sections 3.1.2 and 3.1.3 depend on the derivative of the unit normal with respect to $x$. In differential geometry [17], the *shape operator* (S) is defined as the negative derivative of a unit normal with respect to a direction tangent to the surface. This operator completely describes a differentially small area on a surface. For our computation, the tangent direction of interest is given by the derivative of the ray's intersection point, and thus:

$$\frac{\partial \mathbf{N}}{\partial x} = -\mathrm{S}\left( \frac{\partial \mathbf{P}}{\partial x} \right) \tag{20}$$

For a planar surface, the shape operator is just zero. For a sphere, the shape operator given a unit tangent vector is the tangent vector scaled by the inverse of the sphere's radius. Formulae for the shape operator of both parametric and implicit surfaces may be found in texts on differential geometry (e.g., [17]) and other sources [13], and thus will not be covered here in further detail.

## 3.3 Discussion

One interesting consequence of casting ray differentials in the framework of elementary differential calculus is that we may forgo any understanding of surfaces and differential geometry, even in expressing the derivative of a unit normal. For that matter, we may forgo the geometric interpretation of any calculation, such as the interpretation made for equations (10) and (12). For example, if we know that the equation of a unit normal to a sphere with origin **O** and radius $r$ at a point **P** on the sphere is given by:

$$\mathbf{N} = (\mathbf{P} - \mathbf{O})/r \tag{21}$$

then we may "blindly" differentiate with respect to $x$ to get:

$$\frac{\partial \mathbf{N}}{\partial x} = \frac{\partial \mathbf{P}}{\partial x} \Big/ r \tag{22}$$

This differentiation may be performed on any surface or for any phenomenon. If we know the formula for how a ray is affected by a phenomenon, then we can differentiate it to get a formula for how a ray differential is affected without any understanding of the phenomenon. For example, if we apply an affine transformation to a ray so that we may perform intersections in object space coordinates, then the ray differential is transformed according to the derivative of the affine transformation. If we apply an ad hoc non-linear warp to rays in order to simulate a fish-eye lens effect, then we can derive an expression for warping the ray differentials by differentiating the warping function. This is a large advantage of being based on elementary differential calculus rather than on a physically-based mathematical framework.

In graphics, we often use non-physical surfaces that separate the geometric normal from the shading normal, such as normal-interpolated triangles or bump mapped surfaces. For such surfaces, the use of ray differentials is straightforward. In the case of transfer to the point of intersection, the geometric normal is used for (12) because a neighboring ray would intersect the surface according to the shape defined by the geometric normal. For reflection and refraction, however, the shading normal is used because neighboring rays would be reflected and refracted according to the shading normal. Because of its common use, we derive an expression for the derivative of the shading normal for a normal-interpolated triangle in the box below.

The computational cost of tracing ray differentials is very small relative to the other costs of a ray tracer. Each of the

**Normal-Interpolated Triangles**

The position of a point **P** on the plane of a triangle may be expressed as a linear combination of the vertices of triangle:

$$\mathbf{P} = \alpha \mathbf{P}_\alpha + \beta \mathbf{P}_\beta + \gamma \mathbf{P}_\gamma$$

where the barycentric weights $\alpha$, $\beta$, and $\gamma$ are all positive when **P** is inside the triangle and add up to one when **P** is on the plane of the triangle. These values may be calculated as the dot product between the point **P** expressed in normalized homogeneous coordinates (i.e., $w$=1) and a set of planes $\mathbf{L}_\alpha$, $\mathbf{L}_\beta$, and $\mathbf{L}_\gamma$:

$$\alpha(\mathbf{P}) = \mathbf{L}_\alpha \cdot \mathbf{P}$$
$$\beta(\mathbf{P}) = \mathbf{L}_\beta \cdot \mathbf{P}$$
$$\gamma(\mathbf{P}) = \mathbf{L}_\gamma \cdot \mathbf{P}$$

$\mathbf{L}_\alpha$ can be any plane that contains $\mathbf{P}_\beta$ and $\mathbf{P}_\gamma$ (e.g., one that is perpendicular to the triangle), and its coefficients are normalized so that $\mathbf{L}_\alpha \bullet \mathbf{P}_\alpha = 1$; $\mathbf{L}_\beta$ and $\mathbf{L}_\gamma$ can be computed similarly. The normal at a point is then computed as a linear combination of the normals at the vertices:

$$\mathbf{n} = (\mathbf{L}_\alpha \cdot \mathbf{P})\ \mathbf{N}_\alpha + (\mathbf{L}_\beta \cdot \mathbf{P})\ \mathbf{N}_\beta + (\mathbf{L}_\gamma \cdot \mathbf{P})\ \mathbf{N}_\gamma$$
$$\mathbf{N} = \frac{\mathbf{n}}{(\mathbf{n} \cdot \mathbf{n})^{1/2}}$$

Differentiating, we get:

$$\frac{\partial \mathbf{n}}{\partial x} = \left(\mathbf{L}_\alpha \cdot \frac{\partial \mathbf{P}}{\partial x}\right) \mathbf{N}_\alpha + \left(\mathbf{L}_\beta \cdot \frac{\partial \mathbf{P}}{\partial x}\right) \mathbf{N}_\beta + \left(\mathbf{L}_\gamma \cdot \frac{\partial \mathbf{P}}{\partial x}\right) \mathbf{N}_\gamma$$
$$\frac{\partial \mathbf{N}}{\partial x} = \frac{(\mathbf{n} \cdot \mathbf{n}) \frac{\partial \mathbf{n}}{\partial x} - \left(\mathbf{n} \cdot \frac{\partial \mathbf{n}}{\partial x}\right) \mathbf{n}}{(\mathbf{n} \cdot \mathbf{n})^{3/2}}$$

where a direction (e.g., the derivative of **P**) is expressed in homogeneous coordinates (i.e., $w$=0). The sum of the three barycentric weights for the derivative of **P** add up to zero when the direction is in the plane of the triangle.

Similarly, a texture coordinate can be expressed as a linear combination of the texture coordinates at the vertices:

$$\mathbf{T} = (\mathbf{L}_\alpha \cdot \mathbf{P})\ \mathbf{T}_\alpha + (\mathbf{L}_\beta \cdot \mathbf{P})\ \mathbf{T}_\beta + (\mathbf{L}_\gamma \cdot \mathbf{P})\ \mathbf{T}_\gamma$$

and its derivative is given by:

$$\frac{\partial \mathbf{T}}{\partial x} = \left(\mathbf{L}_\alpha \cdot \frac{\partial \mathbf{P}}{\partial x}\right) \mathbf{T}_\alpha + \left(\mathbf{L}_\beta \cdot \frac{\partial \mathbf{P}}{\partial x}\right) \mathbf{T}_\beta + \left(\mathbf{L}_\gamma \cdot \frac{\partial \mathbf{P}}{\partial x}\right) \mathbf{T}_\gamma$$

interactions in Section 3.1 requires a few dozen floating-point operations. On a very rough scale, this is approximately the same cost as a single ray-triangle intersection, a simple lighting calculation, or a step through a hierarchical acceleration structure, thus making the incremental cost insignificant in all but the simplest of scenes.

# 4 TEXTURE FILTERING

One practical application of ray differentials is texture filtering. If we can approximate the difference between the texture coordinates corresponding to a ray and its neighboring rays, then we can find the size and shape of a filtering kernel in texture space. The texture coordinates of a surface depend on the texture parameterization of the surface. Such a parameterization is straightforward for parametric surfaces, and algorithms exist to parameterize implicit surfaces [14]. In general, the texture coordinates of a surface may be expressed as a function of the intersection point:

$$\mathbf{T} = f(\mathbf{P}) \tag{23}$$

We can differentiate with respect to $x$ to get a function that is dependent on the intersection point and its derivative:

$$\frac{\partial \mathbf{T}}{\partial x} = \frac{\partial [f(\mathbf{P})]}{\partial x} = g\left(\mathbf{P}, \frac{\partial \mathbf{P}}{\partial x}\right) \tag{24}$$

We also derive the expression for the derivative of texture coordinates for a triangle in the box on the previous page.

Applying a first-order Taylor approximation, we get an expression for the extent of a pixel's footprint in texture space based on the pixel-to-pixel spacing:

$$\begin{aligned} \Delta \mathbf{T}_x &= [\mathbf{T}(x+\Delta x, y) - \mathbf{T}(x,y)] \approx \Delta x \frac{\partial \mathbf{T}}{\partial x} \\ \Delta \mathbf{T}_y &= [\mathbf{T}(x, y+\Delta y) - \mathbf{T}(x,y)] \approx \Delta y \frac{\partial \mathbf{T}}{\partial y} \end{aligned} \tag{25}$$

## 4.1 Filtering Algorithms

Assuming texture coordinates are two-dimensional, (25) defines a parallelogram over which we filter the texture. This is illustrated by Figure 2. Given this parallelogram, one of several texture filtering methods can be used. The most common method, mip mapping [19], is based on storing a pyramid of pre-filtered images, each at power of two resolutions. Then, when a filtered sample is required during rendering, a bilinearly interpolated sample is taken from the level of the image pyramid that most closely matches the filtering footprint. There are many ways of selecting this level-of-detail, and a popular algorithm [10] is based on the texel-to-pixel ratio defined by the length of the larger axis of the parallelogram of Figure 2:

$$lod = \log_2\left[\max\left((\Delta \mathbf{T}_x \cdot \Delta \mathbf{T}_x)^{1/2}, (\Delta \mathbf{T}_y \cdot \Delta \mathbf{T}_y)^{1/2}\right)\right] \tag{26}$$

Because the computed level-of-detail can fall in between image pyramid levels, one must round this value to pick a single level. In order to make the transition between pyramid levels smooth, systems will often interpolate between the two adjacent levels, resulting in trilinearly interpolated mip mapping.

Mip mapping is an isotropic texture filtering technique that does not take into account the orientation of a pixel's footprint. When using (26), textures are blurred excessively in one direction

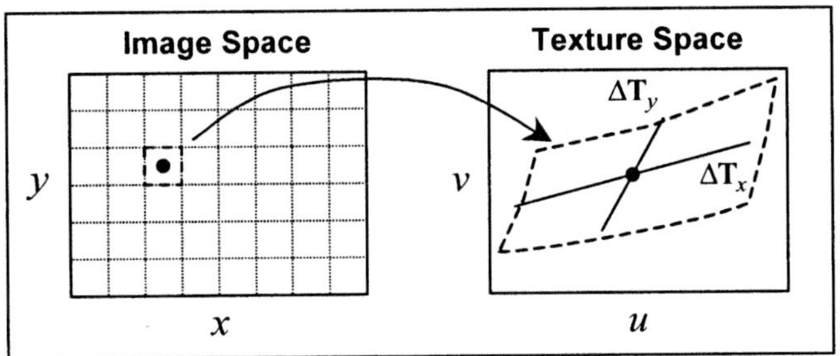


**Figure 2:** Texture Filtering Kernel. A pixel's footprint in image space can map to an arbitrary region in texture space. This region can be estimated by a parallelogram formed by a first-order differential approximation of the ratios between rate of change in texture space and image space coordinates.

if the parallelogram defined by (25) is asymmetric. Anisotropic filtering techniques take into account both the orientation and the amount of anisotropy in the footprint. A typical method [3, 15] is to define a rotated rectangle based on the longer of the two axes of the parallelogram, use the rectangle's minor axis to choose a mip map level, and average bilinear samples taken along the major axis. Again, one may interpolate between mip map levels.

## 4.2 Results

Figure 3 and Figure 4 demonstrate a scene rendered with four approaches towards texture filtering, all generated with a single eye ray per pixel at a resolution of 1000 by 666. In this scene, which consists entirely of texture mapped triangles, we are at a desk that is in a room with a wallpaper texture map for its walls and a picture of a zebra in the woods on the left. We are viewing a soccer ball paper weight on top of a sheet of text, and we are examining the text with a magnifying glass.

In Figure 3a, we perform texture filtering by doing a simple bilinear filtering on the texture map. The text in this image is noticeably aliased in the three places where minification is occurring: on the paper, in the reflection off of the ball, and around the edges of the lens. Additionally, the reflection of the walls and the zebra in the soccer ball is very noisy. This aliasing is also apparent on the frame of the magnifying glass, especially on the left edge as the zebra is minified down to only a few pixels on the $x$ direction. Even at sixteen rays per pixel (not shown), this artifact is visible.

In Figure 3b, mip mapping is performed for texture lookups, and the level-of-detail value is calculated based on the distance a ray has traveled and projection onto the surface. The textures of the image are properly filtered for eye rays, but reflected and refracted rays use the wrong level-of-detail. For the reflections, the divergence of the rays increases because of the surface curvature, and thus the level-of-detail based on ray distance is too low. This results in aliasing off of the ball and the frame. For refraction, the rays converge, making the ray distance-based algorithm cause blurring.

In Figure 4a, we perform mip mapping with the level-of-detail being computed by ray differentials. The limitations of this isotropic filtering are most apparent in the text. In order to address the blurring of the text on the paper, in the reflection off the ball, and around the edges of the lens, we demonstrate anisotropic texture filtering in Figure 4b. This image still has visible aliasing due to silhouette edges and shadowing discontinuities, and Figure 5 demonstrates that a simple super-sampling of 4 rays per pixel combined with anisotropic texture filtering produces a relatively alias-free image.

## 4.3 Discussion

Given the use of ray differentials for texture filtering, two interesting problems arise on how to combine the technique with adaptive edge filtering and with illumination sampling algorithms. First, because the algorithm filters only texture data, some sort of filtering is still necessary for edge discontinuities. The brute-force algorithm used in Figure 5 solves this problem, but an adaptive algorithm would certainly be more efficient. An open question is what kind of adaptive algorithms would work most effectively. It would seem that adaptively super-sampling pixels whose ray trees differ from their neighbors' ray trees would work well, but implementing such an algorithm is challenging.

**Figure 3:** Texture Filtering. The textures in (a) were filtered by taking a bilinearly interpolating an unfiltered texture map, and the textures in (b) were filtered by trilinearly interpolating a mip map at a level-of-detail based on ray distance.

Another open issue with using ray differentials for texture filtering involves surface interactions. Although many surfaces can be described using reflection, refraction, and a localized shading model, one of the large advantages of ray tracing is its ability to implement all sorts of shading and illumination algorithms. For example, a general bi-directional reflectance function (BRDF) is necessary for describing physically correct reflectance models. BRDFs are usually sampled, and an open question is how to combine a ray's footprint with a sampled reflectance model. The idea of dull reflections (as presented for cone tracing [2]) suggests that a large amount of efficiency can be gained by factoring out texture filtering from BRDF sampling.

**Figure 4:** Texture Filtering. The textures in (a) were filtered by trilinearly interpolating a mip map at a level-of-detail based on the ray differential approximation of this paper. To reduce blurring, (b) performs anisotropic texture filtering based on ray differentials.

## 5 CONCLUSION

In this paper, we have presented a novel algorithm for tracking an approximation to a ray's footprint based on ray differentials, the derivatives of a ray function with respect to the image plane. This technique can robustly handle anisotropic pixel spacing and anisotropic texture filtering. Because our algorithm is based on elementary differential calculus, the application of ray differentials to a variety of physical and non-physical graphics algorithms is straightforward. Furthermore, the incremental cost of tracking ray differentials is very small compared to other costs of a ray tracer. Finally, we have demonstrated the use of ray differentials to efficiently perform texture antialiasing without super-sampling the image plane.

## Acknowledgements

We would like to thank Pat Hanrahan, Matthew Eldridge, Matt Pharr, Tamara Munzner, and the reviewers for their assistance with this paper. Financial support was provided by Intel and DARPA contract DABT63-95-C-0085-P00006.

## References

[1] K. Akeley. RealityEngine Graphics. *Computer Graphics* (SIGGRAPH 93 Proceedings), **27**, 109-116, 1993.

[2] J. Amanatides. Ray Tracing with Cones. *Computer Graphics* (SIGGRAPH 84 Proceedings), **18**, 129-135, 1984.

[3] A. Barkans. High-Quality Rendering Using the Talisman Architecture. *1997 SIGGRAPH / Eurographics Workshop on Graphics Hardware*, 79-88, 1997.

[4] M. Born and E. Wolf. *Principles of Optics*. Pergamon Press, New York, 190-196, 1959.

[5] S. Collins. Adaptive Splatting for Specular to Diffuse Light Transport. *Fifth Eurographics Workshop on Rendering*, 119-135, 1994.

[6] R. Cook, T. Porter, and L. Carpenter. Distributed Ray Tracing. *Computer Graphics* (SIGGRAPH 84 Proceedings), **18**, 137-145, 1984.

[7] A. Glassner, ed. *An Introduction to Ray Tracing*. Academic Press, San Diego, 288-293, 1989.

[8] L. Gritz and J. Hahn. BMRT: A Global Illumination Implementation of the RenderMan Standard. *Journal of Graphics Tools*, **1**(3), 1996.

[9] A. Gullstrand. Die reelle optische Abbildun g. *Sv. Vetensk. Handl.*, **41**, 1-119, 1906.

[10] P. Heckbert. Texture Mapping Polygons in Perspective. *NYIT Computer Graphics Lab Technical Memo #13*, 1983.

[11] J. Loos, P. Slusallek, and H. Seidel. Using Wavefront Tracing for the Visualization and Optimization of Progressive Lenses. *Computer Graphics Forum* (Eurographics 98 Proceedings), **17**(3), 1998.

[12] D. Mitchell. Generating Antialiased Images at Low Sampling Densities. *Computer Graphics* (SIGGRAPH 87 Proceedings), **21**, 65-72, 1987.

[13] D. Mitchell and P. Hanrahan. Illumination from Curved Reflectors. *Computer Graphics* (SIGGRAPH 92 Proceedings), **26**, 283-291, 1992.

[14] H. Pederson. Decorating Implicit Surfaces. *Computer Graphics* (SIGGRAPH 95 Proceedings), **29**, 291-300, 1995.

[15] A. Schilling, G. Knittel, and W. Strasser. Texram: A Smart Memory for Texturing. *IEEE Computer Graphics and Applications*, **16**(3), 32-41, 1996.

[16] M. Shinya and T. Takahashi. Principles and Applications of Pencil Tracing. *Computer Graphics* (SIGGRAPH 87 Proceedings), **21**, 45-54, 1987.

[17] D. Struik. *Lectures on Classical Differential Geometry*, Second Edition. Dover Publications, New York, 1961.

[18] T. Whitted. An Improved Illumination Model for Shaded Displays. *Communications of the ACM*, **23**(6), 343-349, 1980.

[19] L. Williams. Pyramidal Parametrics. *Computer Graphics* (SIGGRAPH 83 Proceedings), **17**, 1-11, 1983.

**Figure 5:** Texture Filtering. Here, we demonstrate four rays per pixel with anisotropic texture filtering based on ray differentials.

# A Morphable Model For The Synthesis Of 3D Faces

Volker Blanz Thomas Vetter

Max-Planck-Institut für biologische Kybernetik,
Tübingen, Germany*

## Abstract

In this paper, a new technique for modeling textured 3D faces is introduced. 3D faces can either be generated automatically from one or more photographs, or modeled directly through an intuitive user interface. Users are assisted in two key problems of computer aided face modeling. First, new face images or new 3D face models can be registered automatically by computing dense one-to-one correspondence to an internal face model. Second, the approach regulates the naturalness of modeled faces avoiding faces with an "unlikely" appearance.

Starting from an example set of 3D face models, we derive a morphable face model by transforming the shape and texture of the examples into a vector space representation. New faces and expressions can be modeled by forming linear combinations of the prototypes. Shape and texture constraints derived from the statistics of our example faces are used to guide manual modeling or automated matching algorithms.

We show 3D face reconstructions from single images and their applications for photo-realistic image manipulations. We also demonstrate face manipulations according to complex parameters such as gender, fullness of a face or its distinctiveness.

**Keywords:** facial modeling, registration, photogrammetry, morphing, facial animation, computer vision

## 1 Introduction

Computer aided modeling of human faces still requires a great deal of expertise and manual control to avoid unrealistic, non-face-like results. Most limitations of automated techniques for face synthesis, face animation or for general changes in the appearance of an individual face can be described either as the problem of finding corresponding feature locations in different faces or as the problem of separating realistic faces from faces that could never appear in the real world. The correspondence problem is crucial for all morphing techniques, both for the application of motion-capture data to pictures or 3D face models, and for most 3D face reconstruction techniques from images. A limited number of labeled feature points marked in one face, e.g., the tip of the nose, the eye corner and less prominent points on the cheek, must be located precisely in another face. The number of manually labeled feature points varies from application to application, but usually ranges from 50 to 300.

Only a correct alignment of all these points allows acceptable intermediate morphs, a convincing mapping of motion data from the reference to a new model, or the adaptation of a 3D face model to 2D images for 'video cloning'. Human knowledge and experience is necessary to compensate for the variations between individual faces and to guarantee a valid location assignment in the different faces. At present, automated matching techniques can be utilized only for very prominent feature points such as the corners of eyes and mouth.

A second type of problem in face modeling is the separation of natural faces from non faces. For this, human knowledge is even more critical. Many applications involve the design of completely new natural looking faces that can occur in the real world but which have no "real" counterpart. Others require the manipulation of an existing face according to changes in age, body weight or simply to emphasize the characteristics of the face. Such tasks usually require time-consuming manual work combined with the skills of an artist.

In this paper, we present a parametric face modeling technique that assists in both problems. First, arbitrary human faces can be created simultaneously controlling the likelihood of the generated faces. Second, the system is able to compute correspondence between new faces. Exploiting the statistics of a large dataset of 3D face scans (geometric and textural data, $Cyberware^{TM}$) we built a morphable face model and recover domain knowledge about face variations by applying pattern classification methods. The morphable face model is a multidimensional 3D morphing function that is based on the linear combination of a large number of 3D face scans. Computing the average face and the main modes of variation in our dataset, a probability distribution is imposed on the morphing function to avoid unlikely faces. We also derive parametric descriptions of face attributes such as gender, distinctiveness, "hooked" noses or the weight of a person, by evaluating the distribution of exemplar faces for each attribute within our face space.

Having constructed a parametric face model that is able to generate almost any face, the correspondence problem turns into a mathematical optimization problem. New faces, images or 3D face scans, can be registered by minimizing the difference between the new face and its reconstruction by the face model function. We devel-

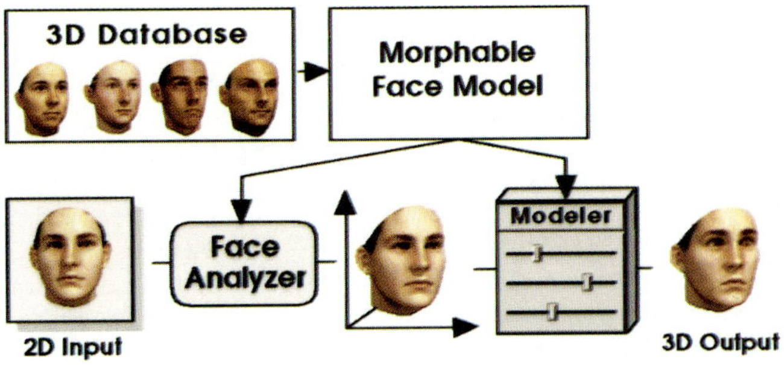


Figure 1: Derived from a dataset of prototypical 3D scans of faces, the morphable face model contributes to two main steps in face manipulation: (1) deriving a 3D face model from a novel image, and (2) modifying shape and texture in a natural way.

*MPI für biol. Kybernetik, Spemannstr. 38, 72076 Tübingen, Germany. E-mail: {volker.blanz, thomas.vetter}@tuebingen.mpg.de

oped an algorithm that adjusts the model parameters automatically for an optimal reconstruction of the target, requiring only a minimum of manual initialization. The output of the matching procedure is a high quality 3D face model that is in full correspondence with our morphable face model. Consequently all face manipulations parameterized in our model function can be mapped to the target face. The prior knowledge about the shape and texture of faces in general that is captured in our model function is sufficient to make reasonable estimates of the full 3D shape and texture of a face even when only a single picture is available. When applying the method to several images of a person, the reconstructions reach almost the quality of laser scans.

### 1.1 Previous and related work

Modeling human faces has challenged researchers in computer graphics since its beginning. Since the pioneering work of Parke [25, 26], various techniques have been reported for modeling the geometry of faces [10, 11, 22, 34, 21] and for animating them [28, 14, 19, 32, 22, 38, 29]. A detailed overview can be found in the book of Parke and Waters [24].

The key part of our approach is a generalized model of human faces. Similar to the approach of DeCarlos et al. [10], we restrict the range of allowable faces according to constraints derived from prototypical human faces. However, instead of using a limited set of measurements and proportions between a set of facial landmarks, we directly use the densely sampled geometry of the exemplar faces obtained by laser scanning ($Cyberware^{TM}$). The dense modeling of facial geometry (several thousand vertices per face) leads directly to a triangulation of the surface. Consequently, there is no need for variational surface interpolation techniques [10, 23, 33]. We also added a model of texture variations between faces. The morphable 3D face model is a consequent extension of the interpolation technique between face geometries, as introduced by Parke [26]. Computing correspondence between individual 3D face data automatically, we are able to increase the number of vertices used in the face representation from a few hundreds to tens of thousands. Moreover, we are able to use a higher number of faces, and thus to interpolate between hundreds of 'basis' faces rather than just a few. The goal of such an extended morphable face model is to represent any face as a linear combination of a limited basis set of face prototypes. Representing the face of an arbitrary person as a linear combination (morph) of "prototype" faces was first formulated for image compression in telecommunications [8]. Image-based linear 2D face models that exploit large data sets of prototype faces were developed for face recognition and image coding [4, 18, 37].

Different approaches have been taken to automate the matching step necessary for building up morphable models. One class of techniques is based on optic flow algorithms [5, 4] and another on an active model matching strategy [12, 16]. Combinations of both techniques have been applied to the problem of image matching [36]. In this paper we extend this approach to the problem of matching 3D faces.

The correspondence problem between different three-dimensional face data has been addressed previously by Lee et al.[20]. Their shape-matching algorithm differs significantly from our approach in several respects. First, we compute the correspondence in high resolution, considering shape and texture data simultaneously. Second, instead of using a physical tissue model to constrain the range of allowed mesh deformations, we use the statistics of our example faces to keep deformations plausible. Third, we do not rely on routines that are specifically designed to detect the features exclusively found in faces, e.g., eyes, nose.

Our general matching strategy can be used not only to adapt the morphable model to a 3D face scan, but also to 2D images of faces. Unlike a previous approach [35], the morphable 3D face model is now directly matched to images, avoiding the detour of generating intermediate 2D morphable image models. As a consequence, head orientation, illumination conditions and other parameters can be free variables subject to optimization. It is sufficient to use rough estimates of their values as a starting point of the automated matching procedure.

Most techniques for 'face cloning', the reconstruction of a 3D face model from one or more images, still rely on manual assistance for matching a deformable 3D face model to the images [26, 1, 30]. The approach of Pighin et al. [28] demonstrates the high realism that can be achieved for the synthesis of faces and facial expressions from photographs where several images of a face are matched to a single 3D face model. Our automated matching procedure could be used to replace the manual initialization step, where several corresponding features have to be labeled in the presented images.

For the animation of faces, a variety of methods have been proposed. For a complete overview we again refer to the book of Parke and Waters [24]. The techniques can be roughly separated in those that rely on physical modeling of facial muscles [38, 17], and in those applying previously captured facial expressions to a face [25, 3]. These performance based animation techniques compute the correspondence between the different facial expressions of a person by tracking markers glued to the face from image to image. To obtain photo-realistic face animations, up to 182 markers are used [14]. Working directly on faces without markers, our automated approach extends this number to its limit. It matches the full number of vertices available in the face model to images. The resulting dense correspondence fields can even capture changes in wrinkles and map these from one face to another.

### 1.2 Organization of the paper

We start with a description of the database of 3D face scans from which our morphable model is built.

In Section 3, we introduce the concept of the morphable face model, assuming a set of 3D face scans that are in full correspondence. Exploiting the statistics of a dataset, we derive a parametric description of faces, as well as the range of plausible faces. Additionally, we define facial attributes, such as gender or fullness of faces, in the parameter space of the model.

In Section 4, we describe an algorithm for matching our flexible model to novel images or 3D scans of faces. Along with a 3D reconstruction, the algorithm can compute correspondence, based on the morphable model.

In Section 5, we introduce an iterative method for building a morphable model automatically from a raw data set of 3D face scans when no correspondences between the exemplar faces are available.

## 2 Database

Laser scans ($Cyberware^{TM}$) of 200 heads of young adults (100 male and 100 female) were used. The laser scans provide head structure data in a cylindrical representation, with radii $r(h, \phi)$ of surface points sampled at 512 equally-spaced angles $\phi$, and at 512 equally spaced vertical steps $h$. Additionally, the RGB-color values $R(h, \phi)$, $G(h, \phi)$,and $B(h, \phi)$, were recorded in the same spatial resolution and were stored in a texture map with 8 bit per channel.

All faces were without makeup, accessories, and facial hair. The subjects were scanned wearing bathing caps, that were removed digitally. Additional automatic pre-processing of the scans, which for most heads required no human interaction, consisted of a vertical cut behind the ears, a horizontal cut to remove the shoulders, and a normalization routine that brought each face to a standard orientation and position in space. The resultant faces were represented by approximately 70,000 vertices and the same number of color values.

## 3 Morphable 3D Face Model

The morphable model is based on a data set of 3D faces. Morphing between faces requires full correspondence between all of the faces. In this section, we will assume that all exemplar faces are in full correspondence. The algorithm for computing correspondence will be described in Section 5.

We represent the geometry of a face with a shape-vector $S = (X_1, Y_1, Z_1, X_2, \ldots.., Y_n, Z_n)^T \in \Re^{3n}$, that contains the $X, Y, Z$-coordinates of its $n$ vertices. For simplicity, we assume that the number of valid texture values in the texture map is equal to the number of vertices. We therefore represent the texture of a face by a texture-vector $T = (R_1, G_1, B_1, R_2, \ldots.., G_n, B_n)^T \in \Re^{3n}$, that contains the $R, G, B$ color values of the $n$ corresponding vertices. A morphable face model was then constructed using a data set of $m$ exemplar faces, each represented by its shape-vector $S_i$ and texture-vector $T_i$. Since we assume all faces in full correspondence (see Section 5), new shapes $S_{model}$ and new textures $T_{model}$ can be expressed in barycentric coordinates as a linear combination of the shapes and textures of the $m$ exemplar faces:

$$\mathbf{S}_{mod} = \sum_{i=1}^{m} a_i \mathbf{S}_i\,, \quad \mathbf{T}_{mod} = \sum_{i=1}^{m} b_i \mathbf{T}_i\,, \quad \sum_{i=1}^{m} a_i = \sum_{i=1}^{m} b_i = 1.$$

We define the morphable model as the set of faces $(S_{mod}(\vec{a}), T_{mod}(\vec{b}))$, parameterized by the coefficients $\vec{a} = (a_1, a_2 \ldots a_m)^T$ and $\vec{b} = (b_1, b_2 \ldots b_m)^T$. [1] Arbitrary new faces can be generated by varying the parameters $\vec{a}$ and $\vec{b}$ that control shape and texture.

For a useful face synthesis system, it is important to be able to quantify the results in terms of their plausibility of being faces. We therefore estimated the probability distribution for the coefficients $a_i$ and $b_i$ from our example set of faces. This distribution enables us to control the likelihood of the coefficients $a_i$ and $b_i$ and consequently regulates the likelihood of the appearance of the generated faces.

We fit a multivariate normal distribution to our data set of 200 faces, based on the averages of shape $\overline{S}$ and texture $\overline{T}$ and the covariance matrices $C_S$ and $C_T$ computed over the shape and texture differences $\Delta S_i = S_i - \overline{S}$ and $\Delta T_i = T_i - \overline{T}$.

A common technique for data compression known as Principal Component Analysis (PCA) [15, 31] performs a basis transformation to an orthogonal coordinate system formed by the eigenvectors $s_i$ and $t_i$ of the covariance matrices (in descending order according to their eigenvalues)[2]:

$$S_{model} = \overline{S} + \sum_{i=1}^{m-1} \alpha_i s_i\,, \quad T_{model} = \overline{T} + \sum_{i=1}^{m-1} \beta_i t_i\,, \qquad (1)$$

$\vec{\alpha}, \vec{\beta} \in \Re^{m-1}$. The probability for coefficients $\vec{\alpha}$ is given by

$$p(\vec{\alpha}) \sim exp[-\frac{1}{2}\sum_{i=1}^{m-1}(\alpha_i/\sigma_i)^2], \qquad (2)$$

with $\sigma_i^2$ being the eigenvalues of the shape covariance matrix $C_S$. The probability $p(\vec{\beta})$ is computed similarly.

**Segmented morphable model:** The morphable model described in equation (1), has $m-1$ degrees of freedom for texture and $m-1$ for shape. The expressiveness of the model can be increased by dividing faces into independent subregions that are morphed independently, for example into eyes, nose, mouth and a surrounding region (see Figure 2). Since all faces are assumed to be in correspondence, it is sufficient to define these regions on a reference face. This segmentation is equivalent to subdividing the vector space of faces into independent subspaces. A complete 3D face is generated by computing linear combinations for each segment separately and blending them at the borders according to an algorithm proposed for images by [7] .

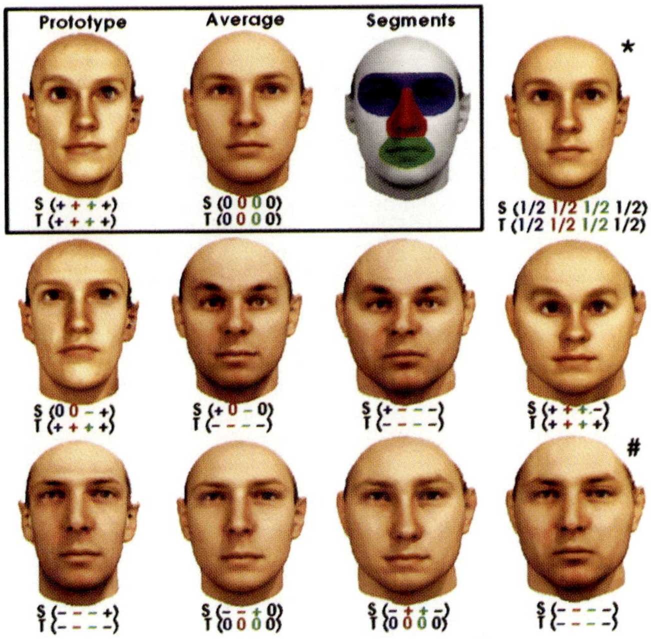


Figure 2: A single prototype adds a large variety of new faces to the morphable model. The deviation of a prototype from the average is added (+) or subtracted (-) from the average. A standard morph (*) is located halfway between average and the prototype. Subtracting the differences from the average yields an 'anti'-face (#). Adding and subtracting deviations independently for shape (S) and texture (T) on each of four segments produces a number of distinct faces.

### 3.1 Facial attributes

Shape and texture coefficients $\alpha_i$ and $\beta_i$ in our morphable face model do not correspond to the facial attributes used in human language. While some facial attributes can easily be related to biophysical measurements [13, 10], such as the width of the mouth, others such as facial femininity or being more or less bony can hardly be described by numbers. In this section, we describe a method for mapping facial attributes, defined by a hand-labeled set of example faces, to the parameter space of our morphable model. At each position in face space (that is for any possible face), we define shape and texture vectors that, when added to or subtracted from a face, will manipulate a specific attribute while keeping all other attributes as constant as possible.

In a performance based technique [25], facial expressions can be transferred by recording two scans of the same individual with different expressions, and adding the differences $\Delta S = S_{expression} - S_{neutral}$, $\Delta T = T_{expression} - T_{neutral}$, to a different individual in a neutral expression.

Unlike facial expressions, attributes that are invariant for each individual are more difficult to isolate. The following method allows us to model facial attributes such as gender, fullness of faces, darkness of eyebrows, double chins, and hooked versus concave noses (Figure 3). Based on a set of faces $(S_i, T_i)$ with manually assigned labels $\mu_i$ describing the markedness of the attribute, we compute

[1] Standard morphing between two faces ($m = 2$) is obtained if the parameters $a_1, b_1$ are varied between 0 and 1, setting $a_2 = 1 - a_1$ and $b_2 = 1 - b_1$.

[2] Due to the subtracted average vectors $\overline{S}$ and $\overline{T}$, the dimensions of $Span\{\Delta S_i\}$ and $Span\{\Delta T_i\}$ are at most $m - 1$.

weighted sums

$$\Delta S = \sum_{i=1}^{m} \mu_i (S_i - \overline{S}), \quad \Delta T = \sum_{i=1}^{m} \mu_i (T_i - \overline{T}). \tag{3}$$

Multiples of $(\Delta S, \Delta T)$ can now be added to or subtracted from any individual face. For binary attributes, such as gender, we assign constant values $\mu_A$ for all $m_A$ faces in class $A$, and $\mu_B \neq \mu_A$ for all $m_B$ faces in $B$. Affecting only the scaling of $\Delta S$ and $\Delta T$, the choice of $\mu_A$, $\mu_B$ is arbitrary.

To justify this method, let $\mu(S, T)$ be the overall function describing the markedness of the attribute in a face $(S, T)$. Since $\mu(S, T)$ is not available per se for all $(S, T)$, the regression problem of estimating $\mu(S, T)$ from a sample set of labeled faces has to be solved. Our technique assumes that $\mu(S, T)$ is a linear function. Consequently, in order to achieve a change $\Delta\mu$ of the attribute, there is only a single optimal direction $(\Delta S, \Delta T)$ for the whole space of faces. It can be shown that Equation (3) defines the direction with minimal variance-normalized length $||\Delta S||^2_M = \langle \Delta S, C_S^{-1} \Delta S \rangle$, $||\Delta T||^2_M = \langle \Delta T, C_T^{-1} \Delta T \rangle$.

A different kind of facial attribute is its "distinctiveness", which is commonly manipulated in caricatures. The automated production of caricatures has been possible for many years [6]. This technique can easily be extended from 2D images to our morphable face model. Individual faces are caricatured by increasing their distance from the average face. In our representation, shape and texture coefficients $\alpha_i, \beta_i$ are simply multiplied by a constant factor.

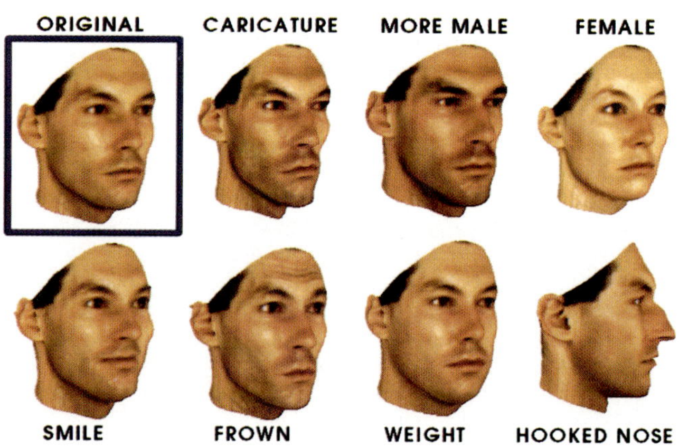


Figure 3: Variation of facial attributes of a single face. The appearance of an original face can be changed by adding or subtracting shape and texture vectors specific to the attribute.

## 4 Matching a morphable model to images

A crucial element of our framework is an algorithm for automatically matching the morphable face model to one or more images. Providing an estimate of the face's 3D structure (Figure 4), it closes the gap between the specific manipulations described in Section 3.1, and the type of data available in typical applications.

Coefficients of the 3D model are optimized along with a set of rendering parameters such that they produce an image as close as possible to the input image. In an analysis-by-synthesis loop, the algorithm creates a texture mapped 3D face from the current model parameters, renders an image, and updates the parameters according to the residual difference. It starts with the average head and with rendering parameters roughly estimated by the user.

**Model Parameters:** Facial shape and texture are defined by coefficients $\alpha_j$ and $\beta_j$, $j = 1, ..., m-1$ (Equation 1). Rendering parameters $\vec{\rho}$ contain camera position (azimuth and elevation), object scale, image plane rotation and translation, intensity $i_{r,amb}, i_{g,amb}, i_{b,amb}$ of ambient light, and intensity $i_{r,dir}, i_{g,dir}, i_{b,dir}$ of directed light. In order to handle photographs taken under a wide variety of conditions, $\vec{\rho}$ also includes color contrast as well as offset and gain in the red, green, and blue channel. Other parameters, such as camera distance, light direction, and surface shininess, remain fixed to the values estimated by the user.

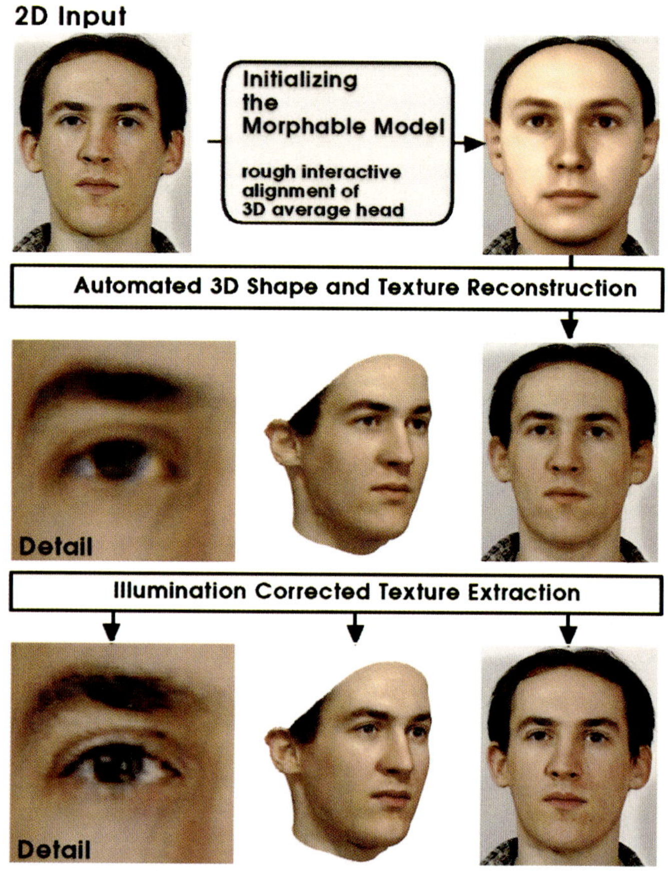


Figure 4: Processing steps for reconstructing 3D shape and texture of a new face from a single image. After a rough manual alignment of the average 3D head (top row), the automated matching procedure fits the 3D morphable model to the image (center row). In the right column, the model is rendered on top of the input image. Details in texture can be improved by illumination-corrected texture extraction from the input (bottom row).

From parameters $(\vec{\alpha}, \vec{\beta}, \vec{\rho})$, colored images

$$\mathbf{I}_{model}(x, y) = (I_{r,mod}(x, y), I_{g,mod}(x, y), I_{b,mod}(x, y))^T \tag{4}$$

are rendered using perspective projection and the Phong illumination model. The reconstructed image is supposed to be closest to the input image in terms of Euclidean distance

$$E_I = \textstyle\sum_{x,y} ||\mathbf{I}_{input}(x, y) - \mathbf{I}_{model}(x, y)||^2.$$

Matching a 3D surface to a given image is an ill-posed problem. Along with the desired solution, many non-face-like surfaces lead to the same image. It is therefore essential to impose constraints on the set of solutions. In our morphable model, shape and texture vectors are restricted to the vector space spanned by the database.

Within the vector space of faces, solutions can be further restricted by a tradeoff between matching quality and prior probabilities, using $P(\vec{\alpha})$, $P(\vec{\beta})$ from Section 3 and an ad-hoc estimate of $P(\vec{\rho})$. In terms of Bayes decision theory, the problem is to find the set of parameters $(\vec{\alpha}, \vec{\beta}, \vec{\rho})$ with maximum posterior probability, given an image $\mathbf{I}_{input}$. While $\vec{\alpha}$, $\vec{\beta}$, and rendering parameters $\vec{\rho}$ completely determine the predicted image $I_{model}$, the observed image $I_{input}$ may vary due to noise. For Gaussian noise with a standard deviation $\sigma_N$, the likelihood to observe $I_{input}$ is $p(\mathbf{I}_{input}|\vec{\alpha}, \vec{\beta}, \vec{\rho}) \sim \exp[\frac{-1}{2\sigma_N^2} \cdot E_I]$. Maximum posterior probability is then achieved by minimizing the cost function

$$E = \frac{1}{\sigma_N^2} E_I + \sum_{j=1}^{m-1} \frac{\alpha_j^2}{\sigma_{S,j}^2} + \sum_{j=1}^{m-1} \frac{\beta_j^2}{\sigma_{T,j}^2} + \sum_j \frac{(\rho_j - \bar{\rho}_j)^2}{\sigma_{\rho,j}^2} \quad (5)$$

The optimization algorithm described below uses an estimate of $E$ based on a random selection of surface points. Predicted color values $\mathbf{I}_{model}$ are easiest to evaluate in the centers of triangles. In the center of triangle $k$, texture $(\bar{R}_k, \bar{G}_k, \bar{B}_k)^T$ and 3D location $(\bar{X}_k, \bar{Y}_k, \bar{Z}_k)^T$ are averages of the values at the corners. Perspective projection maps these points to image locations $(\bar{p}_{x,k}, \bar{p}_{y,k})^T$. Surface normals $\mathbf{n}_k$ of each triangle $k$ are determined by the 3D locations of the corners. According to Phong illumination, the color components $I_{r,model}$, $I_{g,model}$ and $I_{b,model}$ take the form

$$I_{r,model,k} = (i_{r,amb} + i_{r,dir} \cdot (\mathbf{n}_k \mathbf{l}))\bar{R}_k + i_{r,dir} s \cdot (\mathbf{r}_k \mathbf{v}_k)^{\nu} \quad (6)$$

where $\mathbf{l}$ is the direction of illumination, $\mathbf{v}_k$ the normalized difference of camera position and the position of the triangle's center, and $\mathbf{r}_k = 2(\mathbf{nl})\mathbf{n} - \mathbf{l}$ the direction of the reflected ray. $s$ denotes surface shininess, and $\nu$ controls the angular distribution of the specular reflection. Equation (6) reduces to $I_{r,model,k} = i_{r,amb}\bar{R}_k$ if a shadow is cast on the center of the triangle, which is tested in a method described below.

For high resolution 3D meshes, variations in $\mathbf{I}_{model}$ across each triangle $k \in \{1, ..., n_t\}$ are small, so $E_I$ may be approximated by

$$E_I \approx \sum_{k=1}^{n_t} a_k \cdot \|\mathbf{I}_{input}(\bar{p}_{x,k}, \bar{p}_{y,k}) - \mathbf{I}_{model,k}\|^2,$$

where $a_k$ is the image area covered by triangle $k$. If the triangle is occluded, $a_k = 0$.

In gradient descent, contributions from different triangles of the mesh would be redundant. In each iteration, we therefore select a random subset $\mathcal{K} \subset \{1, ..., n_t\}$ of 40 triangles $k$ and replace $E_I$ by

$$E_{\mathcal{K}} = \sum_{k \in \mathcal{K}} \|\mathbf{I}_{input}(\bar{p}_{x,k}, \bar{p}_{y,k}) - \mathbf{I}_{model,k})\|^2. \quad (7)$$

The probability of selecting $k$ is $p(k \in \mathcal{K}) \sim a_k$. This method of stochastic gradient descent [16] is not only more efficient computationally, but also helps to avoid local minima by adding noise to the gradient estimate.

Before the first iteration, and once every 1000 steps, the algorithm computes the full 3D shape of the current model, and 2D positions $(p_x, p_y)^T$ of all vertices. It then determines $a_k$, and detects hidden surfaces and cast shadows in a two-pass z-buffer technique. We assume that occlusions and cast shadows are constant during each subset of iterations.

Parameters are updated depending on analytical derivatives of the cost function $E$, using $\alpha_j \mapsto \alpha_j - \lambda_j \cdot \frac{\partial E}{\partial \alpha_j}$, and similarly for $\beta_j$ and $\rho_j$, with suitable factors $\lambda_j$.

Derivatives of texture and shape (Equation 1) yield derivatives of 2D locations $(\bar{p}_{x,k}, \bar{p}_{y,k})^T$, surface normals $\mathbf{n}_k$, vectors $\mathbf{v}_k$ and $\mathbf{r}_k$, and $\mathbf{I}_{model,k}$ (Equation 6) using chain rule. From Equation (7), partial derivatives $\frac{\partial E_{\mathcal{K}}}{\partial \alpha_j}$, $\frac{\partial E_{\mathcal{K}}}{\partial \beta_j}$, and $\frac{\partial E_{\mathcal{K}}}{\partial \rho_j}$ can be obtained.

**Coarse-to-Fine:** In order to avoid local minima, the algorithm follows a coarse-to-fine strategy in several respects:

**a)** The first set of iterations is performed on a down-sampled version of the input image with a low resolution morphable model.

**b)** We start by optimizing only the first coefficients $\alpha_j$ and $\beta_j$ controlling the first principal components, along with all parameters

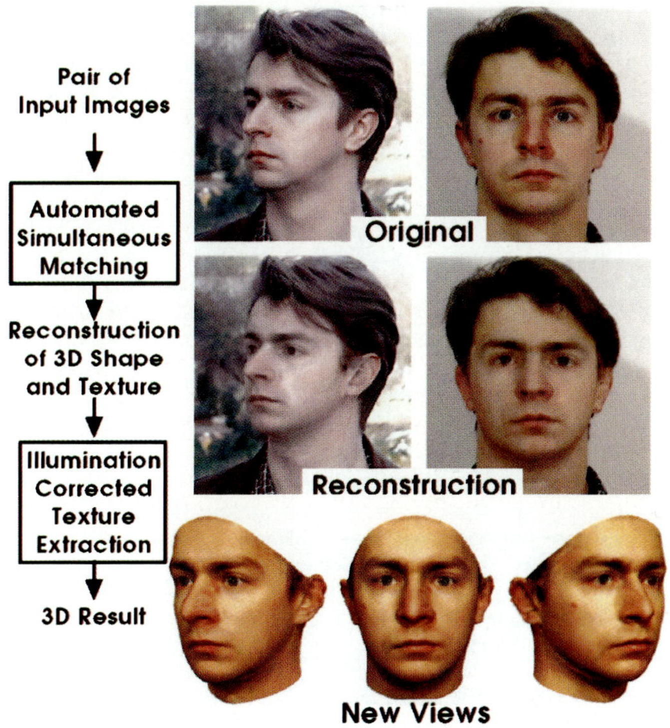


Figure 5: Simultaneous reconstruction of 3D shape and texture of a new face from two images taken under different conditions. In the center row, the 3D face is rendered on top of the input images.

$\rho_j$. In subsequent iterations, more and more principal components are added.

**c)** Starting with a relatively large $\sigma_N$, which puts a strong weight on prior probability in equation (5) and ties the optimum towards the prior expectation value, we later reduce $\sigma_N$ to obtain maximum matching quality.

**d)** In the last iterations, the face model is broken down into segments (Section 3). With parameters $\rho_j$ fixed, coefficients $\alpha_j$ and $\beta_j$ are optimized independently for each segment. This increased number of degrees of freedom significantly improves facial details.

**Multiple Images:** It is straightforward to extend this technique to the case where several images of a person are available (Figure 5). While shape and texture are still described by a common set of $\alpha_j$ and $\beta_j$, there is now a separate set of $\rho_j$ for each input image. $E_I$ is replaced by a sum of image distances for each pair of input and model images, and all parameters are optimized simultaneously.

**Illumination-Corrected Texture Extraction:** Specific features of individual faces that are not captured by the morphable model, such as blemishes, are extracted from the image in a subsequent texture adaptation process. Extracting texture from images is a technique widely used in constructing 3D models from images (e.g. [28]). However, in order to be able to change pose and illumination, it is important to separate pure albedo at any given point from the influence of shading and cast shadows in the image. In our approach, this can be achieved because our matching procedure provides an estimate of 3D shape, pose, and illumination conditions. Subsequent to matching, we compare the prediction $\mathbf{I}_{mod,i}$ for each vertex $i$ with $\mathbf{I}_{input}(p_{x,i}, p_{y,i})$, and compute the change in texture $(R_i, G_i, B_i)$ that accounts for the difference. In areas occluded in the image, we rely on the prediction made by the model. Data from multiple images can be blended using methods similar to [28].

## 4.1 Matching a morphable model to 3D scans

The method described above can also be applied to register new 3D faces. Analogous to images, where perspective projection

$P : \mathcal{R}^3 \to \mathcal{R}^2$ and an illumination model define a colored image $\mathbf{I}(x,y) = (R(x,y), G(x,y), B(x,y))^T$, laser scans provide a two-dimensional cylindrical parameterization of the surface by means of a mapping $C : \mathcal{R}^3 \to \mathcal{R}^2$, $(x,y,z) \mapsto (h,\phi)$. Hence, a scan can be represented as

$$\mathbf{I}(h,\phi) = (R(h,\phi), G(h,\phi), B(h,\phi), r(h,\phi))^T. \quad (8)$$

In a face $(S,T)$, defined by shape and texture coefficients $\alpha_j$ and $\beta_j$ (Equation 1), vertex $i$ with texture values $(R_i, G_i, B_i)$ and cylindrical coordinates $(r_i, h_i, \phi_i)$ is mapped to $\mathbf{I}_{model}(h_i, \phi_i) = (R_i, G_i, B_i, r_i)^T$. The matching algorithm from the previous section now determines $\alpha_j$ and $\beta_j$ minimizing

$$E = \sum_{h,\phi} \|\mathbf{I}_{input}(h,\phi) - \mathbf{I}_{model}(h,\phi)\|^2.$$

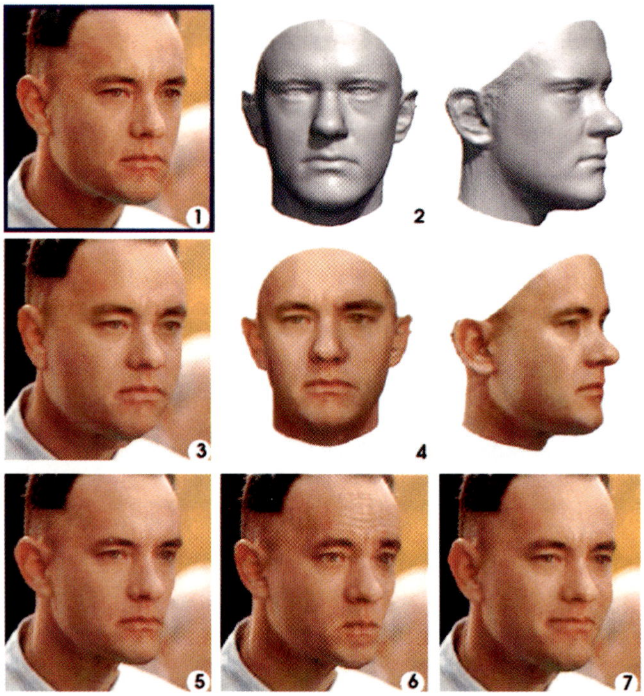

Figure 6: Matching a morphable model to a single image (1) of a face results in a 3D shape (2) and a texture map estimate. The texture estimate can be improved by additional texture extraction (4). The 3D model is rendered back into the image after changing facial attributes, such as gaining (3) and loosing weight (5), frowning (6), or being forced to smile (7).

# 5 Building a morphable model

In this section, we describe how to build the morphable model from a set of unregistered 3D prototypes, and to add a new face to the existing morphable model, increasing its dimensionality.

The key problem is to compute a dense point-to-point correspondence between the vertices of the faces. Since the method described in Section 4.1 finds the best match of a given face only within the range of the morphable model, it cannot add new dimensions to the vector space of faces. To determine residual deviations between a novel face and the best match within the model, as well as to set unregistered prototypes in correspondence, we use an optic flow algorithm that computes correspondence between two faces without the need of a morphable model [35]. The following section summarizes this technique.

## 5.1 3D Correspondence using Optic Flow

Initially designed to find corresponding points in grey-level images $I(x,y)$, a gradient-based optic flow algorithm [2] is modified to establish correspondence between a pair of 3D scans $\mathbf{I}(h,\phi)$ (Equation 8), taking into account color and radius values simultaneously [35]. The algorithm computes a flow field $(\delta h(h,\phi), \delta\phi(h,\phi))$ that minimizes differences of $\|\mathbf{I}_1(h,\phi) - \mathbf{I}_2(h+\delta h, \phi+\delta\phi)\|$ in a norm that weights variations in texture and shape equally. Surface properties from differential geometry, such as mean curvature, may be used as additional components in $\mathbf{I}(h,\phi)$.

On facial regions with little structure in texture and shape, such as forehead and cheeks, the results of the optic flow algorithm are sometimes spurious. We therefore perform a smooth interpolation based on simulated relaxation of a system of flow vectors that are coupled with their neighbors. The quadratic coupling potential is equal for all flow vectors. On high-contrast areas, components of flow vectors orthogonal to edges are bound to the result of the previous optic flow computation. The system is otherwise free to take on a smooth minimum-energy arrangement. Unlike simple filtering routines, our technique fully retains matching quality wherever the flow field is reliable. Optic flow and smooth interpolation are computed on several consecutive levels of resolution.

Constructing a morphable face model from a set of unregistered 3D scans requires the computation of the flow fields between each face and an arbitrary reference face. Given a definition of shape and texture vectors $S_{ref}$ and $T_{ref}$ for the reference face, $S$ and $T$ for each face in the database can be obtained by means of the point-to-point correspondence provided by $(\delta h(h,\phi), \delta\phi(h,\phi))$.

## 5.2 Bootstrapping the model

Because the optic flow algorithm does not incorporate any constraints on the set of solutions, it fails on some of the more unusual faces in the database. Therefore, we modified a bootstrapping algorithm to iteratively improve correspondence, a method that has been used previously to build linear image models [36].

*The basic recursive step:* Suppose that an existing morphable model is not powerful enough to match a new face and thereby find correspondence with it. The idea is first to find rough correspondences to the novel face using the (inadequate) morphable model and then to improve these correspondences by using an optic flow algorithm.

Starting from an arbitrary face as the temporary reference, preliminary correspondence between all other faces and this reference is computed using the optic flow algorithm. On the basis of these correspondences, shape and texture vectors $S$ and $T$ can be computed. Their average serves as a new reference face. The first morphable model is then formed by the most significant components as provided by a standard PCA decomposition. The current morphable model is now matched to each of the 3D faces according to the method described in Section 4.1. Then, the optic flow algorithm computes correspondence between the 3D face and the approximation provided by the morphable model. Combined with the correspondence implied by the matched model, this defines a new correspondence between the reference face and the example.

Iterating this procedure with increasing expressive power of the model (by increasing the number of principal components) leads to reliable correspondences between the reference face and the examples, and finally to a complete morphable face model.

# 6 Results

We built a morphable face model by automatically establishing correspondence between all of our 200 exemplar faces. Our interactive

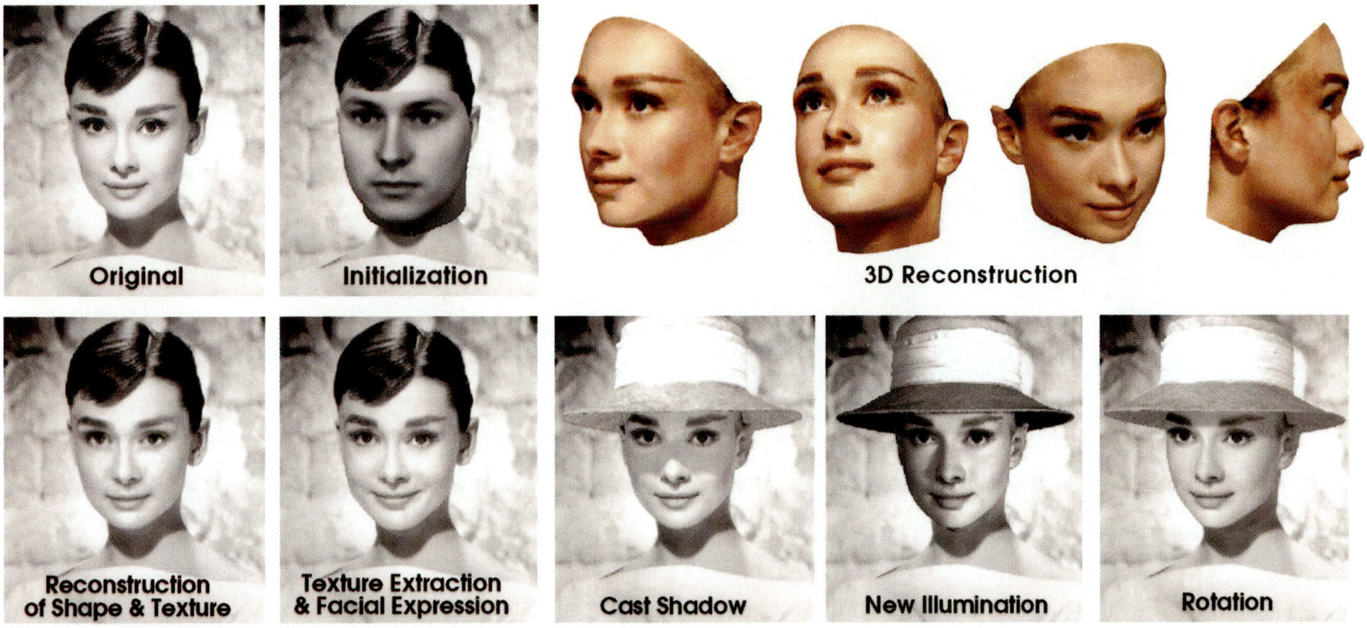


Figure 7: After manual initialization, the algorithm automatically matches a colored morphable model (color contrast set to zero) to the image. Rendering the inner part of the 3D face on top of the image, new shadows, facial expressions and poses can be generated.

face modeling system enables human users to create new characters and to modify facial attributes by varying the model coefficients. Within the constraints imposed by prior probability, there is a large variability of possible faces, and all linear combinations of the exemplar faces look natural.

We tested the expressive power of our morphable model by automatically reconstructing 3D faces from photographs of arbitrary Caucasian faces of middle age that were not in the database. The images were either taken by us using a digital camera (Figures 4, 5), or taken under arbitrary unknown conditions (Figures 6, 7).

In all examples, we matched a morphable model built from the first 100 shape and the first 100 texture principal components that were derived from the whole dataset of 200 faces. Each component was additionally segmented in 4 parts (see Figure 2). The whole matching procedure was performed in $10^5$ iterations. On an SGI R10000 processor, computation time was 50 minutes.

Reconstructing the true 3D shape and texture of a face from a single image is an ill-posed problem. However, to human observers who also know only the input image, the results obtained with our method look correct. When compared with a real image of the rotated face, differences usually become only visible for large rotations of more than $60°$.

There is a wide variety of applications for 3D face reconstruction from 2D images. As demonstrated in Figures 6 and 7, the results can be used for automatic post-processing of a face within the original picture or movie sequence.

Knowing the 3D shape of a face in an image provides a segmentation of the image into face area and background. The face can be combined with other 3D graphic objects, such as glasses or hats, and then be rendered in front of the background, computing cast shadows or new illumination conditions (Fig. 7). Furthermore, we can change the appearance of the face by adding or subtracting specific attributes. If previously unseen backgrounds become visible, we fill the holes with neighboring background pixels (Fig. 6).

We also applied the method to paintings such as Leonardo's Mona Lisa (Figure 8). Due to unusual (maybe unrealistic) lighting, illumination-corrected texture extraction is difficult here. We therefore apply a different method for transferring all details of the painting to novel views. For new illumination, we render two images of the reconstructed 3D face with different illumination, and multiply relative changes in pixel values (Figure 8, bottom left) by the original values in the painting (bottom center). For a new pose (bottom right), differences in shading are transferred in a similar way, and the painting is then warped according to the 2D projections of 3D vertex displacements of the reconstructed shape.

## 7 Future work

**Issues of implementation:** We plan to speed up our matching algorithm by implementing a simplified Newton-method for minimizing the cost function (Equation 5). Instead of the time consuming computation of derivatives for each iteration step, a global mapping of the matching error into parameter space can be used [9].

Data reduction applied to shape and texture data will reduce redundancy of our representation, saving additional computation time.

**Extending the database:** While the current database is sufficient to model Caucasian faces of middle age, we would like to extend it to children, to elderly people as well as to other races.

We also plan to incorporate additional 3D face examples representing the time course of facial expressions and visemes, the face variations during speech.

The laser scanning technology we used, unfortunately, does not allow us to collect dynamical 3D face data, as each scanning cycle takes at least 10 seconds. Consequently, our current example set of facial expressions is restricted to those that can be kept static by the scanned subjects. However, the development of fast optical 3D digitizers [27] will allow us to apply our method to streams of 3D data during speech and facial expressions.

**Extending the face model:** Our current morphable model is restricted to the face area, because a sufficient 3D model of hair cannot be obtained with our laser scanner. For animation, the missing part of the head can be automatically replaced by a standard hair style or a hat, or by hair that is modeled using interactive manual segmentation and adaptation to a 3D model [30, 28]. Automated reconstruction of hair styles from images is one of the future challenges.

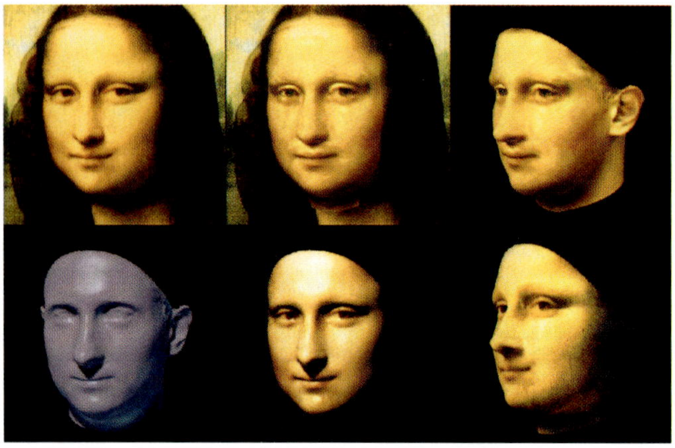

Figure 8: Reconstructed 3D face of Mona Lisa (top center and right). For modifying the illumination, relative changes in color (bottom left) are computed on the 3D face, and then multiplied by the color values in the painting (bottom center). Additional warping generates new orientations (bottom right, see text), while details of the painting, such as brush strokes or cracks, are retained.

## 8 Acknowledgment

We thank Michael Langer, Alice O'Toole, Tomaso Poggio, Heinrich Bülthoff and Wolfgang Straßer for reading the manuscript and for many insightful and constructive comments. In particular, we thank Marney Smyth and Alice O'Toole for their perseverance in helping us to obtain the following. **Photo Credits:** Original image in Fig. 6: Courtesy of Paramount/VIACOM. Original image in Fig. 7: MPTV/interTOPICS.

## References

[1] T. Akimoto, Y. Suenaga, and R.S. Wallace. Automatic creation of 3D facial models. *IEEE Computer Graphics and Applications*, 13(3):16–22, 1993.

[2] J.R. Bergen and R. Hingorani. Hierarchical motion-based frame rate conversion. Technical report, David Sarnoff Research Center Princeton NJ 08540, 1990.

[3] P. Bergeron and P. Lachapelle. Controlling facial expressions and body movements. In *Advanced Computer Animation, SIGGRAPH '85 Tutorials*, volume 2, pages 61–79, New York, 1985. ACM.

[4] D. Beymer and T. Poggio. Image representation for visual learning. *Science*, 272:1905–1909, 1996.

[5] D. Beymer, A. Shashua, and T. Poggio. Example-based image analysis and synthesis. A.I. Memo No. 1431, Artificial Intelligence Laboratory, Massachusetts Institute of Technology, 1993.

[6] S. E. Brennan. The caricature generator. *Leonardo*, 18:170–178, 1985.

[7] P.J. Burt and E.H. Adelson. Merging images through pattern decomposition. In *Applications of Digital Image Processing VIII*, number 575, pages 173–181. SPIE The International Society for Optical Engeneering, 1985.

[8] C.S. Choi, T. Okazaki, H. Harashima, and T. Takebe. A system of analyzing and synthesizing facial images. In *Proc. IEEE Int. Symposium of Circuit and Syatems (ISCAS91)*, pages 2665–2668, 1991.

[9] T.F. Cootes, G.J. Edwards, and C.J. Taylor. Active appearance models. In Burkhardt and Neumann, editors, *Computer Vision – ECCV'98 Vol. II*, Freiburg, Germany, 1998. Springer, Lecture Notes in Computer Science 1407.

[10] D. DeCarlos, D. Metaxas, and M. Stone. An anthropometric face model using variational techniques. In *Computer Graphics Proceedings SIGGRAPH'98*, pages 67–74, 1998.

[11] S. DiPaola. Extending the range of facial types. *Journal of Visualization and Computer Animation*, 2(4):129–131, 1991.

[12] G.J. Edwards, A. Lanitis, C.J. Taylor, and T.F. Cootes. Modelling the variability in face images. In *Proc. of the 2nd Int. Conf. on Automatic Face and Gesture Recognition*, IEEE Comp. Soc. Press, Los Alamitos, CA, 1996.

[13] L.G. Farkas. *Anthropometry of the Head and Face*. RavenPress, New York, 1994.

[14] B. Guenter, C. Grimm, D. Wolf, H. Malvar, and F. Pighin. Making faces. In *Computer Graphics Proceedings SIGGRAPH'98*, pages 55–66, 1998.

[15] I.T. Jollife. *Principal Component Analysis*. Springer-Verlag, New York, 1986.

[16] M. Jones and T. Poggio. Multidimensional morphable models: A framework for representing and matching object classes. In *Proceedings of the Sixth International Conference on Computer Vision*, Bombay, India, 1998.

[17] R. M. Koch, M. H. Gross, and A. A. Bosshard. Emotion editing using finite elements. In *Proceedings of the Eurographics '98, COMPUTER GRAPHICS Forum, Vol. 17, No. 3*, pages C295–C302, Lisbon, Portugal, 1998.

[18] A. Lanitis, C.J. Taylor, and T.F. Cootes. Automatic interpretation and coding of face images using flexible models. *IEEE Transactions on Pattern Analysis and Machine Intelligence*, 19(7):743–756, 1997.

[19] Y.C. Lee, D. Terzopoulos, and Keith Waters. Constructing physics-based facial models of individuals. *Visual Computer*, Proceedings of Graphics Interface '93:1–8, 1993.

[20] Y.C. Lee, D. Terzopoulos, and Keith Waters. Realistic modeling for facial animation. In *SIGGRAPH '95 Conference Proceedings*, pages 55–62, Los Angels, 1995. ACM.

[21] J. P. Lewis. Algorithms for solid noise synthesis. In *SIGGRAPH '89 Conference Proceedings*, pages 263–270. ACM, 1989.

[22] N. Magneneat-Thalmann, H. Minh, M. Angelis, and D. Thalmann. Design, transformation and animation of human faces. *Visual Computer*, 5:32–39, 1989.

[23] L. Moccozet and N. Magnenat-Thalmann. Dirichlet free-form deformation and their application to hand simulation. In *Computer Animation'97*, 1997.

[24] F. I. Parke and K. Waters. *Computer Facial Animation*. AKPeters, Wellesley, Massachusetts, 1996.

[25] F.I. Parke. Computer generated animation of faces. In *ACM National Conference*. ACM, November 1972.

[26] F.I. Parke. *A Parametric Model of Human Faces*. PhD thesis, University of Utah, Salt Lake City, 1974.

[27] M. Petrow, A. Talapov, T. Robertson, A. Lebedev, A. Zhilyaev, and L. Polonskiy. Optical 3D digitizer: Bringing life to virtual world. *IEEE Computer Graphics and Applications*, 18(3):28–37, 1998.

[28] F. Pighin, J. Hecker, D. Lischinski, Szeliski R, and D. Salesin. Synthesizing realistic facial expressions from photographs. In *Computer Graphics Proceedings SIGGRAPH'98*, pages 75–84, 1998.

[29] S. Platt and N. Badler. Animating facial expression. *Computer Graphics*, 15(3):245–252, 1981.

[30] G. Sannier and N. Magnenat-Thalmann. A user-friendly texture-fitting methodology for virtual humans. In *Computer Graphics International'97*, 1997.

[31] L. Sirovich and M. Kirby. Low-dimensional procedure for the characterization of human faces. *Journal of the Optical Society of America A*, 4:519–554, 1987.

[32] D. Terzopoulos and Keith Waters. Physically-based facial modeling, analysis, and animation. *Visualization and Computer Animation*, 1:73–80, 1990.

[33] Demetri Terzopoulos and Hong Qin. Dynamic NURBS with geometric constraints to interactive sculpting. *ACM Transactions on Graphics*, 13(2):103–136, April 1994.

[34] J. T. Todd, S. M. Leonard, R. E. Shaw, and J. B. Pittenger. The perception of human growth. *Scientific American*, 1242:106–114, 1980.

[35] T. Vetter and V. Blanz. Estimating coloured 3d face models from single images: An example based approach. In Burkhardt and Neumann, editors, *Computer Vision – ECCV'98 Vol. II*, Freiburg, Germany, 1998. Springer, Lecture Notes in Computer Science 1407.

[36] T. Vetter, M. J. Jones, and T. Poggio. A bootstrapping algorithm for learning linear models of object classes. In *IEEE Conference on Computer Vision and Pattern Recognition – CVPR'97*, Puerto Rico, USA, 1997. IEEE Computer Society Press.

[37] T. Vetter and T. Poggio. Linear object classes and image synthesis from a single example image. *IEEE Transactions on Pattern Analysis and Machine Intelligence*, 19(7):733–742, 1997.

[38] Keith Waters. A muscle model for animating three-dimensional facial expression. *Computer Graphics*, 22(4):17–24, 1987.

# Creating Generative Models from Range Images

Ravi Ramamoorthi
Stanford University*
ravir@graphics.stanford.edu

James Arvo
California Institute of Technology
arvo@cs.caltech.edu

## Abstract

We describe a new approach for creating concise high-level generative models from range images or other approximate representations of real objects. Using data from a variety of acquisition techniques and a user-defined class of models, our method produces a compact object representation that is intuitive and easy to edit. The algorithm has two inter-related phases: *recognition*, which chooses an appropriate model within a user-specified hierarchy, and *parameter estimation*, which adjusts the model to best fit the data. Since the approach is model-based, it is relatively insensitive to noise and missing data. We describe practical heuristics for automatically making tradeoffs between simplicity and accuracy to select the best model in a given hierarchy. We also describe a general and efficient technique for optimizing a model by refining its constituent curves. We demonstrate our approach for model recovery using both real and synthetic data and several generative model hierarchies.

**CR Categories:** I.3.5 [*Computer Graphics*]: Object Modeling—Curve, surface, solid, and object representations, Object hierarchies, Splines; I.4.8 [*Image Processing and Computer Vision*]: Scene Analysis—Object Recognition, Surface Fitting

**Keywords:** Generative Models, Range Images, Curves and Surfaces, Procedural Modeling

## 1 Introduction

It has recently become feasible to acquire reasonably accurate point-clouds or *range data* from 3D objects [5, 26]. For graphics applications, these point-clouds are usually transformed into polygonal meshes [5, 12], or spline patches [14]. However, these approaches often provide an unintuitive representation that is difficult to manipulate once generated. In addition, a large amount of data is required since the meshes usually contain thousands of triangles. For modeling many man-made objects, *generative models* proposed by Snyder [21, 22] provide an attractive alternative. A generative model is a generalization of a swept surface in which

*Address: Gates Wing 3B-372, Stanford University, Stanford, Ca 94305.

Figure 1: *Generative models recovered from actual range data. Objects were scanned individually, modeled using our algorithm, then composed in this scene with artificial color and shading. A smooth compact representation was generated for each object from a few simple model hierarchies, despite noisy and incomplete data. See figure 7 for a comparison of range data and recovered models.*

the generating curve can be continuously transformed by one or more arbitrary curves. For instance, a banana-like shape is specified parametrically by translating a cross-section while scaling and rotating it. The cross-section, scaling function, and rotation are all described by curves. The modeled object is analytically represented by a tree of operators that provides a logical description of its structure. Designers can easily construct, examine, and modify such a model.

We describe a method for inverting this process to recover generative models from range data or other approximate representations of object geometry. This method requires the user to specify a universe of possible objects by providing a hierarchy of shape operators defining a class of generative models. Given a user-defined hierarchy, such as the ones shown at the bottom of figure 2 and in figure 8, the system automatically selects a parametric model within this hierarchy, and adjusts its parameters to best match data acquired from an actual object. Several models recovered in this way are shown in figure 1.

Our approach for model construction has a number of benefits:

**Simplicity:** Range data may be obtained by several methods, including the *shadow* approach of Bouguet and Perona [2], that requires only a lamp, pencil and checkerboard apart from the camera.

**Robustness:** By exploiting redundancies in the data, accurate models can often be recovered from incomplete and noisy data. Our model-based approach is thus much less sensitive to noise than mesh creation. Many of our examples use only one noisy and incomplete range image, while creation of a polygon mesh generally requires many accurate and properly aligned range images.

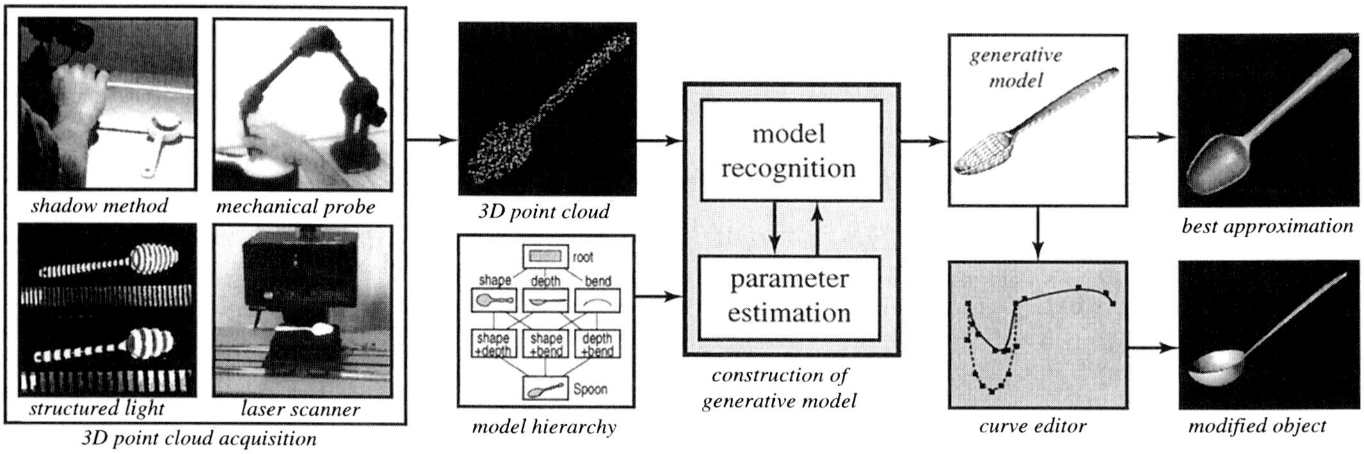


Figure 2: *Overview of generative model creation. The algorithm takes range data in the form of a point-cloud and a generative model hierarchy as input. An appropriate model is then chosen, and parameters are optimized to output an accurate and concise generative model that can subsequently be edited.*

**Compactness:** Generative models provide a concise representation; we need only store an algebraic model description, and control points of the model's parametric curves. This representation can be orders of magnitude smaller than a triangle mesh.

**Intuitiveness:** Since the model is expressed in terms of parametric curves corresponding to logical features of the object, it is easy to understand, manipulate, and edit.

### Related Work

Many methods have been explored, especially in computer vision, for recovering object shape for specific primitives such as generalized cylinders [1, 15], superquadrics [16, 23] and blended deformable models [7]. Terzopoulos and Metaxas [24] have proposed a computational physics framework for shape recovery in which globally deformed superquadrics model coarse shape and local deformations add fine detail. Superquadrics have also been used for model-based segmentation [9, 11], and for recognition of "geons" using relationships between superquadric parameters [19, 27]. DeCarlo and Metaxas [8] introduced shape evolution with blending to recover and combine superquadrics and supertoroids into a unified model. Debevec et a. [6] considered architectural scenes and developed a system for recovering polyhedral models from photographs.

Our approach is somewhat more general than these previous algorithms in that it is based on a general user-specified generative hierarchy rather than a particular parametric model. This allows automatic construction of more complex and varied shapes, without segmentation, than is possible with current computer vision algorithms. Further, many standard primitives used in computer vision can be recovered using our method since generative models are a superset of traditional shape representations such as globally deformed superquadrics, straight homogeneous generalized cylinders, and blended deformable models, all of which have been recovered using our system. Our method is also automatic, with no user intervention required. However, model-specific algorithms, especially those that allow user-intervention, may out-perform our algorithm on the shapes to which they apply by exploiting model-specific information. For instance, by considering only polyhedral models, and having the user manually specify the edges of interest, Debevec et al. [6] are able to work with only photographs, while we require range data.

This paper deals primarily with shapes represented by a single generative model. At present, we do not add local detail [24], nor address automatic model-based segmentation [8, 9, 11] or image interpretation [3]. However, our results suggest that generative models may be useful for these tasks in lieu of superquadrics or generalized cones.

In contrast to some object recognition methods [19, 27],which estimate specific model parameters to classify an object as a member of some class, our method first determines which degrees of freedom in the model hierarchy are most suitable for the acquired data, and then refines the associated parameters.

Recent work on simplifying polygonal meshes shares one of our objectives—providing a more compact representation. For example, Hoppe et al. describe techniques to optimize meshes [13], while Eck and Hoppe [10] and Krishnamurthy and Levoy [14] fit spline surfaces to dense meshes. However, mesh-based methods do not yield compact *high-level* models.

The rest of this paper is organized as follows: Section 2 gives an overview of our algorithm and describes our framework for recovering the appropriate model within a user-specified hierarchy. In section 3, we discuss our methods for optimization. Section 4 briefly outlines the various models used in our tests. In section 5, we discuss our results and section 6 presents our conclusions and directions for future work.

## 2 Algorithm Framework

In this section, we give a high-level overview of the entire algorithm, pictured in figure 2, and describe our method for automatically choosing the appropriate generative model from within a user-defined class. This is essentially a recognition task as it requires the measured data to be classified as one of the models in the user-specified hierarchy. The recognition process is based on a simple tradeoff between accuracy and simplicity. For efficiency, a *greedy algorithm* is employed that starts with the simplest model in the input hierarchy, and then considers more complex models at the next level in the hierarchy. The system selects the model providing the greatest benefit, and repeats the process in a greedy fashion, moving through the hierarchy from simple to more complex models. The process stops when none of the more complex models significantly improves the accuracy, or the most complex model is reached. Although the first model that is fit to the data is trivial, the algorithm then *bootstraps* itself by using information obtained in fitting previous models, improving at each stage until an accurate and suitably complex model is recovered. For illustrative purposes, we will often refer to the specific hierarchy shown at the bottom of figure 2 and on the left of figure 8, which is inspired by the spoon model created by Snyder [21, p. 83].

The model hierarchy has several levels. For our class of models, the root node of the hierarchy is level zero, which consists of a "half-cylinder" with two global parameters controlling width and depth. This object essentially defines a bounding volume for the data. Deeper levels consist of *refining* one or more of the parameters by representing them as curves instead of global values. In general, one curve is added at each level so the number of curves corresponds to the level. For example, the edge to the "depth" node in figures 2 and 8 corresponds to *refining* the depth parameter by representing it as a curve. The hierarchy can also be thought of as a tree; going from parent to child corresponds to adding a single curve. For instance, the *root* is the *parent*, while the model with refined depth is the *child*. The tree representation implies an order in which curves are added. The curve providing the most benefit is added first, and a child node inherits initial parameter estimates from optimized results for the parent node.

**Input to the System:** Part of specifying the model hierarchy is to supply functions that perform the following tasks.

- **Initial Guess for Root Model:** Starting values must be supplied for the parameters of the root model, which typically consists of a simple primitive object. The initial values for both the intrinsic parameters and the extrinsic parameters (translation, rotation, and scale) of the root model may be very crude, since they merely provide a starting point for subsequent refinement and optimization. Parameter estimates for more complex models are obtained automatically from those of the parent model in the tree.
- **Model Evaluation:** A function must be supplied to evaluate any model in the input hierarchy at given $uv$-parameters. Efficient routines can be automatically generated from an algebraic model description.
- **Curve Constraints:** The model hierarchy may optionally contain additional constraints on the curves in the final model, such as fixing their values at specific points, or penalty terms to ensure, for instance, that a particular curve remains positive everywhere.

This information is encapsulated as user-supplied functions along with the code that defines the model hierarchy. Thus, the algorithm may proceed without any manual user intervention.

A summary of our algorithm is shown in figure 3. Below, we discuss each step in detail. The reader may wish to refer to the results in figure 8 and the left of figure 9 for examples of applying the algorithm.

**Step 1. Acquire Range Data:** We have used a number of different methods to acquire range data for our experiments, including two structured light techniques—a method which uses a sequence of alternating dark and light patterns projected onto the object [25], and the highly portable method described by Bouguet and Perona, in which shape is inferred from the shadow of a rod swept over the object [2]. We have also used a mechanical probe and a laser range scanner. This variety of sources demonstrates that our algorithm is amenable to a wide assortment of data acquisition methods.

**Overview of the Algorithm**

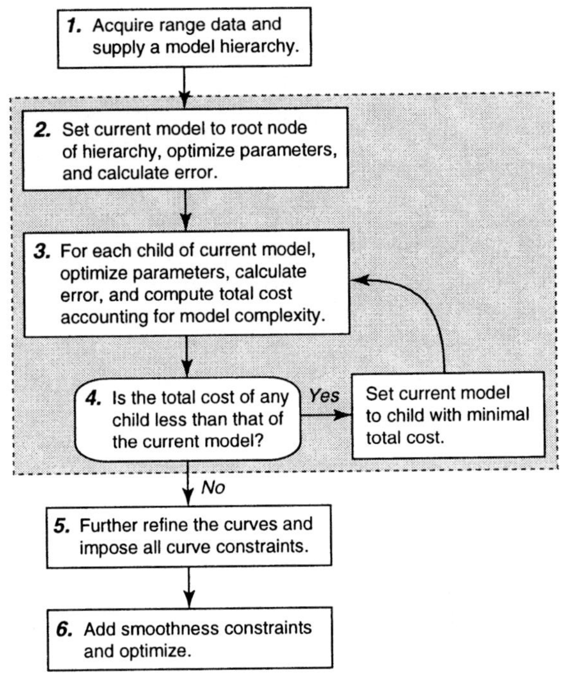


Figure 3: *Overview of the algorithm with the greedy algorithm used for recognition highlighted.*

**Step 2. Fit to root model:**

- **Initialize:** Let $\rho$ denote our current model—initially the root node of the hierarchy. The root node's intrinsic and extrinsic parameters are initialized using a user-specified function.
- **Optimize:** An error-of-fit function $\phi$ is computed based on the spatial deviation between the data and the model as defined in equation 4. Optimization is used to adjust the root node to minimize the error-of-fit. Details are given in the next section.
- **Cost:** After minimization, $\phi$ is used to compute the deviation $D$ which represents the RMS distance between model and data as defined in equation 5. The total cost $C$ is initialized to this deviation.

**Step 3. Fit children to Data:** For each child of the current model $\rho$, denoted by $\gamma_i(\rho)$, we calculate the deviation $D(\gamma_i)$ after optimization. For instance, if $\rho = root$, the children are $\gamma_1 = shape, \gamma_2 = depth, \gamma_3 = bend$. We then calculate a cost function for each child:

$$C(\gamma_i) = D(\gamma_i) + \triangle(\gamma_i), \tag{1}$$

where $\triangle$ is a penalty for model complexity. We use a very simple but effective heuristic to assess the complexity of a model: $\triangle(N) = NQ$ where $N$ is the level in the hierarchy of a specific model and $Q$ is a constant that allows the user to control the trade-off between simplicity and accuracy.

In progressing from the current model $\rho$ to a child $\gamma$, we add a single curve. The entire process is explained in detail with results in subsection 3.3 on curve refinement. The steps are:

- **Initialize:** Initial parameter estimates for $\gamma$ are set to parameter values of its parent $\rho$. The new curve to be added is initialized to a constant inherited from $\rho$, and control points are added at the ends.
- **Optimize:** A first optimization step yields a coarse curve estimate. In all optimization steps, all model parameters are simultaneously varied to minimize the objective function in equation 4.
- **Refine:** A few interior control points are automatically added based on the heuristic defined in equation 16.
- **Optimize:** Optimization is repeated with the additional control points added, which improves the quality of the new model.
- **Cost:** We compute the deviation $D$ using equation 5 as in step 2, and use equation 1 to compute the total cost of $\gamma$.

**Step 4. Reset $\rho$:** The previous stage calculated the cost function for all the children of $\rho$. If the child with lowest cost $C(\gamma_i(\rho))$ has a lower cost than $\rho$, we make it the new best fit ($\rho = \gamma_i$) and go back to step 3. Otherwise, exit to step 5.

For efficiency, we use a **greedy** algorithm to choose the best model. We consider only the descendants of the current model $\rho$ to choose the next model. Conversely, a node is considered only if it is linked to the best guess $\rho$ at some point. Thus, curves are added in order of importance, with the one reducing the objective function the most added first. This approach works best when a particular curve is clearly more important than other choices, or when curves may be refined in any order with similar results. In cases where two curves produce similar results early on, but one branch later proves to be clearly superior, a more exhaustive search algorithm with backtracking would achieve better results.

Steps 2-4 constitute the *Recognition Phase* of the algorithm where an appropriate model is chosen by identifying a path through the model hierarchy as shown in figure 8. The goal is to quickly choose the appropriate model in the hierarchy i.e: to identify which curves and deformations are required to model the data. Since this process merely chooses a suitable model, it is appropriate to represent the curves at a coarse level of detail. However, since we wish to eventually recover an accurate final model, we further refine the "recognized" model $\rho$ in the next step.

**Step 5. Refine curves further and add curve constraints:**

- **Refine:** Using the heuristic in equation 16, control points are automatically added where necessary. More control points are added than in the *refine* phase of step 3 above, as this allows the curve to be represented at a finer resolution; the number of control points used is given by equation 19.
- **Curve Constraints:** We then add user-specified constraints to the curves such as fixing the values at the end-points. Typically, these constraints improve the visual accuracy of the final model, but have little impact on the overall shape.
- **Optimize:** Optimization is used to get a refined model.

**Step 6. Smoothness:** Finally, we add a term given by equation 21 to the objective function, which enforces smoothness of the curves, and repeat the optimization process. This reduces kinks in the model that result from over-fitting noisy input data.

## 3 Optimization

In this section, we describe our optimization techniques for fitting a model to measured data. First, we define an objective function to assess the deviation between data and model, and describe a procedure for efficiently computing the gradient of this function. We then describe methods for refining local features of the model.

### 3.1 Error of Fit

To define a practical measure of fit between a model and the corresponding data, we begin with the notion of such a measure for two arbitrary surfaces. For any point $\mathbf{x} \in R^3$ and subset $S \subseteq R^3$, let

$$\chi(\mathbf{x}, S) = \inf_{\mathbf{y} \in S} || \mathbf{x} - \mathbf{y} || , \tag{2}$$

where $|| \cdot ||$ is the Euclidean 2-norm, which is the distance from $\mathbf{x}$ to the surface $S$. If $S_1$ and $S_2$ are two integrable surfaces in $R^3$, we define a symmetric measure of closeness by

$$\phi(S_1, S_2) = \int_{S_2} \chi^2(\mathbf{x}, S_1)\, d\mathbf{x} + \int_{S_1} \chi^2(\mathbf{x}, S_2)\, d\mathbf{x}, \tag{3}$$

which is zero if and only if $S_1 = S_2$. This function imposes an equal penalty for either surface deviating from the other, or for either surface covering too little of the other. If $S'_1$ and $S'_2$ are discrete point sets with unit weight, this becomes

$$\phi(S'_1, S'_2) = \sum_{\mathbf{x} \in S'_2} \chi^2(\mathbf{x}, S'_1) + \sum_{\mathbf{x} \in S'_1} \chi^2(\mathbf{x}, S'_2). \tag{4}$$

Moreover, if $S'_1 \subset S_1$ and $S'_2 \subset S_2$ are sets of discrete samples from the respective surfaces, then $\phi(S'_1, S'_2)$ can be used to approximate $\phi(S_1, S_2)$. To determine how well a generative model matches an actual object, we employ two point sets in exactly this manner, as equation 3 is typically impossible to evaluate exactly [1]. One point set is obtained from direct measurement, such as a range image, and the other by sampling the parameter space of a model. By optimizing with respect to this objective function, we in effect minimize the RMS deviation of the two surfaces:

$$D(S'_1, S'_2) = \sqrt{\frac{\phi(S'_1, S'_2)}{|S'_1| + |S'_2|}}, \tag{5}$$

where $|S|$ denotes the number of elements in the set $S$.

### 3.2 Computing the Gradient

Since a generative model is typically a nonlinear function of its constituent curves, we use a general optimization technique to estimate the model's shape parameters. For simplicity and ease of implementation, we use a conjugate gradient method [18] to minimize the functional $\phi(S'_d, S'_m)$ with respect to the model parameters. Let $S'_d$ denote the fixed data, and $S'_m$ the model samples, which depend on intrinsic shape parameters as well as extrinsic parameters controlling translation, scale, and pose. Specifically,

$$S'_m = S'_m(c_0, c_1, \ldots, c_k, \mathbf{t}, \mathbf{q}),$$

where $c_0, c_1, \ldots c_k$ are model parameters, such as global deformations and the $y$-components of curve control points, $\mathbf{t} \in R^3$ is the

[1] Simple analytic formulae for $\chi$ are seldom known, and numerical evaluation, though precise, is typically too slow for the inner loop of an optimization algorithm.

global translation, and $\mathbf{q}$ is a quaternion encoding global scale and rotation. Thus, optimization is guided by gradients of the form

$$\nabla\phi = \left[\frac{\partial\phi}{\partial c_0}, \frac{\partial\phi}{\partial c_1}, \ldots, \frac{\partial\phi}{\partial c_k}, \frac{\partial\phi}{\partial \mathbf{t}}, \frac{\partial\phi}{\partial \mathbf{q}}\right]. \qquad (6)$$

To compute this gradient, first observe that

$$\frac{\partial\phi}{\partial c_j}(S'_d, S'_m) = \sum_{i=1}^{|S'_m|} \frac{\partial\phi}{\partial \mathbf{x}_i}\frac{\partial \mathbf{x}_i}{\partial c_j}, \qquad (7)$$

where $\mathbf{x}_1, \mathbf{x}_2, \ldots$ are elements of $S'_m$. Because $\partial\phi/\partial\mathbf{x}_i$ and $\partial\mathbf{x}_i/\partial c_j$ are row and column vectors of dimension three, respectively, the summation is over inner products. We next express the partial derivatives of $\phi$ in equation 7 in terms of the *nearest neighbor function* $\eta_d : S'_m \rightarrow S'_d$, where $\eta_d(\mathbf{x})$ is the element of $S'_d$ nearest to $\mathbf{x} \in S'_m$. The function $\eta_m : S'_d \rightarrow S'_m$ is defined analogously. Then, equation 4 becomes

$$\phi(S'_d, S'_m) = \sum_{\mathbf{x}\in S'_m} ||\,\mathbf{x} - \eta_d(\mathbf{x})\,||^2 + \sum_{\mathbf{y}\in S'_d} ||\,\mathbf{y} - \eta_m(\mathbf{y})\,||^2. \qquad (8)$$

Since the nearest neighbor functions are piecewise constant, their derivatives are zero almost everywhere. Hence

$$\frac{1}{2}\frac{\partial\phi}{\partial\mathbf{x}} = [\mathbf{x} - \eta_d(\mathbf{x})]^T + \sum_{\mathbf{y}\in\eta_m^{-1}(\mathbf{x})} [\mathbf{x} - \mathbf{y}]^T, \qquad (9)$$

for all $\mathbf{x} \in S'_m$, where the inverse relation $\eta_m^{-1}(\mathbf{x})$ denotes the set of points in $S'_d$ whose nearest neighbor in $S'_m$ is $\mathbf{x}$. The nearest-neighbor correspondences are efficiently computed using a $kd$-tree updated at each major iteration of the conjugate-gradient solver.

Suppose now that $c$ is a control point of a curve $\Gamma$. Then, to compute $\partial\mathbf{x}/\partial c$, we must account for the composition of nonlinear transformations that may be applied to the curve as part of the current model. For example, suppose that the point $\mathbf{x}$ is obtained by evaluating the model at the parameter values $u$ and $v$. Then

$$\mathbf{x}(u, v) = \mathbf{F}(u, v, \Gamma(u; c_1, \ldots, c_q)), \qquad (10)$$

where, $\mathbf{F}(u, v, \cdot) : R \rightarrow R^3$ is the parametric mapping defined by previous levels in the model hierarchy and applied to curve $\Gamma$; we assume $\Gamma$ to be a function of the parameter $u$ as well as the control points $c_1, \ldots, c_q$. It follows that

$$\frac{\partial\mathbf{x}(u,v)}{\partial c} = \frac{\partial\mathbf{x}(u,v)}{\partial\Gamma(u)}\frac{\partial\Gamma(u)}{\partial c}, \qquad (11)$$

where $\partial\mathbf{x}/\partial\Gamma(u)$ is the $3\times1$ Jacobian matrix of $\mathbf{F}$ at the parameter values $u$ and $v$. The partial derivative on the right of equation 11 is easily evaluated, given that $\Gamma$ is simply a spline curve. The partial $\partial\mathbf{x}/\partial\Gamma(u)$ can be evaluated symbolically by differentiating the current model. We have found that numerical approximation by a finite difference is equally effective, and may be simpler to compute. Thus, we can also use

$$\frac{\partial\mathbf{x}(u,v)}{\partial\Gamma(u)} \approx \frac{\mathbf{F}(u, v, \Gamma(u) + h) - \mathbf{F}(u, v, \Gamma(u) - h)}{2h}, \qquad (12)$$

where $h$ is a suitably small step. When $c$ is a global parameter, controlling a bending deformation for example, $\partial\mathbf{x}/\partial c$ is obtained directly from the algebraic model specification using either symbolic or numeric differentiation, and the second factor on the right of equation 11 is no longer necessary.

The extrinsic parameters $\mathbf{t}$ and $\mathbf{q}$ map canonical model coordinates, in which the computations are initially performed, into the world-space coordinates of the measured data, in which the gradient $\nabla\phi$ is computed. More precisely,

$$\mathbf{x} = \mathbf{t} + \mathbf{M}(\mathbf{q})\mathbf{x}_0, \qquad (13)$$

where the point $\mathbf{x}_0$ is in canonical coordinates, and $M$ is a scale and rotation matrix parametrized by $\mathbf{q}$. All partials of $\mathbf{x}$ are also transformed by

$$\frac{\partial\mathbf{x}}{\partial\Gamma(u)} = \mathbf{M}(\mathbf{q})\frac{\partial\mathbf{x}_0}{\partial\Gamma(u)}. \qquad (14)$$

Finally, to compute $\partial\phi/\partial\mathbf{t}$ and $\partial\phi/\partial\mathbf{q}$ in equation 6, we substitute partials of $\mathbf{x}$ with respect to $\mathbf{t}$ and $\mathbf{q}$ in place of $\partial\mathbf{x}/\partial c$ in equation 7, where

$$\frac{\partial\mathbf{x}}{\partial\mathbf{t}} = \mathbf{I} \quad \text{and} \quad \frac{\partial\mathbf{x}}{\partial\mathbf{q}} = \frac{d\mathbf{M}}{d\mathbf{q}}\mathbf{x}_0. \qquad (15)$$

Here $\mathbf{I}$ is the $3\times3$ identity matrix, and the derivative of each element in the matrix $\mathbf{M}$ with respect to $\mathbf{q}$ is itself a quaternion. Equation 7 becomes a summation over row vectors or quaternions after the respective substitutions.

```
procedure ComputeGradient
    Use new point correspondences.
    P ← ∅
    for all x ∈ S'_m and y ∈ S'_d do
        add (x, η_d(x)) to P
        add (η_m(y), y) to P
    endfor
    Compute E, extrinsic & global partials.
    g ← 0;  E ← 0
    for all (x, y) ∈ P do
        (u, v) ← parameters of x
        w ← 2(x − y)^T                          Eq. 9
        p ← w [∂x/∂c_0]                          Eq. 7
        g ← g + [p 0 w wṀx_0]                    Eq. 7, 15
        E_u ← E_u + w [∂x/∂Γ(u)]                 Eq. 16
    endfor
    Fill in partials wrt control points.
    for all u samples do
        for each c_j affecting Γ(u) do
            g_j ← g_j + E_u [∂Γ(u)/∂c_j]         Eq. 17
        endfor
    endfor
    return g
```

Figure 4: *Computing the gradient* $\mathbf{g}$ *of the objective function* $\phi$. *We assume a single curve* $\Gamma$ *with control points* $c_1, c_2, \ldots, c_k$, *parametrized with respect to* $u$. *The parameter* $c_0$ *is assumed to be a global shape parameter. The model is sampled at discrete parameter values in* $u$ *and* $v$.

**Efficiency:** From equations 6, 7 and 9, it appears that the gradient computation requires $O(nk)$ time per curve, where $n$ is the number of sample points, and $k$ is the number of shape parameters controlling a curve. By exploiting sparsity, we can reduce the time to essentially $O(n)$ since each sample point of the model is affected by only a small number of shape parameters. In particular, when $c_1, c_2, \ldots$ are control points, their effects are very localized, so each $\partial\Gamma(u)/\partial c$ in equation 11 is nonzero only for a small number of shape parameters $c$.

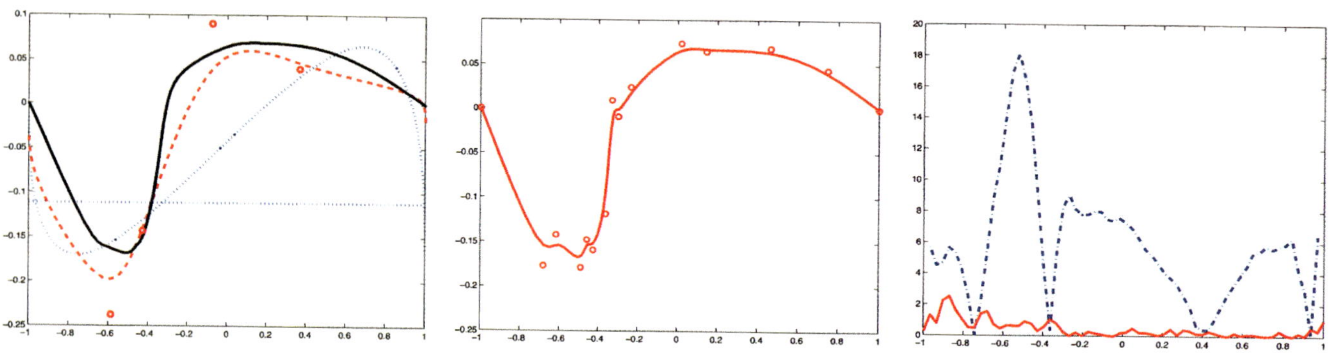

Figure 5: *The process of curve refinement.* **Left:** *Depth curve of spoon model as control points are added in recognition phase. The straight blue dotted line is the global value at root node, and the blue dotted curve is the initial coarse version. The red dashed curve results after adding four control points shown by circles, which greatly improves the approximation. For comparison, the final curve is shown by a black solid curve.* **Middle:** *Further refinement of the depth curve. Constraints force the curve to be 0 at the end-points and additional control points increase the accuracy of the curve, but also introduce undesirable kinks. These are essentially eliminated in the smoothed version shown with a solid line on the left.* **Right:** *The blue dash-dot curve indicates the initial error heuristic before any interior control points are added and the red solid line indicates the error after refinement and optimization. The optimized version has a much lower and flatter error according to the heuristic.*

The pseudo-code in figure 4 summarizes the gradient computation. Here, $\mathbf{g}$ denotes the gradient, which is a row vector, $\mathbf{w}$ is a contribution to the row vector $\partial\phi/\partial\mathbf{x}$, as defined in equation 9, and

$$E_u = \frac{\partial\phi}{\partial\Gamma(u)} = \sum_v \frac{\partial\phi}{\partial\mathbf{x}(u,v)} \frac{\partial\mathbf{x}(u,v)}{\partial\Gamma(u)} \tag{16}$$

is a scalar associated with the parameter value $u$. The summation in equation 16 is over the discrete samples of $v$. Finally, we have

$$\frac{\partial\phi}{\partial c_j} = \sum_u E_u \frac{\partial\Gamma(u)}{\partial c_j}, \tag{17}$$

where the summation is over discrete samples of the $u$ parameter. The computation is broken down in this way for efficiency. Note that the first element of the gradient vector $\mathbf{g}$ is a partial with respect to global parameter $c_0$, while the next $k$ elements of the gradient are partials with respect to curve control points. The construct $[p\ \mathbf{0}\ \mathbf{w}\ \mathbf{w}\dot{\mathbf{M}}\mathbf{x}_0]$ in line 11 of the pseudocode denotes the concatenation of the elements into a single row vector, where the zero vector $\mathbf{0}$ has $k$ entries, and $\dot{\mathbf{M}}$ is the derivative of the scale and rotation matrix with respect to the quaternion $\mathbf{q}$.

In this algorithm, we recompute the point correspondences using a $kd$-tree[2]. We then loop through all the point pairs computing the contributions to $E_u$, the partial with respect to the global parameter $c_0$, and the partials with respect to the extrinsic parameters $\mathbf{t}$ and $\mathbf{q}$. Rather than explicitly computing the set $\eta_m^{-1}(\mathbf{x})$, as shown in equation 9, we simply accumulate the contribution of each data point in a single pass through the point set.

**Discussion:** The objective function $\phi$ described above is fairly crude as it depends on the distribution of sample points, and the nearest neighbor function may fail to make the most meaningful correspondences. Further, we do not interpolate between sample points for greater accuracy, nor do we use connectivity information available in the model. While physically-based heuristics such as momentum and inertia can improve the situation somewhat [24], our simple objective function suffices to guide the traversal of the model hierarchy for the examples described in this paper.

[2] Actually, this is done earlier as a result of evaluating the objective function.

### 3.3 Curve Refinement

Each curve is adaptively refined during optimization. Refinement in this context differs from previous curve-fitting approaches in several ways. First, generative models are composed of spline curves with local control, whereas optimization techniques typically used in computer vision entail global shape parameters. Secondly, the curves of a generative model describe characteristics of a 3-D surface rather than approximating sets of 2-D points [17]. Our approach to curve refinement most closely resembles the techniques for optimizing trajectories used in animation [4, 20].

When a curve is added during the recognition phase in step 3 of figure 3, it is initialized to a constant with a global parameter inherited from the parent node in the model hierarchy. Multiple control points are added at the ends to construct a valid spline curve. After the first optimization pass, four or five additional interior control points are added and optimization is repeated. See figure 5. During recognition, a coarse approximation of the curve suffices, as it is used only to choose a suitable model in the hierarchy.

Our approach to curve refinement is to add control points gradually, and only where needed. We use $E_u$, as defined in equation 16, as an error term for a curve $\Gamma$, and insert new control-points that equidistribute the error; that is, we select the points so segments between them have equal net error.

Since $\nabla\phi = 0$ at a minimum, $\partial\phi/\partial c = 0$ for all $c$. As the number of control-points increases, $E_u$ approaches $\partial\phi/\partial c$ for some control point $c$, and is therefore 0 when the curves are represented exactly. A large $|E_u|$ indicates that the approximating curve needs refinement. We can also use a variational argument. Since $\phi$ at a minimum should be 0 to first order for variations in the curve $\Gamma$, $|E_u|$ is equivalent to the Euler-Lagrange [20, 28] error, which should be 0 when the curve is represented precisely. The error $\phi$ by itself does not necessarily indicate where curves need refining, as the model may be fundamentally incapable of representing the data; this is especially so for simpler models in the hierarchy.

**Producing the Final Curves:** In step 5 of the algorithm shown in figure 3, we refine the curves further and add constraints. First, we compute the total error normalized by the size of the data set separately for each curve:

$$E = \frac{\sum_u |E_u|}{|S'_d \cup S'_m|} \tag{18}$$

Based on this total error, we calculate the number of control-points we wish to add to each curve using the heuristic

$$N_c = \frac{E}{\epsilon}, \tag{19}$$

which adds one control point for each $\epsilon$ of error. We have found that a value of $\epsilon = 10^{-3}$ is suitable for objects of unit dimensions. The control points are again added to equidistribute the error. Then, user-specified constraints such as curve end conditions are added. Refer to the middle of figure 5 for an example. The objective function is minimized again to yield a high-accuracy solution satisfying the constraints.

In the final stage, step 6 in figure 3, we ensure that noise in the data does not lead to extraneous kinks in the model. We do this by introducing a penalty based on the integrated curvature $\beta$ given by

$$\beta = \int_u |\kappa(u)| \, du, \tag{20}$$

where $\kappa(u)$ is the curvature of $\Gamma$ at the parameter value $u$. We estimate $\beta$ using numerical quadrature and approximate the derivatives of $\beta$ with respect to the curve control points using finite differences. These values are summed over all curves in the model. The objective function is then augmented with an extra term

$$\hat{\phi} = \phi + a\beta, \tag{21}$$

where $a$ is a positive weight chosen so that the smoothness term and the original objective function are of approximately the same magnitude. Thus,

$$a = K\frac{\phi_0}{\beta_0}, \tag{22}$$

where the subscript 0 denotes the value after step 5 in the algorithm framework, but before optimizing with respect to the augmented objective function. Here, $K$ is a constant that controls the relative importance of the two terms, which was fixed at 10 in our tests.

## 4 Model Hierarchies Used

This section briefly reviews the model hierarchies used in our experiments. The hierarchy for the spoon is patterned after the model given by Snyder [21, p. 83]. The generative modeling equation is

$$\text{SPOON}(u,v) = \begin{bmatrix} \text{S}_x(v) \\ \text{ARC}_x(\text{S}_y(v), \text{D}_y(v), u) \\ \text{B}_y(v) + \text{ARC}_y(\text{S}_y(v), \text{D}_y(v), u) \end{bmatrix},$$

where S is the width or shape curve, D is the depth curve, and B is the bend, parametrized so $\text{S}_x = \text{D}_x = \text{B}_x$. $\text{ARC}(a,b,u)$ defines a parametric arc passing through $(-a, 0)$, $(0, b)$, and $(a, 0)$ in the $xy$-pane. The above equation is obtained at the deepest level of the hierarchy, regardless of the path, since all the operators commute. In the root model, S and D are global parameters and B is 0. As more complex models are reached, these constants are replaced by curves. Curves are constrained for this model so that S and D are 0 at the end-points, where S is also perpendicular to the $x$-axis; since the model is symmetric about the $x$-axis, this last constraint avoids introducing a kink. To complete the representation, we also require a thickness. Since the thickness is typically small and difficult to discern from range data, we use a constant value derived from the projection of the acquired data in the $yz$-plane.

For a ladle-like shape, the arcs are translated by the bend only after first rotating them about the $y$-axis by an angle equal to that of the bend curve from the horizontal. This forces the arcs to remain perpendicular to the bend curve. A shape suitable for a cup handle is obtained by making the circular cross-section ARC rectangular. [3]

We also used a *rotating generalized cylinder*—the "banana" model defined by Snyder [21, p. 69]—to represent many different objects. This model rotates a cross-section while scaling and translating it, and generalizes common primitives in computer vision known as profile products or simple homogeneous generalized cylinders. The parametric equation is

$$\text{BANANA}(u,v) = \text{YROT}(R(v)) \begin{bmatrix} \text{S}(v)\,\text{C}_x(u) \\ \text{S}(v)\,\text{C}_y(u) \\ \text{Z}(v) \end{bmatrix}$$

where $\text{YROT}(\theta)$ is a rotation of $\theta$ about the $y$-axis, $R$ is the parametric rotation angle, S the scale, and C the 2D cross-section. The root model is a right circular cylinder with unit radius and no rotation. The curves $R$, S, and C are added at more complex levels in the hierarchy. This class of models can also be used to represent surfaces of revolution, such as the bowl example that is shown.

As the previous model hierarchy demonstrates, our approach subsumes some common primitives used in computer vision such as simple homogeneous generalized cylinders. We have also recovered globally deformed superquadrics with our approach.

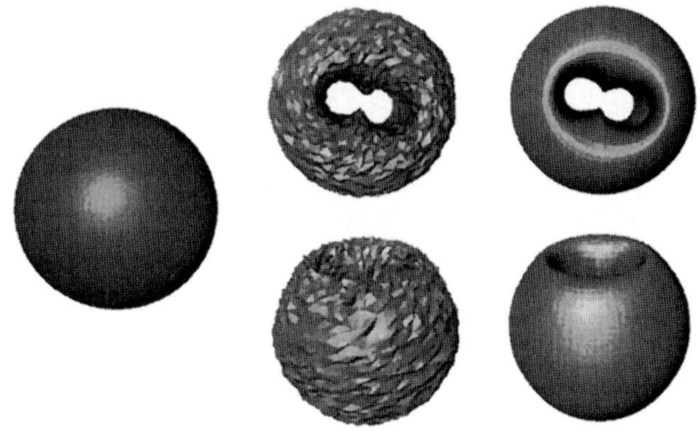

Figure 6: *Fitting of a blended model [7] to synthetic randomly perturbed samples of a sphere/torus blend with variable cross-section. This example shows how blended models fit directly into our framework, with the blend curve being treated like any other generative curve. It also shows that non-spherical and variable topology can be handled. The model eliminates most of the noise in the data without introducing significant errors. The leftmost image is the initial model, which is simply a sphere. To the right are two views of the rough input data and the smooth final model.*

DeCarlo and Metaxas [7] present a method for using blended deformable models. Models of variable topology can be created using their method. Their ideas fit directly into our framework since the *blend curve* is just another curve in the generative model. Since our objective function does not directly consider topology at all, no effort is needed to incorporate variable topology. We note that DeCarlo and Metaxas require certain constraints on the blending function to obtain a consistent model, which are naturally incorporated into the curve constraints phase of our algorithm. The general formula for a blended model [7] is

$$\text{BLEND}(u,v) = \Gamma(u)\text{B}_1(u,v) + (1 - \Gamma(u))\text{B}_2(u,v),$$

[3] The actual handle is not exactly rectangular, leading to the overly *squared* results. The data is also too sparse to reliably estimate the cross-section from scratch.

where Γ is the blending curve that can be treated just as any other curve in the generative model. Here $B_1$ and $B_2$ are simply constituents of the generative model, which can be any shape at all, including as a special case, the superquadrics and supertoroids used in [7]. Figure 6 shows an example of recovering blended models with our approach.

Although this paper deals primarily with shapes that can be represented by a single generative model, we have carried out some experiments on simple articulated objects. The watering-can in figure 1 was modeled by first manually segmenting it into body, handle and spout, and then fitting a rotating generalized cylinder to each part. Minor imperfections are primarily due to errors in segmentation. We may also define a single composite generative model by combining existing parts, each controlled by separate extrinsic and intrinsic parameters. The cup in figure 1 is an example. If the extrinsic transformations of the individual parts are left free—and not constrained to ensure correct connectivity—the user may need to make some minor adjustments at the end to ensure the parts connect properly. While the user-supplied initial guess function can still be crude, it needs to be more accurate for an articulated object since a data point can otherwise be incorrectly associated with the wrong model part.

## 5 Results

**Parameters:** For our tests, the complexity constant $Q$ defined below equation 1 was set to a deviation of .01 after scaling the models to have a major axis range from $-1$ to $+1$. Thus, $Q$ corresponds to a percentage error of approximately .5%. The results demonstrate that the algorithm is not very sensitive to the precise value of $Q$. We report the percentage error using a $64 \times 64$ tessellation of the model. For illustrative purposes only, both range images and the model were meshed to create the final images for display and colors are artificial. Snyder [21] describes alternate methods to image generative models without mesh creation, but at the cost of loss of interactivity.

**Data:** The range data used in our experiments was obtained from a variety of sources. Of the objects in figure 7, the spoon and bowl data are single range images obtained using structured light [25], while 6 cylindrical scans are aligned for the cup data. The ladle is a single range image obtained using the method of Bouguet and Perona [2]. Data for the banana and candle-holder were obtained using a mechanical probe, and the watering-can data is a cylindrical scan obtained from a laser range-scanner. For the data obtained from the probe, connectivity information was not available, so the meshes for the figures were obtained using the approach of Hoppe et al. [12]. Our algorithm operated directly on the range data, and the results demonstrate the benefit of recovering a model as opposed to a mesh, especially in cases of noisy and incomplete data.

**Recognition Trees:** Figure 8 shows recognition trees for two objects—a spoon acquired using structured light, and synthetic data for a banana-like object. Data on errors are given in figure 9. The root models are trivial, and the user-supplied initial guess functions need not specify accurate initial estimates; nonetheless the algorithm is able to *bootstrap* itself to produce an accurate final model. Paths that are not ultimately selected can sometimes produce strange and interesting results as a curve is trying to adjust to match data that it is incapable of matching. This effect will be especially noted in the tree for the banana.

**Accuracy and Robustness:** A visual comparison indicates that the method produces a good match to the data, even when the data is noisy and/or incomplete. As a confirmation of the accuracy of the method, on the synthetic data of the banana shown in figure 8, the technique produces results accurate to within .4%. As shown in the left of figure 10, even if the input hierarchy is unable to adequately represent the object, the algorithm does the best it can, producing a simple model that conveys some of the dominant aspects of the shapes.

Finally, we demonstrate the robustness of the technique by running it on a sparse sampling of the spoon data; after removing 90% of the spoon data, a visually appealing reasonably accurate model is still obtained as shown in figure 9.

**Compactness:** Our models typically had fewer than a hundred parameters, primarily curve control points. This is at least two orders of magnitude smaller than the corresponding meshes.

**Editing:** An example of editing a recovered spoon model into a ladle-like shape is shown on the right of figure 10, demonstrating how easily new models can be constructed by simple and intuitive curve editing from shapes already recovered.

**Computation Time:** The entire algorithm took between 20 and 30 minutes on a 150 MHz SGI MIPS R4400, depending on model complexity and the size of the data set. Each iteration of the conjugate gradient took 1-2 seconds, with each optimization pass taking about 50 iterations. The process was entirely automatic; no manual intervention was required. The total number of points (range data and tessellated model) was typically about 15000.

## 6 Conclusions and Future Work

We have presented a new method for creating concise generative models from incomplete range data, given a user-supplied model hierarchy. Advantages of our approach are simplicity, robustness to noise, and creation of an intuitive compact model. We extend traditional computer vision algorithms for recovery of specific shapes in that curves of a user-supplied generative model are estimated; the user can supply a model of their choice and immediately obtain an automatic recovery algorithm.

Our work currently has many limitations. The fits obtained are not perfect, especially when the model inadequately describes the real object. Even for the synthetic banana-like data used in figure 8, there is some residual error. Our method also does not preserve local detail, and there may be artifacts from under- or over-smoothing, such as the squaring near the ends of the spoon model. Further, the algorithm requires the user to specify an appropriate model hierarchy, and currently does not allow different hierarchies to be combined. If the wrong hierarchy is input, a simple model that mimics the original to the extent possible will be output as shown on the left of figure 10, but those results may not always be useful. Also, while the models shown are complex compared to single parametric models previously used in computer vision, they are still fairly simple for graphics as we do not provide automatic segmentation for recovery of complex articulated objects.

Solving the above problems defines some important directions for future work. Improvements could also be made in using more complex objective functions and minimization algorithms, more flexible tradeoffs between accuracy and simplicity, and more exhaustive non-greedy methods for traversing the input hierarchy. Finally, the model hierarchy used could be learned from examples or created automatically from a model database.

While many challenges remain, we believe that algorithms for recovering high-level models are an important direction of research for both computer vision and computer graphics.

Figure 7: Data (above) and models (below) for the objects in the scene of figure 1. The models are robust to noise and incomplete data, and are a smooth compact representation.

**Acknowledgements:** Special thanks to Jean-Yves Bouguet for reviewing early drafts, and for help with data acquisition. Preliminary discussions with Al Barr were of immense help. We are also grateful to the anonymous Siggraph reviewers (especially #2) and committee for their helpful comments, and to members of the graphics groups at Caltech and Stanford, for their support.

This work was supported by the NSF Science and Technology Center for Computer Graphics and Scientific Visualization (ASC-8920219), an Army Research Office Young Investigator award (DAAH04-96-100077), the Alfred P. Sloan Foundation, and a Reed-Hodgson Stanford Graduate Fellowship. All opinions, findings, conclusions or recommendations expressed here are those of the authors only and do not necessarily reflect the views of the sponsoring agencies and individuals.

## References

[1] T. O. Binford. Visual perception by computer. In *Proceedings of the IEEE Conference on Systems Science and Cybernetics*, 1971.

[2] Jean-Yves Bouguet and Pietro Perona. 3D photography on your desk. In *ICCV 98 proceedings*, pages 43–50, 1998.

[3] R. A. Brooks. Model-based three-dimensional interpretations of two-dimensional images. *IEEE Transactions on Pattern Analysis and Machine Intelligence (PAMI)*, 5(2):140–150, 1983.

[4] M.F. Cohen. Interactive spacetime control for animation. In *SIGGRAPH 92 proceedings*, pages 293–302, 1992.

[5] Brian Curless and Marc Levoy. A volumetric method for building complex models from range images. In *SIGGRAPH 96 proceedings*, pages 303–312, 1996.

[6] Paul E. Debevec, Camillo J. Taylor, and Jitendra Malik. Modeling and rendering architecture from photographs: A hybrid geometry- and image-based approach. In *SIGGRAPH 96 proceedings*, pages 11–20, 1996.

[7] D. DeCarlo and D. Metaxas. Blended deformable models. *PAMI*, 18(4):443–448, Apr 1996.

[8] D. DeCarlo and D. Metaxas. Shape evolution with structural and topological changes using blending. *PAMI*, 20(11):1186–1205, Nov 1998.

[9] S.J. Dickinson, D. Metaxas, and A. Pentland. The role of model-based segmentation in the recovery of volume parts from range data. *PAMI*, 19(3):259–267, Mar 1997.

[10] Matthias Eck and Hugues Hoppe. Automatic reconstruction of B-Spline surfaces of arbitrary topological type. In *SIGGRAPH 96 proceedings*, pages 325–334, 1996.

[11] F. Ferrie, J. Lagarde, and P. Whaite. Darboux frames, snakes, and super-quadrics: Geometry from the bottom up. *PAMI*, 15(8):771–784, 1993.

[12] Hugues Hoppe, Tony DeRose, Tom Duchamp, John McDonald, and Werner Stuetzle. Surface reconstruction from unorganized points. In *SIGGRAPH 92 proceedings*, pages 71–78, 1992.

[13] Hugues Hoppe, Tony DeRose, Tom Duchamp, John McDonald, and Werner Stuetzle. Mesh optimization. In *SIGGRAPH 93 proceedings*, pages 19–26, 1993.

[14] Venkat Krishnamurthy and Marc Levoy. Fitting smooth surfaces to dense polygon meshes. In *SIGGRAPH 96 proceedings*, pages 313–324, 1996.

[15] R. Nevatia. *Structured Descriptions of Complex Curved Objects for Recognition and Visual Memory*. PhD thesis, Stanford, 1974.

[16] A. Pentland. Toward an ideal 3-D CAD system. In *Proc. SPIE Conf. Machine Vision Man-Machine Interface*, 1987. San Diego, CA.

[17] Michael Plass and Maureen Stone. Curve-fitting with piecewise parametric cubics. In *SIGGRAPH 83 proceedings*, pages 229–239, 1983.

[18] W. Press, S. Teukolsky, W. Vetterling, and P. Flannery. *Numerical Recipes in C: The Art of Scientific Computing (2nd ed.)*. Cambridge University Press, 1992.

[19] N. Sriranga Raja and A. K. Jain. Obtaining generic parts from range images using a multi-view representation. *Computer Vision, Graphics, and Image Processing. Image Understanding*, 60(1):44–64, July 1994.

[20] R. Ramamoorthi and A. H. Barr. Fast construction of accurate quaternion splines. In *SIGGRAPH 97 proceedings*, pages 287–292, 1997.

[21] J. Snyder. *Generative Modeling for Computer Graphics and CAD*. Academic Press, 1992.

[22] John M. Snyder and James T. Kajiya. Generative modeling: A symbolic system for geometric modeling. In *SIGGRAPH 92 proceedings*, pages 369–378, 1992.

[23] F. Solina and R. Bajcsy. Recovery of Parametric Models from Range Images: The Case for Superquadrics with Global Deformations. *PAMI*, 12(2):131–147, February 1990.

[24] D. Terzopoulos and D. Metaxas. Dynamic 3D models with local and global deformations: Deformable superquadrics. *PAMI*, 13(7):703–714, July 1991.

[25] Marjan Trobina. Error model of a coded-light range sensor. Technical Report BIWI-TR-164, ETH, Zurich, 1995.

[26] Greg Turk and Marc Levoy. Zippered polygon meshes from range images. In *SIGGRAPH 94 proceedings*, pages 311–318, 1994.

[27] K. Wu and M. D. Levine. Recovering parametric geons from multiview range data. In *CVPR*, pages 159–166, June 1994.

[28] D. Zwillinger. *Handbook of Differential Equations*. Academic Press, 1989.

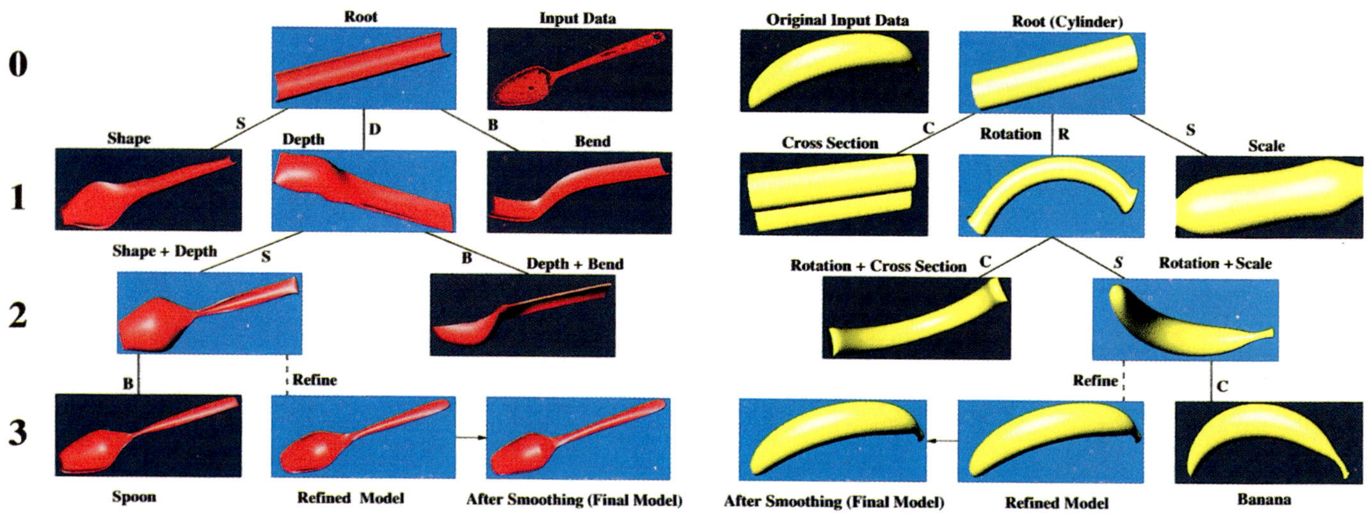


Figure 8: Recognition trees for the spoon (left) and banana (right). Highlighted nodes (lighter background) indicate the best guess at some level, and only nodes reachable from a highlighted node are generated. The algorithm is able to *bootstrap* itself, starting from very crude initial conditions, improving at each stage and finishing with an accurate model.

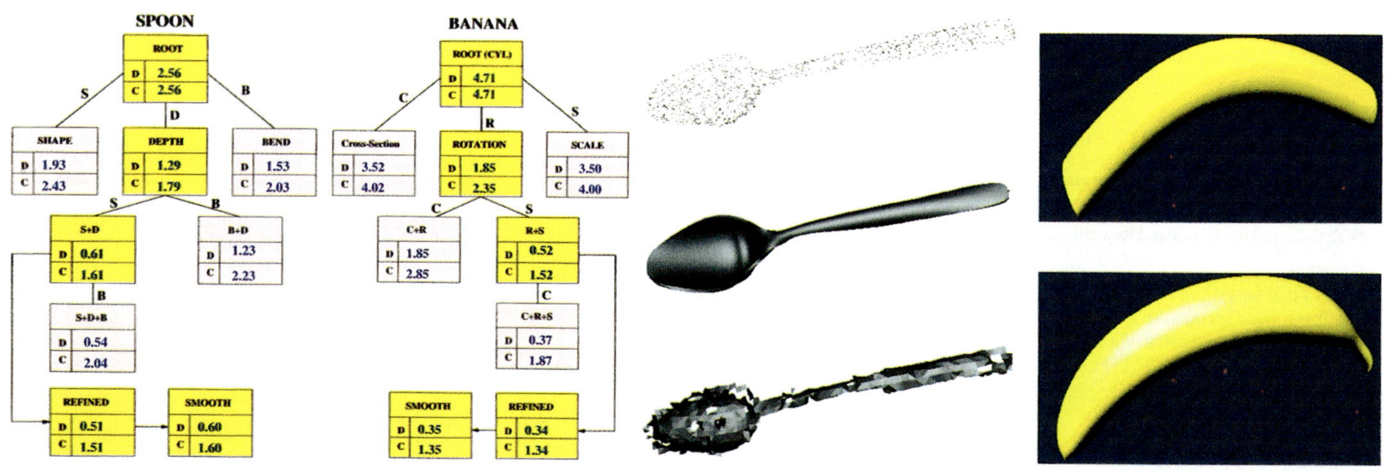


Figure 9: **Left:** Percentage deviation errors (D) and total costs (C) for the spoon (left) and banana (right). **Middle:** Fitting of model to very sparse data. On top is a pointcloud with fewer than 900 points. The middle shows the recovered model while the bottom is a mesh obtained from Hoppe's [12] algorithm on the same data. A comparison indicates the robustness of our approach. **Right:** The top shows a superquadric fit to the banana data while the bottom shows our model, indicating the benefit of generative models.

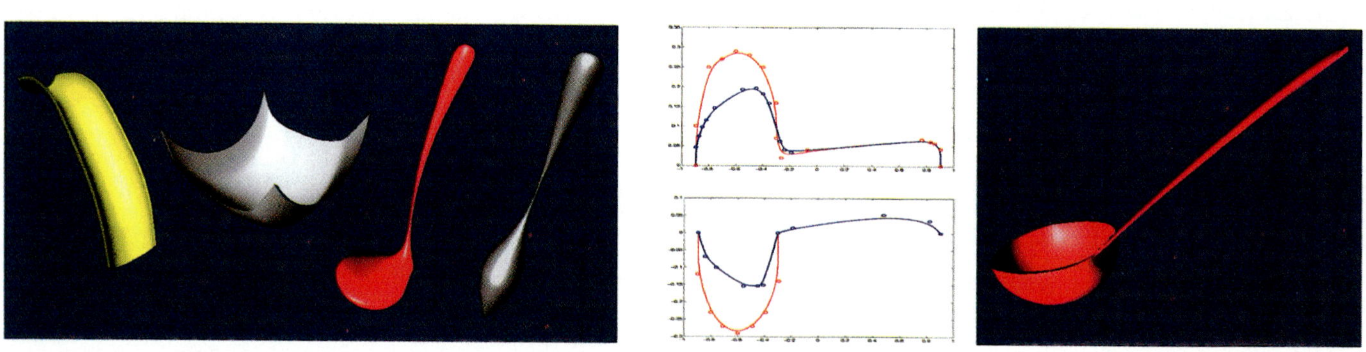

Figure 10: **Left:** Models recovered using a model hierarchy that was a poor match for the actual data since it did not possess the appropriate degrees of freedom to adequately represent the object. The two objects on the left are the banana and bowl recovered using the spoon hierarchy, while the two objects on the right are the ladle and spoon recovered using the rotating generalized cylinder hierarchy. The algorithm did the best that it could, and managed to convey some of the dominant aspects of the shapes. **Middle:** Editing a recovered spoon model into a ladle. Only a few control points need to be moved to get a radically different shape. *Middle Top:* Edited shape curve before (blue) and after (red) editing. Control points are shown as circles. *Middle Bottom:* A similar plot for the depth curve. **Right:** A view of the edited model.

# Environment Matting and Compositing

*Douglas E. Zongker*[1] *Dawn M. Werner*[1] *Brian Curless*[1] *David H. Salesin*[1,2]

[1]University of Washington [2]Microsoft Research

## Abstract

This paper introduces a new process, *environment matting*, which captures not just a foreground object and its traditional opacity matte from a real-world scene, but also a description of how that object refracts and reflects light, which we call an *environment matte*. The foreground object can then be placed in a new environment, using *environment compositing*, where it will refract and reflect light from that scene. Objects captured in this way exhibit not only specular but glossy and translucent effects, as well as selective attenuation and scattering of light according to wavelength. Moreover, the environment compositing process, which can be performed largely with texture mapping operations, is fast enough to run at interactive speeds on a desktop PC. We compare our results to photos of the same objects in real scenes. Applications of this work include the relighting of objects for virtual and augmented reality, more realistic 3D clip art, and interactive lighting design.

**CR Categories:** I.2.10 [**Artificial Intelligence**]: Vision and Scene Understanding – modeling and recovery of physical attributes; I.3.3 [**Computer Graphics**]: Picture/Image Generation – display algorithms; I.3.7 [**Computer Graphics**]: Three-Dimensional Graphics and Realism – color, shading, shadowing, and texture

**Additional Keywords:** environment matte, refraction, reflection, image-based rendering, environment map, augmented reality, interactive lighting design, clip art, alpha channel, blue-screen matting, blue spill, colored transparency

## 1 Introduction

Matting and compositing are fundamental operations in graphics. In the *matting* process, a foreground element of arbitrary shape is extracted from a background image. The *matte* extracted by this process describes the opacity of the foreground element at every point. In the *compositing* process, the foreground element is placed over a new background image, using the matte to hold out those parts of the new background that the foreground element obscures. Matting and compositing were originally developed for film and video production [11], where they are often used, for instance, to place the image of an actor, photographed in a studio in front of a controlled backdrop, into another environment. In 1984, Porter and Duff [20] introduced the digital analog of the matte — the *alpha channel* — and showed how synthetic images with alpha could be useful in creating complex digital images. In 1996, Smith and Blinn [25] described a mathematical framework for extracting alpha channels from real-world scenes, given either a pair of background images or certain assumptions about the colors in the foreground element.

Although matting and compositing have proven tremendously useful in film, video, and computer graphics production, they nevertheless fail to simulate two key effects that are essential for realism:

**Figure 1** A water goblet, digitally composited onto background images, preserving the effects of refraction.

- *refraction*, exhibited by transparent objects; and
- *reflection*, exhibited by shiny objects and objects seen at a grazing angle.

Moreover, in the case of translucent or glossy materials, refraction and reflection are further coupled with various light scattering effects. For colored materials, refraction and reflection may also exhibit selective attenuation and scattering of light, according to wavelength.

In this paper, we generalize the traditional matting and compositing processes to incorporate all of these effects. The resulting processes, which we call *environment matting and compositing*, are capable of capturing not just a foreground object and its traditional matte, but a description of how that object refracts and reflects light, which we call an *environment matte*. The foreground object can then be placed in a new environment, where it will refract and reflect light from that scene. While the environment mattes that we capture provide only an approximation to the way an object truly refracts and reflects light, we have found them to produce convincing results in real scenes. Furthermore, our environment matte representation is such that environment compositing can be performed largely with simple texture mapping. Thus, for environments of reasonable size, this process can be performed at interactive speeds on inexpensive PCs. Figure 1 shows a water goblet captured in this way and composited onto two novel backgrounds.

### 1.1 Related work

The work described in this paper brings together strands of research from many different areas in computer graphics.

Researchers have augmented pixels in a number of ways to enable more flexible image synthesis. Porter and Duff's alpha at each pixel allows for images to be acquired or rendered in layers and then combined [20]. Layers may be modified independently and then simply recombined. As noted above, their compositing method does not account for reflections, refractions, or colored transparency.

Gershbein [12] augments pixels with depth, surface normal, and shading parameters and then performs per-pixel shading calculations for light sources that can be moved at interactive rates. Dorsey *et al.* [10] render a scene under various lighting conditions and then synthesize a new image by taking a linear combination of the renderings. In effect, they store at each pixel the contributions from a set of light sources. Similarly, Nimeroff *et al.* [19] compute linear combinations of images that have been pre-rendered under daylight conditions. By suitably approximating the angular distribution of the daylight, they construct steerable basis functions that model daylight for arbitrary positions of the sun. This approach has been demonstrated on scenes with diffuse surfaces and smoothly varying lighting.

Several researchers have explored the idea of ray tracing a scene while caching the results for efficient re-rendering. Séquin and Smyrl [23] ray trace scenes and store a shading expression at each pixel. After modifying some simple shading parameters for objects in the scene, the shading expression is re-evaluated to generate an image without casting any new rays. Briére and Poulin [3] extend this idea by storing geometric information about the ray paths in a ray tree. Re-shading can be done as before, but changes in scene geometry are handled rapidly through efficient updating of the ray tree. Miller and Mondesir [18] ray trace individual objects and store a ray tree at each pixel for fast compositing into environments consisting of the front and back faces of an environment mapped cube. Each of these methods benefits from the generality of ray tracing and models phenomena such as colored reflection and refraction. However, the scenes are synthetic, and the general effects of glossy and translucent surfaces must be modeled using methods such as distributed ray tracing [7], requiring multiple ray trees per pixel.

Rendering synthetic scenes to augment pixel color is straightforward when compared to the task of acquiring the information from real images. Blue screen matting, pioneered by Vlahos [25], relies on a single-color background sufficiently different from foreground objects. As noted above, Smith and Blinn [25] use two backdrops to lift restrictions on the color of foreground objects. Reflection from the background onto the foreground, called *blue spill*, however, remains troublesome even with two backdrops and results in incorrect object transparency after matte extraction. Our method attempts to model this reflection correctly as a redirection of light from the backdrop.

To acquire our environment matte, we could illuminate one point of light at a time and sweep over the environment around the object. To cover this area would require $O(n^2)$ images where $n^2$ is proportional to the area of an environment around the object. Instead, we take inspiration from the structured light range scanning literature. Using a swept plane of light, $O(n)$ images can give shape through optical triangulation [1]. By projecting a hierarchy of progressively finer stripe patterns, the required number of images can be reduced to $O(\log n)$ [21]. Using intensity ramps, the number of images can be reduced, in theory, to two [5]; however, such methods are highly susceptible to noise. Hybrid methods have been proposed to manage the trade-off between number of images and susceptibility to noise [6, 16]. Our environment matting approach is based on the hierarchical stripe methods. Note, however, that the structured light rangefinders assume a diffuse object and attempt to intersect a line of sight from the sensor with a line of sight from the projected illuminant. In our case, the surface is typically assumed to be relatively shiny, even refractive, and the line of sight of the sensor can be arbitrarily remapped onto a *diffuse* structured light pattern.

Finally, a number of methods have been developed to render reflective and refractive objects into environments. Blinn and Newell [2] introduced the environment (a.k.a. reflection) mapping to model reflections from geometric objects into environments stored as textures. Greene [14] refined the idea to model some limited shading effects. Voorhies and Foran [26] later demonstrated environment mapping at interactive rates using texture mapping hardware. In addition, Kay and Greenberg [17] developed an approximate method for fast rendering of refractive objects. Each of these methods is based on object geometry, and none, to our knowledge, has been demonstrated to represent refraction accurately or model spatially varying translucency and gloss at interactive rates.

Miller and Mondesir's hyper-sprite rendering [18] is closest to our rendering approach; however, it uses supersampling for antialiasing. With summed area tables [8], we can achieve texture antialiasing as well as substantial gloss or translucency at interactive rates.

### 1.2 Overview

The following three sections discuss, in order, our new representation for capturing refraction and reflection properties of a foreground element, the *environment matte* (Section 2); the *environment matting* process, in which an environment matte is extracted from a real-world scene (Section 3); and the *environment compositing* process, in which foreground elements are placed into new environments (Section 4). The discussion of our main results (Section 5) is followed by a sketch of some early results that extend our approach to allow the relative depth of the object and background to be set at compositing time (Section 6). We conclude with some ideas for future research (Section 7).

## 2 The environment matte

We begin with the traditional compositing equation and then augment it with a new structure, the environment matte, which captures how light in the environment is refracted and reflected by a foreground element.

In traditional digital compositing, the color $C$ that results from placing a foreground element with color $F$ and matte $\alpha$ over a background with color $B$ is given by the "Matting Equation" [25], which is computed at each pixel:

$$C = F + (1 - \alpha)B$$

With the Matting Equation, an element's matte, or alpha, has traditionally played a dual role: it is used to represent, simultaneously, both the *coverage* of a pixel by a foreground element, and the *opacity* of that element. In our approach, we use alpha to describe coverage only. Thus, pixels with no foreground element have an alpha of zero, while pixels that are completely covered have an alpha of one—even if the foreground element covering that pixel is semi-transparent or opaque. Similarly, fractional values of alpha are used to represent partial coverage by a foreground element—again, regardless of that element's transparency.

Likewise, in traditional compositing, an element's color can be thought of as a conglomeration of several different components. These include:

1. any emissive component that the foreground object may have;
2. any reflections coming from light sources in the scene; and
3. any additional reflections or transmission of light from the rest of the environment in which the foreground object was photographed.

In our approach, an element's *foreground color* is used to characterize just the first two of these components.[1]

In addition, we use a new structure, the environment matte, to capture how light in an environment is refracted and reflected by a

[1] An alternative would be to represent just the emissive component in the foreground color, and to treat any light sources as just another part of the environment. However, because light sources are generally orders of magnitude brighter than their environments, we have found it to be more practical to separate out their contribution—in much the same way that shaders typically consider the contributions of light sources independently from those of the rest of the environment. (An interesting alternative would be to use the "high dynamic range images" introduced by Debevec and Malik [9].)

foreground element. Thus, the environment matte will capture any transmissive effects of the foreground element—in a manner independent of its coverage, or alpha. The resulting "Environment Matting Equation" will have the following form:

$$C = F + (1-\alpha)B + \Phi$$

where $\Phi$ represents the contribution of any light from the environment that reflects from or refracts through the foreground element.

Our representation for the environment matte should satisfy two requirements. First, the representation should admit a fast compositing algorithm. We therefore choose to represent our environments as sets of texture maps (as in "environment mapping" [2]). Thus, our environment mattes contain indices into these texture maps, along with a small set of additional parameters. Second, we would like the representation to be reasonably concise—that is, to require only a small, constant amount of data per environment map.

We therefore begin with a general formulation for light transport from an environment through the foreground element at each pixel, and then derive an approximation that meets our requirements. This derivation will allow us to bring out each source of error and characterize it explicitly as the approximation is described.

To start, we will assume that the only light reaching the foreground object is light coming from distant parts of the scene. This is essentially the "environment mapping assumption." We use this assumption to create the following simplified model of light transport.

As in Blinn and Newell's original formulation [2], we can describe an environment as light $E(\omega)$, coming from all directions $\omega$. The total amount of light $\Phi$ emanating from the portion $f$ of a foreground element that is visible through a given pixel can then be described as an integral over $f$ of all light from the environment that contributes to point $\boldsymbol{p}$ in the pixel, attenuated by some reflectance function $R(\omega \rightarrow \boldsymbol{p})$:

$$\Phi = \int\!\!\int R(\omega \rightarrow \boldsymbol{p})\, E(\omega)\, d\omega\, d\boldsymbol{p}$$

Note that the reflectance function $R(\omega \rightarrow \boldsymbol{p})$ includes the overall effect of all absorption and scattering as seen through the foreground element. In addition, $\Phi$, $R$, and $E$ all have an implicit wavelength dependence.

Our first approximation is to assume that the reflectance function $R(\omega \rightarrow \boldsymbol{p})$ is actually constant across the covered area of a given pixel, allowing us to write this formula in terms of a new function $R(\omega)$ that is independent of position within the pixel:

$$\Phi = \int R(\omega)\, E(\omega)\, d\omega$$

Next, we break the integral over the environment into a summation over a set of $m$ texture maps $T_i(\boldsymbol{x})$, where each texture map represents light coming from a different part of the environment (for example, from different sides of a cube).

$$\Phi = \sum_{i=1}^{m} \int R_i(\boldsymbol{x})\, T_i(\boldsymbol{x})\, d\boldsymbol{x}$$

Here, the integral is taken over the entire area of each texture map, and $R_i(\boldsymbol{x})$ is a new reflectance function, which describes the contribution of light emanating from a point $\boldsymbol{x}$ on texture map $T_i$ to the pixel $p$.

Finally, we make one more simplifying assumption: that the contribution from a texture map $T_i$ can be approximated by some constant $K_i$ times the total amount of light emanating from some axis-aligned

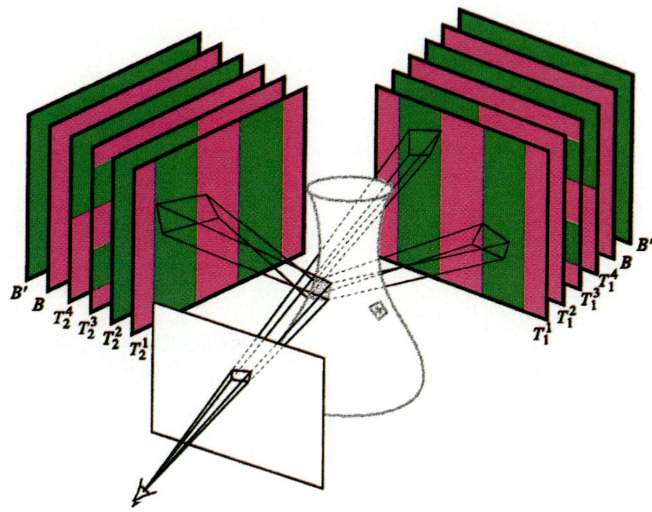


**Figure 2** The environment matting process uses structured textures to capture how light is reflected and refracted from a backdrop (right shaft), as well as from various sidedrops (left shaft). The process also captures light coming from the backdrop that is seen through uncovered portions of a pixel (center shaft).

rectangular region $A_i$ in that texture map. This approximation is reasonable in practice for many specular surfaces. We discuss its limitations in Section 5.

Most standard texture-mapping methods actually compute the *average* value of an axis-aligned region of a texture, so we'll let $R_i = K_i A_i$. Letting $\mathcal{M}(T, A)$ be a texture-mapping operator that returns the average value of an axis-aligned region $A$ of the texture $T$, we have:

$$\begin{aligned} \Phi &= \sum_{i=1}^{m} K_i \int_{A_i} T_i(\boldsymbol{x})\, d\boldsymbol{x} \\ &= \sum_{i=1}^{m} K_i A_i\, \mathcal{M}(T_i, A_i) \\ &= \sum_{i=1}^{m} R_i\, \mathcal{M}(T_i, A_i) \end{aligned}$$

We use the above approximation for $\Phi$. Thus, our overall "Environment Matting Equation" becomes:

$$C = F + (1-\alpha)B + \sum_{i=1}^{m} R_i\, \mathcal{M}(T_i, A_i) \qquad (1)$$

(Note that the reflectance coefficients $R_i$ are essentially "premultiplied," in the sense that they do not need to be multiplied by the element's pixel coverage $\alpha$. This result falls out of our earlier definition of $\Phi$, in which we integrate over only the covered portion of the pixel.)

As mentioned above, light at each wavelength should ideally be treated independently. Instead, we use the standard computer graphics approximation of treating light as having just three color components: red, green, and blue. Thus, in our implementation, the quantities $\Phi$, $R_i$, and $L_i$ are treated as 3-component vectors, while $T_i$ is a 2-D array of the same type. The additions and subtractions in the Environment Matting Equation above are treated as componentwise addition and subtraction.

**Figure 3** A photograph of the experimental setup used to capture environment mattes. The camera in the foreground photographs objects surrounded by structured light patterns displayed on the computer monitors. The image is processed to extract only the area covered by the backdrop pattern, resulting in an image as shown in the inset.

## 3 Environment matting

Here, we consider the problem of extracting, from photos of a real-world object, a foreground color $F$, pixel coverage value $\alpha$, and environment matte $\Phi = \{(R_1, A_1), \ldots, (R_m, A_m)\}$, at each pixel.

Our approach is motivated by the use of structured light systems for acquiring depth. However, unlike these previous systems, in which objects are sampled at individual points, we would like to capture how the collection of *all* rays passing through a pixel are scattered into the environment. (Really, we're interested in the opposite—how all rays in the environment are scattered through an individual pixel toward the eye—but it's easier to think in terms of this "backward ray tracing" approach [13].)

To this end, we use a number of different patterned textures, which we call *backdrops* and *sidedrops*, displayed on monitors behind and to the sides of the foreground object (See Figure 2). Each patterned backdrop is photographed both with and without the foreground object in front of it. In what follows, we will call the image of the backdrop alone the *reference image*, and the image of the foreground object in front of the backdrop the *object image*. We then solve a non-linear optimization problem to determine the set of parameters most consistent with all the image data. We use patterns that vary in only one dimension, thereby decomposing the problem of finding a rectangle into that of finding two one-dimensional intervals. In theory, any linearly-independent arrangement of horizontal and vertical stripes should work for our series of patterns. In practice, though, we felt that using coherent patterns would help reduce the chance that a slight misregistration would cause errors in our interval detection. We therefore chose to use striped patterns corresponding to one-dimensional Gray codes. We chose stripes of magenta and green, since these two colors are orthogonal in *RGB* space and have similar luminance. Our technique also requires views of the object photographed against two solid backdrops.

The dimensionality of the Environment Matting problem is unfortunately quite large: there are three degrees of freedom for the foreground color $F$ and for each reflectance coefficient $R_i$ (one for each color component), four more degrees of freedom for each area extent $A_i$, and one more for $\alpha$. To make this extraction problem more tractable, we separate its solution into four stages. We begin by considering only the backdrop—the face of the environment directly behind the object, which, by convention, we will number as the first in our list of environment textures. In the first stage, we use different backdrops to compute a coarse estimate for $\alpha$. We then determine $F$ and $R_1$ for any pixels covered by the foreground element. Next, we solve for $A_1$, along with a finer estimate of $\alpha$ along the element's boundary. Finally, once we have found $F$, $\alpha$, $R_1$, and $A_1$, we can determine the $R_i$ and $A_i$ values for other faces of the environment.

### 3.1 A coarse estimate of coverage

We begin by computing a coarse estimate of coverage for each pixel. We first partition each pixel of the environment matte into two classes: covered and uncovered. A pixel is considered covered if, for any of the $n$ background images, the colors of the reference and corresponding object images differ by more than a small amount $\epsilon$. Next, we use morphological operations [24] (an *open* followed by a *close*, both with a $5 \times 5$ box as the structuring element) to clean up the resulting alpha channel, removing any stray isolated covered or uncovered pixels.

The uncovered, or *background*, pixels will be assigned an alpha of 0. The covered pixels need to be further partitioned into *foreground* pixels (which have an alpha of 1) and *boundary* pixels at the object silhouette (for which we must determine a fractional alpha). We perform this second partition by eroding the binary image obtained from the first step, and subtracting it from the uneroded image. Computation of the fractional alpha is done at the same time as the rectangle estimation, which is discussed below in section 3.3.

An alternative to this division of the image pixels into three classes ("background," "foreground," and "boundary") would be to independently determine alpha at each pixel from the patterned backdrops—in effect, to treat each pixel as a boundary pixel, and calculate the best alpha for that pixel along with its rectangle. This was indeed the approach we first took, but when working with real photographic data there were inevitably a few single-pixel errors. These errors are generally not noticeable in still composites, but they stand out dramatically when the composited object is in motion with respect to a background. They appear as a "speck of dust" moving in sync with the object, or as a tiny "hole" where the background shines through. Our morphological approach offers cleaner results at the expense of some mathematical elegance. In addition, since it inexpensively determines alpha for most of the pixels in the image, using the morphological approach speeds the acquisition process considerably.

### 3.2 The foreground color and reflectance coefficients

For covered pixels (pixels with $\alpha > 0$), we need to determine the foreground color $F$ and reflectance coefficients $R_i$ for each face of the environment. To do this, we first use photographs of the object in front of two different solid backdrops, and solve for $R_1$ and $F$.

For a given pixel, let $B$ be the color of the first backdrop as seen from the camera, and $B'$ the color of the second. Let $C$ and $C'$ be the colors of the foreground object over these two backdrops, respectively, as seen by the camera. These four colors are related by the Environment Matting Equation (1):

$$C = F + (1-\alpha)B + R_1 B$$
$$C' = F + (1-\alpha)B' + R_1 B'$$

We now have two equations in two unknowns, which are easily solved for $R_1$ and $F$, expressed here as functions of $\alpha$:

$$R_1(\alpha) = (C - C')/(B - B') - (1-\alpha) \quad (2)$$
$$F(\alpha) = C - (1 - \alpha + R_1)B \quad (3)$$

### 3.3 The area extents and a refined estimate of coverage

To refine the alpha values for pixels on the boundary, and to determine the axis-aligned rectangle $A_1$ of the background that best approximates the reflection and refraction in the scene, we minimize an objective function over the series of photographed images for each covered pixel in the scene:

$$E_1 = \sum_{j=1}^{n} \left\| C^j - F(\alpha) - (1-\alpha)B^j - R_1(\alpha)\mathcal{M}(T_1^j, A_1) \right\|^2$$

Here, $B^j$ and $C^j$ are the colors of the pixel in question in the reference image and object image, respectively, when the $j$-th pattern is displayed as a backdrop. Similarly, the texture map $T_1^j$ is obtained by taking a reference photograph of the $j$-th pattern, displayed as a backdrop. The functions $F(\alpha)$ and $R_1(\alpha)$ are computed according to equations (2) and (3) above. Finally, the (squared) magnitude is computed as the sum of squared distances between colors in *RGB* space. Our aim will be to find the rectangular region $A_1$ that minimizes the objective function $E_1$.[2]

This optimization problem still has four degrees of freedom for the unknown rectangle $A_1$: left, right, top, and bottom $(l, r, t, b)$. We can reduce the dimensionality further by using horizontal and vertical stripes for backgrounds. For horizontally striped backgrounds, the area determination is independent of $l$ and $r$; similarly, for vertically striped backgrounds, the area determination is independent of $t$ and $b$. Thus, the five-dimensional problem of minimizing $E_1$ over $(\alpha, l, r, t, b)$ can be effectively reduced to two three-dimensional problems: minimizing over $(\alpha, l, r)$ with one set of patterns, and over $(\alpha, t, b)$ with another.

We begin by assuming a value for $\alpha$: for foreground pixels, $\alpha = 1$; while for boundary pixels we will try out multiple values. We then look for an interval $[l, r]$ that minimizes $E_1$ over the vertically striped patterns by testing a large number of candidate intervals. To speed this search, we apply a multiresolution technique, finding the best interval at some coarse scale, and then repeatedly subdividing to look for better approximations with narrower intervals. We use the same technique with the horizontally striped patterns to find the vertical extents $[t, b]$, and thus determine the rectangle. For boundary pixels, we repeat this search for multiple values of $\alpha$ and output the $\alpha$ and interval $A_1 = (l, r, t, b)$ that together minimize the objective function. This larger search is significantly slower, of course, but is required only at the object silhouette. Moreover a very coarse-grained search of $\alpha$ suffices—we've found that trying just nine values, $\alpha \in \{\frac{1}{8}(0, 1, 2, \cdots, 8)\}$ gives good results.

### 3.4 Sidedrops

The technique we have described allows us to capture information about how an object refracts and reflects light from a backdrop located directly behind the camera. To capture environment mattes for light coming from the other parts of the environment, we photograph the object while illuminating sidedrops, instead of the backdrop, with the same set of structured patterns.

The extraction process is nearly identical. We no longer need to compute $\alpha$ or $F$; these values are the same as before. The computation of $R_i$ is also somewhat simpler. When two different solid colors $S$ and $S'$ are displayed on the sidedrop, the corresponding Environment Matting Equations become:

$$C = F + (1-\alpha)B_1 + R_i S$$
$$C' = F + (1-\alpha)B_1 + R_i S'$$

Here $B_1$ is the color of the backdrop (typically very close to black). Subtracting these two equations gives a solution for $R_i$:

$$R_i = \frac{C - C'}{S - S'}$$

The objective functions $E_i$ to minimize for each additional sidedrop $i$ are then given by

$$E_i = \sum_{j=1}^{n} \left\| C^j - F(\alpha) - (1-\alpha)B_1 - R_i(\alpha)\mathcal{M}(T_i^j, A_i) \right\|^2$$

Since we cannot take reference photographs of each structured pattern on the sidedrop (the sidedrops are not visible to the camera) we instead use the photographs of the corresponding patterns on the backdrop to obtain $B$ and $B'$, as well as the texture maps $T_i^j$.

By placing sidedrops around the object in all directions and illuminating one sidedrop at a time, we can, in theory, obtain a description of all light rays that strike the camera. So far, though, for real objects we have captured environment mattes only for one backdrop and at most two sidedrops.

## 4 Environment compositing

Once we have an environment matte for a foreground object, we can composite it into a new environment in a way that preserves reflections and refractions.

This process, called environment compositing, is just an implementation of Equation (1). It involves summing the contributions of the foreground and background colors, along with a weighted contribution from each of the texture maps describing the environment.

As in any texture mapping process, we need to perform some kind of filtering to avoid aliasing. We use summed area tables [8], which allow us to compute the average value of an axis-aligned rectangle quickly. In order to handle lenticular objects, which magnify, we generally use a higher resolution for storing texture maps of background images than we use for displaying them as backdrops.

## 5 Results

We assembled an imaging system using a digital camera and several monitors to acquire environment mattes from a number of objects to illustrate the capabilities of our method. A photograph of the imaging system appears in Figure 3. We placed three monitors in positions consistent with portions of three faces of a cubical environment. We used identical 20" Trinitron monitors and adjusted the displays so that the magenta and green images were as close as possible on all monitors. We photographed each object with a Kodak DCS 520 digital camera and cycled the images on each monitor, one monitor at a time. Interreflections among monitors did not prove consequential. Enough stripe patterns were used so that the width of the smallest stripe corresponded to a pixel of the final matte. Thus, to extract a $512 \times 512$ matte, we would use 18 stripe images, nine horizontal and nine vertical. The monitors also displayed registration markers enabling the portion of the image containing the structured pattern to be extracted from each photograph. This extraction process includes a simple warp step that attempts to at least partially correct for monitor curvature and lens distortion.

The extraction process took on the order of 10 to 20 minutes per face of the environment map, running on an Intel Pentium II at

[2] Note that if using an axis-aligned rectangle were an exact model of the light transport behavior, then minimizing this objective function would correspond to ascribing a Gaussian error model to the pixel values and solving for the optimal parameters in the "maximum likelihood" sense. In fact, the axis-aligned rectangle is only an approximate model, so we are actually finding a least-squares best fit of the model parameters to the data.

**Figure 4** From left to right: an alpha matte composite, an environment matte composite, and a photograph of an object in front of a background image. The top row shows a ribbed glass candle holder; the bottom row shows a rough-surfaced glass bookend.

400MHz. Compositing is much faster, and can performed at speeds of 4 to 40 frames per second.

In order to obtain consistent colors in our side-by-side comparisons, we photographed the various backgrounds on the monitors and used these digital photos as the backgrounds in our composites. In Figures 4 and 5, the resulting composites are compared against photos of the actual objects against the same backgrounds. Within each row of these figures, the left picture shows the composite obtained using traditional alpha, obtained via the Smith-Blinn triangulation method (Theorem 4 of their paper [25]). The middle picture shows the result of compositing using the environment matte method, and the right picture is a photograph of the actual object in front of a monitor displaying the background image (taken at the same time the environment matte and triangulation data were obtained).

The first object is a glass candle holder. The two ribbed bulges produce a very complex refraction pattern, which is accurately recreated by the environment matte.

The second object is a glass bookend, with a rough textured surface that scatters light passing through it, producing a translucent effect. Note that this object simply disappears with the traditional alpha, since each pixel is judged to be transparent or nearly so.

The third set of images (top row of Figure 5) demonstrates the advantage of representing the reflection/refraction coefficient $R_1$ as an RGB triple. The objects are champagne glasses filled with water tinted red, green, and blue, respectively. The environment matte is able to more accurately reproduce the colors of the background as they appear filtered through the colored water. Note also the success of the environment matte in capturing reflections off the base of each glass, especially as compared to the ordinary alpha image.

The fourth set of images (bottom row of Figure 5) provides an example of glossy reflection. The object is a metal pie tin tilted to a near-grazing angle with respect to the camera. For this object, we used a Gaussian-weighted texture extraction operator, as discussed for the next example in detail.

Figure 6 illustrates how our assumption that light reflecting from an object can be described as a constant-weighted average over a region of a texture map begins to break down when reflections are sufficiently diffuse. The leftmost image reveals noticeable banding due to inaccuracies in this approximation. To ameliorate this effect, we attempted to model the reflection at each pixel as an elliptical Gaussian-weighted average over the texture instead, in a model similar to Ward's [27]. To extract the matte, we first modified the texture operator $\mathcal{M}$ during the acquisition process so that it would return a Gaussian-weighted average of the texture map rectangle, rather than a box-filtered average. The Gaussian is chosen so that each side of the rectangle corresponds to a $3\sigma$ difference from the center. Fast rendering with summed area tables requires a box filter, so for rendering we take each rectangle acquired and shrink it so that it corresponds to a width of $\frac{3}{2}\sigma$, using the box filter as a very rough approximation of the original Gaussian. (A potentially better alternative would be to use an elliptical weighted average (EWA) filter [15], represented as an image pyramid constructed with Gaussian filters [4] for rendering.) Using this Gaussian-filter approximation for acquisition, followed by a box-filter approximation for rendering, improves the results to some extent. However, finding

**Figure 5** From left to right: an alpha matte composite, an environment matte composite, and a photograph of an object in front of a background image. The top row shows three glasses of water tinted red, green, and blue; the bottom row shows a pie tin tilted to reflect light off the backdrop.

an approximation that is general enough to handle both diffuse and specular surfaces and also to provide efficient rendering remains a topic for future research.

Figure 7 shows objects captured using a backdrop and two sidedrops. The objects are a shiny metal candlestick, and a metal vase turned on its side. These objects were chosen and positioned so that as much of their surface as possible was reflecting light off the limited sidedrop area available with our experimental setup. The figure shows the contributions of the foreground color and unoccluded background, followed by the separate contributions of each texture map (back, left, and right). The total composite (bottom left) is made by summing these four images, and is shown along with a photograph for comparison (bottom right). Note that even complex reflections are captured—in the base of the candlestick, we can see light reflecting from the backdrop off the side of the vase facing away from the camera.

Figure 8 illustrates the use of the environment matte technique for novel relighting of objects. Here the objects are shown against a background image, but now the sidedrops are synthetically generated from photographs of actual light sources. As these lights are moved around, the environment matte shows how a light at that position would reflect off the surface of the objects. The figure shows the objects with two different lighting configurations, with the texture maps used for the left and right sidedrops shown in inset.

Figure 9 illustrates some of the ways in which our technique can fail to accurately capture reality. The top row shows an environment matte for a stack of four reflective balls: (a) the composite generated with a butterfly image on each face of the environment, (b) the corresponding photograph. While the composite image recreates the photograph well, it highlights the fact that our current setup is able to capture only a small fraction of the object's environment matte—reflections of the camera and other equipment are visible, having been captured in the foreground color term $F$. This is more a failure of engineering than of theory; with a more elaborate system for surrounding the object with structured patterns a more complete matte could be obtained. The second row of Figure 9 illustrates a more fundamental failure: the result obtained when a single pixel sees two distinct regions of the same backdrop. Here a drinking glass has been tilted so that the single backdrop is visible both through the glass and as a reflection in its surface. This is evident in photograph (d), but the two images of the stripe patterns interfere during the acquisition process. The rectangles obtained are chosen almost arbitrarily, which lead to noise in the composite (c).

## 6 Depth correction

Thus far, we have presented a method that allows us to acquire environment mattes for objects at a fixed distance from the backdrop. As a result. all of the composites we have shown are also in front of backdrops at that same depth. In order to perform composites with a backdrop at an arbitrary distance, we need to capture information about how the light rays travel through space. In this section, we therefore sketch an extension to our method, which models the light refracted or reflected by the foreground object as a 3D beam with axis-aligned rectangles as cross-sections. The rectangular extents for a backdrop at an arbitrary depth can then be constructed

**Figure 6** An object with glossy reflection, captured using an environment matte. From left to right: artifacts produced in composite image when the box filter approximation is used during acquisition, the improvement produced when a Gaussian approximation is used instead, and the actual photograph.

by taking the cross-section of the beam where it is intersected by the backdrop.

To construct a beam for each pixel, we extract two different environment mattes for the foreground object, using a backdrop placed at two different depths. As before, we consider each rectangle's horizontal extent independently of its vertical extent. For a given pixel, let $[l, r]$ and $[l', r']$ be the left and right endpoints of the rectangular extents in the two environment mattes. There are two ways in which these two extents can be connected to form a beam: either $l$ is connected to $l'$, and $r$ to $r'$; or the two endpoints are flipped, and $l$ is connected to $r'$, and $r$ to $l'$. The latter case corresponds to the presence of a focal point between the two backdrop planes. To disambiguate between the two cases, we could extract a third environment matte for a backdrop located in between the two original depths, and test to see whether the extents in that environment matte are most consistent with the straight-through connection or with the flipped connection. Instead, as a proof of concept, we have so far used just a simple flag, set by the user, that controls whether the connections for all the pixels are "straight through" or flipped. (Note that since the flag controls flipping of the beam only *within each pixel*, even if the flag is set incorrectly the refracted image appears in the correct orientation; however, the resulting image may be either too sharp or too blurry due to integration over either too small or too large an area when estimating the contributions of the environment to each pixel.)

Finally, to composite these objects in front of backdrops with arbitrary depth, we use linear interpolation to intersect the beam with a plane at that depth. The resulting rectangle is used as the area extent in the normal environment compositing operation. Figure 10 demonstrates some early results of an environment matte with depth, captured for a magnifying glass.

## 7 Conclusion

In this paper, we have introduced the environment matte and shown how it augments the alpha matte used in traditional image compositing. The environment matte models the effects of reflection, refraction, translucency, gloss, and interreflections. It also handles colored transparency in a manner that more closely approximates reality. We have demonstrated a novel method for acquiring environment mattes for real objects using structured diffuse lighting. To extract the matte from acquired images, we have developed a mathematical framework for analyzing the photographic data. This framework allows us to identify reflection and refraction intervals in a manner that is statistically optimal in the least squares sense and has proven fairly robust for specular and near specular surfaces. Using summed area tables for fast integration over rectangles, we have developed a software rendering system that composites an environment-matted object onto novel backgrounds at interactive rates with modest hardware. By placing images of lights into the environment, we can use the environment compositor as an interactive lighting tool.

This research leads to many areas for future work. First, we have more work to do to accurately calibrate our acquisition process for non-linearities and to compensate for cross-talk in the color channels. Also in the area of acquisition, we would like to explore ways of reducing the number of images required to capture an environment matte. In addition, our method assumes that there is a single region per texture map onto which a pixel maps. This is not the case when there are abrupt changes in reflected and refracted ray directions that map onto the same backdrop. One could imagine increasing the dimensionality of the maximum likelihood problem to identify more than one region, though more backdrops may be necessary to correlate the sets of horizontal and vertical intervals correctly.

As noted in Section 5, we obtain better results for glossy surfaces when estimating axis-aligned elliptical Gaussians instead of rectangles. An area of future work is to find even better functions, such as oriented, possibly steerable, functions for estimating environment mattes. Similarly, at some expense in performance, we could explore more accurate weighted filtering methods when compositing the environment mattes.

To acquire environment mattes with depth, we would like to further investigate methods for extracting the 3D beam for refraction and reflection. As mentioned earlier, we could acquire information at a third depth, and use this to decide, for each pixel, whether there is a focal point between the captured depth extremes. Instead of extracting the rectangle extents independently for each depth, we could optimize over all three depths simultaneously.

For rendering images with depth, we would like to look into methods for compositing on top of backgrounds with varying depth. Permitting the backdrop to rotate away from the camera might be useful for simulating depth of field effects. Also, the depth information might be used to composite onto arbitrary 3D scenes, rather than a 2D background. We could also investigate methods for compositing multiple environment "sprites" into one scene. Miller and Mondesir [18] note that the straightforward method of layering multiple

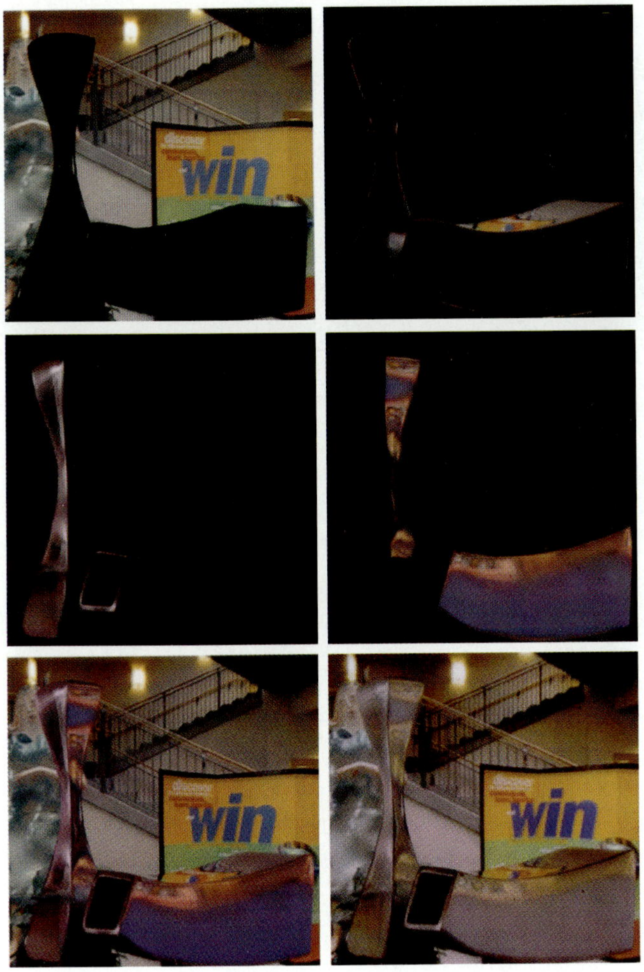

**Figure 7** An environment matte captured using multiple sides. The top left image shows the effects of the foreground color and uncovered pixel terms. The next three images show the light contributed via reflection off the back, left, and right texture maps. The final composite is the sum of these four images, shown at lower left. This is compared with a photograph of the object surrounded by these images at the lower right.

sprites into a background, while not correct, still gives a compelling appearance. Nonetheless, some loss of "depth" must occur. Perhaps our method for capturing depth information could lead to more realistic composites. Indeed, it might be possible to acquire or render our depth environment mattes from many viewpoints, leading to a new rendering primitive: a specular transfer function or specular light field. For each incoming ray, we could quickly determine a set of outgoing rays or prisms.

In other rendering areas, we could explore methods like view morphing [22] to transition among environment mattes acquired from different viewpoints. In addition, images from other viewpoints could be used to cast rays through the object into the environment to create caustics and shadows.

Another interesting area to explore, suggested by this line of research, would include methods for creating and modifying environment mattes for real or synthetic objects, interactively or algorithmically. For instance, one could easily imagine a "paint program" in which the light scattering properties of a scanned object are interactively modified through various paint operations; or texture generation methods, in which its reflectance properties are modified algorithmically.

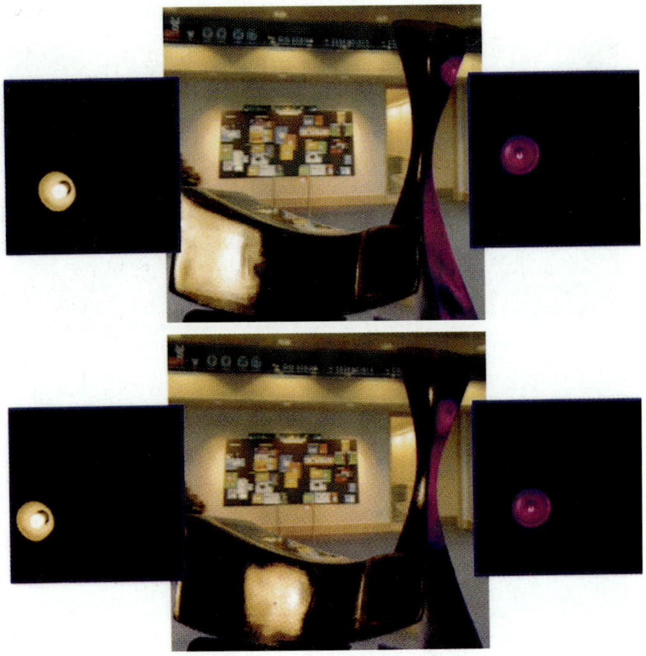

**Figure 8** Interactively relighting an object, using photographs of lights as sidedrops. The left and right sidedrops (shown in insets) are generated by moving a picture of a light source around within the texture map.

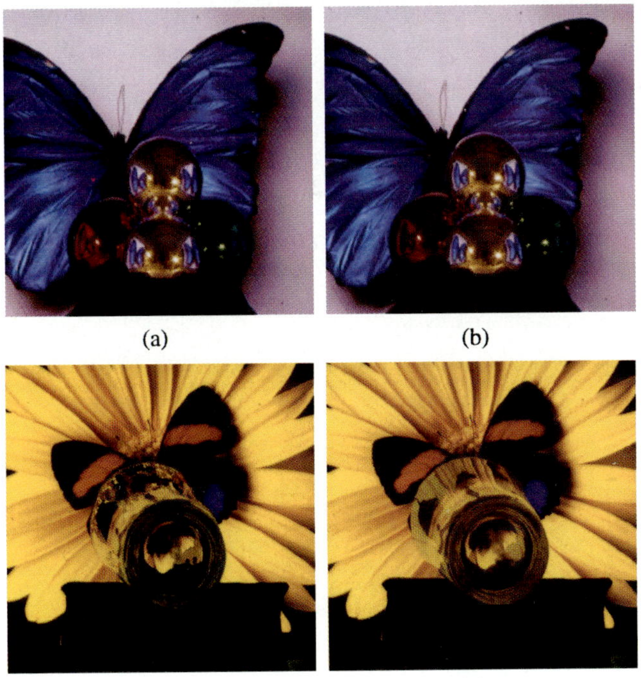

(a) (b)

(c) (d)

**Figure 9** Failure cases.


## 8 Acknowledgements

We would like to thank Steve Wolfman for his valuable contributions at the beginning of this project. Thanks also to Rick Szeliski for providing the panoramic data set used in the environment map composites. This work was supported by NSF grants 9803226 and 9553199, and by industrial gifts from Intel, Microsoft, and Pixar, and by the NSF Graduate Research Fellowship program.

(a) (b) (c) (d)

(e)

**Figure 10** An environment matte rendered at novel depths. Parts (a)–(d) are composites of a magnifying glass in front of a backdrop at four different depths. All four of these depths are different from those of the backdrops in the original object images. For purposes of comparision, (e) and (f) were taken at depths corresponding to (a) and (d), respectively. When the backdrop is moved back, notice how the magnification increases until the image flips both horizontally and vertically. The depth where the inversion occurs corresponds to the presence of a focal point, beyond which magnification decreases.

(f)

## References


[1] Paul Besl. Active optical range imaging sensors. In Jorge L.C. Sanz, editor, *Advances in Machine Vision*, chapter 1, pages 1–63. Springer-Verlag, 1989.

[2] J. F. Blinn and M. E. Newell. Texture and reflection in computer generated images. *Communications of the ACM*, 19:542–546, 1976.

[3] Normand Briére and Pierre Poulin. Hierarchical view-dependent structures for interactive scene manipulation. In *Proceedings of SIGGRAPH 96*, pages 83–90, August 1996.

[4] Peter J. Burt. Fast filter transforms for image processing. *Computer Graphics and Image Processing*, 16:20–51, 1981.

[5] Brian Carrihill and Robert Hummel. Experiments with the intensity ratio depth sensor. In *Computer Vision, Graphics, and Image Processing*, volume 32, pages 337–358, 1985.

[6] G. Chazan and N. Kiryati. Pyramidal intensity ratio depth sensor. Technical Report 121, Center for Communication and Information Technologies, Department of Electrical Engineering, Technion, Haifa, Israel, October 1995.

[7] Robert L. Cook, Thomas Porter, and Loren Carpenter. Distributed ray tracing. *Computer Graphics*, 18(3):137–145, July 1984.

[8] Franklin C. Crow. Summed-area tables for texture mapping. In *Proceedings of SIGGRAPH 84*, volume 18, pages 207–212, July 1984.

[9] Paul E. Debevec and Jitendra Malik. Recovering high dynamic range radiance maps from photographs. In *Proceedings of SIGGRAPH 97*, pages 369–378, August 1997.

[10] Julie Dorsey, James Arvo, and Donald Greenberg. Interactive design of complex time dependent lighting. *IEEE Computer Graphics and Applications*, 15(2):26–36, March 1995.

[11] R. Fielding. *The Technique of Special Effects Cinematography*, pages 220–243. Focal/Hastings House, London, third edition, 1972.

[12] Reid Gershbein. *Cinematic Lighting in Computer Graphics*. PhD thesis, Princeton University, 1999. Expected.

[13] Andrew S. Glassner. An overview of ray tracing. In Andrew S. Glassner, editor, *An Introduction to Ray Tracing*, chapter 1. Academic Press, 1989.

[14] Ned Greene. Environment mapping and other applications of world projections. *IEEE Computer Graphics and Applications*, 6(11), November 1986.

[15] Ned Greene and Paul S. Heckbert. Creating raster omnimax images from multiple perspective views using the elliptical weighted average filter. *IEEE Computer Graphics and Applications*, 6(6):21–27, June 1986.

[16] Eli Horn and Nahum Kiryati. Toward optimal structured light patterns. In *Proceedings of the International Conference on Recent Advances in Three-Dimensional Digital Imaging and Modeling*, pages 28–35, 1997.

[17] Douglas S. Kay and Donald P. Greenberg. Transparency for computer synthesized images. In *Proceedings of SIGGRAPH 79*, volume 13, pages 158–164, August 1979.

[18] Gavin Miller and Marc Mondesir. Rendering hyper-sprites in real time. In G. Drettakis and N. Max, editors, *Proceedings 1998 Eurographics Workshop on Rendering*, pages 193–198, June 1998.

[19] Jeffry S. Nimeroff, Eero Simoncelli, and Julie Dorsey. Efficient re-rendering of naturally illuminated environments. In *Fifth Eurographics Workshop on Rendering*, pages 359–373, June 1994.

[20] Thomas Porter and Tom Duff. Compositing digital images. In *Proceedings of SIGGRAPH 84*, volume 18, pages 253–259, July 1984.

[21] K. Sato and S. Inokuchi. Three-dimensional surface measurement by space encoding range imaging. *Journal of Robotic Systems*, 2:27–39, 1985.

[22] Steven M. Seitz and Charles R. Dyer. View morphing: Synthesizing 3D metamorphoses using image transforms. In *Proceedings of SIGGRAPH 96*, pages 21–30, August 1996.

[23] Carlo H. Séquin and Eliot K. Smyrl. Parameterized ray tracing. In *Proceedings of SIGGRAPH 89*, volume 23, pages 307–314, July 1989.

[24] Jean Paul Serra. *Image Analysis and Mathematical Morphology*. Academic Press, 1982.

[25] Alvy Ray Smith and James F. Blinn. Blue screen matting. In *Proceedings of SIGGRAPH 96*, pages 259–268, August 1996.

[26] Douglas Voorhies and Jim Foran. Reflection vector shading hardware. In Andrew Glassner, editor, *Proceedings of SIGGRAPH 94*, pages 163–166, July 1994.

[27] Gregory J. Ward. Measuring and modeling anisotropic reflection. In Edwin E. Catmull, editor, *Computer Graphics (SIGGRAPH '92 Proceedings)*, volume 26, pages 265–272, July 1992.

# Inverse Global Illumination: Recovering Reflectance Models of Real Scenes from Photographs

**Yizhou Yu, Paul Debevec, Jitendra Malik,** and **Tim Hawkins** *

Computer Science Division
University of California at Berkeley

## ABSTRACT

In this paper we present a method for recovering the reflectance properties of all surfaces in a real scene from a sparse set of photographs, taking into account both direct and indirect illumination. The result is a lighting-independent model of the scene's geometry and reflectance properties, which can be rendered with arbitrary modifications to structure and lighting via traditional rendering methods. Our technique models reflectance with a low-parameter reflectance model, and allows diffuse albedo to vary arbitrarily over surfaces while assuming that non-diffuse characteristics remain constant across particular regions. The method's input is a geometric model of the scene and a set of calibrated high dynamic range photographs taken with known direct illumination. The algorithm hierarchically partitions the scene into a polygonal mesh, and uses image-based rendering to construct estimates of both the radiance and irradiance of each patch from the photographic data. The algorithm computes the expected location of specular highlights, and then analyzes the highlight areas in the images by running a novel iterative optimization procedure to recover the diffuse and specular reflectance parameters for each region. Lastly, these parameters are used in constructing high-resolution diffuse albedo maps for each surface.

The algorithm has been applied to both real and synthetic data, including a synthetic cubical room and a real meeting room. Re-renderings are produced using a global illumination system under both original and novel lighting, and with the addition of synthetic objects. Side-by-side comparisons show success at predicting the appearance of the scene under novel lighting conditions.

**CR Categories:** I.2.10 [**Artificial Intelligence**]: Vision and Scene Understanding—modeling and recovery of physical attributes I.3.7 [**Computer Graphics**]: Three-dimensional Graphics and Realism—color, shading, shadowing, and texture I.3.7 [**Computer Graphics**]: Three-Dimensional Graphics and Realism—Radiosity I.4.8 [**Image Processing**]: Scene Analysis—Color, photometry, shading

**Keywords:** Global Illumination, Image-Based Modeling and Rendering, BRDF Models, Reflectance Recovery, Albedo Maps, Radiance, Radiosity, Rendering

*Email:{yyz,debevec,malik,tsh}@cs.Berkeley.edu, yizhouy@acm.org, Website: http://www.cs.berkeley.edu/~{yyz,debevec,malik,tsh}



## 1 Introduction

Computer graphics is being increasingly used to visualize real objects and environments. Applications in entertainment, architecture, interior design, virtual reality, and digital museums often require that aspects of the real world be rendered realistically from novel viewpoints and/or under novel illumination. For example, one would want to see how a room in a house would look like with different lighting, or how a statue would look at various times of day in a different wing of a museum. Lastly, one might want to realistically render a film location in different lighting, and add in digital props and characters, with the expectation that the rendered results would be the same as what would have happened had it all been for real.

Work in image-based modeling and rendering e.g. [18, 3, 22, 19, 12, 9, 6, 29]) has shown that photographs of a scene can be used along with geometry to produce realistic renderings of diffuse scenes under the original lighting conditions. However, challenges remain in making modifications to such scenes. Whether it is changing the geometry or changing the lighting, generating a new rendering requires re-computing the interaction of light with the surfaces in the scene. Computing this interaction requires knowing the reflectance properties (diffuse color, shininess, etc.) of each surface. Unfortunately, such reflectance property information is not directly available from the scene geometry or from photographs.

Considerable work (e.g. [32, 16, 5, 27, 21]) has been done to estimate reflectance properties of real surfaces in laboratory settings from a dense set of measurements. However, reflectance properties of real scenes are usually spatially varying, and typically change with use and age, making *a priori* laboratory measurements impractical. It would clearly be preferable to estimate the reflectance properties of an entire scene at once, with the surfaces being illuminated *in situ* rather than as isolated samples, and from a relatively sparse set of photographs. This is difficult for two reasons.

The first is that we wish to use only a sparse set of photographs of the scene, rather than exhaustively photographing every point of every surface from a dense set of angles. With such a set of photographs, we can expect to observe each surface point from only a small number of angles. As a result, there will be too little data to determine fully general bi-directional reflectance distribution functions (BRDFs) for each surface. We address this problem in two ways. First, we limit ourselves to recovering low-parameter reflectance models of the surfaces in the scene. Second, we assume that the scene can be decomposed into areas with related reflectance properties. Specifically, we allow the diffuse reflectance, or *albedo*, of the object to vary arbitrarily over any surface; the estimated albedo is computed as an image called an *albedo map*[1]. In contrast, we require that the directional reflectance properties (such as specular reflectance and roughness) remain constant over each area. In this work, such areas are specified as part of the geometry

[1]The commonly used term *texture map* is sometimes used to refer to this same concept. However, texture maps are also sometimes used to store surface radiance information, which is not lighting-independent.

recovery process.

The second problem we face is that in a real scene, surfaces will exhibit mutual illumination. Thus, the light that any particular surface receives will arrive not just from the light sources, but also from the rest of the environment through indirect illumination. As a result, the incident radiance of an observed surface is a complex function of the light sources, the geometry of the scene, and the as-yet-undetermined reflectance properties of all of the scene's surfaces. In this work, we use radiance data from photographs and image-based rendering to estimate the incident radiances of surfaces in the scene. This allows us to estimate the reflectance properties of the surfaces in the scene via an iterative optimization procedure, which allows us to re-estimate the incident radiances. We refer to this procedure as *inverse global illumination.*

Addressing these two problems makes it possible to robustly recover reflectance parameters from the limited radiance information present in a sparse set of photographs, and the accommodations made are appropriate for a wide variety of real scenes. Even when they are not met, the algorithm will compute the reflectance property parameters that best fit the observed image data, which in many cases can still yield a visually acceptable result.

The input to our algorithm is a geometric model of the scene, a set of radiance maps taken under known direct illumination, and a partitioning of the scene into areas of similar non-diffuse reflectance properties. The algorithm outputs a set of high-resolution albedo maps for the surfaces in the scene along with their specular reflectance properties, yielding a traditional material-based model. This output is readily used as input to traditional rendering algorithms to realistically render the scene under arbitrary lighting conditions. Moreover, modifications to the scene's lighting and geometry and the addition of synthetic objects is easily accomplished using conventional modeling methods.

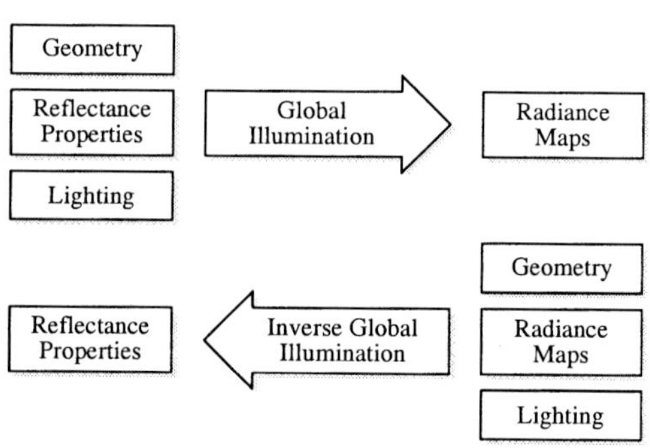


Figure 1: **Overview of the Method** *This figure shows the relationship between global illumination and inverse global illumination. Global illumination uses geometry, lighting, and reflectance properties to compute radiance maps (i.e. rendered images), and inverse global illumination uses geometry, lighting, and radiance maps to determine reflectance properties.*

### 1.1 Overview

The rest of this paper is organized as follows. In the next section we discuss work related to this paper. Section 3 describes *inverse radiosity*, a stepping stone to the full algorithm which considers diffuse scenes. Section 4 presents a technique for recovering specular reflectance properties for homogeneous surfaces considering direct illumination only. Section 5 describes how these two techniques are combined to produce our inverse global illumination algorithm. Section 6 completes the technical discussion by describing how high-resolution albedo maps are derived for the surfaces in the scene. Section 7 presents reflectance recovery results from both real and synthetic data, a description of our data acquisition, and synthetic renderings which are compared to real photographs. Section 8 presents some conclusions and avenues for future work.

## 2 Background and Related Work

The work we present in this paper has been made possible by previous work in BRDF modeling, measurement and recovery, geometry acquisition, image-based rendering, and global illumination.

In graphics, there is a long history of modeling surface reflectance properties using a small number of parameters. Recent efforts in this direction include models introduced in [14, 32, 25, 17]. These models have been shown to yield reasonable approximations to the reflectance properties of many real materials, and they have been used to produce realistic renderings.

On the other hand, considerable recent work has presented methods for measuring and recovering the reflectance properties of materials using imaging devices. [32] and [16] presented techniques and apparatus for measuring reflectance properties, including anisotropic reflection. [5] measured directional reflectance properties of textured objects. [27] and [21] showed that diffuse and specular reflectance properties could be recovered from multiple photographs of an object under direct illumination. [36] recovered reflectance properties of isolated buildings under daylight and was able to re-render them at novel times of day. [7] estimated material properties of parts of a scene so that they could receive shadows and reflections from synthetic objects. [10, 20] used a model of the scene and forward radiosity to estimate diffuse albedos to interactively modify the scene and its lighting. Although mutual illumination has been considered in the problem of shape from shading [23], it has not yet been fully considered for recovering non-diffuse reflectance properties in real environments. A survey of some of the methods is in Marschner [21].

Certain work has shown that changing the lighting in a scene does not necessarily require knowledge of the surface reflectance properties – taking linear combinations of a large set of basis images [24, 35] can yield images with novel lighting conditions.

Recent work in laser range scanning and image-based modeling has made it possible to recover accurate geometry of real-world scenes. A number of robust techniques for merging multiple range images into complex models are now available [34, 30, 4, 27]. For architectural scenes involving regular geometry, robust photogrammetric techniques requiring only photographs can also be employed. The model used in this research was constructed using such a technique from [9]; however, our basic technique can be used regardless of how the geometry is acquired.

Work in global illumination (e.g. [11, 15, 31, 37]) has produced algorithms and software to realistically simulate light transport in synthetic scenes. In this work we leverage the hierarchical subdivision technique [13, 1] to efficiently compute surface irradiance. The renderings in this paper were produced using Gregory Ward Larson's RADIANCE system [33].

Photographs taken by a camera involve nonlinearities from the imaging process, and do not have the full dynamic range of real world radiance distributions. In this work we use the high dynamic range technique in [8] to solve these problems.

## 3 Inverse Radiosity

Most real surfaces exhibit specular as well as diffuse reflection. Recovering both diffuse and specular reflectance models simultaneously in a mutual illumination environment is complicated. In this section, we consider a simplified situation where all surfaces in an environment are pure diffuse (Lambertian). In this case, the global illumination problem simplifies considerably and can be treated in

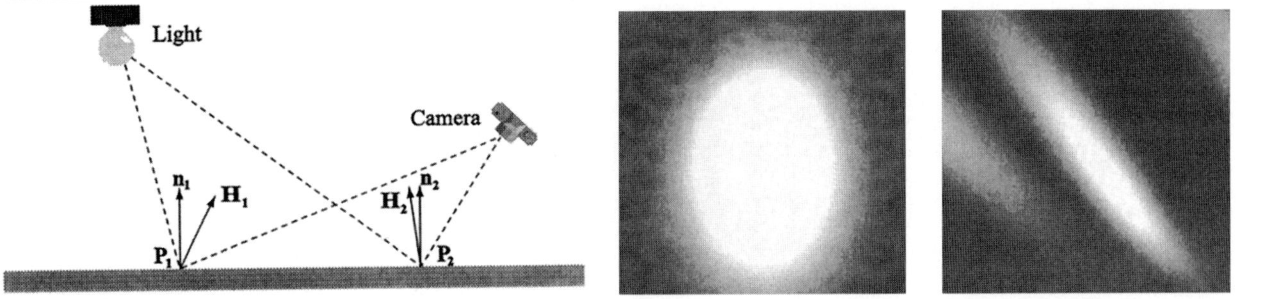


(a) (b) (c)

Figure 2: (a) The lighting and viewing directions at different points on a surface are different with respect to a fixed light source and a fixed viewpoint. This fact can be used to recover a low-parameter BRDF model for the surface from a single image. $\mathbf{n_i}$'s and $H_i$'s are the normals and halfway vectors between lighting and viewing directions at different locations on the surface. We can infer that point $P_2$ on the surface is close to the center of the highlight, and $P_1$ is relatively far away from the center. (b) An example of an isotropic specular highlight, (c) An example of an anisotropic specular highlight.

the radiosity framework [28]. We define *inverse radiosity* as recovering the diffuse albedo at each surface patch in the environment, provided that the geometry, the lighting conditions and the radiance distribution in the scene are known. In the next section we will discuss another simple case — recovering more general reflectance models with specularity considering only direct illumination — and we address the full problem in Section 5.

In the radiosity framework [28], the surfaces in the environment are broken into a finite number of patches. The partitioning is assumed to be fine enough that the radiosity and diffuse albedo of each patch can be treated as constant. For each such patch,

$$B_i = E_i + \rho_i \sum_j B_j F_{ij} \tag{1}$$

where $B_i$, $E_i$, and $\rho_i$ are the radiosity, emission, and diffuse albedo, respectively, of patch $i$, and $F_{ij}$ is the form-factor between patches $i$ and $j$. The form-factor $F_{ij}$ is the proportion of the total power leaving patch $i$ that is received by patch $j$. It can be shown that this is a purely geometric quantity which can be computed from the known geometry of the environment [28].

We take photographs of the surfaces, including the light sources, and use a high dynamic range image technique [8] to capture the radiance distribution. Since Lambertian surfaces have uniform directional radiance distributions, one camera position is sufficient for each surface. Then $B_i$ and $E_i$ in Eqn. (1) become known. Form-factors $F_{ij}$ can be derived from the known geometry. Once these are done, $\rho_i = (B_i - E_i)/(\sum_j B_j F_{ij})$. The solution to inverse radiosity is so simple because the photographs capture the final solution of the underlying light transport among surfaces.

# 4 Recovering Parameterized BRDFs from Direct Illumination

Before tackling the general case of reflectance recovery from photographs of mutually illuminated surfaces with diffuse *and* specular components, we study another special case. Consider a single surface of uniform BRDF which is illuminated by a point light source in known position and photographed by a camera, also in a known geometric position with respect to the surface(Fig. 2). Every pixel in the radiance image provides a measurement of radiance $L_i$ of the corresponding surface point $P_i$ in the direction of the camera, and the known light source position lets us calculate the irradiance $I_i$ incident on that point.

Our objective is to use these data $(L_i, I_i)$ to estimate the BRDF of the surface. Since the BRDF is a function of four variables (azimuth and elevation of incident and viewing directions) it is obvious that the 2-dimensional set of measurements for a single camera/light source pairing is inadequate to do this in general. However for many materials it is possible to approximate the BRDF adequately by a parameterized BRDF model with a small number of parameters (e.g. Ward [32], Lafortune [17], He [14] etc). We use Ward's parameterization in which the BRDF is modeled as the sum of a diffuse term $\frac{\rho_d}{\pi}$ and a specular term $\rho_s K(\boldsymbol{\alpha}, \boldsymbol{\Theta})$. Here $\rho_d$ and $\rho_s$ are the diffuse and specular reflectance of the surface, respectively, and $K(\boldsymbol{\alpha}, \boldsymbol{\Theta})$ is a function of vector $\boldsymbol{\Theta}$, the azimuth and elevation of the incident and viewing directions, and parameterized by $\boldsymbol{\alpha}$, the surface roughness vector. For anisotropic surfaces $\boldsymbol{\alpha}$ has 3 components; for isotropic surfaces $\boldsymbol{\alpha}$ has only one component and reduces to a scalar. The precise functional form of $K(\boldsymbol{\alpha}, \boldsymbol{\Theta})$ in the two cases may be found in Appendix 1.

This leads us to the following equation for each surface point $P_i$,

$$L_i = (\frac{\rho_d}{\pi} + \rho_s K(\boldsymbol{\alpha}, \boldsymbol{\Theta}_i)) I_i \tag{2}$$

where $L_i$, $I_i$ and $\boldsymbol{\Theta}_i$ are known, and the parameters $\rho_d$,$\rho_s$, $\boldsymbol{\alpha}$ are unknowns to be estimated. Depending on whether we are using an isotropic or anisotropic model for the specular term we have a total of 3 or 5 unknown parameters, while there are as many constraining equations as the number of pixels in the radiance image of the surface patch. By solving a nonlinear optimization problem (see Appendix 1 for details), we can find the best estimate of $\rho_d$,$\rho_s$, $\boldsymbol{\alpha}$.

There are two important subtleties in the treatment of this optimization problem. One is that we need to solve a weighted least squares problem, otherwise the larger values from the highlight (with correspondingly larger noise in radiance measurements) cause a bias in parameter estimation. The second is the use of color information which needs to be done differently for dielectrics and metals. Both of these issues are discussed in Appendix 1.

To obtain an obvious global minimum for this optimization problem and achieve robust parameter recovery, the radiance image should cover the area that has a specular highlight as well as some area with very low specular component. If the highlight is missing, we do not have enough information for recovering specular parameters, and can only consider the surface to be diffuse.

# 5 Recovering Parameterized BRDFs in a Mutual Illumination Environment

We are now ready to study the general case when the environment consists of a number of surfaces and light sources with the surface reflectances allowed to have both diffuse and specular components.

Consider a point $P_i$ on a surface patch seen by camera $C_v$ (Fig. 3). The radiance from $P_i$ in the direction of the camera is the re-

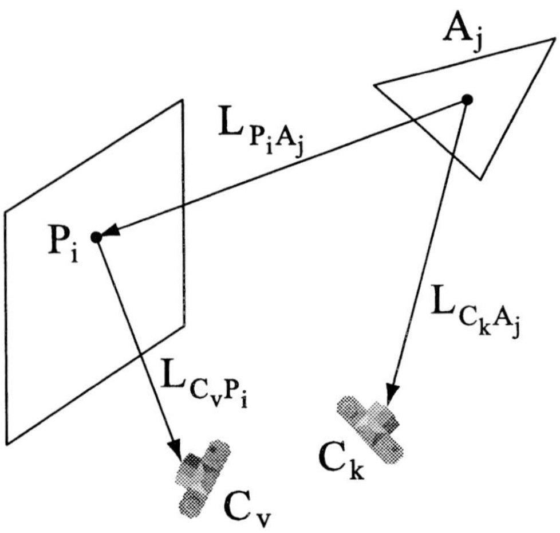


Figure 3: Patch $A_j$ is in the radiance image captured by camera $C_k$. The specular component at $A_j$ in the direction of sample point $P_i$ is different from that in the direction of camera $C_k$. The difference is denoted by $\Delta S$.

flection of the incident light contributed by all the light sources as well as all the surrounding surfaces. Eqn. (2) generalizes to

$$L_{C_vP_i} = E_{C_vP_i} + \rho_d \sum_j L_{P_iA_j} F_{P_iA_j} + \rho_s \sum_j L_{P_iA_j} K_{C_vP_iA_j}, \quad (3)$$

where $L_{C_vP_i}$ is the radiance value in the direction of camera $C_v$ at some sample point $P_i$ on the surface, $E_{C_vP_i}$ is the emission in the direction of camera $C_v$, $L_{P_iA_j}$ is the radiance value along the direction from patch $A_j$ to point $P_i$ on the surface, $F_{P_iA_j}$ is the analytical point-to-patch form-factor [2] between sample point $P_i$ and patch $A_j$, and $\rho_s K_{C_vP_iA_j}$ is the specular term evaluated at $P_i$ for a viewpoint at camera $C_v$ and a light source position at patch $A_j$. The arguments, $\boldsymbol{\alpha}$ and $\Theta$, of $K$ have been dropped to simplify notation.

As before, our objective is to estimate $\rho_d$, $\rho_s$, and specular roughness parameters $\boldsymbol{\alpha}$. Of the other variables in Eqn. (3), $E_{C_vP_i} = 0$ for nonsources, and $L_{C_vP_i}$ can be measured directly from the radiance image at camera $C_v$. In general, the radiances $L_{P_iA_j}$ cannot be measured directly but have to be estimated iteratively. Suppose patch $A_j$ in the environment appears in another radiance image taken by camera $C_k$(Fig. 3). Only if we assume $A_j$ is Lambertian, does $L_{P_iA_j}$ in Eqn. (3) equal $L_{C_kA_j}$, the radiance from $A_j$ to camera $C_k$. Otherwise, the diffuse components will be equal, but the specular components will differ.

$$L_{P_iA_j} = L_{C_kA_j} + \Delta S_{C_kP_iA_j} \quad (4)$$

Here $\Delta S_{C_kP_iA_j} = S_{P_iA_j} - S_{C_kA_j}$ is the difference between the specular components $S_{P_iA_j}$ and $S_{C_kA_j}$ of the radiances in the two directions. To compute the specular differences $\Delta S_{C_kP_iA_j}$, we need the BRDF of $A_j$, which is initially unknown. The estimation of $\Delta S$ (Section 5.1) therefore has to be part of an iterative framework. Assuming that the dominant component of reflectance is diffuse, we can initialize the iterative process with $\Delta S = 0$ (this sets $L_{P_iA_j} = L_{C_kA_j}$).

To recover BRDF parameters for all the surfaces, we need radiance images covering the whole scene. Each surface patch needs to be assigned a camera from which its radiance image is selected. At least one specular highlight on each surface needs to be visible in the set of images, or we will not be able to recover its specular reflectance and roughness parameters. Each sample point gives an equation similar to Eqn. (3). From these equations, we can set up a weighted least-squares problem for each surface as in Appendix 1. During optimization, we need to gather irradiance at each sample point from the surface patches in the environment. One efficient way of doing this is to subdivide each surface into a hierarchy of patches [13, 1] and link different sample points to patches at different levels in the hierarchy. The solid angles subtended by the linked patches at the sample points should always be less than a prescribed threshold. There is a radiance value from the patch to the sample point and a $\Delta S$ associated with each hierarchical link.

For each sample point, we build hierarchical links to a large number of patches, and gather irradiance from these links. The amount of memory and computation involved in this process limits the number of samples for each highlight area. To make a reasonable tradeoff, we note that irradiance from indirect illumination caused by surrounding surfaces generally has little high-frequency spatial variation. Because of this, it makes sense to draw two sets of samples, one sparse set, and one dense set [2]. For the samples in the sparse set, we build hierarchical links and gather irradiance from the environment as usual. For the samples in the dense set, only their irradiance from light sources is computed explicitly, their irradiance from indirect illumination is computed by interpolation.

We are now ready to state the complete inverse global illumination algorithm. First detect all specular highlight blobs falling inside the radiance images using knowledge of the positions of the light sources, the camera poses, and the geometry (Fig. 4). Set the initial $\Delta S$ associated with each hierarchical link to zero. We can then recover an initial estimate of the BRDF parameters for each surface independently by solving a series of nonlinear optimization problems. The estimated specular parameters are used to update all $\Delta S$'s and $L_{P_iA_j}$'s associated with the hierarchical links. With the updated incident radiances, we can go back and re-estimate the BRDF parameters again. This optimization and update process is iterated several times to obtain the final solution of the BRDFs for all surfaces. The overall algorithm is shown in Fig. 5.

```
For each camera position C
  For each polygon T
    For each light source O
      Obtain the intersection P between plane of T and line CO'
        (O' and O are symmetric about T);
      Check if P falls inside polygon T;
      Check if there is any occlusion between P and O;
      Check if there is any occlusion between C and any point
        in a local neighborhood of P;
      /* A highlight area is detected if P passed all the above tests.*/
End
```

Figure 4: The specular highlight detection algorithm.

## 5.1 Estimation of $\Delta S$

Suppose there is a hierarchical link $l_{P_iA_j}$ between a sample point $P_i$ and a patch $A_j$ which is visible to a camera $C_k$ (Fig. 6). The $\Delta S$ for $l_{P_iA_j}$ is defined to be the difference of the specular component in directions $\vec{A_jP_i}$ and $\vec{A_jC_k}$. To estimate this difference, we need to obtain the specular component along these two directions given the BRDF parameters of patch $A_j$. A one-bounce approximation of $\Delta S$ for link $l_{P_iA_j}$ can be obtained by using Monte Carlo raytracing [32]. Because of off-specular components, multiple rays

[2]We choose the two sets of samples as follows. We first find the center of the highlight area in the image plane and rotate a straight line around this center to a number of different positions. The dense set of samples is the set of points on the surface corresponding to all the pixels on these lines. We choose the sparse set of samples on each line by separating two consecutive samples by some fixed distance in the object space.

```
Detect specular highlight blobs on the surfaces.
Choose a set of sample points inside and around each highlight
  area.
Build hierarchical links between sample points and patches in the
  environment and use ray tracing to detect occlusion.
Assign to each patch one radiance image and one average radiance
  value captured at the camera position.
Assign zero to ΔS at each hierarchical link.
For iter=1 to N
  For each hierarchical link,
    use its ΔS to update its associated radiance value;
  For each surface,
    optimize its BRDF parameters using the data
      from its sample points;
  For each hierarchical link,
    estimate its ΔS with the new BRDF parameters.
End
```

Figure 5: The *Inverse Global Illumination* algorithm.

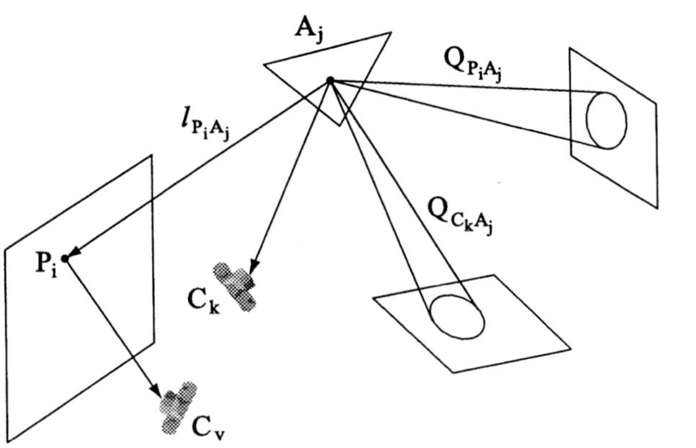


Figure 6: Random rays are traced around the two cones to obtain a one-bounce approximation of $\Delta S$.

should be traced and the direction of the rays is randomized around the mirror directions of $\vec{A_jP_i}$ and $\vec{A_jC_k}$, respectively. For each possible ray direction, the probability density of shooting a ray in that direction is proportional to $K(\boldsymbol{\alpha}_j, \Theta)$ where $\Theta$ encodes the incident and outgoing directions. Intuitively, most of the rays fall inside the two cones $Q_{P_iA_j}$ and $Q_{C_kA_j}$ centered at the two mirror directions. The width of each cone depends on the specular roughness parameters $\boldsymbol{\alpha}_j$ of patch $A_j$. The radiance along each ray is obtained from the patch hit by the ray. Suppose $L_{Q_{P_iA_j}}$ and $L_{Q_{C_kA_j}}$ are the average radiance values of the rays around the two cones, respectively, and $\rho_{s_{A_j}}$ is the specular reflectance of patch $A_j$. Because the average value of Monte Carlo sampling approximates the total irradiance modulated by $K(\boldsymbol{\alpha}_j, \Theta)$, $\Delta S$ can simply be estimated as $\rho_{s_{A_j}}(L_{Q_{P_iA_j}} - L_{Q_{C_kA_j}})$. This calculation could be extended to have multiple bounces by using path tracing [15]; we found that the one-bounce approximation was adequate for our purposes.

### 5.2 Practical Issues

We do not have a formal characterization of the conditions under which the inverse global illumination algorithm converges, or of error bounds on the recovered BRDF parameter values. In practice, we found it worked well (Section 7). Here we give some heuristic advice on how to acquire images to obtain good performance.

- *Use multiple light sources.* A specular highlight directly caused by one of the light sources should be captured on each surface. Having multiple light sources increases the probability that this can be achieved, and lets the whole scene receive more uniform illumination. This also increases the relative contribution of the diffuse component at any particular sample point $P_i$, and supports the $\Delta S = 0$ initialization, since highlights from different sources will usually occur at different locations on the surface.

- *Use concentrated light sources.* If the incoming radiance distribution is not very directional, the specular highlights will be quite extended and it will be difficult to distinguish the specular component from the diffuse one.

## 6 Recovering Diffuse Albedo Maps

In the previous sections, we modeled the reflectance properties as being uniform for each surface. In this section, we continue to do so for specular parameters because a small number of views of each surface does not provide enough information to reliably estimate specular parameters for each point individually. However, we relax this constraint on diffuse albedo and model it as a spatially varying function, an *albedo map*, on each surface. The diffuse albedo for any point $x$ on a surface is computed as:

$$\rho_d(x) = \pi D(x)/I(x) \tag{5}$$

where $\rho_d(x)$ is the diffuse albedo map, $D(x)$ is the diffuse radiance map, and $I(x)$ is the irradiance map.

Suppose there is an image covering the considered surface which gives a radiance map $L(x) = D(x) + S(x)$ where $S(x)$ is the specular radiance map seen from the image's camera position. Then the diffuse radiance map in Eqn. (5) can be obtained by subtracting the specular component from each pixel of the radiance map $L(x)$ using the specular reflectance parameters already recovered. We estimate the radiance due to specular reflection as the sum of specular reflection due to direct and indirect illumination. The specular reflection due to direct illumination is computed from the knowledge of the direct lighting and the estimated reflectance properties, and we estimate the indirect specular reflectance by tracing a perturbed reflected ray into the environment in a manner similar to that in Section 5.1.

The irradiance $I(x)$ can be computed at any point on the surface from the direct illumination and by using analytical point-to-patch form-factors [2] as in previous sections of this paper. For efficiency, we compute the irradiance due to the indirect illumination only at certain sample points on the surfaces, and interpolate these indirect irradiance estimates to generate estimates for all surface points $x$. Of course, care must be taken to sufficiently sample the irradiance in regions of rapidly changing visibility to the rest of the scene.

Something that complicates estimating diffuse albedos in this manner is that in highlight regions the specular component of the reflectance $S(x)$ will be much larger than the diffuse component $D(x)$. As a result, relatively small errors in the estimated $S(x)$ will cause large relative errors in $D(x)$ and thus $\rho_d(x)$. However, just as a person might shift her view to avoid glare while reading a movie poster, we make use of multiple views of the surface to solve this problem.

Suppose at a point $x$ on a surface, we have multiple radiance values $\{L_k(x)\}_{k=1}^{p}$ from different images. The highest value in this set will exhibit the strongest specular component, so we simply remove this value from consideration. For the remaining values, we subtract the corresponding specular estimates $S_k(x)$ from the radiance values $L_k(x)$, to obtain a set of diffuse radiance estimates $D_k(x)$. We compute a final diffuse radiance component $D(x)$ as a weighted average of the $D_k(x)$, with weights inversely proportional to the magnitude of the estimated specular components $S_k(x)$ to minimize the relative error in $D(x)$. We also weight the $D_k(x)$

Figure 7: The complete set of forty radiance images of the room used to recover reflectance properties. Except for a few small areas, every surface in the room was seen in at least one radiance image. Each radiance image was constructed from between one and ten digital pictures depending on the dynamic range of the particular view. Black areas indicate regions which were saturated in all input images, and are not used by the recovery algorithm. The last three radiance images, reproduced ten stops darker than the rest, intentionally image the light bulbs. They were used to recover the positions and intensities of the sources. Full-resolution images are available in the electronic version of this paper.

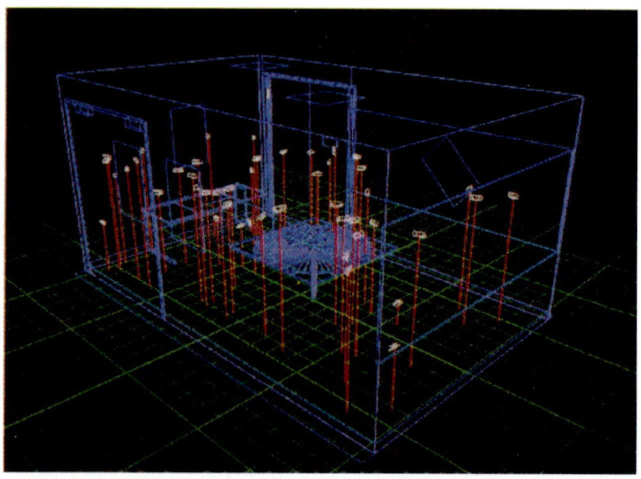

Figure 8: The model of the room, photogrammetrically recovered from the photographs in Fig 7. The recovered camera positions of the forty photographs are indicated.

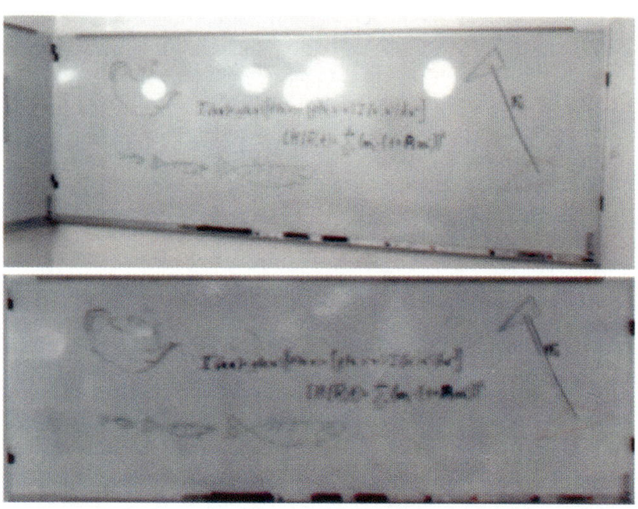

Figure 9: The top picture is a radiance image of a whiteboard, showing strong specular highlights. The bottom picture shows the diffuse albedo map of the whiteboard recovered from several images. Unlike the radiance image, the diffuse albedo map has a nearly uniform background, and is independent of the illumination.

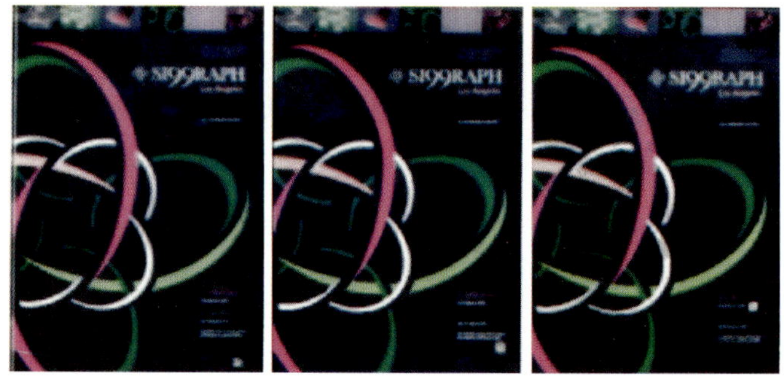

Figure 10: The diffuse albedo maps of three posters with the same texture. The posters were placed at different locations in the scene and thus received significantly different illumination. Nonetheless, the recovered albedo maps are nearly the same. For identification purposes, a small yellow square was placed in a different location on the lower right of each poster.

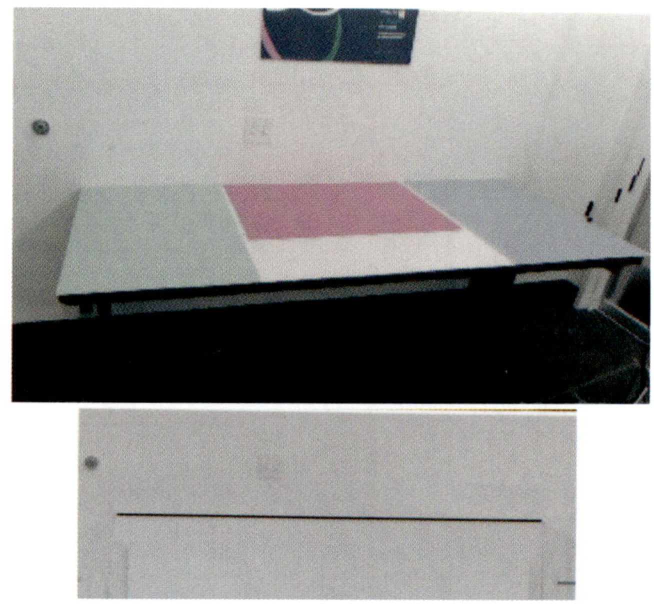

Figure 11: The top image shows a part of a wall that becomes noticeably colored from light reflecting from the cards placed on the table below, an effect known as "color bleeding". The bottom image shows the recovered albedo map of the same part of the wall. It is nearly uniform, showing that the color bleeding was properly accounted for. The black line has been added to indicate where the table top abutted the wall.

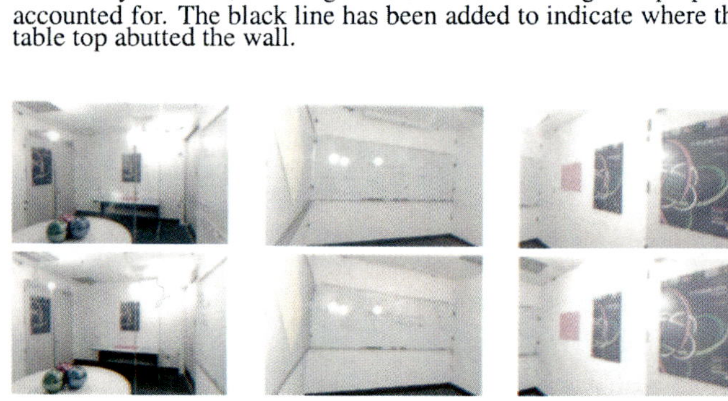

Figure 12: A comparison between real images (top) and synthetic renderings of our room with the recovered reflectance parameters (bottom). The simulated lighting is the same as in the original pictures, and the synthetic viewpoints have been matched to the recovered camera positions of the real images. The images show that good consistency was achieved.

values proportionally to the cosine of the viewing angle of the camera in order to reduce the influence of images at grazing angles; such oblique images typically have poor texture resolution and exhibit particularly strong specular reflection. Since we are combining information taken from different images, we smooth transitions at image boundaries using the image blending technique in [9].

Once diffuse albedo maps are recovered, they could be used to separate the diffuse and specular components in the specular highlight areas. This would allow recovering more accurate specular parameters in the BRDF model. In practice, however, we have found good estimates to be obtained without further refinements.

# 7 Results

## 7.1 Results for a Simulated Scene

We first tested our algorithm on a simple simulated cubical room with mutual illumination. This allowed us to verify the accuracy of the algorithm and compare its results to ground truth. All the six surfaces of the room have monochromatic diffuse and specular components, but each one has a distinct set of parameters. Each of the surfaces has spatially uniform specularity. We assigned two surfaces to be anisotropically specular and added 10-20% zero mean white noise to the uniform diffuse albedo of two surfaces to simulate spatial variations. We used the RADIANCE rendering system [33] to produce synthetic photographs of this scene. Six of the synthetic photographs were taken from the center of the cube with each one covering one of the six surfaces. Another set of six zoomed-in photographs were taken to capture the highlight areas. The scene was illuminated by six point light sources so that specular highlights could be observed on each surface. These twelve images along with the light source intensity and positions were used to solve the BRDF parameters. The images of the specular highlights are shown in Fig. 2(b)-(c). Some of the highlights are visually very weak, but corresponding parameters can still be recovered numerically. The original and recovered BRDF parameters are given in Table 1. For the last two surfaces with noisy diffuse albedo, the recovered albedo values are compared to the true average values. The total running time for BRDF recovery is about half an hour on a SGI $O_2$ 180MHz workstation.

The numerical errors shown in Table 1 are obtained by comparing the recovered parameters with the original ones. There are three sources of error: BRDF modeling error, rendering error, and BRDF recovery error. BRDF modeling error comes from the inability of a given BRDF model to capture the behavior of a real material. By using the same model for recovery that RADIANCE uses for rendering, BRDF modeling error was eliminated for this test. However, because RADIANCE computes light transport only approximately, rendering error is present. We thus cannot determine the exact accuracy of our BRDF recovery. However, the test demonstrates that the algorithm works well in practice.

## 7.2 Results for a Real Scene

In this section we demonstrate the results of running our algorithm on a real scene. The scene we chose is a small meeting room with some furniture and two whiteboards; we also decorated the room with colored cards, posters, and three colored metallic spheres[3]. Once the BRDFs of the materials were recovered, we were able to re-render the scene under novel lighting conditions and with added virtual objects.

[3]The spheres were obtained from Baker's Lawn Ornaments, 570 Berlin Plank Road, Somerset PA 15501, (814) 445-7028.

| | $\rho_d$ | $\rho_s$ | $\alpha_x(\alpha)$ | $\alpha_y$ | $\gamma$ |
|---|---|---|---|---|---|
| True | 0.3 | 0.08 | 0.6 | 0.03 | 0 |
| Recovered | 0.318296 | 0.081871 | 0.595764 | 0.030520 | -0.004161 |
| Error(%) | 6.10 | 2.34 | 0.71 | 1.73 | |
| True | 0.1 | 0.1 | 0.3 | | |
| Recovered | 0.107364 | 0.103015 | 0.300194 | | |
| Error(%) | 7.36 | 3.02 | 0.06 | | |
| True | 0.1 | 0.01 | 0.1 | | |
| Recovered | 0.100875 | 0.010477 | 0.101363 | | |
| Error(%) | 0.88 | 4.77 | 1.36 | | |
| True | 0.3 | 0.02 | 0.15 | | |
| Recovered | 0.301775 | 0.021799 | 0.152331 | | |
| Error(%) | 0.59 | 8.90 | 1.55 | | |
| True | 0.2 | 0.05 | 0.05 | | |
| Recovered | 0.206312 | 0.050547 | 0.050291 | | |
| Error(%) | 3.16 | 1.09 | 0.58 | | |
| True | 0.2 | 0.1 | 0.05 | 0.3 | 45 |
| Recovered | 0.209345 | 0.103083 | 0.050867 | 0.305740 | 44.997876 |
| Error(%) | 4.67 | 3.08 | 1.73 | 1.91 | |

Table 1: Comparison between true and recovered BRDF parameters for the six surfaces of a unit cube. The first and last surfaces have anisotropic specular reflection. They have two more parameters: second roughness parameter $\alpha_y$ and the orientation $\gamma$ of the principal axes in a local coordinate system. The errors shown are the combined errors from both rendering and recovering stages.

### 7.2.1 Data Acquisition

We illuminated the scene with three heavily frosted 3-inch diameter tungsten light bulbs. Using high dynamic range photography, we verified that the lights produced even illumination in all directions. A DC power source was used to eliminate 60Hz intensity fluctuations from the alternating current power cycle.

We used a Kodak DCS520 color digital camera for image acquisition. The radiance response curve of the camera was recovered using the technique in [8]. We used a wide-angle lens with a 75 degree field of view so that we could photograph all the surfaces in the scene from a few angles with a relatively small number of shots. Forty high dynamic range radiance images, shown in Fig. 7, were acquired from approximately 150 exposures. Twelve of the images were taken specifically to capture specular highlights on surfaces.

The radiance images were processed to correct for radial light falloff and radial image distortion. Each of these corrections was modeled by fitting a polynomial of the form $1 + ar^2 + br^4$ to calibration data captured with the same lens settings used for the scene images. To reduce glare and lens flare, we shaded the lens from directly viewing the light sources in several of the images. Regions in the images corresponding to the light stands (which we did not model) or where excessive remaining glare was apparent were masked out of the images, and ignored by the algorithm. The thin cylindrical light stands which appear in the synthetic renderings have been added to the recovered model explicitly.

The radiance images were used to recover the scene geometry and the camera positions (Fig. 8) using the Façade [9] modeling system. Segmentation into areas of uniform specular reflectance was obtained by having each polygon of each block in the model (e.g. the front of each poster, the surface of each whiteboard, the top of each table) have its own uniform specular reflectance parameters.

The positions and intensities of the three light sources were recovered from the final three radiance images. During BRDF recovery, the area illumination from these spherical light sources was computed by stochastically casting several rays to each source.

### 7.2.2 BRDF Recovery

Given the necessary input data, our program recovered the surface BRDFs in two stages. In the first stage, it detected all the highlight regions and recovered parametrized BRDFs for the surfaces. In this stage, even if a surface had rich texture, only an average dif-

| | $\rho_d$(red) | $\rho_d$(green) | $\rho_d$(blue) | $\rho_s$(red) | $\rho_s$(green) | $\rho_s$(blue) | $\alpha$ |
|---|---|---|---|---|---|---|---|
| whiteboard | 0.5794 | 0.5948 | 0.6121 | 0.0619 | 0.0619 | 0.0619 | 0.0137 |
| roundtable top | 0.7536 | 0.7178 | 0.7255 | 0.0366 | 0.0366 | 0.0366 | 0.0976 |
| door | 0.6353 | 0.5933 | 0.5958 | 0.0326 | 0.0326 | 0.0326 | 0.1271 |
| wall | 0.8543 | 0.8565 | 0.8036 | 0.0243 | 0.0243 | 0.0243 | 0.1456 |
| poster | 0.1426 | 0.1430 | 0.1790 | 0.0261 | 0.0261 | 0.0261 | 0.0818 |
| red card | 0.7507 | 0.2404 | 0.3977 | 0.0228 | 0.0228 | 0.0228 | 0.0714 |
| yellow card | 0.8187 | 0.7708 | 0.5552 | 0.0312 | 0.0312 | 0.0312 | 0.1515 |
| teal card | 0.4573 | 0.5951 | 0.5369 | 0.0320 | 0.0320 | 0.0320 | 0.1214 |
| lavender card | 0.3393 | 0.3722 | 0.4437 | 0.0077 | 0.0077 | 0.0077 | 0.1144 |
| red ball | 0 | 0 | 0 | 0.5913 | 0.1862 | 0.3112 | 0 |
| green ball | 0 | 0 | 0 | 0.2283 | 0.3694 | 0.3092 | 0 |
| blue ball | 0 | 0 | 0 | 0.2570 | 0.3417 | 0.4505 | 0 |

Table 2: BRDF parameters recovered for the materials in the test room. All of them are isotropic, and most of them are plastic. The balls are metallic.

fuse albedo was recovered. Surfaces for which no highlights were visible the algorithm considered diffuse. The second stage used the recovered specular reflection models to generate diffuse albedo maps for each surface by removing the specular components.

The running time for each of the two stages was about 3 hours on a Pentium II 300MHz PC. The results show our algorithm can recover accurate specular models and high-quality diffuse albedo maps. Fig. 9 shows how specular highlights on the white board were removed by combining the data from multiple images. Fig. 10 shows the albedo maps obtained for three identical posters placed at different places in the room. Although the posters were originally seen in different illumination, the algorithm successfully recovers very similar albedo maps for them. Fig. 11 shows that the algorithm can remove "color bleeding" effects: colors reflected onto a white wall from the cards on the table do not appear in the wall's diffuse albedo map. Table 2 shows the recovered specular parameters and average diffuse albedo for a variety of the surfaces in the scene. We indicated to the program that all the materials are isotropic, and that the metallic spheres only have ideal specular components[4].

### 7.2.3 Re-rendering Results

We directly compared synthetic images rendered with our recovered BRDF models to real images. In Fig. 12, we show the comparison under the original lighting conditions in which we took the images for BRDF recovery. In Fig. 13, we show the comparison under a novel lighting condition obtained by removing two of the lights and moving the third to a new location, and adding a new object. There are a few differences between the real and synthetic images. Some lens flare appears in the real images of both figures, which we did not attempt to simulate in our renderings. We did not model the marker trays under the whiteboards, so their shadows do not appear in the synthetic images. In Fig. 13, a synthetic secondary highlight caused by specular reflection from the adjacent whiteboard appears darker than the one in the real image, which is likely due to RADIANCE's approximations for rendering secondary specularities. However, in both figures, real and synthetic images appear quite similar.

Fig 14 shows two panoramic views of the rendered scene. (a) shows the entire scene rendered with novel lighting. The original lights were removed and three track lights were virtually installed on the ceiling to illuminate the posters. Also, a strange chandelier was placed above the spheres on the table. The new lights reflect specularly off of the posters and the table. Since the chandelier contains a point light source, it casts a hard shadow around the midsection of the room. The interior of the chandelier shade is turquoise colored which results in turquoise shadows under the spheres. A small amount of synthetic glare was added to this image. (b) shows the result of adding synthetic objects to various locations in the room, including two chairs, a crystal ball, two metal boxes, and a floating diamond. In addition, a very large orange sculpture, was placed at the back of the room. All of the objects exhibit proper shadows, reflections, and caustics. The sculpture is large enough to turn the ceiling noticeably orange due to diffuse interreflection. The video for this paper shows a fly-through of each of these scenes.

[4]For surfaces that have only ideal specular reflection, such as mirrors, there is no diffuse component and the roughness parameter is zero. We can still recover their specular reflectance $\rho_s$ from a single image by noting that the specular reflectance can be computed as the simple ratio between two radiance values. One is the radiance value in the image corresponding to the intersection between the surface and a ray shot from the camera position; the other is the radiance value of the environment along the reflected ray. In practice, we shoot a collection of rays from the camera position to obtain the average reflectance.

## 8 Conclusions and Future Work

In this paper we have presented a new technique for determining reflectance properties of entire scenes taking into account mutual illumination. The properties recovered include diffuse reflectance that varies arbitrarily across surfaces, and specular reflectance parameters that are constant across regions. The technique takes as input a sparse set of geometrically and photometrically calibrated photographs taken under calibrated lighting conditions, as well as a geometric model of the scene. The algorithm iteratively estimates irradiances, radiances, and reflectance parameters. The result is a characterization of surface reflectance properties that is highly consistent with the observed radiances in the scene. We hope this work will be a useful step towards bringing visual spaces from the real world into the virtual domain, where they can be visualized from any angle, with any lighting, and with additions, deletions, and modifications according to our needs and imaginations.

There are a few directions for future research. We wish to apply our technique to more general geometrical and photometric data, such as multispectral radiance images and geometry accquired from laser scanners. It would be of significant practical value to be able to calibrate and use existing or natural illumination in recovering reflectance properties. The algorithm should be more robust to errors in the geometric model, misregistration of the photographs, and errors in the light source measurements. It would also be of theoretical value to obtain conditions under which the algorithm converges.

## Acknowledgments

The authors wish to thank David Culler and the Berkeley NOW (Network of Workstations, http://now.cs.berkeley.edu/) project, and Tal Garfinkel for his help in using the NOW to render the video sequences. Thanks to Gregory Ward Larson for advice in using RADIANCE and estimating reflectance, Carlo Séquin for providing the sculpture model, and the reviewers for their valuable comments. This research was supported by a Multidisciplinary University Research Initiative on three dimensional direct visualization from ONR and BMDO, grant FDN00014-96-1-1200, the California MICRO program, Phillips Corporation, Interval Research Corporation, Pixar Animation Studios and Microsoft Graduate Fellowship.

Figure 13: A comparison between real and virtual, this time with novel lighting. Two of the lights were switched off and the third was moved to a new location. In addition, a real mirrored sphere was placed on the red card. The scene was photographed from two locations and these real views are shown in the top row. To render the bottom row, we recovered the camera positions and light source position in the top views, estimated the reflectance properties and position of the sphere, and added a virtual sphere to the model. The main noticeable difference is lens flare; however, some inaccuracies in the model (e.g. the whiteboard marker tray was not modeled) are also apparent. Otherwise, the illumination of the scene and appearance and shadows of the synthetic object are largely consistent.

(a) Synthetic rendering of room under novel illumination.

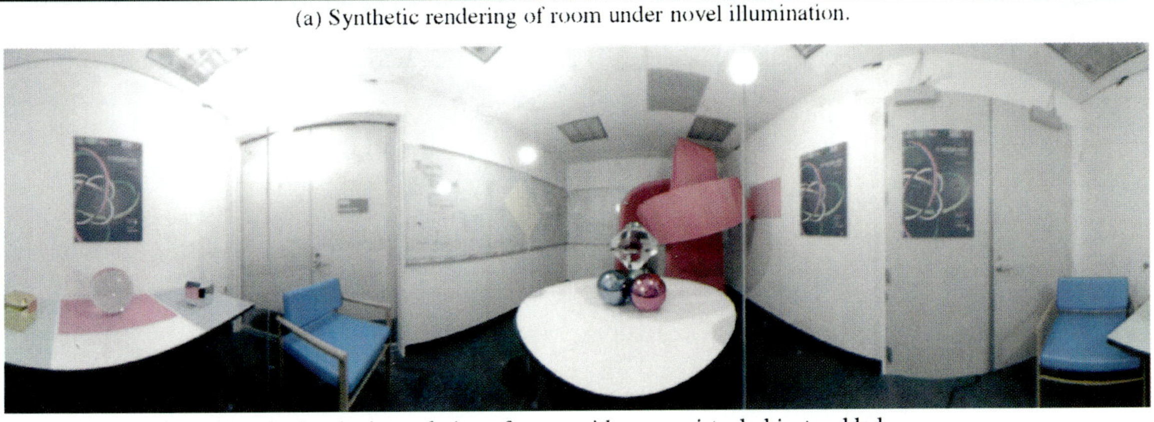

(b) Synthetic rendering of room with seven virtual objects added.

Figure 14: Panoramic renderings of the room, with various changes to lighting and geometry.

# Appendix 1. BRDF Model and Parameter Recovery

In this appendix we present more details on the BRDF model, introduced in Section 4, and how its parameters are recovered. We use Ward's [32] model for the specular term in the BRDF, which could be modeled as either isotropic or anisotropic. In the isotropic case,

$$K(\alpha, \Theta) = \frac{1}{\sqrt{\cos\theta_i \cos\theta_r}} \frac{\exp[-\tan^2\delta/\alpha^2]}{4\pi\alpha^2} \quad (6)$$

where $\alpha$ is a scalar surface roughness parameter, $\theta_i$ is the incident angle, $\theta_r$ is the viewing angle, and $\delta$ is the angle between the surface normal and the halfway vector $H$ between the lighting and viewing directions. $\theta_i$, $\theta_r$ are two components (along with $\phi_i$, $\phi_r$) of the vector $\mathbf{\Theta}$ which represents the incidence and viewing directions.

In the anisotropic case, we need two distinct roughness parameters $\alpha_x$, $\alpha_y$ for two principal axes on the surface and an azimuth angle $\gamma$ to define the orientation of these principal axes on the surface relative to a canonical coordinate system. Then, the parameter vector $\boldsymbol{\alpha}$ actually has three components $(\alpha_x, \alpha_y, \gamma)$ and we have:

$$K(\boldsymbol{\alpha}, \Theta) = \frac{1}{\sqrt{\cos\theta_i \cos\theta_r}} \frac{\exp[-\tan^2\delta(\cos^2\phi/{\alpha_x}^2 + \sin^2\phi/{\alpha_y}^2)]}{4\pi\alpha_x\alpha_y} \quad (7)$$

where $\delta$ is the same as in the isotropic case, and $\phi$ is the azimuth angle of the halfway vector $H$ projected into the local 2D coordinate system on the surface patch defined by the two principal axes. To compute $\phi$, $\gamma$, which relates this coordinate system to the canonical coordinate system, is necessary.

Now to parameter recovery. We wish to find $\rho_d$, $\rho_s$ and $\boldsymbol{\alpha}$ that minimize the squared error between the measured and predicted radiance,

$$e(\rho_d, \rho_s, \boldsymbol{\alpha}) = \sum_{i=1}^{m} (L_i - \frac{\rho_d}{\pi} I_i - \rho_s K(\boldsymbol{\alpha}, \Theta_i) I_i)^2 \quad (8)$$

where $L_i$ is the measured radiance and $I_i$ is the irradiance (computable from the known light source position) at sample point $p_i$ on the surface, and $m$ is the number of sample points.

Note that given a guess of $\boldsymbol{\alpha}$, $K(\boldsymbol{\alpha}, \Theta_i)$ becomes a known quantity, and minimizing the error $e$ reduces to a standard linear least-squares problem for estimating $\rho_d$ and $\rho_s$. Plugging in these values in the right hand side of Eqn. (8) lets us compute $e$ as a function of $\boldsymbol{\alpha}$. The optimization problem thus simplifies to a search for the optimum value of $\boldsymbol{\alpha}$ to minimize $e(\boldsymbol{\alpha})$. This is either a one-dimensional or three-dimensional search depending on whether an isotropic or anisotropic model of the specular term is being used. We use golden section search [26] for the isotropic case, and the downhill simplex method [26] in the anisotropic case. It is convenient that neither method requires evaluating the derivative $e'(\boldsymbol{\alpha})$, and both methods are fairly robust.

To deal with colored materials, we estimate both diffuse and specular reflectance in each of the red, green, blue color channels. The specular roughness parameters $\boldsymbol{\alpha}$ are the same for all color channels. The nonlinear optimization is still over 1 or 3 parameters, since given $\boldsymbol{\alpha}$, $\rho_d$ and $\rho_s$ estimation for each channel remains a linear least squares problem.

To make the parameter estimation additionally robust, we make two simple extensions to the basic strategy derived above. The first is to solve a weighted least squares problem instead of the vanilla version in Eqn. (8). Radiance measurements from the highlight area have much larger magnitude than those from the non-highlight area. Correspondingly the error in those measurements is higher both because of noise in imaging as well as error in the BRDF model. Giving all the terms in (8) equal weight causes biased fitting and gives poor estimation of the diffuse reflectance. From a statistical point of view, the correct thing to do is to weight each term by the reciprocal of the variance of expected error in that measurement. Not having a good model for the error term, we chose a heuristic strategy in which the weight $w_i$ for the $i$-th term in the summation in Eqn. (8) is set to $\frac{1}{K(\boldsymbol{\alpha_c}, \Theta_i)}$ where $\boldsymbol{\alpha_c}$ is some *ad hoc* or iteratively improved roughness vector. Since the roughness of most isotropic materials is less than 0.2, we used an initial value between 0.1 and 0.2 for scalar $\alpha_c$.

The second refinement to improve parameter recovery is to use specular color information. For instance, specular highlights on dielectric and plastic materials have the same color as the light source, while the color of specular highlights on metals is the same as their diffuse components, which is the color of the light modulated by the diffuse albedo. For plastic objects, there would be one distinct variable $\rho_d$ for each color channel, but the same variable $\rho_s$ for all color channels. For metallic objects, there would be one variable $\rho_d$ for each channel and a common ratio between the specular and diffuse reflectance in all channels. Thus, we can reduce the degree of freedom from $2N$ to $N$+1 where $N$ is the number of color channels. For plastic, we can still obtain both analytic and numerical linear least-squares solutions for the $N$+1 variables provided the other parameters are fixed. The program performs a heuristic test to determine whether a material should be estimated with the metal or plastic specular reflectance model. Our program first solves for the specular reflectance of each color channel separately and then checks to see if they are larger than the estimated diffuse components. If they are larger, then the material is considered metallic. Otherwise, the plastic model is used. Then the smaller number of parameters corresponding to these material types are solved.

# References


[1] Aupperle, L., and Hanrahan, P. A hierarchical illumination algorithm for surfaces with glossy reflection. In *SIGGRAPH 93* (August 1993), pp. 155–164.

[2] Baum, D. R., Rushmeier, H. E., and Winget, J. M. Improving radiosity solutions through the use of analytically determined form factors. In *SIGGRAPH 89* (1989), pp. 325–334.

[3] Chen, E. QuickTime VR - an image-based approach to virtual environment navigation. In *SIGGRAPH '95* (1995).

[4] Curless, B., and Levoy, M. A volumetric method for building complex models from range images. In *SIGGRAPH '96* (1996), pp. 303–312.

[5] Dana, K. J., Ginneken, B., Nayar, S. K., and Koenderink, J. J. Reflectance and texture of real-world surfaces. In *Proc. IEEE Conf. on Comp. Vision and Patt. Recog.* (1997), pp. 151–157.

[6] Debevec, P., Yu, Y., and Borshukov, G. Efficient View-Dependent Image-Based Rendering with Projective Texture-Mapping. In *9th Eurographics Workshop on Rendering*, (1998), pp. 105-116.

[7] Debevec, P. Rendering synthetic objects into real scenes: Bridging traditional and image-based graphics with global illumination and high dynamic range photography. In *SIGGRAPH 98* (July 1998).

[8] Debevec, P. E., and Malik, J. Recovering high dynamic range radiance maps from photographs. In *SIGGRAPH 97* (August 1997), pp. 369–378.

[9] Debevec, P. E., Taylor, C. J., and Malik, J. Modeling and rendering architecture from photographs: A hybrid geometry- and image-based approach. In *SIGGRAPH '96* (August 1996), pp. 11–20.

[10] Drettakis, G., Robert, L., and Bougnoux, S. Interactive common illumination for computer augmented reality. In *8th Eurographics workshop on Rendering, St. Etienne, France* (May 1997), J. Dorsey and P. Slusallek, Eds., pp. 45–57.

[11] Goral, C. M., Torrance, K. E., Greenberg, D. P., and Battaile, B. Modeling the interaction of light between diffuse surfaces. In *SIGGRAPH '84* (1984), pp. 213–222.

[12] Gortler, S. J., Grzeszczuk, R., Szeliski, R., and Cohen, M. F. The Lumigraph. In *SIGGRAPH '96* (1996), pp. 43–54.

[13] Hanrahan, P., Salzman, P., and Aupperle, L. A rapid hierarchical radiosity algorithm. In *SIGGRAPH 91* (1991), pp. 197–206.

[14] He, X. D., Torrance, K. E., Sillion, F., and Greenberg, D. P. A comprehensive physical model for light reflection. In *SIGGRAPH 91*, (August 1991).

[15] Kajiya, J. The rendering equation. In *SIGGRAPH '86* (1986), pp. 143–150.

[16] Karner, K. F., Mayer, H., and Gervautz, M. An image based measurement system for anisotropic reflection. In *EUROGRAPHICS Annual Conference Proceedings* (1996).

[17] Lafortune, E.P.F., Foo, S., Torrance, K.E., and Greenberg, D.P. Non-Linear Approximation of Reflectance Functions. In *SIGGRAPH 97*, (1997), pp.117-126.

[18] Laveau, S., and Faugeras, O. 3-D scene representation as a collection of images. In *Proceedings of 12th International Conference on Pattern Recognition* (1994), vol. 1, pp. 689–691.

[19] Levoy, M., and Hanrahan, P. Light field rendering. In *SIGGRAPH '96* (1996), pp. 31–42.

[20] Loscos, C., Frasson, M.-C., Drettakis, G., Walter, B., Granier, X., and Poulin, P. Interactive Virtual Relighting and Remodeling of Real Scenes. Technical Report, iMAGIS-GRAVIR/IMAG-INRIA, (May 1999), http://www-imagis.imag.fr/Membres/Celine.Loscos/relight.html.

[21] Marshner, S. *Inverse Rendering for Computer Graphics*. PhD thesis, Cornell University, August 1998.

[22] McMillan, L., and Bishop, G. Plenoptic Modeling: An image-based rendering system. In *SIGGRAPH '95* (1995).

[23] Nayar, S. K., Ikeuchi, K., and Kanade, T. Shape from interreflections. *International Journal of Computer Vision* 6, 3 (1991), 173–195.

[24] Nimeroff, J., Simoncelli, E., and Dorsey, J. Efficient re-rendering of naturally illuminated environments. In *5th Eurographics Workshop on Rendering* (1994).

[25] Oren, M., and Nayar,S.K., "Generalization of Lambert's Reflectance Model", *Computer Graphics Proceedings, Annual Conference Series*, pp.239-246 (1994).

[26] Press, W., Flannery, B., Teukolsky, S., and Vetterling, W. *Numerical Recipes in C*. Cambridge Univ. Press, New York, 1988.

[27] Sato, Y., Wheeler, M. D., and Ikeuchi, K. Object shape and reflectance modeling from observation. In *SIGGRAPH '97* (1997), pp. 379–387.

[28] Sillion, F. X., and Puech, C. *Radiosity and Global Illumination*. Morgan Kaufmann Publishers, San Francisco, 1994.

[29] Szeliski, R., and Shum, H.-Y. Creating full view panoramic image mosaics and environment maps. In *SIGGRAPH 97* (1997), pp. 251–258.

[30] Turk, G., and Levoy, M. Zippered polygon meshes from range images. In *SIGGRAPH '94* (1994), pp. 311–318.

[31] Veach, E., and Guibas, L. J. Metropolis light transport. In *SIGGRAPH 97* (August 1997), pp. 65–76.

[32] Ward, G. J. Measuring and modeling anisotropic reflection. In *SIGGRAPH '92* (July 1992), pp. 265–272.

[33] Ward, G. J. The RADIANCE lighting simulation and rendering system. In *SIGGRAPH '94* (July 1994), pp. 459–472.

[34] Y.Chen, and Medioni, G. Object modeling from multiple range images. *Image and Vision Computing 10*, 3 (April 1992), pp.145–155.

[35] Wong T.-T., Heng P.-A., Or S.-H. and Ng W.-Y. Image-based Rendering with Controllable Illumination. In *8th Eurographics Workshop on Rendering*, (June 1997), pp.13–22.

[36] Yu, Y., and Malik, J. Recovering photometric properties of architectural scenes from photographs. In *SIGGRAPH 98* (July 1998), pp. 207–217.

[37] Yu, Y., and Wu, H. A Rendering Equation for Specular Transfers and its Integration into Global Illumination. Eurographics'97, In *J. Computer Graphics Forum*, 16(3), (1997), pp. 283-292.

# Modeling and Rendering of Weathered Stone

Julie Dorsey  Alan Edelman  Henrik Wann Jensen  Justin Legakis  Hans Køhling Pedersen

Laboratory for Computer Science
Massachusetts Institute of Technology

## Abstract

Stone is widespread in its use as a building material and artistic medium. One of its most remarkable qualities is that it changes appearance as it interacts with the environment. These changes are mainly confined to the surface but involve complex volumetric effects such as erosion and mineral dissolution. This paper presents an approach for the modeling and rendering of changes in the shape and appearance of stone.

To represent stone, we introduce a *slab* data structure, which is a surface-aligned volume confined to a narrow region around the boundary of the stone. Our weathering model employs a simulation of the flow of moisture and the transport, dissolution, and recrystallization of minerals within the porous stone volume. In addition, this model governs the erosion of material from the surface. To render the optical effects of translucency and coloration due to the composition of minerals near the surface, we simulate the scattering of light inside the stone using a general subsurface Monte Carlo ray tracer. These techniques can capture many aspects of the time-dependent appearance of stone. We demonstrate the approach with models of granite and marble statues, as well as a sandstone column.

**CR Categories:** I.3.7 [Computer Graphics]: Three-Dimensional Graphics and Realism; I.6.3 [Simulation and Modeling]: Applications.

**Additional Keywords:** erosion, material models, natural phenomena, physical simulation, ray tracing, subsurface scattering, texturing, volume modeling, weathering.

## 1 Introduction

A perennial challenge of computer image generation is the depiction of objects with weathered appearances. Much of the visual richness and ambiance of natural scenes is associated with weathered materials, such as mellowed brickwork, moss-covered masonry, and seasoned timber. Unfortunately, the material models widely used in computer graphics assume that the materials are both pristine and immutable, even though real materials are neither. More sophisticated models would allow materials to change over time as they are exposed to the elements. Such models would then allow for the rendering of convincing images of weathered objects by considering a material's structure, its interaction with light, and the physical processes that affect its appearance.

One of the most important materials for such things as buildings and sculptures is stone, which is ubiquitous across time and place in human history, from the Acropolis to the Washington Monument. As a building material, stone is valuable in part because it is durable, but its durability does not mean that its appearance is static. Each stone has a unique structure and mixture of minerals, and these attributes affect the stone's appearance as it interacts with light. Furthermore, the structure and materials also determine how the stone's appearance and shape will change in the face of the elements.

Figure 2 shows a variety of stones in different stages of decay. Such a range of appearances would be very difficult to model and render with current methods. In this paper, we introduce new techniques for the modeling and rendering of weathered stone.

The complex mechanisms of stone weathering are not fully understood based on first principles; our scientific knowledge is incomplete. But even if we had exact knowledge of those mechanisms, the complicated microscopic and macroscopic heterogeneities of the interior pores in stone would make it impossible to describe in full detail the process of weathering. Techniques of time and space averaging of heterogeneities have allowed scientists to derive equations that model flow and transport in porous and fractured rock. These equations form the basis of our simulation model.

Our approach consists of three major components: a surface-aligned, volumetric data structure that represents a region near the boundary of the surface and serves as the basis for simulations; a simulation to model the flow of water, as well as the transport and dissolution of minerals within the volume and erosion of the surface; and a rendering technique to simulate the subsurface scattering of light. Taken together, these techniques are capable of capturing a wide range of time-dependent appearances.

### 1.1 Related Work

Previous related work exists in three categories: volume modeling, surface weathering, and subsurface scattering of light.

In volume modeling, an object is represented as a 3D array of voxels [16]. To accelerate volume rendering and the traversal of a volume, octrees [18] and run-length encoding [17] have been used as means of efficiently storing voxel data, while *shells* have been used to encode the location of high-opacity voxels in the vicinity of the boundary [34]. This latter representation is appealing, as it considers only perimeter voxels, while conveying the impression of a full 3D volume. As stone weathers, the majority of the changes occur in a narrow, volumetric band around the surface. In this work, we introduce a *slab* data structure, which is composed of a thin band of volumetric entities aligned with the surface of an object.

Several different approaches to modeling and/or rendering surface weathering effects have been introduced (see [7] and cited references). Of these techniques, the work of Dorsey and Hanrahan is most closely related to our approach, in that they modeled and rendered both surface and subsurface effects using a stack of layers [7]. In other related work, Curtis *et al.* simulated the effects of watercolor painting on paper fibers [6], and Dorsey *et al.* simulated the effects of water flow on surfaces [8]. Both of these approaches demonstrated the ability to affect the appearance of a surface via water flow simulation. However, all of the above techniques are limited to 2D surface effects. The heuristic model for the erosion of fractal terrains of Musgrave *et al.* [20] also bears relation to the work described here. We move beyond these approaches by simulating changes to both the shape and appearance properties of a material over time.

Methods for modeling the subsurface scattering of light within materials are also relevant [7, 12]. These approaches assume that the surface is composed of a set of homogeneous layers for which one or more simplified transport equations can be solved. As stone is a non-homogeneous mixture of various grains that are not oriented in layers, this assumption is not valid. To render stone we therefore use a general Monte Carlo subsurface ray tracer that treats the stone as a participating medium [26].

### 1.2 Overview

The next section describes stone and how it weathers, and shows several characteristic effects that inspired our work. Section 3 gives an overview of our system. Section 4 presents a volumetric representation for stone and a simulation system that produces a range of weathering effects. Section 5 describes a method for rendering the subsurface scattering of light in stone. Section 6 demonstrates the approach on several models. Finally, Section 7 discusses some ideas for future work.

## 2 Background

In this section, we discuss the nature of stone, the weathering process, and some of the most important characteristic weathering effects.

### 2.1 Rock and Stone

The vast majority of rocks are composed of two or more different minerals joined together in a tight fabric that characterizes the stone and determines in part the physical and chemical properties, color, and durability [36]. "Rock" becomes "stone" when it is shaped by humans. Rocks and stones are classified into three major groups based on their origin and formation:

- *Igneous* rocks crystallize from a silicate melt under intense heat and pressure. As a result, igneous rocks are extremely compact and durable. Granites, which are visibly granular, are the most common of this group.

- *Sedimentary*, or layered rocks, are formed by the accumulation of inorganic or organic debris of variable size and shape, deposited by mechanical means or by chemical precipitation. An important characteristic of sedimentary rocks is their flat, layered structure, known as bedding or stratification. Sandstone and limestone are the most common sedimentary rocks.

- *Metamorphic* rocks are igneous or sedimentary rocks recrystallized by the effects of temperature and pressure. The process is very slow and often associated with intense folding. Limestone and sandstone become marble; clay and shale become slates. Their tightly packed structure makes metamorphic rocks more durable than sedimentary rocks.

### 2.2 Stone Weathering Processes

We confine our study to what is generally termed *chemical weathering* — the erosion or dissolution of a stone surface by water and pollutants [1, 30]. We do not consider other types of stone weathering, such as mechanical or biological deterioration.

In chemical weathering, rainwater dissolves oxides of carbon, sulfur, and nitrogen, and this solution acts at various rates on the minerals in the stone [11]. The solution is absorbed into the stone, where it then transforms the original minerals, such as calcite and silicate, which are fairly stable, into gypsum and other clay-like substances that are more soluble in water. By recrystallization at the surface and in depth, and by the incorporation of environmental soot, a weak crust is formed on the stone. As parts of the crust break off, they carry away with them constituents of the stone, leaving fresh stone open to further chemical attack. Areas that retain water tend to break off first. Thus, horizontal or inclined surfaces erode more rapidly than vertical surfaces [25]. Figure 1 is a schematic diagram of the weathering process.

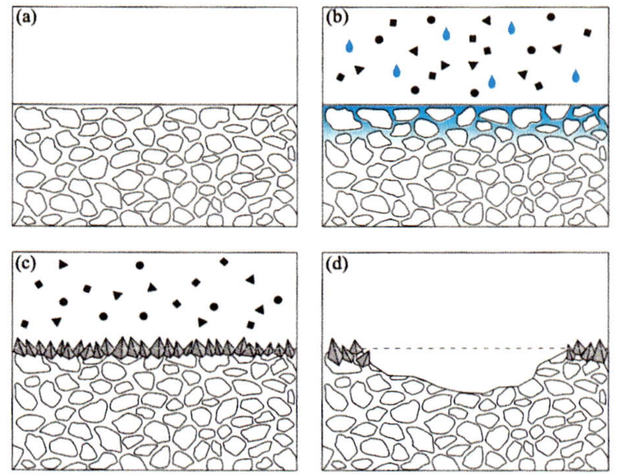


**Figure 1** The mechanism of weathering. After a new stone (a) has been exposed to the weather, it comes under attack by oxides that form a solution with rainwater (b). The solution penetrates into the stone and by recrystallization forms a crust (c). If parts of the crust erode (d), new stone is left open to further chemical attack.

The net effects of weathering, then, are the formation of dirty crusts, the wearing away of the stone surfaces, and, above all, the loss by the aging stone of its capacity to resist decay. Weathering produces a graded zone in which the properties nearest the surface are altered the most and those farthest from the surface resemble the properties of unweathered stone [1].

The basic processes involved in stone weathering are the travel of moisture, dissolution and recrystallization of minerals, chemical transformation of minerals, and deposition of atmospheric pollutants. These factors are described in more detail below.

- *Travel of moisture*: Among the various elements involved in stone weathering, water is the most critical. As stone is a porous material, water is absorbed into the material by capillary pressure and then evaporated back to the surface. The flow of water over a stone surface also plays a role in the weathering of stone. However, in this work, we focus on modeling the movement of water within the stone itself, which is the principal cause of stone decay [1]. We do, however, model the net effect of the flow of water on the surface using a simple probabilistic approach. Given the time scales in which stone weathering occurs, this gives a reasonable approximation.

- *Dissolution and recrystallization of minerals*: When the minerals and salts that constitute stone come into contact with moisture, they begin to dissolve. The rate of dissolution varies greatly depending on the type of mineral, although it is always very slow by human standards. In general, stones composed of fine grains, such as sandstone, weather more quickly than those with larger grains. As the water evaporates, these dissolved minerals recrystallize.

- *Chemical transformation of minerals*: All minerals occurring in stone undergo a continuous process that transforms them into less durable minerals, and eventually into clay. This process results in changes in the appearance, such as fading, increased roughness, and oxidation of iron traces.

**Figure 2** A collection of representative stone weathering effects.

- *Deposition of atmospheric pollution*: The dissolution, recrystallization, and transformation processes are dramatically accelerated in polluted environments, where atmospheric aerosols, such as sulfur and carbon, act as catalysts. Pollutants can arrive either as airborne deposits or via rain.

### 2.3 Stone Weathering Effects

The processes described in the previous section come together to produce a variety of characteristic effects. Figure 2 shows a set of photographs that we have collected to document stone weathering.

- *Corestone weathering* (Figure 2a): Compact stones with tightly packed grains tend to weather from their surface inward by transformation of mineral grains into clay. The low porosity makes the material less susceptible to migration of moisture than more porous rocks. The resulting effect is a gradual rounding of sharp corners and loss of high frequency detail [25, 29].

- *Yellowing* (Figure 2a, c, and d): The minerals that constitute stone often contain traces of iron. During the weathering process, the minerals lose iron, which immediately oxidizes. These oxidation products migrate to the surface with the travel of water and are deposited there. This process results in a patchy, yellowish and brownish discoloration [2, 29].

- *Case hardening* (Figure 2d and f): Evaporation moves transformed calcite and other minerals, in the form of clay, toward the surface, leading to case hardening [36], or the build up of a weakened crust on the surface. A variation of this effect, in which the crusts formed on the surface also contain black deposits, is termed *black scabs* [1].

- *Efflorescence* (Figure 2e): Efflorescences are water-soluble salts that crystallize on the surface, forming white or gray deposits. These salts are either present in the material initially or deposited from the atmosphere. They are carried through or onto the surface by moisture [36].

## 3 System Architecture

Figure 3 presents an overview of our system. The input to our system consists of a polyhedral mesh. We begin by converting the input data into our volumetric slab data structure. From the input mesh, the voxelizer generates a density function for each slab and samples the precomputed dirt and wetness values stored at each mesh vertex. To generate fresh stone, these slabs are passed to the quarry, which samples a 3D stone function for each voxel and scales the result by the density. The simulator operates on the sampled stone data in the slabs to produce weathered stone, affecting both the geometric and chemical makeup of the material.

The volumetric slab data is then used by a subsurface Monte Carlo ray tracer to produce final rendered images. To aid rendering, a polygonal isocontour of the density function is generated to obtain the surface of the weathered stone. In addition, the renderer has direct access to the quarry so that it can sample the various material functions at high resolution.

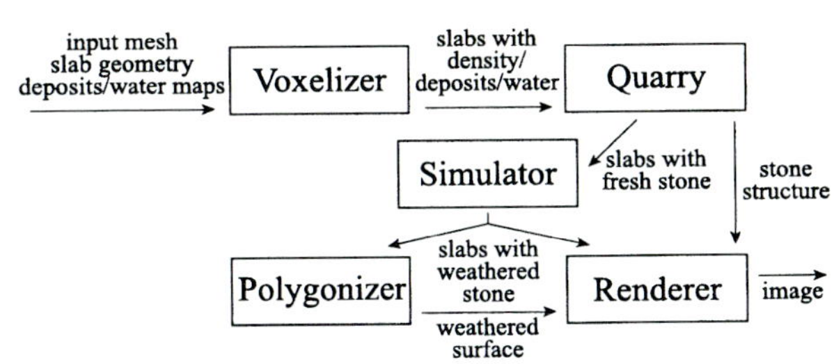


**Figure 3** Architecture of the system.

## 4 Modeling

As we observed in the previous section, the weathering of stone is mainly confined to a thick skin around the surface of an object. In this section, we introduce a volumetric data structure to represent the structure of stone and a simulation model that can be applied to this representation to generate a variety of weathering effects.

### 4.1 Slabs

We parameterize an object with volumetric entities aligned with the boundary of the model, providing for a thick region encompassing the surface and a domain for the simulations. We call each of these

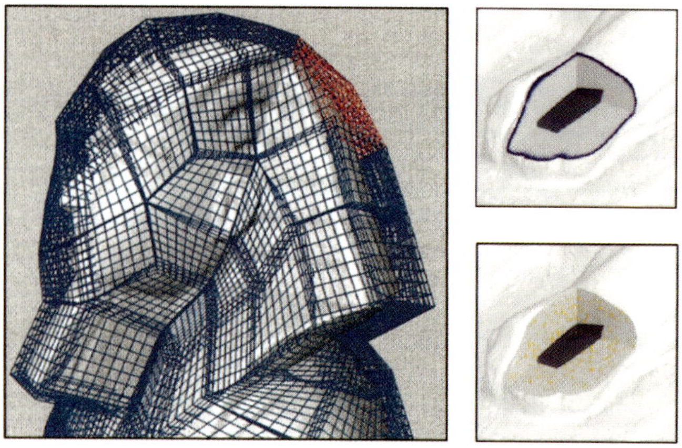

**Figure 4** Slab data structure. (a) Slabs on a scanned mesh, (b) Water diffused into the surface, (c) Iron distributed in grains of mica.

entities a *slab*. Slabs combine benefits of surface- and volume-based object representations. In doing so, slabs allow us to constrain our work to the region near the surface of an object, align the coordinate frame with the local orientation of the surface, sample the object beneath the surface, and model geometric changes.

Each slab is a trilinear volume, similar to volumetric textures [15, 21] (see Figure 4). The geometry of each slab is defined by the positions of its eight corners. Inside, these corners define a local $(u, v, w)$ parameter space based on trilinear interpolation between the corner points. Slabs are arranged so that adjacent slabs share four corners, with bilinear patches as their boundaries.

We fit slabs to an object using a set of simple interactive tools. First, we construct a mesh of quadrilateral faces covering a simplified version of the object. This mesh is then extruded, with each face becoming a slab. For smaller slabs, the mesh can be subdivided first. (Catmull-Clark [5] subdivision works well, as it always produces quadrilateral faces.) The four slab edges in the extruded direction are aligned with the average surface normal in the neighborhood of their intersection with the surface. Finally, the slab vertices are edited by hand, to correct any self-intersections or to align individual slabs with specific features of the object.

### 4.2 Materials

The composition of stone is generated by the *quarry*, in order to provide initial input to the simulations. The input model is first voxelized, creating a sampled density function stored in the slabs. Standard techniques exist for converting meshes into volumetric data sets [28, 35]. As our sampling grid consists of a set of slabs, which are generally distorted and not axis-aligned, this process is slightly more complicated. We sample the density function by computing the signed distance to the input mesh at the corners of each voxel. Voxels completely inside the mesh have density 1, while samples outside the mesh have density 0. Where the surface passes through a voxel, we compute a fractional density value. Given this density function, the quarry generates the remaining parameters to define the fresh, unweathered stone.

To generate the initial stone composition, the quarry uses a combination of standard solid 3D procedural textures [10]. The granular mineral patterns of granite are generated implicitly, similar to Worley's technique for cellular texturing [37]. The veining patterns of marble are created using Perlin's turbulence function [24]. The bedding planes of sandstone are generated using parallel planes distorted by turbulence, to approximate the natural sedimentation processes of layers of different composition building up to form the stone.

### 4.3 Weathering Simulation

In this section, we describe a simulation model that qualitatively captures many of the effects described in Section 2. This model was constructed by incorporating equations used to model flow and transport in porous media [9, 27], as well as techniques from partial differential equations [32, 33].

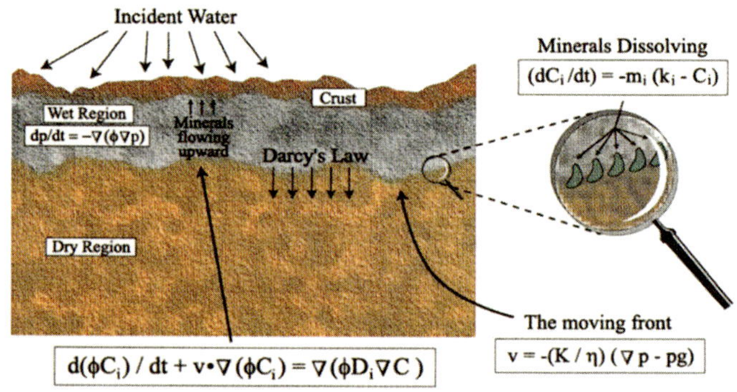


**Figure 5** Overview of the simulation model.

#### 4.3.1 Overview

From outside to inside, three locations have special purpose:

- *The stone surface*: This is the two dimensional exterior interface between the stone and the outside environment where 1) water and other external pollutants meet the stone and penetrate the surface and 2) water from the interior of the stone evaporates forming deposits of minerals and salts. This surface suffers erosion with time.
- *The weathered interior*: This is the three dimensional interior volume where water penetrates into the pores and fractures. The water is assumed to hold dissolved minerals and salts. This volume grows during "wet" cycles as more water enters from the surface, and it gets smaller during "dry" cycles as the water evaporates. The volume also is affected by the surface erosion. The longer an element of stone is inside the weathered interior, the more likely it is to weaken and break off.
- *The interior moist/dry front*: This is the boundary of the weathered interior where dry minerals and salts are dissolved by the water.

For easy reference, we provide a list of all the variables and constants indicating precisely how and where they are used in the simulation (see Table 1).

#### 4.3.2 Travel of Moisture

The porous nature of stone allows moisture to be absorbed by capillary pressure during a wet cycle and then evaporated during a dry cycle. These external weathering conditions are modeled by a boundary condition pressure on the stone surface corresponding to the "push" of the water on this surface. In our simulations, we alternate between wet cycles and dry cycles by setting $p$ according to the surface wetness map during the wet cycle and then $p = 0$ during the dry cycle. More generally $p$ on the surface could be a continuous function such as a sine wave. The penetration of water is simulated by a front below the surface. The boundary condition there is always $p = 0$. The further the water penetrates, the more volume that becomes weakened and weathered. The front moves according to Darcy's law

$$v = -\frac{K}{\eta}(\nabla p - \rho g),$$

| Symbol | Definition | Loc.* | Comment |
|---|---|---|---|
| $C_i$ | mineral/salt concentration | I | computed by a parabolic operator |
| $d$ | decay index | V | computed |
| $e$ | exposure map | S | input and modified |
| $D_i$ | mineral/salt diffusivity | I | input constant |
| $g$ | gravity | F | input for Darcy's law |
| $k_i$ | mineral/salt solubility | I | input constant |
| $m_i$ | maximum saturation | I | input constant |
| $K$ | permeability | F | input material constant |
| $p$ | water pressure | I | computed by evolving parabolic operator |
| | | S | boundary condition derived from exposure map and season |
| $s$ | stone density | V | input and eroded |
| $v$ | fluid velocity | I | computed as a pressure gradient |
| | | F | computed by Darcy's law |
| $\phi$ | porosity | I | input material constant |
| $\rho$ | density of water | F | input constant |
| $\eta$ | viscosity | F | input constant |

*Location key: S=surface, V=volume, F=front, I=interior

**Table 1** Parameters for the weathering simulation.

where the velocity $v$ of the front is computed from $K$, the permeability, $\eta$, the viscosity, $p$, the pressure, $\rho$, the density, and $g$, the acceleration due to gravity. Darcy's law roughly states that the velocity of the front is proportional to the negative pressure gradient at the front. Thus, for example, water penetrates further in sandstone than in granite. This is accounted for by the permeability term $K$.

The location of the water front is computed by evolving the water pressure in time according to the diffusion equation

$$\frac{dp}{dt} = -\nabla \cdot (\phi \nabla p) = -\phi \nabla^2 p - \nabla \phi \cdot \nabla p.$$

The $\phi$ term is a spatially varying material property indicating the porosity. The wet seasons correspond to turning the pressure $p$ on at the surface; the dry seasons correspond to turning the pressure off. These seasons need not be binary, they can vary continuously. We therefore evolve the moisture through iterations whose inner loop consists of the following two steps:

1. Solve $dp/dt = -\nabla \cdot (\phi \nabla p)$ with pressure $p$ specified as Dirichlet conditions, i.e. the pressure condition is imposed as a boundary condition, on the surface and on the front.

2. Update the front by Darcy's law: $v = -\frac{K}{\eta}(\nabla p - \rho g)$.

#### 4.3.3 Dissolution and Recrystallization of Minerals

The front computed above is the site where minerals and salts first come into contact with water. It is therefore at this front that we calculate the dissolution of any number of minerals and salts. These minerals and salts are assumed transported to the surface by an advection term where they recrystallize forming a crust.

Let $C_i$ denote the concentration in the water of a dissolved mineral or a salt. The dissolution at the front is modeled by the equation

$$\frac{dC_i}{dt} = -k_i(m_i - C_i),$$

where $k$ indicates the solubility of the mineral and $m_i$ is the saturated level, i.e., the maximum solubility. The solubility is a rate constant for the dissolution of the material; the quantity $m_i$ cuts off dissolution upon saturation. We point out that this equation does not have a simple closed form solution because it travels with the front.

Now that the minerals are dissolved, we need to model the movement of minerals to the surface. This is accomplished with the convective-diffusion equation:

$$\frac{\partial}{\partial t}(\phi C_i) + v \cdot \nabla(\phi C_i) = \nabla \cdot (\phi D_i \nabla C_i),$$

where $D_i$ is the diffusivity of the mineral, and $v$ is the velocity as obtained from the pressure gradient.

Finally, minerals and salts form a crust on the surface. The material accumulating on the surface at each time step is $\nabla C_i$. Green's theorem preserves conservation of mass.

#### 4.3.4 Erosion: Transformation to Clay

The presence of stone at a voxel is indicated by a three dimensional stone density function $s$, whose value is stored in each voxel. The absence of stone is indicated by $s = 0$ at the voxel. The tendency of the stone to transform into clay is indicated by a decay index $d$ that can impact the stone density $s$ in a probabilistic manner.

At every node, a time average of how much water is present is computed. A weighted average of this and various minerals present "weakens" the stone by adding to the decay index $d$. A large number of erosion events are distributed across the surface with a probability based on the decay index. The density function is reduced within a zone of influence of each event. Once the density hits 0, the stone is no longer present at that site.

#### 4.3.5 Finite Difference Schemes

As the samples inside each slab are arranged in a regular grid, we have chosen a finite difference technique for simplicity. Alternatively, a more complicated finite element method could have been used.

The trapezoidal nature of the lattice of voxels requires special care for the accurate computation of the Laplacian. Carelessly chosen schemes can cause a point source to diffuse into what appears to be more elliptical than an isotropic circle. We have found that a thirteen point scheme is quite adequate.

Our scheme is based on three vectors $u$, $v$, and $w$. The points in the stencil consist of 0, $\pm u$, $\pm v$, $\pm w$ and eight points consisting of sums of any two of $\pm u$, $\pm v$, and $\pm w$.

At the origin, the Laplacian of the functions $x^2$, $y^2$, and $z^2$ is 2, but for other functions such as 1, $x$, $y$, $z$, $xy$, $xz$, $yz$, $x^3$, $x^2y$, $xy^2$, and $z^3$ the value is 0. If we impose these fourteen conditions on the thirteen points in a least squares manner, we find that this is sufficient to achieve reasonably non-distorted results. Of course more points or smaller mesh sizes could have been incorporated for further accuracy.

The gradient is evaluated as an ordinary finite difference.

## 5 Rendering

Stone is primarily composed of transparent crystal grains. When light shines upon a crystal it is both reflected and refracted as described by Fresnel's formulae. Light that is refracted into the stone is scattered further due to the large number of grains and the tiny air bubbles and micro-cracks inside and between these grains. The overall result is stones that look opaque but also show a large degree of translucency in thin sections (see Figure 2b). The color of the stone is determined by the type of minerals present [23]. To capture the effect of translucency and the coloration due to minerals, we need to simulate the scattering of light inside the stone. We ignore effects such as diffraction and interference that cannot be handled using geometrical optics. Instead, we treat stone as a participating medium and focus on the simulation of the subsurface scattering of light.

### 5.1 Subsurface Scattering in Stone

Light transport in a participating medium is described by the following integral-equation [31]:

$$L(x,\vec{\omega}) = \int_{x_e}^{x} \tau(x',x)\,\sigma(x') \int_{\Omega} f(x',\vec{\omega}',\vec{\omega})\,L(x',\vec{\omega}')\,d\omega'\,dx' + \tau(x_e,x)\,L(x_e,\vec{\omega})\,, \qquad (1)$$

where $L(x,\vec{\omega})$ is the radiance at $x$ in the direction $\vec{\omega}$, $\sigma(x)$ is the scattering coefficient, $f(x,\vec{\omega}',\vec{\omega})$ is the phase-function describing how light is scattered in different directions, and $x_e$ is the end point of the medium. The transmittance $\tau(x',x)$ from $x'$ to $x$ is given by

$$\tau(x',x) = e^{-\int_{x'}^{x} \kappa(\xi)\,d\xi}\,, \qquad (2)$$

where $\kappa(\xi)$ is the extinction coefficient.

The phase-function $f$ describes how light is scattered within the stone. Since the cracks and air bubbles are larger than the wavelength of light, the type of scattering is described by Mie theory [3]. To simulate the combined effect of back-scattering and forward-scattering, we use the two-lobed Schlick-approximation [4] of the empirical Henyey-Greenstein phase-function [13], which is a good approximation of Mie scattering.

To simulate subsurface scattering in stone, we need to apply a method that can handle the extreme optical thickness of certain stone minerals, such as mica. If we add to this the non-homogeneous media and the non-diffuse phase-function, then it becomes clear that only a method based on Monte Carlo ray tracing will work. We use a variant of the photon map method in which a volume photon map is used to capture the in-scattered light in a participating medium [14].

The volume photon map is generated by emitting photons from the light sources in the scene and storing them as they scatter inside the stone. We only store photons representing the indirect light; the direct light is computed using standard ray tracing techniques.

The rendering method for the stone medium has been integrated in a Monte Carlo based ray tracer. Whenever a ray enters a stone medium it is decided whether the ray interacts with the medium or continues through the medium. The probability of a ray interacting with medium is given by the following cumulative probability density function:

$$P(x_s) = 1 - e^{-\int_{x}^{x_s} \kappa(x')\,dx'} \qquad (3)$$

As stone is non-homogeneous, we use ray marching to compute the value of the integral in this equation. In practice this works by selecting a uniformly distributed random number $0 < \xi < 1$ and computing $\int_{x}^{x_s} \kappa(x')\,dx'$ using ray marching until it equals $-\log \xi$ or until the back of the stone is reached. If the back of the stone is reached it means that no scattering event happened and the ray is traced through the stone. Otherwise a scattering event happened at $x_s$, and we must compute the radiance $L_s$ scattered in the direction $\vec{\omega}_t$ of the ray at this point. For the extreme optical thickness in stone, this approach is significantly more efficient than the ray marching approach used in [14].

The scattered radiance $L_s(x,\vec{\omega})$ is computed as the sum of out-scattered radiance due to direct illumination $L_d$ and indirect illumination $L_i$:

$$L_s(x,\vec{\omega}) = L_d(x,\vec{\omega}) + L_i(x,\vec{\omega})\,. \qquad (4)$$

The out-scattered radiance due to direct illumination is computed by sending a shadow ray to the light source to test for visibility and also to account for extinction (absorption and out-scattering) as the light passes through the stone. The out-scattered radiance due to in-scattered flux is computed using the volume photon map radiance estimate [14]. This is illustrated in Figure 6.

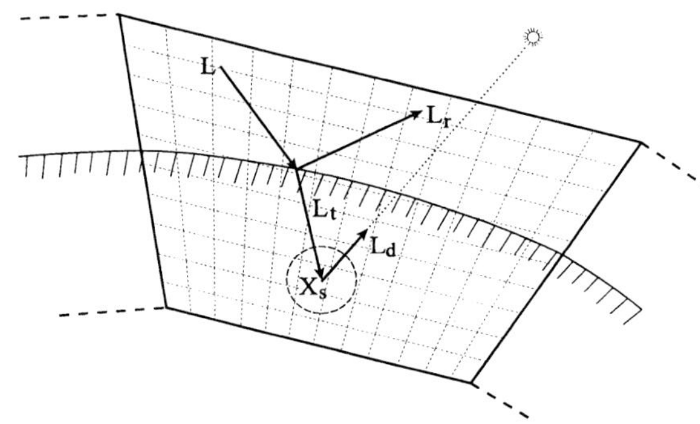


**Figure 6** A subsurface scattering event.

The interaction of light with the stone surface is simulated with Fresnel's formulae for unpolarized light entering a dielectric medium. This formula is described in most standard texts on optics e.g. [3]. We compute the amount of reflected light at a surface as $F_r(x,\vec{\omega})^k$, where $k$ serves as a simple approximation of surface roughness. As the surface roughness is increased, the surface will become less reflective, in particular for light entering the surface in a direction close to the surface normal. This has the effect of forcing more light to be scattered below the surface as the roughness is increased. Whenever a ray intersects the stone surface we use this formula to determine the amount of light reflected; the remaining light is transmitted through the surface.

### 5.2 Integrating the Information in the Slabs

The subsurface rendering method described above does not include the information contained in the slabs. To integrate this information, the ray marcher needs to sample the voxels. The fresh material is still the underlying component since it would be quite costly to make a complete high resolution voxel representation of the stone that is suitable for rendering. Instead, the information in the voxels is used to modify the stone material. This is more efficient since most of the chemical changes within stone are of low frequency.

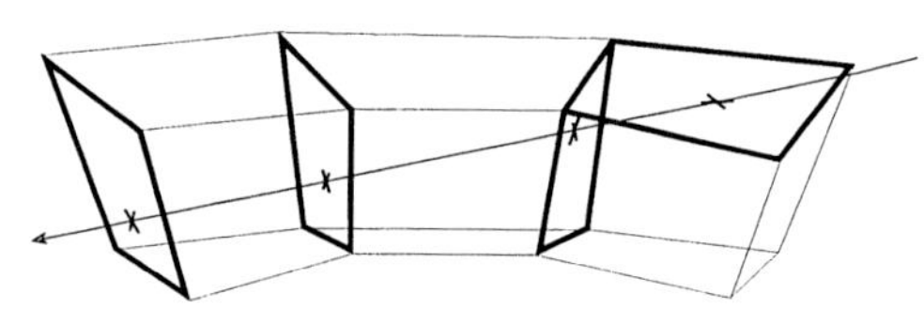

**Figure 7** Ray tracing slabs.

To sample the voxels we need to map the points selected by the ray marcher to voxels inside the slabs. To do this, we first build a sorted list of intersected slabs. This list is created by intersecting the ray with the bilinear patch boundaries. The list of boundary intersections is analyzed to match boundaries of the same slab and to generate a list of slab intervals.

The ray marcher uses the sorted list of slabs to keep track of the slab that contains the current sample point (see Figure 7). The data in each slab is sampled based on a linear interpolation between the entry point and the exit point of the ray with the slab. This is similar to the techniques used in [15] and [21]. Here we ignore that a straight line within a slab is a curved line in the real world. Fortunately this distortion is minimal for reasonably shaped slabs.

## 6 Results

In this section we present results for three models: a granite sphinx, a sandstone column, and a marble statue.

In addition to the models, input to the system consisted of wetness and deposit maps. The deposit maps were computed with accessibility [19] combined with visibility to area deposit sources;

**Figure 8** Granite sphinx.

wetness maps were computed with visibility to a directional rain source.

All simulations were run on a quad 250 MHz R10000 SGI machine, and renderings were computed using a dual 400 MHz Pentium II PC running Linux. Images were rendered with global illumination at a resolution of 1024 in the larger dimension, with four samples per pixel.

### 6.1 Sphinx

Figure 8 shows the weathering of a red granite statue of a sphinx. The model was created from a Cyberware scan and consists of 2.2 million triangles. The model with deposits and wetness maps was then used to initialize 281 slabs, each of which contains $32^3$ voxels. The weathering effects in this sequence were created in approximately 24 hours. Figure 4s b and c show representative cross sections of the sphinx with simulations occurring within the interior of the model.

Figure 8a depicts the original statue prior to the weathering simulation. This is a direct rendering of the original mesh using the stone generated by the quarry; rendering time was 31 minutes.

Figure 8b shows the corestone and yellowing effects. Note the loss of high frequency geometric detail and a general roughening of

(a) (b) (c) (d)

**Figure 9** Sandstone column.

the surface. For this simulation, the rain direction was from above, causing the wetness map to be stronger in the horizontal areas. The greater concentration of water and deposits in these areas caused larger amounts of iron deposits to migrate to the surface. Figure 8c shows erosion and efflorescence effects. Salts were applied to the surface with an exposure map during the simulation process. Note the dulling of the surface due to the decay of minerals and recrystallization of salts. 8d shows a more elaborate simulation with both yellowing and efflorescence.

The rendering times for the weathered sphinx were approximately 80 minutes each. This was due mainly to the sampling of the slabs, which we have observed to increase rendering times by a factor of 1 to 10, depending on the complexity of the model. This is mainly due to the conversion from world coordinates to the parameter space of the slab and the intersection of the bilinear patch boundaries of the slabs, which use costly numerical technique.

### 6.2 Column

Figure 9 shows the weathering of a sandstone column. The column was modeled using AutoCAD and consists of 100,000 triangles. This model consists of 240 slabs, each of which contains $32^3$ voxels.

Figure 9a shows the unweathered column. Rendering time was 30 minutes. The dark horizontal bands are bedding planes that were generated by the quarry. These planes consist of weaker, more porous rock with a higher concentration of iron. The simulations in this example were created in approximately four hours.

Figure 9b and 9c show differential erosion of the front and back sides of the column resulting from the weathering simulation. Because the exposure to water and deposits is greater from the front, the erosion is more dramatic on this side. Note that some of the high frequency detail is still present in the vertical flutes on the back side (9c), while the fluting on front side is more eroded.

The bedding planes of varying porosity have a strong impact on the weathering of the sandstone. Note, for example, the strong correlation between the erosion patterns and the layers of the stone. Because the bedding planes have a higher porosity and thus are more permeable than the surrounding stone, the moisture penetrated more deeply and caused the material in these regions to be more susceptible to erosion.

Figure 9d shows both geometric and optical variations. Note the rust-colored regions at the locus of the bedding planes. These were caused by diffusion and recrystallization of dissolved iron. The black regions indicate black scabs that developed on the surface throughout the simulation and slowly moved inward. Note that protected areas retain more carbon than exposed ones. The less eroded region at the top of the column simulates the appearance of the column in a protected region with very little wetness. This effect was achieved by modulating the input wetness map.

### 6.3 Diana the Huntress

Figure 10 shows simulations on a white marble statue of *Diana the Huntress*, a fourth century B.C. work of art. The model was created from a Cyberware scan and consists of 1.3 million triangles. Figure 11 shows a close-up of the original marble statue prior to the simulations. The light source was placed behind the head to emphasize the simulation of translucency with subsurface scattering. Figure 10a shows the complete model. This image was rendered in 21 minutes. The weathering effects in this example were created in approximately three hours.

Figure 10b shows minor erosion in parts of the statue (concentrated around the right side of the bust, the top of the head, and near the shoulders). Other parts of the sculpture were protected and show less erosion. Note how the yellowing due to dissolved iron is concentrated in the less eroded regions, while whiter, unweathered marble is visible in the more eroded areas. In this example, the case hardening effect is also visible on the surface. Chemical dissolution was the dominant source of erosion in this simulation, although some abrasion also took place in high curvature areas.

(a) (b)

**Figure 10** Marble statue of *Diana the Huntress.*

## 7 Summary and Discussion

We have described new techniques for the modeling and rendering of weathered stone. We use a surface-aligned, volumetric data structure to represent regions near the boundary of the stone surface. This representation resembles the underlying structure of real stone. We present an approach to simulate the flow of water, the transport and dissolution of minerals within the volume, and the erosion of the surface. We also describe a rendering technique to simulate the subsurface scattering of light. These modeling and rendering techniques are capable of capturing a variety of weathered appearances.

Because the state of our scientific knowledge is incomplete, an exact model for stone weathering is not feasible. Therefore, our model is still a phenomenological one. However, we believe that these techniques have many applications in computer graphics, even if they do not perfectly predict real physical processes. By varying the shape of the objects, the material properties, and the initial conditions of the simulations, we can create strikingly different effects. The metaphor of a volumetric surface — a data structure that combines the benefits of surface- and volume-based representations — is easy to understand and could be used to represent the shape and appearance of many materials.

Our system also suggests several interesting areas for future work. In the examples shown in the paper, we do not exploit fully the potential benefits of the slab data structure. Slabs permit a finer sampling of surface detail compared to axis-aligned voxels; however, the efficiency of the representation would be much more apparent when applied to more complex 3D models, such as a building model, where the use of axis-aligned voxels would be impractical. The slab data structure could be extended in many ways. For example, we would like to develop a multiresolution version in which we independently vary tangential and perpendicular sampling resolutions, as well as vary the sampling resolution in different parts of the model. We would also like to extend our simulation techniques to include a fracture model [22]. Finally, the basic simulation framework could also be applied to other types of materials that exhibit complex internal structures.

In our current implementation, we generate initial stone samples with standard procedural texturing techniques. An interesting future direction would be to synthesize 3D stone samples directly from real stone. Alternatively, the simulation and rendering of the stone formation process itself would make for a valuable study that could draw on the geology literature.

The material models widely used in computer graphics today are based on the physics of idealized surfaces. However, such idealized materials rarely exist in real life. What is needed are physically-based models of real materials that can sustain a range of appearances over time. Although our simulations show many effects new to computer graphics and demonstrate — to some extent — the potential of combining simulations with better material representations, a comparison between the real and synthetic examples suggests that many challenging problems lie ahead.

## Acknowledgments

We would like to thank Michael Brenner for many helpful discussions, Steven Gortler for commenting on an early draft, and Britton Bradley and Kurk Dorsey for creative crisis management. Paraform

**Figure 11** Closeup of the unweathered *Diana the Huntress* showing subsurface scattering of light.

provided the Cyberware scan of the Sphinx model; Stephen Duck modeled the column. This work was supported by an Alfred P. Sloan Research Fellowship (BR-3659), an NSF CAREER award (CCR-9624172), an NSF Postdoctoral Research Associates award (EIA-9806139), an NSF CISE Research Infrastructure award (EIA-9802220), and a grant from NTT through the NTT/MIT research collaboration agreement.

## References

[1] Giovanni G. Amoroso and Vasco Fassina. *Stone Decay and Conservation*. Elsevier, New York, NY, 1983.

[2] John Ashurst and Francis Dimes, editors. *Conservation of Building and Decorative Stone*. Butterworth-Heinemann, London, 1990.

[3] Michael Bass, editor. *Handbook of Optics*. McGraw-Hill, Inc., New York, NY, 1995.

[4] Philippe Blasi, Bertrand Le Saec, and Christophe Schlick. A rendering algorithm for discrete volume density objects. In R. J. Hubbold and R. Juan, editors, *Eurographics '93*, pages 201–210, Oxford, UK, 1993. Eurographics, Blackwell Publishers.

[5] E. Catmull and J. Clark. Recursively generated B-spline surfaces on arbitrary topological meshes. *Computer-Aided Design*, 10:350–355, September 1978.

[6] Cassidy J. Curtis, Sean E. Anderson, Joshua E. Seims, Kurt W. Fleischer, and David H. Salesin. Computer-generated watercolor. In *Computer Graphics Proceedings*, Annual Conference Series, pages 421–430. ACM SIGGRAPH, August 1997.

[7] Julie Dorsey and Pat Hanrahan. Modeling and rendering of metallic patinas. In *Computer Graphics Proceedings*, Annual Conference Series, pages 387–396. ACM SIGGRAPH, August 1996.

[8] Julie Dorsey, Hans Køhling Pedersen, and Pat Hanrahan. Flow and changes in appearance. In *Computer Graphics Proceedings*, Annual Conference Series, pages 411–420. ACM SIGGRAPH, August 1996.

[9] F. A. L. Dullien. *Porous Media: Fluid Transport and Pore Structure*. Academic Press, New York, NY, second edition, 1992.

[10] David S. Ebert, editor. *Texturing and Modeling*. Academic Press, New York, 1994.

[11] K. Lal Gauri. The preservation of stone. *Scientific American*, 238(6):126–136, June 1978.

[12] Pat Hanrahan and Wolfgang Krueger. Reflection from layered surfaces due to subsurface scattering. In *Computer Graphics Proceedings*, Annual Conference Series, pages 165–174. ACM SIGGRAPH, August 1993.

[13] L. G. Henyey and J. L. Greenstein. Diffuse radiation in the galaxy. *Astrophysics Journal*, 93:70–83, 1941.

[14] Henrik Wann Jensen and Per H. Christensen. Efficient simulation of light transport in scenes with participating media using photon maps. In *Computer Graphics Proceedings*, pages 311–320. ACM SIGGRAPH, August 1998.

[15] James T. Kajiya and Timothy L. Kay. Rendering fur with three dimensional textures. In *Computer Graphics (SIGGRAPH '89 Proceedings)*, volume 23, pages 271–280, July 1989.

[16] Arie Kaufman, Daniel Cohen, and Roni Yagel. Volume graphics. *IEEE Computer*, 26(7):51–64, July 1993.

[17] Philippe Lacroute and Marc Levoy. Fast volume rendering using a shear–warp factorization of the viewing transformation. In *Computer Graphics Proceedings*, Annual Conference Series, pages 451–458. ACM SIGGRAPH, July 1994.

[18] Marc Levoy. Efficient ray tracing of volume data. *ACM Transactions on Graphics*, 9(3):245–261, July 1990.

[19] Gavin Miller. Efficient algorithms for local and global accessibility shading. In *Proceedings of SIGGRAPH '94*, Annual Conference Series, pages 319–326, July 1994.

[20] F. Kenton Musgrave, Craig E. Kolb, and Robert S. Mace. The synthesis and rendering of eroded fractal terrains. *Computer Graphics*, 23(3):41–50, July 1989.

[21] Fabrice Neyret. Modeling, animating, and rendering complex scenes using volumetric textures. *IEEE Transactions on Visualization and Computer Graphics*, 4(1), January – March 1998.

[22] James F. O'Brien and Jessica K. Hodgins. Graphical modeling and animation of brittle fracture. In *Computer Graphics Proceedings*. ACM SIGGRAPH, August 1999.

[23] Andrew Peckett. *The Colours of Opaque Minerals*. John Wiley and Sons Ltd, Chichester, England, 1992.

[24] Ken Perlin. An image synthesizer. In B. A. Barsky, editor, *Computer Graphics (SIGGRAPH '85 Proceedings)*, volume 19, pages 287–296, July 1985.

[25] D. G. Price. Weathering and weathering processes. *Quarterly Journal of Engineering Geology*, 16(28):243–252, June 1995.

[26] Holly E. Rushmeier. *Realistic Image Synthesis for Scenes with Radiatively Participating Media*. Phd thesis, Cornell University, 1988.

[27] Muhammad Sahimi. *Flow and Transport in Porous Media and Fractured Rock*. VCH, New York, NY, 1995.

[28] William J. Schroeder and William E. Lorensen. Implicit modeling of swept surfaces and volumes. In *Visualization '94*, pages 40–45. IEEE, IEEE Computer Society Press, October 1994.

[29] Walter Schumann. *Handbook of Rocks, Minerals, and Gemstones*. HarperCollins Publishers and Houghton Mifflin Company, New York, NY, 1993.

[30] M. J. Selby. *Hillslope Materials and Processes*. Oxford University Press, Oxford, England, 1993.

[31] Robert Siegel and John R. Howell. *Thermal Radiation Heat Transfer*. Hemisphere Publishing Corporation, Washington, D.C., 3rd edition, 1992.

[32] Gilbert Strang. *Introduction to Applied Mathematics*. Wellesley-Cambridge Press, Wellesley, MA, 1986.

[33] John C. Strikwerda. *Finite Difference Schemes and Partial Differential Equations*. Wadsworth and Brooks, Pacific Grove, CA, 1989.

[34] Jayaram K. Udupa and Dewey Odhner. Shell rendering. *IEEE Computer Graphics and Applications*, 13(6):58–67, November 1993.

[35] Sidney W. Wang and Arie E. Kaufman. Volume-sampled 3d modeling. *IEEE Computer Graphics and Applications*, 14:26–32, September 1994.

[36] Erhard M. Winkler. *Stone in Architecture: Properties, Durablity*. Springer-Verlag, New York, NY, 1997.

[37] Steven P. Worley. A cellular texture basis function. In *SIGGRAPH 96 Conference Proceedings*, Annual Conference Series, pages 291–294. ACM SIGGRAPH, August 1996.

# Pattern-Based Texturing Revisited

Fabrice Neyret Marie-Paule Cani

iMAGIS*/ GRAVIR-IMAG

## Abstract

We present a texturing method that correctly maps homogeneous non-periodic textures to arbitrary surfaces without any of the difficulties usually encountered using existing tools. Our technique requires little redundant designer work, has low time and memory costs during rendering and provides high texture resolution.

The idea is simple: a few triangular texture samples, which obey specific boundary conditions, are chosen from the desired pattern and mapped in a non-periodic fashion onto the surface. Our mapping algorithm enables us to freely tune the scale of the texture with respect to the object's geometry, while minimizing distortions. Moreover, it yields singularity-free texturing whatever the topology of the object. The sets of texture samples may be created interactively from pictures or drawings. We also provide two alternative methods for automatically generating them, defined as extensions of Perlin's and Worley's procedural texture synthesis techniques.

As our results show, the method produces textured objects that look reasonable from any viewpoint and can be used in real-time applications.

**Keywords:** Texture Mapping, Patterns, Texture Synthesis, Non-periodic Tiling

## 1 Introduction

Reproducing the visual complexity of the real world is a dream for many Computer Graphics practitioners. Since every detail cannot be modeled at the geometric level, textures are very useful for adding visual complexity to a synthetic scene. They can for instance be used for representing rocks or vegetation on a distant mountain, for simulating animals' fur or skin, human clothes, or the surface aspect of a material. Most of the textures we need for modeling natural objects, either mineral, vegetable, or animal, have a common feature: they may look homogeneous at a large scale (i.e., large scale statistical properties do not depend on the location), but no visible periodicity can be found anywhere.

Texturing arbitrary shapes with such textures is a challenge for artists, since no CG tool is really adequate to fit real-world constraints: generating the texture directly on the surface is memory and time consuming (either for the CPU or the artist), while using standard image mapping results in pattern distortions, discontinuities, and obvious periodicity.

We present a practical solution to this problem, which involves no increase in computational or memory cost at rendering time over standard image mapping techniques using repetitive patterns. Our method works for arbitrary surfaces. It yields little distortion of the texture, no singularities whatever the topology of the surface, and no periodicity.

### 1.1 Related work

Despite years of CG research and tool development, artists still have difficult (and time consuming) work to do in order to achieve the texturing of complex surfaces. This paper focuses on homogeneous non-periodic textures, such as those we need for natural objects (textures may define any surface attribute, such as color, transparency, normal perturbation or displacement). The two mains problems to solve are *texture generation* and *texture mapping*. Let us review the solutions offered by existing tools:

**Standard 2D texture mapping:** The first solution consists of mapping a single image of the desired texture onto the synthetic object. To do this, a global parameterization of the object surface is required. As a consequence, there will necessarily be discontinuities of the texture somewhere on the surface if the object is closed or has a higher topologic order. Moreover, the texture may be highly distorted if the object has an arbitrary geometry. Optimization techniques such as those in [1, 11] can be used to reduce distortions, either locally, or by allowing the introduction of 'cracks', i.e., discontinuities. Entirely suppressing distortions by editing the mapping is impossible, except if the object's surface can be unfolded onto a plane (such as a cloth). This is not the case for natural shapes. A solution for the user to eliminate apparent texture distortions is to draw a pre-distorted texture that will compensate for the distortions due to the mapping. However, this requires high designer skills[2], and the work needs to be re-done from scratch for every new object.

An alternative is to use pattern-based texture mapping, which consists of repetitively mapping a small rectangular texture patch representing a sample of the desired texture pattern onto the surface. The sample image has to obey specific boundary conditions in order to join correctly with itself. More precisely, it needs to have a toroidal topology: the texture on the left edge must fit the texture on the right, and respectively the top edge has to fit with the bottom. Such texture samples can be created by editing pictures or drawings using interactive 2D painting systems. An advantage with respect to the previous approach is that, being small, the texture sample will be stored at a higher resolution, and will demand less redundant work by the artist. Moreover, it can be re-used for texturing other objects. Discontinuity and distortion problems, however, will be exactly the same as for a single texture map as long as a global parameterization is used to map the texture pattern. See Figure 1.

It should be be noted that these two techniques are the only methods available in current graphics hardware. Thus, other representations or design techniques have to be converted into this representation for rendering if real time constraints apply.

*iMAGIS is a joint project of CNRS, INRIA, Institut National Polytechnique de Grenoble and Université Joseph Fourier.
*Address*: BP 53, F-38041 Grenoble cedex 09, France
*E-mail*: [Fabrice.Neyret|Marie-Paule.Cani]@imag.fr
*WWW*: http://www-imagis.imag.fr/TEXTURES/

[2]This is actually done in practice in industry!

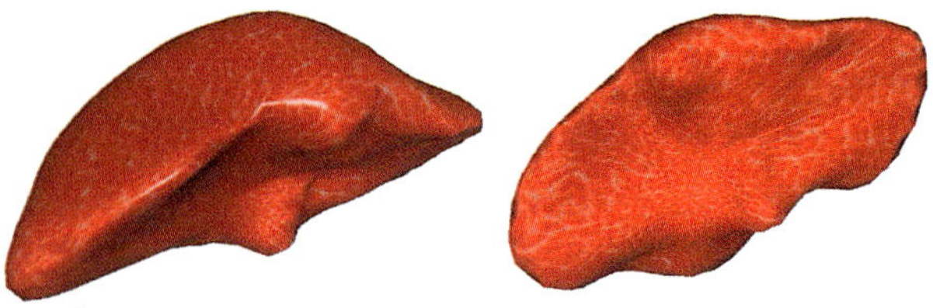

Figure 1: Standard pattern-based mapping used for applying a cellular pattern onto the geometric model of a liver. Distortions are clearly noticeable.

**Interactive techniques:** The problem of finding good local parameterizations for the surfaces is solved in patch-based interactive texturing systems by leaving the user to tile the surface [12, 14, 15]. In [14], the latter interactively subdivides an implicit surface into square patches. Surface geodesics are used for fitting the borders of these patches to the surface. Optimization is then used for deriving a minimally-distorted local parameterization inside each patch. This approach, which can be extended to parametric surfaces as well, can be combined with pattern-based texturing in order to cover an object with a given pattern. However, using a local instead of a global parameterization is not sufficient for avoiding texture discontinuities on closed surfaces (to be convinced, try to map a texture sample with a toroidal topology onto a cube): texture discontinuities will appear across some of the edges, since the neighboring borders of the sample image cannot be those expected everywhere.

Entirely avoiding both distortions and discontinuities can be achieved by using interactive texture painting software [8]. As in the first method, a single texture map corresponding to a global parameterization of the surface is used. However the texture content is directly designed on the object's surface before being stored as a map. The texture map may then appear distorted and discontinuous, but it will be correct when it is rendered. Depending on the user's skills, an homogeneous non-periodic texture may be designed using this method. However, this technique yields a high memory cost (as in the first approach) and consumes lots of user's time since texture details must be drawn all over the surface. Moreover, the user work is almost never re-usable on another shape.

**Texture synthesis techniques:** An alternative to painting the texture onto the surface is to automatically generate it, which has the advantage of saving user's time by replacing the redundant design work by a high level control of the texture features. A wide range of parametric texture synthesis techniques that are convenient for generating natural textures have been proposed [16, 21, 19, 22].

One such method is solid texturing, which involves defining a 3D material field (e.g. marble, wood) which is intersected with the object's surface to create the texture [16, 22]. No distortion nor discontinuity across the object's edges will be produced, since no surface mapping occurs. However the method is restricted to texture patterns that intrinsically come from a 3D phenomenon: it cannot capture surface properties such as the detailed appearance of the skin (e.g. regular scales). Another drawback is that synthesizing the texture during rendering will not allow real-time performance, since it is a per-pixel based computation. An alternative would be to store 3D texture tables at a high memory cost.

Other procedural techniques such as reaction diffusion [21, 19] can be used to generate a pattern-based texture directly on an object's surface. These methods are computationally costly or have a high memory cost, depending whether the texture is generated on the fly or precomputed and stored. We can note that Perlin's and Worley's techniques may also be used on surfaces (as opposed to solid material). However Perlin's noise requires a grid to be generated, so a global parameterization needs to be introduced.

Lastly, all the listed procedural techniques can easily be extended to the automatic generation of square 2D texture samples that have a toroidal topology. The latter can then be used in pattern-based mapping techniques, with the distortion and discontinuity problems discussed above. Moreover, this technique would produce patterns with obvious periodicity, which would probably spoil the natural appearance of the final object.

**Towards non-periodic mapping:** Artistic and mathematical work on tilings such as those of Escher and Penrose (see for instance [3, 5, 6]) can also be a source of inspiration. Escher's drawings include several tilings of the plane with complex shapes such as birds, fishes or reptiles. Penrose studies aperiodic tilings of the plane, and shows that some specific sets of tiles always form non-periodic patterns.

A first attempt to build a practical application of these ideas to texturing in Computer Graphics is Stam's work on "aperiodic textures" [17]. His aim is to render water surfaces and caustics. Stam tiles the plane with a standard grid of square patches, where he maps 16 different texture samples of an homogeneous texture. To do so in a non-periodic fashion, he uses an algorithm for aperiodically tiling the plane with convex polygons of different colors [7] (the colors of the tiles in the mathematical theory correspond to the boundaries of texture tiles). The boundary conditions between texture samples are met by using the same input noise for generating the texture in the rectangular regions that surrounds a shared edge. This method is restricted to applying textures onto a plane, otherwise the usual parameterization problems yielding distortions and discontinuities would appear. Moreover, the problem of synthesizing the texture samples is only addressed for a specific texture, and the algorithm is not explicitly described.

## 1.2 Overview

As shown above, none of the existing tools provides an acceptable solution to the problem of texturing arbitrary surfaces without distortions and discontinuities. With these constraints, previous methods demand too much designer intervention, are not compatible with real-time display, occupy a large memory space, or a combination of the above. This is a critical situation since most applications of Computer Graphics rely on photo-realistic texturing[3]. In this paper, we introduce a full solution to this problem, designed in the spirit of pattern-based texture mapping techniques. Our method avoids discontinuities for all surface topologies, minimizes texture distortions, and avoids the periodicity of the texture patterns.

Our solution is inspired from Escher's work since the surface will not be tiled with square patches as usual, but rather with triangles on which equilateral triangular texture samples will be mapped. It also has connections with Pedersen's geodesics [14], but they are used in our case in an automatic tiling framework, where the user just has to choose the size of the texture triangles with respect to the object's geometry. Our solution to non-periodicity is similar in spirit to the one used by Stam [17], however we have solved the more intricate problem of assigning sets of triangular texture samples onto a curved surface that may be closed, while meeting boundary conditions everywhere. Lastly, our work generalizes Perlin's and Worley's texture synthesis techniques [16, 22] by allowing the automatic generation of adequate sets of triangular texture samples. Solutions using real or hand-made images are also provided.

The remainder of this paper is developed as follows: Section 2 introduces the main features of our approach. Section 3 deals with the mapping of texture samples onto an arbitrary object geometry. Section 4 describes different methods for the generation of texture sample sets, and shows a variety of results. We conclude in Section 5.

[3]Moreover, tools have to cope with real-time constraints for video-games or flight simulators, and artist-time constraints for special effects in movies production, for which designing textures is a huge part.

## 2 Texturing with Triangular Patches

This paper focuses on applying textures that are homogeneous at a large scale. Moreover, as for natural textures, they should be continuous, and no periodicity should be observed. The first feature is obtained by using patterns that capture the short scale surface aspect variations, and by mapping them on the surface with low distortion (see subsection 2.1). The mapping deals with the boundary conditions at the junction between patterns, discussed in subsection 2.2. The final issue concerns the assignment method, explained in subsection 2.3.

The solution described here is designed for isotropic texture patterns, which can be found in many natural objects (for instance in most human and vegetable tissues, in rust, dust, and in numerous bumpy surfaces such as rock, ground, and roughcast wall). A possible extension enabling the introduction and control of some anisotropy is discussed in future work.

### 2.1 Local parameterization with triangles

As we have seen in Section 1.1, the main source of problems in usual mapping techniques is that they generally rely on global surface parameterizations. In most cases, finding a correct global mapping is simply impossible. However, Nature does not need to introduce global parameterizations to 'build' its textures; local parameterizations, together with continuity constraints, are sufficient. A tiling into continuous regions that can be locally parameterized can always be found for the continuous surfaces we wish to texture. Optimization methods will work better when applied to these local regions than to the whole surface.

Rather that defining a tiling with square patches, triangles can be used to tile a surface into regions where a local parameterization will be defined. However, to the authors knowledge, no previous work has used triangular texture patterns to design surface aspect in Computer Graphics. To address the different problem of mesh re-tiling [20], Turk produces a regular triangular surface tiling with controlled size. His algorithm fits precisely our requirements. We claim that if a polygonal tiling adequately captures an object's topology, it can be used for mapping textures. This is the case even if the tiling does not conveniently redefine the geometry, being either too coarse or too precise. Consequently, the first step of our algorithm consists of building a *triangular tiling* of the surface, computed at a user-defined scale. This tiling defines a set of local parameterizations of the surfaces, which will be used for texture mapping. More precisely, a given texture sample is going to be mapped onto each triangular patch of the tiling, whose scale thus controls the texture scale. In the remainder of the paper, we call this tiling the *texture mesh*, as opposed to the *geometric mesh* that is still used to define the shape during rendering.

### 2.2 Texture Samples and Boundary Conditions

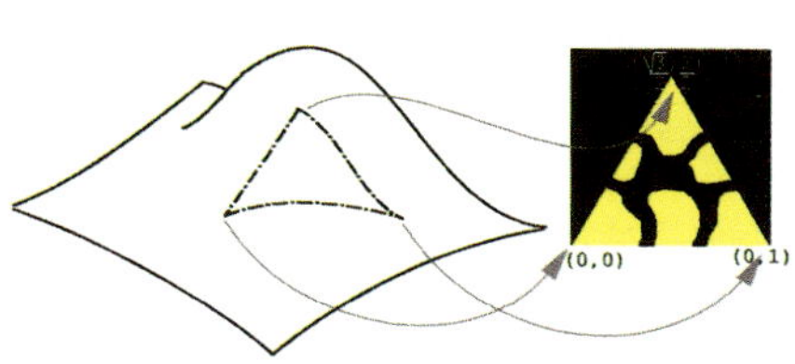


Figure 2: Each triangular patch of the *texture mesh* is mapped onto an equilateral region in a given texture sample.

The idea is to map a triangular image onto each patch of the texture mesh (see Figure 2). As these images are equilateral triangles, there will be no visible distortion if the patches of the texture mesh are approximately equilateral triangles. In order to generate a continuous texture over the entire surface, specific boundary conditions will have to be met between texture samples mapped onto adjacent patches. Basically, the two patterns in the neighborhood of the border separating two patches have to fit, which means that at least both texture values and derivatives are to be the same along a common edge. The methods presented in this paper solve for these local continuity constraints under the hypothesis that the textured patches are equilateral. If a texture sample happened to be mapped on a low quality patch (e.g. with sharp corners), the texture would be distorted and discontinuities of the texture gradient would appear on the patch edges. We have found that our solution is still sufficient in practice, since good quality meshes made of quasi-equilateral triangles can be computed for almost any surface.

Achieving texture continuity constraints using triangular tiles is more intricate than doing it with a square grid of tiles. As soon as a mesh node on a curved surface can be shared by an arbitrary (small) number of neighboring patches (either triangular or square), there is no longer anything equivalent to the 'toroidal topology' that exists when tiling the plane: no global orientation can be defined, so two patches may be connected by any edges. Moreover, this increases a priori the constraints on the texture content near the sample corners. More precisely, this enforces a zero texture gradient at those points, otherwise one would have to manage a continuity constraint between the edges of a triangle. The methods we provide for the generation of texture samples, described in Section 4, will have to cope with these boundary constraints. As our results will show, the gradient constraint at corners does not create any noticeable visual artifacts.

Since our method only relies on local parameterizations and on local continuity constraints between texture patches, it yields singularity free texturing whatever the topology of the object is (see Figure 3). However, the scale of the texture details drawn on the samples must not be too large. Otherwise, unexpected path shapes will appear at the object surface, such as those depicted in Figure 3. A practical solution to this signal processing problem consists of using patterns that are large enough to contain more than a single feature of the texture.

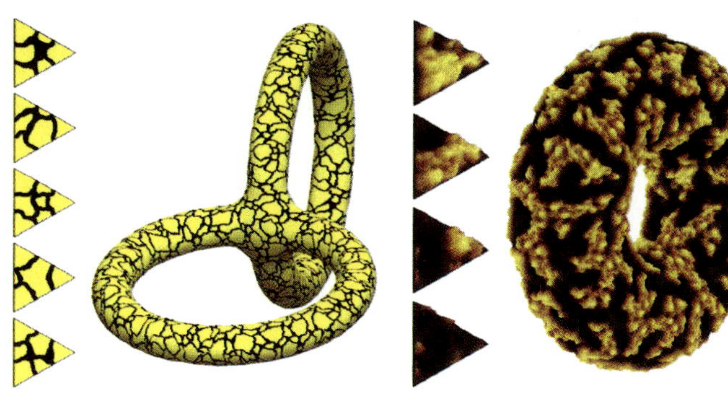

Figure 3: Two cases where unexpected path shapes appear since the lowest frequency of the texture (i.e. the grain size) is too close to the sample scale. *Left:* A naive set of texture samples designed to figure cells onto a surface. *Right:* A set of procedurally generated volumetric textures.

### 2.3 Assignment of Texture Samples

In order to create homogeneous textures that look like those of natural objects, several different texture samples have to be designed and non-periodically mapped onto the surface. The problem is to find how many samples are required in order to guarantee that the continuity constraints at boundaries will be respected, and to allow sufficient variations of the texture. We must also find an algorithm for assigning texture samples to the patches of the texture mesh.

The mathematical expression of this problem is not as simple as in Stam's case [17], where the mathematical theory provided a simple algorithm for achieving aperiodic mapping onto a plane, and linked the number of texture samples to the number of required boundary conditions (e.g. 16). We still have to solve a graph coloring problem (where the triangular patches represent the graph nodes and where the set of three boundaries conditions to assign them correspond to the different colors), but the graph is now a highly non-regular structure, with a varying number of neighbors per node.

A practical method for always providing a solution to continuity constraints is to use texture sample sets that include at least one texture triangle for each possible choice of three edge-constraints. More variation, or more user-control on the large-scale aspect, can be obtained by fixing a material value at each node of the texture mesh. Thus, at least one edge-constraint should be provided for each possible choice of pair of node values. A simple three step stochastic algorithm can then be used to consistently assign the triangular samples onto the surface, in a statistically non-periodic way:

1. randomly[4] choose which material value (among those used at corners of texture triangles in the sample set) is associated with each texture mesh node.

2. randomly choose which edge (among those used in the texture sample set that are compatible with the values at nodes) is associated with each geometrical edge of the texture mesh;

3. randomly assign a texture sample to each patch, among those that obey the three required boundary conditions.

The question now is: how many different texture samples do we need ? Since continuity conditions along an edge between two samples involve the gradient of the color map, the edges used in step 2 must be seen as *oriented edges*: they usually yield different boundary conditions on their two sides (to be convinced, note that a textured triangle does not smoothly weld with its mirror image, except in the special case where the gradient of the image is locally perpendicular to the common edge everywhere along it). Suppose now that we have mapped a single oriented edge $e$ all over the texture mesh. Let us denote by $E$ and $\bar{E}$ the different boundary conditions that the texture samples should fit on both sides of $e$ (see Figure 4). Then, at least four texture triangles respectively obeying the conditions $(E,E,E)$, $(E,E,\bar{E})$, $(E,\bar{E},\bar{E})$, or $(\bar{E},\bar{E},\bar{E})$ must be provided. The other possible values for the boundaries conditions (such as $(E,\bar{E},E)$ for instance) will be met by a rotated instance of one of these triangles.

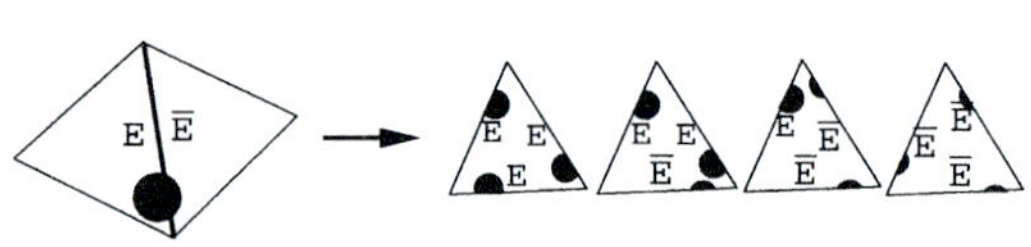

Figure 4: An oriented edge, and the set of four texture samples that need to be created to fit the different boundary conditions it produces.

In the general case of $n$ different boundary conditions (i.e. two times the number of oriented edges), the number of texture triangles needed will be $n + n(n-1) + n(n-1)(n-2)/3$, in which the first term corresponds to the condition where the same edge is used three times, the second one to conditions with two different edge values, and the third one to solutions with three different edge values. For instance, 24 texture triangles will be needed if 2 oriented-edges are used instead of 1 (i.e. 4 boundary conditions instead of $E$ and $\bar{E}$). Since the number of triangles required increases as a power of 3, our algorithm is not convenient for a larger number of edges. Note that if several values at nodes are used in order to constrain possible edge values, the combination of possible triangles is far smaller since edge choices have to be compatible.

In our examples, we use the minimum number of degrees of freedom, with correct results: A single kind of edge (thus two boundary conditions) is used for Figures 10,12,14. We even used the special case of symmetry mentioned above to avoid doubling the boundary condition per edge type in Figures 3(left) and 9. Noticeable repetitivity may happen with some kinds of pattern when using a small number of edge conditions. Our solution consists of providing several completely different texture samples that fit the same boundary conditions. For instance, in Figure 3 left, five texture samples fitting a single symmetric edge constraint are used. The generation of several samples fitting the same boundary conditions can be easily done using the automatic texture synthesis techniques that will be presented in Section 4. Figure 9 illustrates the use of 2 different edge conditions (using symmetry, in order to get only 2 boundary conditions, thus 4 possible triangles). An example where node values are used is presented in Figure 5, with 2 possible values (forest and ground), and symmetric boundary conditions (thus still only 4 triangles to define).

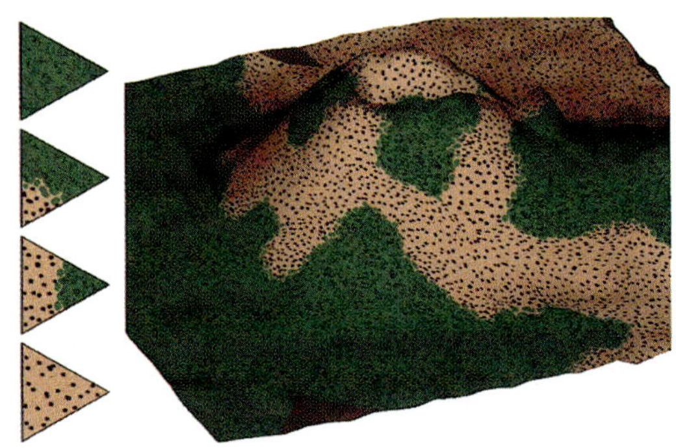

Figure 5: Mountain covered by forest. The location of forest and ground material is controlled by the values at the nodes of the texture mesh. These values are 'painted' by the user with their probability attribute (intensity of presence).

# 3 Mapping

In this section, we assume that we have a set of texture samples obeying adequate boundary conditions, and we describe our method for mapping them on a surface at a user controlled scale.

As suggested above, our solution for providing such control is to map texture samples onto a specifically defined *texture mesh* that tiles the surface, instead of mapping them onto the triangles that describe the object's geometry. This brings several advantages. Firstly, the texture scale becomes completely independent from the object's geometry, which is a very useful property in practice. Secondly, we can compute a high quality mesh in terms of the angular properties of the triangular patches. This will allow the mapping of equilateral texture samples without generating too large texture distortions, whatever the quality of the geometric mesh. Lastly, using a texture mesh that would be too coarse to adequately describe the object geometry is not a problem; the initial geometric mesh will still be rendered. The texture mesh just serves as a set of local parameterizations providing an image identifier and adequate texture coordinates for the geometric mesh vertices.

## 3.1 Overview of the texture mapping algorithm

The user first chooses the set of texture samples he wants to use, with the associated set of possible boundary conditions. He also indicates at which scale texture should be mapped by specifying

[4] This choice can be totally random to provide more variation, totally user defined, or defined with probabilities.

the desired density of texture control points (i.e., points that will be the vertices of the texture mesh) on the object's surface. Then, texture mapping is performed in the following four steps:

1. We randomly generate texture control points of the desired density on the object's surface, let them tune their relative position by simulating a repulsive force, and compute an associated high quality triangular mesh. The code we use for doing this is courtesy of Greg Turk, who uses the same process in his re-tiling algorithm [20].

2. We tile the surface with this mesh, i.e.:

   - we use surface geodesics to compute curved versions of the texture mesh edges;
   - we compute the set of geometric triangles covered by each of the resulting texture patches;
   - we compute the $u, v$ coordinates of each geometric vertex with respect to the texture patch to which it belongs.

3. We use the algorithm described in Section 2.3 to consistently assign a specific texture sample to each patch of the texture mesh.

4. We render the object's geometry using the local $u, v$ coordinates of the mesh vertices to map the texture samples.

A possible solution for implementing step 2 would be to adapt the set of methods introduced in [10]. In our current implementation, we rather compute geodesic curves using a standard length minimization process along a polygonal line, which is constrained to move onto the geometric mesh (the line is made of segments whose ends lie on the mesh edges). Then, we have developed a specific method, described below, for assigning $u, v$ local coordinates to mesh vertices that lie on a texture patch without producing excessively large texture distortions. Alternative (and possibly better) solutions for implementing this part of the process can be found in [10, 4, 11].

## 3.2 Computing texture coordinates for mesh points

The texture mesh may have been designed at either a smaller or a larger resolution than the geometric mesh that describes the object. In the latter case, the local part of the surface that falls into a patch of the texture mesh (i.e., between three connected geodesics) may be highly curved. Computing $u, v$ coordinates for mesh points included in this region must be done while trying to avoid texture distortions. Attention must also be paid to computing coordinates that exactly map the edges of the texture sample onto the geodesic edges of the patch, in order to avoid introducing discontinuities in the large scale texture at the junction between patches. Our solution is as follows:

To get rid of the border problem, we split the geometric triangles that are crossed by a geodesic, in order to be able to specify the exact texture coordinates along the texture patch edges[5].

The problem of computing a good $u, v$ mapping inside each of the texture patches still remains. Since the problem is local, we have developed a simple solution that does not requires an optimization step. The basic idea is to use the three geodesic distances between a mesh vertex and the three edges of the texture patch to estimate the 'barycentric' coordinates of this vertex within the texture patch. Then, conversion into texture coordinates is immediate by analogy with the planar case. The algorithm develops as follows.

[5]The alternative solution that consists of keeping the triangles unsplit, computing a different texturing process (with half-transparent textures) for each texture patch that the triangle intersects does not work well: it does not provide enough control on the $u, v$ coordinates near the edges of a texture patch, yielding texture discontinuities at this location.

For each of the three edges of a texture patch:

1. Use a front propagation paradigm for computing the geodesic distances to the mesh vertices (see Figure 6):

   The front is implemented using a heap that stores the triangles whose three vertices are already provided with a distance value. The heap is initialized by the triangles that lie along the texture patch edge. Each front propagation step consists of taking the most reliable triangle within in the heap, i.e., the triangle which is closest[6] to this curve. The gradient of the distance within this triangle is computed. Then, for each neighboring triangle for which a vertex distance is still missing, we fold the distance gradient onto the plane of this triangle, and use the two already known values plus the gradient for evaluating the missing distance. This neighboring triangle is then inserted into the heap.

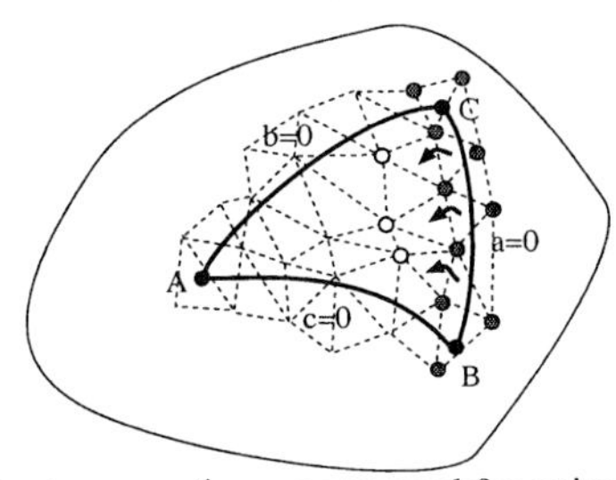


Figure 6: Front propagation process used for estimating the 'barycentric' coordinates of mesh vertices with respect to a texture patch. Distance values at pink points are already computed. The three next points for which the distance will be calculated are marked in white.

   In practice, there may be different ways of propagating distance to a given triangle, coming from several of its already computed neighbors. So we add a quality criterion to the distance value stored in the heap, and we modify a value each time we are sure quality will improve. The best quality is obtained when an vertex to be estimated falls between the two 'gradient lines' passing through the two known vertices. The estimation is less sure when it falls outside this band. The estimation is worst when the gradient is back-propagated, i.e., when the computed distance is smaller than the two known ones (then the result should only be used when no better evaluation is available).

2. Normalize all the distance values by dividing them by the value at the patch vertex that is opposite that edge.

Each vertex of the geometric mesh now stores three numbers $a, b, c \in [0, 1]$. To convert them into barycentric coordinates with respect to the three vertices of the texture patch, we divide them by their sum, so that $a + b + c = 1$. Lastly, we convert barycentric coordinates into texture coordinates with respect to the texture patch (the three corners of the image should map to $(0,0)$, $(\frac{1}{2}, \frac{\sqrt{3}}{2})$, $(1,0)$). The resulting mapping yields good results with only small texture distortions, as shown in Figure 7. However we have to keep in mind that avoiding excessive distortions is only possible 'locally': the surface's radius of curvature should not be too small relative to the patch size.

Figure 8 illustrates the control provided by texture mapping using a texture mesh: the scale of the texture can be increased while leaving the geometry of an object unchanged.

[6]considering the maximum of the three distance values at vertices.

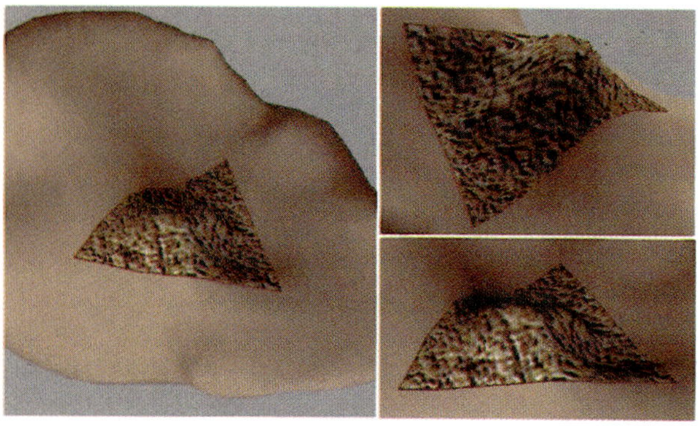

Figure 7: A texture patch mapped onto a curved region of a geometric model (views from three different viewpoints): texture distortions remain reasonable.

Figure 8: From left to right: the geometric mesh, which is rendered; the texture mesh, used for tuning the scale of the texture with respect to the object's geometry; the resulting textured sphere; the sphere with a finer scale texture.

# 4 Texture Samples Generation

## 4.1 Editing pictures or drawings

A first method for generating adequate sets of texture samples is direct editing, under a 2D paint system, of pictures or drawings. An example of hand-drawn texturing of a surface is depicted in Figure 9.

Figure 9: Texture samples drawn by hand, and the resulting image. Two different edge conditions (red, blue), both symmetric, are used.

Although it takes a certain amount of user-time, it is possible to edit real images in order to give them the required boundary conditions. The technique, that consists of copying and smartly pasting rectangular regions along edges and then eliminating texture discontinuities inside the sample, is almost the same as for square images. A single self-cyclical texture triangle, corresponding to a single symmetric edge, can be used. A more complex example of picture editing, where four different texture samples have been created for fitting the constraints associated with a single non-symmetric oriented edge, is depicted on Figure 10. The reference rectangular region figuring the oriented edge has been rotated by 180° or not when copied on the image borders, depending on which of the boundary conditions $(E,E,E)$, $(E,E,\bar{E})$, $(E,\bar{E},\bar{E})$, or $(\bar{E},\bar{E},\bar{E})$ each of the four samples corresponds to.

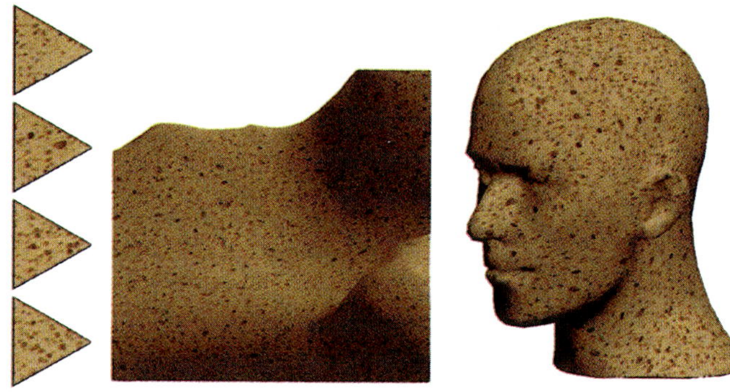

Figure 10: A set of texture samples designed by interactively editing an image of a sponge (left), and the resulting textured surface on a terrain and on a face.

We now describe two procedural synthesis techniques that can be used for automatically generating parameterized sets of texture samples thus saving user's time.

## 4.2 Extending Worley's algorithm

Worley's method [22] is an efficient approach for creating textures depicting small non-periodic cellular patterns such as rocks, scales, or living tissues. When applied in 2D, Worley's method basically consists of computing Voronoï diagrams of noise points randomly distributed on a plane. A square grid is used to accelerate the computation: a noise point is randomly chosen in each cell. Then, determining in which of the Voronoï region each pixel falls can be done efficiently, by only checking the noise points in the 9 closest cells. The portion of the plane covered by the noise points must be slightly larger than the square region to texture, in order to have nice Voronoï regions cross the edges. Worley's method combines the distances from a pixel point to the $N$ nearest noise points to compute the texture value at the pixel (generally, $N \in [1..4]$). We only describe here how to deal with the nearest noise point; the other distance computations are adapted the same way.

Adapting Worley's technique for generating the texture on an equilateral triangle is easy: we just have to tile this triangle with a slightly larger triangular grid as depicted in Figure 11. A noise point is randomly chosen in each of the small triangles, and Voronoï diagrams are computed as in the standard case.

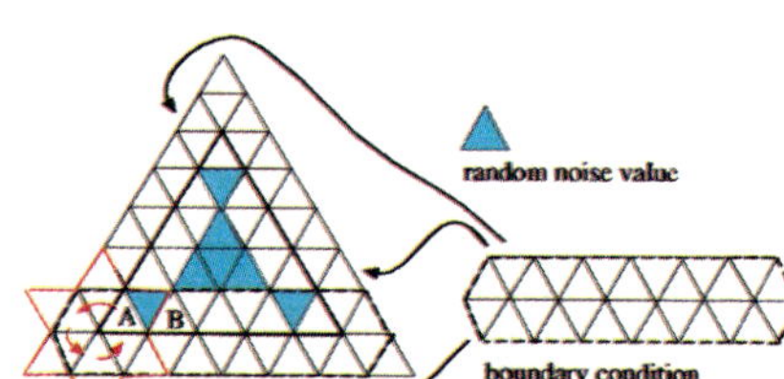


Figure 11: Triangular grid used for extending Worley's algorithm: Noise values that represent a given boundary condition along an edge are surrounded by a dashed line. Values which are the rotated copies of each other in order to maintain continuity constraints at a texture sample corner are indicated in pink.

For our pattern-based texturing application, we need to generate Worley triangles that obey specified boundary conditions along edges. More precisely, we want to be able to control the texture in the neighborhood of each triangle edge in order to ensure continuity between samples. Our solution is similar to the approach suggested in [17], and also to what we have described above for real image editing: we first generate the 'rectangular regions' representing each oriented edge. This rectangular region is implemented here by a two row grid storing the noise points that can influence the border neighborhood, on both parts of the boundary. Once again, we derive the complementary condition by rotating the rectangle that defines a boundary condition by 180°. Then, we duplicate the noise values into the adequate part of the grid, for each texture triangle that must obey this specific condition. Finally, the noise values of the inner unconstrained region of each triangle are chosen at random.

Particular attention must be paid to the achievement of texture continuity near texture sample corners. Two edges meet there, and the noise values they give to the texture triangle should thus be the same. As explained in Section 2.2, the solution is to define a texture with a given value and a zero gradient at these vertices. In terms of the algorithm above, this can be done by copying a rotated version of a given noise value into all the grid cells that surround a given vertex. In a naive implementation, this operation has to be done within two ranks of cells surrounding the corner (figured in pink), since the noise values in the second rank of cells may influence the texture gradient there. A trick for eliminating some possible visual artifacts due to symmetry is to restrict the range of possible noise point values in cells A and B (see Figure 11) so that the Voronoï region generated by the point in the blue cell between them will not intersect the edge of the texture sample. Then, this noise point value will have no influence on the texture at the vertex, enabling a (constrained) random choice for this cell. In Figure 11, all the noise points in the blue triangles can be chosen at random without spoiling boundary conditions.

Two examples of texture sample sets, and the resulting images they produce when mapped on a surface, are depicted in Figure 12.

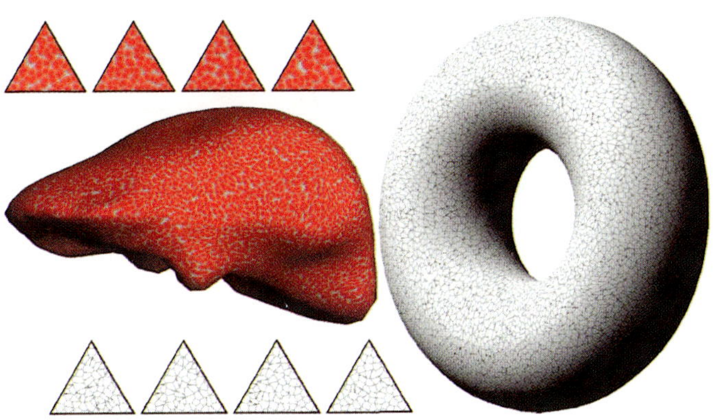

Figure 12: Sets of texture samples generated by our extension of Worley's synthesis technique, and the images produced by non-periodically mapping them onto a surface. *Left:* A human liver. *Right:* A china torus.

### 4.3 Extending Perlin's synthesis technique

Fractal noise based on Perlin's basis function [16] is a self-similar stochastic noise that has become a standard for generating objects that look like wood, marble, or the surface aspect of rock. One of its main features is to ensure continuity of both noise values and gradient at any point of an image (or of a volume, when the method is used in 3D, e.g. to figure smoke).

To adapt it to our texturing methodology, we first have to be able to generate the basis function on 2D equilateral triangles. Since Perlin's standard model is defined on a quadrangular grid, we modify the algorithm in the following way:

1. We first generate a pseudo-periodic noise function on a regular grid that tiles the equilateral triangle into sub-triangles (see Figure 13). This requires two steps:

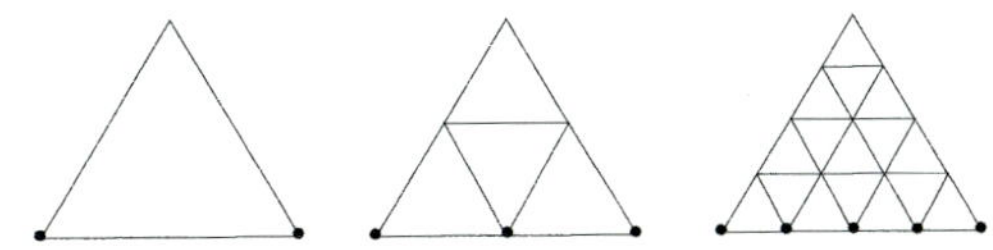

Figure 13: Triangular grids used for generating the noise function at different scales. The noise values that need to be fixed for ensuring boundary conditions are shown in bold.

   - as for textures based on Perlin's technique, we randomly associate a plane to each grid node, defined by its elevation above the node and by its normal vector;
   - we define the noise at any point inside the triangle as the barycentric interpolation of the distances to the three planes that are associated to the vertices of the small triangular cell where the point lies.

2. We define the final noise value at a pixel as the sum of instances of the pseudo-periodic noise function defined above, applied at different scales thanks to recursive subdivision of the triangular mesh, with a scaling factor that is the equal to the scale. This gives the fractal aspect to the noise.

3. The value obtained is used as usual as a seed or a perturbation to define the texture value at the pixel.

Modifying this algorithm to ensure a set of given boundary conditions around each triangle is easy: we just have to model a boundary condition as the set of noise values that control the texture values and derivatives along an edge. These values are those indicated in bold in Figure 13. We then duplicate these boundary values onto the adequate side of the grid, for all the texture samples that have to obey this specific boundary condition. Ensuring continuity at the three corners of texture sample is done as usual by giving the same mean value and zero gradient to the texture there, i.e., using specific noise values at each vertex. As in original Perlin's algorithm, all random values are precomputed in a (small) hash table, and no copy is done: instead we compute at any location which index in the random table should be accessed. To define the same control value at the vertices of two edges, one just has to ensure that the same index is produced, and rotate the built random normal vector on the fly (because adjacent triangles do not use the same frame).

Three examples of texture sample sets and the resulting images they produce are depicted in Figure 14. Note that computing procedural textures on triangular domains while ensuring continuity constraints can also be used on the fly for other kinds of applications. For instance, we have used an algorithm close from above for generating at rendering time a displacement texture modeling the crust of an evolving lava-flow without having to parameterize the flow surface [18].

## 5 Conclusions & Future Work

We have presented a general framework, based on triangular texture tiles, for texturing an arbitrary surface at low rendering time and memory cost. Our method has been designed for covering the surface with an homogeneous non-periodic texture such as those that can be found on many natural objects. The main features of our approach are the following: the texture can be applied at any scale with respect to the object geometry, and whatever the quality of the geometric mesh; no singularity is generated whatever the surface topology, and distortions are minimized. Moreover, using the method demands little user work, by avoiding redundancies. We describe how to use hand-drawing and real images, and we provide two automatic texture synthesis methods that adapt Perlin's and Worley's algorithms to a triangular domain. Adapting other

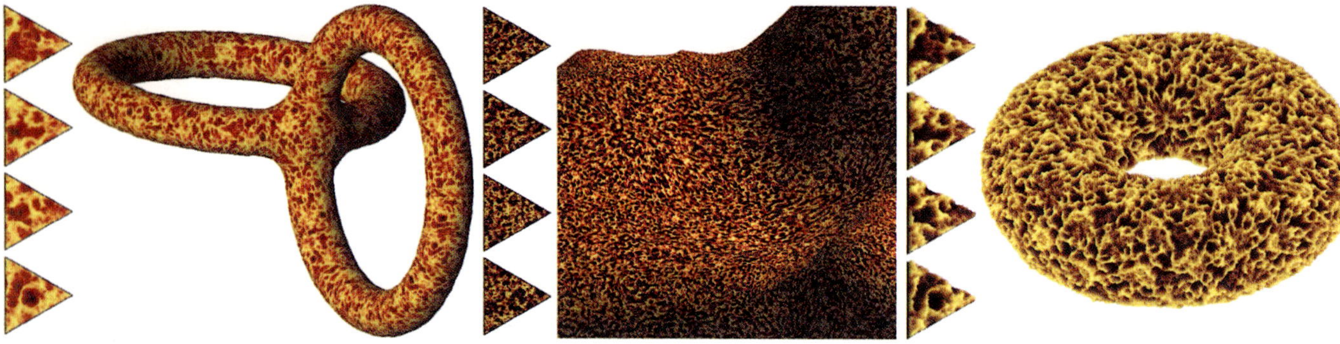

Figure 14: Three sets of texture samples generated by our extension of Perlin's synthesis technique, and the images produced by mapping them onto a surface. In the image on the right, Perlin's texture is used as displacement map, encoded with an OpenGL implementation of volumetric textures [13].

texture synthesis techniques in the same way, such as those based on a pyramidal analysis of real textures [9, 2] should be easy, as filtering kernels and pyramidal constructions can directly be 'translated' to triangular grids. Lastly, our framework is compatible with real-time applications, since the result of the texturing can be represented using classical geometric object formats.

Maintaining $C^1$ continuity of the texture across the surface has been achieved by building texture samples which obey specific boundary conditions, and whose border is mapped exactly onto the geodesic curves that tile the surface onto texture patches. In the current implementation, we ensure the second constraint by splitting the geometric triangles that intersect a geodesic, in order to have enough points for locally controlling the mapping. This is not a problem when large scale texture triangles are used since this splitting process will not greatly increase the number of triangles to render. However, in the case of almost flat surfaces built with a few large triangles, and that need being textured at a small scale, the tiling of the geometry may yield a high increase of rendering time. A solution would be to use a level of details approach for defining texture samples: large samples containing very small patterns would be recursively created by assembling smaller ones. Then, the former would be mapped onto a larger scale texture mesh defined on the surface, which would not split the geometry excessively. Conversely, this would provide a solution to correctly map geometric areas that are smaller than the initial sample size (such as handles or legs), without having to decrease the sample size elsewhere on the surface.

Our future work also includes the introduction of user-controlled pattern anisotropy, which is an important feature of many natural textures. Using anisotropic patterns directly in the scheme we have presented would not be a good idea, since there is no way to ensure continuity of characteristic directions between texture patches. Our idea is rather to rely on the texture mesh itself, to model the kind of anisotropy that corresponds to the stretching of an isotropic pattern: A user-defined tensor field would be used for locally specifying the amount and direction of desired anisotropy all over the surface. This field would be used to influence the generation of texture mesh control points and produce an anisotropic distribution (in the same spirit, Turk suggests in [20] to use the surface curvature). Finally, mapping the usual isotropic texture samples onto this texture mesh would result into adequately deformed patterns, with continuous directional features.

## Acknowledgments

We wish to thank Greg Turk for providing his retiling code and Alexandre Meyer for adapting his volumetric textures to our framework. Thanks to David Bourguignon for creating the sponge texture samples, to Brian Wyvill and Georges Drettakis for rereading this paper, and to Jean-Dominique Gascuel for his help in video editing.

## References

[1] Chakib Bennis, Jean-Marc Vézien, Gérard Iglésias, and André Gagalowicz. Piecewise surface flattening for non-distorted texture mapping. In Thomas W. Sederberg, editor, *Computer Graphics (SIGGRAPH 91 Proceedings)*, volume 25, pages 237–246, July 1991.

[2] Jeremy S. De Bonet. Multiresolution sampling procedure for analysis and synthesis of texture images. In Turner Whitted, editor, *SIGGRAPH 97 Conference Proceedings*, pages 361–368. ACM SIGGRAPH, Addison Wesley, August 1997.

[3] H. S. M. Coxeter, M. Emmer, R. Penrose, and M. L. Teuber, editors. *M. C. Escher: Art and Science*. North Holland, Amsterdam, 1986.

[4] Matthias Eck, Tony DeRose, Tom Duchamp, Hugues Hoppe, Michael Lounsbery, and Werner Stuetzle. Multiresolution analysis of arbitrary meshes. In Robert Cook, editor, *SIGGRAPH 95 Conference Proceedings*, pages 173–182. ACM SIGGRAPH, Addison Wesley, August 1995.

[5] M.c. Escher biography and annotated gallery. http://www.erols.com/ziring/escher_gal.htm.

[6] Andrews Glassner. Andrew Glassner's notebook: Penrose tiling. *IEEE Computer Graphics and Applications*, 18(4):78–86, July/August 1998.

[7] B. Grünbaum and G.C. Shephard, editors. *Tilings and Patterns*. Freeman, New York, 1986.

[8] Pat Hanrahan and Paul E. Haeberli. Direct WYSIWYG painting and texturing on 3D shapes. In Forest Baskett, editor, *Computer Graphics (SIGGRAPH 90 Proceedings)*, volume 24, pages 215–223, August 1990.

[9] David J. Heeger and James R. Bergen. Pyramid-based texture analysis/synthesis. In Robert Cook, editor, *SIGGRAPH 95 Conference Proceedings*, pages 229–238. ACM SIGGRAPH, Addison Wesley, August 1995.

[10] Aaron Lee, Wim Sweldens, Peter Schröder, Lawrence Cowsar, and David Dobkin. MAPS: Multiresolution adaptive parametrization of surfaces. In Michael Cohen, editor, *SIGGRAPH 98 Conference Proceedings*, pages 95–104. ACM SIGGRAPH, Addison Wesley, July 1998.

[11] Bruno Lévy and Jean-Laurent Mallet. Non-distorted texture mapping for sheared triangulated meshes. In Michael Cohen, editor, *SIGGRAPH 98 Conference Proceedings*, pages 343–352. ACM SIGGRAPH, Addison Wesley, July 1998.

[12] Jérôme Maillot, Hussein Yahia, and Anne Verroust. Interactive texture mapping. In James T. Kajiya, editor, *Computer Graphics (SIGGRAPH 93 Proceedings)*, volume 27, pages 27–34, August 1993.

[13] Alexandre Meyer and Fabrice Neyret. Interactive volumetric textures. In G. Drettakis and N. Max, editors, *Rendering Techniques'98, Eurographics Rendering Workshop*, pages 157–168. Eurographics, Springer Wein, July 1998.

[14] Hans Køhling Pedersen. Decorating implicit surfaces. In Robert Cook, editor, *SIGGRAPH 95 Conference Proceedings*, pages 291–300. ACM SIGGRAPH, Addison Wesley, August 1995.

[15] Hans Køhling Pedersen. A framework for interactive texturing operations on curved surfaces. In Holly Rushmeier, editor, *SIGGRAPH 96 Conference Proceedings*, pages 295–302. ACM SIGGRAPH, Addison Wesley, August 1996.

[16] Ken Perlin. An image synthesizer. In B. A. Barsky, editor, *Computer Graphics (SIGGRAPH 85 Proceedings)*, volume 19, pages 287–296, July 1985.

[17] Jos Stam. Aperiodic texture mapping. Technical Report R046, European Research Consortium for Informatics and Mathematics (ERCIM), January 1997. http://www.ercim.org/publication/technical_reports/046-abstract.html.

[18] Dan Stora, Pierrer-Olivier Agliati, Marie-Paule Cani, Fabrice Neyret, and Jean-Dominique Gascuel. Animating lava flows. In *Graphics Interface 99*, June 1999.

[19] Greg Turk. Generating textures for arbitrary surfaces using reaction-diffusion. In Thomas W. Sederberg, editor, *Computer Graphics (SIGGRAPH 91 Proceedings)*, volume 25, pages 289–298, July 1991.

[20] Greg Turk. Re-tiling polygonal surfaces. In Edwin E. Catmull, editor, *Computer Graphics (SIGGRAPH 92 Proceedings)*, volume 26, pages 55–64, July 1992.

[21] Andrew Witkin and Michael Kass. Reaction-diffusion textures. In Thomas W. Sederberg, editor, *Computer Graphics (SIGGRAPH 91 Proceedings)*, volume 25, pages 299–308, July 1991.

[22] Steven P. Worley. A cellular texturing basis function. In Holly Rushmeier, editor, *SIGGRAPH 96 Conference Proceedings*, pages 291–294. ACM SIGGRAPH, Addison Wesley, August 1996.

# Feline: Fast Elliptical Lines for Anisotropic Texture Mapping

Joel McCormack*, Ronald Perry†, Keith I. Farkas*, and Norman P. Jouppi*

Compaq Computer Corporation's Western Research Laboratory and Mitsubishi Electric Research Laboratory

## Abstract

Texture mapping using trilinearly filtered mip-mapped data is efficient and looks much better than point-sampled or bilinearly filtered data. But trilinear filtering represents the projection of a pixel filter footprint from screen space into texture space as a square, when in reality the footprint may be long and narrow. Consequently, trilinear filtering severely blurs images on surfaces angled obliquely away from the viewer.

This paper describes a new texture filtering technique called Feline (for Fast Elliptical Lines). Like other recent hardware anisotropic filtering algorithms, Feline uses an underlying space-invariant (isotropic) filter with mip-mapped data, and so can be built on top of an existing trilinear filtering engine. To texture a pixel, it uses this space-invariant filter at several points along a line in texture space, and combines the results. With a modest increase in implementation complexity over earlier techniques, Feline more accurately matches the desired projection of the pixel filter in texture space, resulting in images with fewer aliasing artifacts. Feline's visual quality compares well against Elliptical Weighted Average, the best software anisotropic texture filtering algorithm known to date, but Feline requires much less setup computation and far fewer cycles for texel fetches. Finally, since it uses standard mip-maps, Feline requires minimal extensions to standard 3D interfaces like OpenGL.

**CR Categories and Subject Descriptors:** I.3.1 [Computer Graphics]: Hardware Architecture – Graphics processors; I.3.7 [Computer Graphics]: Three-dimensional Graphics and Realism – Color, shading, shadowing, and texture

**Additional Keywords:** texture mapping, anisotropic filtering, space-variant filtering

## 1 INTRODUCTION

Ideally, computing a textured value for a pixel involves perspective projecting a filter from screen space (indexed by $x$ and $y$ coordinates) into texture space (indexed by $u$ and $v$ coordinates), then combining this with a reconstruction filter to create a unified filter in texture space. Each texel inside the unified filter's footprint is weighted according to the unified filter's corresponding value in screen space, the weighted samples are accumulated, and the sum is divided by the filter's volume in texture space. Figure 1, inspired by Lansdale [8], gives an intuitive view of this process. A pixel filter is a "window" onto a portion of the texture map; the window's opacity at each point corresponds to the filter's weight. The grid represents a texture map; the shaded rectangle the screen. We view an elliptical portion of the texture map through a round pixel filter. (In degenerate cases, a circle projects to an arbitrary conic section, but for our purposes an ellipse suffices.)

Figure 2 shows a typical pixel filter in screen space—a Gaussian with weighting $e^{-\alpha\,(x^2 + y^2)}$, truncated to zero beyond a radius of one pixel, and with an $\alpha$ of 2. Tick marks on the $x$ and $y$ axes are at one pixel intervals; the $x$-$y$ grid is at $1/10$ pixel intervals. Figure 3 shows an exemplary perspective projection of this filter into texture space, where the tick marks on the $u$ and $v$ axes are spaced at one texel intervals, and the grid is at ½ texel intervals. We normalize all texture filter volumes to one to allow direct comparisons between graphs, then highly exaggerate the vertical axis. Note the distorted filter profile: each contour line is an ellipse, but the ellipses representing lower sample weights are increasingly offset from the filter center.

Mapping the texel positions in Figure 3 back into pixel positions in Figure 2 (let alone creating a unified filter), so that relative weights can then be applied to the texel values, is a gruesome affair. Rather than using a perspective projection, Heckbert and Greene [4][6] suggest using a locally parallel (affine) projection,

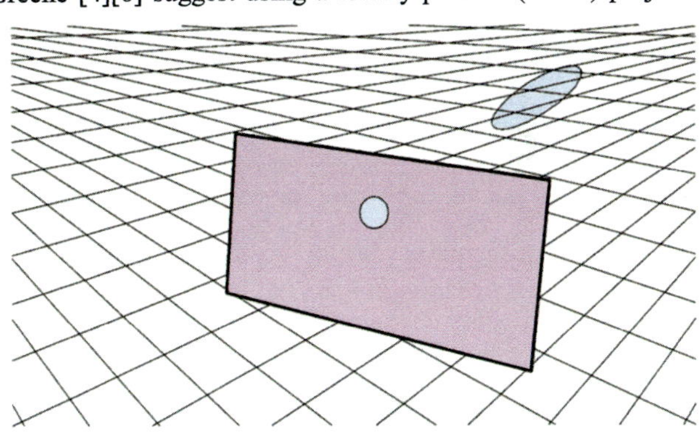

Figure 1: Viewing an elliptical texture area through a circular pixel window.

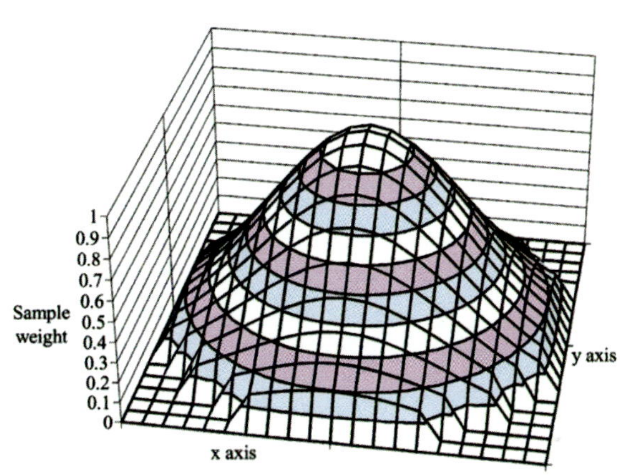


Figure 2: A circular Gaussian filter in screen space.

* Compaq Computer Corporation, Western Research Laboratory, 250 University Avenue, Palo Alto, CA 94301. [Joel.McCormack, Keith.Farkas, Norm.Jouppi]@compaq.com.

† Mitsubishi Electric Research Laboratories, Inc., Cambridge Research Center, 201 Broadway, Cambridge, MA 02139. perry@merl.com.

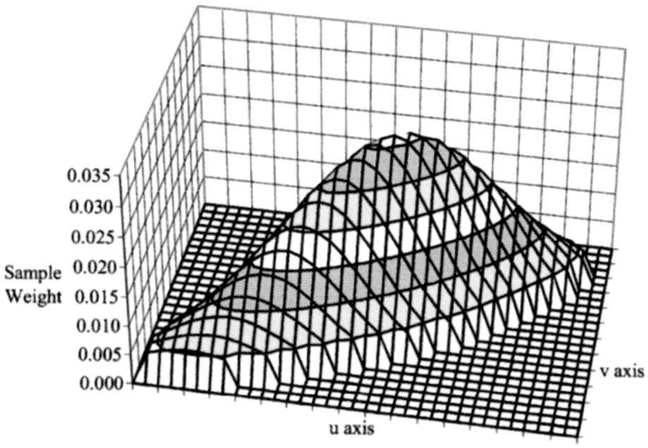


Figure 3: A perspective projection of a Gaussian filter into texture space.

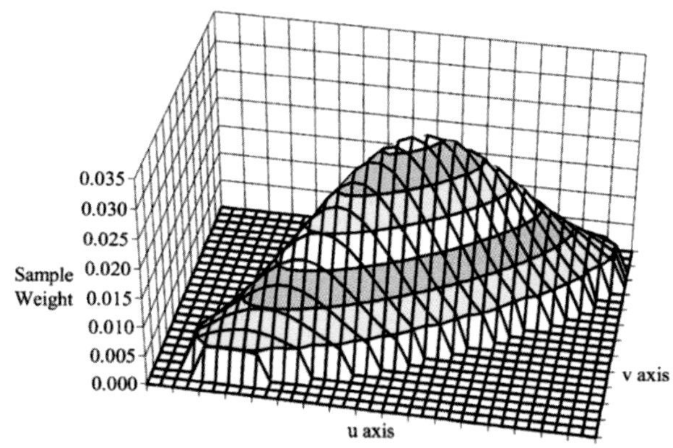


Figure 4: An affine projection of a Gaussian filter into texture space.

as shown in Figure 4. This drastically simplifies computing the footprint and weights of the projected filter. This simplification is visually insignificant. The modest weight differences between Figure 3 and Figure 4 are not detectable in images, and to get the distortion shown in Figure 3 requires a nearly edge-on view of the surface being texture mapped, in which all detail is lost anyway.

Our algorithm approximates the elliptical filter shown in Figure 4 by performing several isotropic (e.g. trilinear, Gaussian) filtering operations, called *probes*, along the major axis of the ellipse. In comparison to other hardware anisotropic filtering methods, Feline better approximates the elliptical filter by more accurately determining the length of the line along which probes should be placed, spacing probes at better intervals, widening probes under certain conditions, and Gaussian weighting the probe results. A more sophisticated algorithm, "Table Feline," described in [10], also better approximates the slope and length of the ellipse's major and minor axes. Both versions of Feline require just a few additional computations over previous algorithms.

In this paper, we first discuss previous work, including the best efficient software technique, and shortcomings of recent hardware anisotropic filtering techniques. We next describe the desired computations for using several probes along a line, show how to make these computations amenable to hardware, and discuss techniques to reduce the number of probes per pixel. Finally, we present several pictures comparing the various methods of filtering. More details about Feline can be found in [10].

## 2 PREVIOUS WORK

We first describe Elliptical Weighted Average (EWA), the most efficient direct convolution method known for computing a textured pixel. This provides a quality benchmark against which to compare other techniques. (We do not describe previous software efforts like [2] and [3], as we feel that EWA either supersedes these algorithms, or that they are so slow as to be in a different class.) We discuss trilinear filtering, which is popular but blurry. We delve more deeply into Texram, a chip that performs anisotropic filtering by repeated applications of an isotropic filter along a line, and discuss its weaknesses. We briefly mention other algorithms apparently similar to Texram, but which are not described in sufficient detail to analyze.

### 2.1 Elliptical Weighted Average

Paul Heckbert's and Ned Greene's Elliptical Weighted Average (EWA) algorithm [4][6] exactly computes the size, shape, and orientation of an elliptical filter like the one shown in Figure 4. If the center of the filter in texture space is translated to (0, 0), then the filter in texture space can be characterized as:

$$d^2(u, v) = Au^2 + Buv + Cv^2$$

The value $d^2$ represents the distance squared from the center of the pixel when the texel position is mapped back into screen space. Thus, $d^2$ can index a table of weights that is unrelated to the affine projection, but depends only upon the pixel filter.

EWA determines $d^2$ for each texel in or near the elliptical footprint. Texels inside the footprint ($d^2 \leq 1$) are sampled, weighted, and accumulated. The result is divided by the sum of the weights, which is the elliptical filter's volume in texture space.

Given the partial derivatives $\partial u/\partial x$, $\partial v/\partial x$, $\partial u/\partial y$, and $\partial v/\partial y$, which represent the rates of change of $u$ and $v$ in texture space relative to changes in $x$ and $y$ in screen space, the biquadratic coefficients for computing $d^2$ are:

$$\begin{aligned}
A_{nn} &= (\partial v/\partial x)^2 + (\partial v/\partial y)^2; \\
B_{nn} &= -2 * (\partial u/\partial x * \partial v/\partial x + \partial u/\partial y * \partial v/\partial y); \\
C_{nn} &= (\partial u/\partial x)^2 + (\partial u/\partial y)^2; \\
F &= A_{nn} * C_{nn} - B_{nn}^2/4; \\
A &= A_{nn}/F; \\
B &= B_{nn}/F; \\
C &= C_{nn}/F;
\end{aligned}$$

Pixels that map to a large area in texture space can be handled by using mip-maps [12], where each level of a mip-map is ½ the height and width of the previous level. Heckbert [6] suggests sampling from a single mip-map level in which the minor radius is between 1.5 and 3 texels, though he later implemented unpublished code in which the minor radius is between 2 and 4 texels, in order to avoid subtle artifacts.

Even using mip-maps, highly eccentric ellipses may encompass an unacceptably large area. This area can be limited by computing the ratio of the major radius to the minor radius, and if this ratio is too large, widening the minor axis of the ellipse and rederiving the coefficients $A$, $B$, and $C$. The combination of mip-maps and ellipse widening allows EWA to compute a textured pixel with a constant time bound.

Choosing a mip-map level and testing for very eccentric ellipses requires computing the major and minor radii of the ellipse:

$$\begin{aligned}
root &= \mathrm{sqrt}((A - C)^2 + B^2); \\
A' &= (A + C - root)/2; \\
C' &= (A + C + root)/2; \\
majorRadius &= \mathrm{sqrt}(1/A'); \\
minorRadius &= \mathrm{sqrt}(1/C');
\end{aligned}$$

Widening an ellipse requires seven multiplies, a square root, an inverse root, and a divide. These setup computations, plus logic to visit only texels in or near the ellipse and compute $d^2$, have thus far precluded hardware implementation of EWA.

The only complaint that can be leveled against EWA's visual quality is its choice of a Gaussian filter. Other filters produce sharper images without introducing more aliasing artifacts (see Wolberg [13] for an excellent discussion). However, these filters have a radius of two or three pixels, which increases the work required to compute a textured pixel by a factor of four or nine. And as Lansdale [8] points out, none of these filters are as mathematically tractable as the Gaussian for unifying the reconstruction filter and projected pixel filter (warped prefilter).

## 2.2 Trilinear Filtering

Trilinear filtering emphasizes simplicity and efficiency at the cost of visual quality. Rather than computing the shape of the projected filter footprint, it uses a square filter in texture space. By blending two 2 x 2 bilinear filters from adjacent mip-map levels, trilinear filtering approximates a circular filter of an arbitrary size. Figure 5 shows a trilinear filter that (poorly) approximates the EWA filter shown in Figure 4. The axis tick marks are spaced one texel apart, while the grid is spaced at ½ texel intervals. Strictly speaking, because it blends two 2 x 2 bilinear filtering operations, a trilinear filter samples a square area of $2^n \times 2^n$ texels. However, most of the filter volume resides inside a circle with the nominal filter radius. In the 2D pictures below, we thus show a trilinear filter's footprint as a circle of the nominal radius.

A trilinear filter blurs or aliases textures applied to surfaces that are obliquely angled away from the viewer. These artifacts arise because the fixed shape of the trilinear filter poorly matches the desired filter footprint, and so the trilinear filter samples data outside the ellipse, doesn't sample data inside the ellipse, or both.

## 2.3 Texram

Texram [11] provides higher visual quality than trilinear filtering with less complexity than EWA. Texram uses a series of trilinear filter probes along a line that approximates the length and slope of the major axis of EWA's elliptical footprint.

The Texram authors considered computation of the ellipse parameters too costly for hardware, and so substituted simplified approximations. These approximations underestimate the length of the major axis of the ellipse, introducing aliasing; overestimate the length of the minor axis, introducing blurring; and deviate from the slope of the major axis, introducing yet more blurring

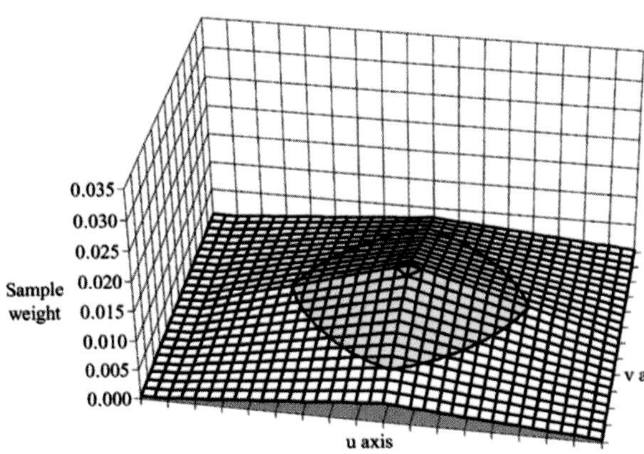


Figure 5: A trilinear filter approximation to Figure 4.

and aliasing. Nonetheless, with the exception of environment mapping, these errors are visually insignificant under typical perspective projections, as discussed further in Section 3.2 below.

Texram has other problems that manifest themselves as aliasing artifacts. Its sampling line is usually much shorter than the ellipse, and the trilinear probes can be spaced too far apart. Texram always uses $2^n$ equally weighted probes, which causes poor high-frequency rejection along the major axis. These problems make Texram's visual quality noticeably inferior to EWA.

Texram uses the four partial derivatives to create two vectors in texture space: $(\partial u/\partial x, \partial v/\partial x)$ and $(\partial u/\partial y, \partial v/\partial y)$. The authors claim to sample roughly the area inside the parallelogram formed by these two vectors, by probing along a line that has the length and slope of the longer of the two vectors. This line can deviate from the slope of the major axis of EWA's elliptical filter by as much as 45°. This is not as bad as it sounds. The largest angular errors are associated with nearly circular filters, which are relatively insensitive to such errors in orientation.

Texram's sampling line can be shorter than the true ellipse's major axis by nearly a factor of four. One factor of two comes from Texram's use of the length of the longer vector as the length of the sample line. Note that if orthogonal vectors are plugged into the ellipse equations in Section 2.1 above, the major radius is the length of the longer vector, and so the ellipse's major diameter is actually *twice* the length of this vector. Texram's error is apparently due to an older paper by Paul Heckbert [5], in which he suggested using a filter diameter that is really a filter radius.

Another factor of two comes from non-orthogonal vectors. If the two vectors are nearly parallel and equal in length, the elliptical footprint is very narrow and has a major radius nearly twice the length of either vector. Again, this is not as bad as it sounds: typical perspective distortions yield a true ellipse radius that is no larger than about 7% of the longer vector.

Texram approximates the radius of the minor axis of the ellipse by choosing the shortest of the two parallelogram side vectors and the two parallelogram diagonals $(\partial u/\partial x + \partial u/\partial y, \partial v/\partial x + \partial v/\partial y)$ and $(\partial u/\partial x - \partial u/\partial y, \partial v/\partial x - \partial v/\partial y)$. If the side vectors are nearly parallel and the shorter is half the length of the longer, this approximation can be too wide by an arbitrarily large factor.

One of the Texram authors was unsure which values round up or down in the division that computes the number of probes. We have assumed values in the half-open interval [1.0 to 1.5) round to one probe, values in [1.5 to 3) round to two probes, values in [3 to 6) round to four probes, etc. Texram does not adjust the probe diameter when it rounds down (as discussed in Section 3.1 below), and so can space probes too far apart. Rather than the smoothly sloped "shield volcano" filter of EWA, Texram can use a "mountain range" filter with individual peaks. These peaks beat against repeated texture patterns to create phantom patterns.

Figure 6 shows an extreme example of these errors, in which $(\partial u/\partial x, \partial v/\partial x)$ is (13, 0) and $(\partial u/\partial y, \partial v/\partial y)$ is (12, 5). The area sampled by EWA is shown as the large heavily outlined ellipse, while Texram's trilinear filter footprints are shown as circles.

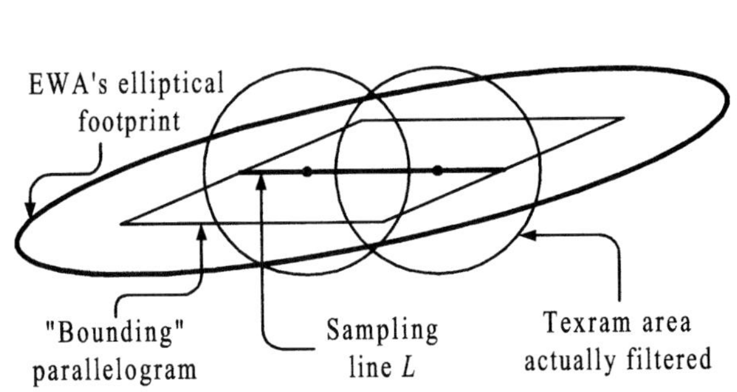


Figure 6: Texram area sampled vs. EWA.

## 2.4 Other Hardware Algorithms

Microsoft's Talisman [1] uses a filtering algorithm "in the spirit of" Texram. Few details are provided, but the aliasing evident in the examples suggest that they may have inherited some or all of Texram's problems. Evans & Sutherland holds U.S Patent #5,651,104 for using space-invariant probes along a line. The patent doesn't describe how to compute the probe line, but the diagrams imply a line that is at most a single pixel in length in screen space, which is once again so short that it will produce visible aliasing artifacts.

# 3 THE FELINE ALGORITHM

Like Texram, Feline uses several isotropic probes along a line $L$ to implement an anisotropic filter. However, we compute a more appropriate length for the sampling line $L$, allow the number of probes to be any integer, don't space probes too far apart, and weight the probes using a Gaussian curve. Feline achieves higher visual quality than Texram with little additional logic.

We first describe the desired computations to yield the locations and weights for a series of probe points along a line. We then describe "Simple Feline," which inherits Texram's approximations of the major and minor radii, after which it implements the desired computations in a fashion suitable for hardware. Under highly distorted perspective projections, which may occur when environment mapping, Simple Feline's major and minor radii approximations result in blurring. "Table Feline," described in [10], uses a table to compute the ellipse axes more accurately. We conclude with techniques to reduce the number of probes, without substantially decreasing Feline's image quality.

## 3.1 The Desired Computations

The combination of multiple isotropic probes should closely match the shape of the EWA filter. Thus, the probe points should occur along the major axis of the ellipse, the probes should be Gaussian weighted, and the probe filter width should be equal to the minor axis of the ellipse.

(Theoretically, the probe filter width should be related to the width of the ellipse at each probe position. We initially did not investigate this because we didn't know how to optimize the trade-off between the probe diameter, probe weighting, probe spacing, and the number of probes. After implementing constant diameter probes, we saw no reason to pursue variable diameter probes. The "improvement" was unlikely to be visible, but would significantly increase the number of probes due to closer spacing of small probes near the ends of the ellipse.)

We compute *majorRadius* and *minorRadius* as in Section 2.1 above, and then the angle *theta* of the major axis:

*theta* = arctan($B/(A-C)$)/2;
// If *theta* is angle of minor axis, make it angle of major axis
if ($A > C$) *theta* = *theta* + $\pi/2$;

If *minorRadius* is less than one pixel (that is, we are magnifying along the minor axis, and possibly along the major axis), the appropriate radii should be widened—there is no point in making several probes to nearly identical locations. Heckbert's Master's Thesis [6] elegantly addresses this situation. He unifies the reconstruction and warped prefilter by using the following computations for $A$ and $C$ rather than the ones shown in Section 2.1 above:

$$A_{nn} = (\partial v/\partial x)^2 + (\partial v/\partial y)^2 + 1;$$
$$C_{nn} = (\partial u/\partial x)^2 + (\partial u/\partial y)^2 + 1;$$

This makes the filter radius sqrt(2) texels for a one-to-one mapping of texels into pixels. (The radius approaches one texel as magnification increases.) While theoretically superior, this wider filter blurs more than the radius one trilinear filter conventionally used for unity mappings and magnifications. In order to match this convention, and to make hardware implementation feasible, we clamp the radii to a minimum of one texel:

*minorRadius* = max(*minorRadius*, 1);
*majorRadius* = max(*majorRadius*, 1);

The space-invariant probes along the major axis have a nominal radius equal to *minorRadius*, and so the distance between probes should also be *minorRadius*. The end probes should be set in from the ellipse by a distance of *minorRadius* as well, so that they don't sample data off the ends of the ellipse. Therefore, the number of probes we'd like (*fProbes*), and its integer counterpart (*iProbes*), are derived from the ratio of the major and minor radii of the ellipse as follows:

*fProbes* = 2*(*majorRadius*/*minorRadius*) – 1;
*iProbes* = floor(*fProbes* + 0.5);
if (*iProbes* > *maxProbes*) *iProbes* = *maxProbes*;

To guarantee that texturing a pixel occurs in a bounded time, we clamp *iProbes* to a programmable value *maxProbes*. An application can use a small degree of anisotropy at high frame rates, and then allow more eccentric filters for higher visual quality when motion ceases.

When *iProbes* > *fProbes*, because *fProbes* is rounded up, we space probes closer than their radius, rather than blur the image by sampling data off the ends of the ellipse.

When *iProbes* < *fProbes*, either because *fProbes* is rounded down, or because *iProbes* is clamped, the ellipse will be probed at fewer points than desired. Spacing the probes farther apart or shortening the line $L$ may cause aliasing artifacts. Instead, we blur the image by increasing *minorRadius* to widen the ellipse. Increasing *minorRadius* increases the level of detail and thus the nominal radius of the probe filter.

if (*iProbes* < *fProbes*)
    *minorRadius* = 2***majorRadius* / (*iProbes*+1);
*levelOfDetail* = $\log_2$(*minorRadius*);

Analogous to clamping *minorRadius* and *majorRadius*, we use a single probe in the smallest 1 x 1 mip-map, which reduces cycles spent displaying a repeated texture in the distance. We don't bother with a similar optimization for the 2 x 2 or 4 x 4 mip-maps. Consider the worst 2 x 2 case, in which a checkerboard is mirror repeated, and an ellipse with a *minorRadius* of 1 is centered at a corner of the texture map. Figure 7 depicts this situation, where the thin lines delineate texels, and the thick lines delineate the (repeated) 2 x 2 mip-map. The circle on the left uses one probe to compute an all-white pixel. The ellipse on the right uses 6 probes to compute the darkest possible pixel of 52% white, 48% shaded. (The white texels apparently inside the ends of the ellipse don't contribute to the pixel's color, as only texel centers are sampled.) Since longer ellipses converge so slowly to an intermediate color, we restrict ourselves to the trivial adjustment:

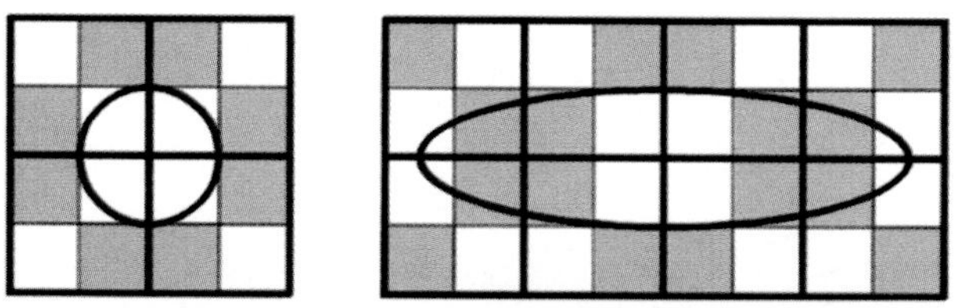

Figure 7: Ellipses in a 2 x 2 texture map oscillate around a blend of the two colors as eccentricity increases.

```
if (levelOfDetail > texture.maxLevelOfDetail) {
    levelOfDetail = texture.maxLevelOfDetail;
    iProbes = 1;
}
```

We compute the stepping vector ($\Delta u$, $\Delta v$), which is the distance between each probe point along the line, as follows:

```
lineLength = 2*(majorRadius – minorRadius);
Δu = cos(theta) * lineLength / (iProbes – 1);
Δv = sin(theta) * lineLength / (iProbes – 1);
```

(The stepping vector is irrelevant if *iProbes* is 1.) The sample points are distributed symmetrically about the midpoint ($u_m$, $v_m$) of the sampling line $L$ in the pattern:

$$(u_n, v_n) = (u_m, v_m) + n/2 * (\Delta u, \Delta v)$$

where $n = \pm1, \pm3, \pm5, \ldots$ if *iProbes* is even, as shown in Figure 8, and $n = 0, \pm2, \pm4, \ldots$ if *iProbes* is odd, as shown in Figure 9.

We apply a Gaussian weight to each probe $n$ by computing the distance squared of the probe from the center of the pixel filter in screen space, then exponentiating:

$$d = n/2 * \mathrm{sqrt}(\Delta u^2 + \Delta v^2) \,/\, majorRadius;$$
$$d^2 = n^2/4 * (\Delta u^2 + \Delta v^2) \,/\, majorRadius^2;$$
$$relativeWeight = e^{-\alpha * d^2};$$

Finally, we divide the accumulated probe results by the sum of all the weights applied.

## 3.2 Implementing Simple Feline

Simple Feline implements the above computations, except it uses Texram's ellipse axes approximations rather than computing the exact values. We use the longer of the two vectors ($\partial u/\partial x$, $\partial v/\partial x$) and ($\partial u/\partial y$, $\partial v/\partial y$) as the major radius, and the shortest of those and the two diagonals ($\partial u/\partial x + \partial u/\partial y$, $\partial v/\partial x + \partial v/\partial y$) and ($\partial u/\partial x - \partial u/\partial y$, $\partial v/\partial x - \partial v/\partial y$) as the minor radius length.

We were surprised that these approximations work essentially as well as the exact values under typical perspective projections. We discovered that the two vectors ($\partial u/\partial x$, $\partial v/\partial x$) and ($\partial u/\partial y$, $\partial v/\partial y$) are more or less orthogonal under typical perspective distortions. In the images shown below, the angle between the two are in the range 90° ± 30°, and the most extreme angles occur with very unequal vector lengths. The simple approximations are tolerably close to the true values under these conditions.

We use a two-part linear approximation for the vector length square root. Without loss of generality, for a vector ($a$, $b$) assume that $a, b > 0$ and $a > b$. The following function is within ±1.2% of the true length $\mathrm{sqrt}(a^2 + b^2)$:

```
if (b < 3a/8) return a + 5b/32
else return 109a/128 + 35b/64
```

We do not compute the stepping vector with trigonometric functions, but instead scale the longer vector directly. Call the longer vector components (*majorU*, *majorV*). Either this vector describes *majorRadius*, or else *iProbes* is one and the stepping vector is irrelevant. By substituting *majorU*/*majorRadius* for cosine, and *majorV*/*majorRadius* for sine, we get:

```
r = minorRadius / majorRadius;
i = oneOverNMinusOneTable[iProbes];
Δu = 2*(majorU – majorU*r) * i;
Δv = 2*(majorV – majorV*r) * i;
```

Finally, we use a triangularish two-dimensional weight table to avoid computing and exponentiating $d^2$. We use the smaller of *fProbes* truncated to a couple fractional bits, or *iProbes*, as the weight table's row index, so that each row of weights applies to a small range of ellipses. The column index is floor((abs($n$)+1)/2). By dividing each of the relative weights in a row by the sum of the weights for that row, the weights in each row sum to 1. Consequently, we need not normalize the final accumulated result. Note that if *iProbes* is odd, the $W_0$ entry in a row should count half as much as the other entries when computing the sum: it is used once, while the other weights are used twice.

Most of the computations specific to Feline can use group scaled numbers with a precision of 8 bits. (The center point ($u_m$, $v_m$) must still be computed with high precision, of course.) Small errors cause sampling along a line at a slightly different angle, and at intervals that are slightly smaller or larger than desired. These arithmetic errors are negligible compared to the inaccuracies caused by the gross approximations to the ellipse axes.

## 3.3 Increasing Efficiency

We investigated how far we could "push the envelope" to reduce the number of probes by shortening and widening the ellipse, and by spreading probe points farther apart than their radius.

We can shorten the ellipse using a *lengthFactor* <= 1:

```
majorRadius = max(majorRadius * lengthFactor,
                  minorRadius);
majorU *= lengthFactor;
majorV *= lengthFactor;
```

The code in Section 3.1 proportionately widens an ellipse more when rounding down a small value of *fProbes* than a large one. We can instead compute *iProbes* so that for all values of *fProbes*, we widen the ellipse to at most a *blurFactor* times the minor radius. We also allow stretching the distance between probe positions by up to *aliasFactor* times the probe filter radius:

```
f = 1 / (blurFactor * aliasFactor);
iProbes = ceiling(f * 2 * (majorRadius/minorRadius)) – 1;
```

If *iProbes* is not clamped to *maxProbes*, we blur (widen the ellipse) by increasing *minorRadius* by up to *blurFactor*:

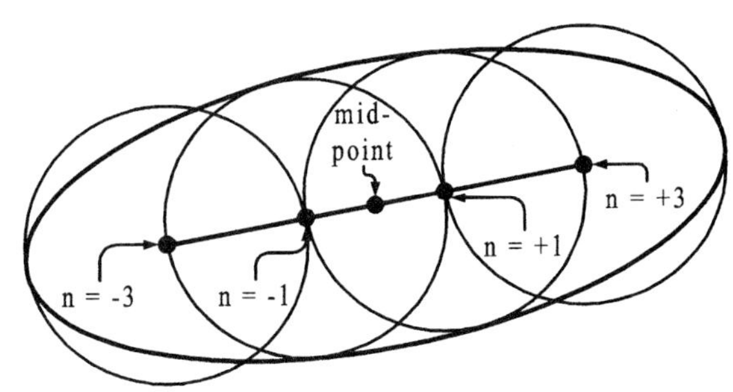


Figure 8: Positioning an even number of probes.

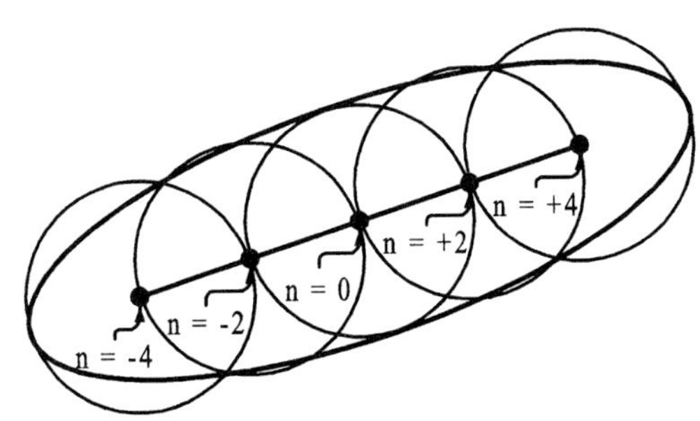


Figure 9: Positioning an odd number of probes.

*minorRadius* = min(2**majorRadius* / (*iProbes*+1), *minorRadius* * *blurFactor*)

The computations of $\Delta u$ and $\Delta v$ automatically make up any remaining difference between *iProbes* and *fProbes* by increasing probe spacing. If *iProbes* is clamped, we blur (in excess of *blurFactor*) to the point where the computations of $\Delta u$ and $\Delta v$ will increase probe spacing by *aliasFactor*:

*minorRadius* = 2 * *majorRadius* / ((*iProbes*+1) * *aliasFactor*);

We chose two sets of parameter values empirically. The "high-quality" set (*lengthFactor* 0.97, *blurFactor* 1.16, *aliasFactor* 1.15) reduces the number of probes by 24% with almost no degradation of image quality, compared to the constant rounding of Section 3.1. The "high-efficiency" set (*lengthFactor* 0.97, *blurFactor* 1.31, *aliasFactor* 1.36) uses the same number of probes as Texram to provide images that contain more artifacts than the "high quality" setting, but are nonetheless much better than Texram.

The high-efficiency *aliasFactor* creates large valleys between the peaks of a trilinear filter, especially along diagonal probe lines. We obtained slightly better images by changing the probe filter from a bilinear filter on each of the two adjacent mip-map levels to a Gaussian filter truncated to a 2 x 2 square. We then linearly combine the two Gaussian results using the fractional bits of the level of detail. (This also makes single-probe magnifications look better.) A hardware trilinear filter tree is easily adapted to implement Gaussian rather than bilinear weightings [9]. Four copies of a small one-dimensional table map the fractional bits of $u$ and $v$ on each of the two mip-maps to Gaussian weights.

## 4 COMPARISONS WITH PREVIOUS WORK

Figure 10 through Figure 14 show various algorithms generating a pattern of curved lines. Figure 15 through Figure 18 show a floor of bricks, and Figure 19 through Figure 22 show magnified texture-mapped text. Texram images use the original algorithm; correcting the errors described in Section 2.3 above results in many more probes *and* degrades visual quality! Aliasing artifacts mostly remain, and images significantly blur due to the equal weighting of probes. Simple Feline images use parameters as described in Section 3.3 above, and a mip-mapped Gaussian for the probe filter. Mip-mapped EWA samples from a mip-map level where the minor radius is between 1.5 and 3 texels; this looks identical to a radius between 2 and 4, but samples about half as many texels. Trilinear, Texram, and Feline images use a radius 3 Lanczos filter to create mip-maps. EWA images use a box filter: the Lanczos filter causes "bluriness banding" artifacts when EWA jumps from using a large ellipse in one mip-map to using a small ellipse in the next.higher mip-map.

Feline with high-quality parameters generates images comparable to EWA, but with slightly stronger Moiré patterns. The only exception occurs if a box filter is used to create mip-maps for textures like checkerboards. Because the base texture and all its

Figure 10: Trilinear paints curved lines with blurring.

Figure 12: Texram paints curved lines with strong Moiré artifacts.

Figure 11: "High-efficiency" Simple Feline paints curved lines with fewer artifacts.

Figure 13: "High-quality" Simple Feline paints curved lines with few artifacts.

Figure 14: Mip-mapped EWA paints curved lines with few artifacts.

mip-maps then contain illegally high frequencies that Feline's relatively narrow filter cannot remove, Feline displays much stronger Moiré artifacts than EWA. Using a better filter, such as the Lanczos, to create the mip-maps makes Feline display *fewer* artifacts than EWA—Feline is more likely to use filtered mip-mapped data, rather than the unfiltered base texture.

Both sets of Feline images are much sharper, and exhibit far fewer Moiré artifacts, than those generated by trilinear filtering. Though not shown here, we note that high-efficiency Feline and Texram are both subject to "probe banding" on repeated textures: some images show a visible line where the number of probes increases from one value to another.

Texram images sometimes seem a little sharper than Feline images, but then, aliased images always seem sharper than antialiased images. Repeated texture patterns amplify Texram's aliasing problems to create strong Moiré patterns, as shown in the curved lines and bricks images. These patterns are even more disturbing in moving images, where they shimmer across the surface. Texram's aliasing is more subtle in non-repeated textures, such as text. Comparing the high-efficiency Feline images to Texram is especially interesting: both use the same number of probes, but the Feline images exhibit far fewer artifacts. Experiments show that Feline's quality is due to the use of a Gaussian probe filter, the Gaussian weighting of probe results, and the end-to-end coverage of the ellipse.

Higher visual quality comes at increased computational cost for setup and sampling. But much of Feline's setup can be performed in parallel with the perspective divide pipeline, and so increases pipeline length over Texram by only a few stages. Feline's setup costs are substantially smaller than mip-mapped EWA's.

Figure 15: Texram paints bricks with herringbone artifacts.

Figure 16: "High-efficiency" Simple Feline paints bricks with fewer artifacts.

Figure 17: "High-quality" Simple Feline paints bricks with few artifacts.

Figure 18: Mip-mapped EWA paints bricks with fewest artifacts.

Both Feline and Texram access eight texels each probe, and probes overlap substantially (especially in the smaller of the two mip-maps). A texel cache [7][9] eliminates most redundant memory fetches. We assume these algorithms can perform one probe per cycle; higher performance requires duplicating large portions (100k to 200k gates) of the texture mapping logic.

Mip-mapped EWA doesn't fetch texels more than once per pixel and samples a substantially larger area. "Optimistic EWA" naively assumes we can sample 8 texels/cycle on all but the last cycle for each ellipse. "Realistic EWA" assumes that hardware traverses the ellipse using a 4 x 2 texel "stamp" for *u*-major ellipses, and a 2 x 4 stamp for *v*-major ellipses. Thus, each cycle several of the stamp's texels usually lie outside the ellipse.

Figure 23 shows how many cycles/pixel each algorithm uses for different viewing angles of one exemplary surface. At 0°, the surface normal is parallel to the viewing angle, and mip-mapped

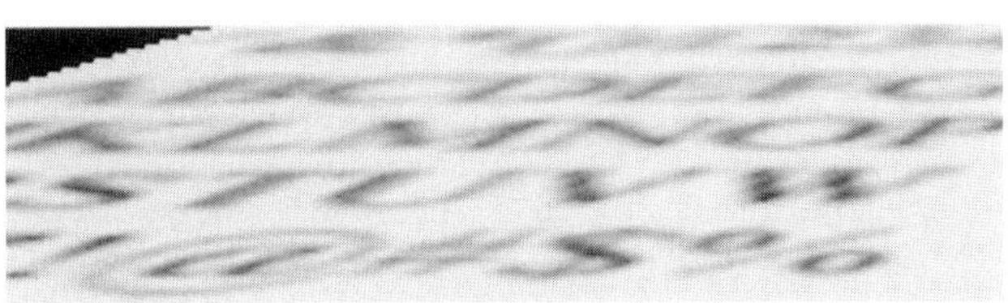

Figure 19: Trilinear paints blurry text.

Figure 21: "High-efficiency" Simple Feline paints smooth text.

Figure 20: Texram paints text with stairstepping.

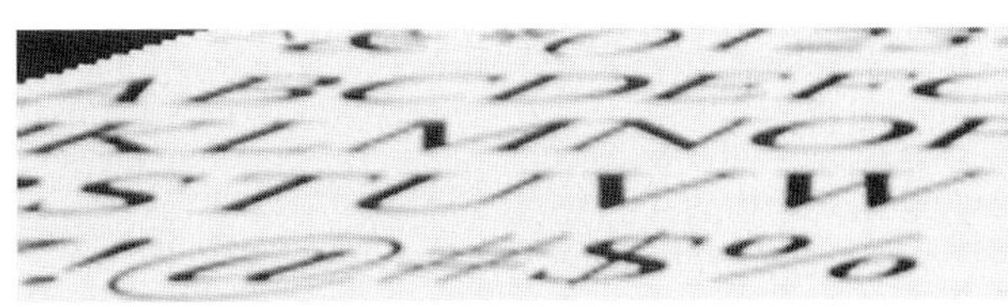

Figure 22: Mip-mapped EWA paints smooth text.

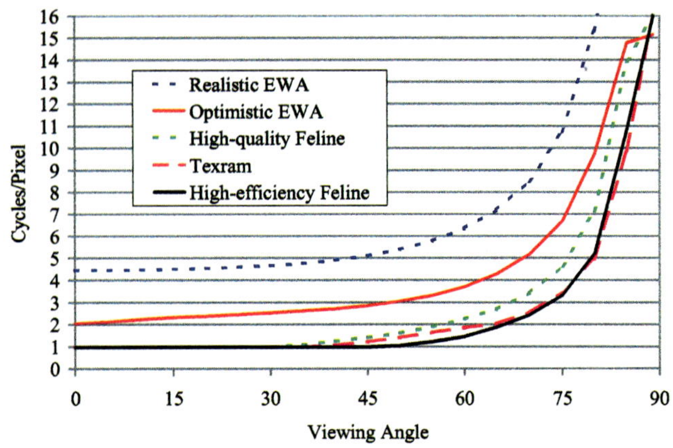


Figure 23: Performance at increasingly oblique viewing angles.

EWA samples the same size circle for each pixel. We made this circle's area the same as would be obtained by averaging results from randomly distributed viewing distances. This graph should be interpreted like EPA gas mileage numbers: it is useful for relative comparisons, but mileage will vary depending upon position on the screen, perspective distortion, etc.

Finally, note that if a scene uses multiple textures per surface, anisotropic texture mapping performance doesn't always slow down by these cycles/pixel ratios. For example, illumination maps tend to be small, so are usually magnified [7], which takes a single probe. They also tend to be blurry (that is, contain mostly low frequencies), so even when minified, an application might limit illumination mapping to one or two probes per pixel.

## 5 CONCLUSIONS

Feline provides nearly the visual quality of EWA, but with much simpler setup and texel visiting logic, and many fewer cycles per textured pixel. Feline provides better image quality than Texram, especially for repeated textures, even when limited to use the same number of probes. Feline requires somewhat more setup and texel weighting logic than Texram, but this cost is small compared to the increase in visual quality. Feline can be built on top of an existing trilinear filter implementation; for better results, the trilinear filter can be converted to a mip-mapped Gaussian at little cost. Since several aspects of Feline are parameterized, Feline can gracefully degrade image quality in order to keep frame rates high during movement. This degradation might accentuate aliasing for irregular textures, in order to preserve image sharpness, and accentuate blurring for repeated regular textures, in order to avoid Moiré artifacts.

In the Sep/Oct 1998 issue of *IEEE Computer Graphics and Applications*, Jim Blinn wrote in his column that "No one will ever figure out how to quickly render legible antialiased text in perspective. Textures in perspective will always be either too fuzzy or too jaggy. No one will ever build texture-mapping hardware that uses a 4x4 interpolation kernel or anisotropic filtering." Feline is simple enough to implement, yet of high enough visual quality, to prove him at least partially wrong.

## 6 ACKNOWLEDGEMENTS

Thanks to Paul Heckbert for answering questions and for providing us with the EWA source code, and to Gunter Knittel for answering questions about Texram.

## References


[1] Anthony C. Barkans. High Quality Rendering Using the Talisman Architecture. *Proceedings of the 1997 SIGGRAPH/EUROGRAPHICS Workshop on Graphics Hardware*, pages 79-88. ACM, August 1997. ISBN 0-89791-961-0.

[2] Frank C. Crow. Summed-Area Tables for Texture Mapping. In Hank Christiansen, editor, *Computer Graphics (SIGGRAPH 84 Conference Proceedings)*, volume 18, pages 207-212. ACM, July 1984.

[3] Alain Fournier & Eugene Fiume. Constant-Time Filtering with Space-Variant Kernels. In Richard J. Beach, editor, *Computer Graphics (SIGGRAPH 88 Conference Proceedings)*, volume 22, pages 229-238. ACM SIGGRAPH, Addison-Wesley, August 1988. ISBN 0-89791-275-6.

[4] Ned Greene & Paul Heckbert. Creating Raster Omnimax Images from Multiple Perspective Views Using the Elliptical Weighted Average Filter. *IEEE Computer Graphics and Applications*, 6(6):21-27, June 1986.

[5] Paul S. Heckbert. *Texture Mapping Polygons in Perspective*, Technical Memo #13, NY Inst. Tech. Computer Graphics Lab, April 1983.

[6] Paul S. Heckbert. *Fundamentals of Texture Mapping and Image Warping* (Masters Thesis), Report No. UCB/CSD 89/516, Computer Science Division, University of California, Berkeley, June 1989.

[7] Homan Igehy, Matthew Eldridge, Kekoa Proudfoot. Prefetching in a Texture Cache Architecture. *Proceedings of the 1998 EUROGRAPHICS/SIGGRAPH Workshop on Graphics Hardware*, pp. 133-142. ACM, August 1998. ISBN 0-89791-1-58113-097-x.

[8] Robert C. Landsdale. *Texture Mapping and Resampling for Computer Graphics* (Masters Thesis), Department of Electrical Engineering, University of Toronto, Toronto, Canada, January 1991, available at ftp://dgp.toronto.edu/pub/lansd/.

[9] Joel McCormack, Robert McNamara, Chris Gianos, Larry Seiler, Norman Jouppi, Ken Correll, Todd Dutton & John Zurawski. *Neon: A (Big) (Fast) Single-Chip 3D Workstation Graphics Accelerator*, WRL Research Report 98/1, Revised June 1999, available at www.research.digital.com/wrl/techreports/pubslist.html.

[10] Joel McCormack, Ronald Perry, Keith I. Farkas & Norman P. Jouppi. *Simple and Table Feline: Fast Elliptical Lines for Anisotropic Texture Mapping*, WRL Research Report 99/1, July 1999, available at www.research.digital.com/wrl/techreports/pubslist.html

[11] Andreas Schilling, Gunter Knittel & Wolfgang Strasser. Texram: A Smart Memory for Texturing. *IEEE Computer Graphics and Applications*, 16(3): 32-41, May 1996. ISSN 0272-1716.

[12] Lance Williams. Pyramidal Parametrics. In Peter Tanner, editor, *Computer Graphics (SIGGRAPH 83 Conference Proceedings)*, volume 17, pages 1-11. ACM, July 1983. ISBN 0-89791-109-1.

[13] George Wolberg. *Digital Image Warping*, IEEE Computer Society Press, Washington, DC, 1990. ISBN 0-8186-8944-7.

# The VolumePro Real-Time Ray-Casting System

Hanspeter Pfister * Jan Hardenbergh † Jim Knittel† Hugh Lauer† Larry Seiler†

Mitsubishi Electric

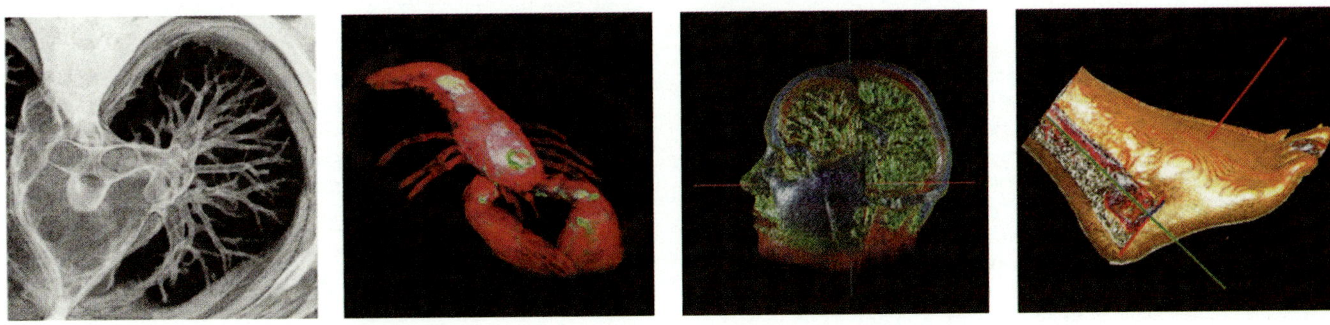

Figure 1: *Several volumes rendered on the VolumePro hardware at 30 frames per second.*

## Abstract

This paper describes VolumePro, the world's first single-chip real-time volume rendering system for consumer PCs. VolumePro implements ray-casting with parallel slice-by-slice processing. Our discussion of the architecture focuses mainly on the rendering pipeline and the memory organization. VolumePro has hardware for gradient estimation, classification, and per-sample Phong illumination. The system does not perform any pre-processing and makes parameter adjustments and changes to the volume data immediately visible. We describe several advanced features of VolumePro, such as gradient magnitude modulation of opacity and illumination, supersampling, cropping and cut planes. The system renders 500 million interpolated, Phong illuminated, composited samples per second. This is sufficient to render volumes with up to 16 million voxels (e.g., $256^3$) at 30 frames per second.

**CR Categories:** B.4.2 [Hardware]: Input/Output and Data Communications—Input/Output DevicesImage display; C.3 [Computer Systems Organization]: Special-Purpose and Application-Based Systems—Real-time and embedded systems; I.3.1 [Computer Graphics]: Hardware Architecture—Graphics processor;

**Keywords:** Graphics Hardware, Hardware Systems, Rendering Hardware, Rendering Systems, Volume Rendering

*MERL, 201 Broadway, Cambridge, MA 02139, pfister@merl.com

†Real Time Visualization, Mitsubishi Electric, 300 Baker Avenue, Concord, MA 01742, [jch,knittel,lauer,seiler]@merl.com



## 1 Introduction

Over the last decade, direct volume rendering has become an invaluable visualization technique for a wide variety of applications. Examples include visualization of 3D sampled medical data (CT, MRI), seismic data from oil and gas exploration, or computed finite element models. While volume rendering is very popular, the lack of interactive frame rates has limited its widespread use. To render one frame typically takes several seconds due to the tremendous storage and processing requirements. The three most promising approaches to achieve real-time frame rates for volume rendering are highly optimized software methods, use of 3D texture mapping hardware, or special-purpose volume rendering hardware.

Optimized software techniques for volume rendering require pre-computation and additional data storage, and they often sacrifice image quality for speed. Shear-warp rendering [11] is currently the fastest software algorithm. It achieves 1.1 Hz on a single 150MHz R4400 processor for a 256 × 256 × 225 volume with 65 seconds of pre-processing time [10]. Unfortunately, pre-processing prohibits immediate visual feedback during parameter changes. It also prevents real-time visualization of dynamically changing volume data.

3D texture mapping hardware can be used for volume rendering using a method called planar texture resampling [4]. A volume is stored as a 3D texture and resampled during rendering by extracting textured planes parallel to the image plane. Interactive rendering rates have been achieved on the SGI Reality Engine [1, 2]. However, texture hardware does not support estimation of gradients that are required to identify surfaces for shading. Efforts to overcome these difficulties either require multi-pass rendering, are limited to iso-surfaces and do not extend to specular illumination [18], or require significant pre-processing [6]. Other restrictions, especially on PC graphics cards, include limited arithmetic precision for blending and interpolation and limited texture memory.

Special purpose hardware for volume rendering has been proposed by various researchers, but only a few machines have been implemented. VIRIM was built at the University of Mannheim, Germany [7]. The hardware consists of four VME boards and implements ray-casting. VIRIM achieves 2.5 frames/sec for $256^3$ volumes. The VIZARD system of the University of Tübingen, Germany, implements perspective ray-casting and consists of two PCI accelerator cards [9]. An FPGA-based system achieves up to 10 frames/sec for $256^3$ volumes. The system, however, uses lossy data compression, and any changes in classification or shading parameters require lengthy pre-processing.

To overcome these limitations, we have developed VolumePro. VolumePro is the first single-chip real-time volume rendering system for consumer PCs. It does not require any pre-processing and performs a brute-force resampling of all voxels for each frame. This makes changes to the volume data immediately visible and allows the integration of VolumePro hardware into simulation systems (e.g., surgical simulation) or real-time acquisition devices (e.g., 3D ultrasound). VolumePro has hardware for gradient estimation, per-sample Phong illumination, and classification, and all parameters can be adjusted in real-time.

A VolumePro system consists of the VolumePro PCI card, a companion 3D graphics card, and software. The VolumePro PCI card contains 128 MB of volume memory and the vg500 rendering chip. The Volume Library Interface (VLI) is a collection of C++ objects and provides the application programming interface to the VolumePro features. The first VolumePro board was operational in April 1999 (see Figure 2). Production shipments started in June 1999 at an initial price comparable to high-end PC graphics cards.

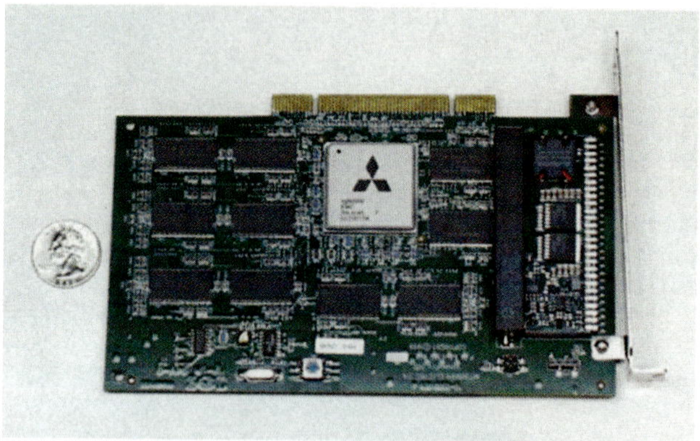

Figure 2: *The VolumePro PCI card.*

VolumePro is based on the Cube-4 volume rendering architecture developed at SUNY Stony Brook [14]. Cube-4 requires, however, a large number of rendering and memory chips, many pins for inter-chip communication, and large on-chip storage for intermediate results. Consequently, we developed Enhanced Memory Cube-4 (EM-Cube) [13] to implement Cube-4 at lower cost.

VolumePro is the commercial implementation of EM-Cube, and it makes several important enhancements to its architecture and design. By giving up scalability we are able to fit four rendering pipelines on one chip (see Section 5). An on-chip voxel distribution network greatly simplifies communication between rendering pipelines (see Section 5.3). A novel block-and-bank skewing scheme takes advantage of the internal organization of modern SDRAM devices (see Section 5.2). VolumePro also implements several novel features, such as gradient magnitude modulation, supersampling, supervolumes, slicing, and cropping (see Section 4).

The reality of a tight production schedule, however, forced us to make compromises. VolumePro supports only 8- and 12-bit scalar voxels and no other voxel formats. It performs orthographic projections of rectilinear volume data sets. Perspective projections and intermixing of polygons and volumes were deemed too complex and were postponed for a future release of the system. This paper is the first detailed description of the VolumePro architecture and system. All images in this paper were rendered on a pre-production version of the VolumePro hardware at 30 frames/sec.

## 2 Rendering Algorithm

VolumePro implements ray-casting [12], one of the most commonly used volume rendering algorithms. Ray-casting offers high image quality and is easy to parallelize. The current version of VolumePro supports parallel projections of isotropic and anisotropic rectilinear volumes with scalar voxels.

To achieve uniform data access we use a ray-casting technique with hybrid object/image-order data traversal based on the shear-warp factorization of the viewing matrix [19, 15, 11] (see Figure 3). The volume data is defined in object coordinates $(u, v, w)$, which are first transformed to isotropic object coordinates by the scale and shear matrix $L$. This allows to automatically handle anisotropic data sets, in which the spacing between voxels differs in the three dimensions, and gantry tilted data sets, in which the slices are sheared, by adjusting the warp matrix. We discuss gradient estimation in anisotropic and sheared volumes in Section 3.2.

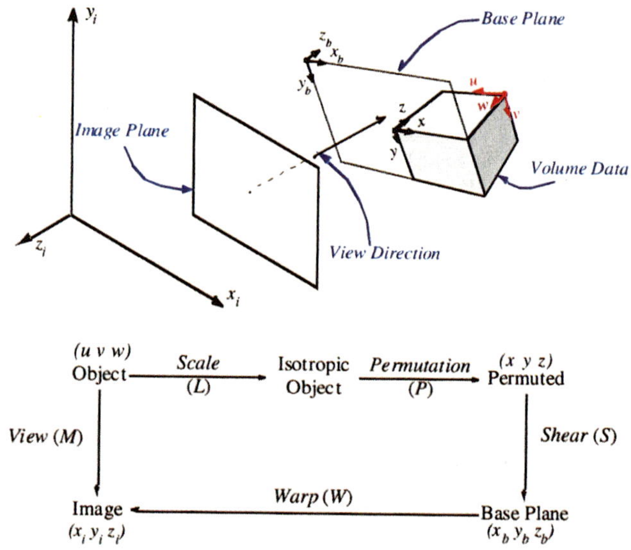


Figure 3: *Shear-warp factorization of the viewing matrix.*

The permutation matrix $P$ transforms the isotropic object to permuted coordinates $(x, y, z)$. The origin of permuted coordinates is the vertex of the volume nearest to the image plane and the z axis is the edge of the volume most parallel to the view direction.

The shear matrix $S$ represents the rendering operation that projects points in the permuted volume space onto points on the base plane. In VolumePro this projection is performed using ray-casting. Instead of casting rays from image space $(x_i, y_i, z_i)$, rays are sent into the data set from the base plane $(x_b, y_b, z_b)$, which is the face of the volume data that is most parallel to the viewing plane. This approach guarantees that there is a one-to-one mapping of sample points to voxels [19, 15].

In contrast to the shear-warp implementation by Lacroute and Levoy [11], VolumePro performs tri-linear interpolation and allows rays to start at sub-pixel locations. This prevents view-dependent artifacts when switching base planes and accommodates supersampling of the volume data (see Section 4.1).

The base plane image is transformed to the image plane using the warp matrix $W = M \times L^{-1} \times P^{-1} \times S^{-1}$. VolumePro uses 2D texture mapping with bi-linear interpolation on a companion graphics card for this image warp (see Section 6). The additional 2D image resampling results in a slight degradation of image quality. It enables, however, an easy mapping to an arbitrary user-specified image size.

The main advantage of the shear-warp factorization is that voxels can be read and processed in planes of voxels, called slices, that are parallel to the base plane. Slices are processed in positive z direction. Within a slice, scanline of voxels (called voxel beams) are read from memory in top to bottom order. This leads to regular, object-order data access. In addition, it allows parallelism by having multiple rendering pipelines work on several voxels in a beam at the same time. This concept is explained further in Section 5. The next section describes a single VolumePro rendering pipeline.

# 3 The Ray-Casting Pipeline

A key characteristic of VolumePro is that each voxel is read from memory exactly once per frame. Therefore, voxel values must be recirculated through the processing stages of the VolumePro pipeline so that they become available for calculations precisely when needed.

A second characteristic of VolumePro is that the reading and processing of voxel data and calculation of pixel values on rays are highly pipelined. One VolumePro processing pipeline can accept a new voxel every cycle and can forward intermediate results to subsequent pipeline stages every cycle. The net effect is that VolumePro can render a volume data set at the speed of reading voxels.

Figure 4 illustrates a flow diagram of an idealized version of the VolumePro processing pipeline. In this figure, the flow and processing of voxel data is shown in black, and control information is shown in red. The figure shows interpolation followed by gradient estimation. In actual practice, the x and y gradients are computed following interpolation, but the z gradients are estimated before interpolation (see Section 3.2).

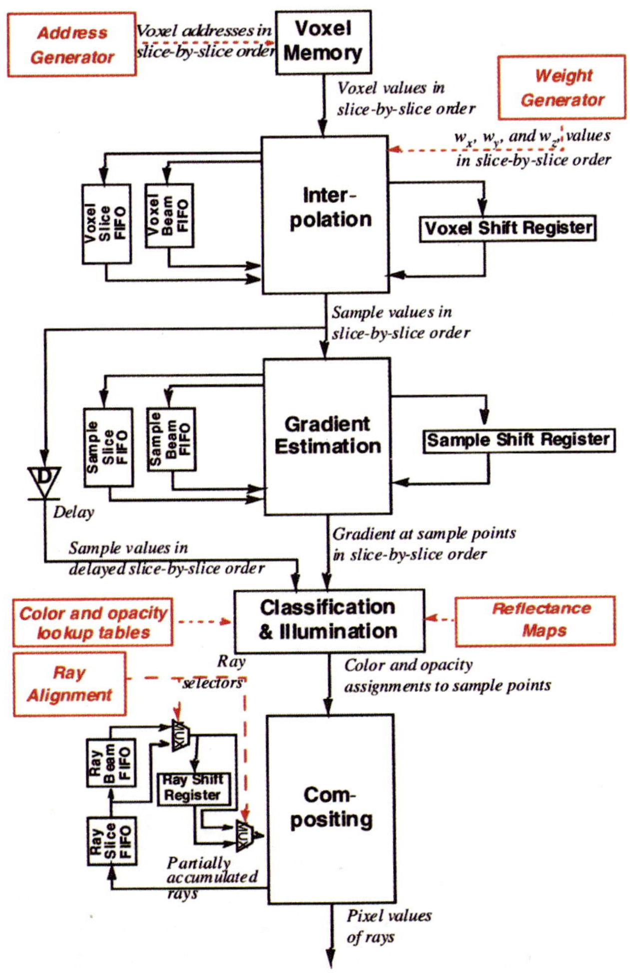


Figure 4: *Conceptual ray-casting pipeline.*

## 3.1 Interpolating Voxel Values

At the top of Figure 4 is Volume Memory, also called Voxel Memory. The current generation of VolumePro supports 8- and 12-bit scalar voxels. All internal voxel datapaths are 12-bits wide. Voxels are read from the memory and are presented to the Interpolation unit in the slice-by-slice, beam-by-beam order described in Section 2, one voxel per cycle. The Interpolation unit converts the stream of voxel values into a stream of sample values, also in slice-by-slice, beam-by-beam order, at the rate of one sample value per cycle. The interpolated samples are rounded to 12-bit values.

Each sample value is derived from its eight nearest neighboring voxels by tri-linear interpolation. Therefore, the Interpolation Unit must have on hand not only the current voxel from the input stream, but also all other voxels from the same tri-linear neighborhood. It does this by storing input voxels and other intermediate values in the Voxel Slice FIFO, Voxel Beam FIFO, and Voxel Shift Register. Each of these is a data storage element sized so that when a newly calculated value is inserted, it emerges again at precisely the time needed for a subsequent calculation.

Trilinear interpolation also requires a set of weights. These are generated by the Weight Generator in Figure 4. This generator is based on a digital differential analyzer (DDA) algorithm to calculate each new set of weights from the previous weights. Since all rays are parallel to each other and have exactly the same spacing as the pixel positions on the base plane (and hence, as the voxels of each slice), a single set of weights is sufficient for all of the samples of a slice.

## 3.2 Gradient Estimation

The output of the Interpolation unit is a stream of sample values, one per cycle in slice-by-slice, beam-by-beam order. This stream is presented to the Gradient Estimation unit for estimating the x, y and z gradients on each sample using central differences.

VolumePro computes gradients in two equivalent ways. In z direction, we interpolate differences between voxels to sample positions, and in x and y direction we take differences of interpolated samples. Both orders of computation yield equivalent results because difference and tri-linear interpolation are commutative linear operators.

The gradient at a particular sample point depends not only on data in the current slice but also on data in the previous and next slice. The next slice, of course, has not been read when the current sample value arrives at the input. Therefore, the Gradient Estimation unit operates one voxel, one beam, and one slice behind the Interpolation unit. That is, when sample $S_{(x+1),(y+1),(z+1)}$ arrives, the Gradient Estimation Unit finally has enough information to complete the estimation of the gradient at sample point $S_{x,y,z}$.

It does this by maintaining two full slices of buffering, plus two full beams of buffering, plus two extra samples. These are stored in the Sample Slice FIFOs, Sample Beam FIFOs, and Sample Shift Registers, respectively, which serve roughly the same functions as the Voxel Slice FIFO, Voxel Beam FIFO, and Voxel Shift Register. Each central difference gradient has signed 8-bit precision, meaning it can represent numbers in the range $[-127 \cdots + 127]$.

VolumePro handles anisotropic and sheared volumes by treating them as isotropic and subsequently adjusting the warp matrix (see Section 2). The different voxel spacing and alignment leads to incorrect gradients, however, because the vector components are not

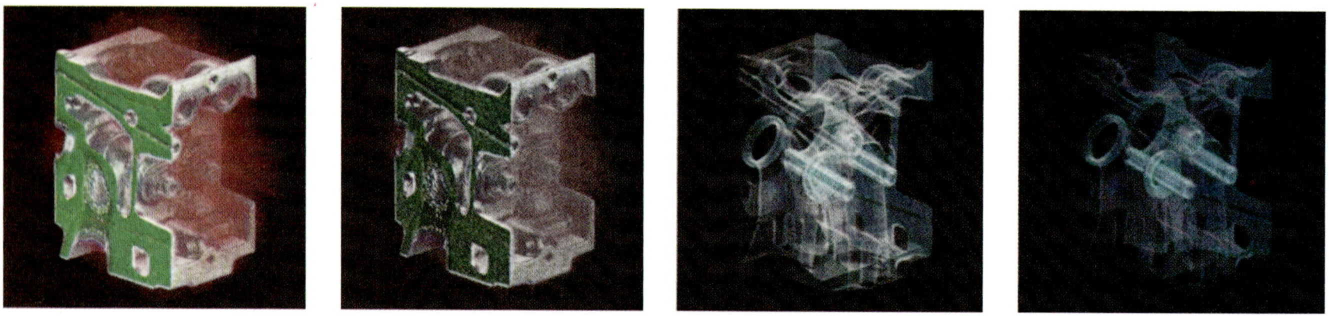

(a) None (b) Illumination (c) Opacity (d) Opacity and illumination

Figure 5: *Images rendered with gradient magnitude modulation of opacity or illumination. Notice how the appearance of surfaces changes.*

orthonormal in object space. We correct for these differences in software by adjusting the light positions every frame to compute the accurate dot product between gradient and light vectors for ambient and diffuse illumination. To correct the specular highlights we adjust the eye vector, used in the reflection vector hardware, every frame (see Section 3.5).

### 3.3 Gradient Magnitude

The gradient magnitude can be used to render multiple semi-transparent surfaces in volumes [12]. In VolumePro the sample opacity and illumination are optionally multiplied with the gradient magnitude. This modulation can be used to emphasize surface boundaries, to reduce the illumination of samples with small gradients, or to minimize the visual impact of noisy data.

Figure 5 shows four renderings of a CT scan of an engine block (256 x 256 x 110). Figures 5(a) and (b) show the difference between no modulation and gradient magnitude modulation of specular illumination. Regions of small gradient magnitude, such as noise, are de-emphasized in Figure 5(b). Figure 5(c) shows gradient magnitude modulation of opacity. Homogeneous regions with small gradient magnitude, such as the walls, are more transparent compared to Figure 5(a). Figure 5(d) shows the combined effect of modulating opacity and illumination by the gradient magnitude. Homogeneous regions are more transparent and the overall illumination is attenuated.

VolumePro derives a sample's gradient magnitude in two phases. First, the square of the gradient magnitude is computed by taking the sum of the squares of the gradient components. Then a Newton-Raphson iteration is used to compute the square-root of this value, resulting in an approximation of the gradient magnitude. The gradient components are in the range of $[-127 \cdots +127]$, making the maximum gradient magnitude value $\sqrt{3 \cdot 127^2}$. It is stored as an unsigned 8-bit number in the range of $[0 \cdots 220]$.

The gradient magnitude is then mapped to the range $[0 \cdots 255]$ by a lookup table (GmLUT). The table stores a user-specified piecewise linear function that can be used to highlight particular gradient magnitude values or to attenuate the modulation effect. The table is also used to automatically correct the gradient magnitudes in anisotropic volumes.

### 3.4 Assigning Color and Opacity

VolumePro assigns RGBA values to interpolated samples as opposed to classifying voxel values first and then interpolating RGBA. This produces the greatest accuracy for nonlinear mappings from data to color and opacity. It also reduces the number of interpolators by a factor of four. Unfortunately, it prevents direct rendering of volumes that have been pre-classified by a software segmentation algorithm into RGBA or material volumes [5].

The classification of sample values to RGBA in VolumePro can summarized as:

$$\alpha = \begin{cases} \mathrm{GmLUT}(|\mathrm{Gradient}|) \cdot \alpha\mathrm{LUT}(\mathrm{Sample}) & \text{if } G_o = 1 \\ \alpha\mathrm{LUT}(\mathrm{Sample}) & \text{if } G_o = 0 \end{cases}$$

$$\mathrm{SampleRGB} = \mathrm{colorLUT}(\mathrm{Sample}).$$

The actual classification of samples is a straightforward table lookup of the 12-bit sample value into a $4096 \times 36$ bit classification lookup table (LUT). The lookup table stores 36-bit RGBA values. Color values are stored with 8-bit precision for each of R, G, and B. $\alpha$ is stored with 12-bits precision for maximum accuracy during ray-casting of low opacity volumes.

The RGBA table is pre-computed and loaded into VolumePro prior to rendering. Color and opacity can be loaded separately. An additional on-chip RGBA table hides the latency of loading the tables through double buffering. Loading a new opacity table with $4k \times 12$ bit entries requires 2k 32-bit PCI transfers, or 246 KB/sec for 30 loads/sec. Updating the table every frame corrects the opacities for non-unit sample spacing during view changes, anisotropic volumes, or supersampling [5]. As mentioned in Section 3.3, the value of $\alpha$ may be optionally multiplied by the gradient magnitude, depending on the value of $G_o$.

### 3.5 Sample Illumination

VolumePro implements Phong illumination at each sample point at the rate of one illuminated sample per clock cycle. The shading calculation can be summarized as:

$$\begin{aligned} \mathrm{RGB} &= ((k_e + (I_d \cdot G_d \cdot k_d)) \cdot \mathrm{SampleRGB}) + \\ & \quad (I_s \cdot G_s \cdot k_s \cdot \mathrm{SpecularColor}), \end{aligned}$$

where:

$$\begin{aligned} I_d &= \mathrm{DiffuseReflectanceMap}(\mathrm{Gradient}), \\ I_s &= \mathrm{SpecularReflectanceMap}(\mathrm{ReflectionVector}), \\ G_{[d,s]} &= \begin{cases} \mathrm{GmLUT}(|\mathrm{Gradient}|) & \text{if } \mathrm{Gmim}_{[d,s]} = 1 \\ 1 & \text{if } \mathrm{Gmim}_{[d,s]} = 0 \end{cases} \end{aligned}$$

and where $k_e, k_d, k_s$, and specularColor are registers of VolumePro. The values of $\mathrm{Gmim}_d$ and $\mathrm{Gmim}_s$ enable or disable Gradient Magnitude Illumination Modulation for diffuse or specular illumination, respectively.

The sample color from the classification LUT is multiplied by $k_e$ to produce the emissive color of the object. The diffuse contribution is obtained by multiplying a user-defined diffuse coefficient $k_d$ with the diffuse illumination value $I_d$ and the sample color. The specular contribution is obtained by multiplying a user-defined specular color with the product of a specular coefficient $k_s$ and the specular illumination value $I_s$.

The diffuse and specular illumination values $I_d$ and $I_s$ are looked up in reflectance maps, respectively. Each reflectance map is a pre-computed table that stores the amount of illumination due to the sum of all of the light sources of the scene. The reflection map implementation supports an unlimited number of directional light sources, but no positional lights. Trading computation for table lookup leads to simpler logic than an arithmetic implementation of shading. The VLI software loads the diffuse and specular reflectance maps into VolumePro prior to rendering a frame.

Reflectance values are mapped onto six sides of a cube, indexed by the unnormalized gradient or reflection vectors [17]. The reflection vector for each sample is computed in hardware from the gradient and eye vectors. Using bi-linear interpolation among reflectance map values keeps the table size small without incurring noticeable visual artifacts [16]. The specular and diffuse map are implemented with 384 32-bit entries each. To load both tables takes 92 KB/sec for 30 loads/sec.

The reflectance maps need to be reloaded when the object and light positions change with respect to each other, or to correct the eye vector in anisotropic volumes (see Section 3.2). Because the reflection vector is computed in hardware, however, the reflectance maps do not have to be reloaded when the eye changes in isotropic volumes.

### 3.6 Accumulating Color Values along Rays

The output of the Classification and Shading unit is a stream of color and opacity values at sample points in slice-by-slice, beam-by-beam order. This stream is fed into the Compositing unit for accumulation into the pixel values of the rays. Samples along rays arrive in front-to-back order. The compositing unit that works on a particular ray also gets samples from other rays, due to the slice-order traversal. Thus, the samples must be buffered until the color and opacity values of the next sample point along the ray arrive in the stream.

The Ray Slice FIFO, Ray Beam FIFO, and Ray Shift Register hold the values of the partially accumulated rays for this purpose. Although these look somewhat like the Voxel Slice FIFO, Voxel Beam FIFO, and Voxel Shift Register, their functions are different because of the cyclical nature of compositing. To understand this, observe that the compositing operation for sample $S_{x,y,z}$ requires as input the result of compositing one of $S_{x,y,(z-1)}$, $S_{(x-1),y,(z-1)}$, $S_{x,(y-1),(z-1)}$, or $S_{(x-1),(y-1),(z-1)}$, depending on the view direction and the value of z. That is, the predecessor value required as input to a particular compositing operation is the result of one of four compositing operations of the previous slice of samples. The selection of which particular one falls under the control of the Ray Alignment unit near the bottom of Figure 4, which drives two multiplexers (labeled MUX in the figure).

The Ray Slice FIFO stores partially accumulated pixel values of rays and makes them available for compositing with color and opacity values from the next slice. The Ray Beam FIFO stores the same values for a further beam time, so that in case the rays angle downward, input values can be obtained from the beam above and before the current sample. Likewise, the Ray Shift Register stores the same value for one additional cycle, in case the input value needs to be obtained from a sample to the left of the current one.

In addition to alpha blending, VolumePro supports Minimum and Maximum Intensity Projections (MIP) (see Table 1). In the table, $C_{acc}$ and $\alpha_{acc}$ are the accumulated color and opacity, respectively. VolumePro uses 12 bits of precision for $\alpha$, $C_{acc}$, $\alpha_{acc}$, and all intermediate compositing values for correct $\alpha$-blending in low-opacity volumes and very large data sets.

| Blend Mode | Functions |
|---|---|
| Front-to-back $\alpha$-blending | $C_{acc} += (1 - \alpha_{acc}) \times (\alpha_{sample} C_{sample})$<br>$\alpha_{acc} += (1 - \alpha_{acc}) \times \alpha_{sample}$ |
| Minimum Intensity | if (sampleValue < minValue):<br>$C_{acc} = C_{sample}$; minValue = sampleValue; |
| Maximum Intensity | if (sampleValue > maxValue):<br>$C_{acc} = C_{sample}$; maxValue = sampleValue; |

Table 1: *Blending modes of VolumePro.*

Finally, after the color and opacity values of all of the sample points on an individual ray have been accumulated, the resulting pixel value of that ray is output. This may occur when a ray passes through the back of the volume – i.e., with a maximum value of z – or when it passes through a side face of the volume. Base plane pixel values are written to Pixel Memory and then transferred to a companion 3D graphics card for the final image warp. The image warp is performed by 2D texture mapping hardware on the companion 3D graphics card. The base plane image is defined as a texture of a polygon corresponding to the base plane bounding box. The 3D graphics card transforms and bi-linearly resamples this textured polygon to the final image position.

Figure 6(a) shows a foot (152 x 261 x 200) of the visible man CT data set rendered with Maximum Intensity Projection (MIP). Figure 6(b) shows the CT scan of a lung (256 x 256 x 115) with low-opacity alpha blending and no illumination. Figure 6(c) shows the same dataset, but with illumination and gradient magnitude modulation of opacity.

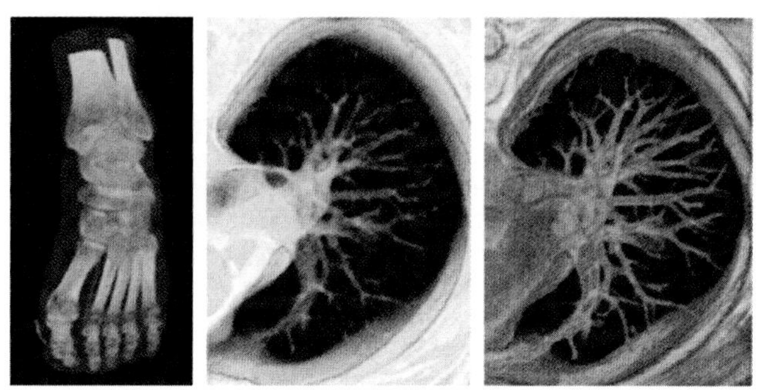

(a) (b) (c)

Figure 6: *(a) MIP. (b) Alpha blending, no illumination. (c) Alpha blending, illumination, gradient magnitude modulation of opacity.*

## 4 Advanced Features of VolumePro

This section describes several additional features that have some impact on the architecture of VolumePro. These include supersampling, supervolumes (volumes larger than 256 voxels in any dimension), subvolumes, cropping and cut planes. We are not aware of any previous implementation of these features in special-purpose volume rendering hardware.

### 4.1 Supersampling

Supersampling [8] improves the quality of the rendered image by sampling the volume data set at a higher frequency than the voxel spacing. In the case of supersampling in the x and y directions, this would result in more samples per beam and more beams per slice, respectively. In the z direction, it results in more sample slices per volume.

VolumePro supports supersampling in hardware only in the z direction. Additional slices of samples are interpolated between existing slices of voxels. The software automatically corrects the opacity according to the viewing angle and sample spacing by reloading the opacity table (see Section 3.4).

Figure 7 shows the CT scan of a foot (152 x 261 x 200) rendered with no supersampling (left) and supersampling in z by 3 (right). The artifacts in the left image stem from the insufficient sampling rate to capture the high frequencies of the foot surface. Notice the reduced artifacts in the supersampled image. VolumePro supports up to eight times supersampling.

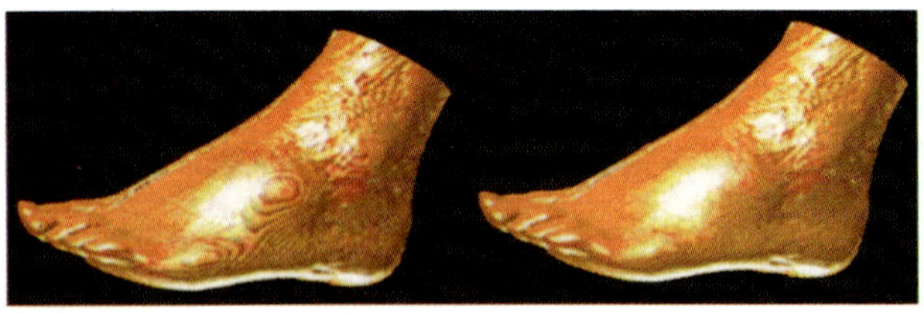

Figure 7: *No supersampling (left) and supersampling in z (right).*

The impact of supersampling on the VolumePro processing pipelines is minimal. Since it is necessary to have voxels from two slices to interpolate in the z direction, it is sufficient to do several of these interpolations from the same pair of slices before moving on to another slice. Since samples pass from the Interpolation unit in slice-by-slice order, the only impact is that the voxel memory stages of the pipeline must stall and wait for the additional, supersampled slices to clear. Thus, if we supersample by a factor of k, the rendering rate in frames per second is reduced by $\frac{1}{k}$.

With the current implementation of VolumePro, supersampling in the x and y directions can be implemented by repeatedly rendering a volume with slightly different ray offsets on the base plane in the x and y dimensions. The VolumePro hardware supports initial ray offsets at sub-pixel accuracy. The VolumePro software provides the necessary support to automatically render several frames and to blend them into a final supersampled image.

## 4.2 Supervolumes and Subvolumes

Volumes of arbitrary dimensions can be stored in voxel memory without padding. Because of limited on-chip buffers, however, the VolumePro hardware can only render volumes with a maximum of 256 voxels in each dimension in one pass. In order to render a larger volume (called a supervolume), software must first partition the volume into smaller blocks. Each block is rendered independently, and their resulting images are combined in software.

The VolumePro software automatically partitions supervolumes, takes care of the data duplication between blocks, and blends intermediate base planes into the final image. Blocks are automatically swapped to and from host memory if a supervolume does not fit into the 128 MB of volume memory on the VolumePro PCI card. There is no limit to the size of a supervolume, although, of course, rendering time increases due to the limited PCI download bandwidth.

Volumes with less than 256 voxels in each dimension are called subvolumes. VolumePro's memory controller allows reading and writing single voxels, slices, or any rectangular slab to and from Voxel Memory. Multiple subvolumes can be pre-loaded into volume memory. Subvolumes can be updated in-between frames. This allows dynamic and partial updates of volume data to achieve 4D animation effects. It also enables loading sections of a larger volume in pieces, allowing the user to effectively pan through a volume. Subvolumes increase rendering speed to the point where the frame rate is limited by the base plane pixel transfer and driver overhead, which is currently at 30 frames/sec.

## 4.3 Cropping and Cut Planes

VolumePro provides two features for clipping the volume data set called cropping and cut planes. These make it possible to visualize slices, cross-sections, or other portions of the volume, thus providing the user an opportunity to see inside in creative ways. Figure 8(a) shows an example of cropping on the CT foot of the visible man. Figure 8(b) shows a cut plane through the engine data.

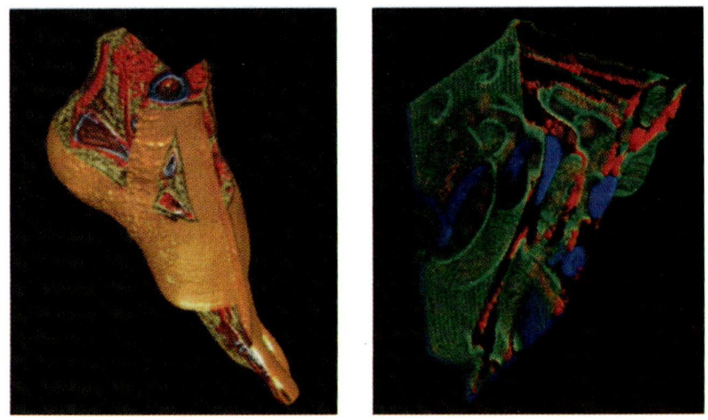

(a) (b)

Figure 8: *(a) Cropping. (b) Cut plane.*

Cropping introduces multiple clipping planes parallel to the volume faces. Figure 9 shows a conceptual diagram and several examples, and Figure 8(a) shows an example image.

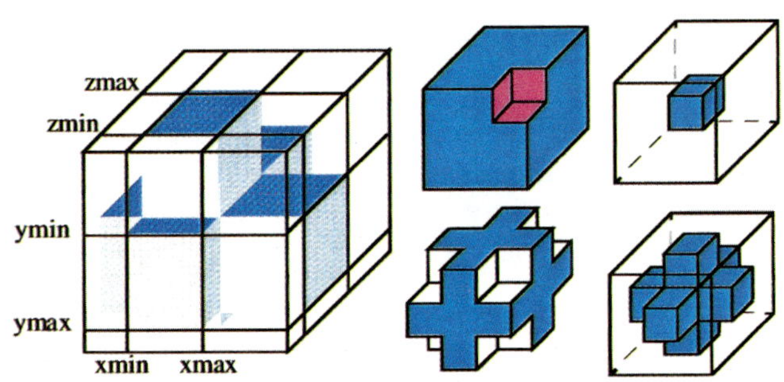


Figure 9: *Cropping of a volume data set and cropping examples.*

Three slabs, one parallel to each of the three axes of the volume data set, are defined by six registers $x_{\min}, x_{\max}, y_{\min}, y_{\max}, z_{\min}$, and $z_{\max}$. Slab $S_x$ is the set of all points (x, y, z) such that $x_{\min} \leq x \leq x_{\max}$, slab $S_y$ is the set of all points such that $y_{\min} \leq y \leq y_{\max}$, and slab $S_z$ is the set of all points such that $z_{\min} \leq z \leq z_{\max}$. Slabs may be combined by taking intersections, unions, and inverses to define regions of visibility of the volume data set. A sample at position (x, y, z) is visible if and only if it falls in this region of visibility. The logic for cropping is implemented in the Compositing unit, which ignores invisible samples.

In Figure 9, the shaded part of the volume remains visible and the remainder is invisible. Alternatively, the same slabs could be combined in a different way so that only the intersection of the three slabs is visible. Note that the cropping planes defining the slabs may fall at arbitrary voxel positions. A side effect is that cropping is an easy way of specifying a rectilinear region of interest (ROI).

The second form of clipping is the cut plane. VolumePro supports a single cut plane with arbitrary thickness and orientation. Samples are visible only if they lie between the two parallel surfaces of the cut plane; alternatively, samples are visible only if they are outside of the cut plane. Figure 10 illustrates a cut plane and its transition region.

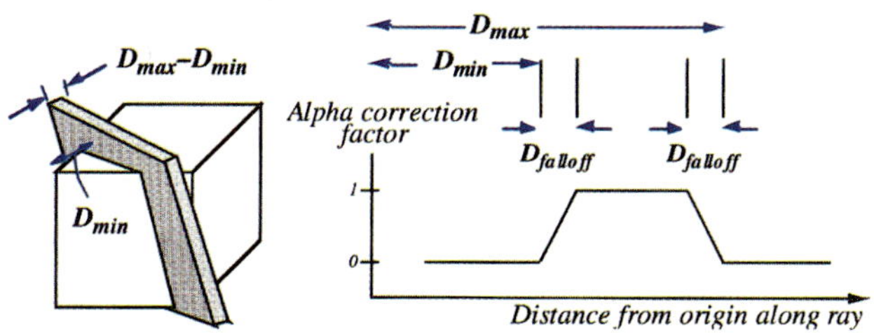


Figure 10: *Cut plane with transition regions.*

The two parallel faces of the cut plane are given by the plane equations:

$$\begin{aligned} Ax + By + Cz - D_{\min} &= 0 \\ Ax + By + Cz - D_{\max} &= 0, \end{aligned}$$

where $D_{\min} \leq D_{\max}$. That is, $D_{\min}$ measures the distance from the origin to one face of the cut plane, and $D_{\max}$ measures the distance from the origin to the other face. The thickness of the cut plane is $D_{\max} - D_{\min}$.

To allow for smooth cuts, a falloff parameter ($D_{\text{falloff}}$) specifies the width of the transition from full opacity to none (see Figure 10). Outside the cut plane, $\alpha$ is forced to zero. In the transition regions, $\alpha$ is multiplied by a correction factor. This correction factor increases linearly from zero to one. In the interior of the cut plane, $\alpha$ is simply the value from the shading stage. The $\alpha$ correction logic for the cut plane is in the Compositing unit.

As shown in Figure 1 on the right, VolumePro also has a 3D cursor feature that inserts a hardware generated, software controlled cursor into the volume data set being rendered. The 3D cursor allows users to explore and identify spatial relationships within the volume data. The samples for the cursor are generated in the Compositing unit and are blended into the volume data by $\alpha$-blending.

## 5 vg500 Chip Architecture

The rendering engine of the VolumePro system is the vg500 chip with four parallel rendering pipelines. It is an application specific integrated circuit (ASIC) with approximately 3.2 million random logic transistors and 2 Mbits of on-chip SRAM. It is fabricated in 0.35 $\mu$ technology and runs at 125 MHz clock frequency. In this section we discuss a number of practical considerations that affect the architecture of the vg500 ASIC and that lead to modifications of the idealized pipeline of Section 3.

### 5.1 Parallel Pipelines

To render a data set of $256^3$ voxels at 30 frames per second, VolumePro must be able to read $256^3 \times 30$ voxels per second – that is, approximately 503 million voxels per second. In the current implementation of VolumePro, each pipeline operates at 125 MHz and can accept a new voxel every cycle. Thus, achieving real-time rendering rates requires four pipelines operating in parallel. These can process $4 \times 125 \cdot 10^6$ or 500 million voxels per second.

The arrangement of the four pipelines in the vg500 chip architecture is illustrated in Figure 11. They work on adjacent voxel or

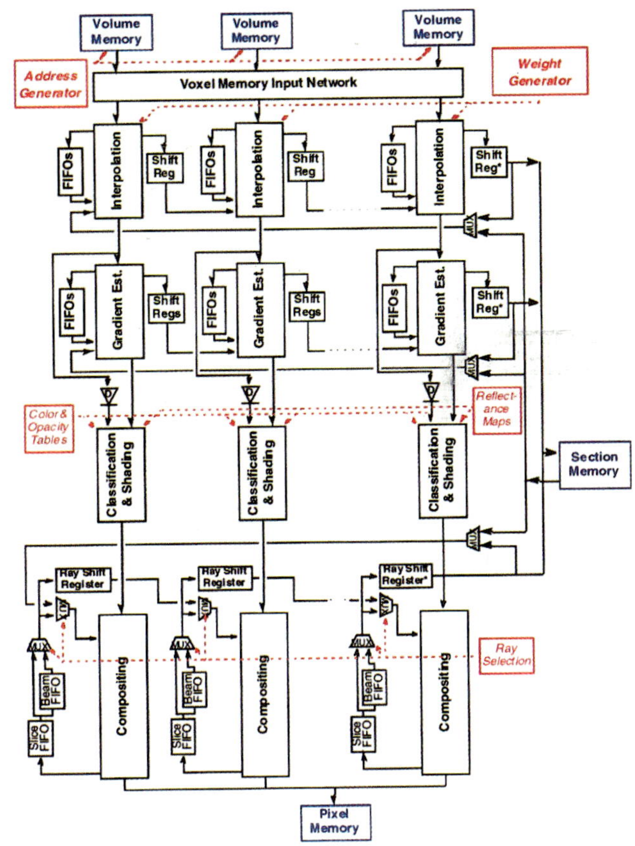


Figure 11: *The four parallel pipelines of the vg500 ASIC. Modules shown in blue are off-chip memory.*

sample values in the x direction. Each pipeline is connected to its neighbor by means of the shift registers in each of the major units. Whereas in Figure 4 the shift registers recirculate values that are needed in the next cycle in the x direction, in Figure 11 they provide values to their neighbors in the same cycle. The exceptions are the shift registers of the rightmost pipeline, each of which is marked with an asterisk. These act as in Figure 4 to recirculate values needed in the next cycle, but they send those values to the leftmost pipeline. An off-chip Voxel Memory supplies data to all of the pipelines, and they all write pixel values to an off-chip Pixel Memory. The additional datapaths on the right and the off-chip Section Memory will be discussed in Section 5.4.

### 5.2 Voxel Memory Organization

The vg500 chip has four 16-bit memory interfaces to Voxel Memory. A typical Voxel Memory configuration consists of four Synchronous Dynamic Random Access Memory (SDRAM) modules. The current implementation of VolumePro uses 64-megabit SDRAMs that provide burst mode access at 125 MHz. Voxel Memory can be extended to four SDRAMs per memory interface. Thus, sixteen SDRAMs provide 1024 megabits (i.e., 128 megabytes) of voxel storage. This is sufficient to hold a volume data set with 128 million 8-bit voxels or four $256^3$ volumes with 12-bit voxels. Four 125 MHz memory interfaces can read Voxel Memory at a burst rate of $4 \times 125$ million (i.e., 500 million) voxels per second, provided that voxels can be organized appropriately in memory.

There are three architectural challenges. First, voxels have to be organized so that data is read from Voxel Memory in bursts of eight or more voxels with consecutive addresses. This is done by arranging voxels in miniblocks. A miniblock is a $2 \times 2 \times 2$ array of voxels stored linearly in a single memory module at consecutive memory addresses. All data is read in bursts of the size of a miniblock. This is much more efficient than the arbitrary memory accesses that resulted from voxel skewing in Cube-4 [14].

Second, miniblocks themselves have to be distributed across memory modules in such a way that groups of four adjacent miniblocks in any direction are always stored in separate memory modules, avoiding memory access conflicts. This is done by skewing [3]. Instead of skewing blocks, as in EM-Cube [13], this skewing technique is applied to miniblocks in VolumePro. It ensures that four adjacent miniblocks, i.e., miniblocks parallel to any axis, are always in different memory modules, no matter what the view direction is.

Third, miniblocks within a memory module must be further skewed so that adjacent miniblocks never fall into the same memory bank of an SDRAM chip. 64-megabit SDRAMs have four internal memory banks. $4 \times 4 \times 4$ cubes of miniblocks are skewed across the four memory banks, thus allowing back-to-back accesses to miniblocks in any traversal order with no pipeline delays.

A voxel with coordinates $(u, v, w)$ has miniblock coordinates $(u_m, v_{\acute{m}}, w_m) = (u/2, v/2, w/2)$, which are mapped to one of the memory modules and memory banks as follows:

$$\begin{aligned} \text{Module} &= (u_m + v_m + w_m) \bmod 4 \\ \text{Bank} &= ((u_m \div 4) + (v_m \div 4) + (w_m \div 4)) \bmod 4, \end{aligned}$$

where mod denotes the modulus operator and $\div$ the integer division operator. This is illustrated in Figure 12.

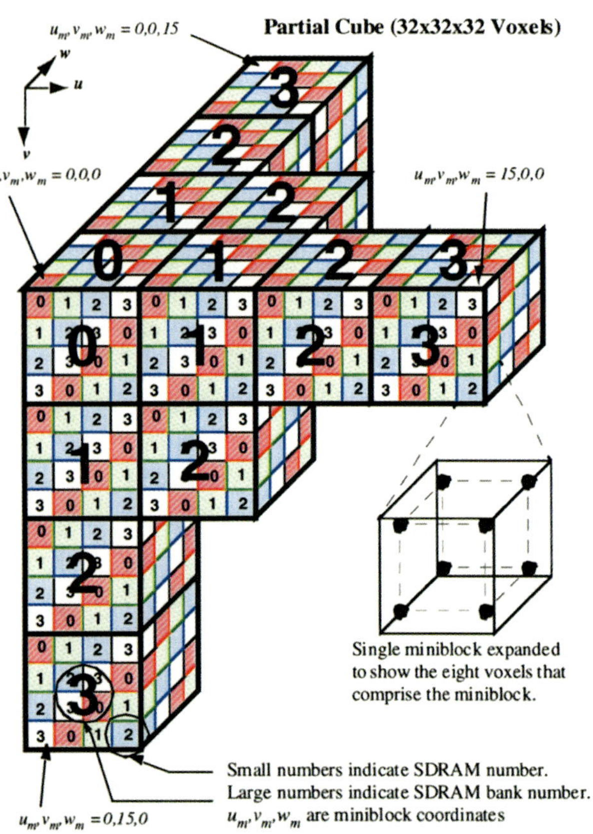


Figure 12: *Organization of miniblocks in Voxel Memory.*

In order to ensure that miniblocks are properly aligned for optimum SDRAM performance, the Voxel Memory must be allocated such that all dimensions of the volume object appear to be multiples of $2 \times 4 \times 4 = 32$ voxels. Arbitrary volumes are stored in Voxel Memory with dimensions that are multiples of 32 voxels; they are then automatically cropped to their original size during rendering. The vg500 ASIC contains all necessary hardware to arrange voxels into miniblocks and to skew and deskew miniblocks during data transfers to and from Voxel Memory.

## 5.3 Voxel Input To Rendering Pipelines

The description of the rendering pipeline in Section 3 assumes that the Interpolation and Gradient Estimation units read voxels in the slice-by-slice, beam-by-beam order described in Section 2. The Voxel Memory Input Network, shown in Figure 11, distributes data from the four Voxel Memory interfaces to the slice buffers. From there it can be read slice-by-slice and beam-by-beam by the four rendering pipelines.

Voxels in a miniblock are always read out of voxel memory in the same order because they are stored sequentially to take advantage of the burst capabilities of the SDRAMs. The miniblocks need to be re-arranged, based on the current view direction, so that the positions of the voxels correspond to the canonical positions assumed for tri-linear interpolation. This is achieved using simple miniblock reorder logic in each memory interface.

Because of the skewing of miniblocks in Voxel Memory, the four miniblocks output by the Voxel Memory controllers must be de-skewed and potentially re-shuffled based upon the chosen view direction. This is required so that the left-most voxel along the x axis flows down the leftmost pipeline and adjacent voxels in x flow down in neighboring pipelines. This is achieved with a global Voxel Memory Input Network that connects the four memory interfaces to the four rendering pipelines.

After the de-skewing network, miniblocks are written into the voxel slice buffers of the four rendering pipelines. Since data is read from voxel memory in miniblocks and processed by the pipelines as slices, a method exists to convert from one to another. The Voxel Memory interface actually reads two slices of voxels at a time because of the memory organization in miniblocks. Three slices of data must be stored so that the z gradients can be computed using central differences. After reading two slices of miniblocks and writing that data into four slice buffers, all necessary data now exists to compute interpolated samples and gradients.

## 5.4 Sectioning

To keep the amount of on-chip memory for the various FIFOs within reasonable limits, the volume data set is partitioned into sections and some intermediate values are off-loaded to external memory between the processing of sections. VolumePro implements sectioning only in the x direction. Each section is 32 voxels wide, corresponding to the memory organization outlined in Section 5.2. Instead of exchanging pixels between sections as in EM-Cube [13], VolumePro exchanges intermediate pipeline values between sections.

The impact of sectioning on the pipeline architecture is illustrated in Figure 11. In the right-hand pipeline of Figure 11 the shift registers are modified to optionally write values to Section Memory at the end of a section. The left-hand pipeline either reads values from Section Memory (at the beginning of a section) or accepts them from the right-hand pipeline. In effect, the Section Memory becomes a big, external FIFO capable of holding values that need to be recirculated in the x direction. Exactly the same values are written to, then read from, Section Memory as would have been passed to the next pipeline. Consequently, no approximation is made and no visual artifacts are introduced at section boundaries.

The voxel traversal order is therefore modified. In particular, voxels are read in slice-by-slice order within a single section. Similarly, within slices, voxels are read in beam-by-beam order, but with beams spanning only the width of a section. The full section is processed front-to-back, and the intermediate values needed for rendering near the right boundary of the section are written to Section Memory. Then the next section is processed. Values are read from the Section Memory in the same order that they had been written, and they are passed through the multiplexers of Figure 11 to the left pipeline. As far as the rendering algorithm is concerned, it is as if the values had been generated on the previous cycle and passed directly. That is, the same values are calculated in either case, but in different orders.

## 6 VolumePro PCI Card

The VolumePro board is a PCI Short Card with a 32-bit 66 MHz PCI interface (see Figure 2). Production shipments started in June 1999 at an initial price comparable to high-end PC graphics cards. The board contains a single vg500 rendering ASIC, twenty 64 Mbit SDRAMs with 16-bit datapaths, clock generation logic, and a voltage converter to make it 3.3 volt or 5 volt compliant. Figure 13 shows a block diagram of the components on the board and the busses connecting them.

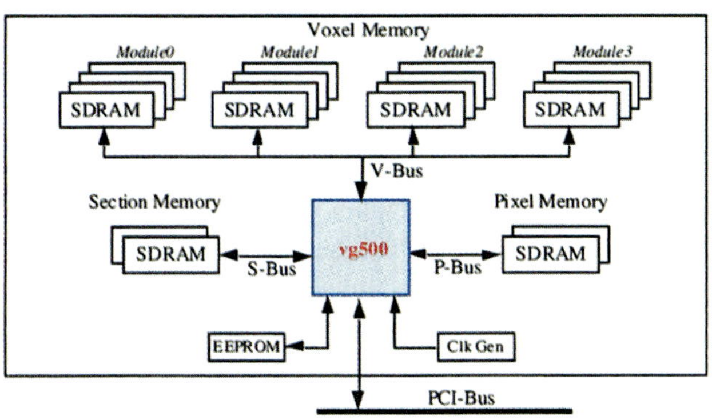


Figure 13: *VolumePro PCI board diagram.*

The vg500 ASIC interfaces directly to the system PCI-Bus. Access to the vg500's internal registers and to the off-chip memories is accomplished through the 32-bit 66 MHz PCI bus interface. The peak burst data rate of this interface is 264 MB/sec. Some of this bandwidth is consumed by image upload, some of it by other PCI system traffic. We currently estimate about 100 MB/sec available bandwidth for loading volume data from main memory.

Most registers are write-only and are memory-mapped via their own PCI base address register. Volume, pixel, and section memory are directly read/write memory-mapped into the PCI address space. The vg500 chip status is checked either by interrupts or by polling an on-chip status register. Alternatively, a copy of the status register gets DMA'ed to host memory when it changes. VolumePro supports many standard 16-bit and 32-bit pixel formats with on-the-fly conversion between formats during reads or writes.

The size of voxel memory is 128 MBytes, organized as four groups with four SDRAMs each. Two 64 Mbit SDRAMs make up Section Memory and two 64 Mbit SDRAMs of Pixel Memory contain the rendered base plane image. They can hold up to sixteen base planes, each with up to 512 × 512 32-bit RGBA pixels. This allows double-buffering of several base planes on the PCI card and pipelined retrieval, warping, and blending of images. The base plane pixels are transferred over the PCI bus to a companion 3D graphics card for the final image warp and display. The transfer of pixels from VolumePro, however, is the only integration with the rest of the graphics system. In particular, the current generation of the system does not perform any intermixing of polygons and volumes.

Several VolumePro PCI cards can be connected to a high-speed interconnect network for higher performance. Alternatively, several vg500 ASICs and their Voxel Memories can be integrated onto a single multi-processing rendering board. Volume data can be rendered in blocks, similar to supervolumes, on different boards or ASICs using coarse-grain parallelism. At the present time, however, we have no plans to implement such a multi-processing system.

## 7 VLI - The Volume Library Interface

Figure 14 shows the software infrastructure of the VolumePro system. The VLI API is a set of C++ classes that provide full access to

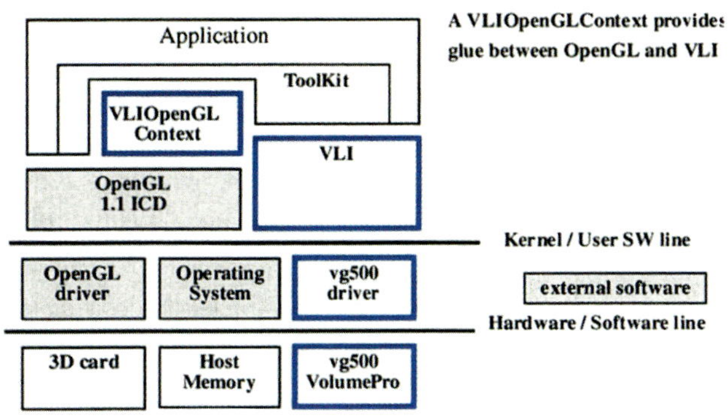


Figure 14: *Software infrastructure of the VolumePro system.*

the vg500 chip features. VLI does not replace an existing graphics API. Rather, VLI works cooperatively with a 3D graphics library, such as OpenGL, to manage the rendering of volumes and displaying the results in a 3D scene. We envision higher level toolkits and scene graphs on top of the VLI to be the primary interface layer to applications. The VLI classes can be grouped as follows:

- Volume data handling. VLIVolume manages voxel data storage, voxel data format, and transformations of the volume data such as shearing, scaling, and positioning in world space.
- Rendering elements. There are several VLI classes that provide access to the features described in Sections 3 and 4, such as color and opacity lookup tables, cameras, lights, cut planes, clipping, and more.
- Rendering context. The VLI class VLIContext is a container object for all attributes needed to render the volume. It is used to specify the volume data set and all rendering parameters (such as classification, illumination, and blending) for the current frame.

The VLI automatically computes reflectance maps based on light placement, sets up $\alpha$-correction based on viewing angle and sample spacing, supports anisotropic and gantry-tilted data sets by correcting the viewing and image warp matrices, and manages supervolumes, supersampling, and partial updates of volume data. In addition, there are VLI functions that provide initialization, configuration, and termination for the VolumePro hardware.

## 8 Conclusions

This paper describes the algorithm, architecture, and features of VolumePro, the world's first single-chip real-time volume rendering system. The rendering capabilities of VolumePro – 500 million tri-linear, Phong illuminated, composited samples per second – sets a new standard for volume rendering on consumer PCs. Its core features, such as on-the-fly gradient estimation, per-sample Phong illumination with arbitrary number of light sources, 4K RGBA classification tables, $\alpha$-blending with 12-bit precision, and gradient magnitude modulation, put it ahead of any other hardware solution for volume rendering. Additional features, such as supersampling, supervolumes, cropping and cut planes, enable the development of feature-rich, high-performance volume visualization applications.

Some important limitations of VolumePro are the restriction to rectilinear scalar volumes, the lack of perspective projections, and no support for intermixing of polygons and volume data. We believe that mixing of opaque polygons and volume data can be achieved by first rendering geometry, transferring z buffer values from the polygon card to the volume renderer, and then rendering the volume starting from these z values. Future versions of the system will support perspective projections and several voxel formats, including pre-classified material volumes and RGBA volumes. The limitation to rectilinear grids is more fundamental and hard to overcome.

We hope that the availability of VolumePro will spur more research in new and innovative interaction techniques for volume data, such as interactive experimentation with rendering parameters. This may lead to new solutions for difficult problems, such as data segmentation and transfer function design. Other areas for future research are hardware support for irregular grid rendering, accurate iso-surface rendering, and integration of polygon rasterization and texturing into volume rendering systems. We are currently working on a next generation system with more features while continually increasing the performance and reducing the cost.

## 9 Acknowledgments

We would like to thank the Volume Graphics Engineering team, especially Bill Peet and Beverly Schultz. Ingmar Bitter, Frank Dachille, Urs Kanus, Chris Kappler, and Dick Waters contributed to the ideas that are implemented in the system. Thanks also to Forrester Cole, voxel wrangler and image master. Thanks to the reviewers for their constructive comments, and to Vikram Simha, Ken Correl, and Jennifer Roderick for proofreading the paper. Special thanks to Arie Kaufman for having a vision 15 years ago and consistently making a dream come true.

## References

[1] K. Akeley. RealityEngine graphics. In *Computer Graphics*, Proceedings of SIGGRAPH 93, pages 109–116, August 1993.

[2] B. Cabral, N. Cam, and J. Foran. Accelerated volume rendering and tomographic reconstruction using texture mapping hardware. In *1994 Workshop on Volume Visualization*, pages 91–98, Washington, DC, October 1994.

[3] D. Cohen and A. Kaufman. A 3D skewing and de-skewing scheme for conflict-free access to rays in volume rendering. *IEEE Transactions on Computers*, 44(5):707–710, May 1995.

[4] T. J. Cullip and U. Neumann. Accelerating volume reconstruction with 3D texture mapping hardware. Technical Report TR93-027, Department of Computer Science at the University of North Carolina, Chapel Hill, 1993.

[5] R. A. Drebin, L. Carpenter, and P. Hanrahan. Volume rendering. *Computer Graphics*, 22(4):65–74, August 1988.

[6] A. Van Gelder and K. Kim. Direct volume rendering with shading via three-dimensional textures. In *ACM/IEEE Symposium on Volume Visualization*, pages 23–30, San Francisco, CA, October 1996.

[7] T. Guenther, C. Poliwoda, C. Reinhard, J. Hesser, R. Maenner, H.-P. Meinzer, and H.-J. Baur. VIRIM: A massively parallel processor for real-time volume visualization in medicine. In *Proceedings of the 9th Eurographics Workshop on Graphics Hardware*, pages 103–108, Oslo, Norway, September 1994.

[8] P. Haeberli and K. Akeley. The accumulation buffer; hardware support for high-quality rendering. In *Computer Graphics*, volume 24 of *Proceedings of SIGGRAPH 90*, pages 309–318, Dallas, TX, August 1990.

[9] G. Knittel and W. Strasser. Vizard – visualization accelerator for real-time display. In *Proceedings of the Siggraph/Eurographics Workshop on Graphics Hardware*, pages 139–146, Los Angeles, CA, August 1997.

[10] P. Lacroute. Analysis of a parallel volume rendering system based on the shear-warp factorization. *IEEE Transactions on Visualization and Computer Graphics*, 2(3):218–231, September 1996.

[11] P. Lacroute and M. Levoy. Fast volume rendering using a shear-warp factorization of the viewing transform. In *Computer Graphics*, Proceedings of SIGGRAPH 94, pages 451–457, July 1994.

[12] M. Levoy. Display of surfaces from volume data. *IEEE Computer Graphics & Applications*, 8(5):29–37, May 1988.

[13] R. Osborne, H. Pfister, H. Lauer, N. McKenzie, S. Gibson, W. Hiatt, and T. Ohkami. EM-Cube: An architecture for low-cost real-time volume rendering. In *Proceedings of the Siggraph/Eurographics Workshop on Graphics Hardware*, pages 131–138, Los Angeles, CA, August 1997.

[14] H. Pfister and A. Kaufman. Cube-4 – A scalable architecture for real-time volume rendering. In *1996 ACM/IEEE Symposium on Volume Visualization*, pages 47–54, San Francisco, CA, October 1996.

[15] P. Schröder and G. Stoll. Data parallel volume rendering as line drawing. In *1992 Workshop on Volume Visualization*, pages 25–31, Boston, MA, October 1992.

[16] J. van Scheltinga, J. Smit, and M. Bosma. Design of an on-chip reflectance map. In *Proceedings of the 10th Eurographics Workshop on Graphics Hardware*, pages 51–55, Maastricht, The Netherlands, August 1995.

[17] D. Voorhies and J. Foran. Reflection vector shading hardware. In *Computer Graphics*, Proceedings of SIGGRAPH 94, pages 163–166, Orlando, FL, July 1994.

[18] R. Westerman and T. Ertl. Efficiently using graphics hardware in volume rendering applications. In *Computer Graphics*, Proceedings of SIGGRAPH 98, pages 169–177, 1998.

[19] R. Yagel and A. Kaufman. Template-based volume viewing. *Computer Graphics Forum, Proceedings Eurographics*, 11(3):153–167, September 1992.

# Deep Compression for Streaming Texture Intensive Animations

Daniel Cohen-Or * Tel Aviv University

Yair Mann ‡ Webglide Ltd.

Shachar Fleishman * Tel Aviv University

## Abstract

This paper presents a streaming technique for synthetic texture intensive 3D animation sequences. There is a short latency time while downloading the animation, until an initial fraction of the compressed data is read by the client. As the animation is played, the remainder of the data is streamed online seamlessly to the client. The technique exploits frame-to-frame coherence for transmitting geometric and texture streams. Instead of using the original textures of the model, the texture stream consists of view-dependent textures which are generated by rendering offline nearby views. These textures have a strong temporal coherency and can thus be well compressed. As a consequence, the bandwidth of the stream of the view-dependent textures is narrow enough to be transmitted together with the geometry stream over a low bandwidth network. These two streams maintain a small online cache of geometry and view-dependent textures from which the client renders the walkthrough sequence in real-time. The overall data transmitted over the network is an order of magnitude smaller than an MPEG post-rendered sequence with an equivalent image quality.

**Keywords:** compression, MPEG, streaming, virtual environment, image-based rendering

## 1 Introduction

With the increasing popularity of network-based applications, compression of synthetic animation image sequences for efficient transmission is more important than ever. For long sequences even if the overall compression ratio is high, the latency time of downloading the compressed file might be prohibitive. A better network-based compression scheme is to partition the compressed sequence into two parts. The first part, or header, is small enough to be downloaded within an acceptable initialization time, while the second part is transmitted as a *stream*. The compressed data is broken up into a stream of data which is processed along the network pipeline, that is, the compressed data is transmitted from one end, and received, decoded and displayed at the other end. Streaming necessarily requires that all the pipeline stages operate in real-time. Clearly, the network bandwidth is the most constrained resource along the pipeline and thus the main challenge is to reduce the stream bandwidth enough to accommodate the network bandwidth constraint.

Standard video compression techniques that take advantage of frame-to-frame coherency, are insufficient for streaming. Given a moderate frame resolution of $256 \times 256$, an average MPEG frame is typically about 2-6K bytes. Assuming a network with a sustained transfer rate of 2K bytes per second, a reasonable quality of a few frames per second cannot be achieved. A significant improvement in compression ratio is still necessary for streaming video in real-time.

Synthetic animations have higher potential to be compressed than general video since more information is readily available for the compression algorithms [2, 12, 22]. Assuming, for example, that the geometric model and the animation script are relatively small, one can consider them as the compressed sequence, transmit them and decode them by simply rendering the animation sequence. By simultaneously transmitting the geometry and the script streams on demand, one can display very long animations over the network (see [19]). However, if the model consists of a large number of geometric primitives and textures, simple streaming is not enough. The texture stream is especially problematic since the texture data can be significantly larger than the geometric data. For some applications, replicated (tiled) textures can be used to avoid the burden of large textures. However, realistic textures typically require a large space. Moreover, detailed and complex environments can effectively be represented by a relatively small number of textured polygons [3, 13, 17, 20, 6, 21, 11]. For such *texture intensive* models the geometry and the animation script streams are relatively small, while the texture stream is prohibitively expensive. Indeed, the performance of current VRML browsers is quite limited when handling texture intensive environments [8].

In this paper we show that instead of streaming the textures, it is possible to stream *view-dependent textures* which are created by rendering nearby views. These textures have a strong temporal coherency and can thus be well compressed. As a consequence, the bandwidth of the stream of the view-dependent textures is narrow enough to be transmitted together with the geometry and the script streams over a low bandwidth network. Our results show that a walkthrough in a virtual environment consisting of tens of megabytes of textures can be streamed from a server to a client over a network with a sustained transfer rate of 2K bytes per second. In terms of compression ratios, our technique is an order of magnitude better than an MPEG sequence with an equivalent image quality.

## 2 Background

Standard video compression techniques are based on image-based motion estimation [9]. An MPEG video sequence consists of intra frames (I), predictive frames (P) and interpolated frames (B). The I frames are coded independently of any other frames in the sequence. The P and B frames are coded using motion estimation and interpolations, and thus, they are substantially smaller than the I frames. The compression ratio is directly dependent on the success of the motion estimation for coding the P frames. Using image-based techniques the optical flow field between successive frames can be approximated. It defines the motion vectors, or the correspondence between the pixels of successive frames. To reduce the overhead of encoding the motion information, common techniques compute a motion vector for a block of pixels rather than for individual pixels. For a synthetic scene the available model can assist in computing the optical flow faster or more accurately [2, 22]. These model-based motion estimation techniques improve the compression ratio, but the overhead of the block-based motion approximation is still too high for streaming acceptable image quality.

A different approach was introduced by Levoy [12]. Instead of compressing post-rendered images, it is possible to render the animation on-the-fly at both ends of the communication. The rendering task is partitioned between the server (sender) and client (receiver). Assuming the server is a high-end graphics workstation, it

*Computer Science Department, Tel-Aviv University 69978, Israel. E-mail: {daniel, shacharf}@math.tau.ac.il

‡Webglide Ltd. E-mail yair@webglide.com

can render high and low quality images, compute the residual error between them, and transmit the residual image compressed. The client needs to render only the low quality images and to add the transmitted residual images to restore the full quality images. It was shown that the overall compression ratio is better than conventional techniques.

If this technique is to be adapted for streaming of the residual images, it would require pre-computing the residual images and downloading the entire model and animation sequence before streaming can take place. It would be possible to transmit only key-frame images and blend (or extrapolate) the in-between frames [4, 14, 15]. However, it is not clear how to treat texture intensive animations, since downloading the textures is still necessary to keep the residual images small enough for streaming. Other related techniques use *imposters* [17, 20] and *sprites* [18, 11] as image-based primitives to render nearby views. When the quality of a primitive drops below some threshold, it is recomputed without exploiting its temporal coherence.

(a) source view (b) mapped view

Figure 1: (a) A source image of a textured cube. (b) A view of the same cube obtained by backmapping into the source image. Note that the texture on the leftmost face is severely blurred, while the other two faces do not exhibit significant artifacts.

## 3 View-dependent Texture Streaming

Assume an environment consisting of a polygonal geometric model, textures, and a number of light sources. Furthermore, assume that the environment is texture-intensive, that is, the size of the environment database is dominated by the textures, while the geometry-space is significantly smaller than the texture-space. Nevertheless, the size of the environment is too large to be downloaded from the server to the client in an acceptable time.

Streaming the environment requires the server to transmit the animation script and, according to the camera viewing parameters, to transmit the visible parts of the model. However, the size of the textures necessary for a single view is too large to be streamed in real-time. Instead of using these original textures, we show that it is better to use nearby views as textures. These views can be regarded as view-dependent textures which are effectively valid only for texturing the geometry viewed from nearby viewing directions.

Given the current camera position, the client generates a new frame based on the data streamed so far, which includes at least the visible polygons from the current camera position and a number of nearby views. The new frame is a perspective view generated by rendering the geometry where the nearby perspective views serve as texture maps. Since the correspondence between two perspective views is a projective map, the model is rendered by applying a projective mapping rather than a perspective mapping. This projective map can be expressed by a linear transformation in homogeneous space, and can be implemented by rational linear interpolation which requires divisions at each pixel [10, 16].

Nearby views are advantageous as textures because (i) they have an "almost" one-to-one correspondence with the current view and therefore, a bi-linear filter, is sufficient to produce quality images, and (ii) they are post-rendered and may include various global illumination effects. Figure 1 shows a simple example of a textured cube. In these views there are three visible polygonal faces. The left image was rendered with a standard perspective texture mapping, while the right image was rendered by applying a backward projective texture mapping from the left image. The projection of each of the cube faces on the left image serves as a view-dependent texture for its correspondence projection on the right image. The size and shape of the source texture is close to its target. This reduces many aliasing problems and hence simplifies the filtering. In this example, for expository reasons, the two views are not "nearby", otherwise they would appear almost indistinguishable. Later we will quantify the meaning of "nearby". Since the view-dependent textures are generated off-line, they can be involved and can account for many global illumination effects, including shadows cast from remote objects. This simplifies the generation of a new frame, since the rendering is independent of the complexity of the illumination model.

View-dependent textures, like view-independent textures are discrete, therefore, when resampled, artifacts are introduced. If the target area is larger than the corresponding source area the result appears blurry, as can be seen on the leftmost face of the cube in Figure 1b. On the other hand, if the target area is smaller than the source area (the rightmost face), by appropriately filtering the source samples, the target image has no noticeable artifacts. Thus, an appropriate view-dependent texture should be (i) created as close as possible to the new view and (ii) created from a direction in which the area is expanded relative to the target. In Section 4 we elaborate on the factor which controls the quality of the view-dependent textures.

One should also consider the visibility, namely that at least part of a polygon can be hidden at the nearby view, while being visible at the current view. This is a well-known problem in image-based rendering [4, 5]. However, in a streaming application where the compressed sequence is precomputed, visibility gaps are known a priori and for each gap there is at least one nearby view that can close that gap. It should be emphasized that the nearby views are not restricted to be from the "past", but can be located near a "future" location of the camera.

As the animation proceeds, the quality and validity of the view-dependent textures decrease as the camera viewing parameters deviate. Thus, new closer view-dependent textures need to be streamed to guarantee that each polygon can be mapped to an appropriate texture. The stream of new view-dependent textures is temporally coherent and thus instead of transmitting the compressed textures, it is possible to exploit this texture-to-texture coherence to get a better compression. The old texture is warped towards the new view and the residual error between the new view and the warped image is computed. The residual image can then be better compressed than the raw texture.

A view-dependent texture is not necessarily a full size nearby view, but may include only the view of part of the environment. Based on a per-polygon amortization factor (see Section 4), a subset of the view-dependent textures, defined by the polygon mesh, is updated. This further reduces the size of texture stream to be optimal with respect to the amortization factor. Thus, a key point is to use a good texture quality estimate.

## 4 The Texture Quality Factor

Given a view and a set of view-dependent textures, it is necessary to select the best quality texture for each visible polygon. As can be seen in Figure 1 for some faces of the cube (in (b)) the view-dependent texture (in (a)) is more appropriate than others. The quality of the source texture is related to the area covered by the projection of each polygon, or cube face in Figure 1, in the two views. Thus, a per polygon local *scaling factor* is required to estimate the areas in the source texture that locally shrink or expand when mapped onto the target image. When the scaling factor is $\leq 1$ we can consider the source image appropriate for generating the target image. As the factor increases above 1, more and more blur appears in the target image, and we should consider the source texture less and less appropriate. This per polygon texture quality factor is used to select the best source texture out of the available set of view-dependent textures. If the best source is above some predetermined threshold, a new texture is required. However, a successful streaming of the textures guarantees that there is always one available texture whose quality factor is satisfactory.

Figure 2 illustrates the per-polygon source selection process. Two examples of nearby views are shown in (a) and (b). The scale factor for the in-between images (f) is visualized using the gray level images (c) and (d), where white is used for low scale factor and black is used for high scale factor. The (c) and (d) columns visualize the scale factor when mapping the textures from (a) and (b) to (f). For each polygon, we select the texture from the image that has the lowest scale factor, this is visualized in (e), where the red levels are the scale factors from (a) and the blue levels are the scale factor from (b).

We are now left with the problem of estimating the maximal value of the scaling factor in a particular polygon in the source image, for a given target image (see also [11]). Note that the factor is defined independently of the visibility of the polygon. We first discuss the case where the polygon is mapped from the source to the target by a linear transformation, and then discuss the more general non-linear case.

Let $A$ be a square matrix corresponding to some linear transformation. The scaling factor of a linear transformation is the 2-norm of the matrix $A$, i.e. the maximum 2-norm of $Av$ over all unit vectors $v$.

$$\max_{||v||_2=1} ||Av||_2$$

It can be shown [7] that the 2-norm of $A$ equals the square root of $\lambda_{max}$, the largest eigenvalue of $A^{\mathrm{T}}A$. In the case of two-dimensional linear transformations, where $A$ is a 2 by 2 matrix, we can write down a closed-form expression for $\lambda_{max}$. Let $a_{ij}$ denote the elements of $A$ and $e_{ij}$ the elements of $A^{\mathrm{T}}A$:

$$A = \begin{pmatrix} a_{11} & a_{12} \\ a_{21} & a_{22} \end{pmatrix} \qquad A^{\mathrm{T}}A = \begin{pmatrix} e_{11} & e_{12} \\ e_{21} & e_{22} \end{pmatrix} \tag{1}$$

The eigenvalues of the matrix $A^{\mathrm{T}}A$ are the roots of the polynomial $\det(A^{\mathrm{T}}A - \lambda I)$, where $I$ is the identity matrix. In the two-dimensional case, $\lambda_{max}$ is the largest root of the quadratic equation

$$(e_{11} - \lambda)(e_{22} - \lambda) - e_{12}e_{21} = 0. \tag{2}$$

Thus,

$$\lambda_{max} = \frac{e_{11} + e_{22} + \sqrt{(e_{11} + e_{22})^2 - 4(e_{11}e_{22} - e_{12}e_{21})}}{2}. \tag{3}$$

Expressing the elements $e_{ij}$ in terms of the elements $a_{ij}$ yields

$$A^{\mathrm{T}}A = \begin{pmatrix} a_{11}^2 + a_{21}^2 & a_{11}a_{12} + a_{21}a_{22} \\ a_{11}a_{12} + a_{21}a_{22} & a_{12}^2 + a_{22}^2 \end{pmatrix}, \tag{4}$$

and finally, defining $S = \frac{1}{2}(a_{11}^2 + a_{12}^2 + a_{21}^2 + a_{22}^2)$, we get

$$\lambda_{max} = S + \sqrt{S^2 - (a_{11}a_{22} - a_{12}a_{21})^2} \tag{5}$$

Dealing with non-linear transformations, such as projective transformations, requires measuring the scaling factor locally at a specific point in the image by using the partial derivatives of the transformation at the given point. The partial derivatives are used as the coefficients of a linear transformation.

Let us denote by $x_0, y_0$, and $x_1, y_1$ the source and target image coordinates of a point, respectively, and by $x, y, z$ the three-dimensional location of that point in target camera coordinates. We have:

$$(x, y, z)^{\mathrm{T}} = \begin{pmatrix} a & b & c \\ d & e & f \\ g & h & i \end{pmatrix} (x_0, y_0, 1)^{\mathrm{T}} \tag{6}$$

$$(x_1, y_1)^{\mathrm{T}} = \frac{1}{z}(x, y)^{\mathrm{T}} \tag{7}$$

or explicitly,

$$x_1 = \frac{ax_0 + by_0 + c}{gx_0 + hy_0 + i} \qquad y_1 = \frac{dx_0 + ey_0 + f}{gx_0 + hy_0 + i} \tag{8}$$

The partial derivatives of the above mapping at $(x_1, y_1)$ define its gradient, which is a linear transformation:

$$A = \begin{pmatrix} \partial x_1/\partial x_0 & \partial x_1/\partial y_0 \\ \partial y_1/\partial x_0 & \partial y_1/\partial y_0 \end{pmatrix} = \frac{1}{z^2}\begin{pmatrix} za - x_1 g & zb - x_1 h \\ zd - y_1 g & ze - y_1 h \end{pmatrix} \tag{9}$$

In cases where the field of view is small, and there is only a little rotation of the plane relative to the source and target views, the following approximation can be used. The transformation of the plane points from source to target image can be approximated by:

$$\begin{aligned} x_1 &= a + bx_0 + cy_0 + gx_0^2 + hx_0y_0 \\ y_1 &= d + ex_0 + fy_0 + gx_0y_0 + hy_0^2 \end{aligned} \tag{10}$$

This is called a pseudo 2D projective transformation and is further explained in [1]. In this case we get:

$$A = \begin{pmatrix} b + 2gx_0 + hy_0 & c + hx_0 \\ e + gy_0 & f + gx_0 + 2hy_0 \end{pmatrix} \tag{11}$$

To estimate the maximal scaling factor, the gradient can be computed at the three vertices of a triangle. In cases where the triangle is small enough, even one sample (at the center of the triangle) can yield a good approximation. Our experiments have shown that a scale factor in the range of [1.3, 1.4], yields high quality images while maintaining high compression ratio.

## 5 Geometry Streaming

We have discussed the strategy for selecting the best view-dependent texture from those available. The system guarantees that at least one appropriate view-dependent texture has already been streamed to the client. If for some reason an appropriate texture is not available on time, some blur is likely to be noticed. However, the error is not critical. On the other hand, a missing polygon might cause a hole in the scene and the visual effect would be unacceptable. Thus, the geometry stream gets a higher priority so as to avoid any geometric miss.

Detecting and streaming the visible polygons from a given neighborhood is not an easy problem. Many architectural models are inherently partitioned into cells and portals by which the cell-to-cell visibility can be precomputed. However, since the geometry stream is computed offline, the visible polygons can be detected by rendering the entire sequence. The set of polygons visible in each frame can be detected by rendering each polygon with ID index color and then scanning the frame buffer collecting all the ID's of the visible polygons. The definition of a polygon that is first visible is transmitted together with its ID. During the online rendering the client maintains a list of all the polygons which have been visible so far, and a cache of the "hot" ID's, i.e., the polygons which are either visible in the current frame or in a nearby frame. The temporal sequence of the hot ID's is precomputed and is a part of the geometric stream. The cache of hot polygons serves as a visibility culling mechanism, since the client needs to render only a small conservative superset of the visible polygons, which is substantially smaller than the entire model.

Table 1: A comparison of the streaming technique (VDS) with an MPEG encoding. The frame resolution is 240 × 180.

| animation (# frames) | size (header) | RMS (0-255) | bits/pix | bits/sec |
|---|---|---|---|---|
| Arts (435) | | | | |
| VDS | 80K (23K) | 18.6 | 0.034 | 29511 |
| MPEG | 1600K | 19.2 | 1.61 | 619168 |
| MPEG | 200K | 31 | 0.085 | 73766 |
| Gallery (1226) | | | | |
| VDS | 111K (30K) | 19.15 | 0.0168 | 14563 |
| MPEG | 1830K | 20.03 | 0.277 | 239436 |
| MPEG | 333K | 27.41 | 0.05 | 43523 |
| Office (1101) | | | | |
| VDS | 177K (72K) | 22.47 | 0.03 | 25722 |
| MPEG | 2000K | 22.60 | 0.336 | 290644 |
| MPEG | 337K | 34.71 | 0.056 | 48937 |

## 6 Results and Conclusions

In our implementation the precomputed sequence of view-dependent textures is streamed to the client asynchronously. The stream updates the set of view-dependent textures from which the client renders the animation. The texture update frequency is defined to guarantee some reasonable quality. The choice of frequency directly effects the compression ratio. Reasonable quality is a subjective jusgement, however we will analyze it quantitatively. We use the *root mean square* (RMS) as an objective measurement to compare MPEG compression and our compression technique (denoted in the following by VDS (View Dependent texture Stream)) with the uncompressed images.

Figure 3 shows five samples of the comparison taken from three sequences that were encoded both in MPEG and VDS. The first two examples, "Arts" and "Gallery", are from two virtual museum walkthroughs, and the third example "Office" is of an animation. The quantitative results are shown in Table 1. Each animation was compressed by MPEG and VDS; we see that when they have about the same RMS, the size of the MPEG is about 10-20 times larger than the VDS. When MPEG is forced to compress the sequence down to a smaller size, it is still 2-3 times larger than the VDS, and its quality is significantly worse. This is evident from the corresponding RMS values in the table and visually noticeable in Figure 3. The VDS is not free of artifacts; some are apparent in the images in Figure 3. Most of them are due to imperfect implementation of the rendering algorithm, rather than being intrinsic to the algorithm. Note that there are slight popping effects when a texture update changes the resolution, which could have been avoided by using a blending technique.

The texture intensive models were generated with 3D Studio Max. The virtual museum "Arts", consists of 3471 polygons and 19.6 Megabytes of texture, and the "Office" animation consists of 5309 polygons and 16.9M Megabytes of 3D Studio Max's textures, that were not optimized for size. Part of the compressed data is the header, which includes the initial data necessary to start the local rendering, that is, the geometry, the animation script, and the first nearby view in JPEG format. Thus, the cost effectiveness of streaming is higher for longer animations. The size of the header appears in parenthesis near the size values in Table 1.

We implemented both the client and the server on a Pentium machine, which was integrated in a browser with ActiveX. The client and the server were connected by a dial-up connection of 14400 bits per second. The download time of the initial setup data, namely the header, is equivalent to the download time of a JPEG image. This means a few seconds on a network with a sustained transfer rate of less than 2K bytes per second. We attached hot-spots (hyperlinks) to the 3D objects visible in the animation, by which the user chooses either high resolution images or precomputed sequences which are streamed online according to his selection.

The offline process that generates the VDS sequence takes a few minutes for animations of several hundred frames as in the above examples. Currently, the client's local rendering is the slowest part of the real-time loop. It should be emphasized that the client uses no graphics hardware to accelerate the rendering which requires a perspective texture mapping. We believe that optimizing the client rendering mechanism will permit streaming sequences of higher resolutions. We are planning to extend our system by allowing some degree of freedom in the navigation, for example, by supporting branching from one movie sequence to others. Currently, we are working on applying computer-vision techniques to reconstruct the geometry of real-world movies and compress them using our geometry-based compression. We believe that the importance of geometry-based compression is likely to play an increasing role in 3D network-based applications.

## References


[1] G. Adiv, Determining three-dimensional motion and structure from optical flow generated by several moving objects. in *IEEE Transactions on PAMI*, 7(4):384-401, July 1985.

[2] M. Agrawala, A. Beers and N. Chaddha. Model-based motion estimation for synthetic animations. *Proc. ACM Multimedia '95*.

[3] D. G. Aliaga. Visualization of complex models using dynamic texture-based simplification. *Proceedings of Visualization 96*, 101–106, October 1996.

[4] S.E. Chen and L. Williams. View interpolation for image synthesis. *Computer Graphics (SIGGRAPH '93 Proceedings)*, 279–288, August 1993.

[5] L. Darsa and B. Costa and A. Varshney. Navigating static environments using image-space simplification and morphing. *1997 Symposium on Interactive 3D Graphics*, Providence, Rhode Island; April 28–30, 1997.

[6] P.E. Debevec, C.J. Taylor and J. Malik. Modeling and Rendering Architecture from Photographs: A Hybrid Geometry- and Image-Based Approach. *Computer Graphics (SIGGRAPH '96 Proceedings)*, 11–20, August 1996.

[7] G.H. Golub, C.F. Van Loan. Matrix Computations. Second edition, pp. 56–60.

[8] J. Hardenberg, G. Bell and M. Pesce. VRML: Using 3D to surf the web. SIGGRAPH'95 course, No. 12 (1995).

[9] D. LeGall. MPEG: A video compression standard for multimedia applications. in *Communications of the ACM*, Vol 34(4), April 1991, pp. 46–58.

[10] P.S. Heckbert and H.P. Moreton. Interpolation for polygon texture mapping and shading. *State of the Art in Computer Graphics: Visualization and Modeling*. pp. 101–111, 1991.

[11] Jed Lengyel and John Snyder. Rendering with Coherent Layers, *Computer Graphics (SIGGRAPH 97 Proceedings)*, 233-242, August 1997.

[12] M. Levoy. Polygon-assisted JPEG and MPEG compression of synthetic images. *Computer Graphics ( SIGGRAPH '95 Proceeding )*, 21–28, August 1995.

[13] P.W.C. Maciel and P. Shirley. Visual navigation of large environments using textured clusters. *1995 Symposium on Interactive 3D Graphic*, 95–102, April 1995.

[14] Y. Mann and D. Cohen-Or. Selective pixel transmission for navigating in remote virtual environments. in *Computer Graphics Forum (Proceedings of Eurographics'97)*, Volume 16(3), 201–206, September 1997.

[15] W.R. Mark, L. McMillan, G. Bishop. Post-rendering 3D warping. *Proceedings of 1997 Symposium on Interactive 3D Graphic*, Providence, Rhode Island; April 28–30, 1997.

[16] M. Segal, C Korobkin, R. van Widenfelt, J. Foran and P. Haeberli. Fast shadows and lighting effects using texture mapping. *Computer Graphics (SIGGRAPH '92 Proceedings)*, 249–252, 1992.

[17] G. Schaufler and W. Sturzlinger. A three dimensional image cache for virtual reality. in *Computer Graphics Forum (Proceedings of Eurographics'96)*, Volume 15(3), 227–235, 1996

[18] G. Schaufler. Per-Object Image Warping with Layered Impostors. in Proceedings of the 9th Eurographics Workshop on Rendering '98, Vienna, 145–156, June 1998.

[19] D. Schmalstieg and M. Gervautz. Demand-driven geometry transmission for distributed virtual environment. *Eurographics '96, Computer Graphics Forum*, Volume 15(3), 421-432, 1996.

[20] J. Shade, D. Lischinski, D.H. Salesin, J. Snyder and T. DeRose. Hierarchical image caching for accelerated walkthroughs of complex environments. *Computer Graphics (SIGGRAPH '96 Proceedings)*,

[21] F. Sillion, G. Drettakis, and B. Bodelet. Efficient impostor manipulation for real-time visualization of urban scenery, in *Computer Graphics Forum (Proceedings of Eurographics'97)*, Volume 16(3), 207–218, September 1997.

[22] D.S. Wallach, S. Kunapalli and M.F. Cohen. Accelerated MPEG compression of dynamic polygonal scenes. *Computer Graphics (SIGGRAPH '94 Proceedings)*, 193–197, July 1994.

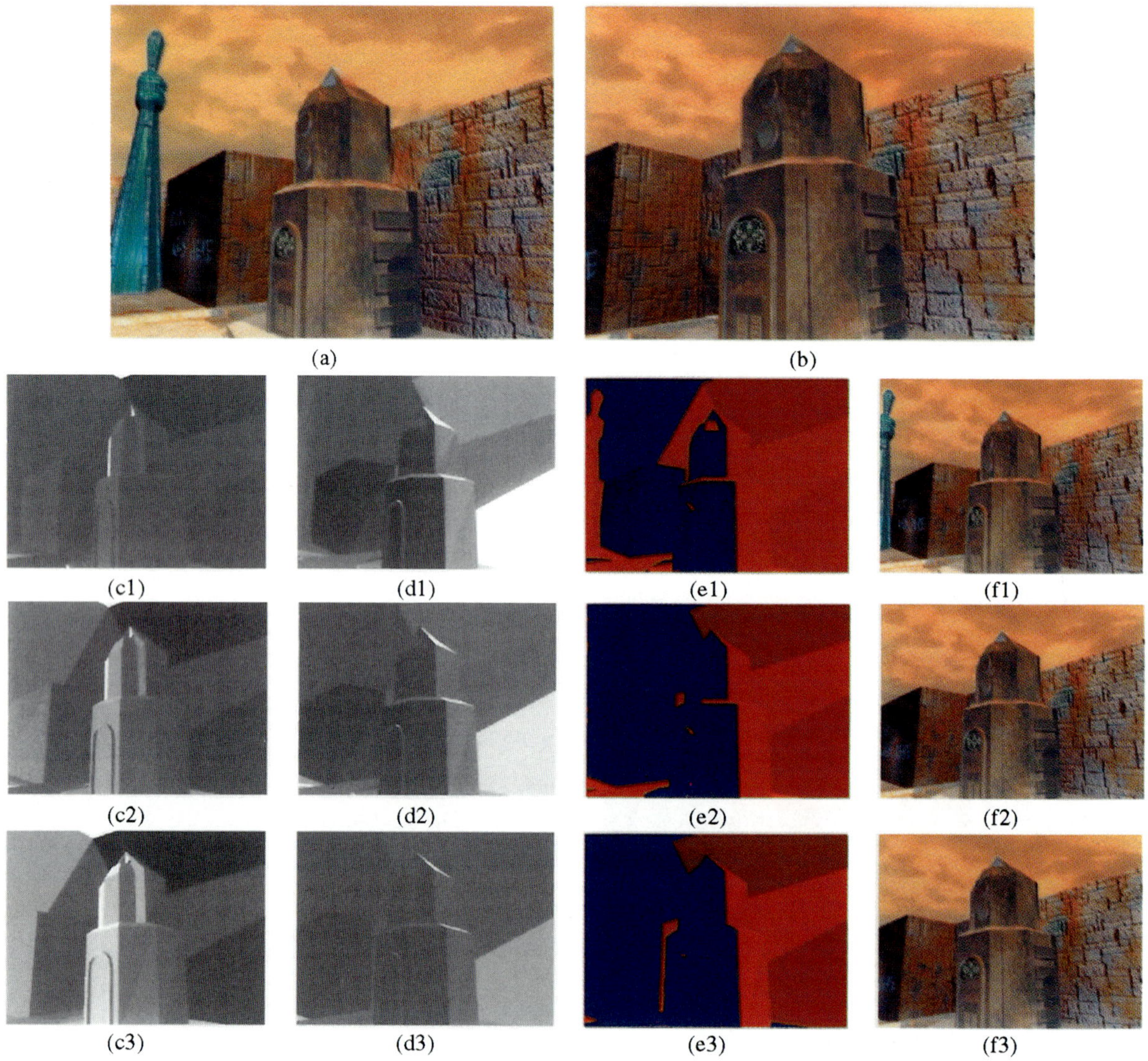


Figure 2: The scale factor. (a) and (b) are the two nearby views, (c) and (d) the per polygon scale factor in gray level from (a) and (b), respectively, (e) the red level and blue level polygons are mapped from (a) and (b), respectively, (f) three inbetween images.

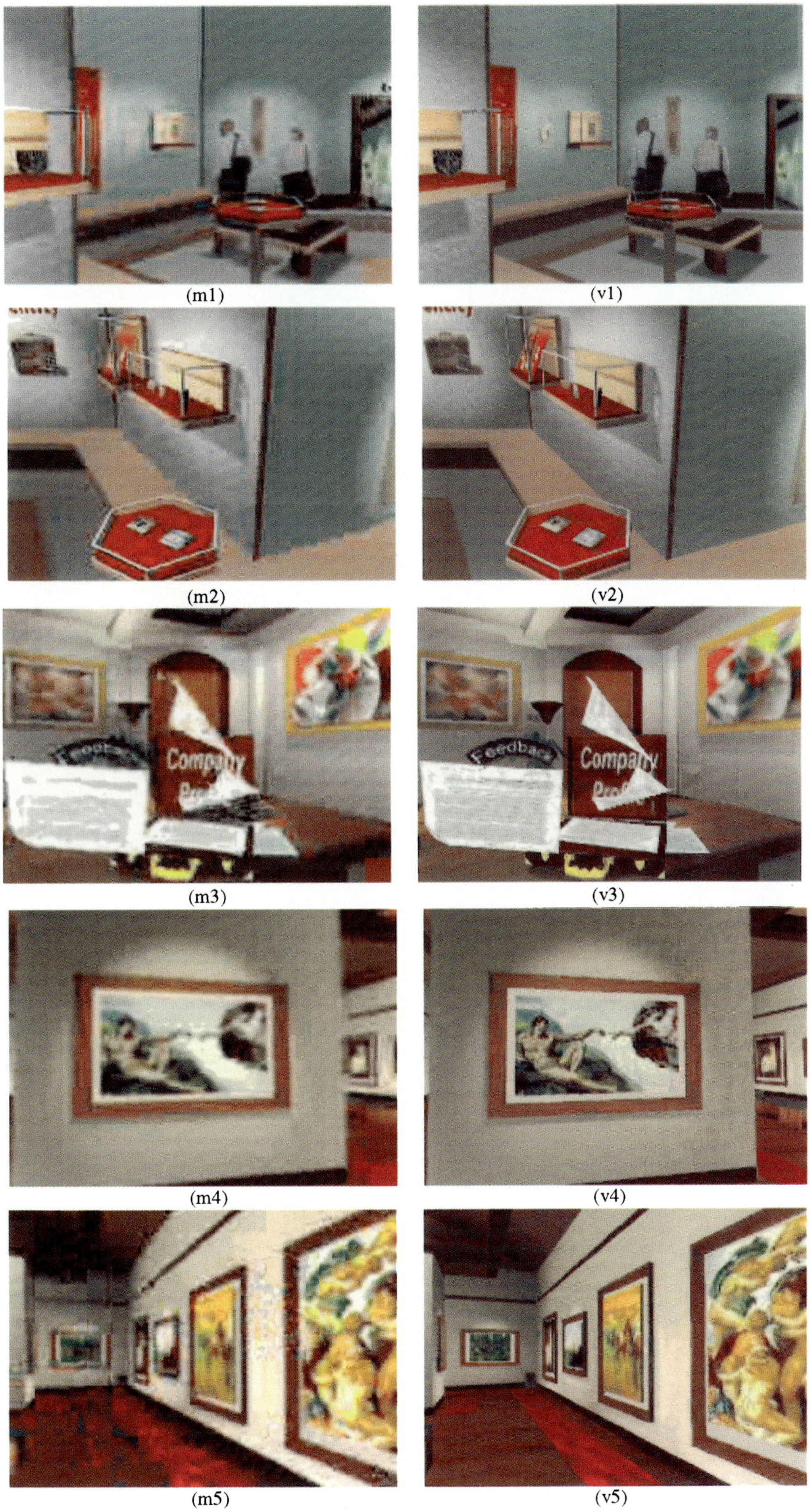


Figure 3: A comparison between VDS and MPEG. The images in the left column are MPEG frames and in the right column are VDS frames. The size of MPEG sequence is about three times larger than the VDS sequence.

# Optimization of Mesh Locality for Transparent Vertex Caching

Hugues Hoppe
Microsoft Research

## ABSTRACT

Bus traffic between the graphics subsystem and memory can become a bottleneck when rendering geometrically complex meshes. In this paper, we investigate the use of vertex caching to transparently reduce geometry bandwidth. Use of an indexed triangle strip representation permits application programs to animate the meshes at video rates, and provides backward compatibility on legacy hardware. The efficiency of vertex caching is maximized by reordering the faces in the mesh during a preprocess. We present two reordering techniques, a fast greedy strip-growing algorithm and a local optimization algorithm. The strip-growing algorithm performs lookahead simulations of the cache to adapt strip lengths to the cache capacity. The local optimization algorithm improves this initial result by exploring a set of perturbations to the face ordering. The resulting cache miss rates are comparable to the efficiency of the earlier mesh buffer scheme described by Deering and Chow, even though the vertex cache is not actively managed.

**CR Categories:** I.3.1 [Computer Graphics]: Hardware Architecture; I.3.3 [Computer Graphics]: Picture/Image Generation - Display algorithms;

**Additional Keywords:** geometry compression, triangle strips.

## 1 INTRODUCTION

Graphics performance in low-end computer systems has recently experienced significant growth due to the integration of 3D graphics functions into custom VLSI graphics processors. The graphics subsystem now shares many similarities with the central processor. Both consist of a massively integrated processing unit, a local memory cache, and a bus to main memory (see Figure 1). Reducing the *von Neumann* bottleneck between the CPU and main memory has been a fundamental problem in computer architecture. The graphics subsystem now experiences a similar bottleneck.

In the traditional polygon-rendering pipeline, the graphics processor must access two types of information from memory: (1) the model geometry and (2) the raster images (e.g. texture map, bump map, environment map) used in shading this geometry. The problem of reducing texture image bandwidth has been studied recently [7]. In this paper, we address the problem of reducing geometry bandwidth.

The model geometry is usually described as a mesh of triangle faces sharing a common set of vertices (Figure 4a). On average, each mesh vertex is shared by 6 adjacent triangles. Vertex data, which may include position, normal, colors, and texture coordinates,

Web: http://research.microsoft.com/~hoppe/



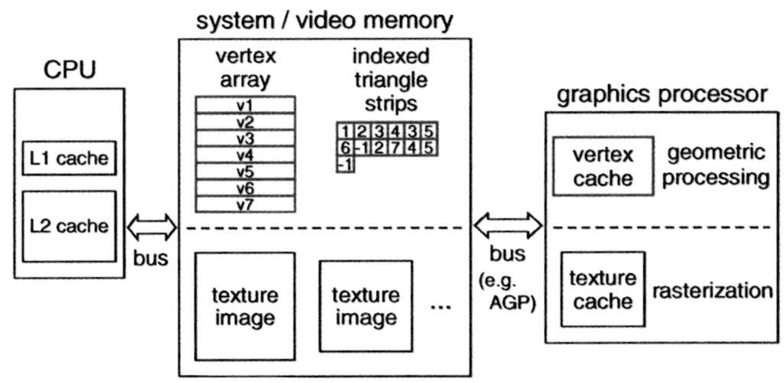


Figure 1: System architecture.

requires on the order of 32 bytes, so it is desirable to minimize the number of times this data must be read from memory. One common technique for reducing the geometry bandwidth (by a factor of almost 3) is to organize faces into triangle strips, so that two vertices are re-used between successive faces [5, 12]. Implementing such triangle strips requires a set of 3 vertex registers in the graphics processor.

The use of a larger vertex register set has the potential to further reduce geometry bandwidth by another factor of nearly 2. The key is to reorder the faces within the triangle mesh so as to maximize references to vertices already loaded in registers. Such an approach was pioneered by Michael Deering [4], and further developed by Mike Chow [3]. In their framework, the vertex data is quantized and delta-encoded into a compressed geometry stream. This geometry stream includes "push bits" to explicitly specify which vertices should be loaded into a first-in-first-out (FIFO) *mesh buffer*. Deering and Chow [3, 4] report excellent compression rates of 3–8 bytes per triangle.

In this paper, our approach is to improve locality of vertex references through a traditional application programming interface (API) for meshes. We investigate the use of a *vertex cache* in the graphics processor to *transparently* buffer data for recently referenced vertices. During a preprocess, the faces of a mesh are reordered to maximize references to vertices in the cache.

Because the traditional mesh API does not compress vertex data, the bandwidth savings in transparent vertex caching are more modest than those obtained by Deering and Chow. However, the framework offers several practical benefits. Because the vertex data is stored in native floating-point format, it can be efficiently modified from frame to frame by the application to create dynamic models. For instance, animated skinned meshes represent a significant portion of geometric bandwidth in some recent computer games [2]. Moreover, an existing application program requires no modification since it continues to use the same API. All that is necessary is to preprocess its geometric models to appropriately reorder the mesh faces. Finally, the approach provides backward compatibility since these preprocessed models still render efficiently using the same API on legacy hardware optimized for triangle strips.

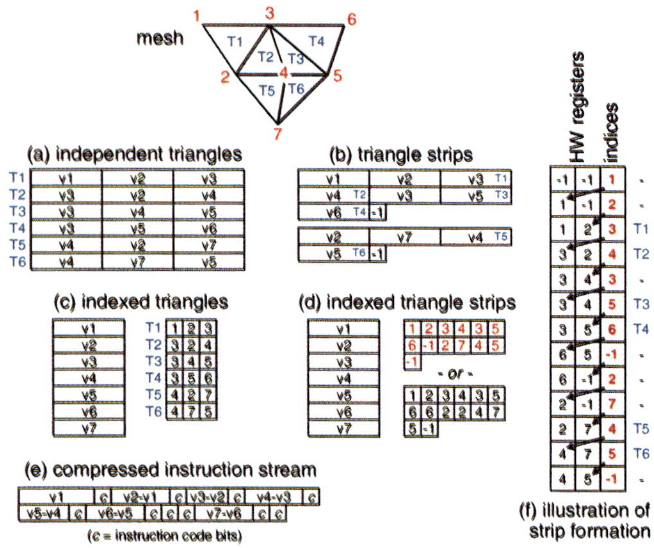


Figure 2: Memory organizations for representing meshes.

| Mesh organization | Memory size | Transfer size |
|---|---|---|
| independent triangles | $96m$ | $96m$ |
| triangle strips | $32bm$ | $32bm$ |
| indexed triangles | $\approx 22m$ | $102m$ |
| indexed triangle strips | $\approx (16+2b)m$ | $34bm$ |

Table 1: Memory and transfer requirements (in bytes).

We cast face reordering as a discrete optimization problem with an explicit cost function corresponding to bus traffic. To approach this problem, we first present a greedy strip-growing algorithm for reordering the faces in a mesh to improve locality. It is inspired by the method of Chow [3]. It differs in that it explicitly simulates the behavior of the vertex cache through a lookahead procedure. The cache miss rates resulting from this algorithm are comparable to those reported by Chow, despite the fact that the mesh interface lacks explicit cache management (e.g. "push bits").

We also explore a local optimization scheme to further improve the result of the greedy strip-growing algorithm. This optimization scheme uses several operators to locally perturb the face ordering. Although the optimization scheme is several orders of magnitude slower, it is effective at further reducing vertex-cache miss rates by several percent.

## 2 REPRESENTATIONS FOR MESHES

In this section we briefly review various memory organizations for representing triangle meshes, and analyze the bus traffic necessary for the graphics processor to render the meshes.

Let $n$ denote the number of vertices in the mesh, and $m$ the number of triangle faces. Often, we use the approximation $m \approx 2n$. Vertex data is assumed to require 32 bytes (3 words for position, 3 words for normal, and 2 words for texture coordinates). Vertex data may be more compact if the normal or texture coordinates are omitted. However, to support multi-texturing, several graphics API's now allow specification of multiple texture coordinates per vertex, so vertex data may also be larger. Some of the representations refer to vertices through indices; each index is assumed to occupy 2 bytes. Although this constrains the maximum mesh size to approximately 128K faces, more complex models are commonly represented as collections of smaller, independent meshes. The mesh representations are illustrated in Figure 2, and a summary of the analysis appears in Table 1.

### 2.1 Traditional representations

**Independent triangles** The mesh is organized as an array of $m$ faces, each containing data for its 3 face vertices, for a total of $m \cdot 3 \cdot 32 \approx 96m$ bytes. Although this organization is seldom used in memory, many graphics drivers convert other representations into such a stream when sending the data to the graphics system.

**Triangle strips** The mesh faces are organized into sequences of contiguous faces called strips. The first face in the strip is specified by three vertices, and each subsequent face uses one additional vertex. Some interfaces (e.g. IRIS GL) allow explicit control over the direction of strip formation in *generalized triangle strips*. More recent, memory-based representations define *sequential triangle strips*, in which the direction of strip formation alternates left/right [12]. The default strip direction can be overriden by duplicating a vertex in the data stream, for instance vertex 3 in Figures 2b,d,f. The overall size of the representation is $32bm$ bytes, where $b$ is a strip "bloat" factor to account for the costs of restarting strips and overriding strip direction. Typically, $1.1 \le b \le 1.5$ . Evans et al. [5] and Xiang et al. [16] present techniques for generating good triangle strips, that is, minimizing $b$.

**Indexed triangles** The mesh is organized as an array of vertices, and an array of faces where each face refers to its 3 vertices through indices. The memory representation has size $n \cdot 32 + m \cdot 3 \cdot 2 \approx 22m$ bytes. Although this representation is more concise than triangle strips, the graphics processor must read more data from memory, a total of $m \cdot 3 \cdot (2+32) = 102m$ bytes.

**Indexed triangle strips** Again, the mesh consists of a vertex array and faces that refer to these vertices through indices, but here the faces are organized into strips. For example, such an interface is implemented in Microsoft Direct3D by the DrawIndexedPrimitiveVB(D3DPT_TRIANGLESTRIP,...) function call. We assume that a strip is restarted using a special vertex index "–1" (or alternatively by duplicating 2 indices) as shown in Figure 2d,f. Memory use is $n \cdot 32 + m \cdot b \cdot 2 \approx (16+2b)m$ bytes, and transfer size is $34bm$ bytes. This will be the mesh API used in the remainder of the paper.

**Edge-based representations** Programs commonly use more general pointer-based data structures (e.g. winged-edge, half-edge, and quad-edge) to allow traversal and topological modification on meshes. However, since many applications may find these operations unnecessary, it is preferable to use a simpler, leaner representation for the API.

### 2.2 Compressed instruction streams

The compression of triangle meshes has recently been an active area of research. Taubin and Rossignac [14] record trees over both the graph and the dual graph of a mesh to compress connectivity to 1–2 bits per triangle, and use a linear predictor to compress vertex data to 5–10 bytes per triangle. Gumhold and Strasser [6] present a fast scheme for encoding mesh connectivity in approximately 2 bits per triangle. Touma and Gotsman [15] encode mesh connectivity by recording the number of neighbors for each vertex, and use a "parallelogram rule" for predicting vertex positions. Hoppe [9], Li et al. [11], and Taubin et al. [13] describe compressed representations that permit progressive transmission of meshes.

While all of these schemes provide significant gains over traditional mesh representations, their decompression algorithms involve data structures that do not easily map onto a graphics processor. Therefore they are most appropriate for transmission and archival purposes. Another limitation is that these schemes currently consider only static geometry, and it would be infeasible to recompress animated geometry changing at every frame.

Bar-Yehuda and Gotsman [1] investigate the use of a vertex stack in reducing the data sent to the graphics system. They show that a stack of size $\theta(\sqrt{n})$ is both necessary and sufficient to render an arbitrary mesh without sending vertices multiple times.

Deering [4] designs a compression scheme specifically aimed at hardware implementation. The scheme makes use of a 16-entry FIFO mesh buffer. The mesh is represented as a stream of variable-length instructions that load vertices into the buffer and use buffer entries to form generalized triangle strips. Vertex data is quantized and delta-encoded to exploit coherence between neighboring vertices. Chow [3] describes several enhancements to this approach, including a *meshification* algorithm and an adaptive quantization technique. As with other compressed stream representations, the scheme is limited to static geometry.

## 3 TRANSPARENT VERTEX CACHING

The transparent vertex caching framework uses the indexed triangle strip memory organization described in Section 2.1. Thus, memory size requirement is still approximately $(16 + 2b)m$ bytes. However, transfer bandwidth is reduced through the introduction of a vertex cache of size $k$, as illustrated in Figure 1. Vertex caching reduces transfer size to $m \cdot b \cdot 2 + m \cdot r \cdot 32 = (r \cdot 32 + b \cdot 2)m$ bytes, where $r$ denotes the average cache miss rate, in misses per triangle. Since each vertex must be loaded into the cache at least once and $m \leq 2n$, the miss rate $r$ has a lower bound of 0.5. The cache replacement policy is chosen to be FIFO as discussed further in Section 7.

As the approach is most closely related to the previous scheme of Deering and Chow, we review here the key differences. Recall the main characteristics of their framework:

- The graphics system reads a linear stream of vertex data and instructions. Vertex data may appear multiple times if it is re-used after being dropped from the cache.
- Vertex data is quantized and delta-encoded.
- The API is a special streaming format.
- Geometry must be static, because (1) duplicated vertices would require additional bookkeeping, (2) delta-encoding prevents random access and modification, and (3) frame-rate re-compression would be infeasible.
- Explicit bits manage allocation within the mesh buffer.

In contrast, with transparent vertex caching:

- The graphics system reads a stream of indices addressing a common array of vertices, so vertex data is not duplicated.
- Vertex data is in native uncompressed format.
- Since the API is a traditional mesh interface, applications can experience speedup without modification, and rendering is still efficient on legacy hardware.
- Geometry can be dynamic, since the application can freely modify the vertex array at video rates.
- Vertex caching is transparent and follows a strict FIFO policy.

## 4 FACE REORDERING PROBLEM

Maximizing the performance of the transparent vertex caching architecture gives rise to the following problem: given a mesh, find a sequence of indexed triangle strips that minimizes the amount of data transferred over the bus. The sequence of triangle strips is uniquely defined by a permutation $F$ of the original sequence of faces $\hat{F}$. Thus, the general optimization problem is

$$\min_{F \in \mathcal{P}(\hat{F})} \mathcal{C}(F)$$

```
function greedy_reorder()
Sequence<Face> F={};        // new face sequence
Face f=0;
loop
  if (!f)                   // restart process at some location
    f=some_unvisited_face_with_few_unvisited_neighbors();
    if (!f) break;          // all faces are visited
  Queue<Face> Q;            // possible locations for strip restarts
  loop                      // form a strip
    if (strip_too_long())   // using lookahead simulation
      f=Q.next_unvisited_face(); // may be 0
      break;                // force a strip restart
    f.mark_visited()
    F.add_to_end(f);
    // Get counter-clockw. and clockwise faces continuing strip
    (fccw,fclw) = f.next_two_adjacent_unvisited_faces();
    if (fccw)               // continue strip counter-clockwise
      if (fclw) Q.push(fclw);
      f=fccw;
    else if (fclw)          // continue strip clockwise
      f=fclw;
    else                    // cannot continue strip
      f=Q.next_unvisited_face(); // may be 0
      break;                // force a strip restart
return F;
```

Figure 3: Pseudocode for the greedy strip-growing algorithm.

where $\mathcal{P}(\hat{F})$ denotes all $m!$ permutations of the faces, and the cost

$$\mathcal{C}(F) = m\left(r(F) \cdot 32 + b(F) \cdot 2\right) \quad (1)$$

corresponds to the number of bytes transferred over the bus. The hardware model is that, for each face, the graphics processor requests 3 vertices from the cache, in the order shown in Figure 2f.

For example, Figure 4 shows the costs for three different orderings of the faces in a simple mesh. The ordering is illustrated using the black line segments (for adjacent faces within a strip) and white line segments (for strip restarts). Within each face, the colors at the three corners indicate if the vertex was present in the cache of size $k = 16$. As shown in Figure 4b, stripification algorithms may produce strips that are too long, resulting in a cache miss rate of $r \approx 1.0$, observed visually as one red corner per triangle. In contrast, our reordering techniques (Figures 4c-d) come closer to the optimal $r = 0.5$, i.e. one cache miss every other triangle.

Since $r \approx 0.6$ and $b \approx 1.5$, the vertex cache miss traffic $(r \cdot 32)$ is generally much more significant than the vertex index traffic $(b \cdot 2)$. Both our face reordering algorithms make some simplifying approximations with respect to this second, less significant term.

## 5 GREEDY STRIP-GROWING TECHNIQUE

Our first approach to solving the face reordering problem is a simple greedy technique. It is fast and can be used to seed the latter local optimization technique with a good initial state. The basic strategy is to incrementally grow a triangle strip, and to decide at each step whether it is better to add the next face to the strip or to restart the strip. This binary decision is made by performing a set of lookahead simulations of the vertex-cache behavior. Pseudocode for the algorithm in shown in Figure 3; we next present it in more detail. The output of the algorithm is shown in Figure 4c.

The algorithm begins by marking all faces of the mesh as unvisited. The first visited face is chosen to be one with the fewest number of neighbors. From this face, the algorithm begins growing a strip. If there are two neighboring unvisited faces, it always continues the strip in a counter-clockwise direction, but pushes the

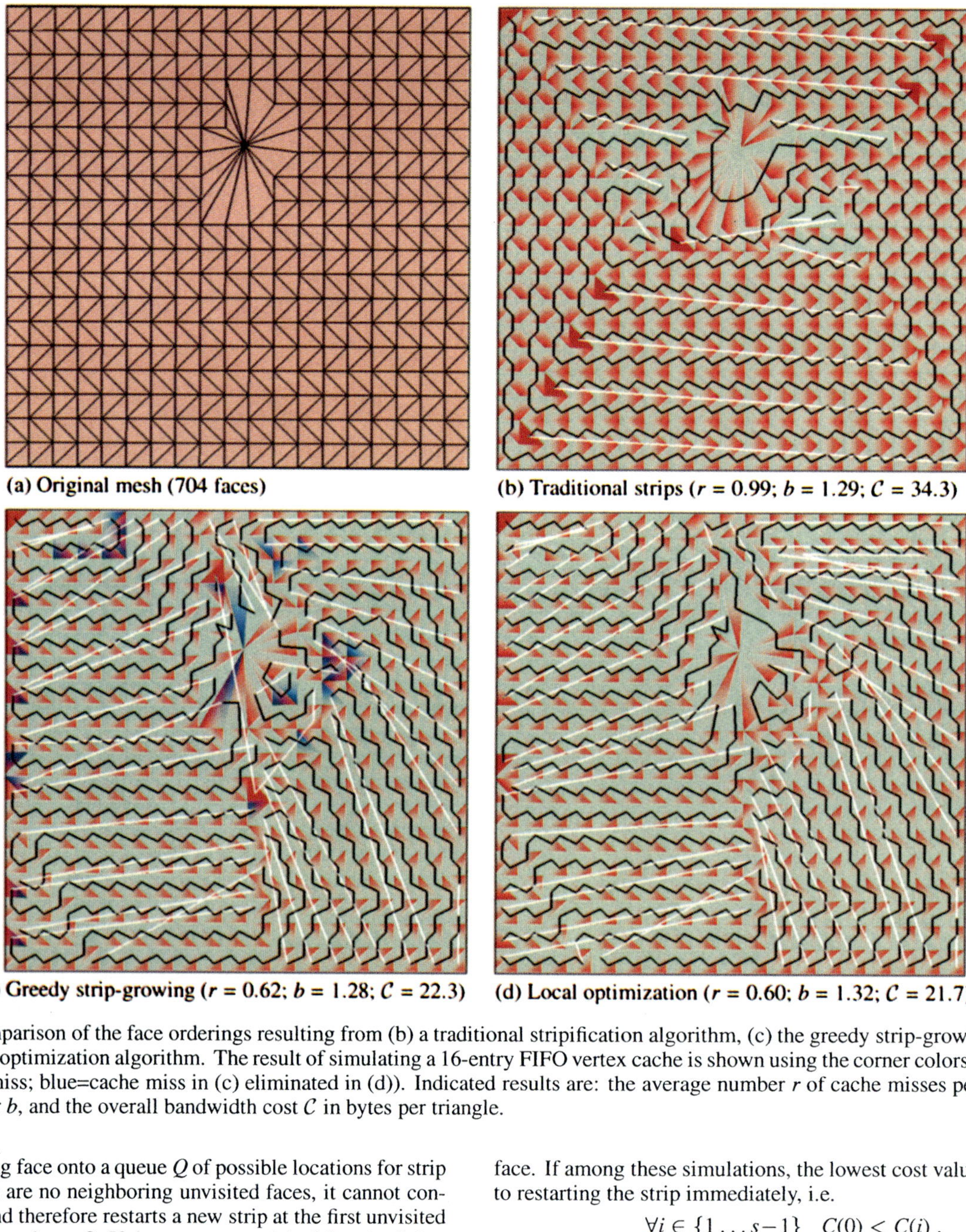

**(a) Original mesh (704 faces)**

**(b) Traditional strips ($r$ = 0.99; $b$ = 1.29; $\mathcal{C}$ = 34.3)**

**(c) Greedy strip-growing ($r$ = 0.62; $b$ = 1.28; $\mathcal{C}$ = 22.3)**

**(d) Local optimization ($r$ = 0.60; $b$ = 1.32; $\mathcal{C}$ = 21.7)**

Figure 4: A comparison of the face orderings resulting from (b) a traditional stripification algorithm, (c) the greedy strip-growing algorithm, and (d) the local optimization algorithm. The result of simulating a 16-entry FIFO vertex cache is shown using the corner colors (green=cache hit; red=cache miss; blue=cache miss in (c) eliminated in (d)). Indicated results are: the average number $r$ of cache misses per triangle, the strip bloat factor $b$, and the overall bandwidth cost $\mathcal{C}$ in bytes per triangle.

other neighboring face onto a queue $Q$ of possible locations for strip restarts. If there are no neighboring unvisited faces, it cannot continue the strip and therefore restarts a new strip at the first unvisited face in $Q$ and then clears $Q$. If there are no unvisited face in $Q$ (i.e. the algorithm has painted itself into a corner), the process must be restarted at a new location on the mesh. In selecting this new location, the primary criterion is to favor unvisited faces with vertices already in the cache. A secondary criterion is to select a face with the fewest number of unvisited neighbors.

Because the algorithm described so far does not constrain the lengths of strips, the strips could overflow the capacity of the cache, thereby preventing re-use of vertices between successive strips. Therefore, before adding each face, the algorithm performs a lookahead simulation to decide if it should instead force the strip to restart. Specifically, it performs a set of $s$ simulations $\{0 \dots s-1\}$ of the strip-growing process over the next $s$ faces. (The choice of $s$ will be given shortly.) Simulation number $i \in \{0 \dots s-1\}$ forces the strip to restart after exactly $i$ faces, and computes an associated cost value $C(i)$ equal to the average number of cache misses per visited face. If among these simulations, the lowest cost value corresponds to restarting the strip immediately, i.e.

$$\forall i \in \{1 \dots s-1\} \quad C(0) < C(i) \,,$$

the strip is forced to restart. Through experimentation, we have found $s = k + 5$ to be a good choice for a FIFO cache.

Note that the local cost function $C$ approximates only the first term of the true bandwidth cost $\mathcal{C}$ of Equation 1. Although $C$ fails to account for vertex index traffic, the greedy algorithm does implicitly attempt to minimize the number of strips, since restarts are only allowed when all the strict inequalities above are satisfied. Within each strip, the algorithm cannot afford to leave isolated faces behind, so it has little choice over the direction of strip formation.

As an optimization, instead of computing all $s$ cost values $\{C(0) \dots C(s-1)\}$ before visiting each face, the algorithm first computes $C(0)$ and then stops as soon as it finds another $C(i) \leq C(0)$. Also, the first cost value computed after $C(0)$ is $C(i_{min})$ where $i_{min}$ was the simulation returning the lowest cost value for the previously visited face. With this optimization, the number of lookahead simulations per face is reduced from $k + 5 = 21$ to 2.9 on average.

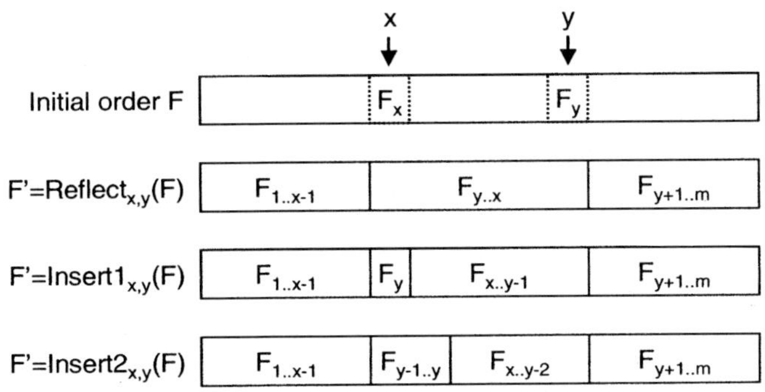


Figure 5: Perturbations to the face ordering.

# 6 LOCAL OPTIMIZATION TECHNIQUE

In this second technique, we start with the initial sequence of faces $F$ produced by the greedy algorithm, and attempt to improve it through a set of ordering perturbations. For each candidate perturbation $P : F \rightarrow F'$, we compute the change in cost $\Delta C(P) = C(F') - C(F)$ and apply the perturbation if $\Delta C(P) < 0$. In the next sections we describe the cost $C(F)$ approximating the true cost $\mathcal{C}$ from Equation 1, the types of reordering perturbations $P : F \rightarrow F'$, the process of selecting candidate perturbations, and several techniques that improve efficiency and quality of results.

**Cost metric** The primary cost function is

$$C(F) = 32 \cdot m \cdot r_k(F) + 6 \cdot \#\text{strips}(F) ,$$

where $m \cdot r_k(F)$ denotes the total number of cache misses for a cache of size $k$, and #strips($F$) is the number of triangle strips induced by the face sequence $F$. This cost function is an approximation of the true cost function $\mathcal{C}$ from Equation 1 in that it does not measure the number of duplicated vertices necessary to override the default direction for strip formation. In our opinion, this difference does not significantly affect results.

**Reordering perturbations** As shown in Figure 5, we define three types of perturbation (subsequence reflection, insertion of one face, and insertion of two faces), each parametrized by two indices $1 \leq x, y \leq m$ into the sequence $F$. We chose these three types of perturbation because they require only two parameters and yet have enough freedom to find many reordering improvements. Let $P^t_{x,y}$ denote a perturbation of type $t$.

**Selection of candidate perturbations** Recall that each candidate perturbation $P^t_{x,y}$ is parametrized by two face indices $x$ and $y$. To determine the index $x$, we simply visit all the faces in a random order. For each visited face $f$, we find its index $x$ in the current ordering, i.e. $F_x = f$.

Having selected $x$, we form a set $Y$ of indices of possible parameters $y$. We could let $Y$ be the exhaustive set $\{1 \ldots m\}$, but that would be wasteful since most faces $F_y$ would be nowhere near $F_x$ and thus unlikely to contribute to an improvement. We therefore let $Y$ contain the indices of faces either vertex-adjacent to $F_x$ in the mesh or adjacent to $F_x$ in the current ordering (i.e. $F_{x-1}$ and $F_{x+1}$).

For each $y \in Y$, we attempt all three types of perturbation, and find the one returning the lowest cost:

$$\min_{y,t} C(P^t_{x,y}(F)) .$$

If $\Delta C(P^t_{x,y}) \geq 0$, we are unable to find a beneficial operation, and therefore proceed to the next $x$. Otherwise, $P^t_{x,y}$ is beneficial and could be applied at this point.

However, before committing $P^t_{x,y}$, we first see if we can find a locally better perturbation. Specifically, we keep the index $y$ and determine the other index

$$z = \underset{z' \in Z}{\operatorname{argmin}} \min_t C(P^t_{y,z'}(F))$$

with the best perturbation from $y$, where the set $Z$ is formed like $Y$. If $z = x$ then we have found a locally optimal perturbation, and we apply it. Otherwise, we replace $x \leftarrow y$ and $y \leftarrow z$, and iterate again until convergence.

**Fast cost re-evaluation** For reasonable performance, the computation of $\Delta C(P^t_{x,y})$ should be fast and independent of the interval length $|x - y|$. Let us first consider just the two perturbations $\text{Insert1}_{x,y}$ and $\text{Insert2}_{x,y}$. One key observation is that the cache behavior for the sequences $F$ and $F'$ is likely to be different only near the interval endpoints $x$ and $y$, since the cache generally resynchronizes within the interior of the interval if $x$ and $y$ are far apart. To exploit this, our approach is as follows.

For each face $F_i$ we store a set $b_i$ of three bits equal to the current cache-miss states of its three vertex references. Given the perturbation $P^t_{x,y} : F \rightarrow F'$, we first load up the expected cache state just prior to location $x$ by moving backwards through $F$ from $x$ until $k$ misses have been detected in the stored bits $b_i$. Next, we simulate the cache from $x$ forwards through $F'$, recording changes in cache misses from those stored in the $b_i$. When $k$ successive cache misses are detected without any intervening cache-miss changes between $F$ and $F'$, the cache state is known to be resynchronized, and thus no more changes will occur until $y$ is reached. Note that the number of faces visited before the caches resynchronize is generally independent of the interval size $|x - y|$.

We then perform the same procedure for the sequence beginning at $y$. Finally, the last element necessary to compute $\Delta C(P)$ is to determine the induced change in the number of triangle strips. For this, we need only consider the face adjacencies at the slice points used by $P$ (shown in Figure 5).

The $\text{Reflect}_{x,y}$ perturbation is more difficult to handle because the entire interval $F_{x \ldots y}$ is reversed. For fast evaluation of its change in cost, we store at each face $F_i$ another three bits $b^R_i$ corresponding to the cache-miss states when traversing the faces of $F$ in *reverse order*, and use those when simulating $F_{y..x} \subset F'$.

**Secondary cost function** Because the cost function $C$ is rather flat and the perturbations do not look very far, we smooth out the cost function by adding a secondary cost function

$$C'(F) = 0.003\, m \cdot r_{k-1}(F) + 0.002\, m \cdot r_{k+1}(F)$$

that examines the number of cache misses for caches with one less entry ($r_{k-1}(F)$) and with one more entry ($r_{k+1}(F)$). The motivation for this function is that it attempts to maximize unused space in the cache whenever possible, in order to preserve "slack" for possible future improvements.

**Search pruning** It is unlikely that a perturbation will be beneficial if its endpoint $x$ lies in the middle of a strip and the surrounding faces have good caching behavior. Therefore, we use the simple heuristic of pruning the search from $x$ if the face $F_x$ is neither at the beginning nor at the end of a strip and the sum of cache misses on the three faces $\{F_{x-1}, F_x, F_{x+1}\}$ is less than 3.

# 7 RESULTS

**Cache replacement policy** Our very first experiments involved a vertex cache with a least-recently-used (LRU) replacement policy, since this policy usually performs well in other contexts. However, as shown in Figure 6, we soon found that an LRU cache cannot support strips as long as a FIFO cache. The reason is that vertices shared between a strip $s-1$ and the next strip $s$ are referenced during the traversal of $s$, and thus "pushed to the front" of the

LRU cache, even though they are no longer used in the subsequent strip $s+1$. (For example, see vertices "2" and "3" in Figure 7.) In contrast, when a FIFO cache reaches steady state, vertices between strips $s-1$ and $s$ are dropped from the cache at precisely the right time — before any vertices used for strip $s$+1 (Figure 7). On a regular mesh, the optimal strip length appears to be only $k-2$ faces for an LRU cache versus $2k-4$ faces for a FIFO cache. We therefore adopted the FIFO policy.

**Cache size** Figure 8 plots cache miss rate $r$ as a function of cache size $k$ using different runs of the greedy strip-growing algorithm. Reordering algorithms depend strongly on the parameter $k$. A mesh preprocessed for a cache of size $k$ will be sub-optimal on hardware with a larger cache, and more importantly, it may completely thrash a smaller cache. For most of our examples, simulating the face orderings optimized for $k = 16$ on a cache of size $k = 15$ increases the average cache miss rate $r$ by 10–30%.

Surprisingly, it is theoretically feasible for an element sequence to perform better on a FIFO cache of size $k$ than on a FIFO cache of size $k + 1$.[1] For instance, in the limit the sequence

$$6, 1, 7, 2, 4, 6, (1, 2, 3, 4, 5, 6, 7), (1, 2, 3, 4, 5, 6, 7), \ldots$$

has twice as many misses on a cache of size 5 than on one of size 4. It might therefore be possible that a super-optimized face ordering would have a similar performance dependency on the precise cache size. However, we have never seen this behavior in practice.

**Greedy strip-growing** The columns labeled "Greedy" in Table 2 show results of the greedy strip-growing algorithm of Section 5. Two of the results are pictured in the first column of Figure 9.

For the mesh buffer scheme [3, 4], Chow reports buffer load rates ranging from 0.62 to 0.70 vertices per triangle. Two of these meshes are the same ours; he reports 0.62 for the "bunny" and 0.70 for the "schooner".[2] The cache miss rates for our greedy algorithm are therefore comparable to those results, even though the cache is not actively managed.

The "gameguy" mesh has a notably high miss rate. It is due to the fact many of its vertices have multiple normals and are therefore artificially replicated in the mesh, resulting in many boundary edges and a low face-to-vertex ratio. Such duplication of vertices also occurs in the "fandisk" and "schooner" meshes. A performance number that better accounts for this variability in $m/n$ is the average number of times each mesh vertex is loaded into the cache (labeled "miss/vertex" in Table 2), which has a lower bound of 1.

The three meshes with the highest miss/vertex ratios are "bunny2000", "bunny4000" and "buddha". These meshes are precisely the ones obtained as the result of mesh simplification. The high miss rates are probably due to the irregular mesh connectivities resulting from the geometrically optimized simplification process.

The execution rate of the greedy algorithm on all of these models ranges from 35,000 to 43,000 faces/second on a 450 MHz Pentium 2 system. So even the most complex mesh is processed in under 6 seconds.

**Local optimization** Results of the local optimization algorithm of Section 6 are presented in the columns labeled "Optimiz." in Table 2 and in Figures 9b,d.

The results show that local optimization is generally able to reduce cache misses by 3–6%. This gain is somewhat disappointing, as we were hoping to see greater improvements. The results seem to indicate, however, that the solution of the greedy algorithm is near a local minimum of the bandwidth cost $\mathcal{C}$.

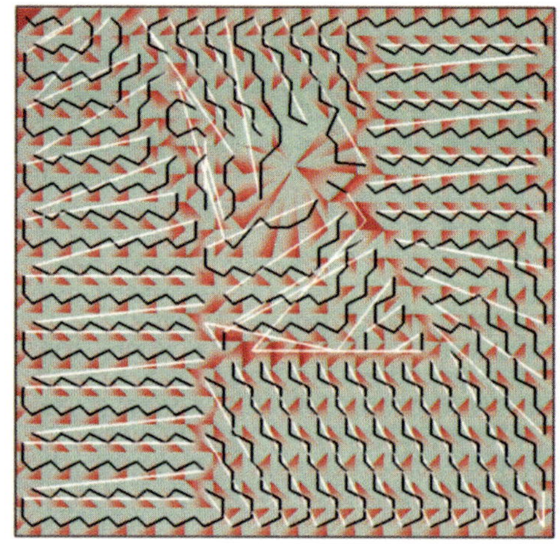

Figure 6: Output of the greedy strip-growing algorithm using an LRU cache replacement policy instead of FIFO, with cache size $k = 16$ ($r = 0.66$; $b = 1.40$; $\mathcal{C} = 23.9$). Compare with Figure 4(c).

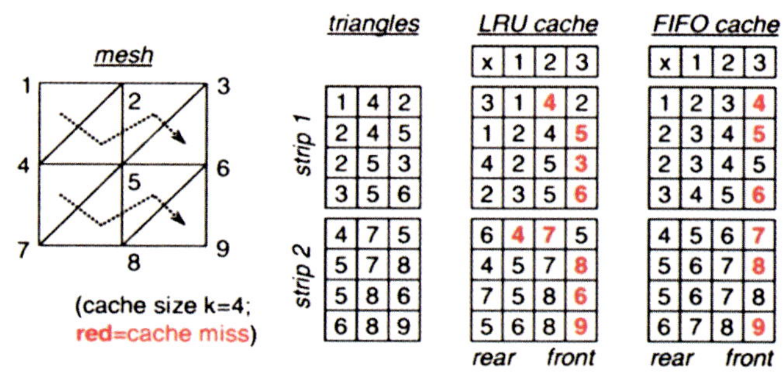


Figure 7: Comparison of LRU and FIFO on a simple mesh.

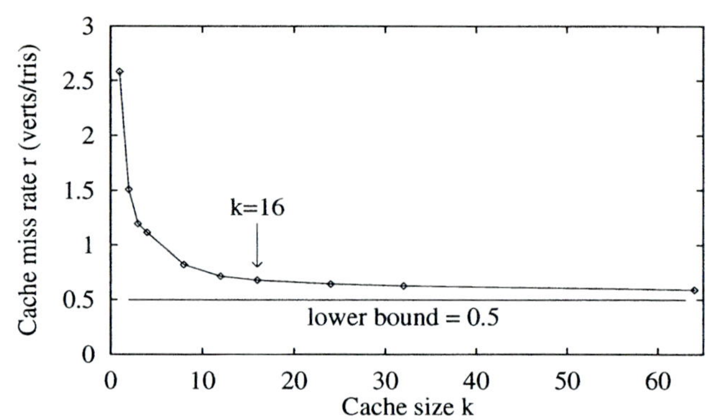


Figure 8: FIFO cache effectiveness as a function of cache size with the greedy strip-growing algorithm on the 4000-face bunny.

Also, one must keep in mind that the cache miss rate has an absolute lower bound of 1 miss per vertex since each vertex must be loaded at least once into the cache. For most meshes, the lower bound is in fact higher because the maximum lengths of strips is bounded by the cache size, and non-boundary vertices on the ends of strips must loaded in the cache more than once. For an infinitely large regular triangulation, the number of misses per vertex therefore has a lower bound of $1 + \frac{1}{k-1}$.

Execution times for the algorithm range from 5 minutes to 4 hours on these meshes. The algorithm finds improvements at a high rate initially, then gets diminishing returns, so it could be stopped earlier.

[1]Thanks to John Miller for pointing this out.

[2]Chow also reports 0.63 for a buddha model of 293,233 faces but it is unfortunately not the same mesh as our simplified 100,000-face buddha.

| Data set | #vertices $n$ | #faces $m$ | Average cache miss rate | | | | Bandwidth (bytes/tri) | | |
|---|---|---|---|---|---|---|---|---|---|
| | | | $r$ = miss/triangle | | miss/vertex | | Triangle strips | Vertex caching | |
| | | | Greedy | Optimiz. | Greedy | Optimiz. | | Greedy | Optimiz. |
| grid20 | 391 | 704 | 0.62 | 0.60 | 1.11 | 1.07 | 36.7 | 22.3 | 21.7 |
| grid40 | 1,075 | 1,999 | 0.67 | 0.63 | 1.25 | 1.17 | 43.9 | 24.7 | 23.6 |
| fandisk | 7,233 | 12,946 | 0.61 | 0.60 | 1.09 | 1.08 | 37.4 | 22.3 | 22.1 |
| gameguy | 7,874 | 10,000 | 0.88 | 0.86 | 1.12 | 1.09 | 46.9 | 31.6 | 30.8 |
| bunny2000 | 1,015 | 1,999 | 0.70 | 0.66 | 1.38 | 1.30 | 45.0 | 25.5 | 24.4 |
| bunny4000 | 2,026 | 3,999 | 0.68 | 0.65 | 1.34 | 1.27 | 44.2 | 24.8 | 23.8 |
| bunny | 34,835 | 69,473 | 0.64 | 0.62 | 1.28 | 1.24 | 39.8 | 23.4 | 22.8 |
| buddha | 49,794 | 100,000 | 0.70 | 0.65 | 1.40 | 1.30 | 45.8 | 25.5 | 24.2 |
| schooner | 105,816 | 205,138 | 0.62 | 0.61 | 1.20 | 1.19 | 41.2 | 22.8 | 22.6 |

Table 2: Cache miss rates using the greedy strip-growing algorithm and the local optimization algorithm (expressed as both miss/triangle and miss/vertex), and overall transfer bandwidth using traditional triangle strips versus transparent vertex caching.

**(a) Greedy ($r$ = 0.70; $b$ = 1.54; $C$ = 25.5)** **(b) Optimization ($r$ = 0.66; $b$ = 1.69; $C$ = 24.4)**

**(c) Greedy ($r$ = 0.70; $b$ = 1.63; $C$ = 25.5)** **(d) Optimization ($r$ = 0.65; $b$ = 1.70; $C$ = 24.2)**

Figure 9: Results of greedy strip-growing (left column) and local optimization (right column) with a 16-entry FIFO vertex cache, for bunny2000 and buddha. (Blue corners on the left indicate cache misses eliminated on the right.) Captions refer to the average number $r$ of cache misses per triangle, the strip bloat factor $b$, and the overall bandwidth cost $C$ in bytes per triangle.

**Analysis** The rightmost columns of Table 2 compare the total bandwidth requirements for a traditional triangle strip representation and for the transparent vertex caching framework. It demonstrates that bandwidth is reduced by a factor of approximately 1.6 to 1.9 .

## 8 DISCUSSION

**Issues in modifying rendering order** Modifying the order in which faces are rendered may alter the final image if faces are coincident, if the Z-buffer is disabled, or if the triangles are partially transparent. This limitation is shared by all schemes that modify the face ordering, including ordinary triangle strip generation.

**Vertex data compression** With the transparent vertex caching framework, vertex data can be compressed by the CPU independently of mesh connectivity. In particular, time-dependent geometry presents a significant opportunity for vertex data compression. As an example, Lengyel [10] describes a scheme that clusters vertices together and predicts their positions by associating to each cluster a local coordinate frame that deforms over time; the resulting residuals are compressed separately. In effect, Lengyel's scheme reorders vertices to improve geometric coherence, and does not concern itself with the order of faces. On the other hand, our framework reorders faces to improve graphics coherence, and does not care about the order of vertices. This demonstrates how vertex data compression could interact elegantly with our framework.

**Memory access pattern for vertex data** As the results in Table 2 indicate, a large percentage of vertices are loaded into the cache only once, i.e. the first and only time they cause a cache miss. In some system architectures, it may be useful to reorder the vertices in the mesh to match the order in which they are first requested, so that the memory access pattern is mostly sequential. The trade-off is that reordering the vertices causes some loss of transparency, since the application may need to be aware that the mesh vertices have been permuted.

In our opinion, the memory access pattern is not a stumbling block. Unlike in a general CPU computation, the memory access pattern from the graphics processor can be predicted by buffering the vertex index stream (which is entirely sequential), so memory latency becomes less important than overall memory bandwidth. Several graphics systems already perform similar buffering when pre-fetching texture memory as triangle fragments make their way to the rasterizer.

## 9 SUMMARY AND FUTURE WORK

We have explored the use of a vertex cache to transparently reduce the geometry bandwidth between the graphics processor and memory in the context of a traditional mesh rendering API. In many cases, it is unnecessary for the application program to be aware of this caching scheme, even if the program applies runtime deformations to the mesh geometry. Maximizing the efficiency of the cache simply involves reordering the faces in the mesh during a preprocessing step.

We have presented a greedy strip-growing algorithm for reordering the faces, and shown that, even without explicit cache management, it is able to achieve comparable results to the previous scheme by Deering and Chow. The greedy algorithm operates at an approximate rate of 40,000 faces/sec and is thus highly practical.

We have also explored a perturbation-based optimization scheme for further improving the face ordering. Although costly in terms of computation time, it succeeds in reducing bandwidth by several percent.

This project suggests a number of areas for future work:

- Exploring more complex reordering perturbations that exploit the strip structure present in the face ordering.
- Examining the interaction with texture caching. Although optimal face orderings for vertex caching and texture caching are likely different, a compromise would be feasible.
- Maintaining cache-efficient face ordering during level-of-detail (LOD) control. While this is straightforward for a precomputed set of LOD meshes, it seems difficult for continuous LOD and particularly for view-dependent LOD [8].

## ACKNOWLEDGMENTS

I am extremely grateful to John Miller. Thanks also to Paolo Sabella and David Kirk of NVIDIA and to Anuj Gosalia of the Microsoft Direct3D group for helpful feedback. The bunny and buddha meshes are courtesy of the Stanford University Computer Graphics Laboratory.

## REFERENCES

[1] BAR-YEHUDA, R., AND GOTSMAN, C. Time/space tradeoffs for polygon mesh rendering. *ACM Transactions on Graphics 15*, 2 (April 1996), 141–152.

[2] BIRDWELL, K. Valve Corp. Personal communication, 1998.

[3] CHOW, M. Optimized geometry compression for real-time rendering. In *Visualization '97 Proceedings* (1997), IEEE, pp. 347–354.

[4] DEERING, M. Geometry compression. *Computer Graphics (SIGGRAPH '95 Proceedings)* (1995), 13–20.

[5] EVANS, F., SKIENA, S., AND VARSHNEY, A. Optimizing triangle strips for fast rendering. In *Visualization '96 Proceedings* (1996), IEEE, pp. 319–326.

[6] GUMHOLD, S., AND STRASSER, W. Real time compression of triangle mesh connectivity. *Computer Graphics (SIGGRAPH '98 Proceedings)* (1998), 133–140.

[7] HAKURA, Z., AND GUPTA, A. The design and analysis of a cache architecture for texture mapping. In *Proceedings of the 24th International Symposium on Computer Architecture* (June 1997), pp. 108–120.

[8] HOPPE, H. View-dependent refinement of progressive meshes. *Computer Graphics (SIGGRAPH '97 Proceedings)* (1997), 189–198.

[9] HOPPE, H. Efficient implementation of progressive meshes. *Computers and Graphics 22*, 1 (1998), 27–36.

[10] LENGYEL, J. Compression of time-dependent geometry. In *Symposium on Interactive 3D Graphics* (1999), ACM, pp. 89–96.

[11] LI, J., LI, J., AND KUO, C. C. Progressive compression of 3D graphics models. In *Multimedia Computing and Systems* (April 1997), IEEE, pp. 135–142.

[12] NEIDER, J., DAVIS, T., AND WOO, M. *OpenGL Programming Guide*. Addison-Wesley, 1993.

[13] TAUBIN, G., GUÉZIEC, A., HORN, W., AND LAZARUS, F. Progressive forest split compression. *Computer Graphics (SIGGRAPH '98 Proceedings)* (1998), 123–132.

[14] TAUBIN, G., AND ROSSIGNAC, J. Geometric compression through topological surgery. *ACM Transactions on Graphics 17*, 2 (April 1998), 84–115.

[15] TOUMA, C., AND GOTSMAN, C. Triangle mesh compression. In *Proceedings of Graphics Interface '98* (1998), pp. 26–34.

[16] XIANG, X., HELD, M., AND MITCHELL, J. Fast and effective stripification of polygonal surface models. In *Symposium on Interactive 3D Graphics* (1999), ACM, pp. 71–78.

# Fast Computation of Generalized Voronoi Diagrams Using Graphics Hardware

Kenneth E. Hoff III, Tim Culver, John Keyser, Ming Lin, Dinesh Manocha

University of North Carolina at Chapel Hill
Department of Computer Science

**Abstract**: We present a new approach for computing generalized 2D and 3D Voronoi diagrams using interpolation-based polygon rasterization hardware. We compute a discrete Voronoi diagram by rendering a three dimensional distance mesh for each Voronoi site. The polygonal mesh is a bounded-error approximation of a (possibly) non-linear function of the distance between a site and a 2D planar grid of sample points. For each sample point, we compute the closest site and the distance to that site using polygon scan-conversion and the Z-buffer depth comparison. We construct distance meshes for points, line segments, polygons, polyhedra, curves, and curved surfaces in 2D and 3D. We generalize to weighted and farthest-site Voronoi diagrams, and present efficient techniques for computing the Voronoi boundaries, Voronoi neighbors, and the Delaunay triangulation of points. We also show how to adaptively refine the solution through a simple windowing operation. The algorithm has been implemented on SGI workstations and PCs using OpenGL, and applied to complex datasets. We demonstrate the application of our algorithm to fast motion planning in static and dynamic environments, selection in complex user-interfaces, and creation of dynamic mosaic effects.

**CR Categories**: I.3.5 [Computer Graphics]: Computational Geometry and Object Modeling; I.3.3 [Computer Graphics]: Picture/Image Generation.

**Additional Key Words**: Voronoi diagrams, graphics hardware, polygon rasterization, interpolation, motion planning, proximity query, medial axis, OpenGL, framebuffer techniques.

## 1 INTRODUCTION

Given a set of primitives, called Voronoi sites, a Voronoi diagram partitions space into regions, where each region consists of all points that are closer to one site than to any other. Voronoi diagrams have been used in a number of applications including visualization of medical datasets, proximity queries, spatial data manipulation, shape analysis, computer animation, robot motion planning, modeling spatial structures and processes, pattern recognition, and locational optimization. The concept of Voronoi diagrams has been around for at least four centuries, and since the

e-mail: {hoff,culver,keyser,lin,dm}@cs.unc.edu
WWW: http://www.cs.unc.edu/~geom/voronoi/

**Cover Plate**: Discrete approximation of the generalized Voronoi diagram of four points, a line, a triangle, and one cubic Bézier curve computed interactively on a PC.

1970s, algorithms for computing Voronoi diagrams of geometric primitives have been developed in computational geometry and related areas.

Good theoretical and practical algorithms are known for computing ordinary Voronoi diagrams of points in any dimension. Ordinary Voronoi diagrams can be generalized in many different ways by using different distance functions and site shapes. A common generalization is to compute the diagram for higher-order sites, such as lines and curves. This greatly increases the complexity since the boundaries of the diagram are composed of high-degree algebraic curves and surfaces, and their intersections; the boundaries of an ordinary point Voronoi diagram are linear. No practically efficient and numerically robust algorithms are known for constructing a topologically consistent, continuous representation of generalized Voronoi diagrams.

Given the practical complexity of computing an exact generalized Voronoi diagram, many authors have proposed approximate algorithms. Interesting approaches include computing the Voronoi diagram of a point-sampling of the sites, adaptively subdividing space to locate the Voronoi boundary, and point-sampling the space to form a volumetric representation of the diagram. In practice, these previous algorithms take considerable time and memory on large numbers of input sites, or are restricted in generality.

**Main Contributions**: In this paper, we present an approach that computes discrete approximations of generalized Voronoi diagrams to an arbitrary resolution using polygon rasterization hardware. Our contributions include:

1. Efficient methods to approximate the distance function, with bounded error, for points, lines, polygons, polyhedra, curves, and curved surfaces using a polygonal mesh that is linearly interpolated by graphics hardware.
2. Efficient algorithms to find Voronoi boundaries and neighbors, and to construct Delaunay triangulations.

3. Techniques to construct weighted and farthest-site generalized Voronoi diagrams in 2D and 3D.
4. Demonstration of the effectiveness of our approach to the following applications:
   - Fast motion planning in static and dynamic environments
   - Selection in complex user-interfaces
   - Generation of dynamic mosaics

The resulting techniques have been effectively implemented on PCs and high-end SGI workstations using the OpenGL graphics library. A 2D example computed in real-time is shown in the cover plate. Our techniques improve upon the state of the art in following ways:

- **Generality**: We make no assumption with respect to input primitives. We only need to mesh the distance function of a site over a grid of point samples.
- **Efficiency**: We show that our approach is quite fast. Its speed arises from using coarse polygonal approximations of the distance functions while still maintaining a specified error bound, using polygon rasterization hardware to reconstruct the distance values, and using the Z-buffer depth comparison to perform distance comparisons. We demonstrate the 2D approach on models composed of nearly 100K triangles in a real-time motion planning application through a complex dynamic scene. We derive efficient meshing strategies for polygonal models in 3D, and show the results of a prototype implementation that demonstrates its potential.
- **Tight Bounds on Accuracy**: Although our approach produces a discretized Voronoi diagram, all sources of error are enumerated and techniques are given to produce output within any specified tolerance.
- **Ease of Implementation**: The approach can be easily implemented on current graphics systems. The special cases are limited and the problem reduces to simply meshing a distance function for any new site.

# 2 RELATED WORK

The concept of Voronoi diagrams has been around for at least four centuries. In his treatment of cosmic fragmentation in *Le Monde de Mr. Descartes, ou Le Traite de la Lumière*, published in 1644, Descartes uses Voronoi-like diagrams to show the disposition of matter in the solar system and its environment. The first presentations of this concept appeared in the work of [Diric50] and [Voron08]. Algorithms for computing Voronoi diagrams have been appearing since the 1970s. See the surveys by [Auren91] and [Okabe92] on various algorithms, applications, and generalizations of Voronoi diagrams.

## 2.1 Voronoi Diagrams of Points

Among the algorithms known for computing Voronoi diagrams of points in 2D, 3D, and higher dimensions are the divide-and-conquer algorithm proposed by [Shamo75] and Fortune's sweepline algorithm [Fortu86]. Numerically robust algorithms for constructing topologically consistent Voronoi diagrams have been proposed by [Inaga92, Sugih94]. A number of implementations in exact and floating-point arithmetic are also available.

## 2.2 Generalized Voronoi Diagrams

Algorithms have been proposed for constructing Voronoi diagrams of higher order sites. Two broad approaches based on incremental and divide-and-conquer techniques have been summarized in [Okabe92]. The set of algorithms includes divide-and-conquer algorithms for polygons [Lee82, Held97], an incremental algorithm for polyhedra [Milen93b], and 3D tracing for polyhedral models [Milen93, Sherb95, Culve99]. Curved sites and CSG objects are handled in [Chian92, Dutta93, Hoffm94]. In all these cases, the computation of generalized Voronoi diagrams involves representing and manipulating high-degree algebraic curves and surfaces and their intersections. As a result, no efficient and numerically robust algorithms are known for computing them.

## 2.3 Approximate Voronoi Diagrams

Many authors compute approximations of generalized Voronoi diagrams based on the Voronoi diagram of a point-sampling of the sites [e.g. Sheeh95]. However, deriving any error bounds on the output of such an approach is difficult, and the overall complexity is not well understood.

[Vleug95] and [Vleug96] have presented an approach that adaptively subdivides space into regular cells and computes the Voronoi diagram up to a given precision. [Laven92] uses an octree representation of objects and performs spatial decomposition to compute the approximation. [Teich97] computes a polygonal approximation of Voronoi diagrams by subdividing the space into tetrahedral cells. All these algorithms take considerable time and memory for large models composed of tens of thousands of triangles, and cannot easily be extended to directly handle dynamic environments.

The idea of using polygon rasterizing hardware and rendering of cones to construct 2D Voronoi diagrams of points is suggested in [Haebe90] and in the OpenGL 1.1 Programming Guide [Woo97].

## 2.4 Graphics Hardware

Polygon rasterization graphics hardware has been used for a number of geometric computations, such as visualization of constructive solid geometry models [Rossi86, Goldf89] and interactive inspection of solids, including cross-sections and interferences [Rossi92]. Algorithms for real-time motion planning using raster graphics hardware have been proposed by [Lengy90].

# 3 OVERVIEW

In this section, we present the basic concepts important to our approach. We give a formal definition of generalized Voronoi diagrams and present a simple brute-force strategy for computing a discrete approximation. We then show how we may greatly accelerate this using graphics hardware.

## 3.1 Generalized Voronoi Diagrams

The set of input sites is denoted as $A_1, A_2, \ldots, A_k$. For any point $p$ in the space, $dist(p, A_i)$ denotes the distance from the point $p$ to the site $A_i$. The dominance region of $A_i$ over $A_j$ is defined by

$$Dom(A_i, A_j) = \{\, p \mid dist(p, A_i) \leq dist(p, A_j) \,\}$$

For a site $A_i$, the Voronoi region for $A_i$ is defined by

$$V(A_i) = \cap_{j \neq i} Dom(A_i, A_j)$$

The partition of space into $V(A_1)$, $V(A_2)$, ..., $V(A_k)$ is called the *generalized Voronoi diagram*. The (ordinary) Voronoi diagram corresponds to the case when each $A_i$ is an individual point. The boundaries of the regions $V(A_i)$ are called *Voronoi boundaries*. For primitives such as points, lines, polygons, and splines, the Voronoi boundaries are portions of algebraic curves or surfaces.

### 3.2 Discrete Voronoi Diagrams

Perhaps the simplest way to compute a discrete Voronoi diagram is to uniformly point-sample the space containing Voronoi sites. For each sample point, we find the closest site and its distance. Associating each point in space with its closest sample point induces a uniform subdivision into rectangular cells. For any point, we know the distance to the closest site to within the maximum distance between a point in space and a sample point, i.e. half the diagonal length of a cell.

A simple brute-force approach to find the closest sites is to iterate through all sample points, computing distances to all sites and recording the closest site and distance. The algorithm can be rearranged to iterate through the sites: for each site, compute distances to all sample points and update the current closest site and distance. The second arrangement is amenable to an implementation in graphics hardware.

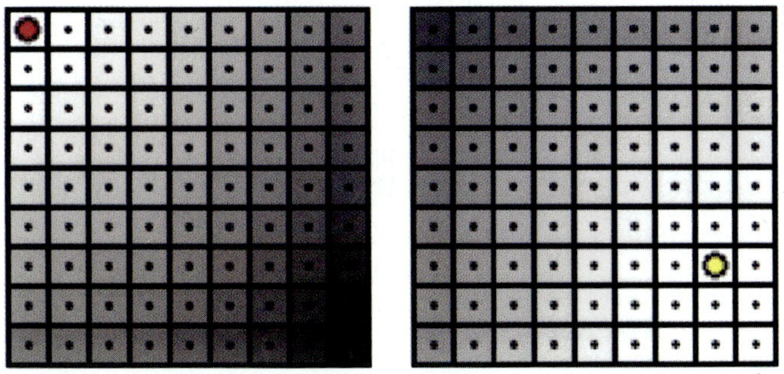

**Figure 1**: Image of the sampled distance functions for two point sites. Uniform point sampling induces a rectangular cell subdivision of space.

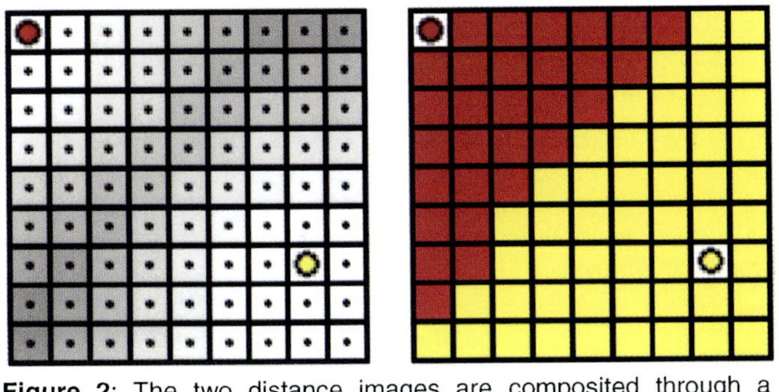

**Figure 2**: The two distance images are composited through a distance comparison operation. The current closest site and the distance to each site is updated based on the lesser distance value. The resulting Voronoi diagram is composed of a distance image (left) and an closest-site ID image (right).

### 3.3 Polygon Rasterization Hardware

Our approach makes use of standard Z-buffered raster graphics hardware for rendering polygons. The frame buffer stores the attributes (intensity or shade) of each pixel in the image space; the Z-buffer, or depth buffer, stores the *z*-coordinate, or depth, of every visible pixel. Given only the vertices of a triangle, the rasterization hardware uses linear interpolation to compute depth values across the triangle's surface. All raster samples covered by a triangle have an interpolated *z*-value.

### 3.4 Our Approach

A key concept for our approach is that of the *distance function* for a site, which gives, for any point, the distance to that site. The main idea of our approach is to render a polygonal mesh approximation to each site's distance function. Each site is assigned a unique color ID, and the corresponding distance mesh is rendered in that color using a parallel projection. We make use of two components of the graphics hardware: linear interpolation across polygons and the Z-buffer depth comparison operation. When rendering a polygonal distance mesh, the polygon rasterization reconstructs all distances across the mesh. The Z-buffer depth test compares the new depth value to the previously stored value. If the new value is less, the Z-buffer records the new distance, and the color buffer records the site's ID. In this way, each pixel in the frame buffer will have a color corresponding to the site to which it is closest, and the depth-buffer will have the distance to that site. In order to maintain an accurate Voronoi diagram, we bound the error of the mesh to be smaller than the distance between two sample points.

Our approach is inspired by an interesting sidenote in the OpenGL 1.1 Programming Guide [Woo97]. In the Section "Now That You Know" on "Dirichlet Domains", the authors briefly discuss a simple method to construct discretized 2D Voronoi diagrams for points using OpenGL graphics hardware. The authors mention the use of cones for Voronoi diagrams of points in 2D, but warn that the technique "might require thousands of polygons." We show that we can render cones using fewer than 100 triangles for a 1K×1K resolution grid and achieve the same level of accuracy. In addition, we generalize this approach to higher-order sites in both two and three dimensions.

## 4 THE DISTANCE FUNCTIONS

For both 2D and 3D, our discrete Voronoi diagram computation has been reduced to finding a 3D polygonal mesh approximation to the distance function of a Voronoi site over a planar 2D rectangular grid of point samples. The error in the approximation must be bounded so that by rendering this mesh using graphics hardware, we can efficiently and accurately compute the distances between the site and all of the point samples.

In this section, we describe the distance functions associated with various sites, and provide efficient methods for meshing these functions within a specified error tolerance.

### 4.1 2D Voronoi Diagrams

Denote the distance from a site $A$ to each pixel location $(x,y)$ by $dist(A,(x,y))$. The *distance function* of $A$ is given by $d(x,y)=dist(A,(x,y))$. Meshing this function corresponds to approximating the graph of $d(x,y)$ with a polygonal model.

The three basic types of 2D sites are points, lines, and polygons. Their corresponding distance functions are shown in the table. In this section, we present algorithms for computing distance meshes for each of them.

| 2D site | Shape of Distance Function | Figure |
|---|---|---|
| Point | Right circular cone | 3a |
| Line segment | "Tent" | 3b |
| Polygon | Cones and tents | 5 |

**Table 1**: Shape of Distance Functions for 2D Sites

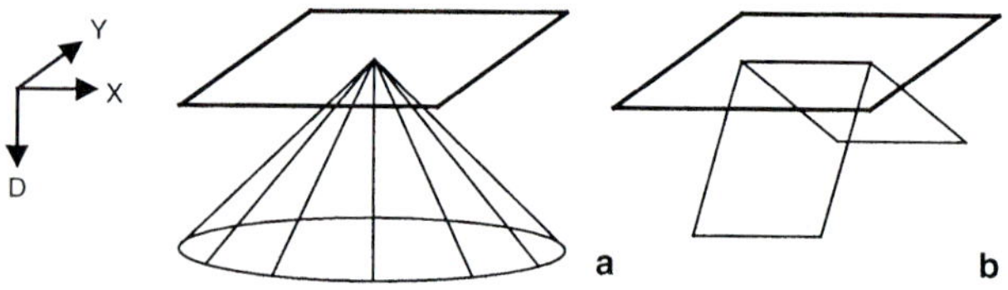


**Figure 3**: The distance meshes used for a point (left) and a line segment (right). The XY-plane containing the site is shown above each mesh.

### 4.1.1 Points in 2D

The distance function for a point in the plane is a right circular cone. We approximate cones as a triangle fan proceeding radially outward from the apex (Figures 3a and 4-left). A point's Voronoi region can potentially extend to any portion of the region of interest, and thus the radius at the cone's base must be of size $M\sqrt{2}$ if the scene is contained in an $M \times M$ square.The mesh's radial lines lie on the cone. The maximum error in distance occurs at the cone base between adjacent vertices. Because the cone is right circular, the error in approximating the circular base as viewed from above is equal to the error in distance.

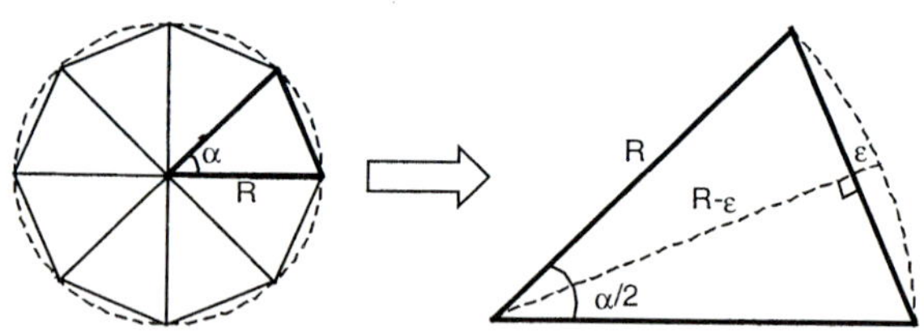


**Figure 4**: A single triangle of the meshed point distance function cone. α is the angle we wish to maximize, R is the radius of the cone (max dist between site and sample pt), and ε is the max error.

From this formulation (see Figure 4), we compute the maximum angle as:

$$\cos(\alpha/2) = \frac{R-\varepsilon}{R} \rightarrow \alpha = 2\cos^{-1}\left(\frac{R-\varepsilon}{R}\right)$$

For example, for a maximum distance error of no more than one pixel's width, a cone mesh for a 512x512 grid will require only 60 triangles. A 1024×1024 grid will require 85 triangles.

### 4.1.2 Line Segments in 2D

The distance function for a line segment is composed of three parts: one for the segment itself and one for each endpoint. The endpoints are treated the same way as points. The distance function for the line segment (excluding the endpoints) is just a "tent" (Figure 3b); its distance mesh is composed of two quadrilaterals. These represent the distance function exactly, so there is no error in the distance mesh representation. The only error for the line segment is in the cone mesh for the endpoint distance functions, as described in the previous section.

### 4.1.3 Polygons and Per-feature Voronoi Diagrams

It is often useful to consider sites as a collection of features, rather than as a single entity. For example, a line segment would be considered as three features: the two endpoints and the linear edge between them. By rendering the distance meshes for different features in different colors, we obtain a discrete approximation of a *per-feature Voronoi diagram*. Such diagrams are useful in several contexts: for example, the computation of a medial axis of a polygon. A picture of a per-feature Voronoi diagram for a polygon is given in Figure 5-left.

**Figure 5**: The per-feature Voronoi diagram of a quadrilateral (left). The corresponding distance mesh (right).

Polygons are rendered as a series of linear segments connected at the vertices. Each edge and vertex is a feature. For the vertices, rendering a triangle fan connecting two adjacent edges, rather than a full point distance mesh cone, saves on the total number of triangles computed and ensures that the distance meshes for adjacent features join smoothly. See Figure 5-right for an illustration.

## 4.2 3D Voronoi Diagrams

Our algorithm computes a 3D discrete Voronoi diagram slice-by-slice. Each slice is parallel to the $(x,y)$-plane and is computed independently.

Consider the slice $z=z_0$. To construct the intersection of the Voronoi diagram with this slice, consider the distance function for a site $A$, restricted to the slice. Denote the restricted distance function by $dist(x,y)=dist(A,(x,y,z_0))$. In this section, we describe $dist(x,y)$ for polygon, line segment, and point sites. As in the 2D case, computing the discrete Voronoi diagram is a matter of meshing the distance function $d=dist(x,y)$ for each site and rendering these meshes.

The distance meshes we give for the 3D problem are for a per-feature Voronoi diagram. Thus, a detached triangle site is treated as seven features: a polygon, three line segments, and three points. As in 2D per-feature diagrams, some features have a restricted region of influence.

| 3D site | Shape of distance function | Figure |
|---|---|---|
| Polygon | Plane | 6 |
| Line segment | Elliptical cone | 7 |
| Point | 1 sheet of a hyperboloid of 2 sheets | 8 |

**Table 2**: Shape of Distance Functions for 3D Sites

### 4.2.1 Polygons in 3D

The influence of this site in 3D is confined to the region formed by sweeping the polygon orthogonally through space, since points outside this region are considered to be closer to an edge or vertex of the polygon. In the slice, this region is a polygon, and $dist(x,y)$ is linear within this region, as illustrated in Figure 6. The distance to the site is computed at the vertices of the region, and a distance mesh composed of a single polygon is rendered. No meshing error is incurred. If the polygon intersects the slice, the intersection is computed and the polygon is decomposed into two sub-polygons. Each sub-polygon is treated as above.

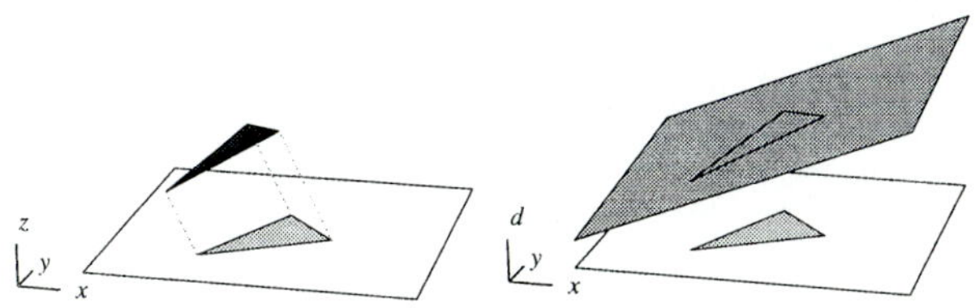


**Figure 6**: A polygonal site and its region of influence in a slice (left). The corresponding linear distance function (right).

### 4.2.2 Line Segments in 3D

The graph of the distance function for a line segment site is an elliptical cone (Figure 7). The apex of the cone lies at the intersection of the segment's line with the slice, and the cone's eccentricity is determined by the relative angle of the line and the slice. The 3D region of influence of a line segment lies between two parallel planes through the endpoints, since a point outside these planes is closer to one of the endpoints than to the segment.

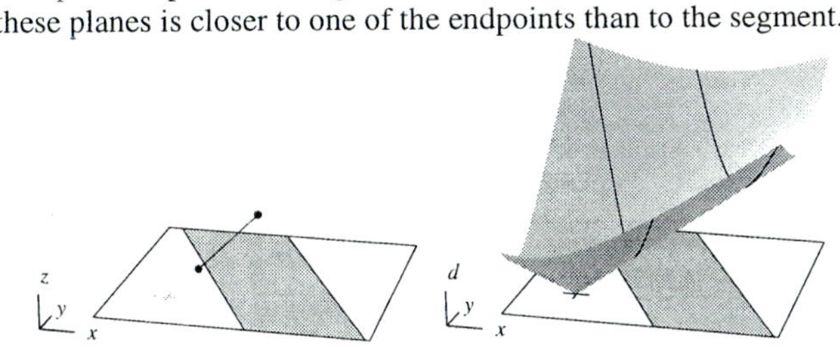


**Figure 7**: A line-segment site and its region of influence in a slice (left). The corresponding conical distance function (right).

### 4.2.3 Points in 3D

The distance function for a point site is shown in Figure 8. Its graph is one sheet of a hyperboloid of revolution of two sheets. If the point lies in the slice, the distance function is a cone rather than a hyperboloid. The region of influence for a single point is the entire slice.

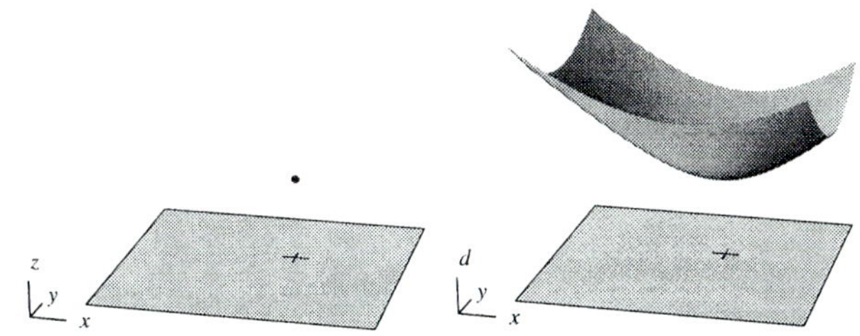


**Figure 8**: A point site and its region of influence in a slice (left). The corresponding hyperbolic distance function (right).

### 4.2.4 Meshes for Line Segments and Points in 3D

The construction of bounded-error meshes for the line-segment and point distance functions is detailed in [Hoff99]. The method attempts to minimize the complexity of the mesh by committing the maximum allowable error $\varepsilon$ in each mesh cell. The structure of the mesh depends only on the *resolution* of the Voronoi diagram, defined by the ratio of the diameter $M$ of the model to the maximum meshing error $\varepsilon$. The mesh structure is precomputed; during the Voronoi diagram construction, the mesh is constructed using table-lookup. Examples of the meshes produced by this method are shown in Figure 9.

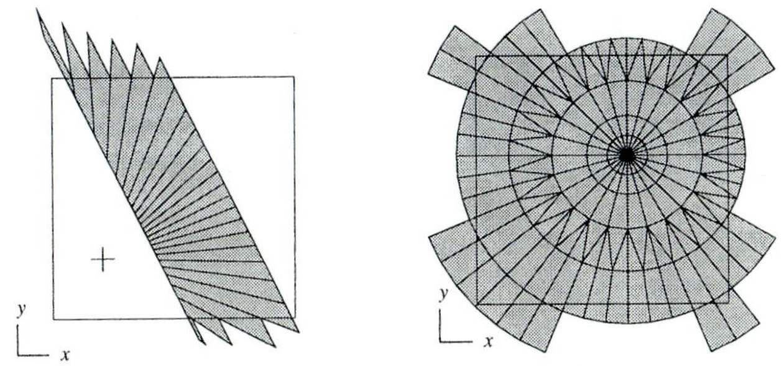


**Figure 9**: A bounded-error distance mesh for the line-segment site (left) and the point site (right).

## 4.3 Generalization to Curved Sites

The exact distance function for a curved site can be rather complicated, and for splines or algebraic curves is a high-degree algebraic function. We simplify this by creating a linear tessellation of the curved site, and then meshing the distance function of this approximation. We can use algorithms such as in [Filip87] and [Kumar96] to obtain bounded-error tessellations.

Figure 10 shows the mesh for a Bézier curve. Since the mesh for a linear segment is exact, the distance error for any of the linear segments is just the error in the deviation of the line from the original curve. The endpoints of the curve must be treated as points, just as for the line segment. The distance mesh for the "joints" between linear segments is a portion of the radial mesh of triangles. An overall maximum error bound of $\varepsilon$ can be obtained for the entire curve by:

- tessellating the curve into linear segments with maximum error bound of $\varepsilon$;
- rendering the distance mesh for the linear segments; and
- treating the endpoints and joints as points, and rendering each point distance mesh with maximum error bound of $\varepsilon$.

This approach generalizes to 3D surfaces, which can be tesselated into a polygonal mesh. The error is bounded in a similar way.

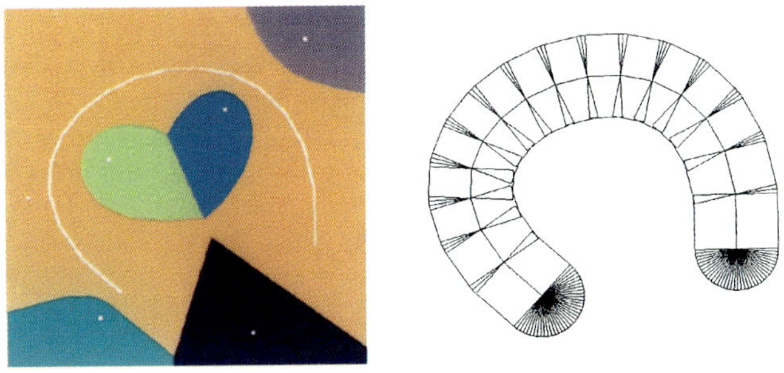

**Figure 10**: The Voronoi diagram of a Bézier curve and 5 points (left). The distance mesh for the Bézier curve that has been tessellated into 16 segments (right).

## 4.4 Weighted and Farthest-site Diagrams

In a *weighted* Voronoi diagram, the distance functions are additively or multiplicatively weighted [Okabe92]. Translation of a distance mesh along the distance axis accounts for additive weights. Linear scaling along the distance axis accounts for multiplicative weights. In 2D, this is equivalent to changing the angle of the cone or tent. Scaling the distance mesh also scales the meshing error.

In a *farthest-site* Voronoi diagram, the farthest site from each point is found. Unlike in the nearest-site diagram, the distance function monotonically decreases as we move away from the site. We obtain the proper distance relationships by negating the distance functions. In practice, however, we need only reverse the depth-test (less-than to greater-than) and change the depth initialization from $\infty$ to 0.

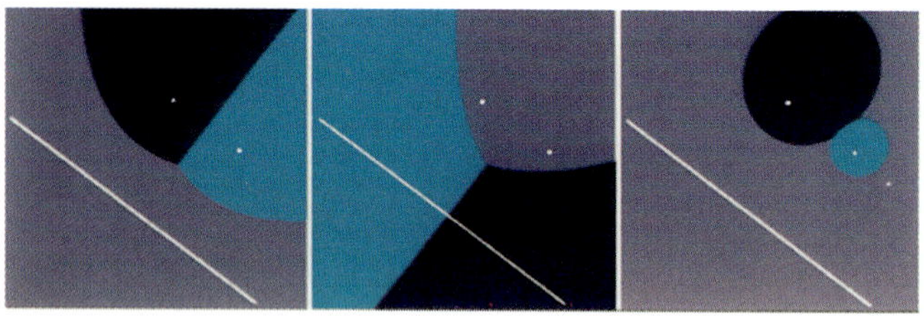

**Figure 11**: Standard nearest-site Voronoi regions (left). Farthest regions for the same sites (middle). Weighted regions (right). Weights: line, 2; dark point, 1; light point, 0.5.

# 5 BOUNDARIES AND NEIGHBORS

A continuous Voronoi diagram representation usually specifies the *Voronoi boundaries* that separate the set of Voronoi regions. In our discrete representation, we must search for the boundaries using approaches similar to iso-surface extraction and root-finding techniques [Bloom97]. However, instead of trying to bracket zero-crossings between sample points where iso-surface functions evaluate to values of opposite sign, we simply find the boundaries in the space between pixel samples of different color. Using the same approaches, we can either point-sample the boundary or compute an approximate mesh representation. In order to increase the precision, we must either use a higher overall resolution or adaptively refine.

One approach is to examine each pair of adjacent cells in 2D or 3D. If the colors are different, the location between the samples is marked as a point on the Voronoi boundary. The operation is very simple and can be accelerated through image operations in graphics hardware.

Another approach is based on a *continuation* method that starts at a point known to be on the boundary and walks along the boundary until all boundary points have been found [Bloom97]. Since we only compare locations near known boundaries, it is output sensitive. The correctness of the continuation method depends on whether the Voronoi boundaries are connected. The boundaries of a generalized Voronoi diagram of a collection of convex sites are always connected, so the method is correct for inputs consisting of point, line-segment, or convex polygonal sites. The method may fail in the presence of curves, curved surfaces, or concave sites where the generalized Voronoi diagram may have isolated components.

In this approach, at least one boundary point must be known as a "seed" value. Assuming convex sites, some Voronoi boundary passes through the edge of the bounded region in which we are computing the diagram, so the method begins by examining every window border pixel. When all Voronoi boundaries are connected only one seed point is needed since all others can be reached from that first point. Starting from a seed point, we recursively check all neighbors that are a different color from the current pixel's. All visited pixels are marked and avoided in the recursion.

This algorithm also finds the *Voronoi neighbors*–pairs of sites that share a Voronoi boundary. This concept is useful in a wide variety of applications, including computing the dual of the ordinary Voronoi diagram–the Delaunay triangulation. The boundary finding algorithms find pairs of adjacent pixels with different colors. The sites corresponding to those two colors are reported to be Voronoi neighbors. Connecting Voronoi neighbors with line segments constructs the Delaunay triangulation.

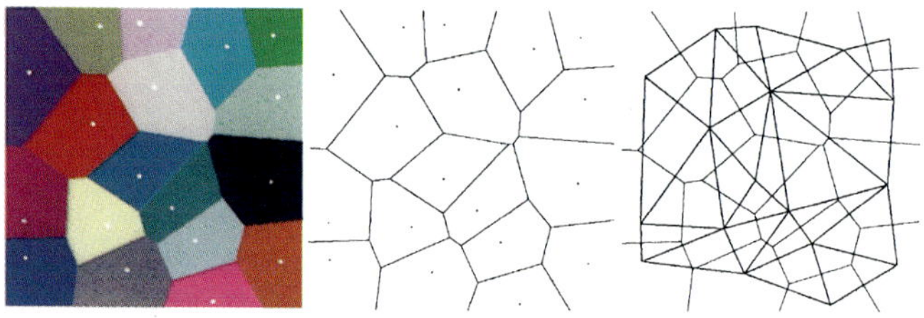

**Figure 12**: Voronoi diagram of set of 2D points (Left). Boundaries found with continuation-based approach (middle). Delaunay triangulation by connecting neighboring sites (right).

# 6 SOURCES OF ERROR

In this section we analyze all sources of error in our approach, and discuss how to reduce this error. We consider two broad categories: error in distance approximation and combinatorial error.

## 6.1 Distance Error

Distance error is the error in the distance computed from a pixel to a site. There are three sources of distance error:

- *Meshing error*, from approximating the true distance function by the distance mesh. We discussed how to bound this error in Section 4.
- *Tessellation error*, from tessellating a curved site into a number of linear sites. The tessellation algorithms presented in [Filip87, Kumar96] give tight bounds. Tessellation error is reduced by using a finer approximation to the site.
- *Hardware precision error,* from the use of fixed-precision arithmetic (integer or floating-point) during rasterization. Hardware precision error cannot be removed without resorting to multiple-precision arithmetic, but hardware error is usually negligible compared to meshing error.

These errors are additive–i.e. the error from one source is not magnified by the other sources. The total distance error is at most the sum of the errors from these three sources.

## 6.2 Combinatorial Error

Combinatorial error refers to qualitative error as opposed to quantitative. For example, a pixel is assigned the wrong color, or the algorithm reports an incorrect pair of Voronoi neighbors. There are three sources that contribute to combinatorial error:

- *Distance error*, as described in the previous section. With significant distance error, depth comparison at a pixel may make a farther site appear closer, causing the pixel to be colored incorrectly.

- *Resolution error*, a result of discrete sampling. If this sampling is too coarse, we may miss some Voronoi regions or find spurious neighbors. Handling resolution error is described below.
- *Z-buffer precision error,* the limitations of the number of bits of precision provided by the Z-buffer. Current graphics systems have 24 bits or 32 bits of precision for each pixel in the Z-buffer, which is more than the 23 bits provided in standard floating-point. If the distances between two pixels cannot be determined within that precision, the Z-buffer cannot accurately choose the correct color. This effect is small when compared to the other two, but can be significant at very high resolutions with very little distance error. A higher-precision Z-buffer can be simulated in software at a significant loss in efficiency.

*Adaptive resolution* allows us to "zoom in" on a region of interest, reducing potential resolution error. This involves identifying a window of interest and applying the appropriate linear transformation for zooming into that region. Figure 13 shows an example. Note that when zooming in, sites outside of the viewing region can still have Voronoi regions inside the region. Thus, the "maximum distance to a site" must be adjusted appropriately when computing the distance error bounds.

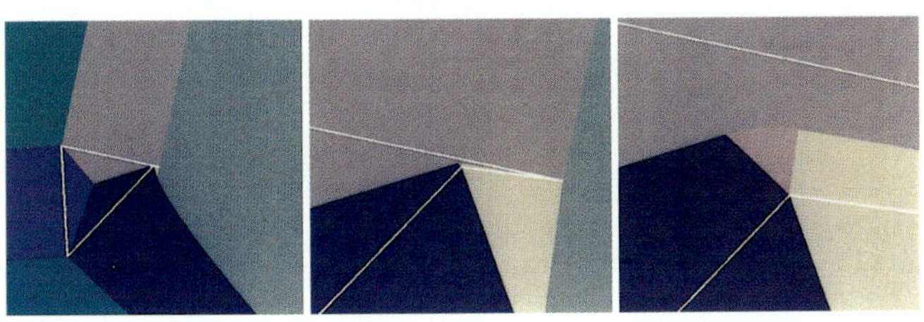

**Figure 13**: Adaptive resolution allows us to zoom in on features that could otherwise be missed.

Resolution error can cause a number of combinatorial problems, such as missing the entire Voronoi region of a site. One such example is shown in Figure 14 (left two images). When no cell has the color of a particular site, we can separately render the site itself, computing the pixels covering that site. By zooming around those pixels, we will find pixels in the Voronoi region of that site. The same technique can be applied to cells in 3D. Another problem arising from resolution error is incorrectly finding Voronoi neighbors (shown in Figure 14 – right two images). This problem (when due solely to resolution error) can be alleviated by adaptively zooming in on all boundary pixels.

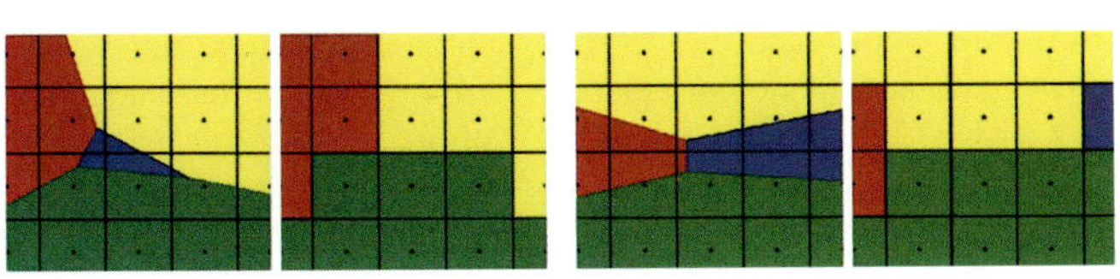

**Figure 14**: Problems caused by resolution error. An entire region in the center will be missed since it does not hit any pixel centers (left two images). The left and right regions, which should meet, become disconnected after rasterization (right two images).

## 6.3 Error Bounds

Distance error occasionally causes a pixel to be colored incorrectly. However, in a certain sense, the pixel is "almost" the right color. Assume that there is no Z-buffer precision error, and that we can bound the maximum distance error by $\varepsilon$, as described earlier. For a pixel $P$ colored with the ID of site $A$ and with a computed depth buffer value of $D$, we know that:

$$D - \varepsilon \leq dist(P,A) \leq D + \varepsilon$$

Furthermore, we know that for any other site $B$,

$$D - \varepsilon \leq dist(P,B)$$

From this information, we easily determine that

$$dist(P,A) \leq dist(P,B) + 2\varepsilon$$

where $dist(X,Y)$ means the distance from the center of pixel $X$ to site $Y$. That is, if a pixel is colored with the ID of $A$, then site $A$ is no more than $2\varepsilon$ farther from the pixel center than any other site. The same bound holds in 3D.

# 7 APPLICATIONS

There are many applications that benefit from fast computation of a discrete Voronoi diagram, an approximation to the distance function, or both. We describe three that we have implemented.

## 7.1 Motion Planning

Motion planning is a fundamental problem in robotics and computational geometry, with applications to the animation of digital actors, maintainability studies in virtual prototyping, and robot-assisted medical surgery. The classic Piano Mover's problem involves finding a collision-free path for a robot moving from one location (and orientation) to another in an environment filled with obstacles. Numerous approaches to this problem have been proposed, some of which are based on generalized Voronoi diagrams [Latom91]. The underlying idea is to treat the obstacles as sites. The Voronoi boundaries then provide paths of maximal clearance between the obstacles. Due to the practical complexity of computing generalized Voronoi diagrams, the applications of such planners have been limited to environments composed of a few simple obstacles.

Our discrete Voronoi computation algorithm can be applied to motion planning in both static and dynamic environments. The Voronoi algorithm computes the approximate distance to the nearest obstacle. The basic approach we implemented is based on the potential field method, which repels a robot away from the obstacles and towards the goal using a carefully designed artificial potential function. Other Voronoi diagram or distance-based approaches are also possible. The details of our motion planning algorithm are provided in [Hoff99].

We demonstrate our planner's effectiveness in a complex environment: the interior of a house, composed of over 100,000 triangles. We use the $x$- and $y$-components of the polygons to give the 2D input primitives for our algorithm. The robot has three degrees of freedom: $x$- and $y$-translation along the ground and rotation about the $z$-axis. Color plate 2 and the video show a sequence of piano motions automatically generated by our motion planner in a static environment. Color plate 2 also shows an image of the distance function for the house. We also apply our planner to environments with moving obstacles. Our video demonstrates the movement of a music stand through a house filled with moving furniture. The entire potential field and the motion planning sequence are computed in real time.

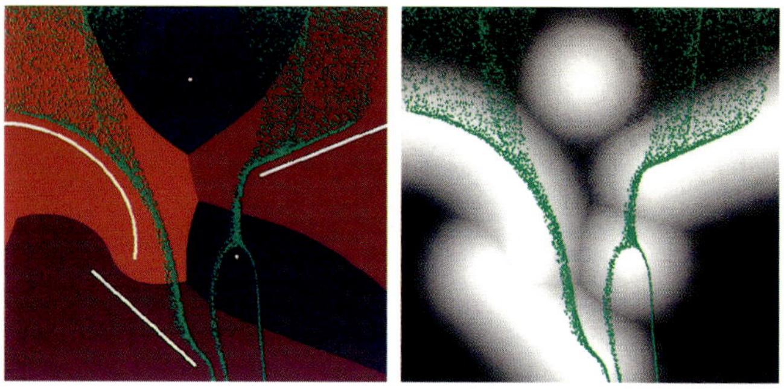

**Figure 15**: Motion planning of falling particles. Sites are avoided by using the Voronoi diagram's distance buffer (right) to create a potential field. This same principle is used in the rigid-body planner.

### 7.2 Selection in Complex User Interfaces

Complex 2D user interfaces sometimes require quick determination of the object nearest to the cursor. The Voronoi diagram of the interface can be used as a nearest-object lookup table indexed by sample points. Given the cursor position, it is simple to find the nearest sample point, and thus the nearest object. In some interfaces it may be desirable to know the distance to the selected object as well. We used this technique in our 2D implementation to allow the user to interactively move sites with the mouse.

### 7.3 Mosaics

We can use our approach for generating Voronoi diagrams to create an interesting artistic effect called mosaicing. A mosaic is a tiled image, where each tile has a single color. The Voronoi diagram of a point set can be used as a tiling [Haebe90]. Each Voronoi tile is colored with a color taken locally from the image. In our implementation, each tile is colored by the image pixel closest to the point site (see color plate 1). Our algorithm can perform this operation very quickly, allowing dynamic mosaics in which the mosaic tiling, the source image, or both may change in real time.

By randomly distributing point sites across an image, we obtain an effect similar to many mosaic filter effects seen in image editing programs. By clustering point sites around areas of higher detail, we obtain a classic tiling seen in many real-life mosaics where smaller tiles are used in areas of greater detail.

## 8 IMPLEMENTATION

For the 2D case, we implemented a complete interactive system incorporating all of the features and applications described here. Example output is shown throughout the paper. The video demonstrates interactive computation of more complex diagrams. In 3D, we show results from a prototype system that uses a simpler distance meshing strategy (see color plate 3 and the video for example output).

We implemented the 2D and 3D systems in C++ using the OpenGL graphics library and the GLUT toolkit. Any graphics API specification that uses a standard Z-buffered interpolation-based raster graphics system is sufficient to support the Voronoi diagram computation. Motion planning and the basic operations of boundary and neighbor finding require reading back of the color and depth buffers. Our system runs, without source modification, on both an MS-Windows-based PC and a high-end SGI Onyx2 with InfiniteReality Graphics. Surprisingly, the performance on a 400 Mhz Intel Pentium II PC with an Intergraph Intense 3D Pro 3410-T graphics accelerator was comparable to the SGI performance. In fact, in boundary finding, neighbor finding, and particle motion planning applications, the performance exceeded the high-end SGI. This was mainly due to intense buffer readback requirements. Each distance mesh must cover every pixel, so performance is bounded by the graphics hardware's pixel fill-rate. For large numbers of input sites, therefore, the SGI outperforms the PC.

When the distance-error tolerance is relaxed, the amount of geometry rendered for each site can be reduced, slightly improving performance. However, the biggest gains are achieved by reducing the number of pixels filled. In many practical cases, we can increase the performance significantly by bounding the site distance functions to a maximum distance. This allows reduction of the size of the distance meshes drawn so that only a portion of the screen is covered for each site. We exploit this observation to obtain interactive rates in the 1,000-point example shown in color plate 1, in the 10,000-point example shown in the video, and in the general case for the computation of the potential field used in the motion-planner. For closed higher-order primitives, such as polygons, we can further increase performance by restricting the distance function to only the inside or outside regions. This is useful in computing potential fields and medial axes.

## 9 CONCLUSIONS AND FUTURE WORK

We have presented a method for rapid computation of generalized discrete Voronoi diagrams in two and three dimensions using graphics hardware. We have presented techniques for creating a mesh of the distance function for each site with bounded error, and described how this distance mesh allows us to compute the Voronoi diagram rapidly. We have analyzed various sources of error, as well as how to bound or reduce those errors. Finally, we have demonstrated a few applications using our approach.

In the future, we would like to extend this work in the following ways: generalizations of distance functions and site geometry, further applications, other distance meshing strategies, and more acceleration techniques for the 3D Voronoi volume computation.

## ACKNOWLEDGEMENTS

Supported in part by ARO Contract DAAH04-96-1-0257 and DAAG55-98-1-0322, NSF Career Award CCR-9625217, NSF grants EIA-9806027 and DMI-9900157, NIH Research Resource Award 2P41RR02170-13, ONR Young Investigator Award and Intel. We would also like to thank Sarah Hoff for extensive help with editing and color plates, Chris Weigle for suggesting mosaicing using 2D point Voronoi diagrams, the UNC-walkthrough group for the house model, and the reviewers for their helpful comments.

## REFERENCES

[Auren91] F. Aurenhammer. *Voronoi Diagrams: A Survey of a Fundamental Geometric Data Structure*. ACM Computing Surveys, 23:345–405, 1991.

[Bloom97] J. Bloomenthal, C. Bajaj, J. Blinn, M-P. Cani-Gascuel, A. Rockwood, B. Wyvill, and G. Wyvill. *Introduction to Implicit Surfaces*. Morgan Kaufmann Publishers, Inc. San Francisco, CA. 1997.

[Chian92] C–S. Chiang. *The Euclidean Distance Transform*. Ph. D. thesis, Dept. Comp. Sci., Purdue Univ., West Lafayette, IN, August 1992. Report CSD-TR 92–050.

[Culve99] T. Culver, J. Keyser, and D. Manocha. *Accurate Computation of the Medial Axis of a Polyhedron*. Proc. of the Fifth Symp. on Solid Modeling and Applications. 1999.

[Dutta93] D. Dutta and C.M. Hoffmann. *On the Skeleton of Simple CSG Objects*. Journal of Mechanical Design, ASME Transactions, 115(1):87–94, 1993.

[Diric50] G.L. Dirichlet. *Uber die Reduktion der Positiven Quadratischen Formen mit Drei Unbestimmten Ganzen Zahlen*. J. Reine Angew. Math., 40:209–27, 1850.

[Filip87] D. Filip and R. Goldman. *Conversion from Bézier-rectangles to Bézier-triangles*. CAD, 19:25–27, 1987.

[Fortu86] S. Fortune. *A Sweepline Algorithm for Voronoi Diagrams*. In Proc. 2nd Annual ACM Symp. on Comp. Geom., pages 313–322, 1986.

[Goldf89] J. Goldfeather, S. Molnar, G. Turk, and H. Fuchs. *Near Real-time CSG Rendering Using Tree Normalization and Geometric Pruning*. IEEE Computer Graphics and Applications, 9(3):20–28, May 1989.

[Haebe90] P. Haeberli. *Paint by Numbers: Abstract Image Representation*. Computer Graphics (SIGGRAPH '90 Proc). vol. 25. pgs 207-214.

[Held97] M. Held. *Voronoi Diagrams and Offset Curves of Curvilinear Polygons*. Computer-Aided Design, 1997.

[Hoff99] K. Hoff, T. Culver, J. Keyser, M. Lin, and D. Manocha. *Fast Computation of Generalized Voronoi Diagrams Using Graphics Hardware*. Technical Report TR99-011, Dept. of Comp. Sci., University of North Carolina at Chapel Hill, 1999.

[Hoffm94] C.M. Hoffmann. *How to Construct the Skeleton of CSG Objects*. In A. Bowyer and J. Davenport, editors. Proc. of the Fourth IMA Conference, The Mathematics of Surfaces, University of Bath, UK, Sept. 1990. Oxford University Press, New York, 1994.

[Inaga92] H. Inagaki, K. Sugihara, and N. Sugie. *Numerically Robust Incremental Algorithm for Constructing Three-dimensional Voronoi Diagrams*. In Proc. 4th Canad. Conf. Comp. Geom., pgs 334-339, 1992.

[Kumar96] S. Kumar, D. Manocha, and A. Lastra. *Interactive Display of Large NURBS Models*. IEEE Trans. on Vis. and Computer Graphics. vol 2, no 4, pgs 323-336, Dec 1996.

[Latom91] J.C. Latombe. *Robot Motion Planning*. Kluwer Academic Publishers, 1991.

[Laven92] D. Lavender, A. Bowyer, J. Davenport, A. Wallis, and J. Woodwark. *Voronoi Diagrams of Set-theoretic Solid Models*. IEEE Computer Graphics and Applications, 12(5):69–77, Sept 1992.

[Lee82] D.T. Lee. *Medial Axis Transformation of a Planar Shape*. IEEE Trans. Pattern Anal. Mach. Intell., PAMI–4:363–369, 1982.

[Lengy90] J. Lengyel, M. Reichert, B.R. Donald, and D.P. Greenberg. *Real-time Robot Motion Planning Using Rasterizing Computer Graphics Hardware*. Computer Graphics (SIGGRAPH '90 Proc.), vol. 24, pgs 327–335, Aug 1990.

[Milen93] V. Milenkovic. *Robust Construction of the Voronoi Diagram of a Polyhedron*. In Proc. 5th Canadian. Conference on Comp. Geom., pgs 473-478, 1993.

[Milen93b] V. Milenkovic. *Robust Polygon Modeling*. Computer Aided Design, 25(9), 1993. (special issue on Uncertainties in Geometric Design).

[Okabe92] A. Okabe, B. Boots, and K. Sugihara. *Spatial Tessellations: Concepts and Applications of Voronoi Diagrams*. John Wiley & Sons, Chichester, UK, 1992.

[Rossi92] J. Rossignac, A. Megahed, and B. Schneider. *Interactive Inspection of Solids: Cross-sections and Interferences*. Computer Graphics (SIGGRAPH '92 Proc.), vol. 26, pgs 353–360, July 1992.

[Rossi86] J.R. Rossignac and A.A.G. Requicha. *Depth-buffering Display Techniques for Constructive Solid Geometry*. IEEE Computer Graphics and Applications, 6(9):29–39, 1986.

[Sheeh95] D.J. Sheehy, C.G. Armstrong, and D.J. Robinson. *Computing the Medial Surface of a Solid from a Domain Delaunay Triangulation*. In Proc. ACM/IEEE Symp. on Solid Modeling and Applications, May 1995.

[Shamo75] M.I. Shamos and D.Hoey. *Closest-point Problems*. In Proc. 16th Annual IEEE Symposium on Foundations of Comp. Sci., pages 151–162, 1975.

[Sugih94] K. Sugihara and M. Iri. *A Robust Topology-oriented Incremental Algorithm for Voronoi Diagrams*. International Journal of Comp. Geom. Appl., 4:179–228, 1994.

[Sherb95] E.C. Sherbrooke, N.M. Patrikalakis, and E. Brisson. *Computation of the Medial Axis Transform of 3D Polyhedra*. In Solid Modeling, pages 187–199. ACM, 1995.

[Teich97] M. Teichmann and S. Teller. *Polygonal Approximation of Voronoi Diagrams of a Set of Triangles in Three Dimensions*. Tech Rep 766, Lab of Comp. Sci., MIT, 1997.

[Vleug95] J. Vleugels and M. Overmars. *Approximating Generalized Voronoi Diagrams in Any Dimension*. Technical Report UU-CS-1995-14, Dept. of Comp. Sci., Utrecht University, 1995.

[Vleug96] J. Vleugels, V. Ferrucci, M. Overmars, and A. Rao. *Hunting Voronoi Vertices*. Comp. Geom. Theory Appl., 6:329–354, 1996.

[Voron08] G.M. Voronoi. *Nouvelles Applications des Paramètres Continus à la Théorie des Formes Quadratiques. Deuxième Mémoire: Recherches sur les Parallélloèdres Primitifs*. J. Reine Angew. Math., 134:198–287, 1908.

[Woo97] M. Woo, J. Neider, and T. Davis. *OpenGL Programming Guide*, Second Edition. Addison Wesley, 1997.

**Plate 1:** We can use the Voronoi diagram to create real-time mosaic effects. Left: Voronoi diagram computed for 1000 2D point sites at a resolution of 512x512. Center: Same diagram using the point locations to index into a 256x256 face texture to obtain the region colors. Right: The final effect at 512x512 with points removed. In the video, we show this same effect in real-time with 10,000 points.

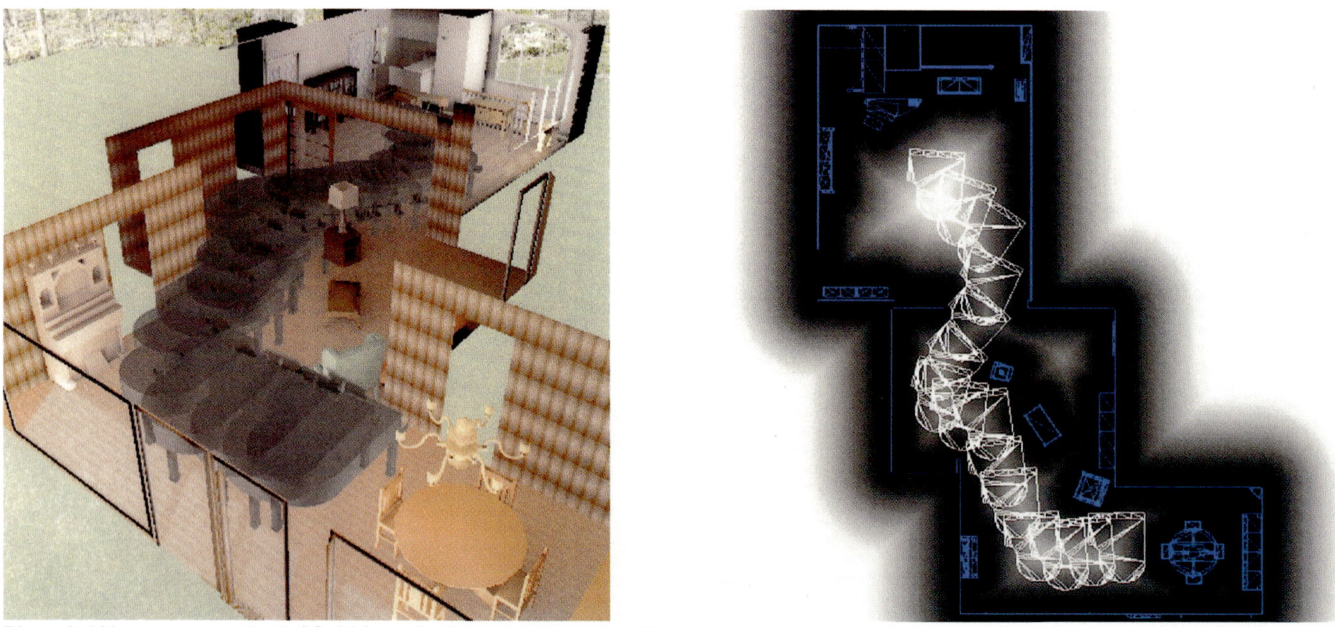

**Plate 2:** We create a potential field from the Voronoi diagram of the house floorplan to plan the motion of a piano through a complex static scene in real-time. Left: The piano motion sequence. Right: Motion sequence overlaying the floorplan distance function. The video demonstrates navigation through a dynamic scene in real-time.

**Plate 3:** We compute the 3D Voronoi diagram of polygonal models by computing one 2D slice at a time. Left: One slice is computed just below the teapot. Center: Complete slice halfway through. Right: Distance image. The colors indicate the Voronoi regions for face edge, and vertex sites. Only the face site colors are shown on the model.

# A Real-Time Low-Latency Hardware Light-Field Renderer

Matthew J. P. Regan, Gavin S. P. Miller, Steven M. Rubin and Chris Kogelnik

Interval Research Corporation.

## Abstract

This paper describes the design and implementation of an architecture for interactively viewing static light fields with very low latency. The system was deliberately over engineered to specifications much tighter than expected necessary to eliminate perceptible latency. This allowed us to relax the specifications to the point at which human users began to detect latency artifacts. We found empirically that when interacting with a light field, human users began to notice latency artifacts when the total system latency is approximately 15 ms. Although the architecture may not be used in practice, this result should prove fundamental for designers of future interactive graphics systems.

**CR Categories and Subject Descriptors:** I.3.3 [Computer Graphics]: Picture/Image Generation - Viewing Algorithms.

## 1 INTRODUCTION

Latency is a serious problem in interactive 3D graphics, particularly in applications such as virtual reality, augmented reality and "Fish Tank" virtual reality, where the user's viewpoint is tracked and used to create the imagery. In virtual reality and augmented reality where the user wears a tracked head mounted display, latency in the graphics system causes objects to "swim" around in the scene. Furthermore, it causes significant dynamic registration problems [Azuma95] and is even believed to be a major contributor to simulator sickness. In "Fish Tank" virtual reality, where the user's head is tracked while viewing a more conventional display [Deering93] or a virtual workbench [Cutler97], latency in the graphics causes objects to "swim" or shear as the result of user head motion. The non-desirable side effects of latency have motivated us to examine techniques for reducing latency and to study how much system latency is perceptible by human users.

The conventional 3D graphics pipeline is not well suited to low-latency interactive graphics. It is inherently frame based and many implementations introduce significant pipelining to improve system throughput at the expense of latency. In a head tracked graphics application running on a conventional graphics pipeline, it is not unusual for the application program to create the geometry from the tracked head location for frame $f$. While simultaneously, frame $f-1$ is being rasterized, frame $f-2$ is being scanned out and frame $f-3$ is decaying on the phosphor. Hence the light actually hitting the user's eyes may be the result of tracking information that was captured some frames ago.

1801 Page Mill Rd. Bldg C.
Palo Alto, CA, 94304
regan@interval.com
miller@interval.com



Techniques such as [Regan94] have been developed specifically to mask the latency introduced by the conventional graphics pipeline. However this particular technique only works for masking the rotational component of the viewing transformation leaving latency in the translational component of the viewing transformations.

Other techniques have been developed to significantly reduce the latency induced by scanning out an image. For a 60 Hz display, the pixels at the bottom of the image are scanned out 16 ms later than the pixels at the top of the image. Olano et al. [Olano95] demonstrated that by changing the viewing transformation during scan out, this latency could be minimized. Their technique called "Just-In-Time Pixels" involves changing the viewing transformation slightly every scan line. It uses prediction and a simple approximation of the viewing transformation to mask scan-out latency. While this approach seems counter-intuitive for those used to dealing with frames, it does actually produce *the right pixel at the right place at the right time*. Provided the transformation is fast enough and smooth enough to avoid tearing, the technique works well.

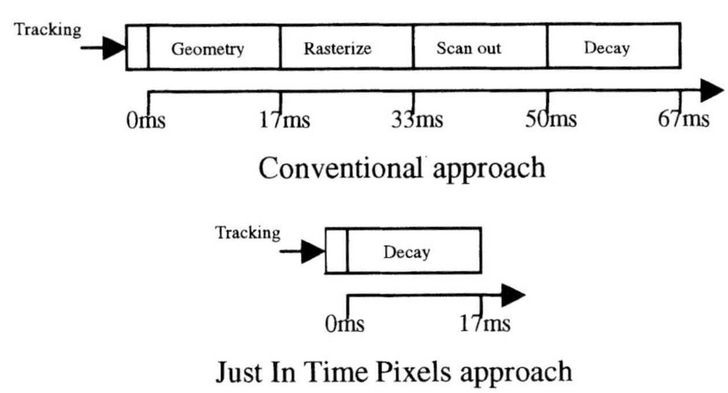


Figure 1 Latency for the bottom scan line in a typical 3D graphics system vs. a "Just In Time Pixel" system.

Images generated with a conventional 3D graphics pipeline have the same camera viewing transformation for all objects in the scene. To use a just-in-time pixels approach directly from a scene's geometry, a real-time ray tracer would be required. Otherwise, the scene's geometry would have to be pre-sorted into scan line order, then transformed and rasterized while "chasing the beam". In fact this in not a new idea as many of the earliest graphics systems used the "chase the beam" approach.

Image-based rendering techniques seem much more appealing for changing the viewing transformation at scan-out rather than operating from geometry. Since pure rotations do not effect the occlusion within an image, image-based techniques have been developed to modify the rotational component of the viewing transformation late in the pipeline or at scan out [Regan94]. Translations do cause changes to occlusions within the scene, so modifying the translational component of the viewing transformation at scan out is much more challenging. Viewpoint interpolation techniques such as [Chen93, McMillan95] have been developed to do this, however these techniques are generally suited to small translations and they can introduce visual artifacts where occlusion information has been lost.

A newer image-based representation known as a "Light Field" [Levoy96] or "Lumigraph" [Gortler96] (from here on in we will use the term light field for convenience) is more suitable for this application than simple viewpoint interpolation. Light fields completely characterize the flow of light through unobstructed space in a static scene with fixed illumination. Hence viewpoint interpolation within a given region from a light field does not suffer from the same occlusion problems mentioned last paragraph.

Section 2 of this paper briefly discusses light fields and the special case of the Levoy - Hanrahan geometry that is used to make the hardware version of the renderer. Section 3 discusses the architecture of the renderer and describes the low-latency hardware implementation. Section 4 discusses and provides the results of a human perception experiment while Section 5 of the paper describes future work and gives a conclusion.

## 2 THE LIGHTFIELD APPROACH

A light field is a 4D function, that captures light rays between two surfaces. Levoy and Hanrahan, and Gortler et al. describe a parameterization method where the light rays are indexed by their intersection with these two surfaces.

If we choose a special case of the Levoy - Hanrahan geometry where the focal plane coincides with the screen, an output image may be generated by re-sampling the light field in orientation but not position. The second projection in the Levoy - Hanrahan scheme is achieved by simply viewing the screen, replacing the quadralinear interpolation with a bi-linear interpolation.

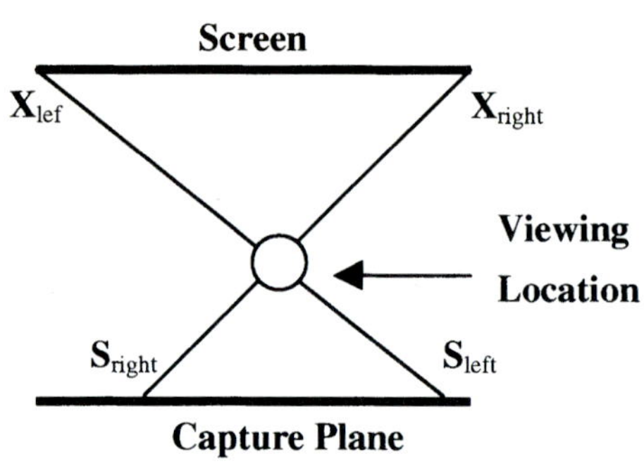


Figure 2. Plan view of the geometry for the special case of the Levoy - Hanrahan light field. The Screen and the Capture Plane are the two surfaces used to create the light field.

Projecting rays from the screen back through the viewing location to the capture plane gives us the s and t parameters for any x, y pixel location. From Figure 2 it can be seen by similar triangles that, s varies linearly with screen location based on the viewing location (t, the other axis not shown in Figure 2 also varies linearly with screen location). Hence for any given location, x and y correspond to the screen space location of a pixel and s and t are simple linear equations derived from the position of the screen and the viewing location. New s and t linear equation coefficients can be computed for every tracking sample.

A disadvantage of the light field representation is the sheer volume of data required to represent a light field, especially when uncompressed. While compression schemes do exist and achieve significant compression ratios, schemes other than Vector Quantization (VQ) [Gersho92] are difficult to implement in real-time hardware. As a result, our initial implementation involves reducing the capture plane to a single axis, which eliminates vertical motion parallax. We refer to this as a 1-axis light field, giving a 3D light field rather than a regular light field which has a 2 axis capture plane resulting in a 4D function.

## 3 LOW LATENCY HARDWARE

In order for a virtual object to appear stationary and accurately registered, two conditions must be satisfied. First, the user's viewpoint must be tracked accurately and with low latency. Secondly, the image must be computed and displayed with low latency. Any latency in the system causes objects to "swim" while the user's head is moving, potentially diminishing the illusion.

A goal of this effort was to implement a low latency rendering scheme for "Fish Tank" virtual reality in order to study the effects of latency. We chose a light field representation for the object to be displayed with low latency. In principle, a light field can be sampled with a different tracking location for each display pixel or each display scan line, rather than just once per frame, making it suitable for the just-in-time pixels approach.

To achieve this goal we actually built a low latency tracking system and a low latency hardware light-field renderer using a combination of custom and off-the-shelf components. We decided to build a "gold standard" system, which was specifically over-engineered to have the lowest latency we could reasonably achieve and significantly lower than we expected necessary. The system is depicted in Figure 3.

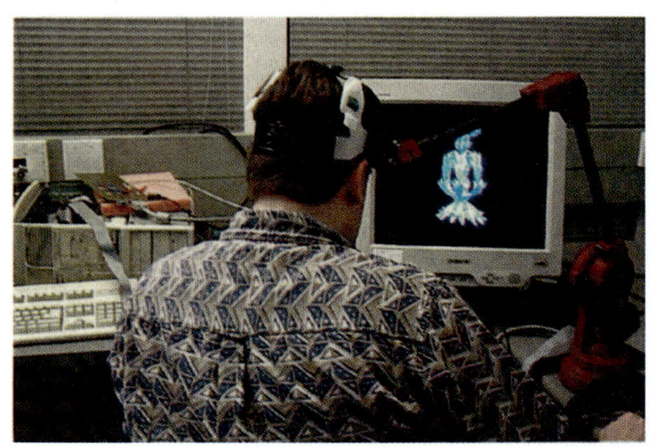

Figure 3. Using the light field renderer. Note the mechanical arm tracking the user's head and the PC in the background which contains the custom hardware for the renderer.

The system was designed to operate at 25 MHz, producing a Standard VGA signal. The user's head can be tracked rapidly and new light field parameters computed, and down-loaded to the hardware, at nearly 100 times per frame.

### 3.1 Tracking

A great deal of work has been done to accurately track a user's head for virtual reality and fish tank virtual reality. Schemes using a plethora of technologies have been developed and many of these systems are commercially available. Technologies used for tracking a user's head include magnetic systems, optical systems such as UNC's hi-ball tracker [Welch97], acoustic systems and mechanical systems. To achieve minimal latency with high accuracy, we decided to use a mechanical system. In practice the main drawbacks of a mechanical system are the limited operating volume and the inertia introduced by the mechanical system. For the purpose of our experiment, where the user sits in front of a screen and moves from side to side, the restrictions of the mechanical tracker were tolerable. The main advantages of the mechanical systems are high accuracy, potentially very low latency and low cost.

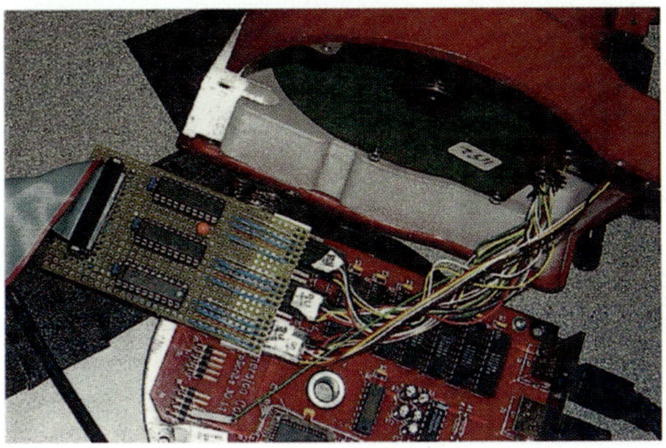

Figure 4. Inside the modified mechanical arm. The interface board allows the rotary encoders to be sampled at high speed.

The tracker used for the light field renderer consisted of a modified MicroScribe mechanical arm from Immersion Corporation [Immersion99]. The arm has relatively low inertia and the manufacturers claim it is accurate to 0.3 mm. The MicroScribe arm uses rotary encoders at each mechanical joint to determine the orientation and location of the tip of the arm. The encoders are connected to counters inside the arm and the encoder readings are transmitted to a PC over an RS232 serial interface. Rather than rely on an RS232 serial link we built a custom interface board that transmits the encoder outputs in parallel to counters in the host PC (see Figure 4). The encoder counters are implemented in a Xilinx-based Field Programmable Gate Array (FPGA) on a custom PCI based board inside the PC. In the test system, the latency of reading the encoders and computing position and orientation information is approximately 64 µs.

## 3.2 Light Field Rendering Architecture

To simplify the implementation of the light field renderer, it was decided that uncompressed light fields should be used. The custom hardware used to implement the architecture has a physical memory limitation of 32 Mbytes, thus as stated earlier, we decided to only implement a 1-axis light field rather than a 2-axis light field. This means vertical motion parallax is eliminated while viewing the light field. Although this is undesirable, it still allows for meaningful latency tests to be carried out. While VQ decompression is well suited to a hardware implementation, even VQ decompression would not free up enough memory for a 2-axis light field on the current system. With 32 Mbytes of memory it is possible to store 128 gray-scale images of 512 by 512 pixels.

The architecture for the light field renderer depicted in Figure 5 is very simple. It consists of a conventional raster generator for counting x and y, a light-field frame buffer, an interpolation unit for $s$, a linear interpolation filter, a stereo management unit and a video DAC. Each clock cycle, the raster generator increments x by one and $s$ by $\delta s$. At horizontal sync, y is incremented by one. Also at the horizontal sync, new values for $s$ and $\delta s$, are loaded into the interpolation unit.

The x, y, s values are concatenated together to form the pixel address within the light field. The pixels at locations (x, y, s) and (x, y, s+1) are fetched simultaneously and blended together using the fractional parts of $s$.

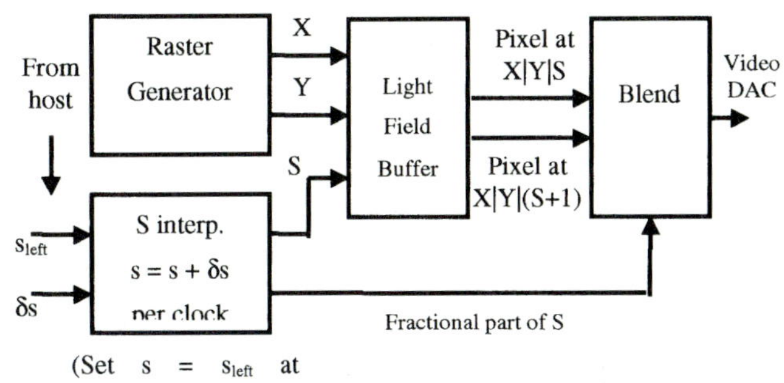


Figure 5. Overview of the hardware light field renderer.

## 3.3 Hardware Implementation

The light field renderer has been implemented using two custom FPGA based rapid prototyping boards referred to as Programmable And Reconfigurable Tool Set (PARTS) boards [Woodfill97] (see Figure 6). Each PARTS board consists of 16 Xilinx 4028 FPGAs arranged in a 4 by 4 grid. The design uses two PARTS boards and operates at 25 MHz to produce a Standard VGA signal (60 Hz). Stereo is currently achieved using a red and green filter. The design can operate in mono mode or in stereo mode. Due to bandwidth limitations, the red green stereo mode operates in an interlaced manner.

Figure 6 The PARTS board. Additional FPGAs are located on the other side of the board.

The main reason for using an FPGA-based approach over a software implementation is that there is no final frame buffer in the system. The light field renderer directly drives the video DAC. The FPGA implementation guarantees data output for every pixel clock. It also guarantees the counters and interpolators will be incremented and updated at the appropriate times. A software-based implementation running on a system with an Operating System (OS) is not suitable for driving the beam directly, as any OS overheads would result in missed pixels. A large First In First Out (FIFO) buffer or a frame buffer would be required to overcome this problem so that the swap time can be amortized over a large number of pixels. However the inclusion of such buffers requires additional hardware and increases latency. Conventional 3D graphics cards are designed to have a fixed viewing transformation for the entire frame and are not suited to the just-in-time pixels approach.

The main tracking loop of the light field rendering system runs on the Pentium II PC host. It reads the rotary encoder counters from the FPGAs, converts these readings to a location for the arm, generates the linear equation for the light field for both the left and the right eyes. These values are then downloaded into the light-field renderer on the PARTS board. The measured end to end latency of the system is 200 μs, with an update rate of 5 kHz. On a sample by sample basis, $s$ and $\delta s$ only change by a small amount. Although the update rate is less than once per scan line, no visual tearing in the light field was observed.

## 4 EXPERIMENTAL RESULTS

We conducted a study to determine the point at which subjects could reliably detect latency in the display. This study involved twelve participants with normal or corrected vision. We ran a 2-interval forced-choice staircase procedure [Levitt71] in which participants were asked to determine which of two intervals contained latency. The 2-down 1-up staircase routine yields the 70.7 percent correct point. Two staircases were randomly interleaved.

The results of this study are depicted in Figure 7. The average latency threshold for the twelve participants was 15.0 ms, with a standard deviation of 3.1ms. Over multiple sessions, the user's threshold tended to decrease.

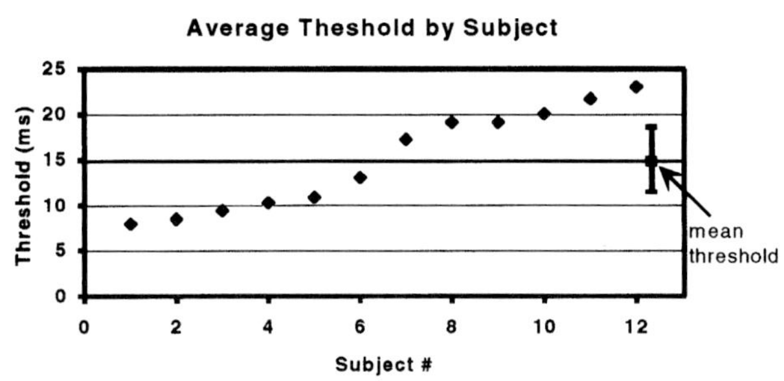


Figure 7. Results from the user test. Note that 0ms latency really means less than 0.5ms.

This experiment determined detectable amounts of system latency, when compared to a negligible latency system. In a practical application, users may tolerate or may not notice higher amounts of latency. When we refer to latency in the experiment, we are only referring to the computational component of the latency, leaving out the mechanical component and phosphor decay component.

## 5 CONCLUSION

We have developed and implemented a graphics system architecture for displaying static light fields with very low latency. A user test of the system revealed an average detectable latency threshold of 15ms, although some users were able to detect 7.5 ms of latency. Below this threshold, the users perceived the graphical objects to be spatially stable. A new version of the system is currently being developed. This will enable the display of 2-axis light fields or motion sequences of 1-axis light fields.

## Acknowledgements

The authors would like to acknowledge Sheryl Ehrlich for designing and conducting the final version of the user study. We would like to thank Michael Bajura for his help with the mechanical tracking system, and Frank Crow and Philip Hubbard for their helpful suggestions. Finally we would like to thank the anonymous reviewers for their constructive criticism of the submission version of the paper.

## References

[Azuma95] Azuma, R., Predictive Tracking for Augmented Reality. UNC Chapel Hill Department of Computer Science PhD Dissertation 1995.

[Chen93] Chen, S.E., Williams L., "View Interpolation for Synthetic Image Synthesis" Computer Graphics (SIGGRAPH '93 Proceedings), Vol. 26, 1992, pp 279-288.

[Cutler97] Cutler, L.D , Frolich, B., and Hanrahan, P., "Two-Handed Direct Manipulation on the Responsive Workbench", 1997 Symposium on Interactive 3D Graphics, pp. 107—114, 1997.

[Deering93] Deering, M., "High resolution virtual reality", Computer Graphics (SIGGRAPH '92 Proceedings), Vol. 26, 1992, pp 195-202.

[Gersho92] Gersho, A., and Grey, R.M., *Vector Quantization and Signal Compression*, Kluwer Academic Publishers, 1992.

[Gortler96] Gortler, S.J., Grzeszczuk, R., Szeliski, R., and Cohen, M., "The Lumigraph", Computer Graphics Proceedings, Annual Conference Series (SIGGRAPH 96), pp43-54.

[Immersion99] Immersion Corporation's web page. www.immerse.com

[Levitt71] Levitt, H., "Transformed Up-Down Methods in Psychoacoutics", The Journal of the Acoustical Society of America, Vol 49. No. 2 (Part 2) 1971 pp467-477.

[Levoy96] Levoy, M., Hanrahan, P., "Light Field Rendering", Computer Graphics Proceedings, Annual Conference Series (SIGGRAPH 96), pp31-42.

[McMillan95] McMillan, L., Bishop, G., "Head-Tracked Stereoscopic Display using Image Warping," Stereoscopic Displays and Virtual Reality Systems II, Proc. SPIE, Vol. 2409, S.Fisher, J. Merritt, B.Bolas eds. 1995, pp21-30

[Olano95] Olano, M., Cohen, J., Mine, M., Bishop, G., "Combatting Rendering Latency" 1995 Symposium on Interactive 3D Graphics, pp. 19—24, 1995.

[Regan94] Regan, M., Pose, R., "Priority Rendering with a Virtual Reality Address Recalculation Pipeline", Computer Graphics Proceedings, Annual Conference Series (SIGGRAPH 94), pp155-161.

[Welch97] Welch, G., Bishop, G., "SCAAT: Incremental Tracking with Incomplete Information," Computer Graphics Proceedings, Annual Conference Series. (SIGGRAPH 97), pp333-344.

[Woodfill97] Woodfill, J., and Von Herzen, B., "Real-Time Stereo Vision on the PARTS Reconfigurable Computer," Proceedings IEEE Symposium on Field-Programmable Custom Computing Machines, Napa, pp. 242-250, April 1997.

# LDI Tree: A Hierarchical Representation for Image-Based Rendering

Chun-Fa Chang Gary Bishop Anselmo Lastra
University of North Carolina at Chapel Hill

## ABSTRACT

Using multiple reference images in 3D image warping has been a challenging problem. Recently, the Layered Depth Image (LDI) was proposed by Shade et al. to merge multiple reference images under a single center of projection, while maintaining the simplicity of warping a single reference image. However it does not consider the issue of sampling rate.

We present the LDI tree, which combines a hierarchical space partitioning scheme with the concept of the LDI. It preserves the sampling rates of the reference images by adaptively selecting an LDI in the LDI tree for each pixel. While rendering from the LDI tree, we only have to traverse the LDI tree to the levels that are comparable to the sampling rate of the output image. We also present a progressive refinement feature and a "gap filling" algorithm implemented by pre-filtering the LDI tree.

We show that the amount of memory required has the same order of growth as the 2D reference images. This also bounds the complexity of rendering time to be less than directly rendering from all reference images.

**CR Categories:** I.3.3 [Computer Graphics]: Picture/Image Generation - Viewing Algorithms; I.3.6 [Computer Graphics] Methodology and Techniques - Graphics data structures and data types; I.3.7 [Computer Graphics]: Three-Dimensional Graphics and Realism.

**Additional Keywords:** image-based rendering, hierarchical representation

## 1. INTRODUCTION

The 3D Image warping algorithm [14] proposed by McMillan and Bishop uses regular single-layered depth images (which are called *reference images*) as the initial input. One of the major problems of 3D image warping is the disocclusion artifacts which are caused by the areas that are occluded in the original reference image but visible in the current view. Those artifacts appear as tears or gaps in the output image. In Mark's Post-Rendering Warping [11], the techniques of splatting and meshing are proposed to deal with the disocclusion artifacts. Both splatting and meshing are adequate for post-rendering warping in which the current view does not deviate much from the view of the reference image.

However, the fundamental problem of the disocclusion artifacts is that the information of the previously occluded area is missing in the reference image. By using multiple reference images taken from different viewpoints, the disocclusion artifacts can be reduced because an area that is not visible from one view may be visible from another. When multiple source images are available, we expect the disocclusion artifacts that occur while warping one reference image to be eliminated by one of the other reference images. However, combining multiple reference images and eliminating the redundant information is a non-trivial problem, as pointed out by McMillan in his discussion of inverse warping [15].

Recently, the Layered Depth Image (LDI) was proposed by Shade et al. [19] to merge many reference images under a single center of projection. It tackles the occlusion problems by keeping multiple depth pixels per pixel location, while still maintaining the simplicity of warping a single reference image. Its limitation is that the fixed resolution of the LDI may not provide an adequate sampling rate for every reference image. Figure 1 shows two examples of such situations. Assuming the two reference images have the same resolution as the LDI, the object covers more pixels in reference image 1 than it does in the LDI. Therefore the LDI has a lower sampling rate for the object than reference image 1. Similar analysis shows the LDI has a higher sampling rate than reference image 2. If we combine both reference images into the LDI and render the object from the center of projection of reference image 1, the insufficient sampling rate of the LDI will cause the object to look more blurry than it looks in reference image 1. When we render the object from the center of projection of reference image 2, the excessive sampling rate of the LDI might not hurt the quality of the output. However, processing more pixels than necessary slows down the rendering.

In this paper, we present the *LDI Tree*, which combines a hierarchical space partition scheme with the concept of the LDI. It preserves the sampling rate of the reference images by adaptively selecting an LDI in the LDI tree for each pixel. While rendering from the LDI tree, we only have to traverse the LDI tree to the levels that are comparable to the sampling rate of the output image. Because each LDI also contains pre-filtered results from its children LDIs, progressive refinement is easy to implement. The pre-filtering also enables a new "gap filling" algorithm to fill the disocclusion artifacts that cannot be resolved by any reference image.

The amount of memory required has the same order of growth as the 2D reference images. Therefore the LDI tree preserves an important feature that image-based rendering has over traditional polygon-based rendering: the cost is bounded by the complexity of the reference images, not by the complexity of the scene.

## 2. RELATED WORK

### 2.1. Inverse Warping

The image warping described in [14] is a forward warping process. The pixels of the reference images are traversed and warped to the output image in the order they appear in the reference images. Some pixels in the output image may receive more than

CB#3175 Sitterson Hall, Chapel Hill, NC 27599-3175, USA.
{chang, gb, lastra}@cs.unc.edu http://www.cs.unc.edu/~ibr

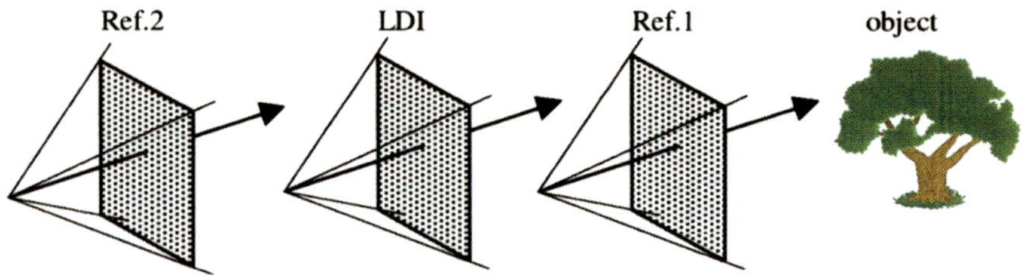


**Figure 1:** The LDI does not preserve the sampling rates of the reference images.

one warped pixel and some may receive none, which causes artifacts.

In [15], McMillan proposed an inverse warping algorithm. For each pixel in the output image, searches are performed in all reference images to find the pixels that could be warped to the specified location in the output image. Although epipolar geometry limits the search space to a one-dimensional line or curve in each reference image and a quadtree-based optimization has been proposed in [10], searching through all reference images is still time consuming.

## 2.2. Layered Depth Image

Another way to deal with the disocclusion artifacts of image warping is to use the Layered Depth Image (LDI)[19]. Given a set of reference images, one can create an LDI by warping all reference images to a carefully chosen camera setup (e.g. center of projection and view frustum) which is usually close to the camera of one of the reference images. When more than one pixel is warped to the same pixel location of the LDI, some of them may be occluded. Although the occluded pixels are not visible from the viewpoint of the LDI, they are not discarded. Instead, separate layers are created to store the occluded pixels. Those extra pixels are likely to reduce the disocclusion artifacts. However the fixed resolution of the LDI limits its use as discussed previously in section 1.

Lischinski and Rappoport used three parallel-projection LDIs to form a Layered Depth Cube [9]. Max's hierarchical rendering method [12] uses the Precomputed Multi-Layer Z-Buffers which are similar to the LDIs. It generates the LDIs from polygons and the hierarchy is built into the model.

## 2.3. Volumetric Methods

The LDI resembles volumetric representations. The main differences between an LDI-based representation and 3D volume data are discussed in [9].

Curless and Levoy presented a volumetric method to extract an isosurface from range images [3]. The goal of their work, however, was to build high-detail models made of triangles. The volume data used in that method is not hierarchical and it relies on a run-length encoding for space efficiency.

There has also been work related to octree generation from range images [1][2][8]. However the octree that is generated in those methods is used to encode the space occupancy information. Each octree cell represents either completely occupied or completely empty parts of the scene.

The multi-resolution volume representation in the Hierarchical Splatting work [6] by Laur and Hanrahan can be considered as a special case of the LDI tree in which the LDIs are of 1×1 resolution. It is however built from a fully expanded octree (which is called a pyramid in their paper). The octree to be traversed during the rendering is also predetermined and does not change with the viewpoint.

## 2.4. Image Caching for Rendering Polygonal Models

The image caching techniques of Shade et al. [18] and Schaufler et al. [17] use a hierarchical structure similar to the LDI tree. Each space partition has an imposter instead of an LDI. The imposter can be generated rapidly from the objects within the space partition by using hardware acceleration. However, the imposter has to be frequently regenerated whenever it is no longer suitable for the new view

In contrast, the information stored in the LDI tree is valid at all times. By generating the LDI tree from the reference images instead of the objects within the space partitions, the LDI tree can be used for non-synthesized scenes as well.

# 3. LDI TREE

The LDI tree is an octree with an LDI attached to each octree cell (node). The octree is chosen for its simplicity but can be replaced by the other space partitioning schemes. Each octree cell also contains a bounding box and pointers to its eight children cells. The root of the octree contains the bounding box of the scene to be rendered[1]. The following is pseudo code representing the data structure:

```
LDI_tree_node =
Bounding_box[X..Z, Min..max]: array of
      real;
Children[0..7]: array of pointer to
      LDI_tree_node;
LDI: Layered_depth_image
```

All LDIs in the LDI tree have the same resolution, which can be set arbitrarily. The height (or number of levels) of the LDI tree will adapt to different choices of resolution. In general, a lower resolution results in more levels in the LDI tree. Ultimately, we can make the resolution of the LDI be 1×1 which makes the LDI tree resemble the volume data in the Hierarchical Splatting [6].

Note that each LDI in the LDI tree contains only the samples from objects within the bounding box of the cell. This is sometimes confusing because the LDI originally proposed by Shade et al. combines the samples from all reference images.

For simplicity, we use one face of the bounding box as the projection plane of the LDI. Orthographic projection is used and the projection direction is perpendicular to the projection plane.

An example of the LDI tree is shown in Figure 7 by viewing the bounding boxes from the top. The following sections discuss the details of constructing the LDI tree from multiple reference images and of rendering a new view from the LDI tree.

[1] For outdoor scenes, background textures can be added to the faces of the bounding box. The bounding box can be extended with little overhead if most of the space is empty.

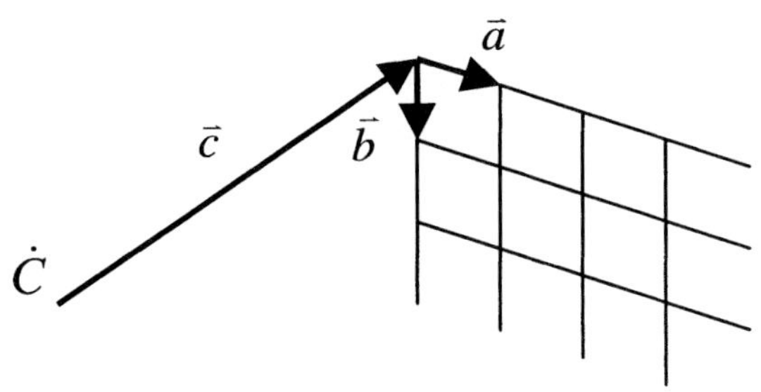


**Figure 2:** The camera model.

## 3.1. Constructing the LDI Tree from Multiple Reference Images

The LDI tree is constructed from reference images by warping each pixel of the reference images to the LDI of an octree cell, then filtering the affected LDI pixels to the LDIs of all ancestor cells in the octree.

In 3D image warping, each pixel of the reference images contains depth information which is either stored explicitly as a depth value or implicitly as a disparity value. This allows us to project the center of the pixel to a point in the space where the scene described by the reference images resides.

We observed that the sampling rate or the "quality" of a pixel of a reference image depends on its depth information. For example, if (part of) a reference image represents a surface that is far away, then those pixels that describe that surface do not provide enough detail when the viewer zooms in or walks toward that surface. Conversely, warping every pixel of a reference image taken near an object is wasteful when the object is viewed from far away.

We characterize the reference image by a pinhole camera model using the notation adopted by McMillan [14][15]. Figure 2 illustrates the camera model. $\dot{C}$ is the center of projection. Each pixel of the reference image has coordinates $(u, v)$ and the vectors $\vec{a}$ and $\vec{b}$ are the bases. Each pixel also contains the color information and a disparity value $\delta$. When a pixel is projected to the 3D object space, we get a point representing the center of the projected pixel and a "stamp size." The center is computed as:

$$\dot{C} + (u\vec{a} + v\vec{b} + \vec{c}) / \delta \qquad (1)$$

and the stamp size $S$ is calculated by:

$$S = S_X \times S_Y \qquad (2)$$
$$S_X = |\vec{a}| / \delta$$
$$S_Y = |\vec{b}| / \delta$$

To simplify our discussion, we do not consider the orientation of the object surface from which the pixel is taken. We also ignore the slight variation of stamp size at the edges of the projection plane.

An octree cell is then selected to store this pixel. The center location determines which branch of the octree to follow. The stamp size determines which level (or what size) of the octree cell should be used. The level is chosen such that the stamp size approximately matches the pixel size of the LDI in that cell.

After an octree cell has been chosen, the pixel can then be warped to the LDI of that cell. The details of the warping are described in [11]. Usually, the center of the pixel will not fall exactly on the grid of the LDI, so resampling is necessary. This is done by splatting [20] the pixel to the neighboring grid points. In this paper we use a bilinear kernel. Four LDI pixels are updated for each pixel of a reference image. More specifically, the alpha values that result from the splatting are computed by:

$$P_X = B_X / N_X$$
$$P_Y = B_Y / N_Y$$
$$Kernel(d, s) = 1 - \frac{d}{s}$$

$$W_X = \begin{cases} Kernel(|Xi - Xc|, \frac{S_X}{P_X}), & S_X > P_X \\ Kernel(|Xi - Xc|, 1) * \frac{S_X}{P_X}, & S_X \le P_X \end{cases} \qquad (3a)$$

$$W_Y = \begin{cases} Kernel(|Yi - Yc|, \frac{S_Y}{P_X}), & S_Y > P_Y \\ Kernel(|Yi - Yc|, 1) * \frac{S_X}{P_X}, & S_Y \le P_Y \end{cases} \qquad (3b)$$

$$\text{alpha} = W_X W_Y \qquad (3)$$

where $B_X$ and $B_Y$ are the sizes of the LDI projection plane (which is a face of the bounding box). $N_X$ and $N_Y$ are the resolutions of the LDI. $S_X$ and $S_Y$ are as defined in equation 2. $(Xc, Yc)$ is the center of splatting in the selected LDI and $(Xi, Yi)$ is one of the grid points covered by the splatting. The conditions in equations 3a and 3b guarantee that the splat size will not be smaller than the LDI grid size, which represents the maximal sampling rate of the LDI.[2]

A pixel also contributes to the parent cell and all ancestor cells of the octree cell that was initially chosen. This is done by splatting the pixel to the LDIs of all the ancestor cells. The result is that the LDI of a cell contains the samples within its descendants filtered down to its resolution. Therefore, later in the rendering stage, we need not traverse the children cells if the current cell already provides enough detail.

We classify the pixels in the LDI tree into two categories: *unfiltered* and *filtered*. The unfiltered pixels are those that come from the splatting to the octree cell that was initially chosen for a reference image pixel. Those pixels that come from the splatting to the ancestor cells are classified as filtered, because they represent lower frequency components of the unfiltered pixels. Note that an unfiltered pixel may be merged with a filtered pixel during the construction of LDI tree. The merged pixel is considered as filtered because better-sampled pixels are in the LDIs of some children cells of the current octree cell.

The classification of unfiltered and filtered pixels is necessary for rendering the output images (as described in section 3.2). Imagine that a cell contains unfiltered pixels of a surface area that is only visible from one of the reference images. When the cell and its children cells are processed during the rendering, we must warp its unfiltered pixels but not its filtered pixels that are filtered from the children cells.

[2] It is similar to how the subpixels are prefiltered in supersampling for antialiasing.

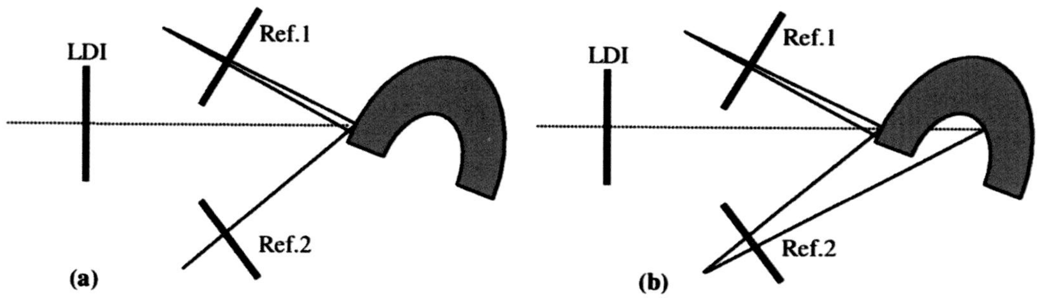


**Figure 3:** Illustrations of pixels that are warped to the same pixel location in an LDI. (a) Two pixels from reference image 1 and a pixel from reference image 2 are taken from the same region of a surface. Blending is used to combine their contribution to the LDI pixel. (b) One of the pixels from reference image 2 is taken from a different surface. A separate layer in the LDI is created to accommodate its contribution to the same LDI pixel.

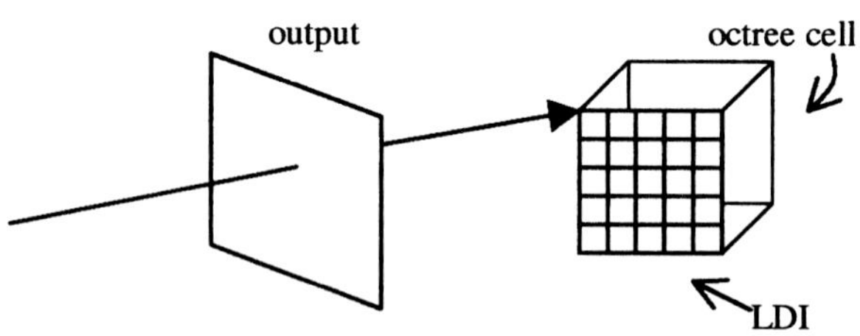


**Figure 4:** To estimate the range of stamp size for all pixels in the LDI, the corners of the bounding box are warped to the output image.

An LDI pixel may get contributions from many pixels of the same surface. They may be neighboring pixels in the same reference image, or pixels in different reference images that sample the same surface. The contributions from those pixels must be blended together. Figure 3a shows an example of those cases. An LDI pixel can also get contributions from many pixels of different surfaces. In those cases, we assign them to different layers of the LDI pixel. Figure 3b shows an example of those cases. To determine whether they are from the same surface or not, we check the difference in their depth value against a threshold. We select the threshold to be slightly smaller than the spacing between adjacent LDI pixels, so that the sampling rate of a surface that is perpendicular to the projection plane of the LDI can be preserved.

## 3.2. Rendering the Output Images

We render a new view of the scene by warping the LDIs in the octree cells to the output image. The advantage of having a hierarchical model is that we need not render every LDI in the octree. For those cells that are farther away, we can render them in less detail by using the filtered samples that are stored in the LDIs higher in the hierarchy.

To start the rendering, we traverse the octree from the top-level cell (i.e. the root). At each cell, we first perform view frustum culling, then check whether it can provide enough detail if its LDI is warped to the output image. If the current cell does not provide enough detail, then its children are traversed. An LDI is considered to provide enough detail if the pixel stamp size covers about one output pixel. Therefore the traversal of the LDI tree during the rendering will adapt to the resolution of the output image. Note that we do not calculate the pixel stamp size for each individual pixel in an LDI. Because all the pixels in the LDI of an octree cell represent samples of objects that are within its bounding box (as shown in Figure 4), we can estimate the range of stamp size for all pixels of the LDI by warping the LDI pixels that correspond to the corners of the bounding box. The corners of the bounding box are obtained by placing the maximal and minimal possible depth at the four corner pixel locations of the LDI. We use equation 2 to compute the stamp size with the vector $\vec{a}$ and $\vec{b}$ of the output image and the disparity value $\delta$ obtained from the warping. Note that a special case exists if the new viewpoint is within the octree cell. When this happens we consider the cell as not providing enough detail and the children are traversed.

The pseudo code for the octree traversal follows:

```
Render (Octree) {
1. If outside of view frustum,
   then return;
2. Estimate the stamp size of the LDI
   pixels;
3. If LDI stamp size is too large or the
   viewer is inside the bounding box then {
4.     Call Render() recursively for each
       child;
5.     Warp the unfiltered pixels in LDI to
       the Output buffer; }
6. else {
7.     Warp both unfiltered and filtered
       pixels in LDI to the output buffer; }
  }
```

Note the difference in step 5 and step 7 of the pseudo code. As mentioned in section 3.1, each LDI in the octree contains both unfiltered and filtered pixels. When we warp both the LDI in a parent cell and the LDI in a child cell, the filtered pixels in the parent cell should not contribute to the output because the unfiltered pixels in the child cell already provide better sampling for the same part of the scene.

One feature of the original LDI is that it preserves the occlusion compatible order in McMillan's 3D warping algorithm [13][14]. However this feature is compromised in the LDI tree. Although the back-to-front order can still be obtained within an LDI and across LDIs of sibling cells of the octree, we cannot obtain such order between LDIs of a parent cell and a child cell. This causes problems when unfiltered samples exist in both parent and child cells. In addition, the warped pixels are semi-transparent due to the splatting process. Therefore, we need to keep a list of pixels for each pixel location in the output buffer. We implement the output buffer as an LDI. At the end of the rendering, each list is composited to a color for display. The details of the compositing are discussed next.

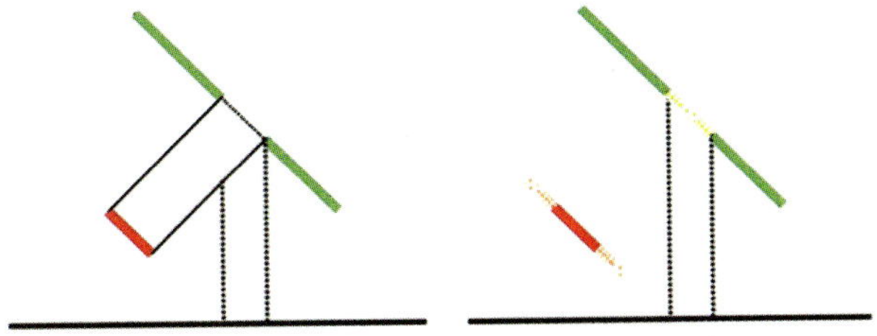

(a) (b)

**Figure 5:** This example shows the different results of gap filling from the meshing method and the method presented in this paper. (a) The meshing method. (b) The gap filling method using filtered samples.

## 3.3. Compositing in the Output Buffer

Given a list of semi-transparent pixels, we sort the pixels in depth and then use alpha blending starting from the front of the sorted list. An exception is that two pixels with similar depth should be merged first and their alpha values summed together before they are alpha-blended with the other pixels. That is because they are likely to represent sampling of the same surface.

Therefore, the pixel merging is also performed in the output LDI, which is similar to the pixel merging in the LDI of the octree cell as discussed in section 3.1. The difference is that a single threshold value of depth difference does not work anymore because the pixels can come from different levels of the LDI tree. This difficulty is solved by attaching the level of octree cell where the pixel comes from to each pixel in the output LDI. The threshold value that is used for that level of octree is then used to determine whether two pixels in the output LDI should be merged.

## 3.4. Progressive Refinement

As discussed in section 3.2, the traversal of the LDI tree during the rendering depends on the resolution of the output image. The simplest method to create the effect of progressive refinement is to render the LDI tree to a low-resolution output image first, then increase the resolution gradually. However, this method does not utilize the coherence between the renderings of two different resolutions.

To utilize the coherence between two renderings, we can tag the octree cells that are traversed in the previous rendering and skip them in the current rendering. Note that some filtered pixels may have been warped to the output buffer if they are from the leaf nodes of the subtree traversed in the previous rendering[3]. Those pixels must also be tagged so they can be removed from the output buffer if the leaf nodes in the previous rendering become interior nodes in the current rendering.

## 3.5. Gap Filling

When we construct the LDI tree from many reference images, chances are we have eliminated most of the disocclusion artifacts. However, it is possible that some disocclusion artifacts still remain. We propose a two-pass algorithm that uses the filtered pixels in the LDI tree to fill in the gaps in the output image. The algorithm consists of the following steps:

1. The first pass is to render the output image from the LDI tree as discussed in section 3.2.
2. A stencil (or coverage of pixels) is then built from the output image.
3. Render the output image from the LDI tree again. But in this pass, splat only the filtered pixels.
4. Use the stencil from step 2 to add the image from step 3 to the image from step 1.

The stencil from step 2 allows the filtered pixels to draw only to the gaps in the output image from step 1. This assumes that the output image would be completely filled if no disocclusion artifact occurred.[4]

Our gap filling method produces different results from the meshing method described in Mark's Post-Rendering 3D Warping [11]. Figure 5 shows an example of the gap that is caused by a front surface occluding a back surface. In the meshing method, the gaps are covered by quadrilaterals stretching between the front surface and the back surface (figure 5a). In contrast, our gap filling method splats the filtered samples from surfaces that surround the gap in the output. As shown in figure 5b, the back surfaces make more contribution to the gap than they do in the meshing method. If we do not have additional surface connectivity information in the original reference image, we believe the methods like ours that are based on the filtering of existing samples are more robust.

## 3.6. Analysis of Memory Requirement

Although a complete, fully expanded LDI tree may contain too many LDIs to be practical for implementation, it is worth noting that only a small subset of a complete LDI tree is used when it is constructed from reference images.

When we construct the LDI tree from reference images, we add a constant number of unfiltered LDI pixels to the octree cell chosen for each pixel of reference images. We also add $O(h)$ filtered LDI pixels to the ancestor cells, where $h$ is the number of ancestors. That means the amount of memory taken by the LDI tree grows in the same order as the amount taken by the original reference images, only if $h$ is bounded.

We can further assume that $h$ is bounded because the maximal height of the LDI tree exists. Let $L$ be the longest side of bounding box of the scene, $N$ be the resolution of an LDI, $d$ be the smallest feature in the scene the human eyes can discern at a minimum distance, and $H$ be the maximal height of the LDI tree. Then we have:

$$H = \left\lceil \log_2 \frac{L}{N \times d} \right\rceil$$

Although we do not include the memory overhead for maintaining the octree, we also do not include the possible saving in memory when pixels are merged in the LDIs. The experimental results will be presented later in this paper to show that amount of memory indeed grows at a slower rate than the number of reference images.

## 3.7. Rendering Time

An advantage that image-based rendering has over traditional polygon-based rendering is that the rendering time does not grow with the complexity of the scene. That advantage is still preserved in the rendering from the LDI tree, even though more layers of LDIs must be rendered. Let us consider the worst case in which we need to render every pixel in the LDI tree. As discussed

[3] See line 7 of the pseudo code in section 3.2.

[4] See previous footnote [1] for special cases such as the windows in the video and figure 11.

previously, the number of pixels grows in the same order as the original reference images. Therefore the time complexity of rendering from the LDI tree is of the same order as warping all reference images in the worst case. Because larger cells are used for farther objects, the worst case rarely happens and usually much fewer pixels in the LDI tree are rendered. The experimental results are presented in the next section.

## 4. RESULTS

We implemented the LDI tree on a Silicon Graphics Onyx2 with 16 gigabytes of main memory. The machine has 32 250 MHz MIPS R10000 processors but we did not exploit its parallel processing capability in our implementation.

We tested our program with a model of the interior of Palladio's Il Redentore in Venice [16]. The reference images are generated by ray tracing using the Rayshade program [5]. Each reference image has 512×512 pixels and 90-degree field of view. Figure 6 shows one of the reference images.

In synthesized scenes, an LDI can be generated directly by ray tracing [19]. We do not include it in our framework because it does not apply to the reference images acquired from non-synthesized scenes, such as the depth images that are acquired by a laser range finder.

Figure 7 shows the top view of the bounding boxes of the LDI tree after two of the reference images are processed. Each cell has an LDI of 64×64 resolution. The left face of each cell is also the projection plane of its LDI. Note that the cells near the center of projection of a reference image have more levels of subdivision. Figure 8 shows a new view rendered from the LDI tree. We disabled the gap filling to let the disocclusion artifacts appear in blue background color. Figure 8 has severe disocclusion artifacts because only four reference images from the same viewpoint are used. Figures 9 and 10 show the same view but with 12 and 36 reference images (from 3 and 9 viewpoints) respectively. Figure 11 is generated from the same LDI tree as figure 10 but with the gap filling enabled.

The memory usage of the LDI trees is shown in chart 1. The first reference image consumes about 30 Mbytes (MB) of memory. About 15 MB is the overhead of the octree. The resampling and filtering (described in section 3.1) generates about 5 LDI pixels for each input pixel. As more reference images are added, the growth of the memory size slows. The last 60 images add less than 1 MB per image in average. Note that the growth of the memory size does not stop completely. That is because more detail near each new viewpoint is still being added to the LDI Tree.

Chart 2 shows the rendering time for various numbers of reference images. Each line represents the rendering times along the path for a given number of reference images. The priority in our experiment is the correctness. Therefore little optimization and hardware acceleration were used to speed up the rendering. For example, the splatting operation is implemented completely in software simulation.

Chart 3 shows the growth of the (averaged) rendering time when the number of reference images increases. It shows that the rendering time grows even slower than the size of memory because some unnecessary details added from additional reference images are not processed during the rendering.

## 5. CONCLUSION AND FUTURE WORK

Using multiple reference images in 3D image warping has been a challenging problem. This paper describes the LDI tree, which combines multiple reference images into a hierarchical representation and preserves their sampling rate of the scene. The LDI tree allows the efficient extraction of the best available samples for any view and uses filtered samples in the hierarchy to reduce the rendering time. The filtered samples also enable the gap filling method presented in section 3.5.

We have assumed that each pixel of reference images provides only the color and depth information. No surface normal or orientation information has been considered. A direction for future work is to incorporate the surface orientation into our framework, for use in the splatting and the calculation of stamp size.

When a surface is sampled in multiple reference images, we should be able to get better sampling of the surface than what we can get from any single image. How to explore this type of cross-image supersampling is another direction of future work.

Like the original LDI, pixels that fall into the same pixel location and have similar depth values are merged together. That is based on the assumption that the surface is diffuse and little view-dependent variance can occur. How to extract view-dependent properties of the surface is yet another direction for future work.

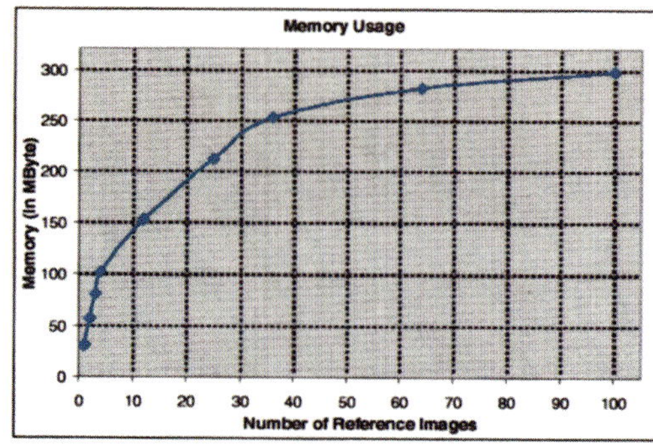


**Chart 1:** The memory usage of LDI trees.

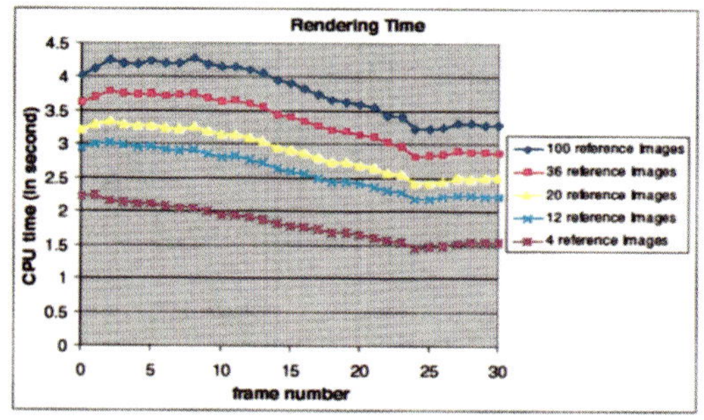


**Chart 2:** The rendering time.

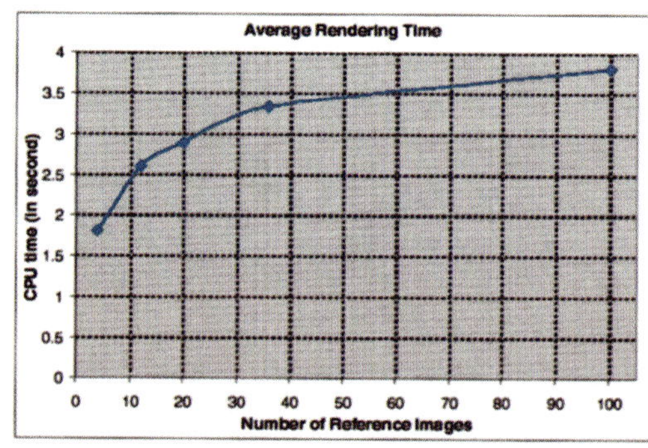


**Chart 3:** The average rendering time per frame.

## 6. ACKNOWLEDGEMENTS

We thank David McAllister for generating the reference images used in this paper, Nathan O'Brien for creating the excellent model of Il Redentore and the permission to use it, and the SIGGRAPH reviewers for their valuable comments. This work is supported by DARPA ITO contract number E278 and NSF MIP-9612643. Generous equipment support was provided by the Intel Corporation.

## 7. REFERENCES

[1] C. H. Chien, Y. B. Sim and J. K. Aggarwal. Generation of Volume/Surface Octree from Range Data. The Computer Society Conference on Computer Vision and Pattern Recognition, pages 254-60, June 1988.

[2] C. I. Connolly. Cumulative Generation of Octree Models from Range Data. Proceedings, Intl' Conf. Robotics, pages 25-32, March 1984.

[3] Brian Curless and Marc Levoy. A Volumetric Method for Building Complex Models from Range Images. In Proceedings of SIGGRAPH 1996, pages 303-312.

[4] Steven J. Gortler, Radek Grzeszczuk, Richard Szeliski and Michael F. Cohen. The Lumigraph. In Proceedings of SIGGRAPH 1996, pages 43-54.

[5] Craig Kolb. Rayshade. http://www-graphics.stanford.edu/~cek/rayshade/.

[6] David Laur and Pat Hanrahan. Hierarchical Splatting: A Progressive Refinement Algorithm for Volume Rendering. Computer Graphics (SIGGRAPH 91 Conference Proceedings), volume 25, pages 285-288.

[7] Marc Levoy and Pat Hanrahan. Light Field Rendering. In Proceedings of SIGGRAPH 1996, pages 31-42.

[8] A. Li and G. Crebbin. Octree Encoding of Objects from Range Images. Pattern Recognition, 27(5):727-739, May 1994.

[9] Dani Lischinski and Ari Rappoport. Image-Based Rendering for Non-Diffuse Synthetic Scenes. Rendering Techniques '98 (Proc. 9th Eurographics Workshop on Rendering).

[10] Robert W. Marcato Jr. Optimizing an Inverse Warper. Master's of Engineering Thesis, Massachusetts Institute of Technology, 1998.

[11] William R. Mark, Leonard McMillan and Gary Bishop. Post-Rendering 3D Warping. Proceedings of the 1997 Symposium on Interactive 3D Graphics, pages 7-16.

[12] Nelson Max. Hierarchical Rendering of Trees from Precomputed Multi-Layer Z-Buffers. Rendering Techniques '96 (Proc. 7th Eurographics Workshop on Rendering), pages 165-174.

[13] Leonard McMillan. A List-Priority Rendering Algorithm for Redisplaying Projected Surfaces. Technical Report 95-005, University of North Carolina at Chapel Hill, 1995.

[14] Leonard McMillan and Gary Bishop. Plenoptic Modeling. In Proceedings of SIGGRAPH 1995, pages 39-46.

[15] Leonard McMillan. An Image-Based Approach to Three-Dimensional Computer Graphics. Ph.D. Dissertation. Technical Report 97-013, University of North Carolina at Chapel Hill. 1997.

[16] Nathan O'Brien. Rayshade - Il Redentore. http://www.fbe.unsw.edu.au/exhibits/rayshade/church/

[17] Gernot Schaufler and Wolfgang Stürzlinger. A Three-Dimensional Image Cache for Virtual Reality. In Proceedings of Eurographics '96, pages 227-236. August 1996.

[18] Jonathan Shade, Dani Lischinski, David H. Salesin, Tony DeRose and John Snyder. Hierarchical Image Caching for Accelerated Walkthrough of Complex Environments. In Proceedings of SIGGRAPH 1996, pages 75-82.

[19] Jonathan Shade, Steven Gortler, Li-wei He and Richard Szeliski. Layered Depth Images. In Proceedings of SIGGRAPH 1998, pages 231-242.

[20] Lee Westover. SPLATTING: A Parallel, Feed-Forward Volume Rendering Algorithm. Ph.D. Dissertation. Technical Report 91-029, University of North Carolina at Chapel Hill. 1991.

**Figure 6:** One of the reference images.

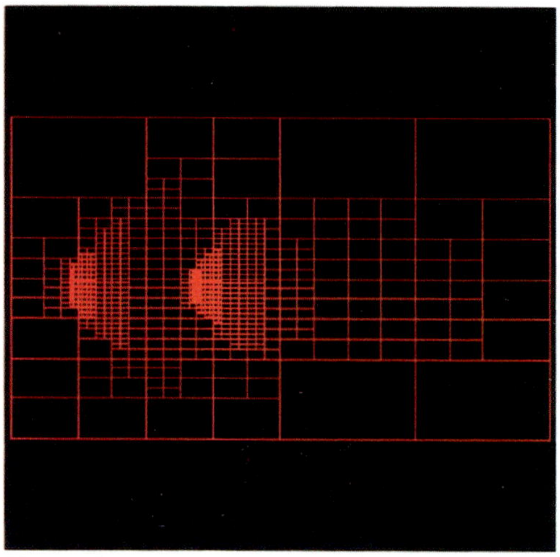

**Figure 7:** Top view of the octree cells after combining two reference images.

**Figure 8:** A new view generated from four reference images (at the same position).

**Figure 9:** A new view generated from 12 reference images (at three different positions).

**Figure 10:** A new view generated from 36 reference images (at 9 different positions).

**Figure 11:** A new view generated from 36 reference images. Gap filling is enabled.

# Rendering with Concentric Mosaics

Heung-Yeung Shum
Microsoft Research, China

Li-Wei He
Microsoft Research

## Abstract

This paper presents a novel *3D* plenoptic function, which we call *concentric mosaics*. We constrain camera motion to planar concentric circles, and create concentric mosaics using a manifold mosaic for each circle (i.e., composing slit images taken at different locations). Concentric mosaics index all input image rays naturally in 3 parameters: radius, rotation angle and vertical elevation. Novel views are rendered by combining the appropriate captured rays in an efficient manner at rendering time. Although vertical distortions exist in the rendered images, they can be alleviated by depth correction. Like panoramas, concentric mosaics do not require recovering geometric and photometric scene models. Moreover, concentric mosaics provide a much richer user experience by allowing the user to move freely in a circular region and observe significant parallax and lighting changes. Compared with a Lightfield or Lumigraph, concentric mosaics have much smaller file size because only a 3D plenoptic function is constructed. Concentric mosaics have good space and computational efficiency, and are very easy to capture. This paper discusses a complete working system from capturing, construction, compression, to rendering of concentric mosaics from synthetic and real environments.

**CR Categories and Subject Descriptors:** I.3.3 [Computer Graphics]: Picture/Image Generation - Viewing Algorithms.

**Additional Keywords:** plenoptic functions, virtual environments, image-based rendering.

## 1 Introduction

The traditional rendering approach to computer graphics starts by constructing a complete geometric and photometric model. Recently, image-based modeling and rendering techniques have been proposed to recover geometric [DTM96, FSL+98, BTZ96] and photometric [SWI97, YM98] models from a collection of photographs. Constructing such models is, in general, time-consuming, and often difficult or even impossible for real environments. Having explicit models makes it simple to add other graphical elements (such as new lights, shadows) later. On the other hand, if we only want to rerender images at a collection of viewpoints, all we need is a complete plenoptic function [AB91], which describes the irradiance perceived from the observer's viewpoints. Other image-based rendering techniques, e.g., view interpolation [CW93] and view morphing [SD96], have also been proposed lately to bypass the difficult and laborious modeling process.



| Dimension | Viewing space | Name | Year |
|---|---|---|---|
| 7 | free | plenoptic function | 1991 |
| 5 | free | plenoptic modeling | 1995 |
| 4 | inside a 3D box | Lightfield/Lumigraph | 1996 |
| 3 | inside a 2D circle | concentric mosaics | 1999 |
| 2 | at a fixed point | panorama | 1994 |

Figure 1: A taxonomy of plenoptic functions.

Indeed, a large thread of image-based rendering work has been based on the plenoptic function. The original 7D plenoptic function was defined as the intensity of light rays passing through the camera center at every location, at every possible viewing angle, for every wavelength and at any time. It has been shown that light source directions can also be incorporated into the plenoptic function for illumination control [WHON97]. By ignoring time and wavelength, McMillan and Bishop [MB95] defined plenoptic modeling as generating a continuous 5D plenoptic function from a set of discrete samples. The Lumigraph [GGSC96] and Lightfield [LH96] systems presented a clever 4D parameterization of the plenoptic function if the scene (or conversely the camera view) can be constrained to a bounding box. If the viewpoint is fixed and only the viewing directions and camera zoom can be altered, the plenoptic function simply becomes a 2D panorama (cylindrical [Che95] or spherical [SS97]).

The dimensionality of each of the various plenoptic functions depends on the space of viewpoints (or images) it represents. A comparison of different plenoptic functions is shown in Figure 1. To represent all possible viewpoints without artifacts, we need to have a complete plenoptic function (5D ignoring time and wavelength) if a complete geometric and photometric model is not used. As long as we stay outside the convex hull of an object, we reduce the dimensionality of the plenoptic function from 5 to 4, thus having a Lumigraph or Lightfield. If we stay at a given point, we can further reduce the dimensionality to only 2 (e.g., a spherical map). The question addressed in this paper is: "if we stay in/near some given region/path, as opposed to a given point (panorama) or a bounding box (Lumigraph/Lightfield), what is a good representation for both space and computational efficiency?".[Coh97]

This paper presents such a good representation, a novel *3D* plenoptic function that we call *concentric mosaics*. We constrain camera motion to planar concentric circles, and create concentric mosaics by composing slit images taken at different locations along each circle. Concentric mosaics index all input image rays naturally in 3 parameters: radius, rotation angle and vertical elevation. Compared with a Lightfield or Lumigraph, concentric mosaics have much smaller file size because only a 3D plenoptic function is constructed. Unlike panoramas in which the viewpoint is fixed, concentric mosaics allow the user to move freely in a circular region and observe significant parallax and lighting changes without recovering the geometric and photometric scene models. Novel views are rendered efficiently by combining appropriate rays that are captured and stored in concentric mosaics. However, rendering with concentric mosaics without depth correction causes vertical distortions in the rendered images, because off-the-plane rays can not be synthesized correctly without knowing corrected depth information.

The usefulness of a plenoptic function also depends on how easily it can be captured. Panoramas have become popular because they are easy to construct. Many previous systems have been built to construct cylindrical and spherical panoramas by stitching multiple images together. [MP94, Sze96, Che95, MB95, SS97] When camera motion is very small, it is possible to put together only small stripes from registered images, i.e., slit images [ZT90, PH97], to form a large panoramic mosaic. Capturing panoramas is even easier if omnidirectional cameras [Nay97], mirrors [Nal96], or fisheye lenses are used.

It is, however, very difficult to construct a continuous 5D complete plenoptic function [MB95, KS96] because it requires solving the difficult feature correspondence problem. The disparity of each pixel in stereo pairs of cylindrical panoramas is computed and used for generating new plenoptic function samples. Similar work on regular stereo pairs can be found in [LF94]. To capture a Lightfield/Lumigraph, precise camera poses have to be known (e.g., using a camera rig [LH96]) or recovered (e.g., using camera calibration [GGSC96]). Walk-throughs of a real scene using Lightfield/Lumigraph have not yet been fully demonstrated because capturing an inside-looking-out Lumigraph or Lightfield is difficult.

Capturing concentric mosaics is as easy as capturing conventional panoramas except that we take more images. We put a video camera on a rotary table, simply spin it slowly around an off-centered circle, and capture a continuous video sequence to form concentric mosaics. 3D reconstruction is not needed, nor do feature correspondences have to be computed. To explore a large environment using conventional panoramas, the user may have to choose a large number of panorama sample nodes and jump between nodes.[Che95] By allowing the user to move continuously (within a circular region) to observe motion parallax and lighting changes, concentric mosaics provide a much richer user experience and require fewer nodes to be sampled.

This paper is organized as follows. We introduce the concentric mosaics in Section 2. Rendering with concentric mosaics, including depth correction, is also discussed in Section 2. Construction of concentric mosaics from synthetic and real environments, along with sampling and interpolation issues, is discussed in Section 3. We present experimental results in Section 4. We conclude the paper with a summary and future work.

## 2 Concentric mosaics

Concentric mosaics are a set of manifold mosaics constructed from slit images taken by cameras rotating on concentric circles. Unlike conventional panoramas, a manifold mosaic[1] [PH97] is composed of images taken by a camera at different viewpoints (or by a set of cameras). In practice, these viewpoints are taken along a continuous path. The composed image is called manifold mosaic because the viewpoints are generally on a continuous surface or curve (a.k.a. manifold). Manifold mosaics have been used in applications such as cel animation [W+97], aerial photogrammetry [GH97], and robot navigation [ZT90].

A possible concentric mosaic capture system setup is shown in Figure 2, where a number of cameras are mounted on a rotating horizontal beam that is supported by a tripod. Each camera is constrained to move continuously and uniformly along its circle. We assume that each camera $C_k$ is a slit camera, i.e., only a vertical line image is taken at the viewpoint $v_j$. The ray going through the pixel in the slit image that is on the plane is tangent to the circle $C_k$ at $v_j$. By putting together all lines from $C_k$ at different rotation angles, we

[1] In this paper we use the term manifold mosaic coined by Peleg. There are, however, many other names referring to images taken from different viewpoints, e.g., multiperspective panorama [W+97], multiple centers of projection image [RG98], pushbroom camera [GH97], and pipe mosaic [RPIA98].

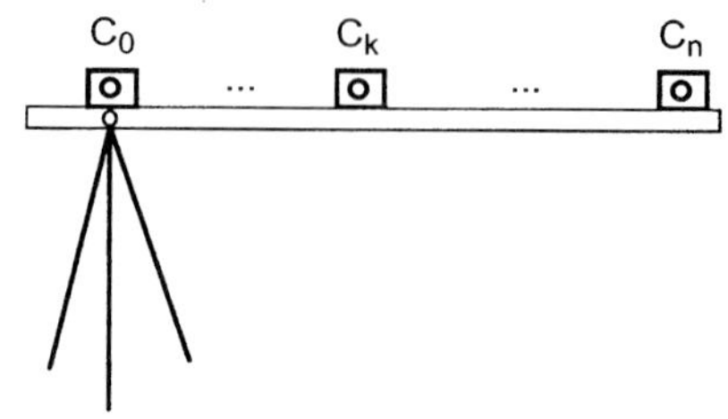


Figure 2: An experimental setup for constructing concentric mosaics.

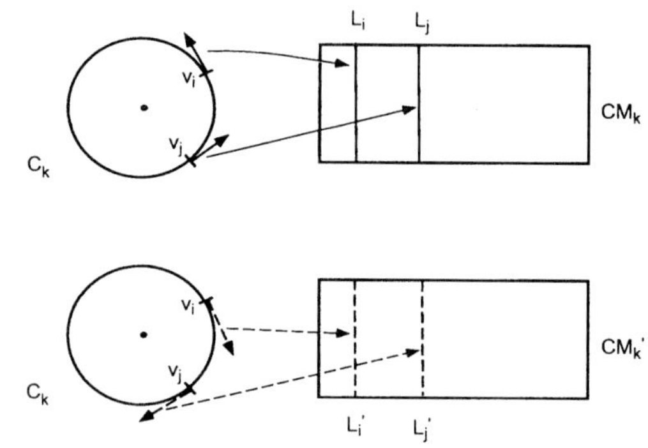


Figure 3: Construction of a concentric mosaic.

obtain a concentric mosaic (manifold mosaic), as shown in the top of Figure 3.

As shown in the bottom of Figure 3, for each circle, we would like to capture both viewing directions at each tangent line. Each line $L_j'$ is at the exact opposite direction of $L_j$. This can be done, for example, with two cameras facing the opposite directions. Therefore, we can capture all the rays going through the circular regions to form a plenoptic function at any point in the region. For clarity, we will only consider concentric mosaic $CM$ from now on. Note that when the camera is located at the rotation center (on the rotation axis), $CM_0$ is the same as $CM_0'$ but shifted by 180 degrees.

By moving the camera further away from the rotation axis, we obtain a collection of concentric mosaics as illustrated in Figure 4. For example, $CM_0$ is the mosaic taken when the camera is coincided with the rotation axis. Three examples of mosaic images are shown in Figure 6, each of which corresponds to $CM_0, CM_k, CM_n$ in Figure 4, respectively.

### 2.1 Rendering a novel view

#### 2.1.1 Rays in the capture plane

Given a collection of concentric mosaics, we can render any novel ray in the capture plane since concentric mosaics have captured most rays in the plane. During the time of rendering, we only need to find out where the rays of the novel view (i.e., a horizontal line image) in the plane are in the previously captured concentric mosaics, or we can bilinearly interpolate them from neighboring mosaics.

This rendering process is illustrated in Figure 5. The ray $PV_j$ is not captured at the novel view point $P$, but at a different point $V_j$ that is located on the concentric mosaic $CM_l$. Because the circular region is a free space, the ray captured on the plane at $P$ is the same as that obtained at $V_j$ [LH96, GGSC96]. Similarly, the ray $PV_i$ is captured at $V_i$ in another concentric mosaic $CM_k$.

#### 2.1.2 Rays off the plane

Only a small subset of the rays off the plane is stored in concentric mosaics because a slit image rather than a regular image is captured. This is why concentric mosaics have a much smaller file size than a Lightfield or Lumigraph. We now have to approximate all rays

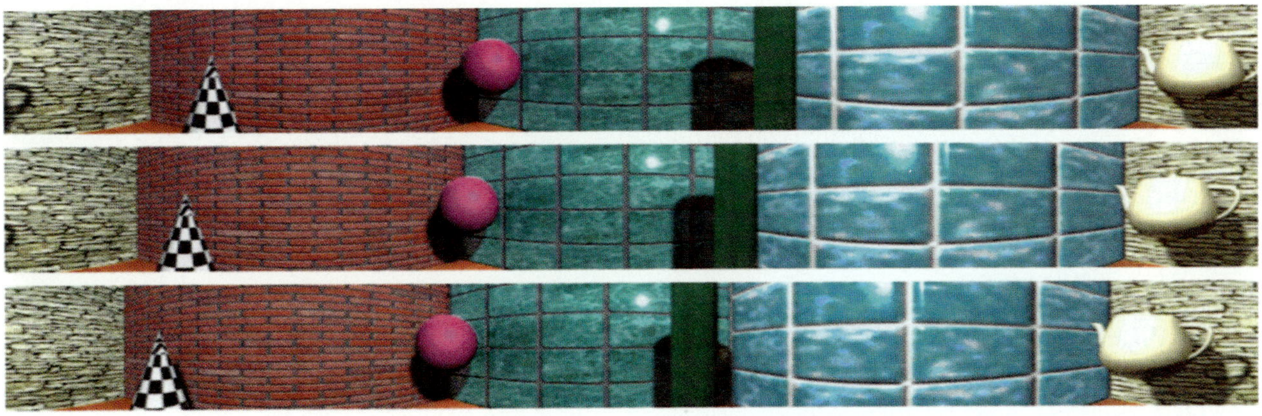

Figure 6: Three examples of concentric mosaics.

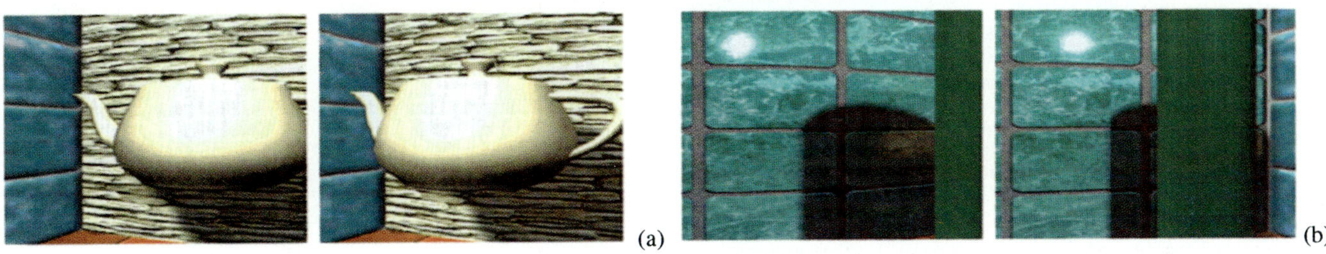


Figure 7: Rendering with concentric mosaics: (a) parallax change; (b) specular highlight and parallax change.

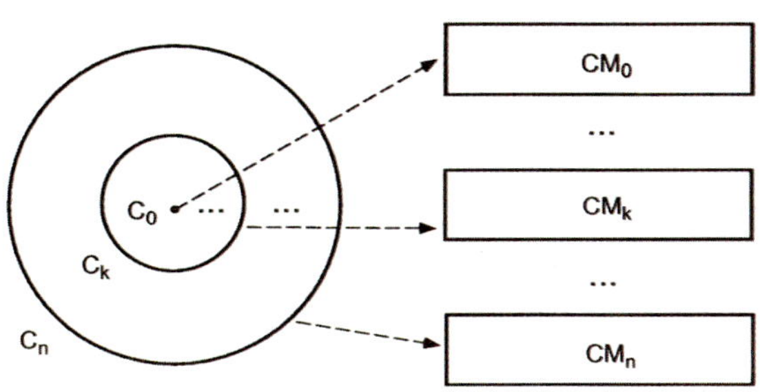


Figure 4: A collection of concentric mosaics.

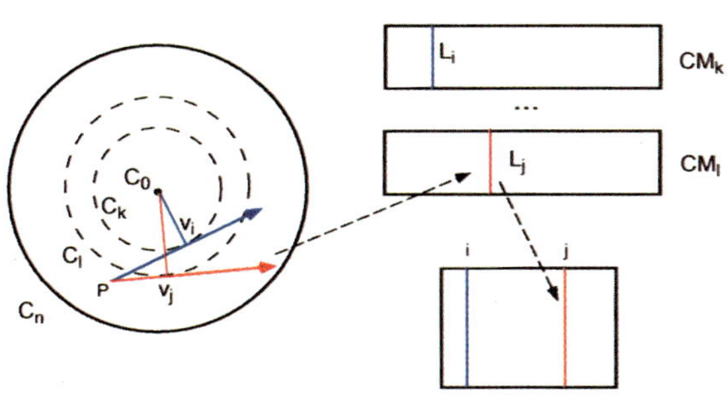


Figure 5: Rendering a novel view with concentric mosaics.

off the plane from only the slit images. As shown in Figure 5, to render a vertical line including rays off the plane at a novel view $P$, we simply take the entire slit line $L_j$ at position $V_j$ from concentric mosaic $CM_l$. $PV_j$ is tangent to the concentric circle $C_k$ on the plane.

The rendering is therefore very efficient because the concentric mosaics are indexed properly for efficient retrieval of each line. Details of rendering equations for concentric mosaics are given in Appendix A. Figure 7(a) illustrates the parallax change near the teapot mouth while Figure 7(b) demonstrates the specular highlight movement on the wall presented in rendered views of a synthetic environment. These novel views are rendered with a set of 12 concentric mosaics (three of them are shown in Figure 6).

By taking the whole line from a different location, however, we are making an implicit infinite depth assumption, i.e., objects that the line of rays meets are at infinity. As shown in Figure 8, parallel rays (pixels with same vertical field of view from two viewpoints $P_{CM}$ and $P_{new}$) only meet at infinity. This approximation will cause vertical distortion in the rendered images.

## 2.2 Depth correction

To alleviate the above vertical distortion problem, several strategies can be used.

### 2.2.1 Full perspective correction

If the distances between the camera optical center and the points in the scene are known, full perspective correction based on distances of individual pixels can be used. The pixel values of the captured rays can be warped to the rendered view using optical flow. However, there are two problems with this approach. First, geometries are usually not known for real scenes and recovering geometries from images is known to be a hard vision problem. Second, hole-filling problems still exist. A method similar to layered-depth image [SGHS98] can be used at the cost of storing more pixels (both color and depth) per sampled ray. For synthetic scenes where precise 3D geometries are known, this approach yields correct novel views and is the preferred approach.

#### 2.2.2 Weak perspective approximation

In many real scenes, it is a reasonable approximation that pixels from a vertical line have the same depth. In that case, we can use a weak perspective approximation. Efficient rendering algorithms exist if weak perspective camera model is used for each line. We only need to estimate a depth value for each vertical line and scale the whole line uniformly. Vertical distortions increase with the amount of depth variation in each vertical line and decrease with the distances of the scene objects from the camera.

#### 2.2.3 Constant depth approximation

The depth information requirement can be further reduced to be a constant for all the captured vertical lines. This approach is essentially a cylindrical environment map that dynamically updates its content based on the location of the novel view. Like the weak perspective case, there are vertical distortions for objects whose depth is different from the assumed depth. The Lumigraph system [GGSC96] uses a similar approach to put the $(u, v)$ plane at the object center. In our system, the user can interactively adjust the assumed depth with a slider control to correct the distortion to the object of interest.

### 2.3 3D plenoptic function

It is now straightforward to show that the concentric mosaics representation is a plenoptic function parameterized by three variables: rotation angle, radius (distance of camera to rotation axis), and vertical elevation or field of view (FOV), as illustrated in Figure 9.

No vertical parallax is captured in concentric mosaics because all the camera views are constrained to a horizontal planar region, and only a slit image is taken at each viewpoint. However, as shown in our real-time rendering experiments and demonstrated years ago by the horizontal parallax only holographic stereograms [Ben83], people still have a strong sense of 3D perception even with only horizontal parallax. Perhaps it is due to the fact that our eyes remain relatively planar and observe mainly horizontal parallax as we move around.

Sloan *et al.*[SCG97] have also derived a 3D parameterization of the Lumigraph by replacing the $(s, t)$ plane with its 1D subset, i.e., constraining the camera motion along a line. A $(s, u, v)$ representation is used where $s$ parameterizes the camera motion (i.e., drop $t$ in the $(s, t)$ plane[2]), and $(u, v)$ parameterizes the plane roughly in the object center. Moving along the line provides parallax in the motion direction. To have a complete coverage of the object, the camera can move on four connected perpendicular lines, i.e., a square. This sampling is not as uniform as concentric mosaics because one has to switch from one line to another. But it has the advantage that straight lines are preserved from 3D Lumigraph to rendered images, therefore has better computational efficiency.

## 3 Construction of concentric mosaics

### 3.1 Synthetic scenes

For synthetic environments, we use a renderer ( 3D Studio Max, www.ktx.com) to render slit images at different concentric circles. These slit images are then put together to construct concentric mosaics. Some examples of concentric mosaics are shown in Figure 6. With the help of a z-buffer plug-in, we are also able to obtain a depth value for each pixel.

How do we sample concentric mosaics in both radial and angular directions to ensure that the user moves uniformly inside a unit circle? It is fair to sample uniformly the angular direction

[2]Here we follow [SCG97] and use the Lumigraph notation. The notation in Lightfield flips $(u, v)$ and $(s, t)$.

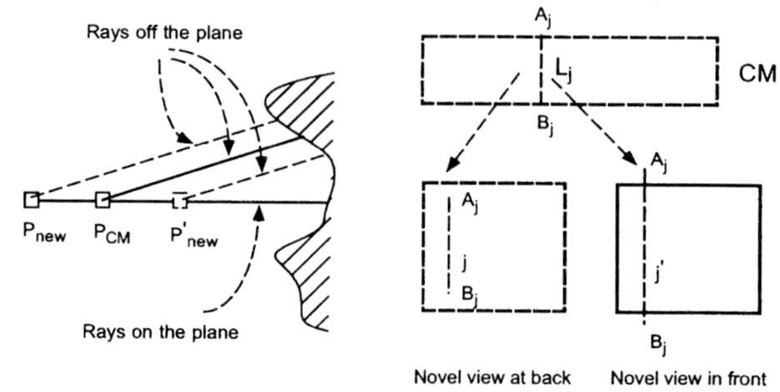


Figure 8: Depth correction with concentric mosaics.

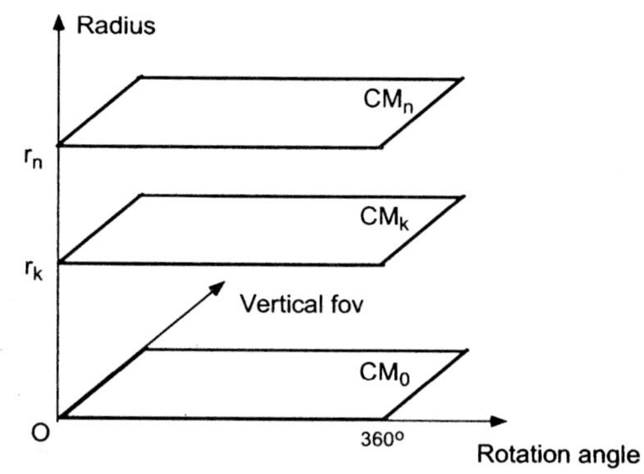


Figure 9: Concentric mosaics represent a 3D plenoptic function.

(e.g., every tenth of a degree). But in the radial direction, the sampled circles should not be at locations $\{0, 1/n, 2/n, ..., 1\}$, but at $\{0, \sqrt{1/n}, \sqrt{2/n}, ..., 1\}$ because the median circle dividing the unit circle into two halves of equal areas is not at $1/2$ but at $\sqrt{1/2}$.

How many samples do we need? In a typical novel view with 36 degrees horizontal FOV and 200 width image, 2000 samples in the angular direction are needed. The more samples taken in the radial direction, the less interpolation is required (therefore better rendering results). Typically, we sample 20 concentric circles in 3000 angular directions, i.e., 20 concentric mosaics with a width of 3000. The width of each slit image is determined according to its horizontal field of view (e.g., 0.12 degree for 3000 samples at each circle).

### 3.2 Real scenes

We considered a number of ways to capture concentric mosaics from a real scene. One design was having many cameras on a beam which rotates, as shown in Figure 2. The problem with this design is that the whole system is bulky and expensive because many cameras are needed. Another design was to use a single camera that shifts to different locations before moving in a new circle. A motorized one-dimensional linear X-stage can be used to control the camera location. However, both designs require synchronization and alignment of multiple mosaics.

A much simpler design is to use a single off-centered camera that rotates along a circle. The rotation is known with the use of a rotary table. At each rotation angle, instead of a slit line image, a regular image with multiple vertical lines (depending on the horizontal FOV of the image) is captured.[PBE99]

As shown in Figure 10a, no matter at which point along the circle $C_n$ the camera is located, the same indexed ray in the plane (e.g., the left most line $r_k$) is always tangent to the same circle $C_k$. A concentric mosaic is formed by putting together the same vertical lines (e.g., the $20th$ vertical scanline) taken at different rotation

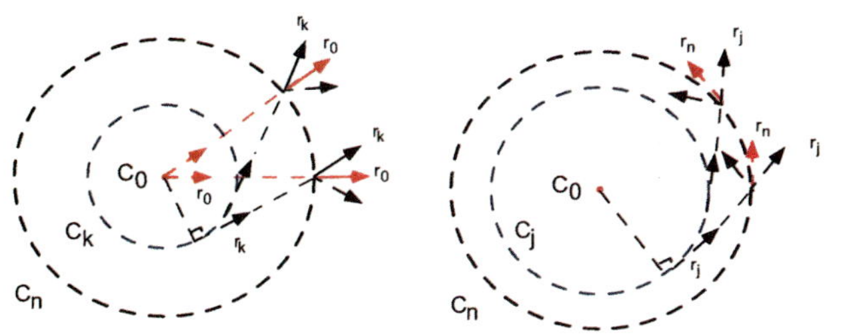


(a) (b)

Figure 10: Construction of concentric mosaics from one circle: camera along (a) normal direction; (b) tangential direction.

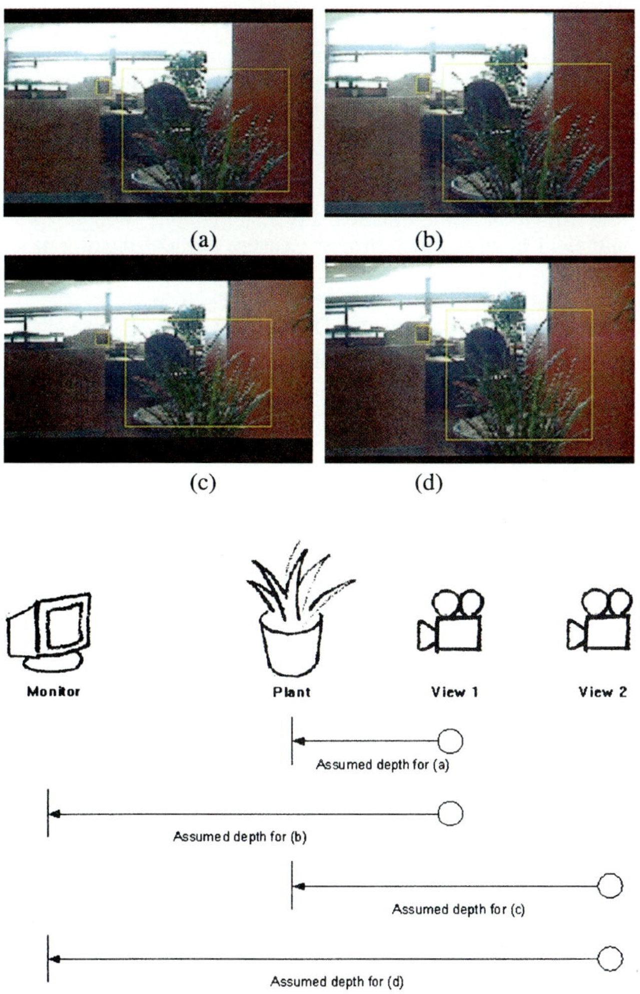


(e)

Figure 11: Rendering with constant depth correction: (a) and (c) front view and back view with depth correction $4R$; (b) and (d) front view and back view with depth correction $16R$; (e) illustration of camera viewpoints, front view A, back view B. The aspect ratio of the plant is preserved in (a) and (c), but not in (b) and (d).

angles. A sequence of $M$ regular images (taken along a circle) with size $H \times (2W-1)$ can be rebinned into $W$ concentric mosaics with size $M \times H$. It is possible to subsample the concentric mosaics by simply dropping columns in the original images. The rebinning process, then, can be skipped to avoid double sampling.

Figure 10 illustrates two possible setups, one along the normal direction[3], the other along the tangential direction. The normal setup covers the inner circle (from $C_0$ to $C_k$), while the tangential setup covers the outer ring (between $C_j$ to $C_n$). Putting all middle vertical lines together, we obtain the concentric mosaic $CM_0$ from the normal setup, but the concentric mosaic $CM_n$ from the tangential setup.

Capturing with one circular motion is easy. However, the resulting visible (or movable) region is significantly limited by the camera's horizontal FOV. For the normal setup, the radius of the visible inner circle $R_k$ depends on the horizontal field of view of the camera ($HFOV$). Indeed,

$$R_k = R_n \sin(HFOV/2). \tag{1}$$

Because vertical lines in an input image have different horizontal FOV's (e.g., the line further away from the middle has smaller FOV than the middle line), they have to be resampled to ensure uniform sampling. This resampling process becomes significant when the camera's horizontal FOV is large. More importantly, the average distance between the novel view (to be rendered) and the captured view (to be used for rendering) is much larger if only one circle is used instead of having multiple circles taken. Longer distance causes bigger depth distortion. This is an important difference between 3D concentric mosaics and 4D Lumigraph: for concentric mosaics, not only do we want to find the captured ray on the plane, but we also want to find the ray as close to the novel view as possible.

A better capturing device is to use a few regular cameras, aligned as shown in Figure 2, with the tangential setup as shown in Figure 10b. Each camera can cover a ring of visible regions.

## 4 Results for real scenes

In our experiments of rendering with concentric mosaics for real environments, we have used a digital video camera (Sony Mini DV digital video camera) with a resolution of 320 by 240. A rotary table (Parker 5″ table and Parker 6104 Indexdrive controller) is used to slowly rotate the camera along an off-centered circle and to provide accurate rotation parameters. If we do not control the rotation precisely, vision techniques such as camera calibration and motion estimation could be used to recover the rotation parameters. There are two reasons why we rotate the camera slowly. The first is to get enough samples along the angular direction. The second is to avoid motion blur. With each full circle motion of about 90 seconds, a total of 1351 frames is recorded. It took a total of only 10 minutes to set up, capture and digitize a complete sequence of video needed for constructing concentric mosaics.

Renderings of a lobby scene from captured concentric mosaics are shown in Figure 14. A rebinned concentric mosaic at the rotation center is shown in Figure 14(a), while two rebinned concentric mosaics taken from exactly opposite directions at the outermost circle are shown in Figures 14(b) and (c), respectively. It has been shown in [PBE99] that such two mosaics taken from a single rotating camera can simulate a stereo panorama.

Rendered images are shown in Figures 14(d)(e)(f). In Figure 14(d), a child can be observed in one view but not the other. In Figure 14(e), strong parallax can be seen between the plant and the poster. In Figure 14(f), lighting changes caused by sunshine can be observed near the ceiling. The dramatic lighting change is partly due to the fact that we have used automatic exposure for the camera during capturing.

[3] In general, the middle ray on the plane is set along the normal direction.

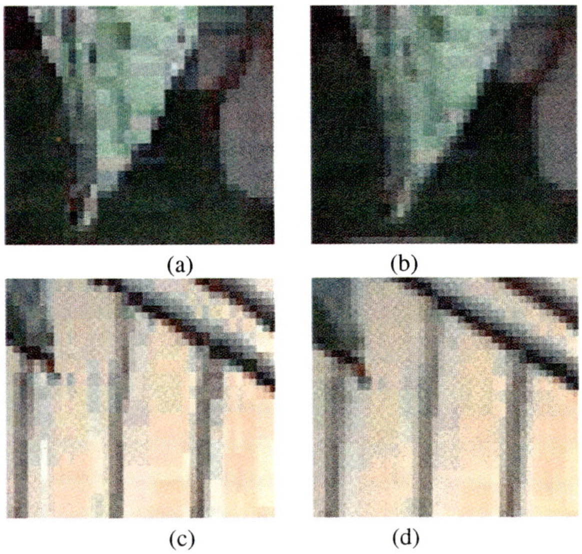


Figure 12: Comparison between point sampling (a)(c) and bilinear sampling (b)(d): blown-up images from rendering the lobby scene in Figure 14.

Constant depth correction is used in the real scene examples. Currently it is the user's responsibility to provide the depth estimation for the region of exploration. If the depth is estimated correctly, we would expect the aspect ratios[4] of objects remain the same after depth correction regardless of the distance between the object and the camera. This is indeed the case. In the lobby scene shown in Figure 14, two views rendered with different depth corrections are shown in Figure 11. The bottom images (c) and (d) are taken at the viewpoint 2, and the top images (a) and (b) at the viewpoint 1. The left images (a) and (c) are depth-corrected using a constant depth at the plant, while the images on the right (b) and (d) at the monitor. Figure 11e shows two viewpoints 1 (in front) and 2 (at back) which point to the same direction. The aspect ratios of the plant using depth correction at the plant are almost identical while they are different using depth correction at the monitor. The reverse is true for the computer monitor.

The input video sequences can be compressed well because of the significant spatial adjacency between frames. We used vector quantization since it is a good choice for selective decoding, as demonstrated in Lightfield compression [LH96]. Using vector quantization, the original video of 1351 frames (of size 320x240) can be compressed to 25M from 415M bytes. Entropy coding can be applied to further reduce the file size to 16M. On a Pentium II PC running at 300 MHz, using the compressed file, we achieved a frame rate of 20 frames per second for rendering with concentric mosaics with bilinear interpolation. Results are shown in Figure 14. Rendering using point sampling is more than twice as fast as using bilinear interpolation, but has lower visual quality, as shown in Figure 12.

We have also applied a standard MPEG4 codec to our video sequences and achieved very high compression ratios. For example, with only 1 I-frame (the first image) and 56k bit rate, the lobby video can be compressed to 640k, which is a compression ratio of 648. At such high compression ratio, block artifacts become visible even though motion parallax and lighting changes are still observed.

[4] Aspect ratio is a good approximation for frontal parallel objects and can be easily computed by identifying the boundary of the object in the image. Ideally, the cross ratio of four co-linear points [Fau93] should be computed to verify if the perspective projection is indeed preserved.

# 5 Conclusion and future work

In this paper we have presented a novel *3D* plenoptic function, which we call *concentric mosaics*. We constrain camera motion to planar concentric circles, and create concentric mosaics by composing slit images taken at different locations of each circle. Concentric mosaics index all input image rays naturally in 3 parameters: radius, rotation angle and vertical elevation. Novel views are rendered by combining the appropriate captured rays in an efficient manner at rendering time. Although vertical distortions exist in the rendered images, they can be alleviated by depth correction. Concentric mosaics have good space and computational efficiency. Compared with a Lightfield or Lumigraph, concentric mosaics have much smaller file size because only a 3D plenoptic function is constructed.

Most importantly, concentric mosaics are very easy to capture. Capturing concentric mosaics is as easy as capturing a traditional panorama except that concentric mosaics require more images. By simply spinning an off-centered camera on a rotary table, we can construct concentric mosaics for a real scene in 10 minutes. Like panoramas, concentric mosaics do not require the difficult modeling process of recovering geometric and photometric scene models. Yet concentric mosaics provide a much richer user experience by allowing the user to move continuously in a circular region and observe significant parallax and lighting changes. The ease of capture makes concentric mosaics very attractive for many virtual reality applications.

It is important, however, to pay attention to vertical distortions while using concentric mosaics. For example, one should capture small field of view environments because vertical distortions increase with larger field of view. Vertical distortions also become more apparent as the user moves backward and forward because significant parallax change occurs. On the other hand, parallax change caused by lateral moves is significantly less, and can therefore be better compensated.

While vertical distortions can be reduced with constant depth correction demonstrated in our experiments, they still exist. The next step in our approach will be to reconstruct 3D depth from the input images using vision techniques such as structure from motion or stereo. Stereo from concentric mosaics is of particular interest because of the special camera configuration and its resulting epipolar geometry. We are currently working on this problem. We are also working on moving from a set of concentric mosaics to another so that the region of motion can be enlarged.

Another important area of future work is the compression of concentric mosaics. Although currently satisfactory, vector quantization will become less and less acceptable as we increase image size and capture more sets of concentric mosaics. Higher compression ratios can be achieved with motion compensated compression techniques. For example, we achieved a very high compression ratio using an MPEG4 codec to compress concentric mosaics. But selectively decoding the compressed MPEG bit stream (depending on the viewing direction) is difficult because of the inter-frame and intra-frame dependency. Better compression algorithms for selective decoding enable us to effectively explore a large environment through the use of multiple sets of concentric mosaics.

# 6 Acknowledgements

This work was inspired by Shmuel Peleg's talk on manifold mosaic at Microsoft Research in 1997 and Michael Cohen's idea to constrain the camera motion. The authors benefited from discussion with Qifa Ke, Anandan, Steve Seitz, Michael Cohen, Rick Szeliski, Jim Kajiya, Mike Sinclair, Peter-Pike Sloan and Steve Gortler. Timely help from Dan Robbins on using 3D Studio Max, Dave Thiel on making Siggraph submission video, Hong-Hui Sun and Min-Sheng Wu on generating pictures in Figure 14 is very much appreciated.

## References


[AB91] E. H. Adelson and J. Bergen. The plenoptic function and the elements of early vision. In *Computational Models of Visual Processing*, pages 3–20. MIT Press, Cambridge, MA, 1991.

[Ben83] S. A. Benton. Survey of holographic stereograms. In *Proc. SPIE Vol. 367 Int. Soc. Eng.*, pages 15–19, 1983.

[BTZ96] P. Beardsley, P. Torr, and A. Zisserman. 3D model acquisition from extended image sequences. In *Fourth European Conference on Computer Vision (ECCV'96)*, volume 2, pages 683–695, Cambridge, England, April 1996. Springer-Verlag.

[Che95] S. E. Chen. QuickTime VR – an image-based approach to virtual environment navigation. *Computer Graphics (SIGGRAPH'95)*, pages 29–38, August 1995.

[Coh97] M. F. Cohen. Personal email communication, September 1997.

[CW93] S. Chen and L. Williams. View interpolation for image synthesis. *Computer Graphics (SIGGRAPH'93)*, pages 279–288, August 1993.

[DTM96] P. E. Debevec, C. J. Taylor, and J. Malik. Modeling and rendering architecture from photographs: A hybrid geometry- and image-based approach. *Computer Graphics (SIGGRAPH'96)*, pages 11–20, August 1996.

[Fau93] O. Faugeras. *Three-dimensional computer vision: A geometric viewpoint.* MIT Press, Cambridge, Massachusetts, 1993.

[FSL+98] O. D. Faugeras, Laveau S., Robert L., Csurka G., and Zeller C. 3-D reconstruction of urban scenes from sequences of images. *Computer Vision and Image Understanding*, 69(3):292–309, March 1998.

[GGSC96] S. J. Gortler, R. Grzeszczuk, R. Szeliski, and M. F. Cohen. The lumigraph. In *Computer Graphics Proceedings, Annual Conference Series*, pages 43–54, Proc. SIGGRAPH'96 (New Orleans), August 1996. ACM SIGGRAPH.

[GH97] R. Gupta and R.I. Hartley. Linear pushbroom cameras. *IEEE Transactions on Pattern Analysis and Machine Intelligence*, 19(9):963–975, September 1997.

[KS96] S. B. Kang and R. Szeliski. 3-D scene data recovery using omnidirectional multibaseline stereo. In *IEEE Computer Society Conference on Computer Vision and Pattern Recognition (CVPR'96)*, pages 364–370, San Francisco, California, June 1996.

[LF94] S. Laveau and O. Faugeras. 3-D scene representation as a collection of images and fundamental matrices. Technical Report 2205, INRIA-Sophia Antipolis, February 1994.

[LH96] M. Levoy and P. Hanrahan. Light field rendering. In *Computer Graphics Proceedings, Annual Conference Series*, pages 31–42, Proc. SIGGRAPH'96 (New Orleans), August 1996. ACM SIGGRAPH.

[MB95] L. McMillan and G. Bishop. Plenoptic modeling: An image-based rendering system. *Computer Graphics (SIGGRAPH'95)*, pages 39–46, August 1995.

[MP94] S. Mann and R. W. Picard. Virtual bellows: Constructing high-quality images from video. In *First IEEE International Conference on Image Processing (ICIP-94)*, volume I, pages 363–367, Austin, Texas, November 1994.

[Nal96] V. S. Nalwa. A true omnidirecional viewer. Technical report, Bell Laboratories, Holmdel, NJ, USA, February 1996.

[Nay97] S. Nayar. Catadioptric omnidirectional camera. In *IEEE Computer Society Conference on Computer Vision and Pattern Recognition (CVPR'97)*, pages 482–488, San Juan, Puerto Rico, June 1997.

[PBE99] S. Peleg and M. Ben-Ezra. Stereo panorama with a single camera. In *Proc. Computer Vision and Pattern Recognition Conf.*, 1999.

[PH97] S. Peleg and J. Herman. Panoramic mosaics by manifold projection. In *IEEE Computer Society Conference on Computer Vision and Pattern Recognition (CVPR'97)*, pages 338–343, San Juan, Puerto Rico, June 1997.

[RG98] P. Rademacher and Bishop G. Multiple-center-of-projection images. In *Computer Graphics Proceedings, Annual Conference Series*, pages 199–206, Proc. SIGGRAPH'98 (Orlando), July 1998. ACM SIGGRAPH.

[RPIA98] B. Rousso, S. Peleg, Finci I., and Rav-Acha A. Universal mosaicing using pipe projection. In *Sixth International Conference on Computer Vision (ICCV'98)*, pages 945–952, Bombay, January 1998.

[SCG97] P. P. Sloan, M. F. Cohen, and S. J. Gortler. Time critical lumigraph rendering. In *Symposium on Interactive 3D Graphics*, pages 17–23, Providence, RI, USA, 1997.

[SD96] S. M. Seitz and C. M. Dyer. View morphing. In *Computer Graphics Proceedings, Annual Conference Series*, pages 21–30, Proc. SIGGRAPH'96 (New Orleans), August 1996. ACM SIGGRAPH.

[SGHS98] J. Shade, S. Gortler, L.-W. He, and R. Szeliski. Layered depth images. In *Computer Graphics (SIGGRAPH'98) Proceedings*, pages 231–242, Orlando, July 1998. ACM SIGGRAPH.

[SS97] R. Szeliski and H.-Y. Shum. Creating full view panoramic image mosaics and texture-mapped models. *Computer Graphics (SIGGRAPH'97)*, pages 251–258, August 1997.

[SWI97] Y. Sato, M. Wheeler, and K. Ikeuchi. Object shape and reflectance modeling from observation. In *Computer Graphics Proceedings, Annual Conference Series*, pages 379–387, Proc. SIGGRAPH'97 (Los Angeles), August 1997. ACM SIGGRAPH.

[Sze96] R. Szeliski. Video mosaics for virtual environments. *IEEE Computer Graphics and Applications*, pages 22–30, March 1996.

[W+97] D. N. Wood et al. Multiperspective panoramas for cel animation. In *Computer Graphics Proceedings, Annual Conference Series*, pages 243–250, Proc. SIGGRAPH'97 (Los Angeles), August 1997. ACM SIGGRAPH.

[WHON97] T. Wong, P. Heng, S. Or, and W. Ng. Image-based rendering with controllable illumination. In *Proceedings of the 8-th Eurographics Workshop on Rendering*, pages 13–22, St. Etienne, France, June 1997.

[YM98] Y. Yu and J. Malik. Recovering photometric properties of architectural scenes from photographs. *Computer Graphics (SIGGRAPH'96)*, pages 207–218, July 1998.

[ZT90] J. Y. Zheng and S. Tsuji. Panoramic representation of scenes for route understanding. In *Proc. of the 10th Int. Conf. Pattern Recognition*, pages 161–167, June 1990.


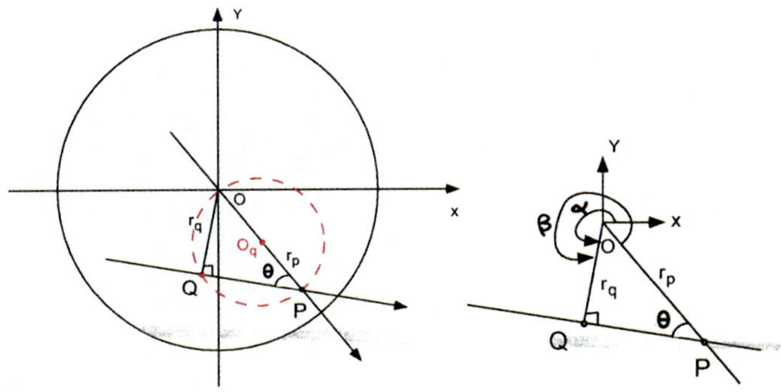


Figure 13: Rendering with concentric mosaics.

## A Rendering equations for concentric mosaics

As shown in Figure 13, given the center of concentric mosaics $O$, a viewpoint $P$, and its viewing direction $\theta$, where is the point $Q$ on the concentric mosaics?

The polar coordinates $(r_p, \theta_p)$ of the viewpoint $P$ are defined as

$$r_p = \sqrt{(P_x - O_x)^2 + (P_y - O_y)^2} \quad (2)$$
$$\theta_p = atan2(P_y - O_y, P_x - O_x) \quad (3)$$

and the polar coordinates $(r_q, \beta)$ of the point $Q$ become

$$r_q = r_p|\sin(\theta)| \quad (4)$$
$$\beta = \theta + \theta_p - \pi/2 \quad (5)$$

where $\alpha = \theta - \pi/2$ and $\alpha - \beta = -\theta_p$.

It is apparent that as $\theta$ increases from 0 to 180 degrees, the trajectory of $Q$ is a circle centered at the middle of $OP$ ($O_q$ in Figure 13) and going through $O$ and $P$. Indeed,

$$Q_x - O_{qx} = -\frac{r_p}{2}\cos(2\theta + \theta_p) \quad (6)$$
$$Q_y - O_{qy} = -\frac{r_p}{2}\sin(2\theta + \theta_p). \quad (7)$$

(a)
(b)
(c)
(d)
(e)
(f)

Figure 14: Rendering a lobby: rebinned concentric mosaic (a) at the rotation center; (b) at the outermost circle; (c) at the outermost circle but looking at the opposite direction of (b); (d) a child is occluded in one view but not in the other; (e) parallax change between the plant and the poster; (f) lighting changes near the ceiling caused by sunshine.

# Automatic Image Placement to Provide A Guaranteed Frame Rate

Daniel G. Aliaga

Lucent Technologies Bell Laboratories

Anselmo Lastra

University of North Carolina at Chapel Hill

## Abstract

We present a preprocessing algorithm and run-time system for rendering 3D geometric models at a guaranteed frame rate. Our approach trades off space for frame rate by using images to replace distant geometry. The preprocessing algorithm automatically chooses a subset of the model to display as an image so as to render no more than a specified number of geometric primitives. We also summarize an optimized layered-depth-image warper to display images surrounded by geometry at run time. Furthermore, we show the results of applying our method to accelerate the interactive walkthrough of several complex models.

## 1. INTRODUCTION

Large and complex three-dimensional (3D) models are required for applications such as computer-aided design (CAD), architectural visualizations, flight simulation, and virtual environments. These models currently contain hundreds of thousands to millions of primitives; more than high-end computer graphics systems can render at interactive rates. Often, the bottleneck for these applications is the geometric transformations required each frame. Thus, rendering acceleration methods endeavor to reduce the number of primitives sent to the graphics pipeline. For our work, we assume that by providing a bound on geometric complexity we can achieve a desired frame rate.

The demand for interactive rendering has brought about many algorithms for model simplification. For example, techniques have been presented for levels of detail [DeH91, Tur92, Coh96, Gar97, Hop97, Lue97], visibility culling [Air90, Tel91, Coo97, Zha97], and replacing objects with images [Mac95, Sha96, Scf96].

In this paper, we present an algorithm for limiting the maximum number of geometric primitives to render from all viewpoints and view directions by dynamically replacing selected geometry with images (Figure 1). We demonstrate our algorithm in a walkthrough system that allows for translation and yaw-rotation of a 60-degree or greater view frustum through several large models. Using images is desirable because we can render them in time proportional to the number of pixels. In addition, increasingly simplified geometric levels of detail, viewed from the same distance, eventually lose shape and color information. A fixed resolution image, on the other hand, maintains an approximately constant display cost and, given sufficient resolution, maintains the apparent visual detail.

Email: aliaga@research.bell-labs.com, lastra@cs.unc.edu


SIGGRAPH 99 Los Angeles CA USA


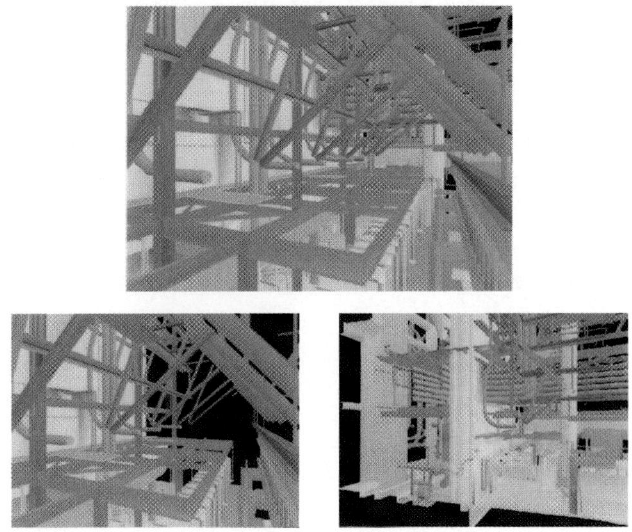

***Figure 1.*** *Geometry+Image Example. These three snapshots illustrate an example rendering of a power plant model. The top snapshot is what the viewer actually sees. In the bottom left snapshot, we render the portion represented as geometry. In the bottom right snapshot, we render the portion represented as a warped image.*

Our results show that we are able to visualize geometric models ranging from 850K to 2M triangles using as little as one-tenth of the geometry and no more than 3.8GB of image data. Based on our empirical results and an analysis of our algorithm, we also predict the expected best case and a near worst-case performance for additional models.

We believe that ultimately a rendering system should combine algorithms such as ours with geometric simplification and other rendering acceleration methods [Ali99]. The system should automatically choose the most appropriate method(s) to use.

## 1.1 Overview

Our approach consists of a preprocessing component to determine the subsets of a model to replace with images and a run-time component for displaying images and conventional geometry.

The preprocessing takes as input a 3D model, stored in a hierarchical spatial partitioning data structure (e.g. octree) [Cla76] and creates a non-uniform grid of points adapted to the local model complexity. At each grid point, an image-placement process selects the smallest and farthest subsets of the model to remove from rendering to meet a fixed geometry budget from that location. Images are then created to represent each selected subset.

At run-time, we select an image from a grid point near the current viewpoint. The geometry behind the projection plane of the image is culled while the remaining geometry is rendered normally. Our grid-point selection algorithm guarantees that we always meet our bound on the amount of geometry to render. We could display the image using texture mapping, but this approach would only yield the correct perspective from the viewpoint where the image was created. Instead, we adopted the strategy of McMillan and Bishop [McM95] to warp images, enhanced with depth, to get proper perspective. Furthermore, to reduce the number of disocclusions that occur because of this technique, we warp layered depth images (LDIs) [Max95, Sha98]. We have observed that, on average, most of the pixel samples of our LDIs are in the first two to four layers [Pop98]. Thus, if we can afford the approximately constant time it takes to warp an image, we can render any size 3D model at a guaranteed frame rate.

## 2. RELATED WORK

A large body of literature has been written on how to reduce the geometric complexity of 3D models. For the purposes of this paper, we can classify related work into three main approaches:

- frame-rate control,
- view-dependent simplification, and
- image caching.

Funkhouser and Sèquin [Fun93] presented a system that, at run-time, selects levels-of-detail (LODs) and shading algorithms, in order to meet a target frame rate. The system maintains a hierarchy of the objects in the environment. It computes cost and benefit metrics for all of the alternative representations of objects and uses a knapsack-style algorithm to find the best set for each frame. If too much geometry is present, detail elision is used.

Maciel and Shirley [Mac95] expanded upon this and increased the representations available for the objects. A set of *impostors*, which include LODs, texture-based representations and colored cubes, can be used to meet the target frame rate.

Flight simulators use several techniques to achieve high frame rates [Sch83, Mue95]. For example, during each frame the system evaluates scene complexity in order to determine the LODs and terrain texture resolutions. When the current selection takes too much time to render, the LOD switching distance and texture resolution are reduced.

View-dependent simplification algorithms support maintaining constant geometric complexity every frame [Hop97, Lue97]. Alternately, they can maintain a bounded screen-space error during simplification. Unfortunately, depending on the amount of simplification needed and on the scene complexity, objects will be merged and details will eventually be lost.

Various systems have been presented that use image-based representations (typically texture-mapped quadrilaterals) to replace subsets of the model. The source images are either pre-computed [Mac95, Ali96, Ebb98] or computed on the fly [Sha96, Scf96]. Metrics are used to roughly control image quality but not the amount of geometry to render. Aliaga and Lastra [Ali97] and Rafferty *et al.* [Raf98] used images to accelerate rendering in architectural models. Doorways (i.e. portals) are replaced with images and only the geometry of the current room is rendered. Both Darsa *et al.* [Dar97] and Sillion *et al.* [Sil97] constructed a simplified mesh to represent the far scene. In the worst case, the complexity of the mesh is proportional to the screen resolution. However, neither system provided control of the number of primitives required to draw the mesh or any nearby geometry.

Regan and Pose [Reg94] created a hardware system that employed large textures as a backdrop. The foreground objects were given a higher priority and rendered at faster update rates. Image composition was used to combine the renderings. Their approach helped to reduce the apparent rendering latency but did not control the number of primitives rendered.

## 3. AUTOMATIC IMAGE PLACEMENT

The goal of our preprocessing is to automatically compute what geometry to replace with images so as to limit the number of primitives to render for an arbitrary 3D model. An image and the subset of the model it culls define a *solution* for a given viewpoint and view direction. We refer to the position of a quadrilateral, corresponding to both the projection and near plane for rendering a model subset, as the *location* of the associated image. Clearly it is impractical to compute a solution for all viewpoints and view directions. Instead, we exploit a property of overlapping view frusta to limit the number of positions and take advantage of hierarchical spatial data structures, used for view-frustum culling, to conservatively sample the view directions. We assume that during preprocessing and run time the same field-of-view (FOV) is used. In this section, we present a recursive method to create a *grid of solution points,* and a process to place the images associated with each of these grid points. Figure 2 provides a summary of the preprocessing pipeline.

```
1. Enqueue all grid points of a uniform grid
2. Repeat
3.   Dequeue grid point
4.   Create view-directions set
5.   While (view direction with most number of
            primitives > geometry budget)
6.     Compute smallest and farthest octree cell
         subset to remove from rendering to meet
         the target geometry budget
7.     If (the resulting image is outside the
          star-shape for the given grid point)
         Discard solution
         Subdivide local grid
         Enqueue new grid points
8.     Else
         Compute a layered-depth image to
           represent the octree-cell subset
       Endif
     Endwhile
9. Until (no more unprocessed grid points)
```

***Figure 2.*** *Preprocessing Algorithm Summary.*

### 3.1 Enclosed View Frusta

Our algorithm exploits the fact that a semi-infinite frustum (A in Figure 3) completely enclosed by another (B in Figure 3), with the same FOV, contains no more geometry than that included in the enclosing frustum. For any viewpoint, such as A, we select the closest grid point contained within the reverse projection of the view frustum (shown in dashed lines). If we have a solution that bounds the total amount of geometry for B, we also have a sufficient solution for a viewpoint such as A (an enclosed frustum with the same FOV and view direction). Since we are considering the total amount of geometry in the view frustum, occlusions are not an issue. Thus, a finite grid of solutions is sufficient to limit the complexity for all viewpoints within the grid. Our preprocessing task reduces to

- finding a good set of the aforementioned grid solution-points to sample the model space (Section 3.2), and
- finding a solution (e.g. the appropriate subsets of the scene to represent as image) for the infinite number of view directions, at each grid point (Section 3.3).

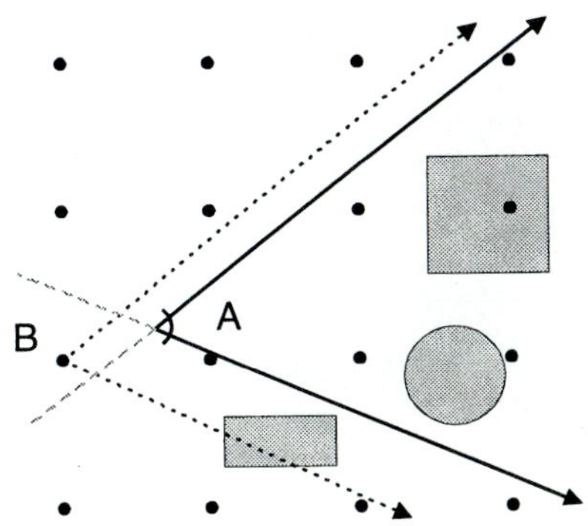


***Figure 3.*** *Enclosed View Frusta. Frustum B has the same FOV and view direction as frustum A. Furthermore, frustum B is centered on the closest grid point contained in the reverse projection of frustum A (as indicated by the lightly dashed lines). Frustum A contains no more geometry than that in frustum B. Hence, we can use an image computed for B to limit rendered geometry from viewpoints such as A.*

## 3.2 Solution Grid

The preprocessing begins by creating a sparse, uniform grid of points that spans the model space. The problem we encounter with this sparse grid is that the image placement may not be valid. Recall that, for a particular point, we choose a solution whose grid point is behind us. It is possible, as shown in Figure 4, that the projection plane used to create the image was placed nearer to its grid point than our current viewpoint (this occurs in areas of the model with complex geometry). We need to ensure that the grid is dense enough to guarantee that the projection plane of selected images will always be in front of any eye location.

### 3.2.1 Star-Shapes

The first step is to determine the locus of eye locations for which a given grid point might be selected (because it's the closest grid point in the reverse projection of the eye's frustum). The left half of Figure 5 depicts a grid of points. This grid has a uniform distribution of points and is defined to be a level 0 grid -- thus an even-level grid. If we allow rotations only about the vertical axis (i.e. *y*-axis) and translations only in the plane, the right half of Figure 5 shows the locus of viewpoints (we refer to this as a *star-shape*) that might have grid point $a_4$ as the closest grid point in the reverse projection of a square view frustum of FOV $2\alpha$. *E* is the farthest eye location from which there is a view direction that still contains $a_4$ as its closest grid point in the reverse view frustum. The distance $s_{2k}$ is equal to $r_{2k}/(2\tan\alpha)$ where $r_{2k}$ is the separation between grid points. As long as the FOV is greater than or equal to 54 degrees (i.e. $2\alpha \geq 54$) $s_{2k}$ is less than or equal to $r_{2k}$. Thus, we can approximate the star-shape with a circle of diameter $4r_{2k}$. Using symmetry, we can conservatively estimate the locus of eye locations with a sphere of diameter $4r_{2k}$.

Hence, for a practical FOV of 60 degrees or greater, we can prevent the problematic situation by ensuring that no grid point has an image placed within its star-shape. If we superimpose the star-shape on the problem case of Figure 4, we see that the image is indeed inside the star-shape. Our algorithm will not work well with narrower fields-of-view because the selected grid point might be too far behind the eye and the star-shape excessively large.

Eye positions near the edge of the model might not contain a grid point in the reverse frustum. We inflate the grid by two points in all the six directions (i.e. positive and negative *x*-, *y*-, and *z*-axes) so that such eye positions have a grid point behind them.

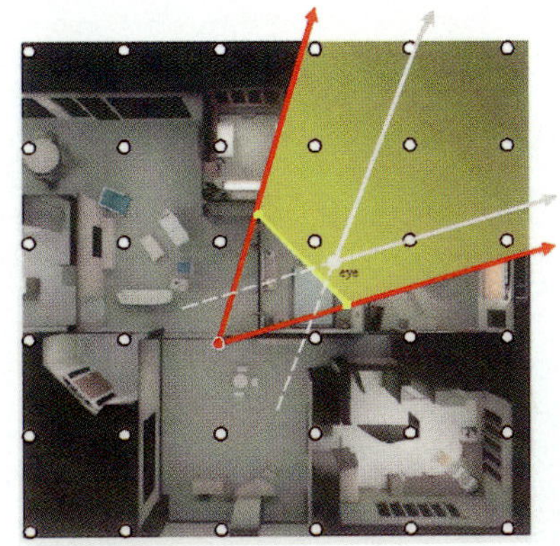

***Figure 4.*** *Image Placed Behind the Eye. We show a top-down view of an architectural model. A plane of points from a uniform grid is shown. The projection plane of the image (yellow line) computed for the closest grid point in the reverse view frustum (dashed lines) is behind the eye. This problem occurs because scene complexity forces the image to be very near its grid point. Geometry replaced by the image is shaded in yellow.*

### 3.2.2 Recursive Subdivision

To ensure that all viewpoints in the model have a valid image solution, we recursively reduce the size of star-shapes by locally subdividing the grid. Our goal is to subdivide until the images computed for all of the grid points are always in front of any possible eye position. The recursion alternates between two sets of rules: one for *even levels* ($2k$) and one for *odd levels* ($2k+1$). We first introduce grid points at the midpoints of the existing points. Then, we introduce the complementary points to return to a denser original configuration. Figure 6 depicts a grid point subdivided through two levels. At each new level, we verify that, for all points, a valid image placement can be produced (Section 3.3). We recursively subdivide points that fail until all have image placements in front of any eye position that can use them. For the odd-level grid, we use a slightly different star-shape that we can approximate with a sphere of diameter $6r_{2k+1}$ (for more details, see [Ali98]). Figure 7 shows a grid automatically computed for one of our test models.

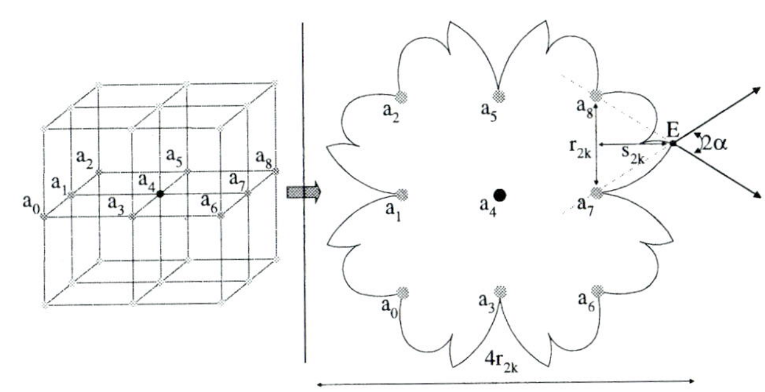


***Figure 5.*** *Star-Shape. To the left, we show a uniform grid of 3x3x3 viewpoints. To the right, we show a top-down view of the horizontal plane defined by grid points $a_0$-$a_8$. If we rotate about the vertical axis and translate a square view frustum, the star-shape represents the plane of locations that might use grid point $a_4$. The distance $s_{2k}$ equals $r_{2k}/(2\tan\alpha)$; thus, for a FOV $2\alpha \geq 54$ degrees, $s_{2k} \leq r_{2k}$. We can approximate the star-shape with a sphere of diameter $4r_{2k}$.*

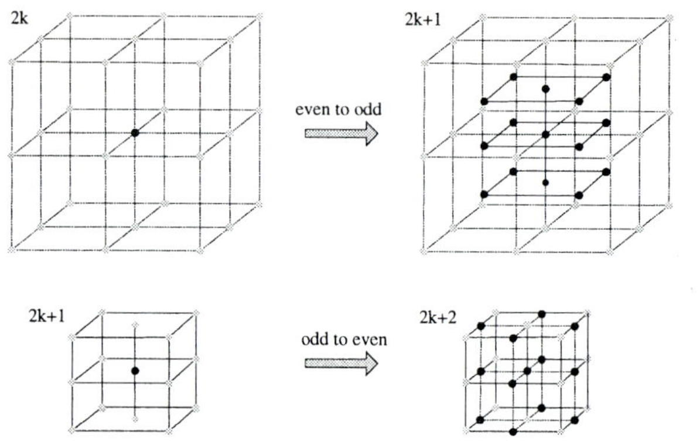


***Figure 6**. Even- and Odd-Level Grid Subdivision. We show even-to-odd and odd-to-even grid point subdivisions. In the upper half, we subdivide a level 2k point, in the middle of a grid, to produce 15 level 2k+1 points. In the lower half, we subdivide a level 2k+1 point to produce 13 level 2k+2 points -- thus returning to an even-level grid.*

To maintain valid star-shapes, we ensure that all neighboring points have a difference of at most one recursion level. This is similar to a problem that occurs when tessellating curved surfaces. If two adjacent patches are tessellated to different resolutions, T-junctions (and cracks) occur at the patch boundary. We must perform an additional tessellation of the intermediate region.

## 3.3 Image Placement at a Grid Point

The goal of our image-placement process is to limit the number of rendered primitives for all view directions centered on a given grid point. The basic approach we have followed is to create a conservative sampling of view directions. Then, for each sampled direction, we ensure that the target primitive count is not exceeded.

### 3.3.1 View-Directions Set

The first step of our image-placement process creates a *view-directions set* for the view directions surrounding a given grid point. The simplest set could be created using a constant sampling of view directions and the same FOV as at run time. But, since there might be a large variation in the amount of geometry surrounding a particular grid point, it is not clear how many samples to produce. Thus, we exploit the fact that the model is stored in an octree (or another hierarchical spatial-partitioning data structure) and create a sampling using the same FOV as at run time but that adapts to the local model complexity.

In an octree, culling is applied on a cell by cell basis, not to the individual geometric primitives. Consider only allowing yaw rotation of a pyramidal view frustum centered on a grid point. The visible set of octree cells remains constant until the left or right edge of the view frustum encounters a vertex from an octree cell, at which point view-frustum culling adds or removes the corresponding octree cell from the set (Figure 8).

The above fact turns the infinite space of view directions into a finite one, consisting of a set of angular ranges. Each angular range is inversely proportional to the model complexity in the view frustum: more complexity will generate more octree cells, hence the visible set of cells will typically remain constant for a smaller angular range. We compute the angular ranges for all grid points by starting with a common initial direction ($z$=-1 axis). Then, we rotate clockwise until the visible set of octree cells changes. We represent the ranges by the view direction at which

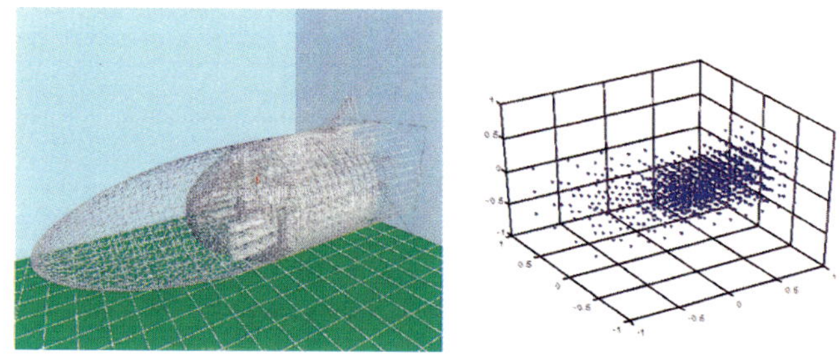

***Figure 7**. Torpedo Room Grid. This figure illustrates an automatically computed solution grid for a torpedo room model. The left snapshot shows an exterior view of the model rendered in wireframe. The right plot shows a grid of 1557 points from where 2333 LDIs are computed to limit the number of primitives per frame to at most 150,000 triangles. Note the cluster of geometry in the middle of the left snapshot and the corresponding cluster in the grid.*

this occurs, thus creating a sampling of view directions with more samples in areas with more model complexity in the view frustum.

If the octree has a large number of leaf cells, we might sample a large number of view directions per grid point, thus increasing the overall number of views and the preprocessing time. Therefore, we select an arbitrary tree depth to act as leaf cells (*pseudo-leaf cells*) and to conservatively represent the views around a grid point. This shallower octree will cause geometry to be more aggressively culled and generate slightly larger and nearer images than strictly necessary.

### 3.3.2 Image Placement

The second step of our image-placement process computes octree-cell subsets to *not* render from a given grid point. Then, at run time images are placed immediately in front of these subsets and the subsets themselves are culled. We define

- a *geometry budget P* – this value represents the maximum number of geometric primitives to render during a frame, and
- an *optimization budget* $P_{opt}$ – this value is slightly less than the actual geometry budget. A larger difference between these two budgets requires fewer images per grid point but increases the overall number of grid points.

For each grid point, the image-placement process starts with the view direction containing the most primitives. If the view exceeds

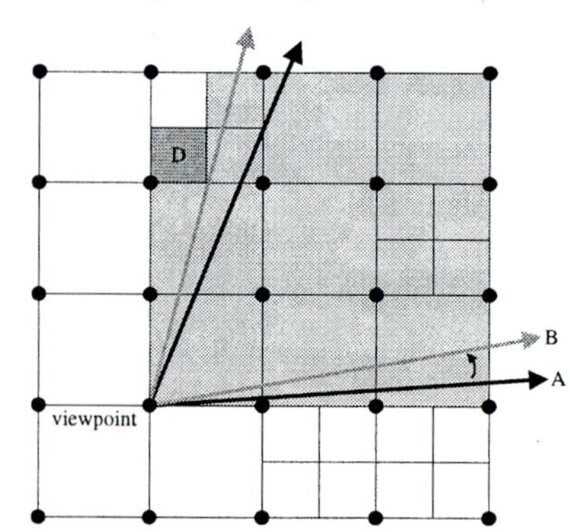


***Figure 8.** View-Directions Set. This example depicts a 2D slice of an octree (i.e. quadtree) and two view frusta. If we rotate counter-clockwise about the viewpoint from view frustum A to view frustum B, the group of octree leaf cells in view remains the same. Only if we rotate beyond B, will cell D be marked visible, thus changing the group of visible octree cells.*

our geometry budget, we perform a binary search through the space of contiguous, visible octree-cell subsets and employ a cost-benefit function to try to select the best subset to remove from rendering in order to meet the optimization budget. We compute one contiguous subset per view because it will require at most one image per frame—this simplifies the run-time system. If, after removing the subset, there is another view that violates the geometry budget, we compute a different subset for that view. The process is repeated until the geometry budget is met for all views.

In the following three sections, we provide more details on our cost-benefit function, our representation scheme for octree cell subsets, and our inner image-placement loop.

### *3.3.2.1 Cost-Benefit Function*

In order to determine which subset of the model to omit from rendering, we define a cost-benefit function *CB*. The function is composed of a weighted sum of the cost and benefit of selecting a given subset. It returns a value in the range [0,1].

The *cost* is defined as the ratio of the number of primitives $g_c$ to render after removing the current subset, to the total number of primitives $G_c$ in the view frustum.

$$Cost = g_c/G_c$$

The *benefit* is computed from the width $I_w$ and height $I_h$ of the screen-space bounding box of the current model subset and the distance *d* from the grid point to the nearest vertex of the subset.

$$Benefit = B_1*(1-max(I_w,I_h)/max(S_w,S_h)) + B_2*d/A$$

The final cost-benefit function *CB* will tend to maximize the benefit component and minimize the cost. A function value near 0 implies a very large-area subset placed directly in front of the eye that contains almost no geometry; 1 implies a subset with small screen area placed far from the grid point that contains all the visible geometry.

$$CB = C*(1-Cost(g_c, G_c)) + B*Benefit(I_w,I_h,d)$$

The constants of the above equation are

- *C, B:* weights of the cost and benefit components
- $B_1$, $B_2$: weights of the image size and depth components,
- *A*: length of the largest axis of the model space, and
- $S_w$, $S_h$: screen width and height.

### *3.3.2.2 Representing Octree-Cell Subsets*

The image-placement process will search through the space of all contiguous, visible subsets of octree cells associated with the current view. This process does not need to create all subsets but does need to enumerate them in order to perform the binary search. Thus, we need a fast and efficient method to represent and enumerate contiguous subsets. Furthermore, the cost-benefit function needs to compute the screen-space bounding box and primitive count of octree-cell subsets.

Our approach is to position a screen-space bounding box to exactly surround the projection of a contiguous group of octree cells. Since a larger number of octree leaf cells are rendered in high complexity areas, we snap between cells to finely change the bounding box in areas of high complexity and to coarsely change the bounding box in areas of low complexity.

We represent an arbitrary, contiguous octree-cell subset with a 6-tuple of numbers. Each number is an index into one of 6 sorted

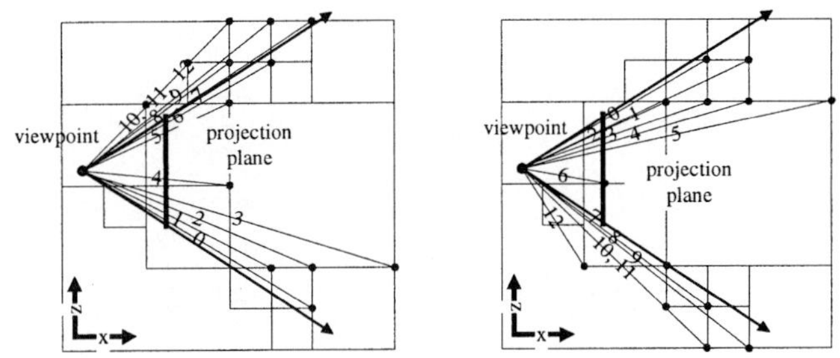


*Figure 9. Octree-Cell Subset Representation. These diagrams show two (of the six) sorted lists of a 2D slice of the octree cells in a view frustum (i.e. quadtree). The left diagram shows the bottom-to-top ordering of the topmost coordinates of the visible octree cells. The right diagram shows the top-to-bottom ordering of the bottommost coordinates. A subset of the visible octree cells can be represented by a minimal index m from the left diagram and a maximal index M from the right diagram. All cells that have a minimal index ≥ m and a maximal index < M are part of the 2-tuple [m,M]. By using this same notation in the XY plane and YZ plane, we can represent an arbitrary contiguous subset in 3D using a 6-tuple of such indices.*

lists representing the leftmost, rightmost, bottommost, topmost, nearest, and farthest borders of a subset (Figure 9). All octree cells whose indices lie within the ranges defined by a 6-tuple are members of the subset. We can change one of the bounding planes of the subset to its next significant value by simply changing an index in the 6-tuple. Furthermore, it is straightforward to incrementally update the screen-space bounding box of the subset as well as the count of geometry.

For example, consider a view with 100 octree cells (each cell is labeled from 0 to 99). The 6-tuple [0,99,0,99,0,99] represents the entire set. To obtain a subset whose screen-space projection is slimmer in the *x*-axis, we increment the "left border" index, e.g. [1,99,0,99,0,99], or decrement the "right border" index, e.g. [0,98,0,99,0,99]. If two or more octree cells share a screen space edge, we consider them as one entry.

### *3.3.2.3 Inner Image-Placement Loop*

Our inner loop uses the cost-benefit function and the 6-tuple subset representation to select the octree-cell subset to remove from rendering in order to meet the optimization budget. The loop starts with the set of all octree (leaf) cells in the view frustum, e.g. [0,99,0,99,0,99]. At each iteration, by moving the border along the *x*-, *y*-, and *z*-axes, we produce five new subsets. Specifically, the

- near border is moved halfway back (e.g. [0,99,0,99,50,99]),
- top border is moved halfway down (e.g. [0,99,0,50,0,99]),
- bottom border is moved halfway up (e.g. [0,99,50,99,0,99]),
- right border is moved halfway left (e.g. [0,50,0,99,0,99]), and
- left border is moved halfway right (e.g. [50,99,0,99,0,99]).

(note: since an image is meant to replace geometry behind the image's projection and near plane, we don't change the far border, the sixth-tuple value, because it will not affect image placement)

To decide which of these subsets to use next, we recurse ahead a few iterations with each of the five subsets. We then choose the subset that returned the largest cost-benefit value. In case of a tie, preference is given to the subsets in the order listed. Iterations stop when the subset no longer culls enough geometry.

We then define the projection plane for the image to be a quadrilateral perpendicular to the current view direction and

*Figure 10. Single- and Multi-Reference-Image LDI. (Left) In this snapshot, we see geometry (foreground) and a 512x384-pixel LDI (background) created from a single reference image. The viewpoint is as far as possible from the center-of-projection before switching to another image. Notice the presence of disocclusions that appear as black gaps. (Right) In this snapshot, we are at the same viewpoint, but we use 9 reference images to construct the LDI. In both cases, we apply a 3x3 convolution-kernel to smooth the warped image.*

exactly covering the screen-space bounding box of the computed subset. The four corners of the quadrilateral, together with the current grid point, determine a view frustum for creating the image to replace the subset. Section 4 explains in more detail how we create the images and display them at run time. For now, we simply associate the computed subset with this view direction and grid point.

Next, we temporarily cull the subset from the model and move on to the next most expensive view from the current grid point. If the total number of primitives in the view frustum is within the geometry budget, we are done with this grid point. Otherwise, we restore the subset to the model and compute another solution for the new view. By using the full model during each pass, we enforce solutions that contain exactly one subset, thus enabling us to warp no more than one image per frame.

## 4. IMAGE WARPING

The preprocessing component has determined the subsets of the model to replace with images—we must now create and display these images. At each grid point, we have the necessary (camera) parameters to create a reference image that accurately depicts the geometry from that position. But each image must potentially represent the selected geometry for any viewpoint within the associated star-shape.

One alternative is to use per-pixel depth values to dynamically warp images to the current viewpoint [McM95]. Unfortunately, warping a single depth image has the limitation that surfaces not visible in the original reference image appear as gaps in the rendered image (Figure 10, left).

Layered Depth Images (or LDIs) [Max95][Sha98] are the best solution to date for the visibility errors to which image warping is prone. They are a generalization of images with depth since, like regular images, they have only one set of view parameters but, unlike regular images, they can store more than one sample per pixel. The additional samples at a pixel belong to surfaces, which are not visible from the original center-of-projection (COP) of the image, along the same ray from the viewpoint. Whenever the LDI is warped to a view that reveals the (initially) hidden surfaces, the samples from deeper layers will not be overwritten and they will naturally fill in the gaps that otherwise appear (Figure 10, right).

LDIs store each visible surface sample once, thus eliminating redundant work (and storage) as compared to warping multiple reference images. An additional benefit is that LDIs can be warped in McMillan's occlusion-compatible order [McM95]. This order guarantees correct visibility resolution in the warped image.

### 4.1 Optimizing LDIs for the Solution Grid

We create the reference images for constructing an LDI from viewpoints within the star-shape surrounding each grid point. Thus, we can do a good job of sampling all potentially visible surfaces. Consider a solution image, *A*. All outward-looking viewpoints from which a view frustum can contain the image quadrilateral are represented approximately by an hemi-ellipsoid centered in front of the grid point. Figure 11 depicts a 2D slice of this configuration. For a more distant image *B*, the region is more elongated (e.g. the dashed hemi-ellipsoid). To construct the LDI, we select reference image COPs that populate this space.

We choose a total of eight construction images and one central image to create a LDI and to eliminate most visibility artifacts. The central LDI image is created using the grid point itself as the

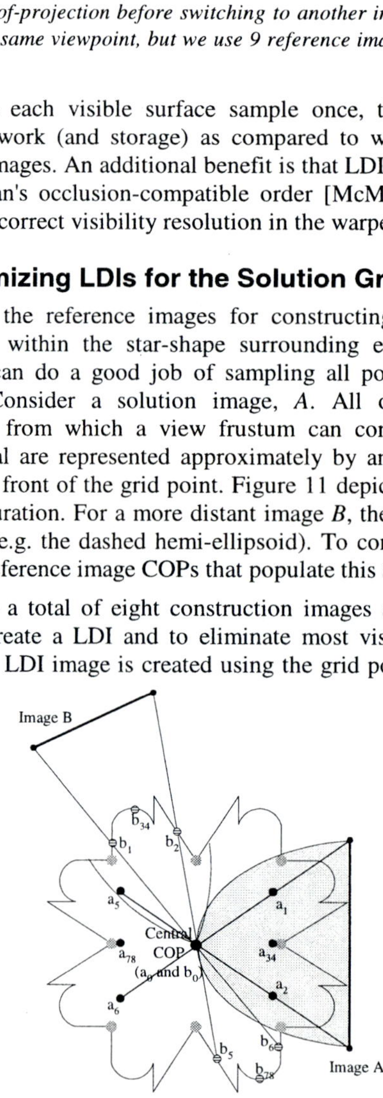


*Figure 11. Construction Images for a LDI. Image A is placed immediately outside a star-shape. Given a fixed FOV, the locus of outward-looking viewpoints within the star-shape from where there exists a view direction that contains the image quadrilateral is depicted by the shaded hemi-ellipsoid. The central COP is placed at grid point $a_0$; the 8 construction-images $a_1$-$a_8$ are placed as indicated. Similarly, $b_0$ and $b_1$-$b_8$ are the COPs for a farther away image B.*

COP ($a_0$ and $b_0$ in Figure 11). Four construction images are created from COPs at the middle of the vectors joining the grid point and the midpoints of each of the four edges of the image quadrilateral ($a_{1\text{-}4}$ and $b_{1\text{-}4}$ in Figure 11). An additional set of four construction images is defined in a similar way but extending behind the grid point ($a_{5\text{-}8}$ and $b_{5\text{-}8}$ in Figure 11). We warp the pixels of the nearest construction image first. This prioritizes the higher quality samples of the nearer images.

Most of the visibility information is obtained from the central image and the first four construction images. They sample most of the potentially visible surfaces. The images behind the grid point help to sample visibility of objects in the periphery of the FOV. In practice, this heuristic method does a good job.

## 5. IMPLEMENTATION

We implemented our program in C++, on a Silicon Graphics (SGI) Onyx2, 4 R10000's @ 195 MHz and Infinite Reality graphics. The program takes as input the

- octree of the 3D model,
- geometry and optimization budget,
- FOV to use for both preprocessing and run time,
- resolution of the initial viewpoint grid (minimum 3x3x3, i.e. the size of an even-level star-shape),
- tree depth to use for the octree (pseudo) leaf cells, and
- cost-benefit constants ($C = 0.4$, $B = 0.6$, $B_1 = 0.1$, $B_2 = 0.9$).

The preprocessing program uses a single processor to create and subdivide the grid; afterwards, multiple processors are used to simultaneously compute the image placements. We use spheres to approximate the star-shapes. If for any view direction, the amount of geometry inside the FOV and within the sphere exceeds the geometry budget, the grid point is subdivided. Once the grid has been created, the grid points are divided among three (of the four) processors. Each processor performs the inner image-placement loop to compute subsets to replace with images.

We empirically determined the constants for the cost-benefit function. In general, we found that LDIs work better the more distant they are (as expected); thus, we bias the function to prefer distant images. Furthermore, the $C$ and $B$ constants are set so that we slightly prefer higher-benefit solutions (i.e. the more distant ones) to ones that cull a little more geometry.

We employ octree pseudo-leaf cells to limit the number of cells for preprocessing. For our test models, we determined that an octree depth of 5 yields a reasonable balance between granularity and performance (thus, a maximum of 32,768 leaf cells per view).

At run time, we find the closest grid point in the reverse view frustum, select the view direction sample for the angular range that contains the current view direction, and check for an image placement. If one was computed, we warp the associated LDI. Our software-based warper distributes the work among three processors and is able to warp near NTSC-resolution LDIs (512x384) at about 8 Hz. We have also pipelined the culling and rendering phases of the system, therefore introducing one frame of latency. Furthermore, we use a 3x3 convolution-kernel to smooth the warped image. Figure 12 summarizes the run-time algorithm.

We create a least-recently-used cache to store image data and to allow us to precompute or dynamically-compute images for an interactive session. All images within a pre-specified radius of the current viewpoint are loaded from disk in near to far order. We either load the additional image data during idle time or use a separate processor to load image data.

```
1. For each frame
2.   Compute the reverse view frustum for the
       current view position and direction
3.   Find the closest grid point contained
       within the reverse frustum
4.   Find the sampled view for the angular range
       that contains the current view direction
5.   If (image was computed)
       Cull octree-cell subset from model
       Cull remaining geometry to view frustum
       Render geometry and warp image to current
         viewpoint
6.   Else
       Cull geometry to view frustum
       Render geometry
     Endif
   Endfor
```

***Figure 12.*** *Run-time Algorithm Summary.*

## 6. PERFORMANCE

We report the performance of our algorithm on four test models:

- a 2M triangle model of a coal-fired power plant (this is the largest model we can fit in memory that leaves space for the image cache and does not require us to page geometry),
- a 850K triangle model of the torpedo room of a notional nuclear submarine,
- a 1.7M triangle architectural model of a house, and
- a 1M triangle model of an array of pipes (procedurally generated by replication and instancing of pipes).

Figure 13 shows the amount of storage required for several maximum primitive counts. In order to display the results in a single graph, we chose to normalize the values to a common pair of axes. We use the horizontal axis to represent the geometry budget as a percentage of model size and the vertical axis to represent the total number of images divided by the total number of model primitives. The non-monotonic behavior of the power plant curve is because our algorithm found a local minimum farther away from the global minimum than the neighboring solutions. The solution at a geometry budget of 23% converged to a cluster of geometry that was large enough to meet the target primitive count but not necessarily the smallest and farthest subset. This occurrence is common with optimization algorithms.

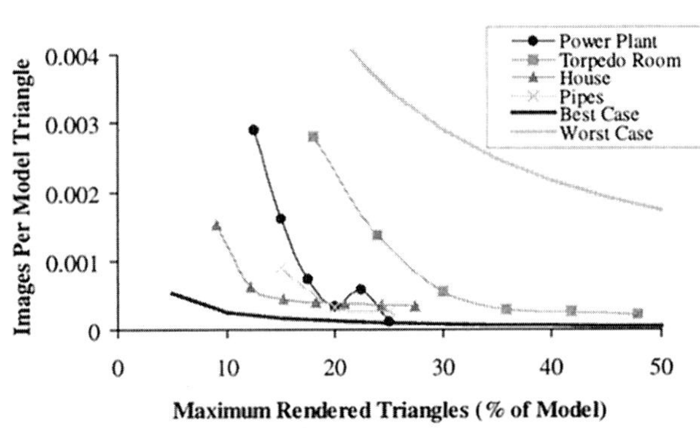


***Figure 13****. Storage Performance. The upper gray line represents the performance of the worst-case scenario. The lower black line represents the best-case scenario. The four test models fall in between these two bounds and in fact tend towards the best-case scenario.*

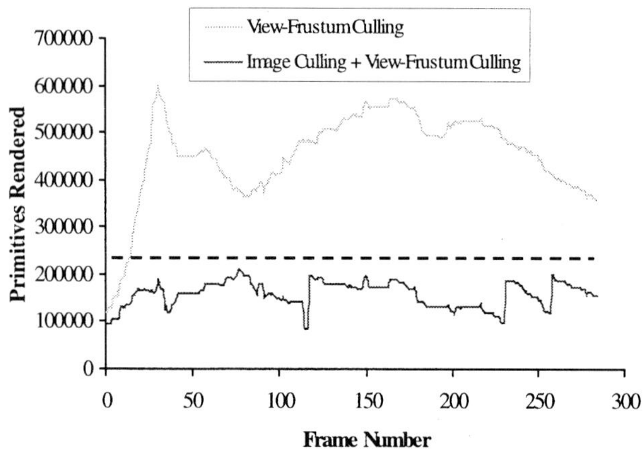


***Figure 14**. Path through Power Plant Model. This graph shows the number of primitives rendered for a sample path through the power plant using a geometry budget of 250,000. We show the results using only view-frustum culling and using image culling plus view-frustum culling. Notice that the primitive count never exceeds our geometry budget; in fact, for this path, it almost never exceeds* $P_{opt}$*=200,000.*

An improvement could be achieved by using a technique such as simulated annealing to move the solution to a "better" minimum.

For comparison with our empirical results, we also show in Figure 13 a curve that corresponds to the theoretical best-case performance of our algorithm. This occurs in models with a uniform distribution of geometry. Figure 13 also shows a curve that corresponds to a theoretical near worst-case performance, as is the case in models with large variations of geometric density. In practice, models fall somewhere in between these two extremes. For more details, we refer you to [Ali98].

Figure 14 shows the number of primitives rendered per frame for a path through the power plant using the solution set for a geometry budget of $P_r$= 250,000 primitives (and an optimization budget of $P_{opt}$ = 200,000 primitives). We have observed that for our test models, a difference between the geometry budget and optimization budget of 5 to 10% of the model primitives yields 1 to 4 images per grid point, on average.

Figure 15 shows a histogram of the number of grid points with the number of images varying from 1 to 5 images. Grid points near the edge usually have fewer images and are generally facing inwards towards the model center. Although images of neighboring grid points are similar, we do not share them. The similarity could be exploited for image compression purposes.

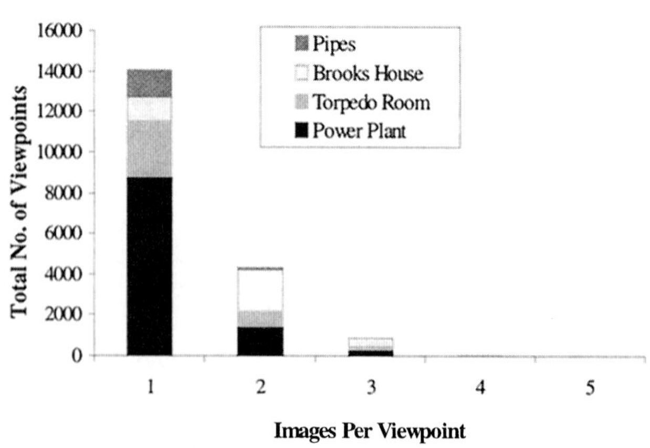


***Figure 15**. Histogram of Images Per Grid Point. Most grid points have between 1 and 3 images; specifically: 14,012 grid points with M=1, 4311 grid points with M=2, 862 with M=3, 40 grid points with M=4.*

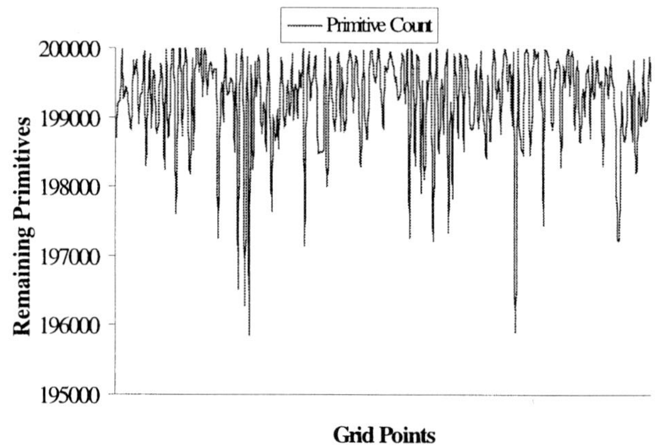


***Figure 16**. Primitive Counts for Solutions at Grid Points. The image-placement process computes image locations that typically produce primitive counts within 2% of the desired value* $P_{opt}$ *= 200,000.*

Figure 16 illustrates how close the solutions computed by the image-placement process (Section 3.3) are to the desired optimization budget. For a given grid-point view, we compute image placements that are conservative and typically fall within 2% of the optimization budget.

Figure 17 compares higher-resolution LDIs to an all-geometry rendering. Both the geometry and NTSC-resolution (640x512) LDI are rendered using 2x2 multi-sampling. This LDI resolution is beyond what we can do interactively today on our SGI workstation, nevertheless we show in our video an animation with these LDIs. To achieve the visual quality of Figure 17, at a frame rate of 30Hz, we would require a graphics performance of at most 7.5M triangles per second plus the ability to warp a multi-sampled NTSC-resolution LDI at 30Hz. The all-geometry approach would require at most 60M triangles per second processing power.

Table 1 summarizes the image-placement results. For each test model, we show the number of images computed and the preprocessing time for grid adaptation and image placement. In addition, we show the estimated space requirement. To determine this, we use an empirically determined average image size. We compress images using *gzip* and use a separate processor to uncompress them at run time—from this information we extrapolate space requirements (at present, we can uncompress an image in under one second).

The preprocessing time of a LDI is dependent on the number of construction images and the model complexity per construction image. First, we render eight construction images and one central image using only view-frustum culling. Second, we create a LDI in time proportional to the number of construction images. For our test models, our (unoptimized) LDI creation process takes 7 to 23 seconds. The total rendering and construction time of 3100 512x384-pixel power plant LDIs is approximately ten hours.

## 7. LIMITATIONS AND FUTURE WORK

Our current implementation only guarantees a rendering performance for translation and yaw rotation. The view-directions set can be easily expanded to include pitch, but it is unclear whether is it worth the extra effort and storage. We have observed that with interactive walkthroughs, gaze is kept nearly horizontal.

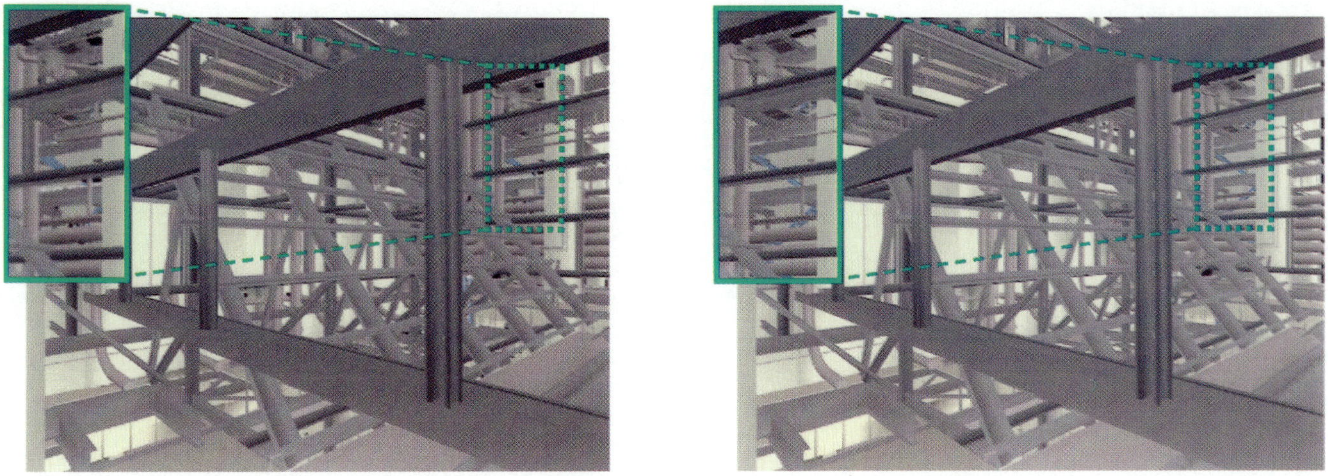

***Figure 17**. LDI+Geometry vs. All-Geometry Comparison. (Left) Snapshot using the same viewpoint as in Figure 10, but with a NTSC-resolution 2x2 multi-sampled LDI. The geometry is rendered using the graphics hardware's single-pass 2x2 multi-sample mode. (Right) For comparison purposes, we show a snapshot of an all-geometry rendering. The LDI does not perfectly reconstruct all surfaces, as can be observed by the pair of insets.*

We have seen a wide range of preprocessing times (from one to 28 hours). Furthermore, we have empirically determined the set of constants and weights required during preprocessing. They have worked well for our test models, but further parallelization (e.g. of the grid creation) and more automatic methods for determining these constants would improve the preprocessing.

Our cost function ignores fill rate. To more accurately achieve a constant frame rate, in particular on midrange systems, we need to take rasterization costs into account. In addition, we could measure the depth complexity (or the total pixel count) of the LDIs to more precisely trade off images for geometry.

| **Model (triangles)** | **Max. No. Tris** | **No. of LDIs** | **Preprocess (hours)** | **Estimated Space (MB)** |
|---|---|---|---|---|
| Power Plant | 250,000 | 5815 | 21.7 | 3802 |
| (2M) | 300,000 | 3224 | 12.4 | 2108 |
| | 350,000 | 1485 | 6.1 | 971 |
| | 400,000 | 706 | 6.5 | 462 |
| | 450,000 | 1169 | 5.9 | 764 |
| | 500,000 | 239 | 1.2 | 156 |
| Torpedo Rm. | 150,000 | 2333 | 11.8 | 933 |
| (850k) | 200,000 | 1160 | 6.0 | 464 |
| | 250,000 | 462 | 2.8 | 185 |
| | 300,000 | 243 | 1.6 | 97 |
| | 350,000 | 212 | 1.3 | 85 |
| | 400,000 | 181 | 1.1 | 72 |
| House | 150,000 | 2492 | 28.4 | 1725 |
| (1.7M) | 200,000 | 994 | 22.0 | 688 |
| | 250,000 | 714 | 10.6 | 494 |
| | 300,000 | 662 | 10.5 | 458 |
| | 350,000 | 629 | 11.2 | 435 |
| | 400,000 | 593 | 12.5 | 410 |
| | 450,000 | 561 | 11.4 | 388 |
| Pipes | 150,000 | 893 | 4.6 | 554 |
| (1M) | 200,000 | 331 | 2.8 | 205 |
| | 250,000 | 282 | 2.4 | 175 |

***Table 1**. Preprocessing Summary for Test Models*

Currently, we cannot perform view-dependent shading with the images at reasonable frame rates; thus, we use precomputed diffuse illumination. Our interactive software warper uses near NTSC resolution images. Higher resolution LDIs (for multi-sample anti-aliasing) are feasible but require proportionally more compute power or processors. Hence, because of our limited warping speed today, we cannot reduce geometric complexity to an arbitrary amount and achieve a high quality rendering.

In general, image warping demands good memory bandwidth. Every frame, we must perform pixel operations on the entire LDI, copy the warped image to the graphics engine and fetch future LDIs. We can transfer a 512x384-pixel image to the frame buffer in less than 3ms. Furthermore, since a single LDI is typically reused for several frames, we expect pixel operations to be performed from cache. The paging of image data from disk and from main memory is the slowest part.

We need to do further investigation of prefetching algorithms for the image data as well as the model geometry. In our current system, we assume the entire model fits in main memory. Moreover, our walking speed is limited by the rate at which we can page data from disk. In addition, we expect to be able to reduce the storage requirement by more sophisticated image representations and by image compression methods.

***Figure 18**. Example View of Pipes Model. Foreground pipes are geometry. Most of the background pipes are a 512x384-pixel LDI.*

## 8. CONCLUSIONS

We introduced a preprocessing algorithm and run-time system for reducing and bounding the geometric complexity of 3D models by dynamically replacing subsets of the geometry with (depth) images. Therefore, if we can afford the approximately constant cost of displaying images and the number of primitives to render dominates our application's rendering performance, we can achieve a guaranteed (minimum) frame rate. We also demonstrated an optimized layered-depth-image approach that yields good visual results and applied our algorithms to several complex 3D models (Figure 18).

The automatic image-placement algorithm we have presented allows us to trade off *space* for *frame rate*. In our case, space is proportional to the total number of images needed to replace geometry and the image size. Higher frame rate is equivalent to reducing the maximum number of primitives to render. Our results, both empirical and theoretical, indicate we can reduce geometric complexity by approximately an order of magnitude using a practical amount of storage (by today's standards).

## 9. ACKNOWLEDGMENTS

We would like to acknowledge the anonymous reviewers for their generous comments and suggestions. We also greatly appreciate the help received from Voicu Popescu, Matthew Rafferty, Bill Mark and the UNC Walkthrough and PixelFlow group.

The power plant model is courtesy of James Close and Combustion Engineering. The Brooks' House model is courtesy of many generations of UNC graduate students. The torpedo room model is courtesy of Electric Boat Division of General Dynamics. The pipes model was created from code written by Lee Westover.

This research was supported in part by grants from the NIH National Center for Research Resources (RR02170), DARPA (E278), NSF (MIP-9612643) and a UNC Dissertation Fellowship. In addition, we thank Intel for their generous equipment support.

## References

[Air90] Airey J., "Towards Image Realism with Interactive Update Rates in Complex Virtual Building Environments", *Symposium on Interactive 3D Graphics*, 41-50 (1990).

[Ali96] Aliaga D., "Visualization of Complex Models Using Dynamic Texture-Based Simplification", *IEEE Visualization*, 101-106 (1996).

[Ali97] Aliaga D. and Lastra A., "Architectural Walkthroughs Using Portal Textures", *IEEE Visualization*, 355-362 (1997).

[Ali98] Aliaga D., "Automatically Reducing and Bounding Geometric Complexity by Using Images", *Ph.D. Dissertation,* University of North Carolina at Chapel Hill, Computer Science Dept., October (1998).

[Ali99] Aliaga D., Cohen J., Wilson A., Baker E., Zhang H., Erikson C., Hoff K., Hudson T., Stuerzlinger W., Bastos R., Whitton M., Brooks F., Manocha D., "MMR: An Interactive Massive Model Rendering System Using Geometric and Image-based Acceleration", *Symposium on Interactive 3D Graphics,* 199-206 (1999).

[Cla76] Clark J., "Hierarchical Geometric Models for Visible Surface Algorithms", *CACM*, Vol. 19(10), 547-554 (1976).

[Coh96] Cohen J., Varshney A., Manocha D., Turk G., Weber H., Agarwal P., Brooks F. and Wright W., "Simplification Envelopes", *Computer Graphics (SIGGRAPH '96)*, 119-128 (1996).

[Coo97] Coorg S. and Teller S., "Real-Time Occlusion Culling for Models with Large Occluders", *Symposium on Interactive 3D Graphics*, 83-90 (1997).

[Dar97] Darsa L., Costa Silva B., and Varshney A., "Navigating Static Environments Using Image-Space Simplification and Morphing", *Symposium on Interactive 3D Graphics,* 25-34 (1997).

[DeH91] DeHaemer M. and Zyda M., "Simplification of Objects Rendered by Polygonal Approximations", *Computer Graphics*, Vol. 15(2), 175-184 (1991).

[Ebb98] Ebbesmeyer P., "Textured Virtual Walls - Achieving Interactive Frame Rates During Walkthroughs of Complex Indoor Environments", *VRAIS '98*, 220-227 (1998).

[Fun93] Funkhouser T., Sequin C., "Adaptive Display Algorithm for Interactive Frame Rates During Visualization of Complex Virtual Environments", *Computer Graphics (SIGGRAPH '93),* 247-254 (1993).

[Gar97] Garland M., Heckbert P., "Surface Simplification using Quadric Error Bounds", *Computer Graphics (SIGGRAPH '97),* 209-216 (1997).

[Hop97] Hoppe H., "View-Dependent Refinement of Progressive Meshes", *Computer Graphics (SIGGRAPH '97),* 189-198 (1997).

[Lue97] Luebke D. and Erikson C., "View-Dependent Simplification of Arbitrary Polygonal Environments", *Computer Graphics (SIGGRAPH '97),* 199-208 (1997).

[Mac95] Maciel P. and Shirley P., "Visual Navigation of Large Environments Using Textured Clusters", *Symposium on Interactive 3D Graphics*, 95-102 (1995).

[Max95] Max N., Ohsaki K., "Rendering Trees from Precomputed Z-Buffer Views", *Rendering Techniques '95: Proceedings of the 6th Eurographics Workshop on Rendering*, 45-54 (1995).

[McM95] McMillan L. and Bishop G., "Plenoptic Modeling: An Image-Based Rendering System", *Computer Graphics (SIGGRAPH '95),* 39-46 (1995).

[Mue95] Mueller C., "Architectures of Image Generators for Flight Simulators", *Computer Science Technical Report TR95-015*, University of North Carolina at Chapel Hill (1995).

[Pop98] Popescu V., Lastra A., Aliaga D., and Oliveira Neto M., "Efficient Warping for Architectural Walkthroughs using Layered Depth Images", *IEEE Visualization*, (1998).

[Raf98] Rafferty M., Aliaga D. and Lastra A., "3D Image Warping in Architectural Walkthroughs", *IEEE VRAIS*, 228-233 (1998).

[Reg94] Regan M., Pose R., "Priority Rendering with a Virtual Reality Address Recalculation Pipeline", *Computer Graphics (SIGGRAPH '94),* 155-162 (1994).

[Sch83] Bruce Schachter (ed.), Computer Image Generation, John Wiley and Sons, 1983.

[Scf96] Schaufler G. and Stuerzlinger W., "Three Dimensional Image Cache for Virtual Reality", *Computer Graphics Forum (Eurographics '96),* Vol. 15(3), 227-235 (1996).

[Sha96] Shade J., Lischinski D., Salesin D., DeRose T., Snyder J., "Hierarchical Image Caching for Accelerated Walkthroughs of Complex Environments", *Computer Graphics (SIGGRAPH '96),* 75-82 (1996).

[Sha98] Shade J., Gortler S., He L., and Szeliski R., Layered Depth Images, *Computer Graphics (SIGGRAPH '98),* 231-242 (1998).

[Sil97] Sillion F., Drettakis G. and Bodelet B., "Efficient Impostor Manipulation for Real-Time Visualization of Urban Scenery", *Computer Graphics Forum Vol. 16 No. 3 (Eurographics),* 207-218 (1997).

[Tel91] Teller S., Séquin C., "Visibility Preprocessing For Interactive Walkthroughs", *Computer Graphics (SIGGRAPH '91),* 61-69 (1991).

[Tur92] Turk G., "Re-Tiling Polygonal Surfaces", *Computer Graphics (SIGGRAPH '92),* 55-64, (1992).

[Zha97] Zhang H., Manocha D., Hudson T. and Hoff K., "Visibility Culling Using Hierarchical Occlusion Maps", *Computer Graphics (SIGGRAPH '97),* 77-88 (1997).

# Implicit Fairing of Irregular Meshes using Diffusion and Curvature Flow

Mathieu Desbrun Mark Meyer Peter Schröder Alan H. Barr

Caltech*

## Abstract

In this paper, we develop methods to rapidly remove rough features from irregularly triangulated data intended to portray a smooth surface. The main task is to remove undesirable noise and uneven edges while retaining desirable geometric features. The problem arises mainly when creating high-fidelity computer graphics objects using imperfectly-measured data from the real world.

Our approach contains three novel features: an *implicit integration* method to achieve efficiency, stability, and large time-steps; a scale-dependent Laplacian operator to improve the diffusion process; and finally, a robust curvature flow operator that achieves a smoothing of the shape itself, distinct from any parameterization. Additional features of the algorithm include automatic exact volume preservation, and hard and soft constraints on the positions of the points in the mesh.

We compare our method to previous operators and related algorithms, and prove that our curvature and Laplacian operators have several mathematically-desirable qualities that improve the appearance of the resulting surface. In consequence, the user can easily select the appropriate operator according to the desired type of fairing. Finally, we provide a series of examples to graphically and numerically demonstrate the quality of our results.

## 1 Introduction

While the mainstream approach in mesh fairing has been to enhance the smoothness of triangulated surfaces by minimizing computationally expensive functionals, Taubin [Tau95] proposed in 1995 a signal processing approach to the problem of fairing arbitrary topology surface triangulations. This method is linear in the number of vertices in both time and memory space; large arbitrary connectivity meshes can be handled quite easily and transformed into visually appealing models. Such meshes appear more and more frequently due to the success of 3D range sensing approaches for creating complex geometry [CL96].

Taubin based his approach on defining a suitable generalization of frequency to the case of arbitrary connectivity meshes. Using a discrete approximation to the Laplacian, its eigenvectors become the "frequencies" of a given mesh. Repeated application of the resulting linear operator to the mesh was then employed to tailor the frequency content of a given mesh.

Closely related is the approach of Kobbelt [Kob97], who considered similar discrete approximations of the Laplacian in the construction of fair interpolatory subdivision schemes. In later work this was extended to the arbitrary connectivity setting for purposes of multiresolution editing [KCVS98].

The success of these techniques is largely based on their simple implementation and the increasing need for algorithms which can process the ever larger meshes produced by range sensing techniques. However, a number of issues in their application remain open problems in need of a more thorough examination.

*{mathieu|mmeyer|ps|barr}@cs.caltech.edu.



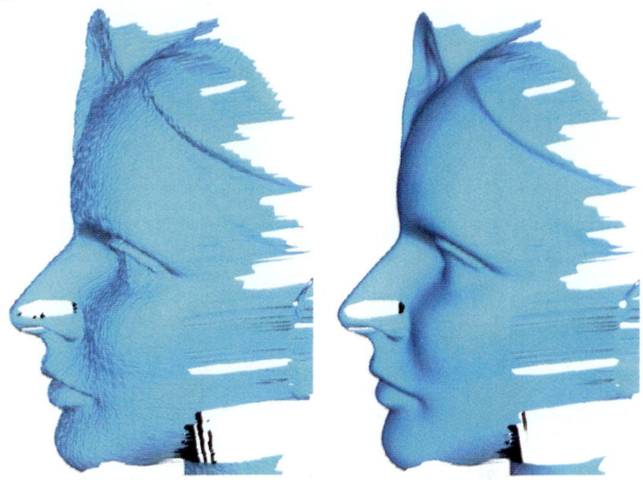

(a) (b)

Figure 1: *(a): Original 3D photography mesh (41,000 vertices). (b): Smoothed version with the scale-dependent operator in two integration step with* $\lambda dt = 5 \cdot 10^{-5}$*, the iterative linear solver (PBCG) converges in 10 iterations. All the images in this paper are flat-shaded to enhance the faceting effect.*

The simplicity of the underlying algorithms is based on very basic, uniform approximations of the Laplacian. For irregular connectivity meshes this leads to a variety of artifacts such as geometric distortion during smoothing, numerical instability, problems of slow convergence for large meshes, and insufficient control over global behavior. The latter includes shrinkage problems and more precise shaping of the frequency response of the algorithms.

In this paper we consider more carefully the question of numerical stability by observing that Laplacian smoothing can be thought of as time integration of the heat equation on an irregular mesh. This suggests the use of *implicit integration* schemes which lead to unconditionally stable algorithms allowing for very large time steps. At the same time the necessary linear system solvers run faster than explicit approaches for large meshes. We also consider the question of mesh parameterization more carefully and propose the use of discretizations of the Laplacian which take the underlying parameterization into account. The resulting algorithms avoid many of the distortion artifacts resulting from the application of previous methods. We demonstrate that this can be done at only a modest increase in computing time and results in smoothing algorithms with considerably higher geometric fidelity. Finally a more careful analysis of the underlying discrete differential geometry is used to derive a curvature flow approach which satisfies crucial geometric properties. We detail how these different operators act on meshes, and how users can then decide which one is appropriate in their case. If the user wants to, at the same time, smooth the shape of an object and equalize its triangulation, a scale-dependent diffusion must be used. On the other hand, if only the shape must be filtered without affecting the sampling rate, then curvature flow has all the desired properties. This allows us to propose a novel class of efficient smoothing algorithms for arbitrary connectivity meshes.

## 2 Implicit fairing

In this section, we introduce *implicit fairing*, an implicit integration of the diffusion equation for the smoothing of meshes. We will demonstrate several advantages of this approach over the usual explicit methods. While this section is restricted to the use of a linear approximation of the diffusion term, implicit fairing will be used as a robust and efficient numerical method throughout the paper, even for non-linear operators. We start by setting up the framework and defining our notation.

## 2.1 Notation and definitions

In the remainder of this paper, $X$ will denote a mesh, $x_i$ a vertex of this mesh, and $e_{ij}$ the edge (if existing) connecting $x_i$ to $x_j$. We will call $N_1(i)$ the "neighbors" (or 1-ring neighbors) of $x_i$, i.e., all the vertices $x_j$ such that there exists an edge $e_{ij}$ between $x_i$ and $x_j$ (see Figure 9(a)).

In the surface fairing literature, most techniques use constrained energy minimization. For this purpose, different fairness functionals have been used. The most frequent functional is the total curvature of a surface $\mathcal{S}$:

$$\mathcal{E}(\mathcal{S}) = \int_{\mathcal{S}} \kappa_1^2 + \kappa_2^2 \, d\mathcal{S}. \quad (1)$$

This energy can be estimated on discrete meshes [WW94, Kob97] by fitting local polynomial interpolants at vertices. However, principal curvatures $\kappa_1$ and $\kappa_2$ depend non-linearly on the surface $\mathcal{S}$. Therefore, many practical fairing methods prefer the membrane functional or the thin-plate functional of a mesh $X$:

$$\mathcal{E}_{membrane}(X) = \frac{1}{2}\int_\Omega X_u^2 + X_v^2 \, dudv \quad (2)$$

$$\mathcal{E}_{thin\ plate}(X) = \frac{1}{2}\int_\Omega X_{uu}^2 + 2X_{uv}^2 + X_{vv}^2 \, dudv. \quad (3)$$

Note that the thin-plate energy turns out to be equal to the total curvature only when the parameterization $(u,v)$ is isometric. Their respective variational derivatives corresponds to the Laplacian and the second Laplacian:

$$\mathcal{L}(X) = X_{uu} + X_{vv} \quad (4)$$

$$\mathcal{L}^2(X) = \mathcal{L} \circ \mathcal{L}(X) = X_{uuuu} + 2X_{uuvv} + X_{vvvv}. \quad (5)$$

For smooth surface reconstruction in vision, a weighted average of these derivatives has been used to fair surfaces [Ter88]. For meshes, Taubin [Tau95] used signal processing analysis to show that a combination of these two derivatives of the form: $(\lambda+\mu)\mathcal{L} - \lambda\mu\mathcal{L}^2$ can provide a Gaussian filtering that minimizes shrinkage. The constants $\lambda$ and $\mu$ must be tuned by the user to obtain this non-shrinking property. We will refer to this technique as the $\lambda|\mu$ algorithm.

## 2.2 Diffusion equation for mesh fairing

As we just pointed out, one common way to attenuate noise in a mesh is through a *diffusion process*:

$$\frac{\partial X}{\partial t} = \lambda \mathcal{L}(X). \quad (6)$$

By integrating equation 6 over time, a small disturbance will disperse rapidly in its neighborhood, smoothing the high frequencies, while the main shape will be only slightly degraded. The Laplacian operator can be linearly approximated at each vertex by the umbrella operator (we will use this approximation in the current section for the sake of simplicity, but will discuss its validity in section 4), as used in [Tau95, KCVS98]:

$$\mathcal{L}(x_i) = \frac{1}{m} \sum_{j \in N_1(i)} x_j - x_i \quad (7)$$

where $x_j$ are the neighbors of the vertex $x_i$, and $m = \#N_1(i)$ is the number of these neighbors (valence). A sequence of meshes $(X^n)$ can be constructed by integrating the diffusion equation with a simple *explicit Euler* scheme, yielding:

$$X^{n+1} = (I + \lambda dt\,\mathcal{L})X^n. \quad (8)$$

With the umbrella operator, the stability criterion requires $\lambda dt < 1$. If the time step does not satisfy this criterion, ripples appear on the surface, and often end up creating oscillations of growing magnitude over the whole surface. On the other hand, if this criterion is met, we get smoother and smoother versions of the initial mesh as $n$ grows.

## 2.3 Time-shifted evaluation

The implementation of this previous explicit method, called *forward Euler method*, is very straightforward [Tau95] and has nice properties such as linear time and linear memory size for each filtering pass. Unfortunately, when the mesh is large, the time step restriction results in the need to perform hundreds of integrations to produce a noticeable smoothing, as mentioned in [KCVS98].

Implicit integration offers a way to avoid this time step limitation. The idea is simple: if we approximate the derivative using the new mesh (instead of using the old mesh as done in explicit methods), we will get to the equilibrium state of the PDE faster. As a result of this time-shifted evaluation, stability is obtained unconditionally [PTVF92]. The integration is now: $X^{n+1} = X^n + \lambda dt\,\mathcal{L}(X^{n+1})$. Performing an implicit integration, this time called *backward Euler method*, thus means solving the following linear system:

$$(I - \lambda dt\,\mathcal{L})X^{n+1} = X^n. \quad (9)$$

This apparently minor change allows the user not to worry about practical limitations on the time step. Consequent smoothing will then be obtained safely by increasing the value $\lambda dt$. But solving a linear system is the price to pay.

## 2.4 Solving the sparse linear system

Fortunately, this linear system can be solved efficiently as the matrix $A = I - \lambda dt\,\mathcal{L}$ is sparse: each line contains approximately six non-zero elements if the Laplacian is expressed using Equ. (7) since the average number of neighbors on a typical triangulated mesh is six. We can use a preconditioned bi-conjugate gradient (PBCG) to iteratively solve this system with great efficiency[1]. The PBCG is based on matrix-vector multiplies [PTVF92], which only require linear time computation in our case thanks to the sparsity of the matrix $A$. We review in Appendix A the different options we chose for the PBCG in order to have an efficient implementation for our purposes.

## 2.5 Interpretation of the implicit integration

Although this implicit integration for diffusion is sound as is, there are useful connections with other prior work. We review the analogies with signal processing approaches and physical simulation.

### 2.5.1 Signal processing

In [Tau95], Taubin presents the explicit integration of diffusion with a signal processing point of view. Indeed, if $X$ is a 1D signal of a given frequency $\omega$: $X = e^{i\omega}$, then $\mathcal{L}(X) = -\omega^2 X$. Thus, the transfer function for Equ. (8) is $1 - \lambda dt\omega^2$, as displayed in Figure 2(a) as a solid line. We can see that the higher the frequency $\omega$, the stronger the attenuation will be, as expected.

The previous filter is called FIR (for Finite Impulse Response) in signal processing. When the diffusion process is integrated using implicit integration, the filter in Equ. (9) turns out to be an Infinite Impulse Response filter. Its transfer function is now $1/(1+\lambda dt\omega^2)$, depicted in Figure 2(a) as a dashed line. Because this filter is always in $[0,1]$, we have unconditional stability.

[1] We use a bi-conjugate gradient method to be able to handle non symmetric matrices, to allow the inclusion of constraints (see Section 2.7).

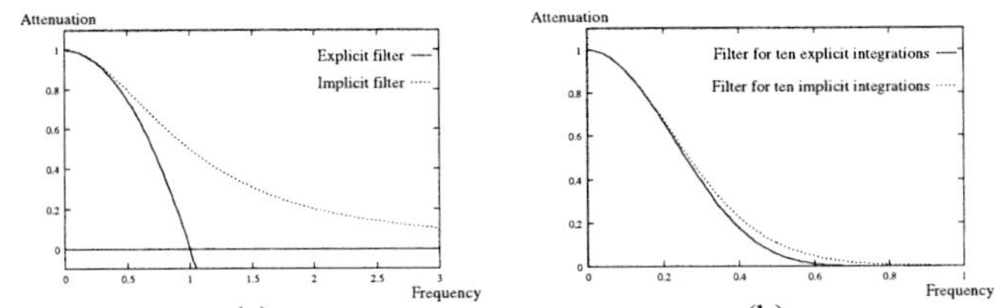


(a) (b)

Figure 2: *Comparison between (a) the explicit and implicit transfer function for $\lambda dt = 1$, and (b) their resulting transfer function after 10 integrations.*

By rewriting Equ. (9) as: $X^{n+1} = (I - \lambda dt \mathcal{L})^{-1} X^n$, we also note that our implicit filtering is equivalent to $I + \lambda dt \mathcal{L} + (\lambda dt)^2 \mathcal{L}^2 + ...$, i.e., standard explicit filtering plus an infinite sequence of higher order filtering. Contrary to the explicit approach, one single implicit filtering step performs global filtering.

### 2.5.2 Mass-spring network

Smoothing a mesh by minimizing the membrane functional can be seen as a physical simulation of a mass-spring network with zero-rest length springs that will shrink to a single point in the limit. Recently, Baraff and Witkin [BW98] presented an implicit method to allow large time steps in cloth simulation. They found that the use of an implicit solver instead of the traditional explicit Euler integration considerably improves computational time while still being stable for very stiff systems. Our method compares exactly to theirs, but used for meshes and for a different PDE. We therefore have the same advantages of using an implicit solver over the usual explicit type: *stability* and *efficiency* when significant filtering is called for.

## 2.6 Filter improvement

Now that the method has been set up for the usual diffusion equation, we can consider other equations that may be more appropriate or may give better visual results for smoothing when we use implicit integration.

We have seen in Section 2.1 that both $\mathcal{L}$ and $\mathcal{L}^2$ have been used with success in prior work [Ter88, Tau95, KCVS98]. When we use implicit integration, as Figure 3(a) shows, the higher the power of the Laplacian, the closer to a *low-pass filter* we get. In terms of frequency analysis, it is a better filter. Unfortunately, the matrix becomes less and less sparse as more and more neighbors are involved in the computation. In practice, we find that $\mathcal{L}^2$ is a very good trade-off between efficiency and quality. Using higher orders affects the computational time significantly, while not always producing significant improvements. We therefore recommend using $(I + \lambda dt \mathcal{L}^2) X^{n+1} = X^n$ for implicit smoothing (a precise definition of the umbrella-like operator for $\mathcal{L}^2$ can be found in [KCVS98]).

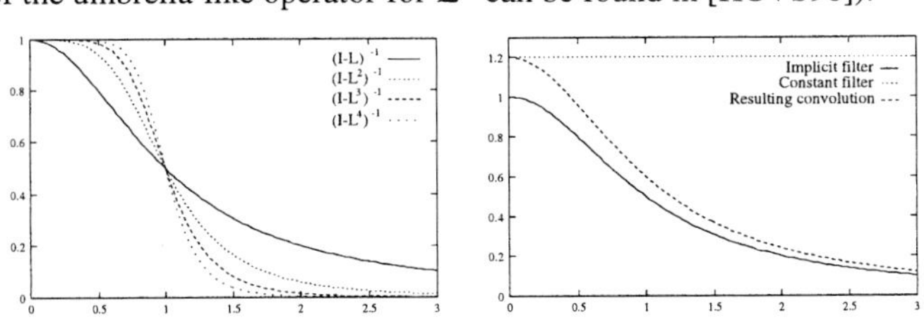


(a) (b)

Figure 3: *(a): Comparison between filters using $\mathcal{L}$, $\mathcal{L}^2$, $\mathcal{L}^3$, and $\mathcal{L}^4$. (b): The scaling to preserve volume creates an amplification of all frequencies; but the resulting filter (diffusion+scaling) only amplifies low frequencies to compensate for the shrinking of the diffusion.*

We also tried to use a linear combination of both $\mathcal{L}$ and $\mathcal{L}^2$. We obtained interesting results like, for instance, amplification of low or middle frequencies to exaggerate large features (refer to [GSS99] for a complete study of feature enhancement). It is not appropriate in the context of a fixed mesh, though: amplifying frequencies requires refinement of the mesh to offer a good discretization.

## 2.7 Constraints

We can put hard and soft constraints on the mesh vertex positions during the diffusion. For the user, it means that a vertex or a set of vertices can be fixed so that the smoothing happens only on the rest of the mesh. This can be very useful to retain certain details in the mesh.

A vertex $x_i$ will stay fixed if we impose $\mathcal{L}(x_i) = 0$. More complicated constraints are also possible [BW98]. For example, vertices can be constrained along an axis or on a plane by modifying the PBCG to keep these constraints enforced during the linear solver iterations.

We can also easily implement *soft constraints*: each vertex can be weighted according to the desired smoothing that we want. For instance, the user may want to smooth a part of a mesh less than another one, in order to keep desirable features while getting a smoother version. We allow the assignment of a smoothing value between 0 and 1 to attenuate the smoothing spatially: this is equivalent to choosing a variable $\lambda$ factor on the mesh, and happens to be very useful in practice. Entire regions can be "spray painted" interactively to easily assign this special factor.

## 2.8 Discussion

Even if adding a linear solver step to the integration of the diffusion equation seems to slow down the problem at first glance, it turns out that we gain significantly by doing so. For instance, the implicit integration can be performed with an arbitrary time step. Since the matrix of the system is very sparse, we actually obtain computational time similar or better than the explicit methods. In the following table, we indicate the number of iterations of the PBCG method for different meshes and it can be seen that the PBCG is more efficient when the smoothing is high. These timings were performed on an SGI High Impact Indigo2 175MHz R10000 processor with 128M RAM.

| Mesh | Nb of faces | $\lambda dt = 10$ | $\lambda dt = 100$ |
|---|---|---|---|
| Horse | 42,000 | 8 iterations (2.86s) | 37 iterations (12.6s) |
| Dragon | 42,000 | 8 iterations (2.98s) | 39 iterations (13.82s) |
| Isis | 50,000 | 9 iterations (3.84s) | 37 iterations (15.09s) |
| Bunny | 66,000 | 7 iterations (4.53s) | 35 iterations (21.34s) |
| Buddha | 290,000 | 5 iterations (13.78s) | 28 iterations (69.93s) |

To be able to compare the results with the explicit method, one has to notice that one iteration of the PBCG is only slightly more time consuming than one integration step using an explicit method. Therefore, we can see in the following results that our implicit fairing takes about 60% less time than the explicit fairing for a filtering of $\lambda dt = 100$, as we get about 33 iterations compared to the 100 integration steps required in the explicit case. We have found this behavior to be true for all the other meshes as well. The advantage of the implicit method in terms of computational speed becomes more obvious for *large meshes* and/or *high smoothing* value. In terms of quality, Figure 4(b) and 4(c) demonstrate that both implicit and explicit methods produce about the same visual results, with a slightly better smoothness for the implicit fairing. Note that we use 10 explicit integrations of the umbrella operator with $\lambda dt = 1$, and 1 integration using the implicit integration with $\lambda dt = 10$ to approximate the same results. Therefore, there is a definite advantage in the use of implicit fairing over the previous explicit methods. Moreover, the remainder of this paper will make heavy use of this method and its stability properties.

# 3 Automatic anti-shrinking fairing

Pure diffusion will, by nature, induce shrinkage. This is inconvenient as this shrinking may be significant for aggressive smoothing. Taubin proposed to use a linear combination of $\mathcal{L}$ and $\mathcal{L} \circ \mathcal{L}$ to amplify low frequencies in order to balance the natural shrinking. Unfortunately, the linear combination depends heavily on the mesh in practice, and this requires fine tuning to ensure both stable

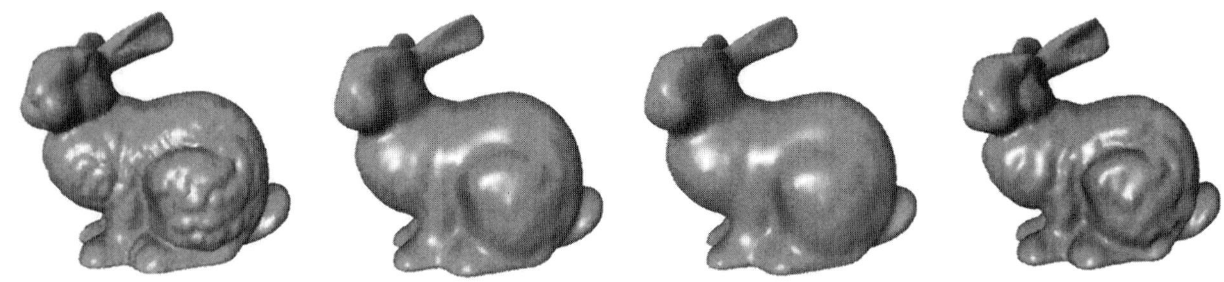

(a) (b) (c) (d)

Figure 4: *Stanford bunnies: (a) The original mesh, (b) 10 explicit integrations with $\lambda dt = 1$, (c) 1 implicit integration with $\lambda dt = 10$ that takes only 7 PBCG iterations (30% faster), and (d) 20 passes of the $\lambda|\mu$ algorithm, with $\lambda = 0.6307$ and $\mu = -0.6732$. The implicit integration results in better smoothing than the explicit one for the same, or often less, computing time. If volume preservation is called for, our technique then requires many fewer iterations to smooth the mesh than the $\lambda|\mu$ algorithm.*

and non-shrinking results. In this section, we propose an automatic solution to avoid this shrinking. We preserve the zeroth moment, i.e., the volume, of the object. Without any other information on the mesh, we feel it is the most reasonable invariant to preserve, although surface area or other invariants can be used.

### 3.1 Volume computation

As we have a mesh given in terms of triangles, it is easy to compute the interior volume. This can be done by summing the volumes of all the oriented pyramids centered at a point in space (the origin, for instance) and with a triangle of the mesh as a base. This computation has a linear complexity in the number of triangles [LK84]. For the reader's convenience, we give the expression of the volume of a mesh in the following equation, where $x_k^1, x_k^2$ and $x_k^3$ are the three vertices of the $k$th triangle:

$$V = \frac{1}{6}\sum_{k=1}^{nbFaces} g_k \cdot N_k \qquad (10)$$

where $g = (x_k^1 + x_k^2 + x_k^3)/3$ and $N_k = \vec{x_k^1 x_k^2} \wedge \vec{x_k^1 x_k^3}$

### 3.2 Exact volume preservation

After an integration step, the mesh will have a new volume $V^n$. We then want to scale it back to its original volume $V^0$ to cancel the shrinking effect. We apply a simple scale on the vertices to achieve this. By multiplying all the vertex positions by $\beta = (V^0/V^n)^{1/3}$, the volume is guaranteed to go back to its original value. As this is a simple scaling, it is harmless in terms of frequencies. To put it differently, this scaling corresponds to a convolution with a scaled Dirac in the frequency domain, hence it amplifies all the frequencies in the same way to change the volume back. The resulting filter, after the implicit smoothing and the constant amplification filter, amplifies the low frequencies of the original mesh to *exactly* compensate for the attenuation of the high frequencies, as sketched on Figure 3(b).

The overall complexity for volume preservation is then linear. With such a process, we do not need to tweak parameters: the anti-shrinking filter is *automatically* adapted to the mesh and to the smoothing, contrary to previous approaches. Note that hard constraints defined in the previous section are applied before the scaling and do not result in fixed points anymore: scaling alters the absolute, but not the relative position.

We can generalize this re-scaling phase to different invariants. For instance, if we have to smooth height fields, it is more appropriate to take the invariant as being the volume enclosed between the height field and a reference plane, which changes the computations only slightly. Likewise, for surfaces of revolution, we may change the way the scaling is computed to exploit this special property. We can also preserve the surface area if the mesh is a non-closed surface. However, in the absence of specific characteristics, preserving the volume gives nice results. According to specific needs, the user can select the appropriate type of invariant to be used.

### 3.3 Discussion

When we combine both methods of implicit integration and anti-shrinking convolution, we obtain an automatic and efficient method for fairing. Indeed, no parameters need be tuned to ensure stability or to have exact volume preservation. This is a major advantage over previous techniques. Yet, we retain all of the advantages of previous methods, such as constraints [Tau95] and the possibility of accelerating the fairing via multigrid [KCVS98], while additionally offering stability and efficiency. This technique also dramatically reduces the computing time over Taubin's anti-shrinking algorithm: as demonstrated in Figure 4(c) and 4(d), using the $\lambda|\mu$ algorithm may preserve the volume after fine tuning, but one iteration will only slightly smooth the mesh. The rest of this paper exploits both automatic anti-shrinking and implicit fairing techniques to offer more accurate tools for fairing.

## 4 An accurate diffusion process

Up to this section, we have relied on the umbrella operator (Equ. (7)) to approximate the Laplacian on a vertex of the mesh. This particular operator does not truly represent a Laplacian in the physical meaning of this term as we are about to see. Moreover, simple experiments on smooth meshes show that this operator, using explicit or implicit integration, can create bumps or "pimples" on the surface, instead of smoothing it. This section proposes a sounder simulation of the diffusion process, by defining a new approximation for the Laplacian and by taking advantage of the implicit integration.

### 4.1 Inadequacy of the umbrella operator

The umbrella operator, used in the previous sections corresponds to an approximation of the Laplacian in the case of a specific parameterization [KCVS98]. This means that the mesh is supposed to have edges of length 1 and all the angles between two adjacent edges around a vertex should be equal. This is of course far from being true in actual meshes, which contain a variety of triangles of different sizes.

Treating all edges as if they had equal length has significant undesired consequences for the smoothing. For example, the Laplacian can be the same for two very different configurations, corresponding to different frequencies as depicted in Figure 5. This distorts the filtering significantly, as high frequencies may be considered as low ones, and vice-versa. Nevertheless, the advantage of the umbrella operator is that it is normalized: the time step for integration is always 1, which is very convenient. But we want a more accurate diffusion process to smooth meshes consistently, in order to more carefully separate high from low frequencies.

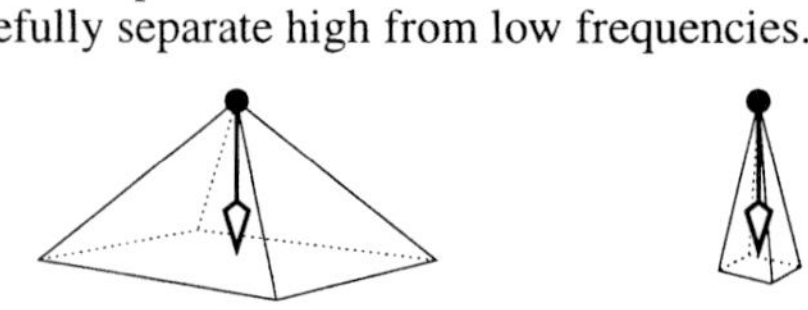

(a) (b)

Figure 5: *Frequency confusion: the umbrella operator is evaluated as the vector joining the center vertex to the barycenter of its neighbors. Thus, cases (a) and (b) will have the same approximated Laplacian even if they represent different frequencies.*

We need to define a discrete Laplacian which is scale dependent, to better approximate diffusion. However, if we use explicit integration [Tau95], we will suffer from a very restricted stability criterion. It is well known [PTVF92] that the time step for a parabolic PDE like Equ. (6) depends on the square of the smallest length scale (here, the smallest edge length $min(|e|)$):

$$dt \leq \frac{min(|e|)^2}{2\lambda}$$

This limitation is a real concern for large meshes with small details, since an enormous number of integration steps will have to be performed to obtain noticeable smoothing. This is *intractable* in practice.

With implicit integration explained in Section 2, we can overcome this restriction and use a much larger time step while still achieving good smoothing, saving considerable computation. In the next two paragraphs we present one design of a good approximation for the Laplacian.

## 4.2 Simulation of the 1D heat equation

The 1D case of a diffusion equation corresponds to the heat equation $x_t = x_{uu}$. It is therefore worth considering this example as a test problem for higher dimensional filtering. To do so, we use Milne's test presented in [Mil95]. Milne compared two cases of the same initial problem: first, the problem is solved on a regular mesh on $[0,1]$, and then on an irregular mesh, taken to consist of a uniform coarse grid of cells on $[0,1]$ with each of the cells in $[\frac{1}{2},1]$ subdivided into two fine cells as depicted in Figure 6(a) and 6(b). With such a configuration, classical finite difference coefficients for second derivatives can be used on each cell, except for the middle one which does not have centered neighbors. Milne shows that if no particular care is taken for this "peripheral" cell, it introduces a *noise term* that creates large inaccuracies — larger than if the mesh was represented uniformly at the coarser resolution! But if we fit a quadratic spline at this cell to approximate the second derivative, then the noise source disappears and we get more accurate results than with a constant coarse resolution (see the errors created in each case in one iteration of the heat equation in Figure 6(c)).

This actually corresponds to the extension of finite difference computations for irregular meshes proposed by Fornberg [For88]: to compute the FD coefficients, just fit a quadratic function at the sample point and its two immediate neighbors, and then return the first and second derivative of that function as the approximate derivatives. For three points spaced $\Delta$ and $\delta$ apart (see Figure 6(d)), we get the 1D formula:

$$(x_{uu})_i = \frac{2}{\delta+\Delta}\left(\frac{x_{i-1}-x_i}{\delta} + \frac{x_{i+1}-x_i}{\Delta}\right).$$

Note that when $\Delta = \delta$, we find the usual finite difference formula.

## 4.3 Extension to 3D

The umbrella operator suffers from this problem of large inaccuracies for irregular meshes as the same supposedly constant parameterization is used (Figure 7 shows such a behavior). Surprisingly, a simple generalization of the previous formula valid in 1D corresponds to a known approximation of the Laplacian. Indeed, Fujiwara [Fuj95] presents the following formula:

$$\mathcal{L}(x_i) = \frac{2}{E}\sum_{j\in N_1(i)} \frac{x_j - x_i}{|e_{ij}|}, \quad \text{with } E = \sum_{j\in N_1(i)} |e_{ij}|. \qquad (11)$$

where $|e_{ij}|$ is the length of the edge $e_{ij}$. Note that, when all edges are of size 1, this reduces to the umbrella operator (7). We will then denote this new operator as the *scale-dependent umbrella operator*.

Unfortunately, the operator is no longer linear. But during a typical smoothing, the length of the edges does not change dramatically. We thus make the approximation that the coefficients of the matrix $A = (I - \lambda dt \mathcal{L})$ stay constant during an integration step. We can compute them initially using the current edges' lengths and keep their values constant during the PBCG iterations. In practice, we have not noted any noticeable drawbacks from this linearization. We can even keep the same coefficients for a number of (or all) iterations: it will correspond to a filtering "relative" to the initial mesh instead if the current mesh. For the same reason as before, we also recommend the use of the second Laplacian for higher quality smoothing without significant increase in computation time. As demonstrated in Figure 7, the scale-dependent umbrella operator deals better with irregular meshes than the umbrella operator: no spurious artifacts are created. We also applied this operator to noisy data sets from 3D photography to obtain smooth meshes (see Figure 1 and 12).

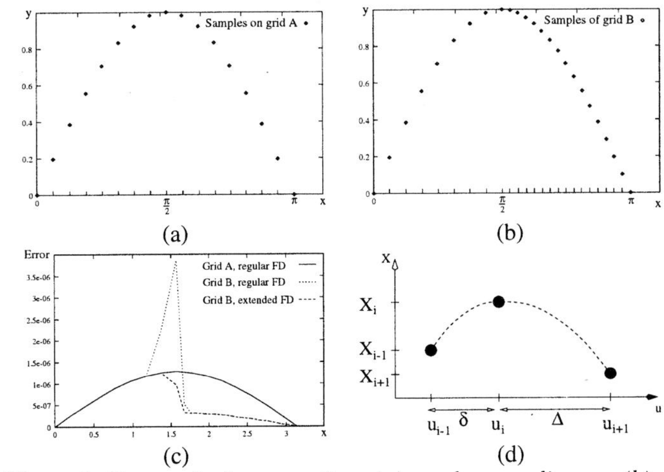


Figure 6: *Test on the heat equation: (a) regular sampling vs. (b) irregular sampling. Numerical errors in one step of integration (c): using the usual FD weight on an irregular grid to approximate second derivatives creates noise, and gives a worse solution than on the coarse grid, whereas extended FD weights offer the expected behavior. (d) Three unevenly spaced samples of a function and corresponding quadratic fitting for extended FD weights.*

The number of iterations needed for convergence depends heavily on the ratio between minimum and maximum edge lengths. For typical smoothing and for meshes over 50000 faces, the average number of iterations we get is 20. Nevertheless, we still observe undesired behavior on flat surfaces: vertices in flat areas still slide during smoothing. Even though this last formulation generally reduces this problem, we may want to keep a flat area *intact*. The next section tackles this problem with a new approach.

# 5 Curvature flow for noise removal

In terms of differential equations, diffusion is a close relative of curvature flow. In this section, we first explore the advantages of using curvature flow over diffusion, and then propose an efficient algorithm for noise removal using curvature flow.

## 5.1 Diffusion vs. curvature flow

The Laplacian of the surface at a vertex has both normal and tangential components. Even if the surface is locally flat, the Laplacian approximation will rarely be the zero vector [KCVS98]. This introduces undesirable drifting over the surface, depending on the parameterization we assume. We in effect fair the parameterization of the surface as well as the shape itself (see Figure 10(b)).

We would prefer to have a noise removal procedure that does not depend on the parameterization. It should use only *intrinsic properties* of the surface. This is precisely what curvature flow does. Curvature flow smoothes the surface by moving along the surface normal $\mathbf{n}$ with a speed equal to the mean curvature $\overline{\kappa}$:

$$\frac{\partial x_i}{\partial t} = -\overline{\kappa}_i\, \mathbf{n}_i. \qquad (12)$$

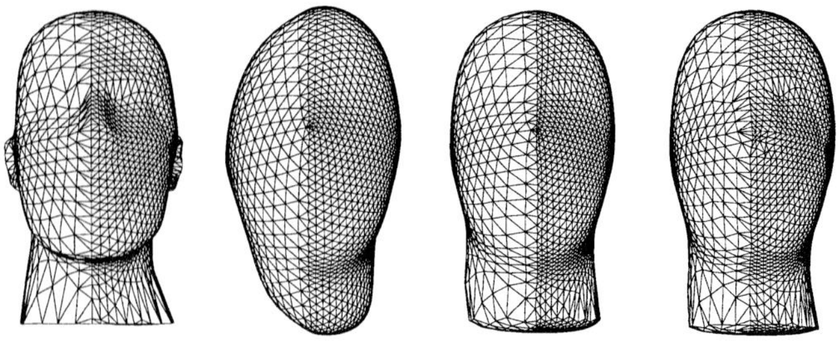

(a) (b) (c) (d)

Figure 7: *Application of operators to a mesh: (a) mesh with different sampling rates, (b) the umbrella operator creates a significant distortion of the shape, but (c) with the scale-dependent umbrella operator, the same amount of smoothing does not create distortion or artifacts, almost like (d) when curvature flow is used. The small features such as the nose are smoothed but stay in place.*

Other curvatures can of course be used, but we will stick to the mean curvature: $\overline{\kappa} = (\kappa_1 + \kappa_2)/2$ in this paper. Using this procedure, a sphere with different sampling rates should stay spherical under curvature flow as the curvature is constant. And we should also not get any vertex "sliding" when an area is flat as the mean curvature is then zero.

There are already different approaches using curvature flow [Set96], and even mixing both curvature flow and volume preservation [DCG98] to smooth object appearance, but mainly in the context of level-set methods. They are not usable on a mesh as is. Next, we show how to approximate curvature consistently on a mesh and how to implement this curvature flow process with our implicit integration for efficient computations.

## 5.2 Curvature normal calculation

It seems that all the formulations so far have a non-zero tangential component on the surface. This means that even if the surface is flat around a vertex, it may move anyway. For curvature flow, we don't want this behavior. A good idea is to check the divergence of the normal vector, as it is the definition of mean curvature ($\overline{\kappa} = div\, \mathbf{n}$): if all the normals of the faces around a vertex are the same, this vertex should not move then (zero curvature). Having this in mind, we have selected the following differential geometry definition of the *curvature normal* $\overline{\kappa}\,\mathbf{n}$:

$$\frac{\nabla \mathcal{A}}{2\,\mathcal{A}} = \overline{\kappa}\,\mathbf{n} \qquad (13)$$

where $\mathcal{A}$ is the area of a small region around the point $P$ where the curvature is needed, and $\nabla$ is the derivative with respect to the $(x, y, z)$ coordinates of $P$. With this definition, we will have the zero vector for a flat area. As proven in Figure 8, we see that moving the center vertex $x_i$ on a flat surface does not change the surface area. On the other hand, moving it above or below the plane will always increase the local area. Hence, we have the desired property of a null area gradient for a locally flat surface, whatever the valence, the aspect ratio of the adjacent faces, or the edge lengths around the vertex.

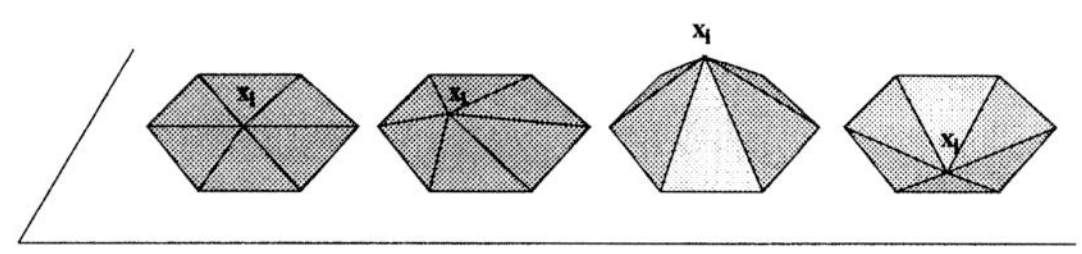

Figure 8: *The area around a vertex $x_i$ lying in the same plane as its 1-ring neighbors does not change if the vertex moves within the plane, and can only increase otherwise. Being a local minimum, it thus proves that the derivative of the area with respect to the position of $x_i$ is zero for flat regions.*

To derive the discrete version of this curvature normal, we select the smallest area around a vertex $x_i$ that we can get, namely the area of all the triangles of the 1-ring neighbors as sketched in Figure 9(a). Note that this area $\mathcal{A}$ uses cross products of adjacent edges, and thus implicitly contains information on local normal vectors. The complete derivation from the continuous formulation to the discrete case is shown in Appendix B. We find the following discrete expression through basic differentiation:

$$-\overline{\kappa}\,\mathbf{n} = \frac{1}{4\,\mathcal{A}} \sum_{j \in N_1(i)} (cot\,\alpha_j + cot\,\beta_j)(x_j - x_i) \qquad (14)$$

where $\alpha_j$ and $\beta_j$ are the two angles opposite to the edge in the two triangles having the edge $e_{ij}$ in common (as depicted in Figure 9(b)), and $\mathcal{A}$ is the sum of the areas of the triangles having $x_i$ as a common vertex.

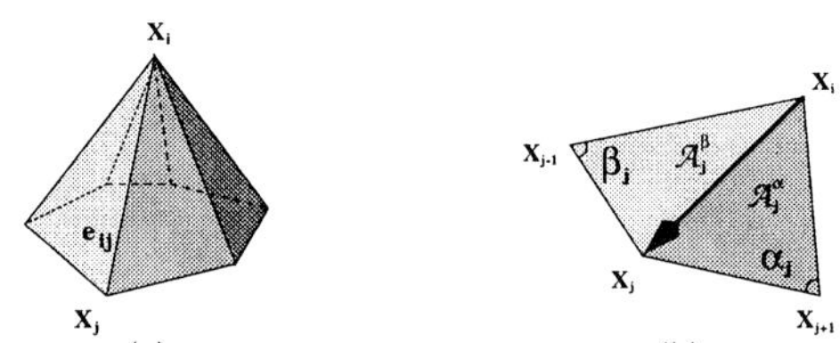

(a) (b)

Figure 9: *A vertex $x_i$ and its adjacent faces (a), and one term of its curvature normal formula (b).*

Note the interesting similarity with [PP93]. We obtain almost the same equation, but with a completely different derivation than theirs, which was using energies of linear maps. The same remark stands for [DCDS97] since they also find the same kind of expression as Equ. (14) for their functional, but using this time piecewise linear harmonic functions.

## 5.3 Boundaries

For non-closed surfaces or surfaces with holes, we can define a special treatment for vertices on boundaries. The notion of mean curvature does not make sense for such vertices. Instead, we would like to smooth the boundary, so that the shape of the hole itself gets rounder and rounder as iterations go. We can then use for instance Equ. (11) restricted to the two immediate neighbors which will smooth the boundary curve itself.

Another possible way is to create a virtual vertex, stored but not displayed, initially placed at the barycenter of all the vertices placed on a closed boundary. A set of faces adjacent to this vertex and connecting the boundary vertices one after the other are also virtually created. We can then use the basic algorithm without any special treatment for the boundary as now, each vertex has a closed area around it.

## 5.4 Implementation

Similarly to Section 4, we have a non-linear expression defining the curvature normal. We can however proceed in exactly the same way, as the changes induced in a time step will be small. We simply compute the non-zero coefficients of the matrix $I - \lambda dtK$, where $K$ represents the matrix of the curvature normals. We then successively solve the following linear system:

$$(I - \lambda dt K)\, X^{n+1} = X^n.$$

We can use preconditioning or constraints, just as before as everything is basically the same except for the local approximation of the speed of smoothing. As shown on Figure 10, a sphere with different triangle sizes will remain the same sphere thanks to both the curvature flow and the volume preservation technique.

In order for the algorithm to be robust, an important test must be performed while the matrix $K$ is computed: if we encounter a face of zero area, we must skip it. As we divide by the area of the face, degenerate triangles are to be treated specially. Mesh decimation to eliminate all degenerate triangles can also be used as suggested in [PP93].

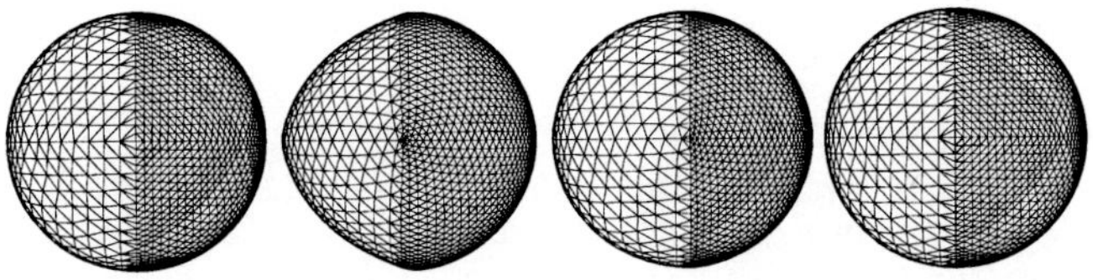

(a) (b) (c) (d)

Figure 10: *Smoothing of spheres: (a) The original mesh containing two different discretization rates. (b) Smoothing with the umbrella operator introduces sliding of the mesh and unnatural deformation, which is largely attenuated when (c) the scale-dependent version is used, while (d) curvature flow maintains the sphere exactly.*

### 5.5 Normalized version of the curvature operator

We can now write the equivalent of the umbrella operator, but for the curvature normal. Since the new formulation has nice properties, we can create a normalized version that could be used in an explicit integration for quick smoothing. The normalization will bring the eigenvalues back in $[-1,0]$ so that a time step up to 1 can be used in explicit integration methods. Its expression is simply:

$$(\bar{\kappa}\,\mathbf{n})_{normalized} = \frac{1}{\sum_j (cot\ \alpha_j^l + cot\ \alpha_j^r)} \sum_j (cot\ \alpha_j^l + cot\ \alpha_j^r)(X_i - X_j)$$

### 5.6 Comparison of results

Figures 7, 10, and 11 compare the different operators we have used:

- For significant fairing, the umbrella operator changes the shape of the object substantially: triangles drift over the surface and tend to be uniformly distributed with an equal size.
- The scale-dependent umbrella operator allows the shape to stay closer to the original shape even after significant smoothing, and almost keeps the original distribution of triangle sizes.
- Finally, the curvature flow just described achieves the best smoothing with respect to the shape, as no drift happens and only geometric properties are used to define the motion.

Knowing these properties, the user can select the type of smoothing that fits best with the type of fairing that is desired. Diffusion will smooth the shape along with the parameterization, resulting in a more regular triangulation. If only the shape is to be affected, then the curvature operator should be used.

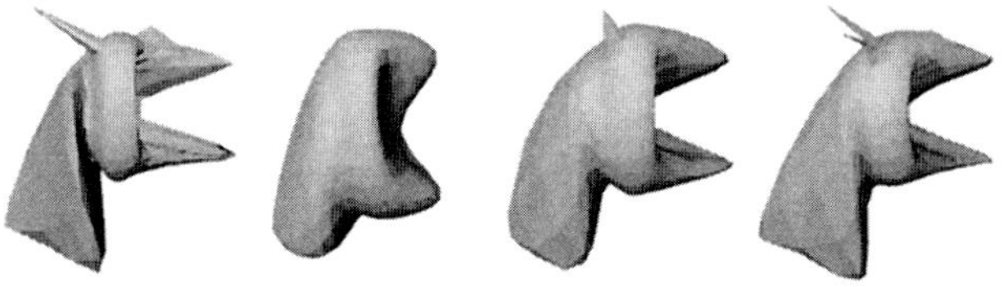

(a) (b) (c) (d)

Figure 11: *Significant smoothing of a dragon: (a) original mesh, (b) implicit fairing using the umbrella operator, (c) using the scale-dependent umbrella operator, and (d) using curvature flow.*

## 6 Discussion and conclusion

In this paper, we have presented a comprehensive set of tools for mesh fairing. We first presented an *implicit fairing* method, using implicit integration of a diffusion process that allows for both efficiency, quality, and stability. Additionally we guarantee volume preservation during smoothing. Since the umbrella operator used in the literature appears to have serious drawbacks, we defined a new scale-dependent umbrella operator to overcome undesired effects such as large distortions on irregular meshes. Finally, since using a diffusion process leads always to vertex "sliding" on the mesh, we developed a curvature flow process. The same implicit integration is used for this new operator that now offers a smoothing only depending on intrinsic geometric properties, without sliding on flat areas and with preserved curvature for constant curvature areas. The user can make use of all these different tools according to the mesh to be smoothed.

We believe the computational time for this approach can still be improved upon. We expect that multigrid preconditioning for the PBCG in the case of the scale-dependent operator for diffusion and for curvature flow would speed up the integration process. This multigrid aspect of mesh fairing has already been mentioned in [KCVS98], and could be easily extended to our method. Likewise, subdivision techniques can be directly incorporated into our method to refine or simplify regions according to curvature for instance. Other curvature flows, for example along the principal curvature directions, are also worth studying.

### Acknowledgements

The original 3D photography mesh was provided by Jean-Yves Bouguet, the mannequin head and spock dataset by Hugues Hoppe, the bunny and buddha models by Stanford University, and additional test meshes by Cyberware. The authors would like to thank John T. Reese for the initial implementation and the dragon mesh, and Konrad Polthier for interesting comments. This work was supported by the Academic Strategic Alliances Program of the Accelerated Strategic Computing Initiative (ASCI/ASAP) under subcontract B341492 of DOE contract W-7405-ENG-48. Additional support was provided by NSF (ACI-9624957, ACI-9721349, DMS-9874082, and ASC-89-20219 (STC for Computer Graphics and Scientific Visualization)), Alias|wavefront and through a Packard Fellowship.

### References


[Bar89] Alan H. Barr. The Einstein Summation Notation: Introduction and Extensions. In *SIGGRAPH 89 Course notes #30 on Topics in Physically-Based Modeling*, pages J1–J12, 1989.

[BW98] David Baraff and Andrew Witkin. Large Steps in Cloth Simulation. In *SIGGRAPH 98 Conference Proceedings*, pages 43–54, July 1998.

[CL96] Brian Curless and Marc Levoy. A Volumetric Method for Building Complex Models from Range Images. In *SIGGRAPH 96 Conference Proceedings*, pages 303–312, 1996.

[DCDS97] Tom Duchamp, Andrew Certain, Tony DeRose, and Werner Stuetzle. Hierarchical computation of PL harmonic embeddings. Technical report, University of Washington, July 1997.

[DCG98] Mathieu Desbrun and Marie-Paule Cani-Gascuel. Active Implicit Surface for Computer Animation. In *Graphics Interface (GI'98) Proceedings*, pages 143–150, Vancouver, Canada, 1998.

[For88] Bengt Fornberg. Generation of Finite Difference Formulas on Arbitrarily Spaced Grids. *Math. Comput.*, 51:699–706, 1988.

[Fuj95] Koji Fujiwara. Eigenvalues of Laplacians on a closed riemannian manifold and its nets. In *Proceedings of AMS 123*, pages 2585–2594, 1995.

[GSS99] Igor Guskov, Wim Sweldens, and Peter Schröder. Multiresolution Signal Processing for Meshes. In *SIGGRAPH 99 Conference Proceedings*, 1999

[KCVS98] Leif Kobbelt, Swen Campagna, Jens Vorsatz, and Hans-Peter Seidel. Interactive Multi-Resolution Modeling on Arbitrary Meshes. In *SIGGRAPH 98 Conference Proceedings*, pages 105–114, July 1998.

[Kob97] Leif Kobbelt. Discrete Fairing. In *Proceedings of the Seventh IMA Conference on the Mathematics of Surfaces '97*, pages 101–131, 1997.

[LK84] S. Lien and J. Kajiya. A Symbolic Method for Calculating the Integral Properties of Arbitrary Nonconvex Polyhedra. *IEEE CG&A*, 4(9), October 1984.

[Mil95] Roger B. Milne. An Adaptive Level-Set Method. *PhD Thesis*, University of California, Berkeley, December 1995.

[PP93] Ulrich Pinkall and Konrad Polthier. Computing Discrete Minimal Surfaces and Their Conjugates. *Experimental Mathematics*, 2(1):15–36, 1993.

[PTVF92] William Press, Saul Teukolsky, William Vetterling, and Brian Flannery. *Numerical Recipes in C, second edition*. Cambridge University Press, New York, USA, 1992.

[Set96] James A. Sethian. *Level-Set Methods: Evolving Interfaces in Geometry, Fluid Dynamics, Computer Vision, and Material Science*. Cambridge Monographs on Applied and Computational Mathematics, 1996.

[Tau95] Gabriel Taubin. A Signal Processing Approach to Fair Surface Design. In *SIGGRAPH 95 Conference Proceedings*, pages 351–358, August 1995.

[Ter88] Demetri Terzopoulos. The Computation of Visible-Surface Representations. *IEEE Transactions on Pattern Analysis and Machine Intelligence*, 10(4), July 1988.

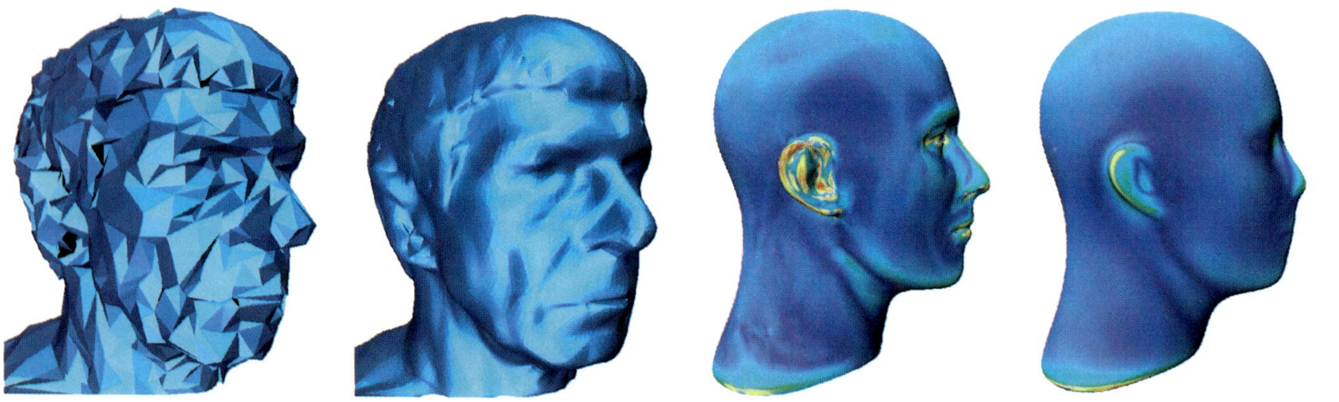

(a) (b) (c) (d)

Figure 12: *Faces: (a) The original decimated Spock mesh has 12,000 vertices. (b) We linearly oversampled this initial mesh (every visible triangle on (a) was subdivided in 16 coplanar smaller ones) and applied the scale-dependent umbrella operator, observing significant smoothing. One integration step was used, $\lambda dt = 10$, converging in 12 iterations of the PBCG. Similar results were achieved using the curvature operator. (c) curvature plot for the mannequin head (obtained using our curvature operator), (d) curvature plot of the same mesh after a significant implicit integration of curvature flow (pseudo-colors).*

[WW94] Willian Welch and Andrew Witkin. Free-form shape design using triangulated surfaces. In *SIGGRAPH 94 Conference Proceedings*, pages 247–256, July 1994.

# Appendix

## A Preconditioned Bi-Conjugate Gradient

In this section, we enumerate the different implementation choices we made for the PBCG linear solver.

### A.1 Preconditioning

A good preconditioning, and particularly a multigrid preconditioning, can drastically improve the convergence rate of conjugate gradient solver. The umbrella operator (7) has all its eigenvalues in $[-1,0]$: in turn, the matrix $A$ is always well conditioned for typical values of $\lambda dt$. In practice, the simpler the conditioning the better. In our examples, we used the usual diagonal preconditioner $\tilde{A}$ with: $\tilde{A}_{ii} = 1/A_{ii}$, which provides a significant speedup with almost no overhead.

### A.2 Convergence criterion

Different criteria can be used to test whether or not further iterations are needed to get a more accurate solution of the linear system. We opted for the following stopping criterion after several tests: $||AX^{n+1} - X^n|| < \varepsilon ||X^n||$, where $||.||$ can be either the $L_2$ norm, or, if high accuracy is needed, the $L_\infty$ norm.

### A.3 Memory requirements

An interesting remark is that we don't even need to store the matrix $A$ in a dedicated data structure. The mesh itself provides a sparse matrix representation, as the vertex $x_i$ and its neighbors are the only non-zero locations in $A$ for row $i$. Computations can thus be carried directly within the mesh structure. Computing $AX$ can be implemented by gathering values from the 1-ring neighbors of each vertex, while $A^T X$ can be achieved by "shooting" a value to the 1-ring neighbors.

With these simple setups, we obtain an efficient linear solver for the implicit integration described in Section 2.

## B Curvature normal approximation

From the continuous definition of the curvature normal (Equ. (13)), we must derive a discrete formulation when the surface is given as a mesh. Let's consider a point $P$ of the mesh. Its neighbors, in counterclockwise order around $P$, are the points $\{Q^n\}$. An adjacent face is then of the form $P, Q^n, Q^{n+1}$. The edge vector $PQ^n$ is the difference between $Q^n$ and $P$:

$$PQ^n = Q^n - P.$$

Now, we take the neighboring area as being the union of the adjacent faces. The total adjacent area $\mathcal{A}$ is then equal to the sum of every adjacent face's area: $\mathcal{A} = \sum_n \mathcal{A}_n$, the area of each adjacent face being: $\mathcal{A}_n = \frac{1}{2}||PQ^n \times PQ^{n+1}||$. So, using Einstein summation notation [Bar89], we have:

$$\mathcal{A}_n^2 = \frac{1}{4}\varepsilon_{ijk}\, PQ_j^n\, PQ_k^{n+1}\, \varepsilon_{ilm}\, PQ_l^n\, PQ_m^{n+1},$$

where $\varepsilon_{ijk}$ is the permutation symbol. Using the Kronecker delta $\delta_{ij}$, and using $\frac{\partial P_i}{\partial P_q} = \delta_{iq}$ as well as $\nabla = \partial/\partial P_q$, we derive:

$$\begin{aligned}
\frac{\partial \mathcal{A}_i^2}{\partial P_q} &= 2\,\mathcal{A}_i \frac{\partial \mathcal{A}_i}{\partial P_q} \\
&= \frac{1}{4}\varepsilon_{ijk}\varepsilon_{ilm}\Big[-\delta_{jq}\, PQ_k^{n+1}\, PQ_l^n PQ_m^{n+1} - \delta_{kq}\, PQ_j^n\, PQ_l^n\, PQ_m^{n+1} \\
&\quad -\delta_{lq}\, PQ_j^n\, PQ_k^{n+1}\, PQ_m^{n+1} - \delta_{mq}\, PQ_j^n\, PQ_k^{n+1}\, PQ_l^{n+1}\Big]
\end{aligned}$$

Using the $\varepsilon$-$\delta$ rule stating $\varepsilon_{ijk}\varepsilon_{ilm} = \delta_{jl}\delta_{km} - \delta_{jm}\delta_{kl}$, we obtain:

$$\begin{aligned}
\frac{\partial \mathcal{A}_i^2}{\partial P_q} &= \frac{1}{2}\Big[-||PQ^{n+1}||^2\, PQ^n + (PQ^n \cdot PQ^{n+1})\, PQ^{n+1} \\
&\quad -||PQ^n||^2\, PQ^{n+1} + (PQ^{n+1} \cdot PQ^n)\, PQ^n\Big]_q \\
&= \frac{1}{2}\Big[(PQ^{n+1} \cdot Q^{n+1}Q^n)\, PQ^n + (PQ^n \cdot Q^nQ^{n+1})\, PQ^{n+1}\Big]_q.
\end{aligned}$$

Consequently:

$$\frac{\partial \mathcal{A}_i}{\partial P} = \frac{1}{4\,\mathcal{A}_i}\Big((PQ^{n+1} \cdot Q^{n+1}Q^n)\, PQ^n + (PQ^n \cdot Q^nQ^{n+1})\, PQ^{n+1}\Big). \tag{15}$$

Using Equ. (13), we find:

$$\frac{\nabla \mathcal{A}}{2\,\mathcal{A}} = \frac{1}{2\,\mathcal{A}} \sum_i \frac{\partial \mathcal{A}_i}{\partial P} \tag{16}$$

From equations (15) and (16), we find the equations used in Section 5.2 since the dot product of $PQ^n$ by $Q^nQ^{n+1}$ divided by their cross product simplifies into a cotangent.

# Multiresolution Signal Processing for Meshes

Igor Guskov
Princeton University

Wim Sweldens
Bell Laboratories

Peter Schröder
Caltech

Figure 1: *Mount Meshmore (Design Khrysaundt Koenig).*

## Abstract

We generalize basic signal processing tools such as downsampling, upsampling, and filters to irregular connectivity triangle meshes. This is accomplished through the design of a non-uniform relaxation procedure whose weights depend on the geometry and we show its superiority over existing schemes whose weights depend only on connectivity. This is combined with known mesh simplification methods to build subdivision and pyramid algorithms. We demonstrate the power of these algorithms through a number of application examples including smoothing, enhancement, editing, and texture mapping.

**CR Categories and Subject Descriptors:** I.3.5 [**Computer Graphics**]: Computational Geometry and Object Modeling - *hierarchy and geometric transformations, object hierarchies*; I.4.3 [**Image Processing and Computer Vision**]: Enhancement - *filtering, geometric correction, sharpening and deblurring, smoothing*; G.1.2 [**Numerical Analysis**]: Approximation - *approximation of surfaces and contours, wavelets and fractals*

**Additional Keywords:** Meshes, subdivision, irregular connectivity, surface parameterization, multiresolution, wavelets, Laplacian Pyramid.



## 1 Introduction

3D range sensing is capable of producing detailed and densely sampled triangular meshes of high quality. Increasing deployment of this technology in the automotive and entertainment industries, as well as many other areas, has fueled the need for algorithms to process such datasets. Examples include editing, simplification, denoising, compression, and finite element simulation.

In the case of regularly sampled data, for example images, basic signal processing tools such as filtering, subsampling, and upsampling exist. These can be used to build subdivision and pyramid algorithms, which are useful in many applications. Our goal is the construction of signal processing style analyses and algorithms for triangle meshes.

Building the elements of a signal processing toolbox for meshes is not immediately straightforward since there are essential differences between images, for example, and meshes. Images are functions defined on Euclidean ("flat") geometry and are almost always sampled on a regular grid. Consequently, algorithms such as subsampling and upsampling are straightforward to define, and uniform filtering methods are appropriate. This makes Fourier analysis an elegant and efficient tool for the construction and analysis of signal processing algorithms.

In contrast, triangle meshes of arbitrary connectivity form an inherently irregular sampling setting. Additionally we are dealing with general 2-manifolds as opposed to a Euclidean space. Consequently new algorithms need to be developed which incorporate the fundamental differences between images and meshes.

A crucial first observation concerns the difference between geometric and parametric smoothness. *Geometric* smoothness measures how much triangle normals vary over the mesh. Geometric

**Terminology**

In order to describe our contribution and its relationship to existing work we need to set some terminology. Among triangulations we distinguish three types

- **Regular:** every vertex has degree six;
- **Irregular:** vertices can have any degree;
- **Semi-regular:** formed by starting with a coarse irregular triangulation and performing repeated quadrisection on all triangles. Coarse vertices have arbitrary degree while all other vertices have degree six.

In all cases we assume that any triangulation is a proper 2-manifold with boundary. On the boundary regular vertices have degree four. Each of these triangulations call for different filtering and subdivision algorithms:

- **Uniform:** fixed coefficient stencils everywhere; typically used only on regular triangulations;
- **Non-uniform:** filter coefficients depend on the connectivity *and* geometry of the triangulation;
- **Semi-uniform:** coefficients of filters depend only on the (local) connectivity of the triangulation; typically used on semi-regular triangulations.

Using our terminology, for example, traditional subdivision [22] uses semi-uniform filters on semi-regular meshes.

smoothness implies that there exists *some* smooth (differentiable) parameterization of the mesh. However, any particular parameterization may well be non-smooth. The smoothness of the parameterizations is important in most numerical algorithms, which work only with the coordinate functions the user provides. The algorithms' behavior, such as convergence rates or the quality of the results, generally depends strongly on the smoothness of the coordinate functions.

In the regular setting of an image, or the knots of a uniform tensor product spline, we may simply use a uniform parameterization and will get parametric smoothness wherever there is geometric smoothness. In the irregular triangle mesh setting there is a priori no such "obvious" parameterization. In this case using a uniformity assumption leads to parametric non-smoothness with undesirable consequences for further processing. One approach to remedy this situation is the use of remeshing [8, 19], which maintains the original geometric smoothness, but improves the sampling to vary smoothly. This enables subsequent treatment with a uniform parameter assumption without detrimental effects. Here we wish to build tools which work on the original meshes directly.

To understand the role of the parameterization further, consider traditional subdivision [22], such as Loop or Catmull-Clark. In the signal processing context, subdivision can be seen as upsampling followed by filtering. One starts with an arbitrary connectivity mesh and uses regular upsampling techniques such as triangle quadrisection to obtain a semi-regular triangulation. The subdivision weights depend only on connectivity, not geometry. Such stencils can be designed with existing Fourier or spectral techniques. These schemes result in geometrically smooth limit surfaces with smooth semi-uniform parameterizations. Because traditional subdivision is only concerned with *refinement* one has the freedom to choose regular upsampling, and semi-uniform schemes suffice.

The picture changes entirely if we wish to compute a mesh pyramid, i.e., we want to be able to *coarsify* a given fine irregular mesh and later *refine* it again. We then need to filter, downsample, upsample and filter again. The downsampling typically involves a standard mesh simplification hierarchy. When subdividing back, we want to build a mesh with the *same* connectivity as the original mesh and a smooth geometry. This time the upsampling procedure is determined by reversing the previously computed simplification hierarchy. We no longer have a choice as in the classical subdivision setting. Consequently the filters used before downsampling and after upsampling should use non-uniform weights, which depend on the local parameterization. The challenge is to ensure that these local parameterizations are smooth so that subsequent algorithms act on the geometry and not some potentially bad parameterization.

## 1.1 Contributions

In this paper we present a series of non-uniform signal processing algorithms designed for irregular triangulations and show their usefulness in several application areas. Specifically, we make the following contributions:

- We show how the non-uniform subdivision algorithm of Guskov [12] can be used for geometric smoothing of triangle meshes. Our scheme is fast, local, and straightforward to implement.
- We use the smoothing algorithm combined with existing hierarchy methods to build subdivision, pyramid, and wavelet algorithms for irregular connectivity meshes.
- We show how these signal processing algorithms can be used in applications such as smoothing, enhancement, editing, animation, and texture mapping.

## 1.2 Related Work

In our approach we draw on observations made by researchers in several different areas. These include classical subdivision [22], which we generalize to the irregular setting with the help of mesh simplification [13] and careful attention to the role of smooth parameterizations. Parameterizations were examined in the context of remeshing [19, 8, 9], texture mapping (e.g., [20]), and variational modeling [16, 28, 21]. One area which employs these elements is hierarchical editing for semi-regular [29] and irregular meshes [18].

Signal processing as an approach to surface fairing in the irregular setting was first considered by Taubin [26, 27]. He defines frequencies as the eigenvectors of a discrete Laplacian generalized to irregular triangulations. The resulting smoothing schemes were used to denoise meshes, apply smooth deformations, and build semi-uniform subdivision over irregular meshes. Our approach is related to Taubin's and can be seen as a generalization to the non-uniform setting. In particular we build a smoothing method by minimizing multivariate finite differences. Together with progressive mesh simplification [14] we use these to define a non-uniform subdivision scheme and pyramid algorithm on top of an irregular mesh hierarchy.

Progressive meshes and a semi-uniform discrete Laplacian were used by Kobbelt et al. [18] to perform multiresolution editing on irregular meshes. Given some region of the mesh, discrete fairing is used to compute a smoothed version with the same connectivity. This smoothed region is deformed and offsets to the original mesh are added back in. Kobbelt discusses the issue of geometric vs. parametric smoothing. Smoothing of irregular meshes based on uniform approximations of the Laplacian results in vertex motion "within" the surface, even in a perfectly planar triangulation. It is geometrically smooth, yet the parameter functions appear non-smooth due to a non-uniform parameterization. This has undesirable effects in a hierarchical setting in which fine levels are defined as offsets ("details") from a coarse level: using the difference between topologically corresponding vertices in the original and smoothed mesh can lead to large detail vectors [18, Figure 4]. To minimize the size of detail vectors they employed a search procedure to find the nearest vertex on the smoothed mesh to a given vertex on the original mesh. This diminishes the advantage of having a smoothed version with the exact same connectivity. In contrast, our non-uniform smoothing scheme affects only geometric smoothness and so does not need a search procedure. We will present two ways in which our scheme can be used for editing: one is based on multiresolution and combines the work of Kobbelt et al. [18] with the ideas of Zorin et al. [29]. The other method relies on defining vector displacement fields with controllable decay similar to the ideas presented in the work of Singh and Fiume [23].

We construct our subdivision scheme by designing a non-uniform relaxation operator which minimizes second differences. This is motivated by the smoothness analysis of the 1D irregular setting [2]. This analysis relies on the decay of divided differences, carefully designed to respect the underlying parameterization. These ideas were extended to the multi-variate setting in [12] and we employ them here. While the schemes we present have many nice properties and work very well in practice, we note that their analytic smoothness is currently unknown.

# 2 Signal Processing Algorithms

Before describing the actual numerical algorithms we begin with some remarks regarding different settings and establish our notation for triangulations and difference operators defined on them.

**Coordinate Functions** To describe our algorithms we must distinguish between two settings: the functional and the surface setting. The *functional setting* deals with a function $g(u, v)$ of two independent variables in the plane. The dependent variable $g$ can be visualized as height above the $(u, v)$ parameter plane. In practice we only have discrete data $g_i = g(u_i, v_i)$. The sample points $(u_i, v_i)$ are triangulated in the plane and this connectivity can be transferred to the corresponding points $(u_i, v_i, g_i)$ in $\mathbf{R}^3$. The canonical example of this is a terrain model.

The *surface setting* deals with a triangle mesh of arbitrary topology and connectivity embedded in $\mathbf{R}^3$ with vertices $p_i = (x_i, y_i, z_i)$. It is important to treat all three coordinates $x$, $y$, and $z$ as *dependent* variables with independent parameters $u$ and $v$, giving us three functional settings. The independent parameters are typically unknown and must be estimated. Algorithms to estimate *global* smooth parameterizations are described in [19, 8, 9, 20]. We require only *local* parameterizations which are consistent over the support of a small filter stencil.

**Triangulations** To talk about local neighborhoods of vertices within the mesh it is convenient to describe the topological and geometric aspects of a mesh separately. We use notation inspired by [24]. A triangle mesh is denoted as a pair $(\mathcal{P}, \mathcal{K})$, where $\mathcal{P}$ is a set of $N$ point positions $\mathcal{P} = \{p_i \in \mathbf{R}^3 \mid 1 \leq i \leq N\}$ (either $p_i = (u_i, v_i, f_i)$ in a functional setting or $p_i = (x_i, y_i, z_i)$ in the surface setting), and $\mathcal{K}$ is an *abstract simplicial complex* which contains all the topological, i.e., adjacency information. The complex $\mathcal{K}$ is a set of subsets of $\{1, \ldots, N\}$. These subsets are called simplices and come in three types: vertices $v = \{i\} \in \mathcal{V}$, edges $e = \{i, j\} \in \mathcal{E}$, and faces $f = \{i, j, k\} \in \mathcal{F}$, so that $\mathcal{K} = \mathcal{V} \cup \mathcal{E} \cup \mathcal{F}$. Two vertices $i$ and $j$ are *neighbors* if $\{i, j\} \in \mathcal{E}$. The 1-ring neighbors of a vertex $i$ form a set $\mathcal{V}_1(i) = \{j \mid \{i, j\} \in \mathcal{E}\}$ (see Figure 2, left). $K_i = \#\mathcal{V}_1(i)$ is the *degree* of $i$. The edges from $i$ to its neighbors form a set $\mathcal{E}_1(i) = \{\{i, j\} \mid j \in \mathcal{V}_1(i)\}$. A 1-ring neighborhood with flaps is shown in Figure 2 (middle). Its vertices except the center vertex form a set $\mathcal{V}_2(i)$ and its interior edges form a set $\mathcal{E}_2(i)$. Finally, the neighborhood $\omega(e)$ of an edge (see Figure 2) is formed by the 4 vertices of its incident triangles.

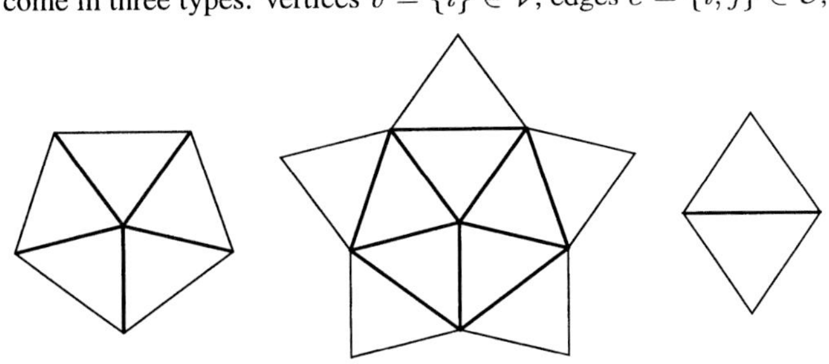

Figure 2: *Left: 1-ring neighborhood. The vertices except the center one form $\mathcal{V}_1(i)$ and the bold edges form $\mathcal{E}_1(i)$. Middle: 1-ring with flaps. The vertices except the center one form $\mathcal{V}_2(i)$ and the bold edges form $\mathcal{E}_2(i)$. Right: Edge neighborhood. The four vertices of the incident triangles form $\omega(e)$.*

The *geometric realization* $\varphi(s)$ of a simplex $s$ is defined as the strictly convex hull of the points $p_i$ with $i \in s$. The polyhedron $\varphi(\mathcal{K})$ is defined as $\cup_{s \in \mathcal{K}} \varphi(s)$ and consists of points, segments, and triangles in $\mathbf{R}^3$.

## 2.1 Divided Differences in the Functional Setting

Our relaxation algorithm relies on minimizing divided differences. In the one dimensional setting divided differences are straightforward to define, but for multivariate settings many approaches are possible (see for example [10, 4, 3]). An approach that was developed specifically with subdivision in mind is described in [12] and we use it here for our purposes.

Consider a face $f = \{i, j, k\}$ and the triangle $t = \varphi(f)$ where $p_i = (u_i, v_i, g_i)$. Then the first order divided difference of $g$ at $f$ is simply the gradient of the piecewise linear spline interpolating $g$ denoted by $\nabla_f g = (\partial g/\partial u, \partial g/\partial v)$. Note that the gradient depends on the parameter locations $(u_i, v_i)$ and converges in the limit to the first partial derivatives. If we create a three vector by adding a third component equal to 1, we obtain the normal $n_f = (-\partial g/\partial u, -\partial g/\partial v, 1)$ to the triangle $t$. Conversely, the gradient is the projection of the normal in the parameter plane. Consequently the gradient is zero only if the triangle $t$ is horizontal ($g_i = g_j = g_k$).

Second order differences are defined as the difference between two normals on neighboring triangles and can be associated with the common edge (see Figure 3, left). Consider an edge $e = \{j, k\}$ with its two incident faces $f_1 = \{j, k, l_1\}$ and $f_2 = \{j, k, l_2\}$ (see Figure 2, right). Compute the difference between the two normals $m_e = n_{f_2} - n_{f_1}$. Given that the two normals are orthogonal to $\varphi(e)$ so is their difference $m_e$ (see Figure 3, right). But the third component of $m_e$ is zero, hence $m_e$ itself lies in the parameter plane, which also contains the segment between $(u_j, v_j, 0)$ and $(u_k, v_k, 0)$. This implies that $m_e$ is orthogonal to the segment and hence only its signed magnitude matters (see Figure 3).

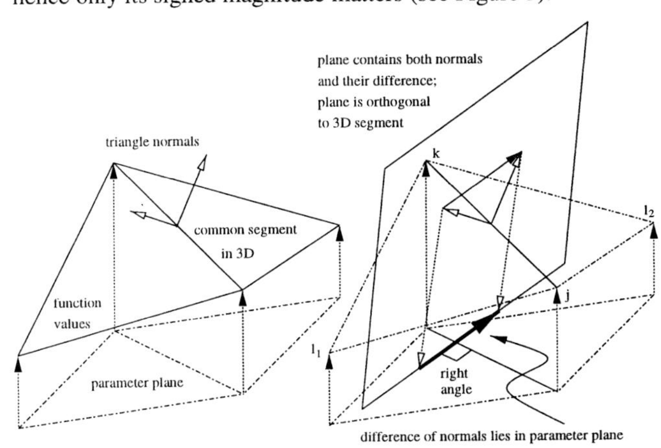


Figure 3: *In the functional setting triangles are erected over the parameter plane. Their normals generate a plane orthogonal to the edge in 3-space. Any vector in that plane which is also in the parameter plane must be at right angles with the parameter plane segment. Hence $D_e^2$ is orthogonal to $(u_j, v_j) - (u_k, v_k)$.*

This argument justifies defining the second order difference $D_e^2 g$ as the component of $m_e$ orthogonal to the segment in the parameter plane. $D_e^2 g$ depends on four function values at vertices $\omega(e) = \{j, k, l_1, l_2\}$. Since all operations to compute $D_e^2 g$ are linear (gradient, difference, and projection) so is the entire expression

$$D_e^2 g = \sum_{l \in \omega(e)} c_{e,l} g_l.$$

The coefficients are given by

$$c_{e,l_1} = \frac{L_e}{A_{[l_1,k,j]}}, \quad c_{e,l_2} = \frac{L_e}{A_{[l_2,j,k]}},$$

$$c_{e,j} = -\frac{L_e A_{[k,l_2,l_1]}}{A_{[l_1,k,j]}\,A_{[l_2,j,k]}}, \quad c_{e,k} = -\frac{L_e A_{[j,l_1,l_2]}}{A_{[l_1,k,j]}\,A_{[l_2,j,k]}}, \tag{1}$$

where $A_{[k_1,k_2,k_3]}$ is the signed area of the triangle formed by $(u_{k_1}, v_{k_1})$, $(u_{k_2}, v_{k_2})$, $(u_{k_3}, v_{k_3})$; and $L_e$ is the length of the segment between $(u_j, v_j)$ and $(u_k, v_k)$ [12]. All the parameterization information is captured in the edge length and signed triangle areas. Given that we later only use squares of $D_e^2$ the actual sign of the areas is not important as long as the orientations prescribed by (1) are consistent. Also, note that the second order difference operator is zero only if the two triangles lie in the same plane.

## 2.2 Relaxation in the Functional Setting

The central ingredient in our signal processing toolbox is a non-uniform relaxation operator. It generalizes the usual notion of a low pass filter. We begin by discussing the construction of such a relaxation operator in the functional setting.

The purpose of the relaxation operation is the minimization of second order differences. To this end we define a quadratic energy, which is an instance of a discrete fairing functional [16]

$$\mathbf{E} = \textstyle\sum_{e \in \mathcal{E}} (D_e^2 g)^2.$$

The relaxation is computed locally, i.e., for a given vertex $i$ we compute a relaxed function value $Rg_i$ based on neighboring function values $g_j$. Treating $\mathbf{E}$ as a function of a given $g_i$ the relaxed value $Rg_i$ is defined as the minimizer of $\mathbf{E}(g_i)$. Given that the stencil for $D_e^2$ consists of two triangles, all edges which affect $\mathbf{E}(g_i)$ belong to $\mathcal{E}_2(i)$ (see Figure 2, middle)

$$Rg_i = \arg\min \mathbf{E}(g_i) = \arg\min \textstyle\sum_{e \in \mathcal{E}_2(i)} (D_e^2 g)^2. \tag{2}$$

Since the functional is quadratic the relaxation operator is linear in the function values. To find the expression, write each of the $D_e^2 g$ with $e \in \mathcal{E}_2(i)$, i.e., all second differences depending on $g_i$, as a linear function of $g_i$

$$D_e^2 g = c_{e,i} g_i + \alpha_e \text{ with } \alpha_e = \textstyle\sum_{l \in \omega(e) \setminus \{i\}} c_{e,l} g_l.$$

Setting the partial derivative of $\mathbf{E}$ with respect to $g_i$ equal to zero yields

$$Rg_i = -\left(\textstyle\sum_{e \in \mathcal{E}_2(i)} c_{e,i}\,\alpha_e\right) / \left(\textstyle\sum_{e \in \mathcal{E}_2(i)} c_{e,i}^2\right), \tag{3}$$

which can be rewritten as

$$Rg_i = \textstyle\sum_{j \in \mathcal{V}_2(i)} w_{i,j} g_j, \quad w_{i,j} = -\frac{\sum_{\{e \in \mathcal{E}_2(i) | j \in \omega(e)\}} c_{e,i} c_{e,j}}{\sum_{e \in \mathcal{E}_2(i)} c_{e,i}^2}.$$

There are two ways to implement $R$ which trade off speed versus memory. One can either precompute and store the $w_{i,j}$ and use the above expression or one can use (3) and compute $R$ on the fly.

Note that if $g$ is a linear function, i.e., all triangles lie in one plane, the fairing functional $\mathbf{E}$ is zero. Consequently linear functions are invariant under $R$. In particular $R$ preserves constants from which we deduce that the $w_{i,j}$ sum to one.

To summarize, given an arbitrary but fixed triangulation in the parameter plane and function values $g_i$ with the associated $(u_i, v_i)$ coordinates, simple linear expressions describe first and second differences. The coefficients of these expressions depend on the parameterization. The relaxation operator $R$ acts on individual function values to minimize the discrete second difference energy over the $\mathcal{E}_2(i)$ neighborhood of a given $p_i = (u_i, v_i, g_i)$, leaving linears invariant.

## 2.3 Relaxation in the Surface Setting

To apply the above relaxation in the surface setting we need to have parameter values $(u, v)$ associated with every point in our mesh. Typically such parameter values are not available and we must compute them. One possible solution is to compute a global parameterization to a coarse base domain using approaches such as those described in [8, 19]. However, specifying parameter values for an entire region is equivalent to flattening that region and thus invariably introduces distortion. Therefore we wish to keep the parameter regions as small as possible. Typically one computes parameter values for a certain local neighborhood like a 1-ring. We propose an even more local scheme in which parameter values are specified *separately* for each of the $D_e^2$ stencils. The two triangles of the $D_e^2$ stencil get flattened with the so-called *hinge map*: using the common edge as a hinge, rotate one triangle until it lies in the plane defined by the other triangle and compute the needed edge lengths and areas from (1). Note that the hinge map leaves the areas of the triangles $\varphi(f_1)$ and $\varphi(f_2)$ unchanged and only affects the faces $\{j, k, l_1\}$ and $\{j, k, l_2\}$. The surface relaxation operator is defined as before, but acts on points in $\mathbf{R}^3$

$$Rp_i = \textstyle\sum_{j \in \mathcal{V}_2(i)} w_{i,j} p_j.$$

Our minimization is similar to minimizing dihedral angles [21]. However, minimizing exact dihedral angles is difficult as the expressions depend non-linearly on the points. Instead one can think of the $D_e^2$ as a linear expression which behaves like the dihedral angle.

**Features** With our scheme it is particularly easy to deal with features in the mesh. Examples include sharp edges across which one does not wish to smooth. In that case the $D_e^2$ associated with those edges are simply removed from the functional.

One may worry what happens with the equations in (1) in case one of the triangles is degenerate, i.e., two of its points coincide and its area is zero. Then the $D_e^2$ that use this triangle are not defined and simply can be left out from the optimization. This is similar to coinciding knots in the case of splines.

**Comparison with Existing Schemes** The approach followed in [18] is to assume that the 1-ring neighborhood of a vertex $i$ is parameterized over a regular $K_i$-gon. Using this approximation a discrete Laplacian, dubbed umbrella, is computed as

$$Lp_i = K_i^{-1} \textstyle\sum_{j \in \mathcal{V}_1(i)} p_j - p_i.$$

This discrete Laplacian was used in a relaxation operator $R = I + L$ which replaces a vertex with the average of its 1-ring neighbors.

In our setting, we can build a 1-ring relaxation scheme by only taking the minimum in (2) over $\mathcal{E}_1(i)$. The relaxation operator is then computed as in (3) with summations over $\mathcal{E}_1(i)$ rather than $\mathcal{E}_2(i)$. Our 1-ring scheme parameterized on a *regular* $K_i$-gon leads to the same relaxation operator as used by Kobbelt. Our scheme can thus be seen as a natural non-uniform generalization of the umbrella which is still linear. In general we use the $\mathcal{E}_2(i)$ (1-ring with flaps) scheme as it yields visually smoother surfaces.

Taubin [26] presents a two step relaxation operator $R = (I + \mu L)(I + \lambda L)$, with $\mu$ and $\lambda$ tuned to minimize shrinkage of the mesh.

Both of these schemes are semi-uniform filters since the weights only depend on $K_i$ and not the geometry. Consequently they affect both geometry and parameterization. Consider again an irregular triangulation of a plane. Semi-uniform schemes try to make each 1-ring look as much as possible like a regular $K$-gon. Thus the triangulation may change globally while the plane remains the same. As we will see, this will lead to unwanted effects in applications such as editing and texture mapping. On the other hand our non-uniform scheme is linearly invariant, leaves the triangles unchanged, and does not suffer from the problems concerning movement "inside" the surface observed in [18, Figure 4].

Figure 4 shows the effect on a non-planar triangulation like the eye of the mannequin head. Our non-uniform scheme (right) smoothes the geometry without affecting the triangle shapes much. The semi-uniform scheme (middle) tries to make edge lengths as uniform as possible which can only be done by effectively destroying the delicate mesh structure around the eye. This effect also applies to any other attributes that vertices may carry such as detail vectors for editing or texture map coordinates causing distortion during smoothing (see Figure 8).

Taubin [26] also uses a non-uniform discrete Laplacian in which the weights vary as the powers of the respective edge lengths. While such an operator can greatly reduce the triangle distortions, it can be shown that such a scheme can never be linearly invariant.

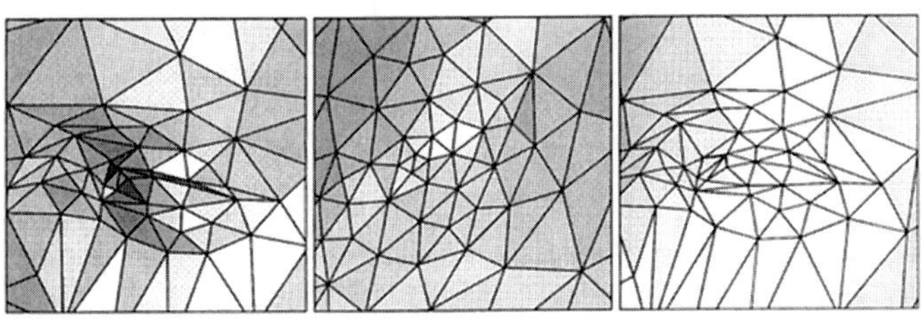

Figure 4: *Smoothing of the eye (left) with our non-uniform (right) and a semi-uniform scheme (middle). The semi-uniform scheme tries to make edge lengths as uniform as possible and severely distorts the geometry, while the non-uniform scheme only smoothes the geometry and does not affect the triangle shapes much.*

# 3 Multiresolution Signal Processing

Up to this point we have only considered operators which act on a scale comparable to their small finite support. To build more powerful signal processing tools we now consider a multiresolution setting.

Multiresolution algorithms such as subdivision, pyramids, and wavelets require decimation and upsampling procedures. For images decimation comes down to removing every other row or column. The situation for meshes is more complex, but a considerable body of work is available [13].

We employ Hoppe's Progressive Mesh (PM) approach [14]. In the PM setting, an edge collapse provides the atomic decimation step, while a vertex split becomes the atomic upsampling step. For simplicity we only employ half-edge collapses in our implementation. As a priority criterion we use a combination of the Garland-Heckbert quadric error metric [11] and edge length to favor removal of long edges (see also [17]).

Each half edge collapse removes one vertex and we number them in reverse so that the one with highest index gets removed first. This gives a sequence of $N$ meshes $(\mathcal{P}^n, \mathcal{K}^n)$, $1 \le n \le N$, and $\mathcal{P}^n = \{p_i \mid 1 \le i \le n\}$. Later we will consider mesh sequences $(\mathcal{Q}^{(n)}, \mathcal{K}^{(n)})$ where the points on coarser meshes do move from their finest mesh position. These are denoted $q_i^{(n)}$, $i \le n$.

In traditional signal processing, downsampling creates a coarser level through the removal of a constant fraction of samples. This leads to a logarithmic number of levels. A PM does not have such a notion of levels. However, one may think of each removed vertex as living on its own level, and the number of levels being linear.

## 3.1 Subdivision

Subdivision starts from a coarse mesh and successively builds finer and smoother versions [22]. In signal processing terms it consists of upsampling followed by relaxation. So far the word subdivision has been associated in the literature with either regular or semi-regular meshes with corresponding uniform or semi-uniform operators. If one only has an original, coarse mesh and cares about building a smooth version, then semi-regular is the correct approach.

Our setting is different. The coarse mesh comes from a PM started at the original, finest level. Hence the connectivity of the finer levels is fixed and determined by the reverse PM. Our goal is to use non-uniform subdivision to build a *geometrically* smooth mesh with the *same* connectivity as the original mesh and with as little triangle shape distortion as possible. Such smoothed meshes can subsequently be used to build pyramid algorithms.

Subdivision is computed one level at a time starting from level $n_0$ in the progressive mesh $\mathcal{Q}^{(n_0)} = \mathcal{P}^{(n_0)}$. Since the reverse PM adds one vertex per level, our non-uniform subdivision is computed one vertex at a time. We denote the vertex positions as $\mathcal{Q}^{(n)} = \{q_i^{(n)} \mid 1 \le i \le n\}$ $(n \ge n_0)$ and use meshes $(\mathcal{Q}^{(n)}, \mathcal{K}^{(n)})$ with the same connectivity as the PM meshes.

Going from $\mathcal{Q}^{(n-1)}$ to $\mathcal{Q}^{(n)}$ involves three groups of vertices. (I) the new vertex $n$, which is introduced together with a point position $q_n^{(n)}$ to be computed. (II) certain points from the $\mathcal{Q}^{(n-1)}$ mesh change position; these correspond to *even* vertices. There is only a small number of them. (III) the remainder of the points of $\mathcal{Q}^{(n-1)}$, typically the majority, remains unchanged. Specifically:

- The new position $q_n^{(n)}$ is computed after upsampling from $\mathcal{K}^{n-1}$ to $\mathcal{K}^n$:

  $$q_n^{(n)} = \sum\nolimits_{j \in \mathcal{V}_2^n(j)} w_{n,j}^{(n)} q_j^{(n-1)}.$$

  The position of the new vertex is computed to satisfy the relaxation operator using points from $\mathcal{Q}^{n-1}$ with weights using areas and lengths of mesh $(\mathcal{P}^n, \mathcal{K}^{(n)})$.

- The even points of $\mathcal{Q}^{n-1}$ form a 1-ring neighborhood of $n$. Their respective $\mathcal{V}_2^n$ neighborhoods contain $n$, which has just received an updated position $q_n^{(n)}$

  $$\forall j \in \mathcal{V}_1^n(n): \;\; q_j^{(n)} = \sum\nolimits_{k \in \mathcal{V}_2^n(j) \setminus \{n\}} w_{j,k}^{(n)} q_k^{(n-1)} + w_{j,n}^{(n)} q_n^{(n)}.$$

  The even vertices are relaxed using the point positions from $\mathcal{Q}^{(n-1)}$ (except for $q_n^{(n)}$), using weights coming from $(\mathcal{P}^n, \mathcal{K}^{(n)})$.

- Finally, the remainder of the positions do not change

  $$\forall j \in \mathcal{V}^{n-1} \backslash \mathcal{V}_1^n(n): \;\; q_j^{(n)} = q_j^{(n-1)}.$$

A central ingredient in our construction is the fact that the weights $w_{i,j}^{(n)}$ depend on parameter information from the mesh $\mathcal{P}^{(n)}$. No globally or even locally consistent parameterization is required. For each $D_e^2$ stencil we use the hinge map as described above. In effect the original mesh provides the parameterizations and in this way enters into the subdivision procedure. The actual *areas* and *lengths*, which make up the expressions for $w_{i,j}^{(n)}$ are assembled based on the connectivity $\mathcal{K}^{(n)}$ of level $n$, and hence induce the level dependence of the weights. As a result all $w_{i,j}^{(n)}$ may be precomputed during the PM construction and can be stored if desired for later use during repeated subdivision. It is easy to see that the storage is linear in the total degree, $\sum_i K_i$, of the mesh.

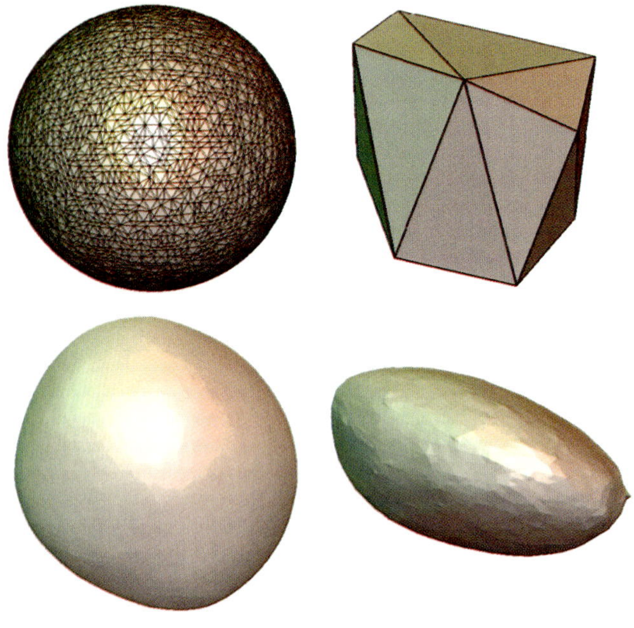

Figure 5: *Starting with the irregular triangulation of a sphere (upper left) we compute a PM down to 16 triangles (upper right). We then compute our non-uniform subdivision scheme back to the finest level (lower left) and obtain a smooth mesh which approximates the original. For comparison the lower right shows the limit surface of a semi-uniform subdivision scheme.*

To illustrate the behavior of uniform functional subdivision schemes one considers the so called *scaling function* or fundamental solution obtained from starting with a Kronecker sequence on the coarsest level. For surface subdivision, there is no equivalent to this. To illustrate the behavior of the surface scheme we perform the following experiment (see Figure 5). We start with an irregular triangulation of a sphere with 12000 triangles (upper left) and compute a PM down to 16 triangles (upper right). Next the non-uniform surface subdivision scheme starting from the 16 triangles back to the original mesh is computed (lower left). We clearly get a smooth mesh. For comparison the lower right shows the limit function using a semi-uniform scheme. It is important to understand that the non-uniform scheme has access to the parameterization information of the original finest mesh whereas the semi-uniform scheme does not use this additional information.

While for uniform and semi-uniform subdivision, extensive literature on regularity of limit functions exists, few results are known for non-uniform subdivision [2, 12]. The goal of our strategy of minimizing $D_e^2$ is to obtain $C^1$ smoothness. However, there is currently no regularity result for our scheme in either the functional or surface setting.

### 3.2 Burt-Adelson Pyramid

The pyramid proposed by Burt and Adelson [1] (BA) is another important signal processing tool. We show how to generalize it to a mesh pyramid. We start from the finest level points $\mathcal{S}^N = \mathcal{P}$ and compute a sequence of meshes $(\mathcal{S}^n, \mathcal{K}^n)$ $(1 \leq n \leq N)$ as well as oversampled differences $d_i^{(n)}$ between levels.

To go from $\mathcal{S}^n$ to $\mathcal{S}^{n-1}$, i.e., to remove vertex $n$, we follow the diagram in Figure 6. The top wire represents the points of $\mathcal{S}^{n-1}$ while the bottom wire represent the points of $\mathcal{S}^n$. There are four

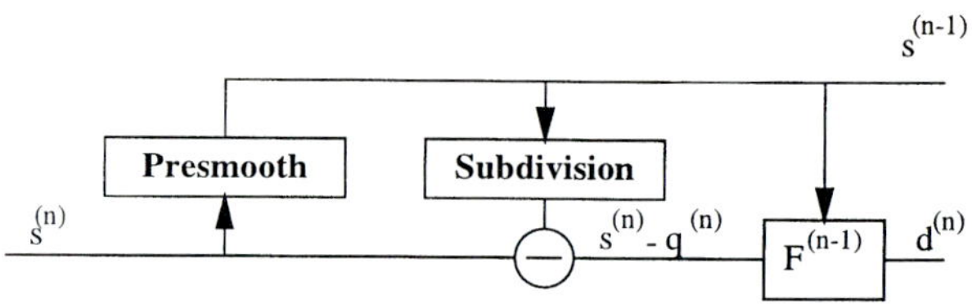


Figure 6: *Burt-Adelson style pyramid scheme.*

stages: presmoothing, downsampling, subdivision, and computation of details.

- **Presmoothing:** Presmoothing in the original BA pyramid is important to avoid aliasing. We have found that in a PM the presmoothing step can often be omitted because the downsampling steps (edge collapses) are chosen carefully, depending heavily on the data. In essence vertices are removed mostly in smooth regions, where presmoothing does not make a big difference. Thus, no presmoothing was used in our implementation.
- **Downsampling:** $n$ is removed in a half-edge collapse.
- **Subdivision:** Using the points from $\mathcal{S}^{n-1}$ we compute subdivided points $q_j^{(n)}$ for the vertex just removed and the surrounding even vertices exactly as described in Section 3.1
- **Detail Computation:** Finally, detail values are computed for all even vertices as well as the vertex $n$. These detail vectors are expressed in a local frame $F_j^{(n-1)}$ which depends on the coarser level:

$$\forall j \in \mathcal{V}_1^n(n) \cup \{n\}: \quad d_j^{(n)} = F_j^{(n-1)}(s_j^{(n)} - q_j^{(n)}).$$

  We refer to the entire group of $d_j^{(n)}$ as an array $d^{(n)}$. In the implementation this array is stored with $n$.

One of the features of the BA pyramid is that the above procedure can always be inverted independent of which presmoothing operator or subdivision scheme is used. For reconstruction, we start with the points of $\mathcal{S}^{n-1}$, subdivide values $q_j^{(n)}$ for both the new and even vertices and add in the details to recover the original values $s_j^{(n)}$.

To see the potential of a mesh pyramid in applications it is important to understand that the details $d^{(n)}$ can be seen as an approximate frequency spectrum of the mesh. The details $d^{(n)}$ with large $n$ come from edge collapses on the finer levels and thus correspond to small scales and high frequencies, while the details $d^{(n)}$ with small $n$ come from edge collapses on the coarser levels and thus correspond to large scales and low frequencies.

**Oversampling factor** A standard image pyramid has an oversampling factor of 4/3, while we have an expected oversampling factor of 7. The advantage of oversampling is that the details are quite small and lead to natural editing behavior [29]. If needed, a technique exists to reduce the oversampling factor. The idea is to use levels with more than one vertex. Say, we divide the $N$ vertices of $\mathcal{V}$ into $M$ levels with $M \ll N$:

$$\mathcal{V} = \mathcal{V}_0 \cup \bigcup_{1 \leq m \leq M} \mathcal{W}_m \quad \text{and} \quad \mathcal{V}_m = \mathcal{V}_{m-1} \cup \mathcal{W}_m.$$

This can be done, for example, so that the sizes of the $\mathcal{V}_m$ grow with a constant factor [7]. The BA pyramid then goes from $\mathcal{V}_m$ to $\mathcal{V}_{m-1}$. First presmooth all even vertices in $\mathcal{V}_m$, then compute subdivided values for all vertices in $\mathcal{W}_m$ and their 1-ring neighbors in $\mathcal{V}_m$. For the subdivided points, which need not be all vertices of $\mathcal{V}_m$, compute the details as differences with the original values from $\mathcal{V}_m$. One can see that the above algorithm with oversampling factor 7 is a special case when $\mathcal{W}_m = \{m\}$. The other extreme is the case with only one level containing all vertices. In that case there is no multiresolution as all details live on the same level. The oversampling factor is 1. By choosing the levels appropriately one can obtain any oversampling between 1 and 7. It is theoretically possible to build a wavelet-like, i.e, critically sampled multiresolution transform based on the Lifting scheme [25]. However, at this point it is not clear how to design filters that make the transform stable.

**Caveat** Often in this paper we use signal processing terminology such as frequency, low pass filter, aliasing, to describe operations on 2-manifolds. One has to be extremely careful with this and keep in mind that unlike in the Euclidean setting, there is no formal definition of these terms in the manifold setting. For example in a mesh the notion of a DC component strictly does not exist. Also in connection with the pyramid we often talk about frequency bands. Again one has to be careful as even in the Euclidean setting the coefficients in a a pyramid do not represent exact frequencies due to the Heisenberg uncertainty principle.

## 4 Applications

The algorithms we described above provide a powerful signal processing toolbox. In this section we demonstrate this claim by considering a variety of applications that use them. These include smoothing and filtering, enhancement, texture coordinate generation, vector displacement field editing, and multiresolution editing.

### 4.1 Smoothing and Filtering

One way to smooth a mesh is through repeated application of the relaxation operator $R$. Numerically this behaves similarly to traditional Jacobi iterations for an elliptic PDE solver. The relaxation rapidly attenuates the highest frequencies in the mesh, but has little impact on low frequencies. Even though each iteration of the operator is linear in the number of vertices, the number of iterations to attenuate a fixed frequency band grows linearly with the mesh size. This results in quadratically increasing run times as the sample density increases relative to a fixed geometric scale. One way to combat this behavior is through the use of appropriate preconditioners, as was done in [18], or through the use of implicit solvers [6].

Using a mesh pyramid we can build much more direct and flexible filtering operations. Recall that the details in a pyramid measure the local deviation from smoothness at different scales. In that sense they capture the local frequency content of the mesh. This spectrum can be shaped arbitrarily by scaling particular details. Multiresolution filtering operators are built by setting certain ranges of detail coefficients in the pyramid to zero. A low pass filter sets all detail arrays $d^{(n)}$ with $n > n_l$ to zero, while a high pass filter annihilates $d^{(n)}$ for $n < n_h$. However, for meshes it makes little sense to put the coarsest details to zero as this would collapse the mesh. More natural for meshes are stopband filters which zero out detail arrays $d^{(n)}$ in some intermediate range, $n_l < n < n_h$.

Figure 7 shows these procedures applied to the venus head ($N = 50000$). On the upper left the original mesh. The upper right shows the result of applying the non-uniform relaxation operator 20 times at the finest level. High frequency ripples quickly diffuse, but no attenuation is noticeable at larger length scales. The bottom left shows the result of a low pass filter which sets all details above $n_l = 1000$ to zero. Finally the bottom right shows the result of a stopband filter, annihilating all details $1000 < n < 15000$. Note how the last mesh keeps its fine level details, while intermediate frequencies were attenuated. If desired all these filtering operations can be performed in a spatially varying manner due to the space-frequency localization of the mesh pyramid. Figure 8 shows the difference between non-uniform (left) and semi-uniform smoothing (right) on the actual vertex positions. By keeping the original finest level texture coordinates for the vertices of both meshes we can

Figure 7: *Smoothing and filtering of the venus head. Original on the top left; 20 finest level relaxation steps on the top right; low pass filter on the bottom left; stopband filter on the bottom right.*

visualize the effect of movement "within" the surface after smoothing. This hints at another application: if one has a scanned mesh with color (r,g,b) attributes per vertex then non-uniform *geometry* smoothing will not distort those colors.

### 4.2 Enhancement

Enhancement provides the opposite operation to smoothing in that it emphasizes certain frequency ranges. As before this can be done in a single resolution manner as well as in the more flexible multiresolution setup.

The single resolution scheme is easy to compute and typically works best for fairly small meshes, such as those used as control polyhedra for splines or semi-regular subdivision surfaces. The main idea is to extrapolate the difference between the original mesh and a single resolution relaxed mesh. The enhanced points are given by

$$Ep_i = p_i + \xi(R^k p_i - p_i),$$

where $\xi > 1$. Figure 9 illustrates the procedure. On the left the original mannequin head, in the middle the result after 20 relaxation steps, and on the right the enhanced version with $\xi = 2$. The first and last models of Figure 1 show the Loop subdivided meshes of the original and enhanced head. By using combinations of the different algorithms peculiar effects can be obtained. The second

Figure 8: *Movement "within" the surface due to smoothing visualized by letting the vertices keep their original finest level texture coordinates. Left non-uniform smoothing and right semi-uniform smoothing.*

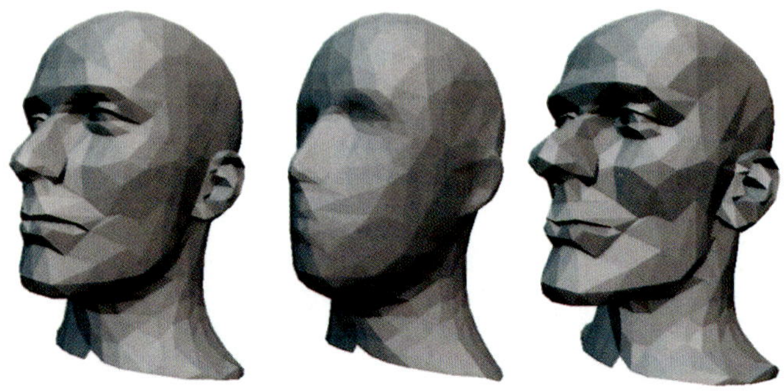

Figure 9: *Enhancement of control mesh. On the left the original, in the middle the smoothed mesh, and on the right the enhanced mesh (see also Figure 1 for the resulting subdivision surfaces).*

model in Figure 1 is obtained by extrapolating from a base model built by 5 semi-uniform relaxation steps followed by 5 non-uniform relaxation steps (needed to recover the parameterization and "pull" features back in place). The third model in Figure 1 is extrapolated from a base built by first simplifying to level 100, then applying 1 relaxation step (which made the chin collapse and ears shrink), and reconstructing.

The single level scheme is simple and easy to compute, but limited in its use. For example, it does not compute offsets with respect to local frames. If the mesh contains fine level detail self intersections quickly appear. As in image enhancement one must be careful not to amplify high frequency noise. For these reasons we need the more flexible setup of multiresolution enhancement. The approach is simple, we compute a mesh pyramid, scale the desired details and then reconstruct. As in the filtering application, the user has control over the different frequency bands. Additionally, the local frames across the many levels of the mesh pyramid tend to stabilize the procedure and lead to a more natural behavior. As a result the multiresolution enhancement scheme deals better with large scanned meshes which usually contain high frequency noise.

Figure 10 shows Loop subdivided versions of the original cow head and an enhanced version obtained by multiplying the details $d^{(n)}$ with $257 < n \leq 2904 = N$ by two (see also Figure 15, right column for an edit of the enhanced model). Finally, Figure 11 shows enhancement on the Stanford bunny ($N = 34835$). Here details with indices $1000 < n < 7000$ were multiplied by 2, and details with indices $7000 < n < 13000$ were multiplied by 1.5.

Figure 10: *Enhancement of cow head (original on the left).*

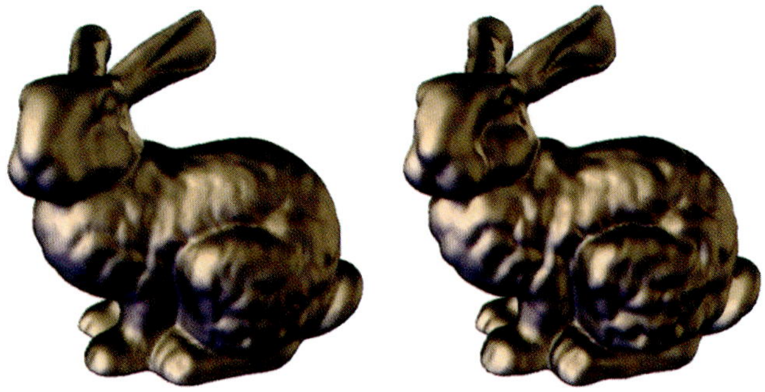

Figure 11: *Enhancement on the bunny. The original is on the left and the frequency enhanced version on the right.*

## 4.3 Subdivision of Scalar Functions on Manifolds

We can use subdivision to quickly build smooth scalar functions defined *on* a manifold. Simply start with scalar values on a coarse level and use non-uniform subdivision to build a smooth function defined on the finest level.

We present two applications. The first creates smoothly varying texture coordinate assignments for the finest level mesh from some user supplied texture coordinate assignments at a coarse level. The second creates a smoothly varying function over a limited region of an irregular mesh and then uses this function to generate a smooth vector displacement field for shape editing purposes.

**Texture Coordinate Generation** DeRose et al. [5] discuss this problem in the context of classical, semi-uniform subdivision. Their goal was the construction of smooth texture coordinates for Catmull-Clark surfaces. Beginning with user supplied texture coordinates at some coarse level they subdivide these parameter assignments to the finest subdivision level using the same subdivision operator for texture coordinates as for the vertices.

Figure 12 shows the application of this idea to our setting. Initial texture coordinate assignments were made using a cylindrical projection of all vertices in $\mathcal{P}^{1000}$. The left image shows a test texture on the coarse polygonal mesh. We then reconstruct the original finest level mesh and concurrently subdivide the texture coordinates to the finest level. The resulting mapping is shown on the right. Even though the geometry has much geometric detail and uneven triangle sizes the final texture coordinates vary smoothly over the entire surface.

**Displacement Vector Field Editing** Singh and Fiume [23] present an algorithm for deformation edits based on vector displacement fields. These fields are defined through a smooth falloff function around a "wire" which drags the surface along. The region of influence is a function of distance in $\mathbf{R}^3$. Controlling this behavior in regions of high curvature or in the vicinity of multiple close objects can be tricky. In our setting we have the opportunity to define the falloff function *only* on the surface itself. A similar idea was used in [15] for feature editing.

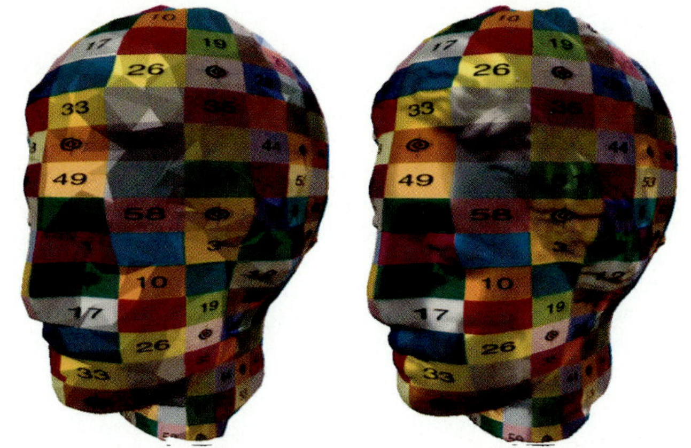

Figure 12: *A test texture is mapped to a coarse level of the mesh pyramid under user control. The resulting texture coordinates are then subdivided to the finest level and the result shown on the right.*

We illustrate this idea with an example. Consider the horse to "giraffe" edit in Figure 13. The user first outlines three regions by drawing closed curves on the mesh. A region that remains unchanged (A); a region that will be gradually stretched (B); and a region that will undergo a translation (C). In our example, region (A) is the back body and the four legs; (B) are the neck and torso; and (C) is the head. The boundary between (A) and (B) consists of three closed curves. Next we define a scalar parameter $\theta$, which is 0 on the boundary between (A) and (B), and 1 on the boundary between (B) and (C). The algorithm computes values for $\theta$ that vary smoothly between 0 and 1 in region (B).

This is accomplished by running a PM on the interior of region (B) to a maximally coarse level. Then the initial value $\theta = 1/2$ is assigned to all interior vertices of the coarse region (B). Next we apply relaxation to $\theta$ on the coarsest level within (B). This converges quickly because there are few triangles; three steps suffice. These $\theta$ values are then used as the starting values for subdivision from the coarsest level back to the original region (B) while keeping the $\theta$ values on the boundary fixed. The resulting $\theta$ values on the finest region (B) vary smoothly between 0 and 1. The only problem is that at the boundary they meet in a $C^0$ and not a $C^1$ fashion. This is because we only imposed Dirichlet like conditions and no Neumann condition. We address this with the following smoothing transformation, $\theta := 1/2 - 1/2\cos(\pi\theta)$.

On the left of Figure 13 the red lines are specified by the user and the black lines show the $\theta$ isolines, visualizing how $\theta$ varies smoothly. The edit is now done by letting the user drag the head. Every vertex in region B is subjected to $\theta$ times the displacement vector of the head. This requires very little computation. The right side of Figure 13 shows the result.

### 4.4 Multiresolution Editing

The displacement vector editing is simple and fast, but has limited use. We next discuss full fledged multiresolution editing for irregular meshes. Our algorithm combines ideas of Zorin et al. [29] and Kobbelt et al. [18]. The former used multiresolution details and semi-regular meshes, while the latter used single resolution details and irregular meshes. We combine the best of both approaches by using multiresolution details with the irregular mesh setting.

The algorithm is straightforward. The user can manipulate a group of points $s_i^{(n)}$ in the mesh pyramid and the system adds the finer level details back in. This is exactly the same use of the pyramid as Zorin et al. only now for irregular meshes. Kobbelt et al. used a *multiresolution/multigrid* approach to define a smoothed mesh over a user selected region, but then compute *single resolution* details between the original and smoothed mesh.

Figure 13: *Horse to giraffe edit using a surface based smooth displacement vector field.*

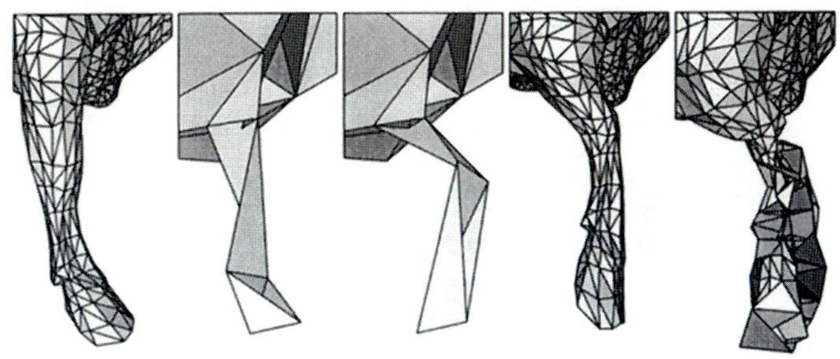

Figure 14: *Cow leg editing sequence: original, coarsest scale, edit, reconstruction with multiresolution details, reconstruction with single resolution details.*

The use of multiresolution details is important when the user wishes to make large scale edits in regions with complicated fine scale geometry. Because the multiresolution details are all described in local frames, they have more flexibility to adjust themselves to a coarse scale edit.

We illustrate this with an edit on the leg of the cow (Figure 14). The sequence shows the original leg, the coarse leg, a coarse edit, and two reconstructions. The first used multiresolution details while the second used single resolution details.

Finally, Figure 15 shows some additional edits. The horse was edited at a level containing only 34 vertices (compare to the original shape shown in Figure 13). The cow edit on the right column involves both manipulation at coarse levels (snout, horns, leg, tail) and overall enhancement.

| Dataset | Venus | Horse | Bunny | Cow | Mann. |
|---|---|---|---|---|---|
| Size (fine) | 50000 | 48485 | 34835 | 2904 | 689 |
| Size (coarse) | 4 | 34 | 19 | 57 | 5 |
| Timings (s) | | | | | |
| Simpl. & Anal. | 79 | 75 | 55 | 3.6 | 0.8 |
| Reconstruction | 9 | 8 | 5.8 | .37 | 0.1 |
| Analysis | 9 | 8 | 5.8 | .37 | 0.1 |

Table 1: *Timings for mesh pyramid computation assuming storage rather then recomputation of all areas and length needed in stencil weight computations. The size field counts the total vertices ($N$). Face counts are generally twice as large. All times are given in seconds on an SGI R10k O2 @175Mhz.*

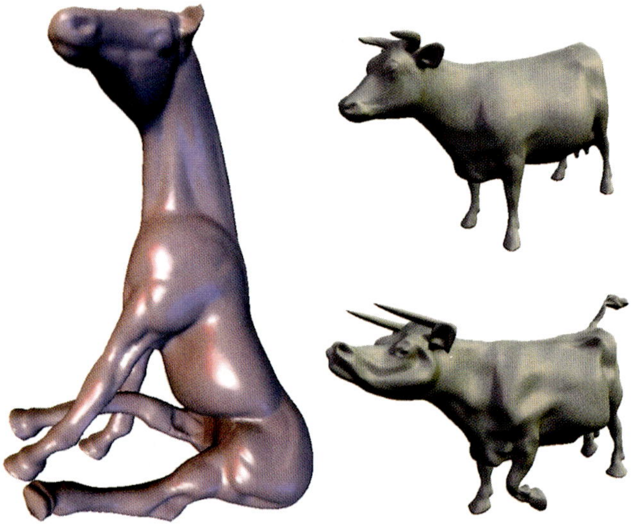

Figure 15: *Multiresolution edits.*

## 5 Conclusions and Future Work

We have shown how basic signal processing tools such as up and down sampling and filtering can be extended to irregular meshes. These tools can be built into powerful algorithms such as subdivision and mesh pyramids. We have demonstrated their use in texturing, editing, smoothing and enhancement.

Further research can be pursued in several directions. On the algorithms side there is incorporation of various boundary conditions, construction of positive weight schemes, and extensions to tetrahedralizations. On the applications side there is adaptive gridding for time dependent PDE's, computing globally smooth parameterizations, extracting texture maps from scanned textures, and space-frequency morphing.

**Compression** Another potential future application is compression. However, one needs to be extremely careful: our subdivision weights depend on the parameterization which in turn depends on the geometry of the original mesh. Thus one cannot use the subdivision scheme as a predictor in a compression framework unless sender and receiver share parameter information, i.e., the needed areas and lengths to compute the subdivision. Only a setting where one repeatedly has to communicate functions or attributes defined over a fixed triangulation would justify this overhead.

This touches upon a deeper issue. In some sense for a geometrically smooth irregular mesh only one dimension can effectively be predicted by a subdivision scheme. Even for a geometrically smooth mesh, no subdivision scheme can compress the information implicitly present in the parameterization. Ideally for smooth surfaces one would like to use meshes with as little parametric information as possible.

A typical example are semi-uniform meshes. This argument strongly makes the case for resampling onto semi-regular meshes using smooth parameterizations [8, 19] before compression.

**Acknowledgments** Igor Guskov was partially supported by a Harold W. Dodds Fellowship and a Summer Internship at Bell Laboratories, Lucent Technologies. Other support was provided by NSF (ACI-9624957, ACI-9721349, DMS-9874082), Alias|wavefront and through a Packard Fellowship. Special thanks to Ingrid Daubechies, Aaron Lee, Adam Finkelstein, Zoë Wood, and Khrysaundt Koenig. Our implementation uses the triangle facet data structure and code of Ernst Mücke, and the priority queue implementation by Michael Garland.

## References


[1] BURT, P. J., AND ADELSON, E. H. Laplacian Pyramid as a Compact Image Code. *IEEE Trans. Commun. 31*, 4 (1983), 532–540.

[2] DAUBECHIES, I., GUSKOV, I., AND SWELDENS, W. Regularity of irregular subdivision. *Const. Approx.* (1999), to appear.

[3] DE BOOR, C. A multivariate divided differences. *Approximation Theory VIII 1* (1995), 87–96.

[4] DE BOOR, C., AND RON, A. On multivariate polynomial interpolation. *Constr. Approx. 6* (1990), 287–302.

[5] DEROSE, T., KASS, M., AND TRUONG, T. Subdivision Surfaces in Character Animation. *Computer Graphics (SIGGRAPH '98 Proceedings)* (1998), 85–94.

[6] DESBRUN, M., MEYER, M., SCHRÖDER, P., AND BARR, A. Implicit Fairing of Irregular Meshes using Diffusion and Curvature Flow. In *Computer Graphics (SIGGRAPH '99 Proceedings)*, Aug. 1999.

[7] DOBKIN, D., AND KIRKPATRICK, D. A Linear Algorithm for Determining the Separation of Convex Polyhedra. *Journal of Algorithms 6* (1985), 381–392.

[8] ECK, M., DEROSE, T., DUCHAMP, T., HOPPE, H., LOUNSBERY, M., AND STUETZLE, W. Multiresolution Analysis of Arbitrary Meshes. In *Computer Graphics (SIGGRAPH '95 Proceedings)*, 173–182, 1995.

[9] FLOATER, M. S. Parameterization and Smooth Approximation of Surface Triangulations. *Computer Aided Geometric Design 14* (1997), 231–250.

[10] FORNBERG, B. Generation of finite difference formulas on arbitrarily spaced grids. *Math. Comput. 51* (1988), 699–706.

[11] GARLAND, M., AND HECKBERT, P. S. Surface Simplification Using Quadric Error Metrics. In *Computer Graphics (SIGGRAPH '96 Proceedings)*, 209–216, 1996.

[12] GUSKOV, I. Multivariate Subdivision Schemes and Divided Differences. Tech. rep., Department of Mathematics, Princeton University, 1998.

[13] HECKBERT, P. S., AND GARLAND, M. Survey of Polygonal Surface Simplification Algorithms. Tech. rep., Carnegie Mellon University, 1997.

[14] HOPPE, H. Progressive Meshes. In *Computer Graphics (SIGGRAPH '96 Proceedings)*, 99–108, 1996.

[15] KHODAKOVSKY, A., AND SCHRÖDER, P. Fine Level Feature Editing for Subdivision Surfaces. In *ACM Solid Modeling Symposium*, 1999.

[16] KOBBELT, L. Discrete Fairing. In *Proceedings of the Seventh IMA Conference on the Mathematics of Surfaces*, 101–131, 1997.

[17] KOBBELT, L., CAMPAGNA, S., AND SEIDEL, H.-P. A General Framework for Mesh Decimation. In *Proceedings of Graphics Interface*, 1998.

[18] KOBBELT, L., CAMPAGNA, S., VORSATZ, J., AND SEIDEL, H.-P. Interactive Multi-Resolution Modeling on Arbitrary Meshes. In *Computer Graphics (SIGGRAPH '98 Proceedings)*, 105–114, 1998.

[19] LEE, A., SWELDENS, W., SCHRÖDER, P., COWSAR, L., AND DOBKIN, D. MAPS: Multiresolution Adaptive Parametrization of Surfaces. In *Computer Graphics (SIGGRAPH '98 Proceedings)*, 95–104, 1998.

[20] LÉVY, B., AND MALLET, J. Non-Distorted Texture Mapping for Sheared Triangulated Meshes. In *Computer Graphics (SIGGRAPH '98 Proceedings)*, 343–352, July 1998.

[21] MORETON, H. P., AND SÉQUIN, C. H. Functional optimization for fair surface design. In *Computer Graphics (SIGGRAPH '92 Proceedings)*, vol. 26, 167–176, July 1992.

[22] SCHRÖDER, P., AND ZORIN, D., Eds. *Course Notes: Subdivision for Modeling and Animation.* ACM SIGGRAPH, 1998.

[23] SINGH, K., AND FIUME, E. Wires: A Geometric Deformation Technique. In *Computer Graphics (SIGGRAPH '98 Proceedings)*, 405–414, 1998.

[24] SPANIER, E. H. *Algebraic Topology.* McGraw-Hill, New York, 1966.

[25] SWELDENS, W. The lifting scheme: A construction of second generation wavelets. *SIAM J. Math. Anal. 29*, 2 (1997), 511–546.

[26] TAUBIN, G. A Signal Processing Approach to Fair Surface Design. In *Computer Graphics (SIGGRAPH' 95 Proceedings)*, 351–358, 1995.

[27] TAUBIN, G., ZHANG, T., AND GOLUB, G. Optimal Surface Smoothing as Filter Design. Tech. Rep. 90237, IBM T.J. Watson Research, March 1996.

[28] WELCH, W., AND WITKIN, A. Free–Form Shape Design Using Triangulated Surfaces. In *Computer Graphics (SIGGRAPH '94 Proceedings)*, 247–256, July 1994.

[29] ZORIN, D., SCHRÖDER, P., AND SWELDENS, W. Interactive Multiresolution Mesh Editing. In *Computer Graphics (SIGGRAPH '97 Proceedings)*, 259–268, 1997.

# Shape Transformation Using Variational Implicit Functions

Greg Turk James F. O'Brien

Georgia Institute of Technology

## Abstract

Traditionally, shape transformation using implicit functions is performed in two distinct steps: 1) creating two implicit functions, and 2) interpolating between these two functions. We present a new shape transformation method that combines these two tasks into a single step. We create a transformation between two $N$-dimensional objects by casting this as a scattered data interpolation problem in $N+1$ dimensions. For the case of 2D shapes, we place all of our data constraints within two planes, one for each shape. These planes are placed parallel to one another in 3D. Zero-valued constraints specify the locations of shape boundaries and positive-valued constraints are placed along the normal direction in towards the center of the shape. We then invoke a variational interpolation technique (the 3D generalization of thin-plate interpolation), and this yields a single implicit function in 3D. Intermediate shapes are simply the zero-valued contours of 2D slices through this 3D function. Shape transformation between 3D shapes can be performed similarly by solving a 4D interpolation problem. To our knowledge, ours is the first shape transformation method to unify the tasks of implicit function creation and interpolation. The transformations produced by this method appear smooth and natural, even between objects of differing topologies. If desired, one or more additional shapes may be introduced that influence the intermediate shapes in a sequence. Our method can also reconstruct surfaces from multiple slices that are not restricted to being parallel to one another.

**CR Categories:** I.3.5 [Computer Graphics]: Computational Geometry and Object Modeling—surfaces and object representations

**Keywords:** Shape transformation, shape morphing, contour interpolation, implicit surfaces, thin-plate techniques.

## 1 Introduction

The shape transformation problem can be stated as follows: Given two shapes A and B, construct a sequence of intermediate shapes so that adjacent pairs in the sequence are geometrically close to one another. Playing the resulting sequence of shapes as an animation would show object A deforming into object B. Sequences of 2D shapes can be thought of as slices through a 3D surface, as shown in Figure 1. Shape transformation can be performed between objects of any dimension, although 2D and 3D shapes are by far the most common cases. Shape transformation has applications in medicine, computer aided design, and special effects creation. We give an overview of these three applications below.

One important application of shape transformation in medicine is contour interpolation. Non-invasive imaging techniques often collect data about a patient's internal anatomy in "slices" of a particular size such as $512 \times 512$ samples. Usually many fewer slices are taken along the third dimension so that a resulting volume might, for example, be sampled at $512 \times 512 \times 30$ resolution. To reconstruct a 3D model of a particular organ, the samples are segmented to create shapes (contours) within the slices. Intermediate shapes are then created between slices in the sparsely sampled dimension. The reconstructed 3D object is formed by stacking together the original and the interpolated contours. This is an example of 2D shape transformation.

turk@cc.gatech.edu, job@acm.org.



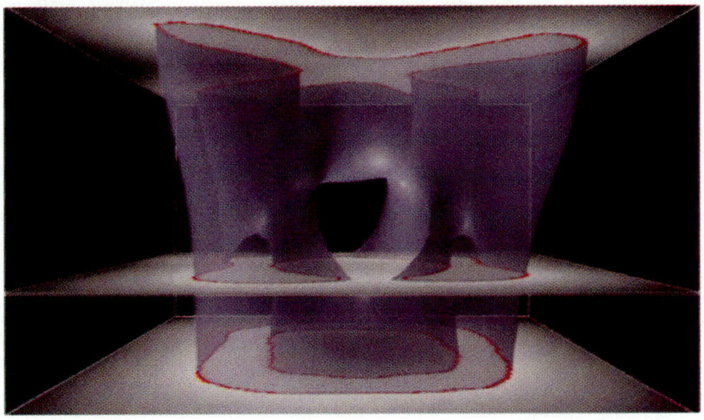

Figure 1: Visualization of transformation between X and O shapes. Top and bottom planes contain constraints for the two shapes. Translucent surface is the isosurface of a 3D variational implicit function, and slices through it give intermediate shapes.

Shape transformation can also be a useful tool in computer aided geometric design. Consider the problem of creating a join between two metal parts with different cross-sections. It is important for the connecting surface to be smooth because those places with sharp ridges or creases are the locations that are most likely to form cracks. The intermediate surface joining the two parts can be created using shape transformation, much in the same way as with contour interpolation for medical imaging. Because of the smoothness properties of variational interpolation methods, we consider them a natural tool to explore for shape transformation in CAD.

Finally, animated shape transformations have been used to create dramatic special effects for feature films and commercials. One of the best-known examples of shape transformation is in the film *Terminator 2*. In this film, a cyborg policeman undergoes a number of transformations from an amorphous and highly reflective surface to various destination shapes. 2D image morphing would not have accurately modeled the reflection of the environment off the surface of the deforming cyborg, hence tailor-made 3D shape transformation programs were used for these effects [9].

In this paper we use variational interpolation in a new way to produce high-quality shape transformations that may be used for any of the previously mentioned applications. Our method allows a user to control the transformation in several ways, and it is general enough to produce transformations between shapes of any topology.

## 2 Previous Work

Most shape transformation techniques can be placed into one of two categories: parametric correspondence methods and implicit function interpolation. Parametric methods are typically faster to compute and require less memory because they operate on a lower-dimensional representation of an object than do implicit function methods. Unfortunately, transforming between objects of different topologies is considerably more difficult with parametric methods. Parametric approaches also can suffer from problems with self-intersecting surfaces, but this is never a problem with implicit function methods. Techniques that use implicit function interpolation gracefully handle changes in topology between objects and do not create self-intersecting surfaces.

A parametric correspondence approach to shape transformation attempts to find a "reasonable" correspondence between pairs of locations on the boundaries of the two shapes. Intermediate shapes are then created by computing interpolated positions between the corresponding pairs of points. Many shape transformation techniques have been created that follow the parametric correspondence approach. One early application of this approach is the method of contour interpolation described by Fuchs, Kedem and Uselton [10]. Their method attempts to find an "optimal" (minimum-area) triangular tiling that connects two contours using dynamic programming. Many subsequent techniques followed this approach of defining a quality measure for a particular correspondence between contours and then invoking an optimization procedure [22, 25]. There have been fewer examples of using parametric correspondence for 3D shape transformation. One quite successful 3D parametric method is the work of Kent et al. [17]. The key to their approach is to subdivide the polygons of the two models in a manner that creates a correspondence between the vertices of the two models. More recently, Gregory and co-workers created a similar method that also allows a user to specify region correspondences between meshes to better control a transformation [12].

An entirely different approach to shape transformation is to create an implicit function for each shape and then to smoothly interpolate between these two functions. A shape is defined by an implicit function, $f(\mathbf{x})$, as the set of all points $\mathbf{x}$ such that $f(\mathbf{x}) = 0$. For contour interpolation in 2D, the implicit function can be thought of as a height field over a two-dimensional domain, and the boundary of a shape is the one-dimensional curve defined by all the points that have the same elevation value of zero. An implicit function in 3D is a function that yields a scalar value at every point in 3D. The shape described by such a function is given by those places in 3D whose function value is zero (the isosurface).

One commonly used implicit function is the *inside/outside function* or *characteristic function*. This function takes on only two values over the entire domain. The two values that are typically used are zero to represent locations that are outside and one to signify positions that are inside the given shape. Given a powerful enough interpolation technique, the characteristic function can be used for creating shape transformations. Hughes presented a successful example of this approach by transforming characteristic functions into the frequency domain and performing interpolation on the frequency representations of the shapes [15]. Kaul and Rossignac found that smooth intermediate shapes can be generated by using weighted Minkowski sums to interpolate between characteristic functions [16]. They later created a generalization of this technique that can use several intermediate shapes to control the interpolation between objects [24]. Using a wavelet decomposition of a characteristic function allowed He and colleagues to create intermediates between quite complex 3D objects [13].

A more informative implicit function can provide excellent intermediate shapes even if a simple interpolation technique is used. In particular, the *signed distance function* (sometimes called the *distance transform*) is an implicit function that gives very plausible intermediate shapes even when used with simple linear interpolation of the function values of the two shapes. The value of the signed distance function at a point $\mathbf{x}$ inside a given shape is just the Euclidean distance between $\mathbf{x}$ and the nearest point on the boundary of the shape. For a point $\mathbf{x}$ that is outside the shape, the signed distance function takes on the negative of the distance from $\mathbf{x}$ to the closest point on the boundary.

Several researchers have used the signed distance function to interpolate between 2D contours [19, 14]. The distance function for each given shape is represented as a regular 2D grid of values, and an intermediate implicit function is created by linear interpolation between corresponding grid values of the two implicit functions. Each intermediate shape is given by the zero iso-contour of this interpolated implicit function. In contrast to the global interpolation methods described above (frequency domain, wavelets, Minkowski sum), this interpolation is entirely local in nature. Nevertheless, the shape transformations that are created by this method are quite good. In essence, the information that the signed distance function encodes (distance to nearest boundary) is enough to make up for the purely local method of interpolation. Payne and Toga were the first to transform three dimensional shapes using this approach [23]. Cohen-Or and colleagues gave additional control to this same approach by combining it with a warping technique in order to produce shape transformations of 3D objects [7].

Our approach to shape transformation combines the two steps of building implicit functions and interpolating between them. To our knowledge, it is the only method to do so. The remainder of this paper describes how variational interpolation can be used to simultaneously solve these two tasks.

# 3 Variational Interpolation

Our approach relies on *scattered data interpolation* to solve the shape transformation problem. The problem of scattered interpolation is to create a smooth function that passes through a given set of data points. The two-dimensional version of this problem can be stated as follows: Given a collection of $k$ constraint points $\{\mathbf{c}_1, \mathbf{c}_2, \ldots, \mathbf{c}_k\}$ that are scattered in the plane, together with scalar height values at each of these points $\{h_1, h_2, \ldots, h_k\}$, construct a smooth surface that matches each of these heights at the given locations. We can think of this solution surface as a scalar-valued function $f(\mathbf{x})$ so that $f(\mathbf{c}_i) = h_i$, for $1 \le i \le k$.

One common approach to solving scattered data problems is to use variational techniques (from the calculus of variations). This approach begins with an energy that measures the quality of an interpolating function and then finds the single function that matches the given data points and that minimizes this energy measure. For two-dimensional problems, thin-plate interpolation is the variational solution when using the following energy function $E$:

$$E = \int_\Omega f_{xx}^2(\mathbf{x}) + 2f_{xy}^2(\mathbf{x}) + f_{yy}^2(\mathbf{x}) \qquad (1)$$

The notation $f_{xx}$ means the second partial derivative in the $x$ direction, and the other two terms are similar partial derivatives, one of them mixed. The above energy function is basically a measure of the aggregate squared curvature of $f(\mathbf{x})$ over the region of interest $\Omega$. Any creases or pinches in a surface will result in a larger value of $E$. A smooth surface that has no such regions of high curvature will have a lower value of $E$. The thin-plate solution to an interpolation problem is the function $f(\mathbf{x})$ that satisfies all of the constraints and that has the smallest possible value of $E$.

The scattered data interpolation problem can be formulated in any number of dimensions. When the given points $\mathbf{c}_i$ are positions in $N$-dimensions rather than in 2D, this is called the $N$-dimensional scattered data interpolation problem. There are appropriate generalizations to the energy function and to thin-plate interpolation for other dimensions. In this paper we will perform interpolation in two, three, four and five dimensions. Because the term *thin-plate* is only meaningful for 2D problems, we will use *variational interpolation* to mean the generalization of thin-plate techniques to any number of dimensions.

The scattered data interpolation task as formulated above is a variational problem where the desired solution is a function, $f(\mathbf{x})$, that will minimize equation 1 subject to the interpolation constraints $f(\mathbf{c}_i) = h_i$. Equation 1 can be solved using weighted sums of the

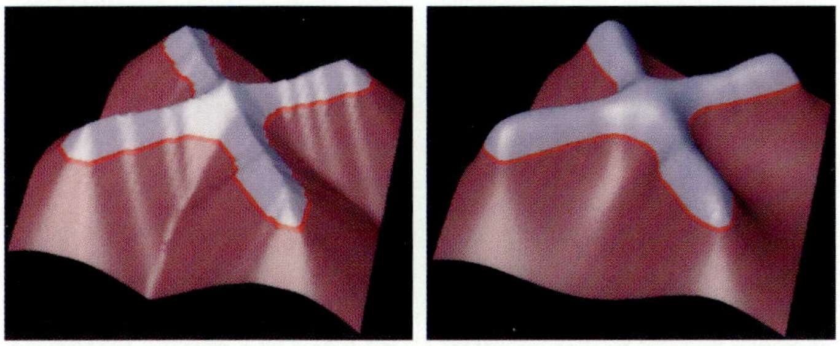

Figure 2: Implicit functions for an X shape. Left shows the signed distance function, and right shows the smoother variational implicit function.

radial basis function $\phi(\mathbf{x}) = |\mathbf{x}|^2 \log(|\mathbf{x}|)$. The family of variational problems that includes equation 1 was studied by Duchon [8].

Using the appropriate radial basis function, we can then express the interpolation function as

$$f(\mathbf{x}) = \sum_{j=1}^{n} d_j \phi(\mathbf{x} - \mathbf{c}_j) + P(\mathbf{x}) \tag{2}$$

In the above equation, $\mathbf{c}_j$ are the locations of the constraints, the $d_j$ are the weights, and $P(\mathbf{x})$ is a degree one polynomial that accounts for the linear and constant portions of $f$. Because the thin-plate radial basis function naturally minimizes equation 1, determining the weights, $d_j$, and the coefficients of $P(\mathbf{x})$ so that the interpolation constraints are satisfied will yield the desired solution that minimizes equation 1 subject to the constraints. Furthermore, the solution will be an exact analytic solution, and is not subject to approximation and discretization errors that may occur when using finite element or finite difference methods.

To solve for the set of $d_j$ that will satisfy the interpolation constraints $h_i = f(\mathbf{c}_i)$, we can substitute the right side of equation 2 for $f(\mathbf{c}_i)$, which gives:

$$h_i \quad = \quad \sum_{j=1}^{k} d_j \phi(\mathbf{c_i} - \mathbf{c_j}) + P(\mathbf{c_i}) \tag{3}$$

Since this equation is linear with respect to the unknowns, $d_j$ and the coefficients of $P(\mathbf{x})$, it can be formulated as a linear system. For interpolation in 3D, let $\mathbf{c}_i = (c_i^x, c_i^y, c_i^z)$ and let $\phi_{ij} = \phi(\mathbf{c}_i - \mathbf{c}_j)$. Then this linear system can be written as follows:

$$\begin{bmatrix} \phi_{11} & \phi_{12} & \dots & \phi_{1k} & 1 & c_1^x & c_1^y & c_1^z \\ \phi_{21} & \phi_{22} & \dots & \phi_{2k} & 1 & c_2^x & c_2^y & c_2^z \\ \vdots & \vdots & & \vdots & \vdots & \vdots & \vdots & \vdots \\ \phi_{k1} & \phi_{k2} & \dots & \phi_{kk} & 1 & c_k^x & c_k^y & c_k^z \\ 1 & 1 & \dots & 1 & 0 & 0 & 0 & 0 \\ c_1^x & c_2^x & \dots & c_k^x & 0 & 0 & 0 & 0 \\ c_1^y & c_2^y & \dots & c_k^y & 0 & 0 & 0 & 0 \\ c_1^z & c_2^z & \dots & c_k^z & 0 & 0 & 0 & 0 \end{bmatrix} \begin{bmatrix} d_1 \\ d_2 \\ \vdots \\ d_k \\ p_0 \\ p_1 \\ p_2 \\ p_3 \end{bmatrix} = \begin{bmatrix} h_1 \\ h_2 \\ \vdots \\ h_k \\ 0 \\ 0 \\ 0 \\ 0 \end{bmatrix}$$

The above system is symmetric and positive semi-definite, so there will always be a unique solution for the $d_j$ and $p_j$ [11]. For systems with up to a few thousand constraints, the system can be solved directly with a technique such as symmetric LU decomposition. We used symmetric LU decomposition to solve this system for all of the examples shown in this paper.

Using the tools of variational interpolation we can now turn our attention to creating implicit functions for shape transformation.

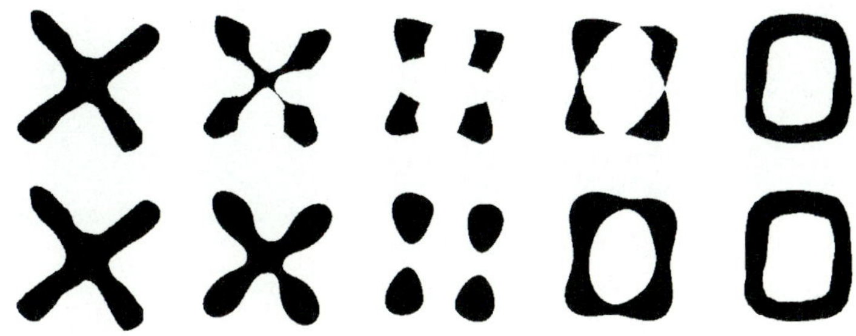

Figure 3: Upper row is a shape transformation created using the signed distance transform. Lower row is the sequence generated using a single variational implicit function.

## 4 Smooth Implicit Function Creation

In this section we will lay down the groundwork for shape transformation by discussing the creation of smooth implicit functions for a single shape. In particular, we will use variational interpolation of scattered constraints to construct implicit functions. Later we will generalize this to create functions that perform shape transformation.

Let us first examine the signed distance transformation because it is commonly used for shape transformation. The left half of Figure 2 shows a height field representation of the signed distance function of an X shape. The figure shows sharp ridges (the *medial axis*) that run down the middle of the height field. Ridges appear in the middle of shapes where the points are equally distant from two or more boundary points of the original shape. The values of a signed distance function decrease as one moves away from the ridge towards the boundaries. Figure 3, top row, shows a shape interpolation sequence between an X and an O shape that was created by linear interpolation between two signed distance functions. Note the pinched portions of some of the intermediate shapes. These sharp features are not isolated problems, but instead persist over many intermediate shapes. The cause of these pinches are the sharp ridges of signed distance functions. In many applications such artifacts are undesirable. In medical reconstruction, for example, these pinches are a poor estimate of shape because most biological structures have smooth surfaces. Because of this, we seek implicit functions that are continuous and that have a continuous first derivative.

### 4.1 Variational Implicit Functions in 2D

We can create smooth implicit functions for a given shape using variational interpolation. This can be done both for 2D and 3D shapes, although we will begin by discussing the 2D case. In this approach, we create a closed 2D curve by describing a number of locations through which the curve will pass and also specifying a number of points that should be interior to the curve. We call the given points on the curve the *boundary constraints*. The boundary constraints are locations at which we require our implicit function to take on the value of zero. Paired with each boundary constraint is a *normal constraint*, which is a location at which the implicit function is required to take on the value one. (Actually, any positive value could be used.) The locations of the normal constraints should be towards the interior of the desired curve, and also the line passing through the normal constraint and its paired boundary constraint should be parallel to the desired normal to the curve. The collection of boundary and normal constraints are passed along to a variational interpolation routine as the scattered constraints to be interpolated. The function that is returned is an implicit function that describes our curve. The curve will exactly pass through our boundary constraints.

Figure 4 (left) illustrates eight such pairs of constraints in the plane, with the boundary constraints shown as circles and the normal constraints as plus signs. When we invoke variational interpo-

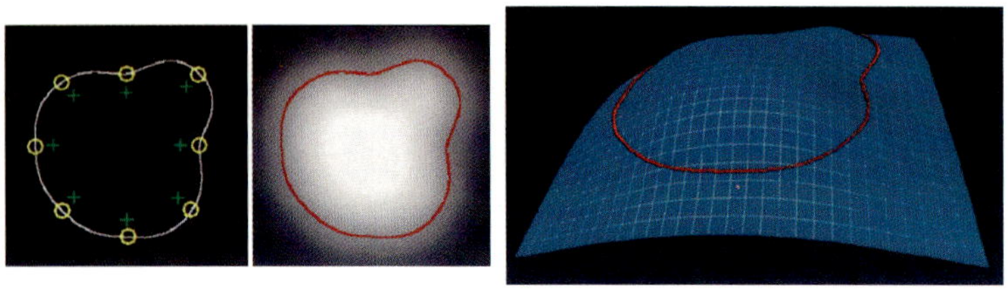

Figure 4: At left are pairs of boundary and normal constraints (circles and pluses). The middle image uses intensity to show the resulting variational implicit function, and the right image shows the function as a height field.

lation with such constraints, the result is a function that takes on the value of zero exactly at our zero-value constraints and that is positive in the direction of our normal constraints (towards the interior of the shape). The closed curve passing through the zero-value constraints in Figure 4 (middle) is the iso-contour of the implicit function created by this method. Figure 4 (right) shows the resulting implicit function rendered as a height field. Given enough suitably-placed boundary constraints we can define any closed shape. We call an implicit function that is created in this manner a *variational implicit function*. This new technique for creating implicit functions also show promise for surface modeling, a topic that is explored in [27].

We now turn our attention to defining boundary and normal constraints for a given 2D shape. Assume that a given shape is represented as a gray-scale image. White pixels represent the interior of a shape, black pixels will be outside the shape, and pixels with intermediate gray values lie on the boundary of the shape. Let $m$ be the middle gray value of our image's gray scale range. Our goal is to create constraints between any two adjacent pixels where one pixel's value is less than $m$ and the other's value is greater. Identifying these locations is the 2D analog of finding the vertex locations in a 3D marching cubes algorithm [21].

We traverse the entire gray-scale image and examine the east and south neighbor of each pixel $I(x,y)$. If $I(x,y) < m$ and either neighbor has a value greater than $m$, we create a boundary constraint at a point along the line segment joining the pixel centers. A boundary constraint is also created if $I(x,y) > m$ and either neighbor takes on a value less than $m$. The value of the constraint is zero, and we set the position of the constraint at the location between the two pixels where the image would take on the value of $m$ if we assume linear interpolation of pixel values. Next, we estimate the gradient of the gray scale image using linear interpolation of pixel values and central differencing. We then create a normal constraint a short distance away from the zero crossing in the direction of the gradient. We have found that a distance of a pixel's width between the boundary and normal constraints works well in practice. Figure 2 (right) shows the implicit function for an X shape that was created using variational interpolation from such constraints. It is smooth and free of sharp ridges.

### 4.2 Variational Implicit Functions in 3D

We can create implicit functions for 3D surfaces using variational interpolation in much the same way as for 2D shapes. Specifically, we can derive 3D constraints from the vertex positions and surface normals of a polygonal representation of an object. Let $(x,y,z)$ and $(n_x,n_y,n_z)$ be the position and the surface normal at a vertex, respectively. Then a boundary constraint is placed at $(x,y,z)$ and a normal constraint is placed at $(x-kn_x, y-kn_y, z-kn_z)$, where $k$ is some small value. We use a value of $k = 0.01$ for models that fit within a unit cube for the results shown in this paper. All of the 3D models that we transform in this paper were constructed by building an implicit function in this manner. Note that we can use this method to build an implicit function whenever we have a collection of points and normals— polygon connectivity is not necessary.

Now that we can construct smooth implicit functions for both two- and three-dimensional shapes, we turn our attention to shape transformation. It would be possible to create variational implicit functions for each of two given shapes and then linearly interpolate between these functions to create a shape transformation sequence. Instead, however, we will examine an even better way of performing shape transformation by generalizing the implicit function building methods of this section.

## 5 Unifying Function Creation and Interpolation

The key to our shape transformation approach is to represent the entire sequence of shapes with a single implicit function. To do so, we need to work in one higher dimension than the given shapes. For 2D shapes, we will construct an implicit function in 3D that represents our two given shapes in two distinct parallel planes. This is actually simple to achieve now that we know how to use scattered data interpolation to create an implicit function.

### 5.1 Two-Dimensional Shape Transformation

Given two shapes in the plane, assume that we have created a set of boundary and normal constraints for each shape, as described in Section 4. Instead of using each set of constraints separately to create two different 2D implicit functions, we will embed all of the constraints in 3D. We do this by adding a third coordinate value to the location of each boundary and normal constraint. For those constraints for the first shape, we set the new coordinate $t$ for all constraints to $t = 0$. For the second shape, all of the new coordinate values are set to $t = t_{max}$ (some non-zero value). Although we have added a third dimension to the locations of the constraints, the values that are to be interpolated remain unchanged for all constraints.

Once we have placed the constraints of both shapes into 3D, we invoke 3D variational interpolation to create a single scalar-valued function over $\mathbf{R}^3$. If we take a slice of this function in the plane $t = 0$, we find an implicit function that takes on the value zero exactly at the boundary constraints for our first shape. In this plane, our function describes the first shape. Similarly, in the plane $t = t_{max}$ this function gives the second shape. Parallel slices at locations between these two planes ($0 < t < t_{max}$) represent the shapes of our shape transformation sequence. Figure 1 illustrates that the collection of intermediate shapes are all just slices through a surface in 3D that is created by variational interpolation.

Figure 3 (bottom) shows the sequence of shapes created using this variational approach to shape transformation. Topology changes (e.g. the addition or removal of holes) come "for free", without any human guidance or algorithmic complications. Notice that all of the intermediate shapes have smooth boundaries, without pinches. Sharp features can arise only momentarily when there is a change in topology such as when two parts join. Figure 5 shows two more shape transformations that use this approach and that also incorporate warping. Warping is an another degree of control that may be added to any shape transformation technique, and is in fact

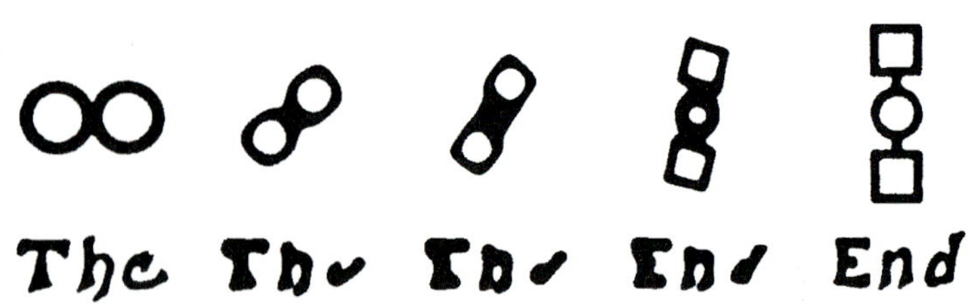


Figure 5: Two shape transformation sequences (using the variational implicit technique) that incorporate warping.

an orthogonal issue to those of implicit function creation and interpolation. Although it is not a focus of our research, for completeness we briefly describe warping in the appendix.

Why has this implicit function building method not been tried using other ways of creating implicit functions? Why not, for example, build a signed distance function in one higher dimension? Because a *complete* description of an object's boundary is required in order to build a signed distance function. When we embed our two shapes into a higher dimension, we only know a *piece* of the boundary of our desired higher-dimensional shape, namely the cross-sections that match the two given objects. In contrast, a complete boundary representation is *not* required when using variational interpolation to create an implicit function. Variational interpolation creates plausible function values in regions where we have no information, and especially in the "unknown" region between the two planes that contain all of our constraints. This plausibility of values comes from the smooth nature of the functions that are created by the variational approach.

### 5.2 Three-Dimensional Shape Transformation

Just as we create a 3D function to create a transformation between 2D shapes, we can move to 4D in order to create a sequence between 3D shapes. We perform shape interpolation between two 3D objects using boundary and normal constraints for each shape. We place the constraints from two 3D objects into four dimensional space, just as we placed constraints from 2D contours into 3D. Similar to contour interpolation, the constraints are separated from one another in the fourth dimension by some specified distance. We place all the constraints from the first object at $t = 0$, and the constraints from the second object are placed at $t = t_{max}$, where $t_{max}$ is the given separation distance. We then create a 4D implicit function using variational interpolation. An intermediate shape between the two given shapes is found by extracting the isosurface of a 3D "slice" (actually a volume) of the resulting 4D function.

Figure 6 shows two 3D shape transformation sequence that were constructed using this method. To extract these surfaces we use code published by Bloomenthal that begins at a seed location on the surface of a model and only evaluates the implicit function at points near previously visited locations [4]. This is far more efficient than sampling an entire volume of the implicit function and then extracting an isosurface from the volume. The matrix solution for the transformation sequence of Figure 6 (left) required 13.5 minutes, and each isosurface in the sequence took approximately 2.3 minutes to generate on an SGI Indigo2 with a 195 MHz R10000 processor. Figure 6 (right) shows a transformation between 3D shapes that used warping to align features.

## 6 Surface Reconstruction from Contours

So far we have only considered shape transformation between pairs of objects. In medical reconstruction, however, it is often necessary to create a surface from a large number of parallel 2D slices. Can't we just perform shape interpolation between pairs of slices and stack the results together to create one surface in 3D? Although this method will create a continuous surface, it is almost certain to produce a shape that has surface normal discontinuities at the planes of the original slices. In the plane of slice $i$, the surface created between slice pairs $i-1$ and $i$ will usually not agree in surface normal with the surface created between slices $i$ and $i+1$. Nearly all contour interpolation methods consider only pairs of contours at any one time, and thus suffer from such discontinuities. (A notable exception is [1]).

To avoid discontinuities in surface normal, we must use information about more than just two slices at a given time. We can accomplish this using a generalization of the variational approach to shape transformation. Assume that we begin with $k$ sets of constraints, one set for each 2D data slice. Instead of considering the contours in pairs, we place the constraints for all of the $k$ slices into

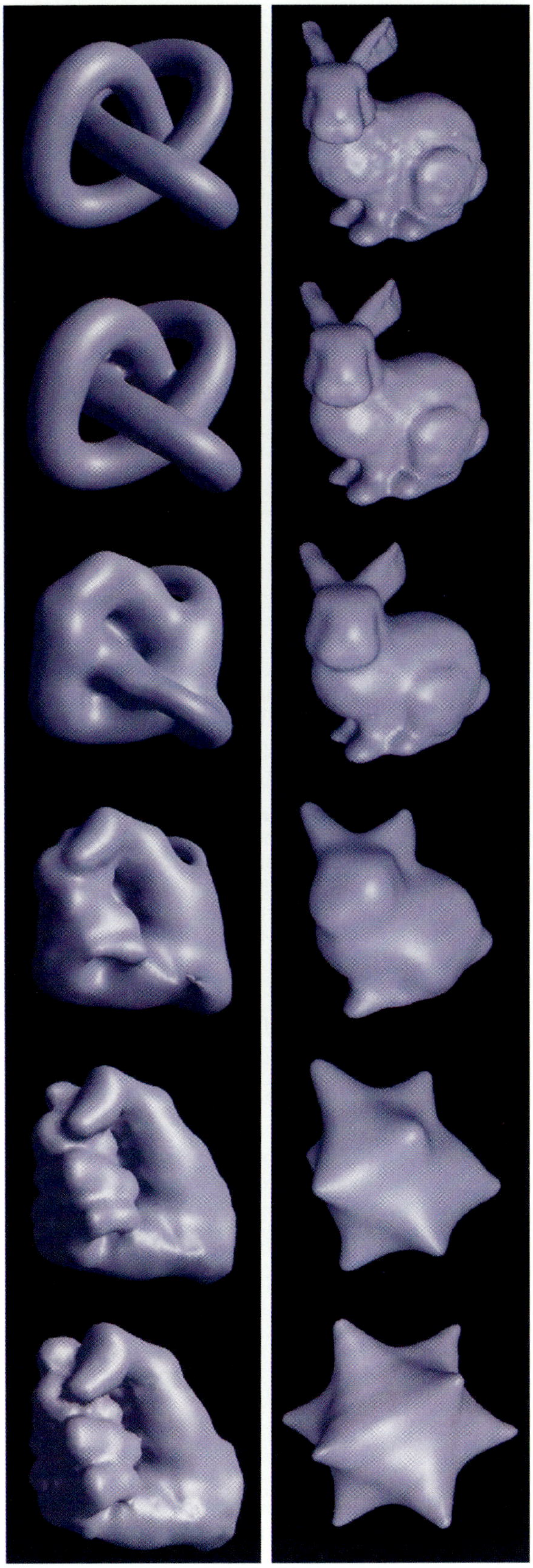

Figure 6: 3D shape transformation sequences.

3D simultaneously. Specifically, the constraints of slice $i$ are placed in the plane $z = si$, where $s$ is the spacing between planes. Once the constraints from *all* slices have been placed in 3D, we invoke

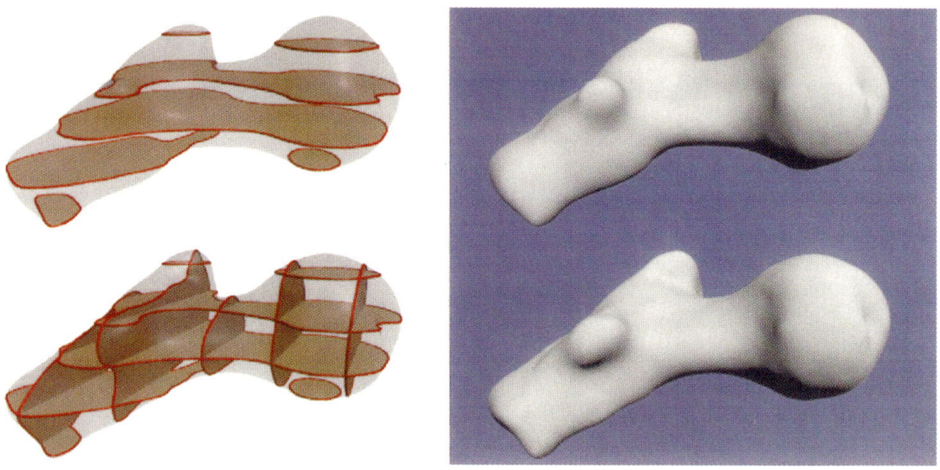

Figure 7: Reconstruction of hip joint from contours. Top row shows the five parallel slices used and the final surface. Bottom row shows intersecting contours and the more detailed surface that is created.

variational interpolation *once* to create a single implicit function in 3D. The zero-valued isosurface exactly passes through each contour of the data. Due to the smooth nature of variational interpolation, the gradient of the implicit function is everywhere continuous. This means that surface normal discontinuities are rare, appearing in pathological situations when the gradient vanishes such as when two features just barely touch. Figure 7 (top row) illustrates the result of this contour interpolation approach. The hip joint reconstruction in the upper right was created from the five slices shown at the upper left.

A side benefit of using the variational implicit function method is that it produces smoothly rounded caps on the ends of surfaces. Notice that in Figure 7 (top left) that the reconstructed surface extends beyond the constraints in the positive and negative $z$ direction (the direction of slice stacking). This "rounding off" of the ends is a natural side effect of variational interpolation, and need not be explicitly specified.

### 6.1 Non-Parallel Contours

In the previous section, we only considered placing constraints within planes that are all parallel to one another. There is nothing special about any particular set of planes, however, once we are specifying constraints in 3D. We can mix together constraints that are taken from planes at any angle whatsoever, so long as we know the relative positions of the planes (and thus the constraints). Most contour interpolation procedures cannot integrate data taken from slices in several directions, but the variational approach allows complete freedom in this regard. Figure 7 (lower row) shows several contours that are placed perpendicular to one another, and the result of using variational interpolation on the group of constraints from these contours.

### 6.2 Between-Contour Spacing

Up to this point we have not discussed the separating distance $s$ between the slices that contain the contour data. This separating distance has a concrete meaning in medical shape reconstruction from 2D contours. Here we know the actual 3D separation between the contours from the data capture process. This "natural" distance is the separating distance $s$ that should be used when reconstructing the surface using variational interpolation. Upon reflection, it is odd that some contour interpolation methods do not make use of the data capture distance between slices. In some cases a medical technician will deliberately vary the spacing between data slices in order to capture more data in a particular region of interest. Using variational interpolation, we may incorporate this information about varying separation distances into the surface reconstruction process.

For both special effects production and for computer aided design, the distance between the separating planes can be thought of as a control knob for the artist or designer. If the distance is small, only pairs of features from the two shapes that are very close to one another will be preserved through all the intermediate shapes. If the separation distance is large, the intermediate shape is guided by more global properties of the two shapes. In some sense, the separating distance specifies whether the shape transformation is local or global in nature. The separation distance is just one control knob for the user, and in the next section we will explore another user control.

## 7 Influence Shapes

In this section we present a method of controlling shape transformation by introducing an *influence shape*. The idea to use additional objects as controls for shape transformation was introduced by Rossignac and Kaul [24]. Such intermediate shape control can be performed in a natural way using variational interpolation. The key is to step into a still higher dimension when performing shape transformation.

Recall that to create a transformation sequence between two given shapes we added one new dimension, called $t$ earlier. We can think of the two shapes as being two points that are separated along the $t$ dimension, and these two points are connected by a line segment that joins the two points along this dimension. If we begin with three shapes, however, we can in effect place them at the three points of a triangle. In order to do so we need not just one additional dimension but two, call them $s$ and $t$.

As an example, we may begin with three different 3D shapes A, B and C. To each constraint that describes one of the shapes, we can add two new coordinates, $s$ and $t$. Constraints from shape A at $(x,y,z)$ are placed at $(x,y,z,0,0)$, constraints from shape B are placed at $(x,y,z,1,0)$ and shape C constraints are placed at $(x,y,z,1/2,1/2)$. Variational interpolation based on these 5-dimensional constraints results in a 5D implicit function. Three-dimensional slices of this function along the $s$-dimension between 0 and 1 are simply shape sequences between shapes A and B when the $t$-dimension value is fixed at zero. If, however, the $t$-dimension value is allowed to become positive as $s$ varies from 0 to 1, then the intermediate shapes will take on some of the characteristics of shape C. In fact, the 5D implicit function actually captures an entire family of shapes that are various blends between the three shapes. Figure 8 illustrates some members of such a family of shapes.

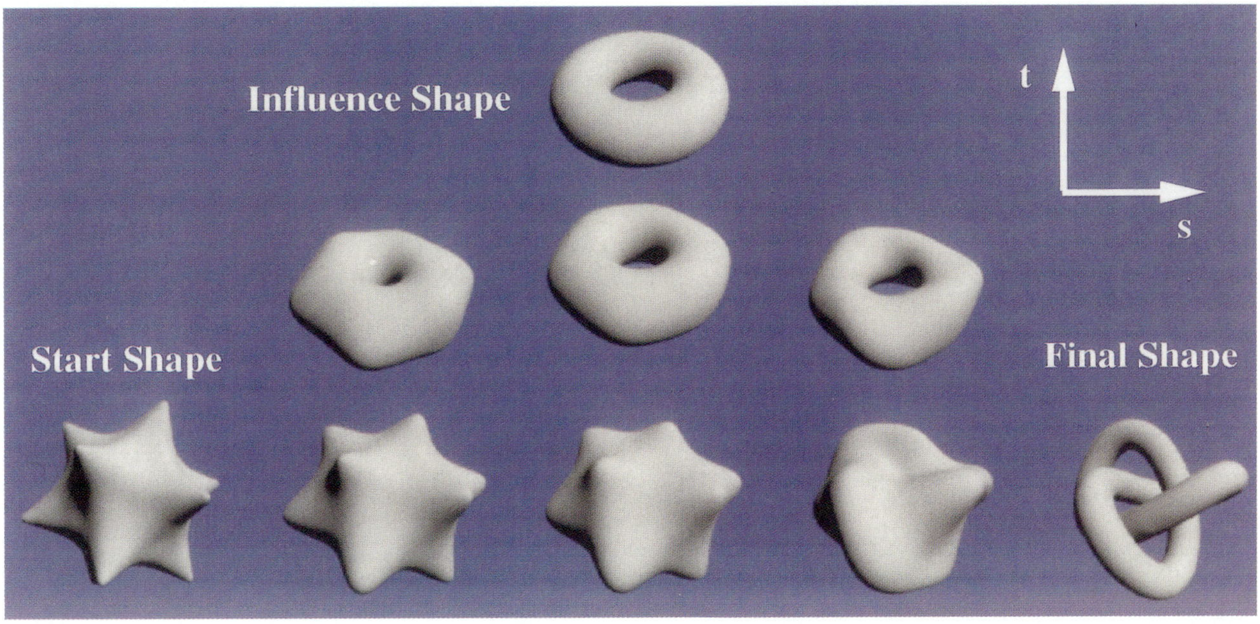


Figure 8: Sequence between star and knot can be influenced by a torus (the influence shape) if the path passes near the torus in the five-dimensional space.

There is no reason to stop at three shapes. It is possible to place four shapes at the corners of a quadrilateral, five shapes around a pentagon, and so on. If we wish to use four shapes, then placing the constraints at the corners of a quadrilateral using two additional dimensions would not allow us to produce a shape that was arbitrary mixtures between the shapes. In order to do so, we can place the constraints in yet a higher dimension, in effect placing the four shapes at the corners of a tetrahedron in $N+3$ dimensions, where $N$ is the dimension of the given shapes.

There are two related themes that guide our technique for shape transformation. The first is that shape transformation should be thought of as a shape-creation problem in a higher dimension. The second theme is that better shape transformation sequences are produced when all of the problem constraints are solved simultaneously— in our case by using variational interpolation. Influence shapes are the result of taking these ideas to an extreme.

## 8 Conclusions and Future Work

Our new approach uses variational interpolation to produce one implicit function that describes an entire sequence of shapes. Specific characteristics of this approach include:

- Smooth intermediate shapes
- Shape transformation in any number of dimensions
- Analytic solutions that are free of polygon and voxel artifacts
- Continuous surface normals for contour interpolation
- Contour slices may be at any orientation, even intersecting

This approach provides two new controls for creating shape transformation sequences:

- Separation distance gives local/global interpolation tradeoff
- May use influence shapes to control a transformation

The approach we have presented in this paper re-formulates the shape interpolation problem as an interpolation problem in one higher dimension. In essence, we treat the "time" dimension just like another spatial dimension. We have found that using the variational interpolation method produces excellent results, but the mathematical literature abounds with other interpolation methods. An exciting avenue for future work is to investigate what other interpolation techniques can also be used to create implicit functions for shape transformation. Another issue is whether shape transformation methods can be made fast enough to allow a user interactive control. Finally, how might surface properties such as color and texture be carried through intermediate objects?

## 9 Acknowledgements

This work owes a good deal to Andrew Glassner for getting us interested in the shape transformation problem. We thank our colleagues and the anonymous reviewers for their helpful suggestions. This work was funded by ONR grant N00014-97-1-0223.

## References

[1] Barequet, Gill, Daniel Shapiro and Ayellet Tal, "History Consideration in Reconstructing Polyhedral Surfaces from Parallel Slices," *Proceedings of Visualization '96*, San Francisco, California, Oct. 27 – Nov. 1, 1996, pp. 149–156.

[2] Barr, Alan H., "Global and Local Deformations of Solid Primitives," *Computer Graphics*, Vol. 18, No. 3 (SIGGRAPH 84), pp. 21–30.

[3] Beier, Thaddeus and Shawn Neely, "Feature-Based Image Metamorphosis," *Computer Graphics*, Vol. 26, No. 2 (SIGGRAPH 92), July 1992, pp. 35–42.

[4] Bloomenthal, Jules, "An Implicit Surface Polygonizer," in *Graphics Gems IV*, edited by Paul S. Heckbert, Academic Press, 1994, pp. 324–349.

[5] Bookstein, Fred L., "Principal Warps: Thin Plate Splines and the Decomposition of Deformations," *IEEE Transactions on Pattern Analysis and Machine Intelligence*, Vol. 11, No. 6, June 1989, pp. 567–585.

[6] Celniker, George and Dave Gossard, "Deformable Curve and Surface Finite-Elements for Free-Form Shape Design," *Computer Graphics*, Vol. 25, No. 4 (SIGGRAPH 91), July 1991, pp. 257–266.

[7] Cohen-Or, Daniel, David Levin and Amira Solomovici, "Three Dimensional Distance Field Metamorphosis," *ACM Transactions on Graphics*, 1997.

[8] Duchon, Jean, "Splines Minimizing Rotation-Invariant Semi-Norms in Sobolev Spaces," in *Constructive Theory of Functions of Several Variables*, Lecture Notes in Mathematics, edited by A. Dolb and B. Eckmann, Springer-Verlag, 1977, pp. 85–100.

[9] Duncan, Jody, "A Once and Future War," *Cinefex*, No. 47 (entire issue devoted to the film Terminator 2), August 1991, pp. 4–59.

[10] Fuchs, H., Z. M. Kedem and S. P. Uselton, "Optimal Surface Reconstruction from Planar Contours," *Communications of the ACM*, Vol. 20, No. 10, October 1977, pp. 693–702.

[11] Golub, Gene H. and Charles F. Ban Loan, *Matrix Computations*, John Hopkins University Press, 1996.

[12] Gregory, Arthur, Andrei State, Ming C. Lin, Dinesh Manocha, Mark A. Livingston, "Feature-based Surface Decomposition for Correspondence and Morphing between Polyhedra", *Proceedings of Computer Animation*, Philadelphia, PA., 1998.

[13] He, Taosong, Sidney Wang and Arie Kaufman, "Wavelet- Based Volume Morphing," *Proceedings of Visualization '94*, Washington, D. C., edited by Daniel Bergeron and Arie Kaufman, October 17-21, 1994, pp. 85–92.

[14] Herman, Gabor T., Jingsheng Zheng and Carolyn A. Bucholtz, "Shape-Based Interpolation," *IEEE Computer Graphics and Applications*, Vol. 12, No. 3 (May 1992), pp. 69–79.

[15] Hugues, John F., "Scheduled Fourier Volume Morphing," *Computer Graphics*, Vol. 26, No. 2 (SIGGRAPH 92), July 1992, pp. 43–46.

[16] Kaul, Anil and Jarek Rossignac, "Solid- Interpolating Deformations: Construction and animation of PIPs," *Proceedings of Eurographics '91*, Vienna, Austria, 2-6 Sept. 1991, pp. 493–505.

[17] Kent, James R., Wayne E. Carlson and Richard E. Parent, "Shape Transformation for Polyhedral Objects," *Computer Graphics*, Vol. 26, No. 2 (SIGGRAPH 92), July 1992, pp. 47–54.

[18] Lerios, Apostolos, Chase Garfinkle and Marc Levoy, "Feature-Based Volume Metamorphosis," *Computer Graphics Proceedings*, Annual Conference Series (SIGGRAPH 95), pp. 449–456.

[19] Levin, David, "Multidimensional Reconstruction by Set-valued Approximation," *IMA J. Numerical Analysis*, Vol. 6, 1986, pp. 173–184.

[20] Litwinowicz, Peter and Lance Williams, "Animating Images with Drawings," *Computer Graphics Proceedings*, Annual Conference Series (SIGGRAPH 94), pp. 409–412.

[21] Lorenson, William and Harvey E. Cline, "Marching Cubes: A High Resolution 3-D Surface Construction Algorithm," *Computer Graphics*, Vol. 21, No. 4 (SIGGRAPH 87), July 1987, pp. 163–169.

[22] Meyers, David and Shelley Skinner, "Surfaces From Contours: The Correspondence and Branching Problems," *Proceedings of Graphics Interface '91*, Calgary, Alberta, 3-7 June 1991, pp. 246–254.

[23] Payne, Bradley A. and Arthur W. Toga, "Distance Field Manipulation of Surface Models," *IEEE Computer Graphics and Applications*, Vol. 12, No. 1, January 1992, pp. 65–71.

[24] Rossignac, Jarek and Anil Kaul, "AGRELs and BIPs: Metamorphosis as a Bezier Curve in the Space of Polyhedra," *Proceedings of Eurographics '94*, Oslo, Norway, Sept. 12–16, 1994, pp. 179–184.

[25] Sederberg, Thomas W. and Eugene Greenwood, "A Physically Based Approach to 2-D Shape Blending," *Computer Graphics*, Vol. 26, No. 2 (SIGGRAPH 92), July 1992, pp. 25–34.

[26] Sederberg, Thomas W. and Scott R. Parry, "Free-Form Deformations of Solid Geometric Models," *Computer Graphics*, Vol. 20, No. 4 (SIGGRAPH 86), pp. 151–160.

[27] Turk, Greg and James F. O'Brien, "Variational Implicit Surfaces," Tech Report GIT-GVU-99-15, Georgia Institute of Technology, May 1999, 9 pages.

[28] Wolberg, George, *Digital Image Warping*, IEEE Computer Society Press, Los Alamitos, California 1990.

## 10 Appendix: Warping

Warping is a commonly used method of providing user control of shape interpolation. Although warping is not a focus of our research, for the sake of completeness we describe below how warping may be used together with our shape transformation technique. Research on warping (sometimes called deformation) include [2, 26, 28, 3, 18, 7].

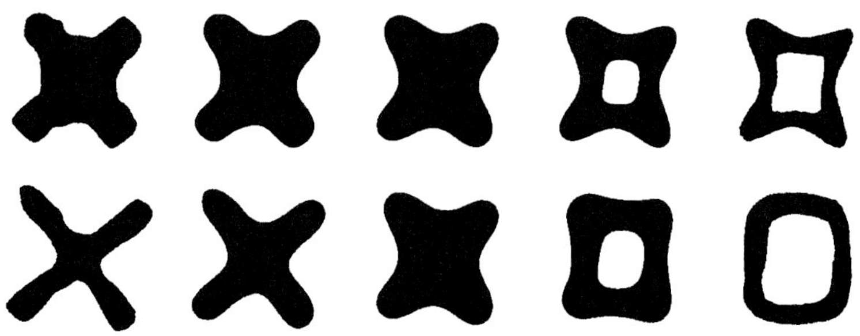

Figure 9: The extreme left and right shapes in the top row have been warped before creating the upper shape transformation sequence. The lower row is an un-warped version of this sequence that gives the final transformation from an X to O.

For symmetry, we choose to warp each shape "half-way" to the other shape. Given a set of user-supplied corresponding points between two shapes $A$ and $B$, we construct two displacement warp functions $\mathbf{w}_A$ and $\mathbf{w}_B$. The function $\mathbf{w}_A$ specifies what values to add to locations on shape $A$ in order to warp it half-way to shape $B$, and the warping function $\mathbf{w}_B$ warps $B$ half of the way to $A$.

In what follows, we will describe the warping process for two-dimensional shapes. Let $\{\mathbf{a}_1, \mathbf{a}_2, \ldots, \mathbf{a}_k\}$ be a set of points on shape $A$, and let $\{\mathbf{b}_1, \mathbf{b}_2, \ldots, \mathbf{b}_k\}$ be the corresponding points on $B$. We construct the two functions $w_A$ and $w_B$ such that $w_A(\mathbf{a}_i) = (\mathbf{b}_i - \mathbf{a}_i)/2$ and $w_B(\mathbf{b}_i) = (\mathbf{a}_i - \mathbf{b}_i)/2$ hold for all $i$. Constructing these functions is another example of scattered data interpolation which we can solve using variational techniques. For 2D shapes, if $\mathbf{a}_i = (a_i^x, a_i^y)$ and $\mathbf{b}_i = (b_i^x, b_i^y)$, then the $x$ component $w_A^x$of the displacement warp $\mathbf{w}_A$ has $k$ constraints at the positions $\mathbf{a}_i$ with values $(b_i^x - a_i^x)/2$. We invoke variational interpolation to satisfy these constraints, and do the same to construct the $y$ component of the warp. The function $\mathbf{w}_B$ is constructed similarly. This is not a new technique, and researchers who use thin-plate techniques to perform shape warping include [5, 20] and others.

In order to combine warping with shape transformation, we use these functions to displace all of the boundary constraints of the given shapes. These displaced boundary constraints are embedded in 3D (as described in Section 5) and then variational interpolation is used to create the implicit function that describes the entire shape transformation sequence. The result of this process is a three-dimensional implicit function, each slice of which is an intermediate shape between two warped shapes. The top row of Figure 9 shows such warped intermediate shapes. We can think of the two "ends" of this implicit function (at $t = 0$ and $t = t_{max}$) as being warped versions of our original shapes. In order to match the two original shapes, the surface of this 3D implicit function needs to be unwarped. To simplify the equations, assume that the value of $t_{max}$ is 2. If $t \leq 1$ the unwarping function $u(x,y,t)$ is:

$$u(x,y,t) = (x + (1-t)w_A^x(x,y), y + (1-t)w_A^y(x,y), t) \tag{4}$$

If $t > 1$ then the unwarping function is:

$$u(x,y,t) = (x + (t-1)w_B^x(x,y), y + (t-1)w_B^y(x,y), t) \tag{5}$$

At the extreme of $t = 0$, the warp $u(x,y,t)$ un-does the warping we used for the first shape. At $t = 2$, the function $u(x,y,t)$ reverses the warping used for the second shape. When $t = 1$ (the middle shape in the sequence), no warp is performed. The bottom sequence of shapes in Figure 9 shows the result of the entire shape transformation process that includes warping. Both sequences in Figure 5 were created using warping in addition to shape transformation.

Although we have described the warping process for 2D shapes, the same method may be used for shape transformation between 3D shapes. For Figure 6 (right), warping was used to align the bunny ears to the points of the star.

# Multiresolution Mesh Morphing

Aaron W. F. Lee* Princeton University

David Dobkin† Princeton University

Wim Sweldens‡ Bell Laboratories

Peter Schröder§ Caltech

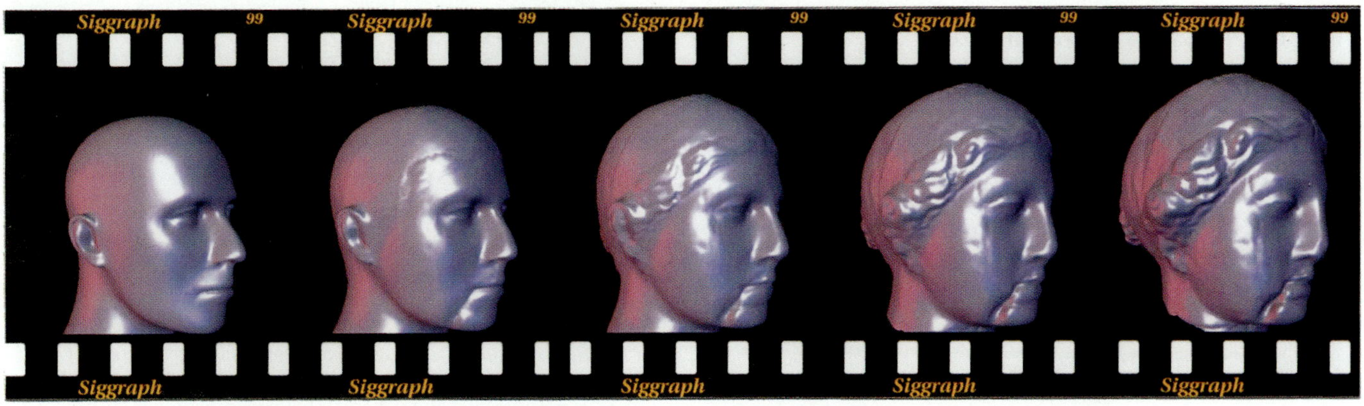


Figure 1: *Morph sequence between two topologically equivalent triangle meshes.*

## Abstract

We present a new method for user controlled morphing of two homeomorphic triangle meshes of arbitrary topology. In particular we focus on the problem of establishing a correspondence map between source and target meshes. Our method employs the MAPS algorithm to parameterize both meshes over simple base domains and an additional harmonic map bringing the latter into correspondence. To control the mapping the user specifies any number of feature pairs, which control the parameterizations produced by the MAPS algorithm. Additional controls are provided through a direct manipulation interface allowing the user to tune the mapping between the base domains. We give several examples of æsthetically pleasing morphs which can be created in this manner with little user input. Additionally we demonstrate examples of temporal and spatial control over the morph.

**CR Categories and Subject Descriptors:** I.3.3 [**Computer Graphics**]: Picture/Image Generation - *Display Algorithms, Viewing Algorithms*; I.3.5 [**Computer Graphics**]: Computational Geometry and Object Modeling - *Curve, Surface, Solid and Object Representations, Hierarchy and Geometric Transformations, Object Hierarchies*; I.3.6 [**Computer Graphics**]: Methodology and Techniques - *interaction techniques*; I.3.7 [**Computer Graphics**]: Three-Dimensional Graphics and Realism - *animation*

**Additional Keywords:** Meshes, surface parameterization, mesh simplification, multiresolution, interpolation, morphing

*wailee@cs.princeton.edu
†dpd@cs.princeton.edu
‡wim@bell-labs.com
§ps@cs.caltech.edu



## 1 Introduction

Advances in 3D scanning and acquisition technology have made dense triangle meshes popular as representations of complex objects. These scanning devices typically create triangulations which form a surface of arbitrary topology. The large size of the meshes makes it difficult to manipulate them efficiently, an issue which can be addressed through the use of multiresolution representations.

Metamorphosis (or morphing) is the process of gradually changing a source object through intermediate objects into a target object. It has numerous applications from modeling to the generation of animation sequences for the movie and advertising industries. Much of the work done in this area has been on 2D metamorphosis, i.e., morphing of filmed or rendered sequences. 3D morphs on the other hand change the geometry of an object independent of subsequent rendering. Such morphs are significantly harder to compute and control.

Most techniques for morphing, both 2D and 3D, are based on a sparse set of user selected feature pairs. These are then used to establish a dense set of correspondences which in turn are used in subsequent interpolation between source and destination. The key to a successful method is its ability to achieve æsthetically pleasing morphs with few such feature pairs while providing means for very detailed control if so desired.

For example, patch based models, if they share the same control mesh, can be gracefully morphed into each other by associating corresponding control points. The underlying smooth surface representation provides the means to extend this sparse set of feature pairs in a predictable fashion to the entire surface. The situation is quite different when the source and destination surfaces are given as dense, irregular connectivity meshes with no obvious coarse level controls.

One possible approach is to transform the meshes into a sampled volumetric representation and apply 3D extensions of image morphing techniques. Instead we work with the meshes directly to avoid issues such as discretization artifacts, high computational cost, and difficulty of control, which volumetric methods generally exhibit.

Specifically we make the following contributions in this paper:

### 3.1 Overview of the Algorithm

In our setting we have two meshes: the *source* mesh $(\mathcal{S}, \mathcal{K}_s)$ with $N_s$ vertices and the target mesh $(\mathcal{T}, \mathcal{K}_t)$ with $N_t$ vertices. Our goal is the construction of a correspondence map $\mathbf{M}$ between $\varphi(\mathcal{S})$ and $\varphi(\mathcal{T})$. The correspondence map has to be a bijection to avoid cracks and folds in the morph. Note that in general the mapping $\mathbf{M}(s_i)$ of a vertex of the source is not a vertex of the target, but instead lies somewhere in a target triangle.

In the first stage we apply the MAPS algorithm [24] to both source and target mesh, constructing coarse base domains $(\mathcal{S}^{(0)}, \mathcal{K}_s^{(0)})$ and $(\mathcal{T}^{(0)}, \mathcal{K}_t^{(0)})$ through a simplification hierarchy, as well as two bijective mappings $\Pi_s : \varphi(\mathcal{S}) \to \varphi(\mathcal{S}^{(0)})$ and $\Pi_t : \varphi(\mathcal{T}) \to \varphi(\mathcal{T}^{(0)})$.

Next we compute a correspondence map $\mathbf{M}^{(0)}$ between the source base domain $\varphi(\mathcal{S}^{(0)})$ and target base domain $\varphi(\mathcal{T}^{(0)})$. Because the base domains are coarse this map can be computed quickly. The final correspondence map between the original meshes is then given as:

$$\mathbf{M} : \varphi(\mathcal{S}) \to \varphi(\mathcal{T}) \text{ with } \mathbf{M} = \Pi_t^{-1}\,\mathbf{M}^{(0)}\,\Pi_s. \qquad (1)$$

The user can control the computation of the correspondence map to the extent desired by specifying features in the original meshes. The MAPS algorithm ensures that these features are mapped to edges in the base domain. The part of the mapping $\mathbf{M}^{(0)}$ that is not determined by the user defined feature pairs is computed automatically but can still be adjusted by the user. Feature pairs can be given by vertices, such as the tip of the nose, and lines which are a sequence of connected edges such as the mouth (see Figure 2). The beginning and end points of a feature lines are also feature vertices.

The overall structure of the algorithm is illustrated by the commutative diagram in Figure 2. On the top row are the source and target meshes. The bottom row shows the corresponding source and target base domains. The user specified feature points and lines are highlighted in red (resp. yellow). All maps respect the corresponding feature pairs.

**A Brief Review of MAPS** The MAPS algorithm uses a mesh hierarchy built through successive removal of a maximally independent set of vertices [10], followed by retriangulation of the resulting holes. By never removing any of the feature points, we can assure that they are contained in the base domain. Say the user specified $U$ feature points and assume the corresponding vertex indices are numbered from 1 to $U$. The parameterization is built so that

$$\Pi_s(s_i) = s_i \text{ and } \Pi_t(t_i) = t_i \text{ for } 1 \le i \le U. \qquad (2)$$

In case of a feature line, the parameterization will map all the points of the original feature line to a sequence of edges (possibly one) in the base domain.

Note that using linear interpolation the maps $\Pi$ are defined for *every* point on the mesh, not only the vertices. The map $\Pi^{-1}$ can also be computed for every point on the base domain using a point location algorithm [24].

### 3.2 The Base Domain Correspondence Map

Construction of the base domain correspondence map consists of the following steps:

- globally align the source and destination base domains and project the source base domain to the target base domain;
- apply an iterative relaxation procedure to improve the mapping;
- user adjustment of the coarse correspondence to produce the final mapping.

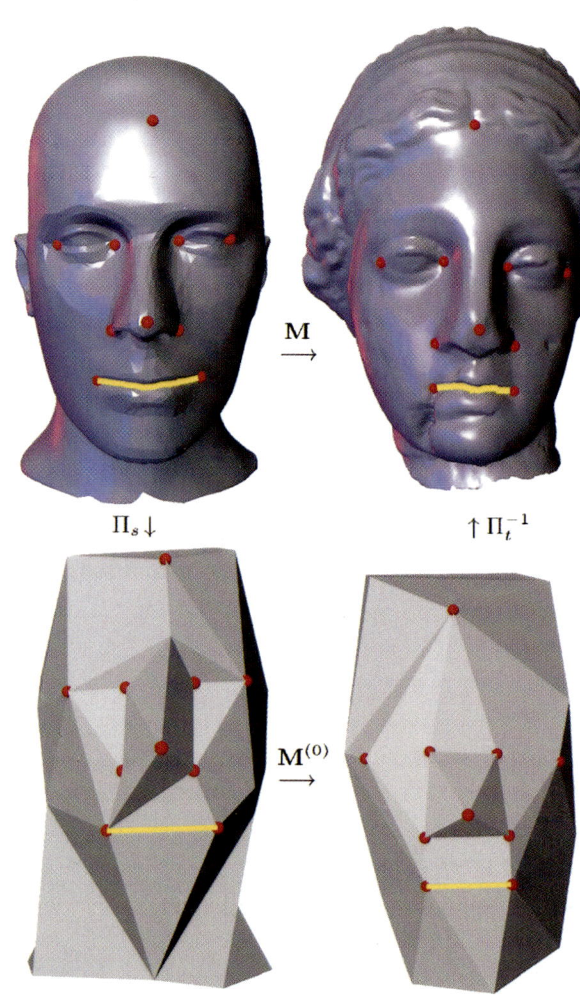


Figure 2: *Overview of the correspondence map computation. The user specifies pairs of feature points (red) and lines (yellow) in the original meshes (top). We then use MAPS to compute mappings $\Pi_s$ and $\Pi_t$ between the original meshes and the respective base domains (bottom). Next we compute the correspondence map $\mathbf{M}^{(0)}$ for the base domains. The final correspondence map $\mathbf{M}$ follows from composing these maps as $\Pi_t^{-1}\mathbf{M}^{(0)}\Pi_s$. As all the individual maps respect the feature pairs, so does the final map $\mathbf{M}$.*

**Global alignment of base domains** Given that feature points are guaranteed to be in the base domain, we can define their correspondence map as $\mathbf{M}^{(0)}(s_i) = t_i$ for $1 \le i \le U$. We still have to establish correspondences for the vertices of the source base domain which are not feature points. Assume that these points have indices $U+1 \ldots N_s^{(0)}$. We now need to find suitable positions for $\mathbf{M}^{(0)}(s_i)$ for $U+1 \le i \le N_s^{(0)}$ on the target base domain. This procedure begins by globally aligning the two base domains and then computing a starting guess for $\mathbf{M}^{(0)}(s_i)$ as the projection of $s_i$ onto the closest triangle of $\varphi(\mathcal{K}_t^{(0)})$.

The global alignment can be done either manually or semi-automatically (see, e.g., [3, 7, 12]), and we have used Chen and Medioni's method with good success. Sometimes user intervention is required for the initial alignment if the source and the target objects are significantly different from each other. The initial projection is improved through an iterative relaxation procedure. Relaxation in planar settings is fairly straightforward and well understood. Computing relaxation *on* a mesh is non-trivial. Indeed,

- **Dense correspondences for arbitrary meshes:** we address the problem of establishing dense correspondences between any two irregular connectivity meshes with the only requirement that they be topologically equivalent. This involves the construction of mappings from the fine meshes to their coarse base domains and of a mapping between the base domains. These mappings are realized through the *metamesh*, a topologically and geometrically merged version of source and destination meshes. The necessary computations are efficient enough to allow us to compute high quality morphs on meshes with thousands of triangles on a low end PC within several minutes.
- **Fine and coarse user control:** we provide easy and effective controls for the mapping from source to destination. In the case of fine features, such as vertices or connected sets of edges ("lines"), simply marking them on each mesh and pairing them up, is sufficient. Coarse control can be exercised by interactively modifying the mapping between the coarse source and destination domains. Providing a small set of feature pairs is generally sufficient to achieve æsthetically pleasing results.

Our algorithm proceeds by first creating parameterizations of the source and destination mesh using the MAPS (Multiresolution Adaptive Parameterization of Surfaces) algorithm of Lee et al. [24]. MAPS controls the parameterization using as few or as many features on the original meshes as the user desires. These two parameterizations are then put into correspondence through the construction of a map between the source and destination domains. This stage provides additional controls to the user to influence the morph in a broad fashion. The composition of these stages is used for subsequent shape interpolation.

## 2 Previous Work

Lazarus and Verroust [23] give an excellent survey of previous work on the 3D morphing problem. As they note, there are an unlimited number of ways to interpolate from one object to another. Such interpolations may be performed for geometry as well as attributes such as color. Algorithms for morphing are evaluated mainly by criteria related to the ease with which the results can be controlled and the æsthetic quality of the results themselves. Ease encompasses both the amount of work an artist has to invest, as well as the predictability of the result. Since æsthetic quality is subjective precise user control is important.

Most methods for morphing 3D objects use either discrete or combinatoric representations for the objects themselves. Discrete representations typically voxelize objects or their distance functions and aim to extend 2D morphing [2, 25, 36] algorithms to 3D.

Lerios et al. [26] extended the work of Beier and Neely [2] and used fields of influence of 3D primitives to warp volumes. Hughes [16] proposed a method working in the Fourier domain. This provided novel controls over the morph by treating individual frequency bands with different functions of time. He et al. [15] extended these ideas to a wavelet setting. Whitaker and Breen [35] performed morphing through the application of evolution equations. Payne [28] described a distance-field volumetric cross-dissolving technique.

The main advantage of volumetric methods is the ease with which they support changing genus. This comes at the price of having to reduce a model to a sampled representation on a finite grid. Since the grid is three dimensional, memory and computation costs can be prohibitive, limiting the visual fidelity of the results.

The alternative is to work directly on boundary representations such as polygonal meshes or patch complexes. Methods for this approach [20, 27, 29, 22, 30, 33, 8, 9, 6, 17, 14] have to first solve the *vertex correspondence* problem, i.e., computing the association of vertices or triangles between the source mesh and the target mesh. Lazarus and Verroust identify this as the key problem and it forms the focus of our paper.

Many approaches to the correspondence problem have been described, but there appears to be no general solution. Kent et al. [20] merged the mesh connectivities under a projection. This works well for star-shaped, swept, or revolutionary objects. Kaul and Rossignac [19] computed the Minkowski sum of scaled versions of the models which works well when the polyhedra are convex. For details of other warping and morphing techniques the reader is referred to [13, 36].

The work closest in spirit to ours is that of Gregory et al. [14] and Kanai et al. [18]. Gregory et al. give a method that allows the user to specify pairs and then decompose the polyhedron into patches. Patches of the source and target meshes are paired and morphed. This approach allows them to morph a broad class of objects. However it requires the user to outline the *entire* network of top level patch boundaries. Especially for large meshes this can be slow and tedious.

Kanai et al. have also extended their previous work [17], which used harmonic maps for morphing, to arbitrary topology triangle meshes. The basic idea is to define reference shapes by using vertex-to-vertex correspondences between the two meshes. The reference shape defines a partition of the mesh and each of the partitioned meshes is embedded into a polygonal region in the plane through a harmonic map. By overlapping those two embedded meshes, they establish correspondence between them. The number of partitions has to be identical so that they can be paired up and mapped to the same plane.

Their harmonic map computations are performed at the finest level while we only invoke such a solver for the coarse base domains. Additionally, we only require a small set of feature pairs and the coarse domain of the two meshes can be quite different to better adapt to the geometries, providing more flexibility. The efficiency of our method allows us to do this for relatively large meshes ensuring that the final surface renderings are of high visual quality.

## 3 Computing the Correspondence Map

As discussed above the key problem in morphing from one mesh to another is the establishment of the correspondence map with suitable user controls. In this section we describe the different stages we employ to compute the correspondence map. To do so we first fix some notation.

**Notation** When describing meshes mathematically, it is useful to separate the topological and geometric information. To this end we introduce some notation inspired by [32]. We denote a triangle mesh as a pair $(\mathcal{P}, \mathcal{K})$, where $\mathcal{P}$ is a set of $N$ point positions $p_i = (x_i, y_i, z_i) \in \mathbf{R}^3$ with $1 \leq i \leq N$, and $\mathcal{K}$ is an *abstract simplicial complex* which contains all the topological, i.e., adjacency information. The complex $\mathcal{K}$ is a set of subsets of $\{1, \ldots, N\}$. These subsets are called simplices and come in 3 types: vertices $v = \{i\} \in \mathcal{K}$, edges $e = \{i, j\} \in \mathcal{K}$, and faces $f = \{i, j, k\} \in \mathcal{K}$, so that any non-empty subset of a simplex of $\mathcal{K}$ is again a simplex of $\mathcal{K}$, e.g., if a face is present so are its edges and vertices.

The *geometric realization* $\varphi(a)$ for $a \in \mathcal{K}$ is the strictly convex hull of all points $p_i$ with $i \in a$. Thus $\varphi(\{i\}) = p_i$, $\varphi(\{i, j\})$ is the open line segment between $p_i$ and $p_j$, and $\varphi(\{i, j, k\})$ is the open triangle between $p_i$, $p_j$, and $p_k$. The geometric realization $\varphi(\mathcal{K})$ is given by $\cup_{a \in \mathcal{K}} \varphi(a)$ and forms a polyhedron embedded in $\mathbf{R}^3$.

Two vertices $\{i\}$ and $\{j\}$ are *neighbors* if $\{i, j\} \in \mathcal{K}$. A set of vertices is *independent* if no two vertices are neighbors. A set of vertices is *maximally independent* if no larger independent set contains it. The 1-ring neighborhood of a vertex $\{i\}$ is the set $\mathcal{V}(i) = \{j \mid \{i, j\} \in \mathcal{K}\}$. The *degree* of a vertex is its number of neighbors.

a linear combination of neighboring points typically no longer lies on the mesh. To address this issue we base our relaxation algorithm on shortest path computations. Our relaxation method is similar to Turk's retiling technique [34]. He retiles a polygonal model by relaxing the new sample points so that they are evenly distributed over the model.

**Relaxation *on* a Mesh** Assume the guess for $\mathbf{M}^{(0)}(s_i)$ lies in a triangle $\varphi(t)$ $(t \in \mathcal{T}^{(0)})$ of the target base domain. The neighbors of $s_i$ as defined by the source base domain connectivity, i.e., the $\mathbf{M}^{(0)}(s_j)$ with $j \in \mathcal{V}_s^{(0)}(i)$, need not lie in $\varphi(t)$. This is illustrated in Figure 3. The center vertex is $v = \mathbf{M}^{(0)}(s_i)$ and its neighbors $\mathbf{M}^{(0)}(s_j)$ are denoted by $v_j$. Compute the shortest paths between $v$ and each of the $v_j$. Denote their lengths as measured on the mesh by $l_j$. The intersection between the boundary of $\varphi(t)$ and each shortest path is given by $v'_j$ which define normalized directions:

$$\vec{d}_j = \frac{v'_j - v}{\|v'_j - v\|},$$

indicated by the bold arrows. The new, relaxed position is given by

$$v := (1-\xi)v + \xi \sum_j \frac{\vec{d}_j}{l_j},$$

where the underrelaxation parameter $\xi < 1$ is chosen to assure that $v$ moves no further than the boundary of $\varphi(t)$. This allows us to gracefully move into a neighboring triangle in the next iteration. Iterating this relaxation procedure will evenly distribute the source domain vertices on the target base domain. For feature

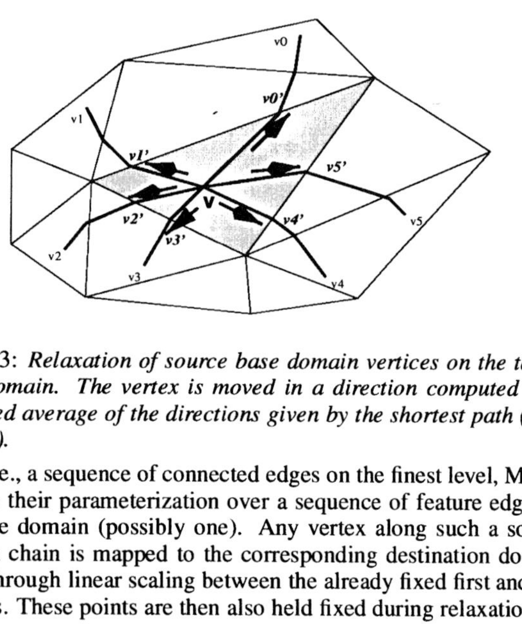


Figure 3: *Relaxation of source base domain vertices on the target base domain. The vertex is moved in a direction computed as a weighted average of the directions given by the shortest path (bold arrows).*

*lines*, i.e., a sequence of connected edges on the finest level, MAPS ensures their parameterization over a sequence of feature edges in the base domain (possibly one). Any vertex along such a source domain chain is mapped to the corresponding destination domain chain through linear scaling between the already fixed first and last vertices. These points are then also held fixed during relaxation.

**Shortest Path Computation** In general computing the exact shortest path between two points on a mesh is a difficult problem. Instead we use the method proposed by Lanthier et al. [21] to approximate the shortest path. Prior to the computation we introduce intermediate edge points (called *Steiner Points*) which subdivide each edge and construct a complete graph within each triangle. We do this for each triangle. Approximate shortest paths are calculated based on this graph using Dijkstra's algorithm [1].

**Boundaries** Notice that the mesh may contain boundaries. A boundary of a mesh $\partial M$ is a closed loop which consists of a set of edges. Such boundaries must also be identified in the same manner as an open chain (feature line). In particular this implies that source and domain should have the same number of holes.

**Caution** We note that this relaxation algorithm depends on the user fixing some feature points in order to reduce the degrees of freedom, e.g., in the mannequin head to Spock head morphing, the user fixes one vertex at the top and four along the neck boundary. This works well in cases where the source and target base domains are similar. If the base domains are highly dissimilar, shortest paths may cross and flipped triangles may appear. The interface can flag them by computing their signed area. The problem can be addressed by fixing more points and repeating the relaxation.

# 4 Additional Controls

We can treat the result of the above relaxation procedure as an initial solution to the base domain correspondence. In general the base domain of the source mesh and the target mesh are quite different and this initial solution may not be what the user desires. The user can exercise further control in the base domain correspondence mapping as we now describe.

We allow the user to map a vertex on the source base domain onto any point on the target base domain to adjust the mapping. This is done by user interface controls that allow the user to map a vertex on one domain to a vertex, point on an edge, or a point in a triangle on the other base domain.

Since the number of base domain vertices is small, adjustment can be done quickly. Our experience is that for similar objects such as two heads, little (if any) further adjustment is needed. In the case of dissimilar objects the adjustment is more involved as illustrated in the horse to rabbit morph in Section 5.

## 4.1 Extending $\mathbf{M}^{(0)}$

At this point we have computed $\mathbf{M}^{(0)}$ only for the vertices of $\mathcal{S}^{(0)}$. We next describe how to compute the map for *any* point of the source base domain (see Figure 4). Consider a triangle $\{i,j,k\} \in \mathcal{K}_s^{(0)}$ of the source base domain. Put its vertices on the target base domain using $\mathbf{M}^{(0)}$ and call them $I = \mathbf{M}^{(0)}(s_i)$, $J = \mathbf{M}^{(0)}(s_j)$, and $K = \mathbf{M}^{(0)}(s_k)$. The points $I$, $J$, and $K$ in general do not lie within a single triangle of the target base domain. We use the already computed shortest paths $\overline{IJ}$, $\overline{JK}$, and $\overline{KI}$ on the target base domain (thick line). This outlines a "triangular shaped" region $IJK$ on the target base domain (shaded). The triangles of the target base domain cut this region $IJK$ into polygons each of which we retriangulate. We next use the piecewise linear harmonic map technique of Eck et al. [11]. By taking the $I$, $J$, $K$ as boundary points and mapping them to $s_i$, $s_j$, and $s_k$ we compute a mapping between $IJK$ and the corresponding source triangle. In this example only one interior vertex needs to be relaxed. In general the computation is fast since only a handful of vertices are involved.

By doing this for every triangle of the source base domain we effectively build the map $\mathbf{M}^{(0)}$ for every point of the source base domain.

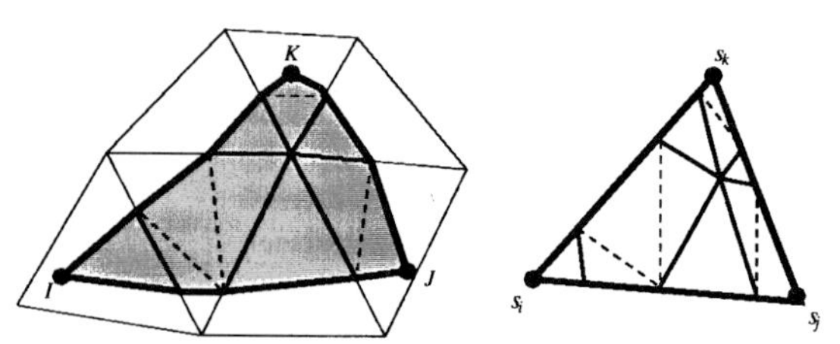


Figure 4: *The source base domain triangle maps to a triangular shaped region (shaded) on the target base domain. We compute the harmonic mapping of this region to a triangle so as to place the target base domain vertices on the source base domain.*

## 4.2 The Final Correspondence Map

Once we have the base domain correspondence map we can place any source mesh point onto the target using the composition $\Pi_t^{-1}\,\mathbf{M}^{(0)}\,\Pi_s$. The inverse map on the target mesh is computed using a point location algorithm [5] on the target base domain. This allows us to map *any* point of $\varphi(\mathcal{S})$ onto $\varphi(\mathcal{T})$.

In the morph we can now interpolate between $s_i$ and $\mathbf{M}(s_i) \in \varphi(\mathcal{T})$. However, the source connectivity $\mathcal{K}_s$ and target connectivity $\mathcal{K}_t$ are quite different. Starting the morph from $(\mathcal{S}, \mathcal{K}_s)$ would get us $(\mathbf{M}(\mathcal{S}), \mathcal{K}_s)$, which are the source vertices placed on the target mesh with the *source* connectivity. This is a fairly arbitrarily remeshed version of the target. Even though it roughly captures the geometry of the target, it will still have numerous artifacts. Our goal is to reach exactly $(\mathcal{T}, \mathcal{K}_t)$, not some remeshed version. Therefore we introduce the notion of a metamesh.

## 4.3 The Metamesh

The purpose of the *metamesh* $(\mathcal{P}, \mathcal{K}_p)$ is to combine the source connectivity $\mathcal{K}_s$ and target connectivity $\mathcal{K}_t$. We want to do this in such a way that for certain metamesh point positions $\mathcal{P} = \mathcal{P}_s$, the geometric realization $\varphi(\mathcal{P}_s)$ coincides with $\varphi(\mathcal{S})$, while for other point positions $\mathcal{P} = \mathcal{P}_t$, the geometric realization coincides with $\varphi(\mathcal{T})$.

To define the abstract complex $\mathcal{K}_p$ we need to find vertices, edges, and faces. We start out by defining the vertices of $\mathcal{K}_p$ as $\mathcal{V}_p = \mathcal{V}_s \cup \mathcal{V}_t \cup \mathcal{V}_i$ where $\mathcal{V}_s$ (resp. $\mathcal{V}_t$) are the vertices of $\mathcal{K}_s$ (resp. $\mathcal{K}_t$) and $\mathcal{V}_i$ are new vertices introduced by intersection of source and target mesh edges.

**Tracing Edge Segments** To find the connectivity of the metamesh we start out by drawing edges *on the target mesh* between the points $\mathbf{M}(\mathcal{S})$. Take two source vertices $s_i$ and $s_j$ with $\{i, j\} \in \mathcal{K}_s$, i.e., an edge of the finest level source mesh, and consider their placement $\mathbf{M}(s_i)$ and $\mathbf{M}(s_j)$ on the target. If they belong to the same target triangle, we can directly connect them with a line. Otherwise we connect them with a segmented line given by $\mathbf{M}(\varphi(\{i, j\}))$. This segmented line can be computed as follows. Start with the segment $\varphi(\{i, j\})$ and trace it through all the different piecewise linear conformal maps that make up the map $\Pi_s$. Each of these conformal maps are used in the MAPS algorithm for flattening a local neighborhood. Thus it is easy to check when the segment $\varphi(\{i, j\})$ breaks into two segments. Put these segments in a list. Start tracing the two new segments and whenever they break add the subsegments to the list. If at any time during this procedure two consecutive segments lie within the same triangle again, we can merge them. Continue this procedure until one arrives at a list of segments connecting $\Pi(s_i)$ and $\Pi(s_j)$ on the source base domain. Because of the merging and the fact that the base domain is so much coarser than the original, almost all lists will contain a single segment.

Given this sequence of segments trace them through $\mathbf{M}^{(0)}$, i.e., from the source base domain to the target base domain. $\mathbf{M}^{(0)}$ is also made up of local "flattenings," this time coming from the base domain correspondence map. Once again it is easy to check when segments break into further subsegments. After this step we have a list of segments connecting $\mathbf{M}^{(0)}(\Pi(s_i))$ and $\mathbf{M}^{(0)}(\Pi(s_j))$ on the target base domain. Finally the same procedure is applied through the mapping $\Pi_t^{-1}$. If at any time two consecutive segments lie within the same triangle we merge them. Finally we arrive at a list of segments connecting $\mathbf{M}(s_i)$ and $\mathbf{M}(s_j)$ on the target mesh. All segments except the first and last connect points that lie on the edges of the target mesh, otherwise they would have been merged. Take those intersection points and add them as vertices to the metamesh. Their position in $\mathcal{P}_t$ is given by the intersection point while their position in $\mathcal{P}_s$ is given by $\mathbf{M}^{-1}$ applied to the intersection point.

In practice it is easiest to find the intersection points in the target base domain and then map them through $\Pi_t^{(0)}$. This is illustrated in Figure 5. The points $\mathbf{M}^{(0)}(\Pi_s(s_i))$ and $\mathbf{M}^{(0)}(\Pi_s(s_j))$ lie in different triangles of the triangle base domain and are connected with a segmented line. Consider neighboring points of the target mesh $\Pi_t(t_k)$. The intersection points (black dots) can easily be found and mapped through $\Pi_t^{-1}$ to form $\mathcal{P}_t$.

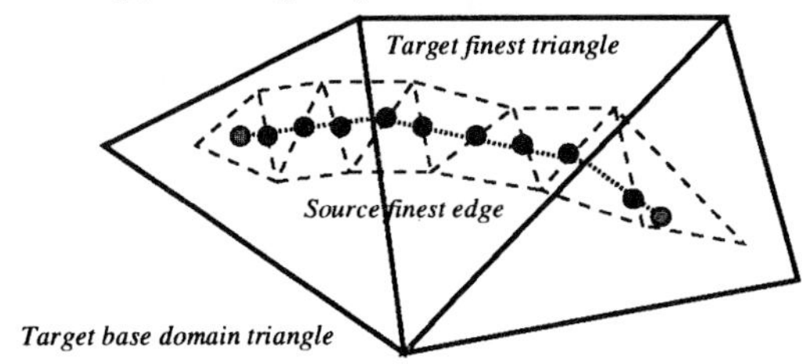


Figure 5: *Building the metamesh. The intersections between the source edge drawn on the target base domain and the target edges on the target base domain define the new vertices of the metamesh.*

Finally these segments have cut the target triangles into polygons. Retriangulate those polygons using a constrained Delaunay triangulation and add the new edges and triangles to $\mathcal{K}_p$. The metamesh is now done.

**Numerical Stability** In order to maintain numerical stability, we employ adaptive precision floating point exact arithematic for robust and fast evaluation of geometric predicates [31]. Also we take *coincidence issues* into account as mentioned in [20, 17]. The idea is fairly simple, instead of representing intersection points in $\mathbf{R}^3$, we represent them as barycentric coordinates in the target triangles. Hence, vertex to vertex correspondence is simply a permutation of $\{1, 0, 0\}$ and vertex to edge correspondence is permutation of $\{\alpha, \beta, 0\}$. This turns out to be very helpful in performing the constrained Delaunay triangulation since the "on-line" predicate does not suffer from numerical round off error.

Finding intersection points is easier if the source mesh contains triangles which are smaller than the target mesh triangles. Then many source edges will lie inside a single triangle of the target mesh and no path needs to be computed. Hence one may need to switch if there is a big difference in size. Once the map is computed one can switch back.

**Properties of the Metamesh** The metamesh has a number of interesting properties. For example, we can make the geometric realization of the metamesh look *exactly* like the geometric realization of both source and target mesh by letting its positions be either $\mathcal{P}_s$ or $\mathcal{P}_t$:

$$\varphi(\mathcal{S}, \mathcal{K}_s) = \varphi(\mathcal{P}_s, \mathcal{K}_p) \text{ and } \varphi(\mathcal{T}, \mathcal{K}_t) = \varphi(\mathcal{P}_t, \mathcal{K}_p).$$

In other words by taking the positions $\mathcal{P}_s$ the triangles of the metamesh line up to form the triangles of the source while by taking the positions $\mathcal{P}_t$ the triangles of the metamesh line up differently to form the triangles of the target.

In the worst case the size of the metamesh can grow as the product of the sizes of the source and target meshes as every edge of each mesh could intersect every edge of the other. In practice this is not the case. As the complexity of the mesh grows, the edge lengths decrease for a fixed geometric size. Since the meshes are about the same density, most of the intersections happen locally and thus are proportional to the degree of vertices which on average is a constant. As shown in Table 1, the metamesh size is no more than 10 times the size of the larger mesh in the examples we have considered.

The positions of intermediate meshes needed in the morph are given by $\mathcal{P} = \theta\mathcal{P}_s + (1-\theta)\mathcal{P}_t, \quad (0 \le \theta \le 1)$ and the connectivity is always $\mathcal{K}_p$. Letting $\theta$ smoothly vary between 0 and 1, these meshes transform from source into target. It is well known that linear interpolation methods can cause self intersections or excessive shape distortion. Some previous 2D work [29] is geared towards avoiding kinks or shrinkage during polygon morphing. Unfortunately these methods work well only for models with similar shape. While we have had success with the our simple interpolation, more sophisticated methods would be desirable.

To time schedule the morph the user can now specify how $\theta$ will vary with time ($t$). The simplest solution is to let $\theta(t)$ vary linearly with time: $\theta = t$. To have a gentle fade-in and fade-out one can let $\theta(t) = 1/2 - 1/2\cos(\pi t)$. The user also has spatial control by letting $\theta$ depend on location: $\theta(t, i)$ with $\{i\} \in \mathcal{K}_p$. This can be used to morph certain regions before others as shown in the mannequin to Spock head example.

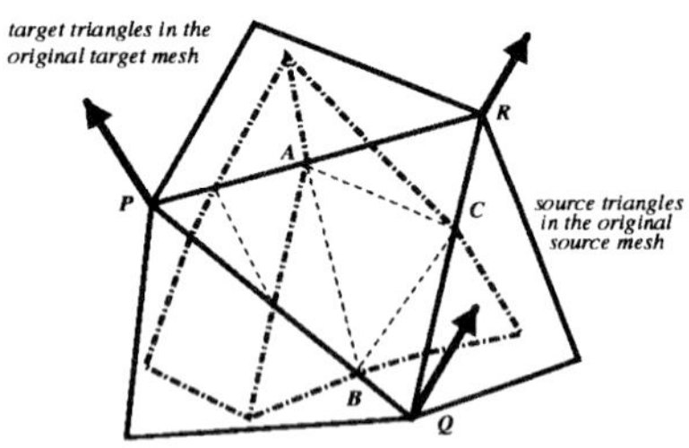


Figure 6: *Intersection between triangles at the source mesh and the target mesh, new edges (broken lines) are introduced for the constrained triangulation which preserves the source and target edges. The attribute vectors (bold arrows) for the target triangle PQR are shown.*

**Attribute Interpolation and Rendering of the Metamesh** We can also interpolate other attributes such as normal, texture and color information between the source and the target. Consider the most general case where the attributes are associated with each vertex per triangle. This allows us to morph between smooth and sharp objects. Consider the case when the metamesh is at the target ($\mathcal{P} = \mathcal{P}_t$). Remember that the metamesh has many more vertices than the original source/target mesh: In Figure 6 triangles (in the metamesh) that are created inside $\Delta PQR$ will have attributes derived from the attribute vector at $P, Q$ and $R$ using barycentric interpolation.

This hints at another application. Assume we have a scanned mesh like a human head with a scanned texture but no texture map. Say we want to put this texture on a model like the mannequin head. Once we have a correspondence map between the two heads, one can simply transfer the texture.

## 5 Results

We have implemented our system on a Pentium Pro 200MHz PC and used it to produce a number of different morphs, described below.

**Mannequin to Venus** Figure 1 shows a number of frames from this sequence. The user only needed 5 minutes to associate the features (Figure 2) and adjust the mapping. Note how ears morph to ears, lips to lips, nose to nose, and eyes to eyes. The source mesh (Mannequin head) is created by using the Loop subdivision scheme to enhance the smoothness. However, its special structure was not used.

**Cup to Donut** This morph illustrates that our system can handle higher genus manifolds as well as morph fairly dissimilar objects. See the color plate (Figure 8 top). The user needed 30 minutes to associate features and adjust the mapping. Note how the cup turns itself inside out to deform to the torus. In morphing two non-zero genus objects, not only do they have to satisfy the homeomorphism condition, they must also be *"tamely homeomorphic"* [4]. $S$ is tamely homeomorphic to $T$ if there is a homeomorphism of $\mathbf{R}^3$ onto itself that carries $S$ onto $T$.

**Mannequin to Spock** Here we show an example of spatial control. See the color plate (Figure 8, middle). We first put the hair of Spock onto the mannequin head (middle frame) and then morph the rest of the face.

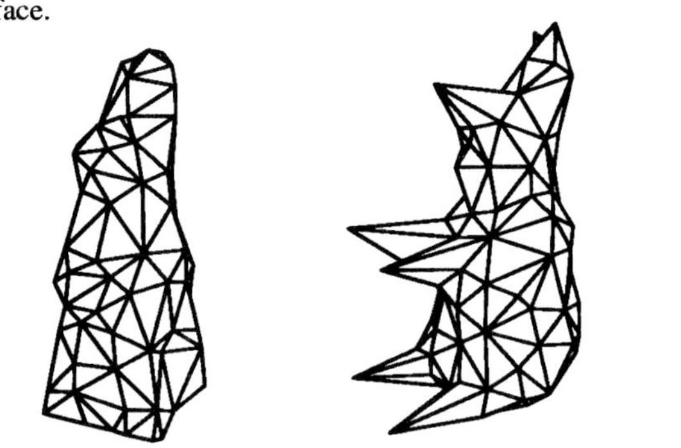

Figure 7: *Modification of the rabbit base domain to more closely match the horse base domain.*

**Horse to Rabbit** This is another example of morphing dissimilar objects. See the color plate (Figure 8 bottom). The user spends almost an hour to establish the base domain correspondences. There are three reasons: there are more feature pairs (60) which the user has to match due to the fact that the rabbit has long ears while the horse has small ones and the horse has a very long neck that the rabbit does not have. Effectively the user has to stretch the horse base domain using the additional control tools to match the rabbit's. Also, the legs of the horse are very noticeable, prominent features. The rabbit has no such features that can be identified. In order to create the morph, we allow the user further control by altering the shape of the rabbit's base domain (see Figure 7). By creating four "legs" on the rabbit base domain the base domain mapping can be quite smooth. These changes induced changes to the finest level correspondence through the MAPS parameterization.

## 6 Conclusions and Future Work

We have demonstrated an effective and easy to use system for user controlled morphing of dense, arbitrary connectivity triangle meshes of arbitrary topology. Future research can be pursued in several directions:

- The main restriction of our method is the requirement that source and target share the same genus. Thus fundamental work on extending MAPS to deal with genus changes is needed.
- Once a dense correspondence map is established the characteristics of the morph can be greatly influenced by the interpolation functions used. We have only explored spatially varying linear interpolation and more sophisticated controls would be desirable in production work.
- We can compute a wavelet transform on the metamesh and give the user the option to schedule different morphing speeds for different scales/frequencies as in [15].
- The user can have even more control over the actual morph by editing the metamesh in certain key frames. The morph will then smoothly adjust itself to those key frames.
- In case the source and target are quite dissimilar, the user needs to spend more time to guide the correspondence map. More tools which naturally combine user control with automated computation are needed.

| Source-Target | Source size (triangles) | Target size (triangles) | Metamesh size (triangles) | Feature pairs | Corresp. map time | Metamesh time | User time |
|---|---|---|---|---|---|---|---|
| mann-venus | 5422 | 90709 | 225502 | 24 | 3' | 19' | 5' |
| cup-donut | 8452 | 2048 | 43188 | 30 | 1'20" | 4' | 30' |
| mann-spock | 5422 | 14100 | 75427 | 24 | 1' | 7' | 5' |
| horse-rabbit | 21130 | 21582 | 220201 | 60 | 22' | 27' | 60' |

Table 1: *Selected statistics for the examples discussed in the text. All times were measured on a 200 MHz PentiumPro.*

**Acknowledgment** Work of David Dobkin and Aaron Lee was supported in part by NSF (CCR-9731535) and the US ARO (DAAH04-96-1-0181). Aaron Lee was also supported by a Wu Graduate Fellowship. Peter Schröder was supported in part by NSF (ACI-9624957, ACI-9721349, and DMS-9874082). Other support was provided by Alias|wavefront and a Packard Foundation Fellowship. Special thanks to Adam Finkelstein for many interesting and stimulating discussions; the University of Washington for providing the Spock and mannequin head; Cyberware for providing the horse and rabbit; Arthur Gregory for providing the cup and donut.

## References


[1] Aho, A. V., Hopcroft, J. E., and Ullman, J. D. *Data Structures and Algorithms*. Addison-Wesley, 1983.

[2] Beier, T., and Neely, S. Feature-based image metamorphosis. In *Computer Graphics (SIGGRAPH '92 Proceedings)*, 35–42, 1992.

[3] Besl, P. J., and McKay, N. D. A Method for Registration of 3-D Shapes. *IEEE Trans. on Pattern Anal. and Machine Intelligence 14*, 2 (Feb. 1992), 239–258.

[4] Boyer, M., and Stewart, N. F. Modeling spaces for toleranced objects. *Int. J. Robotics Research 10*, 5 (1991), 570–582.

[5] Brown, P. J. C., and Faigle, C. T. A Robust Efficient Algorithm for Point Location in Triangulations. Tech. rep., Cambridge University, February 1997.

[6] Eyal Carmel and Daniel Cohen-Or Warp-guided object-space morphing. *The Visual Computer 13*, 9–10 (1998), 46–478. ISSN 0178-2789.

[7] Chen, Y., and Medioni, G. Object Modeling by Registration of Multiple Range Images. *Int. J. of Image and Vision Computing 10*, 3 (Apr. 1992), 145–155.

[8] DeCarlo, D., and Gallier, J. Topological Evolution of Surfaces. In *Graphics Interface '96*, 194–203, May 1996.

[9] Decaudin, P. Geometric Deformation by Merging a 3D-Object with a Simple Shape. In *Graphics Interface '96*, 55–60, May 1996.

[10] Dobkin, D., and Kirkpatrick, D. A Linear Algorithm for Determining the Separation of Convex Polyhedra. *Journal of Algorithms 6* (1985), 381–392.

[11] Eck, M., DeRose, T., Duchamp, T., Hoppe, H., Lounsbery, M., and Stuetzle, W. Multiresolution Analysis of Arbitrary Meshes. In *Computer Graphics (SIGGRAPH '95 Proceedings)*, 173–182, 1995.

[12] Faugeras, O. D., and Herbert, M. The Representation, Recognition, and Locating of 3D Objects. *The Int. J. Robotics Research 5*, 3 (1986), 27–49.

[13] Gomes, J., Darsa, L., Costa, B., and Velho, L. *Warping and Morphing of Graphical Objects*. Morgan Kaufmann, San Francisco, Calif., 1998.

[14] Gregory, A., State, A., Lin, M., Manocha, D., and Livingston, M. Feature-based Surface Decomposition for Polyhedral Morphing. Tech. Rep. TR98-014, Department of Computer Science, University of North Carolina - Chapel Hill, Apr. 14 1998.

[15] He, T., Wang, S., and Kaufman, A. Wavelet-Based Volume Morphing. In *Proceedings of the Conference on Visualization*, 85–92, Oct. 1994.

[16] Hughes, J. F. Scheduled Fourier volume morphing. In *Computer Graphics (SIGGRAPH '92 Proceedings)*, 43–46, 1992.

[17] Kanai, T., Suzuki, H., and Kimura, F. Three-dimensional geometric metamorphosis based on harmonic maps. *The Visual Computer 14*, 4 (1998), 166–176.

[18] Kanai, T., Suzuki, H., and Kimura, F. Metamorphosis of Arbitrary Triangular Meshes with User-Specified Correspondence. *IEEE Computer Graphics and Applications* (to appear).

[19] Kaul, A., and Rossignac, J. Solid-Interpolating Deformations: Construction and Animation of PIPs. In *Eurographics '91*, 493–505, Sept. 1991.

[20] Kent, J. R., Carlson, W. E., and Parent, R. E. Shape transformation for polyhedral objects. In *Computer Graphics (SIGGRAPH '92 Proceedings)*, 47–54, 1992.

[21] Lanthier, M., Maheshwari, A., and Sack, J.-R. Approximating Weighted Shortest Paths on Polyhedral Surfaces. In *6th Annual Video Review of Computational Geometry, Proc. 13th ACM Symp. Computational Geometry*, 485–486, 4–6 June 1997.

[22] Lazarus, F., and Verroust, A. Feature-based shape transformation for polyhedral objects. In *The 5th Eurographics Workshop on Animation and Simulation*, 1–14, 1994.

[23] Lazarus, F., and Verroust, A. Three-dimensional metamorphosis: a survey. *The Visual Computer 14* (1998), 373–389.

[24] Lee, A. W. F., Sweldens, W., Schröder, P., Cowsar, L., and Dobkin, D. MAPS: Multiresolution Adaptive Parameterization of Surfaces. *Computer Graphics (SIGGRAPH '98 Proceedings)* (1998), 95–104.

[25] Lee, S., Chwa, K., Shin, S. Y., and Wolberg, G. Image Metamorphosis Using Snakes and Free-Form Deformations. In *Computer Graphics (SIGGRAPH '95 Proceedings)*, 439–448, 1995.

[26] Lerios, A., Garfinkle, C. D., and Levoy, M. Feature-Based Volume Metamorphosis. In *Computer Graphics (SIGGRAPH '95 Proceedings)*, 449–456, 1995.

[27] Parent, R. E. Shape transformation by boundary representation interpolation: a recursive approach to establishing face correspondences. *The Journal of Visualization and Computer Animation 3*, 4 (Oct.–Dec. 1992), 219–239.

[28] Payne, B. A., and Toga, A. W. Distance field manipulation of surface models. *IEEE Computer Graphics and Applications 12*, 1 (Jan. 1992), 65–71.

[29] Sederberg, T. W., Gao, P., Wang, G., and Mu, H. 2D Shape Blending: An Intrinsic Solution to the Vertex Path Problem. In *Computer Graphics (SIGGRAPH '93 Proceedings)*, vol. 27, 15–18, Aug. 1993.

[30] Shapira, M., and Rappoport, A. Shape Blending Using the Star-Skeleton Representation. *IEEE Computer Graphics and Applications 15*, 2 (1995), 44–50.

[31] Shewchuk, J. R. Adaptive Precision Floating-Point Arithmetic and Fast Robust Geometric Predicates. *Discrete & Computational Geometry 18*, 3 (Oct. 1997), 305–363.

[32] Spanier, E. H. *Algebraic Topology*. McGraw-Hill, New York, 1966.

[33] Sun, Y. M., Wang, W., and Chin, F. Y. L. Interpolating Polyhedral Models using Intrinsic Shape Parameters. In *Pacific Graphics '95*, Aug. 1995.

[34] Turk, G. Re-Tiling Polygon Surfaces. *Computer Graphics (SIGGRAPH '92 Proceedings)* (1992), 55–64.

[35] Whitaker, R., and Breen, D. Level-Set Models for the Deformation of Solid Objects. In *Proceedings of the Third International Workshop on Implicit Surfaces*, 19–35, June 1998.

[36] Wolberg, G. *Digital Image Warping*. IEEE Computer Society Press, 1990. IEEE Computer Society Press Monograph.

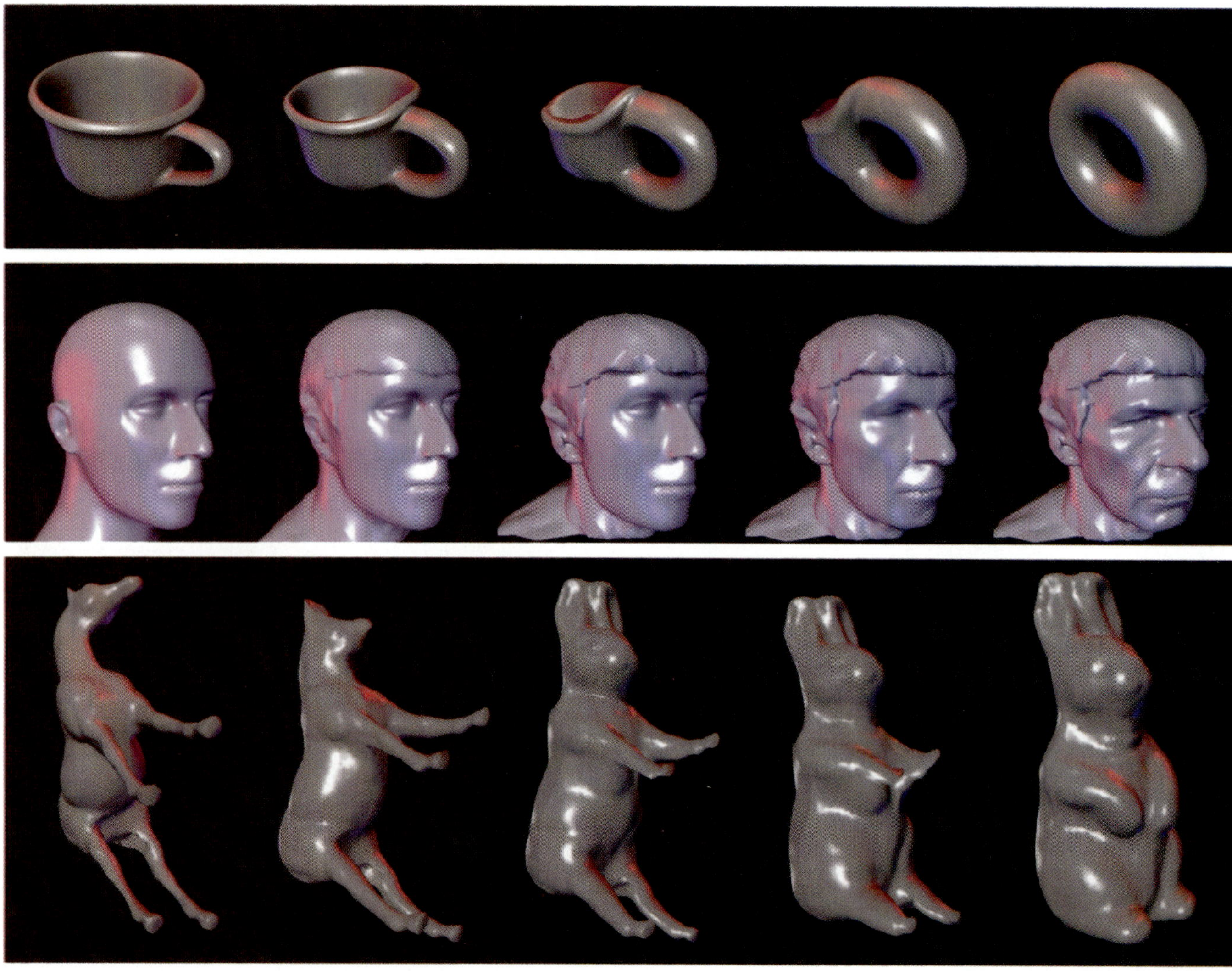

Figure 8: *Morphing gallery.*

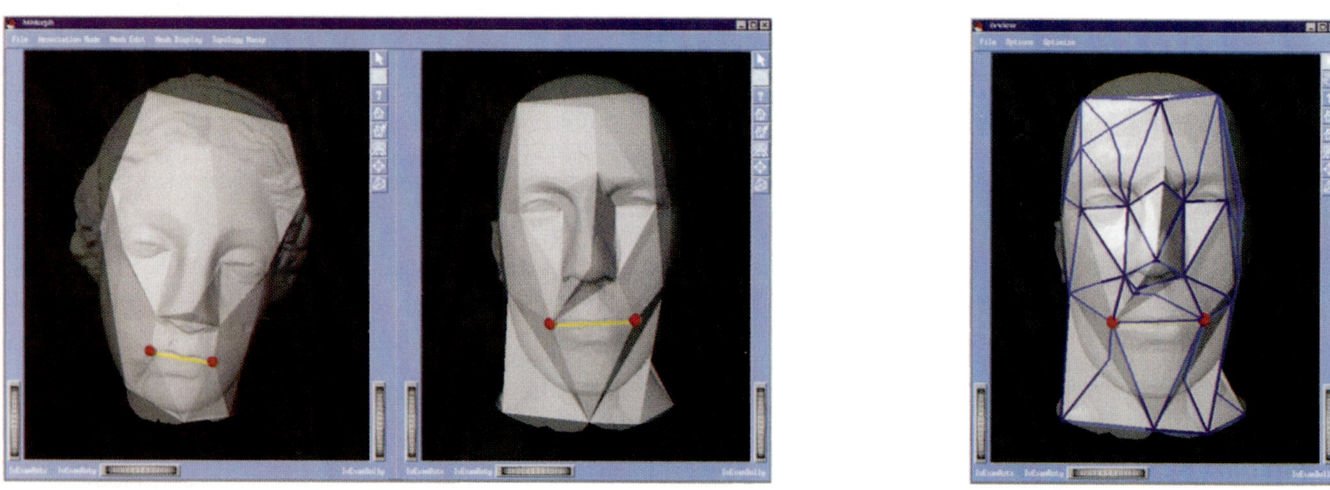

Figure 9: *User interface shows the finest and coarsest resolution of the source (Venus) and the target (Mannequin). It demonstrates the feature vertices and feature edges association (see Section 3.3). The right picture shows the result of mapping the source base domain edges (blue lines) onto the target base domain.*

# Balancing Fusion, Image Depth and Distortion in Stereoscopic Head-Tracked Displays

Zachary Wartell[1], Larry F. Hodges[2], William Ribarsky[3]

GVU Center, College of Computing, Georgia Institute of Technology

## Abstract

Stereoscopic display is a fundamental part of virtual reality HMD systems and HTD (head-tracked display) systems such as the virtual workbench and the CAVE. A common practice in stereoscopic systems is deliberate incorrect modeling of user eye separation. Underestimating eye separation is frequently necessary for the human visual system to fuse stereo image pairs into single 3D images, while overestimating eye separation enhances image depth. Unfortunately, false eye separation modeling also distorts the perceived 3D image in undesirable ways. This paper makes three fundamental contributions to understanding and controlling this stereo distortion. (1) We analyze the distortion using a new analytic description. This analysis shows that even with *perfect* head tracking, a user will perceive virtual objects to warp and shift as she moves her head. (2) We present a new technique for counteracting the shearing component of the distortion. (3) We present improved methods for managing image fusion problems for distant objects and for enhancing the depth of flat scenes.

**CR Categories and Subject Descriptions:** I.3.7 [Computer Graphics] Three-Dimensional Graphics and Realism - Virtual Reality; I.3.6 [Computer Graphics] Methodology and Techniques – Ergonomics; I.3.6 [Computer Graphics] Methodology and Techniques – Interaction Techniques; I.3.3 [Computer Graphics] Picture/Image Generation – Viewing Algorithms
**Additional Keywords:** virtual reality, stereoscopic display, head-tracking, image distortion

## 1 INTRODUCTION

Virtual environments aim to perceptually place the user in an artificial computer-generated world. A key component of creating this illusion is interactive 3D imagery. To generate this imagery, a typical VR system has a location and orientation tracking device, an image generator and one or more displays.

1,2,3 (wartell | hodges | ribarsky)@cc.gatech.edu



The tracking device determines the positions of the user's head and/or eyes and of the displays. The image generator computes the image that each eye would see on a display surface if the eye and the display existed inside the virtual world at their tracked positions. This image is then fed to the physical display. Typical VR systems are configured either as a head-mounted display (HMD) or as a head-tracked display (HTD). In a HMD, the display is attached to a helmet worn by the user, so both the eye points and the display are in continuous motion. In a HTD, the display is stationary, attached to a desk or wall, so only the eye points move. HTD examples are the CAVE [2], the virtual workbench [10] and "fish tank" VR [19].

Most VR systems generate a pair of images, one for each eye. This stereoscopic imagery provides a true 3D image so virtual objects appear to float in front of and behind the physical display surface. Software methods for stereoscopic display are well known [2, 15, 13]. Stereoscopic display for virtual reality has been shown to improve user depth perception and task performance in a variety of tasks [14, 19]. This is not surprising since real world experience shows that stereopsis is an important depth cue especially for objects within the user's personal space (1.5 meters) [3].

Both experience [11] and experimental studies [24, 16] have shown that users with normal stereoscopic vision often have trouble fusing stereo image pairs if the eyes are modeled based on exact eye separation. The common solution is to underestimate the eye separation of the user. This approach solves the image fusion problem but creates a new problem with head-tracked displays.

We observed that underestimating eye separation causes the stereoscopic image to shift and warp with head movement. As the user moves her head forward and back the perceived image will compress and expand. As the user moves her head left and right the perceived image will shift side to side. The images in Figure 1 are indicative of what a user perceives on a stereo HTD with underestimated eye separation. In Figure 1A, a user views a horizontal stereo HTD such as a virtual workbench. The physical display is outlined in black. The gray cube is the model virtual geometry. Figures 1A-1E are a frontal view of this display system. Here the display surface appears as a horizontal black line. While the system internally models a gray cube, the user actually perceives a different shaped object shown in red. Figures 1B and 1C illustrate how the perceived object compresses and expands due to up and down head movement. Figures 1D and 1E illustrate the left/right shifting due to side to side head movement.

This distortion is particularly irksome because the purpose of adding head-tracking to these stereoscopic displays was to remove similar distortions that were observed in earlier *non*-head-tracked systems [9].

It would appear we are stuck between the proverbial rock and a hard place. False eye-separation modeling is necessary to controlling stereo fusion problems and is also instrumental to methods for exaggerating depth of flat scenes [18]. However, when applied to stereo HTD's, false eye-separation reintroduces distortions which the tracking component of HTD's was suppose to remove.

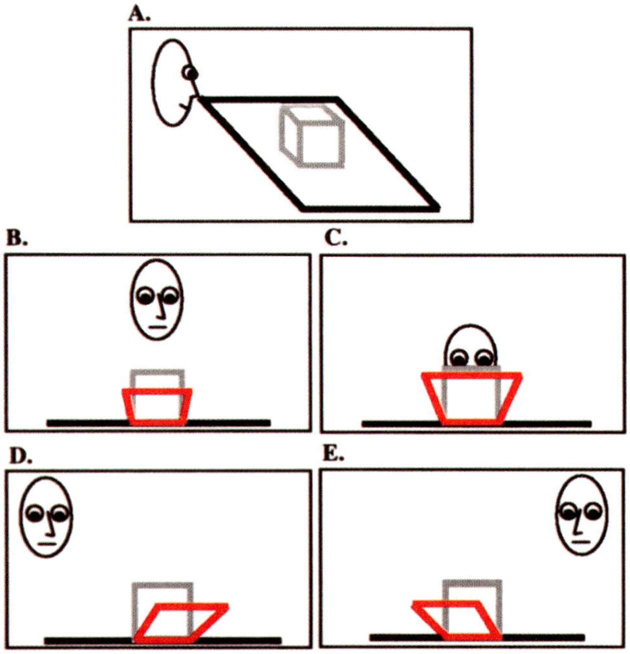


Figure 1: (A) A user viewing a horizontal stereo HTD such as the virtual workbench. The gray cube is a virtual cube. (B-E) are four front views of the user viewing the cube on the stereo HTD. The horizontal black line is the display surface. Underestimated eye separation causes the user to perceive a warped version of the cube shown in red. (A) and (B) illustrate the compression and expansion of the perceived object due to up/down head motion while (C) and (D) illustrate the left/right shifting of the perceived object due to side to side head motion.

This paper presents a novel, highly efficient method for controlling these distortions based on a new analytic description of the distortion. We begin with a geometric construction which describes the distortion and then derive its analytic form, $\Delta$. $\Delta$ subsumes previous work on false eye separation distortion and is more general. Analysis of $\Delta$ shows that the user will perceive virtual objects to warp and shift when she moves her head even with *perfect* head tracking. We present a predistortion technique for counteracting the shearing component of $\Delta$. Based on this technique, we develop a new method to manage image fusion problems for distant objects and a simple but improved method for enhancing the depth of flat scenes.

## 2 BACKGROUND AND PREVIOUS WORK

When a user cannot perceive a single 3D image from a stereo image pair, she experiences diplopia (double vision). In a stereoscopic display the occurrence of diplopia is related to various physical attributes of the display system and the geometry of the display environment [9]. The relevant geometric aspects are:

- the distance of the displayed virtual object relative to the display surface
- the eye separation value used in computing the viewing transform
- the distance of the eyes from the display surface

Figure 2 illustrates the situation and some important measurements. The eyes are on the left and a point on a virtual object is on the right. This point is projected onto two points on the projection plane. The screen parallax, $p$, associated with a virtual point is the distance between the projected points. The distance between the eyes and the virtual point also determine the angle, $\beta$. Associated with the screen itself is another angle, $\alpha$ Research has shown that if the difference, $\alpha$-$\beta$, is outside a limited range, then diplopia occurs and the 3D depth illusion collapses [24, 9, 15]. This range has a negative limit generally associated with points in front of the projection plane and a positive limit generally associated with points behind the projection plane. The negative limit is called the "crossed-parallax" limit while the positive limit is the "uncrossed-parallax" limit.

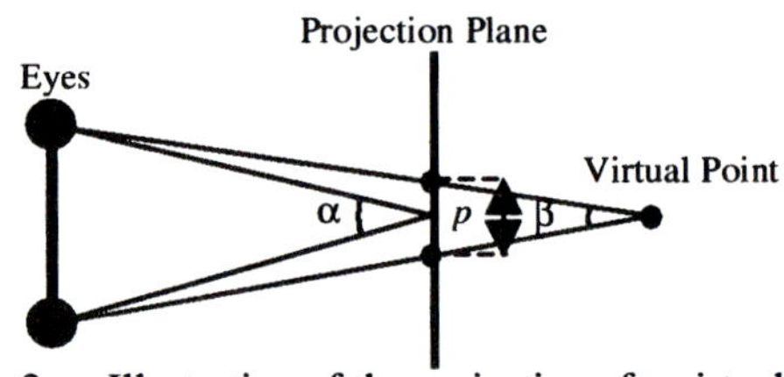


Figure 2: Illustration of the projection of a virtual point onto the projection plane for a user's two eyes. $p$ is the horizontal parallax, or distance on the screen between the stereo images of a virtual point. $\beta$ is the vergence angle of this virtual point. $\alpha$ is the vergence angle of the projection plane itself.

Additional problems with stereoscopic displays are user fatigue and temporary alteration of the visual system's internal coupling of accommodation (eye focus) and convergence (the relative orientation of one eye to the other) [12].

As previously mentioned, the common software technique to minimize these problems in non-head-tracked stereoscopic displays is to model the user's eye separation with a value smaller than the true value. The resulting screen parallaxes and vergence angles are reduced and this minimizes user difficulties. However, when applied to stereo HTD's false eye separation yields the distortions illustrated in Figure 1.

Several researchers find it beneficial to use exaggerated values for the modeled eye separation. Akka [1] reports that users prefer the results of slightly exaggerating the modeled eye separation in a head-tracked stereoscopic display. In Ware [18], the authors dynamically overestimate the modeled eye separation to enhance the perceived depth of terrain. This method was used in a real world application where engineers routed cables along a seabed. Note that this application did not use head-tracking so the stereo distortions introduced by false eye separation modeling would be drowned by the qualitatively similar distortions due to the lack of head tracking.

As discussed in the introduction, these false-eye separation methods induce undesirable distortions in tracked stereo displays. While previous work provides qualitative and quantitative insights into related stereo distortions, none provide a complete description of this distortion.

Researchers [7, 4, 9, 8, 23, 13, 21, 18] investigated various aspects of stereo and monocular distortions. However, none of this previous work describes the stereo distortion due to false eye modeling for stereo HTDs. Ware et al [18] present a brief discussion of the change in the perceived depth of a point for false eye separation modeling in non-headtracked stereo displays. Woods et al [23] derive an analytic description of distortions in stereoscopic tele-operator systems. Woods' treatment assumes the eye axis is parallel to the display plane and that the center of the eyes lies on a line perpendicular to the display and through its center. These assumptions are not true in a stereoscopic HTD system and therefore this previous result does not cover the head-tracked case.

## 3 DESCRIPTION OF DISTORTION

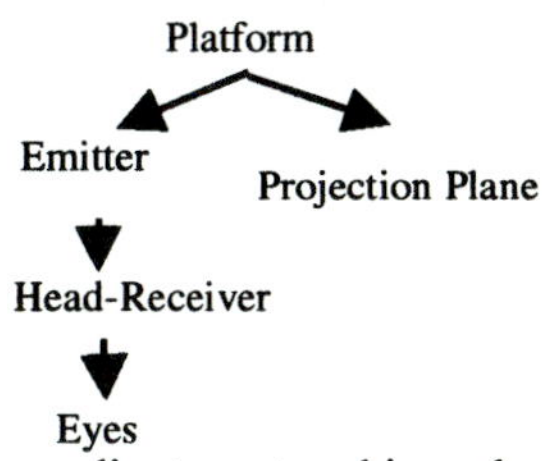


Figure 3: The coordinate system hierarchy for a stereo HTD.

To derive a geometric description of false eye separation distortion, we review and simplify the viewing model used in stereo HTD's. A typical viewing model consists of the coordinate system hierarchy presented in Figure 3. The top coordinate system is the platform coordinate system (PCS). Manipulating this coordinate system moves the user through the virtual space. Directly attached to this coordinate system is the projection plane coordinate system and the emitter coordinate system. The projection plane coordinate system contains the projection plane in its XY plane with the window centered about the origin. The emitter coordinate system simply represents the tracker's emitter. Attached to the emitter coordinate system is the head receiver coordinate system and attached to that is the eye coordinate system. The two eye points are on the x-axis of the eye coordinate system and are symmetric about the origin.

The position and orientation of each child coordinate system relative to its parent are measured physically from the physical display setup along with the view window dimensions. The platform coordinate system's mapping to virtual world coordinates defines the mapping of the physical space of the real world to the virtual space of the virtual world. In addition to specifying the position and orientation, the platform coordinate system can also be uniformly scaled. This causes the virtual world to grow and shrink.

Assuming all the mentioned physical measurements are correct, the virtual eye separation equals the physical separation multiplied by the platform coordinate system's scale. For example, if the modeled eye separation equals the user's true eye separation, say 6 cm, and she views a virtual Earth at a $10^{-6}$ user scale where the planet appears as a large globe, then the virtual eye separation is 60 km. By our definition this case does not represent overestimated eye separation because the modeled physical eye separation equals the veridical 6 cm.

This paper is *not* concerned with this discrepancy between the virtual eye separation and the physical eye separation. This discrepancy, dependent on PCS scaling, merely scales the virtual world up or down. The world may appear as: a small model, such as the Earth as a globe; a true model, such as a telephone at actual size; or a magnified model, such as an atom at the size of a basketball. This uniform scaling always preserves angles, aspect ratios and parallelism, and maintains the perceived rigidity of the virtual world as the head moves. This paper is concerned with the discrepancy between two further distinguishable values for the physical eye separation: the user's true physical eye separation and the system's modeled physical eye separation. A discrepancy between these values will distort the world by a perspective collineation or homology. The virtual world, at whatever scale it is displayed, will shear and warp with head position and neither angles, aspect ratio nor parallelism will be preserved.

We henceforth ignore PCS scale and the virtual eye separation, and we focus on the modeled and true physical eye separations. The term "eye separation" will now always refer to the physical separations.

Figure 4A illustrates geometrically why false eye separation yields distortions. In Figure 4A, two sets of eye points are illustrated in blue. Within each set the true eye points are on the outside (dark blue) and the modeled eye points are on the inside (light blue). Again the projection plane is the horizontal black line. Below this line, a single modeled point is shown in black along with the perceived point as seen by the left and right eye set positions. For each eye set, the modeled point is projected onto the projection plane through the modeled eyes. These projectors are drawn in black. The true eyes reconstruct a perceived image by finding the intersection of the red lines. These red lines are drawn between an eye and its corresponding projected image point. Note how the perceived point (red) moves as the user moves her head. Also the perceived point is closer to the projection plane than the modeled point. This geometric construction can be applied to a set of points to yield all the distortions illustrated in Figure 1.

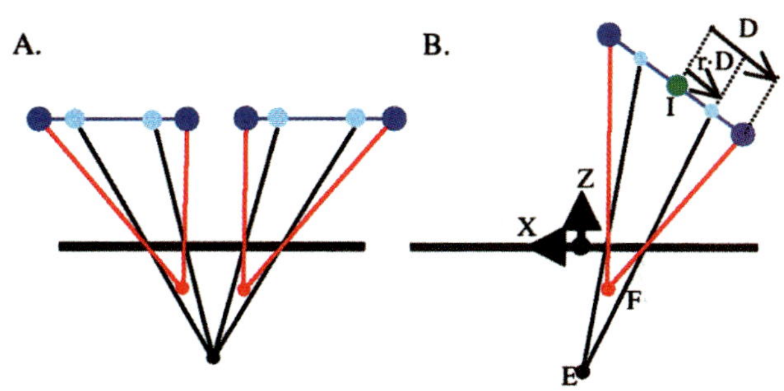


Figure 4: (A) A geometric construction illustrating how false eye modeling distorts the perceived image and how the perceived image moves with head position. (B) A parameterization of geometric construction used to derive the analytic description.

This construction assumes that all the important physical measurements, besides the modeled eye separation, are correct. The construction also assumes any distortion due to curvature of the screen or any optics is negligible or accounted for by other means [4]. Additionally, it assumes that change in the separation of the nodal points of the human eyes during convergence [4] is also negligible or accounted for.

To derive an analytic description of this distortion we parameterized the construction as shown in Figure 4B. First we place the projection plane coordinate system at the center of the projection window with its plane containing the X-Y axes. Next we add a central eye point, $I$. The true left and right eyes (dark blue) are displaced from $I$ by the vectors $D$ and $-D$. $2|D|$ is the true eye separation. The scalar $r$ is the ratio of the modeled eye separation to the true separation. Hence the left and right modeled eyes (light blue) are displaced by $r*D$ and $-r*D$ respectively, and $2r|D|$ is the modeled eye separation. $E$ is the modeled point and $F$ is the perceived point reconstructed by the user's biological visual system.

The above construction defines a transform, Δ, from an arbitrary point $E$ to the point $F$, i.e. $F=\Delta(E)$. In [20], we prove that the transformation is the following homology, or projective transform, expressed in projection plane coordinates:

$$\Delta = \begin{bmatrix} 1 & 0 & \frac{(1-r)(IxIz + Dx\,Dz\,r)}{Dz^2r^2 - Iz^2} & 0 \\ 0 & 1 & \frac{(1-r)(IyIz + Dy\,Dz\,r)}{Dz^2r^2 - Iz^2} & 0 \\ 0 & 0 & \frac{r(Dz^2 - Iz^2)}{Dz^2r^2 - Iz^2} & 0 \\ 0 & 0 & \frac{Iz(1-r)}{Dz^2r^2 - Iz^2} & 1 \end{bmatrix} \quad (1)$$

In the context of a rendering pipeline the distortion acts as follows. Let a matrix, $M_A^B$, denote the coordinate transform from coordinate system A to coordinate system B. Let Screen Coordinates be the coordinates after mapping into the canonical parallel-projection view volume, which is an axis-aligned cube with corners (1,1,0) and (-1,-1,-1) [5, p275]. Then the matrix stack during rendering is:

$$M_{Model}^{Screen} = M_{World}^{Screen} \cdot M_{Model}^{World} \quad (2)$$

Let $[M]_A$ be the representation of a transform M in coordinate system A. Then using false eye separation effectively induces the complete transformation:

$$M'^{Screen}_{Model} = M_{World}^{Screen} \cdot [\Delta]_{World} \cdot M_{Model}^{World} \quad (3)$$

Therefore, using false eye separation will produce the same perceived 3D image as using the true eye separation and adding $[\Delta]_{World}$ on the viewing stack. Note, since equations (2) and (3) describe virtual space, $[\Delta]_{World}$ will include a scale component inherited from the platform coordinate system. However, when analyzing Δ, it is convenient to ignore this scale issue and consider the projection plane coordinate system as it exists in the physical world. We can then discuss the effects of Δ in physical units such as meters and consider how Δ warps the virtual world at whatever scale it is displayed.

# 4 PICTORIAL ANALYSIS OF Δ

Figure 1 provided an intuitive understanding of Δ. Figure 5, illustrates Δ more abstractly. The user is represented by her eye points in blue. The true eyes are dark blue while the modeled eye are light blue. The projection plane is the horizontal black line. The model geometry, a mesh, is in black and the perceived geometry, a warped mesh, is red. For underestimated eye separation ($r$=0.5), 6A and 6B show the compression/expansion effect and 6C and 6D show the side to side shifting. Similar distortions occurs with overestimated eye separation [20].

This distortion has many repercussions. A user designing what she perceives to be as a cube may actually have designed a more general truncated pyramid. Equivalent to Wood's [23] observations in teleoperator environments, perceptions of velocity through the environment will also be distorted given this non-linear distortion. Most importantly static, rigid objects will appear to move as the user moves his head. Qualitatively these results are easily verified on real stereoscopic head-tracked displays.

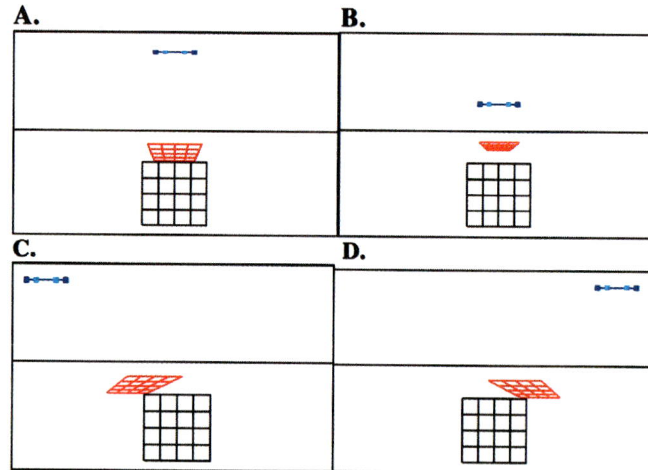


Figure 5: These figures show the that the perceived mesh (red) is a distorted version of the modeled mesh (black). The eye points are in blue and the projection plane is the horizontal black line. For underestimate eye separation (r=0.5), A and B illustrate the compression and expansion while C and D illustrate the side to side shifting.

# 5 QUANTITATIVE ANALYSIS OF Δ

For a quantitative analysis of Δ, we assume neither the modeled eye points nor the true eye points are embedded in the projection plane. These cases lead to degenerate, singular mappings in both Δ and the original construction [20]. Since these embedded cases are rare, ignoring them is permissible.

## 5.1 Maximum Depth Plane

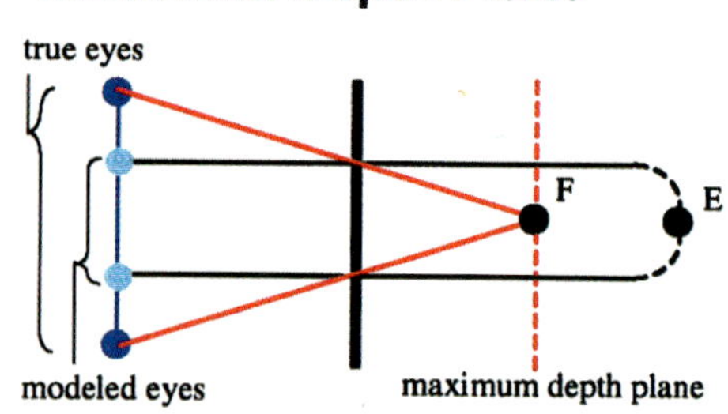


Figure 6: Illustration of the maximum depth plane of perceived space due to underestimating eye separation

We can use $\Delta^{-1}$ to compute the maximum possible depth in perceived space when the modeled eye separation is smaller than the true eye separation ($r < 1$). The existence of a maximum depth in the perceived space has been noted before [23, 18]. Figure 6 illustrates this idea. For a point beyond the projection plane the screen parallax reaches its maximum value, equal to the modeled eye separation, for a point infinitely far away, $E$. This places a limit on the depth of the reconstructed perceived points, $F$.

For a non-degenerate viewing configuration, $\Delta$ is non-singular and hence $\Delta^{-1}$ exists. Like $\Delta$, $\Delta^{-1}$ is a homology so it has a plane, *P*, of ordinary points which are mapped to ideal points (points at infinite). This plane is called the vanishing plane since these points have no image in Euclidean space. $\Delta$ being the inverse of $\Delta^{-1}$ maps these ideal points back to the affine plane *P*. These ideal points represent the points lying infinitely far beyond the projection plane that get mapped to the maximum depth plane. *P* then is precisely this maximum depth plane. The equation for the maximum depth plane is the vanishing plane of $\Delta^{-1}$. It is easy to find the vanishing plane of a perspective matrix [6]. With this insight the maximum depth plane is:

$$z = \frac{r\left(Dz^2 - Iz^2\right)}{Iz\left(1 - r\right)} \tag{4}$$

Equation (4) illustrates how the maximum depth plane position varies with the head position's z-component. This helps explain the head-position dependent squashing of perceived space illustrated in Figure 7. Here the perceived grid compresses as the head moves towards the projection plane. This motion also brings the maximum depth plane (the dash red line) closer in.

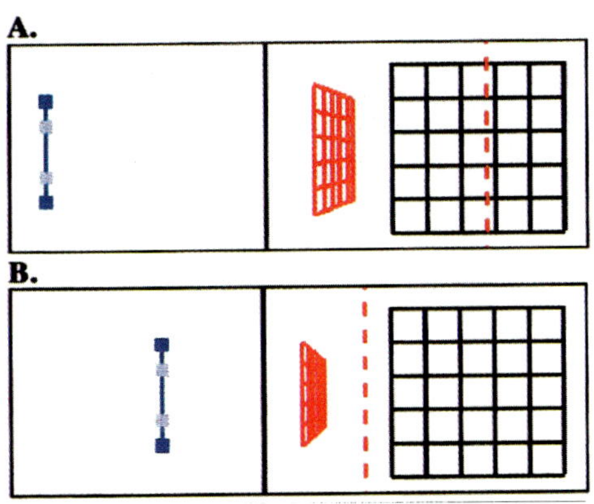


Figure 7: Perceived grid (red) squashed towards view plane. Note maximum depth plane (dashed red line). Again the true eyes are dark blue and the modeled eyes are light blue.

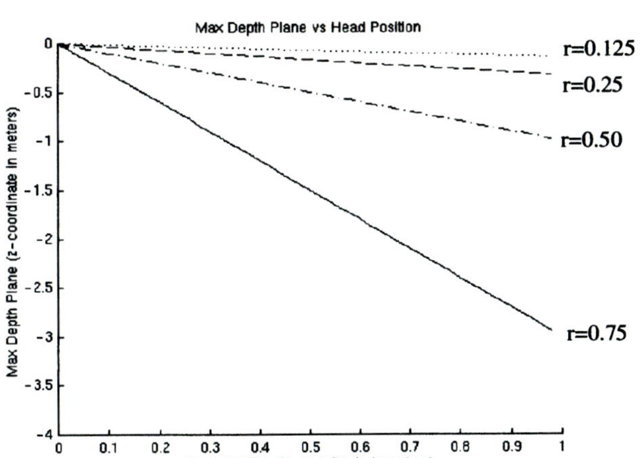


Figure 8: Plot of the position of the maximum depth plane versus user head position for various modeled-to-true eye separation ratios (*r*).

Figure 8 plots the position of the maximum depth plane as a function of viewer head position (Iz) for several eye separations ratios (*r*): 0.75 (solid), 0.5 (dash-dot), 0.25 (dash) and 0.125 (dot). Note, Figure 8 assumes the head is parallel to the projection plane (*dz*=0); however, even for non-parallel case *dz* is typically small compared to *Iz*. In Figure 8, the maximum depth plane position is linear with respect to the head position while it varies non-linearly with *r*. Smaller modeled eye separations produce a closer maximum depth plane and hence a greater compression of the perceived space.

## 5.2 Side to Side Shifting

Previously figures 1C and 1D illustrated the sideways shifting induced by false eye-separation. Here we examine this shifting more rigorously. We plot the x-coordinate difference of a modeled point, *E*, from its distorted point, *F*, as a function of head position. For simplicity, assume the eyes are parallel to the projection plane and are contained in the X-Z plane (dz,dy=0). Fix the central eye's (I) z-coordinate to 1 meter and then vary the central eye's x-coordinate so that the head moves side to side. In this case, *Fx* and hence *Fx-Ex,* varies linearly with *Ix*.

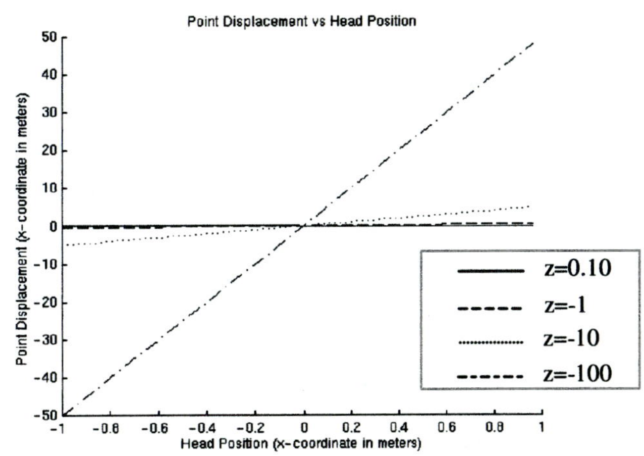


Figure 9: Plot of the displacement of a perceived point from its modeled location versus head position. Head position, *Ix,* varies from –1 to 1; *r* is 0.5; eye-separation is 0.065. Plots are drawn for a model point at various z coordinates.

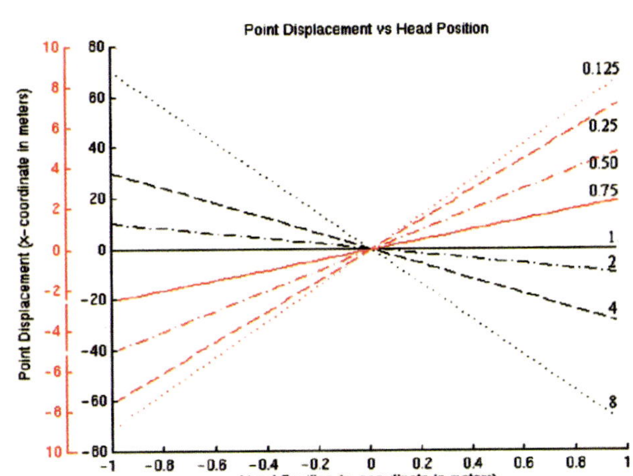


Figure 10: Plot of the displacement of a perceived point from its modeled position (Fx-Ex) versus head position. The modeled point is at (0,0,-10). *r*, the eye separation ratio, is varied over a range of values: 0.125 to 0.75 in red and 1 to 8 in black.

In Figure 9, *Fx-Ex* is plotted against *Ix*. *Ix* varies from –1 to 1; *r* is 0.5; eye-separation is 0.065m. Plots are drawn for a model point a *Ez*=0.10 (solid),*Ez*=-1 (dashed), *Ez*=-10 (dotted) and *Ez*=-100 (dash-dot). Sensitivity to head position grows with object depth, with *Ez*=0.10m ranging up to 0.05m and *Ez*=-100 m ranging up to –50 m.

Figure 10 shows the effect of different values for *r* for a model point at (0,0,-10). In Figure 10 in red, r is 0.75 (solid), 0.5 (dash-dot), 0.25 (dash) and 0.125 (dot). In Figure 10 in black, r is 1 (solid), 2 (dash-dot), 4 (dash) and 8 (dot). Generally, as we move away from using true eye separation, *r*=1, the shifting grows more sensitive to head movement. Note also the change from positive to negative slope as *r* goes from less to greater than one. This represents a reversal in the direction of the shifting.

This discussion illustrates the behavior of the distortions shifting. The plots show the shift grows quite large especially for modeled eye-separations far from the true value (*r*=1).

## 6 REMOVING ARTIFACTS OF Δ

To remove some of the artifacts of false eye modeling while maintaining the effect on screen parallax, we can derive a predistortion transform $Q$ to place on the matrix stack:

$$M_{World}^{Screen} \cdot [Q]_{World} \cdot M_{Model}^{World} \tag{5}$$

With false eye separation, this results in an effective matrix stack:

$$M'^{Screen}_{Model} = M_{World}^{Screen} \cdot [\Delta \cdot Q]_{World} \cdot M_{Model}^{World} \tag{6}$$

$Q$ should cancel the undesirable aspects of Δ while retaining the effect on screen parallax and perceived depth.

$Q = \Delta^{-1}$ is not useful since it cancels all the effects of false eye modeling including the desired ones. The discussion of the maximum depth plane in 5.1, illustrates in that the changes to perceived depth due to false eye separation are inherently perspective in nature. Therefore, the perspective aspect of Δ is not removable. The side to side shifting effect, however, can be removed.

### 6. 1 $\Delta_{Shear}^{-1}$ Predistortion

Predistorting the world by the inverse shear component of Δ will remove the sideways shifting. To extract this component, Δ is first decomposed into a shear of X and Y along Z, $\Delta_{shear}$; a Z scale, $\Delta_{scale}$; and a pure projection, $\Delta_{Project}$ [20]. From the detailed decomposition in [20], we can find the inverse of $\Delta_{shear}$:

$$\Delta_{Shear}^{-1} = \begin{bmatrix} 1 & 0 & \dfrac{-(1-r)(IxIz + Dx\,Dz\,r)}{Dz^2 r^2 - Iz^2} & 0 \\ 0 & 1 & \dfrac{-(1-r)(IyIz + Dy\,Dz\,r)}{Dz^2 r^2 - Iz^2} & 0 \\ 0 & 0 & 1 & 0 \\ 0 & 0 & 0 & 1 \end{bmatrix} \tag{7}$$

The matrix stack we should build at run-time is:

$$M_{World}^{Screen} \cdot [\Delta_{Shear}^{-1}]_{World} \cdot M_{Model}^{World} \tag{8}$$

When using false eye separation, predistorting world space with $\Delta_{Shear}^{-1}$ cancel the shear component of Δ, yielding the complete effective transform:

$$M_{World}^{Screen} \cdot [\Delta_{Project} \cdot \Delta_{Scale}]_{World} \cdot M_{Model}^{World} \tag{9}$$

This technique removes the most objectionable part of Δ, the head dependent shearing. Figure 11 illustrates this. Figures 11A and 11E show the original grid (black) and the perceived grid (red) without predistortion. Next 11B and 11F show the perceived mesh after the original mesh is predistorted into a new mesh (blue) by $\Delta_{Shear}^{-1}$. With the predistortion the perceived mesh is stationary even as the eye moves from left to right (11B to 11F).

### 6.2 α-Predistortion

Experimentally, we find it useful to use a slightly altered version of the $\Delta_{Shear}^{-1}$ technique. If the central eye, *I*, lies on a special curve, $\Delta_{Shear}^{-1}$ is the identity. It is useful to position this curve so that the default viewing position for a given stereo head-tracked display lies on the curve. This locks the perceived objects in place as seen from this standard view position. For the typical viewing position where an eye axis is parallel to the view plane, this curve is a line perpendicular to the display surface.

With a vertical display system, the fixed line could be centered horizontally on the display and then positioned vertically to coincide with the average user's eye level. For a horizontal display, such as the virtual workbench, the fixed line could be centered horizontally on the display and then translated forward perhaps a meter in front of the workbench.

To shift this fixed line we derive the following predistortion matrix,$\alpha$, to replace $\Delta_{Shear}^{-1}$:

$$\alpha = \begin{bmatrix} 1 & 0 & \dfrac{-(1-r)(IxIz + Dx\,Dz\,r - Iz\,Fx)}{Dz^2 r^2 - Iz^2} & 0 \\ 0 & 1 & \dfrac{-(1-r)(IyIz + Dy\,Dz\,r - Iz\,Fy)}{Dz^2 r^2 - Iz^2} & 0 \\ 0 & 0 & 1 & 0 \\ 0 & 0 & 0 & 1 \end{bmatrix} \tag{10}$$

*where*

*Fx and Fy are the x and y coordinates of the fixed line*

Figure 11 illustrates the use of the predistortion $\alpha$ with different fixed lines (dash gray). The top row illustrates eyes on the left while the bottom row illustrates eyes on the right. In the first column, $\alpha$ is not used. In the next 3 columns $\alpha$ is used with the fixed line in at center, on the left, and on the right. Using $\alpha$ with the fixed line on the left, the perceived grid for the left head position *is not altered* by $\alpha$ (compare C to A), while the perceived grid for the right head position *is altered* by $\alpha$ (compare E to G). On the other hand, using $\alpha$ with a fixed line on the right, the perceived grid for the left head position *is altered* by $\alpha$ (compare D to A), while the perceived grid for the right head position *is not altered* by $\alpha$ (compare H to D). Hence changing the position of the fixed line determines which viewpoints are locked in place. This fixed line can be positioned to contain the typical viewing position in a given head-tracked stereo display system.

In OpenGL [22], $\alpha$-predistortion can be implemented as follows. At every frame compute $\alpha$. Next compute $[\alpha]_{view}$. $[\alpha]_{view}$ is $\alpha$ relative to the OpenGL view coordinate system.

Recall OpenGL combines the affine model and view transforms on a single "ModelView" matrix stack while the projective frustum transform goes on the "Projection" matrix stack. Typically, the first transform placed on the ModelView stack is that which maps world coordinates to view coordinates. This transform consists of a rotation and a translation accounting for the location of the eye point and the orientation of the view plane. Since the orientation of the view coordinate system and the projection plane coordinate system are the same, $\alpha$ is mapped from projection plane coordinates to view coordinates as follows: $[\alpha]_{view}= T^{-1} \bullet \alpha \bullet T$ where $T$ is a translation by the coordinates of the eye in projection plane coordinates. $[\alpha]_{view}$ must be placed between the last transform on the Projection stack and the first transform on the ModelView stack. To avoid affecting lighting, place $[\alpha]_{view}$ on the Projection matrix stack as the last transform. Also note that for applications with application level bounding-box to view-volume culling, the $\alpha$ transform must be taken into account.

## 7 APPLICATIONS OF $\alpha$-PREDISTORTION

False-eye separation modeling is used either to avoid diplopia by underestimating the eye separation or to enhance stereoscopic depth by exaggerating eye separation. For head-tracked displays, this induces a distortion $\Delta$. While we tested and verified that $\alpha$-enhanced false-eye modeling removes the shearing for both underestimated and overestimated eye separation, we argue that exaggerated eye separation, even with $\alpha$-predistortion, is not useful.

With exaggerated stereo two choices exist:

- produce a distorted image that shears with head-movement and does not preserve parallelism

or

- produce a distorted image that does not shear but still does not preserve parallelism (using $\alpha$-predistortion)

In the best case exaggerated stereo still distorts the image by a homology about the projection plane. But why use a depth enhancing distortion that will necessarily map cubes to truncated frustums (i.e. not-preserve parallelism)? We are better off simply scaling the world perpendicular the projection plane in order to enhance the depth.

However, underestimating eye separation to minimize diplopia is still useful. Because $\Delta$ is a homology it has the effect of bringing points at infinity to some fixed plane beyond the projection plane. So by underestimating user eye separation we can map the *entirety* of space beyond the projection plane to a finite region between the projection plane and some maximum depth plane (5.2). (No affine transform can do this). Now we can set this maximum depth plane to the maximum fusible depth plane, the plane that delimits the farthest points that typical users can fuse. Rewriting Southard's [15] equation (6) for the maximum fusible depth plane using our nomenclature:

$$far\_fusible = Iz - \frac{2|D|Iz}{2|D| - Iz\theta_{\max}} \qquad (11)$$

where $\theta_{\max}$ is the positive uncrossed vergence angle limit

Now from equation (4) we can solve for the eye separation ratio, $r$, that will bring all points infinitely beyond the view plane into the fusible region delimited by *far_fusible*:

$$r = \begin{cases} \dfrac{far\_fusible \cdot Iz}{Dz^2 - Iz^2 + far\_fusible \cdot Iz}, & \text{if } 2|D| - Iz\theta_{\max} > 0 \\ 1, & \text{otherwise} \end{cases} \qquad (12)$$

The r=1 case occurs when the user is far enough from the projection plane so that the maximum depth plane is at infinity, i.e. all far space is fusible. In this case we use the true eye separation (r=1). Finally, applying $\alpha$-predistortion removes the left/right shearing.

The first virtue of this technique over previous methods is that it does not throw out geometry that the user cannot fuse. Previous methods set the far clipping plane to *far_fusible* [15]. In contrast, the new method throws out nothing; instead it maps the *entire* geometry data set into the fusible depth range. Additionally compared to [18], the technique does not require computing scene depth at every frame and it does not have the left/right shearing.

## 8 CONCLUSIONS

We have presented a novel analytic description of the distortion induced by false eye-separation modeling for a head at an arbitrary position and orientation. We analyzed the effects of this distortion as it relates to head-tracked stereoscopic displays. We then presented the $\alpha$-predistortion technique for counteracting the removable artifacts of this distortion. Finally we described new methods for controlling uncrossed diplopia and enhancing depth.

## 9 FUTURE WORK

An analytic description of the distortion due to false-eye separation can aid studies of the effects of a change in eye-separation due to convergence [4]. Second, further interface development, exploration and user study is warranted for $\alpha$-predistortion and for the techniques presented for depth enhancement and diplopia control. Issues are:

- What value to use for $\theta_{max}$ for a variety of display technologies? (Yeh and Silverstein's 1.57 is very conservative and is based on color CRT's with a particular phosphor set).
- Extensions for managing crossed-parallax diplopia.
- How these techniques interact with the wide variety of HTD applications?
- How these techniques affect user performance in basic and more applied tasks in HTD's?

## Acknowledgements

This work was performed in part under contracts N00014-97-1-0882 and N00014-97-1-0357 from the Office of Naval Research. Support was also provided under contract DAKF11-91-D-004-0034 from the U.S. Army Research Laboratory.

## References

[1] Robert Akka. Utilizing 6D head-tracking data for stereoscopic computer graphics perspective transformations. *Proceedings of the SPIE - The International Society for Optical Engineering, Stereoscopic Displays and Applications IV*, 1915: 147-154, Feb. 1993.

[2] C. Cruz-Neira, D.J. Sandin, , T.A. DeFanti, Surround-screen projection-based virtual reality: the design and implementation of the CAVE. In *SIGGRAPH 93 Conference Proceedings*, Annual Conference Series, pages 135-42. ACM SIGGRAPH, Addison Wesley, August 1993.

[3] James E Cutting. How the eye measures reality and virtual reality. *Behavioral Research Methods, Instruments & Computers*, 29(1): 27-36, February 1997.

[4] Michael Deering. High Resolution Virtual Reality. In *Computer Graphics (SIGGRAPH 92 Conference Proceedings)*, volume 26, pages 195-202. Addison Wesley, July 1992.

[5] James D. Foley, Andries Van Dam, Steven K. Feiner, John F. Huges. *Computer Graphics: Principles and Practice*. Addison-Wesley Publishing Company. 1992.

[6] Ronald N Goldman. Decomposing Projective Transformations. In David Kirk, editor, *Computer Graphics Gems III*. Boston : Harcourt Brace Jovanovich, 1992.

[7] Larry F. Hodges, David F. McAllister. Rotation algorithm artifacts in stereoscopic images. *Optical Engineering*. 29(8): 973-976, August 1990.

[8] Larry F. Hodges, Elizabeth Thorpe Davis. Geometric Considerations for Stereoscopic Virtual Environments. *Presence*, 2(1): 34-42, Winter 1993.

[9] Larry F. Hodges. Tutorial: Time-Multiplexed Stereoscopic Computer Graphics. *IEEE Computer Graphics and Applications*. 12(2): 20 –30, March 1992.

[10] W. Krüger, B. Fröhlich. The Responsive Workbench (virtual work environment). *IEEE Computer Graphics and Applications*. 14(3):12-15. May 1994.

[11] Lenny Lipton. *Foundations of the Stereoscopic Cinema: A Study in Depth*. Van Nostrand Reinhold, 1982.

[12] M. Mon-Williams, J.P. Wann, S. Rushton. Design factors in stereoscopic virtual-reality displays. *Journal of SID*, 3/4: 207-210. 1995.

[13] Warren Robinett, Richard Holloway. The Visual Display Transformation for Virtual Reality. *Presence*, 4(1): 1-23. Winter 1995.

[14] Louis B. Rosenberg. The Effect of Interocular Distance upon Operator Performance using Stereoscopic Displays to Perform Virtual Depth Tasks. In Proceedings of *IEEE Virtual Reality Annual International Symposium 93*, 27-32. Sept. 1993.

[15] David A. Southard. Viewing model for virtual environment displays. *Journal of Electronic Imaging*, 4(4): 413–420. October 1995.

[16] R. Troy Surdick, Elizabeth T. Davis, Robert A. King, Larry F. Hodges. The Perception of Distance in Simulated Displays. *Presence*, 6(5): 513-531, October 1997.

[17] John P. Wann, Simon Rushton, Mark Mon-Williams. Natural Problems for Stereoscopic Depth Perception in Virtual Environment. *Vision Research*. 35(19): 2731-2736, 1995.

[18] Colin Ware, Cyril Gobrecht and Mark Paton. Algorithm for dynamic disparity Adjustment. In *Proceedings of the SPIE - The International Society for Optical Engineering. Stereoscopic Displays and Virtual Reality Systems II*, 2409:150-6, Feb. 1995.

[19] Colin Ware, Kevin Arthur and Kellogg S. Booth. Fish Tank Virtual Reality. In proceedings of *InterChi '93*, pages 37-41. April 1993.

[20] Zachary Wartell, Larry F. Hodges, William Ribarsky. The Analytic Distortion Induced by False-Eye Separation in Head-Tracked Stereoscopic Displays. Georgia Institute of Technology, GVU Technical Report, no. 99-01, 1999. (See also *Computer Graphics Proceedings CD-ROM SIGGRAPH 99*).

[21] B.A. Watson, L. F. Hodges. Using texture maps to correct for optical distortion in head-mounted displays. In proceedings of *IEEE Virtual Reality Annual International Symposium 95* (VRAIS '95), pages 172-178.

[22] Mason Woo, Jackie Neider, Tom Davis. *OpenGL Program Guide*. Addison-Wesley Developers Press. Reading, Massachusetts. 1997.

[23] Andrew Woods, Tom Docherty, Rolf Koch. Image Distortion in Stereoscopic Video Systems. In *Proceedings of the SPIE – The International Society for Optical Engineering, Stereoscopic Displays and Applications IV*, 1915: 36 – 48, 1993.

[24] Yei-Yu Yeh and Louis .D. Silverstein. Limits of Fusion and Depth Judgements in Stereoscopic Color Displays. *Human Factors*, 32(1): 45-60, Feb. 1990.

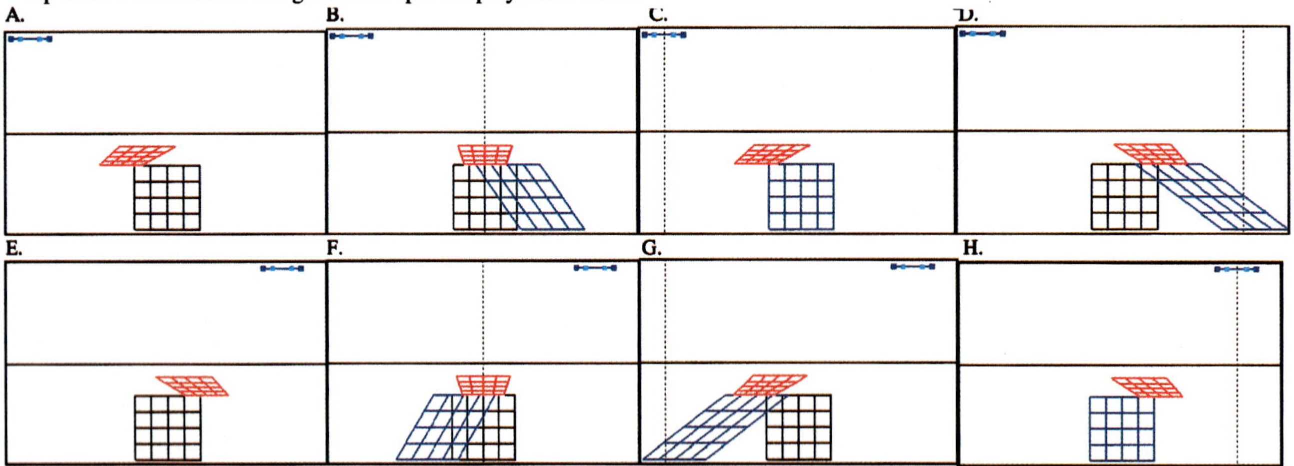


Figure 11: Comparison of non-predistorted perceived mesh (A,E) to a $\Delta_{shear}{}^{-1}$-predistorted mesh (B,F) and a $\alpha$-predistorted mesh with the fixed line on the left (C,G) and the fixed lined on the right (D,H). The fixed line is the dashed, gray vertical line. The true eyes are dark blue and the modeled eyes are light blue. The perceived mesh is red. The modeled mesh is black and the predistorted mesh is blue. Comparing (A) and (E) to their corresponding rows, note that both predistortion methods remove the sideways shifting of the perceived mesh. Using $\alpha$-predistortion (C,D,G,H) allows relocation of the fixed line which represents the set of viewpoints whose views are unaffected by $\alpha$-predistortion.

# Walking > Walking-in-Place > Flying, in Virtual Environments

Martin Usoh[†] Kevin Arthur[‡] Mary C. Whitton[‡] Rui Bastos[‡] Anthony Steed[†] Mel Slater[†] Frederick P. Brooks, Jr.[‡]

[†]Department of Computer Science, University College London
[‡]Department of Computer Science, University of North Carolina at Chapel Hill

## Abstract

A study by Slater, *et al.,* [1995] indicated that naive subjects in an immersive virtual environment experience a higher subjective sense of presence when they locomote by walking-in-place (*virtual walking)* than when they push-button-fly (along the floor plane). We replicated their study, adding real walking as a third condition.

Our study confirmed their findings. We also found that real walking is significantly better than both virtual walking and flying in ease (simplicity, straightforwardness, naturalness) as a mode of locomotion. The greatest difference in subjective presence was between flyers and both kinds of walkers. In addition, subjective presence was higher for real walkers than virtual walkers, but the difference was statistically significant only in some models. Follow-on studies show virtual walking can be substantially improved by detecting footfalls with a head accelerometer.

As in the Slater study, subjective presence significantly correlated with subjects' degree of association with their virtual bodies (avatars). This, our strongest statistical result, suggests that substantial potential presence gains can be had from tracking all limbs and customizing avatar appearance.

An unexpected by-product was that real walking through our enhanced version of Slater's visual-cliff virtual environment (Figure 1) yielded a strikingly compelling virtual experience—the strongest we and most of our visitors have yet experienced. The most needed system improvement is the substitution of wireless technology for all links to the user.

**CR Categories and Subject Descriptors**: I.3.7 [Computer Graphics]: Three-Dimensional Graphics and Realism — *Virtual Reality*; I.3.6 [Computer Graphics]: Methodology and Techniques — *Interaction techniques*; H.5.2 [Information Interfaces]: User Interfaces — *Evaluation/Methodology.*

**Keywords:** Presence, Locomotion, Virtual Reality, Virtual Walking, Human Factors, Neural Networks, Visual Cliff

[†] Gower Street, London WC1E 6BT, UK
{m.usoh|a.steed|m.slater}@cs.ucl.ac.uk
[‡] CB #3175, Chapel Hill, NC 27599-3175, USA
{arthur|whitton|bastos|brooks}@cs.unc.edu

Figure 1. View over virtual ledge.

## 1. BACKGROUND AND OBJECTIVES

A crucial problem in virtual environments research is the development of natural and effective virtual surrogates for user interactions with physical spaces and objects. Locomotion through virtual spaces is the most primitive and important special case [Iwata, 1999; Bowman, 1997].

Most people believe, and studies confirm, that active usage of the participant's body, with the real proprioceptive sensations matched by synthetic visual and aural data, strongly affects virtual presence [Slater, 1994; Slater, 1997]. Therefore research in locomotion has proceeded in two dimensions: development of wide-area trackers so users can really walk about [Ward, 1992], and development of body-active surrogates for walking: treadmills, bicycles, wheelchairs, roller skates, and walking-in-place [Brooks, 1986; Christensen, 1998; Darken, 1997; Iwata, 1999; Slater, 1993].

In immersive virtual environments the most common mode of locomotion is local walking limited by tracker range, combined with button-controlled flying of the whole local neighborhood to a different virtual location [Robinett, 1992]. This can be likened to walking about on a flat-bed truck that is independently navigated for global motions. Slater, *et al.*, developed a simple and economical walk-in-place technique, a *virtual treadmill*, that uses a neural net to analyze the tracked head motion to detect steps [Slater, 1993; Hertz, 1991]. A 1995 study indicated that virtual walking using this technique significantly enhanced the subjective rating of presence compared to flying, for subjects who subjectively associated with their avatars. Avatar association did not significantly enhance presence for flying subjects [Slater, 1995].

In the present study we brought the two streams of locomotion research together, using a wide-area ceiling tracker and replicating the Slater 1995 study of virtual walking, and adding real walking as a third condition.

The objectives were:

- To see if the results of the earlier study hold true, given more recent technology.
- To compare flying, virtual walking, and real walking with respect to ease of locomotion and subjective presence.

If virtual walking is indeed better than flying, it is so economical to implement as to become the technique of choice for most applications that today use flying. If, and this was our hope, virtual walking is essentially equivalent to real walking, wide-area tracking can be reserved for very specific applications where physical motion is essential.

## 2. ENHANCEMENTS TO THE ORIGINAL STUDY

We tried to maintain the integrity of the original study. However, we amended the procedure and scenario to accommodate restrictions of physical space and to add real walking, improve the visual fidelity of the model, and enhance the measure of presence.

### 2.1 Real Walking

Participants were free to walk around the entire virtual scene in the same manner as in a real environment. We tracked the user's head and one hand using a custom optical tracker [Ward, 1992; Welch, 1997]. This tracker works over a range of approximately 10 m by 4 m with millimeter precision. Two optical sensors view blinked infrared LEDs on the ceiling tiles. The tracking system updates position and orientation at approximately 1.5 kHz. These reports are fed to the application at 70 Hz. We set tracker filtering to result in tracker latency of 25 ms. Total latency, taking into account network and graphics delays as well, was approximately 100 ms. Allowing participants to walk freely around a large area required care so that participants would not snag or trip on cables, or collide with real obstacles in the laboratory. One of the experimenters walked behind the user handling cables and preventing collisions.

### 2.2 Virtual Walking

Virtual walking requires participants to reproduce the physical head motions generated during actual walking but without physically locomoting. The changes in head position are fed to a neural network previously trained to recognize walking. The network discriminates when participants are walking-in-place from when they are doing anything else. When virtual walking is detected, they are moved forward in virtual space in the direction of head-facing. This appears to be intuitive; participants are able to navigate without being told they will move in the gaze direction. We used the same feed-forward neural network as the 1995 study (see [Slater, 1993] for details). Streaming position data to the neural network at 10 Hz gives good discrimination.

As with the 1995 study we used a neural network trained for *standard* virtual walking. This standard net was derived from the gait of the principal author. It has been effective in recognizing the walking-in-place motion. Casual visitors to the laboratory were able to replicate the movements; it was not necessary to train the system on the gaits of individual subjects.

The neural network can make two types of errors. Type I is judging users to be walking when they are not; Type II is judging them to be not walking when in fact they are. The Type II errors typically occur on motion starting, Type I errors on cessation, and they manifest themselves as overshooting—sometimes causing virtual collisions. Type II errors are generally not so severe, since they manifest as momentary breaks in performance, giving a general slowness in locomotion. Type I error is more disturbing to users.

### 2.3 Flying

In the original experiment, flying was in the direction the hand pointed. This decoupled the head and hand so that subjects could freely look around while flying. However, subjects generally found it more difficult than flying in the direction of gaze. To make the flyer and virtual walker groups match, we chose locomotion along gaze (actually, head direction). A mismatch of movement along gaze direction can also occur when subjects look down at their virtual feet. Hence we forced the forward direction of the virtual feet to correspond to head direction.

### 2.4 The Virtual World and Scenario

The 1995 scenario consisted of a virtual corridor about 10 m long with an open doorway leading to another room. The corridor contained a number of boxes on the floor. Subjects could travel to a certain point along the corridor without being able to see through the doorway; instructions and training were given in this part of the scene (Figure 2a). This was mainly for acclimatization and for practice in locomotion and grasping of virtual objects.

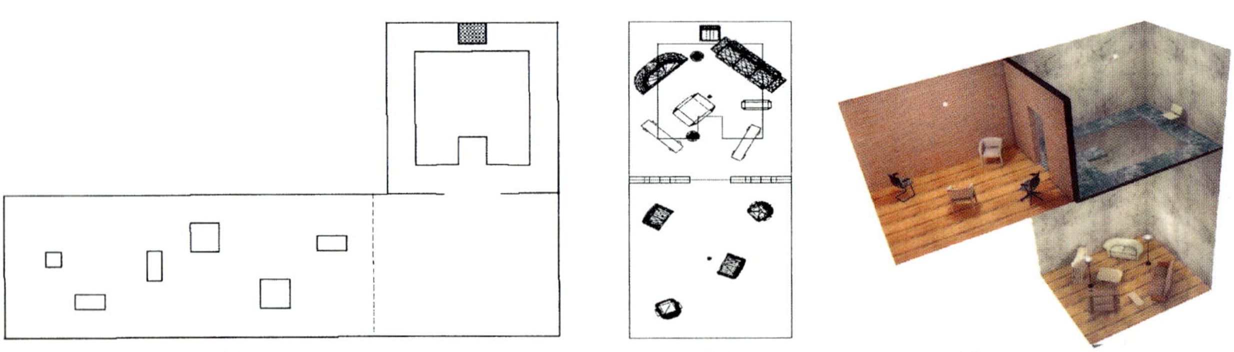

(a) (b) (c)

Figure 2. (a) Original Slater environment, 1,000 polygons; (b, c) environment for current study, 40,000 polygons.

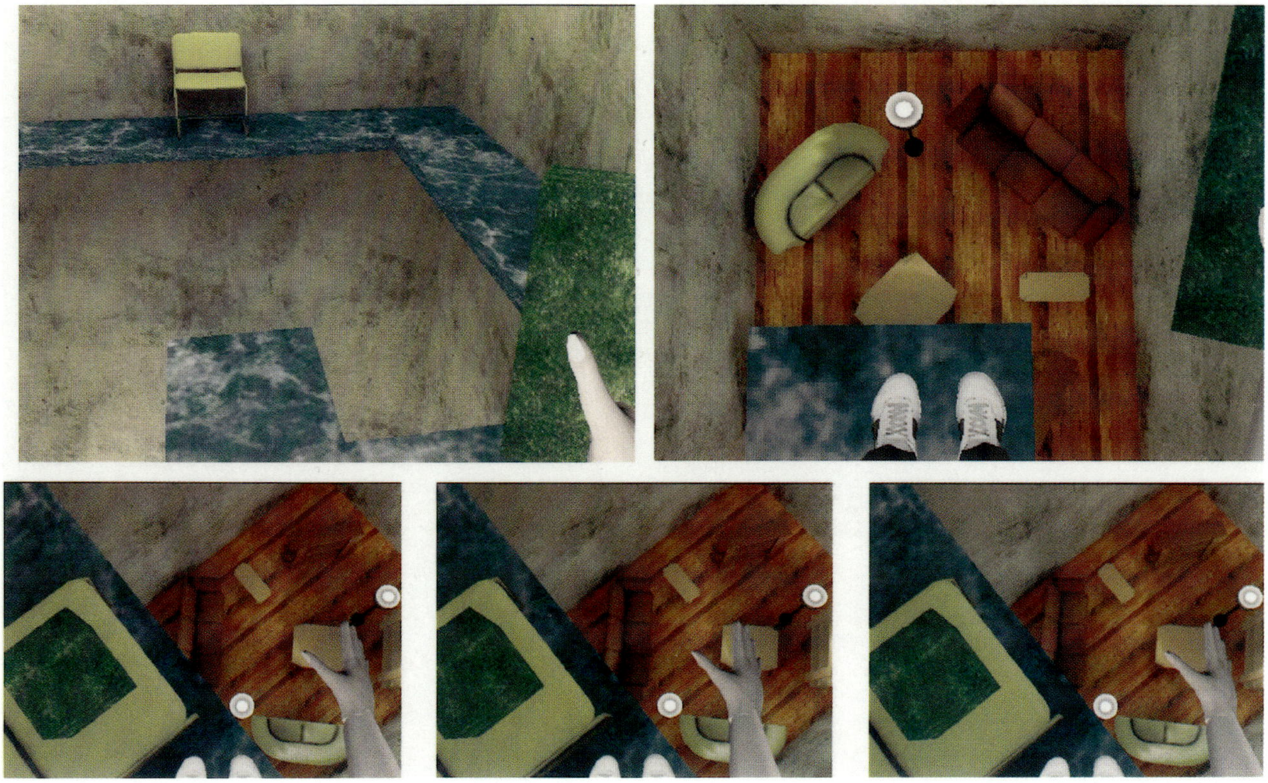

**Figure 3.** Sequence of images of the environment. The top left image shows a subject's view when entering the pit room. The top right shows the view when standing on the "diving board" on the ledge. The bottom images form stereo pairs of the view when looking down from beside the target chair (the left two images are for wall-eyed viewing; the right images are for cross-eyed viewing).

When a user enters the virtual room leading off the corridor, he or she is on a 0.7 m wide ledge 6 m above the floor of the room. The ledge goes all the way around the room and there is a chair on the ledge on the far side. The floor below is populated with living room furniture. A direct path from the doorway to the chair would mean walking out onto "empty space". However, it is possible to get to the chair "safely" by going along the edge of the room. This scene is inspired by Gibson's visual cliff experiment [Gibson, 1960] and fear-of-heights work by other researchers [Rothbaum, 1995].

Although we are using wide-area tracking, the virtual scene still must fit into a finite area. We therefore divided the tracked space into a training area and an experimental area, each of 5 x 4 meters. In virtual space these areas corresponded to a training room and the room containing the virtual pit. A virtual door prevents subjects from seeing the virtual pit room during training. We maintained the dimensions of the 1995 virtual pit room, and used a smaller virtual training area (Figures 2b, 2c).

A modern graphics engine (SGI Infinite Reality System) enabled us to use a much enhanced visual scene—about 40 times as many polygons (some 40,000 total), radiosity lighting, and texturing for almost half the polygons (Figure 3).

Because the 1995 study showed the importance of user association with the virtual body, we invested over 11,000 of the polygons in a detailed avatar (Figure 4). The subject was able to see his tracked virtual right hand connected by a virtual arm to his body. A subject looking down could see his virtual body and feet, and an untracked virtual left hand. The virtual body was oriented in the head direction. Consequently if one looked at one's virtual feet while swiveling the head, the virtual body shifted correspondingly. However, this effect was not always noticeable and only 10% of subjects reported it as a distraction.

## 2.5 MEASURES AND DATA COLLECTION

Several researchers have undertaken the quantification of presence [Slater, 1994; Ellis, 1996; Pausch, 1997]. Subjective reporting using questionnaires is the most common method. This method, however, relies on eliciting responses about subjects'

Figure 4. View showing avatar.

experiences *after* the event. Subjects must retain detailed memories of each part of the experience. An ideal measure would require recordings from subjects *while* immersed in the environment. A recent approach depends on gestalt psychology to record presence levels without interfering with the VE experience [Slater, 1998]. This relies on subjects indicating when they have a *break in presence* (BIP) from the virtual environment.

We retained the 1995 questionnaire-based method for determination of the virtual presence, but enlarged it substantially. The enlarged set of questions asks about various aspects of the virtual experience such as the sense of "being there", frequency of dominance of the virtual world over the real one, sense of visiting versus viewing a scene, etc. These were interspersed with questions on the ease and effectiveness of locomotion and padded with filler questions. All presence and performance related questions were rated on a scale of 1-7; the total number of 6 and 7 scores was taken as the overall score. We augmented the questionnaire with an oral debriefing, inquiring into factors reinforcing the experience or causing BIPs. We encouraged free-form comments.

Both real and virtual views of sessions were videotaped. Debriefing sessions were audio taped. Tracking information and button-push events were recorded. Investigator observation of user foot motion and corresponding neural net judgments were recorded for virtual walkers, so as to yield goodness scores for the net.

## 3. THE EXPERIMENT

The experiments used a Silicon Graphics Onyx2 with one graphic pipe, two raster managers, four 195 MHz R10000 processors and 2 GB of main memory. The scene was rendered using OpenGL and locally developed software; the system maintained a frame rate of 30 Hz stereo. Viewing used a Virtual Research V8 head mounted display with true VGA resolution of (640x3) x 480 pixels per eye — 307,200 triads. This display consists of two 1.3 inch active matrix LCDs with a field of view of 60 degrees diagonal at 100% overlap and aspect ratio 4:3.

The input device was a joystick with four buttons; the experiment used two. The joystick and HMD were tracked by the ceiling tracker. The system had an overall latency of about 100 ms with a lag of about 500 ms for walking-in-place.

A total of 33 "naive" subjects participated in the study. The requirement was that they have no knowledge of the goals of the experiment. Each subject was paid $10. Naive subjects were grouped into flyers, virtual walkers, and real walkers, each with 6 men and 5 women. Another 11 subjects (10 men, 1 woman) were "expert" users who had experienced immersive virtual reality on several occasions and were generally working in the area of computer graphics. We included this group's results in the analysis, and tested if expertise was a significant variable in the results. It was not.

The experiment consisted of a simulator sickness questionnaire with 16 categories [Kennedy *et al.*, 1993], the virtual experience, a repeat simulator sickness questionnaire, the presence questionnaire, and then an oral debriefing session. An investigator trained the subject in the training room, which had some chairs, a blue box, and a green box. Subjects practiced locomotion and picking up the blue box until they were comfortable with both. Boxes fell when dropped. Subjects were told to proceed with the experiment whenever they felt ready. The investigator did not speak again until they had completed the task. This task was to grasp the green box in the training room and carry it to the chair in the virtual pit room. Picking up the green box automatically opens the door between the two virtual rooms. Subjects were free to choose the path to the chair, either going along the ledge, left or right, or moving directly to the chair over the pit. Objectively we associate a path over the virtual pit with a lower sense of presence than one along the ledge.

## 4. ANALYSIS

To enable the comparison with the 1995 study an analysis was done using the original questions followed by one with our enhanced set. Another analysis was done on behaviors, observed and reported: consciousness of background noise, vertigo, actual path to the chair, willingness to walk out over the pit, etc.

We used the same binomial logistic regression analysis as was used in 1995 for presence, behavior, and locomotion responses [Cox, 1970]. We fitted a baseline model that uses only locomotion method as the independent variable. We then tested a number of other explanatory variables by starting from the baseline model and adding or deleting terms according to their significance level as judged against the Chi-squared distribution. We were most interested in degree of association with the virtual body, since in the 1995 study it was the dominant explanatory variable for extent of presence.

We present the questionnaire data, behavioral data, debriefing comments, and the details of the statistical analysis on the web page http://www.cs.unc.edu/~walk/walking_expt/.

## 5. RESULTS

### 5.1 Overall Conclusions

The experiment confirms the 1995 result that presence correlates highly with the degree of association with the virtual body. This seems to hold irrespective of anything else. The evidence suggests that presence is higher for virtual walkers than for flyers, and higher for real walkers than for virtual walkers. However, the difference between groups diminishes when oculomotor discomfort is taken into account. Oculomotor discomfort is one of the three diagnostic subscales measured by the simulator sickness questionnaire [Kennedy, 1993]. We found that it reduces presence for the virtual walkers and flyers, but does not do so for the real walkers. This likely has to do with the match between presence and proprioception—the greater match in the real walking case overcoming the disadvantages of discomfort. This result is very much in line with previous findings. Finally, if the goal is to have people assess locomotion as natural, easy, and uncomplicated, then real walking is better than the other methods.

### 5.2 User Reports

Subjective reports of the sense of "being there" were generally strong across all three groups. Although subjects were intellectually aware that they are in a simulation, the power of the human visual system triggers innate responses. One commented, "I was afraid to experience the falling sensation I might have had if I'd walked straight ahead [over the virtual pit]."

Subjects were also asked what factors, if any, broke them out of the simulation. Reports included incorrect behavior of the environment and avatar, background noise, and interference by the hardware. About 30% reported awareness of the cables as causing breaks-in-presence. About 15% of subjects commented on becoming more immersed in the experience once the investigator stopped giving instructions.

## 5.3 Locomotion

We found a strong significant difference between real walking and the other methods. Figure 5 illustrates mean responses to the three questions on locomotion.

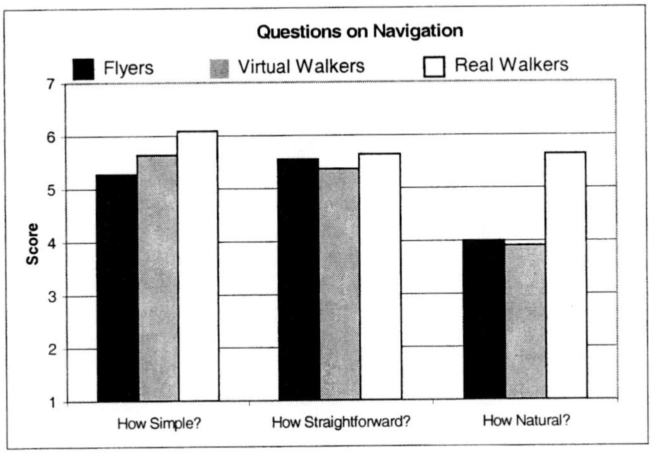


Figure 5: Ease of locomotion across groups.

Real walking associates with greater overall ease of locomotion as measured by the combination of the three locomotion questions. The overall model is not a good fit, and clearly other variables are needed to explain the variation among the subjects. No other variable in the experiment is significant. If each of the three questions about locomotion is considered separately, then the differences among the groups are not significant. This indicates that the three component results cluster together.

## 5.4 Behavioral Presence

By behavioral presence we mean the extent to which actual behaviors or internal states and perceptions indicated a sense of being in the situation depicted by the VE rather than being in the real world of the laboratory. A score was constructed from five components:

- A reported indicator of the extent to which the subject was aware of background sounds in the real laboratory (on a scale of 1 through 7);
- The extent to which their reaction when looking down over the pit was self-assessed as being similar to what it would have been in a similar situation in real life (on a scale of 1 through 7);
- The extent to which they had any vertigo or fear of falling when looking down over the virtual pit (on a scale of 1 to 7);
- Their willingness to walk out over the pit (on a 1 to 7 scale);
- The path they actually took to the chair on the other side of the pit – if they walked across the chasm the score was 0, if they went around the edge the score was 1.

This measure of behavioral presence correlates highly (and positively) with the subjective presence treated in the next section. Previous game playing is not significant, and otherwise an excellent fitted model depends on the same variables as that for subjective presence.

There is no significant difference in the impact of locomotion type on this behavioral presence score.

Oculomotor discomfort has a significant impact in conjunction with locomotion type. In particular, higher discomfort reduces behavioral presence for the flyers, but has no impact for the virtual or real walkers.

Association with the body contributes significantly to behavioral presence.

## 5.5 Subjective Presence

Using the original basic 1995 presence scoring method, we confirmed the principal results of that study:

- There were no significant differences at all between the groups (flyers; virtual walkers; and, in our study, real walkers).
- Association with the virtual body is positively associated with presence rating.

We also found that females had a higher sense of presence than males. However, since females also played computer games significantly less than males, substituting game playing for gender yields a better fitting model. Greater game playing is associated with lower presence. No other variables were significant.

Using the enhanced questionnaires, with four new questions added to the original three, produced richer results:

- There was a significant difference between flyers, virtual walkers and real walkers. However, the major significant difference was between the first group and the second two, with the virtual and real walkers reporting a significantly higher sense of presence than the flyers. If nothing else is taken into account, then the real walkers have a higher sense of presence than the virtual walkers.
- The higher the association with the virtual body, the greater the sense of presence, irrespective of other variables.
- Game playing is negatively associated with presence, irrespective of anything else. However, there is the same confounding of game playing and gender.

When oculomotor discomfort is brought into the model, then an interesting result occurs. There is then essentially no difference between real and virtual walkers, although these groups still have a significantly higher presence than for the flyers. However, there is a different impact of discomfort across the three groups. For the flyers and virtual walkers, higher discomfort is associated with decreased presence, whereas this is not the case for the real walkers.

# 6. UNEXPECTED RESULT — A COMPELLING VIRTUAL ENVIRONMENT EXPERIENCE

An unexpected by-product of this study was that real walking (and, to a lesser extent, virtual walking) through our enhanced version of Slater's virtual environment yields a strikingly compelling virtual experience. "Wow!" "Whoa!" "Uh-oh!" are typical reactions of participants upon finding themselves at the open door to the ledge above the pit.

We have demonstrated the scenario to over 200 people. A few refuse to go through the door into the pit room at all. Others will make their way around the ledge to the chair, but refuse to come back. Many refuse to venture out over the pit. For those that do, it requires an obvious act of will, even after they have repeated the experience several times. As Gibson taught us, the visual cliff evokes deep instincts; violating it is a gut-wrenching experience. The total experience is substantially better than anything previously achieved in our laboratory; it sets a new standard.

confluence of many factors:

- The visual cliff environment itself, the depth of the pit, the narrowness of the ledge
- Almost imperceptible end-to-end system lag, on the order of 100 ms
- Real walking about in a significant space
- The reasonably realistic avatar
- The visual fidelity of the detailed, textured, radiosity-lit scene
- The excellent resolution and color saturation of the V8 HMD
- The 30 Hz stereo frame rate achieved by the Onyx 2 Infinite Reality engine
- Stereopsis
- The precision and crispness of the tracker

It is quite beyond us to guess, much less measure, the contribution of each factor.

## 7. OBSERVATIONS, LESSONS, AND FUTURE WORK

**Cables** are without doubt the most unsatisfactory part of the VE experience. Some 30% of the subjects commented on this difficulty. We are working on wireless links.

**Real walking** is best for human-scale spaces, though not cheap.

**Virtual walking** seems clearly better than flying for exploring human-scale spaces, if one wants heightened presence or a visceral estimate of spatial extents. It is very inexpensive to implement.

**Substantially improved virtual walking** can be had. The present neural net implementation requires a somewhat exaggerated gait, which can distract participants. The lag on walking cessation creates fake virtual collisions and other BIPs. A miniaturized accelerometer on the head tracker is a promising alternate implementation. Results from early studies show Type I errors to be only 1%, Type II errors 11%; versus 3%, 32% for the neural net. We shall also investigate foot-floor contact sensing.

**Avatar realism** is worth a lot of work and investment, since user identification with the virtual body is such a strong factor in presence. In our experiment, the limp left hand and non-walking feet were disconcerting, but were not major BIPs. We are working on extending tracking to each hand and foot, and trusting inverse kinematics to do the rest of limb realism.

**Clothing identification** was surprisingly important to some subjects. We have experimented with video-fed image-based rendering to achieve visual realism for a viewer's own avatar. It is very promising.

**Investigator location incongruity** caused many BIPs, but fortunately they occurred only during training phases, not the experimental phases. Subjects reported that looking at the experimenter's voice location and seeing no one caused a BIP. We plan hereafter to have investigator instructions given only via the HMD headphones, and not localized. The headphones will also attenuate other incongruous laboratory noise.

**Ambiguous and erroneous interpretations** of questionnaire questions will not all be exorcised by pilot experiments. Questions require great care. Oral debriefing of subjects resolves many ambiguities.

We thank the UNC Chapel Hill Tracker project for the wide-area tracker that enabled us to do this experiment. We also thank Phil Winston for tracker software support, Zac Kohn for accelerometer testing, Neil Golson for help with model creation, David Harrison and Kurtis Keller for hardware support, and Todd Gaul for video support.

This work was partially supported by NIH National Center for Research Resources number RR02170. Intel generously donated equipment used in this research. Anthony Steed is funded by the European ACTS project, COVEN (Collaborative Virtual Environments). Rui Bastos was funded by CNPq/Brazil, PRAXIS XXI, and SGI.

## REFERENCES

Bowman, D., D. Koller, and L. Hodges, 1997: "Travel in Immersive Virtual Environments: An Evaluation of Viewpoint Motion Control Techniques," Proc. *Virtual Reality Annual International Symposium*, Albuquerque, NM, *IEEE Computer Society*, 45-52.

Brooks F.P., Jr., J. Airey, J. Alspaugh, A. Bell, R. Brown, C. Hill, U. Nimscheck, P. Rheingans, J. Rohlf, D. Smith, D. Turner, A. Varshney, Y. Wang, H. Weber, and X. Yuanet, 1992: "Six Generations of Building Walkthrough," Final Technical Report to the National Science Foundation (Number TR92-026), Department of Computer Science, University of North Carolina at Chapel Hill.

Brooks, F.P., Jr., 1986: "Walkthrough — A dynamic graphics system for simulating virtual buildings," *Proc. of 1986 ACM Workshop in Interactive 3D Graphics*, Chapel Hill, NC, October, 1986, 9-21.

Christensen, R., J.M. Hollerbach, Y. Xu, and S. Meek, "Inertial force feedback for a locomotion interface," *Symp. on Haptic Interfaces, Proc., ASME Dynamic Systems and Control Division*, DSC-Vol. 64, Anaheim, CA, Nov. 15-20, 1998, 119-126.

Cox, D.R., 1970: *Analysis of Binary Data*, London: Menthuen.

Darken, R.P, W. R. Cockaybe, and D. Carmein, 1997: "The Omni-Directional Treadmill: A Locomotion Device for Virtual Worlds," *Proc. of UIST'97*, Banff, Canada, ACM Press, October 14-17, 1997, 213-221.

Ellis, S.R., 1996: "Presence of mind: a reaction to Thomas Sheridan's, 'Further musings on the psychophysics of presence,' " *Presence*, **5**, 2: 247-259.

Gibson, E.., and R.D. Walk, 1960: "The visual cliff," *Scientific American*: 202:64-71.

Hertz, J.. A. Krogh, and R.G. Palmer, 1991: *Introduction to the Theory of Neural Computation*, Addison-Wesley Publishing Company.

Iwata, H, 1999: "Walking About on an Infinite Floor," *Proc. of Virtual Reality '99, March 13-17, Houston, Texas, IEEE Computer Society Press*, 286-293.

Kennedy, R.S., N.E. Lane, K.S. Berbaum, and M.G. Lilienthal, 1993: "A Simulator Sickness Questionnaire (SSQ): A New Method for Quantifying Simulator Sickness," *International Journal of Aviation Psychology*, **3**, 3: 203-220.

Pausch, R., D. Proffitt, and G. Williams, 1997: "Quantifying Immersion in Virtual Reality," *Proc. of SIGGRAPH 97*, Computer Graphics Proceedings, Annual Conference Series, 1997, 13-18.

Robinett, W., and R. Holloway, 1992: "Implementation of Flying, Scaling and Grabbing in Virtual Worlds," *Proc. of the 1992 Symposium on Interactive 3D Graphics*, Computer Graphics **25**, 2: 189-192.

Rothbaum, B.O., L.F. Hodges, and M. North, 1995: "Effectiveness of Computer-Generated (Virtual Reality) Graded Exposure in the Treatment of Acrophobia," *American Journal of Psychiatry*, **152**, 4: 626-628.

Slater, M., A. Steed, and M. Usoh, 1993: "The Virtual Treadmill: A Naturalistic Metaphor for Navigation in Immersive Virtual Environments," *First Eurographics Workshop on Virtual Reality*, ed. M. Goebel, 71-86.

Slater, M., M. Usoh, and A. Steed, 1994: "Depth of Presence in Virtual Environments," *Presence: Teleoperators and Virtual Environments*, MIT Press, **3**, 2: 130-144.

Slater, M., M. Usoh, and A. Steed, 1995: "Taking Steps: The Influence of a Walking Technique on Presence in Virtual Reality," *ACM Trans. on CHI*, Special Issue on Virtual Reality Software and Technology, **2**, 3: 201-219, September.

Slater, M., A. Steed, J. McCarthy, and F. Marinelli, "The Influence of Body Movement on Presence in Virtual Environments," *Human Factors: The Journal of the Human Factors and Ergonomics Society*, **40**, 3: September: 469-477.

Slater, M., A. Steed, 1998: "A Virtual Presence Counter," *submitted for publication*.

Ward, M., R. Azuma, R. Bennett, S. Gottschalk, and H. Fuchs, 1992: "A demonstrated optical tracker with scalable work area for head-mounted display systems." *Proc. of the 1992 Symposium on Interactive 3D Graphics*, Computer Graphics **25**, 2: 43-52.

Welch, G., and G. Bishop, 1997: "SCAAT: Incremental tracking with incomplete information." *Proc. of SIGGRAPH 97*, Computer Graphics Proceedings, Annual Conference Series, 1997, 333-344.

# Real-Time Acoustic Modeling for Distributed Virtual Environments

Thomas Funkhouser
Princeton University

Patrick Min
Princeton University

Ingrid Carlbom
Bell Laboratories

## Abstract

Realistic acoustic modeling is essential for spatializing sound in distributed virtual environments where multiple networked users move around and interact visually and aurally in a shared virtual world. Unfortunately, current methods for computing accurate acoustical models are not fast enough for real-time auralization of sounds for simultaneously moving sources and receivers. In this paper, we present three new beam tracing algorithms that greatly accelerate computation of reverberation paths in a distributed virtual environment by taking advantage of the fact that sounds can only be generated or heard at the positions of "avatars" representing the users. The *priority-driven beam tracing* algorithm performs a best-first search of a cell adjacency graph, and thus enables new termination criteria with which all early reflection paths can be found very efficiently. The *bidirectional beam tracing* algorithm combines sets of beams traced from pairs of avatar locations to find reverberation paths between them while requiring significantly less computation than previous unidirectional algorithms. The *amortized beam tracing* algorithm computes beams emanating from box-shaped regions of space containing predicted avatar locations and re-uses those beams multiple times to compute reflections paths as each avatar moves inside the box. Cumulatively, these algorithms enable speedups of approximately two orders of magnitude over previous methods. They are incorporated into a time-critical multiprocessing system that allocates its computational resources dynamically in order to compute the highest priority reverberation paths between moving avatar locations *in real-time* with graceful degradation and adaptive refinement.

**Key Words:** Virtual environment systems, virtual reality, acoustic modeling, auralization, beam tracing.

## 1 Introduction

Distributed virtual environment (DVE) systems incorporate computer graphics, sound, and networking to simulate the experience of real-time interaction between multiple users represented by avatars in a shared three-dimensional virtual world. They allow a user to "explore" information and "interact" with other users in the context of a virtual environment by rendering images and sounds of the environment in real-time while the user "moves" through the 3D environment interactively. Example applications for DVE systems include collaborative design [4], distributed training [35], teleconferencing [29], and multi-player games [27].

A difficult challenge in implementing a DVE system is to render realistic sounds spatialized according to the virtual environment in real-time on every participating user's computer. Sound waves originating at a source location travel through the environment along a multitude of reverberation paths, representing different sequences of reflections, transmissions, and diffractions. The different arrival times and amplitudes of sound waves traveling along these paths provide important auditory cues for localization of objects, separation of simultaneous speakers (i.e., the "cocktail party effect"), and sense of presence in a virtual environment [11].



The goal of our work is to build a DVE system in which multiple users can communicate with each other in a 3D virtual world with realistic spatialized sound. User generated sounds and avatar movements are transmitted via network messages to an audio server which spatializes sounds according to impulse responses encoding the reverberations computed for every pair of avatars (see Figure 1). The new research challenge is to develop geometric acoustic modeling algorithms to compute reverberation paths between every pair of avatar locations *in real-time* as they move through a 3D environment.

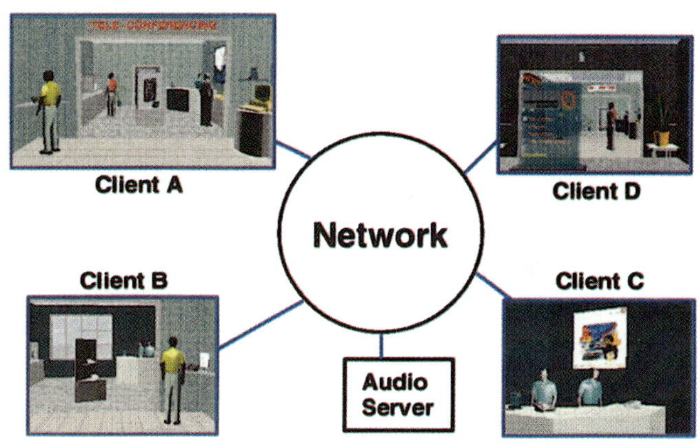


Figure 1: Distributed virtual environment system.

Acoustic modeling algorithms for DVE systems must be efficient, adaptive, predictive, and asynchronous so that appropriate impulse responses are ready for use without delay as avatars move. Since the numbers and locations of avatars inhabiting the virtual environment can be highly variable, it is not practical to preallocate a fixed amount of computational resources to the update of reverberation paths between any pair of avatars. Some avatars may be moving very closely to one another within the same room, requiring impulse response updates at more than 10Hz to avoid noticeable localization artifacts, while others may be separated by great distances and require less frequent and/or less accurate acoustic simulations (people can detect angular differences in sound source locations separated by 5 degrees [3]). Similarly, the quality of the computed results should degrade gracefully as the computational demands increase (e.g., when more users inhabit the environment), and it should refine adaptively as more resources become available (e.g., when all the users remain stationary). Time critical algorithms must be used to guarantee update rates and allocate computational resources effectively and adaptively so that the overall quality of computed impulse responses is the best possible.

In this paper, we describe geometric beam tracing algorithms to compute reverberation paths between moving avatar locations at very high rates. The primary research contributions are embodied in the three methods we introduce for accelerating computation of reverberation paths: 1) priority-driven beam tracing, 2) bidirectional beam tracing, and 3) amortized beam tracing. We have integrated these methods into a time-critical computing framework to build a complete DVE system incorporating realistic imagery and spatialized sound for real-time communication between multiple networked users.

## 2 Previous Work

There has been decades of work in *off-line* acoustic modeling for applications such as concert hall design. Previous methods include path tracing [22], image source methods [1, 5], boundary element methods [26, 33], and beam tracing [8, 18]. Surveys of work in this area appear in [3, 21, 23]. In general, current off-line systems compute reverberation paths for a small set of pre-specified source and receiver locations, and they allow interactive evaluation only for precomputed results. Unfortunately, it is usually not possible to store precomputed impulse responses or reverberation paths over all possible avatar locations for use by a distributed virtual environment system, as the storage requirements of this approach would be prohibitive for all cases except very simple environments or very coarse samplings.

There have also been many advances over the last decade in distributed virtual environments systems supporting visual interactions between networked users in a shared 3D virtual environment (an early example is Reality Built for Two [4]). The most common examples include multi-player games (e.g., Quake [27]), military battle simulations (e.g., NPSNET [35]), and multi-user chat environments (e.g., Sony's Community Place [29]). These programs display images in real-time with complex global illumination and textures to produce visually compelling immersive experiences.

On the other hand, there has been relatively little progress in real-time acoustic modeling. Current on-line systems generally consider only simple geometric arrangements and low-order specular reflections. For instance, the Acoustetron [13] computes only first- and second-order specular reflections for box-shaped virtual environments, while video games provide spatialized sound with ad hoc localization methods (e.g., pan effects), rather than with realistic acoustic modeling methods. Almost all DVE systems attenuate sound with distance, and many support user-specified "regions of influence" (e.g., ellipsoids) for each sound source [16]. However, to quote the 1995 National Research Council Report on Virtual Reality Scientific and Technological Challenges [12], "current technology is still unable to provide interactive systems with real-time rendering of acoustic environments with complex, realistic room reflections."

The new algorithms presented in this paper are based on the beam tracing method described in [14]. To review, beams are traced from the position of each *stationary* sound source along paths of transmission and specular reflection via a depth-first traversal of an adjacency graph of polyhedral cells (see Figure 2). The algorithm starts in the cell containing the source with a beam representing the entire cell (labeled 'D'). Then, it recursively traces convex pyramidal beams through intersected cell boundaries into adjacent cells, incrementally trimming the beams by convex polygons at traversed cell boundaries ($u$, $o$, $p$, $t$, and $s$), and mirroring the beams at reflecting cell boundaries ($o$ and $p$). The recursion of each depth-first traversal is captured and stored in a beam tree, representing all the traced reverberation paths emanating from the source. Later, during an interactive session, the precomputed beam trees are used to generate reverberation paths to a moving receiver position. For every beam containing the receiver, a reverberation path is constructed by iterative intersection with the reflecting cell boundaries stored with the ancestors of the corresponding beam tree node (as shown in Figure 2).

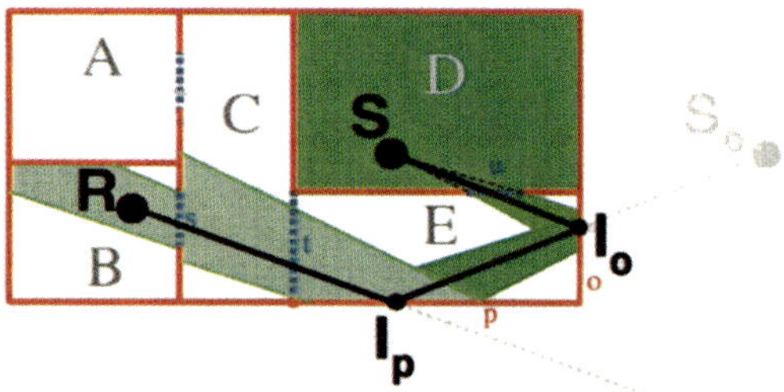


**Figure 2: Beam tracing.**

The key idea in this previous method is that it is possible to use an off-line precomputation to construct a data structure (a beam tree) encoding potential reverberation paths from each static source location and use that precomputed data structure to compute reverberation paths to a moving receiver quickly for auralization. Since the off-line beam tracing algorithm takes up to 50 seconds for each new source location [14], this method is not directly applicable for computing reverberation paths in real-time between *moving* avatars in a distributed virtual environment. Other data structures proposed for interactive updates of global illumination solutions are best suited for handling changes to materials and geometry in primarily diffuse environments [6, 10], and they would generally not perform well for viewpoint changes in highly specular environments.

The focus of our new work is developing beam tracing algorithms that can be used to compute reverberation paths *in real-time* with update rates suitable for auralization in distributed virtual environment applications (up to 100Hz). Achieving this goal requires acceleration of current beam tracing methods by two or three orders of magnitude.

## 3 Overview of Approach

Our approach is to take advantage of the fact that DVE systems must only compute reverberation paths between avatar locations,[1] and not between all points in 3D space. Since avatars are located at a discrete set of positions, and they tend to move along continuous paths, beam tracing algorithms for DVEs can utilize directed searches and temporal coherence to find reverberation paths very efficiently. In this paper, we propose the following three beam tracing algorithms that exploit these properties:

- **Priority-driven beam tracing** uses psychoacoustically motivated priorities and termination criteria to trace only beams that can represent the most significant reverberation paths from one avatar location to another.

- **Bidirectional beam tracing** combines two sets of beams traced from different avatar locations to find reverberation paths efficiently.

- **Amortized beam tracing** utilizes beams traced from a region of space to compute reverberation paths quickly for a sequence of nearby avatar locations.

The following three sections contain detailed descriptions of these new algorithms, while Sections 7 and 8 describe how they are integrated into our adaptive, real-time DVE system.

[1] We extend the notion of an avatar to include anything that can be a source or receiver of sound.

## 4 Priority-Driven Beam Tracing

The first algorithm is motivated by priority-driven search methods. For a given avatar location, all reverberation paths are not equally important. Some paths are psychoacoustically very significant (e.g., direct paths to other avatars), while others follow complex sequences of reflections towards empty regions of space.

Our priority-driven beam tracing algorithm exploits knowledge of avatar locations to compute only the most significant reverberation paths efficiently. Specifically, the algorithm considers beams in *best-first* order, rather than depth-first order as in previous beam tracing algorithms (e.g., [14]). As beam trees are constructed, the leaf nodes are stored in a priority queue, and the highest priority node is iteratively popped for expansion at each step. The benefit of this approach is that the most significant beams are considered first, enabling methods based on adaptive refinement and dynamic termination criteria.

The first issue in implementing the priority-driven algorithm is to assign relative priorities to different beam tree nodes. Following accepted practice of the acoustics literature, we partition the reverberation paths represented by the beams into two categories: 1) early reflections, and 2) late reverberations. Early reflections are defined as the ones that arrive at the receiver within some short amount of time, $T_e$, after the most direct sound, while late reverberations comprise the rest ($20ms \leq T_e \leq 80ms$ [3, 17]). Since localization in the human brain is most sensitive to the early reflections, and the late reverberations are characterized by many paths arriving from all directions after being multiply scattered by many surfaces, geometric acoustic modeling systems generally compute only early specular reflections, while late reverberations and diffractions are modeled with statistical approximations (see Figure 3). In our current system, we use this approach, assigning higher priorities to beam tree nodes representing shorter reflection paths.

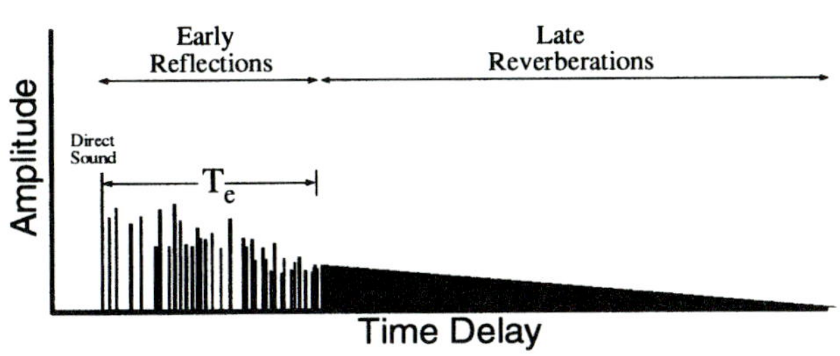


Figure 3: Impulse response.

The second issue is how to guide our priority-driven algorithm to find early specular reflection paths efficiently. Previous algorithms have traced beams in depth-first order up to some termination criteria based on the maximum number of reflections, maximum path length, and/or maximum attenuation. One problem with this approach is that it is impossible to select a priori a termination criterion that guarantees finding all early specular reflection paths. In general, the length of the longest early reflection path cannot be predetermined, since it depends on the length of the shortest one, which is not known until it is found.

Priority-ordered search helps us overcome this problem. We assign the priority , $f(B)$, of each beam tree node, $B$, to the length of the shortest path from the beam source to the last traversed cell boundary, $g(B)$, plus the length of the shortest path from that cell boundary to the closest avatar location, $h(B)$ (see Figure 4). Since $f(B)$ underestimates the length of any path through $B$ to an avatar, we can be assured that all early specular reflection paths are found if we terminate the traversal when the value of $f(B)$ for all nodes remaining in the priority queue corresponds to an arrival time at least $T_e$ later than the most direct path found to every avatar location.

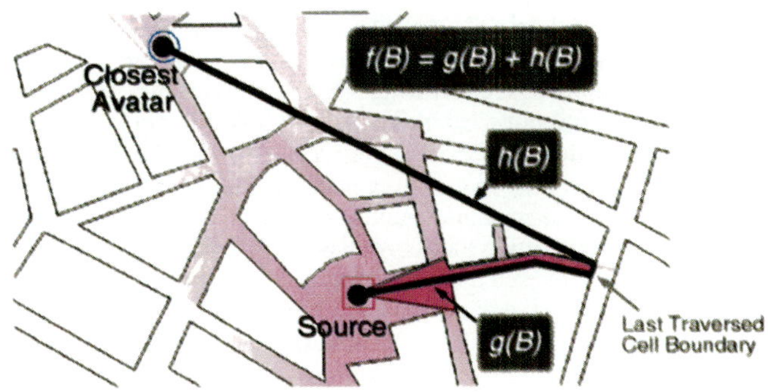


Figure 4: The priority heuristic, $f(B)$, underestimates the distance traveled so far, $g(B)$, plus the distance to the closest avatar, $h(B)$.

Our implementation of this approach is closely related to the classical $A^*$ algorithm from the artificial intelligence literature [15]. The difference is that the search for each avatar locations has multiple goals (i.e., the early reflection paths to all other avatar locations). Thus, we must remember the shortest path to each avatar when we find it, and we must remember for which avatars we have already considered all potential early reflection paths.

The primary advantage of the priority-driven beam tracing method is that it avoids geometric computations for many beams representing insignificant reverberation paths, and therefore it is able to compute the significant ones more rapidly. It can also be used to allocate resources dynamically in a real-time system (see Section 7). The disadvantage is that there is extra overhead in computing priorities and maintaining priority queues of beam tree nodes.

## 5 Bidirectional Beam Tracing

The second algorithm uses a bidirectional approach to combine beam trees traced independently from two different avatar locations to find reverberation paths between them.

The primary motivation for a bidirectional approach is that the computational complexity of beam tracing algorithms grows exponentially with increasing reflections. Consequently, tracing one set of beams up to $k$ reflections usually takes far longer than tracing two sets of beams up to $k/2$ reflections.

A second motivation is that DVE systems must find reverberation paths between all pairs of avatars. In this situation, unidirectional approaches are inherently redundant, since beams must be traced fully from all except one avatar locations to insure that reverberation paths are found between all pairs. But then almost every reverberation path is traced twice, once in each direction. With a bidirectional approach, we can avoid this redundant work by combining beams traced from one avatar location with beams traced from another to find the same reverberation paths more efficiently.

Bidirectional path tracing approaches have been investigated for decades in ray tracing (e.g., [7, 24, 34]), radiosity (e.g., [20, 28]), and other fields (e.g., [9, 25]). Generally, for every ray found impinging upon a surface, a data structure associated with the surface is both updated and queried to compute the energy traveling forwards and backwards along the ray. The main challenge of the bidirectional approach is to find a data structure that efficiently and accurately represents the directional energy radiating from every surface of the environment. Previous data structures for bidirectional path tracing have mostly been based on storing discrete radiance samples (e.g., "illumination maps" [2] and "radiosity textures" [19]), and thus they suffer from aliasing artifacts. An important observation is that beam tree data structures [18] are an object-space representation of the directional energy radiating from each surface, and they are well-suited for implementing a bidirectional approach.

Our bidirectional beam tracing algorithm computes reverberation paths by combining beam trees traced independently from different avatar locations. The key contribution of our algorithm is the method we use for determining which beams, $B_1$ and $B_2$, traced independently from avatar locations, $P_1$ and $P_2$, combine to represent viable reverberation paths. We base our method on the following observations, which apply for common ray propagation models comprising specular reflections, diffuse reflections, transmissions, and diffractions over locally reacting surfaces.[2]

- **Condition A:** There is a reverberation path if $B_1$ contains $P_2$ (see Figure 5a).

- **Condition B:** There are (usually an infinite number of) reverberation paths containing a diffuse reflection at surface $S$ if both $B_1$ and $B_2$ intersect the same region of $S$ (see Figure 5b).

- **Condition C:** There is a reverberation path containing a straight-line transmission through surface $S$ if: 1) both $B_1$ and $B_2$ intersect the same region of $S$, 2) $B_1$ intersects the virtual source of $B_2$, and 3) $B_2$ intersects the virtual source of $B_1$ (see Figure 5c).

- **Condition D:** There is a reverberation path containing a specular reflection at surface $S$ if: 1) both $B_1$ and $B_2$ intersect the same region of $S$, 2) $B_1$ intersects the mirrored virtual source of $B_2$, and 3) $B_2$ intersects the mirrored virtual source of $B_1$ (see Figure 5d).

- **Condition E:** There is a reverberation path containing a diffraction at an edge $E$ if: 1) $B_1$ and $B_2$ both intersect the same region of $E$ (see Figure 5e).

To accelerate determination of these conditions, we construct lists of beam tree nodes intersecting each cell and face of the spatial subdivision as the beams are traced. We traverse these lists to determine efficiently which pairs of beam tree nodes potentially combine to represent viable reverberation paths, avoiding consideration of all $n(n-1)/2$ pairwise combinations of traced beams. First, for each pair of beam tree nodes considered, we check to see if both nodes are either the root or a leaf of their respective beam trees. If not, the pair can be ignored, as it surely represents a reverberation path that will be found by another pair of nodes. Otherwise, we check the beams intersecting each cell containing an avatar to see if they satisfy Condition A. We check pairs of beams intersecting the same transmissive face to see if they satisfy Condition C. We check pairs of beams intersecting the same reflecting face to see if they satisfy Conditions D. Finally, we use the first node meeting one of these criteria to compute an underestimating distance heuristic to another avatar location, which can be used to aid early termination when searching for early reflection paths in an integrated bidirectional and priority-driven beam tracing algorithm.

As compared to unidirectional beam tracing methods, the main advantage of our bidirectional algorithm is that paths with up to R reflections can be found by combining two beam trees representing up to $R_1$ and $R_2$ reflections, respectively, where $R_1 + R_2 - 1 = R$. Since $c^{R_1} + c^{R_2} << c^R$ for most c, fewer beams must be traced. The main disadvantage is that extra bookkeeping and processing is required to combine beams from different beam trees.

[2] So far, we have implemented the methods only for specular reflections.

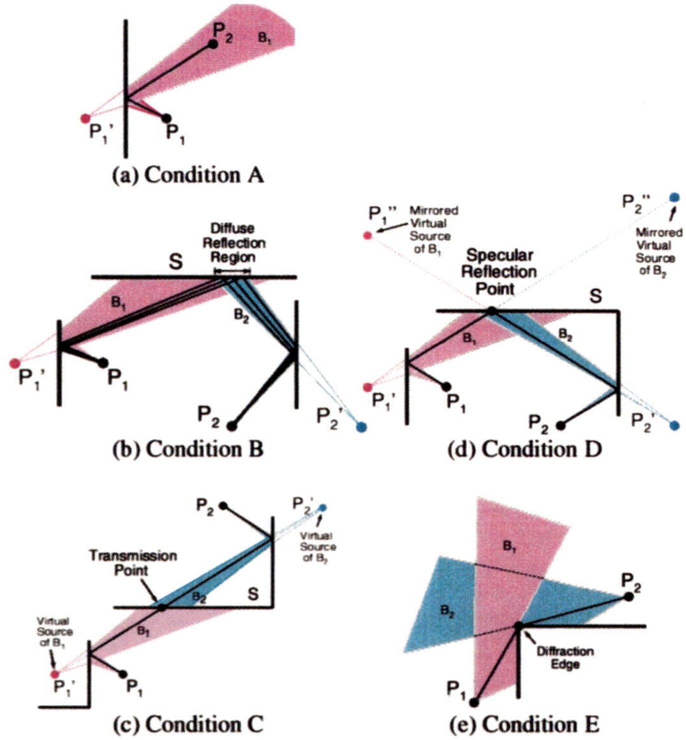


Figure 5: Combining bidirectional beams.

## 6 Amortized Beam Tracing

The third algorithm accelerates computation of reflection paths between moving avatars by amortizing the cost of a single beam tracing computation over several receiver locations.

The paths taken by people as they move through a virtual environment generally exhibit a large amount of spatial and temporal coherence. People usually do not jump from point to point arbitrarily. Rather, they tend to move along continuous paths. User interfaces may even impose bounds on their speeds, rotations, and directions of movement. Moreover, a person's two ears are nearby one another at fixed relative positions. By utilizing temporal coherence and spatial constraints we can model reverberation paths more efficiently for a sequence of receiver locations than for a set of unrelated locations. Specifically, we extend the notion of a beam tree to include *conservative beams* traced from a region of space, rather than just a point. Since these beams over-estimate the set of reverberation paths emanating from any point within the region, we can usually re-use them for a sequence of receiver locations inside the region to identify potential reverberation paths more rapidly than tracing beams from scratch for every avatar movement.

Our approach is motivated by algorithms originally proposed for conservative visibility determination (visibility is tracing 0th-order paths) [30, 32]. These algorithms do not solve the visibility problem exactly. Instead, they simply reduce the size of the polygon set to be processed by a later hidden-surface algorithm (e.g., z-buffer). In the same way, a conservative beam tree does not exactly represent the reflection paths for any point. Instead, it encodes a superset of the possible sequences of reflections and transmissions from all points within its source region. Thus, to find exact reflection paths from such a point to another point, we must only check a relatively small set of potential polygon sequences encoded in the beam tree to see which of them admits a "valid" reflection path. These relatively simple checks can be executed very quickly for each pair of avatar locations, while the much longer time required for beam tracing is amortized over multiple avatar movements.

Our amortized beam tracing algorithm is integrated with the priority-driven and bidirectional methods as shown in Figure 6. From top to bottom, we first use motion prediction to update a set of *source regions* that we expect to contain future avatar locations. Then, in the second step, we trace conservatively over-estimating polyhedral beams in priority order from each source region and store them in a *conservative beam tree*. Next, for every pair of source regions, we use our bidirectional methods to combine the conservative beam trees to form a set of *polygon sequences*, each of which describes how a ray traveling from one region to the other can potentially reflect off and/or transmit through an ordered list of polygons. Finally, for each time an avatar moves within one of the source regions, we generate exact reflection paths to every other avatar simply by processing the appropriate set of polygon sequences. This last step is the only one repeated for every avatar movement, and it is usually very fast.

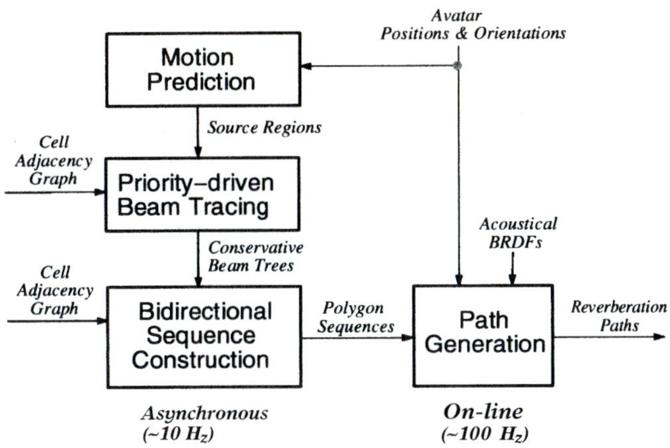


Figure 6: Amortized beam tracing phases.

The key challenges in implementing this algorithm are: 1) selecting effective source regions, 2) efficiently tracing a set of tightly over-estimating beams emanating from a region of space, 3) forming polygon sequences by combining beams traced from two regions of space, and 4) checking polygon sequences quickly to see if they admit valid reflection paths for a specific pair of avatar locations.

First, to select effective source regions, we must balance competing goals. Each one should contain as many future avatar locations as possible so that its conservative beam tree can be re-used many times. However, they cannot be too large (e.g., a whole room). Otherwise, the beams traced from the region are "too over-estimating," which not only slows down the beam tracing computation, but also puts undue processing burden on the subsequent steps. Our current method updates a source region associated with each avatar by predicting its motion with a second-degree polynomial curve and detecting collisions with obstacles in the environment. The source region is always an axis-aligned box with user-specified dimensions ("Box Size"). We are currently extending this method to adapt the size of each source region according to the locations of other avatars and the geometric complexity of the local environment.

Second, to trace beams from a box-shaped source region efficiently, we over-estimate the set of paths emanating from the source by a polytope comprising the intersection of at most six halfspaces, with two halfspaces bounded by planes parallel to each of the X, Y, and Z axes. Each of the three pairs of halfspaces form a wedge bounding the beam in one dimension, and the intersection of the three wedges form a polytope over-estimating the potential reverberation paths from any point within the source region. As cell boundaries are traversed in the beam tracing algorithm, the halfspaces are updated incrementally by a gift-wrapping step, in which the plane bounding each halfspace is rotated around an extremal edge of the source box until it hits an extremal vertex of the cell boundary, as shown in Figure 7. Although this beam tracing method is slightly more over-estimating than previously described approximations (e.g., [32]), it is very fast, requiring constant time per cell boundary, and it provides a fairly tight over-estimate for the paths traced in typical virtual environments.

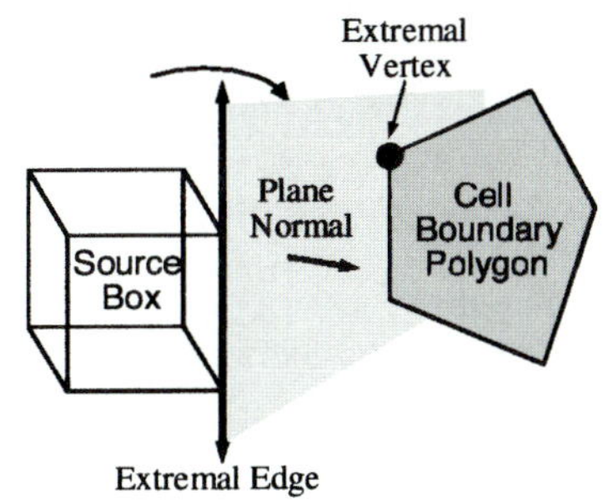


Figure 7: Conservative beam tracing gift wrapping step.

Third, to form polygon sequences, we extend the bidirectional method described in Section 5 to combine beams whose sources are boxes rather than points and to construct polygon sequences rather than specific reverberation paths. In particular, for each pair of beam tree nodes meeting one of the conditions, A-E, listed in Section 5 (with beam sources extended to include axis-aligned boxes), we construct a polygon sequence by concatenating the ordered lists of reflections and transmissions at cell boundaries encoded in the ancestor nodes of the two beam trees, as shown in Figure 8. Every polygon sequence constructed in this way provides a recipe for how a ray potentially can travel from a point in one source region to a point in the other.

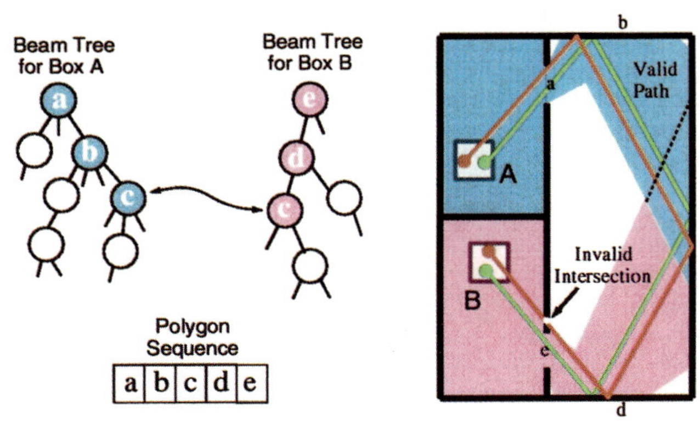


Figure 8: Constructing a polygon sequence by linking beam tree nodes, and determining its validity for specific pairs of avatar locations by checking polygon intersections.

Finally, to find paths between a specific pair of avatar locations, $P_1$ and $P_2$, we simply check each polygon sequence, $S$, associated with the appropriate pair of source regions to see whether a ray traveling from $P_1$ traveling along the prescribed sequence of reflections and transmissions can possibly reach $P_2$. We first traverse the polygon sequence in backwards order to construct a stack of mirror images of $P_2$, where $P_2^i$ corresponds to the image resulting from mirroring $P_2$ over the last $i$ of the $n$ reflecting polygons in the sequence. Then, we construct the reverberation path by traversing the polygon sequence in forwards order, while iteratively checking

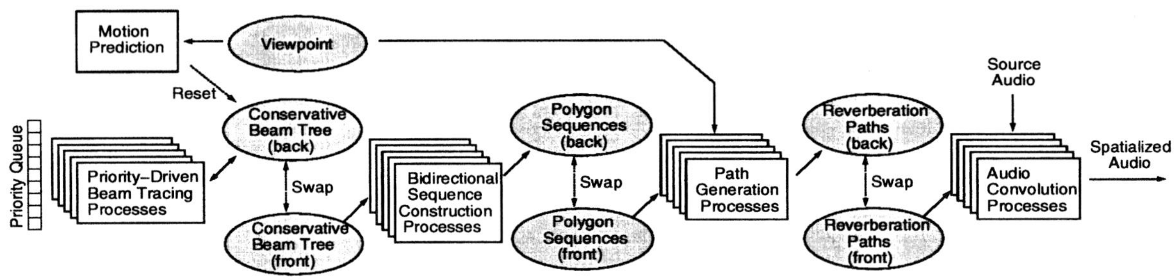


Figure 9: Multiprocessing system organization.

to see whether the ray starting from $P_1^i$ to $P_2^{n-i}$ intersects every polygon, $S_i$, in the sequence (see Figure 8). If so, we have found a valid reflection path from $P_1$ to $P_2$ along $S$ (shown as a green line in Figure 8). The length of the path is given by the distance from $P_1$ to $P_2^{n-1}$, and the attenuation of sound traveling along the path is given by the product of the attenuations at each polygon in the sequence. Otherwise, if a ray fails to intersect one of the polygons (e.g., the red line in Figure 8), the sequence is determined to be in the over-estimating portion of the conservative beams, and it is ignored.

One advantage of conservative beam tracing is that the cost of computing each beam can be amortized over all points within its source region. However, tracing beams from a larger region of space is generally more expensive. So, the sizes of source regions must be chosen carefully to maximize the effective speedups. Another advantage is that beam trees and polygon sequences can be constructed asynchronously (or even off-line), and then reflection paths can be found at very high rates. This feature is exploited in the multiprocessing system described in the next section.

## 7 Time-Critical Multiprocessing

Motivated by the principles of time-critical computing, we have developed an adaptive, real-time multiprocessing system that uses multiple asynchronously executing processes and allocates computational resources dynamically in order to perform the highest priority beam tracing computations in a timely manner. We expand the notion of priority-driven beam tracing to include multiple processors working together on the beam trees for all avatars at once. Rather than updating the beam tree for each avatar independently, the system computes beam tree nodes in global priority order, and thus the system can trade-off computational resources between different avatars dynamically. For instance, if many avatars enter the virtual environment, available resources for computing beam tree nodes for each avatar decreases, and the quality of computed reverberation paths degrades gracefully. Conversely, when avatars leave the environment or become stationary, the quality of spatialized sounds is adaptively refined. In the limit, if there is just one avatar in the environment, all available processors concurrently expand its beam tree nodes in priority order.

Our multiprocessor implementation executes as shown in Figure 9. Each data structure (oval) is stored as a pair of "front" and "back" buffers. Just as in computer graphics, the back buffer is used for updates, while other processes access the front buffer. Updates to all data structures are synchronized by mutual exclusion locks that allow multiple readers, but only a single writer. As a result, a high degree of concurrent processing is possible, as mutual exclusion is required for front buffers only when the buffers are swapped.

As every avatar moves through the environment, a motion prediction process determines when to swap an avatar's beam trees (e.g., when it has moved significantly). When the beam trees are swapped, the new "back" beam tree is emptied and then prepared for expansion: a new source region is assigned and a root node is created and put on the priority queue. Asynchronously and continuously, multiple beam tracing processes work on expanding "back" beam tree nodes in global priority order. Each process iteratively pops a node from the priority queue, computes the children of the node, and pushes them onto the priority queue. Meanwhile, multiple bidirectional polygon sequence construction processes monitor the arrival of new beam trees in the front buffer of any avatar. When one arrives, the "front" and "back" buffers of the appropriate polygon sequences are swapped, and new "back" buffers of polygon sequences are updated from the new beam tree. Similarly, each time an avatar moves, or a new polygon sequence becomes available, path generation processes access the polygon sequences to form reverberation paths. Finally, source audio signals are spatialized via software convolution with binaural impulse responses computed for each avatar. The responses are derived by adding a pulse for each computed reverberation path, where the delay is determined by $L/C$, where $L$ is the length of the path, and $C$ is the speed of sound, and the amplitude is set to $1/2(1 + \cos\theta)A/L$, where $\theta$ is the angle of arrival of the pulse with respect to the normal vector pointing out of the ear, and $A$ is the product of all the frequency-independent reflectivity and transmission coefficients for each of the reflecting and transmitting surfaces along the corresponding reverberation path.

The nicest feature of this implementation is that it provides a framework in which each component of the system can "do the best it can" without slowing down the other components. In particular, the path generation processes continue to compute reverberation paths even when an avatar moves out of its beam tree's source region. This feature provides "extrapolation" of reverberation paths from nearby points and is critical to providing a seamless auditory experience when the beam tracing processes become overloaded.

## 8 Experimental Results

We have implemented the algorithms described in the preceding sections in C++ and integrated them into a DVE system supporting communication between multiple users in a virtual world with spatialized sound. Our current implementation supports specular reflections and transmissions in 3D polygonal environments, and it runs on PCs and SGIs connected by a 100Mb/s TCP network.

The system uses a client-server design. Each client provides an immersive audio/visual interface to the shared virtual environment from the perspective of one avatar. As the avatar "moves" through the environment, possibly under interactive user control, images and sounds representing the virtual environment from the avatar's simulated viewpoint are updated on the client computer in real-time. Communication between remote users on different clients is possible via network connections to the server(s). Any client can send messages to the server(s) describing updates to the environment (e.g., the position and orientation of avatars) and the sounds occurring in the environment (e.g., voices associated with avatars). When a server receives these messages, it processes them to determine which updates are relevant to which clients, it spatializes the sounds for all avatars with the beam tracing algorithms described in the preceding sections, and it sends appropriate messages with updates and spatialized audio streams back to the clients so that they may update their audio/visual displays.

To evaluate the effectiveness of our new beam tracing methods in the context of this system, we executed a series of experiments with a single server spatializing sounds on an SGI Onyx2 with four 195MHz R10000 processors. In each experiment, we used different beam tracing algorithms to compute specular reflection paths from a source point (labeled 'A') to each of the three receiver points labeled 'B,' 'C,' and 'D' in the 3D model shown in Figure 10.

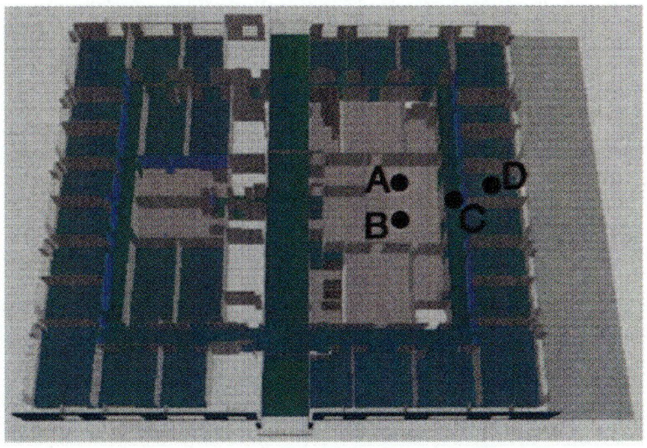


Figure 10: Test model geometry and avatar locations.

## 8.1 Priority-Driven Beam Tracing Results

We tested the relative benefits and costs of priority driven beam tracing by running a series of tests using the following three different beam tracing algorithms based on different search methods for traversing the cell adjacency graph and different termination criteria:

- **DF-R:** Depth-first search up to a user-specified maximum number of reflections.
- **DF-L:** Depth-first search up to a user-specified maximum path length.
- **P:** Priority-driven search (our algorithm).

In each set of tests, we computed all early specular reflection paths ($T_e$ = 20ms) from a source point (labeled 'A') to one of three receiver points (labeled 'B,' 'C,' and 'D') in the 3D model shown in Figure 10. The depth-first search algorithms, DF-R and DF-L, were aided by oracles in these tests, as the termination criteria were chosen manually to match the exact maximum number of reflections, R, and the maximum path length, L, respectively, of known early reflection paths, which were predetermined in earlier tests. In contrast, the priority-driven algorithm, P, was given no hints, and it used only the dynamic termination criteria described in Section 4.

The bar chart in Figure 11 shows the wall-clock times (in seconds) required to find all early specular reflection paths for each combination of the three receiver points and the three beam tracing algorithms. Although all three algorithms find exactly the same set of early reflection paths from the source to each receiver, the computation times for the priority-driven approach (the blue bars) were between 2.6 and 4.3 times less than the next best. The reason is that the priority-driven algorithm considers beams representing earliest paths first and terminates according to a metric utilizing knowledge of the receiver location, and thus it avoids computing most of the useless beams that travel long distances from the source and/or stray far from the receiver location.

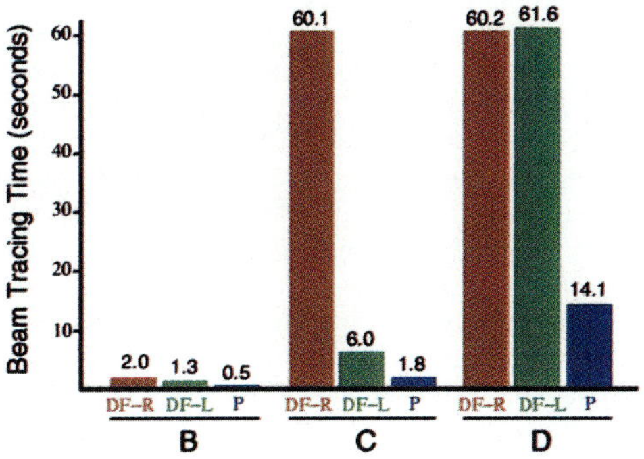


Figure 11: Beam tracing times with different traversal algorithms and termination criteria.

The relative value of the priority-driven approach depends on the geometric properties of the environment. For instance, all early reflection paths to the receiver point 'B,' which was placed in the same room as the source, required less than or equal to 3 specular reflections, and the longest path was only 623 inches. These relatively tight termination criteria were able to bound the complexities of the depth first search algorithms, so the speedup of the priority-driven algorithm is only around 2.6x over the next best. In contrast, for receiver point 'D,' some early reflection paths required up to 7 specular reflections, and the longest early reflection path was 1046 inches. In this case, the priority-driven algorithm is far more efficient (speedup is 4.3x) as it directs the beam tracing search towards the receiver point almost immediately, rather than computing beams extending radially in all directions.

The benefits of directed search are shown visually in Figure 12, which contains two images of 10,000 beams (pink) traced in a 2D map of Boston from a source point (square) to two different receiver locations (circles). In this case, the distance heuristic directs beams towards each receiver location enabling it to find complex reflection paths (blue).

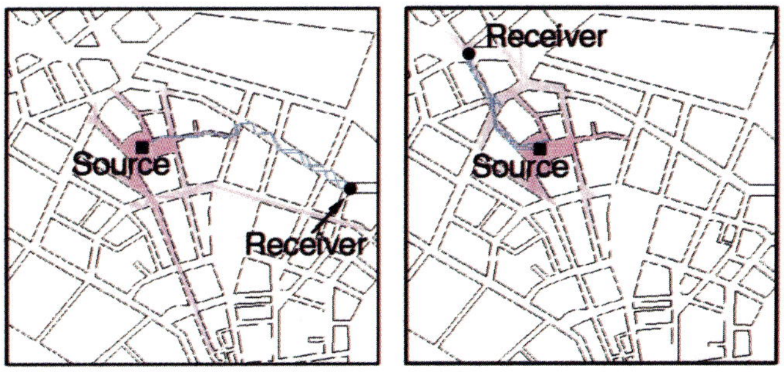


Figure 12: Visualization of beams traced for different receiver points with priority-driven beam tracing.

## 8.2 Bidirectional Beam Tracing Results

To test the relative benefits and costs of the bidirectional beam tracing algorithm described in Section 5, we ran a series of tests with comparable unidirectional and bidirectional beam tracing implementations on an SGI workstation with a 195MHz R10000 processor.

In each set of tests, we computed all specular reflection paths from a source point (labeled 'A') to one of three receiver points (labeled 'B,' 'C,' and 'D') up to a specified maximum number of reflections ('R') in the 3D model shown in Figure 10. The unidirectional algorithm constructed a single beam tree containing all paths with up to $R$ specular reflections from the source point, and then it reported a specular reflection path for each beam containing the specified receiver point. In contrast, the bidirectional algorithm constructed two beam trees for each source-receiver pair, the first containing beams up to $R/2 + 1$ specular reflections from the source, and the second containing beams up to $R/2$ specular reflections from the receiver. The two beam trees were combined to find all Rth-order specular reflections. In this experiment, the unidirectional and bidirectional algorithms find exactly the same set of paths with up to $R$ specular reflections. The goal of the experiment is to determine which algorithm takes less total computation time.

Table 1 contains statistics collected during these tests. From left to right, the first column (labeled 'P') lists which receiver point was used. The second column (labeled 'R') indicates the maximum number of specular reflections computed. Then, for both the unidirectional and bidirectional algorithms, there are three columns which show the times (in seconds) required to compute the beam trees ("Beam Time"), find the reflection paths ("Path Time"), and the sum of these two ("Total Time"). Finally, the last column (labeled "Speedup") lists the total time for unidirectional beam tracing algorithm as a ratio over the total bidirectional beam tracing time.

| | | Unidirectional | | | Bidirectional | | | |
|---|---|---|---|---|---|---|---|---|
| P | R | Beam Time | Path Time | Total Time | Beam Time | Path Time | Total Time | Speed Up |
| B | 3 | 2.02 | 0.01 | 2.03 | 1.04 | 0.03 | 1.07 | 1.9 |
| | 4 | 5.79 | 0.03 | 5.82 | 2.55 | 0.10 | 2.65 | 2.3 |
| | 5 | 15.01 | 0.07 | 15.08 | 4.23 | 0.50 | 4.73 | 3.5 |
| | 6 | 31.53 | 0.14 | 31.66 | 8.02 | 1.31 | 9.33 | 3.9 |
| | 7 | 60.26 | 0.24 | 60.50 | 11.95 | 4.43 | 16.39 | 5.0 |
| | 8 | 100.82 | 0.41 | 101.22 | 21.12 | 9.52 | 30.64 | 4.8 |
| C | 3 | 2.03 | 0.01 | 2.03 | 0.96 | 0.01 | 0.98 | 2.1 |
| | 4 | 5.81 | 0.01 | 5.82 | 2.49 | 0.04 | 2.54 | 2.3 |
| | 5 | 14.83 | 0.02 | 14.86 | 3.92 | 0.20 | 4.12 | 3.8 |
| | 6 | 31.38 | 0.05 | 31.42 | 7.82 | 0.54 | 8.37 | 4.0 |
| | 7 | 60.82 | 0.08 | 60.90 | 11.23 | 1.97 | 13.20 | 5.4 |
| | 8 | 100.89 | 0.14 | 101.03 | 20.56 | 4.13 | 24.69 | 4.9 |
| D | 3 | 2.03 | 0.00 | 2.03 | 0.62 | 0.01 | 0.62 | 3.3 |
| | 4 | 5.81 | 0.01 | 5.81 | 2.17 | 0.03 | 2.20 | 2.7 |
| | 5 | 14.94 | 0.01 | 14.95 | 2.47 | 0.12 | 2.59 | 6.0 |
| | 6 | 31.88 | 0.02 | 31.90 | 6.24 | 0.29 | 6.53 | 5.1 |
| | 7 | 60.31 | 0.04 | 60.35 | 7.10 | 0.92 | 8.02 | 8.5 |
| | 8 | 100.68 | 0.06 | 100.75 | 16.27 | 1.83 | 18.10 | 6.2 |

Table 1: Bidirectional beam tracing statistics.

The results of this experiment show the trade-offs of the bidirectional approach very clearly. First, comparing the "Beam Times" in Table 1, we see that the bidirectional algorithm spends significantly less time tracing beams than the unidirectional algorithm. This is because it constructs beam trees with less depth, thereby avoiding the worst part of the exponential growth. A visualization of this effect appears in Figure 13, which shows a comparison of 2D beams traced (a) unidirectionally and (b) bidirectionally to find the same reflection paths (shown in blue). Note how many more beams are traced in the unidirectional case. Second, comparing the "Path Times," we see that the bidirectional algorithm spends significantly more time generating reverberation paths. This is because it must perform intersection tests for each pair of beams reflecting off the same surface. Overall, the bidirectional beam tracing algorithm is significantly faster than the unidirectional algorithm, with speedups ranging from 4.8x to 6.2x for 8 specular reflections in these experiments.

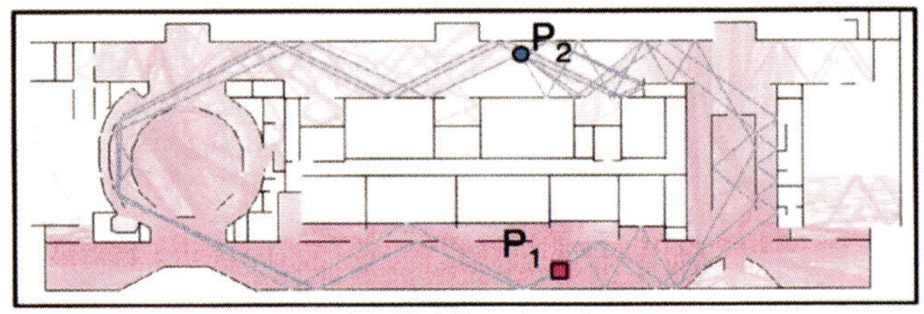


(a) Unidirectional
(59,069 beams)

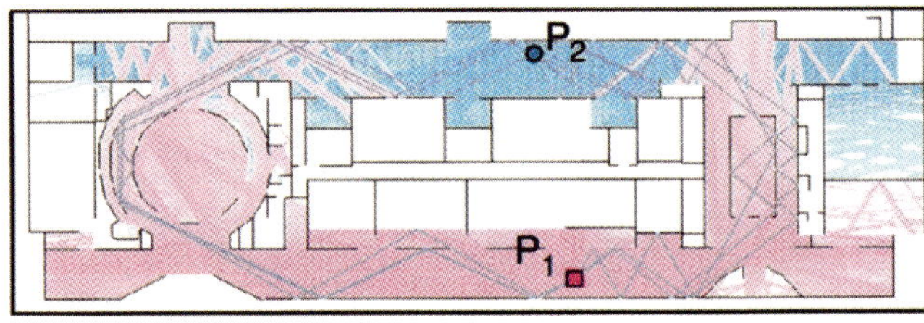


(b) Bidirectional
(15,078 pink beams + 24,665 blue beams)

Figure 13: Visualization of beams traced to find specular reflection paths between points P1 and P2 with (a) unidirectional and (b) bidirectional methods. The beams emanating from location P1 are shown in pink, while the ones from P2 are shown in cyan. The blue lines represent specular reflection paths.

## 8.3 Amortized Beam Tracing Results

We studied the trade-offs of the amortized beam tracing approach described in Section 6 by running a set of tests in which conservative beams were traced from source regions with varying sizes to find specular reflection paths between a source point (labeled 'A') and one of the three receiver points (labeled 'B,' 'C,' and 'D') in the 3D model shown in Figure 10.

During each test, cubes with width "Box Size" were constructed around both the source point and one of the receiver points. Then, the following three steps were used to compute specular reflection paths between the two points.

1. Trace conservative beams from both source regions up to 3 specular reflections.
2. Combine the beams to form polygon sequences containing potential paths with up to 5 specular reflections.
3. Process the polygon sequences to find all valid 5th-order specular reflection paths from the source point to the receiver.

Table 2 shows times (in seconds) measured during each test. The first column ("P") lists the receiver point, and the second ("Box Size") indicates the source box width in inches. The next four columns show the times required for beam tracing ("Beam Time"), polygon sequence construction ("Seq Time"), and path generation ("Path Time"), respectively. The column labeled "Amort Time" represents the average wall-clock time required for the amortized algorithm to compute all 5th-order specular reflection paths from the source to the receiver at even intervals separated by 1/2 inch, while the last column (labeled "Speedup") lists the speedup of the amorized beam tracing algorithm as compared to the bidirectional algorithm described in the previous section (i.e., "Box Size" = 0).

Scanning down the rows of the table, we see that the times required for all three steps increase with larger source regions, first slowly, and then very rapidly. This growth pattern matches the number of beams traced in each test. As the source region grows larger, a larger portion of the space can be reached by reflection paths, and

| P | Box Size | Beam Time | Seq Time | Path Time | Amort Time | Speedup |
|---|---|---|---|---|---|---|
| B | 0 | 4.2 | 0.48 | 0.004 | 4.691 | 1.0 |
| | 2 | 4.6 | 0.57 | 0.006 | 2.593 | 1.8 |
| | 4 | 5.1 | 0.64 | 0.006 | 1.423 | 3.3 |
| | 8 | 5.9 | 0.81 | 0.008 | 0.840 | 5.6 |
| | 16 | 8.9 | 1.48 | 0.013 | 0.651 | 7.2 |
| | 32 | 83.3 | 5.89 | 0.054 | 2.787 | 1.7 |
| C | 0 | 3.9 | 0.20 | 0.001 | 4.116 | 1.0 |
| | 2 | 4.3 | 0.23 | 0.001 | 2.264 | 1.8 |
| | 4 | 4.6 | 0.27 | 0.002 | 1.214 | 3.4 |
| | 8 | 5.4 | 0.39 | 0.005 | 0.730 | 5.6 |
| | 16 | 8.2 | 0.73 | 0.012 | 0.561 | 7.3 |
| | 32 | 13.9 | 3.07 | 0.049 | 0.531 | 7.8 |
| D | 0 | 2.5 | 0.12 | 0.000 | 2.597 | 1.0 |
| | 2 | 2.7 | 0.12 | 0.000 | 1.405 | 1.8 |
| | 4 | 2.8 | 0.14 | 0.001 | 0.739 | 3.5 |
| | 8 | 3.4 | 0.20 | 0.001 | 0.448 | 5.8 |
| | 16 | 5.2 | 0.35 | 0.004 | 0.344 | 7.5 |
| | 32 | 10.1 | 1.55 | 0.021 | 0.364 | 7.1 |

Table 2: Amortized beam tracing statistics.

more beams must be traced (see Figure 14). Accordingly, more polygon sequences are constructed, and they all must be processed for each path generation step. We must be careful not to choose source regions that are so big that the resulting beam tree and the list of polygon sequences are grossly over-approximating.

The benefits of conservative beam tracing are reaped by amortization as the beam trees and polygon sequences are re-used for more and more nearby avatar locations as the source regions grow. The result of this trade-off between extra processing versus amortization is shown in the right-most column of the table (labeled "Speedup"). In this experiment, we see that the competing factors are balanced most advantageously when the box sizes have width around 16 inches. In this case, the conservative beams do not overestimate exact ones by too much, and thus they require only 2.1x more time to compute, while the benefits of amortization can be realized over 16 distinct avatar locations separated by 1/2 inch as the avatar walks from the center of the box, resulting in an effective 7x speedup.

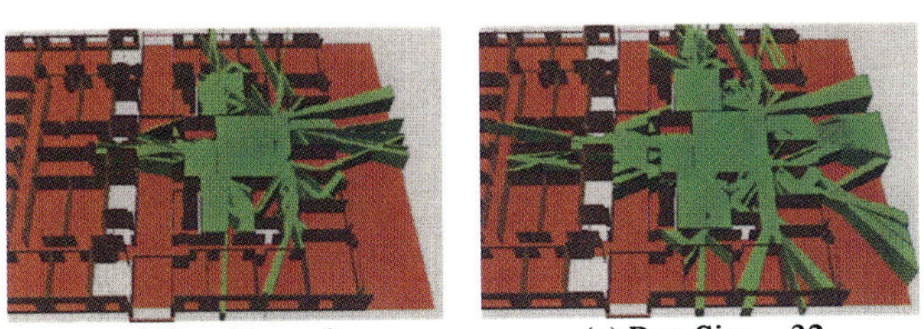

(a) Box Size = 0 (4,686 beams)

(c) Box Size = 32 (12,242 beams)

Figure 14: Beams traced for up to 2 reflections from source regions of different sizes centered at point 'A.'

## 8.4 Time-Critical Multiprocessing Results

We studied the time-critical multiprocessing aspects of our system by running tests with multiple avatars moving simultaneously through a virtual environment (shown in Figure 15) while logging statistics regarding the system's performance. During these tests, each of four avatars moved autonomously along a path which caused it to pass very close to other avatars sometimes, and to wander alone at others.

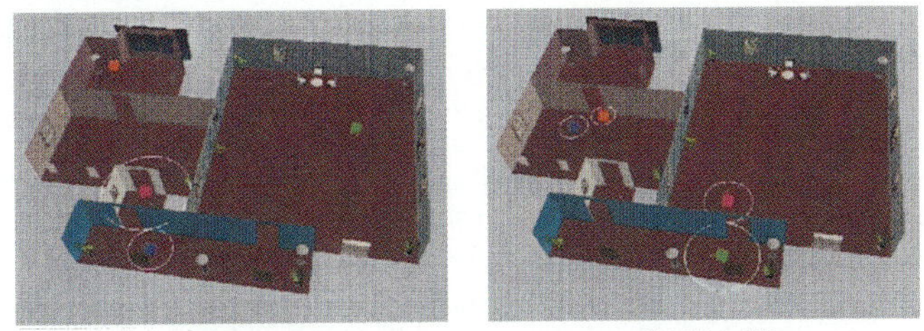

(a) T = 65

(b) T = 90

Figure 15: Visualization of adaptive real-time beam tracing (circles represent number of beam tree nodes).

Figure 16 contains a plot indicating the number of nodes in each of four avatars' beam trees during a test executing on an SGI Onyx2 workstation with 4 195 MHz R10000 processors. Each of the four curves represents a single avatar, and the vertical position of the curve at every time step indicates the amount of computation the system is expending updating the beam tree for the avatar. Figure 15 shows the status of the simulation at (a) T=65 and (b) T=95. For visualization purposes, the radius of the circle around each avatar in these images matches the corresponding height in the plot.

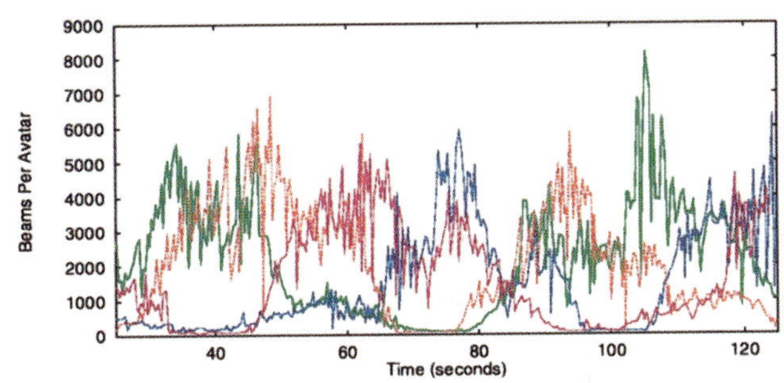


Figure 16: Plot of number of nodes in the beam tree for each avatar showing adaptive real-time beam tracing.

The plot clearly shows the adaptive and time-critical natures of our multiprocessing system. In some situations, such as the one occurring at T=65, two avatars are in close proximity, while the others are off by themselves. Accordingly, the system allocates most of its resources to computing beam trees for those two avatars (blue and purple) as they interact (i.e., the blue and purple lines are relatively high). At other times in the simulation, different avatars are interacting and the system adapts dynamically. Yet, the total number of beams traced for all avatars (i.e., the sum of the heights for all lines in the plot) remains approximately constant across all time steps. This feature reflects the time-critical nature of our real-time algorithm.

# 9 System Limitations

Our system is a research prototype, and it has several limitations. First, the 3D model must comprise only planar polygons because we do not model the transformations for beams as they reflect off curved surfaces. Nor do we trace beams along paths of refraction, diffraction, or diffuse reflection, which are very important acoustical effects. However, we think that the conservative beam tracing approach may be an appropriate framework for extending our system to handle these situations.

Second, our methods are only practical for coarse 3D models without highly faceted surfaces, such as the ones often found in acoustic modeling simulations. The difficulty is that beams get fragmented by cell boundaries as they are traced through a cell adjacency graph. For this reason, we are not optimistic that our implementation can be easily adapted to model light transport for photorealistic image synthesis. However, the algorithms probably can be applied effectively in other application areas concerned with simulation of wave phenomena (e.g., radio frequency propagation).

Third, the major occluding and reflecting surfaces of the virtual environment must be static through the entire execution. If any acoustically significant polygon were to move, the cell adjacency graph would have to be updated incrementally.

Finally, our implementation does not include sophisticated models for acoustical reflectance distribution functions or for directionality of audio sources and receivers. For instance, we currently represent the reflectance of each surface with an angle-independent and frequency-independent absorption coefficient. However, since we compute reverberation paths explicitly, adding these auralization features is relatively straight-forward.

## 10 Conclusion

In this paper, we have described three beam tracing algorithms well-suited for geometric acoustic modeling in a distributed virtual environment system. These algorithms offer two important advantages over previous approaches: 1) they are much faster, and 2) they support real-time computing.

To summarize the speedup results, the priority-driven algorithm accelerates searches for early reflection paths by 2.6x – 4.3x; the bidirectional approach runs 4.8x – 6.2x faster than a comparable unidirectional algorithm; and, amortized beam tracing achieves speedups of 7.2x – 7.5x. Moreover, our multiprocessing system achieves nearly linear speedups for up to at least four processors. Overall, the speedup achieved combining all these algorithms is approximately two orders of magnitude over previous beam tracing systems.

Our adaptive multiprocessing system utilizes these new beam tracing algorithms to support many features essential for a real-time system, including time-critical updates, graceful degradation, and adaptive refinement. Moreover, the system performs asynchronous beam tracing computations, while reverberation paths are generated, and even extrapolated, at very high update rates. Overall, our system is able to match the accuracy of many previous off-line acoustic modeling systems while executing in real-time.

## Acknowledgements

The authors thank Gary Elko, Mohan Sondhi, Jim West, and Perry Cook for their valuable discussions. We would also like to acknowledge Nadia Magnenat-Thalmann, Daniel Thalman, and Eric Petajan for use of the images in Figure 1.

## References

[1] Allen, J.B., and D.A. Berkley, Image Method for Efficiently Simulating Small-Room Acoustics, *J. Acoust. Soc. Am.*, 65, 4, Apr 1979, 943-950.

[2] Arvo, James. Backward Ray Tracing. *Developments in Ray Tracing Course Notes*, SIGGRAPH 86, 1986.

[3] Begault, Durand, *3D Sound for Virtual Reality and Multimedia*, Academic Press, 1994.

[4] Blanchard, C., S. Gurgess, Y. Harvill, J. Lanier, A. Lasko, M. Oberman, and M. Teitel, Reality Built for Two: A Virtual Reality Tool. *ACM SIGGRAPH Special Issue on 1990 Symposium on Interactive 3D Graphics*, (Snowbird, Utah), 1990, 35-36.

[5] Borish, Jeffrey. Extension of the Image Model to Arbitrary Polyhedra. *J. Acoust. Soc. Am.*, 75, 6, June, 1984, 1827-1836.

[6] Briere, Normand, and Pierre Poulin, Hierarchical View-Dependent Structures for Interactive Scene Manipulation, *Computer Graphics* (SIGGRAPH 96), 83-90.

[7] Chattopadhyay, Sudeb, and Akira Fujimoto, Bi-directional Ray Tracing, *Computer Graphics 1987 (Proceedings of CG International '87)*, Springer-Verlag, Tokyo, 1987, 335-343.

[8] Dadoun, N., D.G. Kirkpatrick, and J.P. Walsh. The Geometry of Beam Tracing. *Proceedings of the Symposium on Computational Geometry*, Baltimore, June, 1985, 55-61.

[9] Davison, B. *Neutron Transport Theory.* Oxford University Press, London, 1957.

[10] Drettakis, George, and Francois Sillion. Interactive Update of Global Illumination Using a Line-Space Hierarchy. *Computer Graphics* (SIGGRAPH 97), 1997, 57-64.

[11] Durlach, N.I., R.W. Pew, W.A. Aviles, P.A. DiZio, and D.L. Zeltzer. *Virtual Environment Technology for Training (VETT).* Report No. 7661, Bolt, Beranek, and Newmann, Cambridge, MA, 1992.

[12] Durlach, N.I, and A.S. Mavor, editors, *Virtual Reality Scientific and Technological Challenges*, National Research Council Report, National Academy Press, Washington, D.C., 1995.

[13] Foster, S.H., E.M. Wenzel, and R.M. Taylor. Real-time Synthesis of Complex Acoustic Environments. *Proc. IEEE Workshop on Applications of Signal Processing to Audio and Acoustics,* 1991.

[14] Funkhouser, Thomas A., Ingrid Carlbom, Gary Elko, Gopal Pingali, Mohan Sondhi, and Jim West A Beam Tracing Approach to Acoustic Modeling for Interactive Virtual Environments. *Computer Graphics* (SIGGRAPH '98), Orlando, FL, July, 1998, 21-32.

[15] Hart, P.E., N.J. Nilsson, and B. Raphael, A Formal Basis for the Heuristic Determination of Minimum Cost Paths, *IEEE Transactions on SSC*, Vol. 4, 1968.

[16] Hartman, Jed, Josie Werneck, *VRML 2.0 Handbook*, Addison-Wesley, ISBN 0-201-47944-3, August 1996.

[17] Hartmann, W.M., Listening in a Room and the Precedence Effect, *Binaural and Spatial Hearing in Real and Virtual Environments*, edited by Robert H. Gilkey and Timothy R. Anderson, Lawrence Erlbaum Associates, 1997.

[18] Heckbert, Paul, and Pat Hanrahan. Beam Tracing Polygonal Objects. *Computer Graphics* (SIGGRAPH 84), 18, 3, 119-127.

[19] Heckbert, Paul. Adaptive Radiosity Textures for Bidirectional Ray Tracing. *Computer Graphics* (SIGGRAPH 90), 24, 4, 145-154.

[20] Immel, David S., Michael F. Cohen, and Donald P. Greenberg. A Radiosity Method for Non-Diffuse Environments. *Computer Graphics* (SIGGRAPH 85), 19, 3, 133-142.

[21] Kleiner, Mendel, Bengt-Inge Dalenback, and Peter Svensson. Auralization – An Overview. *J. Audio Eng. Soc.*, 41, 11, Nov 1993, 861-875.

[22] Krockstadt, U.R. *Calculating the Acoustical Room Response by the Use of a Ray Tracing Technique*, J. Sound and Vibrations, 8, 18, 1968.

[23] Kuttruff, Heinrich *Room Acoustics*, 3rd Edition, Elsevier Science, London, England, 1991.

[24] Lafortune, E.P., and Y.D. Willems, Bi-directional path tracing, *CompuGraphics*, Alvor, Portugal, 1993, 145-153.

[25] Lewins, Jeffery. *Importance, The Adjoint Function: The Physical Basis of Variational and Perturbation Theory in Transport and Diffusion Problems.* Pergamon Press, New York, 1965.

[26] Moore, G.R. *An Approach to the Analysis of Sound in Auditoria.* Ph.D. Thesis, Cambridge, UK, 1984.

[27] *Quake*, id Software, Mesquite, TX, 1996.

[28] Smits, Brian, James R. Arvo, and David H. Salesin. An Importance-Driven Radiosity Algorithm. *Computer Graphics* (SIGGRAPH 92), 26, 2, 273-282.

[29] Sony Corporation, *Community Place Browser Manual*, 1996.

[30] Teller, Seth., and Carlo Séquin, Visibility Preprocessing for Interactive Walkthroughs, *Computer Graphics* (SIGGRAPH 91), 25, 4, 61-69.

[31] Teller, Seth Computing the Antiumbra Cast by an Area Light Source. *Computer Graphics* (SIGGRAPH 92), 26, 2, 139-148.

[32] Teller, Seth *Visibility Computations in Densely Occluded Polyhedral Environments.* Ph.D. thesis, Computer Science Division (EECS), University of California, Berkeley, 1992. Also available as UC Berkeley technical report UCB/CSD-92-708.

[33] Tsingos, Nicolas, and Jean-Dominique Gascuel. A General Model for Simulation of Room Acoustics Based On Hierarchical Radiosity. Technical Sketches, *SIGGRAPH 97 Visual Proceedings*, 1997.

[34] Veach, Eric, and Leonidas Guibas, Bidirectional Estimators for Light Transport, *Fifth Eurographics Workshop on Rendering*, Darmstadt, Germany, June, 1994, 147-162.

[35] Zyda, Michael J., David Pratt, John Falby, Chuck Lombardo, and Kristen Kelleher, The Software Required for the Computer Generation of Virtual Environments. *Presence*, 2, 2 (March 1993), 130-140.

# Creating a Live Broadcast from a Virtual Environment

Chris Greenhalgh, Steve Benford, Ian Taylor,[1] University of Nottingham, UK

John Bowers[2], Royal Institute of Technology (KTH), Stockholm, Sweden

Graham Walker[3], BT Laboratories, UK

John Wyver[4], Illuminations Television, UK

## Abstract

"Inhabited Television" combines multiuser virtual environments with television, so that online audience-members can participate in TV shows staged in a virtual world. It is presented simultaneously both to conventional passive viewers and to on-line participants. In many cases it benefits from being broadcast live. This paper is based on our fourth major experiment with Inhabited TV, a live virtual game show called "Out Of This World". For this event we adopted non-automated approaches to camera control and mixing to allow an exploration of appropriate forms of presentation for inhabited television. We describe the techniques which were used to create and enhance the live video output which was produced during the show: appropriate world design; dynamic constraints on participant movements; and a performance-oriented virtual camera control interface. This camera control interface includes explicit support for a range of spatial and temporal control styles. We also give evaluative feedback on the camera control interface and the event's (television-based) approach to mixing and directing, drawing on a social scientific field study conducted on-site during the preparation for, and performances of, the show.

**CR Categories and Subject Descriptors:** I.3.8 [Computer Graphics]: Applications; I.3.6 [Computer Graphics]: Methodology and Techniques – Interaction Techniques; I.3.7 [Computer Graphics]: Three-Dimensional Graphics and Realism – Virtual Reality.

**Additional Keywords:** Multi-User, Networked Apps, Video, Viewpoint control.

## 1 INTRODUCTION

Multiuser virtual environments are shared 3D audio-graphical worlds in which distributed users can communicate, interact, compete and undertake other tasks and activities. We are interested in the use of these environments to create "inhabited television"; this combines multiuser virtual environments with television, so that online audience-members can participate in TV shows staged in a virtual world. We believe that this may become the "killer application" for multiuser virtual environments. Inhabited TV goes beyond the capabilities of traditional broadcast television (and more recent interactive TV systems) by allowing the online audience to interact socially with one another and to become directly involved in the content, e.g. becoming a participant in a game show or debate. Inhabited television offers broadcasters access to new formats, structures and audiences; it offers existing virtual environments a motivation for participation, an impetus for development, and a route to potential exploitation.

One of the distinctive characteristics of inhabited television is that it is presented simultaneously both to conventional passive (or interactive) viewers and to on-line participants, i.e. "inhabitants". The online participants may interact with the virtual environment through a networked PC or future set-top box. The viewers watch a traditional (or digital or interactive) broadcast television program.

There are two major benefits to making an inhabited television broadcast live rather than pre-recorded:

- interactive TV viewers can directly influence events in the virtual world as the program unfolds, for example by voting for particular changes or outcomes; and
- during the program viewers can choose to become inhabitants and vice-versa (assuming that they are using suitable equipment to view the program).

Consequently, one of the key requirements for Inhabited TV is to create live broadcasts from within a virtual environment. This paper describes the approaches and techniques which we have used to create an effective live broadcast (into a theatre space) from a multiuser virtual environment during a unique public experimental Inhabited TV show, "Out Of This World" (OOTW). This was staged at isea98revolution, part of the International Symposium of Electronic Arts, at the Green Room, Manchester, England, on the 5th and 6th September 1998.

Section 2 describes some of our previous experiences with Inhabited TV and the particular problems which we encountered in combining multiuser virtual environments with television-style broadcasting. Section 3 describes and contrasts related work. Section 4 gives further information about the structure and nature of the OOTW event, and also describes the first two techniques which we used to enhance the broadcast potential of the show: appropriate world design; and managed participant constraints. Section 5 describes the third technique: a virtual camera control interface tailored for real-time performance. Section 6 contains our evaluation of the camera control interface and the event's (television-based) approach to mixing and directing, based on a social scientific field study conducted on-site. Finally, section 7 contains our conclusions and describes areas for future work.

[1]School of Computer Science and IT,
Email: {cmg, sdb, imt}@cs.nott.ac.uk
[2]Centre for User-Oriented IT-Design (CID),
Email: bowers@nada.kth.se
[3]Email: graham.walker@bt-sys.bt.co.uk
[4]Email: john@illumin.co.uk

## 2 EXPERIENCES WITH INHABITED TELEVISION

The authors have been involved in three previous experiments in inhabited television [2]:

- "MASSIVE" [3], a virtual poetry performance, occurring simultaneously in a physical theatre and in a virtual world. This was staged by the University of Nottingham, in collaboration with VR artist Sean Varney and poets from Chocolate Art, as part of Nottingham's NOWninety6 arts festival.
- "The Mirror" [18], six public online virtual worlds run along-side the UK BBC television series "The Net". This was created by BT and Illuminations, in association with the BBC and Sony. The broadcast in this case was based on edited recorded footage.
- "Heaven & Hell - Live", a live 1-hour television broadcast on the UK's Channel 4 from inside a public virtual world. This was also created by BT and Illuminations, in association with Sony.

In each event there were four types of participants (or "levels of participation"):

- passive viewers, either watching broadcast television or watching a single projected view in a theatre (in the case of MASSIVE);
- online inhabitants, embodied within the virtual worlds, and able to interact and take part;
- professional performers or correspondents, also embodied in the virtual worlds, providing content and coordination; and
- the production team, including camera operators, director and technical support, who worked behind the scenes to make each event happen.

These experiments raised a number of significant issues with the creation of inhabited television. The issues relevant to this paper are described below.

- It is typically very difficult to achieve precise and coordinated movement within a multiuser virtual environment. In a normal television show the positions and movements of the participants are tightly controlled, to support its presentation and timing. In a virtual environment movement is typically comparatively clumsy and uncontrolled. So it was hard for inhabitants (untrained members of the public) and even for performers to be in the right place at the right time.
- There is a huge difference in natural pace between virtual environments (as they exist now) and television. Television is typically tightly scripted and directed to give an intense viewing experience. General-purpose multiuser virtual environments, on the other hand, tend towards a much more sedate pace of interaction. This is especially true when interaction is text-based, as was the case in The Mirror and Heaven & Hell – Live (here we are ignoring specialized quick-reaction game environments, e.g. first-person shooting games or virtual racing, because we wish to explore a broader range of genres and richer forms of social interaction).
- There were significant problems with camera control and navigation. In particular, Heaven & Hell – Live and The Mirror used the normal user navigation interface to control the virtual cameras; this was a "body-centered" or flying vehicle control metaphor [19]. This meant that the virtual cameras had difficulty keeping up with the action and got lost on occasion, even giving shots of empty space. They also had trouble coping with occlusion in the scene – it was extremely difficult to adjust the shot to avoid, for example, a passing inhabitant, while maintaining the shot.

These problems combined to create a final broadcast which was often incoherent, and sometimes incomprehensible to watch as a normal viewer. These problems are demonstrated most clearly in Heaven & Hell – Live because it combines a truly live broadcast with a relatively complex and densely populated world.

As described in this paper, we have sought to alleviate these problems by using three techniques: appropriate world design (section 4.1); managed movement of inhabitants and performers (section 4.2); and a new performance-oriented virtual camera control interface (section 5).

## 3 RELATED WORK

Multiuser virtual environments, and film and television each have their own distinct bodies of literature. However, in this paper we are focusing on the boundary between the two: shaping and enhancing a live video output from a shared 3D audio-graphical environment.

In this event we adopted non-automated approaches to camera control and mixing, relying instead on established human skills and patterns of working, i.e. a director and camera operators. In this way we could explore how these activities were influenced by the change of technology and medium, rather than simply recreating and automating existing techniques which may not be appropriate for 3D virtual worlds.

This may be contrasted with attempts to automate the whole presentation process, including camera work, direction and mixing. For example, He, Cohen and Salesin [12] created the "Virtual Cinematographer", also used in realtime multiuser virtual worlds. However, in their case, camera placement and cutting are fully automated. Their virtual environment also uses a constrained set of high-level actions (e.g. "go to the bar") whereas our worlds are based largely on free navigation and interaction. This approach might be applicable in some situations, although it would need to extract likely semantics from more primitive activities (e.g. free navigation).

As our understanding of Inhabited TV matures it will become possible to integrate automation in a principled and informed way. This will allow us to draw on work such as the following. Drucker et al. [7] defined a procedural interface for expressing shots and integrating other techniques, which was then extended in [8] to use constraint-satisfaction, including path planning. Seligmann and Feiner [9] address automated placement of cameras and composition of shots for conveying information in semantically specified situations. They do not address live performance issues, although they indicate that their methods could be combined with interactive manipulation.

All of these approaches might be used to enhance or (perhaps partially) automate camera operation for Inhabited TV. However the realtime and the performance nature of the medium would have be carefully considered (an area which is not addressed in these papers).

Some of these, and others (notably Karp and Feiner [14], and He et al. [12]), have considered how cinematic principles (e.g. [1]) can be applied in computer graphics. In this work we are exploring how inhabited television and 3D graphical environments may actually differ from established experience with the physical world.

At a more conceptual level, this work can be compared to interactive digital artworks and installations, which combine computer graphics with aspects of live performance (see, for example, [17]). These same pieces might be made available through an inhabited television medium, although with an increased concern for the experiences of non-interacting (traditional TV) viewers.

## 4 OUT OF THIS WORLD

The Out Of This World event may be regarded as a follow on to Heaven & Hell – Live, taking into account the issues highlighted in section 2 (and issues relating to other aspects of the Inhabited TV). Like Heaven & Hell – Live, Out Of This World was a live game show staged in a multiuser virtual world. The game show was "broadcast" live into a theatre space, where it was projected onto a large screen which can be seen in figure 3.

The show featured a competition between two teams (the "aliens" and the "robots"), to escape a doomed space station (figure 5). Each team was led by a professional performer who was wearing an immersive VR headset and was tracked (head and both hands) using electromagnetic trackers. The team leaders are visible at the sides of the main projection screen in figure 3. Each team comprised four members of the public (drawn from those entering the theatre) seated at networked PCs in the back-stage production area, as in figure 4. In "real" Inhabited TV these people would be at home. These inhabitants could navigate on the ground plane using a standard PC joystick, and took part in four collaborative games. The show was fronted by a virtual host who appeared in the world as a live video texture on a large virtual screen (visible in figure 6). The inhabitants and performers all wore microphone-headsets and were able to talk to one another using packetised network audio (c.f. IP telephony). The host also had a microphone, and audio spot effects were triggered automatically at various points in the games. The multiuser virtual environment used was MASSIVE-2 [11].

To create the live audio/video feed into the theatre we made use of standard outside broadcast (field production) methods. Part of the back-stage area, including the director, is shown in figure 1. The video-related components of this are shown schematically in figure 2. There were four virtual cameras, each with its own operator. These fed into a video mixing desk (with input, preview and transmission monitors), together with a direct view of the host and a video tape (VT) player for additional linking footage. An experienced television director was responsible for directing and video mixing. An additional technician operated the VT, and audio was mixed separately by an audio engineer through the house PA. All of these people were on a wired talk-back circuit to allow them to coordinate their actions.

In this way we sought to exploit established methods of working and human skills (e.g. of the director and the camera operators) within a new context – 3D virtual worlds.

In the show's finale the theatre audience were able to "save" one of the losing inhabitants using an interaction system inspired by Loren Carpenter's CINEMATRIX Interactive Entertainment System [6], waving colored pieces of card to vote for their favorite player.

There were a total of four rehearsals and four performances over a period of three days, each lasting approximately 40 minutes.

Figure 1: The director, VT operator and world manager at work, during a show.

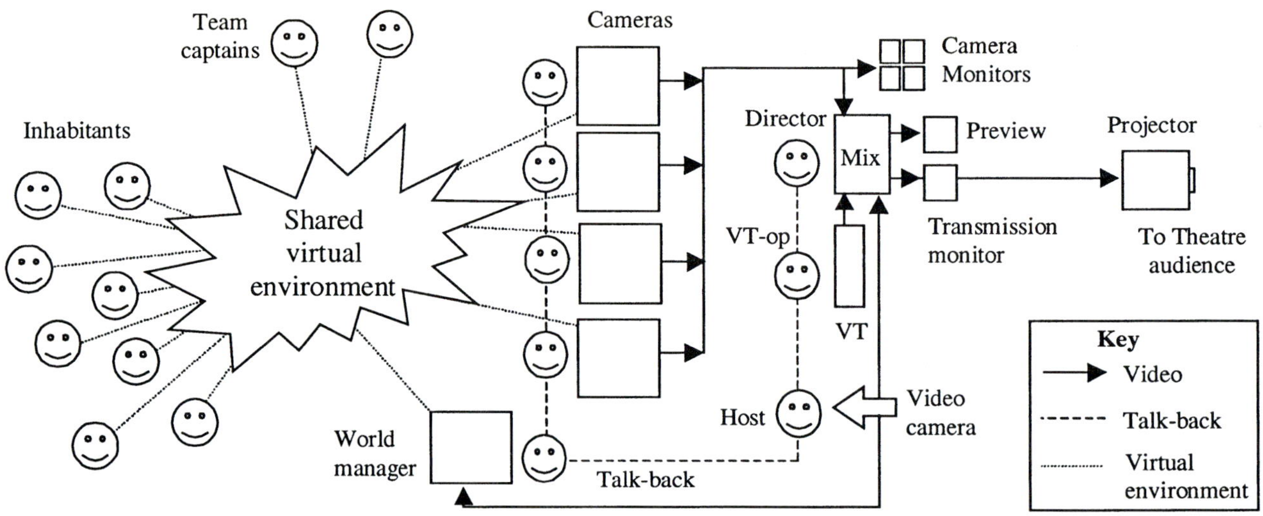


Figure 2: Video production infrastructure for OOTW.

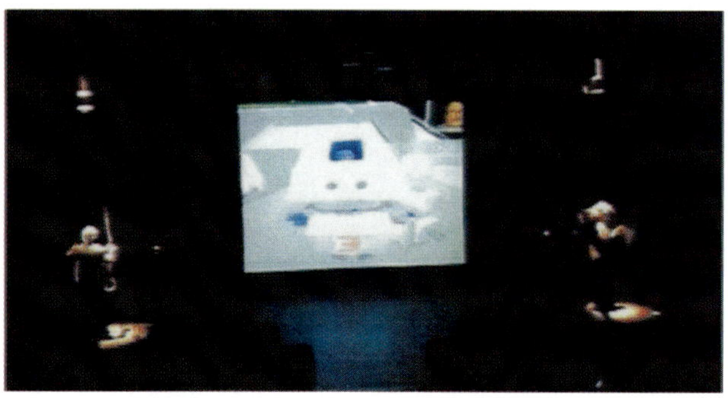

Figure 3: The front of the theatre.

Figure 4: The inhabitants, “at home”, in the production area.

## 4.1 World Design Principles

In creating the world and games for OOTW we sought to enhance legibility, presentation and the effectiveness of the virtual cameras. To these ends we employed the following principles and guidelines:

- use simple representations, and simplify games and concepts wherever possible;
- exploit the system’s realtime audio capabilities for interaction and effects;
- use an open world design with few visual barriers and no external walls (facilitating overview and context shots, such as figure 6) and use significant virtual separations to establish the different playing arenas (visible in figure 5);
- place most of the action at ground level; and
- use game interaction methods which rely on proximity, so that participants will be close to their effects in the environment (e.g. in one game – shown in figure 9 – inhabitants have to run up to “space frogs” to herd them towards their team captain; in another game the inhabitants all have to stand in a “jet car” and collectively guide it through a race course), rather than selection at a distance or shooting, for example.

In more constrained applications or genres some or all of these may not be possible or appropriate. We anticipate that, as the technology and common concepts of inhabited television evolve, many of these heuristics could be relaxed, or compensated for by additional automated assistance.

Figure 5: The virtual world, looking back past the final arena.

Figure 5 shows the scale and linear form of the virtual world. The camera is looking back past the host/scoreboard in the final arena (with the spaceship ready to leave), towards the race arena, with the previous (quiz) arena just visible in the distance. Figure 6 shows an aerial view of the quiz game (the third game arena). The host is visible as a video texture, overseeing the event. When the teams answer questions correctly their leader is raised up through the hoops by the world manager. Figure 7 shows the fish game in action (the second game arena). The inhabitants are collaboratively guiding their team leaders through the arena, to allow them to hook "space fish" down from the sky.

Figure 6: The quiz arena.

Figure 7: Inhabitants guide their team leaders in the fish game.

## 4.2 Participant Constraints

One of the key innovations of OOTW was the use of an event management and control interface which allowed us (amongst other things) to apply a positional constraint to each participant (inhabitant, performer or host). This constraint could be time-varying, allowing us to move participants from one part of the game world to another, for example creating virtual "travellators" between the different game arenas (visible in figures 5 and 6). These constraints could also vary in size, allowing us to "root" participants to the spot during interview segments or release them to explore a whole game arena (but not the whole world) during the actual games.

Specifically, each constraint consisted of a bounding box restricting movement in space, plus a forward (look) vector and permitted angular deviation. Constraints were defined in pairs, and linearly interpolated between, at a rate specified in each constraint-pair. The positional component and forward vector of each constraint were normally extracted automatically from annotations in the world definition files.

New constraints could be specified for every "phase" of the game, with the whole OOTW event comprising more than fifty phases, including contingencies and alternatives. The world manager (who was listening to directions on talk-back) was responsible for triggering phase changes from a list in the management interface. This management interface then informed each participant's client program of any new constraints, and triggered any required reconfigurations of objects within the virtual world (e.g. resetting game objects).

This allowed us to ensure that all participants kept up with the game – by dragging them if necessary – and were in the right place at the right time. In this way we addressed (at least partially) two of the issues from section 2:

- we could enforce coordinated movements and "crowd" control within the virtual environment, avoiding inhabitants getting lost or running out of control; and
- we could increase the pace of the event by enforcing time limits and by rapidly shuttling participants to new locations or elements of the show.

In addition, the use of constrained positioning meant that potential shots could be established in advance and the director and virtual camera operators could plan for them accordingly (e.g. establishing tailored camera positions and settings for different stages of the show, in relation to these pre-set constraints). For example, figure 8 shows the alien team being constrained to line up at the end of the final race. The inhabitants were visually alerted when their movement was constrained to avert frustration and confusion.

This same management interface also allowed the world manager to change the audio level of each participant within the virtual world, either to make them louder or quieter, or to virtually gag them, if necessary.

Figure 8: Participant constraints in action – lining up the aliens.

# 5 REAL-TIME CAMERA CONTROL INTERFACE

The previous section has described how appropriate world design plus constrained and managed participant movement were used to enhance the imageability of Out Of This World. In addition we created a specialized real-time camera control interface for the four camera operators. The characteristics of this interface reflect the real-time performance-oriented control requirements which derive from a live broadcast. In this section we consider the capabilities, construction and operation of this interface.

Figure 9 shows a screen image from one of the virtual cameras, showing both the normal flying vehicle-style controls (the arrow buttons at the bottom of the screen) and the custom camera interface (the dialog box at the right of the screen). The 3D window is sent to the mixing desk using the system's normal video output capabilities (SG Octane, Impact and O2 machines, with standard video options, were used for the cameras). The 3D view is taken from the "space frogs" game: robot number one, in the background, has just chased a space frog towards the robot team leader, ready for it to be impaled on the team leader's spiky hat.

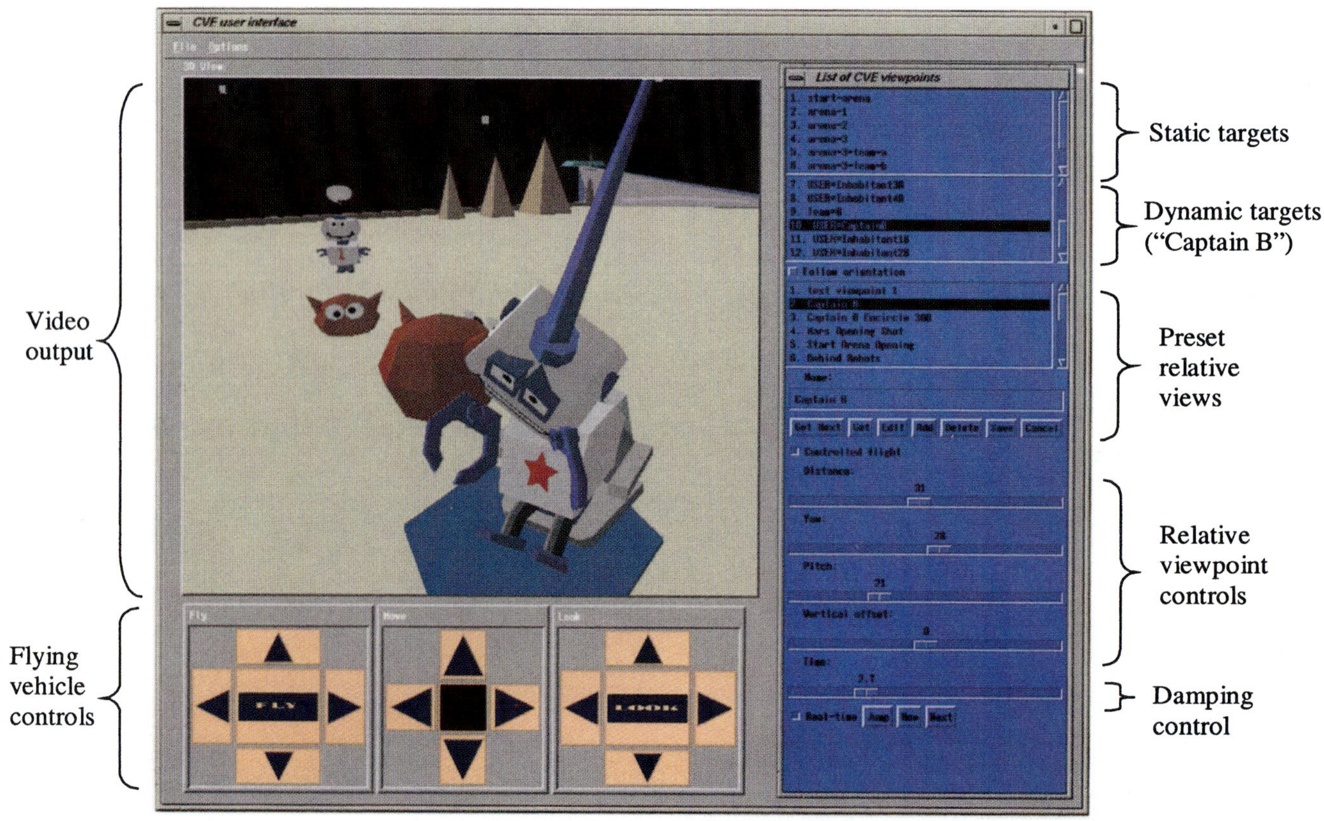


Figure 9: Camera interface for Out Of This World.

## 5.1 Flying Vehicle Control

The basic flying vehicle controls allow the camera to be moved in five degrees of freedom; the horizon was constrained to be horizontal at all times due to previous problems users had found with reorienting the viewpoint when rolling around the look vector. The main method of use is to control the camera's forwards/backwards velocity and left/right pan using the central black drag-box (which uses a cubic mapping from mouse displacement to vehicle velocity). Ware and Osborne [19] found this kind of view-relative navigational style (in their case controlled with a 3D tracker) to be good for "movie making", with its smooth control and perceived flexibility. The flying vehicle controls can also be used in concert with the object-centered controls described in the next section.

As noted in section 2, using only this type of interface in Heaven & Hell – Live produced a number of problems, such as failing to keep up with the action, getting lost, and difficulties coping with occlusion in the scene. Section 6 describes how it was used in Out Of This World.

## 5.2 Object-Centered Control

The flying vehicle metaphor controls both the position and orientation of the camera. The alternative object-centered controls allow the camera operator to specify independently the target of the camera (the look-at point as in [4]), and the relative viewing attitude and distance of the camera. This interface also provides additional temporal controls, as described below.

### 5.2.1 Look-at Point Control

The look-at point can be controlled in three ways:

- Vehicle-based free navigation, as described above, except that it is the target point rather than the camera itself which is being moved. This offers direct control over positioning in 3D space.
- Jump to preset fixed points in the virtual environment (derived from reference point artefacts included in the world

specification), for example, game arenas and player starting positions.

- Continuously track a single participant or a group of participants (e.g. team A or team B). The camera process continually monitors the activities of objects within the virtual world and adjusts the target as they move.

Note that the last two options are semantic choices expressed in terms of named objects or regions within the space. Their inclusion allows the camera operator to jump to key locations or track participants or activities irrespective of their speed (both of which were problems in previous experiments). In this respect the system introduces elements of constrained and automated camera control, as in [7] and [9], except that it is in the context of real-time control for performance.

The selected target can also optionally determine the reference orientation for the camera in the XZ plane (the ground plane). For example, when used with the tracking option it allows the camera to adopt first-person perspectives (as the participant sees the world), locked facing shots (keeping the participant full-face at all times) and a range of other possibilities.

### 5.2.2 Relative Viewing Control

In the object-centered control mode the position of the camera is not specified directly. Instead, it is specified relative to the position (and optionally the orientation) of the camera's current target. The relative position is specified primarily in terms of spherical polar coordinates, an approach which we first made use of in [3]. Specifically, the camera operator uses independent sliders to specify:

- the yaw of the camera relative to the reference orientation;
- the elevation of the camera;
- the distance of the camera from the target (including the option of going beyond the target to show an out of the eyes view for a participant); and
- a vertical offset relative to the target, to allow the operator to create views over or under the reference point, or to compensate for movements away from the ground plane.

A logarithmic control mapping has been used for the distance from the target, allowing controlled transitions between close and distant shots as proposed in [15]. These degrees of control are illustrated in figure 10.

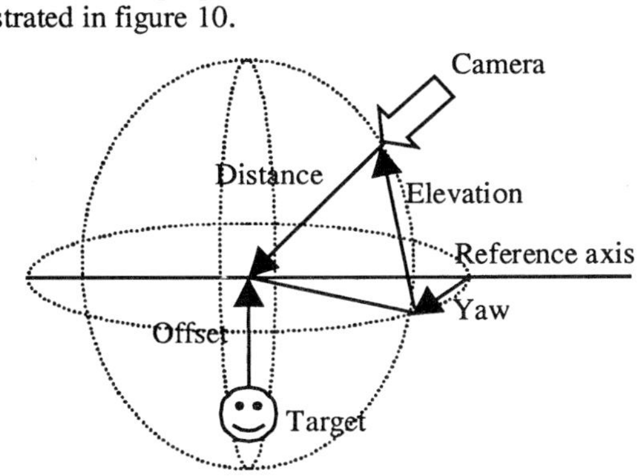


Figure 10: Relative viewing controls.

We suggest that this simple slider-based control over rotation is appropriate because it has been observed to be effective for single axis manipulation [5], and in our system we cannot use controls which overlap the 3D view because we cannot allow the mouse cursor to enter the graphical view (since it would be seen on the final broadcast).

These controls together allow the camera operator significant (but not complete) control over the framing of the target within the shot. They also (we hope) make it relatively difficult to create incomprehensible or empty shots.

### 5.2.3 Temporal Control

The final significant aspect of this control interface is its support for various forms of temporal control. In the current system the target point is controlled directly and interactively. However the relative viewing parameters can be controlled in three different ways, described below (and which may be compared to the automated mix-down capabilities of a modern digital recording studio).

- Real-time: the camera moves as each slider is moved, subject to a controllable damping coefficient which allows the operator to trade responsiveness against smoothness of movement.
- "Just-in-time": the camera operator can temporarily "disconnect" the sliders from the camera, make coordinated adjustments to all aspects of the relative view control and then trigger those changes as a single atomic operation. Again, the damping control determines the rate at which the camera interpolates between old and new settings.
- Pre-programmed: the camera operator can define complete sets of viewpoint parameters and store them for later recall. These preset viewpoints can then be selected by the operator as a single action, triggering an interpolation to that new viewpoint (with the rate determined by the damping value in the viewpoint being recalled).

The just-in-time and pre-programmed modes also allow the operator to specify a sequence of camera movements, to be executed one after another. Alternatively the operator can jump directly to the new viewpoint, or immediately start a new interpolation.

## 6 EVALUATION AND REFLECTION

As part of our evaluative reflection on OOTW a social scientific field study (of the type widely applied in the CSCW community, e.g. [13]) was conducted, with an ethnographer on-site during the performances of the show and the production and preparation work surrounding them. Here, we report on those aspects of the study concerned with the camera control software which forms a main focus of this paper.

### 6.1 Camera Use and Roles

The director of OOTW (RB) allocated the four camera operators to different basic tasks. One operator was to follow the activities of one team, another was to follow the other. A third was to get overall views of the environment ("geography shots"). A fourth was given a freer rein, instructed to seek out "relationships of interest, like the hand held camera would do". This division of labor maps well to the different forms of camera control provided for in the design we have discussed. The relationship operator, for example, might be expected to utilize the 5 DOF flying vehicle mode, while the team-oriented operators might be expected to use the option to track team-members and leaders. Finally, the operator seeking geography shots could adopt positions based on the static targets defined in the world definitions.

Interestingly, RB divided up the labor of camera operation in this fashion because this would be a standard division of labor for real television analogues of OOTW, a division of labor which was appropriately embodied in the software, and *not* because she saw these as the constraints built into the camera control technology. Clearly, future systems should also consider distinctive support for these same roles: geography or context shots; main characters or teams; and interest or relationship shots. Of course, this list cannot claim to be comprehensive.

During the later performances and as the operators' experience in virtual camera control increased, all operators were observed using the less constrained control modes (e.g. the 5DOF flying vehicle) more commonly. A manually controlled shot in pursuit of a team-leader might even be preferred over automatically targeting them. At least two reasons can be suggested for this. First, manual control can give the right amount of "camera shake" (as the target slips to one side or even momentarily out of shot) to convey a sense of frenetic activity. Second, manual control can enable the camera operator to follow the action in more flexible ways. For example, shots that were not directly supported by the camera control software could be achieved manually.

However, the controlled and preprogrammed shots we have discussed remained useful, especially in three contexts. First, when there were more scripted and recognizably repeatable moments in the action. For example, just after each game, the reactions of team leaders were asked for by the show's presenter (as in figure 8). Clearly, having standard methods to obtain such predictable shots is appropriate. Second, tracking shots were needed to follow rapid transitions, such as the movements between the different game arenas. Third, as RB said in a briefing meeting for the camera operators: "If it all goes pear-shaped [badly wrong], I can always say go back to your terms of reference". Having a known responsibility for each operator and a series of standard shots associated with it provided the camera operators with "escape routes" and a "safety net" in times of trouble, which wouldn't be available from higher DOF navigation vehicles alone.

Perhaps this should not come as a surprise, since it echoes common ideals of user-interface design: that the interface should be accessible to relatively novice users; that it should make common jobs easy; and that it should allow experienced users to exploit further levels of flexibility and customization.

## 6.2 Camera Coordination and Embodiment

One of RB's "worst nightmares" was that all cameras at a specific moment would head for the same shot and that she would have "nothing to cut to". For example, something especially remarkable at a particular location might catch the eye of all operators. In real television, the physical embodiment of the cameras and their operators militates against this to some extent: if a camera physically moves in a certain direction to get a shot, it is often clear to others what is going on. Conventional cameras also have facilities for operators to check out the views from other cameras without having to release their own current shot. Furthermore, operators typically have visual access to a "TX monitor" (showing the transmitted shot) commonly placed on the studio floor. In this way, operators can have an awareness of what each other are doing and check what is being transmitted. This can all help find an optimal shot or angle and avoid this problem.

However, in OOTW, it was decided not to graphically represent the cameras in the game worlds for other, good reasons (e.g. to avoid distracting the participants or occluding their views). Also, the only way the operators could see what others were capturing was by physically looking over to their workstations. Additionally, the operators had no TX monitor. This led to a number of occasions where RB had a sub-optimal selection of shots available to her, especially during the less scripted, more free-form action components of the show. Some clear enhancements suggest themselves, for example, access to a TX monitor and to the viewpoints of other cameras. Note that this is not concerned so much with an individual operator's camera control application or interface, but with how a set of cameras work together in the cooperative activity of inhabited television direction and camera work.

Also, the disembodiment of the cameras meant that performers and inhabitants did not know when and in what way they were being filmed, and so could not produce their speech and actions with reference to the cameras. In a future event it might be possible to use "subjective" views, to allow performers and inhabitants (and also camera operators and the director) to see the cameras, while removing them from the final broadcast output.

Finally, in OOTW both the director and crew only had visual access to the world through what the cameras were picking up, so there was no way to "have a quick look round" (e.g. to find who is speaking). This suggests the provision of extra views to camera crew and director may be necessary, so that they can explore the environment for their own purposes without this being made available for transmission.

## 6.3 Camera Interface and Video Output

In OOTW the 3D graphical views of the camera operators were directly output as the final broadcast material. This created five significant limitations:

- It was not possible to allow the camera operators to see the other cameras embodied without them also appearing on the final broadcast.
- The camera operators had very limited screen space available for additional interface controls or feedback mechanisms (such as an embedded TX monitor).
- The camera operators had to use a primarily 3D graphical view of the world, rather than, for example, a schematic or plan view of the environment, which might have been more effective in some situations.
- The camera operators had to avoid getting their mouse in the main graphical view because it would have appeared in the broadcast. Consequently they could not use image space controls such as Gleicher and Witkin's [10] "through-the-lens" method of incremental camera control.
- The image quality and frame-rate of the final broadcast was exactly that of the camera machine currently being broadcast. This meant that camera machines were a critical limitation in the broadcast quality, and motivated against additional computational or rendering complexity (and, therefore, capability) in the camera interfaces.

We have recently prototyped a "software mixing" solution which avoids this problem, and opens up opportunities to directly address the limitations described above.

In this approach, the final broadcast is generated by a single (typically high-performance) rendering machine, which runs the same multiuser virtual environment software. The viewpoint of this rendering machine is controlled directly by the currently selected camera, i.e. the camera machines output sequences of viewpoints rather than actual video. Note that the director also requires an additional machine to provide camera and preview monitors, and has to cut between cameras using the computer interface, rather than a traditional video mixer.

## 6.4 Manual Control

We believe that the design strategy to facilitate manual control rather than to automate shots and their transitions was appropriate. In particular, for research purposes, preferring enhanced manual control at this stage of research allows the users, as part of their actual interaction with the technology, to express in an occasioned and natural way the benefits and difficulties they experience in practice. It is these expressions which we have summarized in this section and are able to use as a source of future requirements.

Furthermore, limiting the degree of automation has allowed the director we have worked with to experiment with different ways of directing inhabited television. She can vary the pace of cutting, give different sets of instructions to the camera crew, get into the midst of the action or view it from the side, and so forth. Indeed, she consciously experimented with different direction styles during the course of the four OOTW shows, deciding to make fewer cuts but getting the cameras closer in for the last two shows. Again, it seems appropriate to design software at this stage which will enable such experimentation from television personnel, permitting them to address issues about the nature of inhabited television from their own professional viewpoint (e.g. how should one cut between virtual cameras?) rather than mandating an answer through excessive automation in software design.

## 6.5 Live Performance Issues

From section 5.2.3 it is apparent that temporal control over viewpoint in live performance settings can be more complicated than in non-realtime or non-performance applications. For example, in both computer animation and interactive exploration compound camera movements can be made incrementally (e.g. using a version of the real-time interface); it does not matter if the camera passes through intermediate "incomplete" states. However in a live performance, every placement of the camera must be acceptable in itself, since it may be part of the broadcast. To address this, the just-in-time mode of the camera control interface allowed the camera operator to compose complex camera movements to be executed as a single action. Similarly, the pre-programmed control interface allowed the camera operator to recall complete viewpoints which were established in advance.

Both of these facilities are motivated by the live performance nature of the interface's use. In a general sense, they address the extremely time-limited nature of live performance, by allowing the operator to exploit work done during less constrained periods of time. The pre-programmed interface allows the operator to use time in rehearsal or training to establish viewpoints for time-critical use in the performance. Similarly, the just-in-time mode allows the operator to accumulate unseen work in order to define a complex viewpoint transition.

We suggest that any live performance of significant richness will need to draw upon a significant body of previously established resources (e.g. script, training, understanding, virtual world definitions, geometry, computer programs). This work points to the potential for directly supporting this within the production and broadcast infrastructure.

# 7 CONCLUSIONS AND FUTURE WORK

From audience feedback and our own reviewing of the show video tapes we find that the broadcast output was legible and coherent (unlike some of our previous experiences) and the pace of the event was much closer to television than to normal interactive virtual environments. We ascribe this success to the following factors: relatively simple world geometry, structures and games; management controls to constrain the movements of participants; a specialized realtime performance camera interface; and increasing experience with events of this kind and their appropriate visual form (for example, reducing the cutting rate).

Having demonstrated the ability to create pace and legibility in an established and cliched game show format we now intend to develop this work in the areas of richer content, more complex narrative forms, more expressive avatars and new forms of interaction. We plan to stage our next major experimental event late-1999. The final sections describe some of the areas in which this work could be taken forward.

**Camera Mixing**
In OOTW we performed the final video mix in the analogue video domain using standard video mixers. However, using a software mixing approach (as described in section 6.3) we can use a single "broadcast" machine to render all of the final broadcast. The main advantages of this approach are that: the broadcast machine can be more powerful than the cameras, giving a better quality output (e.g. higher framerate); automated or semi-automated mixing can be integrated and used in parts of the broadcast (see also the next section); and the camera operators can have more specialized interfaces, for example including direct manipulation within their view (e.g. using the methods of [10]). In future experiments we plan to make use of this approach.

**Automation**
In Out Of This World, we did not attempt to define camera shots or transitions automatically. However there are many situations in which partial or full automation of camera positioning and/or mixing would be advantageous. We are particularly interested in using techniques for automated viewpoint control and/or mixing to reduce production costs, with a view to supporting long running, possibly permanently available, inhabited television experiences. Alternatively, automation might be used some of the time or for some aspects, supplemented by human expertise and aesthetic guidance.

**Mix Your Own**
With a traditional broadcast the individual viewer has no control over what they see. If the image from each camera was individually broadcast then the viewer would be able to "mix their own" final program by switching between the individual camera channels. Alternatively, if the virtual world data itself is broadcast then the viewer could choose between the director's

mix, their own mix, or controlling their own independent viewpoint. With a suitable network back-channel, they could also make the transition to become an inhabitant, becoming embodied, active and visible within the event itself.

**For Those Watching at Home…**

The staging of OOTW fell short of "real" Inhabited TV in one important respect: neither the viewers nor the inhabitants were actually at home, in front of their TV/set-top box. In our next set of experiments we will return to domestic viewers and inhabitants, as in The Mirror and Heaven and Hell – Live. For viewers, the removal of the social context of the theatre space is likely to make them more demanding of the broadcast in and of itself. For the inhabitants, use from home raises major issues of heterogeneity and reliability of hardware and software, and of trust, accountability, control and governance for the individual inhabitants.

**Audio**

This paper has focused on the visual aspects of inhabited television. However, audio also plays a critical role. In film and television there is typcally a very rich and complex relationship between sound and vision, and it will be a significant challenge to support some of this richness in an Inhabited TV system. By analogy with virtual cameras, we also plan to explore approaches to virtual microphones and appropriate sound design, production and presentation for inhabited television.

## Acknowledgements

We acknowledge the support of the European Community for the eRENA project under the ESPRIT IV Intelligent Information Interfaces (I3) programme and also the EPSRC for the Multimedia Networking for Inhabited Television project under the Multimedia Networking Applications programme. Additional support for Out of this World was provided by the UK's FACT and North West Arts.

We would like to thank all those who helped to design, create and stage Out Of This World – especially Mike Craven, Jason Morphett, CJ, Gareth, Jules and Rena – and all those who took part as inhabitants and viewers.

## References

[1] D. Arijon. *Grammar of the Film Language.* Communication Arts Books, Hastings House, New York, 1976.

[2] Steve Benford, Chris Greenhalgh, Chris Brown, Graham Walker, Tim Reagan, Paul Rea, Jason Morphett and John Wyver. Experiments in Inhabited TV. *CHI'98 Late Breaking Results (Conference Summary)*, pp. 289-290. ACM, 18-23 April 1998. ISBN 1-58113-028-7.

[3] Benford, S.D., Greenhalgh, C.M., Snowdon, D.N., and Bullock, A.N.. Staging a Poetry Performance in a Collaborative Virtual Environment. *Proceedings ECSCW'97*, Lancaster, UK. Kluwer, 1997.

[4] Blinn, J.. Where am I? What am I looking at? *IEEE Computer Graphics and Applications*, July 1988, pp. 76-81.

[5] Michael Chen, S. Joy Mountford and Abigail Sellen. A Study in Interactive 3-D Rotation Using 2-D Control Devices. *Computer Graphics*, 22(4), August 1988, pp. 121-129.

[6] CINEMATRIX, Interactive Entertainment System, http://www.cinematrix.com/ (verified April 28, 1999)

[7] Steven M. Drucker, Tinsley A. Galyean and David Zeltzer. CINEMA: A System for Procedural Camera Movements. *Proc. 1992 Symposium on Interactive 3D Graphics*, Cambridge MA: ACM Press, March 29-April 1, 1992, pp. 67-70.

[8] Steven M. Drucker and David Zeltzer. Intelligent Camera Control in a Virtual Environment. *Proceedings Graphics Interface '94*, pp. 190-199, 1994.

[9] Dorée Duncan Seligmann and Steven Feiner. Automated Generation of Intent-Based 3D Illustrations. *Computer Graphics (SIGGRAPH 91 Conference Proceedings)*, 25(4), July 1991.

[10] Michael Gleicher and Andrew Witkin. Through-the-Lens Camera Control. *Computer Graphics*, 26(2), July 1992, pp. 331-340.

[11] Greenhalgh, C. M. and Benford, S. D.. Supporting Rich And Dynamic Communication In Large Scale Collaborative Virtual Environments. *Presence: Teleoperators and Virtual Environments*, Vol. 8, No. 1, February 1999, pp. 14-35, MIT Press.

[12] Li-wei He, Michael F. Cohen and David H. Salesin. The Virtual Cinematographer: A Paradigm for Automatic Real-Time Camera Control and Directing. *SIGGRAPH 96 Conference Proceedings*, Annual Conference Series, pp. 217-224, Addison Wesley, August 1996.

[13] John Hughes, Val King, Tom Rodden, and Hans Anderson. Moving Out from the Control Room: Ethnography in System Design. *Proc. CSCW'94*, October 22-26 1994, Chapel Hill, NC, USA, pp. 429-439, ACM Press.

[14] Peter Karp and Steven Feiner. Issues in the Automated Generation of Animated Presentations. *Proceedings Graphics Interface '90*, 14-18 May 1990, Halifax, Nova Scotia, pp. 38-48.

[15] Jock D. Mackinlay, Stuart K. Card and George G. Robertson. Rapid Controlled Movement Through a Virtual 3D Workspace. *Computer Graphics*, 24(4), August 1990, pp. 171-176.

[16] Cary B. Philips, Normal I. Badler and John Granieri. Automatic Viewing Control for 3D Direct Manipulation. *1992 Symposium on Interactive 3D Graphics*, ACM Press, March 29-April 1, 1992, pp. 71-74.

[17] Ritter, D. The Intersection of Art and Interactivity. *Ars Electronica Festival 96*, Vienna: Springer, pp. 274-285, 1996.

[18] Walker, G.R.. The Mirror – reflections on Inhabited Television. *BT Technology Journal*, 16(1), pp. 29-38, 1997.

[19] Colin Ware and Steven Osborne. Exploration and Virtual Camera Control on Virtual Three Dimensional Environments. *Proceedings of the 1990 Symposium on Interactive 3D Graphics*, Special Issue of Computer Graphics, Vol. 24, pp. 173-183, 1990.

# Emancipated Pixels: Real-World Graphics In The Luminous Room

**John Underkoffler, Brygg Ullmer, and Hiroshi Ishii**

**Tangible Media Group, MIT Media Laboratory**

## ABSTRACT

We describe a conceptual infrastructure – the *Luminous Room* – for providing graphical display and interaction at each of an interior architectural space's various surfaces, arguing that pervasive environmental output and input is one natural heir to today's rather more limited notion of spatially-confined, output-only display (the CRT). We discuss the requirements of such real-world graphics, including computational & networking demands; schemes for spatially omnipresent capture and display; and issues of design and interaction that emerge under these new circumstances. These discussions are both illustrated and motivated by five particular applications that have been built for a real, experimental Luminous Room space, and by details of the current technical approach to its construction (involving a two-way optical transducer called an *I/O Bulb* that projects and captures pixels).

**CR Categories and Subject Descriptors:** H.5.2 [User Interfaces] Input devices and strategies; H.5.1 [Multimedia Information Systems] Artificial, augmented, and virtual realities; B.4.2 [Input/Output and Data Communications] Input/Output Devices – Image display; I.4.8 [Image Processing and Computer Vision] Scene Analysis – Tracking, Applications; I.3.6 [Methodologies and Techniques] – Interaction Techniques

**Additional keywords:** real-world graphics, luminous-tangible interfaces, projection, computer vision, architectural space, CAD

## 1 INTRODUCTION

For the three decades of Computer Graphics's so-far existence, the graphics in question have been confined to screens: vectorscopes, raster-scanned CRTs, head-mounted displays, and – when budget, technology, or Hollywood permits – the cinema screen. We suggest that it is time for computer-driven graphical constructs to escape the strictures of the rectangular screen and take their place as denizens of real-world architecture. Specifically, we introduce the concept of the Luminous Room: an interior architectural space whose surfaces have been made capable both of displaying visual information and of performing visual capture. By insisting on this collocated pairing of optical input and output, we make of each room surface – floor, walls, ceiling, tabletops, assorted furniture – a potential site for interaction. These are sites at which the 'room itself' can react to what's happening within its bounds, sites at which otherwise inert physical objects can become digital implements visibly surrounded by computational appendages.

This document, then, concerns the Luminous Room, dovetailing discussion of the general with the specific. Overarching questions – of appropriate technical means for achieving what we propose, of the role played by physical objects in the interactions that result, of the ways design for such a space must differ from traditional computer-visual design – are paralleled by corroborating ideas from experiments in which we have built pieces of a Luminous Room and some applications that live there.

20 Ames St. Cambridge MA 02139 / jh@media.mit.edu



We'll begin by presenting five such examples: working Luminous Room applications that, while hardly encompassing the full set of 'things to do with graphics in the real world', should provide background and basis for the ensuing discussion of some large-scale issues. Specifically, we explore (1) approaches to distributing visual information throughout and extracting spatial information from a room; (2) the computational and networking needs related to input, i.e. analysis of the environment; and (3) design issues attending the deployment of and interaction with computer graphics in a real-world setting.

## 2 EXAMPLE APPLICATIONS

One major intent of our research has been to find ways in which the facilities of a Luminous Room – pretending for a moment that the formidable challenges of its basic technical realization are already met – can be usefully employed. If every room surface really is capable of display, what interactions does it make sense to pursue there? The following five applications will serve as grounding for our later discussion of large-scale implementation issues; they also illustrate one class of problem that we've found nicely susceptible to treatment by reactive real-world computer graphics.

### 2.1 Illuminating Light

Designed as a rapid prototyping tool for optical engineers, *Illuminating Light* provides a collection of simple objects representing real-world optics: lenses, mirrors, lasers, beamsplitters, and recording film. The system acts to imbue these models with the same meaning and function as their real-world counterparts [13], so that placing the laser-model on the ordinary table that is the application's arena results in a graphical beam of light, apparently emanating from the laser's front aperture. This beam remains registered with the laser as it is rotated and moved about the workspace. Other optics models placed in an existing beam's path have the expected effects: a mirror-model reflects the beam; a lens-model spreads one beam into a fan of many; a beamsplitter-model reflects part of the beam and transmits the

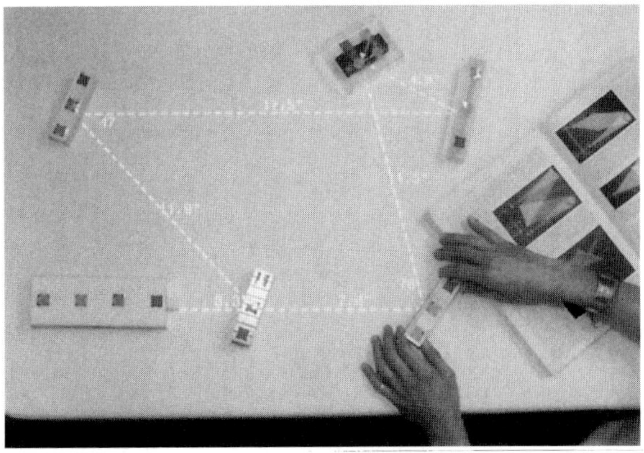

**Fig 1:** ***Illuminating Light*: physical optics, digital light beams**

remainder; and a recording-film-model absorbs incoming beams to form an eventual image. Ancillary information – the length of each beam and the angle of beam-bounce at each mirror and beamsplitter surface – is presented as a collection of numerical annotations that float in the vicinity of the beams and optical elements to which they refer.

Additional domain knowledge concerning holography is built into the application: as an experimenter works at arranging a hologram-recording layout, a nearby display shows optical path-length-matching information (critical for successful recording). Similarly, once a viable setup has been achieved a simulated holographic reconstruction appears in the workspace. *Illuminating Light* has aroused a great deal of interest in our local optics and physics communities. The students and professionals who

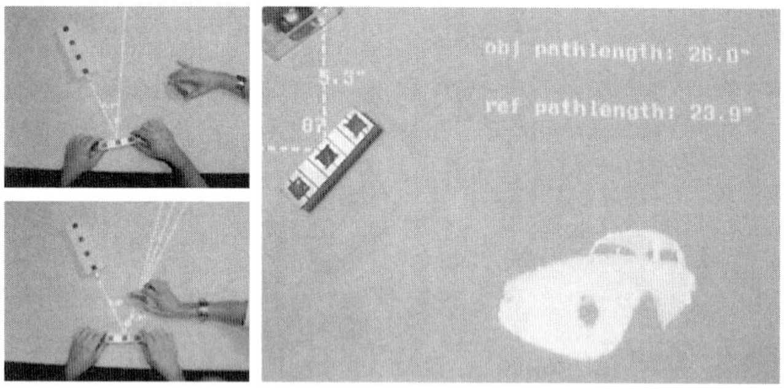


**Fig 2a: collaborative optics design; 2b: simulated hologram**

have experimented with it affirm that its direct manipulation style – "like working with the real thing" – both fosters and takes advantage of the spatial understanding inherent to work with real optics. Their comments have also indicated that for many tasks the system is easier and faster to use than the on-screen CAD-style applications that are the other alternative to prototyping directly in the lab.

## 2.2 Chess-&-Bottle

An application that involves a vertical rather than horizontal surface, this collection of design experiments covers an entire wall in a small office. Placing a large chessboard anywhere on the wall engages a chess system that rapidly populates the board with animated pieces; moving the board induces the individual pieces to scramble into the appropriate new positions. In the same space (and at the same time, if desired), digital artifacts can be stored in a physical container. Images, numbers, text, and even regions of live video can be brought into loose association with a glass vase, which extends graphical springs to capture any of these 'documents' in its proximity. A simple gesture – rotation about its vertical axis – causes the vase to fully ingest its collection of documents. The vase can then be moved to a new location and twisted once more, whereupon (like any good physical

**Fig 3a: physically stored digital elements; 3b: chess**

container whose exterior location does not alter what is contained) it disgorges those same documents.

Individual documents (live video windows, at the moment) are created with a colored paddle that's used as a spatial pointer. The same paddle is used to move existing documents over the wall, to bring them into or out of association with the container-vase, and ultimately to dispose of them in a physical trash can.

## 2.3 seep

A cellular automata system is used as the basis for *seep*, an interactive simulation that allows physical objects placed in a workspace to act as obstacles in a purely computational fluid flow. The flow is depicted as a grid of field lines whose orientation and length show the local direction and speed of fluid transport. A lattice gas laid out on a hexagonal grid – the FHP formulation [5] – expresses fluid behavior as an aggregate of individual particle motions; particle interactions are dictated by a small set of collision rules that accurately lead to the dynamics predicted by the *Navier-Stokes* equations. Physical objects placed in this graphical

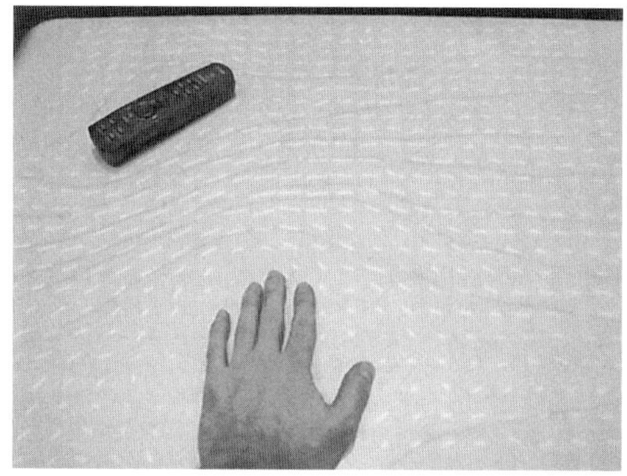

**Fig 4: *seep*'s fluid diverted by physical obstacles**

flow are tracked and reduced to a two-dimensional silhouette, whose interior region is then analyzed into the grid of FHP cells as a collection of obstacle cells. The result is an engaging tool for experimenting with basic fluid physics.

## 2.4 Urp

We have built a second 'professional' application, expanding on many of the ideas we'd been exploring with *Illuminating Light*, to address the field of urban design and planning. The resulting system, called *Urp*, also permits direct manipulation of basic objects – in this case architectural models – to affect an underlying simulation. One part of this simulation attaches computational solar shadows to each building model in its purview. The buildings are continuously tracked and each shadow is closely registered to the structure that is its source, so that a convincing

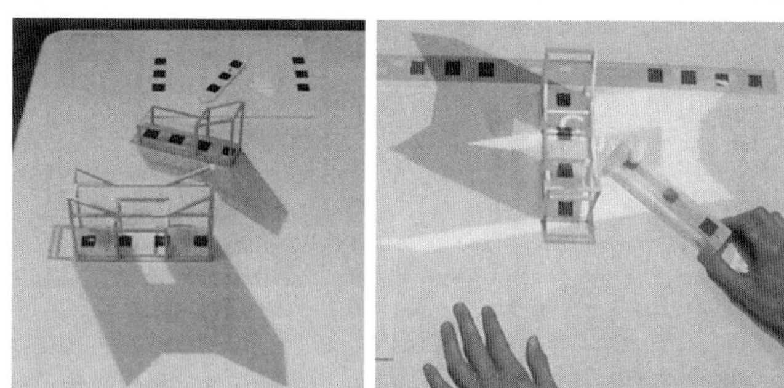

**Fig 5a: shadows; 5b: material wand makes a building glass**

illusion of the shadows' authenticity results for many experimenters (despite the incongruity of a wireframe construction casting a solid shadow!).

But where *Illuminating Light* provides essentially a single class of object – i.e. each object is a stand-in for some optical element, designed to closely emulate the behavior of that real-world counterpart – *Urp* expands the repertoire. So while the architectural models are in their 'literalness' clearly analogous to the earlier optics models, *Urp* also provides tool-objects: objects that act on other objects in the simulation, or that act on the global state of the simulation. Thus, experimenters can rotate the hour hand of a simple clock-object placed on the table to change the system's time – and thereby the current solar position; the shadows swing around accordingly. This adjustable time, together with the graspable physicality of the architectural models, provides a straightforward mechanism for performing shadow studies.

Similarly, a measuring-tool can be used to 'draw' a distance measurement between any two structures; the line that represents this metric connection persists as the models are moved about the workspace, always updating the displayed distance. A material tool, brought into contact with any building, changes its 'facade' from brick to glass: the simulation then additionally displays the calculated solar reflection from each exterior surface. This makes possible planning for the interaction between glass-faced structures and nearby freeways, which can become significantly hazardous when low-angle sunlight is reflected into oncoming drivers' eyes. Finally, a wind tool placed into the workspace at some particular angle summons a windflow simulator – the same FHP lattice gas underlying *seep* – that blows from the chosen direction and takes into account the obstruction of any buildings in its path. The resulting field, as with *seep*, is projected down into alignment with the workspace, enabling straightforward wind-flow studies.

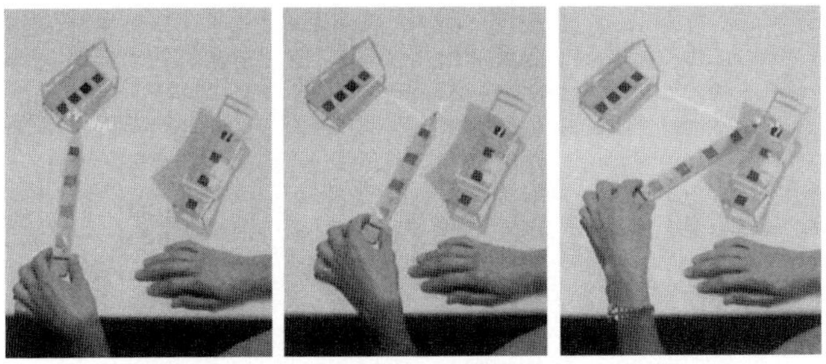

**Fig 6: A measurement line is wigglingly established**

Reaction to *Urp* from practicing and academic urban planners and architects has been emphatically positive. Plans are already under way to duplicate the system several times over for a new design studio in our university's architecture school. This new version will also include a distribution mechanism (discussed in §5.2.4) that allows several planners, each at a separate workspace, to simultaneously see and collaborate on an evolving design.

## 2.5 Distributed Illuminating Light

Finally, the ongoing expansion of our Luminous Room infrastructure has allowed the integration of multiple *Illuminating Light* workspaces. Our distribution scheme (§5.2.4, again) permits two workspaces to be physically juxtaposed, leading simply to a larger workspace. For the alternate case, in which the workspaces are not adjacent, we have implemented two distinct modes of operation. In the first, each workspace is a 'window' onto a continuous optics workbench that's rigidly isomorphic and -metric with real space. Thus, a laser shined off the edge of one table will reappear on another if aimed properly (Fig. 7). In the second mode, all workspaces are understood as instances of the same underlying space; this is the 'I-see-what-you-see' case. Here, optics models present on one table will be graphically represented on the others, but will not be directly manipulable by experimenters there. Beams, of course, are identically represented on each table; and so each experimenter views (and has a role in constructing) the same optical layout.

# 3 CONTEXT

## 3.1 Historical

The idea of incorporating live computer-generated imagery into architectural spaces is not nearly new, of course.

**Fig 7: distributed *Illuminating Light***

Myron Krueger's decades-long series of experiments, including notably the many faces of *VideoPlace*, used simultaneous video projection and capture to embed the human participant (in silhouette form) in a variety of games and simulations [7]. This same video-acquired silhouette, subjected to simple geometric- and gesture-analysis, was itself also the input to VideoPlace.

MIT ArcMac offered in 1979 the notion of the 'Media Room', an office-sized space in which an entire wall was in fact a rear-projection video system [2]. The room's occupants were able to interact with wall-displayed applications like *World of Windows* and *Put-That-There* by way of a multiplicity of input mechanisms, including physical gesture (Polhemus-style magnetic tagging), verbal commands (voice recognition), visual attention (eye tracking), and a set of more ordinary buttons & joysticks.

Most inspiring and aesthetically potent is the work of Michael Naimark, who since the 1970s has worked with immersive video and film projections schemes. Among them, especially germane is his 1984 piece *Displacements*, in which a central rotating camera had earlier captured actors' antics in a mocked-up living room; the room was then painted entirely white (furniture, props, and all) and the developed film placed in a rotating projector precisely registered with the original camera. Visitors who entered the room watched a finite frame of color and life sweeps around, animating the otherwise sterile environment.

## 3.2 Contemporary

Viewed broadly, the Luminous Room shares certain individual aspects with a handful of other research projects, including the CAVE [3]; augmented reality systems such as Karma [4]; 'smart rooms' as in [10]; several desk- and workbench-based VR systems such as [1]; and, more recently, projective environments such as [11]. Our research differs from these systems in several key respects. We seek to 'paint on' the physical objects and surfaces that constitute the real world, bypassing the encumbering mediation of see-through displays and tethered tracking technologies. Our work is also distinguished by its reliance upon systems of physical artifacts both as representations of and as mediums of interface with the digital world.

This latter concern is shared by much of the 'Tangible Bits' work of MIT's Tangible Media Group [6], but where the 'phicons' of these systems are typically endowed with *symbolic correspondences* between digital meanings and physical manifestations, Luminous Room objects have more often demonstrated a *direct correspondence* with pre-existing physical artifacts (e.g. optics and buildings), along with a corresponding faithfulness to the original interaction modalities of these items.

Perhaps closest in spirit to our present work is Wellner's DigitalDesk system, which used projection and video-capture techniques to merge (literally) the computer desktop with the physical office desktop [14].

## 4 GETTING PIXELS IN AND OUT

What means are plausibly available for realizing a Luminous Room? How can display and capture actually be distributed *pervasively* throughout a room?

### 4.1 Display

There are three basic ways to enable display at an architectural surface. A first requires replacement or occlusion of the surface in question by a planar emissive structure, varieties of which include the hoary CRT (whose applicability seems dubious, given the significant thickness involved) and the more credible flat-panel display technologies. A second approach involves projection; rear projection is often implausible because of the large 'under-surface' distances demanded, but projection from within the space remains a possibility. Finally, just-emerging active-contrast technologies hold interesting promise. These can take the form (among others) of 'electronic toner', as with Jacobsen's E-Ink work [8]: electrically rewritable but optically passive (black or white) pixels that may be affixed to various surfaces.

### 4.2 Capture

Similarly, we may identify several basic schemes for the acquisition and spatial tracking of the room's contents and inhabitants. Note that, in addition to the tracking of inanimate objects and humans (or perhaps other bits of biology), we may also wish to apprehend the Luminous Room's own displayed graphics – e.g. in order to employ auto-calibration schemes of the sort described in [11].

Approaches to capture include *tethered tagging schemes* (e.g. Polhemus) in which position and orientation information is reported for any object or human to which a 'receiver' has been attached. A second approach is 'Electric Field Sensing' (described in [12]), which is an *electronic non-contact tagless scheme* in which an object modifies an electric field generated and sensed by a fixed transceiver; the position and orientation of the interposed object emerge from calculations based on the characteristics of the received field. Another approach is video capture, followed by the application of any machine vision algorithm(s) – an *optical non-contact tagless scheme*. The final approach, an *electronic non-contact tagging scheme*, is any – like [9] – that affixes untethered tags (RF cavity tag, magnetic tag, etc.) to objects and then uses a set of sensors fixed under a surface to discover the spatial particulars of each tag.

### 4.3 I/O Bulb

We have established the dyad of optical input and projective output as our approach – for the moment, at least – to building Luminous Rooms. This decision is multiply predicated. Critically for actual implementation, camera-in and projector-out are the schemes most clearly within the current realm of the attainable. The proposition of carpeting and wallpapering a room with flat-panel displays is not only prohibitively expensive but engenders structural (in the load-bearing sense) difficulties, leading as well to slightly smaller rooms or slightly larger houses. The present immaturity of E-Ink technology precludes its use. Polhemus-style input too is expensive and does not scale well, and its signal-wire-tethers are antithetical to the non-encumbering aims of the project. Electric field sensing techniques are not yet capable of satisfactory object disambiguation and essentially require objects to be partially conducting (flesh, usually). RF tagging approaches also suffer limits on the number and material composition of objects that can be recognized.

Equally important to our decision is a philosophical consideration: using optical input and projective output is the only configuration that is largely 'non-invasive'. Although future homes and workspaces may incorporate embedded display and sensing facilities in their surfaces as a matter of course, there is for now a strong appeal to schemes that do not require laying down extra surfaces or burrowing beneath existing ones to install electronic hardware.

The particular tack we endorse involves close physical integration of the optical input and output functions. In particular, we have proposed the evolution of the ordinary lightbulb, as follows. If we first generously consider a present-day lightbulb to be an extremely low-resolution digital projector – a 1x1 pixel(s) projector, in fact, typically also sporting a 1 bit dynamic range – then the necessary evolution is easy to see. We must increase the resolution of the bulb, so that its current angularly independent output (roughly the same intensity throughout the full $4\pi$ steradian surface that surrounds it) becomes an output of angularly dependent intensity (with, say, 8 bits of dynamic range). To this high resolution bulb structure we now also add a tiny video camera, so that the bulb not only concerns itself with the light that flows *outward* through its familiar glass shell, but also collects the light from the outside environment that flows through the shell *inward*.

The result is a two-way optical information device that we call the *I/O Bulb*. The applications presented in this paper have so far made use of various I/O Bulb mockups built from off-the-shelf components (described below in §4.4). Building a 'real' I/O Bulb is itself a tangible engineering goal, an ongoing research project that we have been pursuing with an outside industrial partner (an early prototype is shown in Fig. 13b). But the I/O Bulb is also

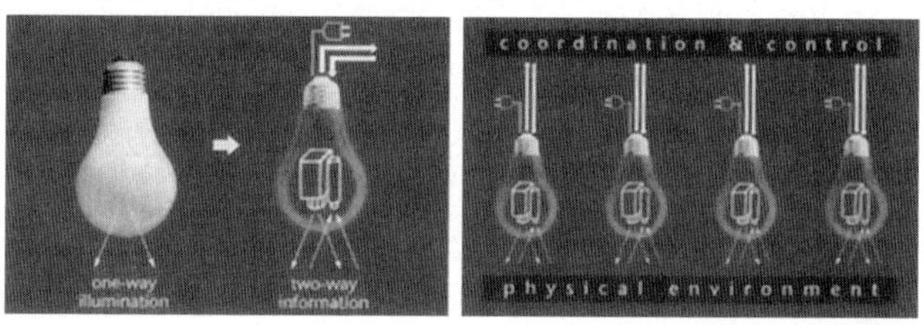


**Fig 8a: from lightbulb to I/O Bulb; 8b: a Luminous Room**

useful as a conceptual unit. If an individual I/O Bulb is capable of treating some finite region with display and scene capture, then we can build a Luminous Room in the same way that an ordinary architectural space is illuminated: through a multiplicity of bulbs. By placing enough I/O Bulbs in a room (most in the ceiling, mimicking one traditional style of illumination) and by supporting their coordination and intercommunication, we can 'tile' the entire space with graphical interactivity – and thereby build a proper Luminous Room.

### 4.4 Projective Geometries

Several optical-geometric issues pervade any attempt to build an I/O-Bulb-like structure using off-the-shelf components.

#### 4.4.1 Anti-Keystoning

Projector manufacturers in 1998-9 tend to assume that their products are used more or less exclusively in business presentations, and will thus only ever be placed on conference-room tables or mounted on ceilings. The anti-keystoning mechanism that is consequently integrated into every modern data projector means that its projection expands along a frustum not centered on the normal to the lens – although each parallel focus plane of this frustum is of course still properly orthogonal to the lens normal (Fig. 9). Thus a projector that points toward the horizon, straight ahead, will deposit its image well above the 'horizon-aim' of its lens, but that image will be properly rectangular and wholly in focus. This is in contrast to, say, a standard slide projector, whose projected image center will always coincide with the aim-point of its lens; moving the image higher on the wall necessitates propping up the front end of the apparatus, but the

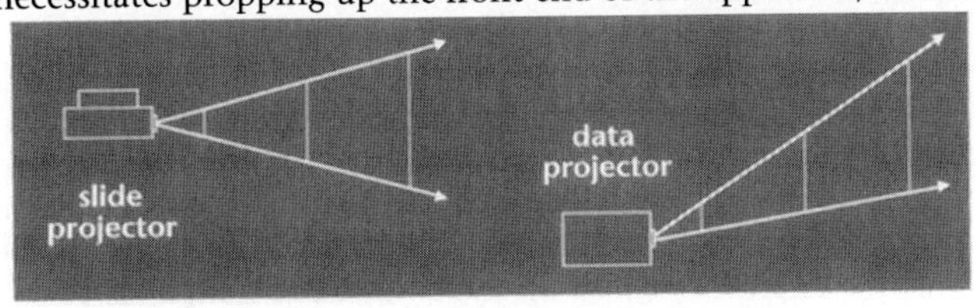


**Fig 9: Normal v. 'anti-keystoned' projection**

image then becomes trapezoidal ('keystoned').

An I/O Bulb, meanwhile, is clearly only useful if the region observed by its input-camera is the same as the region painted by its output-projector. Given that available projectors cannot truly project 'forward', we are left with two prospective geometries for achieving coincidence of input and output. We can either separate the camera and the projector, so that the regions treated by each are precisely the same; or we can keep the camera and projector together (at least as close as is geometrically possible) and tip the projector downward to bring the center of the projection into alignment with the center of the camera's view. The significant shortcoming of this latter arrangement is

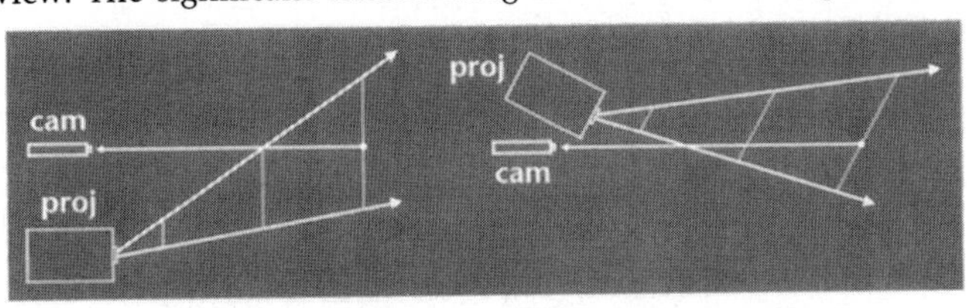


**Fig 10: Geometries for aligned I/O coverage**

that not only is the resulting projection trapezoidally distorted – requiring software clients to apply a final counterdistortion transformation to any imagery before display – but the plane of projective focus is now also tipped with respect to an orthogonal projection surface: correct focus is no longer possible over the extent of the image.

### 4.4.2 Coincidence and Coaxiality

Equally serious is the issue of whether the two system components are optically coaxial or not: is there parallax between the camera's view and the projection axis? Early thought maintained that a true 'zero-parallax' (precisely coaxial, with camera and projector essentially coincident) system would be optimal; indeed there are reasons that minimizing parallax is advantageous. The fact is, however, that for an arrangement in which all objects and projections are restricted to a single plane – which frequently is the desired arrangement (e.g. an overhead I/O Bulb addressing a table surface) – the parallax issue is moot. Indeed, simply-calculated offsets can precisely account for the positions of objects that 'depart the plane', as long as the geometry of the responsible I/O Bulb is well known.

Barring the availability of a single chip with an active surface that both emits and collects light, the only way to achieve a true zero-parallax optical input-output system is through the use of a partially-silvered mirror. But a version of the I/O Bulb built early in the research using this technique quickly revealed the fundamental drawback that renders such an approach largely unworkable: optical scatter. Even an absolutely clean beamsplitter scatters a small fraction of the light that's incident upon it. Since output visibility in a normal work environment requires the projection component of the I/O Bulb to be substantially high-intensity (the more so because the beamsplitter 'throws away' part of the light that would normally reach the projection surface), a fair amount of light is unavoidably scattered from the beamsplitter surface. The camera must look through this surface as well, and whatever it might have seen of the environment beyond the I/O Bulb assembly is now drowned out by this scattered projection light.

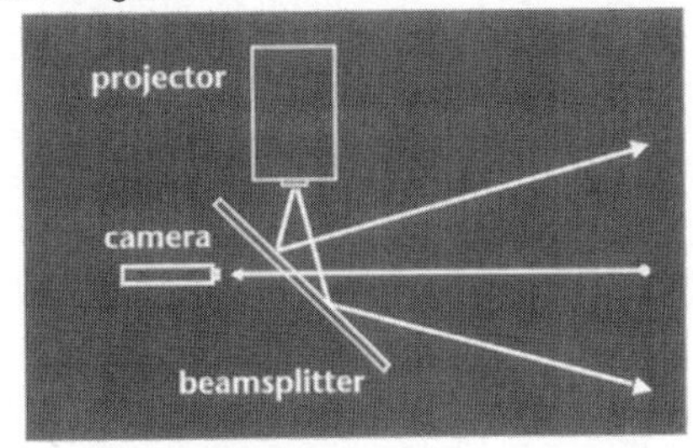


**Fig 11: Scatter-crippled approach to zero-parallax**

### 4.4.3 The Current I/O Bulb

With all this in mind we embrace (temporarily) the spatially-separated-camera-and-projector option, so that most of our functioning 'I/O Bulbs' to date have been built as shown below. Although a long-term objection to this configuration exists – we ultimately intend the I/O Bulb to be a compact device, suitable for unobtrusive and large-scale deployment – the ideological disparity is tolerable in the short term as we develop the applications that are an equally important part of the Luminous Room investigations. Too, despite our original misgivings about such a large amount of camera-projector parallax, it works quite well.

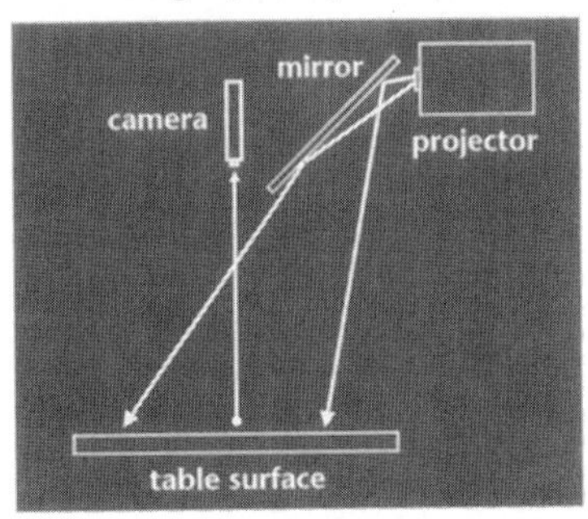


**Fig 12: The currently prevalent I/O Bulb geometry**

An unforeseen advantage of this physically distributed design quickly emerged. For typical 'workbench' applications in which operators stand or sit at the front of the table (i.e. on the left side in the diagram above) and at its sides, occlusion by an operator is *less* of a problem than would be the case with a zero-parallax system: shadows from an operator's hands and arms tend to be thrown forward – that is, back toward the operator herself.

## 5 PARSING THE ENVIRONMENT

Whether the Luminous Room acquires 'raw' information about the presence, position, and movements of the objects and people inside its confines by way of a video camera, an electric-field sensing setup, or some tagging scheme, a great challenge is always the compilation and interpretation of this low-level data into the form of 'recognized phenomena'. So, for example: a high-velocity arc has been recorded; is someone waving, or has *Illuminating Light*'s beamsplitter just been thrown in anger?

### 5.1 Distributed v. Centralized Approach

No matter what scheme or collection of schemes is used to implement a Luminous Room, decisions about how to distribute the resulting computational load will arise. In particular, because any currently plausible scheme involves juxtaposition of many finite-purview input and output mechanisms (i.e. no single device can 'cover the whole room'), some amount of coordination among these more basic spatial 'tiles' is required. What happens, for example, when a graphical construct needs to straddle or cross the boundary between adjacent tiles?

A central question thus concerns the granularity of the computation that reflects and is responsible for the room's tiling. The two extremes would see (1) an individual process, probably running on its own dedicated CPU, assigned to each tile, with the smallest possible amount of intercommunication keeping the tiles synchronized – viz., the fully distributed approach – or (2) a single 'omniscient' process whose massive job it is to attend to all tiles in aggregate and simultaneously; sharing of information between tiles is then not merely effortless but in fact unnecessary. In between, we may imagine a largely distributed approach that assigns individual processes to each tile but manages these via a master, supervisory process: a tack perhaps understandable as an 'Operating System for the Luminous Room'.

In §5.2.4 we present an implementation of the first (maximally fine-grained) option.

## 5.2 Luminous Room Vision Techniques

Here we present the fundamental choices made and techniques employed that allow our current Luminous Room implementation to track objects within its purview.

### 5.2.1 glimpser

Early stage, low-level vision is accomplished by the *glimpser* program, which simply identifies colored dots in its visual input. *glimpser* accepts commands from its master application to define, create, destroy, and condition 'finders'. Each finder is an independent directive to locate within the input frame a specific-sized region of some particular color. Finders, once created, can be restricted to a certain subregion of the input field, can be temporarily deactivated or fully reactivated, and can be 'de-emphasized' to be evaluated less frequently in order to streamline the search when input movements are known to be slow or very sporadic. Finally, each finder may be instructed to report only one color-spot location per frame, to report up to some fixed number of spot locations per frame, or to report fully as many spot locations as may be found per frame.

*glimpser* is implemented as an isolable server in which requests and directives are received and resulting reports are transmitted over a TCP/IP connection. In this way *glimpser*'s predictably heavy computational demands may be fobbed off onto another CPU altogether, leaving the 'main' CPU freely available for the full simulation and rendering needs of the application in question; or, for lighter tasks, glimpser's low-level vision efforts as well as the application-specific calculations can be assigned to the same machine. *glimpser* has been used with satisfactory results in both guises.

### 5.2.2 Seeing Spots

The point of this color-dot-finding is that, in most of the applications built so far for the Luminous Room, individual physical objects are tagged with unique colored-dot patterns. For a variety of reasons, not least of which is the desire to maximize reliability and stability while minimizing per-frame computational cost, we decided at the outset of all our implementation to eschew higher-level machine vision techniques (like template-matching) that attempt to identify objects through shape and other per-object attributes.

Instead, the intent is a kind of object-independent tagging scheme that – while enjoying the benefits of machine vision, like inherent multiplexing – would exhibit a special flexibility. For example, if we decide that an application needs to be able to recognize a new object, we need only declare the unique dot pattern that will be affixed to this object. Depending on the structure of the application and the intended function of the new object, this addition may not require recompilation (or indeed even restarting the application). An object-centric vision scheme would, on the other hand, typically require some form of 'retraining'. At the same time, the dot-pattern vocabulary is highly extensible, limits being imposed only by available physical space (obviously, we need the patterns to be small enough to fit on the object they identify), camera resolution, and the syntactic richness of the pattern space we establish.

An important implementation issue is the reliable isolation of genuine color dots from an unpredictable background. To wit: even with highly saturated colors chosen as pattern-dot 'primaries', the dots are at best still Lambertian reflectors. Thus there is no way to guarantee (1) that the same hue will not be present in garments, skin pigments, or unrelated objects in the environment, or (2) that brightly-illuminated surfaces in the environment may become isomers of the dots' hues through aliasing of the CCD's chromatic response curves. So irrespective of the sophistication of *glimpser*-level algorithms, false positives will be reported and genuine dots ignored with crippling frequency. Making the dots self-luminous (say, by embedding small LEDs) could solve the problem by boosting the luminance of each to an unambiguous level in the video input field, but would uncomfortably breach the maxim that objects used by Luminous Room applications should be passive.

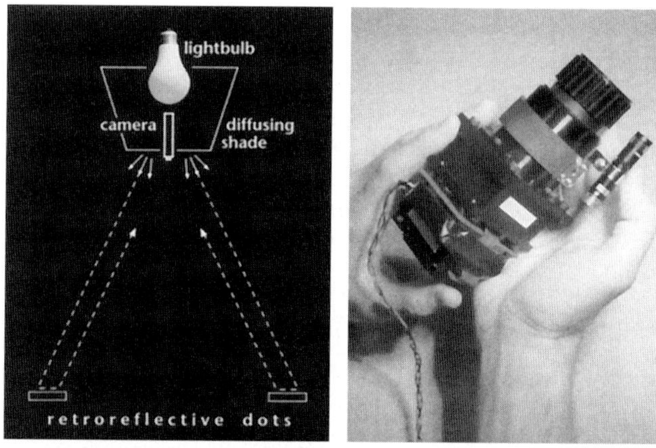


**Fig 13a: retroreflective tagging; 13b: real I/O Bulb prototype**

Instead, we've elected to use retroreflective dots complemented by a low-intensity, diffuse light source around the I/O Bulb's camera. A first round of dot-design employed a disk of panchromatic 3M ScotchLite material covered with a colored gel (red, green, or blue). At the same time, a moderate 60W (old-fashioned) lightbulb was incorporated into the I/O Bulb structure, placed directly above the slim video camera. A diffusive shade was constructed around the whole, with the lens of the camera protruding from the bottom.

Each dot is then illuminated by this annular diffuser and, irrespective of the angle of the light's incidence on it, reflects a gel-filtered version of most of this light directly back into the camera's lens. Because of this angularly selective reflection, human operators do not perceive the dots as other than normal surfaces; they seem no brighter than anything else. But from the privileged position of the camera, the dots glow fiercely: typically 2–4 stops brighter than any other part of the visual field. The critical result of all this is that it is now necessary to stop down the camera (either optically or electronically) in order to bring the high-luminance dots back within its dynamic range – and but doing so renders most of the rest of the input field black. Reliable dot isolation is thereby assured.

New, even more chromatically selective dots are now being constructed as a single layer, cut directly from recently available 3M tinted ScotchLite sheets. The color selectivity of these materials is good enough that we are also adding yellow and brown to our corral of recognized dot colors, extending *glimpser* accordingly.

### 5.2.3 voodoo

An application-independent geometric parsing toolkit called *voodoo* interprets the simple colored-dot-location output of the *glimpser* program. *voodoo* analyzes each unorganized per-frame collection of found color dots into a list of the unique patterns that have been registered with it by the application it serves. These patterns specify a sequence of colors; associated with each pair of adjacent color dots in a pattern is a distance, and with each contiguous triplet of dots an angle. These two parameters – the distance between each pair of dots and the angle through each triplet, along with the dots' color sequence – are enough to uniquely define any arbitrary pattern; as discussed earlier, we

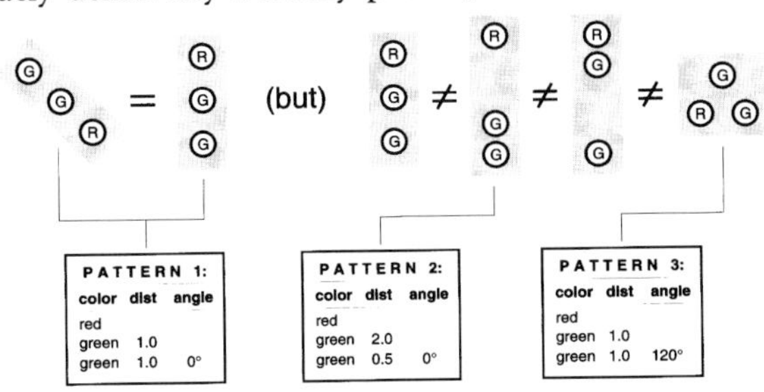


**Fig 14: dot-pattern definitions in *voodoo***

assign one such pattern to each of the client system's known objects, both physically (colored dots are affixed to the top of the object) and computationally (the pattern is registered with *voodoo*).

An adjustable tolerance, definable for each distance and angle specification, permits *voodoo* to absorb the inevitable inaccuracies and occasional single-pixel indecisions of machine vision algorithms. This tolerance mechanism further makes possible the definition of 'parametric' patterns: patterns that are correctly recognized throughout a range of angles or spacings, but which may then use the particular value of angle or spacing to set some flexible parameter (the variable curvature of a lens, etc.) [13].

*voodoo* also provides an 'object persistence' scheme, so that when low-level vision fails for a frame or two – or when users' hands intermittently occlude dots – the affected objects exhibit a bit of 'temporal inertia'. Objects can thus continue to exist for a short while even in the absence of positive visual data.

### 5.2.4 dee-voodoo

*voodoo* in its 'solitary' guise is responsible for reporting to its master application the identities and locations of all objects seen by its I/O Bulb. Making the same report to every other I/O Bulb as well is one way of connecting together multiple such instances in the same room. Thus *dee-voodoo* ('distributed *voodoo*') is a set of extensions to the existing software – entirely transparent to the higher-level implementer – whose first task is to connect over a dedicated TCP/IP port to all other *dee-voodoo* processes that can be found in close network proximity. Each of the various resulting links is then used to effect a bidirectional transfer of geometry information: the initiating (newest) *dee-voodoo* describes its I/O Bulb's position, orientation, and associated surface dimensions, all with respect to some globally acknowledged reference, and receives in return the distant I/O Bulb's complementary particulars.

Following that preliminary exchange, every object recognized by the *dee-voodoo* process serving I/O Bulb **A** is not only reported to application **A**, but is also relayed to I/O Bulb **B**'s (and **C**'s and **D**'s and ...) *dee-voodoo* process, which in turn reports the object to application **B** *as if the object had been seen by I/O Bulb* ***B***. This entails a small preparatory step in which **A** first transforms the reported object's geometric description into **B**'s local coordinate system. The object-exchange is also of course reciprocated from **B** to **A**, and so on, in an ongoing relay mesh with $n^2 - n$ links.

Although we have at present only two I/O Bulbs, we have tested use of *dee-voodoo* to synchronize up to five independent application processes, using 'manual' mouse-and-keyboard manipulation for objects of the three bulb-less processes. Even with the consequent twenty point-to-point links in simultaneous operation, the participating systems evinced negligible lag (less than or equal to one frame-update time) between the movements of local objects and those of distant objects.

Naturally, an $O(n^2)$ communication scheme like this one is unlikely to scale very well. With this in mind we've recently begun to experiment with alternate connection topologies, including centralized (star-shaped) and annularly-distributed (shift-ring) approaches.

It is through the use of *dee-voodoo* that we finally begin to assemble individual I/O Bulbs – the atomic units of our graphical-display-and-capture world – into a true Luminous Room structure.

## 6 DESIGN FOR LUMINOUS ROOMS

If the visual aspect of computation to date is theatrical – the screen an empty proscenium whose contextless nothing can be filled with anything, and therefore filled with the luxury of very few inherent expectations – then visual design for the Luminous Room must be more like narrative filmmaking or cinema verite: graphical co-occupation of a world already filled with people, things, and assumptions. Thus: design that's about accommodation and cooperation.

The future of reactive, real-world graphics will surely have its own Rands and Tuftes, Leacocks and Gilliams. For now, however, we have identified a few general guidelines.

### 6.1 Physical Objects

A central characteristic of all the applications we've built for the Luminous Room thus far is their extensive use of physical objects. This is an element curiously absent from nearly all other graphics-in-the-real-world research systems, which tend rather to rely for input either on gestural or symbolic means (mediated by VR suits & gloves, 'Twiddlers', etc. – things that are part of the computer's world but fundamentally *not* part of the real world). A single notable exception is – again – Pierre Wellner's superb DigitalDesk project [14].

Objects, usefully, are an excellent way to represent complex state. The distribution of optics models in the *Illuminating Light* application, for example, itself contains a great deal of information (irrespective of the graphical/digital parts of the system). If we imagine implementing the same system, on the same physical tabletop, but without the optics models, and relying instead solely on 'hand-tracked' gestural input: it's clear that the optics must then be represented graphically – and that simply moving them around is suddenly much harder for the operator.

We find further that proper deployment of physical objects in Luminous Room interfaces manifests itself in the tight cognitive binding of these implements with the attending projective information. One facet of this physical/digital association is a strong sense of causality: *Illuminating Light*'s optics seem to act directly on the beams they modify. The resulting interactions thus extend the illusion of a tight causality (rotating a mirror causes the beam it's reflecting to sweep across the workspace) even though there is an *implementational* distinction between input and output.

### 6.2 Graphical Dynamism

Each of the five applications discussed at the paper's outset is marked by a constant graphical dynamism. Indeed, pains have been taken to incorporate subtle motion into every graphical construct that does not, by the nature of its content and meaning, demand stasis (shadows, for example, are obviously not free to dance around; but even laser beams, which clearly must not translate laterally, are represented by a dashed line that swims ever forward). We find that, as a general design principle for Luminous Room interactions, these small visual gestures are desirable for the following reasons:

- *Apparent life.* Slight ongoing motions reassure the Luminous Room occupant that the room is still respondingly alive. They also lend a modicum of personality to the application: not strictly necessary, but always welcome.
- *Disambiguation of the real and the virtual.* Early tests with largely static graphical systems showed that with fairly dense, interpenetrating collections of physical objects and digital projections, confusions could sometimes arise over the status of the projections. Slight motions of a sort unlikely to attend physical objects help to signal graphics' identity.
- *Increased resolution.* Because the resolutions at which our current Luminous Room applications operate (32 dpi down to 4 dpi) are significantly lower than those commonly provided by other displays, human parsing of text is often hampered. But – since these glyphs are anti-aliased – even sub-pixel motions can dramatically increase their comprehensibility. Text aside, the perceived resolution of all projected Luminous Room graphics is increased when these constructs are in motion.
- *Aesthetics.* If we understand the aesthetics of an interaction to be a function of clarity and detail, then the combination of the three effects just described certainly leads to a 'pleasanter experience'. More ineffably, applications that apply subtle motions to different parts of their graphical apparatus simply look better than those whose elements are static.

## 6.3 Boundarylessness

The history of computer-based display is a history of bounding rectangles: buttons, text-blocks, panels, frames, windows, desktops, and – ultimately – the CRT screen itself. Real-world graphics must be deployed with a significantly different philosophy. Painting a projector's-worth of rectangular frame onto the floor or wall makes the framed region a *window onto* something else; our goal, contrariwise, is to make projected graphical constructs *part of* the physical surround, to gracefully integrate these graphics with (possibly mobile) parts of the physical world.

Considered another way, the question is one of compositing. Screen-based pixels lie only over the blackness of the screen. But real-world pixels must be composited with reality; thus, as with any compositing task, the irrelevant but literal rectangular shape of the *ground* in which the intended *figure* pixels lie must be hidden by making all *ground* pixels transparent.

In the end, any boundaries must belong to the room itself: the edge of a table, the join of a wall with the floor, the moulding near the ceiling: for graphics in the Luminous Room, *these* are the borders that count and that must be respected.

## 6.4 Kinds of Applications

Four of the five applications described in this paper have subscribed to a remarkably similar characteristic: with the exception of the Chess-&-Bottle system, each has addressed a domain or phenomenon whose concerns are directly spatial in nature. Optical design is a question of the proper geometric arrangement of component elements; urban planning deals with the positioning and orienting of large architectural structures to solve both aesthetic and pragmatic problems; and so on.

Generalizing from the current set of examples, and acknowledging that the Luminous Room's basic nature encourages interactions that involve physical objects arrayed and moved through space, we feel confident that a broad range of spatial applications will map naturally to similar workbench-style Luminous Room configurations.

While the Chess-&-Bottle application begins in a modest way to explore more abstract manipulations, understanding how to properly formulate non-spatial problems for treatment in a Luminous Room setting remains a longer-term challenge.

## 7 CONCLUSION

We have presented a broad overview of the Luminous Room, an infrastructure for distributing digitally-generated graphics and interaction throughout an architectural space. With one particular set of hardware and software techniques implementing the pervasive display and capture needs of the Luminous Room, and a handful of illustrative applications, we've described a small initial foray into an alternative graphical interaction field we believe to be extremely fertile.

## ACKNOWLEDGEMENTS

Dean William Mitchell of MIT's School of Architecture and Planning, for unassailable enthusiasm for each part of the project and for the informed conviction that each'd be worth doing in the first place; Andy Dahley, Peter Underkoffler, and Paul Yarin, who collectively applied the steel-toed kick of design to occasional physical artifacts that really deserved it; Nicholas Negroponte; Gustavo Santos and Dan Chak, whose future we expect to transcend our mere present; and – most of all – Wendy Plesniak, who in 1996 catalyzed the entire project idea with a short sentence and whose influence has hovered over it ever since.

## REFERENCES

[1] Agrawala, M., Beers, A., Frohlich, B., et. al. The Two-User Responsive Workbench: Support for Collaboration Through Individual Views of a Shared Space, in *Proceedings of SIGGRAPH*, 1997, 327-332.

[2] Bolt, R. "Put-That-There": Voice and Gesture at the Graphics Interface. *Proceedings of SIGGRAPH*, 1980, 262-270.

[3] Cruz-Neira, C., Sandin, D., and DeFanti, T. Surround-Screen Projection-Based Virtual Reality: The Design and Implementation of the CAVE, *Proceedings of SIGGRAPH*, 1993, p. 193.

[4] Feiner S, MacIntyre B, Seligmann D. Knowledge-Based Augmented Reality. *Communications of the ACM*, Vol. 36, No. 7, July 1993

[5] Frisch, E., Hasslacher, B., and Pomeau, Y. Lattice-Gas Automata for the Navier-Stokes Equation. *Physical Review Letters*, 56, 1505-8

[6] Ishii, H. and Ullmer, B. Tangible Bits: Towards Seamless Interfaces between People, Bits and Atoms. *Proceedings of CHI '97*, March 1997.

[7] Krueger, M. Artificial Reality II. Addison-Wesley, 1991.

[8] Jacobsen, J., Comiskey, B., et al. The Last Book. *IBM Systems Journal*, Vol. 36, No. 3, International Business Machines Corporation, 1997.

[9] Paradiso, J., and Hsiao, K.-Y. Swept-Frequency, Magnetically-Coupled Resonant Tags for Realtime, Continuous, Multiparameter Control. *Proceedings of CHI '99, Late Breaking Results*, May 1999.

[10] Pentland, A. Smart Rooms. *Scientific American*, v. 274 no. 4, pp. 68-76. April 1996.

[11] Raskar, R., Welch, G., Cutts, M., et al. The Office of the Future: A Unified Approach to Image-Based Modeling and Spatially Immersive Displays. *Proceedings of SIGGRAPH*, 1998, 179-188.

[12] Smith, J., White, T., Dodge, C., Allport, D., Paradiso, J., and Gershenfeld, N. Electric Field Sensing for Graphical Interfaces. To Appear in *Computer Graphics and Animation*, Special Issue on Novel Input Devices.

[13] Underkoffler, J. and Ishii, H. Illuminating Light: An Optical Design Tool with a Luminous-Tangible Interface. *Proceedings of CHI '98*, April 1998.

[14] Wellner, P. Interacting with Paper on the DigitalDesk. *Communications of the ACM*. Vol. 36, No. 7: 87-96, July 1993.

# Skin: A Constructive Approach to Modeling Free-form Shapes

*Lee Markosian* *Jonathan M. Cohen* *Thomas Crulli* *John Hughes**

Brown University site of the NSF and Technology Center for
Computer Graphics and Scientific Visualization,
Box 1910, Providence, RI 02912

## Abstract

We present a new particle-based surface representation with which a user can interactively sculpt free-form surfaces. The particles maintain mesh connectivity and operate under rules that lead them to form triangulations with properties that make them suitable for use in subdivision. A user interactively guides the particles, which we call *skin*, to grow over a given collection of polyhedral elements (or *skeletons*), yielding a smooth surface (through subdivision) that approximates the underlying skeletal shapes. Skin resembles blobby modeling in the constructive approach to modeling it supports, but allows a richer vocabulary of skeleton shapes, supports sharp creases where desired, and provides a convenient mechanism for adding multiresolution surface detail.

**CR Categories and Subject Descriptors:** I.3.5 [Computer Graphics]: Computational Geometry and Object Modeling I.3.6 [Computer Graphics]: Methodology and Techniques

**Additional Key Words:** Free-form modeling, meshes, subdivision, multiresolution

## 1 Introduction

The algorithm described in this paper derives from our ongoing effort to build a free-form modeling system with a direct interface – that is, one in which the user defines shapes by sketching them directly as they would appear from a given viewpoint. In particular, we seek to extend the principles developed in the SKETCH system [26] – rapid construction of approximate shapes via direct interaction – to the problem of free-form modeling. The Teddy system presented in these proceedings [11] targets similar goals, though we seek to provide more fine-grained control over the resulting shape, including the ability to add surface detail at multiple scales. An important goal is that the interface should allow a user with skill at drawing on paper to apply this skill to model compelling 3D forms.

With that in mind, we seek to build a system in which the user models complex surfaces by first constructing simplified representations of the underlying masses that give them their form, then "oversketches" these masses with a smooth surface that approximates their collective shape. We chose this approach because of its tractability (SKETCH and Teddy, as well as our system for sketching 3D curves [6], describe techniques that could be applied to define the "underlying masses"), and because it is natural – that is, it resembles techniques commonly used by artists and recommended in books on art instruction [1, 5, 7, 8, 16, 18, 22].

*{lem,jmc,tc,jfh}@cs.brown.edu



This paper describes our solution to a sub-problem that arises in implementing our approach: given a collection of "masses" (or *skeletons*) represented as polygon meshes, each with an associated offset (typically small), construct a smooth surface that approximates the distance surface defined by the skeletons and their offsets. Distance surfaces, discussed in [3] and defined in section 3 below, typically have sharp creases that are not desired. Thus the final surface should smoothly approximate the distance surface, not fit it exactly. The solution should work in an interactive setting, continually updating the surface as skeletons are added, manipulated, or removed.

Our solution, the *skin* algorithm, works by constructing a subdivision surface control mesh that roughly fits the shape of the distance surface. The control mesh in turn defines a smooth surface with a similar shape. A key contribution of this paper is to provide an algorithm for generating a *suitable* control mesh for use in subdivision. Simply matching a given shape is not sufficient – the triangulation of the control mesh has a strong influence on the qualities of the resulting surface. Smaller triangles provide less "smoothing" effect, yielding a surface that more closely fits the control mesh, and – more importantly – irregular triangulations can greatly reduce the fairness of the limit surface. This can be seen in figure 1.

The skin algorithm is good for *rapid* construction of *approximate* free-form shapes. It is not suitable for applications that require exact control of the final shape. Skin supports fast, intuitive editing of features at multiple resolutions and produces piecewise smooth surfaces with creases or sharp corners where desired. Since the algorithm manipulates a polygon mesh, rendering can be done efficiently on common graphics hardware.

Together with these advantages, the skin algorithm has some drawbacks: it is based on an iterative algorithm that is not guaranteed to converge to a fixed triangulation – and sometimes doesn't. The exact results depend not just on the primitives used to define the surface, but also on the order of the user's operations. Finally, the behavior of the skin depends on the size of its triangles (which the user can control). It would be preferable not to expose the user to the issue of triangle size as a means of controlling surface shape. The other difficulties can be alleviated by providing tools to let the user control the skin's behavior, as we will illustrate. Because we designed skin for use in an interactive setting, we do not consider any of these problems to be severe.

## 2 Related work

The skin algorithm resembles the methods for iteratively evolving a triangulation described in [9, 10, 20, 23, 24]. It has much in common with Miller *et al.*'s "volumetrically deformed models" [14] in which a balloon-like surface is inflated under constraints to match a volumetrically defined implicit function. Also, because the skin al-

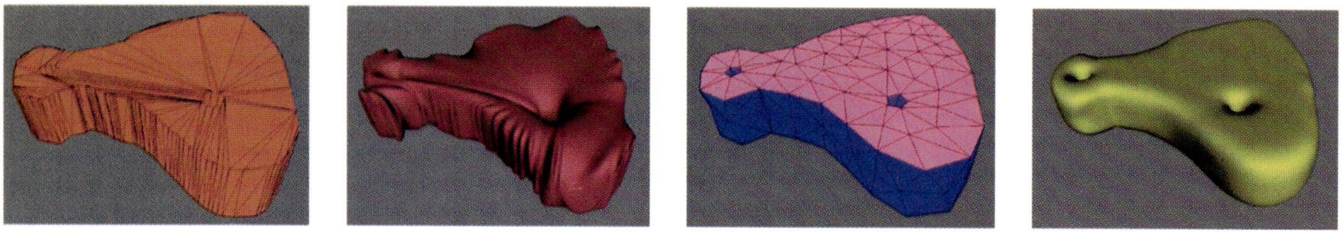

(a) (b) (c) (d)

**Figure 1** Triangulation matters. Two triangulations of the same shape ((a) and (c)) produce different results when subdivided ((b) and (d)). The skin algorithm produces even triangulations, avoiding skinny triangles like those in (a) that lead to unexpected wiggles and bumps when subdivided.

gorithm treats vertices as particles that interact with their neighbors while being guided by an implicit function, it resembles the particle system methods described in [21, 25]. (An important difference is that skin particles have explicit connectivity information.) Skin is related to the large body of work on implicit surfaces, particularly offset and convolution surfaces [3, 17] and blobby modeling [2, 4], in the constructive approach to modeling it provides.

For multiresolution editing, we use Loop subdivision meshes [13], including the rules for defining creases and corners described in [9, 19]. Previous work on subdivision surfaces has primarily focused on specifying subdivision rules and analyzing properties of the limit surface, *given a control mesh*. Hoppe *et al.* [9] present a means to construct a good-quality control mesh for a subdivision surface that approximates a given polygon mesh (typically scanned from a real model). We are not aware of any work that discusses ways to construct suitable control meshes for subdivision surfaces *from scratch*. Recently Zorin *et al.* [27] and Pulli [15] presented systems that let the user add detail to a subdivision surface (given the control mesh). With these systems the user edits details of the subdivision surface (at a given resolution) by manipulating individual vertices directly. The skin algorithm, though originally designed to construct a good-quality control mesh in the first place, is readily extended to provide a mechanism for adding detail at finer scales more conveniently than by individual control point manipulations.

## 3 Terms and definitions

Our meshes are triangle meshes, represented in the usual way: each consists of a collection of vertices, edges and faces with local connectivity information. That is, each vertex stores pointers to its adjacent edges; each edge stores pointers to the two vertices that define it and to at most two adjacent faces; each face stores pointers to the three edges and vertices that define it. *Skeletons*, represented with this mesh data structure, may be non-self-intersecting closed surfaces, surfaces with boundary, polylines or even isolated points. With each skeleton is associated a positive real-valued *offset*. The skin algorithm iteratively modifies the *skin* mesh (a closed surface) to roughly fit the distance surface defined by the skeletons and their offsets. Each skeleton also has an associated *target length* that specifies the desired size of triangles the skin should generate when growing over that skeleton. We refer to vertices of the skin mesh as *particles*. It is convenient to associate with each particle a *reference length* that measures the scale of the skin mesh near that particle. We take the reference length to be the average length of the particle's adjacent edges.

Let $S$ denote the set of skeletons. For a given skeleton $s \in S$ with associated offset $r_s$, and a point $\mathbf{x}$ in space, let $d_s(\mathbf{x})$ denote the signed distance from $\mathbf{x}$ to $s$. That is, $d_s(\mathbf{x})$ is the distance from $\mathbf{x}$ to the nearest point on $s$, but if $s$ is a closed surface and $\mathbf{x}$ is inside it, the "distance" is taken to be negative. Now let $f_s(\mathbf{x}) = d_s(\mathbf{x}) - r_s$. The *distance surface* defined by a single skeleton and its offset is just the implicit surface defined by $f_s(\mathbf{x}) = 0$. The distance surface defined by the collection of skeletons and their offsets is the implicit surface defined by $F(\mathbf{x}) = 0$, where $F$ is the continuous function given by:

$$F(\mathbf{x}) = \min\{f_s(\mathbf{x}) : s \in S\}.$$

The rules for positioning particles described in section 4.1 are designed so that the skin approximates this surface. They also allow us to evaluate the implicit function efficiently.

## 4 The skin algorithm

At a high level, the skin algorithm closely resembles algorithms described in [10] and [24] for iteratively evolving a triangle mesh. The primary difference is in the implementation of step (1) of the main loop:

```
repeat
    (1) reposition particles
    (2) modify the skin's connectivity
until no changes occur
```

Intuitively, in step (1) particles move toward the implicit surface while tending to distribute themselves more evenly and smoothing out wrinkles and bumps in the skin. In step (2), the connectivity of the skin is modified to produce triangles that are more nearly equilateral and whose size is roughly the target length specified by nearby skeletons. We now describe steps (1) and (2) in detail.

### 4.1 Repositioning particles

The rules for repositioning particles are designed to allow the skin to grow adaptively to conform to the changing implicit surface as skeletons are added, repositioned, removed, or their offsets are edited. In step (1) of the skin algorithm, each particle is visited in turn. The new position $\mathbf{x}'_p$ of particle $p$ is computed as a weighted sum of its current position $\mathbf{x}_p$, the centroid $\mathbf{c}_p$ of its neighbors' positions, and a target position $\mathbf{t}_p$ chosen to bring the particle closer to the implicit surface:

$$\mathbf{x}'_p = \alpha\mathbf{x}_p + \beta\mathbf{c}_p + \gamma\mathbf{t}_p.$$

The weights $\alpha$, $\beta$, and $\gamma$ are non-negative and sum to one. We always take $\alpha = 0.3$, and choose $\beta$ according to how smooth the skin is near $p$. (Then $\gamma$ is taken to be $1 - \alpha - \beta$.) We estimate the smoothness of the skin near $p$ by calculating the minimum, over each edge adjacent to $p$, of the dot product of the normals of the two faces adjacent to that edge. This value (call it $m$) lies between 1 and $-1$. When $m$ is close to 1, the skin is smooth near $p$; when

$m$ is close to $-1$, the skin contains one or more sharp edges near $p$. A large value for $\beta$ results in a greater smoothing effect, so we choose $\beta = (1-\alpha)\beta_{scale}$, where $\beta_{scale}$ is the function of $m$ shown in figure 2. This function, chosen heuristically, seems to produce good results. It has the effect of letting the skin move briskly toward the implicit surface where the skin is reasonably smooth. Where the skin is bumpy or uneven, it slows or stops moving until it smooths out again, then resumes its motion toward the implicit surface.

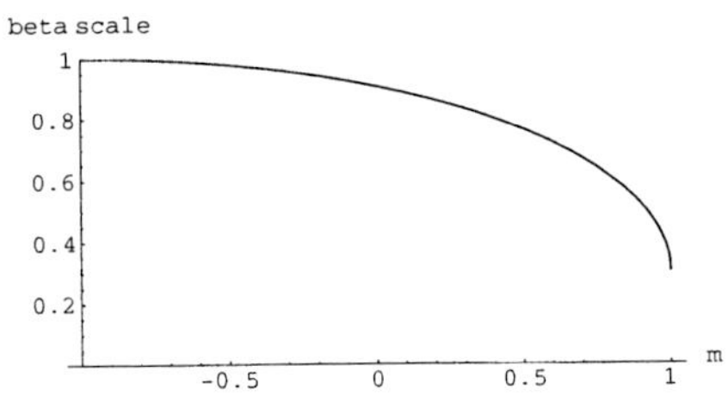


**Figure 2** The coefficient $\beta_{scale}$ chosen as a function of the minimum dot product $m$. This function is a quarter ellipse.

The target position $\mathbf{t}_p$ is chosen so that the skin tends to expand when inside the implicit surface, stay fixed when on it, and contract when outside it. We can determine whether the particle is inside, on, or outside the implicit surface according to whether $F(\mathbf{x}_p)$ is negative, zero, or positive, respectively. Also, by definition, the magnitude of this value specifies a lower bound on the distance from the particle to the nearest point on the implicit surface. We thus set the target position to be a displacement along the particle's surface normal $\vec{\mathbf{n}}_p$ by an amount $d$ determined by $F(\mathbf{x}_p)$:

$$\mathbf{t}_p = \mathbf{x}_p + d\vec{\mathbf{n}}_p.$$

We can take $d = -F(\mathbf{x}_p)$ unless this value is large (that is, the particle is far from the implicit surface). To prevent the particle from taking excessively large steps, we restrict the magnitude of $d$ to be no more than the reference length of the particle.

Because $\beta$ is always nonzero, skin particles tend not to arrive exactly at the implicit surface. (Where it is concave they lie outside it, and where it is convex they lie inside it.) As mentioned earlier, we prefer this behavior, since the distance surface defined by the skeletons typically has unwanted sharp creases. For this reason, we can think of the implicit function as guiding rather than defining the skin's final shape.

### 4.2 Evaluating the implicit function

The skin algorithm is intended to work with skeletons that may be finely tessellated (as when representing muscle masses, such as those in figure 15). For the algorithm to be usable in an interactive setting, it is important to evaluate the implicit function efficiently. The particles do this by exploiting locality in two ways. To explain this, let's first assume there is only a single skeleton, $s$. Each particle $p$ tracks a point $\mathbf{y}_p$ on $s$ that is locally closest to $p$.[1] We refer to $\mathbf{y}_p$ as $p$'s *track point*.[2] After updating its position $\mathbf{x}_p$, $p$ updates its track point using the LOCAL-SEARCH procedure (figure 3), passing in a face $f$ containing the track point:

$$\mathbf{y}_p \leftarrow \text{LOCAL-SEARCH}(f, \mathbf{x}_p).$$

Evaluating $f_s(\mathbf{x}_p)$ is now simple: For a non-closed skeleton surface, we evaluate the distance $d$ from $\mathbf{x}_p$ to $\mathbf{y}_p$, and subtract $r_s$. For a closed surface, we negate $d$ if the particle is inside it, and then subtract $r_s$. (Each skeleton surface is checked in a pre-process step to determine whether it is closed.) For closed surfaces, we can determine when a particle is inside provided that the particle has actually tracked the globally closest point $\mathbf{y}_p$ on the skeleton. For then the plane containing $\mathbf{y}_p$ that is perpendicular to the vector from $\mathbf{y}_p$ to $\mathbf{x}_p$ divides space into two parts. The skeleton locally near $\mathbf{y}_p$ lies all in one part and the particle lies in the other. An examination of the face normals around $\mathbf{y}_p$ determines whether $p$ is inside or outside the surface.

[1] By locally closest, we mean that all points on $s$ in a neighborhood of $\mathbf{y}_p$ are farther away.

[2] In fact, $p$ stores a pointer to a face of $s$ containing $\mathbf{y}_p$.

```
LOCAL-SEARCH(f, x)
    y ← closest point to x on f
    if y is on boundary of f
        foreach adjacent face f_i containing y
            if closest point to x on f_i ≠ y
                return LOCAL-SEARCH(f_i, x)
    return y
```

**Figure 3** The LOCAL-SEARCH algorithm, starting from face $f$ on a mesh $M$, traverses faces of $M$, always moving closer to point $\mathbf{x}$, to reach a point $\mathbf{y}$ on $M$ that is locally closest to $\mathbf{x}$.

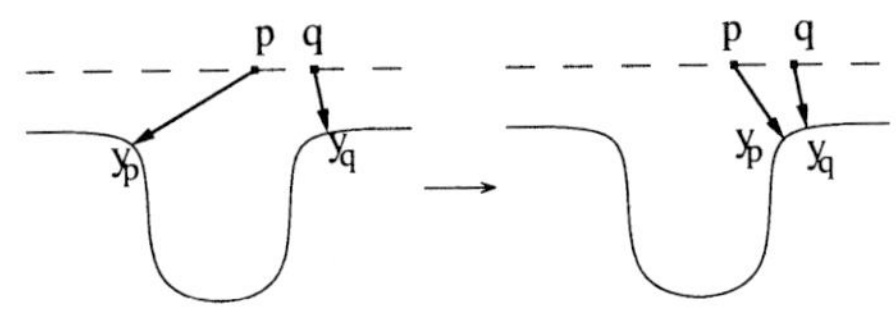


**Figure 4** A particle $p$ can use its neighbor's track point $\mathbf{y}_q$ to get out of a local minimum.

Of course, the LOCAL-SEARCH procedure may return a point on the skeleton that is only *locally* closest to $p$ (see figure 4). To overcome this, particles exploit a second kind of locality: they share information with their immediate neighbors. Thus, to evaluate $f_s(\mathbf{x}_p)$, $p$ runs the LOCAL-SEARCH procedure starting from its own track point, and then again starting from the track points of each of its neighbors in turn. The particle selects the result yielding the smallest distance, and stores this as its new track point.

When there are multiple skeletons, $p$ can switch to a track point on a different skeleton if doing so yields a smaller *value* for the implicit function. It can switch to a different track point on the same skeleton, though, only if doing so yields a smaller *distance*. The distinction between these cases occurs only when the skeleton is a closed surface. In this case, the particle should first find the closest point on the skeleton, then evaluate the implicit function from the signed distance to this point. Figure 5 shows examples of these two cases.

When a new skeleton is added, it is sufficient for a single particle (lying inside the skeleton's distance surface) to begin tracking its closest point on the skeleton. That particle will then recruit its neighbors to track points on the new skeleton, and in the next iteration they will recruit their neighbors, and so on.

It sometimes happens that a particle has no track point: for example, when a skeleton is removed, particles tracking points on it forget their track points. In this case particles simply take $\beta = 1-\alpha$, which causes them to move towards the centroids of their neighbors. The region of skin that covered that skeleton will wither away, until all of its particles are either destroyed in edge collapses (described in the next section) or acquire new track points on other skeletons from their neighbors.

There are two other cases in which particles forget their track points. If a particle is outside of the implicit surface but its surface normal points toward its track point, the particle would, according to the rules described above, tend to back away from the track point,

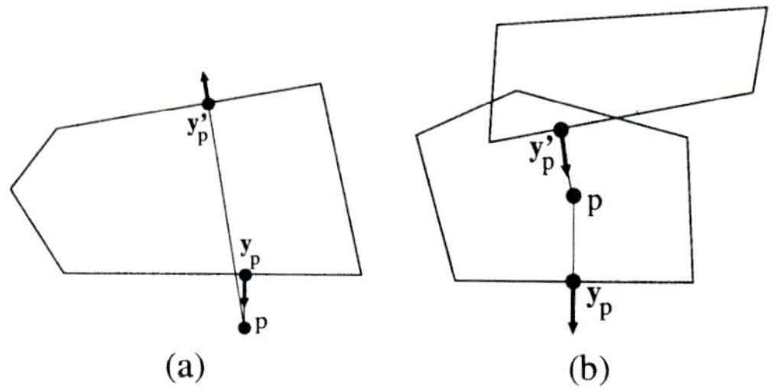


**Figure 5** In (a), $p$ is deciding between tracking $\mathbf{y}_p$ or $\mathbf{y}'_p$. Since both points lie on the same skeleton, it will choose $\mathbf{y}_p$. Note that the surface normal at $\mathbf{y}'_p$ is facing away from $p$, so tracking $\mathbf{y}'_p$ would yield a negative value for the implicit function, while $\mathbf{y}_p$ would yield a positive value. In (b), $\mathbf{y}'_p$ is closer. However, $\mathbf{y}_p$ is on a different skeleton, and will yield a lower implicit function value because its surface normal is facing away from $p$. $p$ should therefore choose to track $\mathbf{y}_p$.

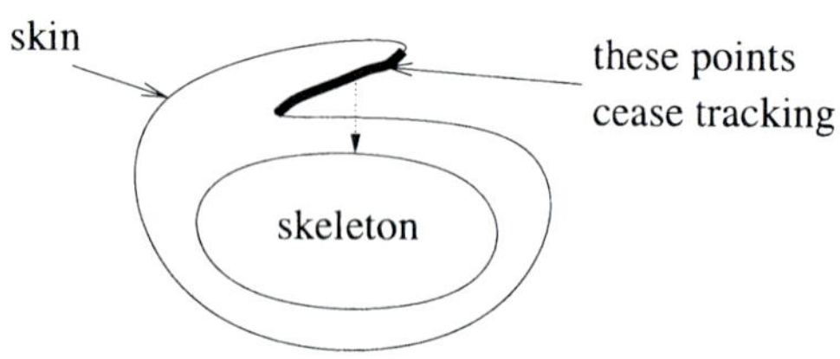


**Figure 6** When the skin folds over so that an exterior particle's normal points towards the skeleton, the particle ignores the track point to avoid "backing away."

moving farther and farther from the implicit surface (see figure 6). To prevent this, particles in this case simply forget their track points and take $\beta = 1-\alpha$ as above. The second case occurs when a particle is adjacent to a *stressed* edge – that is, an edge whose two adjacent faces form an angle of less than 60 degrees. We discuss this case further in section 5.

### 4.3 Modifying the mesh connectivity

In step (2) of the skin algorithm we modify the skin's connectivity by performing the edge operations shown in figure 7. These operations were described in [10, 24]; conditions under which the operations are valid are discussed in [10].

We swap an edge when doing so increases the minimum angle within its adjacent faces. As noted by Welch and Witkin [24], repeated application of this swap operation (always increasing the minimum angle) computes a constrained Delaunay triangulation. That is, it maximizes the minimum angle over all the triangles of the mesh.

Each edge has an associated target length. We split an edge if it is longer than 1.5 times its target length, and collapse the edge if it is less than half its target length. These numbers are chosen in part so that a collapse operation will not immediately be invoked on an edge that has just been split. We compute the target length for each edge as follows.

As mentioned in section 3, each skeleton has an associated target length that the user can set. This specifies the desired size of triangles for portions of skin growing over that skeleton. We also store a target length value in each particle. In the repositioning step, each particle sets its target length to a weighted sum of its current value, the average target length of the particle's neighbors, and the target length of the skeleton currently tracked by the particle. (We use weights of 0.4, 0.4 and 0.2, respectively.) The target length of an edge is taken to be the average of the target lengths of its two adjacent particles.

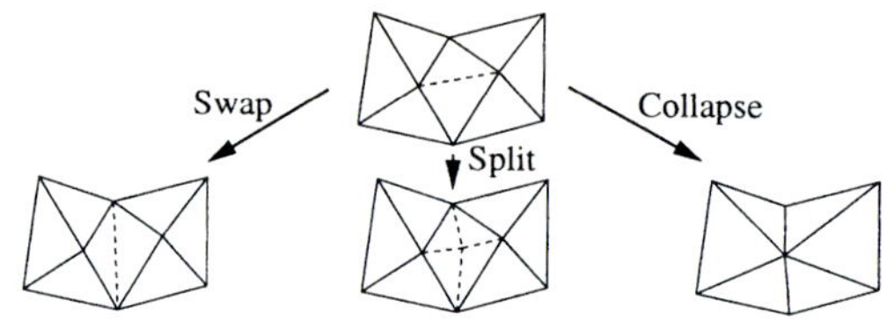


**Figure 7** We *swap* to improve the minimum angle of a triangle. A *split* introduces a new vertex by splitting a long edge. A *collapse* removes a vertex by destroying a short edge.

Splitting and collapsing edges as described tends to produce edges of approximately the desired length. Interleaving steps (1) and (2) of the skin algorithm further tends to equalize edge lengths, allowing particles to redistribute themselves more evenly after edge operations are performed. In fact, we control the number of split and collapse operations that can occur between repositioning steps by sorting edges by the ratio of their actual length to their target length, then considering split operations just on the last 5% of edges and collapse operations just on the first 5% of edges. Any edge that is too long (or too short) is still guaranteed to be split (or collapsed) eventually.

Each edge operation affects the valence of nearby vertices. Since Loop subdivision performs best on meshes with a majority of valence-six vertices, we modify the rules slightly to favor the formation of such vertices. For example, a proposed edge swap is evaluated according to: (1) how much it will increase or decrease the minimum angle interior to its adjacent faces, and (2) the extent to which it will increase (or decrease) the number of valence-six vertices around it. The other operations are "handicapped" in a similar way. Such handicapping yields a small but noticeable improvement in the quality of the resulting subdivision surfaces.

### 4.4 Geometric constraints – creases

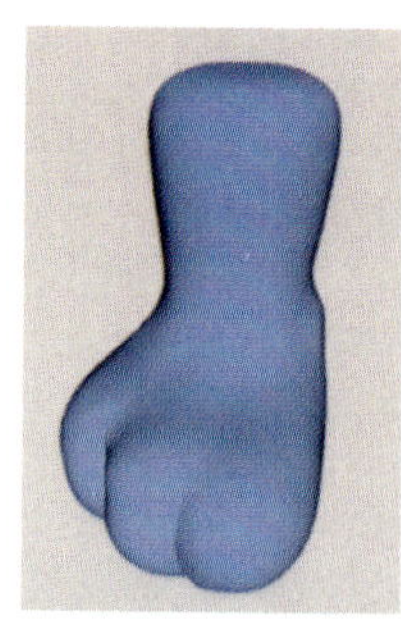

**Figure 8** Indentations were created in the foot model using crease curves.

The user might want to constrain the skin's triangulation to include a sequence of edges aligned along some curve. Such an ability is required to model piecewise-smooth surfaces that include sharp "creases." Many organic forms, including human figures, can be described as having such features. To support this, we let the user first create a curve interactively by drawing onto the skin surface. We then split the triangles of the skin through which the curve passes to produce a sequence of edges aligned along this curve. Finally, the skin retriangulates in the neighborhood of the curve to maintain a good triangulation subject to the constraint that edges remain aligned along the curve. The user can then interact with the curve to change the shape of the surface. The foot model in figure 8 was created by drawing curves to model the creases between the toes, and then interactively pushing each curve into the foot to create the indentations. In this way, the user can create features that are not present in the implicit surface. Because the rules for repositioning vertices do not force them to interpolate the implicit surface, the region of skin around the crease blends smoothly to meet it.

For particles and edges lying on a crease, we modify the skin algorithm as follows. First, edges lying along a crease are not allowed to swap. Second, a particle $p$ lying on a crease curve $C$ is constrained to stay on $C$. If $p$ lies on an endpoint of $C$, its position is constrained to remain at that endpoint. Otherwise, it computes its target position $\mathbf{t}_p$ by taking a convex combination of its current position $\mathbf{x}_p$ and the midpoint $\mathbf{c}_p$ between its two neighboring particles on the crease curve. Then, instead of moving under the influence of the implicit function, $p$ sets its new position $\mathbf{x}'_p$ to be the point on the curve that is closest to $\mathbf{t}_p$:

$$\mathbf{x}'_p = \underset{\mathbf{x} \in C}{\operatorname{argmin}} |\mathbf{t}_p - \mathbf{x}|.$$

We use a global search to compute this point, but a number of other techniques, such as gradient descent, could be applied depending on the underlying curve representation.

### 4.5 Termination

In the repositioning step, we actually assign a particle its new position only if it is appreciably different from the current position. Specifically, the new position must differ from the current one by more than .01 times the particle's reference length. This prevents the skin from continuing to make visually unnoticeable adjustments to the particle's positions after the surface is essentially stable.

Still, we have observed two cases in which the algorithm does not terminate. The first can occur when the topology of the skeletons' distance surface differs from that of the skin. The rules for modifying the skin's connectivity do not change its surface topology. If the user grows a skin over two skeletons that are initially close together, and then pulls them far apart, the skin does not spontaneously separate into two pieces. (In section 7 we describe how the user can explicitly invoke this type of topological change.) Instead, it remains joined by a thin strand, along which particles continue to move as edges are repeatedly split and collapsed. If the strand is cut, the skin heals itself and stabilizes.

The other case can occur when adjacent regions of skin have very different target lengths. In this case particles may continuously "swim" out from the region with small triangles toward the one with larger ones. This happens when a particle between the regions drifts toward the centroid of its neighbors in the region with larger triangles. As this happens, the particle's shorter edges are stretched, leading them to split and create new particles that repeat the process. We do not currently provide a solution to this, other than letting the user "freeze" the skin in that region.

Another problem involves premature termination. This can occur when the target length associated with a skeleton is large relative to one of its dimensions. In that case, the region of skin attempting to grow over the skeleton may necessarily have sharp edges. The tendency for particles to move to their neighbors' centroids may then outweigh their tendency to move toward the implicit surface, and the skin stops. An effective remedy is for the user to reduce the target length associated with the skeleton.

## 5 Preventing self-intersection

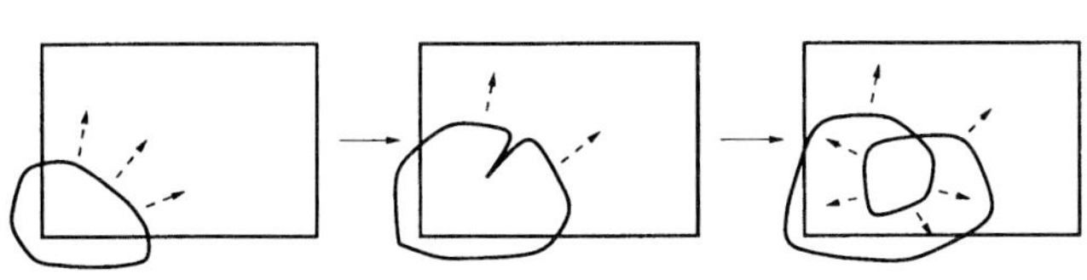

**Figure 9** Uneven expansion of a skin can lead to self-intersection.

One problem with the skin algorithm as stated is shown in figure 9. During rapid expansion, one region of the skin may grow at a different rate from a neighboring region. The skin begins to buckle, and

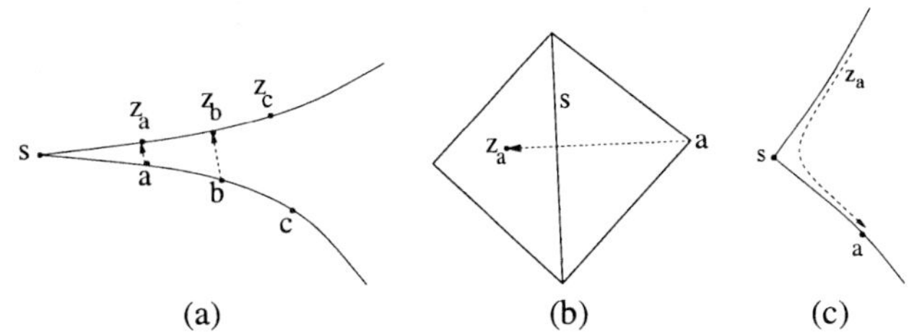


**Figure 10** In (a), $a$ and $b$ track their penetration points $\mathbf{z}_a$ and $\mathbf{z}_b$. $c$ is too far away from $\mathbf{z}_c$, so it has no penetration point. In (b), the stressed edge $s$ tells adjacent particle $a$ to track $\mathbf{z}_a$. In (c), the surface has smoothed out, so $a$'s LOCAL-SEARCH returns to $a$.

soon two adjacent regions of skin interpenetrate, forming a "bubble" that expands to produce a second, unwanted layer of skin.

In this section we discuss how we can prevent such self-intersection efficiently by reusing the particles' abilities to track a locally closest point on some mesh, and by sharing information as in section 4.2. A key observation is that local interpenetration typically occurs between two portions of surface separated by a chain of stressed edges. Our strategy is to initiate a non-penetration behavior only as needed, starting at stressed edges and propagating along opposing surface regions. We illustrate the idea in figure 10.

In figure 10(a), we see the skin surface, in cross section, starting to buckle along the stressed edge $s$. Particle $a$, which shares a face with $s$, receives notification from $s$ to begin tracking its closest point $\mathbf{z}_a$ on the opposite face, shown in figure 10(b). We call $\mathbf{z}_a$ the *penetration point* of $a$.

As particles are repositioned, each updates its penetration point using the LOCAL-SEARCH procedure starting from its previous penetration point, as well as each of its neighbors' penetration points, if they have them. If a local search starting from any of these points returns a point that is not the particle's location, but is at a distance of less than 1.5 times the particle's reference length, the particle stores this point as its new penetration point. Particles are in this way always attempting to borrow penetration points from their neighbors.

Thus, $b$ acquires a penetration point $\mathbf{z}_b$ by using the LOCAL-SEARCH starting from $\mathbf{z}_a$. When $c$ does the same – borrowing from $b$ – the result $\mathbf{z}_c$ is too distant (more than 1.5 times $c$'s reference length) so $c$ "forgets" the penetration point.

Whenever a particle with a valid penetration point passes through the surface containing its penetration point, it suspends the normal repositioning rules and moves back to the correct side of the surface. The result is that a crease temporarily forms in the skin but then resolves itself (figure 11). As the surface flattens out, particles track their penetration points back to themselves (figure 10(c)), upon which they forget their penetration point and revert to the normal repositioning rules.

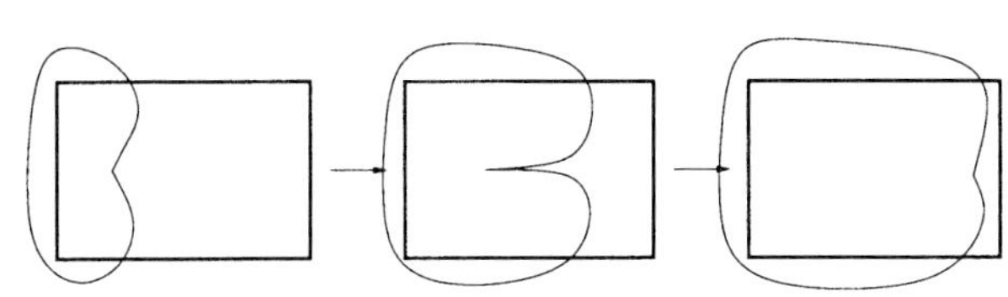

**Figure 11** With the non-penetration behavior, a crease forms along the stressed edge, and then resolves itself as the skin grows.

## 6 Multiresolution editing

The approach to modeling we have targeted – sculpting complex surfaces by constructing the underlying masses that define their shape – naturally allows the user to work in a coarse-to-fine manner. That is, the user can begin with a coarse cylindrical shape to represent a torso, and then refine the surface, adding masses to define the shapes of individual muscles, bones, and tendons. The subdivision surface framework is naturally compatible with such an approach. With each level of refinement, the surface can effectively "resolve" detail at finer scales. The systems described in [15, 27] allow the user to add detail to a subdivision surface at multiple scales by manipulating vertices individually. We now explain how to extend the skin algorithm with little modification to support *subdivision skeletons*. A subdivision skeleton is like a regular skeleton except that it is active only at specific levels of subdivision. When the skin is subdivided, its vertices act as *subdivision particles* that track points on the subdivision skeletons active at that level.

Intuitively, subdivision particles that lie inside the implicit surface of a skeleton should move in the normal way (toward the implicit surface). A particle far from any subdivision skeleton should remain at the position it was initially assigned through subdivision, which we call its *base point*. In some range near the skeleton, a particle should smoothly blend between its base point and the displacement induced by the skeleton in the region of skin near the particle.

We achieve this as follows. Each particle evaluates the implicit function $F$ as before, sharing information with its neighbors and tracking a point on some skeleton active at the current level of subdivision. Each particle has an associated "cutoff distance" $M$, equal to 3 times its reference length, beyond which it is unaffected by any skeleton. As before (section 4.1), its new position is computed from a weighted average of its current position, the centroid of its neighbors, and its target position:

$$\mathbf{x}'_p = \alpha \mathbf{x}_p + \beta \mathbf{c}_p + \gamma \mathbf{t}_p.$$

| $F(\mathbf{x}_p)$ | $\alpha$ | $\gamma$ | $\mathbf{t}_p$ |
|---|---|---|---|
| 0 | .3 | .4 | $\mathbf{x}_p$ |
| $\geq M$ | 0 | 1 | $\mathbf{b}_p$ |

We now choose the target position and weights $\alpha$, $\beta$, and $\gamma$ according to the value of the implicit function: when $F(\mathbf{x}_p) < 0$, the particle sets its target as before and uses weights $\alpha = 0.3$, $\beta = 0.3$, and $\gamma = 0.4$. When the implicit function is 0 or $M$ we choose values for $\alpha$ and $\gamma$ according to the above table, setting $\beta = 1 - \alpha - \gamma$. For values of $F(\mathbf{x}_p)$ between 0 and $M$ we choose the target position and weights by interpolating the corresponding values listed in the table.

## 7 Topology changes

At each iteration, the skin evolves through local operations, using local information. Global properties of the skin surface, such as its genus, are not taken into account (or modified). Consequently, we do not automatically detect topological changes to the implicit surface. Figure 12 shows an example of a skin growing over a toroidal skeleton. When the new skeleton is first added, it changes the genus of the implicit surface. The skin grows around the torus and through itself in an attempt to fit the implicit surface. We could perhaps detect this interpenetration and prevent it. However, since it is global and not local, the method given in section 5 will not work.

Instead, we allow the user to explicitly change the genus of the skin by joining two sections of surface or by cutting a region of skin into two parts. Because the skin will evolve a poor triangulation into a good one, we can perform these operations without worrying about leaving a good triangulation.

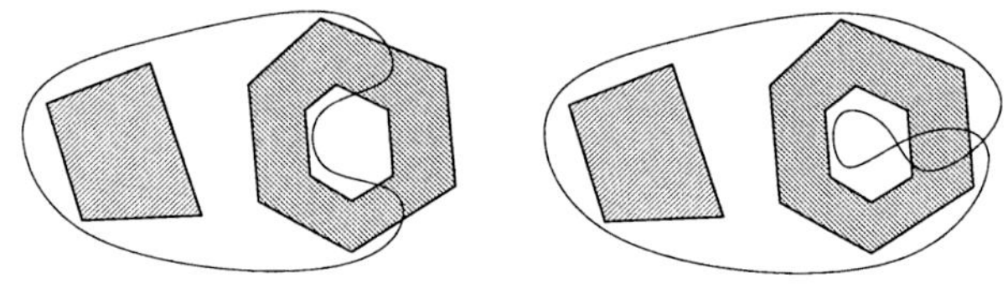

**Figure 12** The skin does not detect the topology of the isosurface, which is toroidal, and hence will interpenetrate unless the user intervenes.

To cut the skin, we split the edges and faces that cross a user-specified cutting plane, and stitch up the resulting holes with a simple triangulation. (If desired, we can place crease curves along the cut to preserve its shape.) To join two portions of skin surface, we remove a face on each portion to create two holes, then connect the holes with a bridge of triangles. In either case, when editing the topology of the skin it's important to edit the skeletons accordingly so that the implicit surface matches the skin's new topology.

## 8 Software framework

We developed the skin algorithm within a larger system consisting of a collection of C++ libraries that provide extensive support for 3D modeling and interaction. The mesh class consists of a collection of vertices, edges, and faces (generically called simplices) that store connectivity information as described in section 3. To implement skin, we first introduced a separate class, Tessellator, that operates on a mesh's simplices according to some procedure, typically by editing connectivity and vertex positions. We made a small modification to the existing simplex classes to allow a tessellator to store arbitrary data directly on them.

The skin algorithm is implemented by a skin tessellator, which is a type of 2D tessellator – that is, it operates on a region of surface. Other types of tessellators include point tessellators and curve tessellators, which are 0D and 1D tessellators, respectively. Each Tessellator receives a callback every frame in which it iterates over its simplices and edits them according to its procedure. We enforce the rule that if multiple tessellators attempt to edit the same simplex, the tessellator with the lowest dimension wins. For example, we represent a curve constraint with a 1D tessellator that acts on its vertices and edges to approximate the curve. A skin tessellator operating on the surrounding surface is not allowed to edit the vertices and edges of the curve.

A vertex is considered active only if it has moved within the last 32 frames. Edges and faces are considered active if some contained vertex is active. We also activate simplices when the user performs an operation that could cause particles to move, such as changing a skeleton's offset distance or target length, or interactively moving a constraint curve. Tessellators operate only on simplices that are active. Since users typically edit just a local region of a surface at a time, this can significantly increase the interactivity of the system – particularly when the user edits a subdivision skin, which may have a large number of inactive vertices.

## 9 Discussion

As stated in the introduction, skin was designed to be used in an interactive free-form modeling setting. Since our ultimate aim is to create high-quality models, we believe our results should be judged by what types of models we can create within this framework. Although we have not designed the final interface for our system, we do have a preliminary implementation that lets the user create primitives either using SKETCH [26] or by importing them from other modeling packages. The user can interactively create a ball of skin and grow it over a primitive. Editing operations include instructing the skin to grow over a new skeleton, adjusting a skeleton's offset distance or target length, drawing and editing crease curves, and changing the genus of the skin surface.

With this system we have created the models shown in figures 8, 13, 14, and 15. The torso model was created by growing skin over the skeleton shown in the top image of figure 15. The skeletons were created by a user with no artistic training using SKETCH. Some skeletons were created by growing skin over a sketched primitive. The skin surface was edited at both one and two levels of subdivision. For example, the muscles of the neck were added as subdivision skeletons. The foot and hand models demonstrate how skin can be used to create cartoonish effects. Both models are expressive, yet were built by growing skin over simple skeletons. The face model is more complex. Note the use of crease curves to delineate the mouth, nose, and eye sockets. This model would be difficult to create using a surface patch representation. The skeletons, created by a skilled computer artist using a conventional modeling system, are shown in the top image of figure 13.

## 10 Future work

Future work will proceed in two directions. We are continuing to design an end-to-end interface to allow a skilled artist to create expressive 3D scenes. This will include facilities for defining underlying skeletons and stick figures, along the lines of [6, 11, 26], an interface for creating and guiding the skin, an interface for editing the surface at fine levels of detail, and an interface for assigning and customizing procedural textures for rendering, some of which are described in these proceedings [12].

We have also begun to investigate modifying the skin algorithm to perform mesh optimization, remeshing for subdivision connectivity, and mesh decimation.

## 11 Acknowledgments

We thank Michael LeGrand for creating the skeletons for the face model. Thanks also to Andy van Dam and the Graphics Group, and to our sponsors: the NSF Graphics and Visualization Center, Advanced Network and Services, Alias/Wavefront, Autodesk, IBM, Intel, Microsoft, National Tele-Immersion Initiative, Sun Microsystems, and TACO. Lee Markosian received support for his graduate education from Intel through the Intel Foundation Ph.D. Fellowship program.

## References

[1] Greg Albert, editor. *Basic Figure Drawing Techniques*. North Light Books, Cincinnati, Ohio, 1994.

[2] James F. Blinn. A generalization of algebraic surface drawing. *ACM Transactions on Graphics*, 1(3):235–256, July 1982.

[3] Jules Bloomenthal and Ken Shoemake. Convolution surfaces. In *SIGGRAPH 91 Conference Proceedings*, pp. 251–257. ACM SIGGRAPH, July 1991.

[4] Jules Bloomenthal and Brian Wyvill. Interactive techniques for implicit modeling. In *Proceedings of the 1990 Symposium on Interactive 3D Graphics*, pp. 109–116, March 1990.

[5] George B. Bridgman. *Constructive Anatomy*. Dover Publications, Inc., New York, 1973.

[6] Jonathan M. Cohen, Lee Markosian, Robert C. Zeleznik, John F. Hughes, and Ronen Barzel. An interface for sketching 3d curves. In *Proceedings of the 1999 Symposium on Interactive 3D Graphics*, pp. 17–21, 1999.

[7] Louise Gordon. *How to Draw the Human Figure*. Penguin Books, New York, 1979.

[8] Burne Hogarth. *Dynamic Anatomy*. Watson-Guptill Publications, New York, paperback edition, 1990.

[9] Hugues Hoppe, Tony DeRose, Tom Duchamp, Mark Halstead, Hubert Jin, John McDonald, Jean Schweitzer, and Werner Stuetzle. Piecewise smooth surface reconstruction. In *SIGGRAPH 94 Conference Proceedings*, pp. 295–302. ACM SIGGRAPH, July 1994.

[10] Hugues Hoppe, Tony DeRose, Tom Duchamp, John McDonald, and Werner Stuetzle. Mesh optimization. In *SIGGRAPH 93 Conference Proceedings*, pp. 19–26. ACM SIGGRAPH, August 1993.

[11] Takeo Igarashi, Satoshi Matsuoka, and Hidehiko Tanaka. Teddy: A sketching interface for 3d freeform design. In *SIGGRAPH 99 Conference Proceedings*. ACM SIGGRAPH, August 1999.

[12] Michael A. Kowalski, Lee Markosian, J.D. Northrup, Lubomir Bourdev, Ronen Barzel, Loring S. Holden, and John F. Hughes. Art-based rendering of fur, grass, and trees. In *SIGGRAPH 99 Conference Proceedings*. ACM SIGGRAPH, August 1999.

[13] C. Loop. Smooth subdivision surfaces based on triangles. Master's thesis, University of Utah, 1987.

[14] J. V. Miller, D. E. Breen, W. E. Lorensen, R. M. O'Bara, and M. J. Wozny. Geometrically deformed models: A method for extracting closed geometric models from volume data. In *SIGGRAPH 91 Conference Proceedings*, pp. 217–226. ACM SIGGRAPH, July 1991.

[15] Kari Pulli and Michael Lounsbery. Hierarchical editing and rendering of subdivision surfaces. Technical report, University of Washington, 1997.

[16] Walt Reed, editor. *The Figure: An Approach to Drawing and Construction*. North Light Books, Cincinnati, Ohio, 2nd edition, 1984.

[17] A.A.G. Requicha. Toward a theory of geometric tolerancing. *International Journal of Robotics Research*, 2(4):45–49, 1983.

[18] Fritz Schider. *An Atlas of Anatomy for Artists*. Dover Publications, Inc., New York, 3rd american edition, 1957.

[19] J. Schweitzer. *Analysis and application of subdivision surfaces*. PhD thesis, University of Washington, 1996.

[20] Barton T. Stander and John C. Hart. Guaranteeing the topology of an implicit surface polygonization for interactive modeling. In *SIGGRAPH 97 Conference Proceedings*, pp. 279–286. ACM SIGGRAPH, August 1997.

[21] Richard Szeliski and David Tonnesen. Surface modeling with oriented particle systems. In *SIGGRAPH 92 Conference Proceedings*, pp. 185–194. ACM SIGGRAPH, July 1992.

[22] Hal Tollison. *Cartooning*. Walter Foster Publishing, Inc., Laguna Hills, CA, 1989.

[23] C.W.A.M van Overveld and B. Wyvill. Shrinkwrap: an adaptive algorithm for polygonizing an implicit surface. Technical report, University of Calgary, 1993.

[24] William Welch and Andrew Witkin. Free–Form shape design using triangulated surfaces. In *SIGGRAPH 94 Conference Proceedings*, pp. 247–256. ACM SIGGRAPH, July 1994.

[25] Andrew P. Witkin and Paul S. Heckbert. Using particles to sample and control implicit surfaces. In *SIGGRAPH 94 Conference Proceedings*, pp. 269–278. ACM SIGGRAPH, July 1994.

[26] Robert C. Zeleznik, Kenneth P. Herndon, and John F. Hughes. SKETCH: An interface for sketching 3D scenes. In *SIGGRAPH 96 Conference Proceedings*, pp. 163–170. ACM SIGGRAPH, August 1996.

[27] Denis Zorin, Peter Schröder, and Wim Sweldens. Interactive multiresolution mesh editing. In *SIGGRAPH 97 Conference Proceedings*, pp. 259–268. ACM SIGGRAPH, August 1997.

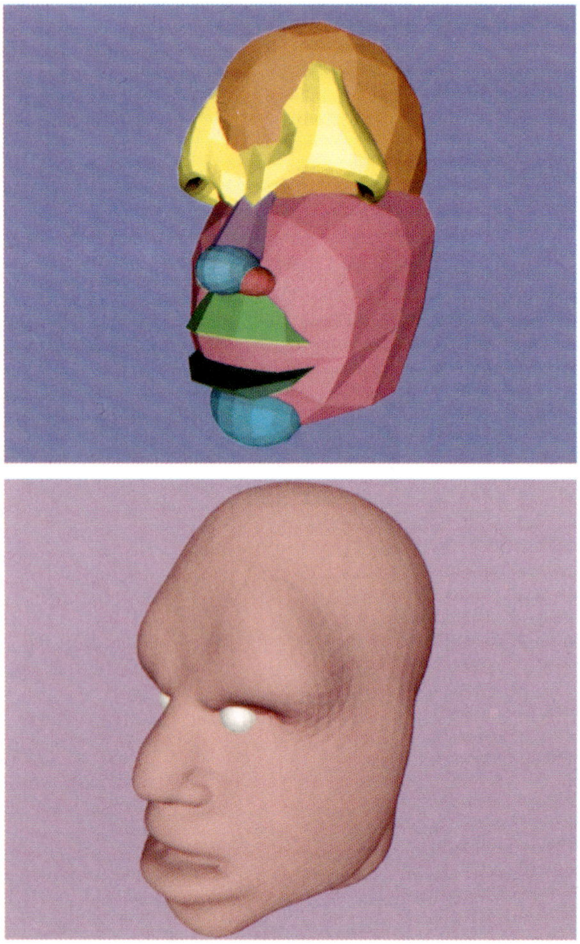

**Figure 13** This face model consists of a skin surface with about 3500 particles. The skeleton, shown in the upper image, was created using a commercial modeling package. Notice the fine detail around the nose and eyes, which was created using creases in the base mesh, and subdivision skeletons.

**Figure 14** This frog hand is based on an image from a children's book. It was made from 10 skeleton meshes. Notice the smooth webbing between the fingers.

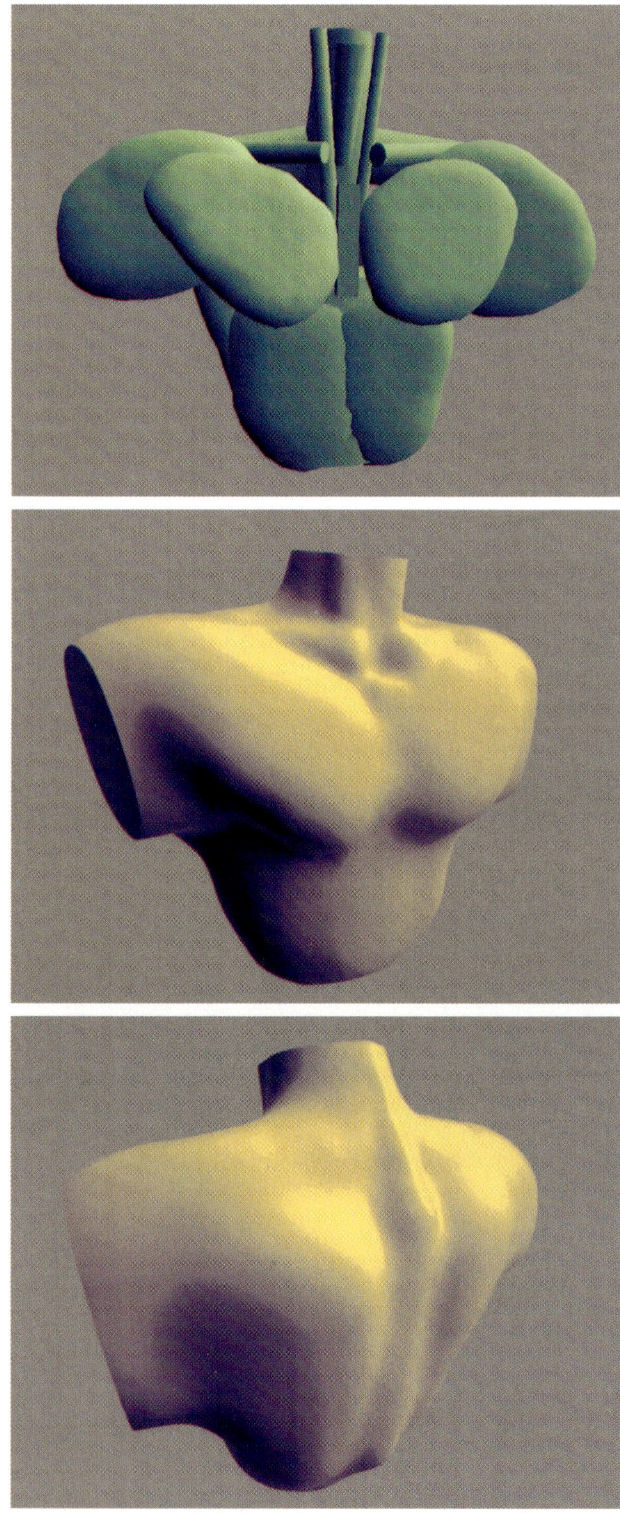

**Figure 15** The torso model was edited at 2 levels of subdivision. For example, the vertical neck muscles and the spine were added as subdivision skeletons. Notice the indications of underlying muscles, especially around the neck.

# Six Degree-of-Freedom Haptic Rendering Using Voxel Sampling

**William A. McNeely** **Kevin D. Puterbaugh** **James J. Troy**

The Boeing Company*

## Abstract

A simple, fast, and approximate voxel-based approach to 6-DOF haptic rendering is presented. It can reliably sustain a 1000 Hz haptic refresh rate without resorting to asynchronous physics and haptic rendering loops. It enables the manipulation of a modestly complex rigid object within an arbitrarily complex environment of static rigid objects. It renders a short-range force field surrounding the static objects, which repels the manipulated object and strives to maintain a voxel-scale minimum separation distance that is known to preclude exact surface interpenetration. Force discontinuities arising from the use of a simple penalty force model are mitigated by a dynamic simulation based on virtual coupling. A generalization of octree improves voxel memory efficiency. In a preliminary implementation, a commercially available 6-DOF haptic prototype device is driven at a constant 1000 Hz haptic refresh rate from one dedicated haptic processor, with a separate processor for graphics. This system yields stable and convincing force feedback for a wide range of user controlled motion inside a large, complex virtual environment, with very few surface interpenetration events. This level of performance appears suited to applications such as certain maintenance and assembly task simulations that can tolerate voxel-scale minimum separation distances.

**CR Categories and Subject Descriptors:** H.5.2 [User Interfaces]: Haptic I/O, I.3.5 [Computational Geometry and Object Modeling]: Physically Based Modeling.

**Additional Keywords:** force feedback, voxel representations, virtual environments.

## 1. INTRODUCTION

The problem of simulating real-world engineering tasks — for example, objectives like design-for-assembly and design-for-maintenance — has been exacerbated by the modern transition from physical mockup to virtual mockup. Physical mockup provides natural surface constraints that prevent tools and parts from interpenetrating, whereas virtual mockup requires the user to satisfy such constraints by receiving collision cues and making appropriate body postural adjustments, which is usually tedious and may yield dubious results. In order to emulate the natural surface constraint satisfaction of physical mockup, one must introduce force feedback into virtual mockup. Doing so shifts the burden of physical constraint satisfaction onto a haptic subsystem, and the user becomes free to concentrate on higher-level problems such as path planning and engineering rule satisfaction.

Tool and part manipulation inherently requires six degree-of-freedom (6-DOF) haptics, since extended objects are free to move in three translational and three rotational directions. Affordable high-bandwidth 6-DOF devices are becoming available, but 6-DOF haptic rendering remains an outstanding problem. It is considerably more difficult than 3-DOF point-contact haptic rendering. One can compare haptics with collision detection, since they share some technical similarity. Real-time collision detection is a challenging problem [13], but 6-DOF haptics adds stringent new requirements such as:

- Detect all surface contact (or proximity, for a force field), instead of stopping at the first evidence of it.
- Calculate a reaction force and torque at every point or extended region of contact/proximity.
- Reliably maintain a 1000 Hz refresh rate, independent of position and orientation of the manipulated object.
- Control geometry driven haptic instabilities, such as forcing an object into a narrow wedge-shaped cavity.

To address the needs of our targeted engineering applications, we adopt the following additional goals:

- Minimize the interpenetration of exact surface representations.
- Handle complex static scenes, e.g., those containing several hundred thousand triangles, with reasonable memory efficiency.
- The haptic rendering algorithm should parallelize easily.

Furthermore, we accept the limitation of voxel-scale accuracy. For example, a common engineering rule is to design at least 0.5 inch clearance into part removal paths, whenever possible, in order to accommodate tool access and human grasping and to serve as a cushion against assembly tolerance buildup.

We describe an approach that formally meets most of these requirements. It demonstrates the ability to drive a commercially available 6-DOF prototype device at a reliable 1000 Hz haptic refresh rate without the aid of asynchronous physics and haptic rendering loops. It supports the manipulation of a single rigid object within an arbitrarily rich environment of static rigid objects by rendering a half-voxel-deep force field that surrounds the static objects and serves to block potential interpenetration of the exact surface representations, as described in section 4.2. Given a predetermined spatial accuracy (i.e., voxel size), rendering performance depends linearly on the total exposed surface area of the manipulated object. There is also a relatively minor dependence on the instantaneous amount of contact/proximity, with a worst-case performance (e.g., maximum contact/proximity) of about half that of the best-case performance.

* Bill McNeely, The Boeing Company, P.O. Box 3707, M/S 7L-43, Seattle, WA 98124, (bill.mcneely@boeing.com)

Our approach is distinguished primarily by its high haptic rendering speed, which is derived primarily from:

- A simple penalty force scheme called the tangent-plane force model, explained in section 3.
- A fixed-depth voxel tree, explained in section 4.3.
- A voxel map that collectively represents all static objects, explained in section 4.4.

Although the simplicity of our force model is critically important to performance, it is so simple that it generates force magnitude discontinuities (but not force direction discontinuities), especially under sliding motion. In 3-DOF point-contact haptics, force discontinuities can be devastating to force quality and stability, but under our 6-DOF approach there is a stochastic effect that lessens their impact. However, it proved necessary to introduce various measures to explicitly enhance force quality and stability, such as:

- A single-body dynamic model based on virtual coupling
- Pre-contact braking forces

All such measures are explained in section 5.

Data storage is often a secondary consideration in haptics work, because it is tempting to trade memory efficiency for higher performance. However, voxels are so relatively inefficient as geometric modeling elements that we improve their memory efficiency by generalizing the octree method, as explained in section 4.3.

## 2. PREVIOUS WORK

Although largely the result of unpublished work, there are numerous examples of 6-DOF haptic rendering for scenarios containing a very limited number of geometrically well behaved virtual objects, for example [6,7,24]. Our approach differs from this work primarily in its ability to render considerably more complex 6-DOF scenarios with no formal constraints on object shape, although at reduced accuracy.

Our approach includes a collision detection technique based on probing a voxelized environment with surface point samples. Voxel-based methods have been applied to non-haptic collision detection [12,15,16] and to 3-DOF haptics [3,18]. Sclaroff and Pentland [22] apply surface point sampling to implicit surfaces.

Intermediate representations for haptics were suggested by Adachi et al. [1], and have been subsequently elaborated [17]. This involves using a simple haptics proxy that approximates the exact scene and is simple enough to update the forces at the required high refresh rate, while a slower but more exact collision detection and/or dynamic simulation runs asynchronously and updates the proxy's parameters. Our work differs by tightly integrating collision detection, the force model, and the dynamic model into a single loop that updates forces directly at 1000 Hz.

There has been much work in multibody dynamic simulation for physically based modeling, for example [4,23]. Mirtich and Canny [19] track the contacts found from an iterative collision detection method and use this information to generate constant-size impulses. In general, such work is characterized by its emphasis on accuracy over rendering performance, and consequently it relies on methodology such as exact-surface collision detection and simultaneous surface constraint satisfaction, which currently fall far short of 6-DOF haptics performance requirements.

Our dynamic model adopts the practice of using an artificial coupling between the haptic display and virtual environment, as originally proposed by Colgate et al. [10] and recently elaborated by Adams and Hannaford [2]. We also adopt a version of the "god object" concept suggested by Zilles and Salisbury [25] and others [21], generalized to 6-DOF and modified to use penalty forces that only approximately satisfy surface constraints. In addition, we use the concept of pre-contact braking force suggested by Clover [9].

Hierarchical techniques, such as employed by Gottschalk [13], can be used to alleviate convex-hull bounding box limitations for objects in very close proximity by recursively generating a tree of bounding volumes around finer features of the object. While this technique speeds collision detection, it also introduces indeterminacy in the cycle rate due to the varying cost of traversing the tree structure to an unknown depth to check each colliding polygon against object polygons. Cycle-rate should not only be fast but should also have a rate that is as constant as possible.

Temporal and spatial coherence can also be exploited [4,5,8] by assuming that objects move only slightly within each time step, thus allowing extrapolation from the previous state of the system. The number of polygon tests carried out at each time step is effectively reduced, increasing cycle-rate at the cost of introducing indeterminacy. With certain configurations or motions of objects, however, there are often noticeable drops in performance — a situation which is unacceptable in a real-time simulation.

## 3. TANGENT-PLANE FORCE MODEL

In our tangent-plane force model, dynamic objects are represented by a set of surface point samples, plus associated inward pointing surface normals, collectively called a point shell. During each haptic update the dynamic object's motion transformation is applied to every point of the point shell. The environment of static objects is collectively represented by a single spatial occupancy map called a voxmap, which is illustrated in Figure 1. Each haptically rendered frame involves sampling the voxmap at every point of the point shell.

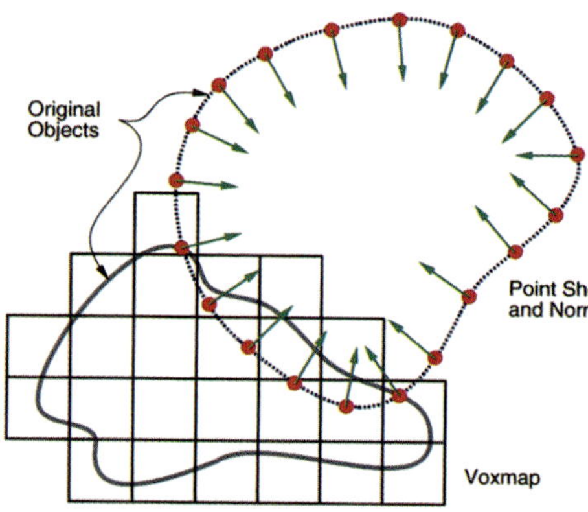


**Figure 1.** Voxmap colliding with point shell.

When a point interpenetrates a voxel (assumed for now to be a surface voxel) as shown in Figure 2, a depth of interpenetration is calculated as the distance $d$ from the point to a plane within the voxel called the tangent plane.

The tangent plane is dynamically constructed to pass through the voxel's center point and to have the same normal as the point's associated normal. If the point has not penetrated below that plane (i.e., closer to the interior of the static object), then $\boldsymbol{d}$ is zero. Force is simply proportional to $\boldsymbol{d}$ by Hooke's law ($\boldsymbol{F} = K_{ff}\boldsymbol{d}$). We call $K_{ff}$ the "force field stiffness," since the voxel represents a half-voxel-deep force field. The net force and torque acting on the dynamic object is obtained as the sum of all force/torque contributions from such point-voxel intersections.

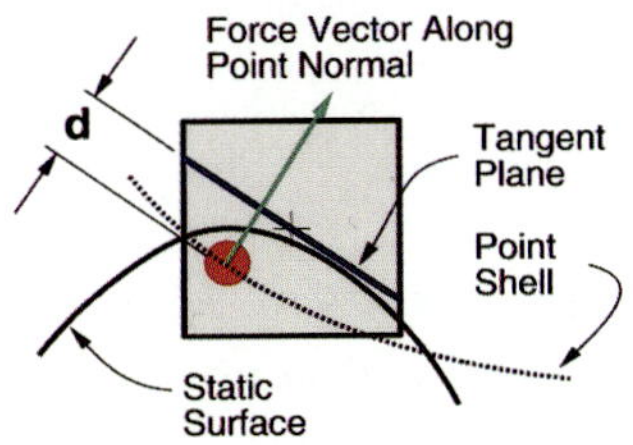


**Figure 2.** Tangent-plane force model.

The tangent-plane force model was inspired by the fact that the surfaces of contacting objects are tangent at an osculation point. It is important that the force takes its direction from a precomputed surface normal of the dynamic object. This proves to be considerably faster than the common practice of dynamically computing it from the static object's surface, or in the case of a force field, dynamically taking the gradient of a potential field.

One can see that this simple model has discontinuities in force magnitude when a point crosses a voxel boundary, for example, under sliding motion. Section 5 describes how discontinuities can be mitigated for haptic purposes.

## 4. VOXEL DATA STRUCTURES

This section outlines the creation and usage of voxel-based data structures that are required under our approach. Exact (polygonal) surface penetration and memory usage will also be discussed.

### 4.1 Voxmap and Point Shell

One begins by selecting a global voxel size, $s$, that meets the virtual scenario's requirements for accuracy and performance. The performance aspect is that the force model requires traversing a set of point samples, and $s$ determines the number of such points. Consider a solid object such as the teapot in Figure 3(a). It partitions space into regions of free space, object surface, and object interior. Now tile this space into a volume occupancy map, or voxmap, as in Figure 3(b). The collection of center points of all surface voxels constitutes the point shell needed by the tangent-plane force model, as in Figure 3(c).

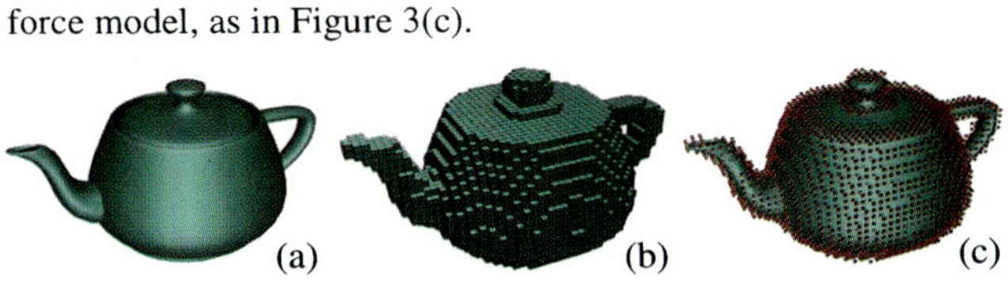


**Figure 3.** Teapot: (a) polygonal model, (b) voxel model, (c) point shell model.

This method for creating the point shell is not optimal, but it is convenient. Its accuracy may be improved by choosing points that lie on the exact geometrical representation.

Each voxel is allocated two bits of memory that designate it as a free space, interior, surface, or proximity voxel. The 2-bit voxel types are defined in Table 1 and illustrated by an example in Figure 4.

A neighbor voxel is defined as sharing a vertex, edge, or face with the subject voxel. Each voxel has 26 neighbors. It is important that each static object be voxelized in its final position and orientation in the world frame, because such transformations cause its voxelized representation to change shape slightly.

**Table 1.** Voxel types (2-bit)

| Value | Voxel type | Description |
|---|---|---|
| 0 | Free space | Encloses only free-space volumes |
| 1 | Interior | Encloses only interior volumes |
| 2 | Surface | Encloses a mix of free-space, surface, and interior volumes |
| 3 | Proximity | Free-space neighbor of a surface voxel |

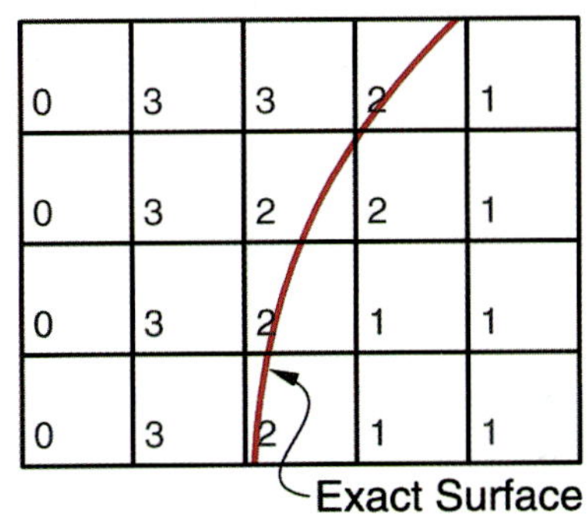


**Figure 4.** Assignment of 2-bit voxel values.

By the nature of 3D scan conversion, voxmaps are insensitive to surface imperfections such as gaps or cracks that are smaller than the voxel width. However, identifying the interior of a voxmap can be difficult. We adopt the practice of (1) scan-converting to create surface voxels, (2) identifying free-space voxels by propagating the voxelized walls of the object's bounding box inward until surface voxels are encountered, and (3) declaring all other voxels to be interior voxels. This ensures that objects with open surfaces will be voxelized instead of "leaking" and filling all voxels.

### 4.2 Avoiding Exact Surface Interpenetration

In the tangent-plane force model shown in Figure 2, the exact surfaces of colliding objects are allowed to interpenetrate by voxel-scale distances during a point-voxel intersection. While this may be acceptable for some applications, we seek instead to preclude exact-surface interpenetration. We do this by offsetting the force field outward away from the surface by two voxel layers, as shown in Figure 5. (In this figure, the rotated boxes represent the surface voxels associated with the points of a pointshell, viewed as surface bounding volumes.) The offset force layer then serves to maintain a minimum object separation that provably precludes exact-surface interpenetration.

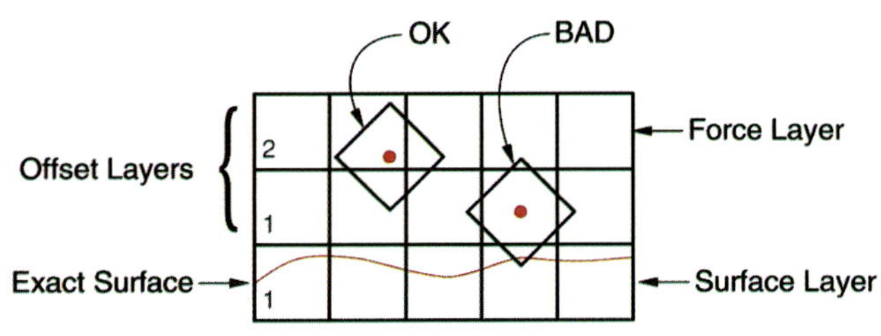


**Figure 5.** Criterion for exact-surface interpenetration.

The voxel legend described by Table 1 and Figure 4 is correspondingly redefined so that "surface" and "value 2" now refer to the offset force-layer voxels instead of geometric surface voxels, and similarly for the other voxel types. (Offset proximity voxels and free-space voxels are omitted from Figure 5, but they would occupy additional layers at the top of the figure.)

Force-layer offsetting is implemented as a final step of voxelization, in which the geometric surface voxel layer is grown outward by a process of promoting proximity voxels to surface values and demoting original surface voxels to interior values. This process is repeated to achieve the desired two-layer offset. (If voxels were allocated more than two bits, it would not be necessary to "recycle" voxel values in this manner, and there are other advantages to wider voxels that we are beginning to explore.)

Force-layer offsetting also serves to prevent any spike-like feature in the static object from generating a linear column of voxels that the point shell could completely fail to penetrate for certain orientations of the dynamic object. The force layer has no such features, because voxel values are propagated to 26 connected neighbors during the offsetting process.

### 4.3 Voxel Tree

A natural next step is to impose an octree organization on the voxels for the sake of memory efficiency and scalability. However, the need for a consistently fast haptic refresh rate is at odds with the variability in the tree traversal time. To address this, we have devised a hierarchy that represents a compromise between memory efficiency and haptic rendering performance. It is a generalization of octree with a tree depth that is limited to three levels, explained as follows.

At each level of the tree, the cubical volume of space is divided into $2^{3N}$ sub-volumes, where $N$ is a positive integer. ($N$ is unity for an octree.) We have discovered that the most memory-efficient value for $N$ may be at higher values, depending on the sparseness of the geometry. Figure 6 illustrates a study of the total memory consumed by a $2^{3N}$-tree as a function of $N$ for geometry that is typical to our work. It has a minimum at $N$=3, which might be called a 512-tree.

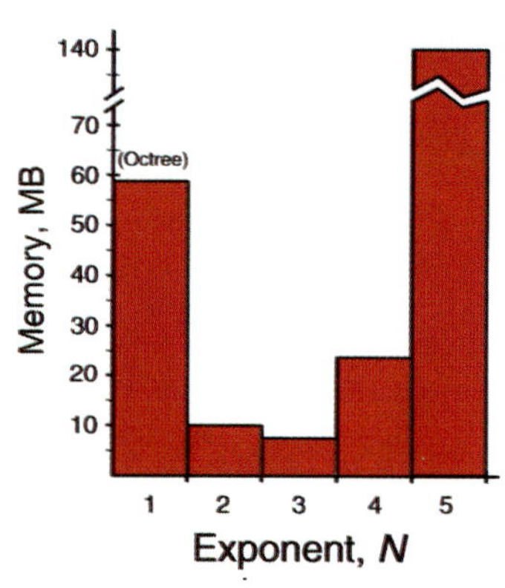


**Figure 6.** Memory usage of $2^{3N}$ tree as a function of $N$.

We further limit tree depth by fixing both the minimum and maximum dimensions of the bounding volumes in the tree. The minimum dimension is the size of voxels at the leaf level, and the maximum dimension is given implicitly by creating only three levels above the leaf level. The minimum-size requirement means that smaller features may not be adequately represented, but we fundamentally accept a global accuracy limitation, analogous to the practice of accepting a fixed tessellation error in polygonal surface representations. The maximum-size requirement impacts memory efficiency and scalability, because one must cover all remaining space with the largest-size bounding volumes. However, these effects are mitigated by the use of $2^{3N}$-tree, since for a fixed number of levels, higher values of $N$ increase the dynamic range of the bounding volume dimensions.

### 4.4 Merged Scene Voxmap

Our approach is limited to the case of a single dynamic rigid object interacting with an arbitrarily rich environment of static rigid objects. If it were necessary to separately calculate the interaction force for each of $N$ static objects, then the computing burden would grow linearly with $N$. However, there is no inherent need to separately compute such interactions on a pairwise basis. For example, there is no need to identify the type of a contacted object in order to apply different material properties, since all static objects are treated as rigid. Furthermore, under our force-field approach, objects are never actually contacted in the sense of undergoing surface intersections. Therefore, we merge all static-object voxel representations together as if they were a single static object, applying straightforward precedence rules to merged voxel values and recalculating a voxel tree for the voxmap.

## 5. DYNAMIC MODEL

For the dynamic model, we use an impedance approach, in which user motion is sensed and a force/torque pair is produced. We further adopt what is called the "virtual coupler" scheme, which connects the user's haptic motions with the motions of the dynamic object through a virtual spring and damper. This is a well known method for enhancing haptic stability [2].

To solve for the motion of the dynamic object, we perform a numerical integration of the Newton-Euler equation, using a constant time step $\Delta t$ corresponding to the time between force updates, e.g., $\Delta t$ =1 msec for 1000 Hz haptic refresh rate. We also must assign a mass $m$ to the dynamic object equal to the apparent mass for the dynamic object that we want to feel at the haptic handle (in addition to the haptic device's intrinsic friction and inertia, and assuming that its forces are not yet saturated). The net force and torque on the dynamic object is the sum of contributions from the spring-damper system, explained in section 5.1; stiffness considerations, explained in section 5.2; and the pre-contact braking force, explained in section 5.3.

### 5.1 A 6-DOF Spring-Damper System

Conceptually, a copy of the haptic handle is placed in the virtual scene and is coupled to the dynamic object through a spring-damper connection, as shown in Figure 7.

The real haptic handle controls the position and orientation of its virtual counterpart. This influences the spring's displacement, which generates a virtual force/torque on the dynamic object and an opposite force/torque on the real haptic handle. Spring displacement also includes rotational motion, as shown in Figure 7 by the spiral at the center of the dynamic object (suggestive of a clock mainspring). Spring force is proportional to displacement, while spring torque is proportional to the angle of rotation from an equivalent-angle analysis and directed along an equivalent axis of rotation [11].

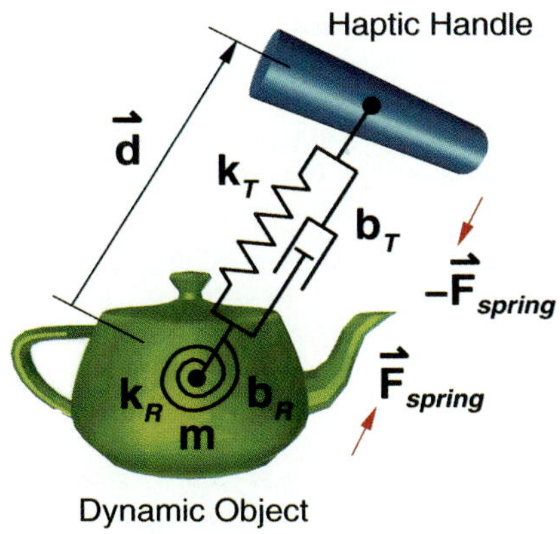


**Figure 7.** Dynamic model based on virtual coupling.

This 6-DOF spring makes the dynamic object tend to acquire the same position and orientation of the virtual haptic handle, assuming that the two objects are initially registered in some manner, e.g., with the center of the handle located at the dynamic object's center of mass and the handle's main axis aligned with one of the dynamic object's principal axes. The virtual object is assigned mass properties, which are reflected at the haptic interface as apparent mass that is added to the haptic device's intrinsic inertia. We operated at a small reflected mass of 12 g. The force and torque equations used here are:

$$\boldsymbol{F}_{spring} = k_T\boldsymbol{d} - b_T\boldsymbol{v}$$

$$\vec{\tau}_{spring} = k_R\vec{\theta} - b_R\vec{\omega}$$

where

$k_T$, $b_T$ = spring translational stiffness and viscosity

$k_R$, $b_R$ = spring rotational stiffness and viscosity

$\vec{\theta}$ = equivalent-axis angle (including axis direction)

$\boldsymbol{v}$, $\vec{\omega}$ = dynamic object's relative linear and angular velocity.

Spring stiffness is set to a reasonably high value that is still comfortably consistent with stable numerical behavior at the known time sampling rate. Stiffness and viscosity are straightforwardly related to obtain critically damped behavior. A limitation of this simple formalism is that it is only valid for a dynamic object having equal moments of inertia in every direction, such as a sphere of uniform mass density. Since we were not interested in reflected moments of inertia, and indeed sought to minimize them, this was an acceptable limitation. It represents an implicit constraint on the virtual object's mass density distribution but not on its geometrical shape.

## 5.2 Virtual Stiffness Considerations

When the virtual object is in resting contact with the half-voxel-deep force field described by stiffness $K_{ff}$, we want to prevent the user from stretching the spring so far as to overcome the force field and drag the dynamic object through it. The spring force is clamped to its value at a displacement of *s/2*, where *s* is the voxel size. In the worst case, this contact force is entirely due to a single point-voxel interaction, which therefore determines an upper limit on the spring force. This can be viewed as a modification of the god-object concept [25], in which the god-object is allowed to penetrate a surface by up to a half voxel instead of being analytically constrained to that surface.

Whenever many point-voxel intersections occur simultaneously, the net stiffness may become so large as to provoke haptic instabilities associated with fixed-time-step numerical integration. To cope with this problem, we replace the vector sum of all point-voxel forces by their average, i.e., divide the total force by the current number of point-voxel intersections, *N*. This introduces force discontinuities as *N* varies with time, especially for small values of *N*, which degrades haptic stability. We mitigate this side effect by deferring the averaging process until $N = 10$ is reached:

$$F_{Net} = F_{Total} \quad \text{if } N < 10$$

$$F_{Net} = \frac{F_{Total}}{N/10} \quad \text{if } N \geq 10$$

and similarly for torque. $K_{ff}$ is adjusted to assure reasonably stable numerical integration for the fixed time step and at least 10 simultaneous point-voxel intersections. While this heuristic leads to relatively satisfactory results, we are investigating a hybrid of constraint-based and penalty-based approaches that formally address both the high-stiffness problem and its dual of low stiffness but high mechanical advantage. Forcing an object into a narrow wedge-shaped cavity is an example of the latter problem.

Dynamic simulation is subject to the well studied problem of non-passivity, which might be defined as the unintended generation of excessive virtual energy [2,10]. In a haptic system, non-passivity manifests itself as distracting forces and motions (notably, vibrations) with no apparent basis in the virtual scenario. Non-passivity is inherent in the use of time-sampled penalty forces and in the force discontinuity that is likely to occur whenever a point crosses a voxel boundary. Another potential source of non-passivity is insufficient physical damping in the haptic device [10]. Even a relatively passive dynamic simulation may become highly non-passive when placed in closed-loop interaction with a haptic device, depending on various details of the haptic device's design, its current kinematic posture, and even the user's motion behavior.

The most direct way to control non-passivity is to operate at the highest possible force-torque update rate supported by the haptic device, which for our work was the relatively high value of 1000 Hz. We also investigated the technique of computationally detecting and dissipating excessive virtual energy. While this had some success, it was eventually replaced by the simpler technique of empirically determining the largest value of $K_{ff}$ consistent with stable operation over the entire workspace of the haptic device. As a further refinement, we discovered some residual instability in the dynamic object when it lies in free space. Whenever that occurs, therefore, we apply zero force and torque to the haptic device (overriding any non-zero spring values). A free-space configuration is trivially detected as every point of the dynamic object intersecting a free-space voxel of the environment.

## 5.3 Pre-Contact Braking Force

The treatment of spring-force clamping in section 5.2 ignored the fact that the dynamic object's momentum may induce deeper instantaneous point-voxel penetration than is possible under resting contact, thereby overcoming the force field. Currently, we do not attempt to avoid this outcome in every instance. Instead, we generate a force in the proximity voxel layer that acts to reduce the point's velocity, called the pre-contact braking force. In order to avoid a surface stickiness effect, the force must only act when the point is approaching contact, not receding from a prior contact. To determine whether the point is approaching or receding, consult its associated inward-pointing surface normal, $\hat{n}_i$, and then calculate the force:

$$F_i = -bv_i(-\hat{n}_i \cdot \hat{v}_i), \text{ if } \hat{n}_i \cdot \hat{v}_i < 0$$

$$F_i = 0, \text{ if } \hat{n}_i \cdot \hat{v}_i \geq 0$$

where $b$ is a "braking viscosity," $v_i$ is the velocity of the $i^{th}$ point in the point shell, and $\hat{v}_i$ is a unit vector along $v_i$.

As a simple heuristic, therefore, adjust $b$ so as to dissipate the object's translational kinetic energy along the direction of approaching contact within one haptic cycle:

$$b = \frac{(\frac{1}{2}mv^2)/\Delta t}{v \cdot \Sigma_i v_i(-\hat{n}_i \cdot \hat{v}_i)}$$

where $m$ and $v$ are the dynamic object's mass and velocity component along $\Sigma F_i$, respectively, and the sum over $i$ is understood to traverse only points for which $\hat{n}_i \cdot \hat{v}_i < 0$.

We have not yet implemented a braking torque. Calculating this type of torque would be similar in form to the translational braking viscosity equation above.

A weakness of the braking technique is that an individual point's velocity may become so large that the point skips over the proximity voxel in a single haptic cycle, or even worse, over all voxels of a thin object. We call this the "tunnelling problem." This is particularly likely to happen for points of a long dynamic object that is rotated with sufficient angular velocity. One possible solution is to constrain the dynamic object's translational and angular velocities such that no point's velocity ever exceeds $s/\Delta t$.

## 6. RESULTS

The system configuration for our preliminary implementation is illustrated in Figure 8. Haptic rendering is performed on a dedicated haptics processor, which asserts updated force and torque information to the haptic device and reads position and orientation of the haptic handle in a closed loop running at 1000 Hz.

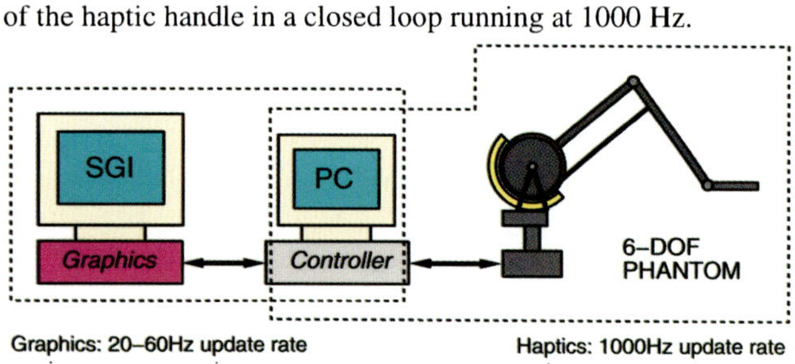


**Figure 8.** System Configuration.

In a separate asynchronous open loop, the haptics processor transmits UDP packets containing position and orientation information to a dedicated graphics processor, which renders the updated scene at about 20 Hz. This section provides more details on the system components and presents some preliminary results.

### 6.1 Haptics Device

We used a desk-mounted system called the PHANTOM™ Premium 6-DOF Prototype (shown in Figure 9), made by SensAble Technologies, Inc. This system includes the mechanism, its power electronics, a PCI interface card, and the GHOST® Software Developer's Kit (SDK). Force feedback in three translational degrees-of-freedom is provided by a vertical 2-link planar structure, with a third orthogonal rotational axis at the base. Cable transmission actuators drive linkages from the base. Its peak force is 22 N and the nominal positioning resolution is 0.025 mm at the end effector. The translational range of motion is about 42×59×82 cm, approximating the natural range of motion of the entire human arm. Torque feedback in three rotational degrees of freedom is provided by a powered gimbal mechanism that provides torques in yaw, pitch, and roll directions. Its peak torque is 0.67 Nm and the nominal resolution is 0.013° in each axis. The rotational range of motion is 330° in both yaw and roll, and 220° in pitch.

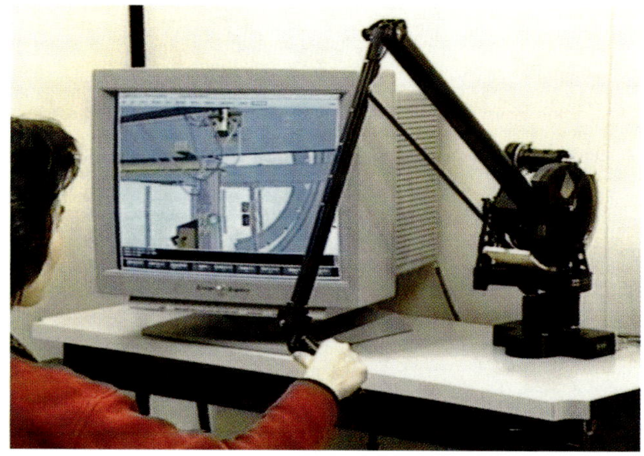

**Figure 9.** User with the 6-DOF haptic device.

Low-level interactions with the PCI interface card are handled by the PHANTOM device drivers provided with the system. The GHOST SDK transparently provides real-time motion control, including the use of a proprietary mechanism that guarantees a 1 kHz servo rate. A kinematic model that deals with conversions between joint space and Cartesian space, and dynamics algorithms that optimize the feel by compensating for device dynamics. Although the GHOST SDK supports numerous high-level interactions with the system, our usage is currently limited to (1) querying for global position and orientation of the end effector as a 4×4 homogeneous transformation matrix and (2) asserting the desired global force and torque.

### 6.2 Haptics and Graphics Processing

The dedicated haptics processor of our prototype system was a 350 MHz Pentium® II CPU with 128 MB of RAM running Windows NT®. The functions of voxelization, voxel-sampling, and force generation were provided by Boeing developed software known as Voxmap PointShell™, which implements the approach presented in this paper. Voxmap PointShell is interfaced with the GHOST SDK, which manages the 1 kHz servo loop. Within this loop, the haptic handle's position and velocity information is received, a haptic frame is rendered, and updated force and torque information is sent to the device. GHOST monitors the time consumption of each loop and interrupts operation whenever a 1 kHz servo loop constraint is violated. Outside the servo loop, a separate, asynchronous loop samples the transformation matrices for the dynamic object and haptic handle, and sends them via UDP to a dedicated graphics processor.

Our dedicated graphics processor was an SGI Octane™ with one 250 MHz R10000 processor, 256 MB of RAM, and SI graphics. For visualization we use FlyThru®, a proprietary high-performance visualization system. This system was first used to virtually "preassemble" the Boeing 777 and is now employed on commercial, military, and space programs throughout Boeing. FlyThru can maintain a frame rate of ~20 Hz, independent of the amount of static geometry. This is achieved by rendering the static geometry once to the color and Z-buffers, then reusing those images for subsequent frames [20]. This visualization scheme provided smooth motion with no noticeable lag.

One disadvantage of using two separate computers is that setup and usage tend to be cumbersome. In light of this, we have also implemented our approach on an Octane with two processors — one used strictly for haptics and the other for graphics.

### 6.3 Virtual Scenario

The static environment of our virtual scenario consisted of simulated aircraft geometry, with beams, tubes, wires, etc., voxelized at 5 mm resolution. Its polyhedral representation contains 593,409 polygons. Its FlyThru representation consumed 26 MB of memory, and its voxelized representation consumed 21 MB. Voxelization time on a 250 MHz SGI Octane was 70 sec. A closeup shot of a dynamic object (a teapot) maneuvering through a portion of this environment is shown in Figure 10.

The dynamic object for much of our testing was a small teapot (75 mm from spout to handle), logically representing a small tool or part, which when voxelized at 5 mm resolution yielded 380 points in its pointshell for the PC haptics processor. The dedicated haptics processor of the two-processor Octane system was able to achieve a maximum of 600 points for the same object.

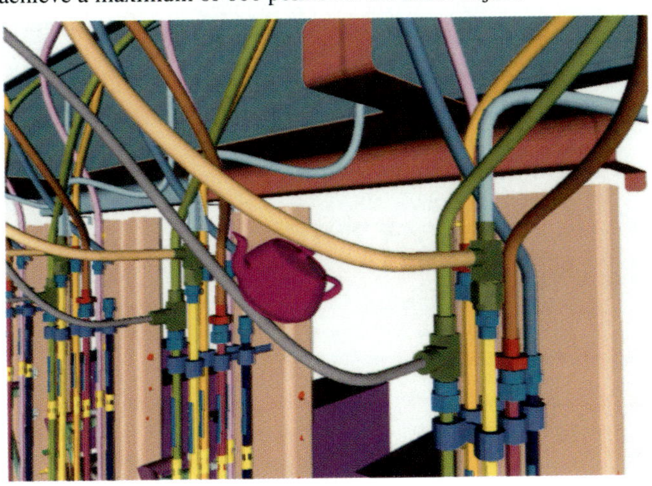

**Figure 10.** Dynamic object in the test environment.

### 6.4 Preliminary Test Results

We haptically rendered the motion of the teapot through the simulated aircraft geometry, paying particular attention to motion behavior and quality of force feedback. We evaluated the feeling of free space as well as resting and sliding contact (with the force field). In an attempt to explore the system's limits, we sought to induce haptic instabilities and exact-surface interpenetrations by trapping the teapot in congested areas and by staging high-speed collisions.

Subjectively, the observed free-space behavior was indistinguishable from power-off operation, for translational as well as rotational motion. Sliding behavior on a flat or slowly curving surface was notably smooth. A relatively slight surface roughness was felt when sliding in contact with two surfaces. Torques were clearly felt. We were able to move the teapot easily through congested areas where combinations of rotation and translation were required to find a path through the area, similar to path planning for maintenance access.

Throughout such investigation, a 1 kHz update requirement was maintained. We were unable to cause the teapot to pass completely through any of the environment surfaces, including relatively thin ones, even at maximum collision speed. There were remarkably few potential exact-surface interpenetration events. One natural metric is the ratio of penetration to collision events (PR) defined as the number of haptic frames registering one or more potential exact-surface penetrations divided by the number of haptic frames registering contact with the force-field layer (including penetration events).

We evaluated the benefit of the pre-contact braking force by selectively disabling it and re-measuring PR. The effect of this was fewer exact-surface penetrations, as shown in Table 2.

**Table 2.** Penetration ratio

| Test | Braking | Penetrations | Contacts | PR |
|---|---|---|---|---|
| 1 | No | 70 | 69,000 | $1.0 \times 10^{-3}$ |
| 2 | Yes | 6 | 108,000 | $6 \times 10^{-5}$ |

All such work was done with the haptic device limited to 15 N force and 0.1 Nm torque. At these limits we found the device to be stable for every possible type of motion.

## 7. CONCLUSIONS AND FUTURE WORK

The voxel-based approach to haptic rendering presented here enables 6-DOF manipulation of a modestly sized rigid object within an arbitrarily complex environment of static objects. The size of the moving object (i.e., the number of points in the point shell) is limited by the processor speed, while the size of the static environment is limited by memory. A force model was described in which the interaction of the moving object's surface normals with the static voxmap was used to create haptic forces and torques. Results of testing an implementation of our approach on a 6-DOF haptic device showed that the performance appears to be acceptable for maintenance and assembly task simulations, provided that the task can tolerate voxel level accuracy.

It is apparent to us that we are just beginning to discover all the potential uses for the voxmap sampling method in haptics and other fields. Our primary focus will be to enhance the performance of the system for use in complex environments.

The voxel sampling method can be easily parallelized, using clones of the static environment and cyclic decomposition of the dynamic object's pointshell. We intend to take advantage of this by investigating parallel computing environments, specifically low-latency cluster computing. This will allow haptic simulation of larger and more complex dynamic objects.

Another area of interest that we are pursuing involves using wider-bit-width voxel types (4-bit, 8-bit, etc.). This enhancement will allow for an extended force field range to model compliance when simulating varying material types.

We also intend to continue investigating solutions to problematic situations, like the wedge problem and tunnelling (moving through a thin object without detecting collision), as well as further reducing non-passivity.

## Acknowledgments

The authors express their thanks to colleagues Karel Zikan for the idea of voxel sampling, Jeff A. Heisserman for the idea of normal-aligned force direction, Robert A. Perry for creating simulated aircraft geometry, and Elaine Chen of SensAble Technologies, Inc. for literature research and technical information about the PHANTOM device and GHOST software support.

## References

[1] Adachi, T., Kumano, T., Ogino, K., "Intermediate Representations for Stiff Virtual Objects," *Proc. IEEE Virtual Reality Annual Intl. Symposium*, pp. 203-210, 1995.

[2] Adams, R.J. and Hannaford, B., "A Two-Port Framework for the Design of Unconditionally Stable Haptic Interfaces," *Proc. IROS*, Anaheim CA, 1998.

[3] Avila, R.S. and Sobierajski, L.M., "A Haptic Interaction Method for Volume Visualization," *Proc. Visualization'96*, pp. 197-204, Oct. 1996.

[4] Baraff, D., "Curved Surfaces and Coherence for Non-Penetrating Rigid Body Simulation," *Computer Graphics (proc. SIGGRAPH 90)*, vol 24, no. 4, pp. 19-28, Aug. 1990.

[5] Baraff, D., "Fast Contact Force Computation for Nonpenetrating Rigid Bodies," *Computer Graphics (proc. SIGGRAPH 94)*, pp. 23-42, July 1994.

[6] Berkelman, P.J. and Hollis, R.L., "Dynamic performance of a hemispherical magnetic levitation haptic interface device," in *SPIE Int. Symposium on Intelligent Systems and Intelligent Manufacturing, (Proc. SPIE)*, Vol. 3602, Greensburg PA, Sept. 1997.

[7] Brooks, F.P., Ouh-Young, M., Batter, J.J., Jerome, P., "Project GROPE — Haptic Displays for Scientific Visualization," *Computer Graphics (proc. SIGGRAPH 90)*, pp. 177-185, Aug. 1990.

[8] Cohen, J.D., Lin, M.C., Manocha, D., and Ponamgi, M.K., "I-COLLIDE: An Interactive and Exact Collision Detection System for Large-Scale Environments," *Computer Graphics (proc. SIGGRAPH 95)*, pp. 189-196, Aug. 1995.

[9] Clover, C.L., *Control system design for robots used in simulating dynamic force and moment interaction in virtual reality applications,* Ph.D. thesis, Iowa State University, Ames, IA, Apr. 1996.

[10] Colgate, J.E., Grafing, P.E., Stanley, M.C., and Schenkel, G., "Implementation of Stiff Virtual Walls in Force-Reflecting Interfaces," *Proc. IEEE Virtual Reality Annual International Symposium (VRAIS)*, Seattle, WA, pp. 202-208, Sept., 1993.

[11] Craig, J.J., *Introduction to Robotics: Mechanics and Control.* 2nd ed., Addison-Wesley, Reading MA, 1989.

[12] Garcia-Alonso, A., Serrano, N., and Flaquer J., "Solving the Collision Detection Problem," *IEEE Computer Graphics and Applications*, vol. 14, no. 3, pp. 36-43, 1994.

[13] Gottschalk, S., Lin, M.C., Manocha, D., "OBBTree: A Hierarchical Structure for Rapid Interference Detection," *Computer Graphics (proc. SIGGRAPH 96)*, pp. 171-180, Aug. 1996.

[14] Jackins, C., and Tanimoto, S.L., "Oct-Trees and Their Use in Representing Three-Dimensional Objects," *Computer Graphics and Image Processing*, vol. 14, no. 3, pp. 249-270, 1980.

[15] Kaufman, A., Cohen, D., Yagle, R., "Volume Graphics," *IEEE Computer*, 26(7), pp. 51-64, July, 1993.

[16] Logan, I.P., Wills D.P.M., Avis N.J., Mohsen, A.M.M.A., and Sherman, K.P., "Virtual Environment Knee Arthroscopy Training System," *Society for Computer Simulation, Simulation Series*, vol. 28, no. 4, pp. 17-22, 1996.

[17] Mark, W.R., Randolph, S.C., Finch, M., Van Verth, J.M., and Taylor II, R.M., "Adding Force Feedback to Graphics Systems: Issues and Solutions," *Computer Graphics (proc. SIGGRAPH 96)*, pp. 447-452, Aug. 1996.

[18] Massie, T.H. and Salisbury, J.K., "The Phantom Haptic Interface: A Device for Probing Virtual Objects," *Proc. of the ASME International Mechanical Engineering Congress and Exhibition*, Chicago, pp. 295-302, 1994.

[19] Mirtich, B. and Canny, J., "Impulse-based Dynamic Simulation." *Proceedings of Workshop on Algorithmic Foundations of Robotics*, Feb. 1994.

[20] OpenGL Architecture Review Board, Woo, M., Neider, J., and Davis, T. *OpenGL Programming Guide*, 2nd, Addison-Wesley, Reading, MA, 1997.

[21] Ruspini, D.C., Kolarov, K., and Khatib, O., "The Haptic Display of Complex Graphical Environments," *Computer Graphics (Proc. SIGGRAPH 97)*, pp. 345-352, Aug. 1997.

[22] Sclaroff, S. and Pentland, A., "Generalized Implicit Functions for Computer Graphics," *Computer Graphics (Proc. SIGGRAPH 96)*, pp. 247-250, July, 1991.

[23] Witkin A. and Welch, W., "Fast Animation and Control of Nonrigid Structures," *Computer Graphics (Proc. SIGGRAPH 90)*, pp. 243-252, Aug. 1990.

[24] Yokokohji, Y., Hollis, R.L., and Kanade, T., "What you can see is what you can feel. Development of a visual/haptic interface to virtual environment," *Proc. IEEE Virtual Reality Annual Int. Symposium (VRAIS)*, pp. 46-53, Mar., 1996.

[25] Zilles, C.B. and Salisbury, J.K., "A Constraint-based God-object Method for Haptics Display," *Proc. IEEE/RSJ Int. Conf. on Intelligent Robots and Systems*, Pittsburgh, PA, pp. 146-151, 1995.

# Teddy: A Sketching Interface for 3D Freeform Design

Takeo Igarashi†, Satoshi Matsuoka‡, Hidehiko Tanaka†

† University of Tokyo, ‡ Tokyo Institute of Technology

## Abstract

We present a sketching interface for quickly and easily designing freeform models such as stuffed animals and other rotund objects. The user draws several 2D freeform strokes interactively on the screen and the system automatically constructs plausible 3D polygonal surfaces. Our system supports several modeling operations, including the operation to construct a 3D polygonal surface from a 2D silhouette drawn by the user: it inflates the region surrounded by the silhouette making wide areas fat, and narrow areas thin. Teddy, our prototype system, is implemented as a Java™ program, and the mesh construction is done in real-time on a standard PC. Our informal user study showed that a first-time user typically masters the operations within 10 minutes, and can construct interesting 3D models within minutes.

**CR Categories and Subject Descriptions:** I.3.6 [Computer Graphics]: Methodology and Techniques – Interaction Techniques; I.3.5 [Computer Graphics]: Computational Geometry and Object Modeling – Geometric algorithms

**Additional Keywords:** 3D modeling, sketching, pen-based systems, gestures, design, chordal axes, inflation

Figure1: Teddy in use on a display-integrated tablet.

Figure 2: Painted models created using Teddy and painted using a commercial texture-map editor.

## 1 INTRODUCTION

Although much progress has been made over the years on 3D modeling systems, they are still difficult and tedious to use when creating freeform surfaces. Their emphasis has been the precise modeling of objects motivated by CAD and similar domains. Recently SKETCH [29] introduced a gesture-based interface for the rapid modeling of CSG-like models consisting of simple primitives.

This paper extends these ideas to create a sketching interface for designing 3D freeform objects. The essential idea is the use of freeform strokes as an expressive design tool. The user draws 2D freeform strokes *interactively* specifying the silhouette of an object, and the system automatically constructs a 3D polygonal surface model based on the strokes. The user does not have to manipulate control points or combine complicated editing operations. Using our technique, even first-time users can create simple, yet expressive 3D models within minutes. In addition, the resulting models have a hand-crafted feel (such as sculptures and stuffed animals) which is difficult to accomplish with most conventional modelers. Examples are shown in Figure 2.

We describe here the sketching interface and the algorithms for constructing 3D shapes from 2D strokes. We also discuss the implementation of our prototype system, Teddy. The geometric representation we use is a standard polygonal mesh to allow the use of numerous software resources for post-manipulation and rendering. However, the interface itself can be used to create other representations such as volumes [25] or metaballs [17].

Like SKETCH [29], Teddy is designed for the rapid construction of approximate models, not for the careful editing of precise models. To emphasize this design goal and encourage creative exploration, we use the real-time pen-and-ink rendering described in [16], as shown in Figure 1. This also allows real-time interactive rendering using Java on mid-range PCs without

{takeo, tanaka}@mtl.t.u-tokyo.ac.jp, matsu@is.titech.ac.jp

http://mtl.t.u-tokyo.ac.jp/~takeo

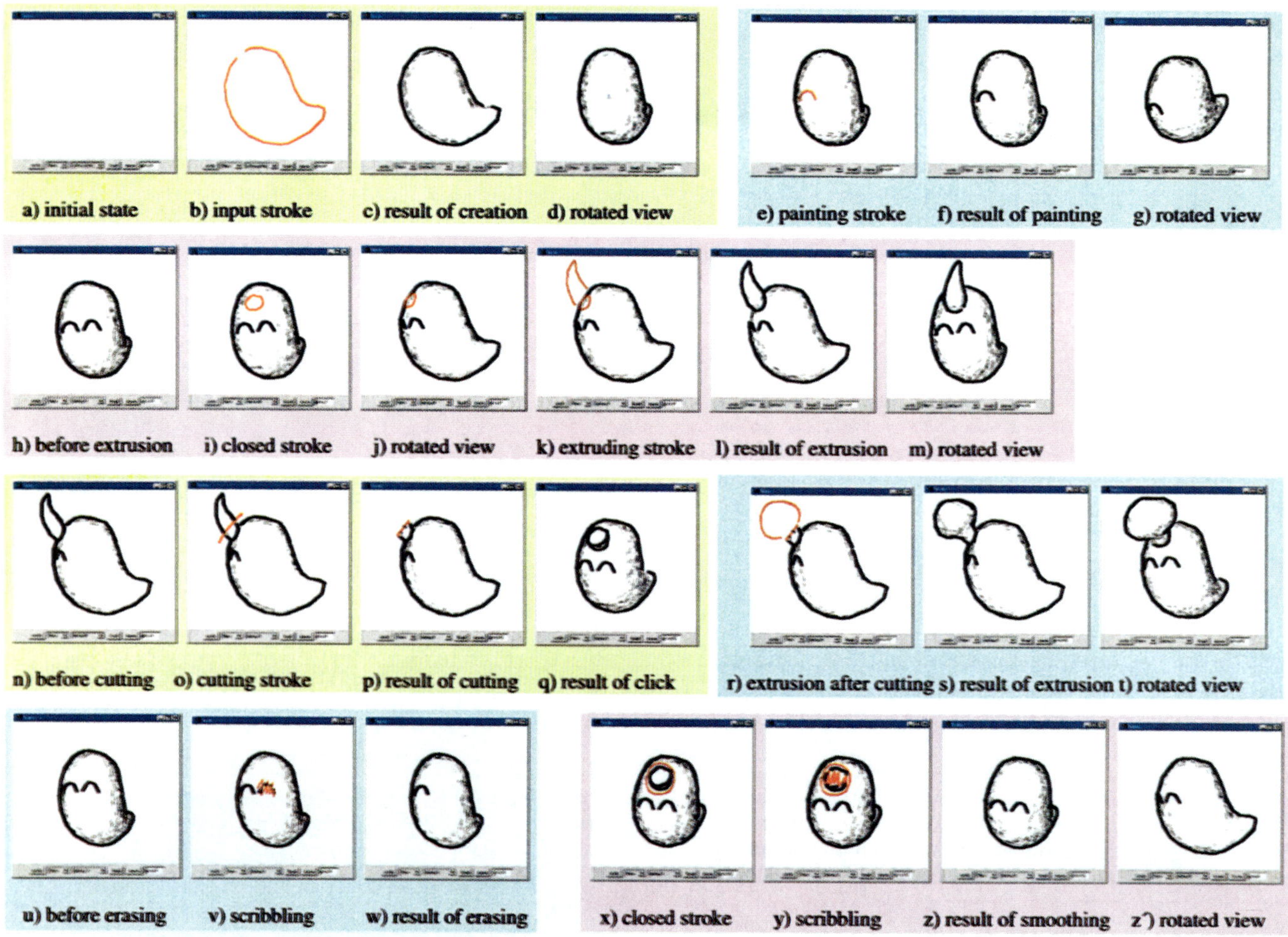


Figure 3: Overview of the modeling operations.

dedicated 3D rendering hardware.

An obvious application of Teddy is the design of 3D models for character animation. However, in addition to augmenting traditional 3D modelers, Teddy's ease of use has the potential to open up new application areas for 3D modeling. Possibilities include rapid prototyping in the early stages of design, educational/recreational use for non-professionals and children, and real-time communication assistance on pen-based systems.

The accompanying videotape demonstrates Teddy's user interface. Teddy is available as a Java applet at the following web site. http://www.mtl.t.u-tokyo.ac.jp/~takeo/teddy/teddy.htm

## 2 RELATED WORK

A typical procedure for geometric modeling is to start with a simple primitive such as a cube or a sphere, and gradually construct a more complex model through successive transformations or a combination of multiple primitives. Various deformation techniques [15,23] and other shape-manipulation tools [8] are examples of transformation techniques that let the user create a wide variety of precise, smooth shapes by interactively manipulating control points or 3D widgets.

Another approach to geometric modeling is the use of implicit surfaces [3,18]. The user specifies the skeleton of the intended model and the system constructs smooth, natural-looking surfaces around it. The surface inflation technique [17] extrudes the polygonal mesh from the skeleton outwards. In contrast, our approach lets the user specify the silhouette of the intended shape directly instead of by specifying its skeleton.

Some modeling systems achieve intuitive, efficient operation using 3D input/output devices [6]. 3D devices can simplify the operations that require multiple operations when using 2D devices.

Our sketching interface is inspired by previous sketch-based modeling systems [7,29] that interpret the user's freeform strokes and interactively construct 3D rectilinear models. Our goal is to develop a similar interface for designing rounded freeform models.

Inflation of a 2D drawing is introduced in [27], and 3D surface editing based on a 2D painting technique is discussed in [28]. Their target is basically a 2D array with associated height values, rather than a 3D polygonal model.

The use of freeform strokes for 2D applications has recently become popular. Some systems [10,14] use strokes to specify gestural commands and others [2] use freeform strokes for specifying 2D curves. These systems find the best matching arcs or splines automatically, freeing the users from explicit control of underlying parameters.

We use a polygonal mesh representation, but some systems use a volumetric representation [9,25], which is useful for designing topologically complicated shapes. Our mesh-construction algorithm is based on a variety of work on polygonal mesh manipulation, such as mesh optimization [12], shape design [26], and surface fairing [24], which allows polygonal meshes to be widely used as a fundamental representation for geometric

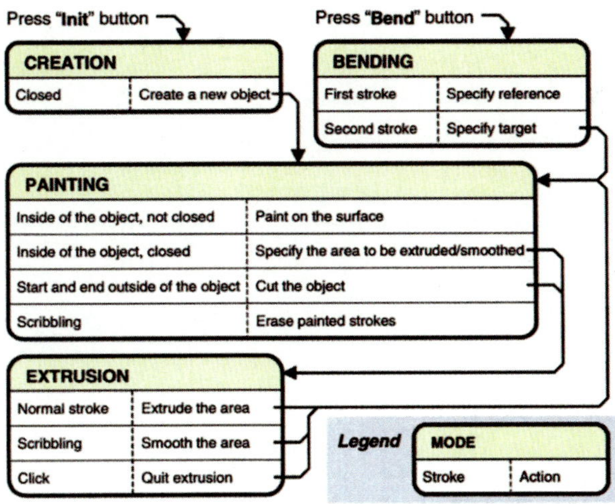


Figure 4: Summary of the gestural operations.

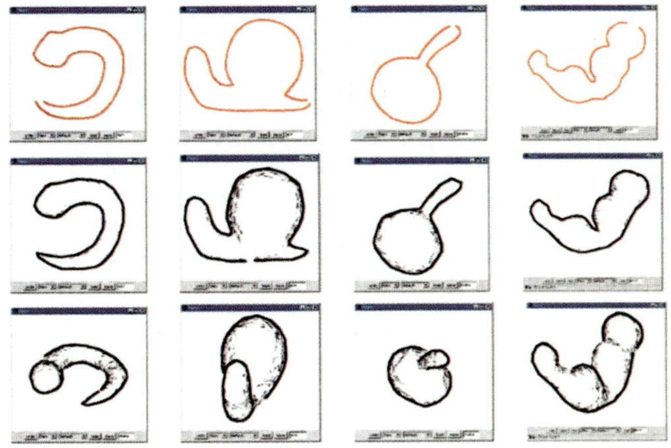

a) snake b) snail c) cherry d) muscular arm

Figure 5: Examples of creation operation (top: input stroke, middle: result of creation, bottom: rotated view).

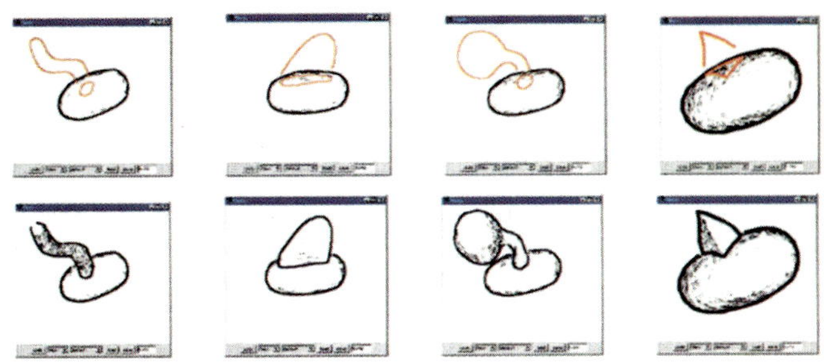

a) long b) thin c) fat d) sharp

Figure 6: Examples of extrusion (top: extruding stroke, bottom: result of extrusion).

a) digging stroke b) result c) rotated d) closed stroke e) after click

Figure 7: More extrusion operations: digging a cavity (a-c) and turning the closed stroke into a surface drawing (d-e).

modeling and computer graphics in general.

# 3 USER INTERFACE

Teddy's physical user interface is based upon traditional 2D input devices such as a standard mouse or tablet. We use a two-button mouse with no modifier keys. Unlike traditional modeling systems, Teddy does not use WIMP-style direct manipulation techniques or standard interface widgets such as buttons and menus for modeling operations. Instead, the user specifies his or her desired operation using freeform strokes on the screen, and the system infers the user's intent and executes the appropriate editing operations. Our videotape shows how a small number of simple operations let the users create very rich models.

In addition to gestures, Teddy supports direct camera manipulation using the secondary mouse button based on a virtual trackball model [13]. We also use a few button widgets for auxiliary operations, such as save and load, and for initiating bending operations.

# 4 MODELING OPERATIONS

This section describes Teddy's modeling operations from the user's point of view; details of the algorithms are left to the next section. Some operations are executed immediately after the user completes a stroke, while some require multiple strokes. The current system supports neither the creation of multiple objects at once, nor operations to combine single objects. Additionally, models must have a spherical topology; e.g., the user cannot create a torus. An overview of the model construction process is given first, and then each operation is described in detail.

The modeling operations are carefully designed to allow incremental learning by novice users. Users can create a variety of models by learning only the first operation (creation), and can incrementally expand their vocabulary by learning other operations as necessary. We have found it helpful to restrict first-time users to the first three basic operations (creation, painting, and extrusion), and then to introduce other advanced operations after these basic operations are mastered.

## 4.1 Overview

Figure 3 introduces Teddy's general model construction process. The user begins by drawing a single freeform stroke on a blank canvas (Figures 3a-b). As soon as the user finishes drawing the stroke, the system automatically constructs a corresponding 3D shape (c). The user can now view the model from a different direction (d). Once a model is created, it may be modified using various operations. The user can draw a line on the surface (e-g) by drawing a stroke within the model silhouette. If the stroke is closed, the resulting surface line turns red and the system enters "extrusion mode" (h-i). Then the user rotates the model (j) and draws the second stroke specifying the silhouette of the extruded surface (k-m). A stroke that crosses the silhouette cuts the model (n-o) and turns the cut section red (p). The user either clicks to complete the operation (q) or draws a silhouette to extrude the section (r-t). Scribbling on the surface erases the line segments on the surface (u-w). If the user scribbles during the extrusion mode (x-y), the system smoothes the area surrounded by the closed red line (z-z´).

Figure 4 summarizes the modeling operations available on the current implementation. Note that the appropriate action is chosen based on the stroke's position and shape, as well as the current

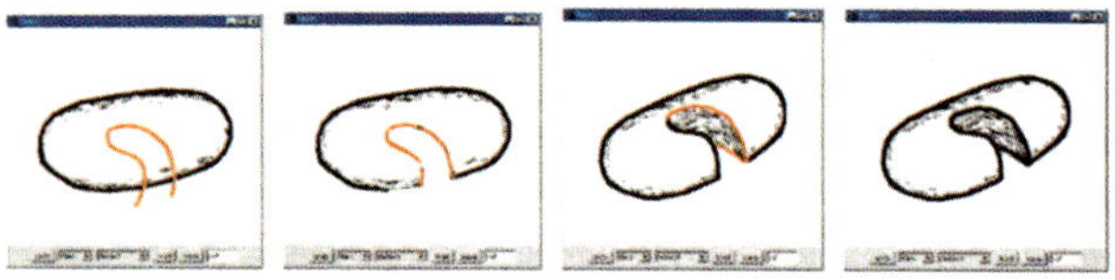

a) biting stroke b) result c) rotated view d) after click

Figure 8: Cutting operation.

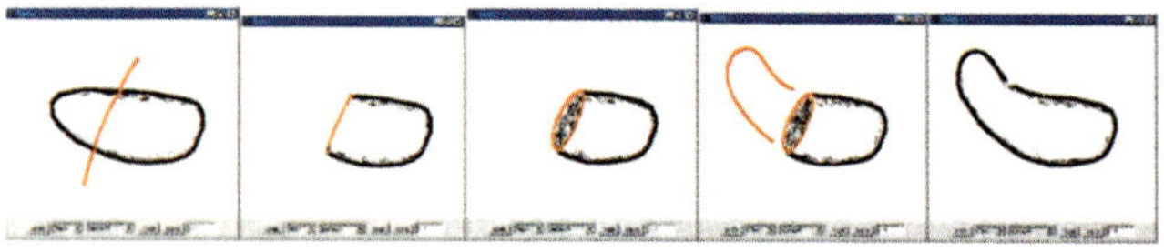

a) cutting stroke b) result c) rotated d) extruding stroke e) result

Figure 9: Extrusion after cutting.

mode of the system.

## 4.2 Creating a New Object

Starting with a blank canvas, the user creates a new object by drawing its silhouette as a closed freeform stroke. The system automatically constructs a 3D shape based on the 2D silhouette. Figure 5 shows examples of input strokes and the corresponding 3D models. The start point and end point of the stroke are automatically connected, and the operation fails if the stroke is self-intersecting. The algorithm to calculate the 3D shape is described in detail in section 5. Briefly, the system inflates the closed region in both directions with the amount depending on the width of the region: that is, wide areas become fat, and narrow areas become thin. Our experience so far shows that this algorithm generates a reasonable-looking freeform shape. In addition to the creation operation, the user can begin model construction by loading a simple primitive. The current implementation provides a cube and a sphere, but adding more shapes is straightforward.

## 4.3 Painting and Erasing on the Surface

The object surface is painted by drawing a freeform stroke within the object's silhouette on the canvas (the stroke must not cross the silhouette) [11]. The 2D stroke is projected onto the object surface as 3D line segments, called surface lines (Figure 3e-g). The user can erase these surface lines by drawing a scribbling stroke[1] (Figure 3u-w). This painting operation does not modify the 3D geometry of the model, but lets the user express ideas quickly and conveniently when using Teddy as a communication medium or design tool.

## 4.4 Extrusion

Extrusion is a two-stroke operation: a closed stroke on the surface and a stroke depicting the silhouette of the extruded surface. When the user draws a closed stroke on the object surface, the system highlights the corresponding surface line in red, indicating the initiation of "extrusion mode" (Figure 3i). The user then rotates the model to bring the red surface line sideways (Figure 3j) and draws a silhouette line to extrude the surface (Figure 3k). This is basically a sweep operation that constructs the 3D shape by moving the closed surface line along the skeleton of the silhouette

[1] A stroke is recognized as scribbling when `sl/pl > 1.5`, where `sl` is the length of the stroke and `pl` is the perimeter of its convex hull.

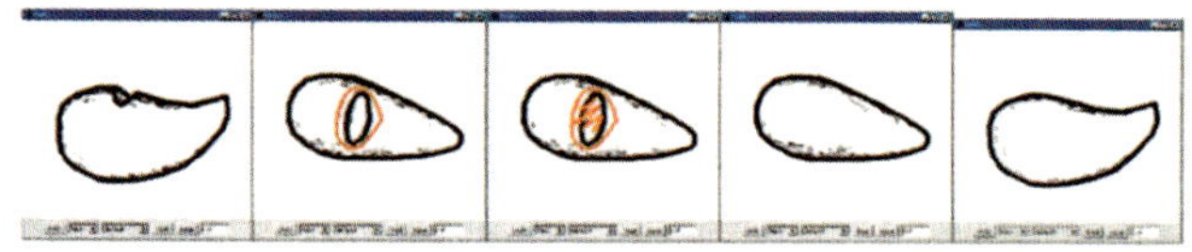

a) cleaning a cavity

b) smoothing a sharp edge

Figure 10: Smoothing operation.

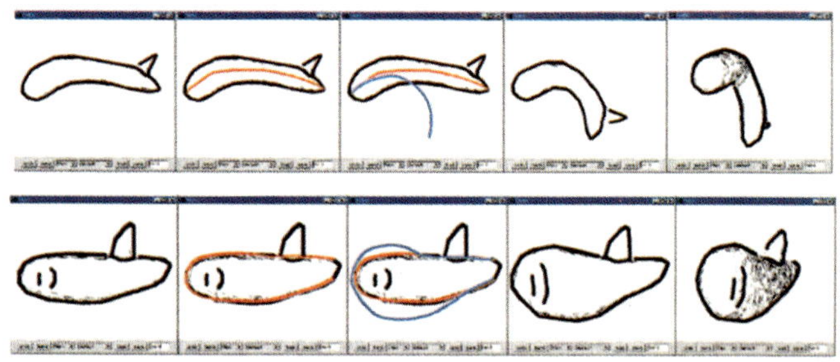

a) original b) reference stroke c) target stroke d) result e) rotated

Figure 11: Examples of transformation (top: bending, bottom: distortion).

(Figure 3l-m). The direction of extrusion is always perpendicular to the object surface, not parallel to the screen. Users can create a wide variety of shapes using this operation, as shown in Figure 6. They can also make a cavity on the surface by drawing an inward silhouette (Figure 7a-c). The current implementation does not support holes that completely extend to the other side of the object. If the user decides not to extrude, a single click turns the red stroke into an ordinary painted stroke (Figure 7d-e).

## 4.5 Cutting

A cutting operation starts when the user draws a stroke that runs across the object, starting and terminating outside its silhouette (Figure 3o). The stroke divides the object into two pieces at the plane defined by the camera position and the stroke. What is on the screen to the left of the stroke is then removed entirely (Figure 3p) (as when a carpenter saws off a piece of wood). The cutting operation finishes with a click of the mouse (Figure 3q). The user can also `bite' the object using the same operation (Figure 8).

The cutting stroke turns the section edges red, indicating that the system is in "extrusion mode". The user can draw a stroke to extrude the section instead of a click (Figure3r-t, Figure 9). This "extrusion after cutting" operation is useful to modify the shape without causing creases at the root of the extrusion.

## 4.6 Smoothing

One often *smoothes* the surface of clay models to eliminate bumps and creases. Teddy lets the user smooth the surface by drawing a scribble during "extrusion mode." Unlike erasing, this operation modifies the actual geometry: it first removes all the polygons surrounded by the closed red surface line and then creates an entirely new surface that covers the region smoothly. This operation is useful to remove unwanted bumps and cavities (Figure 3x-z', Figure 10a), or to smooth the creases caused by earlier extrusion operations (Figure 10b).

## 4.7 Transformation

We are currently experimenting with an additional "transformation" editing operation that distorts the model while preserving the polygonal mesh topology. Although it functions properly, the interface itself is not fully gestural because the modal transition into the bending mode requires a button push.

This operation starts when the user presses the "bend" button and uses two freeform strokes called the *reference stroke* and the *target stroke* to modify the model. The system moves vertices of the polygonal model so that the spatial relation between the original position and the target stroke is identical to the relation between the resulting position and the reference stroke. This movement is parallel to the screen, and the vertices do not move perpendicular to the screen. This operation is described in [5] as *warp*; we do not discuss the algorithm further.

Transformation can be used to bend, elongate, and distort the shape (Figure 11). We plan to make the system infer the reference stroke automatically from the object's structure in order to simplify the operation in a manner similar to the mark-based interaction technique of [2].

# 5 ALGORITHM

We next describe how the system constructs a 3D polygonal mesh from the user's freeform strokes. Internally, a model is represented as a polygonal mesh. Each editing operation modifies the mesh to conform to the shape specified by the user's input strokes (Figure 12). The resulting model is always topologically equivalent to a sphere. We developed the current implementation as a prototype for designing the interface; the algorithms are subject to further refinement and they fail for some illegal strokes (in that case, the system indicates the problem and requests an alternative stroke). However, these exceptional cases are fairly rare, and the algorithm works well for a wide variety of shapes.

Our algorithms for creation and extrusion are closely related to those for freeform surface construction based on skeletons [3,18], which create a surface around user-defined skeletons using implicit surface techniques. While our current implementation does not use implicit surfaces, they could be used in an alternative implementation.

In order to remove noise in the handwriting input stroke and to construct a regular polygonal mesh, every input stroke is re-sampled to form a smooth polyline with uniform edge length before further processing [4].

## 5.1 Creating a New Object

Our algorithm creates a new closed polygonal mesh model from the initial stroke. The overall procedure is this: we first create a closed planar polygon by connecting the start-point and end-point of the stroke, and determine the spine or axes of the polygon using

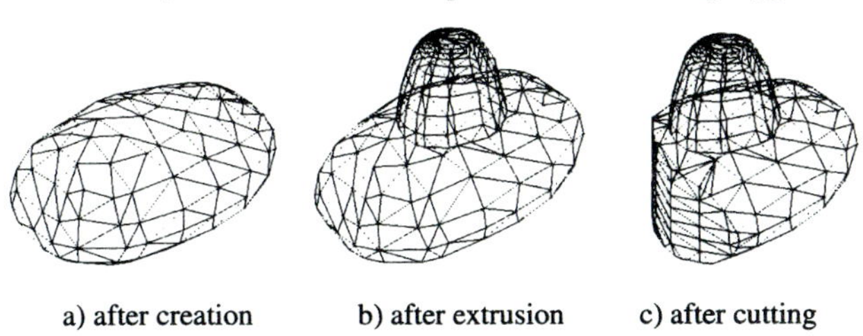

a) after creation b) after extrusion c) after cutting

Figure 12: Internal representation.

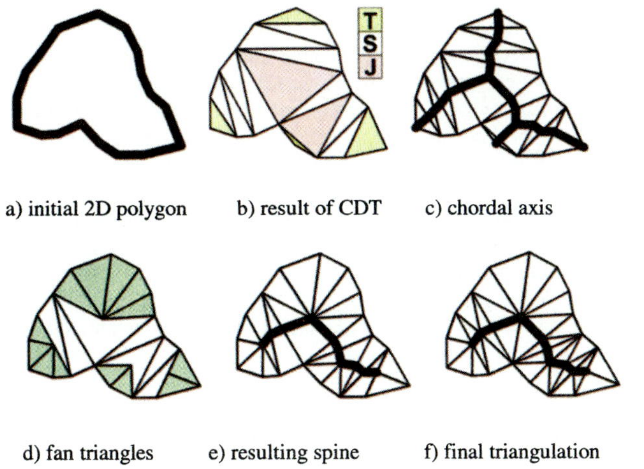


a) initial 2D polygon b) result of CDT c) chordal axis

d) fan triangles e) resulting spine f) final triangulation

Figure 13: Finding the spine.

the *chordal axis* introduced in [21]. We then elevate the vertices of the spine by an amount proportional to their distance from the polygon. Finally, we construct a polygonal mesh wrapping the spine and the polygon in such a way that sections form ovals.

When constructing the initial closed planar polygon, the system makes all edges a predefined unit length (see Figure 13a). If the polygon is self-intersecting, the algorithm stops and the system requests an alternative stroke. The edges of this initial polygon are called *external edges*, while edges added in the following triangulation are called *internal edges*.

The system then performs constrained Delaunay triangulation of the polygon (Figure 13b). We then divide the triangles into three categories: triangles with two external edges (terminal triangle), triangles with one external edge (sleeve triangle), and triangles without external edges (junction triangle). The chordal axis is obtained by connecting the midpoints of the internal edges (Figure 13c), but our inflation algorithm first requires the *pruning* of insignificant branches and the retriangulation of the mesh. This pruning algorithm is also introduced in [21].

To prune insignificant branches, we examine each terminal triangle in turn, expanding it into progressively larger regions by merging it with adjacent triangles (Figure 14a-b). Let X be a terminal triangle; then X has two exterior edges and one interior edge. We erect a semicircle whose diameter is the interior edge, and which lies on the same side of that edge as does X. If all three vertices of X lie on or within this semicircle, we remove the interior edge and merge X with the triangle that lies on the other side of the edge.

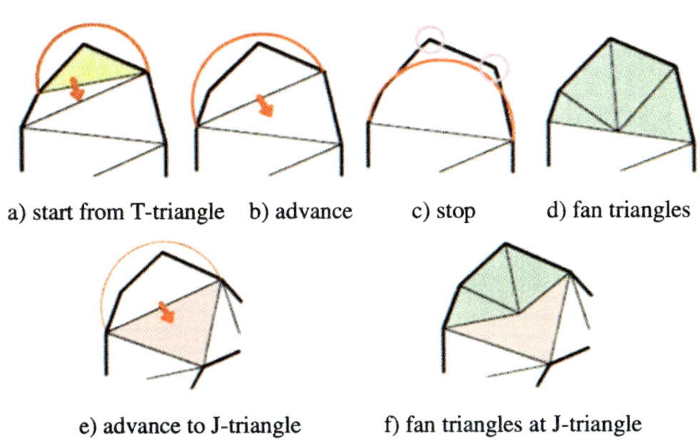

a) start from T-triangle b) advance c) stop d) fan triangles

e) advance to J-triangle f) fan triangles at J-triangle

Figure 14: Pruning.

If the newly merged triangle is a sleeve triangle, then X now has three exterior edges and a new interior edge. Again we erect a semicircle on the interior edge and check that all vertices are within it. We continue until some vertex lies outside the semicircle (Figure 14c), or until the newly merged triangle is a junction triangle. In the first case, we triangulate X with a "fan" of triangles radiating from the midpoint of the interior edge (Figure 14d). In the second case, we triangulate with a fan from the midpoint of the junction triangle (Figure 14e-f). The resulting fan triangles are shown in Figure 13d. The pruned spine is obtained by connecting the midpoints of remaining sleeve and junction triangles' internal edges (Figure 13e).

The next step is to subdivide the sleeve triangles and junction triangles to make them ready for elevation. These triangles are divided at the spine and the resulting polygons are triangulated, so that we now have a complete 2D triangular mesh between the spine and the perimeter of the initial polygon (Figure 13f).

Next, each vertex of the spine is elevated proportionally to the average distance between the vertex and the external vertices that are directly connected to the vertex (Figure 15a,b). Each internal edge of each fan triangle, excluding spine edges, is converted to a quarter oval (Figure 15c), and the system constructs an appropriate polygonal mesh by sewing together the neighboring elevated edges, as shown in Figure 15d. The elevated mesh is copied to the other side to make the mesh closed and symmetric. Finally, the system applies mesh refinement algorithms to remove short edges and small triangles [12].

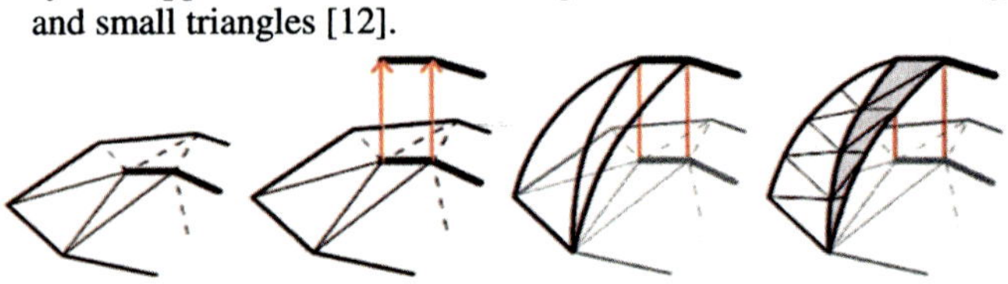

a) before b) elevate spines c) elevate edges d) sew elevated edges

Figure 15: Polygonal mesh construction.

## 5.2 Painting on the Surface

The system creates surface lines by sequentially projecting each line segment of the input stroke onto the object's surface polygons. For each line segment, the system first calculates a bounded plane consisting of all rays shot from the camera through the segment on the screen. Then the system finds all intersections between the plane and each polygon of the object, and splices the resulting 3D line segments together (Figure 16). The actual implementation searches for the intersections efficiently using polygon connectivity information. If a ray from the camera crosses multiple polygons, only the polygon nearest to the camera position is used. If the resulting 3D segments cannot be spliced together (e.g., if the stroke crosses a "fold" of the object), the algorithm fails.

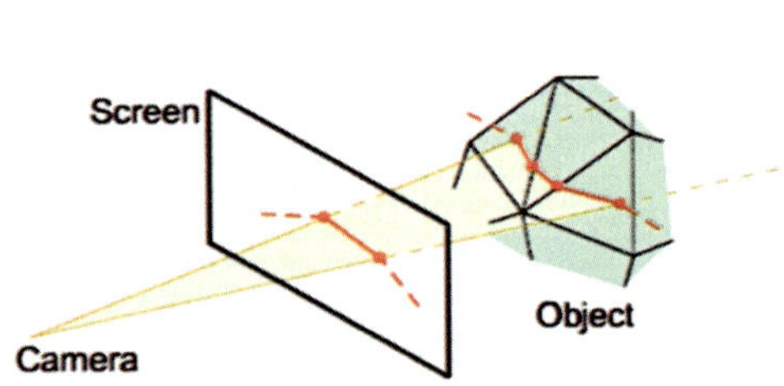


Figure 16: Construction of surface lines.

## 5.3 Extrusion

The extrusion algorithm creates new polygonal meshes based on a closed base surface line (called the base ring) and an extruding stroke. Briefly, the 2D extruding stroke is projected onto a plane perpendicular to the object surface (Figure 17a), and the base ring is swept along the projected extruding stroke (Figure 17b). The base ring is defined as a closed 3D polyline that lies on the surface of the polygonal mesh, and the normal of the ring is defined as that of the best matching plane of the ring.

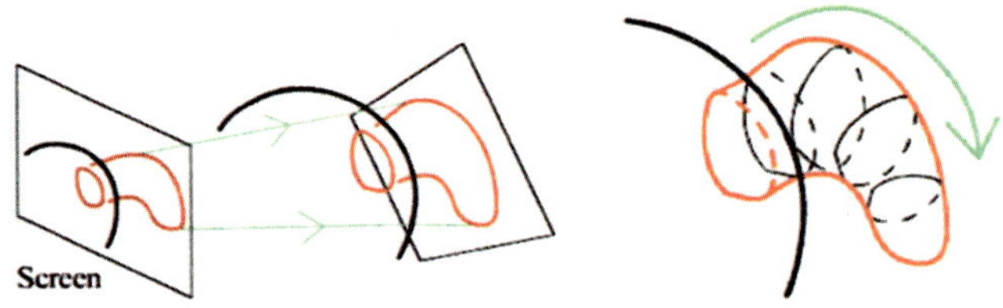


a) projection of the stroke b) sweep along the projected stroke

Figure 17: Extrusion algorithm.

First, the system finds the plane for projection: the plane passing through the base ring's center of gravity and lying parallel to the normal of the base ring[2]. Under the above constraints, the plane faces towards the camera as much as possible (Figure 17a).

Then the algorithm projects the 2D extruding stroke onto the plane, producing a 3D extruding stroke. Copies of the base ring are created along the extruding stroke in such a way as to be almost perpendicular to the direction of the extrusion, and are resized to fit within the stroke. This is done by advancing two pointers (left and right) along the extruding stroke starting from both ends. In each step, the system chooses the best of the following three possibilities: advance the left pointer, the right pointer, or both. The *goodness* value increases when the angle between the line connecting the pointers and the direction of the stroke at each pointer is close to 90 degrees (Figure 18a). This process completes when the two pointers meet.

Finally, the original polygons surrounded by the base ring are deleted, and new polygons are created by sewing the neighboring copies of the base ring together [1] (Figure 18b). The system uses the same algorithm to dig a cavity on the surface.

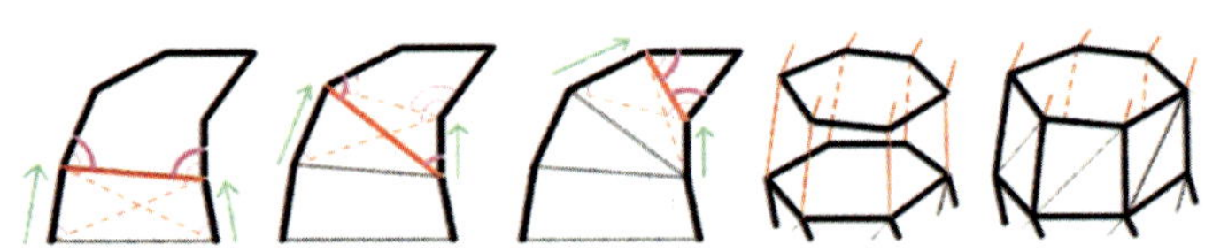

a) pointer advancing b) sewing adjacent rings

Figure 18: Sweeping the base ring.

This simple algorithm works well for a wide variety of extrusions but creates unintuitive shapes when the user draws unexpected extruding strokes or when the base surface is not sufficiently planar (Figure 19).

[2] The normal of the ring is calculated as follows: Project the points of the ring to the original XY-plane. Then compute the enclosed "signed area" by the formula:
`Axy = 0.5*sum(i=0, i=n-1, x[i]*y[i+1]-x[i+1]*y[i])`
(indices are wrapped around so that `x[n]` means `x[0]`).
Calculate `Ayx` and `Azx` similarly, and the vector
`v=(Ayz,Azx,Axy)` is defined as the normal of the ring.

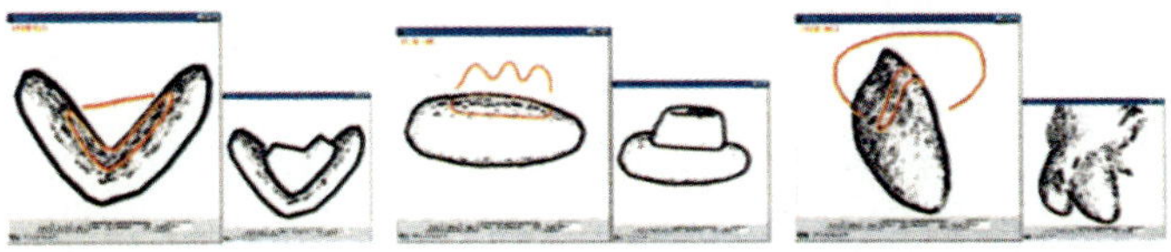

a) flat extrusion b) wavy extrusion c) wrapping extrusion

Figure 19: Unintuitive extrusions.

## 5.4 Cutting

The cutting algorithm is based on the painting algorithm. Each line segment of the cutting stroke is projected onto the front and back facing polygons. The system connects the corresponding end points of the projected edges to construct a planer polygon (Figure 20). This operation is performed for every line segment, and the system constructs the complete section by splicing these planer polygons together. Finally, the system triangulates each planer polygon [22], and removes all polygons to the left of the cutting stroke.

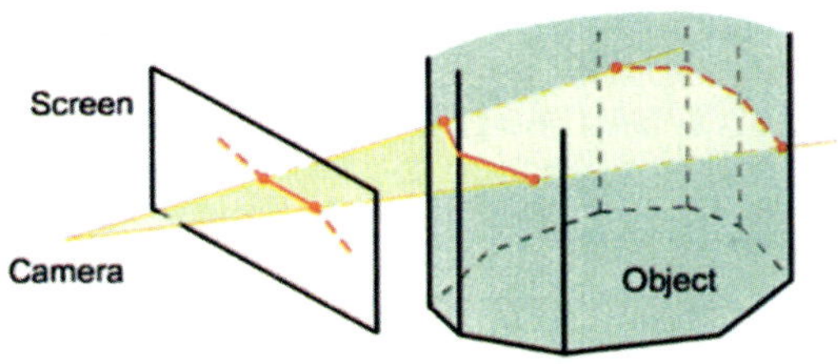


Figure 20: Cutting.

## 5.5 Smoothing

The smoothing operation deletes the polygons surrounded by the closed surface line (called a ring) and creates new polygons to cover the hole smoothly. First, the system translates the objects into a coordinate system whose Z-axis is parallel to the normal of the ring. Next, the system creates a 2D polygon by projecting the ring onto the XY-plane in the newly created coordinate system, and triangulates the polygon (Figure 21b). (The current implementation fails if the area surrounded by the ring contains creases and is folded when projected on the XY-plane.) The triangulation is designed to create a good triangular mesh based on [22]: it first creates a constrained Delaunay triangulation and gradually refines the mesh by edge splitting and flipping; then each vertex is elevated along the Z-axis to create a smooth 3D surface (Figure 21d).

The algorithm for determining the Z-value of a vertex is as follows: For each edge of the ring, consider a plane that passes through the vertex and the midpoint of the edge and is parallel to the Z-axis. Then calculate the z-value of the vertex so that it lies on the 2D Bezier curve that smoothly interpolates both ends of the ring on the plane (Figure 21c). The final z-value of the vertex is

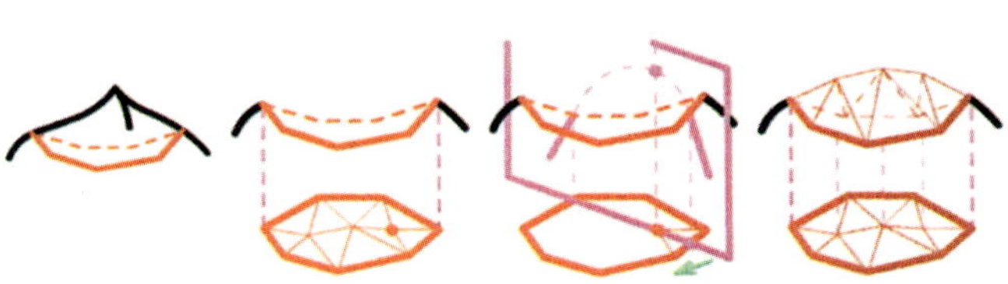

a) before b) triangulation c) calculating Z-value d) result

Figure 21: Smoothing algorithm.

the average of these z-values.

Finally, we apply a surface-fairing algorithm [24] to the newly created polygons to enhance smoothness.

## 6 IMPLEMENTATION

Our prototype is implemented as a 13,000 line Java program. We tested a display-integrated tablet (Mutoh MVT-14, see Figure 1) and an electric whiteboard (Xerox Liveboard) in addition to a standard mouse. The mesh construction process is completely real-time, but causes a short pause (a few seconds) when the model becomes complicated. Teddy can export models in OBJ file format. Figure 2 shows some 3D models created with Teddy by an expert user and painted using a commercial texture-map editor. Note that these models look quite different from 3D models created in other modeling systems, reflecting the hand-drawn nature of the shape.

## 7 USER EXPERIENCE

The applet version of Teddy has undergone limited distribution, and has been used (mainly by computer graphics researchers and students) to create different 3D models. Feedback from these users indicates that Teddy is quite intuitive and encourages them to explore various 3D designs. In addition, we have started close observation of how first-time users (mainly graduate students in computer science) learn Teddy. We start with a detailed tutorial and then show some stuffed animals, asking the users to create them using Teddy. Generally, the users begin to create their own models fluently within 10 minutes: five minutes of tutorial and five minutes of guided practice. After that, it takes a few minutes for them to create a stuffed animal such as those in Figure 2 (excluding the texture).

## 8 FUTURE WORK

Our current algorithms and implementation are robust and efficient enough for experimental use. However, they can fail or generate unintuitive results when the user draws unexpected strokes. We must devise more robust and flexible algorithms to handle a variety of user inputs. In particular, we plan to enhance the extrusion algorithm to allow more detailed control of surfaces. We are also considering using implicit surface construction techniques.

Another important research direction is to develop additional modeling operations to support a wider variety of shapes with arbitrary topology, and to allow more precise control of the shape. Possible operations are creating creases, twisting the model, and specifying the constraints between the separate parts for animation systems [20]. While we are satisfied with the simplicity of the current set of gestural operations, these extended operations will inevitably complicate the interface, and careful interface design will be required.

## 9 ACKNOWLEDGEMENTS

This project was not possible without the support and encouragement of people. We would especially like to thank Marshall Bern, Lee Markosian, Robert C. Zeleznik, and Hiromasa Suzuki for their invaluable advice in the development of the system, and we thank John F. Hughes, Randy Pausch, Jeffrey S. Pierce, Joe Marks, Jock D. Mackinlay, Andrew Glassner, and Brygg Ullmer for their help in the preparation of this paper. We also thank the SIGGRAPH reviewers for their thoughtful comments. This work is supported in part by JSPS Research Fellowship.

## References


1. G. Barequet and M Sharir. Piecewise-linear interpolation between polygonal slices. *ACM 10th Computational Geometry Proceedings*, pages 93-102, 1994.
2. T. Baudel. A mark-based interaction paradigm for free-hand drawing. *UIST'94 Conference Proceedings*, pages 185-192, 1994.
3. J. Bloomenthal and B. Wyvill. Interactive techniques for implicit modeling. *1990 Symposium on Interactive 3D Graphics*, pages 109-116, 1990.
4. J.M. Cohen, L. Markosian, R.C. Zeleznik, J.F. Hughes, and R. Barzel. An Interface for Sketching 3D Curves. *1999 Symposium on Interactive 3D Graphics*, pages 17-21, 1999.
5. W.T. Correa, R.J. Jensen, C.E. Thayer, and A. Finkelstein. Texture mapping for cel animation. *SIGGRAPH 98 Conference Proceedings*, pages 435-456, 1998.
6. M. Deering. The Holosketch VR sketching system. *Communications of the ACM*, 39(5):54-61, May 1996.
7. L. Eggli, C. Hsu, G. Elber, and B. Bruderlin, Inferring 3D models from freehand sketches and constraints. *Computer-Aided Design*, 29(2): 101-112, Feb.1997.
8. C.Grimm, D. Pugmire, M. Bloomental, J. F. Hughes, and E. Cohen. Visual interfaces for solids modeling. *UIST '95 Conference Proceedings*, pages 51-60, 1995.
9. T. Galyean and J.F. Hughes. Sculpting: an interactive volumetric modeling technique. *SIGGRAPH '91 Conference Proceedings*, pages 267-274, 1991.
10. M.D. Gross and E.Y.L. Do. Ambiguous intentions: A paper-like interface for creative design. *UIST'96 Conference Proceedings*, pages 183-192, 1996.
11. P. Hanrahan, P. Haeberli, Direct WYSIWYG Painting and Texturing on 3D Shapes, *SIGGRAPH 90 Conference Proceedings*, pages 215-224, 1990.
12. H. Hoppe, T. DeRose, T. Duchamp, J. McDonald, and W. Stuetzle. Mesh optimization. *SIGGRAPH 93 Conference Proceedings*, pages 19-26, 1993.
13. J. Hultquist. A virtual trackball. *Graphics Gems* (ed. A. Glassner). Academic Press, pages 462-463, 1990.
14. J.A. Landay and B.A. Myers. Interactive sketching for the early stages of user interface design. *CHI'95 Conference Proceedings*, pages 43-50, 1995.
15. R. MacCracken and K.I. Joy. Free-form deformations with lattices of arbitrary topology. *SIGGRAPH 96 Conference Proceedings*, pages 181-188, 1996.
16. L. Markosian, M.A. Kowalski, S.J. Trychin, L.D. Bourdev, D. Goldstein, and J.F. Hughes. Real-time nonphotorealistic rendering. *SIGGRAPH 97 Conference Proceedings*, pages 415-420, 1997.
17. H. Nishimura, M. Hirai, T. Kawai, T. Kawata, I. Shirakawa, K. Omura. Object modeling by distribution function and a method of image generation. Transactions of the Institute of Electronics and Communication Engineers of Japan, J68-D(4):718-725, 1985
18. L. Markosian, J.M. Cohen, T. Crulli and J.F. Hughes. Skin: A Constructive Approach to Modeling Free-form Shapes. *SIGGRAPH 99*, to appear, 1999.
19. K. van Overveld and B. Wyvill. Polygon inflation for animated models: a method for the extrusion of arbitrary polygon meshes. *Journal of Visualization and Computer Animation*, 18: 3-16, 1997.
20. R. Pausch, T. Burnette, A.C. Capeheart, M. Conway, D. Cosgrove, R. DeLine, J. Durbin, R. Gossweiler, S. Koga, and J. White. Alice: Rapid prototyping system for virtual reality. *IEEE Computer Graphics and Applications*, 15(3): 8-11, May 1995.
21. L. Prasad. Morphological analysis of shapes. *CNLS Newsletter*, 139: 1-18, July 1997.
22. J.R. Shewchuk. Triangle: engineering a 2D quality mesh generator and Delauny triangulator. *First Workshop on Applied Computational Geometry Proceedings*, pages 124-133, 1996.
23. K. Singh and E. Fiume. Wires: a geometric deformation technique. *SIGGRAPH 98 Conference Proceedings*, pages 405-414, 1998.
24. G. Taubin. A signal processing approach to fair surface design. *SIGGRAPH 95 Conference Proceedings*, pages 351-358, 1995.
25. S.W. Wang and A.E. Kaufman, Volume sculpting. *1995 Symposium on Interactive 3D Graphics*, pages 109-116, 1995.
26. W. Welch and A. Witkin. Free-form shape design using triangulated surfaces. *SIGGRAPH 94 Conference Proceedings*, pages 247-256, 1994.
27. L. Williams. Shading in Two Dimensions. Graphics Interface '91, pages 143-151, 1991.
28. L. Williams. 3D Paint. *1990 Symposium on Interactive 3D Graphics*, pages 225-233, 1990.
29. R.C. Zeleznik, K.P. Herndon, and J.F. Hughes. SKETCH: An interface for sketching 3D scenes. *SIGGRAPH 96 Conference Proceedings*, pages 163-170, 1996.

# Digital Facial Engraving

*Victor Ostromoukhov*[1]
Ecole Polytechnique Fédérale de Lausanne (EPFL), Switzerland

## Abstract

This contribution introduces the basic techniques for digital facial engraving, which imitates traditional copperplate engraving. Inspired by traditional techniques, we first establish a set of basic rules thanks to which separate engraving layers are built on the top of the original photo. Separate layers are merged according to simple merging rules and according to range shift/scale masks specially introduced for this purpose. We illustrate the introduced technique by a set of black/white and color engravings, showing different features such as engraving-specific image enhancements, mixing different regular engraving lines with mezzotint, irregular perturbations of engraving lines etc. We introduce the notion of engraving style which comprises a set of separate engraving layers together with a set of associated range shift/scale masks. The engraving style helps to port the look and feel of one engraving to another. Once different libraries of pre-defined mappable engraving styles and an appropriate user interface are added to the basic system, producing a decent gravure starting from a simple digital photo will be a matter of seconds. The engraving technique described in this contribution opens new perspectives for digital art, adding unprecedented power and precision to the engraver's work.

**Keywords:** photorealistic rendering, nonphotorealistic rendering, halftoning, dithering, digital engraving

## 1. Rationale

Engraving is among the most important traditional graphical techniques. It first appeared in the fifteenth century as an illustrative support for budding book-printing, but very quickly became an art in its own right, thanks to its specific expressive power. Actually, four main classes of engraving are used by artists: letterpress or relief printing, intaglio or in-hollow printing, silk screen process and lithography, with several different techniques in each class. The history of printmaking was punctuated by prosperous periods of techniques which later declined for various reasons. Facial engraving is one such example. Extremely popular in seventeenth and eighteenth centuries, when photography did not exist, this wonderful art became almost unused, due to the extreme technical demands that it made on the engraver. Professional copperplate engravers are rare today, and the cost of true engravings is simply too prohibitive to be used in everyday printing. At the same time, traditional facial engraving has no doubt very specific appeal: its neat, sharp appearance distinguishes it advantageously from photos. To appreciate the graphical impact of engravings it's enough to compare the engraved portraits in the Wall Street Journal with portraits in other newspapers produced with traditional impersonal screening.

Does it mean that this enjoyable art is condemned to disappear for purely economical reasons? We don't think so. We do believe that computer graphics can transform traditional engraving into a digital art. Already in the past, considerable effort has been made to transform traditional pen-and-ink illustrations into digital form [24], [22], to make digital watercolors [3], various line art drawings [5], [6], [7], [8], [9], [15], [21], woodcut imitations [18], and expressive painting [13], [17].

**Fig. 1** Traditional copperplate engravings: an enlargement of a modern post stamp (left) and an enlargement of a modern banknote (right).

In the present contribution, we shall try to establish the basis for digital engraving, and more specifically, for facial engraving. Our goal is very precise: starting from a digital photo of a person, to be able to reproduce it faithfully, relying on the technical achievements and techniques that traditional engravers used in the past. The resulting digital engraving should be visually pleasant, and the person must be recognizable. We limit our study to one particular type of facial engraving: copperplate engraving. Although the terms "etching", "mezzotint," "aquatint" and others designate different traditional techniques, we shall sometimes use these terms as well.

Many authors who tried to produce digital gravures in the past were too influenced by their scientific background: they tried to put engraving layers or similar lineart stuctures on 3D parametric surfaces directly attached to the 3D objects (see for example [7], [8], [9], [16]). Notwithstanding the extreme complexity of such an approach, it leads to results of a relative value for facial engraving: simple geometrical objects look too striped, while more sophisticated objects like human face are too complicated to be manipulated easily.

Instead, we tried to reuse the graphical techniques at the disposal of traditional artists who did not know anything about parametric surfaces (see Fig. 1). Visibly, the main rule for creating facial engravings was: the directions of the engraving lines should somehow follow facial features. Somehow means: just loosely related to large facial surfaces. Long curves traversing several features were very welcome (see for example [2], [14]). This rough figure-hugging layered engraving, combined with cross-etching, forms the basis for our approach.

Technically, the micro-photography of the copperplate engraving process shown in Fig. 2a gives us an important insight. The width of the furrows produced by the tip of the graver will influence the engraving line width. The furrows have a specific triangular shape clearly visible in Fig. 2a (please note: they are concave, not convex). Based on this observation, we could build a virtual "univer-

1. http://lspwww.epfl.ch/~victor

sal" copperplate as shown in Fig. 2b. This "universal" copperplate can be cut at different heights thus producing furrows of different widths. By putting ink into the furrows we imitate the true copperplate engraving printing process. But at the same time the process described here is nothing other than conventional dithering, well-known in computer graphics [23]. Simply, the term of virtual "universal" copperplate stands for the threshold matrix (threshold levels corresponding to the height of our "universal" copperplate), while cutting and inking stands for comparison between the input signal level and the current threshold value, thus producing a black or white output signal. The analogy is so perfect that the art of digital copperplate engraving may be resumed as the art of building appropriate threshold structures looking like the "universal" copperplate in Fig. 2b. Once this threshold structure is built, the rendering may be done using conventional dithering software.

In section 2, we establish the basic rules for building separate layers containing elementary engraving lines, as well as the rules for merging separate layers together in order to produce the resulting threshold structure. In section 3, we show how the proposed technique may be applied to black and white engraving. In section 4, simple color extensions are proposed. The perspectives for future work are discussed in section 5. Finally, we draw some conclusions in section 6.

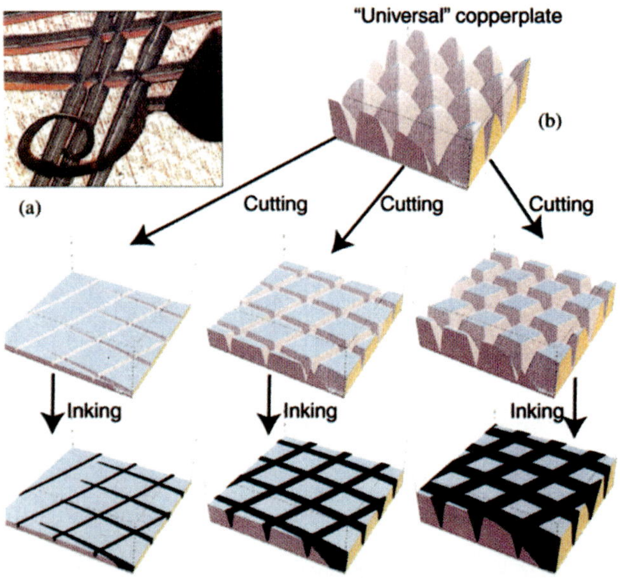


**Fig. 2** (a) A micro-photography of the graver's tip making a furrow in the copperplate showing a shaving lifted by the bevel. (b) Virtual "universal" copperplate cut at different heights, producing furrows of different widths. Putting ink into the furrows imitates the true copperplate engraving printing process.

## 2. Basic rules

Our goal is presently to develop a technique for building separate engraving layers, to transform them in order to follow the desired directions and finally to superimpose these layers, thus forming various cross-etching and smooth transitions between different parts of the artwork rendered by different engraving layers.

In this section we develop a simple and straightforward technique based on the most regular support for any line art: a sequence of equidistant straight lines defined on a given region. We call such a sequence the basic engraving layer. After appropriate morphing, the basic engraving layer roughly corresponds to the main etching technique used in traditional engraving. Later, we shall see how this relatively simple technique may be extended to imitate more sophisticated etching techniques such as irregular lines or mezzotint.

### 2.1 Building separate layers

Let us suppose that the basic (non-transformed) engraving layer is defined on a unit square in the *uv* coordinate system, as shown in Fig. 3. The layer is built of a sequence of threshold structures made up of uniformly spaced waves, as shown in Fig. 3b. The cross-section of each wave has a simple saw shape, directly inspired by the shapes of the furrows in Fig. 2a. The directions of the waves are not necessarily parallel to axes *u* and *v*.

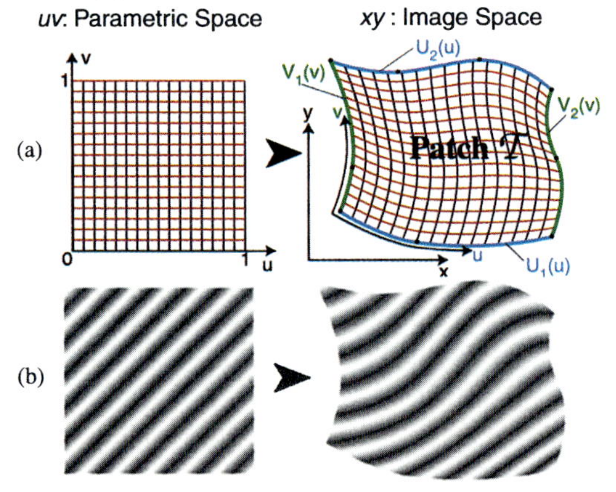


**Fig. 3** Parametric grid defined on a unit square in parametric space *uv* is transformed into morphed parametric grid inside the patch $\mathcal{T}$ in image space *xy* (upper row). This transformation maps Basic Engraving Layer onto Transformed Layer (lower row).

The basic engraving layer can easily be transformed into a warped layer (Fig. 3). There are many ways to perform such a transformation (see for example [11], [12], or [25]). We have chosen a very simple and intuitive way to define the transformation by means of *Coons patches* [4]. The main advantage of this construction consists in the fact that the border curves $\boldsymbol{U}_1(u)$, $\boldsymbol{U}_2(u)$, $\boldsymbol{V}_1(v)$ and $\boldsymbol{V}_2(v)$, which delimit the Coons patch, can easily be created on top of the source photo to be rendered by the engraving, using popular powerful tools such as Adobe Illustrator. As we want the engraving lines to somehow follow the directions of the features in the original image, we naturally build the border curves taking into account the borders of the features such as nose, eyes, cheeks, lips etc. The process of building the border curves becomes more clear by observing a concrete example of building an engraving style shown in the top row of Fig. 5.

The border curves are built of an arbitrary number of straight line and/or Bézier curve segments (two segments for the curves $U_1(u)$, $V_1(v)$, $V_2(v)$, and three segments for the curve $U_2(u)$ in Fig. 3). Each curve has to be re-parametrized in order to preserve the uniformity of the curve's Euclidean length when the parameter uniformly walks in the range $[0..1]$ (see for example [10], section 9.4). The re-parametrization permits a smooth and uniform interpolation between the curves built of a different number of segments, of different lengths.

We suppose that our parametric curves $\boldsymbol{U}_1(u)$, $\boldsymbol{U}_2(u)$, $\boldsymbol{V}_1(v)$ and $\boldsymbol{V}_2(v)$ form the interior of the closed quadrilateral patch $\mathcal{T}$: $\boldsymbol{U}_1(0)=\boldsymbol{V}_1(0)$, $\boldsymbol{U}_1(1)=\boldsymbol{V}_2(0)$, $\boldsymbol{U}_2(0)=\boldsymbol{V}_1(1)$ and $\boldsymbol{U}_2(1)=\boldsymbol{V}_2(1)$. Any point $\boldsymbol{P}(u,v)=(x,y)$ inside the patch $\mathcal{T}$ can be defined as a function of parameters *u* and *v* (after re-parametrization), by applying the linear interpolation between the curves $\boldsymbol{U}_1(u)$ and $\boldsymbol{U}_2(u)$, taking into account the correction terms $\boldsymbol{L}(v)$ and $\boldsymbol{R}(v)$ due to deviations by left and right curves $\boldsymbol{V}_1(v)$ and $\boldsymbol{V}_2(v)$:

$$\begin{aligned} \boldsymbol{P}(u,v) &= (1-v)\cdot \boldsymbol{U}_1(u) + v\cdot \boldsymbol{U}_2(u) + (1-u)\cdot \boldsymbol{L}(v) + u\cdot \boldsymbol{R}(v) \\ \boldsymbol{L}(v) &= \boldsymbol{V}_1(v) - (1-v)\cdot \boldsymbol{V}_1(0) - v\cdot \boldsymbol{V}_1(1) \\ \boldsymbol{R}(v) &= \boldsymbol{V}_2(v) - (1-v)\cdot \boldsymbol{V}_2(0) - v\cdot \boldsymbol{V}_2(1) \end{aligned} \tag{1}$$

$$\text{where } 0 \le u, v \le 1$$

A uniform grid defined in the parametric space *uv* is transformed using the transformation (1) into a warped grid, as shown in Fig. 3. Any basic engraving layer defined in the parametric space is accordingly transformed into a warped engraving layer in the image space.

## 2.2 Superimposition of separate layers

Now, our task is to establish basic rules for the superimposition of several transformed engraving layers, each of which is a simple matrix of threshold values. For the sake of simplicity, we consider that the threshold values are in the range between 0 and 1; one entry of this threshold matrix corresponds to one pixel of the resulting image. We assume that there is a one-to-one correspondence between the matrix of threshold values representing the engraving layer and the resulting image. No geometrical transformation is performed at this stage, only the threshold values may be affected.

The superimposition of several layers is performed sequentially, one layer after another. For this reason, it is important to define a set of basic rules for superimposing *two* layers, the extension to several layers being straightforward. Each engraving layer, before the superimposition, may undergo two range transformations: it may be scaled (range scale) and raised or lowered (range shift):

$$T'(x, y) = T(x, y) \cdot S(x, y) + D(x, y)$$

where range scale values $S(x,y)$ and range shift values $D(x,y)$ are two matrices of the same dimensions as the matrix of threshold values $T(x,y)$ which forms the transformed engraving layer. We build the range scale and range shift matrices using popular image-manipulation tools such as Adobe Photoshop on top of the feature borders in the original image. A trimming operation may be needed when the resulting threshold value $T(x,y)$ goes beyond the range $[0..1]$. Trimming may be performed either after every layer superimposition operation, or at the very end of the whole sequence of superimpositions.

As we see, superimposing engraving layers consists in consecutively merging the current layer (CL) into the resulting layer (RL). Once merged, the current engraving layer disappears as an independent entity. The merging is performed according to the merging mode. Table 1 enumerates some merging modes, among the most important ones. This list in not exhaustive: additional modes may be added if needed.

**Table 1: Merging (superimposition) modes**

| merging mode | description |
|---|---|
| .. **copy** CL | $T_{RL}(x,y) = T_{CL}(x,y) * S(x,y) + D(x,y)$ |
| .. **smaller** CL | $T_{RL}(x,y) = \mathrm{MIN}(T_{RL}(x,y), T_{CL}(x,y) * S(x,y) + D(x,y))$ |
| .. **bigger** CL | $T_{RL}(x,y) = \mathrm{MAX}(T_{RL}(x,y), T_{CL}(x,y) * S(x,y) + D(x,y))$ |
| .. **multiply** CL | $T_{RL}(x,y) = T_{RL}(x,y) * (T_{CL}(x,y) * S(x,y) + D(x,y))$ |
| .. **add** CL | $T_{RL}(x,y) = T_{RL}(x,y) + (T_{CL}(x,y) * S(x,y) + D(x,y))$ |

Fig. 4 illustrates the use of merging modes. The sample image contains two parts: a uniform gray ramp and four flat patches whose respective intensities are 1/8, 3/8, 5/8 and 7/8. It may be noticed that the "copy" "smaller" and "bigger" modes are by far the most useful for engraving purposes. In fact, the "copy" mode serves to initialize the resulting engraving layer for the very first merging operation. The "smaller" mode produces cross-etching which is very close to traditional cross-etching known in the art. Please note that in the dark area this mode does not produce continuous lines. The "bigger" mode is complementary to the "smaller" mode: it produces continuous lines in the dark areas, and discontinuous ones in highlights. Finally, as can be observed in the bottom line of Fig. 4, a judicious combination of appropriate merging mode with individual layer range shift may produce very interesting technical effects: one particular layer may become apparent only in a desired subrange of gray.

## 2.3 Equilibration

One may notice that the tone reproduction curve of two superimposed layers is no longer linear, even if both layers forming the superposition have a linear curve reproduction behavior. This means that when several layers are superimposed, the resulting engraving may appear locally darker or lighter than what is expected. In order to cope with this phenomenon, we have to equilibrate the resulting threshold structure: when the dithering process is applied, this modified threshold structure must produce visually uniform gray for a uniform input signal of any intensity, independently of the number of layers and the superposition rules that have been used. A simple histogram equalization will not work because of its global nature. Instead we need local model-based histogram equalization, taking into account the dot gain of the printing engine and the characteristics of the human visual system. This dramatically improves the quality of the result because the engraving lines are often very thin, and their visual impact should be carefully taken into account. The equilibration process has been described in detail in another publication [19]. Let us outline it in a few words.

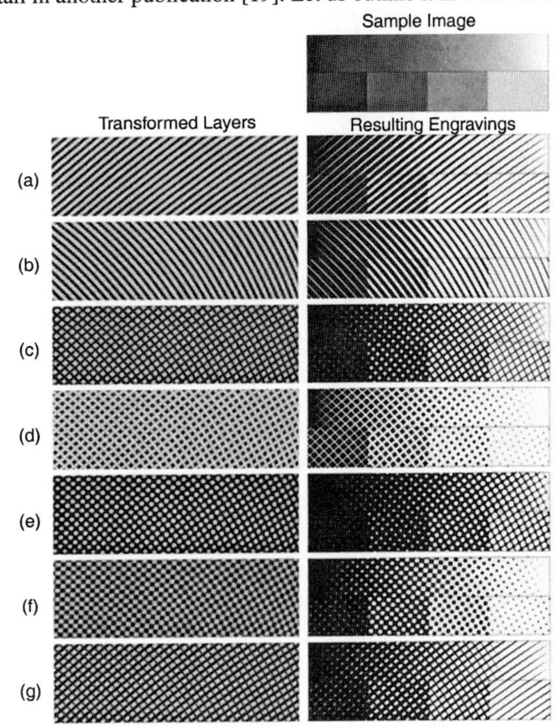


**Fig. 4** Merging modes. Left column: the threshold structure obtained by superimposing threshold structures L1 and L2 using different merging modes. Right column: a sample image (the topmost image) rendered using the threshold structures shown in the left column. Used merging modes were: row a: **copy** L1, row b: **copy** L2, row c: L1 **smaller** L2, row d: L1 **bigger** L2, row e: L1 **multiply** L2, row f: (L1 scaled 1/2) **add** (L2 scaled 1/2), row g: L1 **smaller** (L2 raised 3/16).

The threshold matrix to be equilibrated is corrected separately, for different input signals (flat uniform surfaces). For each input level, standard dithering is performed in order to obtain the bitmap to be sent to the printing device that we modelize. After applying dot-gain correction and low-pass filtering which simulates the human visual system, we get the model approximation of the printed and perceived surface corresponding to the uniform input signal of a given intensity. The response of the model is usually non-uniform. According to the local discrepancies between the input and model-based output, we locally modify the threshold matrix, then redo the whole cycle of the output model-based simulation described before. After a few iterations, we obtain the threshold matrix which produces a reasonably uniform output. Various parameters of the model are adjusted using the measurements of real test prints. Once all correction terms for the threshold matrix have been calculated for all input intensities, the resulting corrected threshold matrix may be calculated. For performance reasons, we calculate the correction terms only for a few (16) input intensity levels spread uniformly throughout the whole intensity range, the rest being linearly interpolated.

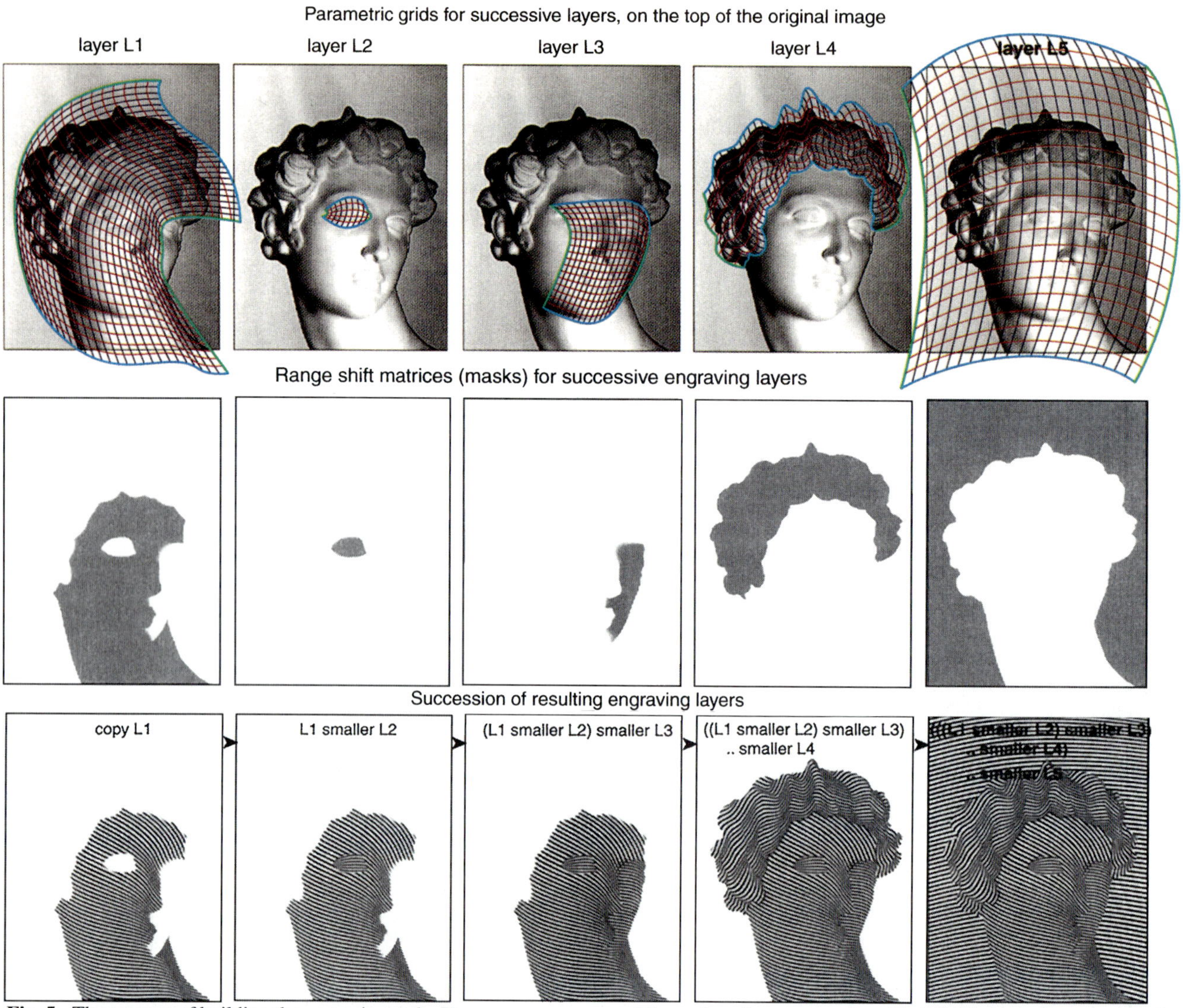


**Fig. 5** The process of building the engraving style. Upper row: sequence of figure-hugging parametric grids. Middle row: the corresponding range shift masks. Lower row: the succession of resulting engraving layers during the superimposition process. The merging rules are indicated on the top of each layer.

The results of our equilibration technique are very satisfactory for the digital engraving presented in this article, as well as for other dithering techniques.

## 3. Black and white facial engraving

Now, let us illustrate the techniques described in the previous section showing an example of black and white engraving of the head of Michelangelo's Giuliano de Medici. Five separate engraving layers for various parts of the face have been created (see Fig. 5, upper row). The borders of the patches are arranged in such a way that the patches' grids loosely follow the key features of the image: the nose line, the cheek profile, the eye shape etc.

The middle row of Fig. 5 shows the range shift matrices associated with the corresponding engraving layers. Here we use the following convention: mid-gray corresponds to a zero range shift, white corresponds to a full-range raise ($D(x,y)=+1$) and black corresponds to a full-range lowering ($D(x,y)=-1$), and the gradations between these three states mean intermediate range shifts. It may be noticed that the pixels whose range shift values in a given layer are +1 (white in our convention) do not participate in building the resulting engraving layer. In such a way, the range shift matrices act as transfer masks between the current and the resulting engraving layers. Smoothness of gradation between the areas where shift $D(x,y)=0$ and $D(x,y)=1$ determines the nature of the fusion between several layers: abrupt boundaries define neat junctions between layers whereas smooth boundaries determine a very progressive fusion between the layers. In our example, the boundaries of the area where $D(x,y)=0$ in layer L2 (around the right eye) are relatively abrupt; the corresponding engraving shows a pretty neat junction between layers L1 and L2, as can be seen in Fig. 6b. On the contrary, the junction between layers L1 and L3 in the area of the left eyebrow is more progressive - and the resulting engraving shows some overlapping between these layers (Fig. 6b). It's according to the artist's taste that the degree of smoothness between the layers may be determined.

In the building process shown in Fig. 5 we used only the "copy" and "smaller" merging rules between successive layers. For all layers, the scale values $S(x,y)=1$ (i.e. no scaling).

Fig. 6 shows the resulting engraving achieved using the engraving style shown in Fig. 5 (the only difference between the engraving layers shown in Fig. 5 and Fig. 6 consists in dividing by two all etching frequencies in the former, for the sake of visibility). It may appear quite surprising that a relatively simple technique described here produces such a decent result.

Furthermore, the visual quality of the engraving may be improved by applying more sophisticated techniques, and especially various cross-etchings, as shown in Fig. 7. The principle of cross-etching shown in Fig. 7a and enlarged in Fig. 7b is very simple: from the same patch $\mathcal{T}$ we generate two engraving layers: in the first one, the engraving crests are oriented following the curvilinear coordinate $u$, and in the second one - following the curvilinear coordinate $v$.

**Fig. 6** The engraving produced using the engraving style shown in Fig. 5.

Fig. 7c shows that the "bigger" rule for superimposition of the layers may play an additional role.

## 3.1 Mixing etching and mezzotint

Fig. 7 illustrates another expressive tool traditionally used by some engravers: mixing regular etching and mezzotint. In this example, the entire layer L5 has been replaced by a specially designed mezzotint engraving layer. Enlargement in Fig. 7d shows that our simulated mezzotint is a relatively good match for the traditional aquatint texture shown in micro-photography in Fig. 7e. We implemented our mezzotint following the description in [20], slightly modified. Let us note the specifically warm appearance of such an engraving, as well as the acute contrast between regular and "stochastic" parts. Traditional engravers in the past often made the most of the additional expressive power of such juxtapositions.

## 3.2 Real photos

Compared to the photographs of sculptures, real-people photos may present some additional difficulties: the contrast of the key features such as the profile line, the nose, lips and eye contours may be insufficient. Real people may have some particular traits and features that one may wish to hide or stress. Typically, the wrinkles in female portraits often become almost invisible, whereas the vigorous lines on the male portraits are sometimes stressed.

Also, special features such as glasses, moustaches, earrings etc. may require special technical attention. Real photos may need an additional pre-processing phase which would perform traditional cosmetic arrangements, contrast and edge enhancements, as well as engraving-specific enhancement techniques.

## 3.3 Engraving-Specific Enhancement

Engraving offers a large set of expressive tools for visual contrast enhancement. We have already mentioned the effect of mixing mezzotint and regular etching. Further examples are shown in Fig. 8. The contrast between the glasses and the face is achieved by an abrupt change of the direction and frequency of the etching. As we explained before, such an effect can very easily be obtained by designing appropriate engraving layers, and by abrupt borders in the range shift masks.

Another tool for stressing particular features like a contour line or a small detail is illustrated in Fig. 8c. Here, a small additional layer has been added in order to accentuate the nasolabial fold. It may be noticed that additional engraving strokes parallel to the feature did not modify the impression of the gray level of this particular area: our equilibration process made the other lines locally thinner. On the contrary, the feature itself (nasolabial fold) appears much more contrasted.

**Fig. 7** The engraving produced using the engraving style shown in Fig. 5 enriched by the cross-hashing and the mezzotint. The upper enlargement shows cross-etching using "smaller" rule, whereas the lower enlargement shows another engraving which uses both "smaller" and "bigger" rules. The enlargement in the middle of the upper row is compared with the micro-photography of a real aquatint copperplate.

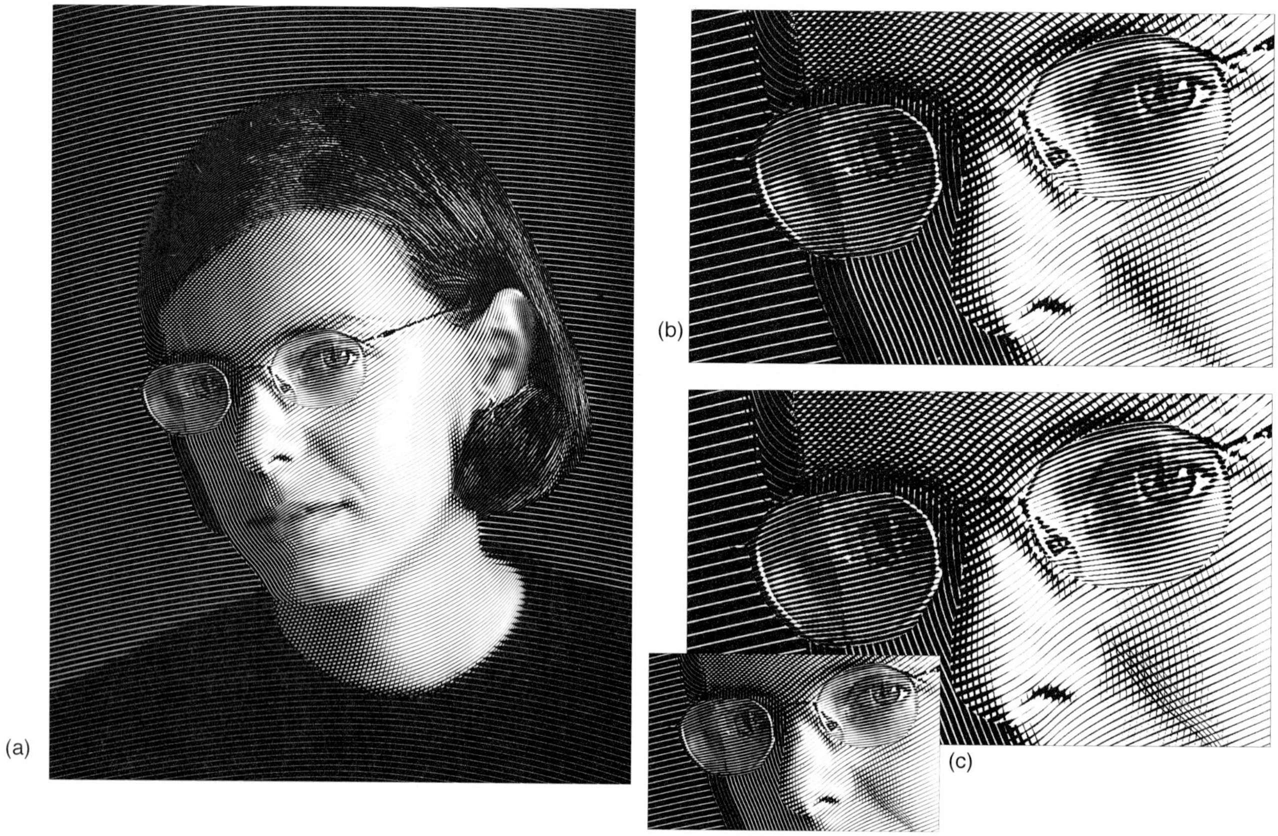

**Fig. 8** This engraving shows various enhancement techniques: an abrupt change of the orientation and frequency of the etching (in glasses), or an additional layer for sharper appearance of the nasolabial fold in (c).

Yet another, more subtle enhancement technique consists in irregular perturbation of regular engraving layers. The simplest case is visible in the background layer of the bottom-left color engraving in Fig. 9, where the engraving lines have been unevenly disturbed. This effect provides a feeling of tension, especially when compared with the mezzotint background of the bottom-right color engraving in Fig. 9.

### 3.4 Engraving Style

The set of layers which form the engraving together with range shift and scale matrices form what may be called *the engraving style*. The usefulness of this notion consists in the possibility of using the same engraving layers for different photos of the same person, as well as for producing engravings of different persons, with minimal modifications. Engravings shown in Fig. 6 and Fig. 8 represent two different (although quite close) engraving styles. On the contrary, engravings in Fig. 6 and Fig. 9 use almost identical styles for the face itself, for the same person (two lower engravings in Fig. 9), as well as for different persons (two left engravings in Fig. 9). Only minor modifications were needed in order to adapt the engraving style from one person to another.

The engraving styles in Fig. 6 and Fig. 9 have been adjusted to the photos manually. Another possibility of making such an adjustment automatically or semi-automatically would be to use the technique of feature-based image metamorphosis described in [1]. In fact, the resulting engraving layer for person A is a two-dimensional threshold structure, rich enough to be subjected to some morphing which would map the features of person A to those of person B. This work is under way.

## 4. Color engraving

Traditional engraving is essentially black and white art. This does not remove the temptation to experiment with colors. Color raster images like digital photos are usually stored in Red-Green-Blue (RGB) or Cyan-Magenta-Yellow-Black (CMYK) representation. For the sake of simplicity let us consider the first case.

The simplest color scheme would be to use the same resulting engraving layer for all three RGB components: it is known as in-phase color printing. It certainly works but the achieved visual effect is not very different from black and white gravure.

One may expect a more advanced visual effect when the different color layers use different orientations. A simple but efficient scheme has been experimented: for the Red and Blue color planes, we use the engraving layers with line orientation along the parametric axis $u$, whereas for the Green color plane, we use the same engraving layers but with line orientation along the parametric axis $v$. This produces very nice color cross-etching visible in the engravings in Fig. 9. This technique may be called engraving by orthogonal (in parametric space) color lines.

Yet another possibility is to mix normal regular engraving for some color planes with the mezzotint for the others. The enlargement in the middle of Fig. 9 shows a detail where all three color engraving techniques enumerated here are shown in the same picture: the bluish background is done using in-phase engraving with the same slightly disturbed lines for all three RGB color planes; the boy's forehead has been produced with orthogonal color lines, whereas the boy's hair is a mixture of regular engraving (Red and Blue color planes) with mezzotint (Green color plane). We hope that more advanced color mixing / texture mixing schemes may introduce unexpected, beautiful visual effects.

## 5. Future Work

The technique presented in this contribution may be extended in several directions.

The first direction, and probably the most important one, is to build libraries of pre-defined mappable engraving styles. As we mentioned before, the feature-based image metamorphosis presented by Beier and Neely, or a similar algorithm may work: in our case, as well as in [1] we have to deal with 2D structures only. With such libraries of pre-defined styles, one will be able to chose one style among several proposed, and the whole job of engraving production will be a matter of seconds. The engraving styles of the samples shown in this contribution contain 5 to 10 separate layers, rate layers. If needed, specific image-dependent features can be added on top of the basic style.

Another promising direction is experimentation with color engraving as well as with different engraving textures. The techniques for color engraving shown in this contribution are relatively straightforward extensions of black and white engraving. Although the results shown in Fig. 6 to Fig. 9 may be considered satisfactory, we see a good opportunity to go beyond the imitation of existing techniques. Computers offer us unlimited computational power, and one may experiment with very sophisticated graphical techniques, inaccessible to traditional engravers for purely technical reasons.

Finally a substantial effort to provide an appropriate user interface has to be made. In the current implementation we have developed a very rudimentary user interface. To be attractive for a final user who, we hope, will be an artist rather then a programmer, the engraving system should have ergonomics comparable to that of the best lineart products such as Adobe Illustrator. Feature-based layer construction guidance, inter-layer constraint control, simple and intuitive mapping of the pre-defined styles - all these function should be incorporated into a powerful GUI.

## 6. Conclusions

We have presented a very simple technique for producing digital engravings. The proposed system is based on the analogy between the "universal" copperplate which imitates the true copperplate engraving technique and conventional dithering. The art of digital copperplate engraving may be resumed as the art of building appropriate threshold structures.

We have developed the basic technique for building separate engraving layers (threshold structures) which roughly follow the features of the original image, as well as the rules for merging them together. The resulting threshold structure is equilibrated in such a way that it generates a visually uniform output for a uniform input signal of any intensity. Applied on an input digital photo, using a standard dithering algorithm, such a threshold structure generates a reasonably faithful reproduction, which imitates traditional engraving. Several enhancement techniques, specific to engraving, have been proposed. The important notion of engraving style which comprises a set of separate engraving layers together with range shift and scale masks has been introduced. Engraving styles make it easier to adapt the look and feel of an engraving of person A to an engraving of person B. Finally, a simple color extension has been proposed.

With this contribution, we consider that the main goal that we set ourselves – starting with a digital photo, to be able to make a digital engraving of reasonable quality in a reasonably short time – has been achieved. In perspective, additional features such as libraries of pre-defined mappable engraving styles, special color and texture effects and an appropriate user interface will certainly make such a system attractive and usable by most of graphists.

## 7. ACKNOWLEDGEMENTS

I would like to express my gratitude to several people who participated in discussions touching the subject of this article: Roger Hersch, Nicolas Rudaz, Isaac Amidror, David Salesin, Frédéric Pighin, Catrin Petersen, Gershon Elber, among many others. Special thanks come to Monique Lazega, a professional engraver, who initiated me to the traditional engraving art. Also, many thanks to my kids, Bella, David and Michael, for lending their nice faces. Finally, many thanks to anonymous SIGGRAPH reviewers for their helpful suggestions and comments.

## REFERENCES

[1] T. Beier and S. Neely, Feature-based image metamorphosis. In *Computer Graphics (SIGGRAPH'92 Proceedings)*, 26(2), pp. 35-42, 1992.

[2] F. Brunner, *A Handbook of Graphic Reproduction Process*, Hasting House Publ., New York, 1984.

[3] C. Curtis, S. Anderson, J. Seims, K. Fleischer, D. H. Salesin. Computer-Generated Watercolor, Proceedings of SIGGRAPH 97, in *Computer Graphics Proceedings,* Annual Conference Series, pp. 421-430, 1997.

[4] S. A. Coons, *Surfaces for Computer Aided Design of Space Forms*, MIT Project TR-41, MIT, Cambidge, MA, 1967.

[5] O. Deussen, J. Hamel, A. Raab, S. Schlechtweg, T. Strothotte. An illustration technique using intersections and skeletons, *Graphics Interface 99*, Kingston, Ontario,1999 (to appear) .

[6] D. Dooley and M. F. Cohen. Automatic illustration of 3D geometric models: Lines. *Computer Graphics,* Vol. 24, No. 2, pp 77-82, 1990.

[7] G. Elber. Line Illustrations in Computer Graphics. *The Visual Computer,* Vol. 11(6), pp 290-296, 1995.

[8] G. Elber. Line Art Rendering via a Coverage of Isoparametric Curves, *IEEE Transactions on Visualization and Computer Graphics,* Vol. 1, No 3, pp 231-239, September 1995.

[9] G. Elber., Line Art Illustrations of Parametric and Implicit Forms, *IEEE Transactions on Visualization and Computer Graphics,* Vol 4, No 1, pp. 71-81, 1998.

[10] G. Farin, *Curves and Surfaces for Computer Aided Geometric Design,* Academic Press, 1990.

[11] J. D. Foley, A. van Dam, S. K. Feiner, J. F. Hughes, *Computer Graphics, Principles and Practice,* Second Edition, Addison-Wisley Publ., 1990.

[12] J. Gomes, L. Darsa, B. Costa, L. Velho, *Warping And Morphing Of Graphical Objects,* Morgan Kaufman Press, 1998.

[13] P. Haeberli, Paint by numbers: Abstract image representation. in *Computer Graphics (SIGGRAPH'90 Proceedings)*, Vol. 24, pp. 207-214, 1990.

[14] W. M. Ivins, Jr., *How Prints Look,* John Murray Publ., London, 1988.

[15] J. Lansdown, S. Schofield, Expressive Rendering: A Review of Nonphotorealistic Techniques, *IEEE Computer Graphics and Applications,* Vol. 15(3), pp. 29-37, May 1995.

[16] W. Leister, Computer Generated Copper Plates, *Computer Graphics Forum,* Vol.13(1), pp. 69-77, 1994.

[17] B.J.Meier, Painterly Rendering for Animation. Proceedings of SIGGRAPH 96, in *Computer Graphics Proceedings,* Annual Conference Series, pp. 477-484, 1996.

[18] S. Mizuno, M. Okada and J. Toriwaki. Virtual Sculpting and Virtual Woodcut Printing, in *Visual Computer,* 10, pp. 39-51, 1998.

[19] V. Ostromoukhov, R. D. Hersch, Multicolor and Artistic Dithering, Proceedings of SIGGRAPH'99, In *ACM Computer Graphics,* Annual Conference Series, 1999.

[20] V. Ostromoukhov, R. D. Hersch, Stochastic Clustered-Dot Dithering. In Proc. SPIE Vol. 3648, *Color Imagig: Device-Independent Color, Color Hardcopy, and Graphic Arts IV,* pp. 496-505, 1999.

[21] Y. Pnueli, A. M. Bruckstein, Digidürer - a digital engraving system, The Visual Computer, Vol. 10, pp. 277-292, 1994.

[22] M. P. Salisbury, M. T. Wong, J. F. Hughes, and D. H. Salesin. Orientable Textures for Image-Based Pen-and-Ink Illustration, Proceedings of SIGGRAPH 97, in *Computer Graphics Proceedings,* Annual Conference Series, pp. 401-406, 1997.

[23] R. Ulichney, *Digital Halftoning,* The MIT Press, Cambridge, Mass., 1987.

[24] G. Winkenbach, D. H. Salesin. Rendering parametric surfaces in pen and ink. Proceedings of SIGGRAPH 96, in *Computer Graphics Proceedings,* Annual Conference Series, pp. 469-476, 1996.

[25] G. Wolberg, *Digital Image Warping,* IEEE Computer Society Press, 1990.

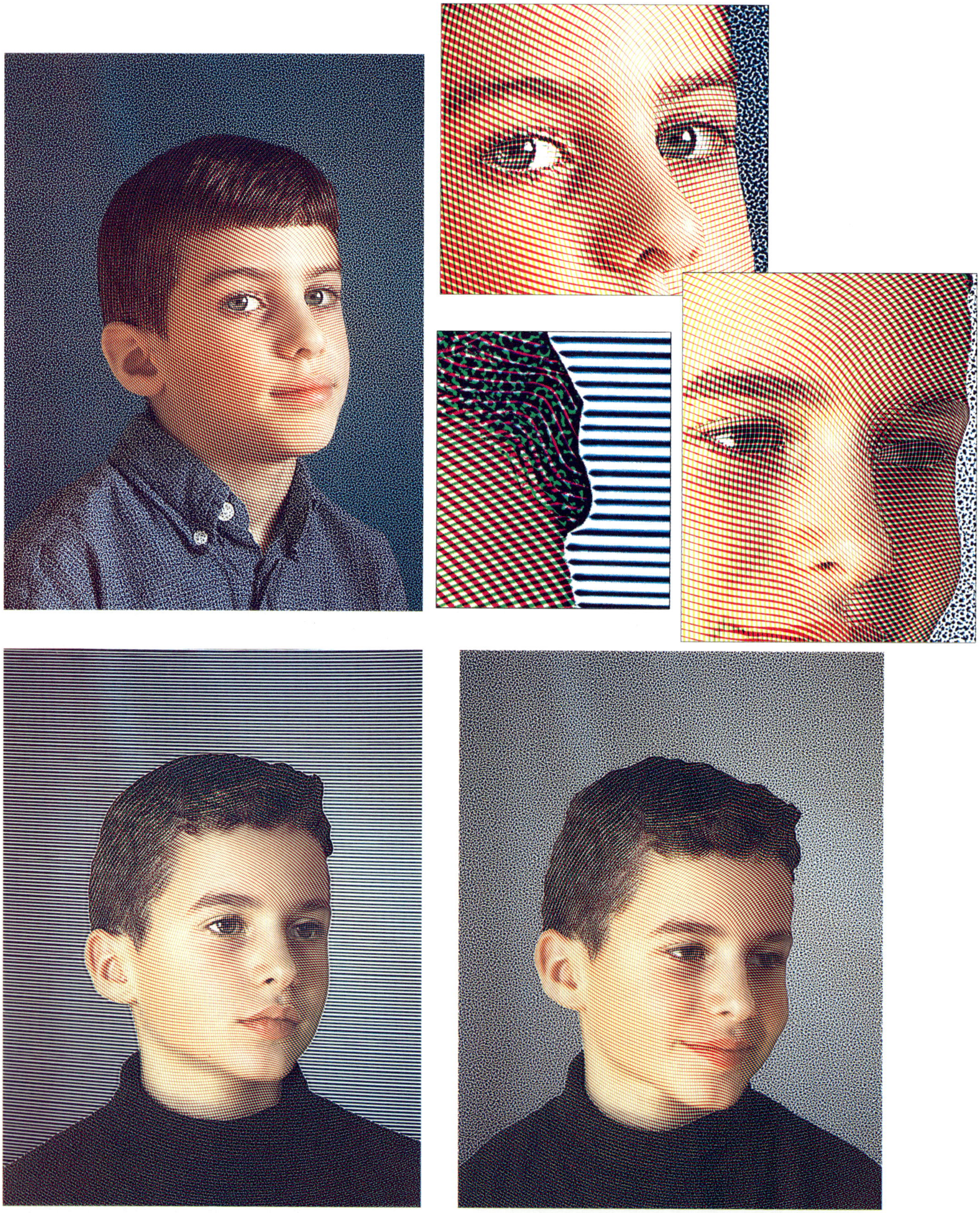

**Fig. 9** Examples of color engraving.

# Multi-Color and Artistic Dithering

*Victor Ostromoukhov, Roger D. Hersch*
*Ecole Polytechnique Fédérale de Lausanne (EPFL), Switzerland*
*{victor, hersch}@di.epfl.ch*


## Abstract

A multi-color dithering algorithm is proposed, which converts a barycentric combination of color intensities into a multi-color non-overlapping surface coverage. Multi-color dithering is a generalization of standard bi-level dithering. Combined with tetrahedral color separation, multi-color dithering makes it possible to print images made of a set of non-standard inks. In contrast to most previous color halftoning methods, multi-color dithering ensures by construction that the different selected basic colors are printed side by side. Multi-color dithering is applied to generate color images whose screen dots are made of artistic shapes (letters, symbols, ornaments, etc.). Two dither matrix postprocessing techniques are developed, one for enhancing the visibility of screen motives and one for the local equilibration of large dither matrices. The dither matrix equilibration process corrects disturbing local intensity variations by taking dot gain and the human visual system transfer function into account. Thanks to the combination of the presented techniques, high quality images can be produced, which incorporate at the micro level the desired artistic screens and at the macro level the full color image. Applications include designs for advertisements and posters as well as security printing. Multi-color dithering also offers new perspectives for printing with special inks, such as fluorescent and metallic inks.


**Keywords:** color halftoning, artistic dithering, dither matrix equilibration, non-standard inks, side by side printing

## 1. Introduction

The reproduction of color images requires in the general case (1) separating the image colors (for example red, green and blue) into the set of available printable colors (for example cyan, magenta, yellow and black), (2) halftoning each of the printable color layer and (3) possibly calibrating the system to ensure that the printed colors are close to the original image colors.

Most existing color halftoning techniques are based on the independent halftoning of each of the contributing color layers. In offset and in many electrographic printers, the color layers are generated independently at angles of 15, 45, 75 degrees in order to avoid interferences between the cyan, magenta and black layers ([24], chapter 13). Ink-jet printers often use error-diffusion to halftone each of the color layers independently.

Existing approaches for color separation with non-standard inks[1], for example the segmentation of the CIE-XYZ color space into a set of tetrahedra having as a common edge the black-white axis [14], the creation of correspondence tables between input colors and combination of output inks [1], or the selection of an optimal subset of inks according to an objective function [19] consider that color layers can be printed independently one from another. This is true as long as the inks are transparent and as long as the dots of each screen are randomly positioned with respect to the dots of the other screens, as assumed by the Neugebauer equations [17].

If these assumptions are not true, halftoning each of the color layers independently may generate color shifts depending on the amount of superposition between screen dots of individual halftone layers. As long as the inks are transparent, the color shifts are small and the reproduction fidelity can be ensured by calibrating the printing device [6], for example, in the case of process colors, by establishing a 3D mapping between CIE-XYZ coordinates and the output Cyan, Magenta, Yellow and Black surface coverage values [5].

Some applications however require that different inks are always printed side by side without overlapping. This is for example the case when printing with opaque inks [9], [10]. Manufacturers of valuable documents, such as banknotes, identity cards and checks often make use of the high registration accuracy of their original printing equipment to create a graphic design which is both visually pleasant and difficult to imitate using standard printing processes ([22], chapter 6).

We propose a multi-color dithering method which automatically enforces *side by side printing* of several color layers. Combined with color separation by tetrahedral interpolation, multi-color dithering makes it possible to print images made of non-standard inks. In addition, we explore ways of creating large dither matrices to produce artistically screened color images, i.e. color images whose screen elements are made of artistic color shapes (letters, symbols, ornaments, etc.).

In section 2, we present the new multi-color dithering method, which is a generalization of standard black and white dithering. We show how multi-color dithering can be used for the color separation of non-standard inks. In section 3, we describe the synthesis of dither matrices improving the visibility of screen motives in areas of high ink coverage. In section 4, we describe an equilibration process which improves the quality of large dither matrices by compensating for local uneven motive distribution and dot gain. In section 5, we apply the previously described dither matrix synthesis methods to generate screens representing freely chosen artistic shapes. We show the results in the form of color pictures which comprise at the micro level the desired artistic screens and at the macro level the global color image. The conclusions and perspectives are presented in section 6.

## 2. Multi-color dithering and color separation.

Error-diffusion in color space [20] may be used for side by side printing with non-standard colors, i.e. for ensuring that different inks are always printed side by side. Error-diffusion in color space is a straightforward extension of standard error-diffusion [21]: given an input color vector (for example in RGB space) the closest printable color is selected and printed on the current output pixel. The 3D difference vector (error) between input and selected color is distributed among the current pixel's neighbors [7]. A disadvantage of color error diffusion are the classical error-diffusion artifacts and the fixed dot size which in case of dot gain may induce a strongly non-linear tone reproduction behavior [8].

The new multi-color dithering method we introduce here has the same advantages as standard dithering. It enables the creation of dither matrices of the desired size and orientation and the genera-

1. Inks which differ from the standard cyan, magenta, yellow and black process colors

tion of dither threshold levels according to the desired dot growth behavior. Furthermore, small individual dither matrices can be assembled to form large super-matrices incorporating many intensity levels ([6], chapter 9).

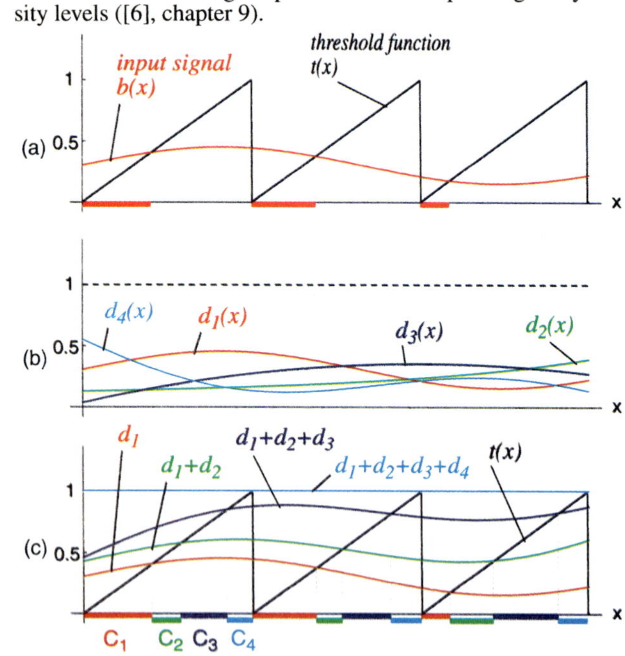


**Fig. 1** (a) Black-white dithering of a variable darkness input signal, (b) relative color intensities, (c) multi-color dithering.

### 2.1 Standard black-white dithering

Before explaining multi-color dithering, let us describe the basics of standard dithering for black-white (two colors). To simplify the explanations we assume that an input grayscale image with normalized darkness values between *0* (white) and *1* (black) is dithered by comparing at each output location corresponding input darkness and dither threshold values[1]. If the darkness $b(x)$ is higher than the dither threshold value $t(x)$, then the output location is marked as black, else it is marked as white (Fig. 1a).

Standard dithering converts a darkness value into a surface coverage. Conceptually, we can look at a given darkness value $b$ as a percentage $b$ of black and as percentage of $(1\text{-}b)$ of white. The dithering process converts an input signal of darkness $b$ to a surface coverage $b$ of black and $(1\text{-}b)$ of white.

### 2.2 Multi-color dithering

Let us now extend dithering to color. Suppose that we would like to print with 4 different color inks $C_1$, $C_2$, $C_3$, $C_4$ (called basic colors). At each pixel of the output pixmap, the color separation we use gives us the relative percentages of each of the basic colors (Fig. 1b), for example $d_1$ of color $C_1$, $d_2$ of color $C_2$, $d_3$ of color $C_3$ and $d_4$ of color $C_4$. One of the basic colors, for example $C_4$, may be white.

Extending dithering to multiple colors consists in intersecting the relative cumulative amounts of colors $d_1$, $d_1+d_2$, and $d_1+d_2+d_3$ with the dither function $t$ (Fig. 1c). In the interval where $d_1(x) > t(x)$, the output location will be printed with basic color $C_1$ (Fig. 1c). In the interval where $d_1(x)+d_2(x) > t(x)$ and $d_1(x) \le t(x)$, the output location will be printed with basic color $C_2$. In the interval where $d_1(x)+d_2(x)+d_3(x) > t(x)$ and $d_1(x)+d_2(x) \le t(x)$, the output location will be printed with basic color $C_3$. In the remaining interval where $d_1(x)+d_2(x)+d_3(x)+d_4(x) > t(x)$ and $d_1(x)+d_2(x)+d_3(x) \le t(x)$, the output locations are printed with basic color $C_4$. Multi-color dithering therefore converts the relative amounts $d_1$, $d_2$, $d_3$, $d_4$ of basic colors $C_1$, $C_2$, $C_3$, $C_4$ into relative coverage percentages and ensures by construction that the contributing colors are printed side by side.

Color dithering is generally applied with 4 basic colors, since a point in 3D color space within the printer's gamut can be described by a barycentric combination of 4 colors.

### 2.3 Color Separation

When given a set of basic colors (inks), each specified by its tri-stimulus value in a given 3D color space (RGB or CIE-XYZ space), the 3D volume covered by these basic colors, called the printable gamut, can be segmented into a set of mutually adjacent tetrahedra [4]. The vertices of each tetrahedron correspond to four neighboring basic colors. Many tetrahedrizations of a point set in 3D exist; there is however only a single tetrahedrization which ensures that the enclosing sphere of a tetrahedron does not include another tetrahedron. Properties of tetrahedrizations and methods of construction are well described in the literature ([12], chapter 20).

Color separation of an input tristimulus value (RGB or CIE-XYZ) is obtained by locating in the selected color space the tetrahedron enclosing the given tri-stimulus value and by finding the barycentric coefficients $d_1$, $d_2$, $d_3$, $d_4$ used to express the input tristimulus value as a linear combination of the tetrahedron's vertices. These barycentric coefficients give the relative amounts of basic colors $C_1$, $C_2$, $C_3$ and $C_4$ used to reproduce the input tristimulus value.

As an illustration for tetrahedral decomposition and interpolation, let us consider an RGB color cube whose vertices correspond to the basic colors black, red, green, blue, cyan, magenta, yellow and white (Fig. 2a). A color wedge (Fig. 2b) with vertices close to cyan, blue, red and yellow is reproduced by multi-color dithering using the available set of basic colors. This color wedge, a planar slice in RGB space (Fig. 2a), intersects all tetrahedra into which the RGB cube is decomposed. In each tetrahedron, the corresponding color wedge part is reproduced using the 4 basic colors associated with the tetrahedron's vertices.

The dither matrix used for producing Fig. 2b has been obtained by discretizing and renumbering an egg crate function ([6], section 9.3.1, Fig. 9.6a). The resulting dithered color wedge incorporates ring shaped screen elements. All contributing basic colors are printed side by side.

If color reproduction fidelity is an issue, a calibrated input device (for example a scanner) is needed which provides a mapping from RGB input device values to CIE-XYZ device-independent values. Color separation in CIE-XYZ space is possible by tetrahedral decomposition of the volume formed by the measured CIE-XYZ values of the basic colors (inks + paper white). Colors close to the basic colors will be reproduced correctly. However, colors requiring the combination of several basic colors may deviate from their desired CIE-XYZ value, depending on various parameters such as printer registration accuracy, dot gain and ink density distribution of printed screen dots. The present contribution does not deal with printer color calibration. However, a possible printer calibration may be achieved by printing a large number of samples covering the printer's gamut and by measuring their CIE-XYZ values in order to build a 3D calibration table providing a mapping between device independent input CIE-XYZ values and output space "predicted" CIE-XYZ values (CIE-XYZ values predicted by linear interpolation within each tetrahedron).

When printing with transparent inks, we may want to use the superposition of one or sevral pairs of selected inks as additional basic colors. This is easily done by measuring for each pair its CIE-XYZ tristimulus values and incorporating the superposition of the two inks as a new color $C_j$ into the set of available basic colors.

In this paper, we generally assume that input color values are within the range of printable colors. If the input color values are not located within the range of printable colors, a gamut mapping method must be applied. Several gamut mapping methods are known to produce convenient results [19].

Appendix I gives an example of a color separation with a set of non-standard offset inks (see single color page insert).

1. The darkness of an image pixel is one minus its normalized intensity value (in the graphic arts, a maximal intensity value is white and a minimal intensity value is black).

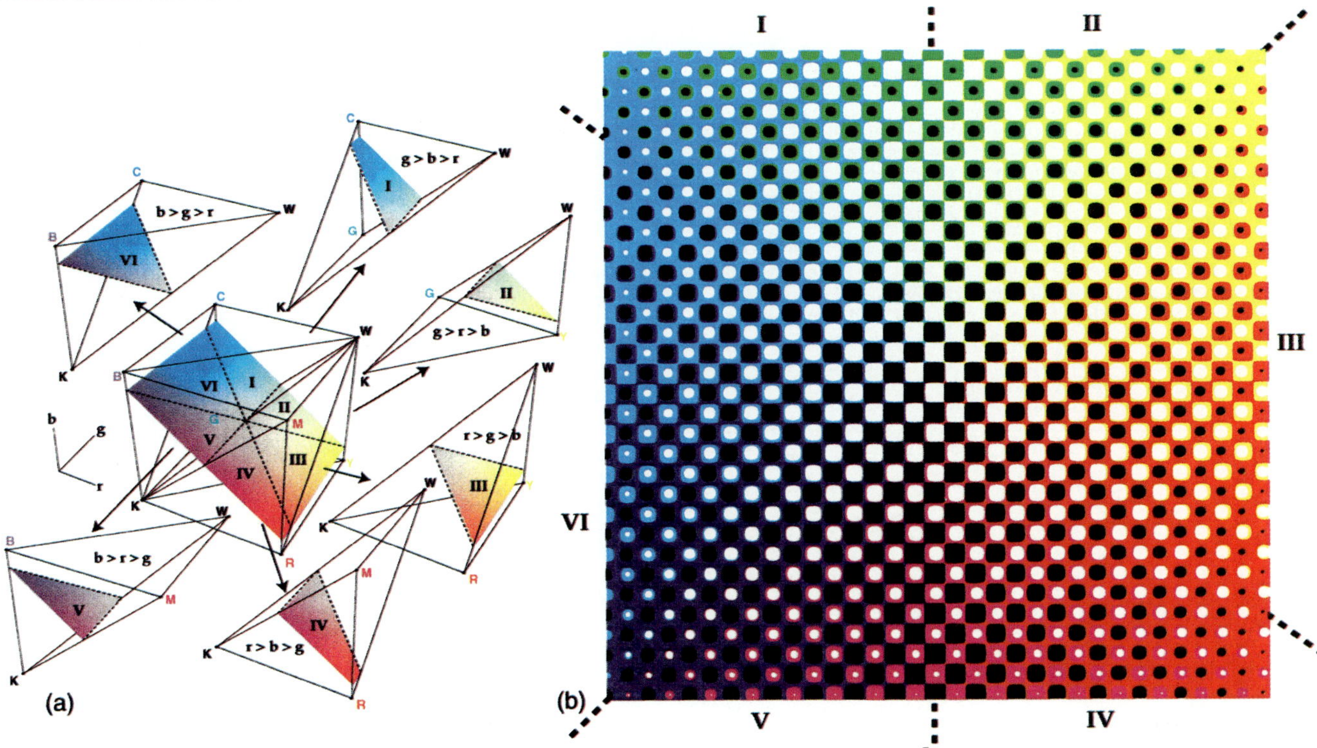


**Fig. 2** (a) Color separation by tetrahedral decomposition of the RGB cube, (b) example of color dithered cyan - blue - red- yellow wedge with all basic colors printed side by side.

## 3. Synthesis of partially continuous, partially random dither matrices

For the purpose of artistic color screening, we need to generate dither matrices incorporating visually appealing symbols and ornamental motives. At low intensities however, one process color (for example black) may become very dominant and the corresponding screen motive may become too large to be recognized.

In order to solve this problem, we propose to generate dither matrices which produce partially ordered and partially random screen dots. To avoid enlarging the screen motive too much when strongly increasing the color surface coverage, we allow the background to contribute to the corresponding color. In the case of a black screen motive, from a certain darkness level, the background becomes successively darker. Thus instead of enlarging the motive shape, its contrast to the background becomes successively less pronounced, until it finally vanishes (Fig. 4b). One may observe that with a partially random screen, the desired screen motive remains visible over a larger intensity range than with a standard clustered screen. The final result however depends on dot gain: if dot gain is small, this effect is clearly visible. When dot gain is important, this effect is counterbalanced by the decreased contrast due to dot gain at high ink surface coverages.

It is relatively easy to create dither matrices generating partially clustered, partially random screens. One may first generate a continuous screen function representing the clustered part of the screen dot and sample it at each dither matrix cell (Fig. 3a). Then a very small amplitude noise[1] can be applied either to all dither matrix cells or to dither matrix cells having low dither values (Fig. 3b). Dither matrix cells are successively numbered according to their respective dither values (histogram equalization). Their ordinal numbers represent, after normalization, their dither threshold levels (Fig. 3c).

A color image dithered with such a mixed dither matrix preserves the screen motive better than with a standard dither matrix, see for example the still visible screen motive in the dark hair of the girl (Fig. 7b)

1. For the sake of simplicity, we apply white noise.

## 4. Equilibration of large dither matrices

In order to create artistically screened color images incorporating sophisticated screen shapes, we need to synthesize large dither matrices which may cover surfaces of several square millimeters. Since the motives incorporated into such dither matrices may not be well balanced, i.e. specific regions within a large dither matrix may not have a flat histogram of threshold values, alternations of dark and light within the produced screen dots may generate light and dark strips over the resulting dithered color image. This phenomenon is accentuated by dot gain since middle and dark tones tend to become darker.

The dither matrix equilibration method we propose compensates the uneven local surface coverage of the screen motive. It takes into account the dot gain and the human visual system transfer function ([23], chapter 7). It is related to model-based halftoning methods [16], but instead of modifying the final halftone image, it modifies the dither matrix used to produce the final image.

We assume that dot gain is similar for all contributing inks. We therefore equilibrate the dither matrix for a single ink, the black ink. Dither matrix equilibration is an iterative process. We start with the initial dither matrix containing the desired screen motive. We define a number of uniform gray patches equally spread throughout the available intensity range, for example patches at 16 representative intensity levels $g_1$ to $g_{16}$. These grayscale patches undergo a transformation comprising dithering, application of dot gain, and application of the human visual system transfer function. The transformation includes the following detailed steps:

(1) With the dither matrix, generate the halftone patches corresponding to the desired representative grayscale values

(2) For each generated halftone patch, take dot gain into account by adding into each pixel a darkness value representing the dot gain of the black neighboring pixels. In our model and for our target electrographic printer we consider that, due to dot gain, each black pixel adds 20% of blackness to its vertical and horizontal neighbors, and 5% of blackness to its diagonal neighbors [18]. We limit the maximal blackness of any pixel to 100%.

(3) Apply to the resulting grayscale images a Gaussian low-pass filter approximating to some extent the low pass behavior of the human transfer function. Based on the estimation of about 30 cycles per degree for the cutoff frequency of the human visual system ([13], chapter 7), we approximate the human visual system

transfer function by the Gaussian function $F(q) = Exp(-\pi q^2)$, where the unit on the frequency axis (q-axis) corresponds to the cutoff frequency of 30 cycles per degrees. The corresponding impulse response, i.e. the inverse Fourier Transform of $F(q)$, is also a Gaussian function, $f(r)=Exp(-\pi r^2)$, whose unit (r-axis) corresponds to 1/30 degree of visual angle. Considering a large observation distance (25", twice the normal observation distance), where details of the screen motive should disappear, 1/30 degree corresponds, at 1200 pixels/inch, to 17.45 pixels. To produce the discrete convolution kernel, this Gaussian impulse response function is sampled on a 5σ x 5σ grid, where $\sigma=1/Sqrt(2\pi)$ corresponds on our pixel grid to 7 pixels. Please note that for different printing resolutions, as well as for different observation distances (e.g. for posters to be observed from far away) the discrete convolution kernel needs to be recomputed accordingly.

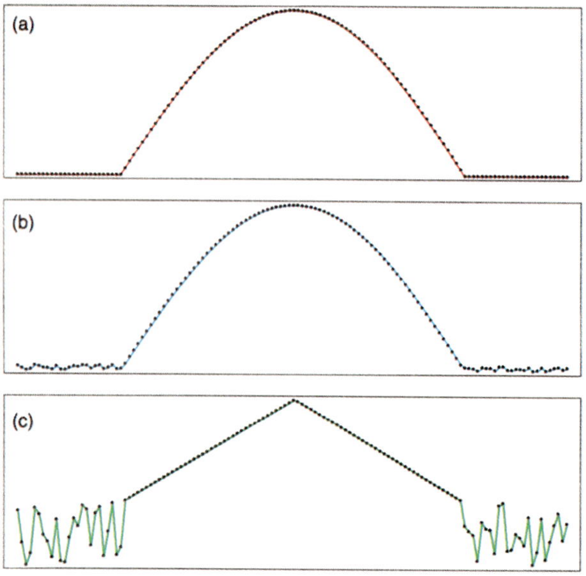


**Fig. 3** Producing a dither matrix comprising partially continuous, partially random threshold levels.

The resulting transformed gray patches $h_1$ to $h_{16}$ correspond to the original uniform grayscale images perceived by a human observer under given conditions (dot gain, resolution, distance).

The difference in gray values between the original uniform grayscale patches and the resulting halftoned patches specify the modification to be applied to the original dither matrix $d(x,y)$ in order to produce a modified dither matrix $d'(x,y)$ which compensates for the locally uneven motive distribution, i.e. the locally non uniform distribution of dither levels. The compensated dither matrix $d'(x,y)$ is obtained by successively compensating the differences associated with the different representative grayscale levels.

In a first step, a subset of threshold levels of the compensated dither matrix $d'(x,y)$ is computed by scaling the threshold levels of dither cells between $0$ and the first representative grayscale value $g_1$ according to a value proportional to the difference between the desired grayscale level $g_1$ and grayscale level $h_1$ obtained by the previously described transformation:

```
if d(x,y) <= g1 then d'(x,y) = d(x,y) + k (h1(x,y)-g1)
```

where $d(x,y)$ represents the original dither threshold matrix, and $k$ a scaling factor, chosen between 1/2 and 1.

This compensation is repeated in further steps for all successive representative grayscale levels and finally all dither cells of the original threshold matrix are corrected to yield the compensated dither matrix $d'(x,y)$.

The resulting algorithm can formulated as follows in pseudo-code:

```
for all successive representative intensity levels gi
  for all cells (x,y)
     if gi-1 < d(x,y) <= gi) then
         d'(x,y) = d(x,y) + k (hi(x,y)-gi);
  endfor;
endfor;
```

Fig. 5 graphically shows the application of the equilibration process to a one dimensional dither function $d(x)$.

Further equilibration passes, starting from the resulting corrected dither function $d'(x,y)$ may bring further improvements. The convergence is fast and a small number of passes is sufficient.

The effect of the equilibration process on the produced dither matrix can be observed in Fig. 6b and Fig. 6c. Small surfaces of low dither levels (white) surrounded by large surfaces of high dither levels tend to become larger. Correspondingly, the large surfaces with the high dither levels (black) tend to shrink. As an example, look at the internal cavities within the Allah motive ( الله )

Fig. 7a shows a color image produced without equilibration (dither matrix of Fig. 6b) and Fig. 7b a color image with equilibration (dither matrix of Fig. 6c). The equilibration process considerably improves the quality of the resulting image and enables the generation of large dither matrices incorporating visually significant ornamental patterns without explicitly taking care of the pattern's local distribution of dither threshold levels (ideally, i.e. without taking into account dot gain, dither threshold levels over a given surface should be uniformly distributed).

(a)

(b)

**Fig. 4** Grayscale wedge produced (a) with a standard continuous dither matrix and (b) with a mixed dither matrix made of partially continuous, partially random threshold levels.

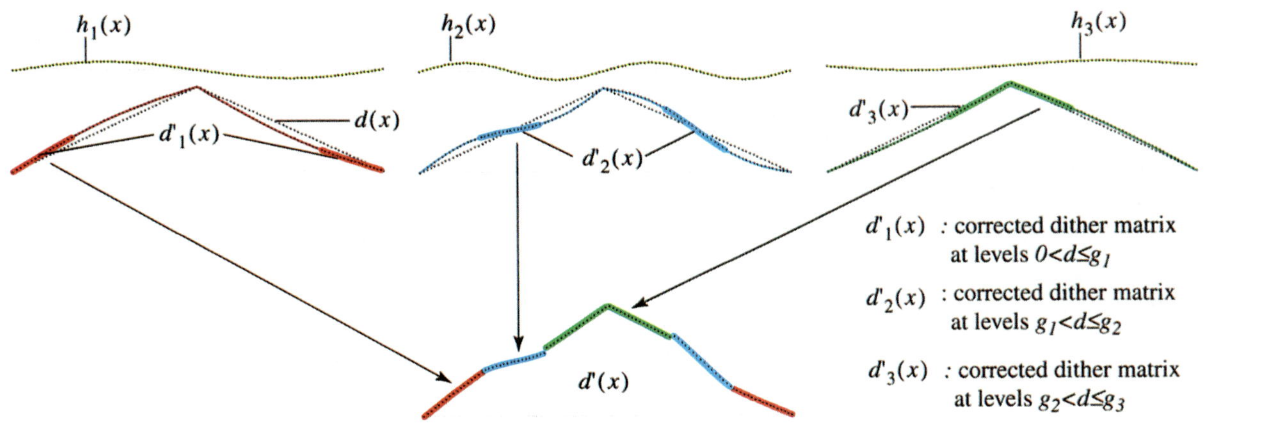


**Fig. 5** Equilibrating a 1D dither function *d(x)* to produce the equilibrated dither function *d'(x)*

## 5. Artistically dithered images

By creating large size artistic dither matrices and by equilibrating them appropriately, one may create artistic color screens which enable the generation of color images incorporating two layers of information: a macro layer, i.e. the global image, and a micro layer formed by the artistic color screens. As a characteristic design example, we would like to render an image using the square Kufi arab script style for "Allah", which can be found on the mosque of Badra, Azerbaijan ([3], page 182). The first step consists in designing a continuous screen made of several functions: paraboloid cylinders for the horizontal and vertical segments and half-spheres at segments ends (Fig. 6a). This continuous screen is sampled at the center of dither matrix cells and converted into an array of dither values. A small random value (noise) is added. The consecutive renumbering of cells according to their dither values yields a dither matrix (Fig. 6b), to which the equilibration process is applied (Fig. 6c). The resulting dither matrix is used to produce an output image (Fig. 7b) with red, green, blue, cyan, magenta, yellow, black and white basic colors. One can observe from a certain distance that the produced halftoned image is smooth despite the large size of the screen element and the uneven surface coverage behavior of the original screen function.

The next example shows the generation of a screen element of high aesthetic value laid out according to the beautiful *Cairo tessellation* ([11], page 119). Fig. 9a to Fig. 9e show how this threshold matrix is constructed. First, we define a simple analytical bell function on a unit square (Fig. 9a). Then, we take five halves of this bell function (Fig. 9b) that we project, by a set of linear transformations on a unit square as shown in Fig. 9c. We obtain a five-petals flower pattern. We take twelve such patterns, and, by applying twelve different linear transformations according to [11], we superpose them on a unit square thus obtaining the final analytical function shown in Fig. 9d. This analytical function is converted as in the previous examples into a set of discrete threshold values - our final dither matrix represented in Fig. 9e.

The example shown in Fig. 8 consists of an image rendered with a parallelogram dither array whose dither values form the shape of a celtic spiral motive. The thickness of the spiral varies from very thin in light tones to relatively thick in dark tones. Beyond a certain darkness level, the motive doesn't become thicker, but thanks to a partially ordered, partially random dither matrix, the background of the motive becomes darker. Please note the perfectly smooth transitions between the red spirals in light tones and the black spirals in dark tones.

The final example shown in Appendix I illustrates a real example of a graphic design, dithered either with typographic character shapes or with an oriental motive and printed with non-standard inks on an offset press.

At a first glance, the produced artistically dithered color images have some resemblance with images produced by black-white artistic screening [15]. The applied techniques however are completely different and significant differences between images produced by black-white artistic screening and by artistic color dithering exist. In dark tones, artistically screened black-white images have motives which nearly fill up the screen element space, whereas with color dithering, the size of the visible screen motive grows up to a certain limit; after that limit, the contrast between background and foreground is successively reduced until it vanishes.

In addition, artistic color dithering is able to render any color image and therefore has a much larger application range than artistic screening, which is limited to black-white or duo-tone.

Regarding implementation issues, artistic dither matrices can be designed in different ways, either by programming continuous 2D functions and sampling them into discrete threshold values or by starting from bi-level shape designs, transforming them into grayscale intensity images (with PhotoShop for example) and applying histogram equalization to generate the dither threshold levels. Once the initial dither matrix is produced, the remaining part of the work is rather automatic. Dither matrix equilibration is slow, but is done only once. After having prepared the final dither matrix, reproducing the image requires color separation by tetrahedral interpolation and dithering. To improve image rendition speed, one can build a 3D look-up table establishing a pre-computed mapping between input tri-stimulus values and output color percentages of the contributing basic colors. With such a look-up table, we expect that multi-color dithering of images using pre-computed dither matrices can be made as fast as other color reproduction techniques (color error diffusion).

## 6. Conclusions and perspectives

Multi-color dithering is a generalization of standard bi-level dithering. Combined with tetrahedral color separation, multi-color dithering makes it possible to print images made of a set of non-standard inks. In contrast to most previous color halftoning methods, multi-color dithering ensures by construction that the different selected basic colors are printed side by side.

In this contribution, we extended bi-level dithering to multi-color dithering and explored multi-color dithering in the context of artistic color screening. To generate high-quality dithered color images incorporating artistic screen motives, we developed two dither matrix postprocessing techniques, one for enhancing the visibility of screen motives and one for the local equilibration of large dither matrices. By combining within the same dither matrix continuous threshold levels for the screen motive and randomly distributed dither threshold levels for the background, we enhance the visibility of the generated screen shapes at high ink saturation levels. The dither matrix equilibration process we propose to avoid disturbing local intensity variations takes both the physical behavior of the printer, i.e. the dot gain and the human visual system modulation transfer function into account.

Thanks to the combination of the presented techniques, high quality images can be produced, which incorporate at the micro level the desired artistic screens and at the macro level the full color image. Possible applications include innovative designs for publicity and posters.

Multi-color dithering clears the way for further color reproduction applications. It is known that some electrographic printing processes [2] require that different toners be placed beside one another (no overlap allowed). Security printing may make use of multi-color dithering in order to print side by side with non-standard inks at a high registration accuracy. In that context, many new issues arise, such as the selection of the inks and the design of screen motives making the original very difficult to replicate, both by professional craftsmen and by simple color photocopying. Multi-color dithering also offers new perspectives for printing with special inks, such as fluorescent and metallic inks.

## 7. Acknowledgement

We would like to thank Orell Füssli Security Printing Ltd, Zürich, Switzerland, for collaborating with us on this project. Thanks also to David Salesin, Eric Stollnitz and Nicolas Rudaz for helpful discussions. This work was partly supported by the Swiss CTI (Grant 3776.1) and by the Swiss National Science Foundation (Grant 21-54127.98).

## 8. References

[1] H. Boll, "A Color to Colorant Transformation for a Seven Ink Process", in *Device Independent Color Imaging* (Ed. E. Walowit), SPIE Proceedings, Volume 2170, pages 108-118, 1994.

[2] J. Geraedts, S. Lenczowski, "Océ's productive colour solution based on the Direct Imaging Technology", Proceedings IS&T International Conf. on Digital Printing Technologies (NIP-13), pages 728-733, 1997.

[3] I. Hargittai, M. Hargittai, *Symmetry, A Unifying Concept,* Shelter Publ., 1994.

[4] P.C. Hung, Colorimetric calibration in electronic imaging devices using a look-up-table model and interpolations, *Journal of Elecronic Imaging,* 2 (1), pages 53-61, 1993.

[5] International Color Consortium. Specification ICC.1:1998-09. http://www.color.org.

[6] H.R. Kang, *Color Technology for Electronic Imaging Devices,* SPIE Publication, 1997.

[7] R.V. Klassen, R. Eschbach, K. Bharat, Vector Error Diffusion in a Distorted Colour Space, Proc. of IS&T 47th Annual Conference, 1994, Reprinted in *Recent Progress in Digital Halftoning,* (Ed. R. Eschbach), IS&T Publication, pages 63-65, 1994.

[8] K.T. Knox, Printing with Error Diffusion, in *Recent Progress in Digital Halftoning* (Ed. R. Eschbach), IS&T Publication, pages 1-5, 1994.

[9] H. Küppers. *Die Farbenlehre der Fernseh-, Foto- und Drucktechnik: Farbentheorie der visuellen Kommunikationsmedien.* DuMont Buchverlag, Köln, 1985.

[10] US Patent 4,812,899, issued March 14, 1989, filed Dec 19, 1986, Inventor: H. Kueppers.

[11] G.E. Martin, *Transformation Geometry. An Introduction to Symmetry.* Springer-Verlag, 1982.

[12] G.M. Nielson, H. Hagen, H. Müller, *Scientific Visualization,* IEEE Computer Society, 1997.

[13] L. Olzak, J.P. Thomas, Seeing spatial patterns, in *Handbook of perception and human performance, (*Eds. K. R. Boff, L. Kaufman, J. P. Thomas), Chapter 7, J. Wiley, pages 7-1 to 7-55, 1986.

[14] V. Ostromoukhov, Chromaticity Gamut Enhancement by Heptatone Multi-Color Printing, in *Device-Independent Color Imaging and Color Imaging Systems Integration*, Proc. SPIE, Vol. 1909, pages 139-151, 1993

[15] V. Ostromoukhov, R.D. Hersch, Artistic Screening, *Proceedings of SIGGRAPH 95,* Annual Conference Series, pages 219-228, 1995.

[16] T. N. Pappas, Model-based halftoning of color images, IS&T 8th International Congress on Advanced in Non-Impact Printing Technologies, 1992, reproduced in *Recent Progress in Digital Halftoning* (Ed. R. Eschbach), IS&T Publication, pages 144-149, 1994.

[17] G.L. Rogers, "Neugebauer Revisited: Random Dots in Halftone Screening", *Color Research and Applications,* 23 (2), pages 104-113, 1998.

[18] C.J. Rosenberg, "Measurement based verification of an electrophotographic printer dot model for halftone algorithm tone correction", IS&T 8th International Congress in Non-Impact Printing Technologies, Oct. 25-30, 1992, Reprinted in *Recent Progress in Digital Halftoning,* (Ed. R. Eschbach), IS&T Publication, pages 159-163, 1994.

[19] E. J. Stollnitz, V. Ostromoukhov, D. H. Salesin, Reproducing Color Images Using Custom Inks, *Proceedings of SIGGRAPH 98,* Annual Conference Series, pages 267-274, 1998.

[20] J. R. Sullivan, R. L. Miller, T. J. Wetzel, *Color digital halftoning with vector error diffusion,* US Patent 5,070,413, 1991.

[21] R. Ulichney, *Digital Halftoning,* The MIT Press, Cambridge, Mass., 1987.

[22] R. L. Van Renesse (Ed.), *Optical Document Security,* Artech House, 1998.

[23] B.A. Wandell, *Foundations of Vision*, Sinauer Associates, Inc. Publishers, Sunderland, Mass., 1995.

[24] J.A.C. Yule. *Principles of Color Reproduction.* John Wiley & Sons, New York, 1967.

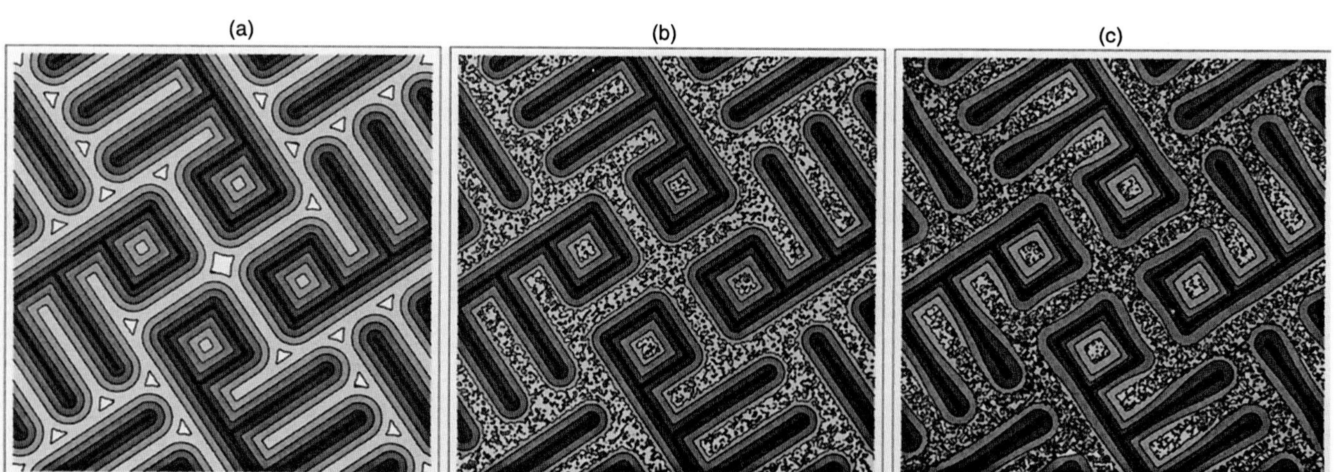


**Fig. 6** "Allah" motive, from Mosque of Badra, Azerbaijan: (a) the initial dither matrix, (b) the mixed dither matrix incorporating continuous and random dither levels and (c) the equilibrated mixed dither matrix.

**Fig. 7** (a) Color image produced without and (b) with the equilibration process

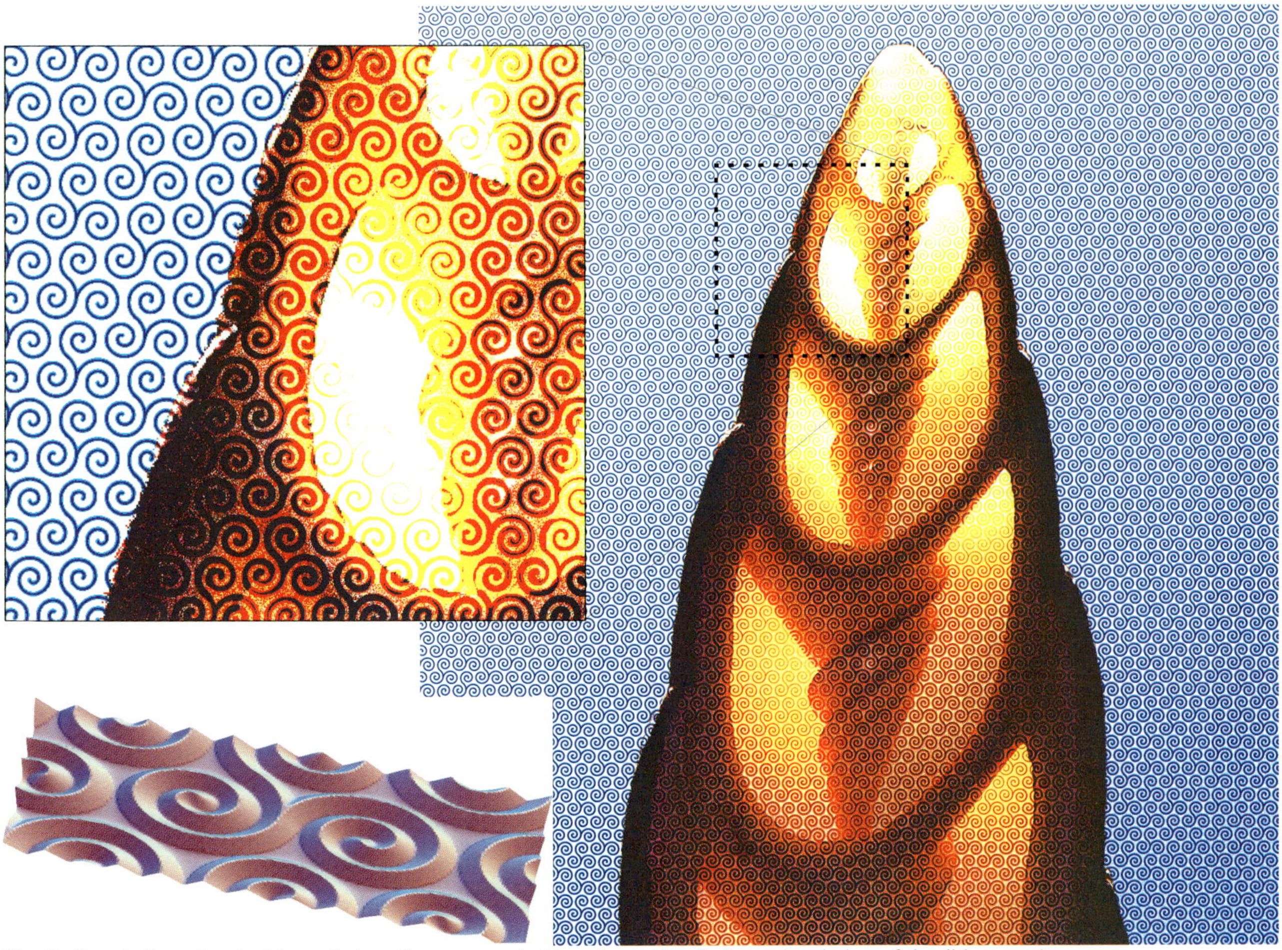

**Fig. 8** See shell rendered with a spiral motive, represented together with a 3-dimensional view of the dither matrix.

**Fig. 9** A sample image produced using a threshold matrix inspired by the *Cairo tessellation*. Figures (a)-(e) show the building process of the threshold matrix.

**Appendix I.** Examples printed with 4 non-standard inks on an offset press

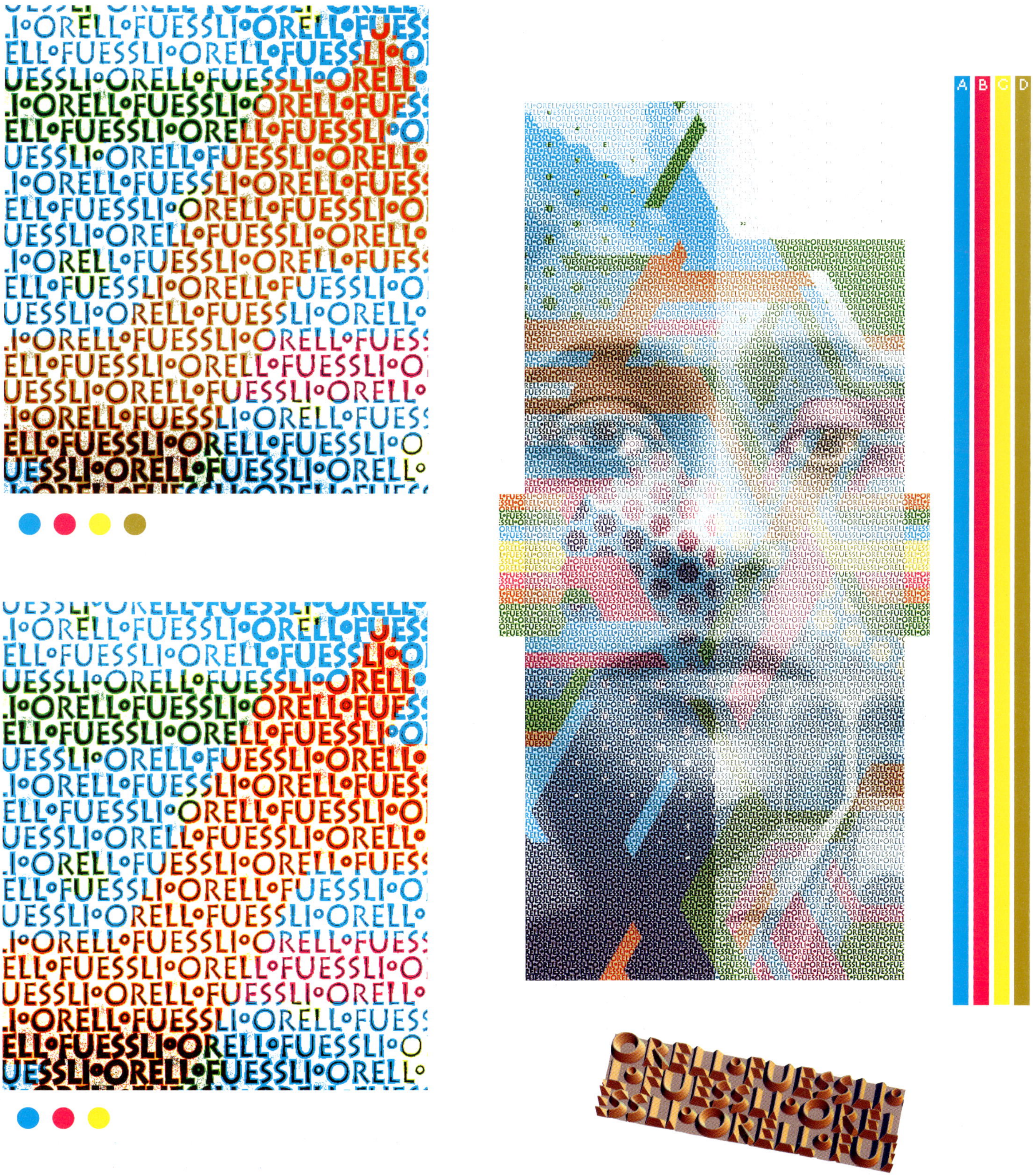


**Fig. A1.** Graphic design made by Roger Pfund for Orell Füssli Security Printing Ltd., printed with non-standard inks A,B,C and D. The enlargment on the top left is printed with all 4 inks. For comparison, the enlargment on the bottom left is printed with only 3 inks, A (close to cyan), B (close to Magenta) and C (close to yellow). The bottom right part shows a 3D view of the dither matrix created for artistic dithering.

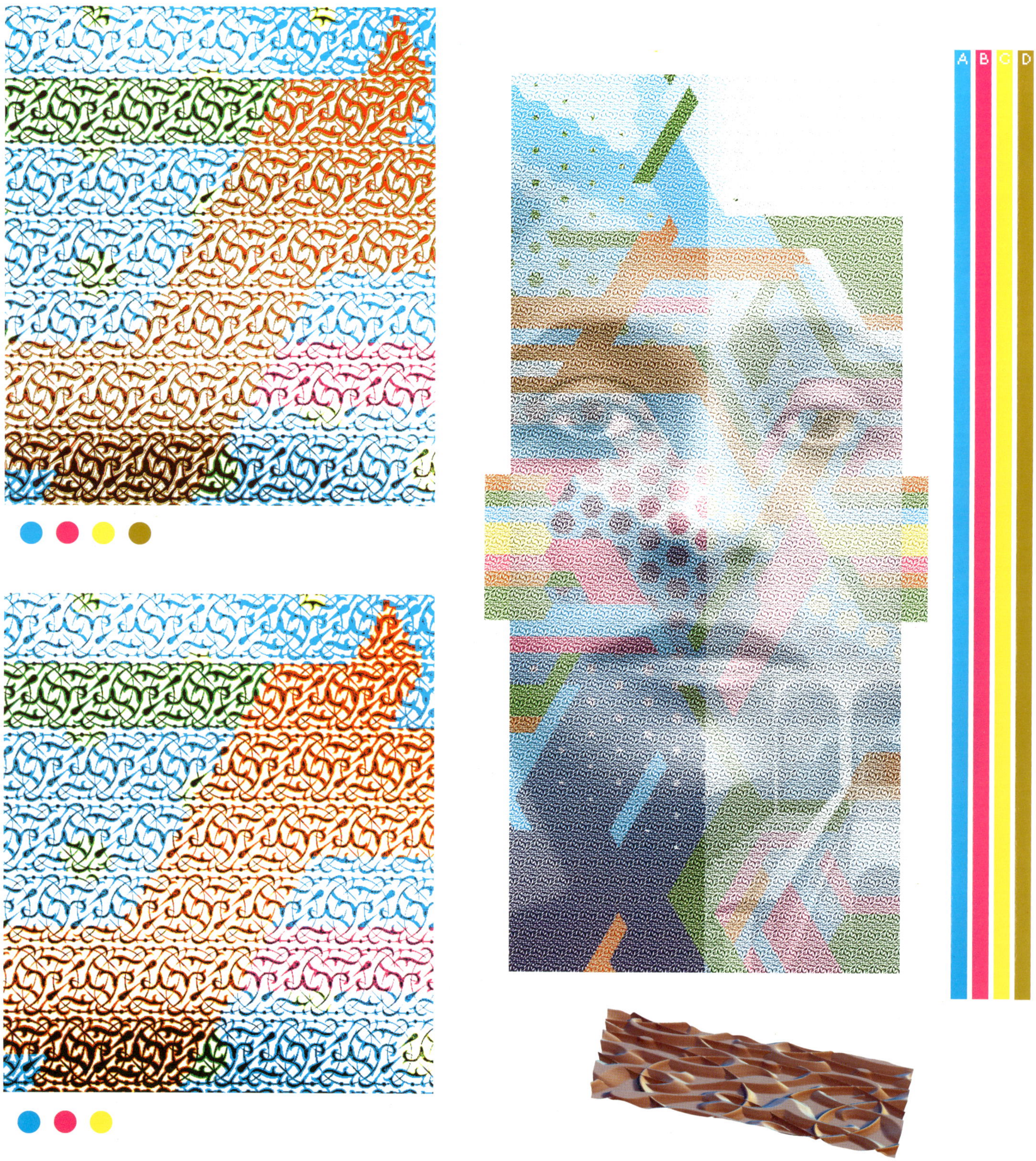


**Fig. A2.** Same design, dithered with an arabesque motive, printed with non-standard inks A,B,C, and D. The enlargment on the top left is printed with all 4 inks. For comparison, the enlargment on the bottom left is printed with only 3 inks, A, B, and C. The bottom right part shows a 3D view of the arabesque dither matrix.

# Art-Based Rendering of Fur, Grass, and Trees

*Michael A. Kowalski*[◇*] *Lee Markosian*[◇] *J.D. Northrup*[◇] *Lubomir Bourdev*[†]
*Ronen Barzel*[‡] *Loring S. Holden*[◇] *John F. Hughes*[◇]

[◇]Department of Computer Science
Brown University
{mak,lem,jdn,lsh,jfh}@cs.brown.edu

[†]Advanced Technology Group
Adobe Systems
lbourdev@adobe.com

[‡]Pixar
ronen@pixar.com

## Abstract

Artists and illustrators can evoke the complexity of fur or vegetation with relatively few well-placed strokes. We present an algorithm that uses strokes to render 3D computer graphics scenes in a stylized manner suggesting the complexity of the scene without representing it explicitly. The basic algorithm is customizable to produce a range of effects including fur, grass and trees, as we demonstrate in this paper and accompanying video. The algorithm is implemented within a broader framework that supports procedural stroke-based textures on polyhedral models. It renders moderately complex scenes at multiple frames per second on current graphics workstations, and provides some interframe coherence.

**CR Categories and Subject Descriptors:** I.3.3: Computer Graphics: Picture/Image Generation; line and curve generation; bitmap and frambuffer operations; I.3.5 Computer Graphics: Computational Geometry and Object Modeling: curve, surface, solid, and object representations; I.3.7: Three-Dimensional Graphics and Realism: Color, shading, shadowing, and texture. **Additional Key Words:** Non-photorealistic rendering, graftals, procedural textures.

## 1 Introduction

Any art student can rapidly draw a teddy bear or a grassy field. But for computer graphics, fur and grass are complex and time-consuming. Even so, the artist's few-stroke rendering may have greater persuasive or evocative power than the usual computer-graphics rendering.

How does the artist effectively communicate the teddy bear or grass? By rapidly creating an impression of free-form shape – difficult to do with conventional 3D modeling systems – and then drawing a few well-chosen strokes. This paper describes some of our efforts to expand the expressive power of 3D graphics by adopting techniques for depicting complexity from the centuries-old disciplines of art and illustration.

Three goals in our work on art-based graphics are to give the designer of a scene control over the style of rendering; to ease the burden of modeling complex scenes by treating the rendering strategy as an aspect of modeling; and to provide interframe coherence for the kinds of stylized renderings we've developed. Other goals, less directly related to the work in this paper, include the development of systems for rapidly creating free-form shapes [9], and the control of scene composition.

Our approach to creating complex expressive renderings is to target the kinds of images made by artists and illustrators and reproduce the effects and techniques we observe in those images. Much 2D art and illustration is created by making strokes on a flat surface (paper, canvas), so we have based our work on what we call "stroke-based textures." We started from the drawings of Theodore Geisel ("Dr. Seuss") [4, 5], in part because they are such an extreme departure from the domain of conventional computer graphics.

**Figure 1** A furry creature, after Dr. Seuss. The fur is generated in a view-dependent way by a procedural stroke-based texture that places it near silhouettes, varying the style of the tufts according to how much the underlying surface faces the viewer.

*Currently at ATR Media Integration & Communications Research Laboratories, Kyoto, 619-0288, Japan.

**Figure 2** A more complex scene, again based on the style of Dr. Seuss. The grass, bushes, and truffula treetops are implemented with graftal textures that use the same basic algorithm to place graftals with a variety of shapes and drawing rules. The truffula tree trunks are drawn by stroke textures (not graftal textures) assigned to ribbon-like surfaces that always face the viewer. The treetops use the same type of graftal as seen in the previous figure, but with a different orientation rule: they always circulate clockwise around the treetop, no matter what the point of view. This cannot be modeled with any fixed geometry, of course.

There are two main research challenges: the development of algorithms and a software framework in which procedural stroke-based textures can be rendered, and the development of a user interface (within the context of a free-form modeling system) that allows a designer to assign and customize such procedural textures. In this paper, we describe our approach to the first of these challenges.

We have developed a system to generate and render stroke-based textures that mimic the styles of two artists, and a framework for generalizing this to other techniques. The system renders the images shown in this paper at several frames per second on a Sun Sparc Ultra 2 model 2/300 with Creator 3D graphics, and even faster on a high-end PC. Our main contributions are the system architecture, the (partial) temporal coherence of the texture elements, and the particular methods used to mimic Dr. Seuss's and Geoffrey Hayes's [7] styles.

## 2 Prior Work

Using art as a motivation for computer graphics techniques is not new, and our work builds on the efforts of many others. Fundamental to our ideas are the particle systems of Reeves [12, 13], which he used to create trees, fireworks, and other complex imagery from relatively simple geometry. Alvy Ray Smith's later use of particles, together with recursively defined L-systems that he called "graftals," extended this to more biologically accurate tree and plant models [15]. His "Cartoon Tree" is a direct precursor to the work in this paper. Graftals have since come to be described more generally: according to Badler and Glassner [1], "Fractals and graftals create surfaces via an implicit model that produces data when requested." We use the word "graftal" in this much more general sense.

We use a modified version of the "difference image" stroke-placing algorithm of Salisbury *et al.* [14] to place procedural texture elements at specific areas of the surface. Winkenbach and Salesin [17] described the use of "indication" (showing a texture on part of an object) in pen-and-ink rendering. And Strothotte *et al.* [16] extensively discuss the use of artistic styles to evoke particular effects or perceptions.

At a more mechanical level, Meier's work on particle-based brush strokes [11] was a major inspiration in two ways: first, her use of particles to govern strokes that suggest complexity in her Monet-like renderings showed that not all complexity need be geometric; second, the fixed spacing of the particles on the objects, which limited how closely one could zoom into the scene, inspired us to seek a similar but hybrid screen/object space technique.

The present work builds on our earlier efforts [10] to produce nonphotorealistic effects at interactive frame rates. One limitation of our earlier system was that it supported just one "style" at any given time – applying the style equally to every object in the scene. A more flexible system would allow the designer of a virtual scene to assign different nonphotorealistic "textures" to different surfaces within the scene. The framework we describe in the next section makes this possible. For instance, the fur texture on the creature in figure 1 is applied over most of the body but not the face, even in profile. Our other images show more examples of the selective use of distinct nonphotorealistic textures applied to objects in a scene according to what each represents.

**Figure 3** The same scene as in figure 2 rendered without graftal textures or the stroke-based textures on the truffula trunks.

## 3 Software Framework

Our procedural stroke-based textures are implemented within a general system for rendering polyhedral models using OpenGL [2]. In our system models are divided into one or more surface regions (called *patches*), to each of which the user can assign one or more procedural textures (called *textures*) – although just one is active at a time. The "procedure" that defines a texture needn't be complicated – many simply draw their patch in some conventional style (e.g., smooth-shaded or wireframe). One of our textures performs Floyd-Steinberg dithering [3]. Others perform a variety of hatching effects.

An important component of the system is the provision of *reference images*. These are off-screen renderings of the scene, subsequently read from frame-buffer memory to main memory and made available to the procedural textures. We currently use two kinds of reference images: a *color reference image* and an *ID reference image*.

To prepare the color reference image, the active texture of each patch is asked to render into it in some appropriate way, depending on how the texture will use the image. For example, the graftal textures described in the next section use the color reference image in a special way to decide where to draw tufts of fur, grass, or leaves. For the ID reference image, triangles (or edges) are each rendered with a color that uniquely identifies that triangle or edge. Lighting and blending are disabled so that the colors are preserved exactly.

After the ID reference image is prepared, all of its pixels are checked in one pass: when a pixel contains the ID of a triangle or edge, that pixel location is stored in a list on the patch that contains the triangle or edge. Later, the active texture of the patch can access the list of pixel locations in its main rendering loop. For example, the dithering texture simply runs the Floyd-Steinberg algorithm on the pixels of its patch.

The ID reference image can be used to determine the visibility of a point on a known triangle – the details of how to make this work robustly, even for triangles whose screen dimensions are less than a pixel, are beyond the scope of this paper (see [8]). If the triangle belongs to a patch of a convex surface, a simple test can be used: If the point (in screen space) is more than one pixel from the boundary of the patch, and also from any visible silhouette curve in the scene, then it is visible if and only if its triangle is front-facing and the value in the ID reference image at the point's screen position identifies a triangle of the same patch.

## 4 Graftal Textures

The textures described in this section place fur, leaves, grass or other geometric elements into the scene procedurally, usually to achieve a particular aesthetic effect (e.g., indicating fur at silhouettes but tending to omit it in interior surface regions). We'll call this class of textures *graftal textures*. They all share the same basic procedure for placing tufts, leaves, grass, etc., all of which we call *graftals*. The key requirements are that graftals be placed with controlled screen-space density in a manner matching the aesthetic requirements of the particular textures, but at the same time seem to "stick" to surfaces in the scene, providing interframe coherence and a sense of depth through parallax.

### 4.1 Placing graftals with the difference image algorithm

To meet these requirements, we have adapted the "difference image" algorithm (*DIA*) used by Salisbury *et al.* [14] to produce pen-and-ink-style drawing from grayscale images. Their algorithm controls the density of hatching strokes in order to match the gray tones of the target image. For each output stroke drawn, a blurred image of the stroke is subtracted from a "difference" image (initially the input image). The next output stroke is placed by searching in the difference image for that pixel most (proportionally) in need of darkening, and initiating a stroke there. The resulting image consists of marks whose density conveys the gray tones of the original.

The DIA meets our first requirement of placing marks (or in our case, graftals) with a controlled screen-space density. To control graftal placement according to a particular aesthetic requirement, each graftal texture simply draws its patch into the color reference image so that darker tones correspond to regions requiring a denser distribution of graftals. We call the result the *desire image*, and the value at a pixel in that image measures the *desire* that graftals be placed there. For example, to render the furry creature in figure 1, the reference image is drawn darker near silhouettes – easily done by placing a point light near the camera position. Also, some regions (e.g., the feet) can be explicitly darkened by the designer to promote a greater density of graftals there.[1]

To meet the requirement that graftals appear to stick to surfaces in the scene, we must convert the 2D screen position of a graftal (assigned to it by the DIA ) to a 3D position on some surface. This is achieved in $O(1)$ time (per graftal) by using the ID reference image to find the triangle (and the exact point on the triangle with a ray-test) corresponding to a given screen position.

This now allows graftals to be distributed over surfaces in the scene to achieve a desired screen-space density – for a single frame. To create some interframe coherence, we modify the algorithm:

- In the first frame, graftals are placed according to the DIA.
- In each successive frame, the graftal texture first attempts to place the graftals from the preceding frame.
- Then, when all the "old" graftals have been considered for placement and accepted or rejected, the graftal texture executes the DIA to place new graftals into the scene as needed.

An existing graftal may fail to be placed in a frame for two reasons: (i) the graftal is not visible (it is occluded or off-screen); (ii) there is insufficient desire in the desire image at the graftal's screen position. This can happen if the original desire value at the graftal's screen position was small (e.g. the graftal is far from a silhouette).

[1] To further encourage drawing near silhouettes, we filter the desire image, replacing each desire value $d$ with $2d - d^2$, where $d$ ranges from 0 (no desire) to 1 (maximum desire).

**Figure 4** A tree rendered in the style of Geoffrey Hayes [7]. The leaves are drawn with graftals based on OpenGL triangle fans, rather than the triangle strip-based type of graftal shown in figure 5. The interior is shaded with the technical-illustrator shader of Gooch *et al.*[6].

It can also happen if the camera has zoomed out and the graftal's neighbors, now closer to it in screen space, have already subtracted the available "desire" in the vicinity. When a graftal fails to be placed in a frame, it is discarded. Otherwise it updates its attributes (as described below) and is drawn.

We make a final modification to the DIA: we use a bucket-sort data structure to find the pixel with the greatest desire. This key step can be completed in $O(1)$ time rather than the $O(\log(n))$ quad-tree method of Salisbury *et al.*, where $n$ is the number of pixels.[2] This lets the algorithm run at interactive speeds on simple scenes.

### 4.2 Subtracting the blurred image

When a graftal is placed in the scene (either initially or in subsequent frames) it subtracts a blurred "image" of itself from the difference image. For this, graftals are treated as points with a given (variable) screen size, so the blurred image is just a Gaussian dot.

Pixels in the desire image are encoded with values ranging from zero (no desire) to one (maximum desire). Each graftal has an associated "volume" that determines how much total "desire" it subtracts from the desire image. This volume is proportional to the graftal's approximate screen space area. Intuitively, a visually large graftal subtracts a large volume, corresponding to a wide blurred dot: this eliminates desire in a wide region near the graftal, preventing others from being placed there.

Graftals can scale their geometry and volume so that they tend to maintain a desired screen-space size and relative density. For example, strictly adhering to the laws of perspective when zooming away from the model could result in graftals being drawn too small to be individually discernible. An artist might choose to draw them larger than they would realistically appear in this case. In any case, graftals that appear smaller in screen space should scale their volume accordingly in the DIA , or they will be placed too sparsely.

To perform such compensatory scaling, each graftal must keep track of its approximate screen space size. It does so by first converting its object-space length $L$ to a screen-space measurement $s$ in every frame (ignoring foreshortening). Then it chooses a scale factor $r$ by which to multiply $L$ as follows. As part of its definition, the graftal is given a desired screen space length $d$ and corresponding volume $v_0$ (chosen by the user). At one extreme the graftal could take $r = d/s$, so that it always appears the same size on the screen regardless of distance. At the other extreme it could take $r = 1$, which would be strictly realistic. In our examples, we have taken a weighted average between the two extremes:

$$r = w(d/s) + (1 - w),$$

with weight $w = 0.25$. This approach moderates the degree to which the graftal scales with distance, providing a measure of resistance to change from its ideal size. Finally, the volume in each frame is calculated as $v = v_0(rs/d)^2$ to keep it proportional to the graftal's current screen size.

Now let $d_0$ be the value in the desire image at the graftal's screen position $\mathbf{x}_0$ (which has been verified as visible). Let $v > 0$ be the volume of the graftal. We seek a 2D Gaussian function $g$ such that

$$g(\mathbf{0}) = d_0 \quad \text{and} \quad \int_{-\infty}^{\infty}\int_{-\infty}^{\infty} g(\mathbf{x})\,dxdy = v.$$

This is given by $g(\mathbf{x}) = d_0 e^{-\pi d_0 |\mathbf{x}|^2/v}$. Thus, to subtract the "blurred image" at $\mathbf{x}_0$, we subtract $g(\mathbf{x} - \mathbf{x}_0)$ from each pixel location $\mathbf{x}$ in the desire image. Of course, outside of some radius values of $g$ are negligible. If we take $m$ to be the minimum value we can represent in the 8 bits we use to store desire, then this radius is $(v \log(2d_0/m)/(\pi d_0))^{1/2}$. We only subtract $g$ from pixel locations within this radius of the graftal's screen position.

As the graftal subtracts this Gaussian from the desire image, it records the total desire subtracted. (It can't subtract more from a pixel than is stored there.) When all goes well, this quantity should equal the volume $v$ (ignoring discretization errors and the small portion of the Gaussian outside the maximum radius above). If the total is less than $v$, the graftal may draw itself with a reduced level of detail. If the total is too low (below 0.5 in all our examples), the graftal reports failure to its texture and is removed from the scene. To avoid "popping" when graftals appear and disappear, they may initially be drawn with reduced detail, quickly increasing to full detail over a short time, and reversing the process when they are removed. This has its limitations, though, as we discuss below.

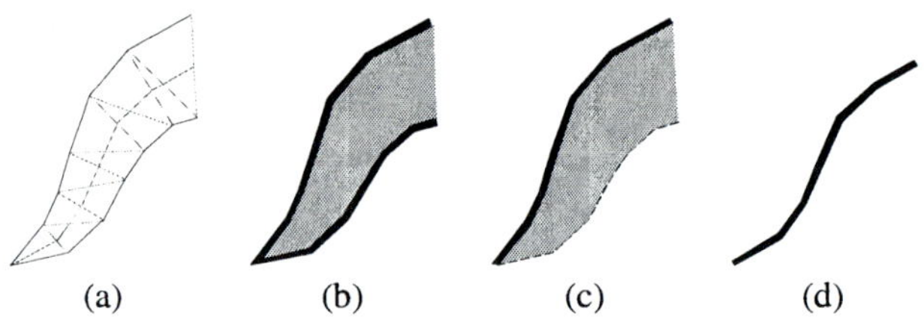

**Figure 5** A fur graftal is based on a planar polyline and table of widths, used to construct a GL triangle strip (a). The graftal can render itself in three ways: It can draw a set of filled polygons with strokes along both borders (b) or just one (c); or it can draw just the spine (d).

### 4.3 Details of fur graftals

A fur graftal – the kind used for the furry creature in figure 1, and for the truffula tufts and grassy mounds at the base of the trees in figure 2 – is not particularly complex. It is based on a flat tapering shape by a gradually reducing width about a central spine (see figure 5). The central spine is a planar polyline, and the taper widths are recorded in an array. For the model in figure 1, just a few taper

[2]We thank Ken Lao for suggesting this idea.

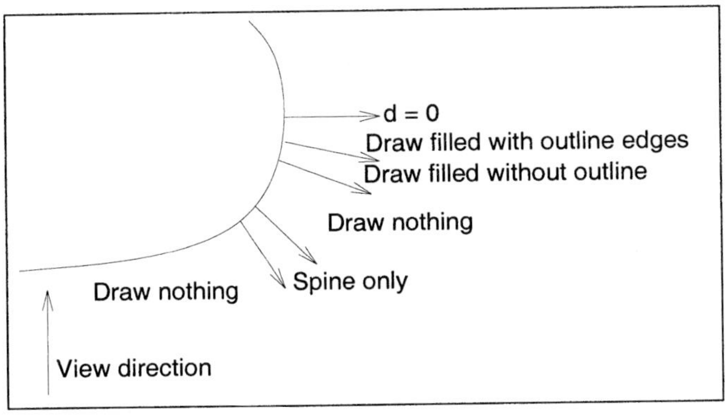


**Figure 6** The dot product $d$ of the view vector and surface normal determines a graftal's drawing style. In figure 1 the "Draw filled without outline" region is empty: we transition directly from "filled with outline" to "draw nothing."

widths were assigned; for the truffula tufts there were about seven. The shape of the central spine was drawn on graph paper and entered by hand.

After being placed with the DIA, each fur graftal determines how to orient and draw itself by computing the dot product $d$ of the unit surface normal $\vec{n}$ at the graftal's position with the unit view vector $\vec{v}$ from the camera to its position (see figure 6). For varying values of $d$, the tuft may be drawn filled, filled with one edge, filled with both edges, as a spine only, or not at all. For the fur in figure 1, we draw just the spine for $-0.75 < d < -0.6$. We draw the filled tuft with both edges for $-0.55 < d < 0$. Other schemes are possible, and we believe that adjusting the thresholds and drawing styles during "fade-in" and "fade-out" might help smooth these transitions.

Finally, the fur graftals are oriented to face the camera – that is, to lie in the plane containing the underlying surface normal and most nearly orthogonal to the view vector. They're placed so that in general they bend down. This behavior can be modified (as in the truffula tufts) so that they point clockwise, or so that they follow directions that have been "painted" onto the graftal texture's patch, as in the feet in figure 1.

## 5 Results and Future Work

Our system can produce scenes that evoke a remarkable sense of complexity, in a style that's new to 3D graphics, and at interactive rates. Figures 2, 4 and 8 show the kinds of results that can be achieved with graftal textures. In each case the underlying geometry was simple to produce, yet the renderings have an expressiveness often lacking in computer graphics imagery. With our system, even the truffula scene can be rendered at several frames per second on a high-end PC.

The accompanying video[3] shows our system in action. It includes sequences captured in real-time and animation sequences rendered off-line and played back at significantly higher frame rates. The problem of poor frame-to-frame coherence stands out most noticeably in the latter case. Graftals that persist from frame to frame maintain geometric coherence (if we simply redistributed graftals at every frame, the flicker would be overwhelming); unfortunately, the DIA has no inherent interframe consistency, so it's easy for a graftal to be "crowded out" in one frame, replaced in the next, and so on, causing the flickering artifacts that are so noticeable in the video.

We have recently begun experimenting with some strategies to address this problem. One possibility is to make much greater use of fading and alpha blending when introducing graftals into the scene and taking them out. The degree to which this approach is usable depends quite a lot on the specific style being targeted. Fading in a large yellow truffula tuft outlined in black against a blue sky may be just as jarring as introducing it suddenly; but fading in semi-transparent blades of grass rendered with a watercolor-like effect over green terrain might seem perfectly acceptable.

One problem we have encountered in our early experiments with fading in tufts of fur like those in figure 1 occurs when all the tufts along a silhouette are newly introduced, and thus nearly transparent. The model then appears (briefly) to be missing its fur along that silhouette. A possible solution that we have not yet implemented is to maintain a separate population of tufts drawn on back-facing surfaces. This requires an auxiliary ID reference image prepared with front-facing triangles culled. It also requires two separate calls to our modified DIA each frame – one to place front-facing tufts, another to place back-facing ones. The point is that tufts emerging into view from behind a silhouette (as the object turns) would already be drawn and thus would not "pop in." Each frame might take twice as long to render – possibly a worthwhile trade-off if the resulting animations are significantly more watchable.

Another strategy we have experimented with is to use *static* graftals (see figure 7). With this approach, graftals are assigned fixed positions on the surface, rather than being generated each frame as needed. They still draw in a view-dependent way – those far from a silhouette, say, may not draw at all. This works quite well as long as the camera does not zoom out too far: in that case the graftals are drawn too densely in screen space. We can overcome this by assigning graftals several levels of priority – say numbered 0 through 2. Each level is distributed evenly over the surface, with those in a given level outnumbering those in the next lower level by a factor of about four. In a given frame, every graftal at level 0 "draws" itself view-dependently (possibly not at all if far from a silhouette). Each also subtracts its blurred image from the desire image, as in the DIA , and measures its success rate. If, collectively, this rate is high enough, the next level is given the chance to draw, and goes through the same procedure to decide whether the last level should also have the chance to draw. This strategy is suitable for localized objects -– we have tested it on versions of the truffula treetops – but not for landscapes where the choice of what level graftal to draw must vary over the surface according to distance from the camera. Our preliminary results indicate the effectiveness of this strategy. We demonstrate this in the accompanying videotape. Figure 7 shows a truffula tree top with static graftals drawn at three levels of detail.

A separate area for future work is to explore a range of new styles. For example, we have begun to explore rendering fur using two layers, one light and one dark, on a neutral background (see figure 8). This is a common technique in traditional drawing that can suggest more complex lighting effects (such as glossiness) while omitting unnecessary detail: nothing is drawn in midtone regions, which are represented by the unaltered background color.

## 6 Acknowledgments

We thank Michael LeGrand for creating the "furry creature" model, and Cynthia B. Rubin and Scott Klemmer for advice on preparing the images. Thanks also to Andy van Dam and the Graphics Group, and to our sponsors: the NSF Graphics and Visualization Center, Advanced Network and Services, Alias/Wavefront, Autodesk, IBM, Intel, Microsoft, National Tele-Immersion Initiative, Sun Microsystems, and TACO. Lee Markosian received support for his graduate education from Intel through the Intel Foundation Ph.D. Fellowship program.

[3] See the Siggraph 99 Conference Proceedings Video Tape.

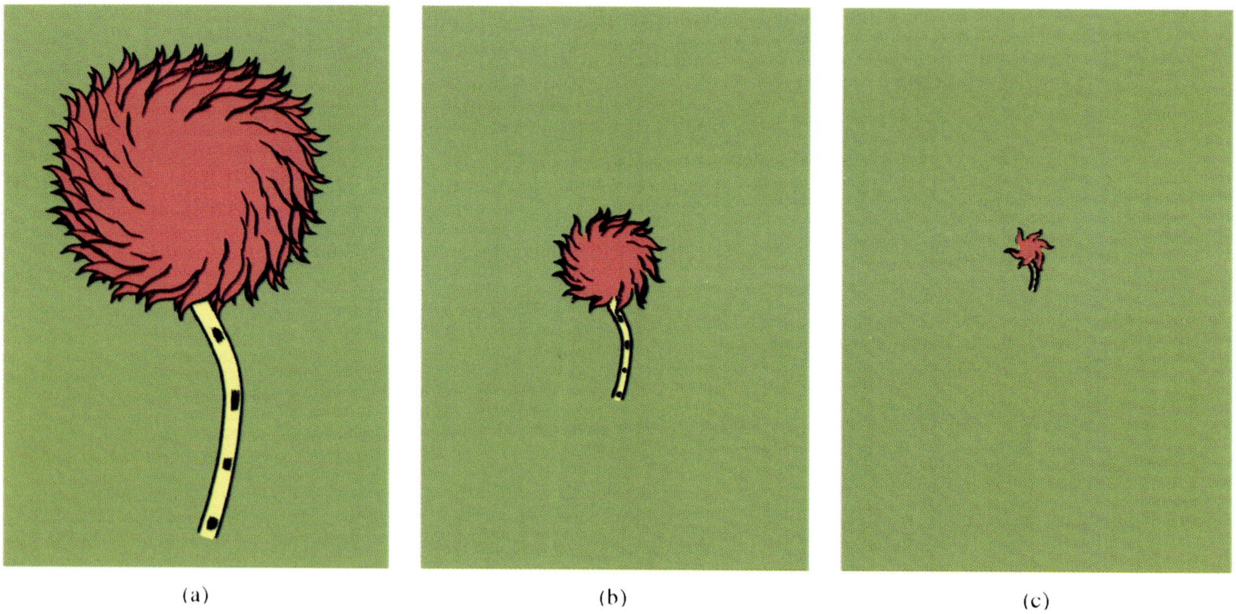

Figure 7 A truffula treetop with static graftals organized in a three-level hierarchy. When the camera is close, all three levels are drawn (a). As the camera zooms out, only two levels are drawn (b), and finally just the base level is drawn (c).

**Figure 8** Fur rendered in light and dark layers on a neutral background. Model courtesy of Stanford University.

## References


[1] Norman I. Badler and Andrew S. Glassner. 3D object modeling. In *SIGGRAPH 97 Introduction to Computer Graphics Course Notes*. ACM SIGGRAPH, August 1997.

[2] OpenGL Architecture Review Board. *OpenGL Reference Manual, 2nd Edition*. Addison-Wesley Developers Press, 1996.

[3] J. D. Foley, A. van Dam, S. K. Feiner, and J. F. Hughes. *Computer Graphics: Principles and Practice*. Addison-Wesley, Reading, MA, 2nd edition, 1992.

[4] Dr. Seuss (Theodor Geisel). *The Lorax*. Random House, New York, 1971.

[5] Dr. Seuss (Theodor Geisel). *The Foot Book*. Random House, New York, 1988.

[6] Amy Gooch, Bruce Gooch, Peter Shirley, and Elaine Cohen. A non-photorealistic lighting model for automatic technical illustration. In *SIGGRAPH 98 Conference Proceedings*, pp. 447–452. ACM SIGGRAPH, July 1998.

[7] Geoffrey Hayes. *Patrick and Ted*. Scholastic, Inc., New York, 1984.

[8] Lee Markosian. *Art-based Modeling and Rendering for Computer Graphics*. PhD thesis, Brown University, November 1999 (expected completion).

[9] Lee Markosian, Jonathan M. Cohen, Thomas Crulli, and John Hughes. Skin: A constructive approach to modeling free-form shapes. In *SIGGRAPH 99 Conference Proceedings*. ACM SIGGRAPH, August 1999.

[10] Lee Markosian, Michael A. Kowalski, Samuel J. Trychin, Lubomir D. Bourdev, Daniel Goldstein, and John F. Hughes. Real-time nonphotorealistic rendering. In *SIGGRAPH 97 Conference Proceedings*, pp. 415–420. ACM SIGGRAPH, August 1997.

[11] Barbara J. Meier. Painterly rendering for animation. In *SIGGRAPH 96 Conference Proceedings*, pp. 477–484. ACM SIGGRAPH, August 1996.

[12] W. T. Reeves. Particle systems – a technique for modeling a class of fuzzy objects. *ACM Trans. Graphics*, 2:91–108, April 1983.

[13] William T. Reeves and Ricki Blau. Approximate and probabilistic algorithms for shading and rendering structured particle systems. In *SIGGRAPH 85 Conference Proceedings*, pp. 313–322. ACM SIGGRAPH, July 1985.

[14] Michael P. Salisbury, Michael T. Wong, John F. Hughes, and David H. Salesin. Orientable textures for image-based pen-and-ink illustration. In *SIGGRAPH 97 Conference Proceedings*, pp. 401–406. ACM SIGGRAPH, August 1997.

[15] Alvy Ray Smith. Plants, fractals and formal languages. In *SIGGRAPH 84 Conference Proceedings*, pp. 1–10. ACM SIGGRAPH, July 1984.

[16] T. Strothotte, B. Preim, A. Raab, J. Schumann, and D. R. Forsey. How to render frames and influence people. In *Computer Graphics Forum*, volume 13, pp. 455–466. Eurographics, Basil Blackwell Ltd, 1994. Eurographics '94 Conference issue.

[17] Georges Winkenbach and David H. Salesin. Computer-generated pen-and-ink illustration. In *SIGGRAPH 94 Conference Proceedings*, pp. 91–100. ACM SIGGRAPH, July 1994.

# View-Dependent Geometry

Paul Rademacher
University of North Carolina at Chapel Hill


## ABSTRACT

When constructing 3D geometry for use in cel animation, the reference drawings of the object or character often contain various view-specific distortions, which cannot be captured with conventional 3D models. In this work we present a technique called View-Dependent Geometry, wherein a 3D model changes shape based on the direction it is viewed from. A view-dependent model consists of a *base model*, a set of *key deformations* (deformed versions of the base model), and a set of corresponding *key viewpoints* (which relate each 2D reference drawing to the 3D base model). Given an arbitrary viewpoint, our method interpolates the key deformations to generate a 3D model that is specific to the new viewpoint, thereby capturing the view-dependent distortions of the reference drawings.


**Keywords:** Cartoon animation, 3D animation, rendering, animation systems, non-photorealistic rendering, 3D blending

**CR Categories:** I.3.5 surface and object representations; I.3.3 display algorithms

## 1 INTRODUCTION

Cartoon animation has continually taken advantage of developments in computer graphics. Three-dimensional elements have been used to render crowds, buildings, scenery, and even main characters. When these 3D objects are created, the modelers typically begin with a set of reference drawings of the object (the *model sheet*) showing it from different viewpoints. Unlike photographs or technical illustrations, these hand-created images do not correspond to a precise physical space – the artists who draw them try to achieve the best *aesthetic* effect, and are not bound to geometric precision. As a result, these drawings typically contain many subtle artistic distortions, such as changes in scale and perspective (also noted by [Zori95]), or more noticeable effects such as changes in the shape or location of features (e.g., the face, hair, and ears of Figure 1). Because these distortions differ in each drawing and do not correspond to a 3D geometric space, conventional 3D models are unable to capture them all. As a result, these view-specific distortions are often lost as we move from the artistic 2D world to the geometric 3D world.

One might attempt to remedy this problem using existing 3D modeling and animation tools by directly modifying the object at selected keyframes of the final animation, to match the drawings better. However, this approach is only feasible if the camera path is fixed, and might be prohibitively expensive if the object is replicated many times from different angles (e.g., in a crowd).

In this paper, we propose to make the view-dependencies an *inherent* part of the model, defining them only once during the modeling phase. The appropriate distortions can then be generated automatically for any arbitrary viewpoint or camera path.

We accomplish this with a technique we call View-Dependent Geometry – geometry that changes shape based on the direction it is seen from. A view-dependent model consists of a base model (a conventional 3D object) and a description of the model's exact shape as seen from specific viewpoints. These viewpoints are known as the key viewpoints (which are independent of the camera path that will be used during rendering), and the corresponding object shapes are the key deformations. The key deformations are simply deformed versions of the base model, with the same vertex connectivity. Given an arbitrary viewpoint or camera path, the deformations are blended to generate a new, view-specific 3D model.

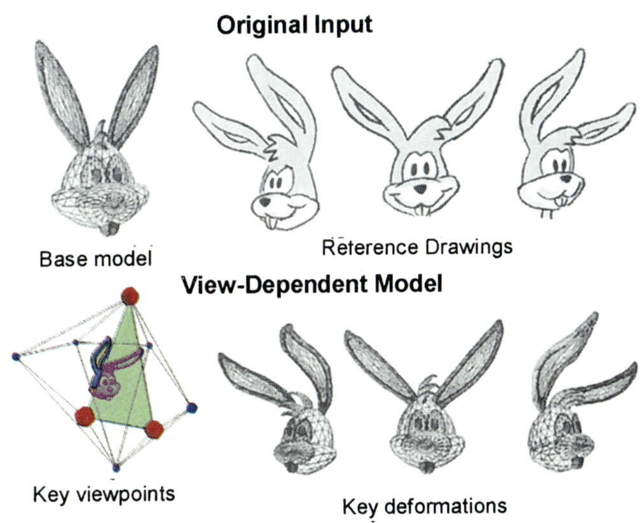


**Figure 1** Example components of a view-dependent model

View-dependent models are able to capture different looks for an object from different viewing directions. By creating a key deformation for each reference drawing, we can create models that automatically respond to any given viewing direction or camera path, yielding the proper artistic distortions.

This paper describes how to construct and render view-dependent models, both static and animated. It discusses the various interpolation issues, and shows how to deal with sparse deformations. Several examples of the technique's applicability to animation are given. We note, however, that View-Dependent Geometry is not limited to the specific driving problem of artistic distortions, but rather presents a general method – that of allowing an object's shape to vary in response to view direction – which may be of use in other areas of computer graphics as well.

UNC Department of Computer Science, Sitterson Hall, CB #3175, Chapel Hill, NC, 27599-3175. Email: rademach@cs.unc.edu

## 2 PREVIOUS WORK

The problem of cartoon animation was addressed very early in computer graphics, for example by [Levo77, Hack77, Reev81]. Many computer systems have since been designed to aid in traditional animation. [Dura91] provides an overview of many of the issues and tradeoffs involved. [Litw91] describes the Inkwell system, based on 2-D geometric primitives. [Feke95] describes TicTacToon, which mimics the workflow of a traditional animation studio. [Robe94b] presents an overview of different commercial software packages for cartoons, and [Robe94a] describes Disney's CAPS system, the most successful usage of computers in cel animation to date. Many techniques of cartoon animation were introduced to the graphics literature by [Lass87].

The above papers describe general cel animation systems; there have also been many recent publications describing specific methods for graphics in cartoons. [Libr92] describes a system which takes as input a set of vector-based drawings, and parametrically blends them to interpolate any number of defined features. [Pfit94] describes the wildebeest scene in Disney's *The Lion King*. [Guag98] describes similar techniques in Disney's *Mulan*, as well as their enhanced 2.5-D multiplane system, Faux Plane. [Wood97] shows how to render multiperspective panoramas of backgrounds for use in cartoons. Finally, Correa demonstrates a method for integrating texture mapping with cel animation [Corr98]. Our method is similar in nature to Correa's. The common philosophy is that one should not discard the inherent expressiveness of the 2D artist as 3D computer graphics are incorporated into the animation. In their work, they apply textures to hand-drawn animated sequences (thereby retaining the artistry of the drawn animation) whereas in our method we create 3D models that are able to capture the artistic distortions in multiple drawings of an object.

Our method involves issues in 3D interpolation and deformations. Related work includes [Beie92, Lee95, Lerios95]. Our method is also similar to [Debe98], where textures – rather than geometry – are blended in response to the current viewpoint.

## 3 CREATING AND RENDERING VIEW-DEPENDENT GEOMETRY

A view-dependent model is composed of a base model and a set of deformations specifying the model's shape as seen from specific viewpoints. This section discusses how to determine these key viewpoints, how to construct the corresponding deformations, and how to blend between the different deformations as the object is viewed from an arbitrary location.

### 3.1 Creating View-Dependent Models

The inputs to our system are a conventional 3D model of an object (the base model) and a set of drawings of the object from various viewpoints (Figure 2 shows an example model created as a polygonal mesh in 3D Studio Max, and a single hand-drawn image). The base model is created using standard 3D modeling software. It represents the best-fit geometry to the complete set of drawings (since the context is artistic animation, "best-fit" can be interpreted in an intuitive – and not necessarily numerical – sense). In this section we assume the base model is rigid (animated models are discussed in Section 4).

#### 3.1.1 Aligning the base model and the images

The first step is determining a viewpoint for each drawing. That is, we find a camera position and orientation relative to the base model, with a projection that best matches the given drawing (the current implementation uses perspective cameras, although this discussion also applies to parallel projections). Because of the artistic distortions, exact alignment of the model with the drawing is not possible. We therefore cannot use standard linear correspondence methods such as in [Faug93] (although non-linear methods might prove useful in future work). Note, however, that exact alignment is not actually necessary in our context, since the features in the 3D model that cannot be aligned will be deformed to match the image in the next step.

In the current implementation the user manually aligns the model with each drawing by rotating and translating the camera until the main features match. Figure 3 shows the model superimposed over a drawing after it has been manually aligned.

#### 3.1.2 Deforming the base model

There are many existing techniques for deforming 3D models. For example, one may use free-form deformation lattices [Sede86], "wires" [Sing98], or various other existing methods. These all operate in 3D space, thereby permitting arbitrary changes to the object's shape.

For our application, however, full 3D deformations are not always necessary. Since we are ultimately concerned with the model's shape as seen from only a single fixed viewpoint (for each reference image), we can perform the majority of the deformations in 2D, parallel to the image plane of the camera. This makes the deformation step considerably easier than the full 3D modeling required to originally build the base model.

The current implementation of the deformation system is quite straightforward. Given a polygonal mesh representation of the model, the user picks a vertex. All vertices within a specified

**Figure 2** A reference drawing of a character, and the base model. The model is constructed using standard 3D modeling software.

**Figure 3** Construction of the view-dependent model. We first align the base model to the drawing – this establishes the *key viewpoint*. We then deform the model to match the drawing (the drawing is not altered). On the right we see the final *key deformation*.

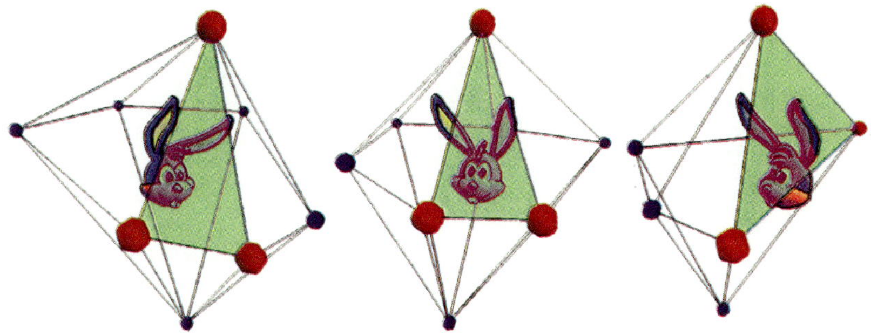

**Figure 4** Viewpoints for each key deformation are shown as spheres around the model. To compute the shape as seen from the current viewpoint, we find the nearest three key viewpoints (indicated in red) and interpolate the corresponding 3D deformations.

distance $\boldsymbol{r}$ in 3D of the selected vertex are then also selected. As the user drags the original vertex across the image plane, the other vertices are dragged in the same direction with a scaling factor of $(1-d/r)^2$, where $\boldsymbol{d}$ is the distance of a given vertex to the originally-chosen point, and $\boldsymbol{r}$ is the selection radius, both in world units. The vertices' Z-distances from the camera remain unchanged. This simple method permits relatively smooth deformations (dependent on the resolution of the underlying mesh). The middle still in Figure 3 shows a deformation on the example model. The currently-selected group of vertices is shown in red.

Besides dragging vertices across the image plane, our implementation also allows the user to push and pull vertices in the Z direction (towards or away from the camera). This is necessary to fix vertices that accidentally pass through the mesh as they are translated on the image plane. A more sophisticated implementation should provide an entire suite of tools including arbitrary rotations and scalings of groups of vertices – as with any modeling application, the quality of the interface can greatly influence the quality of the resulting mesh.

Note that *the topology (vertex connectivity) of the model does not change* during the deformation; only the vertex locations are altered. This greatly simplifies the subsequent interpolation step. Also note that the *drawings are not altered* – only the base model is deformed.

The last image in Figure 3 shows the model after the deformation process. Comparing this with Figure 2, we see that the deformed model matches the reference drawing's shape more closely than the base model.

After the object and image are matched to the user's satisfaction, the deformed object is saved to file as a key deformation, and the aligned camera location is saved as a key viewpoint.

## 3.2 Rendering View-Dependent Models

In the previous step we saw how to specify what the model should look like when seen from specific, discrete viewpoints. These viewpoints and deformations are independent of the final camera path (they are inherent components of the model itself), and are constructed *a priori* in the modeling phase. At rendering time we need to determine – given an arbitrary camera direction relative to the model – what the object's 3D shape should be. The rendering process proceeds as follows:

1) Find the three nearest key viewpoints surrounding the current viewpoint.
2) Calculate blending weights for the associated key deformations.
3) Interpolate the key deformations to generate a new 3D model for the current viewpoint.
4) Render the resulting interpolated 3D model.

This process is similar to the view-dependent texture mapping of [Debe98], in which three textures (on a regular grid called a "view map") are blended to capture reflectance and occlusion effects in multiple images of an object.

### 3.2.1 Finding the nearest surrounding key viewpoints

First we must find the nearest key viewpoints surrounding the current viewpoint. In this paper we consider only the viewing *direction* for the key and current viewpoints, and not the distance from the cameras to the object (we also assume, without loss of generality, that the view directions point towards the centroid of the object). Since we do not differentiate between distances, we can map the viewing directions to points on a *viewing sphere* around the object. To find the surrounding key viewpoints, we find the three points on this sphere whose spherical triangle contains the current viewpoint (Figure 5).

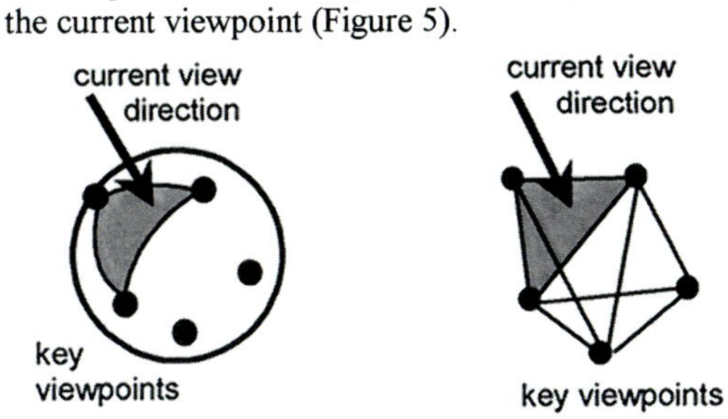


**Figure 5** The key viewpoints surrounding the current viewpoint are given by the intersected spherical triangle on the viewing sphere. This is equivalent to the corresponding planar triangle on the convex hull of sphere points.

However, we can avoid working in the spherical domain by noting that a spherical triangle is simply the projection onto the sphere of the *planar* triangle between the three vertices. Therefore, if the current viewpoint maps to the spherical triangle between three given keys, it also maps to the corresponding planar triangle. This leads to the following simple method for finding the surrounding viewpoints: as a preprocess, project the key viewpoints to a sphere around the object, and then compute the convex hull of these points; this gives a triangulation around the object (any convex hull algorithm that avoids creating long, splintery triangles can be used. Our current implementation uses

**Figure 6**

Top row: Different views generated as we rotate our camera about the model. They are created by interpolating the three key deformations nearest to the camera viewpoint.

Bottom row: The interpolated 3D model seen formed.
Texture extraction – It is straightforward to extract texture coordinatestop row's viewpoint changes

[Wats81]). At rendering time, find the face in the convex hull which is intersected by a ray from the current camera to the sphere center. The intersected triangle denotes the three key viewpoints surrounding the current camera (note that the result of the intersection test may be zero or two points if the key viewpoints do not fully enclose the object - discussed further in Section 3.3).

Figure 4 shows the key viewpoints of our example view-dependent model, projected onto a sphere. The convex hull for these points is displayed in wireframe. For each rendered view, we project a ray from the eye towards the sphere center; the intersected triangle of the hull is shown in green. The vertices of this triangle (shown in red) correspond to the three nearest key viewpoints for the current view.

### 3.2.2 Calculating the blending weights

Given the intersection of a viewing ray with one of the triangles from the previous section, the blending coefficients are given directly by the barycentric coordinates $w_1$, $w_2$, $w_3$ of the intersection point. These weights are continuous as the camera is moved within and across triangles. Furthermore, one of the barycentric coordinates will reach a value of one – and the other two weights will equal zero – when the current viewpoint exactly matches a key viewpoint (i.e., when the intersection point is at a triangle vertex). When this occurs, the blended model will exactly match the one key deformation corresponding to that viewpoint.

The blending weights can be scaled exponentially to alter the sharpness of the transition between adjacent deformations. We define these new, scaled weights as:

$$w_i' = \frac{w_i^\alpha}{w_1^\alpha + w_2^\alpha + w_3^\alpha}$$

where $\alpha$ is the sharpness factor. As $\alpha$ grows >1, the resulting blended model moves more quickly towards the nearest key deformation. As $\alpha$ becomes <1, the blend is more gradual. The next section discusses the actual interpolation of the deformed models' vertices, given the three blending weights $w_1'$, $w_2'$, and $w_3'$.

### 3.2.3 Interpolating the key deformations

The final deformed model for the current viewpoint is generated by interpolating corresponding vertices from the three nearest key deformations. Since the key deformations all share the same vertex connectivity, the vertices correspond directly – and interpolation is a simple matter of computing a weighted blend of the corresponding vertices' positions in 3-space.

Since the interpolation is computed independently for each vertex in the final model, we can limit our discussion here to a single vertex $v$. We denote the vertices corresponding to $v$ at each of the $N$ key deformations as $\{v^1, v^2, \ldots, v^N\}$. Each of these vertices is the 3-space location of $v$ under the deformation corresponding to one particular image. We now denote the three vertices from the nearest key deformations as $v^i$, $v^j$, $v^k$. Our current implementation uses a linear interpolation scheme, and thus the vertex $v$ is given as:

$$v = v^i w_1' + v^j w_2' + v^k w_3'$$

where $w_1'$ is the weight corresponding to the first key deformation, $v^i$, and similarly for $w_2'$ and $w_3'$.

One could obtain smoother blends by applying higher-order interpolation. This would consist of taking the set of vertices $v^1 \ldots v^N$ and fitting a higher-order surface to it, yielding a smooth tri-patch (with the vertex connectivity given by the convex-hull triangulation). This tri-patch would be locally parameterized by two of the weights $w'$ (since the third is always one minus the sum of the first two). Given an arbitrary viewing direction, a single point is computed on this surface and used as the current location for $v$.

Another interpolation scheme worth investigating for future work is that of Radial Basis Functions, a multidimensional learning-based technique. These are used by [Libr92] to generate artistic images interpolated from vector-based drawings.

Note that the above discussion only deals with the *vertex-wise* smoothness of the interpolation. We do not enforce any *global* constraints on the deformations or on the resulting interpolation (e.g., ensuring the mesh doesn't pass through itself, enforcing mesh curvature constraints, etc.). Doing so would involve a tradeoff between the quality of the resulting meshes and the extent of allowable deformations.

### 3.2.4 Rendering the resulting 3D model

In this paper, we display the resulting model using non-photorealistic rendering techniques, consisting of a non-standard lighting scheme and a silhouette-rendering scheme. The object is lit and shaded with a method similar in nature (though not identical) to [Gooc98]. Our lighting equation is:

$$C_{final} = k_a C_{base} + (\hat{l}_1 \bullet \hat{n})(C_{warm} - (C_{base} * k_1)) * k_2 + (\hat{l}_2 \bullet \hat{n})(C_{cool} - (C_{base} * k_3)) * k_4$$

where $l_1$ and $l_2$ are the positions of two lights on opposite sides of the surface, $n$ is the surface normal, $C_{final}$ is the final color for the surface, $C_{base}$ is the base color of the surface (e.g., the diffuse color), and $C_{cool}$ and $C_{warm}$ are cool and warm colors (e.g., blue and orange). The parameter $k_a$ controls how much of the base color the surface receives as ambient light (the given examples use $k_a = .9$). The parameters $k_1$ and $k_3$ are used to prevent the lights from oversaturating the surface (since it has a strong ambient component), and $k_2$ and $k_4$ control the intensity of the warm and cool lights. A value of 1.0 can be used as a default for $k_1$ through $k_4$.

In contrast with the Gooch method, the values of $k_1$ through $k_4$ are *varied for each surface*, based on the hue of $C_{base}$. For example, we disable the warm (orange) light when rendering white-ish surfaces – yielding soft, cool whites. For purple surfaces, we set $k_4$ to 2.0 (intensifying the cool light component), while for red colors we increase the cool light while also decreasing the warm light – yielding rich purples and brilliant reds. There are many other hues that can be handled, and varying the parameters leads to many interesting effects (e.g., letting the parameters extend to negative values yields fluorescent surfaces).

The above equation can be implemented in OpenGL by setting the global ambient light to $C_{base} * k_a$, setting the per-light ambient and specular components to zero, and using the second and third terms in the above equation as the diffuse component for the first and second lights, respectively.

Our silhouette algorithm is based on [Rask99] (the techniques of [Mark97] can also been applied). In the former paper, silhouettes are generated by rendering the model in two passes: first a regular backface-culled rendering pass, with lit and shaded polygons, then a second pass with front faces culled and back faces rendered in thick black wireframe (using the OpenGL commands `glDepthFunc(GL_LEQUAL)`, `glCullFace(GL_FRONT)`, and `glPolygonMode(GL_BACK, GL_LINE)`). This method is easy to implement, and operates on unstructured "polygon soup" models as well. In our implementation, we also optimize by first detecting adjacent faces which span a silhouette edge (that is, one face is front-facing and the other back-facing). We then only render these faces – rather than all the backfaces – in the second pass. In addition, we render these faces a third time as points using `glPolygonMode( GL_BACK, GL_POINT)`, to eliminate cracks that can appear between adjacent thickened edges.

### 3.2.5 Example View-Dependent Model

In Figure 6 we show a static view-dependent model, rendered from a series of viewpoints. This model was created by applying the three deformations shown in Figure 1, along with 5 other minor deformations about the viewing sphere. As we rotate around the head, we see the ears and hair shift to match the original drawings (from Figure 1). In the bottom row (in blue) we show the model from an independent, fixed viewpoint. This clearly shows the 3D changes in the model as the camera rotates.

## 3.3 Unspecified Regions in Viewing Sphere

Our method has assumed that the key viewpoints entirely surround the base object. Then there will always be three key viewpoints surrounding any arbitrary new viewpoint. However, if the hull of the key viewpoints does not enclose the center of the viewing sphere, then there will be areas on the sphere that have no associated key deformations. This may happen, for example, if there are fewer than four deformations, or if the key viewpoints all lie on one side of the object.

We can deal with these unspecified regions by interpolating the deformations with the original base model. For example, if the key viewpoints all lie on one side of the sphere, we can insert dummy "deformations" – simply copies of the base model – in order to fully enclose it. Equivalently, we can revert to the base model without explicitly inserting dummy keys by using a cosine or cosine-squared falloff on the available deformations as the current viewpoint moves into unspecified regions.

For example, in Figure 7 we show a building model, to be used as a background object. Since backgrounds are often only seen from a single viewpoint, we only apply one deformation (from the front of the building). As the current camera moves away from the front, we gradually revert to the base model by blending the single deformation and the base model with:

$$\begin{aligned} new\_model \; &= \mathbf{max}\left(0, \left(\hat{V}_{key} \bullet \hat{V}_{eye}\right)\right) * deformed\_model \\ &+ \mathbf{max}\left(0, 1 - \left(\hat{V}_{key} \bullet \hat{V}_{eye}\right)\right) * base\_model \end{aligned}$$

where $V_{key}$ is the view vector for the single key deformation, and $V_{eye}$ is the view vector for the current eye point. This formula blends smoothly between the single deformation and the base model as the viewpoint changes.

## 4 ANIMATED VIEW-DEPENDENT MODELS

The basic view-dependent method described above only handles static base models. This can be useful for background objects, props, vehicles, etc. In this section, we demonstrate how to deal with objects whose shape changes non-rigidly over time.

We note that if the animation will be used for only a single shot, or if the camera path for the final render is fixed, then it may be easier to match the animation and artwork directly using conventional keyframe methods. However, if we have an animation that will be used repeatedly from arbitrary angles (e.g., a walking cycle), in large numbers (e.g., crowds), or from an unknown camera path (e.g., a real-time application), then it may be more efficient to use view-dependent geometry. The animation can then be rendered from any arbitrary viewpoint, automatically yielding the proper distortions.

**Figure 7** The base model in this example is a simple rectangular building. We applied a single deformation, from a viewpoint directly facing the building. The output model is fully deformed when the current camera faces the building front, and reverts to the original shape as the camera moves towards the sides.

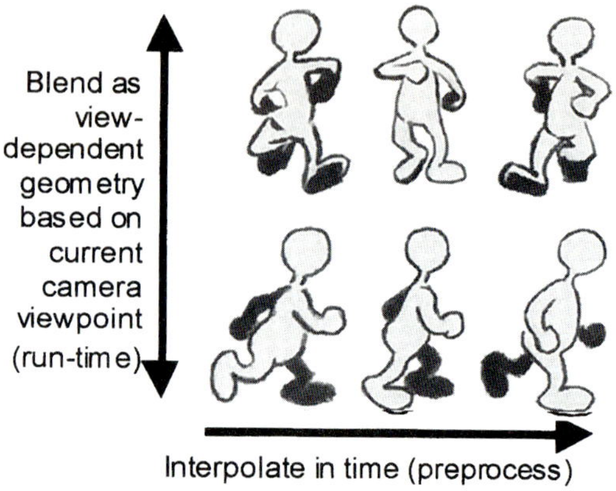


**Figure 8** A set of drawings showing the object at different frames, from different viewpoints. We interpolate across time (horizontally) to generate deformations for each frame. We blend between different deformations at a given frame (vertically) to render from an arbitrary viewpoint.

## 4.1 Animated Base Models

A set of key deformations indicates what an object should look like from various viewpoints, but does not show change over time. When the base model is non-rigidly animated, then a single set of deformations no longer suffices. Instead, we will need a different set of deformations *for each frame of the model's animation*, which are then blended on a per-frame basis in response to the current viewpoint.

However, the user does not have to *explicitly* specify the set of key deformations for every frame – a tedious and error-prone task. Instead, the user only needs to define a small number of deformations, at different times in the animation and from various viewpoints (Figure 8). All the deformations from the same viewpoint are then interpolated over time (discussed in the next section). This yields, for each viewpoint on the viewing sphere, a deformation at every frame. Once this interpolation is applied for all key viewpoints, we will have a full set of deformations for each frame. We can then directly apply the basic view-dependent geometry method on a per-frame basis.

## 4.2 Interpolating the Key Deformations Over Time

Let us consider a single key viewpoint. We need a deformation of the base model from this viewpoint for every frame in the animation, but are given only a small number of them at selected frames. Because the deformations are given sparsely and do not necessarily correspond to the underlying animation keyframes, we cannot interpolate between them directly (doing so would lead to the typical problems of object blending discussed in [Beie92, Leri95, Witk95, Sede93]).

Instead of interpolating directly, we propagate the deformations throughout the underlying animation by factoring out the deformation offsets at the given frames, interpolating between these offsets, then adding the interpolated deformation offsets to the original animated model. This preserves the underlying motion while propagating the changes due to deformation.

For example, let $v$ be a vertex in an animated base model, with deformations at two given frames. We denote $v$'s original 3D location at the first given frame as $v_a$, and its original position at the next keyframe as $v_b$. We denote the *deformed* vertex locations at those two frames as $v_a'$ and $v_b'$. Instead of interpolating directly from $v_a'$ to $v_b'$, we decompose the 3D locations into:

$$v_a' = v_a + o_a$$
$$v_b' = v_b + o_b$$

where $o_a$ and $o_b$ are the offsets (3D vectors) by which the vertices are deformed in each given frame. We then interpolate the *offsets* (the current implementation uses natural cubic splines), and add each new offset vector $o_i$ (at frame $i$, between the two keyframes) to the undeformed vertex $v_i$, yielding the final interpolated vertex position.

## 4.3 Example Animated View-Dependent Model

Figures 9-12 show an animated base model of a 40-frame walk cycle. We applied a total of 4 key deformations to the original walking model: one from the front and one from the side at frame 10, and another two from the front and side at frame 30 (these deformations simply exaggerate the pose of the model,

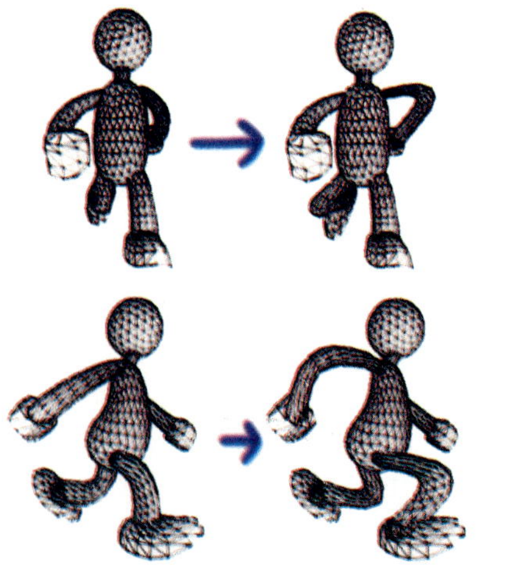

**Figure 9** Two different deformations applied to an animated model. On the left is the base model, on the right is the deformed version.

**Figure 10** This sequence shows different views of the animated model, *at a single moment in the model's animation* (time is not changing, only the viewpoint). The object's shape varies depending on the viewpoint. Top row: view-dependent model as seen from the main (rotating) camera. Bottom row: model as seen from independent, fixed camera. The bottom row clearly shows the distortions in the arms and legs as the camera rotates.

making the arms and legs swing out more). We therefore have 2 key viewpoints (a front view and a side view), and two deformations in time per viewpoint (the two deformations at frame 10 are shown in Figure 9). These deformations are first offset-interpolated in time as a preprocess, yielding deformations at *every* frame, for each key viewpoint. These key deformations are then blended at run-time using the view-dependent geometry method. In Figure 10 we show a *single frame* of the walk cycle, seen from various viewpoints around the model. The blue model (seen from a fixed, independent viewpoint) shows how the object distorts as we view it from different angles. Figure 11 and 12 compare the original model against the view-dependent model as they are animated over time. Figure 11 is the original model, without view-specific distortions. Figure 12 shows the view-dependent model, clearly showing the effects of the distortions.

# 5 PUTTING IT ALL TOGETHER

In Figure 13 we bring together the different methods discussed in this paper. The rabbit's head is a static view-dependent model, the body is an animated view-dependent model, and the buildings are static view-dependent models with a single deformation applied. We can see the ears differ in the first and last viewpoints. We also see the distortions of Figure 9 in the middle two viewpoints. Finally, we see the buildings are distorted when seen face-on, but otherwise revert to their original rectangular shape.

# 6 FUTURE WORK

Both the current implementation and the general method of view-dependent geometry are open to many avenues of further investigation:

- Semi-automatic alignment and deformation based on feature correspondence. For example, one might adapt standard image morphing techniques such as [Beie92].
- Automatic construction of the 3D base model from the 2D drawings.
- Better deformations might be achieved by applying higher-order interpolation, and by ensuring vertices do not pass through the mesh as it is deformed.
- Texture extraction – It is straightforward to extract texture coordinates from each reference drawing, and then use view-dependent textures [Debe98]. However, drawings are difficult to blend due to contour lines and differences in the shading, line style or coloring of each drawing.
- Key viewpoints at different distances. Instead of a triangulation of the viewing sphere, a tetrahedralization of space would be required.
- Interface tools and model formats – The current implementation could be greatly enhanced by refining the selection tools, the deformation methods, and by operating on NURBS and other curved surfaces.

# 7 CONCLUSION

It is an established fact in computer graphics that the camera viewpoint plays an important role in determining the appearance of an object. From Phong shading to microfaceted reflections to view-dependent texture mapping, graphics research has shown that gaze direction is an important parameter in rendering objects. Our work extends this progression by modifying the actual *shape* of an object depending on where it is viewed from. In doing so, we directly address a problem in 3D-enhanced cel animation – the loss of view-specific distortions as an object moves from the artistic 2D world to the geometric 3D world. By employing view-dependent geometry in cartoon animation, we can render 3D models that are truer in shape to their original 2D counterparts.

# ACKNOWLEDGEMENTS

The author would like to thank Gary Bishop, Susan Thayer, Nick England, Mark Mine, Michael Goslin, Gary Daines, and Matt Cutts for helpful discussions throughout the progress of this work, the reviewers for their feedback, and Todd Gaul for video editing assistance. This project was funded by DARPA ITO contract number E278, NSF MIP-9612643, DARPA ETO contract number N00019-97-C-2013, and an NSF Graduate Fellowship. Thanks also to Intel for their generous donation of equipment.

**Figure 11** The base (undeformed) model animated over time, viewed by a rotating camera. At each frame, both the base model and the viewpoint changes. Since this is a conventional animated model, there are no viewpoint-specific distortions.

**Figure 12** The view-dependent model animated over time, viewed by a rotating camera. The animated model's shape changes based on the viewpoint. The distortions of Figure 9 are seen in the 2nd and 7th frames – all other frames use offset-interpolated deformations.

## REFERENCES


[Beie92] Thaddeus Beier and Shawn Neely. Feature-Based Image Metamorphosis. In *Proceedings of SIGGRAPH 92*, pages 35-42. New York, July 1992. ACM.

[Blai94] Preston Blair. *Cartoon Animation.* Walter Foster Publishing, Laguna Hills, California, 1994.

[Corr98] Wagner Toledo Correa, Robert Jensen, Craig Thayer, and Adam Finkelstein. Texture Mapping for Cel Animation. In *Proceedings of SIGGRAPH 98*, pages 435-446. New York, July 1998. ACM.

[Debe98] Paul Debevec, George Borshukov, and Yizhou Yu. Efficient View-Dependent Image-Based Rendering with Projective Texture-Mapping. In *9th Eurographics Rendering Workshop*, Vienna, Austria, June 1998

[Dura91] Charles Durand. The "Toon" Project: Requirements for a Computerized 2D Animation System. In *Computers and Graphics* 15 (2), pages 285-293. 1991.

[Faug93] Olivier Faugeras. *Three-Dimensional Computer Vision: A Geometric Approach.* MIT Press, Cambridge, Massachusetts, 1993.

[Feke95] Jean-Daniel Fekete, Erick Bizouarn, Eric Cournarie, Thierry Galas, and Frederic Taillefer. TicTacToon: A Paperless System for Professional 2D Animation. In *Proceedings of SIGGRAPH 1995*, pages 79-90. July 1995. ACM.

[Gooc98] Amy Gooch, Bruce Gooch, Peter Shirley, and Elaine Cohen. A Non-Photorealistic Lighting Model for Automatic Technical Illustration. In *Proceedings of SIGGRAPH 98*, pages 447-452. New York, July 1998, ACM.

[Guag98] Eric Guaglione, Marty Altman, Kathy Barshatzky, Rob Bekuhrs, Barry Cook, Mary Ann Pigora, Tony Plett, and Ric Sluiter. The Art of Disney's Mulan. In *SIGGRAPH 98 Course Notes #39*. New York, July 1998. ACM.

[Hack77] Ronald Hackathorn. Anima II: a 3-D Color Animation System. In *Proceedings of SIGGRAPH 77*, pages 54-64. New York, 1977. ACM.

[Lass87] John Lasseter. Principles of Traditional Animation Applied to 3D Computer Animation. In *Proceedings of SIGGRAPH 87*, pages 35-44. New York, July 1987. ACM.

[Lee95] Seung-Yong Lee, Kyung-Yong Chwa, Sung Yong Shin, and George Wolberg. Image Metamorphosis Using Snakes and Free-Form Deformations. In *Proceedings of SIGGRAPH 95*, pages 439-448. New York, July 1995. ACM.

[Leri95] Apostolos Lerios, Chase Garfinkle, and Marc Levoy. Feature-Based Volume Metamorphosis. In *Proceedings of SIGGRAPH 95*, pages 449-456. July 1995. ACM.

[Levo77] Marc Levoy. A Color Animation System Based on the Multiplane. In *Computer Graphics,* vol. 11, pages 65-71. New York, July 1977.

[Libr92] Stephen Librande. Example-Based Character Drawing. M.S. Thesis, MIT. September 1992.

[Litw91] Peter Litwinowicz. Inkwell: A 2½-D Animation System. In *Proceedings of SIGGRAPH 91*, pages 113-122. New York, July 1991. ACM.

[Mark97] Lee Markosian, Michael Kowalski, Samuel Trychin, Lubomir Bourdev, Daniel Goldstein, and John Hughes. Real-Time Nonphotorealistic Rendering. In *Proceedings of SIGGRAPH 97*, pages 415-420. July 1997. ACM.

[Pfit94] Gary Pfitzer. Wildebeests on the Run. In *Computer Graphics World*, pages 52-54. July 1994.

[Rask99] Ramesh Raskar and Michael Cohen. Image Precision Silhouette Edges. To appear in *Proceedings of Interactive 3D Graphics 99.*

[Reev81] W. T. Reeves. Inbetweening For Computer Animation Utilizing Moving Point Constraints. In *Proceedings of SIGGRAPH 81*, pages 263-269. July 1981. ACM.

[Robe94a] Barbara Robertson. Disney Lets the CAPS Out of the Bag. In *Computer Graphics World*, pages 58-64. July 1994.

[Robe94b] Barbara Robertson. Digital Toons. In *Computer Graphics World*, pages 40-46. June 1994.

[Sede86] Thomas Sederberg and Scott Parry. Free-Form Deformation of Solid Geometric Models. In *Proceedings of SIGGRAPH 86*, pages 151-160. New York, Aug 1986. ACM.

[Sede93] Thomas Sederberg, Peisheng Gao, Guojin Wang, and Hong Mu. 2-D Shape Blending: An Intrinsic Solution to the Vertex Path Problem. In *Proceedings of SIGGRAPH 93*, pages 15-18. New York, July 1993. ACM.

[Sing98] Karan Singh and Eugene Fiume. Wires: A Geometric Deformation Technique. In *Proceedings of SIGGRAPH 98*, pages 405-414. New York, July 1998. ACM.

[Wats81] David Watson. Computing the N-Dimensional Delaunay Tessellation With Application to Voronoi Polytopes. In *The Computer J.*, 24(2), p. 167-172. 1981.

[Witk95] Andrew Witkin and Zoran Popovic. Motion Warping. In *Proceedings of SIGGRAPH 95*, pages 105-108. New York, July 1995. ACM.

[Wood97] Daniel Wood, Adam Finkelstein, John Hughes, Craig Thayer, and David Salesin. Multiperspective Panoramas for Cel Animation. In *Proceedings of SIGGRAPH 97,* pages 243-250. New York, July 1997. ACM.

[Zori95] Denis Zorin and Alan Barr. Correction of Geometric Perceptual Distortions in Pictures. In *Proceedings of SIGGRAPH 95*, pages 257-264. July 1995. ACM.

**Figure 13** We combine the various techniques into one scene. The rabbit's head is a static view-dependent model. Note the different tilt of the ears between the first and last viewpoints. The body is an *animated* view-dependent model. It incorporates the view-specific distortions of Figure 9. The background buildings are view-dependent models with a single key deformation. They distort when seen front-on, and appear rectangular as the viewing angle increases.

## SIGGRAPH 99 Committee

SIGGRAPH 99 Conference Chair
Warren Waggenspack
Louisiana State University

SIGGRAPH Conference Chief Staff Executive
Dino Schweitzer
Capstone

Accounting / Conference Management / Copy Coordination / Marketing and Media / Registration
Smith, Bucklin, & Associates, Inc.

Art Gallery: technOasis
Marla Schweppe
Rochester Institute of Technology

Audio/Visual Support
AVW Audio Visual, Inc.

Computer Animation Festival
Brian Blau
SGI

Conference Administration
Capstone

Courses
Barb Helfer
The Ohio State University

Creative Applications Lab: The Digital Cafe
Gudrun Enger
SGI

Electronic Schoolhouse: Educators Program | sigKIDS | Community Outreach
Jodi Giroux
The Allen-Stevenson School
Anne Richardson
StarMedia
Jill Smolin
Cinesite Visual Effects

Emerging Technologies: The Millennium Motel
Kathryn Saunders
Royal Ontario Museum

Exhibition Management
Hall-Erickson, Inc.

Graphic Design / Editing / Web Site
Q LTD

International Services
Linda Hersom
James Scidmore
Scidmore, Hersom, & Others Inc.

GraphicsNet
David Spoelstra
MediaMachine

Organizational Development
Gayle Magee
Independent Consultant

Panels
Jeff Jortner
Sandia National Laboratories

Papers
Alyn Rockwood
Power Take-Off Software, Inc.

Pathfinders
John Fujii
Hewlett-Packard Company

Publications
Stephen N. Spencer
The Ohio State University

Service Contractor
Freeman Decorating Company

Sketches & Applications
Richard Kidd
Cinesite Visual Effects

Student Volunteers
Ron Roff
California Microwave, Inc.

The Studio
Anshuman Razdan
Arizona State University

Travel Agent
Travel Technology Group, Ltd.

SIGGRAPH 98 Conference Chair
Walt Bransford
Thrillistic

SIGGRAPH 2000 Conference Chair
Jackie White
California State University, Los Angeles

SIGGRAPH 2001 Conference Chair
Lynn Pocock
New York Institute of Technology

SIGGRAPH Chair
Steve Cunningham
California State University Stanislaus

## SIGGRAPH Executive Committee

Chair
Judith R. Brown
The University of Iowa

Vice Chair
Alan Chalmers
University of Bristol

Director for Communications
John C. Hart
Washington State University

Director for Education
Mike McGrath
Colorado School of Mines

Director for Professional Chapters
Scott Lang
Academy for the Advancement of Science & Technology

Director for Publications
Stephen N. Spencer
The Ohio State University

Directors-at-Large
Nick England
University of North Carolina Chapel Hill

Theresa-Marie Rhyne
Lockheed Martin Technical Services/
US EPA Scientific Visualization Center

Treasurer
Garry M. Paxinos
Metro Link Incorporated

Past Chair
Steve Cunningham
California State University, Stanislaus

SIGGRAPH 99 Conference Chair
Warren Waggenspack
Louisiana State University

SIGGRAPH Conference
Chief Staff Executive (ex officio)
Dino Schweitzer
Capstone Management Group, Inc.

## Conference Advisory Group

Conference Advisory Group Chair
John Fujii
Hewlett-Packard Company

SIGGRAPH 98 Conference Chair
Walt Bransford
Thrillistic

SIGGRAPH 99 Conference Chair
Warren Waggenspack
Louisiana State University

SIGGRAPH 2000 Conference Chair
Jackie White
California State University Los Angeles

SIGGRAPH 2001 Conference Chair
Lynn Pocock
New York Institute of Technology

SIGGRAPH Conference
Chief Staff Executive (Ex officio)
Dino Schweitzer
Capstone Management Group, Inc.

Executive Committee Representative
Steve Cunningham
California State University Stanislaus

Executive Committee Representative
Theresa-Marie Rhyne
Lockheed Martin Technical Services/
US EPA Scientific Visualization Center

## Papers Committee

Kurt Akeley
Silicon Graphics, Inc.

Chandrajit Bajaj
Department of Computer Sciences and TICAM

Alan H. Barr
California Institute of Technology

Ronen Barzel
Pixar

Gary Bishop
University of North Carolina

Kellogg Booth
The University of British Columbia

Michael Cohen
Microsoft

Rob Cook
Pixar

Andries van Dam
Brown University

Tony DeRose
Pixar Animation Studios

David Dobkin
Princeton University

George Drettakis
iMAGIS/GRAVIR

Eugene Fiume
Alias|Wavefront - University of Toronto

Adam Finkelstein
Princeton University

Henry Fuchs
University of North Carolina

Markus Gross
Swiss Federal Institute of Technology

Chuck Hansen
University of Utah

Hugues Hoppe
Microsoft

Michal Irani
Dept. of Applied Math and Computer Science

Thomas Jensen
think3

Michael Lounsbery
Alias|Wavefront

Leonard McMillan
MIT

Jitendra Malik
University of California at Berkeley

Joe Marks
MERL

Nelson Max
Lawrence Livermore National Laboratory

Gary Meyer
University of Oregon

Gavin Miller
Interval Research Corporation

Steve Molnar
NVIDIA

Tomoyuki Nishita
University of Tokyo

Dan Olsen
Brigham Young University

Michiel Van de Panne
University of Toronto

Randy Pausch
Carnegie Mellon University

Ken Perlin
NYU Media Research Lab

Alyn Rockwood
Power Take-Off Software, Inc.

Pete Shirley
University of Utah

Mel Slater
University College London

Greg Turk
Georgia Institute of Technology

Luiz Velho
Instituto de Matematica Pura e Aplicada

## SIGGRAPH 99 Visionary Papers Jury

Frederick Brooks, Jr.
University of North Carolina

Nick England
University of North Carolina

James Foley
ITA - Mitsubishi Electric Information Technology Center America

Robin Forrest
University of East Anglia

Andrew Glassner
Microsoft Corporation

Jim Kajiya
Microsoft Corporation

Gary Watkins
Evans & Sutherland

Turner Whitted
Microsoft Corporation

# Paper Reviewers

Gregory Abowd
Maneesh Agrawala
John Airey
Kiyoharu Aizawa
Daniel G. Aliaga
John Amanatides
Nina Amenta
P. Anandan
John Anderson
Ken Anjyo
Remi Arnaud
Jim Arvo
Ian Ashdown
Peter Astheimer
Matt Ayers
Ronald Azuma
Norman Badler
Wyeth Bair
Chandrajit Bajaj
Mike Bajura
Harlyn Baker
Kavita Bala
David C. Banks
Gill Barequet
Woodrow Barfield
Tony Barkans
Al Barr
William Barrett
Brian Barsky
Richard Bartels
Joseph Bates
Dan Baum
Ben Bederson
Andrew Beers
Thad Beier
Walter Bender
Jim Bergen
Michael J. Black
Andrew Blake
Jim Blinn
Jules Bloomenthal
Bruce Blumberg
Aaron Bobick
Bobby Bodenheimer
Silviu Borac
Jan Borgerson
James Boritz
Paul Borrel
Rachael Brady
David Breen
Normand Briere
John Bronskill
Armin Bruderlin
Steve Bryson
Richard Bukowski
Andreas Butz
William Buxton
Brian Cabral
Sharon Calahan
Tom Calvert
Swen Campagna
Marie-Paule Cani-Gascuel
Rikk Carey
Loren Carpenter
Gianpaolo U. Carraro
Ed Catmull
Tom Caudell
Bernard Chazelle
Cindy Chen
Eric Chen
Vernon Chi
Norishige Chiba
Eng Wee Chionh
Insook Choi
Peter Chou
Mike M. Chow
Lilian Chu
Paolo Cignoni
Robert Clear
Jeff Close
Elaine Cohen
Jonathan Cohen
Michael Cohen
Danny Cohen-Or
D'nardo Colucci
Perry R. Cook
Satyan Coorg
Sabine Coquillart
Mike Cosman
Michelle Covell
William Cowan
Michael Cox
Alan Craig
Roger Crawfis
Jim Cremer
Carolina Cruz-Neira
Davor Cubranic
Tim Cullip
Brian Curless
Bena Currin
Cassidy Curtis
Niels da Vitoria Lobo
Morten Daehlen
Kristin Dana
Trevor Darrell
Lucia Darsa
Katja Daubert
Larry S. Davis
David Dean
Jeremy De Bonet
Paul Debevec
D. DeCarlo
Michael Deering
Leila DeFloriani
Tony Derose
Rod Deyo
Sven Dickinson
Paul Diefenbach
Suzana Djurcilov
David Dobkin
Steve Dollins
Bruce Rondall Donald
Judith S. Donath
Walt Donovan
Julie Dorsey
George Drettakis
Mark Duchaineau
Tom Duff
Aude Dufresne
Fredo Durand
Charles R. Dyer
David Ebert
Herbert Edelsbrunner
John T. Edmark
Gershon Elber
Matt Eldridge
Steve Ellis
Jihad El-Sana
Nick England
J. Robert Ensor
Carl Erikson
Mark D. Fairchild
Gerald Farin
Olivier Faugeras
Sidney Fels
James A. Ferwerda
Adam Finkelstein
Russ Fish
Eugene Fiume
Kurt Fleischer
Michael Fong
Michael Forkheim
David Forsey
David A. Forsyth
Nick Foster
Farhad Fouladi
Alain Fournier
William Freeman
Henry Fuchs
John Funge
Thomas Funkhouser
Jean Gallier
Michael Garland
Jean-Dominique Gascuel
Simon Gibson
Andrew Glassner
Mike Gleicher
Martin Goebel
Martin Goebel
Jeff Goldsmith
Steven Gortler
Phil Gossett
Ed Granger
Sebastian Grassia
Ned Greene
Guenther Greiner
Cindy Grimm
Larry Gritz
Markus Gross
Brian Guenter
Andre Gueziec
Mukul Gupta
Paul Haeberli
Tom Hahn
James Hahn
Eric Haines

Roy Hall
Mike Halle
Pat Hanrahan
Diane Hansford
Andy Hanson
John Hart
David Haumann
Barbara Hayes-Roth
Christopher Healey
Paul Heckbert
Wolfgang Heidrich
Alan Heirich
Sheila Hemami
Travis Heppe
Roger Hersch
Lambertus Hesselink
Terry Higgins
Shaun Ho
Larry F. Hodges
Jessica Hodgins
Murray Hodgson
Tobias Hoellerer
Kenny Hoff
Dave Holliday
Robert Holt
Michael Hopcroft
Youichi Horry
Jim Hourihan
Donald H. House
Alex Hsu
Philip Hubbard
David Huffman
Zahid Hussain
Katsushi Ikeuchi
Kori Inkpen
Victoria Interrante
Hiroshi Ishii
Thomas W. Jensen
Dan Jobson
Stephen Johnson
Michael Jones
Ken Joy
Zafer Kadi
Jim Kajiya
Ioannis A. Kakadiaris
Michael Kass
Henry Kaufman
Arie E. Kaufman
Alexander Keller
John Kender
Jim Kent
Scott Kim
Kwansik Kim
David Kirkpatrick
R. Victor Klassen
Reinhard Klein
Brian Knep
Gunter Knittel
Leif Kobbelt
Visa Koivunen
E. Kokkevis
Klaus Kremer
David Kriegman
Paul Kruszewski
Subodh Kumar
Andrew Kunz
Alexandra Kuswik
Kiriakos Kutulakos
Phil Lacroute
David Laidlaw
James Landay
Anselmo Lastra
Jean-Claude Latombe
Asish Law
Mark Leather
Yuencheng Lee
Seungyong Lee
Justin Legakis
Jed Lengyel
David Levin
Hongbo Li
Ming Lin
Erik Lindholm
Peter Lindstrom
Dani Lischinski
James Little
Zicheng Liu
Mark Livingston
Yarden Livnat
N. Lobo
Suresh Lodha
Gerald Lohse
Jack Loomis
Charles Loop
Bill Lorensen
David Lowe
Mark Lucente
David Luebke
Tom Lyche
Kwan-Liu Ma
Carl Machover
Blair MacIntyre
Christine L. MacKenzie
Bruce Madsen
Nadia Magnenat-Thalmann
Mark Manca
Steve Mann
Dinesh Manocha
Martti Mantyla
Bill Mark
Lee Markosian
Paul Martin
Kenji Mase
Nelson Max
David McAllister
Michael McAllister
Michael McCool
Tim McInerney
Leonard McMillan
G. Medioni
Barbara Meier
Christopher Migdal
Victor Milenkovic
Gavin Miller
Tim Miller
Mark Mine
Brian Mirtich
Neelkanth Mishra
Don Mitchell
Joe Mitchell
David Mizell
Steve Molnar
Michael Monks
John Montrym
Henry Moreton
Dave Morgan
Bryan Morse
Mike Moshell
Amitabha Mukerjee
Michael Nagy
Marc Najork
Shree Nayar
Shawn Neely
Ulrich Neumann
Fabrice Neyret
Tom Ngo
Wayne Niblack
Jeffry Nimeroff
Alan Norton
Ryutarou Ohbuchi
Drew Olbrich
Kirk Olynyk
Joseph O'Rourke
Eben Ostby
Victor Ostromoukhov
Dinesh K. Pai
James S. Painter
Alex Pang
Matt Papakipos
Richard Parent
Tony Parisi
Frederic Parke
Steven Parker
Kannan Parthasarathy
Velerios Pascucci
Alexander Pasko
Sumant Pattanaik
Randy Pausch
Darwyn Peachey
Hans Køhling Pedersen
Mark Peercy
Catherine Pelachaud
Shmuel Peleg
Joseph Penn
Sandy Pentland
Ken Perlin
B. Peroche
Bernard Peroche
Hanspeter Pfister
Matt Pharr
Cary Phillips
Frederic Pighin
John Platt
Jean Ponce
Jovan Popovic
Zoran Popović

Hanna-Oskar Porr
Tom Porter
Frits H. Post
Helmut Pottmann
Pierre Poulin
Joanna Power
Apurva Prakash
Gill A. Pratt
Hartmut Prautzsch
John Princen
Dennis Proffitt
Przemyslaw Prusinkiewicz
Kari Pulli
Hong Qin
Sudeep Rangaswamy
Ari Rappaport
Matt Regan
Jun Rekimoto
Sandy Ressler
Craig Reynolds
Bill Ribarsky
George Robertson
Charles Rose
Lawrence J. Rosenblum
Dan Rosenthal
Jarek Rossignac
Holly Rushmeier
Paolo Sabella
Malcolm Sabin
Georgios Sakas
Tim Salcudean
Mike Salisbury
Nick Sapidis
Dietmar Saupe
Harpreet Sawhney
Gernot Schaufler
Andreas Schilling
Christophe Schlick
Bengt-Olaf Schneider
Robert Schneider
Chris Schoeneman
Will Schroeder
Peter Schroeder
Robert Schumacker
Stan Sclaroff
Roberto Scopigno
Mark Segal
Steve Seitz
Doree Seligmann
Carlo Sequin
Jonathan Shade
Mubarak Shah
Rob Shakespeare
Michael Shantz
Michael Shantzis
Linda Shapiro
Chris Shaw
Qin Shen
S. Shin
Peter Shirley
Ken Shoemake
Harry Shum
Kwanak-ku Sillim-dong
Bruno Silva
Michael Siminovitch
Karl Sims
Karan Singh
Mukesh P. Singh
Phil Skolmoski
Mel Slater
Peter-Pike Sloan
Kenneth Sloan
Philipp Slusallek
Brian Smits
Scott Snibbe
Cyril Soler
Bob Sproull
Pierre St. Hilaire
Jos Stam
Marc Stamminger
John Stasko
Andrei State
Anthony Steed
Eckehard Steinbach
Eric Stollnitz
Maureen Stone
Wolfgang Straßer
Paul Strauss
Timothy Strotman
Wolfgang Stürzlinger
Wim Sweldens
Richard Szeliski
Tapio Takala
Steven Tanimoto
Gabriel Taubin
Seth Teller
Patrick Teo
Daniel Thalmann
Craig Thayer
Carlo Tomasi
Ken Torrance
Nicolas Tsingos
Xiaoyuan Tu
Mihran Tuceryan
Jack Tumblin
Greg Turk
Ken Turkowski
Sam Uselton
Michiel van de Panne
Kees van Overveld
Mark VandeWettering
Amitabh Varshney
Eric Veach
Luiz Velho / Gomes
Vivek Verma
Anne Verroust
Lev Virine
Doug Voorhies
James Waldrop
Bruce Walter
Jack Walther
Wenping Wang
Colin Ware
Joe Warren
Keith Waters
Richard C. Waters
Greg Welch
Will Welch
Pierre Wellner
Stephen Westin
Lee Westover
Turner Whitted
Lance Williams
John Willinsky
Andrew Willmott
Georges Winkenbach
Stephanie Winner
Andrew Witkin
George Wolberg
George Wolberg
Hans Wolters
Michael Wong
Daniel Wood
Adam Woodbury
Brian Wyvill
Yaser Yacoob
Hussein Yahia
Harold Zatz
Robert Zeleznik
David Zeltzer
Hansong Zhangh
Jianmin Zheng
Michelle Zhou
Ben Zhu
Andrew Zisserman
Douglas Zongker
Denis Zorin
Michael Zyda

**Courses Committee**

Steve Anderson
sgi

Lou Harrison
North Carolina State University

Barb Helfer
The Ohio State University

Alyce Kaprow
THE-NEW-STUDIO

Kathy Kershaw Barshatzky
Walt Disney Feature Animation, Florida

Anselmo Lastra
UNC-Chapel Hill

Kris Laszlo
With Nature In Mind

Steve May
Pixar

Harry Smith
UNC-Wilmington

**Courses Reviewers**

David B. Anderson
Steve Anderson
David Backer
Mike Bailey
William H. Bares
Paul Barham
Kathy Barshatzky
David Bennett
Jack Bresenham
Wolfgang Broll
Charles Callaway
Michael Capps
Wayne Carlson
Loren Carpenter
Peter G. Carswell
Jonathan Corson-Rikert
Carolina Cruz-Neira
Tim Davis
Mark A. DeLoura
Hank Driskill
Martin Dulberg
James W. Durkin
David S. Ebert
Rich Ehlers
Nick England
Steven Feiner
Sebastian Fernandez
Ken Flurchick
Nick Foster
Bill Garrett
Kevin Geiger
Robert Geitz
Priamos Georgiades
Steve Ghee
Andrew Glassner
Michael Gleicher
Brian Green
Chris Greenhalgh
Lou Harrison
David Hart
Christopher G. Healey
Barb Helfer
Leo Hourvitz
Donald H. House
Tom Hudson
Steve Hwan
Gil Irizarry
Jason James Jerald
David E. Johnson
Alyce Kaprow
Scott King
Don Krug
Anselmo Lastra
Joseph J. LaViola Jr.
Wm Leler
James C. Lester
Matthew Lewis
Martin Livesey
Sean Locke
Shaun Love
David Luebke
Kevin Luster
David F. McAllister
Michael Macedonia
William R. Mark
Steve May
Michael Miller
Bryon Nordquist
Lars Nyland
Ken O'Connell
Marc Olano
Manoj Patel
Keith S. Pickens
Saty Raghavachary
Sudhakar Rao
Dave Reed
Timothy Richards
Dave Robertson
Kevin Rodgers
Elizabeth Rosenzweig
Eddie Saxe
Nan Schaller
Ferdi Scheepers
Scott Senften
Mel Slater
Harry F. Smith
Gary Stelling
Ed Swan
Russell M. Taylor II
Dawn Truelsen
Ben Trumbore
Gregory J. Wiet
Len Wanger
Benjamin Watson
Patricia Wenner
Mary Whitton

# Exhibitors

(as of 03 March 1999)

3D Design
3D Pipeline Corporation
The 3D Shop
3Dlabs, Inc.
3Name3D
5D Ltd.

A K Peters Ltd.
Academic Press, Inc.
Accom Inc.
Addison Wesley Longman
Adobe Systems
Advanced Imaging Magazine
Advanced Media Production
Advanced Rendering Technology
AIST Inc.
AJA Video
Alias | Wavefront
Alien Skin Software
Alpha Processor, Inc.
Amazon/Interactive Effects
American Cinematographer
Ampex Corporation
ANDATACO
Animation Magazine
Anthro Corporation
Appian Graphics
The Art Institutes International
Artbeats
ARTBYTE
Artel Software Inc.
Ascension Technology Corporation
auto.des.sys, Inc.
Autologic Information International
AutoMedia Ltd.
Autometric, Inc.
AV Video & Multimedia Producer

B & H Photo Video-Pro Audio
B & L Engineering
Balboa Capital
BE, Inc.
Blossom Technologies Corporation
Blue Sky | VIFX

CADALYST
Caligari Corporation
Cambridge University Press
CamSys, Inc.
Catalogic
CELCO
Charles River Media
Chromatek Inc.
Ciprico Inc.
Cogswell College
Communication Arts
Compaq Computer Corporation
Computer Graphics Systems Development Corporation
Computer Graphics World

The Coriolis Group
Crater Software
CREATION ENGINE, LLC
Cutting Edge Technology
Cybelius Software
Cyberware
Cycore Computers

Daily Variety
Dataram Corporation
DCC
Dell Computer Corporation
Desktop Engineering Magazine
Desktop Images
DHIMA
Diamond Multimedia
Digibotics, Inc.
DigiEffects
Digimation, Inc.
Digital Domain
Digital Firepower
Digital Producer Magazine
Digital Production
Digital Video
Digits 'n Art Software Inc.
DIMENSION 3D-Systems GmbH
DISC, Incorporation
Discreet Logic
DPS (Digital Processing Systems)
Dreamworks Feature Animation
Dynamic Graphics, Inc.

ELSA Inc.
Emedia Weekly
Ensemble Designs Inc.
EUROGRAPHICS
Evans & Sutherland Computer Corporation
Exabyte Corporation

Fakespace
Film & Video
FORE Systems
Fraunhofer CRCG

Game Developer
General Reality
Gentle Giant Studios, Inc.
Geometrix, Inc.

Hash Inc.
Hewlett-Packard Company

IBM Corporation
ICE
I.D. Magazine
ID8 Media
IdN
IEEE Computer Society
IMAGICA Corporation of America
Imagina
Immersion Corporation

In-Harmony Technology Corporation
Industrial Light + Magic
InSpeck inc.
Intel Corporation
Intergraph Computer Systems
International Fine Arts College
InterSense, Inc.
Islip Media, Inc.

John Wiley & Sons
Journey Education Marketing

Kaydara Inc.
Kinetix
Kingston Technology Company

LambSoft, Inc.
LEGASYS International
Leitch
Lightwave Communications, Inc.
LightWork Design
Linker Systems, Inc.
Lips, Inc.
Logitech Inc.

Macmillan Computer Publishing
MacWorld
Management Graphics, Inc.
Matrox Video Products Group
Maxon Computer Inc.
MAXSTRAT Corporation
Measurand Inc.
Media 100 Inc.
MetaCreations Corporation
Microboards Technology, Inc.
Microsoft Corporation
Millimeter
Minicomputer Exchange, Inc.
Minolta Corporation
Miranda Technologies Inc.
Mitsubishi Electric
mms-Multi Media Systems GmbH
The Motion Factory
MotionAnalysis Corporation
MultiGen, Inc.
Multimedia Content Association of Japan (MMCA)
Muse Technologies Inc.

n-Vision, Inc.
NASA Tech Briefs
National Animation & Design Centre
New Media
New Tekniques
NewTek
Nichimen Graphics Inc.
Northern Digital Inc. (NDI)
Nothing Real, LLC

# Exhibitors

Odyssey Productions
Okino Computer Graphics
ORAD Hi Tech Systems
Orphan Technologies
Oxberry LLC

Panasonic Broadcast & Digital Systems Company
ParaForm
PC Video Conversion
Peak Performance Technologies, Inc.
Pepper's Ghost
Phoenix Technologies Inc.
Photron USA
Pixar Animation Studios
PixelFusion
Polhemus, Incorporated
Post Magazine
Producción & Distribución
Professional Marketing Services, Inc.
Publicidad & Comerciales
Puffin Designs
Purdue University

Quantel Inc.
Quantum Corporation
Questar Productions

Raindrop Geomagic
Raycer Graphics
Real 3D
REALViZ
REM INFOGRAFICA, SA
Research Systems
RGB Spectrum
Rhythm & Hues Studios
Roland DGA Corporation
RT-SET Ltd

San Francisco Imaging Services Inc.
Savannah College of Art and Design
SBS Bit 3 Operations
Scitex Digital Video
Screen Actors Guild
SensAble Technologies, Inc.
Sharp Electronics Corporation
Side Effects Software
Sierra Design Labs
Silicon Gear Corporation
Silicon Grail/GW Hannaway
Silicon Graphics, Inc.
Silicon Graphics World
Society of Motion Pictures and TV Engineers (SMPTE)
Softimage
The Software Video Company
Sony Electronics Inc.
Springer-Verlag
Square USA, Inc.
StorageTek
Stratasys, Inc.
Sun Microsystems Inc.
SunExpert Magazine
Sven Technologies
SynaPix, Inc.

TechImage Ltd.
Tektronix, Inc.
Texas Memory Systems, Inc.
TGS, Inc.
TNT Technologies
Toonboom Technologies Inc.
Tri-Star Computer
Trimension Systems
Trinity Animation

UCLA Center for Digital Innovation
University of Advancing Computer Technology

Vancouver Film School
Variety
ViaGrafix
Vicon Motion Systems
Video Systems
Videography
Videonics, Inc.
Viewpoint DataLabs
ViewSonic Corporation
Virtual 3D Incorporated
Volume Graphics Association

Wacom Technology Corporation
The Walt Disney Company
Web Techniques
Western Micro Technology
Wicks and Wilson Limited

# SIGGRAPH Professional Chapters

**California**

Los Angeles ACM SIGGRAPH
Genny Yee
PO Box 9399
Marina del Rey, CA 90295
los_angeles_chapter@siggraph.org
http://www.siggraph.org/chapters/los_angeles

San Diego ACM SIGGRAPH
Nancy Collier
4822 Santa Monica Ave, Suite 179
San Diego, CA 92107
san_diego_chapter@siggraph.org
http://www.siggraph.org/chapters/san_diego

San Francisco ACM SIGGRAPH
Walter Beer
100 First St., Suite 100 - Box 347
San Francisco, CA 94105
san_francisco_chapter@siggraph.org
http://www.siggraph.org/chapters/sf

Silicon Valley ACM SIGGRAPH
Alesh Jancarik
PO Box 804
Mountain View, CA 94042-1205
silicon_valley_chapter@siggraph.org
http://www.siggraph.org/chapters/siliconv

**Colorado**

Denver/Boulder ACM SIGGRAPH
Mike McCarthy
PO Box 61402
Cherry Creek Station
Denver, CO 80206-8402
denver-boulder_chapter@siggraph.org

**District of Columbia**

Washington, D.C. ACM SIGGRAPH
Mary Higgins
SAIC/Telefusion
8301 Greensboro Drive, Suite T-10, M/S E-T-2
McLean, VA 22102-3600
washington_dc_chapter@siggraph.org
http://www.dcsiggraph.org

**Florida**

Ft. Lauderdale ACM SIGGRAPH
Garry M. Paxinos
Metro Link Inc
4711 N. Powerline Road
Fort Lauderdale, FL 33309
fort_lauderdale_chapter@siggraph.org
http://www.siggraph.org/chapters/ftlsig/

Orlando ACM SIGGRAPH
Lynn R. Finch
PO Box 2208
Winter Park, FL 32790-2208
orlando_chapter@siggraph.org
http://www.siggraph.org/chapters/orlando/

Tampa Bay ACM SIGGRAPH
Blake Barr (acting chair)
12001 Ninth St. N. #2901
St. Petersburg, FL 33716
tampa_bay_chapter@siggraph.org

**Georgia**

Atlanta ACM SIGGRAPH
Jason Key
PO Box 769182
Roswell, GA 30076-9182
atlanta_chapter@siggraph.org
http://www.acm.org/chapters/atlanta

**Massachusetts**

Boston ACM SIGGRAPH
Olin Lathrop
PO Box 194
Bedford, MA 01730
boston_chapter@siggraph.org
http://www.siggraph.org/chapters/boston

**Minnesota**

Minneapolis/St. Paul ACM SIGGRAPH
Stan Bissinger
5401 Elliot Ave. S.
Minneapolis, MN 55417
minneapolis-stpaul_chapter@siggraph.org
http://www.pixel8.com/siggraph/

**New Jersey**

Princeton ACM SIGGRAPH
Douglas Dixon
P.O. Box 1324
Princeton, NJ 08542
princeton_chapter@siggraph.org
http://www.siggraph.org/chapters/princeton/

**New Mexico**

Rio Grande ACM SIGGRAPH
Gwen Sylvan
P.O. Box 8352
Albuquerque, NM 87108-8352
rio_grande_chapter@siggraph.org

**New York**

New York City ACM SIGGRAPH
Scott Lang
NYC ACM SIGGRAPH Chapter
ACM/Local Activities
1515 Broadway
New York, NY 10036
new_york_city_chapter@siggraph.org
http://www.siggraph.org/chapters/nyc

**North Carolina**

NC Research Triangle ACM SIGGRAPH
Randy Brown
SAS Campus Drive RA 459
Cary, NC 27513
research_triangle_chapter@siggraph.org
http://www.siggraph.org/chapters/research_triangle/

**Pennsylvania**

Pittsburgh
David Egts
Concurrent Technologies Corporation (CTC)
1450 Scalp Ave.,
Johnstown, PA 15904-3374
pittsburgh_chapter@siggraph.org
http://www.vr.ctc.com/siggraph

**Texas**

Dallas ACM SIGGRAPH
Ben Chan
4315 Durango Lane
McKinney, TX 75070
dallas_area_chapter@siggraph.org
http://acm.org/~aaronh/das.html

Houston ACM SIGGRAPH
Christine Rosso Paige, Acting Chair
The Art Institute of Houston
1900 Yorktown
Houston, TX 77056
houston_chapter@siggraph.org
http://www.siggraph.org/chapters/houston/

**Washington**

Seattle ACM SIGGRAPH
Steve Hollasch
Microsoft
One Microsoft Way
Redmond, WA 98052-6399
seattle_chapter@siggraph.org
http://www.siggraph.org/chapters/seattle/

# SIGGRAPH Professional Chapters

**Argentina**

Buenos Aires ACM SIGGRAPH
Alejandro Beviglia
TucumBn 1625 PB "B"
1050 Buenos Aires, Argentina
buenos_aires_chapter@siggraph.org

**Bulgaria**

Sofia ACM SIGGRAPH
Gospodin Jelev
Dept of Prog & Computer Appl
Technical Univ. of Sofia
1756 Sofia,
Bulgaria
sofia_chapter@siggraph.org

**Canada**

Vancouver B.C. ACM SIGGRAPH
Graeme Gish, chair
Vancouver Film School
420 Homer Street,
Vancouver, B.C.
V6B 2V5
Canada
vancouver_bc_chapter@siggraph.org
http://fas.sfu.ca/cs/research/groups/GMRL/ACM-SIGGRAPH

**France**

Paris ACM SIGGRAPH
Thierry Frey
c/o SUPINFOCOM - Terita 3000
2, rue Henri Matisse
59300 Aulnoye-lez-Valenciennes,
France
paris_chapter@siggraph.org
http://www.siggraph.org/chapters/paris/

**Israel**

Central Israel ACM SIGGRAPH
Ayellet Tal
Dept. of Electrical Engineering
Technion - Israel Institute of Technology
Haifa, Israel, 32000
Phone: +972-4-8294651
Fax: +972-4-8323041
central_israel_chapter@siggraph.org
http://www.cs.technion.ac.il/~sudar/icgf.html

**Japan**

Tokyo ACM SIGGRAPH
Masa Inakage
c/o Yukiko Ozaki
Image Systems Engineering Division
IMAGICA Corporation
2-14-1,Higashi-Gotanda,Shinagawa-ku
Tokyo,141
Japan
tokyo_chapter@siggraph.org
http://www.siggraph.org/chapters/tokyo

**Mexico**

Mexico City ACM SIGGRAPH
Gonzalo Leon
Calzada de las Aguilas #1124-E-202
Col. San Clemente
Mexico City 01740 D.F.
Mexico
mexico_city_chapter@siggraph.org
http://www.spin.com.mx/sigmex/sighome.htm

**Singapore**

Singapore ACM SIGGRAPH
Hock Soon Seah
Nanyang Technological University
Nanyang Avenue
Singapore 639798
Republic of Singapore
singapore_chapter@siggraph.org
http://www.ntu.edu.sg/siggraph

**In-Formation Chapters**

Brussels ACM SIGGRAPH - In Formation
Jean-Yves Roger, acting chair
Project Officer
European Commission
Directorate General III - Industry
Rue de la loi/Wetstraat 200
B-1049 Bruxelles/Brussel
Belgium
brussels_chapter@siggraph.org

Milano ACM SIGGRAPH - In Formation
Maria Grazia Mattei, acting chair
MGM Digital Communication s.r.l.
via Vivaio 23
20122 Milano Italia
+39 2 798760 (Voice)
+39 2 798701 (Fax)
milano_chapter@siggraph.org

Oktibbeha ACM SIGGRAPH - In Formation
Paras Kaul, acting chair
P.O. Box 5275
Portland, OR 97215
+1-503-234-6377 (Voice)
oktibbeha_chapter@siggraph.org

Portland ACM SIGGRAPH - In Formation
Hercules Silverstein, acting chair
5631 SE Salmon Street
Mississippi State, MS 39762
+1-612-332-3361 Ext. 131 (Voice)
oktibbeha_chapter@siggraph.org

Rotterdam ACM SIGGRAPH - In Formation
Richard E. Ouwerkerk
Department of Arts and Architecture
Hogeschool Rotterdam & Omstreken
Scheepmakersstraat 7
PO Box 1272
3000 BG Rotterdam
The Netherlands
rotterdam_chapter@siggraph.org

Toronto ACM SIGGRAPH - In Formation
Adele Newton
Newton Associates
6338 Snowflake Lane
Mississauga, Ontario
L5N 6G9
Canada
toronto_chapter@siggraph.org
http://www.siggraph.org/chapters/to

# Author Index

# Cover Image Credits

**Front Cover**

To render this virtual landscape we borrowed techniques from the drawings of Dr. Seuss. The leaves and tufts of grass are suggested with a few strokes – our eyes fill in the rest. In fact, the underlying geometry is simple – the leaves and grass are generated just as needed each frame in our interactive system. Realistic depiction of trees or bushes is hard to do in conventional graphics, and yet a simple, stylized rendering can be more persuasive than the realistic one. This is one example of how techniques from art and illustration can be applied to expand the expressive power of 3D computer graphics.

Reference: "Art-Based Rendering of Fur, Grass and Trees," *Michael A. Kowalski, Lee Markosian, J. D. Northrup, Lubomir Bourdev, Ronen Barzel, Loring S. Holden, John F. Hughes, pp. 433-438.*

**Frontispiece**

"Tree and Streetlight on a Foggy Night"
Jack Tumblin

An LCIS hierarchy made this low contrast (~20:1) display image from pixels of a high contrast (>100,000:1) floating-point scene. Despite severely reduced display contrast, LCIS preserves details everywhere, even within strong shadows, highlights and image intensity gradients. Original scene intensities were gathered using 11 photographs (note tracks of flying insects) and Debevec's radiance map method. Though long radial fog streaks were plainly visible at the scene, they were not apparent on the source photos. Thanks to Huong Q. Dinh for crucial image alignment work for this scene.

Reference: "LCIS: A Boundary Hierarchy For Detail-Preserving Contrast Reduction," *Jack Tumblin, Greg Turk, pp. 83-90.*

**Back Cover**

**Upper Left:**

Reference: "Digital Facial Engraving," *Victor Ostromoukhov, pp. 417-424.*

**Upper Right:**

"Novel Views of Mona Lisa"

Reconstructing Leonardo's Mona Lisa with a morphable face model, which is derived from 3D scans of 200 example faces, yields a colored 3D model of the face (top right). Based on this estimate of the underlying 3D structure (bottom left), novel views of Mona Lisa can be generated using a warping technique which retains characteristics of the painting (bottom right).

Reference: "A Morphable Model for the Synthesis of 3D Faces," *Volker Blanz, Thomas Vetter, pp. 187-194.*

**Lower Left:**

This picture is a snapshot from our two-dimensional stable fluid solver. The texture is created interactively by applying forces to a fluid which our simulator animates in real time. The distortions are created by moving the texture coordinates through the fluid. The grid resolution for the fluid is 100 x 100 for this picture.

Reference: "Stable Fluids," *Jos Stam, pp. 121-128.*

**Lower Right:**

Reference: "Computational Fluid Dynamics in a Traditional Animation Environment," *Patrick Witting, pp. 129-136.*